LESTER A. LEFTON

University of South Carolina

SECOND EDITION

Psychology

ALLYN AND BACON, INC.

Boston, London, Sydney, Toronto

This book is dedicated to the people who help make my life joyful—
Linda, Sarah, and Jesse.

Production Editor: David Dahlbacka
Cover Designer: Christy Rosso
Series Editor: Bill Barke

Library of Congress Cataloging in Publication Data

Lefton, Lester A., 1946–
  Psychology.

  Bibliography: p.
  Includes index.
  1. Psychology. I. Title.
BF121.L424 1982   150   81-10940
ISBN 0-205-07590-8   AACR2

Printed in the United States of America.

10 9 8 7 6 5 4 3 2   86 85 84 83 82

CREDITS

Endpapers: FRONT ENDPAPER (left)—John Running/After Image; (right top)—Ira Berger/Black Star; (right center)—Nicholas Devore/Bruce Coleman Inc.; (right bottom)—Doug Wilson/Black Star. BACK END-PAPER (right)—Adapted from W. McKinley (ed.), *IES Lighting Handbook*, New York: Illuminating Engineering Society, 1947.

Chapter 1: CO DUOTONE p.1—Anamarie Sarazin, Principal Dancer with The Boston Ballet. QUOTE p.2—From Edwin Arlington Robinson, *The Children of the Night.* Copyright under the Berne Convention (New York: Charles Scribner's Sons, 1897). Reprinted with the permission of Charles Scribner's Sons. PHOTO p.7—Ed Malitsky/The Picture Cube. PHOTO p.8—Leonard Freed/Magnum. PHOTO p.9—Charles Gatewood. PHOTO p.10—Ron Alexander/Stock, Boston. PHOTO p.10—Charles Gatewood. PHOTO p.11 (top left)—Courtesy The Bettmann Archive, Inc. PHOTO p.11 (top center)—Courtesy of The Library of Congress. PHOTO p.11 (top right)—Courtesy The Bettmann Archive, Inc. PHOTO p.12—Courtesy of Culver Pictures, Inc. FIG.1.2, p.12—From The mind body problem by Jerry A. Fodor, copyright © 1981 by Scientific American, Inc. All rights reserved. PHOTO p.14—Abigail Heyman/Magnum. PHOTO p.15—John Running/Stock, Boston. PHOTO p.15—Alex Webb/Magnum. CARTOON p.20—© King Features Syndicate, 1972. BOX p.24—"Baboons too use tools." *Science News*, Feb. 3, 1973, pp. 71–72. Reprinted with permission from *Science News*, the weekly news magazine of science, copyright 1973 by Science Service, Inc. PHOTO p.26—Margaret Thompson/The Picture Cube. PHOTO p.27 —Eugene Richards/The Picture Cube.

Chapter 2: CO DUOTONE p.31—E. Michael Barley. QUOTE p.32— From pp. 4–6 in *Brave New World.* Copyright 1932, 1960 by Aldous Huxley. Reprinted by permission of Harper & Row, Publishers, Inc. CARTOON p. 35—THE WIZARD OF ID by permission of Johnny Hart and Field Enterprises, Inc. FIG. 2.1, p.37—Courtesy Dr. P.S. Gerald and K.D. Dale, Children's Hospital Medical Center, Boston. FIG. 2.2, p.38— From Carlson, N.R. *Physiology of behavior.* Boston: Allyn and Bacon, 1977, p.290. BOX p.39—"The Gene Transplanters," *Newsweek*, June 17, 1974, p.54. Copyright 1973, by Newsweek, Inc. All Rights Reserved. Reprinted by Permission. PHOTO top p.40—Charles Gatewood. PHOTO top p.40—Margaret Thompson/The Picture Cube. PHOTO p.42—© Harvey Stein 1978. PHOTO p.42—Cary Wolinsky/Stock, Boston. FIG.2.3, p.43—Adapted from Erlenmeyer-Kimling, L. and Jarvik, L.F., *Science*, 1963, 142, 1477–1479, Copyright 1963 by the American Association for the Advancement of Science. FIG.2.6, p.48—From Carlson, N.R., *Physiology of behavior.* Boston: Allyn and Bacon, 1977. FIG.2.14, p.54—From Carlson, N.R., *Physiology of behavior.* Boston: Allyn and

(Continued after Subject Index)

Contents

CHAPTER 6 DEVELOPMENT

CHAPTER 7 INTELLIGENCE

Preface

THE GOAL: A BALANCED PRESENTATION

THE AIM OF THIS text is to achieve a balance between scientific accuracy and student accessibility. At the same time, I have tried to show how many psychologists have applied their knowledge in ways relevant to individuals and society.

I feel that psychology can be shown as a rigorous and comprehensive science and still be focused so that students see how its fundamental aspects apply to their lives. My aim as a teacher and writer has been to work out the best possible balance between two sides of a teaching dilemma—to give an interesting and understandable, yet thorough and accurate, picture of the most significant features of psychological science. The most important task has been to portray this often confusing and diverse science with the level of scientific accuracy necessary if a student is to fully understand it. Meaningfulness and scientific rigor are not mutually exclusive goals.

NEW CHALLENGES

To a great extent the first edition of this book accomplished many of these goals. The text was adopted at scores of universities and colleges. Instructors considered the first edition teachable; students learned easily from it and generally liked it. The student guide supplement to the text, *Keeping Pace*, has been hailed as one of the best student guides ever written. Even with these successes, instructors and students asked for more. They wanted expanded content, more detail, and increased coverage of the research process. From these needs have grown a slightly different format and a broadened scope based on extensive feedback from users and specialists.

A UNIQUE SYSTEM OF FEEDBACK

The manuscripts for both editions of this book have been extensively tested in the classroom; the entire book as well as individual chapters were critically evaluated by students and instructors. Their responses were taken very seriously; many changes are directly due to this student and instructor feedback. Readers included graduate students, lecturers at state colleges and universities, and professors of psychology who have been teaching this discipline for many years. In addition, detailed reviews were provided by research specialists. All have offered useful and constructive criticism. Even as the final manuscript was being prepared, the dialogue was continuing.

An even more distinctive system of feedback was provided by the Allyn & Bacon field staff, who interviewed adopters to ascertain which features of the first edition they found most useful in teaching psychology. At several schools the field staff also arranged for written student feedback; I have a file drawer of evaluations from hundreds of students. While encouraging a clear and concise presentation of the details of sophisticated issues, these individuals also helped me keep a high level of scientific accuracy.

FEATURES OF THE NEW EDITION

The comprehensive feedback system provided clear suggestions for changes in six main areas. This new edition reflects these suggestions.

- MORE TOPICS—There has been an increase in the number and type of topical coverage. Previous coverage was expanded (e.g., testing) and many new topics were added (e.g., environmental psychology).
- RESEARCH COMPLEXITY—In key areas, the complexity of research is dealt with in more detail (e.g., schizophrenia), from alternative viewpoints, and at a slightly higher level of sophistication.
- CONNECTING THEMES—The use of connecting, interweaving themes was used more extensively to ensure a sense of thematic unity and integrity.
- STUDENT INTEREST—Applications, human interest examples, opening vignettes, and a running glossary were provided to arouse and maintain the interest of students.
- APPLICATION—A new chapter has been added to show how psychology is applied in the fields of industrial psychology, environmental psychology, and criminal behavior. Throughout the text, real-life applications of psychology are shown in *IMPACT* panel inserts.
- UPDATING—The comprehensive feedback system allowed up-to-the-minute information on current issues and research problems. Knowledgeable researchers provided extremely detailed critiques to ensure the timeliness and thoroughness of the presentation.

NEW TOPICS. Some topical coverage from the first edition was expanded. Some totally new coverage was introduced. In some cases, coverage of older data and theories was reduced. Nearly every chapter has been increased in length and breadth, but some received special emphasis. For example, the areas of testing and intelligence have been expanded greatly. The study of abnormal psychology reflects the new *DSM-III* classification system. The chapter on learning has been expanded dramatically without increasing its level of difficulty. Motivation and emotion were expanded greatly and with a new emphasis; so were the chapters on social psychology and development.

Although by no means complete, the following list contains some of the new topics in this edition:

Forgetting	Alfred Adler
Cognitive Control of Motivation	Biological Causes of Depression
Day Care Centers	Autism
Gifted Children	Satisfaction in the Workplace
The Nature of Consciousness	Crowding
Acupuncture	Causes of Criminal Behavior

Many previously covered topics were greatly expanded. For example:

Brain Lateralization	Psycholinguistics
Classical Conditioning	Meditation
Social Learning Theory	Bystander Intervention
Intrinsic Motivation	Learned Helplessness
Gestalt Views of Perception	Schizophrenia
Kohlberg's Views of Morality	Hyperactivity
Bonding	Systematic Desensitization
Intelligence Testing	Locus of Control

TEACHING AND LEARNING AIDS. Panel inserts on a variety of topics are used to keep student interest levels high. Under the headings *IN THE NEWS* and *IMPACT*, the relevance of psychology to people's lives is presented *and* evaluated. Panel inserts headed *RESEARCH PROFILE* are used to examine some research problems in depth from at least two viewpoints, describing data, theory, and methods in detail to show how data are collected, reported, and interpreted. These research profiles are a diversion from the textual prose and, at the same time, supplement it with further examples and additional information. They attempt to show the nature and diversity of psychology and also how it continues to evolve as a science. The profiles should be an excellent teaching tool; they stress the intricacies of research without making the complex sound difficult.

STUDENT INTEREST. Because maintaining student interest is a high priority, devices such as chapter opening vignettes, chapter opening outlines, and a marginal glossary have been carried over from the previous edition, with strengthening and extending where appropriate.

INSTRUCTIONAL ART. Art can be used to accomplish many ends in a textbook; in this book art has a specific clear goal—to help teach psychology. Photographs were chosen with care to help illustrate important ideas. Special new pieces of instructional art were drawn to prompt student thought about complicated issues. Graphs and figures were drawn simply, clearly, and with the aim of bringing clarity, not confusion, to psychology. Students will find especially useful a series of building tables that grow in size as the chapter progresses, helping them organize their ideas in meaningful ways. Psychologists, artists, designers, and photo researchers worked with me to help develop a meaningful, clear, and pedagogically useful art program that is more than a mere embellishment of the text.

DOMINANT THEMES. Because psychology represents so many subdisciplines, it is not surprising that introductory students often have difficulty at first understanding how such diverse fields can be placed together under one umbrella. This need not be the case. Psychology is an unified discipline, unified through certain recurring and dominant themes that appear over and over again. One such theme is nature vs. nurture; this issue is raised prominently in 11 chapters. Another such theme, the role of learning in behavior, is stressed repeatedly in 12 chapters. In every chapter, there is an important focus on the development of psychology as a science and on the idea that old ideas spawn new ones. Acknowledged fully is the idea that today's theories may soon become obsolete and that this is part of the evolution of psychology. A number of chapters show how a person's developing behavior patterns and inherited abilities (like intelligence) may or may not modify day-to-day living patterns. As students read about these issues and themes, and become familiar with them, their understanding increases.

THE BALANCING ACT

My goal in this second edition has been to revise the first edition of this textbook in a way that would enhance its strengths and eliminate its weaknesses. Further, I have attempted to use the feedback provided to me by students, instructors, researchers, and technical specialists to build upon previous successes and strengths. All of this had to be accomplished while presenting to students an easy to read, understandable, and accessible book. The goal was to present psychology in the most understandable way possible without oversimplifying, and to show a diversity of viewpoints without introducing confusion. To a great extent, this is a balancing act. I have been fortunate that so many of my friends, colleagues, and newly-made friends have helped me in my attempt to achieve this goal. I would like to thank them here.

ACKNOWLEDGEMENTS

During the last three years I have kept up a correspondence with a number of instructors who used the first edition of *Psychology*. They have been particularly helpful in providing me with information as to the strongest and weakest components of the first edition. Some made technical comments; others, global reviews. Some provided a single postcard with an important comment; others wrote extensively and frequently. Their efforts are those of dedicated teachers and scholars; I thank these individuals:

Helene Ballmer	California State University, Fullerton
William L. Curry	Wesleyan College
John Driscoll	Holy Cross Junior College
Janet Dunkle	California State University at Northridge
George E. Field	Marshalltown Community College
Judith Green	William Patterson College of New Jersey
Ray Johnson	Hardin-Simmons University
Henry L. Kaplowitz	Kean College of New Jersey

John Kenny	Rockford College
Arlene Kestner	Southern University
Myrna Lane	Southern University
A. Bryan Laver	Carleton University
Donna Lis	College of St. Rose
Barbara P. Losty	Stephens College
Sheldon Malev	Westchester Community College
George T. Martin	Mt. San Antonio College
Richard E. Miller	Navarro College
Leslie E. Moser	Baylor University
David L. Novak	Lansing Community College
Thomas G. O'Brien	Lincoln University
Harvey Pennington	Williamsport Area Community College
Clark Presson	Indiana University
Gary Schaumburg	Cerritos College
Wayne G. Slife	Henderson State University
Joseph A. Smith	Shippensburg State College
Tom Vilberg	University of Scranton
Roger Woodbury	Wilson County Technical Institute
R. A. Yocum	Williamette University

As part of a comprehensive package of teaching materials for the psychology instructor, Terry Pettijohn has developed an excellent *Instructor's Manual*. In doing so he was helped by a number of psychologists who provided alternative views and reviews of selected high-interest research pieces. These teachers and researchers helped further broaden the scope of this textbook and I am thankful for their help. Among these individuals were a number of senior graduate students at the University of South Carolina. They are: David A. Balota, Janet M. Balota, Kimberly J. Davis, Joseph B. Denneny, Gerald S. Drose, John W. Galbary, Linda L. Hernandez, Cheryl McDonnell, Katherine H. Mills, Ryan Ramsey, Ruth Striegel-Moore, and Gwendolyn Whitley. I especially thank these contributors from various colleges and universities throughout the country:

Ilene L. Bernstein	University of Washington
Rose Boltz	Ohio State University at Marion
Mary Lou Cheal	McLean Hospital and Harvard Medical School
Daniel J. Christie	Ohio State University at Marion
Janis Wiley Driscoll	University of Colorado at Denver
Anita Ekren	Community College of Denver, Red Rocks Campus
Susan G. Forman	University of South Carolina
John C. Gurski	Fort Hays State University
Elaine Hatfield	University of Wisconsin at Madison
Margaret C. Hazelett	Ohio State University at Marion
Tamra Lehman	Ohio State University at Marion
Joel Macht	University of Denver
Karen S. Miller	University of Toledo
Roger A. Page	Ohio State University at Lima
Dennis H. Passe	Florida State University
Chris E. Paterson	Ohio State University At Marion
Robert Rosenthal	Harvard University
John Paul Scott	Bowling Green State University

Susan Sprecher	University of Wisconsin
Sara Staats	Ohio State University at Newark
Thomas S. Szasz	State University of New York at Syracuse
Elizabeth Decker Tanke	University of Santa Clara
Margaret E. Vaughan	Harvard University
Bruce Walsh	Ohio State University
Mary M. Webster	University of Washington
Leonard J. Williams	Wittenberg University
Stanley D. Winter	Laradon Hall School

I have been fortunate that so many individuals have helped me write this textbook by providing critical evaluations. Some were friends and colleagues; others were anonymous. Some read the entire manuscript; others read single chapters. Each has made a substantive contribution. I thank each of these teachers and researchers, all scholars, for their efforts in helping produce a better text:

Roger C. Bailey	East Tennessee State University
William W. Beatty	North Dakota State University
William M. Beneke	Lincoln University
Michael Best	Southern Methodist University
Samuel W. Cochran	East Texas State University
B. Theodore Cole	University of South Carolina
Charles Crowell	University of Notre Dame
Ann Cydell	San Diego City College
William O. Dwyer	Memphis State University
Eleanor Fahle	City College of San Francisco
Barry Fish	Eastern Michigan University
Frank Ted Friedberg	University of Southwestern Louisiana
William Heater	Lansing Community College
William Holliman	University of Southern Mississippi
William G. Johnson	University of Mississippi Medical Center
James Johnston	Madison Area Technical College
Curtis S. McKee	Black Hills State College
Lynn Peterson	Los Angeles Pierce College
Robert E. Pryjula	Middle Tennessee State University
James Roach	College of San Mateo
Judy Sims-Knight	Southeastern Massachusetts University
Leighton E. Stamps	University of New Orleans at Lake Front
Richard Stone	Kean College
Henry Janpol	Lane Community College
Lawrence B. Wallnau	State University of New York at Brockport
Barry Weber	Private Practitioner, Chicago, Illinois
Leonard J. Williams	Wittenberg University
William C. Williams	Eastern Washington University
Jerry Wisner	Florida Junior College/North College
Carol Woodward	Moorpark College

I have been helped in many valuable ways by many psychologists. However, a few went far beyond providing excellent reviews; these individuals provided me detailed, line-by-line comments. They provided insights, alternative interpretations, and, in doing so, challenged me and truly helped change the shape of the text. These people deserve special thanks:

Robert Arkin	University of Missouri
John Best	Eastern Illinois University
David H. Dodd	University of Utah
Karen Duffy	State University of New York at Geneseo
Leslie E. Fisher	Cleveland State University
Russell Geen	University of Missouri
E. Scott Geller	Virginia Polytechnic Institute & State University
Gary Greenberg	Wichita State University
John F. Hall	Pennsylvania State University
Yvonne V. Hardaway	Louisiana State University
Sherry Kermis	Canisius College
Margaret Matlin	State University of New York at Geneseo
Terry F. Pettijohn	Ohio State University at Marion
Ronald Rogers	University of Alabama
Jerome Sattler	San Diego State University
William H. Tedford	Southern Methodist University
Laura Valvatne	Community College of Denver/Red Rocks
Fred H. Wallbrown	Kent State University

During the development of this text, I called upon many of my friends and colleagues in the Psychology Department of the University of South Carolina to help me in their special areas of expertise. They were generous with their time and comments and I wish to thank them collectively for their collegial support.

Several students were a great help to me. I thank Rhonda Whitley for helping me do library research and for keeping track of references. I thank Marina Yartzeff, Lauren Hertz, Ann Macaluso, and Sandra Rausch who all assisted in typing and keeping track of references.

I especially thank Gwendolyn Whitley, my assistant, secretary, and all-around helper. Gwen typed the manuscript repeatedly; she kept track of a seemingly endless number of details. Working with me on a day-to-day basis, she read the manuscript like a professional editor and provided many important comments that encouraged me to change many sections of the book.

The entire staff at Allyn & Bacon are the best. The production team was incredibly skillful. I thank Nancy Murphy for her skilled efforts in managing the entire production process. Designer Dorothy Thompson provided an exceptionally tasteful and pleasing design; cover designer Christy Rosso created a superb cover. I especially thank production editor David Dahlbacka who throughout the entire production process carefully coordinated the extraordinary number of details that were involved in producing this textbook.

The field staff of Allyn & Bacon were especially helpful to me in talking with instructors about the first edition of my book. Many of them interviewed instructors at length and set up phone calls for me with instructors and students. Over 55 dedicated men and women in the field have helped me enormously. Working closely with them, Ray Short and Sandi Kirshner deserve my special thanks.

The editorial staff at Allyn & Bacon were the men and women with whom I had the most contact. I thank editorial assistant Wendy Ritger for her coordination of the supplements that accompany the book. Basic book editor Allen Workman is a consummate developmental editor. He critically read the manuscript; on some pages of text I would often find more of his blue pencil marks than my own typed words. His comments were always lengthy, incisive, and—most important—usually correct. Series editor Bill Barke belongs on the All-Pro team; Bill has had the extraordinary responsibility of being accountable for everything associated with this book. Helping me as well as orchestrating all of the people, schedules, ideas, and plans for an introductory textbook was a herculean task; Bill Barke handled all of this with skill, gusto, and good humor.

Although many psychologists, friends, colleagues, and students have been important in shaping this book, none have had more of an impact than my wife and children. My wife, Linda, served as a wellspring of support throughout the writing of the first edition. Her love, encouragement, and friendship have made possible my continued efforts on this book. Few people share a partnership like ours; I am very grateful for it. My daughters, Sarah and Jesse, ages 8 and 5, have also been a source of inspiration. I am fortunate that my children have learned well the good habits that Linda and I share while at the same time have tended to ignore our bad ones. As they have developed and blossomed into unique, very special human beings, I have been inspired and have gained greater insight into psychology, my own behavior, and that of others. They have truly made my life more productive and meaningful. For these reasons, I dedicate this book to the people who bring joy to my life—my wife, Linda, and my daughters, Sarah and Jesse.

LAL

PSYCHOLOGISTS STUDY BEHAVIOR so they can understand it, predict it, and eventually manage it. Psychology seeks to better understand behavior in order to benefit our lives. Information about behavior is used in such fields as clinical and counseling psychology to treat patients, as well as in research and teaching. Psychologists have developed controlled methods to study behavior so that they can continue to develop and apply behavior principles. The purpose of this chapter is to present an overview of psychology showing its origins, how it evolved, and the broad range of activities in which psychologists are involved.

What is Psychology?

RICHARD CORY

Whenever Richard Cory went down town,
We people on the pavement looked at him:
He was a gentleman from sole to crown,
Clean favored, and imperially slim.

And he was always quietly arrayed,
And he was always human when he talked;
But still he fluttered pulses when he said,
'Good-morning,' and he glittered when he walked.

And he was rich—yes, richer than a king—
And admirably schooled in every grace:
In fine, we thought that he was everything
To make us wish that we were in his place.

So on we worked, and waited for the light,
And went without the meat, and cursed the bread;
And Richard Cory, one calm summer night,
Went home and put a bullet through his head.

EDWIN ARLINGTON ROBINSON

Discovering the truth about yourself or others can be a disturbing experience. To some, it may seem tempting to put aside those uncomfortable questions about why people behave or feel as they do. Why not be like Richard Cory's admirers, building your life around the outer appearance of things? But this sort of concealment and self-deceit is obviously dangerous—almost as much so for the average "people on the pavement" as for the Richard Corys of this world who are unable to discover a sense of self they can live with. We all eventually need some insight into our own behavior and human potential; we also need a way to share feelings, hopes, and capabilities, as well as problems.

How can people best try to learn about their feelings and personal resources or to feel comfortable about expressing them? Often social situations seem to make such understandings more difficult. How many times has a father reached out to hug his son but stopped because he felt it unmanly? How many times were tears held back at funerals because of feelings of social impropriety? How many times have people not taken a chance in life because they felt unworthy? If all of us were able to face the truth about our feelings in situations like these, perhaps such knowledge would give us a greater freedom to choose a better kind of life.

Psychologists try to discover and understand truths about behavior in order to help people understand themselves and to improve the human condition. By understanding the principles of behavior it is possible to lead happier lives, make better adjustments to society, and truly fulfill oneself. Psychology can't provide all the answers, nor will it make people happy overnight, but studying it can give some insight into why people act in certain ways. Behavior is complex and no single rule, theory, or explanation can account for everything a person feels, thinks, or does. Still, psychology tries to provide a framework and a careful analysis of how and why people behave the way they do. Psychology tries to discover some of the truths that will make you free.

Human **behavior** encompasses everything a person feels, thinks, and does, and **psychology** is the science of behavior. Since psychologists examine all aspects of a person's behavior, we will be studying a wide range of activities, including topics such as thought processes, prejudice, and sexual behavior. While many psychologists specialize in mental health, others concentrate on the study of perception, physiology, hypnosis, dreams, or learning. These seemingly diverse topics are all part of behavior and, therefore, part of psychology.

Many people think that psychology is all Sigmund Freud, couches, and therapy. While Freud and therapy are an important part of psychology, they are only one relatively small aspect. Psychology is the science of all behavior, animal and human. This book is a survey of psychology with each chapter considering a different aspect of psychological investigation. It is important to remember that psychologists, because they are scientists, try to examine behavior through carefully controlled research methods. To discuss this in a clear and direct way, a whole new vocabulary of terms will be used, many of which will be a part of most readers' everyday language by the time they finish reading this book. As you go through the text, it will be crucial to keep in mind that the central goal of psychologists is to understand behavior. This is really the challenge of psychology: to *understand* behavior with all of its facets. This means understanding what people feel, think, and do, and why they respond to the world as they do. Behavior is not always directly observable; the psychologist must understand thinking processes, emotions, and motivations as well. This is no easy task, and many theories and explanations have been devised to explain all of these aspects of behaviors. As you study these different approaches to behavior, try to evaluate them and decide if they help give people an understanding of behavior and how people cope with life and respond to its demands. For most of us the day-to-day adaptations are fairly simple; yet, we know that for some people such changes take a heavy toll. The psychologist's task is to study behavior with the goal of understanding it; in doing so they can help individuals learn how to cope better with the demands of living.

Since psychologists study behavior to understand *why* people behave the way they do and *how* they behave the way they do, the goals of psychology are to measure and describe behavior in a scientific manner. By being careful observers psychologists can eventually predict behavior and help people to manage it; prediction and management go hand-in-hand. Psychologists would like to be able to manage the rate at which people learn new information; similarly, they would like to help people better manage the way they handle their aggressive behaviors. Guiding behavior is also important in the mental health fields; a psychologist may try to manage the behavior of a person who is having emotional problems or is severely disturbed. For example, a seriously depressed student may be threatening to jump out of a dormitory window. If a psychologist knows the appropriate things to say to help change this person's behavior, then the study of psychology is clearly worthwhile. To help people cope effectively, a psychologist first needs to be able to predict that certain behaviors will occur.

Equally important to being able to help people cope more effectively with life is the goal of helping people help themselves. Psychologists study behav-

Behavior Every aspect of an organism's actions including thought, emotional, and physical activities; some of these actions may not be directly observable.

Psychology The science of behavior.

ior and try to predict difficult situations so as to teach people how to help manage their own behavior. People often need to learn to express sadness when they are sad; they need to learn to shout and let their feelings out in manageable and reasonable ways. Psychologists try to teach people to manage their behavior effectively to make their lives happier and more meaningful.

WHAT IS A PSYCHOLOGIST?

Psychologist One who studies behavior and uses behavior principles in scientific research or in applied settings for the treatment of emotional problems. Psychologists have advanced graduate training and usually hold Master's and PhD degrees.

Everyone knows a little bit about behavior and what makes people tick, but not all are called psychologist. A **psychologist** studies behavior and uses behavioral principles in scientific research or in settings which make direct use and application of this knowledge, for example, in a mental health center. Typically, psychologists are university graduates who continue their education toward a Master's degree; most psychologists then study for four or five years toward a PhD (Doctor of Philosophy). Very often, psychologists have additional training for a year or two in a particular area. Psychologists have training in research and acquiring knowledge, and they generally specialize in some area and confine their research and applied interests to that area. With all of this specialized training in one area of psychology, researchers are able to provide the scientific community and individuals with reliable data. The data can then be used to make accurate statements and predictions about the likelihood of certain situations and how people are apt to respond.

Psychiatrist A medical doctor who has done a residency to study behavior and treats patients with emotional and physical problems.

Many people do not know the difference between a psychologist and a psychiatrist. **Psychiatrists** are physicians, medical doctors. Like all physicians, psychiatrists attend undergraduate school, medical school, and do an internship; then they generally do a residency in psychiatry and specialize in the treatment of disturbed behavior. Psychiatrists and psychologists often have different approaches to behavior problems. Psychiatrists often see patients who have medical problems in conjunction with emotional problems. They usually treat the mentally disturbed who are in hospitals and in need of medication. Psychologists usually treat such individuals as well; they focus on patients' psychological disturbances. They do this alongside a physician who treats a patient's medical problems. In mental hospitals it is common to see physicians, psychologists, and other mental health practitioners working side-by-side and with one another. In contrast to psychiatrists' training and practice, psychologists generally have had more extensive experience in testing, evaluating, and treating emotional disturbances and in addition they must be trained in research. A psychiatrist may have had little research experience with behavior problems. This is an important distinction because psychologists are researchers and consider research one of their most important activities. Regardless of the area within which a psychologist specializes, the discipline's focus on research is usually apparent. New research findings are constantly updating psychologists' conceptions of behavior. The experiments that are necessary in this research run the full gamut of human behavior; some studies deal with the treatment of emotional disorders and how this should best be done, while others deal with techniques such as how to teach children with reading difficulties to use a dictionary.

Psychoanalyst One who has studied the technique of psychoanalysis (usually a psychiatrist) and uses it as a primary method of treating emotional problems.

Most psychiatrists and psychologists are not psychoanalysts. A **psychoanalyst** is generally a psychiatrist who has gone on for additional study using a very specific approach to treating emotional problems, that is, psychoanalysis. Psychoanalysis involves special techniques, including the study of unconscious motivation and dream analysis, and often requires many years of daily sessions of therapy. The use of the term psychoanalyst must be restricted only to those people who have been trained to use the technique.

For a person seeking therapy, the choice of a psychiatrist or a psychologist is usually determined by availability and the type of problem that a person has. If a person is having emotional problems, then the practitioner of choice should be the psychologist. In treating emotional problems, the psychologist has generally had more extensive training and experience. As will be discussed in chapter 13, when group therapy, marital therapy, and extensive testing are involved, psychologists are usually sought out. When most people think of obtaining some type of help for emotional problems, they often first think of a psychiatrist rather than a psychologist. It is important to evaluate these two types of practitioners; as you will see, psychologists look at behavior somewhat differently than psychiatrists. Psychiatrists and psychologists are both important mental health practitioners, but the medical approach of psychiatrists involves certain assumptions about behavior which the psychologist may not necessarily accept. Trained first as physicians, psychiatrists adopt a view of maladjustment that is quite different from their usually better trained psychological counterpart, the psychologist. This issue will be discussed again in chapter 12.

WHAT PSYCHOLOGISTS DO

Psychologists are not just concerned with the treatment of emotional disturbances. Some psychologists do see clients who are in need of emotional help, but some are totally engaged in research, while still others are teaching. A survey of the American Psychological Association showed that 33% of its members were clinical psychologists, and an additional 23% were in the fields of community, counseling, and school psychology. So, all together 56% of the membership of the American Psychological Association were in the human service fields that deal with helping people cope (Boneau & Cuca, 1974; Gottfredson & Dyer, 1978). As can be seen from Figure 1.1, the remaining 44% of psychologists are involved in research and teaching.

Human Service Fields 56%

CLINICAL PSYCHOLOGY. Clinical psychologists specialize in helping clients who are experiencing behavior problems. These clients may be exhibiting anxiety or fear, or may be having trouble adjusting to the stress of living, home, and family. Most clinical psychologists counsel clients in private practice or at a hosptial, mental institution, or social service agency. Clinical psychologists give psychological tests, interview potential clients, and treat emotional problems by psychological means. Many clinicians are employed by universities and help patients with psychological problems. In this setting they often continue their research into the causes of normal and abnormal behavior. Presently, of all areas in psychology, there are more job opportunities in clinical psychology than in any other area.

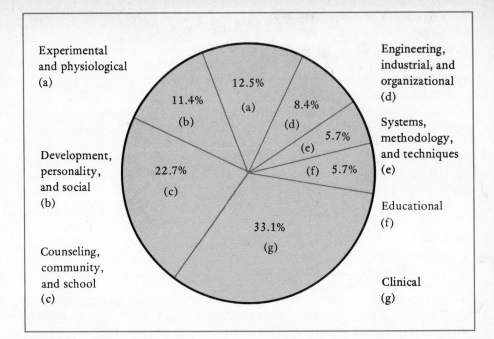

Figure 1.1 Where do psychologists work? The pie chart shows the relative number of psychologists (PhDs and MAs) in different areas of psychology

— less serious nature

COUNSELING PSYCHOLOGY.   Like a clinical psychologist, a counseling psychologist works with people who have emotional problems, but the problems are often of a less serious nature. A person might seek the help of a counseling psychologist for information about vocational rehabilitation, choice of jobs, or adjustment to a new life-style. While clinical psychologists are often in private practice, counseling psychologists usually work for mental health agencies, hospitals, and universities. Many colleges and universities have counseling bureaus for their students to help them adjust to a university atmosphere and to provide vocational and educational guidance. Like clinical psychologists, many counseling psychologists often continue their research into the causes and treatment of maladjustment.

COMMUNITY PSYCHOLOGY.   Community psychology is a relatively new area and generally focuses on community mental health. Community psychologists work for mental health agencies, state governments, and private organizations. They help the community and its institutions adjust to problems and try to find answers. For example, a community psychologist might be concerned with establishing outpatient mental health treatment centers in rural communities. A community psychologist might also be involved in analyzing the misuse of drugs or in proposing a program of drug rehabilitation. The evaluation of current programs as well as their redirection has developed into a focus of community psychology.

SCHOOL PSYCHOLOGY.   School psychologists work in educational systems. Their role is to establish a relationship among parents, teachers, administrators, and other psychologists. A school psychologist provides information to teachers and parents about a student's progress and counsels them on how to help the student and the faculty do a better job. Many school psychologists feel that their job is to help students, teachers, parents, and others understand each other.

Experimental psychology is the other major subfield of psychology. Experimental psychologists are concerned with the basic processes involved in behavior. For example, an experimental psychologist may be interested in visual perception or with how individuals learn language or solve problems. Experimental psychology is not a single area but is really made up of areas that overlap with fields of specialization outside of psychology.

Because behavior is so complex, some psychologists feel that to understand it, they should first study simple elements of behavior which can be examined in animals as well as humans. Many of these psychologists study the behavior of animals and generalize the behavior principles they observe to human beings. Sometimes those who work with animals are concerned with the physiological processes underlying behavior; they examine the nature of the nervous system and how it is related to behavior. A psychologist who works with animals might be concerned with the learning process; rats, pigeons, and a variety of other species might be placed in situations where they are required to learn certain tasks. Psychologists who study learning hope to use these studies to find some of the basic principles of learning in order to apply them to human learning.

Psychologists who work with human **subjects** are often concerned with the same processes as those who use animals. However, they frequently require their subjects to perform different tasks. Learning psychologists who use humans as subjects look at more complex tasks. They often try to study the methods by which humans learn or the way humans remember information as compared with the way animals do.

To some extent, the use of animals rather than humans in research studies is a convenience for isolating some simple aspect of behavior and eliminating all of the complex distractions that arise in human subjects. Testing animals allows for carefully controlled situations, and in some studies, an examination of the previous health of the animals after they die. Animals generally have a shorter life span than humans; this enables a researcher to study completely one or more generations in a relatively short period of time. A researcher can better control the life history of an animal than a human. Furthermore, animal behavior is intrinsically interesting. Whether psychologists work with animals or humans, their aim is the same: to find the basic components of behavior and to understand them. Animal and human behaviors have great similarities and differences. By studying how both animals *and* humans react under different circumstances, psychologists can gain insight into the basic principles of behavior.

There are a number of other subfields of psychology. For example, *developmental psychologists* are concerned with the changes that take place in organisms as they develop from conception to death. *Social psychologists* are concerned with attitude formation, the behavior of groups, and aggression. *Educational psychologists* are concerned with how learning proceeds in the classrooms. Increasing production and keeping good management-labor relations are a focus of *industrial psychologists.* These are just a few of the increasing number of subspecialties growing within the psychological domain.

Many people may not have realized the wide range of activities in which psychologists are involved. Many of these activities and areas of study are usually not thought of as psychological. By the end of this text you will see that all aspects of behavior are part of psychology. For example, it is impor-

Subject An individual who participates in an experiment and from whose behavior data are collected.

A psychologist studies all ages and all stages in a human life, from infancy through old age. A psychologist studies the development of the infant. . . .

. . . and the further growth, mental and emotional, of the child.

tant to understand the biology of hormones, chemicals that dramatically affect behavior. Therefore, to understand why people act the way they do, we have to know a little about a lot of seemingly unrelated topics. To really understand behavior, we have to be aware of all kinds of activities.

PSYCHOLOGY YESTERDAY AND TODAY

When a young individual is having trouble coping with a changing social role, it is fairly easy to see that behavior is affected by many things. He or she is undergoing physical growth changes and has been influenced by parents, peer group, and religious upbringing. If we wish to use psychology to help, we have to examine all of these aspects of the situation. A psychologist trying

Choosing a Therapist

Many people who experience emotional disorders are hesitant to seek help because of misconceptions and lack of knowledge about the kinds of therapists who are available. The idea of going to a "shrink" suggests images of forbidding medical figures who might analyze, dissect, and diagnose. In reality, there is a wide variety of people who can provide emotional help to people desiring it. Counselors, psychologists, and psychiatrists all provide therapy and counseling to troubled individuals. When a person is having trouble coping with the everyday demands of life, home, or family, he or she often seeks out the help of a professional. Yet, a bewildering array of people can provide therapy. Choosing among these therapists can be difficult, but there are a few guidelines.

College students can usually seek the help of a therapist through a psychological service center located on their campus, or perhaps through a counseling bureau. If these centers do not have appropriate facilities, staff members can usually refer a student to appropriate qualified mental health professionals. In larger cities, the community at large can seek the help of therapists through the outpatient branch of hospitals; many of today's best mental health centers are outpatient divisions of psychiatry departments of medical centers. The telephone directory will also contain a list of people who provide therapy services, usually referred under psychologists or psychiatrists.

Sallie Adams, a member of Ralph Nader's health research group, has written a consumers' guide to therapy called *Through the Mental Health Maze.* While this report on the status of mental health services and how to find them has been highly criticized, it does provide some guidelines for finding therapy in your community and deciding if a therapist is a competent and well-trained individual. No one wants to be treated by a quack. A therapist should have training from an accredited institution of higher learning. A friend or relative can act as a therapist but is not trained to provide mental health services.

Even after choosing a therapist a person should be relatively cautious. It is reasonable to ask what the therapist hopes to achieve and how he or she hopes to achieve it. As you will learn as you read this text, there are a variety of therapies available that vary significantly in approach.

A warning: If you don't like your therapist or the way he or she is treating you, speak up. You are paying for those services and have the right to evaluate them and to discontinue therapy in the same way that you have the right to evaluate the services of a painter, carpenter, or teacher.

---

to help such a person realizes the young individual's development, motivation, and learning experiences, as well as members of the family, must be considered. Psychologists have recognized that people's biological makeup is important, their early experiences are important, and their current life situation is important as well. As the study of psychology developed, the complex interplay of people's biological heritage and their life's experiences has come into sharp focus. Researchers have become especially aware that one's biological heritage and one's experiences affect day-to-day behavior. You will see as we study psychology that these two co-determinants of behavior are in a delicate balance with one another; they are mutually dependent.

When a person comes to a psychologist for help in coping with an emotional situation, the psychologist considers the full range of variables that might be affecting current situations, biological and environmental variables. Such a thorough evaluation of a person's background was not always considered necessary, appropriate, or within the domain of psychology. Psychology has undergone vast changes in the last century.

The formal discipline of psychology did not exist until the late 1800s. Until that time, any psychological question was considered within the realm of philosophy, medicine, or theology. However, as understanding of how the body functions developed, the importance of the brain in managing behavior became evident.

A psychologist studies also the adolescent and the mature adult, at work . . .

. . . at play . . .

Structuralism School of psychology founded by Wilhelm Wundt (1832–1920) who believed the proper subject matter of psychology was the study of the contents of consciousness. Structuralists developed and used the technique of introspection.

Introspection The technique of examining the contents of one's mind through self-report and careful examination of what one is thinking and feeling.

Functionalism School of psychology which grew out of structuralism and was concerned with how and why the conscious mind works the way it does.

As groups of scientists gathered to exchange ideas about behavior, true psychological investigations were beginning. More often than not, psychologists at the turn of the century adopted a specific approach toward the study of behavior. For example, the first widely accepted approach was presented by Wilhelm Wundt (1832–1920). Wundt founded the **structuralist** school and the first psychological laboratory in 1879 at Leipzig, Germany. Wundt and his followers considered the proper subject matter of psychology to be the study of the contents of consciousness. Rather than looking at the broad range of behavior that psychologists consider today, Wundt tried to study the contents of the mind through self-examination of what one is thinking and feeling. This process is called **introspection**. The focus of Wundt and these early psychologists was really quite limited by today's standards, and they made little headway in describing the nature of people's behavior.

By and large, the early psychologists were in a constant state of change, so it didn't take long for a new school of thought to develop. One new school developed around the concept of **functionalism,** which was an outgrowth of structuralism that was concerned not only with the contents of consciousness but also with the "how and why" the brain works the way it does. While the functionalists, like the structuralists, also used introspection, they were closer in approach to modern psychologists because they tried to understand the "hows and whys" of behavior. One of the better known functionalists of the day was William James (1842–1910).

. . . and in love.

Structuralist   Functionalism   psychoanalysis

Three founding fathers of modern psychology: (*left*) Wilhelm Wundt (1832–1920); (*center*) William James (1842–1910); (*right*) Sigmund Freud (1856–1939).

At the same time, other approaches to psychology were developing in Europe and the United States. These different ways of looking at behavior presented still other vantage points. For example, practitioners of **Gestalt psychology** looked not at conscious experience but at the process of perception and analyzing the world in terms of a perceptual framework. Eventually Gestalt psychology became a major influence in the field of perception.

Although most psychologists at this time were not concerned with a person's emotional troubles, psychoanalytic theory came about from efforts to help people cope with personal problems. Sigmund Freud (1856–1939) developed an approach to help people who were overcome with anxiety; this approach was called **psychoanalysis.** Psychoanalysts use techniques such as free association to thoughts and dream interpretation to unravel unconscious experiences. Psychoanalysts were far more concerned with the treatment of emotional disturbances than with the functioning of the brain.

As the discipline of psychology was developing, dramatically different approaches were being used simultaneously. Structuralists, Gestaltists, and psychoanalysts felt that they had little in common, but this really was not the

Gestalt psychology School of psychology which argues that behavior cannot be studied in parts but must be viewed as an interdependent whole.

Psychoanalysis A technique used by trained individuals to help people cope with personal problems by overcoming anxiety. This theory and technique were developed by Sigmund Freud (1856–1939), who was concerned with how the personality develops.

Gestalt psychologists argue that behavior cannot be studied in parts but must be viewed as an interdependent whole

case. All were concerned with the workings of the brain, or as they called it, the mind. All were concerned <u>not so much with observable behavior</u>, but with|private perceptions|and|conscious or unconscious activities|

In contrast with many of the psychologists of his day, John B. Watson (1878–1958) led a new movement and approach that became the cornerstone of modern American psychology: **behaviorism.** Like the functionalists, Watson argued that the private contents of consciousness were not appropriate for psychologists. As a behaviorist, he argued that the proper subject matter of psychology is overt behavior. Introspection is a waste of time; each individual's conscious experience is different and this is not the way to measure and describe behavior. Watson's method was to observe the type of stimuli that brought about different behaviors. However, Watson overreacted to Wundt's introspection theory; he argued that *only* actions or overt performances can be objectively observed and measured. Watson served as the founder of a major school of psychology that considered|only measurable stimuli and responses| The approach of behaviorism has been extended and further developed by Harvard psychologist B. F. Skinner. As a modern psychologist Skinner has attempted to explain the causes of behavior by cataloging and describing the relationships between stimuli and responses. The old philosophical questions and techniques have been excluded by such behaviorists. <u>Modern American psychology is rooted in principles of|behaviorism|</u> Even so, by the 1940s there was a distinct division between behaviorists and nonbehaviorists. In many ways this division still exists today (Fodor, 1981).

In studying behavior, psychologists have searched for explanations; they have sought to understand why people act in characteristic ways and what the factors are that make people unique as well as similar to one another. In the history of psychology there are some psychologists who have taken a view that has favored learning and environmental experiences as the princi-

John B. Watson (1878–1958), the founder of behaviorism.

Behaviorism School of psychology that rejects the notion that the proper subject of psychology is the contents of consciousness and argues instead that psychology can only describe and measure what is observable, either directly or through the use of instruments.

Figure 1.2 In extreme forms of behaviorism, the idea that cognitive or thought processes enter into behavior is excluded. The strict behaviorist considers the behavior of an organism to be its response to a stimulus; psychology is to catalogue the relationship between stimuli and responses (Fodor, 1981)

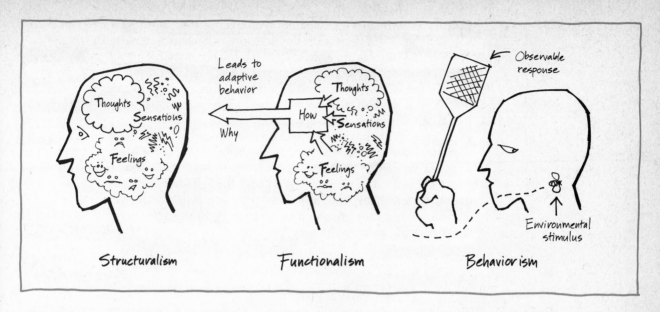

Structuralism   Functionalism   Behaviorism

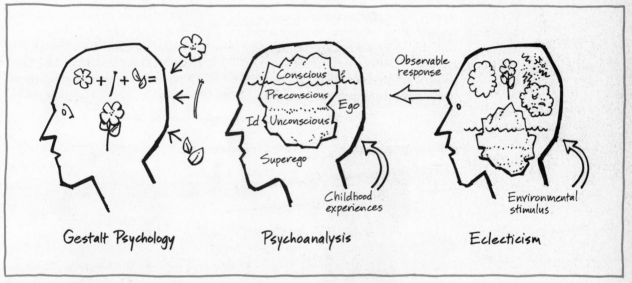

Gestalt Psychology   Psychoanalysis   Eclecticism

Each of the various schools of psychology has a special and unique focus.

pal determinants of behavior. At the same time, other psychologists have been especially sensitive to the role of heredity and the biological variables that might be responsible for certain behavior patterns. As the study of behavior has grown more sophisticated, psychologists have realized that there is a complex relationship between biological and environmental influences. They have recognized that a person's biological heritage sets the foundation for future learning experiences; in addition, they have realized that through the course of development many situations can occur which may modify an established or about-to-be established set of behaviors.

When we study the history of psychology, we see that the focus of individual psychologists has shifted. Initially, psychologists studied the mind; later, psychologists studied only overt behavior. While Gestalt psychologists were studying conscious perceptions, psychoanalysts were examining unconscious thought processes. Recognizing the complex interplay of the po-

Eclecticism The combining of theories, facts, or techniques. This term usually describes the practice in clinical psychology of using whatever therapy techniques are appropriate for an individual client rather than relying only on the techniques of a particular branch of psychology.

tential determinants of behavior has been a developing process; in many ways, this process has been the maturing of psychology as a discipline.

Modern American psychologists have been heavily influenced by behaviorism. Watson's behaviorism has been modified, and in its newer forms it is used in the laboratory as well as with patients who are in need of emotional help. Psychology in the United States has been influenced by all of the traditional schools of psychology. Today, there are practicing psychoanalysts, there are strict behaviorists, and Gestalt psychology still thrives in some laboratories. Most modern American psychologists are **eclectic;** they are willing to use a variety of different approaches toward data, theory, and therapy. This is a great step for psychology and the human condition. Psychologists are no longer restricting themselves to one aspect of behavior or one approach; rather, they are using many avenues of investigation to find out what makes people behave the way they do.

HOW PSYCHOLOGISTS STUDY BEHAVIOR

The study of behavior is a systematic one that tries to consider all of the potential aspects of a situation that might cause an organism to behave the way it does. If we were to observe a college student engaged in deep concentration and note taking in the library, we might assume that the student was writing a term paper. Or, she might be involved in preparing for an exam. But she might be employed by some faculty member and be collecting background information on some important event in history. The possibility

A psychologist studies animal behavior to reveal human behavior . . .

even exists that the individual is researching her hobby, antique furniture. Just by observing behavior we cannot be appraised of all of the potential components and motivations that are involved. Only one obvious fact emerges from our observation of the library note taker and that is that she was actively studying and taking notes; we can infer little else.

Psychologists try to gather systematic data about behavior, even note-taking behavior, so as to be able to predict behavior in certain given instances. The mere association of some events with others does not establish any facts other than showing a relationship. Two events show a relationship if when the probability of one event increases, the probability of the other also changes. For example, there is a relationship between a person's height and weight; as height increases, so does weight, generally. Similarly, there is a relationship between use of narcotic drugs, like heroin, and crime; this relationship shows that people who use narcotic drugs are far more likely to be involved in crime than those who are not using such drugs. A person's height does not cause him to weigh more, for there are very thin tall people who weigh far less than some obese short people. In the same manner, the use of narcotic drugs does not by itself cause someone to be a criminal. It is very likely that expensive drug use necessitates theft for some people to raise money, but the actual drug addiction does not *cause* the crime. When such relationships exist, we say that a correlation exists. We will be discussing correlation later in this chapter.

. . . human work to reveal human motivation . . .

While psychologists are concerned with finding relationships between certain characteristics of people and behavior, they are far more concerned with finding the cause of those relationships. This is usually far more easily said than done. Some social and behavioral patterns are hard to pin down and establish an exact cause for. There are so many social, political, and economic reasons for many of people's problems that finding *the* cause is sometimes impossible. Psychologists then rely on strong relationships. When these relationships occur repeatedly from person to person, psychologists are far more likely to believe that there may be a real cause-and-effect situation.

A primary aim of psychological research, then, is to gather systematic and reliable knowledge about behavior which shows strong and regular relationships. Armed with such reliable data psychologists can apply and use this knowledge in therapy and counseling to help clients who are experiencing emotional difficulty. Finding such reliable knowledge is not easy; researchers have to use carefully planned methods and very specialized techniques. In the same way that many physical diseases have been conquered in the hospital, researchers have attempted to explore behavior systematically in the laboratory through carefully controlled experimentation.

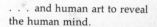

. . . and human art to reveal the human mind.

There are other important and useful techniques in addition to the laboratory experiment. Each of these techniques is useful because it allows the psychologists to make some reliable statements about the subjects involved. However, none of the statements can be *cause*-and-*effect* statements. For example, we may find that children from broken homes have more emotional problems than children who do not come from broken homes; the researcher can state this fact. It is most likely that broken homes provide an atmosphere that is conducive to emotional stress and turbulence in the child and in later years this stress leads to greater emotional crises. However, the researcher is not able to draw any such causal statement from his data; he is not able to say that broken homes cause emotional disturbances later in life. *why?*

Research Can Solve Important Day-to-Day Problems

As with any discipline, when we look closely at psychology we find a number of subareas and specialities. Even though these areas are quite divergent, all of these specialities look at behavior and use scientific methods for their examination. The way psychologists go about using the scientific method is, of course, through research. Psychologists conduct research to further understand behavior, to explain why and under what circumstances it occurs, as well as to solve a number of real problems. Let us take a closer look at some problems, and in doing so, we can see how wide a range of behaviors psychologists observe. At the same time, we can see some of the methods these psychologists use.

Problem #1

Obesity is a difficult problem for Americans. More and more people are overweight; this is one of the contributing causes of heart disease and strokes. The overweight person has long been known to eat too much and too often; this is in part due to internal physiological conditions like hunger and in part due to psychological and emotional reasons.

Since eating behavior involves both physiological and psychological aspects, it is a question perfectly suited for psychological investigation. Some psychologists have monitored eating behavior to see how often and how much the obese eat compared to normal thin people. These studies have shown that the obese eat not only more often, but they also eat more at individual eating session.

Schachter (1971) has reported a series of studies in which experimenters manipulated cues such as the presence or absence of food. In one study subjects were in a room with food, and a clock on the wall was made to work faster so that it seemed as if more time had passed than really had. So, if 1 hour had passed, the clock showed 2 hours passing. Obese subjects who were exposed to the fast clock ate more and sooner than obese subjects exposed to the normal slow clock or than normal thin people. These are some experimental evidence to show that these obese subjects were eating in response to the clock on the wall, not to internal physiological factors. Eating behavior and studies like the one just described will be discussed in Chapter 4 on Motivation.

Problem #2

A bank teller has been arrested in New York City; he has just murdered his wife, two children, and a neighbor. The court has referred him for psychological testing because it feels that he may be experiencing emotional problems and his behavior may be a result of his severe emotional disturbance. The court asks psychologists to decide if this person knew what he was doing and is responsible for his behavior.

"Not guilty by reason of insanity" is frequently the judgment of a court of law. Judges and juries have taken the word of professional psychologists that an individual in question may not be responsible for his or her own behavior. Psychologists make these decisions through a long process of psychological evaluation. First, the person is interviewed. This is often extensive interviewing lasting for an hour or two each day for 2 or 3 weeks. Second, the person is tested. This includes personality tests, tests of intelligence, achievement, and motivation, and tests of the ability to perceive reality. After all of these data are collected, analyzed, and interpreted, psychologists can report to the court with some degree of accuracy whether the person on trial is aware of the difference between right and wrong and to what extent the crime is a direct consequence of emotional disturbance.

Problem #3

Your ability to learn about psychology may be determined by what you ate for breakfast this morning! For years nutritionists have been arguing that breakfast is the most important meal of the day. The impact of this

Correlation A measure of the degree of a relationship between two variables; it expresses how changes in one variable relate to changes in the other. A correlation is expressed in terms of the correlation coefficient, which varies in extent from −1 to +1.

Many research techniques provide data showing **correlations** or relationships between two variables. We are constantly bombarded with correlations. There are correlations between educational level and money earned in a lifetime, between IQ scores and race, between height and weight, between eye and hair color. Although there is a correlation between IQ scores and race, this correlation does not say that because a person is of a particular race, his or her IQ score is high or low. The low IQ may be because of educational

idea has recently been felt in the classroom because psychologists and physicians are suspecting that certain behavioral and learning problems may be caused by what we eat.

In classrooms there have always been children whose behavior has been disruptive to teachers and other more serious students. Frustrated by these students, teachers often place them apart from the other children and frequently discipline them. In the past decade or two researchers have found that some of these children are suffering from a behavioral problem called hyperactivity. Hyperactivity describes a group of behavioral symptoms including restlessness, inability to concentrate, inattention, and seemingly boundless energy. At first psychologists thought these children were emotionally disturbed, but subsequent investigations have shown that at least some of these children can be treated by controlled diets and drugs. (In chapter 6, one such study is presented. In chapter 3, techniques are discussed to help modify some of the more specific outbursts in a classroom.) Some researchers are claiming that the intake of certain substances in excessive amounts may account for hyperactivity. For example, a diet too high in sugar and too low in protein may play a contributing role in hyperactivity. The results are not yet in, but initial research efforts suggest that for some children at least a change in diet brings about a change in behavior.

Problem #4

Many psychological researchers have taken on the challenge of finding out how children learn to think, talk, and develop intellectually. In studying language development some researchers have recorded the verbal output of children from birth to age 4, tape recording everything that children say. Later they take these tapes and try to analyze if there is any meaningful pattern in the way speech develops. As will be shown in chapters 6 and 8, such efforts have proven very fruitful.

Other researchers have focused on intellectual development and asked how and when children can develop certain thinking abilities. For example, when can a child best be taught to read? Can we teach a newborn to read? Decidedly not, but why? Psychologists have found that a certain readiness factor has to develop before a child can be taught to read. Once this ability to read matures, then teaching a child to read is relatively easy. Before then it is relatively impossible.

As with intellectual development, researchers have found that certain kinds of social development occur at fairly typical ages and stages of development. These insights have helped shape child guidance books and provided insight for parents so they can encourage their children's social development.

Problem #5

How can a child who has temper tantrums be treated? Many children learn at an early age that their parents are fairly easy to manipulate. Sometimes just a short bout of crying produces the desired results; sometimes it takes yelling, screaming, kicking, and throwing themselves down on the ground to get what they want. Children use these manipulations, and learning psychologists provide some insight as to how these behaviors are learned; even more important, they can provide information on how to "unlearn" them.

Early research attempts in helping children eliminate tantrumlike behavior came from the laboratory and studies of animals. Psychologists found that when animals were not rewarded they stopped exhibiting certain behaviors. If the researchers started rewarding the behaviors, then they occurred again. If tantrums are rewarded by a parent giving in to the child's insistent wishes, it is likely that the tantrums will continue. By contrast, researchers argue if parents do not give in to tantrums, and thus stop rewarding them, they will eventually decrease in intensity and disappear. Here data from the laboratory have been applied directly to the home.

level achieved, discrimination, or a myriad of other variables. There is a positive correlation between heroin addiction and frequency of marijuana use during teenage years. This correlation only says that heroin addicts have smoked marijuana. The correlation does not imply that smoking marijuana causes heroin addiction. Correlation data are important; however, they are often misinterpreted by nonpsychologists and are used to make causal and inferential statements. Such inferences are very tempting, but inappropriate.

A correlation shows a relationship but it *does not* show cause and effect as an experiment can.

When psychologists study behavior and suggest that some situation *causes* another, they attempt to make accurate conclusions. In such attempts they are extremely careful to evaluate the type of data they have collected, how they have been collected, and if the phenomenon under study is repeatable. Researchers have tried to be sure that differences they find among people or behaviors are significant differences. The term *significant difference* has a special meaning for a psychologist; it refers to the likelihood that a behavior has not occurred by chance alone. In the next section and in the appendix (p. 675) you will see that psychologists try to create situations in which they can limit the likelihood that a result is a chance occurrence. They do this in a number of ways. They study a specialized topic; they focus on different aspects of a problem separately. Then they often examine competing or alternative explanations to rule out other possibilities. The setting for the development of ideas and the ruling out of other ones is usually in the experiment. It is in the experiment that a researcher can make statements about the probability of an occurrence happening by mere chance; within the experiment the results can be interpreted and extended to other situations.

The Experiment

Experiment A situation in which an observer systematically manipulates certain variables to describe objectively a relationship between the variable of concern and the resulting behavior. Influences about causes and effects can be drawn from well-designed experiments.

Variables The potentially changeable conditions or characteristics of a situation or experiment.

Results are safely interpreted with cause-and-effect statements in a controlled experiment. An **experiment** is a situation in which a researcher systematically manipulates certain variables to describe relationships among them. **Variables** are the characteristics of a situation that can change. Because psychologists are interested in cause-and-effect relationships, psychological journals are full of experimental studies in which certain elements or variables are manipulated. Consider a simple drug such as caffeine, a drug contained in coffee. We might be interested in the effects of this drug (variable) on behavior. The variable that we would manipulate would be the amount of caffeine coffee drinkers have in their bloodstream. Let us conduct a simple experiment. Assume we have two groups of high school students who run a mile and both groups run at about the same speed. We take one group of students and give them an injection of neutral salt water (which has been shown to have no effects on behavior). We take another group of students and give them an injection of caffeine; the amount of caffeine is equivalent to three cups of coffee. We know that caffeine is a stimulant, so the hypothesis of our experiment is that students who are given caffeine will run faster than students who have not been given caffeine. Both groups had injections of a substance and both have probably had similar experiences previous to the experiment. The results show that the students who were given the injection of caffeine were able to run the mile 25 seconds faster than the students who were given the neutral salt water injections. In our experiment we feel justified in concluding that caffeine acts as a stimulant for someone running the mile. Figure 1.3 depicts the results of such an experiment.

A similar experiment might be to test the effect of the lack of sleep on the speed with which students can respond to a light. The student's task is to push a button as quickly as possible when a light is flashed on. He sleeps in the laboratory for four successive nights and is allowed to sleep only 8 hours each night. He is tested each morning in a reaction time task. On the fourth day he is allowed to sleep only 4 hours; he is then tested on the reaction time task. Any slowing of reaction time to the light is inferred to be due to sleep deprivation.

One of the most important characteristics of a controlled experiment is that the two groups of individuals being compared are essentially the same before the experiment begins. Knowing that all of the students in our first experiment ran the mile at about the same speed before the experiment began means that they are comparable. By providing one group with a drug and the other with a nondrug, we can assess the effect of this drug on behavior. In a controlled experiment we have manipulated the drug and measured running speed. The strength of the controlled experiment is that it allows us to make direct observation and infer cause-and-effect relationships. The weakness of the controlled experiment is that the experimenter is manipulating the situation. Because the experimenter is involved in the experiment, he or she may contaminate the results.

One of the most important aspects of good experiments is that a control group is used for comparison purposes. A **control group** is a group of sub-

Control group In an experiment, the group of subjects that does not receive the treatment under investigation and that is used for purposes of comparison.

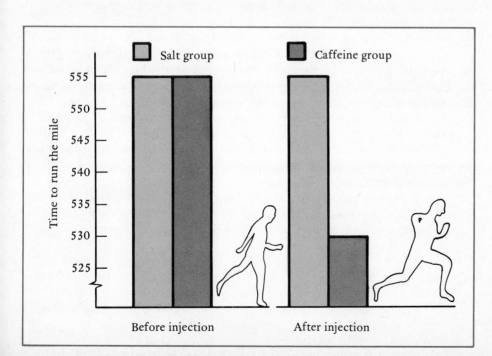

Figure 1.3 How a control group is used. When injected with a salt solution, control-group subjects showed no change in their time to run the mile. By contrast, experimental group subjects injected with caffeine decreased their running time by 25 seconds

The dependent variable is the behavior measured in an experiment

Experimental group In an experiment, the group of subjects that receives the treatment under investigation.

jects who are tested in the same way as the **experimental group** but who have not had a treatment applied to them. Our mile-running high school students were divided into an experimental and a control group. The control group members were given a neutral solution of salt water, which research has shown has no effect on behavior; the experimental group students were given the injection of caffeine. When a difference was found in running speed between the experimental group (caffeine) and the control group (salt water), researchers concluded that differences in running speed had to be due to the variable that the researchers were manipulating, the injection of the caffeine.

Control groups are important because without them few real conclusions can be drawn from data. The high school students who were running the mile needed to be similar in all respects to each other. When comparing these groups it is important that both the experimental and control groups be about the same age, weight, and of the same sex. It is also important that the subjects have had similar experiences before the study began; thus we might try to test only students who came from the same community and belonged to the same church.

Independent variable The variable in an experiment that is directly and purposely manipulated by the experimenter.

The variable that is manipulated from subject to subject in controlled experiments is called the **independent variable.** It is directly and purposely manipulated by the experimenter. Before the study begins, subjects are usually assigned to the different groups, experimental or control, by some arbitrary or chance process. In our mile-running high school students case, the independent variable was whether the drug was given or not. Any effects on running speed that are obtained are assumed to be caused only by this independent variable. All other factors have been controlled, so if there is a difference in running speed, it seems most reasonable that it was caused by the independent variable. The behavior or change in the organism that is being measured is called the **dependent variable.** In our fictitious study the dependent variable was running speed. The effects of providing a drug (independent variable) produce changes in running speed (the dependent variable).

Dependent variable The behavior measured in an experiment to assess whether changes in the independent variable affect the behavior under study.

WHAT MAKES A GOOD EXPERIMENT? A good experiment tests some expectations and provides the experimenter with direct and conclusive evidence as to whether these expectations have been met or not. A good experiment must therefore have a control group with which its observers can compare experimental groups.

For data from an experiment to be considered conclusive, there must be some statistical evidence that the control and experiment groups differ only with respect to the dependent variable. One important consideration is to make sure that the group of subjects is large enough. Assume that there is a 10-second difference between the control and experimental groups in our running study. If we had tested only three students, we would probably not be convinced that this 10-second difference is a real difference. By contrast, if we had tested 2,000 students in the control group and 2,000 students in the experimental group, we would probably be more convinced that any difference in running speed is real. The larger the number of subjects, the more confident we are that an experiment is repeatable and accurate. We make the assumption that if an effect is obtained with a large number of subjects, then it could not be due to mere chance. With only five or six subjects, one subject might show an extreme score; this could change the set of conclusions that might be made. With a large number of subjects (if properly chosen) the chances of one or two people affecting the overall result are small. Our assumption is that with a large sample of subjects they will represent the entire population—not just a couple of extreme individuals. This idea is explored in greater length in the appendix (see p. 680).

Good experiments generally do not depend on just two groups. Most studies in the laboratory are done with several groups, at least one of which is a control group. Other groups being used may have different dosage levels of a drug or several different treatment procedures. For example, in a study of the effect of sleep deprivation on reaction time, there might be a control group and four or five experimental groups, each of which will have to do without sleep for a different length of time. With several experimental groups researchers can examine the effects of these different periods on reaction time. A good experimenter looks at the independent variable and considers such factors as duration or the time without sleep. The shortest duration, perhaps 1 hour, may not have an effect, but moderate and long durations will probably have a dramatic effect. Consider the sleep deprivation–reaction time example. A researcher might find that a short amount of sleep deprivation may have no effect on the subject's reaction time. A slightly longer sleep deprivation may have only a modest effect of slowing reaction time. However, the researcher may find that beyond 2 hours of sleep deprivation, each additional hour produces a great change in reaction time. We thus see that sleep deprivation acts in a way that is especially dependent on the duration of the deprivation (see Figure 1.4 on p. 22). By using several groups, experimenters are able to gain a better idea as to how the independent variable (sleep deprivation) affects reaction time (dependent variable).

There is little debate as to the importance of careful experimentation in scientific research. However, experiments are not the only way to collect data about human behavior. While the experiment—with all of its control and manipulations—allows for cause-and-effect statements, other techniques that show relationships between variables are also important. To review some of these other techniques, let us start with the interview, an in-depth look at a person and his or her problems.

Interviews

An **interview** with a person is a face-to-face meeting in which the psychologist asks a series of standardized question. Responses are either tape-recorded or written by the interviewer. The advantage of an interview over a

Interview A series of open-ended questions used to gather basic and detailed information about a person. Although time consuming, this technique allows a psychologist to probe a potentially important issue or problem in depth.

Figure 1.4 An experimenter can manipulate the number of hours of sleep deprivation among several groups of subjects. The independent variable is, of course, hours of sleep deprivation. The behavior being observed and measured, the dependent variable, is the subjects' average reaction time to respond to a light. By having several groups of subjects a researcher can observe whether changes in the independent variable cause changes in the dependent variable. In this case, a researcher can observe whether each increasing hour of sleep deprivation brings about a similar increase in reaction time. In this hypothetical example we can see that each additional hour of sleep deprivation affected reaction time to a greater and greater extent. Short amounts of sleep deprivation would produce minimal changes. However, many hours of sleep deprivation would produce significantly greater increases

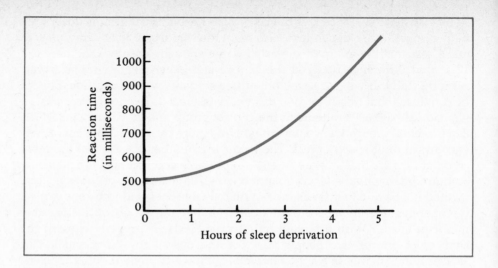

questionnaire approach is that it allows the interviewer to ask additional questions where appropriate. For example, if an interviewer asks a 16-year-old boy, "Have you ever had sexual intercourse?" the boy may respond with bravado, "Sure, lots of times." The interviewer may note this bravado in the boy's tone and instead of just recording the single response may continue to ask him other questions about his sexual experiences. Therefore, the interview approach allows the psychologist to explore fully an area which seems to be in question or particularly important. The bravado of our 16-year-old may even suggest that he has not had as many sexual experiences as he indicated.

Following are some typical questions asked in an interview. Notice how they allow respondents to answer in almost any way they choose. They can be characterized as open-ended questions.

- Describe yourself briefly.
- What does your mother say when she compliments you?
- What nicknames have people called you? What do the names mean?
- What do you want to be at maturity?
- What do you like most about yourself?
- What do you like least about yourself?
- Have you ever been in trouble?
- What was your favorite childhood story?
- How do you think you might die? At what age?
- What would "heaven on earth" be for you?
- If by magic you could change anything about yourself, what would you change?
- What do you want most out of life?
- What is your biggest problem?

Interviews can be anonymous. For example, the interviewer and the client may be in separate rooms and converse through an intercom system. This approach is not used often but can be when anonymity is required. While interviews do have the advantage of providing detailed information on specific areas, they have the weakness of taking a considerable amount of time and gaining a relatively small amount of data.

Questionnaires

While interviews collect in-depth information, they are time-consuming and expensive. But if we sent a survey—or, as it is sometimes called, a **questionnaire**—to all of the students who are enrolled in an elementary psychology course this year, we would probably be talking about over a million people. We might ask each student to list age, sex, weight, previous courses taken, grades in high school, grades in college, SAT scores, number of brothers and sisters, parents' financial status, and a myriad of other questions. From this large survey we could gain a considerable amount of information about what the typical student of psychology is like. We need not confine our questions to data about age, height, and sex; we might ask questions about personal preferences, sexual relations, career goals, and personal likes and dislikes. The advantage of the survey technique is that a large amount of information can be gained from a large number of people in a relatively short time.

Questionnaire A printed form with questions. Usually given to a large group of people, a questionnaire can gather a substantial amount of data in a short amount of time.

One of the aims of surveys and questionnaires is to find if some groups of questions show a relationship. Very often a person's family background or socioeconomic status is related to his or her personal preferences in regard to employment, marital status, and number of children. For example, it might be found that respondents from low socioeconomic status homes tend to have more brothers and sisters. Similarly, children from parents of high socioeconomic status tend to have career goals that lead toward graduate school and professional training. By examining the answers on questionnaires one can gain this kind of information about clusters of traits of individuals.

If the strength of questionnaires is that they gather large amounts of information in a relatively short time, their weaknesses are that they are impersonal and can gather only the information asked in questions. Because the subject's range of responses is limited, relationships may be observed between two facts but no cause-and-effect statements can be drawn from these correlations. No causal relationships can be established from a questionnaire, and questions about a specific person's motivation cannot be asked.

Naturalistic Observation

Probably the simplest way to find out about behavior is to watch it. In **naturalistic observation,** the psychologist tries to record behavior without letting subjects know that they are being observed. When you tell people you are going to observe their drinking, eating, or smoking behavior, they become self-conscious and alter their behavior. In naturalistic observation, the experimenter solves this problem by observing the way people behave in their natural setting. Bird watchers, for example, use naturalistic observation; they watch their birds through telescopes *at a distance*. In fact, many scientists spend a good portion of their lives in the jungles of the world examining the behavior of animals at a distance. One notable example is the work of Jane van Lawick-Goodall, who has spent years in the forests of East Africa observing the behavior of apes. Slowly, almost imperceptibly, van Lawick-Goodall became a part of the environment. Eventually she was approached by the animals as a part of the jungle. She observed the behavior of these apes, making notes about everything they did. In her naturalistic observation studies she did not try to interact with the animals, nor did she try to affect their behavior. The purpose of her studies was to gain information about the way these animals behaved *naturally*.

Naturalistic observation Careful and objective observation of events as they occur in nature, without their experimental control or manipulation.

Baboons Too Use Tools

When scientists want to know the answer to a research question, they use the most appropriate techniques available. In researching the question "Do animals use tools in the same way humans do?" a naturalistic observation study was conducted in East Africa.

SCIENCE NEWS Since 1960, Jane van Lawick-Goodall, a protégé of the late Louis S. B. Leakey, has been studying the behaviors of chimpanzees in their natural habitat. Working in the Gombe National Park in Tanzania, East Africa, van Lawick-Goodall and her husband, photographer Hugo van Lawick, have received wide attention for their descriptive studies of animal behaviors—especially tool-making and tool-use among wild chimpanzees. But the tool-use studies are not confined to chimpanzees. In the journal *Nature* she, her husband, and C. Parker describe two incidents of tool-use by free-living baboons in Gombe National Park.

To feed on the seeds of a certain fruit, baboons must break open a pod in which the seeds are surrounded by a white glutinous juice that dries to a consistency of rubber cement. When this food is in season the hair around the baboons' lips frequently becomes matted by the juice. Usually they attempt to remove the juice by rubbing their mouths against a tree or large rock. One three-year-old female, however, was observed picking up a stone and repeatedly and forcibly rubbing it across her muzzle in an attempt to remove the dried juice.

In a separate incident, an adult male of a different troop cut his lip during a fight. Blood and saliva ran down his chin. When the blood began to coagulate, the baboon looked around, picked up an old piece of corn cob and used it to wipe the blood from his lower lip. "Whilst we cannot draw conclusions from one episode," say the authors, "it is interesting that, although there were several stones nearby, this baboon selected a softer, more porous and generally more suitable material." Some baboons, it seems, have learned to use napkins.

Tool-use, using an object as a functional extension of the hand, claw, mouth, or beak in the attainment of an immediate goal, is not entirely unknown among baboons. Previous researchers have noted that these primates break open hard-shelled fruits with rocks, use stones to squash scorpions before eating them, and use sticks to stir up termite nests. In these reports, however, few details of the behaviors or the conditions under which they were observed are given. The van Lawick-Goodall studies, because of their long-term nature, are able to document the amount of tool-use by baboons and chimpanzees and to view tool-use within the context of a variety of behaviors and situations. "As knowledge is gradually accumulated about a variety of different monkey and ape species," says van Lawick-Goodall, "it is possible to trace certain evolutionary trends of increasing complexity, culminating in man."

Naturalistic observation is not only used to examine the behavior of animals. When people get together in groups, new behavior patterns often emerge. For example, when a riot is taking place, psychologists may try to observe this special type of group behavior. They cannot manipulate the group and suggest that there are too many people of one race compared with another. In the same way, psychologists cannot say that they are only trying to examine the behavior of riots in cities rather than on college campuses. Because they are naturalistic observers, psychologists have to take their riots where and how they find them!

The naturalistic observation approach to collecting data is an important one, but it is a tedious and slow process. In addition, the type of behavior that the psychologist might wish to examine is not always exhibited. The animals might not show mating behavior; the group may not develop a riot. While naturalistic observation has its strengths because the researcher does not contaminate the results, its weakness is that the behavior under investigation may not always be readily evident. It is a slow and tedious process, and variables cannot be manipulated by the psychologist. Thus, like the interview and questionnaire, naturalistic observation does not allow for cause-and-effect statements.

Perhaps no more intensive method for collecting data about a behavior has been devised than the **case study.** This method really has its roots in other disciplines. For example, when we walk into a physician's office for a medical checkup, one of the first things she does is ask for a history. Generally the physician will go all the way back to our childhood and ask about childhood diseases. She then may ask us about any present symptoms of recurring problems that we might be having. After gathering all of this information, she does a physical examination.

A psychologist uses the same approach in the case study method. Typically, the psychologist takes a case history and tries to find out as much about the person's early life as possible. He then asks about symptoms and current problems, and does in-depth interviews. A diagnosis of the person's emotional problems might then be made and a course of treatment suggested.

Sometimes people with emotional problems exhibit seemingly strange types of symptoms. Some people become jittery; others develop nervous tics; still others develop needs to eat or drink. A case study is a report of the specifics of a single individual, and it is an important research tool. The case study can describe in detail the specific problem, symptoms, and method of treatment of a particular individual. While no two people have exactly the same problems or cope with them in precisely the same way, case studies allow researchers to see commonalities among people with similar emotional problems. Ruth Langley, described in the case study to follow (Leon, 1974, pp. 127–128), exhibited ritualistic compulsive behavior typical of a certain kind of maladjustment. We will discuss this specific problem later in chapter 12, but for now, observe how a case study detailed information about how this woman responded to the world:

Ruth Langley was thirty years old when she sought the help of a behavior therapist. She had been in treatment since childhood with a succession of therapists who had used other treatment methods. The client had read about some recent developments in the field of behavior modification, and after a period of indecision, she made an appointment to see Dr. M.

Ruth was extremely thin. She sat rigidly in her chair, with her hands tightly folded, and she maintained an expressionless gaze and tone of voice. She revealed that she was troubled by a longstanding feeling of contamination which compelled her to carry out cleansing activities numerous times each day. She stated that she became intensely uncomfortable if she noticed any dirt on her person or in her immediate environment, and she responded to this feeling by thoroughly washing her hands and arms. If she detected some dirt in her house, she was compelled to completely and methodically scrub her apartment, in addition to showering in a rigidly specified manner. The client reported that she also felt contaminated after going to the bathroom and after doing housework or cooking, and again, she was compelled to thoroughly wash herself.

Ruth complained that her life was extremely restricted because she was spending most of her time engaged in some type of behavior she felt driven to carry out. In addition, each ritual activity was becoming more involved and time consuming. At the time of the interview, she was washing her hands at least three or four times an hour, showering six or seven times a day, and thoroughly cleaning her apartment at least twice a day.

The client was white and came from a Protestant, upper socioeconomic class background. Ruth was unmarried and she lived alone in a studio apartment. She had an independent income which provided her with comfortable financial support, and she spent her free time painting. However, she had done very little art work over the past few years, because her time had been so occupied with the performance of various ritualistic behaviors.

A psychologist's treatment is usually some kind of therapy. In therapy the patient and the psychologist try to explore the individual's problems, understand them, and place them in a reasonable framework so that the client is no longer troubled by the problem. Once a resolution to the problem is achieved, therapy is discontinued. A psychologist writing up a case study reports the history of the individual, the diagnosis, the treatment, and techniques that were used. The case study method is a good way of providing information about a single individual and how his or her treatment proceeded. By examining many case studies one can find certain commonalities in emotional problems and in treatment procedures.

The strength of a case history is that it provides intensive information about an individual, his or her problems, and treatment. The problem with a case study is that it provides information *only* about one individual and his or her unique problem. It is impossible to generalize from one case study to an entire population. The behavior of one person may be like others, but it may be unique to that person. Generalizing from a single person to an entire population is too risky to consider, and psychologists must be very cautious when generalizing even from a large number of case histories.

A Diversity of Approaches

Five important ways by which researchers gather information about behavior have been presented along with their strengths and weaknesses. These research methods produce data and research reports. They do not bring about instant applications in mental hospitals or classrooms. In reading through each of the chapters of this text, it is likely that you will see a wide range of applications for psychology. There will be applications for emotion-

A psychologist deals with both the mind . . .

. . . and the heart.

ally disturbed patients. There will be ways that psychology can be used in the classroom, on the job, and in the treatment of the handicapped. In each chapter of this text, I will present a series of *IMPACT* panels that will highlight some of the applications of psychological studies. You will see that psychology has direct and immediate ways of affecting your daily behavior. Many psychological areas overlap. Perception, motivation, and learning have elements in common. Personality, motivation, and abnormal psychology have common elements. In some cases, overlapping areas have merged and developed new subdisciplines within psychology. In chapter 14 we will consider some of these overlapping subfields, which have emerged as applied disciplines within psychology.

The application of psychology to our everyday lives has not developed quickly or easily. Before actual problems can be solved in meaningful ways, much research and experimentation needs to be done. We do not have all of the answers; in fact, we have not yet defined all of the questions that have to be answered. Psychology is an evolving science. With each new decade, we see new findings, new theories, and reevaluation of older theories and findings. The development of new theories and explanations is dependent upon conducting new research and collecting new data.

The process of collecting data carefully is a slow one. Research must be repeated to ensure that the findings are reliable. Even then, after the research is published and read by professionals, possible applications are used cautiously at first and with small numbers of people. Overzealous researchers sometimes wish that more direct applications could be tested in the real world sooner than they are, but good research stands the test of time and rigorous scientific testing. Like the laws of physics, if they are orderly and regular, the laws of behavior will unfold and be scrutinized experimentally for years to come. The laws of behavior are not simple and so easily stated. Behavior is complex, and no single law, rule, or theory is going to explain how each person behaves at all times. However, each chapter of this text examines a different aspect of human behavior and tries to present some of the basic components that describe how and why people behave the way they do.

SUMMARY

Often when people come to a psychologist they are looking for help. Why might a psychologist be a better choice than a minister or physician and in what situations? The most likely answer is that psychologists have a wide range of skills and ways of dealing with emotional problems; they have studied motivation, emotion, learning, and development. Psychology covers all aspects of behavior. Even so, every psychologist has a specialty; some treat people with emotional problems, while others focus on studying basic behavioral principles to advance the science of psychology.

Contemporary psychology is not like the psychology of the structuralists. Each of the early schools of psychology adopted a specific point of view toward the mind, but today, even the use of the term *mind* does not fit in with the behavioristic approaches of most psychologists. Psychologists have attempted to adapt modern technology and thinking to the study of behavior through the use of carefully controlled experiments, surveys, and other techniques. More than anything else, psychologists realize that psychology is the study of behavior: everything that people feel, think, and do. No activity can be excluded; all *must* be subject to scientific inquiry. The reflex behavior of a newborn infant is as much a part of psychology as reading disorders, hyperactivity, and mental retardation.

Since behavior is so diverse and varied, many techniques and approaches have been developed to study, treat, and understand behavior. This book divides psychology, perhaps arbitrarily, into 14 chapters, each examining a different aspect of behavior. At first, some areas may not seem related to each other, but all are part of psychology—the science of behavior.

CHAPTER REVIEW

1. Psychology is the science of behavior. Behavior includes everything a person feels, thinks, and does.
2. By carefully studying why, how, and when people behave as they do, psychologists attempt to predict and control behavior.
3. A psychologist is a person who has obtained a graduate degree in psychology, typically a PhD; psychiatrists are medical doctors who have specialized in the treatment of disordered behavior.
4. Fifty-six percent of psychologists in the American Psychological Association are in the human service fields such as clinical, counseling, community, and school psychology.

5. Experimental psychology represents a large group of psychologists whose interests cover a wide range of topics and whose focus is usually teaching and research.

6. Psychology did not appear as a field of study until the mid 1800s, and it has since developed into specific areas of interest.

7. Structuralism, founded by Wundt, was the first school of psychology and the contents of consciousness was its focus of study.

8. Functionalism, with James and others as its spokesmen, stressed *how* and *why* the mind works the way it does.

9. Gestalt psychology was a reaction to structuralism and functionalism; the early Gestalt psychologists studied perception.

10. John B. Watson led the revolt in psychology that was to be called behaviorism. Watson argued that the proper subject matter in psychology was overt actions and behavior.

11. Psychoanalysis, which was developed by Freud, came to be a theory of personality and a treatment procedure to help people to cope with their problems.

12. Psychologists use a number of techniques to help them investigate behavior, including the case study method, naturalistic observation, surveys, questionnaires, interviews, and controlled experiments.

13. The controlled experiment more readily allows an investigator to make cause-and-effect statements. If psychologists are to describe, measure, predict, and control behavior, then they need to be able to indicate what situations *cause* certain behaviors.

14. The variables of an experiment are the conditions or characteristics that can change.

15. The independent variable in an experiment is the variable that is directly and purposefully manipulated by the experimenter.

16. The dependent variable is the behavior measured in an experiment to assess whether changes in the independent variable affect the behavior under study.

17. Psychology represents a diverse group of people all studying different aspects of behavior. Behavior is such a large group of activities that many fields of psychology have developed, each investigating a different aspect of human activity. All of these investigations have as their central theme the study of what people feel, think, and do—their behavior.

SUGGESTIONS FOR FURTHER READING

A career in psychology. American Psychological Association, 1200 17th Street, N.W., Washington, D.C. 20036. A free booklet that can be written for.

BONEAU, C.A. AND CUCA, J.M. An overview of psychology's human resources. *American Psychologist*, 1974, 29, 821–839.

BORING, E.G. *A history of experimental psychology* (2nd ed.). New York: Appleton-Century-Crofts, 1950.

SARBIN, T.R., AND COE, W.C. *The student psychologist's handbook: A guide to sources.* Cambridge, Mass.: Schenkman, 1969.

VAN LAWICK-GOODALL, J. *In the shadow of man.* New York: Dell, 1971.

AS LONG AS WE ARE ALIVE our nervous systems are active; whether we are moving, thinking, or asleep, our bodies are responding to voluntary and involuntary commands. An understanding of the biological bases of behavior is important because the way in which our bodies function dramatically affects our behavior. The purpose of this chapter is to present an overview of how our biology creates a potential for behavior which then affects our daily lives. Genetics, hormones, and physiology are discussed, along with techniques by which we can alter the ways our bodies work.

Biological Bases of Behavior

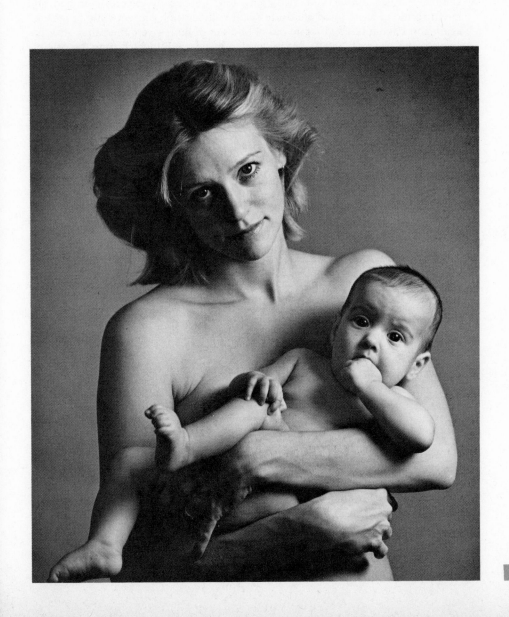

"Bokanovsky's Process," repeated the Director, and the students underlined the words in their little notebooks.

One egg, one embryo, one adult—normality. But a bokanovskified egg will bud, will proliferate, will divide. From eight to ninety-six buds, and every bud will grow into a perfectly formed embryo, and every embryo into a full-sized adult. Making ninety-six human beings grow where only one grew before.

"Essentially," the Director concluded, "bokanovskification consists of a series of arrests of development. We check the normal growth and, paradoxically enough, the egg responds by budding."

Responds by budding. The pencils were busy.

He pointed. On a very slowly moving band a rack-full of test-tubes was entering a large metal box, another rack-full was emerging. Machinery faintly purred. It took eight minutes for the tubes to go through, he told them. Eight minutes of hard X-rays being about as much as an egg can stand. A few died; of the rest, the least susceptible divided into two; most put out four buds; some eight; all were returned to the incubators, where the buds began to develop; then, after two days, were suddenly chilled and checked. Two, four, eight, the buds in their turn budded; and having budded were dosed almost to death with alcohol; consequently burgeoned again and having budded—bud out of bud out of bud—were thereafter—further arrest being generally fatal—left to develop in peace. By which time the original egg was in a fair way to becoming anything from eight to ninety-six embryos—a prodigious improvement, you will agree, on nature. Identical twins—but not in piddling twos and threes as in the old viviparous days, when an egg would sometimes accidentally divide; actually by dozens, by scores at a time.

"Scores," the Director repeated and flung out his arms, as though he were distributing largesse. "Scores."

But one of the students was fool enough to ask where the advantage lay.

"My good boy!" The Director wheeled sharply round on him. "Can't you see? Can't you see?" He raised a hand; his expression was solemn. "Bokanovsky's Process is one of the major instruments of social stability!"

Major instruments of social stability.

Standard men and women; in uniform batches. The whole of a small factory staffed with the products of a single bokanovskified egg.

"Ninety-six identical twins working ninety-six identical machines!" The voice was almost tremulous with enthusiasm. "You really know where you are. For the first time in history." He quoted the planetary motto. "Community, Identity, Stability." Grand words. "If we could bokanovskify indefinitely the whole problem would be solved."

ALDOUS HUXLEY
Brave New World

Huxley's futuristic tale of a "brave new world" seems to raise the nightmare of genetic control of people's lives and behavior. The creation of biological robots and uniform, stable behavior for all people was the aim of Huxley's director. Today, people are concerned more than ever that there could be genetic manipulation of their children and their behavior. With the birth of test-tube babies, such possibilities seem to be rapidly increasing. Recent research on brain chemistry, hormones, and drug effects receives much attention in the popular press. People are concerned about how our behavior might be manipulated and controlled because of the results of such research. How are we to judge such possibilities? What are the limits and possibilities of our biological bases for behavior, and how much can these be manipulated or controlled? The study of psychology involves us in this issue, but psychologists' concern for biology and genetics is not based on a desire for such control. Their only desire is to understand what people do and why they do it in order to help us manage our own lives better. An important part of understanding the influences on behavior is understanding a person's genetic makeup and biology. This chapter considers the influences that genetic heritage has on our day-to-day activities. Similarly, the ways we treat our bodies and how this treatment affects our behavior will be reviewed.

Whatever their feelings on the possibilities of genetic control of behavior, people have a basic concern for the limitations and potentialities our bodies place on our behavior. We can spend years working in a gym, building our bodies and maximizing our physical potentials, but our body structure still limits what we are capable of doing. Even the strongest 170-pound man cannot lift a 2,000-pound weight without the help of a mechanical instrument. In the same way people can try to maximize their intellectual gifts through training and education; but again, some people have limited intellectual abilities. Much of a psychologist's interest in biology lies in the relationship between a person's basic bodily and intellectual capacities and the extent to which these shape or even determine day-to-day behavior. The focus of a psychologist's interest in biology is, therefore, the interrelationship of the body and behavior and how one potentially affects the other.

Most people recognize that a person's performance levels can suddenly change. For example, a runner may have a sudden spurt of energy during the last lap of a race; a television announcer may say that the runner's adrenalin is flowing. Adrenalin is a chemical or hormone released in the bloodstream that allows a runner to sprint with newfound energy. There are, of course, many other hormones that change people's behavior; there are hormones that affect menstrual cycles, eating, drinking, and sexual activity. Psychologists study hormones as well as other aspects of biology to gain insight and develop technology so they can intervene when behavior has gone out of control. Some people's behavior needs management through drugs and hormones. The emotionally disturbed sometimes need drugs to help keep them calm. The management of diabetics' hormone levels is of clear concern to both their health and their ability to function normally in society. Later in this chapter you will see that people can learn to monitor and even alter their bodies' abilities and functions through special techniques like biofeedback.

There is little you can do to influence the way your hormones affect you, but you do exert some control over your body and behavior when you take drugs like aspirin to relieve pain, or when you drink coffee to help you stay awake, or when you meditate to help yourself relax. Although a discussion of drugs and how they affect behavior will be taken up in another chapter, it is clear that people can alter their bodies and the way they work. Even though you can train in a gym, study endlessly, or take drugs, some parts of your behavior and capabilities still seem to be fixed. These fixed capabilities are a basic part of your individuality and are passed on to you by your parents through heredity.

Nature vs. Nurture

Mozart, Picasso, and Hepburn share a rare quality—talent. Special creative abilities are usually the product of a person's basic inborn characteristics *combined* with learning experiences in life. The talented do not express their abilities at birth; instead, these special abilities unfold as they mature and interact with the environment. While a great many factors influenced their development, the especially creative do seem to have been born with something special. Critics, historians, and psychologists have tried to pinpoint this something special, but the source of these artists' genius remains elusive. However, you need not be born with extraordinary talents to be different from the man or woman down the block. People are all different and have developed unique abilities and interests.

A look at a current controversy may help us understand the complex interplay between inborn and developed potentialities. Minorities in the United States have lower scores on standardized intelligence tests than the general population. This fact is substantiated, but the reason and the significance of the difference in scores create the controversy. Some suggest that the difference is due to biological endowment and potential; their view is that these minorities have an inferior intellectual endowment as measured by the test scores. Others argue that the tests are made for the general middle-class population and are based on middle-class experiences, and that this accounts for the intelligence test score differences. Once again the relationship between a person's inherited characteristics and how they affect behavior including talent or even intelligence test scores is of great concern to psychologists. A person's inborn characteristics will clearly affect behavior, but we must remember that each individual may or may not express his or her abilities and talents. The use of inborn abilities is up to individuals and the environment in which they develop.

While biology may confer some special ability on a child, the child must be placed within an environment in which this ability might be expressed. In looking at a concept like intelligence, we recognize that a child born to exceptionally bright individuals may have inherited characteristics which will lead to a high measured IQ; however, this IQ will only be seen *if* the child is reared in an environment in which intelligent behavior is given a chance to operate.

If left unattended, most plants (or people) will grow, but when they are nurtured with attention and care they blossom and mature beautifully.

A talented basketball player or concert pianist is often asked how much he or she practices each day. In this case, interviewers are trying to find out how much of such a person's behavior is due to natural inherited abilities and how much has been nurtured by parents, teachers, and coaches. Most people recognize that the behavior of ordinary *and* exceptional people is determined by their inherited nature and by the nurturing of parents and teachers. Some scientists believe that heredity is the main determinant in a person's behavior; they are said to advocate a **nature** position. Other scientists focus on the idea that a person's experiences shape behavior; they are said to advocate a **nurture** position.

Nature The inherited characteristics of an individual that are determined by genetics.

Nurture The experiences of an individual in an environment.

Most all psychologists agree that both *nature* and *nurture* are operating in the development of a person's behavior. Where they fail to agree is the extent to which one affects the other. There is no question that one's biological makeup affects one's intelligence; the real question is, To what extent can the environment modify one's intelligence? Phrased differently, we might ask, Does the environment act in a dynamic way with our biological makeup, or are the nature and nurture components fixed and unmodifiable? Psychologists have learned that inherited traits depend upon the environment; such traits are not evident in behavior unless they are expressed in the environment. If the trait that we are considering is intelligence, then an environment that can allow for intelligent behavior must be available. If the biological trait is musical talent, then the individual must be given opportunities to express and develop such a talent—perhaps by being given an instrument or music lessons.

Are traits like intelligence based more on nature than on nurture? The answer must be phrased in terms which recognize that (1) both nature and nurture affect the expression of a trait like intelligence, (2) the environment must be appropriate for an inherited trait to be expressed in behavior, (3) there is a complex interplay between nature and nurture such that one must be evident for the other to have its effect. An optimal "musical environment" cannot guarantee musical talent unless there is the biological trait of musical talent; in the same way, a biological gift of potential for high intelligence must have an environment in which this trait might be expressed. Thus, (4) there is a complex and constantly changing relationship between biological and environmental influences which will affect behavior.

Neither heredity nor environment can totally account for behavior because both factors determine it. Both heredity *and* environment determine intelligence, talent, and ability to get along with others. Much of people's behavior seems to be affected by their biological functioning *and* by their environment. It is the relationship between inherited characteristics and expe-

THE WIZARD OF ID by permission of Johnny Hart and Field Enterprises, Inc.

Your biological makeup sets the framework for your behavior, and your experiences shape it further . . .

riences that is the focus of this chapter. Your biological makeup sets the framework for your behavior, your experiences shape it further, but your inherited abilities with your experiences and learned skills ultimately shape everything you feel, think, and do. As you continue to read, ask yourself how these basic biological facts affect day-to-day behavior. It is important to remember, though, that most behavior is affected by both heredity *and* environment, nature *and* nurture.

Genetics

Heredity is the potential given to people by their parents through the transmission of genes. Of course, heredity is unique because each set of parents is unique, and passes their individual potential on to each child. **Chromosomes** carry the basic genetic information; they are made up of strands of deoxyribonucleic acid (DNA) and proteins. The basic or functional unit of the chromosome is the **gene.** The genes are lined up on the chromosomes which are contained in the nucleus (or center) of a cell. In humans, each cell in the body normally contains 23 pairs of chromosomes, a total of 46. The genes on these chromosomes control some aspect of a person's body structure or behavior. For example, genes influence eye color, hair color, height, and basic intellectual traits.

A child is born with chromosomes contributed from both the father and mother. The sperm and ova which combine each contain not 46 chromosomes, but only 23; these sex cells are made up of only one-half of each pair of chromosomes. At the moment of conception when the sex cells combine to form a new individual and the chromosomes rejoin to form pairs, the sperm and ovum each contribute one-half the chromosome makeup of the person being formed.

Just one pair of chromosomes is all it takes to determine the sex of a newborn. Of the 23 pairs, the first 22 chromosomes are responsible for the same characteristics in males and females, but the 23rd pair is different in men and women. The 23rd pair in women contains two X-type chromosomes; the 23rd

Genetics The study of heredity.

Heredity The potential transmitted from parents to offspring through genes.

Chromosome Strands in the nuclei of cells that carry genes. They are composed of a DNA core and are responsible for hereditary transmission of traits. Found in pairs, they represent genes of both the mother and father.

Gene The unit of heredity transmission carried in chromosomes and made up of deoxyribonucleic acid (DNA) and protein.

pair in men contains one X-type and one Y-type chromosome. When the man's sperm are formed (and the chromosomes are not in pairs), the 23rd pair has split into an X-type and a Y-type sperm cell. Since females only have X-type cells in their 23rd pair, the ova resulting from splitting will always contain just one X-type 23rd chromosome. When fertilization unites the sperm and the ova, the chromosomes recombine. If the male X sperm combines with a female X cell, this produces a female, XX; if the male Y cell combines with the female X cell, this produces a male, XY. Thus, the 23rd pair of chromosomes is special because it alone determines the sex of a newborn.

You can see why everybody is different if you think that when the 23 pairs of chromosomes from one parent split, there are 8,388,608 possible combinations of genes. With the combination of genes from two parents, the total number of possibilities is huge: 70,368,744,000,000. Thus, while many people look alike and share common characteristics, except for identical twins no two individuals are exactly alike genetically.

GENETIC DEFICIENCIES.   We already know that a person's chromosomes determine his or her potential, but it is possible that some behavioral problems are completely determined by a person's biological characteristics. Most people will agree that the problems of the mentally retarded are not a consequence of their behavior, but of the fact that they were born with less ability. Let us look at some cases where genetics has brought about mental retardation.

Some people are born with too few or too many chromosomes. The result is usually dramatic. For example, in **Down's syndrome,** or mongolism, there are three chromosomes in pair 21; a child afflicted with Down's syndrome is often physically deformed and mentally retarded. However, extra chromosomes need not exist for behavioral and physical abnormalities to result. For

Down's syndrome Also known as mongolism, a genetic defect in humans in which there are three number 21 chromosomes. Individuals with Down's syndrome are usually physically deformed and mentally retarded.

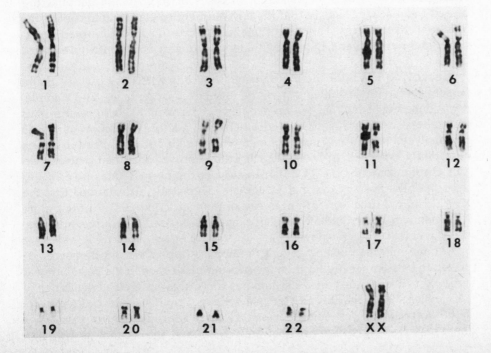

Figure 2.1 What determines sex? The 46 chromosomes that occur in each cell come in pairs. The first 22 pairs in both males and females are alike and transmit similar kinds of characteristics. The 23rd pair determines sex. In this pair females carry two X-type chromosomes, while males carry one X-type and one Y-type chromosome.

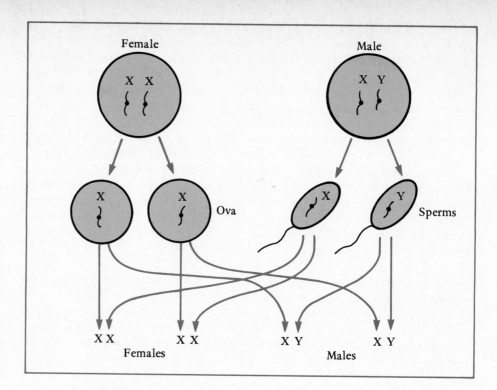

Figure 2.2 The sex of a new person depends on whether the sperm cell carries an X or a Y chromosome (Carlson, 1981, p. 319)

Phenylketonuria (PKU) A genetic defect that creates an inability to metabolize an amino acid, phenylalanine. This usually brings about mental retardation shortly after birth if the condition is not detected. It can successfully be treated by a diet low in phenylalanine (an amino acid present in milk).

example, **phenylketonuria** (PKU) is caused by a recessive gene. In cases of PKU, individuals have inherited an inability to process a certain amino acid, phenylalanine, and this can cause irreparable mental retardation. In the United States infants are given a PKU test shortly after birth since some of the consequences of PKU can be averted by placing the child on a diet containing low levels of phenylalanine. In cases of PKU, while genetics has caused the disorder, we see that the environment (diet) can help control the harmful consequences. Thus, resulting behavior is in part determined by genetics and heredity and in part by the environment; both contribute to and influence behavior.

In studying behavior there are many situations where we can see that a person's behavioral problems might be influenced by genetics. For example, it was once suggested that certain people were far more likely to be criminals than others and that this was genetically based. A study was reported in 1965 that analyzed the chromosomes of men who were institutionalized in a state hospital for criminals in Scotland. The study showed that men who had an XYY chromosome for the 23rd pair instead of the normal XY were 6 inches taller than the average, normal XY inmate. This study also claimed that the XYY's criminal involvement began earlier than XY criminals'. Further, more XYY men were described as impulsive, aggressive, and disruptive, and they were generally underachievers.

At one time, the percentage of XYY subjects in penal institutions was reported to be 20 times higher than the number of XY men in the population at large. Yet in one study of 2,538 inmates there was no greater incidence of XYY males. Other studies of XYY males have shown similar conflicting results. For example, on some personality tests administered to XYY males there have been no differences between these men and XY males. Although

The Gene Transplanters

Many people fear that scientists are going too far with research. Sometimes this fear is generated because of brief journalistic reporting of complicated studies. Too often, speculation from preliminary results leads to anxiety and sometimes false hopes.

NEWSWEEK   It used to be assumed that heredity couldn't be tampered with. You could make any number of alterations in a single organism, but when it reproduced itself, only the original characteristics would pass to the offspring. But when the structure of the DNA molecule, the fundamental building block of genetics, was discovered twenty years ago, biologists could for the first time imagine transplanting genes, the small lengths of DNA that specify individual hereditary characteristics, from one organism to another. And now a group of California-based researchers has turned the trick.

At present, the genetic transplanters are chiefly concerned with the simplest organisms, such as bacteria. But the method is extremely general in application. One group has incorporated into bacteria genetic material from creatures much higher on the evolutionary ladder, and many teams are using the approach in an effort to equip bacteria with nonbacterial functions that might solve problems in medicine and agriculture.

Most genes are grouped together in large circular chains known as chromosomes. A few, however, are linked in smaller rings called plasmids. These plasmids have been the basic ingredients of the transplantation studies. First, Herbert Boyer and Howard Goodman of the University of California Medical Center in San Francisco discovered an enzyme that splits DNA at specific sites. Then Stanley Cohen and Annie Chang of Stanford University Medical School, in cooperation with Boyer and his colleague Robert Helling, devised a method of using the enzyme to split plasmids and introduce foreign genes into them, without affecting the plasmids' ability to reproduce and issue their genetic instructions. The same team also perfected a technique of inserting doctored plasmids into bacteria.

Freak

Combining these techniques, the two groups managed first to transplant genes from one type of bacteria to a related type. Then, in the *Proceedings of the National Academy of Sciences,* Cohen and Chang announced that they had transplanted genes from *Staphylococcus* bacteria into the completely unrelated bacteria known as *Escherichia coli,* producing hybrids that possessed genetic characteristics of both species. Now, in another issue of the *Proceedings,* the same group, together with John Morrow, who is at the Carnegie Institution, reports an even more startling success: incorporation of genes from an animal, a South African toad, into *Escherichia coli* bacteria.

Much of the value of these studies will come from the understanding they provide of basic cell chemistry and biology. In addition, Cohen's group is trying to incorporate into *Escherichia coli* the genes responsible for producing the antibiotic streptomycin, because *Escherichia coli* are far easier to cultivate than the bacteria that produces streptomycin naturally. A similar medical goal is to introduce into simple bacteria the genetic ability to produce insulin which is currently obtained from the pancreases of animals. And Cohen hopes that by treating bacteria associated with such food grains as corn and wheat, they can be given the ability to convert the nitrogen in the air into chemicals that stimulate the grains' growth. This would substantially reduce the need for high-price fertilizers.

further research is necessary, XYY men are probably no more aggressive than other males. Such data must be interpreted with great care because they have strong implications for genetic counseling and screening, two issues of highly emotional content with strong moral implications (Kessler & Moos, 1973).

TWINS.   In trying to determine the contribution of nature and nurture in a person's behavior, psychologists have often relied on studies of twins. Everybody knows that identical twins look alike, but most people never really understand how twins develop or the differences between identical twins and fraternal twins. Psychologists are particularly interested in twins,

Creative talent can express itself
early in life.

Birth defects can make learning
even simple skills difficult.

not because of their looks, but because twins share a special genetic heritage. Brothers and sisters share similar genes, as do a parent and child. But twins are raised in the same uterine environment, at the same time, and share the same nutrition and other influences before birth. Since twins are potentially so much alike in inherited abilities, psychologists often use them to determine the relative contribution of a person's inherited abilities to his behavior.

Let us look at how twins develop. Fraternal twins share a genetic heritage; identical twins have exactly the same genes. To create fraternal twins, two ova are released by the female and are fertilized by two sperm. The two zygotes (fertilized eggs) are then implanted in the uterus and grow alongside each other. **Fraternal twins** can, therefore, be either males, females, or a male and a female. They are children sharing a genetic heritage, like brothers and sisters; their genes are not identical. Genetically, fraternal twins are as alike (and dissimilar) as brothers and sisters born a year apart.

Identical twins have exactly the same genes. In ordinary conception, when an ovum has been fertilized and the zygote is formed, the cells split and multiply; this multiplication eventually forms an entire human being. However, in the formulation of identical twins, upon splitting the zygote produces two identical cells which do not stay together but separate and become two organisms. The multiplication of cells then proceeds naturally. If the two cells which make up identical twins should also split, there is a possibility of identical quadruplets! Twins are not an everyday phenomenon and identical twins are fairly rare. In 250 births, there are 3 sets of fraternal twins, but only 1 set of identical twins.

Psychologists have closely examined the behavior of identical twins because of their unique genetic makeup. It is important to remember that while identical twins have the same heredity, their environment may be significantly different. For example, one child may be raised by his or her parents and the other child may be raised at a school, be adopted at birth, or merely interact with different people. If we give intelligence tests to identical twins who have had dramatically different social experiences, and there are differences in intelligence, we must infer that experience and the environment account for the differences in intelligence, not their genes.

Studies of identical twins are also important in examining abnormal behavior. For example, when the severe behavior disorder schizophrenia occurs in a twin, both members of a pair of identical twins are likely to have schizophrenia, whereas only one member of a pair of fraternal twins may show the disorder. This finding suggests that heredity is important in schizophrenia because if experience were the only cause, then identical twins would be no more likely to have schizophrenia than fraternal twins. Genetic studies conducted with twins show the tremendous part genetics plays in our attempts to understand human behavior.

Our day-to-day experiences do not affect our genetic makeup because the DNA that makes up our genes is fixed. However, through tens of thousands of years and the process of evolution, animals and especially human beings have developed a highly organized brain that allows for experiences to affect them through the process of learning. The brain can learn and act as a library of information. With each new learning experience we humans are able to change the ways in which we respond in the future. So, while genetic

Fraternal twins Double births resulting from the release of two ova in the female that are then fertilized by two sperm. Their genetic makeups are not exactly the same.

Identical twins Double births resulting from the splitting of a zygote into two identical cells that then separate and develop independently. Identical twins have the same genetic makeup.

When reared in the same environment, identical twins can often share interests.

Inborn talents are important, but practice makes perfect.

makeup is fixed and unmodifiable, behavior is modifiable because of recorded experiences.

This structure of a fixed biology and a brain sensitive to experiences provides humans with the wonderful capacity to experience the world in unique ways, to develop new technology, and, with each new generation, to better the human condition. Because of our brain development, human beings have become more than just reflexive organisms whose lives are controlled solely by genetics. Our love for other humans, our desire to do good, and our ability to develop high levels of creativity, communication, and technology are a reflection of our genetics and especially of our ability to remember, think, combine, recall, and invent new ways of thinking. While our genetics acts as the foundation for our development, our experiences in the environment also shape our day-to-day destiny.

Psychologists study the biological mechanisms that underlie behavior because they recognize that there is a complex interplay between genetics and the environment. A person's genetic heritage provides the framework for behavior. This doesn't mean that genes necessarily determine behavior, but that they do influence a person's basic potentialities and capabilities. However, some have suggested that our potential can be stretched dramatically like a rubber band. We don't have to be limited by our genetic endowment because through experience, training, and a little hard work that rubber band can be stretched to amazing lengths. So, while genetics lays down the foundation of behavior, other factors such as experience and learning affect exactly what we feel, think, and do.

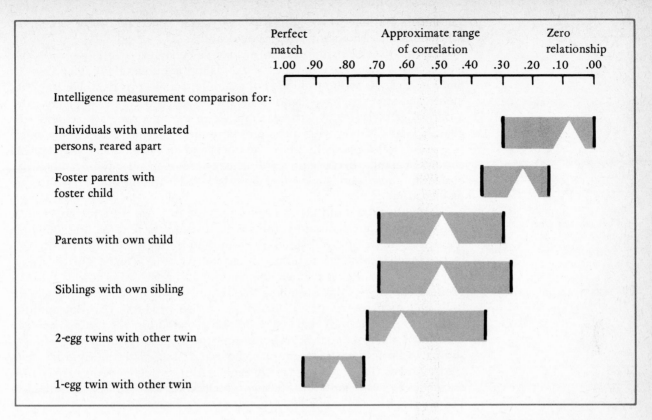

Figure 2.3 How closely matched (correlated) are intelligence measurements? The rectangles show the range of correlation (over several studies), with the triangles pointing to the average. There is little or no correlation between measurements for unrelated people, but identical twins show very high correlations. These data suggest that intelligence is in part genetically determined

HORMONES AND GLANDS

Almost all aspects of a person's behavior are determined by inherited characteristics and learning experiences. Eating, especially overeating, is a behavior that is most dramatically affected by our bodily states and by past experiences with food. When people overeat and become fat, they often try to diet to cope with their problem. But dieting is difficult, and, for some people, close to impossible. Could it be that for some, dieting is actually impossible or at least useless? Look at the case of Rita.

During most of Rita's adult life people have tried to be nice by commenting on her pretty face; they hate to mention the obvious: Rita is 5 feet 5 inches tall and weighs 220 pounds. Whenever friends talk about Rita's weight they comment that everyone in her family is overweight. They imply that there may be some genetic reason for this weight problem, and someone usually suggests that Rita has a glandular problem. Rita's real problem is that she eats too much and has done so for years. But her friends' comments about glandular malfunctions do have some basis, because glandular deficiencies can help produce obesity.

Although Rita is not one of them, some people are overweight because of glandular deficiencies. In these cases, the gland that might be malfunctioning is the *thyroid*. The thyroid gland is responsible for producing thyroxin, a chemical that partly controls metabolism. Too much thyroxin produces highstrung, nervous, thin people; too little thyroxin produces people who lose their appetites, are often lethargic, are limited in their growth potential, and sometimes become overweight. Rita's physician might be concerned about Rita's thyroxin production *and* her overeating.

Since glands are so important to a person's behavior, a closer look at them is necessary. There are two types of glands in the human body: glands with ducts and glands without ducts. For example, certain organs, including the mouth and stomach, have glands with specific ducts that carry substances to a particular place for a particular job; there are also tear, sweat, and sex glands. While glands with ducts are important, psychologists are far more interested in the glands that have no ducts and are called ductless glands or **endocrine glands,** because their influence on a person's behavior can be very dramatic. These glands secrete chemicals called **hormones** directly into the bloodstream.

Although the thyroid gland is very important, if we were forced to pick the one most important endocrine gland, it would have to be the *pituitary,* the body's master gland. Secretions from the pituitary not only produce direct changes in bodily functions, but also affect other glands. The pituitary gland is divided into two lobes, the anterior and posterior. The *anterior lobe* produces hormones that stimulate the thyroid gland and the adrenal gland, both of which control other behaviors. It also produces gonadotrophins, which are involved in sexual behavior, and growth hormones, which control the body's development. Secretions from the anterior pituitary have been shown to be influenced by the psychological state of the individual; one study showed that viewing sexually explicit films brought about increases in hormones from the anterior pituitary which were related to sexual behavior

Endocrine glands Ductless glands that secrete hormones directly into the bloodstream.

Hormone A chemical that regulates the activities of specific organs or cells. Hormones are produced by the endocrine glands and are transported to their site of action by the bloodstream.

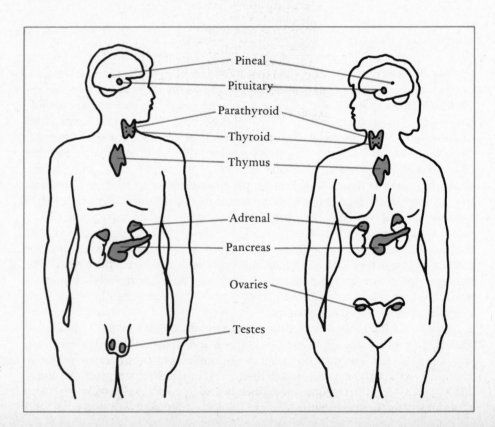

Figure 2.4 The endocrine glands are situated throughout the body. Though small in size, they exert enormous influences on behavior

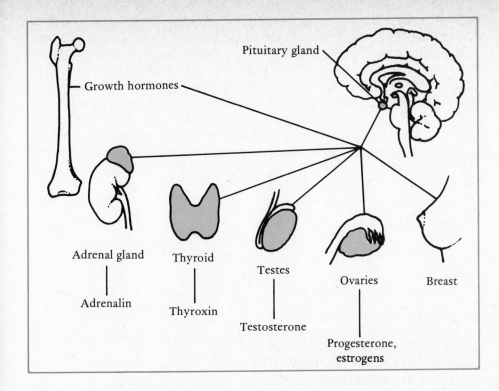

Growth hormones

Pituitary gland

Adrenal gland

Adrenalin

Thyroid

Thyroxin

Testes

Testosterone

Ovaries

Progesterone, estrogens

Breast

Figure 2.5 The pituitary is a small gland with direct effects on behavior through the control of other glands as well as the secretion of hormones into the bloodstream

(LaFerla, Anderson, & Schalch, 1978). Thus, the anterior lobe controls not only specific behavior but other glands as well.

The *posterior lobe* of the pituitary secretes two major hormones, an antidiuretic hormone and oxytocin. The antidiuretic hormone (ADH) acts on the kidneys to increase fluid absorption and thus decrease the amount of urine formed. Oxytocin stimulates uterine contractions and causes labor to begin in a pregnant woman. When a woman has difficulty giving birth because her labor contractions are not strong enough, injections of oxytocin are often very effective. Oxytocin also causes the release of milk in a nursing mother.

It has recently been suggested that the endocrine system in general and the pituitary system in particular may be crucially involved in depression; depressed patients often have abnormalities in their hormonal levels, particularly from the pituitary (Van Praag, 1978). The pituitary is of great importance because of its impact on specific glands and behaviors. This small gland weighs very heavily in the balance of nature and nurture.

A gland which in part manipulates blood sugar levels is the *pancreas*. Sugar substances in the blood greatly determine energy levels and their effect on behavior is very obvious. When blood sugar is high, people have energy; when it is low, they feel weak and tired. The pancreas controls the production of **insulin,** which aids the body in putting sugars where they can be metabolized into energy. If someone has **diabetes mellitus,** or diabetes, an insufficient amount of insulin is being produced. If there is not enough insulin in a person's system, there is an excess of sugar in the blood. This condition is known as **hyperglycemia,** and a severe case can bring about coma and death. People who have diabetes take daily doses of insulin to ensure that the sugar in their blood is being used properly. Of course, a pancreas may

Insulin A hormone produced by the pancreas that allows the body to transport sugar from the blood into body cells to be metabolized.

Diabetes mellitus A condition in which too little insulin is present in a person's blood to allow sufficient quantities of sugar to be transported into body cells. This can result in hyperglycemia.

Hyperglycemia A condition in which too much sugar is present in the blood.

Hypoglycemia A condition resulting from the overproduction of insulin, causing very low blood sugar levels. It is usually characterized by a lack of energy, and often faintness and dizziness.

produce too much insulin, resulting in the opposite condition; this is called **hypoglycemia,** very low blood sugar. Hypoglycemic patients have no energy and often feel faint; but this condition can also be controlled. The effects of the pancreas on behavior are usually evident only when there is an abnormality; yet, we can see why the pancreas's role in controlling bodily functions is important. An individual's performance on the job, in school, and even in the family setting is greatly determined by his or her energy levels and ability and desire to interact with others. Because of low blood sugar a person is liable to be labeled lazy and punished by people who assume he lacks motivation. Again, we see that a person's bodily systems affect behavior in very direct ways, highlighting the nature-nurture controversy.

Table 2.1 The glands of the human body with the substances they secrete and their effects

GLAND	SECRETES	EFFECTS
Pituitary		
Adenohypophysis (anterior pituitary)	Growth hormone	Controls rate of protein synthesis; promotes release of fat from fat stores
	Adrenocorticotrophic hormone (ACTH)	Regulates cortex of adrenal gland
	Thyrotrophin	Regulates thyroid gland
	Follicle stimulating hormone	Regulates sex organs
	Luteinizing hormone	Promotes secretion of sex hormones
	Prolactin	Milk production
Neurohypophysis (posterior pituitary)	Arginine vasopressin	Antidiuretic action
	Oxytocin	Uterine contractions; stimulates lactation
Pancreas	Insulin	Regulates use of sugar
		Regulates storage of carbohydrates
	Glucagon	Acts synergistically with insulin
Thyroid	Thyroxin	Regulates metabolic rate
Parathyroid	Parathyroid hormone	Regulation of calcium levels
Pineal	Melatonin	Regulates reproduction and growth
Adrenal		
Cortex	Steroids	Resistance to stress
		Regulation of carbohydrate metabolism
Medulla	Adrenalin (Epinephrine)	Changes metabolic activity
	Noradrenalin (Norepinephrine)	Inhibitory effect on CNS generally
Reproductive Glands		
Female	Estrogens	Control of menstrual cycle
	Progestins	Maintenance of pregnancy
Male	Androgens	Promotion of male sex characteristics and growth

The hormonal system is very complicated and no single description of its functioning will suffice, but its role in the control of many behaviors is readily apparent. Even sexual behavior in human beings is controlled, at least in part, by hormones. One study of the sexual hormones and frequency of intercourse among married couples showed that there was a significant relationship between frequency of intercourse and hormone level (Persky, 1978). Although such a finding is not surprising, we know that the sexual behavior of animals is to a great extent under hormonal control; the extent to which human behavior is under hormonal control is still under active investigation.

Other glands that control behavior are shown in Table 2.1. One of the most important, as we have seen, is the adrenal gland, which produces adrenalin (epinephrine), a substance that can dramatically alter energy levels. As can be seen in Table 2.2, the effects of adrenalin production can greatly alter a person's behavior and physiology.

If we return to Rita and her weight problem for a moment, we will remember that sympathetic friends tried to explain Rita's problem as a genetic one (her whole family is fat) or as a result of a glandular disorder (the thyroid gland). While Rita should probably see a physician before embarking on a serious weight-reducing program, we can probably bet that her problem is not glandular. This is the case because serious glandular disorders affect many types of behavior, not just weight. The glandular system is interactive; this means that each hormone affects behavior *and* eventually other glands. If there is a disorder in the thyroid, it will affect not only metabolic rate, but it will also affect the pituitary, which in turn will affect other behaviors. Of course, being fat or short is not a behavior, but the negative treatment one receives because of these problems can result in problem behaviors. Because the glandular systems do not work alone, we can see that their effect on behavior can be dramatic.

Up until now we have dealt with relatively large organs and complex behaviors. A close examination of some of the basic components of the nervous system can also provide insight into *how* we do what we do.

Table 2.2 Adrenalin affects different organs and systems of the body with dramatic behavioral outcomes

ORGAN OR SYSTEM	ADRENALIN AFFECTS THE SYSTEM TO . . .
Heart rate	Increase
Cardiac output	Increase
Blood pressure	Raise
Respiration	Stimulate
Skin vessels	Constrict
Muscle vessels	Dilate
Metabolism	Increase
Oxygen consumption	Increase
Blood sugar	Increase
Central nervous system	Arouse
Uterus in late pregnancy	Inhibit
Kidney	Vasoconstrict

We just saw that the glandular system is very complicated. For example, the pituitary controls other glands that affect specific behaviors, which in turn affect the pituitary itself. Hormones are just one controlling mechanism; the brain, with all its subdivisions, is linked to groups of subsystems that affect and to some extent control behavior. Think of all the brain mechanisms involved in the simple act of walking. The visual areas of the brain are activated so that we can see where we are going. Motor areas help make our legs move. One area, called the cerebellum, helps us keep our balance as we walk. We already know that our glandular systems help in the conversion of sugar to provide energy. The brain is far more complex; any activity involves the combined efforts of many brain cells, sometimes thousands.

When looking at the contribution of nature to behavior we have to consider the vast complexity of all of the centers of control involved. Perhaps the puzzle which we call the brain will never be fully understood! Yet its influence on behavior is potentially so great that psychologists and physiologists continually try to assess it. So, to analyze the brain and how it controls behavior we begin at the smallest unit of analysis, the neuron. We will build upon our knowledge steadily to show that the structure and functions of the brain weigh heavily in the nature-nurture debate.

The Basic Unit—The Neuron

Neuron The basic unit of the nervous system. Typically, a neuron is a single cell composed of *dendrites*, which receive information; a *cell body*, which generates electrical signals; and an *axon*, which transmits neural signals.

The basic building block of the nervous system is the **neuron.** Typically, a neuron is composed of *dendrites*, which receive information and carry it to a *cell body*. The cell body generates electrical signals, and a long slim *axon* carries the impulse to the next neuron.

There are about 100 billion neurons in the human brain; approximately 10 billion of them are contained in the covering of the brain called the cortex (Hubel & Wiesel, 1979). Neurons are of different shapes and sizes; they have

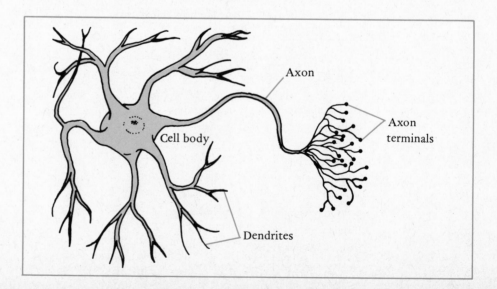

Figure 2.6 The basic components of a neuron with dendrites, cell body, and a long slim axon are shown

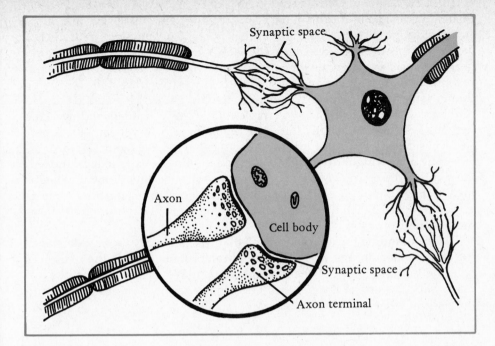

Synaptic space

Axon

Cell body

Synaptic space

Axon terminal

Figure 2.7 The synaptic space is very small. Chemicals released by the axon terminal cross the synaptic space to stimulate the cell body or dendrites of another neuron

different functions and are found throughout the body and brain. One property that almost all neurons share is that the end branches of the axon terminate close to and sometimes almost touch the dendrites or cell body of another neuron. The small amount of space between the end branches of the axon and the dendrite or cell body of another neuron is called a **synapse.** This space is so small that it cannot be seen without a very high powered microscope. Figure 2.7 depicts this relationship (Hubel, 1979; Stevens, 1979).

We do not have a complete understanding of how electrical signals are transferred at the synapse. The most reliable explanation suggests that chemicals are released from the end branches of the axon and are transferred to the dendrites of the next neuron. The release of chemicals at the synapse can be excitatory or inhibitory; this means that at some synapses the release of chemicals excites the next neuron, but others inhibit or decrease the firing of the next neuron. One of the most well known excitatory chemicals in the central nervous system is acetylcholine. Others that are well known are norepinephrine, serotonin, and dopamine. If the change in excitatory chemical activity at a cell body is great enough, an electrical signal called a spike is generated. A **spike discharge** is an electrical current of constant strength transmitted along the axon. When a spike is generated the cell does so in an **all-or-none** fashion. This means that the cells generate a spike at full strength or not at all. As a rule, neurons cannot fire or generate spikes more than 1,000 times per second because there is a recovery period of a few thousandths of a second. This period is called the **refractory period.** During this quiet period the chemical balance between the axon and the area around it is being reestablished.

Through the firing of these neurons, information is transferred from the senses to the brain and from the brain to the muscular system and the glands. Consider all the advances that could be made if we knew how the nervous

Synapse The small space between the end branches of the axon of one neuron and the receptive site (dendrite, cell body, or neural membrane) of another neuron.

Spike discharge An electrical current sent down the axon of a neuron.

All-or-none The principle by which a neuron will either fire at full strength or not fire at all.

Refractory period The recovery period of a neuron after it fires, during which time it cannot fire again. This period allows the neuron to reestablish its electrical balance with its surroundings.

system passes along information. For one thing, psychologists could more successfully predict and manage the behavior of people with neurological damage. Consider the hope such knowledge would provide the blind and deaf; if physicians knew how neuronal signals were transmitted, they could potentially help them see and hear. Since many learning disabilities may be due to some type of neural dysfunction, they might be alleviated or treated differently. These are just a few examples of the way an understanding of the nervous system may directly influence the management of behavior. A person's basic body structure directly affects behavior. Behaviors are also affected by a growing individual's environment and life experiences. Indeed, the combined working of basic body structure and the environment will ultimately shape day-to-day behavior. Many behavioral problems have biological components. When the body is not working normally, this often produces the behavior problem.

If understanding the neuron were all that was necessary to an understanding of behavior, things would be complicated enough—but the neuron is only the building block of the nervous system. We still must consider two major subdivisions of the nervous system: the central nervous system and the peripheral nervous system.

The Central Nervous System

Central nervous system (CNS) The part of the nervous system consisting of the brain and spinal cord.

Afferent The term used to denote pathways and signals of the peripheral nervous system that run toward the central nervous system.

Efferent The term used to denote neural pathways or signals that run away from the central nervous system to other structures of the body.

Convolutions Folds in tissues that are a characteristic of the cerebral hemispheres and overlying cortex in humans.

The **central nervous system** is made up of the brain and the spinal cord. The brain is a highly complex group of structures that function together to coordinate the receiving and sending of two types of electrochemical signals. **Afferent signals,** the first type, are signals coming to the brain. The second type, called **efferent signals,** go from the brain and the spinal cord to other structures in the body.

On the first examination, it is easy to see that the brain is composed of two large *cerebral hemispheres.* The exterior covering of the brain, the *cortex,* constitutes the major component of the cerebral hemispheres. The cortex is made up of several thin layers of cells and looks like material that has been crumpled together, or **convoluted.** This convoluting provides more surface area to the brain—the brains of humans contain nearly 20 square feet of cortical area. The cortex is involved in control of emotion, the senses, and complex cognitive activities. A large thick tissue that connects the two cerebral hemispheres is called the *corpus callosum.* The corpus callosum makes it possible for information to be transferred from one cerebral hemisphere to the other.

We can best describe the working of the brain by dividing it into three separate sections: the hindbrain, the midbrain, and the forebrain.

HINDBRAIN.   The *hindbrain* consists of three main structures: the medulla, the pons, and the cerebellum. The *medulla,* through which many incoming signals to the brain must pass, lies just above the spinal cord and controls heartbeat and breathing. Within the medulla there is a system of latticelike networks of nerve cells, called the *reticular formation.* A person's state of arousal is directly controlled by the reticular formation. This network of cells controls waking, sleeping, and other bodily functions and, if damaged, can bring about coma and death. The reticular formation also extends into and through the pons and the midbrain. The *pons* also controls sleeping, while the *cerebellum* influences balance and movement.

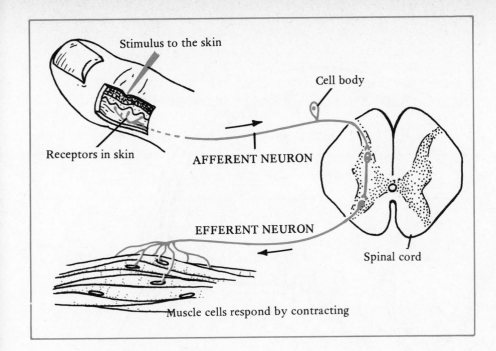

Figure 2.8 *Afferent* neurons carry signals to the spinal cord and the brain; *efferent* neurons carry signals to the muscles and the glands

MIDBRAIN. The *midbrain* is made up of a number of nuclei, or cell bodies, that accept afferent signals, interpret them, and either relay this information to a more complex part of the brain, or cause the body to act at once. The midbrain continues the reticular formation system and, again, its damage or disruption can bring about coma or death.

FOREBRAIN. The forebrain is composed of two main structures, the first of which is the *diencephalon*. The diencephalon is made up of two structures, the hypothalamus and the thalamus. The *thalamus* acts mainly to send information to other parts of the brain, although it probably also has some interpretive function. The *hypothalamus* seems to be involved in many complex behaviors, including motivation, emotion, and eating and drinking, as well as sexual appetite.

The second portion of the forebrain, the *telencephalon*, is composed of three main structures: the basal ganglia, the corpus callosum, and the cortex. The *basal ganglia* are a series of nuclei located deep within the brain that control movement, posture, and have been shown to be involved in Parkinson's disease. The *corpus callosum*, as has already been suggested, conveys information between cerebral hemispheres and when damaged results in essentially two separate brains. The cerebral *cortex*, the covering of the cerebral hemisphere, has been mentioned as being involved in complex cognitive processes.

The human cortex can be divided into different areas. The *motor cortex* is associated with movement and when portions of it are removed, there is a loss of ability to make fine motor movements, such as movement of the fingers. The *sensory cortex* receives information from lower structures about sensory systems. Thus, the visual and auditory system both connect into the visual and auditory cortex. Additional areas of the cortex do not have such

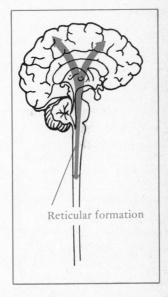

Figure 2.9 Many afferent and efferent signals pass through the reticular formation

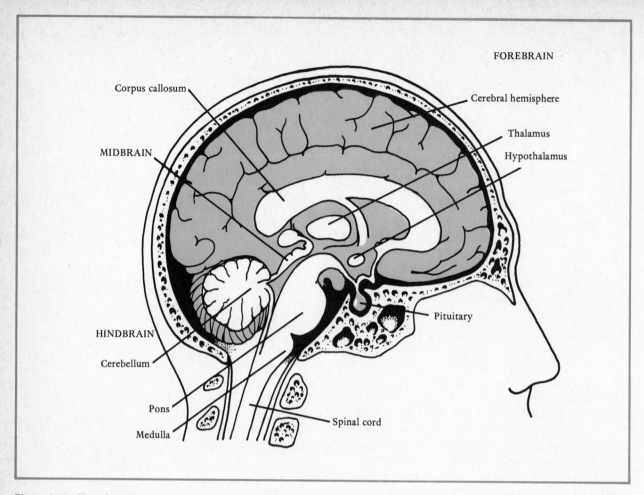

FOREBRAIN

Corpus callosum

Cerebral hemisphere

MIDBRAIN

Thalamus

Hypothalamus

HINDBRAIN

Pituitary

Cerebellum

Pons

Medulla

Spinal cord

Figure 2.10 This diagram shows the three major sections of the brain: hindbrain, midbrain, and forebrain

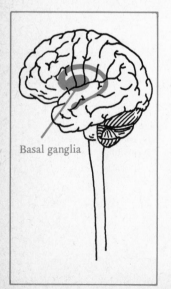

Basal ganglia

specific functions, but they are involved in certain visual functions. We speak of these areas not as primary sensory areas, but as association areas. The *association cortex* is thought to be involved in more complex behaviors. These activities may not be strictly visual, auditory, or motor, but they will involve some complex combinations of many different systems.

Probably one of the least understood areas of the brain is the *limbic system.* This is an interconnected group of structures throughout the brain (including parts of the cortex, thalamus, and hypothalamus) which forms a system that is involved in emotional behavior, memory, and even epilepsy and alcoholism. Within the limbic system are the hippocampus and the amygdala. In humans, the *hippocampus* is integrally involved in memory functions. In past decades the *amygdala* has been thought to be an area that modulates emotional behavior; it has been a target for "psychosurgery" in certain extremely violent patients. Some fascinating studies have shown that there are even "pleasure centers" in the limbic system. For example, Olds and Milner (1954) discovered areas of the brain which when stimulated brought extremely pleasurable sensations to rats.

Figure 2.11 The basal ganglia found deep within the brain is involved in the regulation and control of gross movement. Damage to this important center can have severe behavioral consequences

SPLIT BRAINS. Scientists know that the two cerebral hemispheres of the human brain are connected by the corpus callosum. Over the past decade or two, a number of operations have been performed on humans in which the corpus callosum has been severed. This operation has generally been performed on people who have had uncontrollable epilepsy. The purpose of surgery was to confine the epileptic seizures to one hemisphere rather than let the seizures spread from one hemisphere to the other. These operations have generally proved successful but they have also shown that the human brain is, in a sense, two brains, each capable of different functions and largely independent of the other.

The left cerebral hemisphere is usually dominant and controls speech and language behavior. When the left hemisphere is not provided certain information, experimental subjects do not respond in normal ways. For example, when stimulus information is presented to the left cerebral hemisphere, **split-brain patients** are able to describe it, match it, and deal with it in essentially normal ways. By contrast, when this same stimulation is presented to the right cerebral hemisphere, although subjects are able to do matching tasks, they are unable to describe the stimuli verbally. The left hemisphere usually controls speech and language, and since it is cut off from the right hemisphere, the split-brain subject is unable to use speech and language to describe the activities carried out by the right hemisphere. This same result occurs in learning situations. If the right cerebral hemisphere is provided a learning situation involving language or speech, the left cerebral hemisphere is essentially isolated and has no information about that learning.

Split-brain patients Term applied to people whose corpus callosum—which normally connects the two cerebral hemispheres—has been surgically severed.

Figure 2.12 Diagrammatic representation of the two basic divisions of the nervous system and their major subdivisions

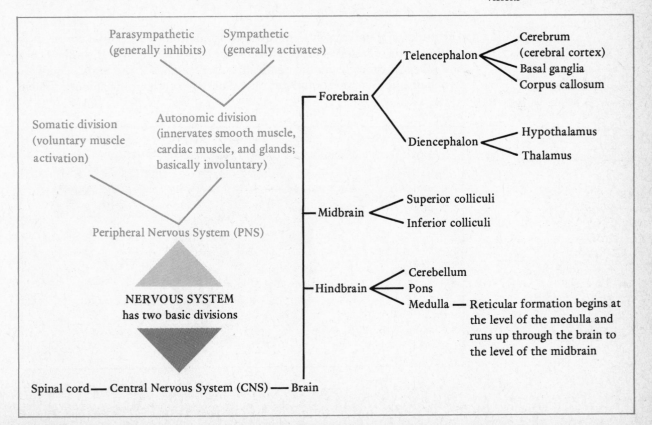

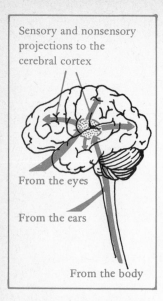

Sensory and nonsensory projections to the cerebral cortex

From the eyes

From the ears

From the body

Figure 2.13 The thalamus acts as a relay station for sensory information and sends afferent input to higher centers

Peripheral nervous system Parts of the nervous system that are not part of the central nervous system. Its two main subdivisions are the somatic and autonomic nervous systems.

Somatic nervous system The part of the peripheral nervous system that controls skeletal muscles and, in turn, bodily movement.

Figure 2.14 In most individuals, speech and language are lateralized to the left hemisphere. Body functions are controlled by the hemisphere of the brain that is on the opposite side of the body from the energized body part (Carlson, 1981, p. 10)

We have discussed a number of complex structures in the brain, and it is easy to see that the functions of these structures are very involved. These functions are so complicated that we cannot simply say that a particular area of the brain exclusively controls a specific behavior. We do know that certain structures are definitely primarily involved in vision or movement, *but* most behaviors involve the combined working of several areas of the brain. The system is complex, and different areas of the brain all receive input from the senses and muscles and try to process it correctly.

The reason psychologists (and students) study the structure of the brain so closely is that the brain holds so many important answers to behavioral problems. For example, we know that the limbic system may be involved in alcoholism. We are forced to wonder, then, whether alcoholism may be caused, at least in part, by a damaged, diseased, or faulty limbic system. Similarly, certain groups of brain cells seem to influence eating behavior; perhaps the obese have a different functioning hypothalamus than thin people. Perhaps the most compelling biological inference that can be made is within the realm of schizophrenia. There is significant evidence that the severe behavior disorder of schizophrenia (at least in part) has a biological basis. We will be examining this evidence in chapter 12, Abnormal Psychology. Of course, the answer to every behavior problem cannot be traced to the structure of the central nervous system, but without understanding how the brain works, we will never fully understand normal or abnormal behavior. Now, let us take one step further by looking at the second major division of the nervous system, the peripheral nervous system.

The Peripheral Nervous System

The peripheral nervous system carries information to the spinal cord and to the brain via (1) a series of fiber tracts that run up and down the spinal cord and (2) a system of 12 cranial nerves that carry signals to the brain. There are two main subdivisions of the **peripheral nervous system:** the **somatic system**

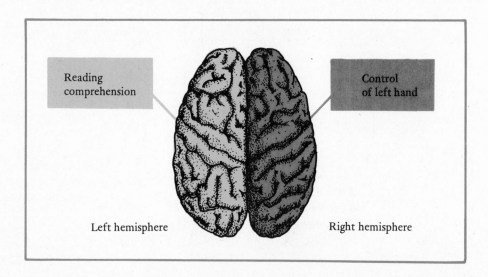

Reading comprehension

Control of left hand

Left hemisphere

Right hemisphere

Figure 2.15 How the brain divides its work

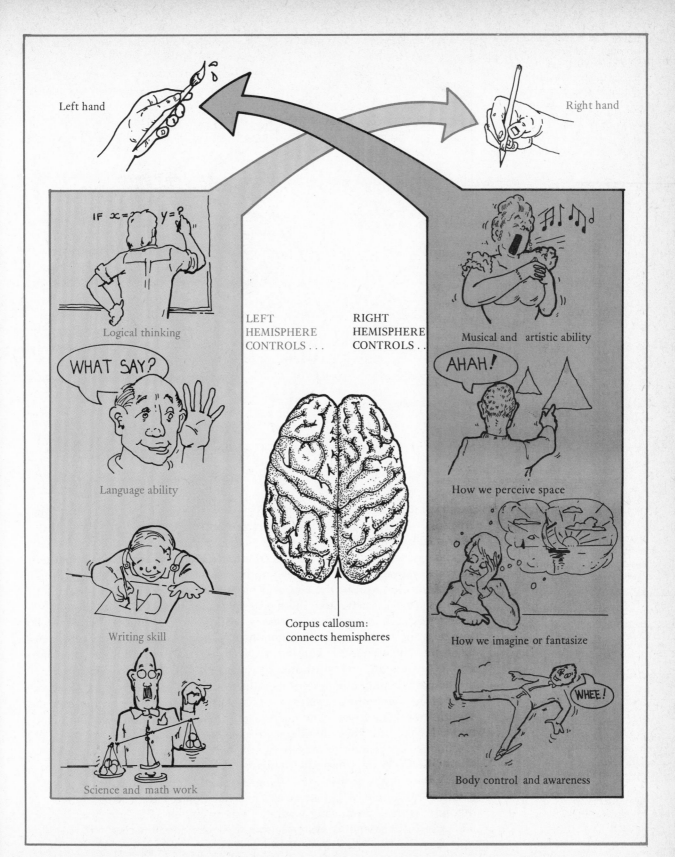

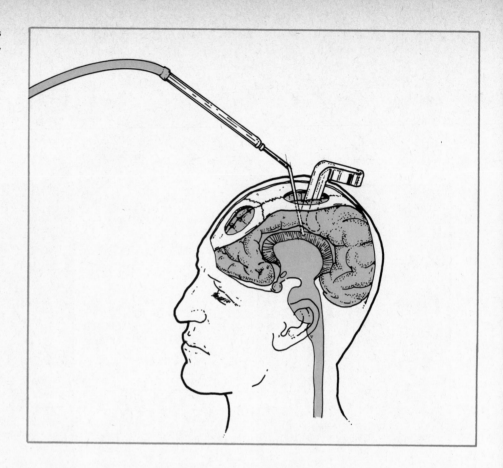

Figure 2.16 When the corpus callosum is severed surgically, the two cerebral hemispheres are separated permanently and no further information can be exchanged between them (Carlson, 1981, p. 9)

Autonomic nervous system The part of the peripheral nervous system that controls the vital processes of the body, such as heart rate, digestive processes, blood pressure, etc. Its two main divisions are the sympathetic and parasympathetic systems.

Sympathetic nervous system The part of the autonomic nervous system that responds to emergency situations. It is active only on occasion; sympathetic activity calls up bodily resources as needed.

Parasympathetic nervous system The part of the autonomic nervous system that is generally conservatory, storing up bodily resources when they are not needed. Its activities are balanced by those of the sympathetic nervous system.

and the **autonomic nervous system.** The somatic system includes nerves that are involved in movement and muscle control.

The autonomic nervous system is made up of two parts: the sympathetic nervous system and the parasympathetic nervous system. The **sympathetic nervous system** controls the speed of the heart, secretion of digestive fluids, dilation of the pupil in the eye, and blood pressure. When the sympathetic nervous system is activated, there is an increase in heart rate and blood pressure, a decrease in digestive processes, a dilation of the pupil, and generally a preparation for emergencies, sometimes called the fight-or-flight reflex. Activation of the sympathetic nervous system often brings about an increased flow of adrenalin, the hormone produced by the adrenal glands.

The **parasympathetic system** has functions that counterbalance the functions of the sympathetic system. This system is active most of the time and controls normal digestion and heart rate. The parasympathetic system is suppressed when the sympathetic system is activated. (See Figure 2.18 on p. 59.)

Changes in the autonomic nervous system bring about changes in the somatic system. When the sympathetic system is activated and the organism is in a fight-or-flight posture, the somatic system becomes sensitized and activated. For example, when a runner's adrenal glands have been stimulated so that adrenalin is produced, a burst of energy is felt. This increased energy will affect the somatic system, and the runner's muscles will respond

Two "Brains" in One

Understanding the complex structures of the brain is no easy task. Yet researchers have been studying both brain and behavior so as to gain further insight into brain functioning.

Psychologist Michael Gazzaniga (1967) has done studies of patients who have had their corpus callosums severed. This operation essentially yields a person with two brains which cannot talk to each other. Gazzaniga and other scientists have shown that most humans have a dominant hemisphere which is specialized for the processing of speech and language. The other hemisphere seems better organized to process spatial tasks, musical, and perhaps creative abilities.

Using simple tests, researchers like Gazzaniga have shown that a subject whose corpus callosum has been severed may hold a pencil in one hand behind a screen and not be able to describe it. If the subject switches hands, the task then becomes simple. The left hand is connected neurologically to the right hemisphere, which has little or no speech and language ability. By contrast, the right hand is neurologically connected to the left language-dominant hemisphere. The pencil is thus easily described when held in the right hand.

Going beyond Gazzaniga's studies, research on brain functioning is done with normal as well as split-brain patients. In some studies brain wave activity is monitored while different kinds of stimuli are exposed to the subjects. Certain characteristic brain wave activity is produced on the left side of the brain when subjects are asked to look at letters, think about them, or perhaps rehearse a speech. By contrast, brain wave activity becomes apparent on the right side of the brain when creative tasks are asked for or the subject is told to reorganize some spatial pattern.

While this evidence suggests there are highly specialized brain functions which are organized by hemispheres, it is still unclear how permanently isolated these functions are. Before a person reaches the age of about 4, the left and right hemispheres seem equally proficient with language information. Yet, with each year past the age of 4, the left cerebral hemisphere becomes increasingly involved in the use of language. By the time the brain has matured at the age of 13, individuals generally have a distinctly dominant hemisphere that is responsible for speech and language.

With all of the evidence that has been gathered on brain functions and the differences between left and right hemispheres, researchers are still not all of one mind. For example, some researchers contend that much of the learning that many people refer to when they talk about intelligence takes place in the left hemisphere. If this is the case, the tests of intelligence should examine left-hemisphere processing (to include logical, verbal, and language skills) as well as right-hemisphere processing. At present most intelligence tests examine only left-hemisphere functioning. In making such arguments, researchers like Alan Kaufman argue that if a psychologist has evidence to suggest that a person is using his or her right hemisphere more than the left, this needs to be taken into consideration in examining their intelligence test scores. Kaufman has gone so far as to suggest that for practical purposes one can consider learning-disabled children right-brain learners (Kaufman, 1979; Rappoport, 1979). There is some anatomical evidence to suggest that learning-disabled children do indeed have a lack of normal brain lateralization. However, not all researchers agree. Some researchers, like Drake Duane, argue that to speak of "left-brain" individuals in contrast with "right-brain" individuals is misleading; their argument is that the brain works as a unit and the two sides work together to produce adaptive intelligent behavior.

All of the data are not yet in. Many of the research studies show important left- vs. right-side differences; others suggest that these differences are rather trivial. There is much to be learned about brain function from studies of the left side and the right side of the brain, because they do process information differently. Whether this is a cause of certain problems or not is yet to be firmly established. We will be exploring some of the issues involved in brain lateralization again in chapter 8 on Language and Thought and chapter 9 on Altered States of Consciousness.

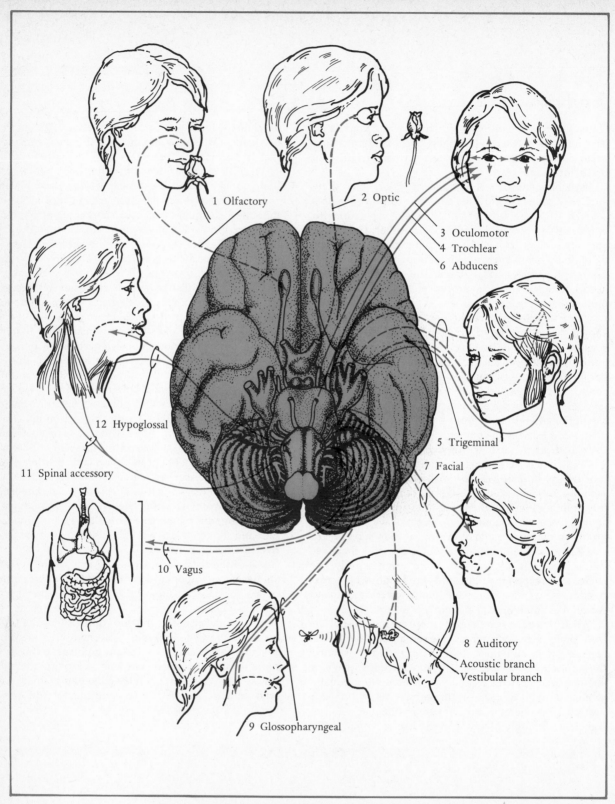

1 Olfactory

2 Optic

3 Oculomotor
4 Trochlear
6 Abducens

5 Trigeminal

7 Facial

8 Auditory
Acoustic branch
Vestibular branch

9 Glossopharyngeal

10 Vagus

11 Spinal accessory

12 Hypoglossal

Figure 2.17 There are 12 cranial nerves, each of which sends information directly to the brain. The locations and functions of these nerves are shown (Redrawn from Carlson, 1981, p. 130)

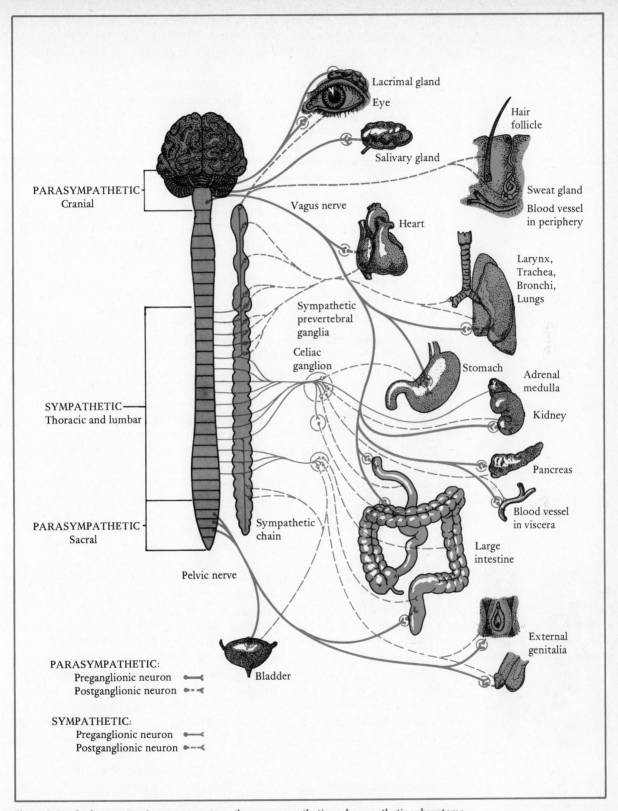

Figure 2.18 In the autonomic nervous system, the parasympathetic and sympathetic subsystems each control different aspects of bodily functions. (Carlson, 1981, p. 132)

strongly and rapidly. We see that our bodies can alter our behavior very quickly. Increased adrenalin flow can dramatically change the outcome of a race. In the next section we will see if we can alter our biological function to eventually affect behavior.

The peripheral and central nervous systems work in harmony. When the central nervous system is provided information by the peripheral nervous system, it acts upon the information and then sends out efferent signals. These efferent signals can either modify the nature of the somatic system or leave it exactly as it is operating. When the complex interactions of the central and peripheral nervous systems are considered in relation to the large number of our bodies' structures, it is clear that the biological reasons for our behavior are very complicated.

We have outlined the major structures and subdivisions of the nervous system but have spent little time looking at the way information is analyzed and transmitted. The nature of electrical activity in the nervous system is our next area of exploration.

ELECTRICAL ACTIVITY IN THE NERVOUS SYSTEM

Stop for a moment and review. You know that the brain and spinal cord are very complex structures and that all of the structures of the nervous system are involved in behavior. Furthermore, you know that the hormones our glands secrete affect our behavior, and that you can affect your body through drug consumption. The structure of the nervous system and its functions have also been referred to. One very important question, though, has not been examined. How does the nervous system convey messages to muscles and glands and vice versa? Although researchers know less about electrical activity in the nervous system than about structures and functions, what they do know is intriguing. Much of this knowledge has come from hospitals and laboratories where researchers have tried to assess abnormalities in brain structures and function. For example, some of our knowledge about electrical activity in the brain has come from the diagnosis and treatment of epilepsy.

The nervous system is constantly active, so even as we sleep neurons are firing. The activity of the nervous system can be measured through two basic procedures, the first of which is called single unit recording. With this technique, a thin wire or needle is placed next to or within a single cell. Long wires are attached to this recording needle and sent to an amplifier that records and amplifies changes in the electrical activity at the cell. These data are then followed on an oscilloscope, a device used for recording changes in electrical voltage. Since neurons fire so rapidly, it is very often necessary to feed data into a computer that averages the number of times the cell fires within a single second or within a single minute. Most of the work in recording single units or single cells is done with animals. For example, when examining the extent to which cells in the visual cortex fire to visual stimulation, researchers have often used single unit techniques. Human experimentation in this research is limited since it involves placing wires within the skull; cats, rats, and monkeys are typical species that have been examined.

A second widely used technique for examining electrical activity in the nervous system of both humans and animals is called electroencephalog-

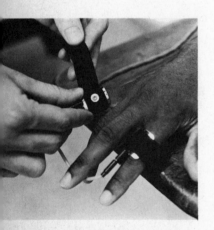

Monitoring the electrical activity in the skin is one way of measuring the emotional responses of subjects.

raphy. This technique produces a record of activity called the **electroenceph-alogram** or, as it is better known, the EEG. An EEG is recorded by placing a small electrode on the scalp of a subject. The electrode is usually less than one-quarter inch in diameter and, although rather small, records the activity from thousands of cells beneath the skin.

EEGs are recorded for a variety of purposes, including the assessment of brain damage, epilepsy, tumors, and other kinds of abnormalities. Although the exact nature of brain waves is not yet fully understood, we do know enough to say that certain brain waves are common to everyone. Awake, healthy human beings, who are relaxed and not engaged in directed thinking when an EEG is recorded, show brain waves that are called *alpha waves*. Alpha waves occur at a rate of about 8 to 12 cycles per second. The brain waves of a person who has become excited change dramatically from alpha waves to waves of high frequency and low amplitude. These are *beta* and *gamma waves*. When people are asleep during different times in the night, their brain waves show a pattern of both high-frequency–low-amplitude bursts as well as low-frequency waves. We will be explaining these brain waves when we study sleep in chapter 9.

Individuals can manipulate their EEGs by changing their level of excitation. A relaxed individual showing alpha waves on a polygraph can change those alpha waves to high-frequency waves just by becoming more alert and paying attention. Since subjects can change their brain wave activity by changing their bodily states, they might be able to control other aspects of their behavior while their brain waves are being monitored. This notion is supported by a series of studies in the rather new area of psychological interest called biofeedback. One of the aims of biofeedback is to help people cope with life and manage their own bodies in competent, successful ways. While psychologists try to help people to manage aspects of their behavior, their aim is to help people cope more effectively, not to control their behavior.

Electroencephalogram (EEG) The record of an organism's electrical brain patterns. EEGs are recorded by placing electrodes on the scalp of a subject; they pick up the electrical activity of the brain.

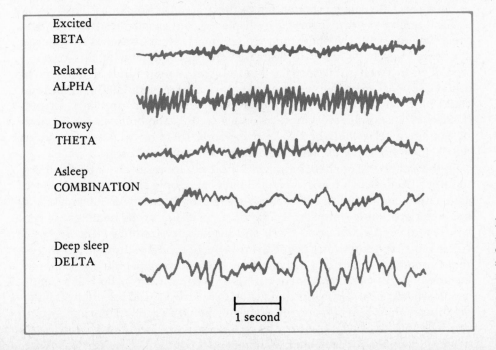

Excited
BETA

Relaxed
ALPHA

Drowsy
THETA

Asleep
COMBINATION

Deep sleep
DELTA

1 second

Figure 2.19 Human electrical activity patterns. Note that different states of excitation show characteristic EEG activity. High frequency on this record is shown by a large number of waves occurring within a single unit or period of time

Biofeedback and Muscle Tension

From time to time you may have a problem that makes you tense—so tense, in fact, that you may get a headache. Some people suffer from these tension-caused headaches far too often. Research on biofeedback has shown that it helps people with such headaches.

It is very easy to monitor the level of muscle tension in an individual and give immediate feedback to the subject. Haynes, Moseley, and McGowan (1974) have reported a study in which subjects were presented with information on the technique of biofeedback in an effort to reduce the muscle tension of their foreheads or were taught to relax these muscles through standard procedures such as relaxation training. In relaxation training, groups of subjects were instructed to passively allow the muscles of their forehead to become relaxed. A second relaxation group was told to relax the muscles in their forehead by alternately tensing and relaxing muscles. A

control group was told to relax but given no specific instructions on how to do it. The fourth group, the biofeedback group, was given a tone via earphones through which listeners could assess how relaxed their individual foreheads were by the pitch of the tone.

The results of the study showed that biofeedback not only effectively aided muscle relaxation, but also was significantly more effective than the relaxation procedures or the control procedure.

All studies do not find that biofeedback is more effective than other techniques; however, in this experiment subjects were tested for only one session and there were significant results. These results provided strong support for the effective use of biofeedback in the reduction of stress-related symptoms. (See chapter 13 on psychotherapy for a discussion of the potential uses of biofeedback to treat behavior disorders.)

Biofeedback

Studies are now being completed in which subjects are trying to control functions of their bodies not previously considered controllable. Neal Miller (1969) found that individuals can monitor and control the activity of certain organs and functions of their bodies. Miller trained rats to control certain glandular responses and suggested that these techniques can be used with humans. For example, one might attach electrodes over different organs of the body and allow subjects to monitor these activities on an oscilloscope. A subject might see her heart rate displayed on an oscilloscope. As she breathed more quickly, she would see her heart rate increase; as she relaxed she would see her heart rate decrease. The eventual aim of this training would be to teach subjects what kind of bodily states they should try to achieve so as to make their bodies work the way they should. This technique could be particularly useful for people with high blood pressure, tension headaches, insomnia, and chronic backaches. By using biofeedback they can be taught to relax their bodies; consequently their blood pressure can go down, their backache go away, and sleep come more easily.

Biofeedback The general technique by which individuals can monitor the "involuntary" activity of certain organs and bodily functions and thereby learn to control them.

In the last few years there has been a great deal of research on **biofeedback** training. The research has involved all kinds of people and problems. For example, there have been studies on the use of biofeedback with alcoholics as a treatment procedure (Johnson, 1978; Lenigan, 1977), for the treatment of certain skin diseases (Manuso, 1977), and in memory training (Mapes, 1977). While biofeedback training is not always effective, some studies have shown some important results that can affect the lives of many people. For example, Dietvorst (1977) used biofeedback training with patients who had recently had heart attacks; these people tend to be very anxious and are often afraid of the future. Their nervousness often gets in the way of their recovery. Everyone tells the heart attack victim to take it easy and relax; with each such warning, they often become more anxious. Dietvorst trained heart attack patients to decrease the level of arousal by monitoring a measure of autonomic activity, hand temperature. The patients were able to lower their level of arousal and thus their anxiety. While the results are complicated and affected by a number of variables, it seems that the use of biofeedback to help certain subject populations (like heart attack victims) to relax is a most reasonable possibility. Of course, one need not be a heart attack victim to use biofeedback; it has been used successfully to treat hyperactivity in children (Hampstead, 1977; Whitmer, 1977), nearsightedness (Trachtman, 1978), and even depression (Delk, 1977). By using basic research from the laboratory, researchers have been able to apply this knowledge to treat a whole array of disorders that have varied from speech pathology (Davis & Drichta, 1980), the acquisition of fine motor movements (French, 1980), to the control of sexual arousal (Hoon, 1980).

Biofeedback revolves around the notion that people can repeat or recall behavior or bodily states that they find pleasurable or reinforcing. People with tension headaches monitor the muscle tension in their necks, and when they relax the headaches are reduced. By monitoring tension in their necks, the subjects learn what they can do to reduce their muscle tension and, therefore, reduce their headaches (see Adams, Feuerstein, & Fowler, 1980). By monitoring skin temperature a patient may be able to lower his or her overall level of arousal and reduce anxiety. Although the effectiveness of the technique is still controversial (e.g., Raskin, Bali, & Peeke, 1980; Surwit & Keefe, 1978), the potential of biofeedback is great because the patient may eventually be able to use it at home.

Figure 2.20 Patients can be taught to use biofeedback to monitor the electrical activity of their bodies in order to reduce muscle tension

SUMMARY

We study the biological bases of behavior because of the important influence our bodies have on behavior. If a person is having emotional problems and is tense, high-strung, and nervous, it may be because of some hormonal imbalance that could be easily treated. Alternatively, stress, tension, or fear might alter the person's hormone system and thus his or her behavior. Certainly, an understanding of the hormonal system is essential to an understanding of the behavior of humans and animals.

In addition to our concern with behavior, we realize that it is important to know about the potentialities that each person is born with. A person's behavior is certainly going to be determined by his or her potential as well as by heredity. Studies of twins can be used to assess many aspects of behavior, including intelligence and behavior disorders. For example, twin studies have shown that schizophrenia is more likely in both members of a pair of identical twins than in both members of a pair of fraternal twins or siblings. However, even in identical twins, if one twin develops schizophrenia, the other twin will not necessarily develop it. This means that heredity cannot answer all of the questions, but it is certainly involved.

We are forced to conclude that both heredity and environment are involved in intelligence, schizophrenia, and other aspects of behavior. The big question still remains—how much of behavior can be accounted for by heredity? The answer to this question is still unclear, but with further studies into the nature of DNA and chromosomes, psychologists are gaining a greater understanding of the basic building blocks of heredity.

The nervous system is so complex that it sometimes seems that no one will ever be able to fully understand it. This will not always be the case because scientists are answering many questions about how the brain is structured and how it functions. Different areas of the brain have been mapped out, and their roles in seeing, hearing, and thinking are being examined. Many questions remain unresolved, but electrophysiological studies, as well as anatomical studies of the nervous system, are providing important data about the structure of the brain and how its functions might control or influence behavior.

Psychologists try to understand biological bases of behavior to help people live happier lives. For example, hormones and drugs are used in the treatment of hyperkinetic or overly active children to help control their erratic behavior. Similarly, the use of biofeedback is being expanded each day to help people get rid of their tension headaches, backaches, and high blood pressure. If biofeedback fulfills its potential, it may be a quick and easy way of treating patients with stress-related problems.

The use of drugs and biofeedback is a direct way of having control over our bodies. In addition, through the study of the nervous system, genetics, and hormones, we are coming ever closer to understanding how our bodies naturally control our behavior. The biological bases of behavior are important because many emotional problems and day-to-day behaviors are determined by our bodies. Each area of psychology in one way or another comes back to the basic abilities that each person is born with. Each time psychology asks the question, nature vs. nurture, we need to know each person's basic abilities. The study of the biological bases of behavior serves as a firm foundation on which psychologists examine other aspects of everything that people think, feel, and do. A critical concept to be remembered is that behavior is affected by both nature and nurture, heredity and environment. These two factors affect each other and the resulting behavior of the individual.

CHAPTER REVIEW

1. Heredity is the potential given to each person by his or her parents through the transmission of genes.
2. A person's heredity is unique because the genetic contributors, his or her parents, each have a unique genetic makeup.
3. Chromosomes are the carriers of genes, the basic unit in heredity.
4. The 23 pairs of chromosomes contain many genes made up of DNA.
5. All of the inherited potential of people is carried by chromosomes.
6. The 23rd pair of chromosomes determines sex.
7. In Down's syndrome there are three number 21 chromosomes.
8. Conflicting results have surrounded studies of XYY chromosomes in men.
9. Identical twins share exactly the same genetic heritage; they come from one ovum and one sperm. Fraternal twins are produced by two ova and two sperm and can, therefore, be either males, females, or a male and a female.
10. The endocrine glands secrete hormones into the bloodstream that affect behavior.
11. The pituitary gland, or master gland, is made up of anterior and posterior lobes.
12. The pancreas, which produces insulin, helps the body metabolize sugar.
13. Each gland controls a different aspect of behavior, but all are in one way or another related to the pituitary.
14. The basic building block of the nervous system is the neuron, which is made up of dendrites, a cell body, and a long slim axon. The neuron fires in an all-or-none manner and has a refractory period during which it cannot fire. The space be-

tween the end branches of an axon and the dendrite of another neuron is called the synapse.

15. The nervous system is composed of two subsystems, the central and peripheral nervous system.

16. The central nervous system is made up of the brain and spinal cord. The brain can be divided up into three separate sections: the hindbrain, midbrain, and forebrain. The spinal cord joins the brain at its base.

17. The peripheral nervous system carries information to the spinal cord and the brain through a series of nerve fibers that run up and down the spinal cord. It is divided into the somatic and autonomic nervous systems. The autonomic nervous system is made up of two parts, the sympathetic and parasympathetic nervous systems, each having a different function.

18. The cerebral hemispheres each have control over different aspects of behavior, and some individuals have been identified whose brains have been actually split in half, surgically or in accidents.

19. The nervous system is constantly active, and the electrical activity in it can be recorded through techniques such as the electroencephalogram or EEG. The EEG can be used to assess disease as well as the types of activity taking place in thought or other types of behavior.

20. Biofeedback is the technique that allows people to monitor the activity of their bodies so that they can eventually have some control over a particular activity.

SUGGESTIONS FOR FURTHER READING

CARLSON, N. R. *Physiology of behavior* (2nd ed.) Boston: Allyn & Bacon, 1981.

GAZZANIGA, M. S. *The bisected brain.* New York: Appleton-Century-Crofts, 1970.

HEBB, D. O. *The organization of behavior.* New York: John Wiley & Sons, 1949.

THOMPSON, R. *Introduction to physiological psychology.* New York: Harper & Row, 1975.

REGULARITIES IN THE ENVIRONMENT allow the world to be understood; without certain systematic events, people would be confused. Animals need to know where to find and how to stalk their prey; similarly, humans need to nurture their young, to work to find food and shelter, and, in modern society, to understand a complex and everchanging world. All organisms need to understand and interpret their environment so that they can learn its regularities and eventually come to have some control over it. When we study the process of learning, we are studying the changes that take place in the behavior of an organism because of previous experience. Through learning we begin to establish control over ourselves, our environment, and perhaps other people. The purpose of this chapter is to describe some of the basic principles that underlie learning and memory processes in both animals and humans. Learning is a fundamental process and a concept repeatedly used by psychologists in every aspect of the study of behavior.

CHAPTER 3

Learning

If you put a rat in front of a bunch of tunnels and put cheese in one of them, the rat will go up and down the tunnels looking for the cheese. If every time you do the experiment you put the cheese down the fourth tunnel, eventually you'll get a successful rat. This rat knows the right tunnel and goes directly to it every time.

If you now move the cheese out of the fourth tunnel and put it at the end of another tunnel, the rat still goes down the fourth tunnel. And, of course, gets no cheese. He then comes out of the tunnel, looks the tunnels over, and goes right back down the cheeseless fourth tunnel. Unrewarded, he comes out of the tunnel, looks the tunnels over again, goes back down the fourth tunnel again, and again finds no cheese.

Now the difference between a rat and a human being is that eventually the rat will stop going down the fourth tunnel and will look down the other tunnels, and a human being will go down the tunnel with no cheese forever. Rats, you see, are only interested in cheese. But human beings care more about going down the right tunnel.

It is the belief which allows human beings to go down the fourth tunnel *ad nauseam*. They go on doing what they do without any real satisfaction, without any nurturing, because they come to believe that what they are doing is *right*. And they will do this forever, even if there is no cheese in the tunnel, as long as they believe in it and can prove that they are in the right tunnel.

ADELAIDE BRY
EST: Erhard Seminars Training

Human beings are not rats, and cheese as well as other things affects what they do. Some consider cheese seeking a vice; others see it as a virtue. The important point of this story is that human beings can learn how to behave like rats, for rewards; but unlike rats, they also have the ability to make decisions based on abstract ideas. Human behavior is far more complex than that of an animal like a rat, but basic learning processes do underlie rat learning and human learning. Learning represents changes in a person's behavior; some people learn well and others do not.

Chances are good that you learned and can remember the name of your first grade teacher. You are also likely to remember the names of your second and third grade teachers, but in contrast, you probably don't remember the name of the author of this textbook. Why do we remember some things but forget or never learn others? Remembering, forgetting, and learning are words which seem to indicate that there has been some change in our ability to recall. So much of our everyday behavior is learned that we take it for granted. We learned to read, write, and talk in the early years of our life. In addition, some have learned to speak French, Spanish, and computer language; we have also learned such social niceties as table manners, polite language, and how to interact with others.

No one will argue that people learn thousands of things in a lifetime, but knowing *what* a person learns tells us little about the process of learning. Psychologists want to know *how* people learn, not what they learn. The process of learning itself cannot be seen or measured; in order to study learning we have to study a person's overt behavior, or performance. Performance is what a person does, and from it a psychologist can infer that learning has taken place. If after teaching a child to multiply, you hear her recite the multiplication tables, you can infer that she has learned the process. So learning can be measured through behavior. On the other hand, people learn many things in life that may be stored in memory but may not consistently be shown through performance. For example, an emotionally disturbed child may not use proper table manners even though he may have learned them. Thus, while performance changes are the easiest way to tell if learning has taken place, performance of a behavior is not always seen. Think of how many times you may have learned something for an exam that you forgot during the exam. In the same way, a 4-year-old may be able to identify her A, B, Cs, but unless asked to do so by a caring adult, this learning may not be shown.

While remembering that learning may or may not be shown in performance, let's define it. Learning is a relatively permanent change in behavior that occurs as a result of experience. This means that inborn **reflexes** (for example, the knee jerk) are not learned because the organism can respond reflexively without having prior experience. People learn to ride a bicycle, to speak Hebrew, to argue, to think logically, and to fear dentists.

When psychologists first studied learning, they looked at simple behaviors that seemed related, such as learning new skills and remembering or learning new information. The basic idea leading these investigators was that certain stimuli seemed to be associated with certain responses. Early researchers in learning, therefore, looked at the relationship of performance to stimuli; sometimes these experiments were examining the responses of animals to signals like bells and lights. These were conditioning experiments. Other early studies were attempts to investigate how well people could remember new ideas or concepts.

We have learned much about the way humans learn by studying animal learning. Some psychologists have made a distinction between animal and human learning, but this distinction is arbitrary because learning underlies both human and animal behavior. In some cases, this distinction may be brought about because of verbal factors—animals cannot take part in learning experiments in which spoken answers are necessary.

In our investigation of learning, we shall first consider the basic learning process known as conditioning, then consider higher level learning which typically involves verbal components and memory. As you read and *learn* new terms and concepts, try to figure out how these concepts have helped or hindered you in learning a new language, your first grade teacher's name, a basic skill, or how they have influenced your habits.

Learning A relatively permanent change in behavior that occurs as a result of experience.

Reflex An involuntary behavior that occurs in response to stimuli without prior learning.

Awkward at first, preteenagers learn the skills for successful social exchanges.

Paper training a puppy is often difficult because we are taking an animal of only moderate intelligence and trying to make it control its bladder and bowel functions. The puppy must recognize that its bladder needs to be emptied and then must indicate that it needs to empty it (and then must do it only in the designated place). The dog has little motivation to learn, so people resort to different techniques that include punishing it as well as coaxing it with love and affection. Such techniques can be effective if those who use them keep in mind some simple learning principles.

The first learning principles we will study are those of conditioning. **Conditioning** is the procedure through which conditioned responses are learned. We are all familiar with conditioning, although we may not have used the term. Most of us respond predictably when we walk into a dentist's office. Through conditioning, we have learned to associate the dentist's office with drilling and subsequent pain. The stimulus of the office brings about a definite set of learned fear responses. Psychologists refer to these learned responses as *conditioned responses*.

When the first psychologists began to study learning, they realized that many of the learned responses that both animals and humans make are similar to reflexive behavior. This means that like reflexes, they happen involuntarily. Reflexive behaviors are elicited or brought about by a stimulus; each time the stimulus occurs, the reflexive response occurs. So, food in the mouth leads to salivation; a tap to the knee leads to a knee jerk; and a bright light in the eye leads to the pupil contracting. When any of these stimuli are presented, they elicit a particular reflexive response. Many people have come to respond almost reflexively to dentists and their offices. We all know that dentists are human beings who have families and love their children; they should not elicit a set of fear responses. However, some of us have become conditioned to respond to the sight of a dentist's drill; for some people even the thought of entering a dentist's office elicits fear. Our fears of dentists and their offices occur so automatically in response to specific stimuli (that is, the dentist's drill and the thought of the dentist's office) that they appear reflexive. Like reflexes, these responses are involuntary; unlike reflexes, these responses are learned. To better understand how people learn or become conditioned, let us explore the pioneering experiments of the Russian biologist turned psychologist, Pavlov.

Process

Ivan Pavlov (1927) reported a series of experiments in which he used conditioning to teach dogs. Pavlov knew that it was normal for dogs to salivate when they ate. Salivation is a reflexive, involuntary behavior. But he noticed and was amazed to see that salivation was occurring even before the dogs tasted their food. He thought that perhaps the early salivation was occurring because the dogs had made an association between food and the trainers who brought them their food. This insight led Pavlov to see if he could condition or teach dogs to salivate to a new stimulus, a bell.

Since food is a natural or unlearned stimulus that produces salivation, Pavlov called it an **unconditioned stimulus.** He called salivation the **unconditioned response** because salivation is the natural, unlearned, involuntary re-

Conditioning A systematic procedure through which conditioned responses are learned.

Unconditioned stimulus A stimulus that normally produces an involuntary measurable response.

Unconditioned response The unlearned or involuntary response to an unconditioned stimulus.

sponse to food in the mouth. The unconditioned stimulus, food, brought about the unconditioned response, salivation. Pavlov attached tubes inside the dogs' mouths to measure the amount of saliva produced. After establishing the amount of salivation that was produced by food, Pavlov introduced a new stimulus, a bell. The bell, which normally has no relationship to salivating, was called a *neutral stimulus.* Pavlov measured the amount of saliva produced by the dogs when a bell alone was rung and found the amount of saliva to be negligible. Then he began the conditioning process. He rang the bell and *immediately* blew food powder into the dog's mouths. After a few days of hearing the bell (neutral or conditioning stimulus) along with presentation of the food powder, the dog's normal response of salivating (unconditioned response) was easily evoked by the bell. At this point, when the bell on its own was able to elicit salivation, things had changed. The dogs had learned a new response—that of salivating to the sound of a bell. The bell was then called a **conditioned stimulus** because, through learning, it elicited salivation.

Salivation to the sound of a bell is a learned response called a **conditioned response.** Pavlov discovered that although the conditioned stimulus evoked a response similar to the unconditioned response, the conditioned response was somewhat weaker. Food produced a few more drops of saliva than the bell was able to produce. This entire process is called **classical conditioning;** sometimes it is called *Pavlovian conditioning*—the names are interchangeable.

A key characteristic of classical conditioning is that a formerly neutral stimulus *elicits* or brings about a response; this result is achieved by repeatedly pairing the neutral stimulus with one that naturally elicits a response, the unconditioned stimulus. A bell doesn't naturally elicit salivation, but food does; however, if a bell is presented along with food, it can become a conditioned stimulus and bring about a conditioned response—salivation. Again, a formerly neutral stimulus comes to elicit a reflexive-like response.

Conditioned stimulus The stimulus that, through repeated association with an unconditioned stimulus, becomes capable of eliciting a response.

Conditioned response The response brought about by a conditioned stimulus.

Classical conditioning A conditioning process where, by being paired with a stimulus that naturally elicits a response, a neutral stimulus also comes to elicit a similar or even identical response; sometimes called *Pavlovian conditioning.*

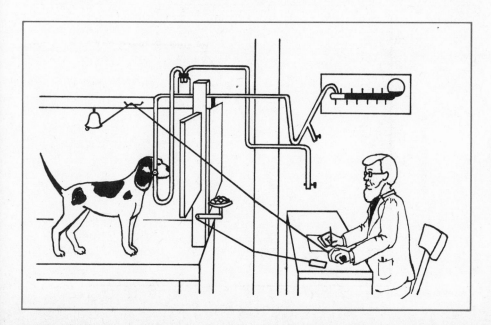

Figure 3.1 Pavlov measured the salivary responses of dogs when he paired food with a bell and when the bell was presented alone. Drops of saliva were collected by a tube connected to the dog's cheek. When a bell was rung, food was presented and these two events became associated. This kind of association is a fundamental component of classical conditioning

Figure 3.2 In classical conditioning, there are three basic stages by which a neutral stimulus eventually leads to a conditioned response, such as salivating

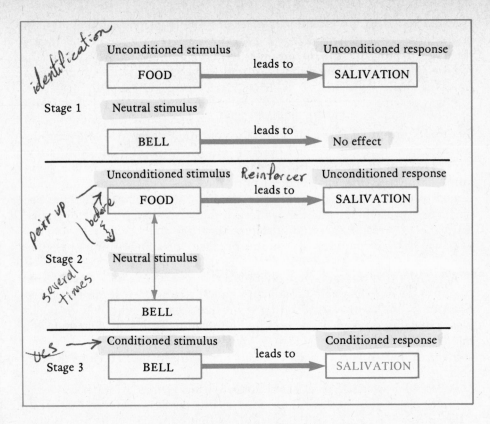

Figure 3.3 In classical or Pavlovian conditioning, the first pairings of the conditioned stimulus with the unconditioned stimulus do not bring about a conditioned response. Thus, if presented with the conditioned stimulus alone, an organism in the early days of conditioning might make few if any conditioned responses. However, over a period of many days or trials, the probability increases significantly. If a light were paired with food powder and the conditioned response were salivation, an organism (such as a dog) would not salivate when presented with the light alone near the end of a feeding session. However, after many days of such pairings, the probability of a conditioned response, such as salivation occurring in response to a light only, is markedly higher. This kind of graph is sometimes called an *acquisition curve;* it shows the course of acquisition of a conditioned response

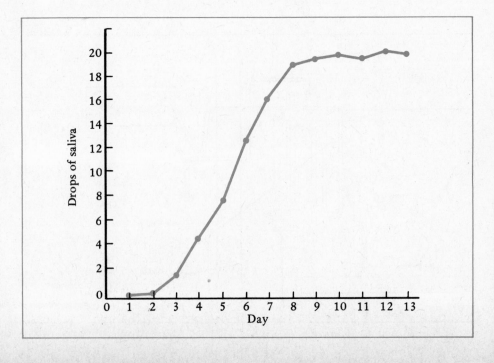

Classical conditioning can be shown with responses like salivation in dogs; it can also be seen in a variety of ways with humans. Let's take a look at how conditioning can affect a human infant. When an infant's lips are touched with an object, the infant immediately starts sucking. The object that touches the lips is usually the nipple of a breast or bottle, and the infant sucks to get milk. The nipple's touch is an unconditioned stimulus that elicits sucking (an unconditioned response). By repeated pairing of a sound or light with the nipple, infants suck at the mere introduction of the sound or light. Marquis (1931) showed this effect in infants after only 9 days of conditioning.

The inborn reflexes of sucking and salivating are only two of a series of reflexive behaviors that human infants have. Newborns show reflexive responses to loud noises, pain, falling, and even strange people or surroundings. When a loud noise is made, newborns exhibit a startle response—outstretching of the arms and legs and associated changes in heart rate, blood pressure, and respiration. These responses as a group are considered fear responses. Infants and children naturally respond with fear to loud noises, pain, or strange people.

Whenever a stimulus can naturally elicit a response, psychologists have learned that other neutral stimuli can be conditioned to elicit them also. One's heart rate, breathing, blood pressure, and sweating are examples of responses that can be tied to a neutral stimulus during conditioning. How many times have we seen automobile commercials on television featuring an exceptionally attractive model or movie personality? The commercial's producers are trying to get us to associate their car (a neutral stimulus) with a response of excitement or pleasure. They do this by pairing their product with a stimulus (an exceptionally attractive model) that elicits an emotional response. They hope that each time we see their automobile on subsequent occasions, it too will elicit a pleasant reaction.

It is easy to see how stimuli become associated with naturally occurring pleasant reactions. Humans and animals also respond to stimuli in defensive ways—for example, by showing a startle response to pain and loud noises. Psychologists have studied extensively a number of stimuli that bring about such defensive reactions. Electric shock is a stimulus that elicits a defensive reaction. If applied to one's fingertips, electric shock normally elicits an avoidance response. Similarly a particularly bitter taste or nauseating smell elicits avoidance. Imagine the situation in which a dog is shocked a few times every minute. As it is shocked, a light comes on and is paired with the shocks. Within just a few pairings of the light and the electric shock, one sees a conditioned response. The dog retracts its paw upon presentation of the light alone.

Not as dramatic as the effects on an electric shock, the effects of a puff of air on the eye blink have been extensively studied over the years. When a puff of air is delivered to the eye, the natural unconditioned response on the part of the organism is to blink. If a light or buzzer is paired with the delivery of puffs of air, the light or buzzer can come to elicit the eye blink. This effect has been found in a wide range of animals as well as in humans and even infants (Hilgard & Marquis, 1935; Lintz et al., 1967). We must note that not all stimuli can be easily conditioned to elicit a response. Some responses work well with certain types of stimuli but not with others. For example, certain orga-

Research in conditioning is often carried out with rats and with equipment like this.

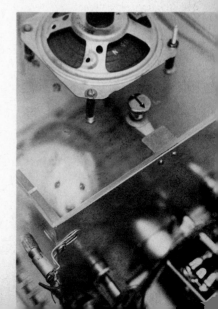

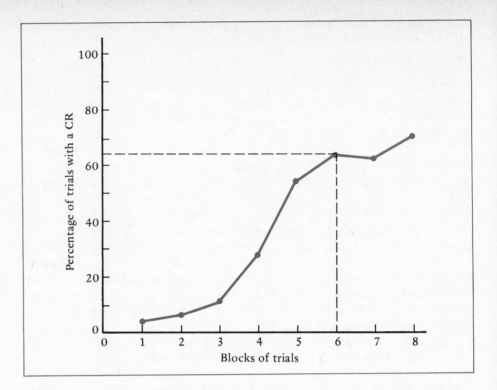

Figure 3.4 The development or acquisition of a conditioned eye blink response in a rabbit is shown. The percentage of trials that showed a conditioned eye blink response is plotted for a series of 8 blocks of trials. While initially there were few conditioned responses, by the 6th block eye blinks were made 65% of the time (data from Schneiderman, Fuentes, and Gormezano, 1962)

nisms can learn to associate being sick with certain smells or tastes; however, a response of nausea is very difficult to elicit by using lights or bells.

CONDITIONING EMOTIONAL RESPONSES.   Some psychologists believe that all emotional responses are classically conditioned to the stimuli that bring them about. Let's consider an example of how this can come about. A child may be playing with a cat, a rabbit, or dog. Suddenly, a loud noise occurs and the child is frightened. If this sequence occurs repeatedly, the child will become conditioned to be afraid each time he or she sees the former friend. Thus, the emotional response, fear, has been classically conditioned.

People who deliver mail in suburban neighborhoods may have had the experience of being bitten by an angry or violent dog. Needless to say such bites are painful and certainly frightening. Bites induce pain; an unconditioned stimulus has brought about an unconditioned response. Since dogs bring about the pain, they can become conditioned stimuli that can in turn bring about a series of defensive reactions associated with fear and pain. Each time people who deliver mail see a dog, any dog, they may exhibit the classically conditioned response to fear—increased heart rate, respiration, and sweating. We also recognize that other neutral stimuli like children, cats, and employers are equally capable of becoming conditioned stimuli and of eliciting defensive reactions.

Once a formerly neutral stimulus has taken on conditioning value, it is likely to evoke a conditioned response each time it is presented to the subject. So, if a specific person has always been associated with the delivery of pain, it is not unlikely that upon seeing that person on another occasion a conditioned response of fear is likely to be emitted. The mere presence of a formerly neutral person, such as a dentist, physician, or mortician, who has become associated with pain or painful experiences may cause a rush of fear. In the same way, even such a person's office may come to be associated with pain and a fear response.

The impact of Pavlovian conditioning on our everyday lives is also illustrated when one considers that the conditioned stimulus need not be available directly to get a conditioned response; we call this higher order conditioning. **Higher order conditioning** is a situation where a neutral stimulus that has been associated with a well-established conditioned stimulus takes on conditioning properties. Let us consider an example. A light becomes a conditioned stimulus that brings about a set of fear responses in a dog. In such a situation, the light is paired with electric shocks, so upon seeing the light (conditioned stimulus), the dog exhibits a conditioned response (fear). After repeated sessions and a well-established response, suppose that on certain occasions we present a bell along with the light and that such pairings occur without the shocks. The new stimulus (the bell) could also elicit a fear response—it too would have the potential to take on conditioned stimulus properties. While it would take repeated pairings for such conditioning to happen, the organism would learn to associate the two events. Now suppose another variation: What if the new stimulus event were an experimenter in a white lab coat? The organism could then associate the experimenter in the white lab coat with the bell or light. It is possible that after enough trials, the organism would begin to make conditioned fear responses not only to the light, but also to the bell and to people in white lab coats. Thus, the experimenter, the bell, or the light could elicit a fear response; the organism now has three stimuli to which it is conditioned (Pavlov, 1927; Rescorla, 1977).

Over the last decade some of classical conditioning's principles have been applied to help treat people with behavior problems. While we will be exploring the techniques more fully in chapter 13 (p. 604), the technique of systematic desensitization uses the ideas of classical conditioning. The basic idea is that people who are fearful and tense in certain situations can be taught a *new* response to whatever was making them fearful. So, a person who is fearful of snakes, dentists, or even members of the opposite sex can be *taught* through conditioning procedures a new, more adaptive response. If the old conditioned response was fear, the newly conditioned response might be relaxation. So, upon seeing a snake (initially at a distance), the person might be taught to elicit a response of relaxation rather than fear. Eventually, the aim of such therapy is to allow the person to replace the old maladaptive (fearful) response with a new realistic response (relaxation).

The association of events during the process of classical conditioning is a regular aspect of our everyday lives. Conditioning with humans is easily seen when we watch television and movies. We have been conditioned to associate villains who commit heinous crimes with certain types of music, which in turn elicit automatic responses from us. So, even before a villainous character appears on the screen, we can be cued as to how we might respond by the initiation of the "villainous" music.

Higher order conditioning
The process by which a neutral stimulus that is paired with a conditioned stimulus takes on conditioned stimulus properties.

Important Variables in Classical Conditioning

Classical conditioning is not a simple process, although the effect is easily produced with many stimuli in the laboratory and is readily apparent in everyday life. Like many psychological phenomena, many important characteristics of a situation will affect if, when, and under what conditions classical conditioning will occur.

CONTIGUITY. If an unconditioned stimulus is to be paired with a conditioned stimulus, it must occur close in time. Conditioning would hardly be evident if the bell and the food powder in Pavlov's experiment were presented an hour apart. The unconditioned stimulus and the neutral stimulus to be conditioned must be presented close enough in time that they can be associated. They may be separated by a short duration or they may even be presented simultaneously; however, if strong conditioned responses are to occur, then only a brief duration may separate them. How brief is brief? The actual time varies from study to study and is dependent upon a number of circumstances; however, as a general guideline, the neutral (conditioned) stimulus should occur about $\frac{1}{2}$ second *before* the unconditioned stimulus.

It is important to remember that without such pairings, associations between conditioned and unconditioned stimuli cannot occur. We therefore say that the unconditioned stimulus (for example, food powder) acts as a reinforcer; for now, let us call a *reinforcer* some event that acts to increase the likelihood that a response will occur. So, food powder acts as a reinforcer because it acts to increase the likelihood that salivation will occur when a bell or light is presented just before it. A puff of air acts as a reinforcer because its presentation increases the likelihood that a light or tone will elicit a conditioned response, the eye blink. So, in classical conditioning, the unconditioned stimulus acts as a reinforcer, and without it conditioning cannot occur. You will see later that a reinforcer becomes the central element of instrumental conditioning, which will be presented later in the chapter.

FREQUENCY OF PAIRINGS. The mere pairing of the neutral stimulus with the unconditioned stimulus does not generally bring about conditioning—frequent pairings are necessary. The more frequently the bell and food powder appear together, the more quickly can a dog be conditioned to respond with salivation. Once salivation has reached its maximum strength in response to a conditioned stimulus like a bell, further pairings of the bell and food powder do not strengthen the conditioned response any further. It is easy to see that the frequency of pairing must also be considered in relation to the total number of times the unconditioned stimulus is presented. If the bell and food powder are paired on every trial, a dog is conditioned much more quickly than if the bell and food powder are paired on every other trial.

MAGNITUDE OF THE UNCONDITIONED STIMULUS. When the unconditioned stimulus is very weak, it is unlikely that it will elicit a reflexive unconditioned response. Certainly pairing a neutral stimulus with a weak unconditioned one will not lead to conditioning. By contrast, when the unconditioned stimulus is strong and elicits a quick and regular reflexive unconditioned response, then conditioning of the neutral stimulus is more likely and will probably take place in fewer trials. Puffs of air delivered to an

Figure 3.5 The conditioned stimulus (for example, a bell) can be presented before, during, or even after the unconditioned stimulus (for example, food). However, the best conditioning occurs when the conditioned stimulus precedes and overlaps in time with the unconditioned stimulus

Presentation of the Conditioned Stimulus (CS) in relation to the Unconditioned Stimulus (UCS)	Relationship of CS to UCS over time	Conditioning produced
Early and overlapping	CS (Bell) ... 0 1 2 3 4 5 Seconds ... UCS (Food)	Superior
Early	CS (Bell) ... 0 1 2 3 4 5 Seconds ... UCS (Food)	Good to superior
Simultaneous	CS (Bell) ... 0 1 2 3 4 5 Seconds ... UCS (Food)	Poor to none
Delayed	CS (Bell) ... 0 1 2 3 4 5 Seconds ... UCS (Food)	None

organism's eye elicit a conditioned reflex easily, but only when the air puff is sufficiently strong.

Extinction The process whereby the probability of an organism emitting a conditioned response is reduced when the unconditioned stimulus (the reinforcer) is withheld.

Spontaneous recovery The reoccurrence of a conditioned response following a rest period after extinction.

EXTINCTION AND SPONTANEOUS RECOVERY. There is no question that the contiguity of the unconditioned stimulus and the neutral stimulus is important; similarly, the frequency of pairing determines the nature of conditioning. Assume that after conditioning has occurred, we no longer present the unconditioned stimulus (such as food powder). In such a situation the chances of a conditioned response occurring decrease. In classical conditioning, **extinction** is the process of reducing the probability that an organism will respond with a conditioned response by withholding the reinforcement of the unconditioned stimulus. Imagine an eye blink study in which a puff of air has been associated with a buzzer and the buzzer will consistently elicit the conditioned response of an eye blink. If the unconditioned stimulus (the puff of air) is no longer delivered, the likelihood that the buzzer will elicit an eye blink decreases consistently. On the first series of trials, eye blinks will still be elicited when the puff of air is not delivered; after many series the presentation of the buzzer will not elicit an eye blink. We say that the conditioned response of eye blinks has undergone extinction.

A conditioned response that has undergone extinction by the failure to deliver the unconditioned stimulus (such as food powder) will reoccur after a rest period; we call this phenomenon spontaneous recovery. **Spontaneous recovery** is the reoccurrence of a conditioned response after a rest period. Imagine a dog that has been classically conditioned to elicit a salivary response to the sound of a bell. If after a long series of trials food is no longer paired with the bell, the dog will show a decreased likelihood of responding —extinction. However, if the dog is placed in the experimental situation again after a rest period of 20 minutes, the salivary response will reoccur for a brief period of time (though probably not as strongly).

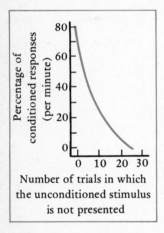

Figure 3.6 The process of extinction. Organisms that have developed a conditioned response to a conditioned stimulus (such as a bell) decrease the percentage of times they emit the conditioned response when they are no longer presented with the unconditioned stimulus (such as food)

STIMULUS GENERALIZATION AND DISCRIMINATION. When an organism responds to a stimulus that is similar—but not the same as—a training stimulus, we say that **stimulus generalization** has taken place. A person responds with an eye blink to a loud tone that has been paired with a puff of air delivered to the eye. If the next time the tone is presented it is just a bit less loud, the person will still respond. If the tone is presented and it is quite soft, it is unlikely to elicit an eye blink. The extent to which an organism will respond with a conditioned response depends on how similar the stimulus is to the training stimulus. Tones that are very similar will produce conditioned responses; tones less similar will produce them to a lesser extent. Tones that are not similar will not elicit conditioned responses at all.

Although similar stimuli will elicit conditioned responses, humans and animals can be trained to discriminate efficiently between conditioned stimuli and to respond only to the conditioned stimulus, not to other ones similar to it. The procedure used to make organisms efficient at **stimulus discrimination** is to pair *only* the exact neutral stimulus with the unconditioned stimulus.

Some of Pavlov's early work points to some of the ways that people in modern day society respond. In studies of stimulus discrimination, Pavlov showed that animals can learn to tell the difference between pairs of stimuli.

Stimulus generalization Responding to stimuli similar to, but not the same as, the training stimulus.

Stimulus discrimination The process by which an organism learns to respond to a specific stimulus and to no other similar stimulus; the complementary process to stimulus generalization.

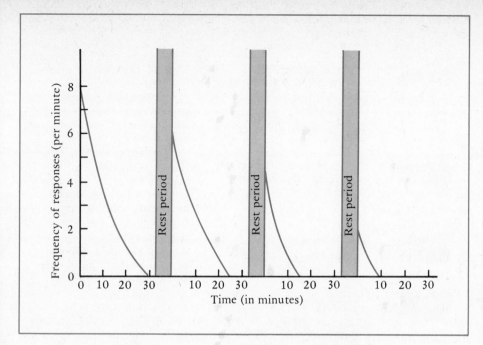

Figure 3.7 A nonreinforced behavior extinguishes; however, after a rest interval an animal will show the response again. The rate of responding will not be as high after a series of rest intervals, and extinction will take place more quickly. This reoccurrence of a conditioned response after a rest period is called *spontaneous recovery*

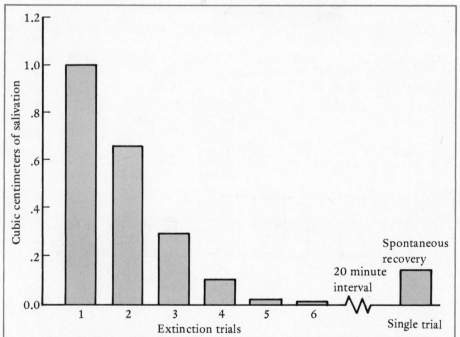

Figure 3.8 In spontaneous recovery, the reoccurrence of a conditioned response takes place after a rest interval. When Pavlov's dogs were producing a salivary response to a conditioned stimulus and were not provided with reinforcement, the amount of salivation decreased over successive trials taking place at 3-minute intervals. After a rest interval of 20 minutes, the salivary response reoccurred; however, it was not as strong as in previous trials (data from Pavlov, 1927, p. 58)

For example, an animal may learn in a conditioning experiment to discriminate between a circle and an ellipse. In some experiments reported by Pavlov (1927), researchers changed the shape of the ellipse so that on each trial it looked more and more like the circle next to it. Eventually, the ability of the animal to discriminate between the circle and the ellipse disappeared. Instead, the animal randomly chose the circle or the other figure that was prac-

Table 3.1 Four important properties of classical conditioning

PROPERTY	DEFINITION	EXAMPLE
Extinction	The process whereby the probability of an organism emitting a conditioned response is reduced when the unconditioned stimulus (the reinforcer) is withheld.	An infant who has been conditioned to suck in response to a light is no longer given the unconditioned stimulus of stroking the lips; the infant stops sucking in response to the conditioned stimulus.
Spontaneous recovery	The reoccurrence of a conditioned response following a rest period after extinction.	A dog conditioned to salivate that has undergone extinction salivates in response to the conditioned stimulus after a rest period.
Stimulus generalization	Responding to stimuli similar to but not the same as the training stimulus.	A dog that has been conditioned to salivate in response to a high-pitched tone salivates also to a lower pitched tone.
Stimulus discrimination	The process by which an organism learns to respond to a specific stimulus and then to no other similar stimulus; the complementary process to stimulus generalization.	A goat that salivates in response to a light can be conditioned to respond *only* to lights of high intensity, not to lights of low intensity.

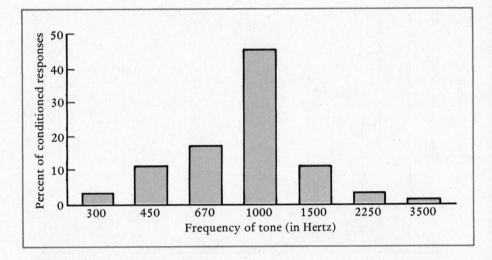

Figure 3.9 Stimulus generalization occurs when an organism elicits a conditioned response to other similar stimuli. In the figure, when an organism was trained with a 1,000-Hertz tone and later was presented with tones of different frequencies, the organism's probability of responding decreased as the tone's frequency became increasingly different (data from Jenkins & Harrison, 1969)

tically a circle. In a situation where the discrimination becomes difficult, if not impossible, animals can become agitated and upset, and they act fearful and aggressive. When an animal is unable to decide which shape to respond to, its normal behavior breaks down. When human beings are placed in similar situations to which they feel forced to make a response but to which they do not know how to respond correctly, they sometimes exhibit the same kind of agitated, aggressive behavior; sometimes their behavior becomes stereotyped and limited in scope. In these cases, people are choosing not to respond to stimuli or to always respond in the same way (Lundin, 1961; Maier & Klee, 1941).

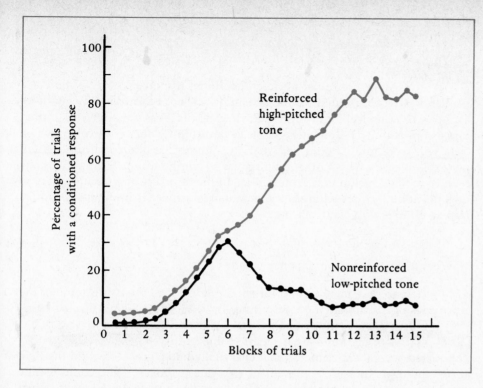

Figure 3.10 In stimulus discrimination, two stimuli initially elicit a conditioned response from an organism. However, when one stimulus continues to be reinforced with the unconditioned stimulus (such as food) and the other is not, stimulus discrimination takes place. In this case, we see conditioned responses being produced for the proper conditioned stimulus but decreasing in frequency for the nonreinforced one (adapted from Schwartz, 1978)

Table 3.2 Types of learning: classical conditioning

TYPE OF LEARNING	PROCEDURE	RESULT	EXAMPLE
Classical Conditioning	A neutral stimulus (such as a bell) is paired with an unconditioned stimulus (such as food).	The neutral stimulus becomes a conditioned stimulus—it elicits the conditioned response.	A bell elicits a salivary response in a dog.

Summary of Key Concepts

In classical conditioning, a stimulus that naturally elicits a response is paired with a neutral stimulus so that the neutral stimulus can become conditioned and elicit the same response. A key idea is that stimuli are eliciting responses. A stimulus brings about a response naturally, reflexively, and involuntarily. The response may be salivating, sweating, increased heart rate, blood pressure, or groups of these characteristics which might be called fear responses. By pairing neutral stimuli with the unconditioned ones that elicit these responses, they too take on the properties necessary to elicit these same responses. The organism is not active in this process; it does not actively participate because the responses are involuntary.

It is important to remember that classical conditioning has certain essential components. Among them are (1) an unconditioned stimulus, (2) an unconditioned response, (3) a neutral (conditioning) stimulus, (4) a closeness in time between the presentation of the neutral stimulus and the unconditioned stimulus, (5) the formation of a conditioned stimulus, and (6) the acquisition of a conditioned response.

While many responses, especially emotional responses, can be shown to be classically conditioned, other behaviors are not reflexive and cannot be explained by classical conditioning. Pavlov and his ideas explain well a limited range of phenomena; however, classical conditioning does not explain why a clerk will work for 40 hours per week in a store. Classical conditioning will not explain easily why a pigeon will press a lever hundreds of times an hour to have food delivered to it. You will see in the next section that another type of conditioning exists wherein the organism's activity is particularly important in establishing conditioning.

INSTRUMENTAL CONDITIONING

Instrumental conditioning A conditioning procedure in which responses that organisms emit are increased or decreased in probability of reoccurring by delivery of a reinforcer or punisher; sometimes called *operant conditioning*.

Each time parents praise a child for good grades, they are using some of the principles of instrumental conditioning. In **instrumental conditioning**, a response is rewarded or punished selectively so that its occurrence will be increased or decreased. In the early part of the century, E. L. Thorndike (1932) conducted several experiments that eventually had a great effect on the field of psychology. Thorndike placed hungry cats in boxes. They could escape from the boxes to get food by hitting a lever on the box which would open the door and allow the food to become available. The behavior that Thorndike was trying to condition (hitting the lever) was quickly performed because upon hitting the lever (usually by accident) the hungry cats received food.

Process

In instrumental conditioning, an animal emits or shows a behavior and then this behavior is followed by a consequence of reward or punishment. You will see shortly that one of the most important components of instrumental conditioning is the consequence of the organism's behavior; consequences usually come in terms of rewards or punishments. Let us focus for the moment on rewards as a consequence.

Reinforcer Any event that increases the probability of the reoccurrence of a response that precedes it.

We call a reward a reinforcer and the actual process of delivering the reward the process of reinforcement. A **reinforcer** is any event that increases the chances of the reoccurrence of a response similar to the one that preceded the reinforcing event. If the response is hitting a lever, then any stimulus event that follows the response and increases the chance of that response happening again would be defined as a reinforcer. In Thorndike's experiment, food served as the reinforcer. It is important to recognize that the delivery of rewards or punishers enables organisms to be conditioned. As in classical conditioning, the amount, delay, and type of these consequences are the chief variables that will determine the extent of conditioning. Instrumental conditioning is sometimes called *operant conditioning;* the two terms will be used interchangeably.

The key concept in instrumental conditioning is that a behavior must first be shown or emitted and then a consequence is delivered. The behavior is

Our pets will jump, roll over, and beg for primary reinforcements.

Skinner box   Named for its developer, B. F. Skinner, this hollow box contains a responding mechanism (usually a lever) capable of delivering a reinforcer (often food or water) to the organism.

B. F. Skinner is one of the most noted behavioral psychologists in the world today.

usually voluntary and, after it is shown, its consequence determines the likelihood of its being emitted again.

Procedures

Much of the research on instrumental or operant conditioning carried out after Thorndike's time has used an apparatus called a Skinner box. The **Skinner box** was named for its developer, the noted psychologist and researcher B. F. Skinner. The box is generally constructed so that whenever an organism (such as a rat) makes a readily identifiable response that the experimenter has decided on beforehand, a consequence, often a reward, will be provided. For example, a small lever or bar may be placed through a hole in the side of the box; whenever the rat presses it, this constitutes a "desired" response that can be rewarded (Skinner, 1938, 1956).

A traditional experiment is one in which a rat that has been deprived of food is placed in a one-cubic foot box. The rat moves around the box, often seeking escape, and eventually it stumbles upon the lever and depresses it. This action delivers a pellet of food into a cup. The rat moves about some

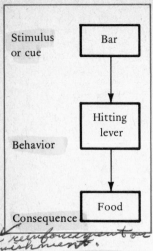

Stimulus or cue — Bar

Behavior — Hitting lever

Consequence — Food

either reinforcement or punishment.

Figure 3.11 In instrumental conditioning—unlike classical conditioning—an organism emits a behavior such as hitting a lever and *then* the behavior is reinforced

more and happens to press the lever again; another pellet of food is delivered. After a few more trials, the rat quickly learns that pressing the lever brings food. A hungry rat will learn to press the lever many times and in rapid succession to obtain the reinforcer.

In both classical and instrumental conditioning, consequences are necessary. In Pavlov's classical conditioning experiments, the food acts as the reinforcer because the sound of a bell would not bring about salivation without food. So, the food or reinforcer increases the probablity that the organism will show the conditioned response (salivation). Food also acts as the reinforcer in instrumental conditioning, for unless the lever-pressing response produces a reinforcer such as food, the animal will make no effort to press the lever at all.

Counting lever presses or measuring salivary responses is a tedious yet necessary part of the process of studying conditioning. Although it is not a problem primarily of psychologists, record keeping has always been difficult in working with animals and doing research. When an animal is placed in a Skinner box, it may press the bar many times within an hour. How is this behavior to be measured or counted? One possibility is to pay an undergraduate student by the hour to sit and count the number of bar presses. This is an inefficient way to collect data. More practical is a simple device called a *cumulative recorder*, which psychologists use to measure animal behavior. In a cumulative recorder, an ink pen is placed on a piece of paper that is constantly moving sideways from right to left, although at a slow rate. If the animal does not make a response, a straight line is drawn on the paper. If the animal makes a response, the pen moves upward toward the top of the page, and the response record begins to appear like a series of steps. As is shown in Figure 3.12, when the recording pen reaches the top of the page, it will automatically return to the bottom of the page and start another sequence of steps. This technique of recording instrumental animal behavior is in wide use today. In fact, it is because of instrumentation like the cumulative recorder that so much progress has been made in animal learning laboratories. Without such devices the work of an experimental psychologist would be slowed down considerably.

Figure 3.12 The cumulative recorder marks each time an organism makes a bar pressing response. The paper in a cumulative recorder moves constantly; if the organism doesn't respond, the pen makes a straight line

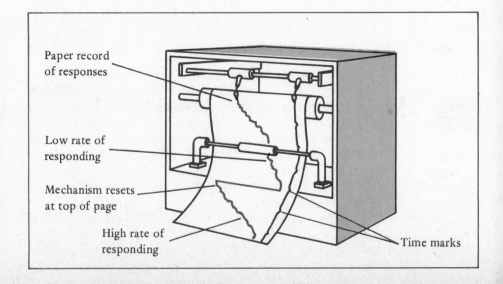

Paper record of responses

Low rate of responding

Mechanism resets at top of page

High rate of responding

Time marks

REINFORCEMENT. The delivery of consequences, reinforcers or punishers, is a critical part of conditioning. Let us look closer at this process, starting with reinforcement. There are two kinds of reinforcers that increase the probability of a response: positive and negative reinforcers. In **positive reinforcement** we increase the likelihood of a response by the delivery of a reward; behavior is established or maintained because a reinforcer is delivered.

Most of us use positive reinforcement in our daily lives. When we teach a dog new tricks, we give him a bone or a pat on the head upon completing the task; these generally work as positive reinforcements. In toilet training a 2-year-old, a parent often applauds when the child has successfully completed a bowel movement; this applause is intended to be a reinforcer. After a week of working a clerk receives a paycheck; this pay is the reinforcer. Why should our dog stand on its hind legs, our 2-year-old control her bowel movements, or the clerk work hard for a week? These behaviors are carried out because they are rewarded, and if the reward is great enough, people will continue to behave in a similar manner for the same reward. Of course, what is considered a reinforcer for one person may not have reinforcing value for another; certainly events that are reinforcing for a white rat are going to be different from those that are reinforcing for a college student. So, in general, we say that a **reinforcer** is any event that increases the probability of the reoccurrence of a response that preceded it.

The delivery of food pellets to a hungry rat that has just pressed a lever increases the likelihood that it will do so again. Psychologists and even nonpsychologists have recognized this phenomenon for many years. They have also recognized, however, that the delivery of these reinforcers only works if the rat is hungry; rats who have just eaten do not find food pellets reinforcing. This means that a rat (or a human being) must need or want food if it is to act as a reinforcer. A number of different needs allow events like food delivery to act as reinforcers. In the next chapter on motivation you will see that hunger motivates organisms to seek food and that needs for achievement motivate people in other ways. Thus, the needs, desires, and general conditions of the organism play an important role in determining what can be considered a reinforcer. In studying learning and conditioning, psychologists have been able to study reinforcement by depriving animals of food or water for a period of time; in doing so they motivate them and allow food delivery to take on reinforcing properties. So, in general, you will see that in most of the experiments that psychologists conduct, the organism is in one way or another motivated; often the motivation comes from hunger or thirst, but other needs motivate behavior as well.

Reinforcers that do not have to be taught are considered **primary reinforcers.** Food serves as a primary reinforcer for a hungry rat, and water serves as a primary reinforcer for a thirsty one. In psychology laboratories, animals are generally deprived of food or water for 24 hours and thus are willing to work for their rewards. But animals and humans don't always work for just food and water. People will work for a paycheck, a pat on the head, or an approving smile. How do these reinforcements work? These reinforcers are **secondary reinforcers,** neutral stimuli that have no intrinsic value for the organism. However, in pairing the neutral stimulus with a reinforcing stimulus, the neutral stimulus becomes a reward too. Consider an example. Neither a pat on the head nor money is a primary reinforcer. They do not

Positive reinforcement Reinforcement that acts to increase the probability of a response reoccurring by the introduction of a rewarding or pleasant stimulus.

Reinforcer Any event that increases the probability of the reoccurrence of a response that precedes it.

Primary reinforcer Any stimulus or event that by its mere delivery or removal acts naturally (without learning) to increase the likelihood of a response that precedes it. For example, food acts as a reward for a hungry organism; similarly, the removal of a painful stimulus acts naturally as a reward.

Secondary reinforcer A neutral stimulus that has no value to the organism, which through pairings with a reinforcing stimulus has taken on reinforcement value.

provide a direct contribution to the survival of the organism, nor do they reduce its hunger or thirst. Money, however, has taken on an important value as a secondary reinforcer, because it can take the value and reward properties of a primary reinforcer such as food. Many pleasures in life are secondary reinforcers that have acquired value, including things such as leather coats that keep us no warmer than cloth ones and racy sports cars that transport us no more quickly than utilitarian four-door sedans.

The basic behavior principles that deal with the process of reinforcement have been known for centuries. A clerk who works hard does so because hard work has brought reinforcement. People are often paid by the hour; the longer they work the more money they make. There are obviously many reasons why a clerk works hard at a law firm, but the most important is the weekly reinforcer, for without it, he or she would most likely quit. Reinforcers can clearly take on many forms, and they will help maintain behaviors for long periods of time if they are strong enough, if they are delivered often enough, and if they are important to the organism involved. Clearly, reinforcement acts to ensure an increase in the likelihood that an organism will repeat the same behavior again (Postman, 1947).

The delivery of reinforcers helps establish behaviors and maintain them. Humans have been known to work very long hours when their rewards are significant. Indeed, successful salespeople usually work 70-hour weeks to reach their sales objectives. Often management will offer salespeople an added bonus during a slow month if they can increase their sales by a certain percentage. Management people are using a little basic psychology; they are reasoning that if the reinforcer (money) is increased, they may be able to get higher sales from their salespeople. The bosses are correct, at least up to a point, because changing the amount of a reinforcer can alter an individual's behavior significantly.

Positive reinforcement is reinforcement in which the probability of a response will be increased because of the presentation of a reward. Now let us consider another kind of reinforcement, negative reinforcement. Consider what happens when a rat is placed in a Skinner box with an electrified grid. The shock is delivered every 50 seconds but can be avoided if the rat presses the bar. The behavior being conditioned is bar pressing. What is the reinforcement? The reinforcement is the avoidance of a painful stimulus. So, **negative reinforcement** is reinforcement that acts to increase the probability of a response due to the removal of an aversive stimulus. Negative reinforcement increases the probability of bar pressing because the shock is avoided.

Both positive reinforcement and negative reinforcement act to increase the likelihood of a response. Positive reinforcements provide pleasant stimuli and rewards; negative reinforcements increase the likelihood of a response by the removal of an aversive stimulus. So, the removal of a shock reinforces a previously emitted behavior like bar pressing. The animal will press the bar to avoid the shock. In the same way, people can learn to take a drug by injection when they find that their pain and suffering are diminished after the injection. The behavior that is established and maintained, self-injection, is learned because it removes or relieves an existing painful condition.

Noxious, aversive, or unpleasant stimuli are often used in experiments with animals to study escape and avoidance patterns. So, negative reinforcement is the principal mode of an organism's learning escape and avoidance behavior patterns. Both of these behaviors are learned through negative rein-

Negative reinforcement Reinforcement that acts to increase the probability of a response by the removal of an aversive event.

forcement. In an escape study, an animal is placed in a Skinner box and the floor of the box is electrified. When the electricity is turned on and the rat is given a mild shock, it generally thrashes around the Skinner box until it bumps against the bar—stopping the shock. In just a few trials a rat will quickly learn to press the bar to escape a shock.

In a similar experiment, a rat is placed in a Skinner box, and a buzzer precedes the shock by a few seconds. A rat will learn that upon hearing the buzzer, it should press the bar, for pressing the bar allows it to avoid the shock. Avoidance conditioning of this type usually involves some kind of escape conditioning. The animal first learns how to escape the shock by pressing the bar; then, when a buzzer is introduced to signal the oncoming shock, avoidance conditioning is easily learned. Most children have mastered both escape and avoidance conditioning at an early age. Appropriate signals from a disapproving parent often bring about an avoidance response so that punishment does not follow. Similarly, a grimace from a disgruntled teacher often proves to be an effective stimulus to a sensitive student. In escape learning, the organism is actually exposed to the unpleasant stimulus and responds to stop it from continuing to annoy or hurt. In avoidance learning, the organism is not exposed to the unpleasant stimulus provided it responds in a manner that prevents the stimulus from ever being delivered.

An easy way to distinguish between positive and negative reinforcement is to think about the addition or subtraction of an event that attempts to increase the likelihood of a behavior (Chance, 1979). In positive reinforcement we add or introduce an event that increases behavior; a reward like food or money is reinforcing. In negative reinforcement, we subtract an event or remove an aversive stimulus and this removal is reinforcing; so, removing an electric shock delivered to a rat's foot is reinforcing. Reinforcement always increases the likelihood of a behavior occurring again—positive reinforcements do so through the addition of a stimulus and negative reinforcements do so through the removal of a stimulus.

Offering a child a cookie only increases the likelihood of future temper tantrums or crying jags.

Punishment The process by which a response that is followed by an undesirable or noxious stimulus decreases in probability of reoccurring.

Primary punisher Any stimulus or event that, by its mere delivery or removal, acts naturally (without learning) to decrease the likelihood of a response that preceded it. For example, the delivery of electric shocks acts as a punishment to a rat; similarly, the removal of food acts naturally to decrease the likelihood of a behavior that preceded it.

Secondary punisher A neutral stimulus with no value to the organism that, through repeated pairings with a punishing stimulus, has taken on punishing qualities.

PUNISHMENT.   We established earlier that when an organism emits a behavior and the behavior is followed by reinforcement, the behavior will be maintained. With reinforcement a researcher or parent is trying to increase the probability of a response; with punishment we try to decrease the probability of a response. Punishment is one of the most commonly used techniques in teaching children and pets to control their behavior. When a pet is nasty to strangers, its owners slaps it; when a child is found writing on the walls with crayons, her mother spanks her. In both cases people are trying to indicate their displeasure with a behavior and are attempting to suppress it.

In **punishment** we are trying to *decrease* the probability of a behavior reoccurring; a noxious or unpleasant stimulus is delivered to the organism when it emits a certain undesirable behavior. A noxious stimuli is one an organism will attempt to avoid. If an animal is punished each time for a specific behavior, the probability that it will continue to emit that behavior decreases. In punishment, the delivery of a noxious stimulus like a slap on the hand, an electric shock, or a spanking will suppress a behavior. Punishment techniques have been used to control the behavior of those who are too young to understand the consequences of some of their potentially dangerous behaviors and of those who are self-destructive or profoundly retarded. A **primary punisher** like electric shock is naturally painful to the organism. A **secondary punisher** is a neutral stimulus that takes on punishing qualities. When a person is given an electric shock or spanking upon emitting some behavior, this is primary punishment. Usually associated with the delivery of the punishment is a verbal command like the word "No." Such verbal stimuli initially have no intrinsic punishing qualities; however, through association with primary punishers, words, frowns, and indifference take on punishing qualities. So, secondary reinforcers and punishers can effectively control behavior. There are probably as many secondary punishers as there are secondary reinforcers, but psychologists know that to establish behavior and maintain it, reinforcement techniques should be used. When reinforcers are used in combination with punishers, then the most effective behavior management technique is possible.

In other forms of punishment, the removal of some pleasant stimulus is noxious to the organism. If a child finds that removal of television watching is unpleasant, it can be used as a punishment; each time a child misbehaves, the privilege of television watching might be taken away. A common punishment procedure that has proved to be very effective is *time-out*. In time-out a person is removed from a situation in which reinforcers might be found; so, a child who hits and kicks is placed in a room where there are no toys, televisions, or people. The behavior that the parent is trying to suppress is hitting and kicking; by removing the child from an environment where positive things can happen, it helps suppress hitting and kicking. The removal of the child from the fun environment is noxious. With teenagers the removal of the family car keys serves as a form of punishment; if the gas tank is left empty, a parent will try to suppress that behavior (leaving the tank empty) by removing the car keys and making the automobile unavailable for a period of time. This form of punishment can be very effective.

Try to think of punishment in terms of addition or subtraction of events to suppress a behavior; we may add a noxious event, like a slap, or we may subtract an event or stimulus, like television watching. In both cases our aim is to *decrease* the likelihood of a behavior.

Table 3.3 Positive and negative reinforcement increase the likelihood of a behavior, whereas punishment decreases its likelihood.

POSITIVE REINFORCEMENT (BEHAVIOR ESTABLISHMENT)	NEGATIVE REINFORCEMENT (BEHAVIOR ESTABLISHMENT)	PUNISHMENT (BEHAVIOR SUPPRESSION)
The introduction of a rewarding and usually pleasant stimulus.	An aversive stimulus is removed and thus the organism is rewarded.	The introduction of an aversive stimulus like an electric shock or a slap on the hand.

Punishment, like reinforcement, is dependent upon a number of important variables. For example, a more intense punishing stimulus has a greater effect than a weak one; delayed punishment is not as effective as immediate punishment. There is no question that punishment can suppress simple behavior patterns; however, it has been shown that once punishment is removed, animals return to the behavior exhibited before punishment was delivered. According to Appel and Peterson (1965), for punishment to remain effective, it must continue to be given. Appel and Peterson argue that punishment by itself is essentially an ineffective way to control or eliminate behavior. However, this does not mean that punishment should not be used. If punishment is used in combination with positive reinforcement for correct behavior, it can be an effective and lasting way of modifying the behavior of an organism. It must be emphasized that punishment *by itself* is not the most effective way to control and change behavior. Punishment suppresses behavior—that is its goal, and that is what it does. However, punishment has its limitations, and we do not always wish to choose punishment when trying to control behavior.

A serious limitation in the use of punishment is that it only suppresses existing behaviors. If a behavior already exists and we want to decrease its frequency, we use punishment; but we can't use punishment to establish a new desired behavior.

Punishment has some serious social consequences. It may cause social disruption (Azrin & Holz, 1966). People who are punished tend to try to escape from the source of punishment. If punishment is used in the home as a means of controlling a child's behavior, the child may try to escape from the home so that future punishment cannot be delivered. Here, punishment may control the child's behavior, but it may also alienate him or her from the home.

Punishment can also bring about aggression. A child or institutionalized patient may try to strike out at the person who provides punishment. This type of behavior is an attempt to eliminate or remove the punisher, and thus eliminate punishment. Punishment can also bring about aggression toward others who are not involved in the delivery of punishment as well. For example, if two rats in a Skinner box both receive painful shocks, they will strike out at one another. In the same way, children or institutionalized patients who are being punished as a group are often hostile and aggressive toward other members of the group. If punishment is going to be used as a means of controlling behavior, then the consequences of punishment to a human as a social animal must be considered since punishment may lead to aggressive or other antisocial behaviors.

SHAPING AND SUPERSTITIOUS BEHAVIORS. Training an animal to press a lever or bar, to jump through a hoop, or to control its bowel movement is usually done in stages. This process of reinforcing behavior that approximates a desired response is called **shaping;** gradually an animal is taught new responses. For example, in teaching a hungry rat to press a bar in a Skinner box, one of the first stages is to get it to come over to the correct side of the box. With an imaginary line, we divide the Skinner box into two halves. Each time we observe the rat crossing over the imaginary line into half where the bar is located, we give it a pellet of food. It doesn't take long for the rat to learn that to get food it must be on one side of the box. In the next stage of shaping, we give the rat food only when it touches the wall where the bar is located. Now the animal must not only cross over to the proper side of the box, but it must also touch the wall. This process can be further refined so that it must touch the middle portion of the wall and then the bar itself. Eventually, the animal must press the bar to receive the food.

This shaping process is very effective in teaching animals new tricks and in helping humans learn new behaviors as well. The behavior that we may wish to shape in a child may be bed making. At first, a child may make the bed very sloppily, but we still reinforce the attempt. Over successive weeks, though, we reinforce only the better attempts. Eventually the child learns that only "good" bed making gets reinforced and so makes the bed well to get the praise, treats, or allowance that we call a reinforcer. An important aspect of shaping is that we cannot expect too much too soon. We must be patient and reinforce all steps, no matter how small, toward the desired behavior (see Fischer & Gochros, 1975).

The technique of shaping is used not only in the laboratory but also in the treatment of emotional disturbances. It will be pointed out in later chapters that psychologists often try to help people cope with their lives by teaching them new, realistic, and acceptable behaviors. The technique of helping the person through small steps, each somewhat closer to the desired behavior or response, is, of course, the use of the basic learning principle called shaping.

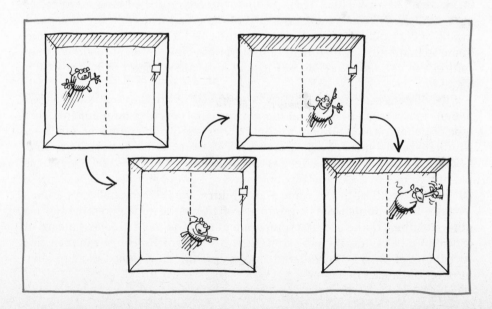

Shaping is the technique of helping an organism through small steps, each somewhat closer to the desired behavior

Many of us often exhibit behaviors that have superstitious origins. When writing a term paper we may always play a certain record, or on going out on a first date we may always wear a certain shirt or pair of shoes. How do these **superstitious behaviors** begin? Generally, superstitious behaviors come about because reinforcement occurred after an activity. On a second instance we happened to be wearing the same clothes and the same reinforcement came about. So we may feel that there is causal relationship; we may feel that wearing a particular pair of shoes ensured a successful date or that playing a certain record made it easier to write a term paper.

Superstitious behavior Behavior learned through coincidental association with reinforcement.

Animals can learn superstitious behaviors while being trained in Skinner boxes. A hungry rat may turn its head to the upper righthand corner of the cage before pressing a bar to receive reinforcement. On trials in which it was learning the bar-pressing response, it came to turn its head to the right before pressing the bar and it always received reinforcement. Of course, this reinforcement was only contingent upon pressing the bar; yet, as long as it turned its head to the right and pressed the bar, it was reinforced. For the rat, both head turning and pressing the bar seemed to be necessary responses (Skinner, 1948).

INTRINSICALLY MOTIVATED BEHAVIOR. Clearly, organisms work for primary and secondary reinforcements, and these reinforcements sometimes establish and usually maintain their work rates. A hungry rat works steadily for food pellets, and a piece worker in a factory similarly works at a steady rate so as to be productive and remain employed. There is no question that reinforcements are effective in establishing and maintaining behavior. But some behaviors are intrinsically rewarding, performed not for any direct immediate reinforcement, but because they are fun and pleasurable to do in and of themselves. For example, crossword puzzles are enjoyable to do and people do them with no reward other than their own pleasure. Indeed, it has been shown that if you offer reinforcement for crossword puzzle solving, a persons's performance decreases. So, some people's behavior is intrinsically motivated, and it will likely be done again. *Extrinsically motivated* behavior is done for reinforcements. When we work for a paycheck, our work is extrinsically motivated; when we work because we love our work, we say that it is *intrinsically motivated*. It has been shown that offering reinforcements for intrinsically motivated work can decrease performance!

Probably all people are intrinsically motivated in some way or another. The question to be answered is why some people are intrinsically motivated to do crossword puzzles and others to climb the highest mountain first. The answer is probably that as a child the former was reinforced, or praised, for accomplishing small tasks that were challenging, while the latter was reinforced for small competitive feats. Each learned to feel pleasure, or intrinsic reinforcement, for behaviors that brought challenge or competition.

Earlier the idea was presented that a reinforcer like food or money only becomes a reinforcer if an organism is motivated; hungry rats find food reinforcing and ambitious lawyers find winning court cases reinforcing. Psychologists have suggested a number of reasons why people find certain behaviors reinforcing; this is especially interesting when we consider intrinsically motivated behaviors where there is no obvious directly observable reinforcer. We will explore the conditions that allow for intrinsically motivated behavior in greater detail in the next chapter on motivation (p. 166).

In studying the basic procedures involved in instrumental conditioning, we see that the delivery of consequences, either reinforcements or punishments, is crucial. Indeed, without these consequences the behaviors would not be maintained or established. Like Pavlovian conditioning, instrumental conditioning is affected by a number of important characteristics of situations that can change. Among these variables are the magnitude and delay of the reinforcements and punishments that are delivered as well as their discriminability. Let us examine some of these properties more closely.

MAGNITUDE OF CONSEQUENCES. Researchers can change the amount of a reinforcer they give an animal and record how frequently it presses a bar for a large reinforcer as compared with a small one. Similarly, psychologists might watch the productivity of workers when they are given a few cents for each piece of machinery assembled as compared to when they are given a few dollars for each piece assembled. Generally, studies like this show that as the amount of the reward increases, the more desirable it becomes and so the subjects work harder, longer, or faster to complete their task. As shown in Figure 3.13, the time a hungry rat takes to run down an alley to reach its goal decreases when more reinforcer is provided.

Food and money can serve as positive reinforcers and their magnitude can be manipulated; the magnitude of a punishment can be changed in similar ways. A more intense punishment will suppress behavior more quickly and maintain that suppression for a longer time. If a child is put in a time-out room and removed from positive reinforcements, the duration of this stay in the time-out room affects the suppression of the unacceptable behavior. A 2-minute stay is certainly not as effective in suppressing temper tantrums as is a 10-minute stay. In the same way, a slap on the wrist is not as effective in suppressing behavior as is a swift hard slap to the rear end. The magnitude of a consequence is only one element that determines an organism's behavior. The process of the delivery of consequences is complex, and variables such as when the consequence is provided are also important.

DELAY OF CONSEQUENCES. Students will study long hours for the goal of achieving good grades at the end of a semester. Medical students put off the practice of medicine for over 10 years before they can achieve the reinforcer that they desire. How long can one delay a reinforcer and still expect continuous behavior? We saw that in classical conditioning the time between the conditioning stimulus (the bell) and the unconditioned stimulus (the food) is important. If the bell is presented 2 hours before the food, there will be little association between the event and thus no conditioning; if the bell is presented 10 minutes before food, there probably won't be conditioning; however, if the time between the bell and the food is relatively short, perhaps $\frac{1}{2}$ second, we expect conditioning. In instrumental conditioning, the time between the behavior (for example, pressing the bar) and the delivery of food is also critical. If a hungry rat works and is not given a reinforcer for an hour, it is unlikely that it will learn the task or emit the behavior again; however, if the time between the behavior and the reinforcer is short, the chances that it will learn are better. Generally, an increase in the time between the behavior and the reward causes a decrease in performance. Contiguity in time of the

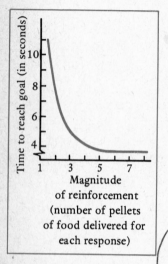

Figure 3.13 As the amount of a reinforcer like food increases, a hungry organism's time to reach a goal usually decreases. Thus, large reinforcers usually bring faster running speeds or more bar presses to achieve the reinforcer

two events is critical. This has been shown in numerous experiments in many kinds of conditions (Tarpy & Sawbini, 1974).

FREQUENCY OF CONSEQUENCES. It is obvious that both the immediacy of a consequence like reinforcement and its magnitude are important. In some cases if a reward is delayed, the same work rate can be achieved by increasing the amount of the reward (Logan, 1965). To make matters a bit more complex, another variable that can be manipulated is the frequency of the delivery of consequences. In the studies we have seen so far, it has generally been assumed that each response is followed by a consequence, but this is not always the case. An organism does not always have to be reinforced or punished each time it emits a behavior in order to achieve conditioning.

While initially establishing a new behavior, reinforcement after each response is usually necessary; once a response is established, a researcher can manipulate how frequently the organism is to be reinforced. For example, a hungry rat that presses a bar for reinforcement can be trained to press the bar three times before being reinforced. In this case, reinforcement is delivered not after every bar press but after every three bar presses. Reinforcement can be delayed still further by having the delivery of the reinforcement come after long delays or after more bar pressings or both. Let us look more closely at schedules of reinforcement.

How often do you need to be reinforced? Is a paycheck once a year or once a month sufficient? Would you rather be paid weekly, daily, or perhaps hourly? Will people work better if they are reinforced often or if they do not know when they will be reinforced? In most situations, people are not reinforced continually. Two basic schedules of reinforcement are based upon time, and two are based upon the frequency of the organism's response.

Assume that in a Skinner box a hungry rat is working by pressing a bar and being reinforced with food. In a **fixed-interval** schedule the rat is rewarded as soon as a response occurs after some interval of time. This means that whether the rat works a great deal or just a little, after every time interval it will be given a reinforcer if it has pressed the bar at least once. This schedule is fixed because the animal doesn't control how often it will be reinforced. Animals in this situation typically respond slowly just after a reinforcement. As you can see by checking the record shown in Figure 3.15 on p. 94, the work rate shows a "scalloping" pattern for the rat's performance in this situation.

The reinforcing interval need not be fixed. With a **variable-interval** schedule an animal is reinforced after varying amounts of time, provided it has made a response after that time has elapsed. For example, it will be reinforced for a response occurring after a 40-second period, then a 6-second period, then 25 seconds, and so on. In this situation rats work at a relatively steady rate, and they do not show scalloping as they do in a fixed-interval schedule. However, because the delivery of a reinforcer is tied more to time than to work output, their work rate is still slow. For example, rats who are placed on a variable-interval schedule have a lower overall rate of response than those in a fixed-interval schedule.

While an interval schedule deals with time, ratio schedules deal with work output. In a **fixed-ratio** schedule an organism is reinforced for a particular amount of work. For example, a rat in a Skinner box may be reinforced for every tenth bar press; it will work at a fast, steady, and regular rate because it

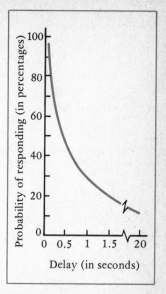

Figure 3.14 As a delay is introduced between a response and reinforcement, the probability of that behavior decreases. Short delays (or even no delays) between a response and the reinforcer maximize the chances of the behavior occurring again

Fixed interval A schedule of reinforcement where a reinforcer occurs after a specified interval of time providing the required response has occurred at least once after the interval has elapsed.

interval - time

Variable interval A schedule of reinforcement in which a reinforcer occurs after intervals of different lengths of time providing the required response has occurred at least once since the interval has elapsed.

ratio - frequency # of responses

Fixed ratio A schedule of reinforcement in which a reinforcer occurs after a set number of responses

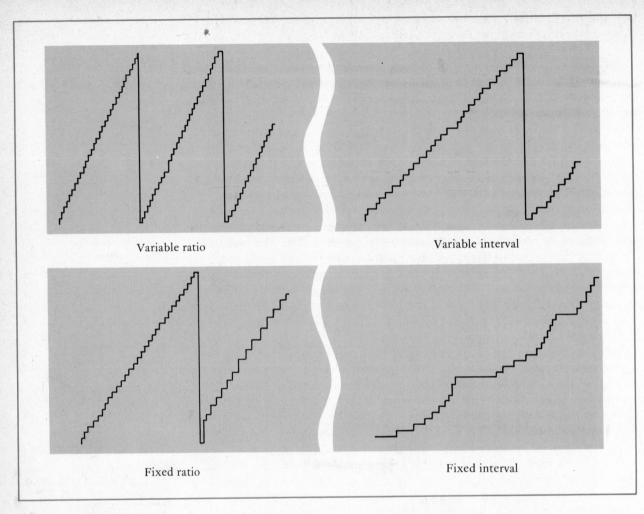

Variable ratio

Variable interval

Fixed ratio

Fixed interval

Figure 3.15 The four basic types of reinforcement schedules. Note the scalloping of responses in the fixed-interval schedule and the high performance rates in the variable-ratio schedule. High work rates are indicated by steep slopes

Variable interval:

Fixed ratio

Variable ratio

Variable ratio A schedule of reinforcement in which a reinforcer occurs after varying number of responses.

has learned that hard work brings about the delivery of a reinforcer on a regular basis. Figure 3.15 shows that the work output of a rat on a fixed-ratio schedule is very high as compared with a rat on interval schedules.

Very high rates of response are achieved with a variable-ratio schedule as well. As in the fixed-ratio schedule, on a **variable-ratio** system work output determines how frequently the organism will be reinforced. Unlike the fixed-ratio schedule, however, the amount of work output required before a reinforcer is given varies from trial to trial. Our rat learns that hard work produces a reinforcer; however, it also learns that it cannot predict when this reinforcer might come about. The rat's best bet is to work at a very even rate; the variable-ratio schedule, therefore, produces very high rates of response.

Other schedules of reinforcement can be easily derived, for example, a combination of the fixed-ratio and the fixed-interval schedules. A rat in a Skinner box might have to make a certain number of responses *and* have to wait 30 seconds for reinforcement. If 30 seconds should go by and the rat has not made the correct number of responses, it is not reinforced. Still other schedules of reinforcement have been devised in which the animal must not respond for a period of time and then must respond with a certain amount of work; if it works before the fixed time has elapsed, it is not rewarded. These are complex schedules and an animal requires considerable training to learn them. However, with many days of patient training most animals can be taught.

Whether they realize it or not, people are all on different schedules of reinforcement. If you were a piece worker in a factory, your schedule of reinforcement would be of particular importance to you. You would want to know if you were being paid on an interval or ratio schedule. It is probable that you would do less work on an interval schedule than on a ratio schedule. In college, how often are students reinforced for studying? After each examination, or after each semester? Reinforcement with grades comes on a regular basis, and its magnitude is usually determined by the amount and quality of work done. The more you study, the higher your grade. So, a college schedule is based on both interval and ratio. Every semester (interval) you are

Table 3.4 Schedules of reinforcement

SCHEDULE	DESCRIPTION	EFFECT
Fixed Interval (FI)	Reinforcement given for first response that follows after a fixed time has elapsed.	Response rate drops right after reinforcement but shows scalloping and thus increases as the interval nears its end; then the response rate is rapid.
Variable Interval (VI)	Reinforcement given for the first response after a determined but variable lapse of time.	Response rate is steady.
Fixed Ratio (FR)	Reinforcement given after a fixed number of responses have occurred.	Response rate is rapid.
Variable Ratio (VR)	Reinforcement given after a determined variable number of responses.	Response rate is high and steady.

rewarded with As and Bs that can vary in number depending on studying effort (ratio).

97

Learning

STIMULUS DISCRIMINATION AND GENERALIZATION.   In many animal-learning experiments, the animals have to learn to tell the difference between two stimuli, perhaps a vertical and a horizontal line, a square and a circle, or high- and low-pitched tones. In learning to make these judgments, an animal is learning to discriminate between stimuli. This process is called **stimulus discrimination.** While making such discriminations is rather easy for a human adult, young animals and even young children find discriminations difficult at first. Of course, children learn to discriminate between vertical versus horizontal lines and black versus white stimuli very easily and at a very young age. Teaching a white rat or a pigeon to make such a discrimination often involves repeated presentation of the different stimuli with reinforcements given only when the animal indicates that the two stimuli are different. An experimental situation might be set up as follows: an organism is presented with either two vertical lines, two horizontal lines, or a vertical and a horizontal line. Two keys are presented with one key to be pressed if the lines are the same, the other if they are different. The organism is reinforced only if it makes a correct response. A rat in such a situation usually makes errors at first; initially the rat may indicate that a pair of vertical lines are the same or different an equal number of times; however, after repeated presentations of the vertical and horizontal pairs and reinforcements only when the rat presses the correct key, discrimination learning will occur. Such stimulus discrimination is established not only with lines, but also with colors, tones, and far more complex situations.

What happens when we present a tone with a pitch that is not quite the same as the training stimulus? Let us say that we train a college student or even a pigeon to press a bar when it hears a high-pitched tone (see Hovland,

Stimulus discrimination The process by which an organism learns to respond to a specific stimulus and then to no other similar stimulus; the complementary process to stimulus generalization.

Table 3.5 Four important properties of instrumental conditioning

PROPERTY	DEFINITION	EXAMPLE
Extinction	The process whereby the probability of an organism emitting a conditioned response is reduced when the reinforcement is withheld.	A rat trained to bar press stops pressing when it is no longer reinforced after each bar press.
Spontaneous recovery	The reoccurrence of a conditioned response following a rest period after extinction.	A rat that has stopped responding by bar pressing due to extinction starts to bar press again after a rest interval.
Stimulus generalization	Responding to stimuli similar to, but not the same as, the training stimulus.	A cat presses a bar in response to an ellipse or a circle.
Stimulus discrimination	The process by which an organism learns to respond to a specific stimulus and then to no other similar stimulus; the complementary process to stimulus generalization.	A pigeon presses a key only in response to red lights, not to blue ones or green ones.

Stimulus generalization Responding to stimuli similar to, but not the same as, the training stimulus.

1937). What happens when the tone is a different pitch? As in classical conditioning, responding to a stimulus that is similar but not the same as the training stimulus is called **stimulus generalization** (see p. 78). An animal's bar-pressing behavior is determined by how similar the test tone is to the training tone. If the test tone is just slightly lower in pitch than the training stimulus, it's likely that the animal will respond but not as frequently. An animal's bar-pressing behavior depends upon pitch, and it will respond with the most bar pressing to the tone to which it was originally trained. As pitch differs to a greater and greater extent, the amount of responding decreases dramatically (Honig, 1966; Pavlov, 1927; Stebbins, 1970).

EXTINCTION AND SPONTANEOUS RECOVERY. It has been suggested repeatedly that behavior that is followed by some consequence increases or decreases in its likelihood of occurrence. What has not been explained is what happens to behavior that is not followed by a consequence. Let's focus on reinforced behavior that occurs more frequently because it is rewarded and look at it the way a psychologist does. Suppose that we train a pigeon to respond by pecking on a key whenever it hears a high-pitched tone. Pecking to the high-pitched tone brings reinforcement, but pecking at a low-pitched tone doesn't. We already know that this type of training isn't particularly difficult.

But what happens if we no longer reinforce pecking to the high-pitched tone? Or what happens if a person stops getting paid every week? The answer is simple—eventually the organism involved, either the pigeon or the person, will stop working. If the animal is on a variable-ratio schedule, chances are it will work for a very long time before it stops; it has been trained to work for long periods before reinforcement occurs. In contrast, a pigeon that has been trained on a fixed-interval schedule (and has come to expect reinforcement in a relatively brief period of time) will stop pecking at a key after a few nonreinforced trials.

Extinction The process whereby the probability of an organism emitting a conditioned response is reduced when reinforcement is withheld.

In instrumental conditioning, **extinction** is the process of withholding a reinforcement and thus reducing the probability that an animal or human will respond with a conditioned response. In fact, one way to measure how well an animal has learned a task is to measure how long it takes or how many trials are necessary to achieve extinction. The behavior of an animal on a schedule where it is normally reinforced after every trial will extinguish quickly if reinforcers are no longer delivered after a large number of reinforced trials. Obviously, then, the way to eliminate a behavior that is normally reinforced is to have a long series of nonreinforced trials (see, for example, Pavlov, 1927; Braun & Geiselhart, 1959).

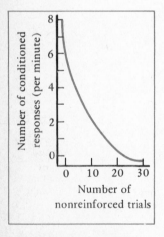

Figure 3.16 The process of extinction. When an animal that has learned a procedure is first placed in a Skinner box, it responds rapidly. If the animal is not reinforced, after a few trials the likelihood of responding decreases. After many trials the animal does not respond at all

Let's go back to the pigeon that pecks when it hears a high-pitched tone. It is rewarded each time it pecks correctly and is tested each day over a period of 60 days for 30 minutes. On day number 61 the pigeon is placed in the Skinner box and is not reinforced for its correct behavior. For the first few minutes the pigeon continues to work normally. However, after a few minutes its work rate decreases, and by the end of its half-hour session, it is not pecking at all. On day number 62, when we bring the pigeon back to the Skinner box and present a tone, it responds with pecking, but again, we don't deliver a reinforcer. Within a relatively short period of time, the pigeon's conditioning shows the process of extinction. The decrease in responding does not happen immediately upon withholding a reinforcer. In fact it has often been seen that initially upon withholding a reinforcer, organisms work harder and show an increase in performance. So, the process of extinction may sometimes show a small increase in performance followed by a decrease (see Allen, Turner, & Everett, 1970).

Extinction follows principles similar to classical conditioning, so spontaneous recovery occurs in instrumental conditioning, too. After a rest interval it is typical for a conditioned response, like pecking, that has undergone extinction to reoccur. If an organism is subjected to extinction procedures, given a rest period, then tested again, it will show **spontaneous recovery.** If it is brought through this sequence several times with several rest periods, the work rate in each session of spontaneous recovery will decrease. After one rest period, spontaneous recovery will bring the organism's work rate back close to what it was when the conditioned response was reinforced. However, after a dozen or so rest periods (and no reinforcements) the organism may only make one or two responses; that is, the level of spontaneous recovery has decreased markedly. Eventually the behavior will disappear completely.

People, too, show spontaneous recovery. When students speak up in class and offer answers to questions, reinforcement usually follows. Instructors usually comment on the adequacy of the response. If an instructor does not reinforce correct answers or does not call on students to answer, their willingness to show such behavior decreases. After a few classes of not being called on, most students stop raising their hands. Yet, after a spring break, the same hand-raising behavior typically reoccurs—spontaneous recovery. Of course, extinction will follow again if the hand raising is not reinforced.

ELECTRICAL BRAIN STIMULATION. For many years, psychologists have recognized that different types of consequences can affect an organism's be-

Spontaneous recovery The reoccurrence of a conditioned response following a rest period after extinction.

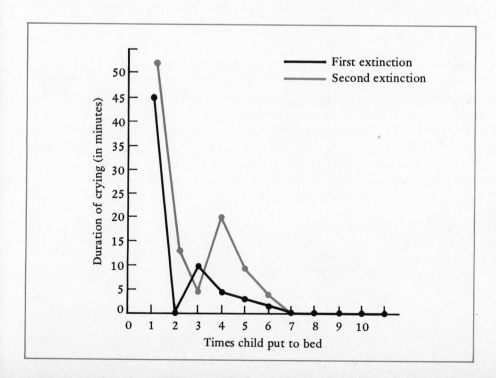

Figure 3.17 A child emitted tantrums at bedtime so as to have attention paid to him. Williams (1959) counted the number of minutes the child cried. The parents were instructed to no longer pay attention to his tantrums. After several days of the number of minutes the child cried decreased to zero. A week later when an aunt put the child to bed, the child made a fuss (spontaneous recovery); the aunt reinforced the child with attention. The child then had to go through a second series of extinction trials

havior. In a hungry rat, food acts as a reinforcer and can easily establish a conditioned response like bar pressing. Thirsty rats press bars for water. In humans, money, a pat on the back, or even an approving smile can serve as a reinforcer for certain behaviors. Many years ago a type of reinforcer was found that did not conform to the usual form of reinforcers. It was suggested earlier that the reason reinforcers establish or maintain a behavior is that they satisfy some need or drive in the organism; remember, food acts as a reinforcer only in a *hungry* rat, not in one that has just eaten. In the 1950s it was found that electrical stimulation of certain areas of the brain seemed to be rewarding.

In a fascinating series of studies, Olds (1955, 1969) found that rats will press a bar in order to receive an electrical stimulation to their brains. Each rat had an electrode implanted in its hypothalamus, and these electrodes were attached to a stimulator that provided a small voltage. The stimulator was activated only when the rat pressed a lever in a Skinner box. Olds pointed out that rats will not only work to achieve electrical stimulation, but that such animals will perform better in a maze and will run faster and with fewer errors. Rats will even cross an electrified grid in order to obtain this electrical stimulation; hungry rats will often choose brain stimulation over food! When provided with hypothalamic stimulation, rats will go so far as to press a bar hundreds and thousands of times to continue the self-stimulation. In one such study, rats pressed a bar at a rate of 1,920 times per hour (Olds & Milner, 1954).

Thousands of jolts of electricity have been delivered to the brains of thousands of rats. These rats have found the brain stimulation reinforcing and will work hard at bar pressing to achieve stimulation. Yet, today we are still not sure how electrical stimulation acts to reinforce a behavior like bar pressing. There is no question that the particular area of the brain stimulated is important and that the state of the organism and its particular physiological needs are important. For example, although a hungry rat chooses electrical

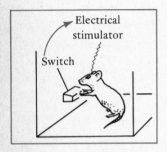

Figure 3.18 Rats will press a bar hundreds of times per hour to be stimulated electrically. Olds and Milner's 1954 finding led to volumes of studies on electrical brain stimulation

Table 3.6 Types of learning: classical conditioning and instrumental conditioning

TYPE OF LEARNING	PROCEDURE	RESULT	EXAMPLE
Classical Conditioning	A neutral stimulus (such as a bell) is paired with an unconditioned stimulus (such as food).	The neutral stimulus becomes a conditioned stimulus—it elicits the conditioned response.	A bell elicits a salivary response in a dog.
Instrumental Conditioning	A behavior is followed by a consequence of reinforcement or punishment.	The behavior increases or decreases in frequency.	A pigeon will peck on a key 20 times per hour to achieve a reward or avoid punishment.

brain stimulation over food, the rat will not starve to death by always choosing brain stimulation instead of food (see, for example, Routtenberg & Lindy, 1965).

The issue is complex. For example, we know that when certain areas of the brain are stimulated, other drives and activities are initiated. Furthermore, you will see in the next chapter that when organisms are stimulated in certain areas of the brain, they start to eat, drink, or even have sex. So, electrical brain stimulation acts in some cases to reinforce behavior like bar pressing, but in other cases it acts to increase eating, drinking, or sexual behavior. Considering these diverging views, psychologists acknowledge that our understanding of electrical brain stimulation is far from complete; furthermore, they recognize that they must know more about the chemistry of the brain and how different areas affect each other before they can understand fully the nature of electrical brain stimulation.

Summary of Key Concepts

Instrumental conditioning focuses heavily on the consequences of an organism's behavior. Behavior that is followed by a reinforcer tends to occur again, while behavior that is followed by a punisher is suppressed. As in classical conditioning, there are several variables. The consequence, be it a reinforcer or punisher, must be clear and of sufficient magnitude to establish the conditioned response. In the same way, if the reinforcer is not delivered over a series of trials, extinction will occur. As in classical conditioning, there is stimulus generalization and discrimination, and the timing of the behavior and the reinforcer is important. While consistent reinforcement is not necessary once a conditioned response is established, certain schedules of reinforcement produce higher rates of conditioned responses. Perhaps most important is the concept that a behavior is first emitted and then reinforcement or punishment is delivered. There is a contingency—consequences follow behavior and are not given unless and until the behavior is shown.

Comparison of Classical and Instrumental Conditioning

Both classical and instrumental conditioning are considered basic learning procedures. The basic distinction between them is that the unconditioned stimulus in classical conditioning (such as food) is presented along with the neutral or conditioning stimulus (such as a bell); in instrumental conditioning, however, the consequence (such as food) is dependent or contingent upon the organism's behavior. This is a very important distinction because in instrumental conditioning the organism must show the behavior before a reinforcer (or punisher) is given. Parents reinforce or reward good table manners when their children emit or show those manners. Similarly, people reinforce their dogs for sitting or rolling over *only* when they sit or roll over. By contrast, in classical conditioning, the neutral stimulus is always paired and thus associated with the unconditioned stimulus. In instrumental conditioning the animal will get the food only *if* it emits the correct behavior. It must, therefore, be stressed that in instrumental conditioning a definite contingency is involved; the delivery of a reinforcer or punishment is contigent on the organism's behavior. Another major distinction between classical and instrumental behaviors is the type of behavior involved. Classically conditioned behaviors are usually reflexive and involuntary. By contrast, behaviors conditioned through instrumental procedures are usually voluntarily emitted.

It becomes apparent that a reinforcer is of critical importance in both classical and instrumental conditioning. In classical conditioning the unconditioned stimulus (such as food) is presented before the organism may make a conditioned response, whereas in instrumental conditioning it is contingent or dependent upon the organism's behavior (Skinner, 1937, 1938). Many learning theorists have tried to distinguish between classical and instrumental conditioning based on differences in the use of reinforcers, but they all agree that a reinforcer is important in any learning situation.

OBSERVATIONAL LEARNING

We have discussed at length how the procedures of reinforcement and punishment establish, suppress, and maintain various behaviors. The conditioning procedures of classical and instrumental conditioning have used these ideas extensively and have served as the foundation of learning theory for many years. Today we recognize that Pavlov's ideas explain only a limited range of behaviors; so when learning theorists developed and expanded upon the ideas of instrumental conditioning, a major conceptual breakthrough was made. New theories were generated which explain a much wider range of phenomena. Psychologists were now able to explain not only reflexive behaviors but also a much wider range of behaviors, from bar pressing in a Skinner box to the suppression of tantrums with time-out procedures. In the last 20 years a new way to think about learning has developed which expands still further the range of behaviors that learning theory can explain. This relatively new approach to learning is called **observational learning** or sometimes *social learning;* we will use the terms interchangeably.

Albert Bandura (1969, 1977) presented the idea that people can learn by observing the behavior of others and then by imitating it. Research supports Bandura's ideas. Children were shown films that involved aggressive content and were later compared with children who saw films that were neutral in terms of aggressive content. The children were compared on how much aggression they exhibited in play activities. It was found that children who observed aggressive, violent films tended to be aggressive and violent after viewing them. A great deal of research has been generated on this subject because researchers are particularly interested to know if merely watching a behavior is sufficient to learn it. In particular, psychologists have focused on people's viewing violent behavior on television. This research does not stand alone because even anecdotal reports inform us that people imitate the behavior of others they hold in high esteem (Bandura, Ross, & Ross, 1963; Bandura & Walters, 1963).

There are many situations from which people have opportunities to observe and learn new behaviors. Certainly a young child who observes others involved in aggressive behaviors has an opportunity to observe and learn about aggressive acts. However, as observers we do not always act out those events we observe. This raises two issues. *First,* do we have to be engaged in a behavior to learn it, or, rephrased, can we learn by merely observing? *Second,* can we learn new behaviors without reinforcement? You will see that

Observational learning The learning procedure by which organisms learn new responses by observing the behavior of a model and then imitating it; also called social learning theory.

Albert Bandura is one of the leading researchers in the field of observational learning.

Often we learn the most just by observing others.

the research answers these questions affirmatively. New behaviors can be learned by merely watching others; furthermore, reinforcement is not absolutely necessary for a new behavior to be established.

Both children and adults learn new behaviors by observing the behaviors of others (sometimes called *models*). Many times people learn how to respond to a specific situation by watching other people, yet they do not have the opportunity to express this newly learned behavior. Thus, the behaviors that people learn through observation are not always shown in directly observable behavior. For example, people learn how to express grief at the loss of a loved one by watching others grieve. When people who have never been exposed to death are faced with the loss of someone close to them, they may not know what to say or how to act. While most people feel that they grieve naturally in such situations, our experiences in watching others provide a variety of alternatives for grieving.

Any parent knows that children learn by observing; similarly, common sense explains many behaviors that may be learned by the observational learning approach. However, psychologists have been slow to follow this approach in explaining behavior patterns. There are probably several reasons for this; Bandura (1971) has suggested that one reason may be because describing and explaining observational learning is so much more complex than simple classical conditioning. Another reason that there has been little experimentation in observational learning is that early laboratory attempts were not initially successful. Perhaps most important is that the study of observational learning requires that psychologists study a topic that for years they have avoided—thinking.

When observational learning has been subjected to study in the laboratory, results have been generally positive. For example, some support for observational learning of a classically conditioned response has been found by Bernal and Berger (1976). They had subjects watch a film of other subjects being conditioned. A tone was paired with a puff of air to the eyelids of the filmed subjects. After a number of trials, the subjects in the film showed an eye blink to the tone alone. The experimental subjects who watched the film also developed an eye blink to the presentation of a tone. In studies of instrumental conditioning, by watching reinforced behavior, observers also learned the behavior. In one classic study, children who observed models being reinforced for aggressive behavior tended to show aggressive behavior later (Bandura, Ross, & Ross, 1963). Studies with cats have shown that they too learned by observing; a study by John (John et al., 1968) has shown that cats will learn to avoid receiving a shock through a grid floor if they watch other cats who could avoid the shocks by performing a task. Manipulations of verbal learning have shown that college students can be conditioned to respond with certain kinds of responses (Kanfer & Marston, 1963). Stutterers can decrease stuttering by watching others decrease their stuttering (Martin & Haroldson, 1977). Even children who are afraid of animals can learn to become less afraid by watching other children interact with animals (Bandura & Menlove, 1968).

Table 3.7 Types of learning: classical conditioning, instrumental conditioning, and observational learning.

TYPE OF LEARNING	PROCEDURE	RESULT	EXAMPLE
Classical Conditioning	A neutral stimulus (such as a bell) is paired with an unconditioned stimulus (such as food).	The neutral stimulus becomes a conditioned stimulus—it elicits the conditioned response.	A bell elicits a salivary response in a dog.
Instrumental Conditioning	A behavior is followed by a consequence of reinforcement or punishment.	The behavior increases or decreases in frequency.	A pigeon will peck on a key 20 times per hour to achieve a reward or avoid punishment.
Observational Learning	Observer attends to a model to learn a behavior.	Observer learns the sequence of behaviors and becomes able to perform it at will.	After watching television violence, children are more likely to show aggressive behaviors.

Bandura's explanation of learning through observation has filled a large gap in the learning literature (1977). But, in some ways, it has made new gaps —we now need to know the variables involved in observational learning. Because observational learning involves more than just simple stimuli and responses, the task for the psychologist is great. We need to learn all about what people think and how they think about events to be able to understand how they might learn an observed behavior. Bandura suggests that observational learning takes place because a person may rehearse an observed behavior; such rehearsal is not overt and directly observable and thus is difficult for a psychologist to investigate. Yet, increasingly, psychologists are suggesting that observational learning combined with traditional classical and instrumental conditioning approaches can account for nearly all learned behavior. Bandura's observational learning approach does not discount reinforcement, but rather suggests that reinforcement in combination with observational learning can account for most behaviors. Later in discussing personality and therapy we will again see the extent to which Bandura's research has been important in helping discover how people learn.

HUMAN MEMORY

If only Robin could remember the name of her old roommate in Brooklyn, she knew that she would have a place to stay over the holidays. Robin hadn't seen her college roommate in 12 years and while she remembered her name, Linda Somers, she couldn't remember her married name. Robin went through the alphabet, the phone book, and then finally gave up. She knew the name but couldn't remember it. At one time or another, we all find ourselves in this frustrating situation.

Think about the time that you took an examination for which you were well prepared, yet still did poorly. There are several reasons why you may not have done well. First, you might not really have studied enough. It is also possible you learned the material but forgot it when you needed it—this was Robin's problem. Third, you may have learned the material, kept it in memory, but still have been unable to show your learning on the specific test you were given. The first excuse, lack of studying, deserves no comment. But, Robin's problem, memory failure, is quite common, and we will talk about that more in a while. The lack of performance on well-learned material is problematic.

Accountants often study for years to learn and understand their discipline, but when faced with the test to become a CPA (certified public accountant), they often fail, sometimes due to faulty learning, sometimes due to forgetting, and sometimes due to confusing information. Psychologists have long recognized that recalling supposedly well learned facts is not easy. People forget and confuse previously learned material. In the same way, conditioned responses that humans make do not *always* occur to a stimulus; it is for this reason that we talk about the *probability* of a conditioned response. Behavior is very complex, and we recognize that a number of variables will affect a person's memory for facts and even for conditioned responses. Part of the challenge of those who study learning is to separate those factors that are involved in initial learning and those in remembering the learning.

Through the process of studying learning and memory, psychologists

People can remember the events of their childhood with great detail.

Memory The ability to recall or remember information, events, or skills learned in the past.

have focused on differences between learning and performance that were presented earlier. Psychologists usually infer learning through some change in behavior, in performance. In conditioning experiments, they infer learning when an organism responds when presented with a conditioned stimulus, like a bell. With animals there are no ways other than by performance to determine if learning has occurred. However, humans are verbal. Humans can tell you if they have learned something, and they can show their learning through verbal performance.

When humans learn something, it means that there will be some change in ability or performance. In motor learning this means that some new skill might be mastered; in verbal learning this means that some new idea or thought might be acquired. Both skills and ideas might easily be shown in human behavior. When individuals exhibit the ability to remember or maintain these skills, we say that they show memory for them. **Memory** is the ability to recall or remember information, events, or skills learned in the past. Humans can remember previous learning over long periods of time. You shouldn't think that animals don't have memories, though, because animals can remember a great deal. Some remember for a few minutes, others for a few hours, still others for a few days, and in some instances for relatively long periods of time.

Because humans can tell a psychologist about their learning and memory, much more complex learning processes can be studied in humans than in animals. Psychologists can analyze a human's response as evidence of recall of past events. Our ability to remember for long periods of time, and our special ability to be able to verbally report our memories, makes possible the study of complex learning tasks in humans.

Studying the process of memory has important applications in daily life. Clearly, teachers are concerned with maximizing a student's performance by presenting material in ways that are easy to remember. Similarly, in studying material either for school or for a hobby, we often try to organize it and learn it in efficient ways so as to maximize our later recall of information.

Aspects of Memory

The year was 1885; Hermann Ebbinghaus was the researcher; Hermann Ebbinghaus was also the subject. The task was to learn lists of letters in order of presentation. The actual items that this early memory researcher used were called *nonsense syllables* because they were made up of three letters that when strung together had no meaning—such as NAK, DUB, MIP, DAF. Ebbinghaus presented himself with lists of items to learn and in many of his studies recorded how many times he needed to present the lists to himself until he could remember them perfectly. When the lists were short and consisted of only a few nonsense syllables, learning was nearly perfect in a single trial or two. However, when the lists exceeded about seven items, repeated presentations of the list were necessary for accurate recall of the list. In his research Ebbinghaus was studying an important component of memory— memory span. *Memory span* is the number of digits, letters, or, in general, items that can be remembered without special rehearsal or techniques. It would be a full 70 years before George Miller (1956) would rediscover and popularize the idea that memory span is seven, plus or minus two, items. Miller even suggested that seven was like a "magic number" in that so many events happened in sevens plus or minus two. Thus, memory span has generally been taken to be in chunks of five to nine items. You will see that the number of items subjects can remember depends upon the subject, the task, the specific items, and the difficulty of the items.

Research on memory has practical implications. It has been found that when a number of items are presented in a list and one item in that list is different from all the others, it is often learned more easily. This is called the *Von Restorff effect*. In some learning experiments a subject is presented with a stimulus and has to learn a specific response. A subject may be presented with and have to respond to 20 stimuli on flash cards. Samuels (1970) found that printing the stimulus in red on one trial while all the other stimuli were printed in black helped subjects to learn the response. Samuels suggests that educational innovations which use color cues to facilitate learning may be helpful; but Samuels also showed that any gain in learning would probably be lost when the relevant cues are removed. This type of memory study can provide direct and important information for teachers who are trying to be innovative and help students learn and remember.

Unlike the white rat, humans have the ability to remember events, discuss them, and place them in other contexts so as to apply newly learned knowledge. Our memory is the ability to recall or recognize skills, events, or ideas that were learned in the past. Not only do human beings have incredibly good memory for previous events, but we have different kinds of memory. Some people have exceptionally good memory for faces, others for names, and still other people can remember story lines from old movies for long peri-

Figure 3.19 In a paired-associate learning task, the subjects may be shown flash cards in which there is a stimulus (left side) and a response (right side). After showing the cards to the subjects, experimenters present just the stimulus side and the subject must answer with the response side. The dependent variable in these studies is often the number of times the study list must be presented for the subjects to do at least 90% correct in the test list. In the Samuels (1970) study, printing the words on the left (the stimulus words) in a different color facilitated recall performance

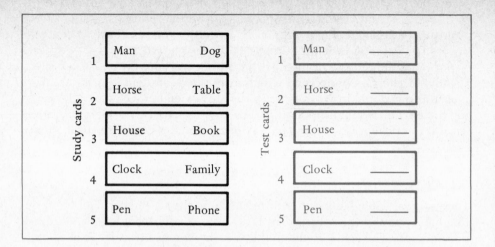

ods of time. Remembering a story line involves a different type of memory than remembering a person's name. Both of these types of memory are different from remembering whether or not you have been to a certain restaurant before. In the process of studying different types of memory, it has been convenient to separate memories into two classes, *recall* and *recognition*. In a recognition task, a person must remember if he or she has seen some material before or if it is familiar. In a recall task, the person must remember the details of a situation or idea, place them together in a meaningful framework, and present them, usually without any kinds of cues or aids. In recall the person is required to remember more information than in recognition. It is different to ask someone if William Shakespeare wrote the lines, "Romeo, Romeo, wherefore art thou . . ." than to ask the person to recite the lines from Juliet's balcony soliloquy to Romeo. So recognition and recall both examine memory, but they ask for different levels of information.

Over the years, psychologists have attempted to understand potential differences between recognition and recall. They have generally found that recognition is a more sensitive measure than recall. This means that it is easier to pick up small differences in memory ability through recognition tasks than it is through recall tasks. A person may recognize a previously studied fact but may not be able to recall the fact if asked for the same piece of information. Some psychologists feel that this difference is important (Flexser & Tulving, 1978); others suggest that these differences are not very important and that both tap a general memory system but perhaps in different quantities or at different levels (Anderson & Bower, 1974; Murdock, 1974; Rabinowitz et al., 1977). While debates still take place, psychologists agree that by using different tasks they can examine memory in different ways. Furthermore, they all agree that the task given to the subject clearly affects his or her accuracy; one task may not necessarily examine a subject's memory any better, but it may change a subject's score dramatically.

Important Variables in Memory

Psychologists have studied recall to a greater extent than recognition. Let us look more closely at some of the tasks involved in recall and recognition so that we can explore our memory system to a greater extent.

ORDER OF RECALL.   Two of the most widely used techniques that have been used in studying recall are *free recall* and *serial recall*. In recall tasks, subjects have to remember previously presented information. Often laboratory subjects have to remember strings of digits or letters. A typical study might ask subjects to remember a string of words or nonsense syllables such as WUG, RAI, DAQ, CIZ, MYG. This list might be presented on a screen at the rate of one syllable every $\frac{1}{2}$ second; given that there are 10 syllables, at the end of about 5 seconds the subject then has to tell the researcher the names of the syllables. The difference between a free recall task and a serial recall task is that in the free recall task the subjects can recall the syllables in any order they want. In a serial task the syllables have to be remembered in the order of their presentation. In free recall, if a subject remembers seven out of 10 syllables (in correct order or not) the subject receives a score of 70% on that trial. In serial recall, if only 3 of the 10 syllables were recalled in order and another 4 were recalled but in the wrong order, the subject's score would be only 30%. Thus, serial recall tasks are more stringent—they're harder.

ORGANIZATIONAL FACTORS IN RECALL.   Psychologists have investigated procedures to make memory tasks easier for subjects. There are many ways to make tasks easier. One can provide retrieval cues to help subjects retrieve or remember information. One way is to help the subjects by presenting the information to be remembered in an organized manner, for example, by grouping all the names together and grouping all the birds together, or by presenting the material in some organized alphabetical scheme. This helps subjects organize their memory, which generally is shown to facilitate retrieval (see Buschke, 1977).

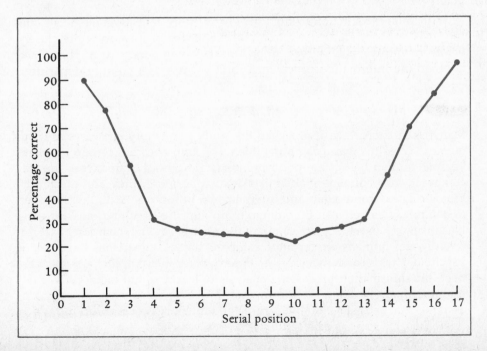

Figure 3.20   In studies of memory, the items in the list are examined for accuracy of recall. Such data are usually presented as percent accuracy as a function of the serial position of the item in the list. In this sample data, accuracy is presented for a 17-item list

VARIABLES IN RECOGNITION.   Recognition tasks require different experimental situations and different task demands. If a researcher were to present a string of letters, XBDFMPG, to a subject and then ask, "Did I present the letter *M*?", the task would be too easy; subjects would virtually always be correct. To get around this problem, researchers present more complicated tasks when recognition accuracy is used as the dependent variable. Some incredible data have accumulated with respect to recognition accuracy! In a series of studies replicated in other laboratories, it has been shown that human beings have amazingly good abilities to recognize pictures that have been shown previously. Researcher Ralph Haber, now at the University of Illinois, Chicago Circle, has shown that when presented with hundreds or even thousands of pictures, subjects can recognize those pictures virtually all of the time. Standing, Conezio, and Haber (1970) conducted studies where subjects were shown thousands of slides, each for a few seconds. Later they were shown pairs of slides, one of which they had seen before. The subject's task was to identify which of the pair of slides they had previously seen. The basic results were that with better than 95% accuracy, subjects were able to recognize which pictures they had seen before. These results have been repeated and have been shown to hold up with the presentation of as many as 10,000 different pictures (Standing, 1973) and in situations where pictures were presented *very* quickly (Intraub, 1980).

Where have you seen this face before? (For answer, see p. 69.)

Many other types of recognition memory can be studied. One type is people's ability to recognize other people they have seen before. In the last decade, researchers have been focusing on how well individuals remember others. We will be looking at this more closely when we study social psychology. For now, it is instructive to point out that in studies of eyewitness testimony where people say that a specific individual is the one who committed a crime, they are often wrong! Eyewitnesses often name the wrong people and recall events incorrectly. Loftus (1979) has shown that they not only recall events incorrectly but they often cannot even use recognition memory accurately.

With this introduction to the kinds of memory that psychologists examine, it is appropriate that we examine the stages of memory more closely. While not universally agreed upon, most contemporary researchers have adopted the information-processing point of view as a point of departure.

Stages in Memory: An Information-Processing Approach

Many researchers have approached the study of memory processes as if our memory acted the way a computer does. This approach has certain problems because human beings are not computers, nor do our brains work the way computers do. Humans make mistakes; furthermore, they are affected by biological, environmental, and interpersonal influences. Still, there are certain similarities between the human brain and the computer, and for these reasons many psychologists compare them. Even though computers act differently and humans are far more complex, these comparisons have helped psychologists research memory. An outgrowth of the computer approach has been the information-processing analysis to learning and memory. We will examine memory using the information-processing analysis; this approach assumes that each stage of the learning and memory process is an individual one. The first stage is called the sensory register and our examination will begin there.

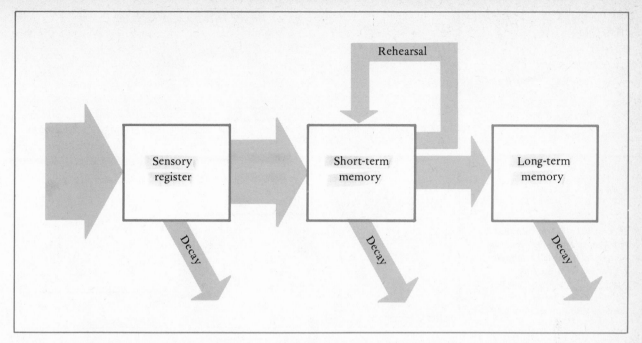

Rehearsal

Sensory register

Short-term memory

Long-term memory

Decay

Decay

Decay

Figure 3.21 When information enters the memory-processing system, it proceeds from the sensory register to short-term memory into long-term memory. At each stage, decay can take place and there is a loss of information. The information-processing approach stresses this analysis by stages wherein each level can be examined separately

Sensory register The process and mechanism by which initial coding and brief storage of stimuli occur. The duration of the visual sensory register is $\frac{1}{4}$ second.

SENSORY REGISTER.   For learning to occur, there must be a stimulus. When you read a textbook, the stimuli are words on a page; when you are listening to a lecture, the stimuli are auditory. The very first stage of the learning process must be the first representation of the stimulus, and herein lies the role of the **sensory register.** This process, which lasts only about one-quarter of a second, is the mechanism by which initial coding and brief storage of stimuli occur.

Consider the visual system as an example. When stimuli are presented to the visual system, they are briefly stored in the sensory register for $\frac{1}{4}$ second in an almost photographic manner, with little neural interpretation. This visual sensory register is sometimes called the *icon.*

Why is the visual sensory register necessary? For any stimulus to be seen or learned the receiver has to establish it first in an electrical or neural form; the visual sensory register does precisely this. Once information is established in the sensory register, it must be transferred into some other coding place or it will be lost in the system. Consider what happens when you examine a telephone book. You look for the number of the local pizza parlor, read the seven digits, then make your way to the phone. In the time that you go from the phone book to the phone, either you rehearse the number by saying it over and over or you forget the number. The information that was established in your visual sensory register will be lost if it is not rehearsed and transferred into some kind of memory, usually short-term memory.

SHORT-TERM MEMORY.   After stimuli are entered into the sensory register, they either decay or are transferred into short-term memory. In **short-term memory,** information is maintained for about 30 seconds and there is a great deal of coding. In coding, stimuli are no longer represented in the way that they were presented to the eye or ear. For example, visual stimuli are often coded as sounds. If a string of letters is presented for a subject to learn and she makes errors when reporting them back, these errors often occur be-

Short-term memory The memory process that temporarily stores information for immediate or short-term use. The duration of short-term memory is about 30 seconds and has a limited capacity of 5 to 9 items.

111

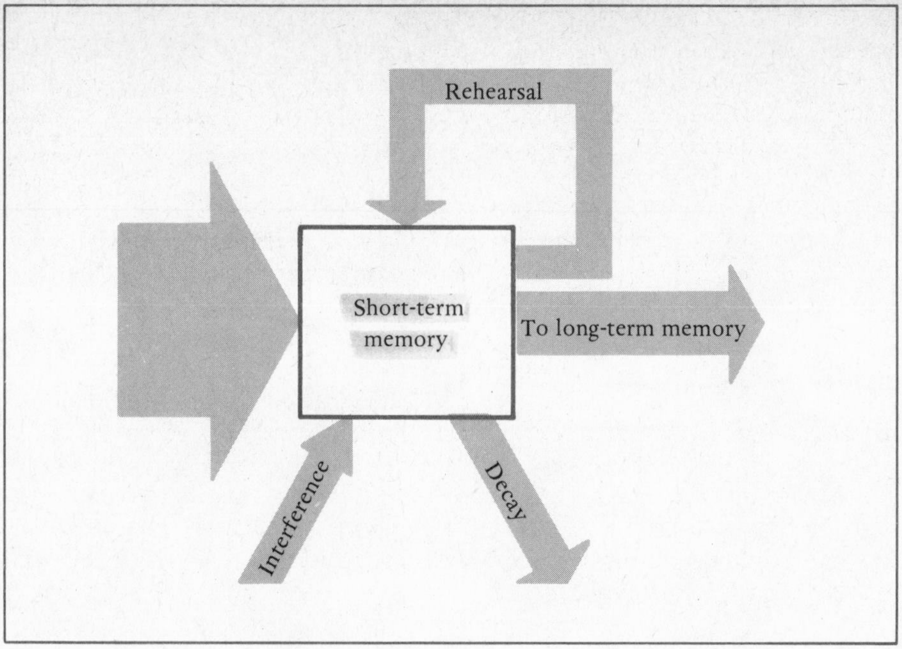

Figure 3.22 When information enters a person's memory system, it is initially entered into short-term memory where it is subject to decay, interference, rehearsal, or a transfer into long-term memory

cause the person reports back letters that sound like the letters she is trying to remember. If the letters to be reported were X, B, D, P, F, the subject might say X, E, D, B, F. She has reported letters that sound similar but are not the same letters; this shows that auditory coding is involved in short-term memory.

Short-term memory is not always coded auditorially; studies have shown that it has visual components as well (Fisher & Karsh, 1971; Fisher, Jarombek, & Karsh, 1974). Let's go back to our example of remembering a phone number. After visually examining a telephone book, how do you remember the phone number you have examined? Generally you repeat this number over and over to yourself to remember it. While you still have a visual representation of the digits, you generally recite them.

Much like the sensory register, information in short-term memory is either transferred into a subsequent coding mechanism (long-term memory) or it is forgotten. The concept of short-term memory is an important one because information that people receive daily enters short-term memory.

Long-term memory The mechanism by which a relatively permanent record of information is kept; being relatively permanent, long-term memory resists the loss of information.

LONG-TERM MEMORY.   Information stored in **long-term memory** is coded in a relatively permanent form and will be remembered. Recalling our first grade teacher's name, we are convinced that we are able to remember information for long periods of time. People remember names, dates, and places; they remember other people, things, and smells; they remember important events as well as trivial ones. Most people have been required to learn certain poems or literary messages by heart; generally, after many years they can still remember much of this material. For example, almost everyone can remember the first few lines of Mark Antony's speech from *Julius Caesar*. "Friends, Romans, countrymen, lend me your ears; I come to . . . "

Although we are often able to remember information for many years, we sometimes forget it. Even infomation that is stored in long-term memory is subject to forgetting. Perhaps for a year or two after learning Mark Antony's speech you were able to report the whole speech, while a few years later you can only remember just a few lines. This inability to remember all the information that was once stored in long-term memory may be due to the passage of time, or it may be the result of interference. We have many speeches and events to remember and learning new ones may interfere with our ability to remember old ones. Most of us are aware that events from the past are not recalled completely. We take notes during a lecture as an aid in recalling information that was presented; by taking notes in class we are admitting that our long-term memories are fallible. Our inability to recall lectures or people's names is often considered a problem of retrieval. *Retrieval* is the process by which we use our memory to recall something previously learned or to recognize something as familiar. Problems in retrieval, of course, suggest that the information is contained in long-term memory, but it is difficult to get at, for whatever reason.

We often assume that excellent memories are the unique ability of highly intelligent people. Yet this is not the case. Researchers have identified people considered retarded in overall level of functioning but who have a special talent. These individuals are called *idiot savants*, and their special talent is usually an extraordinary memory. They may also perform very well in mathematics, music, or art. A typical idiot savant is an individual who has an IQ of 60, but who also has the ability to tell the day of the week that a particular date fell upon many years ago. The question to the idiot savant might be, "'On what day of the week was July 26, 1946?'' ''Saturday,'' he or she would correctly respond.

Entering the facts and theories into long-term memory can be time consuming and tedious.

How Our Memories Work

Researchers know that there are different stages in memory, each one of which is responsible for different functions. Obviously, information that is in the sensory register is treated differently from information in long-term memory. In this section we shall see how these different stages in memory have been discovered, how they operate, and why they are important. Again, the obvious place to start is with the sensory register.

SENSORY REGISTER. In the early 1960s, George Sperling conducted a series of studies that was eventually to show the existence of the sensory register. In one of the studies three rows of letters, each four letters long, were briefly presented to subjects, who were then asked to report as many of the letters as they could remember. The subjects could only report an average of about $3\frac{1}{2}$ letters. In another study the subjects were told that they would have to report only one row of the three-row array. The row that they were to report would be signaled by a tone: a high-pitched tone meant that they should report the top row; a low-pitched tone, the bottom row; a tone of medium pitch, the middle row. The tone was either presented simultaneously with the letters or else delayed by a fraction of a second. Sperling found that when the tone was presented simultaneously, the subjects could report just as many letters as when they were allowed to report the entire three-row array. However, when the tone was delayed, accurate reporting decreased. These data were taken as support for the existence of a rapidly decaying memory— a sensory register.

113

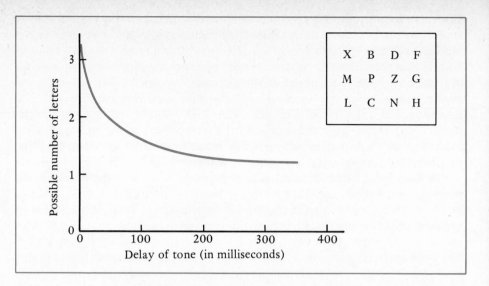

Figure 3.23 In Sperling's (1960) experiments, subjects were shown an array of 12 letters. They were to report one row. The row they were to report was signalled by a tone that was delayed by various intervals. Accuracy was plotted as function of the delay of the tone. Note how there are no further decreases in accuracy after 250 milliseconds

According to Sperling (1960), information established in a sensory register can easily be reported; however, as time passes, the information will decay. Most researchers believe the significance of the sensory register lies in its being the first stage in the process of coding and remembering information. While the existence of the sensory register has been acknowledged for over 20 years, some researchers still challenge its existence (Holding, 1975) and its physiological base (Sakitt & Long, 1979). Still, taken together the literature suggests that the sensory register is indeed the very first stage of coding (Dick, 1974; DiLollo, 1980).

SHORT-TERM MEMORY. An important study done in 1959 by Lloyd and Margaret Peterson changed the course of memory research. The Petersons asked subjects to remember a three-consonant sequence, such as XBD. The letters were to be recalled after 0, 3, 6, 9, 12, 15, or 18 seconds, during which the subjects were required to count backwards by threes. Counting backwards, or some other distracting task, does not allow the subjects to rehearse the syllable they are supposed to remember. The aim of the study was to examine recall when rehearsal was not allowed, and the results are presented in Figure 3.24. As the interval increased before recall, accuracy of recall decreased. These results had an important impact: the data showed that there was a loss of information over the first 18 seconds of memory. These results were initially interpreted as evidence for the existence of a brief short-term memory.

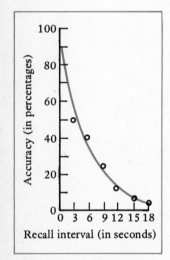

Figure 3.24 The principal finding of the study by Peterson and Peterson (1959) was that when report of 3-letter syllables is delayed by having subjects count backwards, accuracy decreases over the first 18 seconds

Short-term memory is different from other types of memory in a number of ways. First and most important is its *duration*—short-term memory is short in duration. The Peterson's experiment showed that after just a few seconds, information contained in memory is unavailable. We distinguish between short-term memory and long-term memory on the basis of how long information can be stored. In the first few seconds after a nonsense syllable or a telephone number is presented, it is contained in short-term memory; after those first few seconds it must be remembered permanently or lost.

A second and important distinguishing characteristic of short-term memory is its *capacity*. Short-term memory is limited in capacity and holds only a small amount of information. Human beings can remember only a limited number of items—about seven. In 1956, George Miller argued convincingly that humans can remember about seven, plus or minus two, items in memory. So, between five and nine items were supposedly the limit of short-term memory; this is quickly seen when we give long lists to subjects to learn. Depending on the type of material, the subjects are only able to remember seven, plus or minus two, items. Of course, some items are remembered more easily and in greater numbers than others, particularly if they are organized in some meaningful way such as alphabetically.

A third critical aspect of short-term memory is that *rehearsal* of the items in it allows them to be maintained. Given the list of letters XBDFMPG, subjects will forget them quickly unless they try to maintain them in short-term memory by rehearsing them. Rehearsal is the process of repeating over to ourselves in some active way the items to be remembered. Actively rehearsed items can be maintained in short-term memory almost indefinitely. Usually, however, the information entered into short-term memory is transferred to long-term memory or it is lost.

Before being transferred into long-term memory, most items in short-term memory go through some type of coding. A fourth property of short-term memory is that information contained in it is *coded* in some way; this coding is usually assumed to be visual or acoustic. When a series of letters are presented visually to a subject to learn or remember, the subject must transfer them out of the sensory store into short-term memory; yet, it is unlikely that their representation in short-term memory is the same as when they were stored in the sensory store. Indeed, we know that some information that is stored in short-term memory is stored in a visual way while other times information seems to be stored in an acoustic way. It has been shown that errors subjects make on information to be recalled, for example, are often acoustic in nature. If a subject is to recall orally the letters B A T, the subject might confuse these letters with P A C—an acoustic confusion. Other times, depending upon the task we give to the subject, the error that the subject makes in recalling the letters is visual—we present C O S and the subject responds with Q U B. In this case, the subject is confusing the shapes of the letters and making errors (Conrad & Hull, 1964).

One of the most prominent ways that we have been able to identify and study short-term memory is through retrieval processes. When an item to be remembered is to be recalled, it may be searched for in short-term memory in various ways. One way is by searching through all of the items in short-term memory in a complete or exhaustive way. Another way would be to limit our search for items and terminate our search when we find the needed item. This difference between exhaustive, complete searches and self-terminating, limited searches has shown us that short-term memory is quickly and very rapidly examined for information to be remembered.

Perhaps the most studied of all aspects of short-term memory is the loss of information from it—that is, *forgetting*. We lose information from short-term memory if it is not rehearsed, and in this process psychologists gain a great deal of information about the nature of memory. We will again consider forgetting as a topic in a few paragraphs. However, for now let us examine two of the major explanations for why people forget information from short-term memory—decay and interference. *Decay* suggests that information is

Memory: The Unreliable Witness

When people experience an event, study for an exam, or attempt to learn a new language, they rely heavily on their memory. Psychologists have often assumed that people's memories are extensive, reliable, and generally accurate. The following news article shows that even commonplace events are subject to decay and interference. People's memories in many ways are not as reliable as we would like them to be.

TIME Psychologist Jean Piaget vividly remembered an attempt to kidnap him from his baby carriage along the Champs Elysées. He recalled the gathered crowd, the scratches on the face of the heroic nurse who saved him, the policeman's white baton, the assailant running away. However vivid, Piaget's recollections were false. Years later the nurse confessed that she had made up the entire story.

Many social scientists believe that most early childhood memories are dreamlike reconstructions of stories told by parents and friends. Now Elizabeth Loftus, a psychologist at the University of Washington at Seattle, has a sobering message for grownups: their memories are almost as unreliable as children's—so encrusted with experiences, desires and suggestions that they often resemble fiction as much as fact. In *Eyewitness Testimony*, a book she published a year ago, Loftus made a strong case against the reliability of remembrances of court witnesses. In her latest work, *Memory*, she indicts human recollections in general.

One problem with memory, says Loftus, is that people do not observe well in the first place. Surprisingly often, people fail a simple test: picking out the exact copy of a real penny coin in a group of 15 possible designs (*see* [Figure 3.25]). More important, people forget some facts and "refabricate" the gaps between the ones they do remember accurately; they tend to adjust memory to suit their picture of the world. One example: in tests involving observations of a black man with a hat and a white man carrying a razor, people often recall the razor being in the black's hands. "We fill in gaps in our memory using chains of events that are logically acceptable," says Loftus. "Our biases, expectations and past knowledge are all used in the filling-in process, leading to distortions in what we remember."

Hypnosis and "truth serums" can also produce as much fiction as fact. Far from dredging up reality, writes Loftus, "hypnosis encourages a person to relax, to cooperate, and to concentrate." Suggestibility is so heightened that people may remember events that never occurred. Studies show that after taking truth drugs, people can lie competently, garble facts and invent stories to please their questioners. Other Loftus arguments:

- Hearing memory is apparently stronger in humans than touch, sight or smell memory. Patients who have been under total anesthesia can sometimes recall words spoken during an operation.
- Most people can easily remember no more than six or seven items in a series—a fact that bodes ill for the postal service's plan to replace five-digit zip codes with nine-digit ones. A Loftus tip: mental shopping lists should be set up with the important purchases at the beginning or the end, because as memory dims, the items in the middle tend to fade first.
- Slight stress improves memory; heavy stress erodes it. People who are about to subject themselves to danger—mountain climbing, parachute jumping. etc.—perform poorly at mental tasks.
- Booze and pot seem to affect information storage more than retrieval. That is, memory may work well at the time, but some things that occur while a person is under the influence may not be recalled. Senility works in a similar way, eroding ability to store new information.
- Any severe shock can produce memory loss. Rats forget tricks when given electric jolts. Amnesia, which can be the result of physical or emotional shock, is often selective. One woman, a professor of English, forgot the events and dates of her own life, but remembered those of English literature well enough to teach.
- For a few people, sexual intercourse brings sudden loss of memory lasting several hours. Dr. Richard Mayeux, of New York's Neurological Institute, has reported treating two cases of one-time memory loss and confusion after sex. Mayeux believes that this phenomenon may be related to hypertension, but is not particularly worrisome. Says he, soothingly: "One need not discourage patients from resuming their normal sexual activities."

One of the questions in memory research is whether long-term memories are held permanently in the brain. Freud thought so, believing that these memories lie deep in the unconscious, undisturbed by surface mental distortions. The late neurosurgeon Wilder Penfield agreed. His famous discovery, found accidentally while examining an epileptic woman, proved that electrical stimulation of the brain could trigger a re-experience of past events. Penfield took this as an indication of a "permanent imprint" of experience on the brain.

Loftus argues otherwise, finding that electrical stimulation of the brain produces the same mix of fiction and fact found in most unassisted attempts at recollection. Her conclusion: there is no evidence that "true" memories exist, like Platonic essences, beneath confused and adapted ones. "Unfortunately," she writes, "we are simply not designed that way." All memories, even those dredged up by psychoanalysis or hypnosis, are apt to be skewed. Or, as Santayana might have put it, those who remember the past are condemned to revise it. (By John Leo)

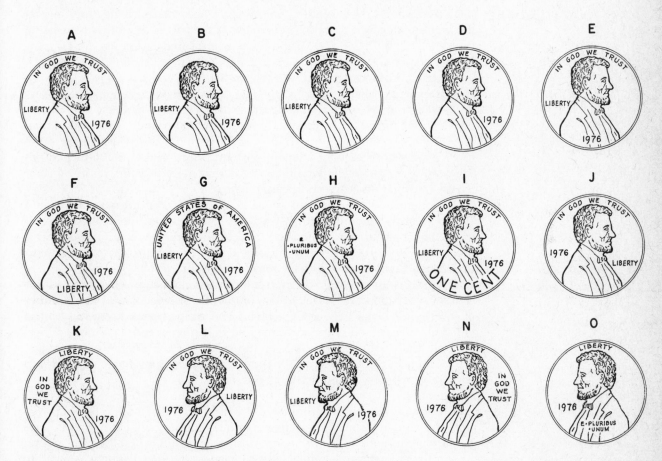

Figure 3.25 A simple recollection test: Which drawing of the penny is accurate?

Interference The suppression or confusion of one bit of information with another received either earlier or later.

lost just because of the passage of time; another term might be *disuse*. **Interference** suggests that since short-term memory is limited in capacity, items contained in it are interfered with and confused with other newly learned items.

If we could say the loss of information from short-term memory were only due to time and decay, the analysis would be simple. However, things are not that simple. Consider what would happen if you looked up a telephone number and then someone else gave you another telephone number to remember. What is the probability that you will remember the first number correctly? Chances are fairly good that the second number will interfere with your ability to remember the first one. There will have been no decay of information from short-term memory, but rather, interference or confusion.

Consider an experiment to investigate whether decay or interference is the primary factor in forgetting within short-term memory. Waugh and Norman (1965) did a study in which subjects listened to lists of single digits. One of the digits in the list was repeated; simultaneously, a tone that had special significance was sounded. The tone told the subject that the number that was just heard was also heard earlier. The subject's task was to tell the experimenter the name of the digit that occurred just *after* the earlier digit. So, if the list of digits were 3, 5, 7, 1, 2, 4, 6, 7, and the tone appeared on the last digit (7), the correct response would be 1. A 1 occurred just after the digit 7.

Waugh and Norman let the subjects listen to the list at two different speeds. Subjects heard the list at the rate of either one or four digits per second. Waugh and Norman reasoned that if forgetting was caused by decay, the slow rate of presentation would create a greater chance of forgetting than the fast rate of presentation. There would be more forgetting because the items were presented over a longer period of time. If the results turned out this way, the researchers would conclude that decay was the main cause of losing information from short-term memory.

The other possible result might be that both rates of presentation would show the same amount of forgetting. It might turn out that the number of items between the item to be reported and the tone was more important. If the results were like this, then interference or the number of items in memory rather than time would be most important.

The results are depicted in Figure 3.26. The data show similar recall for *both* presentation speeds. Regardless of the rate of presentation, the number of interfering items between the target and probe seems to be the critical variable. Waugh and Norman concluded that interference is a more critical variable than decay in the loss of information from short-term memory.

In summary, reconsider what happens to information that is entered into short-term memory. There are three possibilities. The *first* is that information will decay (be lost over time) and be forgotten. The *second* possibility is that the information in short-term memory will be confused with other information of a similar nature (interference) and, therefore, will get mixed up and be partially forgotten. The *third* and most likely result is that the information in short-term memory is rehearsed and used or rehearsed and transferred to long-term memory.

LONG-TERM MEMORY. You might think that with all of the coding that takes place in the sensory register and short-term memory, there is not much left for long-term memory to do. This is not the case at all because any impor-

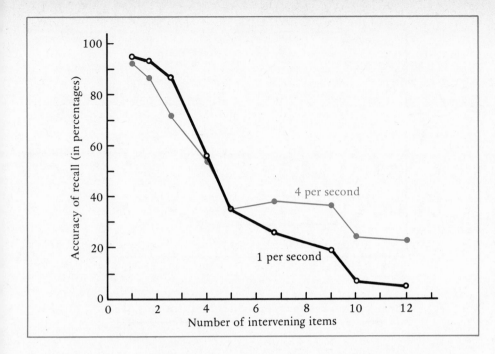

Figure 3.26 Waugh and Norman (1965) manipulated the number of items between the target items and the probe indicating to the subject the item to be recalled. They also manipulated the rate of presenting the items. Regardless of presentation speed, the accuracy of recall from short-term memory seems to be determined by the number of interfering items. Notice the large decrease in recall when the number of interfering items is large

tant or significant event we may wish to recall is stored in long-term memory. One of the critical variables that determines whether an item will be transferred into long-term memory is its importance. So, a trivial item such as the cost of a bunch of bananas will probably not be entered into long-term memory. In contrast, the cost of a gallon of gasoline may be etched into long-term memory because gasoline is so expensive.

Rehearsal of an item is a second important determinant of long-term memory. Events that are often repeated are etched into long-term memory. If we buy strawberry preserves every day, we are likely to remember their cost. We remember the name of our first-grade teacher because she had an important place in our lives, and we used her name repeatedly. Information in long-term memory is retained because of its meaning and salience and because it has been actively rehearsed.

Consider some experiments done in long-term memory. A typical experiment might be one in which a subject is asked to study a list of 30 or 40 words. The list of words will be presented at a rate of one word every 2 seconds and, at the end of the list, the subject is asked to recall the items. The results from such an experiment show an overall recall of 20% of the words. Recall is not the same for words at the beginning, middle, and end of the list. Look at recall of words in the beginning and end positions of Figure 3.27, p. 120: Words in the middle of the list are recalled relatively few times compared with words at the beginning and end of the list.

Why are results typically like those in Figure 3.27? When people are presented with a long list of words to learn, one or more of these three processes may take place:

Process #1: The stimuli enter the sensory register.
Process #2: The stimuli enter short-term memory.
Process #3: The stimuli enter long-term memory.

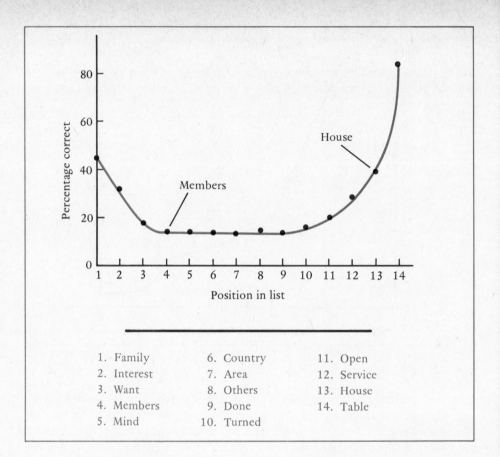

Figure 3.27 The accuracy of a subject's recall for each of the 14 words in a list is shown by this graph. Each subject recalls the word correctly or incorrectly; when a group of subjects is tested and their data added together, they are plotted in percentages correct as a function of each position. Sometimes this presentation of the data is called a serial position curve

1. Family
2. Interest
3. Want
4. Members
5. Mind
6. Country
7. Area
8. Others
9. Done
10. Turned
11. Open
12. Service
13. House
14. Table

In the hypothetical experiment just described, the stimuli may be described as going through Process #1, the sensory register. The stimuli would also proceed to Process #2, entering short-term memory. *However*, a long list of items will overload the short-term memory system. Most people cannot maintain 30 or 40 items in short-term memory (they have difficulty remembering a 7-digit phone number). Recall, therefore, must be from long-term memory (Process #3).

How well will items in long-term memory be remembered? Some data from an experiment by Glanzer and Cunitz (1966) are presented in Figure 3.29. For most of the items in the list, accuracy of recall is only about 25%. Items at the beginning of the list and particularly at the end were recalled with significantly higher accuracy. But why?

All of the items in the list have gone through the sensory register (Process #1), have been entered into short-term memory (Process #2), and have proceeded on to long-term memory (Process #3). However, the last items in the list were not necessarily transferred out of short-term memory into long-term memory. They were the last items stored in short-term memory, and they were not followed by any other items. Subjects had time to rehearse these last items, to keep them active in short-term memory, and to report them accurately. These data led Glanzer and Cunitz to suggest that both short-term and long-term memory were involved in the recall of lists of items. They suggested that the early and middle portions of the data were reflecting long-

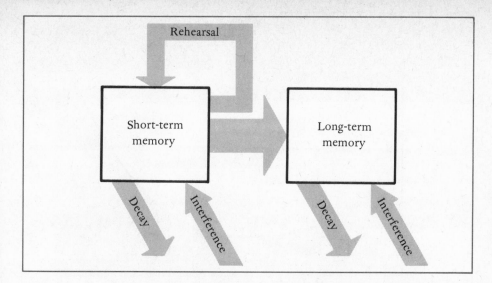

Figure 3.28 Information maintained in short-term memory can be transferred into a more permanent, lasting storage, long-term memory. Long-term memory is subject to both decay and interference

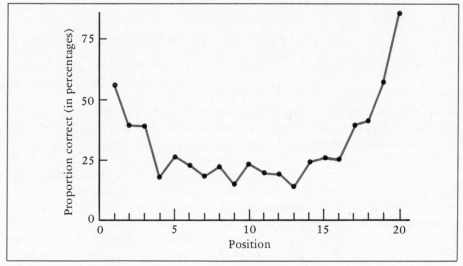

Figure 3.29 Some typical serial position function data from an experiment by Glanzer and Cunitz (1966). Note how the percentage of items reported correctly is higher at the beginning and end of the list. This serial position curve is typical of the data that memory studies produce

term memory, while the data from the end of the list were recalled principally from short-term memory (see Figure 3.30, p. 122).

We are rarely placed in situations in which we have to remember long lists of items. However, we are often presented with large amounts of information and later asked to recall portions of it. In the serial position curves in Figures 3.20 and 3.27 we saw that initial and end items were recalled better than other items. We generally see that the material from the end of long amounts of information will be recalled with the greatest accuracy; this **recency effect** is due to the information being actively rehearsed in short-term memory. It is also likely that information given at the beginning will also be remembered with slightly greater accuracy. This ability to remember information better that is presented at the beginning is called a **primacy effect**. Primacy effects result because there is no information in the short-term storage mechanism, the task is new, and the subject's attention to the stimuli is probably at its peak. Thus, primacy and recency effects account for the increased recall at the beginning and end of lists. It is interesting to note that

Recency effect Phenomenon in which items presented to the subject more recently are more accurately recalled.

Primacy effect Phenomenon in which items presented first in a list or series are more accurately recalled.

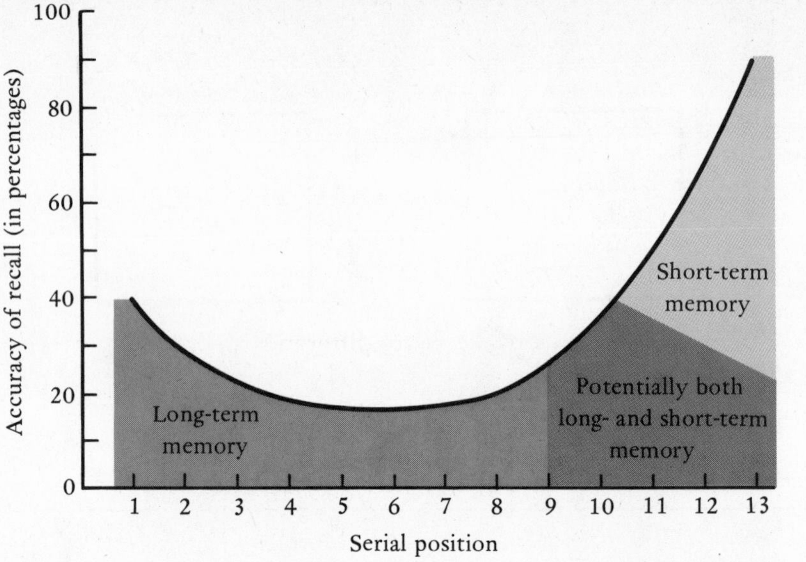

Figure 3.30 According to Glanzer and Cunitz (1966), primarily the last items in a list are kept in short-term memory. All other recalled items have been transferred into long-term memory, and this might or might not include the last item.

very often the stressed parts of plays, symphonies, art exhibitions, and political rallies are the beginning and the end. A politician's opening and closing remarks are often the ones that are quoted and remembered.

Long-term memory (in which all past events are stored) has generally been considered unitary in nature. However, in 1972 Tulving suggested that there are two kinds of information stored in long-term memory, episodic and semantic. *Episodic* memory is memory for events, objects, and situations that are specific in nature. This might be what you had for breakfast, the movie you saw last night, or what you did on vacation last summer. *Semantic* memory is memory for ideas, rules, concepts, and general conceptions about the world. To develop semantic memory, one first must go through many events and have a developed episodic memory. Most research has supported the idea of a distinction between episodic and semantic memory (Herrmann & Marwood, 1980), but not all research has been supportive (Anderson & Ross, 1980).

Research has supported the idea of semantic memory by doing studies that show that there seems to be a hierarchy of information in semantic memory. This means that certain information is contained at a particular level of memory, and if a person needs more information, she or he must go to another level of memory to access this information. For example, if one were presented with the sentence "a canary is a bird that has feathers and can sing" and were asked if this sentence were true or false, we might measure how long it takes a subject to make this judgment. One theory of semantic memory organization suggests that we know certain things about all birds, of which canaries are one class. As we try to verify information in the sample sentence, we must examine and try to access different levels of information, for example, about animals, birds, and canaries. An individual's response time will depend on the number of levels the person must examine to verify the accuracy of the sentence. Like short-term memory, long-term memory has its subdivisions and varying nature (Collins & Quillian, 1972).

STAGES OF MEMORY: A SUMMARY.   By now it should be apparent that there are differences between the three components of learning and memory: the sensory register, short-term memory, and long-term memory. Each of the components will have a different duration and be affected by different variables. For example, short-term memory is subject to rapid decay and to interference from other new information, while information in long-term memory is less likely to be forgotten and does not need to be rehearsed to be maintained. Furthermore, information in long-term memory can be episodic or semantic in nature. Although there are differences of opinion as to how our memories function, we can still derive a generalized model of memory.

In examining how our memories work, we have used the *information-processing* approach. This approach divides memory into a series of stages and has allowed us to consider how each stage works and how it might relate to other stages. Many psychologists who have studied learning and memory have tried to build theories of how memory works. They use different terms and suggest different ways each process might operate. There have been those who do not make a distinction between short- and long-term memory, as well as those who attribute different aspects of learning to different memory systems. The weight of the evidence today suggest that there are three memory processes. How each of the systems works and how information is transferred from one system to the next is still under active consideration. Indeed, there is much to dispute about in the details of how each mechanism operates. Many psychologists see these same mechanisms operating in very different ways. As you will soon read, some have even gone to the physiology laboratory to support their contentions. Yet almost all agree on the three basic principles. First, the sensory register is considered a brief representation of the original stimulus with minimal neural coding taking place. Second, short-term memory is considered a storage mechanism that is acoustic in nature (although it may have visual components) and lasts for less than 30 seconds. Rehearsal helps maintain information in short-term memory, but the major losses of information in short-term memory are caused by interference and decay. Third, long-term memory is the final coding mechanism of our memory system; it is the memory mechanism that is sensitive to the importance of an event, its meaningfulness, and degree of rehearsal.

Why are psychologists so concerned about the way our memories work? The answer lies in the title of this chapter, Learning. Humans have great capacities to learn and understand. By gaining insight into our learning and memory processes, psychologists might be able to maximize performance. Teachers are concerned about students' ability to remember recently learned information. Similarly, those designing computer-aided instruction are equally concerned with what and how people learn. Through studying learning, psychologists can maximize human abilities to deal with the world effectively and cope with its complexities ingeniously.

Forgetting: The Loss of Memory

The early psychologists and contemporary researchers have used the idea that studying what we don't remember must tell us something about mem-

LAG, MUG, DAX, and GIP

For years, psychology laboratories have been ringing bells at dogs and allowing rats to push levers to obtain food. In the same way, humans have been presented nonsense syllables; these made-up nonsense words like LAG, MUG, DAX, and GIP have been used as stimuli in studies of human learning since before the turn of the century. They have been popular because they are meaningless, and when researchers have tried to study memory, they have tried to separate memory processes from our memories of specific events, ideas, or words.

In Ebbinghaus's laboratory, subjects were presented with made-up nonsense syllables in lists that they were to repeat. When presented with a short list the task is easy—LAG, MUG, DAX, for example, is easy to remember. However, when there are 14 items presented in such a list, subjects have difficulty remembering the nonsense syllables. Through this technique, people's memory span can be established. Memory is often defined as the number of items that can be remembered 50% of the time.

Widely used in the early part of the century, the memory span technique was replaced in 1959 with a new task—the one presented by Peterson and Peterson. The task had been used by Bigham even as early as 1894.

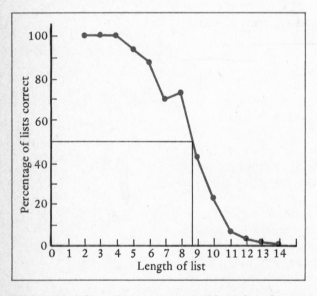

Figure 3.31 When subjects are presented lists of numbers to learn, their ability to recall them depends on the length of the list. The 50% point (often defined as memory span) in this experiment is the list between eight and nine items long (data from Oberly, 1928; after Hintzman, 1978)

In its present form, credit is usually given to the Petersons and another researcher, Brown (1958), who independently used the task. The *distractor task* (sometimes called the Brown-Peterson task) is one in which a stimulus like a nonsense syllable is presented to a subject and then is followed with some other kind of task that distracts the subject from rehearsing the item to be remembered. We examined this task earlier (p. 114 and especially Figure 3.24).

Probe tasks were another method of investigating short-term memory. In these tasks, lists given to a subject are supposed to be remembered. At some point in the list the subject is given a cue or probe, which indicates that the subject is to recall the item that followed it on an earlier presentation. We examined a probe task in the study by Waugh and Norman (1965) (see p. 118 and especially Figure 3.26).

To assess memory over long periods still newer techniques have been devised. In a *continuous task* method, subjects are presented with items to be remembered as part of a long series of items that may span a few minutes, a few hours, or a few days. Consider the task used by Begg and Wickelgren (1974). In their experiment, they had subjects study short sentences like "The ice cream is on the table" and then had them indicate if they had seen the sentence before. In the long series of sentences, some of the sentences were repeated; this allowed the subjects to indicate "Yes, this is the same sentence." On all other sentences, the subjects were to indicate that the sentence was new. The amount of time between the presentation of a sentence and its repetition was varied. By manipulating this interval, Begg and Wickelgren assessed memory loss over longer time periods. In fact, they tested their subjects over a 4-day period and presented over 6,000 sentences. Shown in Figure 3.32 are the results of their study. Shown is the percentage of sentences recognized as a function of the time between a sentence and its repetition. We see from the figure that there is a consistent and steady loss of information over these larger time periods.

In a new attempt to study forgetting from short-term memory, Muter (1980) used a modified distractor task and found *very* rapid forgetting; in fact, his forgetting rates were far more rapid than ever found before. Essentially the Muter (1980) experiment used a distractor task just like the one used by Peterson and Peterson (1959); the difference was that the subjects were rarely or never asked to recall the item presented after the distracting retention interval. Subjects saw letters and then counted backwards by 3s. They were not asked to recall the letters. However, on two trials per session, the subjects

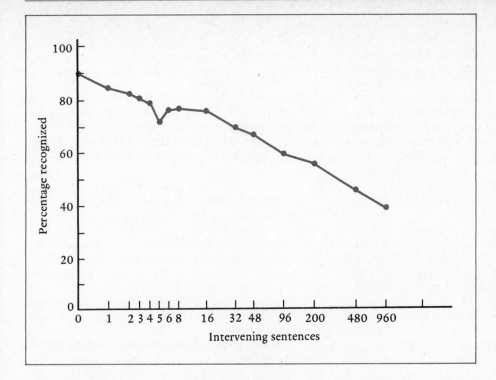

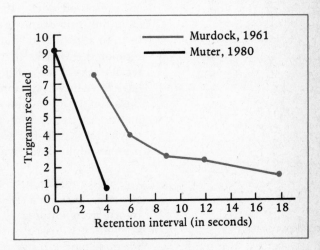

Figure 3.32 In continuous tasks, subjects are presented with items to be remembered over long periods of time. In these situations, subjects might respond with an indication if the item had been seen or heard before. In Begg and Wickelgren's study (1974), sentences were presented over many days, and if one was repeated, the subjects were to indicate this to the experimenter. Their results show a steady decline in accuracy of recall as the number of interfering sentences and time increases (data from Table 3 of Begg & Wickelgren, 1974)

were asked to recall the earlier presented letters; this thus became a Peterson and Peterson task. The results showed that after 4 seconds subjects were very poor at recalling the letters; they performed far worse than did the subjects in the experiments performed by Peterson and Peterson or other similar studies. From Muter's view, when subjects are told they will have to remember an item and then are given a distractor task, the results are *very* different from when they are to recall the item but are not aware that they are to do so. Thus, a subject's expectations about retention and the retention interval change the nature of forgetting curves.

From Muter's view, when people are given the task of looking up a telephone number and then are distracted, the loss from memory is less rapid than the situation where the person looks up the telephone number, decides not to use it, and goes on to something else. After 10 seconds in the first case some memory for the telephone number will still be available, but in the second case (Muter's example) the number would be virtually lost.

Modern memory research has spanned more than eight decades, and its tasks have varied with the questions that its researchers have asked. Each task has provided new information that answers different questions. We know much more about learning, memory,

and forgetting now than we did several years ago. It is likely that our evolving science of psychology will provide more information about the nature of forgetting in the next few years.

Figure 3.33 In Muter's experiment (1980), the proportion of trigrams recalled decreased to a low level much more quickly during a retention interval than previous studies have shown (data from Muter, 1980)

125

Improving Your Memory

Have you ever tried to remember a list of names for an exam or a list of procedures for a job by saying the first letters of the words over and over? Sometimes people organize these letters into a word; their aim is to remember the letters of the word and let letters act as a cue for memory. For instance, SSL could stand for Sensory register, Short-term memory, and Long-term memory, the three major stages of memory. As a memory aid for this chapter just remember SSL, which could be made meaningful by recoding it to Sam Solomon Lane.

This memory aid of coding words through letters is an example of a *mnemonic*. A mnemonic is one of several ways to improve your memory without expensive or time-consuming memory aids. Laird Cermack, a noted learning psychologist, has written a paperback book on this subject called *Improving Your Memory* (McGraw-Hill, 1978) in which he outlines a how-to-do-it approach.

The Cermack method involves two basic steps and three techniques. First, you have to pay close attention to what you want to remember. Second, you have to organize your thoughts, and it takes time to do so.

Assuming that you are attending and organizing, then you can use three techniques to help you remember: mediation, imagery, and mnemonics. *Mediation* is the technique of hooking up two items to be remembered with a third that ties them together. *Soup* and *letter* need to be remembered, so you remember the word *alphabet*. Cermack uses as examples the names John and Tillie. How do we remember their names? John reminds you of *bathroom*, which can then be associated with *tiles*, which sounds and looks like Tillie. The system of mediation uses this bridging technique.

The second technique is imagery. *Imagery* is making pictures in our memory of events or things to be remembered. Imagining items in special situations is a big help for recall. Try to form images that involved *you* in them!

Mnemonics is Cermack's third recommendation. *Mnemonics* is the combining of items into a preestablished format or the creation of a rhyme or jingle which contains the information to be remembered. For instance, most children learn the notes of the musical scale, EGBDF, through a mnemonic jingle, "Every Good Boy Deserves Fudge." Mnemonics is the most creative form of organization, but the technique is very effective.

All three techniques work, but they require practice and repeated use. Do you remember what the mnemonic SSL stands for?

---

ory. To study forgetting, researchers have manipulated how quickly subjects are presented with lists to learn. They have manipulated the length of the lists, the content of the lists, as well as the confusability of the items in the lists. In addition to changes in the stimulus materials, researchers have manipulated the tasks that subjects have been involved in—free recall, serial recall, tasks of recognition, and even tasks of delayed memory where subjects have to remember information for long periods of time. Our examination of the structure of memory has pointed to two main approaches to how information is lost or forgotten—decay and interference—but there are other ways that it is lost as well. Let us briefly review decay and interference and present some other ways in which information can be forgotten.

DECAY. Information that is entered into memory can be forgotten because of decay. This idea suggests that strictly due to a passage of time, events or information entered in memory will be lost. Some researchers have described such losses in terms of a fading memory trace, where the memory trace is some kind of physiological representation of the event in memory. There is some limited evidence to show that the passage of time is involved in forgetting. The Petersons' experiment described earlier (p. 114) showed that after 18 seconds, information is unavailable from short-term memory. As time passes, events that are not important to individuals seem to fade from long-term memory; the details become fuzzy, confused, or lost (Bartlett, 1932). Support for decay notions comes from Conrad and Hille (1958), who presented a list to adult subjects at one of two rates, either 30 or 90 words per minute. With a faster rate of presentation, less time is taken to present a list of fixed length. According to decay theory, this faster rate of presentation should allow for less decay and therefore better accuracy of recall. This was their finding.

There is other support for the decay explanations of information from memory (see, for example, Reitman, 1974). Many of the early findings that suggested that decay is the principal reason for the loss of information have been shown to be problematical; some of these early studies did not take into consideration many important variables that affect memory processes in general. Still, the idea has been popular for many years; although not widely accepted as the explanation for forgetting, there is enough evidence to suggest that it cannot be discounted and is probably at least part of what will be the final explanation of forgetting.

INTERFERENCE: Human beings have limited abilities to remember everything that they are presented; in addition, they are often presented with a great deal of new information about the same topic within a short period of time. In these situations, there is likely to be interference or confusion of information in memory. Both research and personal experience support the interference claim. Studies such as those presented earlier by Waugh and Norman (1965) show that interference plays a much greater role than decay does. When presented with long lists of digits to learn, the number of items in the list (the number of confusing items) seemed to affect recall more than how quickly they were presented. As students know, when too much information is presented, they often feel swamped with ideas and become confused. Too much information in too short a time creates interference rather than organized ideas.

Interference implies that other information will affect a person's memory. Over the years, research has agreed with this general finding, but in addition it has found that the extent and nature of a person's experiences *before,* as well as after, learning is also particularly important. Assume a subject is given a list of nonsense syllables to learn. Let us call this list the *target* list. We might find that the subject's recall of the items is 75% correct. However, if we had given the subject 20 other lists to learn before this target list, we would find that recall of the target list would be lower. The previous lists interfered with current list learning. Furthermore, if after we presented our list, we gave the subject other lists to learn, the subject's later recall of the target list would be still lower. We call these effects proactive and retroactive inhibition. *Proactive inhibition* is the decrease in accuracy of a target list due to previous events, while *retroactive inhibition* is the decrease in accuracy of a target list due to material learned after the target list was presented. Both effects have been studied extensively and have been found to be very important in recalling information from both short- and long-term memory (Keppel & Underwood, 1962; Underwood, 1957).

The information-processing point of view of information storage and retrieval accepts both decay and interference explanations of information loss from memory. Furthermore, this view accepts the idea that information rehearsed in either short- or long-term memory is less likely to be forgotten.

Generally, however, the information-processing view overlooks two other kinds of forgetting, which we shall now examine.

MOTIVATED FORGETTING.   Decay and interference are related to the structure of memory and physiological processes; they have little or nothing to do with the feelings, desires, or wants of a person living within a specific environment. Because human beings are affected by more than just physiology, psychologists have recognized that there may be certain events, facts, or memories that people do not want to remember; that is, they are motivated to forget.

In 1933, Freud was the first psychologist to suggest formally that unwanted or unpleasant events might be lost in memory because people wanted to lose them. Freud spoke of repression, or the burying of unpleasant ideas where they are dismissed to the unconscious and are inaccessible. Freud's idea was that during the course of a person's life it is likely that certain unpleasant circumstances are sufficiently uncomfortable and awkward that people are motivated to forget them. Freud was to develop a formal theory of behavior based in part on the ideas of repressed memories motivating later behavior. Freud's idea is appealing, and indeed there are many anecdotal reports of therapists who will recount how people seem to choose to forget important and painful events in their lives. Even as people are going through a difficult circumstance, they report that they wished it were over so that they might forget about it.

In trying to investigate motivated forgetting in the laboratory, researchers have provided little support for the idea. While most researchers recognize that motivated forgetting probably exists in some form, they have been unable to provide even modest support for it as a formal mechanism by which people forget.

AMNESIA.   While television soap operas are constantly portraying people who have developed the condition, the actual occurrence of amnesia in the population is relatively rare. **Amnesia** is the inability to remember events from the past, usually because of physiological trauma. Amnesia is more than just a loss of ability to remember—it is typically associated with loss of memory for any and all events over a certain period of time. There are two basic kinds of amnesia—retrograde amnesia and anterograde amnesia. *Ret-*

Amnesia A loss of memory, usually due to traumatic injury.

How quickly we forget!

rograde amnesia is the inability to remember events that preceded the injury (this is what might be called the "soap-opera loss"). After an auto accident, a blow to the head, or a fall from a tree, a person cannot remember events that preceded the incident. Sometimes the inability to remember only covers the time period just before the accident; other times the memory loss covers a period of years. Retrograde amnesia may be caused by injuries to the head, but it is also associated with carbon monoxide poisoning and has been associated with certain kinds of shock therapy in patients with depressive problems. While the recovery from amnesia is generally gradual, older events usually are remembered first (see McGaugh & Herz, 1970).

Anterograde amnesia is the inability to remember events that have taken place since the time of injury or brain damage. In studying patients with brain damage or patients who have had surgery for major epileptic attacks, researchers have found that a region of the brain called the *hippocampus* may be responsible for the transfer of new information into a permanent memory store. Brenda Milner (1966) argued that if certain regions of the brain are damaged or removed, humans have an inability to store *new* information. Their ability to remember old information is intact; it is new information that cannot be remembered (Milner, Corkin, & Teuber, 1968). People who are severe, chronic alcoholics show similar kinds of symptoms in a disease called Korsakoff's syndrome. It has been assumed that the extra amounts of alcohol affect the same portions of the brain and that Korsakoff's syndrome and anterograde amnesia have a common base.

Recent studies have challenged the conclusions of Milner and the studies of Korsakoff's patients. These studies (see, for example, Albert, Butters, & Levin, 1979) have shown that such patients have retrograde amnesia as well as anterograde amnesia; they have trouble remembering events in the past as well as new information (Marslen-Wilson & Teuber, 1975). The memory system of such patients has clearly been impaired; we might speculate that the process whereby new traces are called up has been impaired or perhaps the ability to convert new neural traces into permanent ones is impaired (Milner, 1968). Our data are far from complete; furthermore, they do not speak directly or conclusively to the idea that separate places or processes in the brain account for short-term and long-term memory.

The problems of the amnesiac and those of the person trying to forget an unpleasant childhood experience are clearly different from those of a sophomore college student trying to remember a list of nonsense syllables. However, taken together, the research in all of these areas helps psychologists piece together our limited but growing understanding of memory. Studies of forgetting are providing clues to how we remember.

Physiology of Memory

If psychologists knew the exact physiological basis of learning and memory, they would have a much better understanding of how these elements work and how learning takes place. But the brain is very complex and our partial understanding of it keeps us from a complete understanding of learning. Nevertheless, there are some physiological data, and a variety of researchers have attempted to define the physiological basis of memory. New findings are presented all the time, and important breakthroughs are becoming more frequent. We shall examine only a couple of these research attempts, but their thrust is important.

One of the major psychological and physiological theories of memory is that put forth by Canadian psychologist Donald Hebb (1949). Hebb suggested that when groups of neurons are stimulated, they form patterns of activity. If this same pattern of neural activity fires frequently, then a reverberating and regular neural circuit is established. According to Hebb, this "cell assembly" serves as the basis of short-term memory. If this neural circuit is stimulated frequently, a structural change takes place in the brain; information is thus coded into long-term memory.

Consolidation is the term used to describe the change from a temporary neural circuit that has evolved over time to a more permanent structure. If Hebb is correct, then initially there are only temporary changes in neurons when people see or hear a new stimulus. Hebb argues that, with repetition, consolidation will take place—the temporary circuit will become a permanent structure.

Attempts have been made to stop consolidation processes; for example, electroconvulsive shock has been used to disrupt consolidation and thus impair learning. Results of studies in which both animals and humans were given electroconvulsive shock show impaired memory in both groups. Many psychologists feel that the consolidation process holds the key to our understanding of learning and memory. Perhaps differences in ability to learn or remember are due to our ability to consolidate new information properly! Consolidation may be responsible for differences in learning ability, remembering, or even intelligence.

Unfortunately, physiological studies of memory have not unearthed dramatic or startling answers. However, studies of patients who have had accidents or operations that have allowed for a precise physiological diagnosis have provided support for a distinction between short- and long-term memory. Baddeley and Warrington (1970) worked with amnesiac subjects with certain types of brain damage. They compared these amnesiac subjects with normal ones in a variety of memory experiments. Their results showed that amnesiac patients have intact short-term memories but grossly defective long-term memories; thus their studies lend support to the distinction between short-term and long-term memory.

Milner (1966) reported a case of a specific memory deficit in a brain-damaged adult. She showed that this patient had an inability to form new long-term memories, yet his short-term memory was intact. As long as the subject was able to rehearse information and keep it within short-term memory, his memory behavior was normal. As soon as the subject was put in a situation in which he could no longer rehearse (and long-term memory was necessary), his performance was very poor. While these data are actively being challenged, there are neurological data to support a distinction between short- and long-term memory (see, for example, Drachman & Arbit, 1966).

Advances in knowledge concerning the physiological basis of memory will most likely be in terms of how information is coded in the consolidation process. Do the changes take place at synaptic junctions? Are the changes that take place due to new memory traces established in the structure of protein molecules? Psychologists can only hint at these answers at the present time. The weight of the evidence suggests that there is a distinction between

Consolidation The term used to describe the change from a temporary neural circuit to one that has evolved over time to a more permanent circuit.

short- and long-term memory and the process of consolidation may provide critical clues to the nature of coding.

SUMMARY

We have been examining both learning and memory and have defined a number of important principles. First, we have shown that reinforcement is a critical property in conditioned learning. Second, we have shown how punishment can be used to control behavior, although it is probably not the best way to do it. Third, we have shown how information proceeds from the sensory register to short-term and long-term memory by analyzing the coding processes, including the physiological mechanisms, which might underlie memory.

Human and animal learning overlap in many ways. Central to both is the concept of reinforcement; only reinforced behaviors tend to occur again in both animals and humans. Admittedly, most human behaviors are not performed in order to obtain a primary reinforcer such as food or water. Rather, people emit behaviors for a secondary reinforcer such as money. Reinforcement increases performance in a classroom setting, at work, for a dieter, and for an artist. Reinforcement is central to animal learning *and* human learning; it is a basic learning process.

Once an organism learns something, we can study its memory. Studying memory in humans is fairly easy because we can ask humans questions about what they remember; with animals, studying memory is more difficult. Even so, we are able to study what effect new activity has on the subject's ability to remember events learned earlier. Again, some basic learning processes are evident in both humans *and* animals. Primacy and recency effects, for example, are apparent for both in long-term memory. While humans may be easier to communicate with, animals are more appropriate subjects for the study of the physiological bases of memory. The process of consolidation and the psychology that underlies learning and memory are being investigated now, and we are just beginning to understand the physiology of memory.

To what extent can psychologists compare animal studies and human studies? Are studies done with rats appropriate to human behavior? It would be nice if psychologists could answer this question with a simple yes or no, but that cannot be done at present. Many basic behavior principles studied with animals are appropriate to humans. But, at the same time, many animal behaviors have little to do with human behavior. Therefore, generalizations based upon animal data must be made carefully. The areas in which we must be most conservative in comparing animal data to human data are those involving complex perceptual and learning processes. Animal data are most useful in studying basic behavior principles and how the organisms respond to basic learning situations. In the same way, human data are probably most useful for studying memory processes. The complete process of learning will only be understood when psychologists know about the behavior of *both* humans and animals.

CHAPTER REVIEW

1. Learning is a relatively permanent change in behavior that occurs as a result of experience.
2. Classical conditioning involves the pairing of a neutral stimulus (such as a bell) with an unconditioned stimulus (such as food) so that the unconditioned response (such as salivation) will become a conditioned response.
3. A key characteristic of classical conditioning is that a formerly neutral stimulus elicits or brings about a response.
4. The impact of Pavlovian conditioning on our everyday lives is illustrated when one considers that the conditioned stimulus need not be available directly to get a conditioned response; we call this higher-order conditioning.
5. If an unconditioned stimulus is to be paired with a conditioned stimulus, they must occur close in time for conditioning to occur.
6. The probability of a response reoccurring is directly related to the magnitude of the reinforcement and is inversely related to its delay.
7. Extinction is the process whereby the probability of an organism emitting a conditioned response is reduced when reinforcement is withheld.
8. Spontaneous recovery is the reoccurrence of a conditioned response following a rest period after extinction.
9. Stimulus generalization is the conditioned response to stimuli similar to, but not the same as, the training stimulus.
10. In instrumental conditioning, an animal emits or shows a behavior, and then this behavior is followed by a consequence of reward or punishment.
11. A reinforcer is any event that increases the probability of the reoccurrence of a response that precedes it.
12. Secondary reinforcers are originally neutral stimuli that have no intrinsic value for the organism but take on reinforcing properties by virtue of being paired with primary reinforcers.
13. Positive reinforcement is reinforcement that acts to increase the probability of a response reoccurring by the introduction of a rewarding or pleasant stimulus.
14. Negative reinforcement increases the probability that an organism will emit a certain behavior. Thus, an animal may press a bar to avoid a painful electric shock.
15. In punishment, we try to decrease the probability of a behavior being emitted, whereas with reinforcement we try to increase the probability that a behavior will be emitted.
16. When a person is given an electric shock or a spanking upon emitting some behavior, this is a primary punishment. Through association with primary punishers, words, frowns, and indifference take on punishing qualities (become secondary punishers).
17. A common punishment procedure that has proved to be very effective is time-out; in time-out a person is removed from a situation in which reinforcers might be found.
18. Shaping is the training of an animal or human to make a certain response; this process is usually done in stages.
19. Organisms will work to achieve reinforcement on interval and ratio schedules that are fixed or variable.
20. In instrumental conditioning, extinction is the process of reducing the probability that an animal or human will respond with a conditioned response by withholding a reinforcement.
21. In classical conditioning, the organism's behavior (whether or not it responds to the conditioned stimulus) is not considered; by contrast, the unconditioned stimulus (the reinforcer) in instrumental conditioning only occurs *if* the organism emits the correct behavior.
22. Classically conditioned behaviors are usually reflexive and involuntary; by con-

trast, behaviors conditioned through instrumental procedures are usually voluntarily emitted.

23. Observational learning is the process by which organisms learn new responses by observing the behavior of a model and then imitating it; it is also called social learning theory.
24. Memory is the ability to recall or remember information, events, or skills learned in the past.
25. The difference between a free recall task and a serial recall task is that in the free recall task the subject can recall the syllables in any order.
26. The sensory register contains the initial representation of a stimulus in memory.
27. In short-term memory, stimuli that have gone through the sensory register are further coded and maintained for about 30 seconds.
28. Short-term memory has visual and auditory components and is subject to interference and decay.
29. Long-term memory is the coding mechanism for storing information permanently.
30. Episodic memory is memory for events, objects, and situations that are specific in nature; semantic memory is memory for ideas, rules, concepts, and general conceptions about the world.
31. Primacy and recency effects increase the accuracy of lists recalled at the beginning and end of a list, respectively.
32. Proactive inhibition is the decrease in accuracy of a target list due to *previous* events; retroactive inhibition is the decrease in accuracy of a target list due to material being learned *after* the target list was presented.
33. The information-processing point of view of information storage and retrieval accepts both decay and interference explanations of the loss of information from memory.
34. Amnesia is a loss of memory, usually due to a traumatic injury.
35. Consolidation is the term used to describe changes from a temporary neural circuit to a more permanent circuit that has evolved due to structural changes.
36. Physiological data have been collected to strengthen the belief that there is a distinction between short- and long-term memory; however, this view is regularly challenged.
37. While animal and human learning can be considered separately, both are sensitive to basic learning processes.

SUGGESTIONS FOR FURTHER READING

BANDURA, A. *Social learning theory*. Englewood Cliffs, NJ: Prentice-Hall, 1977.

CERMAK, L. S. *Improving your memory*. New York: McGraw-Hill, 1976.

HILGARD, E. R., AND BOWER, G. H. *Theories of learning* (4th ed.). Englewood Cliffs, NJ: Prentice-Hall, 1975.

LAHEY, B. B., AND JOHNSON, M. S. *Psychology and instruction*. Glenview, IL: Scott, Foresman, 1978.

LOFTUS, E. F., AND LOFTUS, G. R. *Human memory*. New York: John Wiley & Sons, 1976.

NORMAN, D. A. *Memory & attention: An introduction to human information processing*. New York: John Wiley & Sons, 1969.

PAVLOV, I. *Conditioned reflexes*. Oxford, England: Clarendon Press, 1927.

SKINNER, B. F. *Walden Two*. New York: Macmillan, 1948.

SKINNER, B. F. *About behaviorism*. New York: Knopf, 1974.

IN STUDYING MOTIVATION, psychologists examine the drives or needs within an organism that direct it toward a goal. Organisms have physiological needs which arouse them and initiate behavior; for example, hungry or thirsty animals will work for food or fluids. Physiological drives are usually based upon an imbalance, and whenever an imbalance exists the organism becomes motivated. However, not all states that initiate human behavior are physiological. People learn to have desires for mastery, achievement, and affiliation. They also learn to control their anxiety, desires, and needs. Thus, a number of factors, including a person's physiological and learned motives, direct behavior on an hour-to-hour and day-to-day basis. This chapter not only reviews the physiological and learned components of motivation, but also examines emotional behavior. Human behavior is likely to be affected by motivations, emotional states, and abilities.

CHAPTER 4

Motivation and Emotion

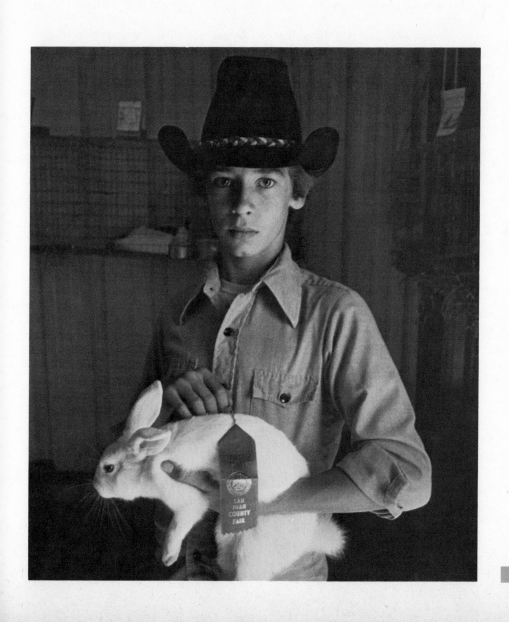

"THE SELF-STARVERS"

At seventeen, Susan looked alarmingly emaciated, with sunken eyes and fragile, sticklike arms and legs. Though she was 5 feet 5 inches tall, she weighed only 70 pounds and scorned all but the tiniest morsels of food. Amazingly, Susan believed herself to be too fat and maintained a frenzied level of physical exercise to help keep any weight off her scrawny frame.

Susan was a victim of anorexia nervosa, "the starvation disease" or "Twiggy syndrome," a rare and bizarre emotional disorder that has been occurring more frequently in the past few years. Of those affected, 80 percent are female, mostly in their early teens. Typically they are intelligent, ambitious, middle- and upper-class girls who are perfectionists and eager to please their mothers and fathers. Suddenly they start to diet and then simply stop eating, sometimes losing 50 pounds or so in a few months. Some, like Susan, now twenty-one, seek treatment and manage to get back to a normal weight. Others, with or without treatment, may start eating enough to survive, yet remain rail-thin and undernourished. Still 5 percent to 15 percent of known victims of anorexia nervosa have starved to death despite treatment.

Researchers generally agree that the disease has purely psychological origins. Some therapists believe that young girls become anoretics out of fear of sexuality; by reducing their body weight to childlike proportions, they stall the process of becoming a woman. (Menstruation almost invariably ceases, or in the case of younger girls does not begin, after such severe weight loss.) Other therapists see the disease as a symbolic "oral rebellion" against overcontrolling and troubled parents.

"There is a terrible fear of not being good enough, or not doing what is expected of them," says Dr. Hilde Bruch, professor of psychiatry at Baylor College of Medicine in Houston. "Anoretics want to reassure themselves that they are really in control. There is an obsession with slimness and achievement." Bruch believes that the incidence of anorexia will continue to increase as greater demands are made on women.

Some doctors hospitalize anoretic patients and take away privileges like watching television till they gain weight. But, says Bruch, "they lose it again as soon as they leave." She believes that psychiatric therapy is necessary.

Time

Anorexia nervosa is one side of the motivation story; it tells of a psychological condition that directs a person to become incredibly thin. The story of Jose tells of a psychological condition of a different nature.

Stardust Motel, 3 miles ahead. Jose had driven 11 miles, across the river, and was quietly making his way on Highway 215 toward the dimly lit Stardust. Few of his friends or neighbors were likely to be found on this side of town. His rendezvous was only a few minutes ahead. With both hands on the wheel he stepped down hard on the gas and was breathing quickly. He parked his car in an unobtrusive spot and signed the register in a pseudonym. A handmade sign behind the desk indicated that he could rent by the hour; he estimated 2 hours.

He adjusted the lighting, turned on the TV, and prepared himself. The long-awaited moment had arrived. Jose's eyes opened wide as he withdrew from a shopping bag a dozen assorted doughnuts, a half gallon of chocolate almond ice cream, and two jars of toasted almonds. As he had many times in the past, Jose was about to begin a binge. A compulsive eater, Jose needed periods during which he could be alone without any disapproving friends or family; occasionally, he would check into a motel and feast on his favorites.

This Tuesday night was going to be the beginning of a difficult period. With much pleasure he finished his goodies and smiled. As he stood up to change TV channels, he saw a reflection of himself in a full-length mirror. His head fell into his hands, he collapsed back into a chair and started to cry. At 327 pounds Jose had entered a never-ending circle of eating. He seemed unable to control his desires for food. His repeated diets seemed to do no good because with each loss of 10 pounds, a subsequent binge would put back that 10 plus an additional 10. Jose wanted to lose weight, yet he felt uncontrollable urges to eat. He desired to lose weight but was constantly eating. He asked himself that night, "Why?" This was a constant question in this fat man's mind, "Why?" Jose had long recognized his problem and had sought the help of a clinical psychologist about 4 weeks before this binge. They were exploring the why of Jose's eating. Although they had only met together four times, Jose began to realize that people eat for a variety of reasons, physiological and learned, and sometimes people eat for strictly emotional reasons.

Jose knew, of course, that people have to eat to live. There are physiological drives that tell people they need to eat. Yet, for Jose, the act of eating had acquired a value. A compulsive eater like Jose needs to learn to separate physiological needs from emotional ones, and in so doing, learn about the why of behavior.

More often we ask ourselves why we did something. We are concerned about *why* we go out Saturday nights instead of studying. Or we ask *why* we feel dependent on our parents. The causes of behavior are usually not clear just from observing our own actions. When we look at a compulsive eater like Jose, we infer that something within him is causing him to be directed toward the goal of food. **Motivation** is any internal condition within an organism that appears (by inference) to produce goal-directed behavior. Motivation or motivated behavior may develop because of physiological needs and drives, or because of more complex desires. In Jose's case, if he had not eaten in some time, his goal-directed behavior would have risen from a physiological imbalance in his body. Any such state of physiological imbalance is termed a **need.** In a strict sense, the term need is often limited to a state or condition of physiological imbalance.

Motivation A general condition within an organism that produces goal-directed behavior. It is an inferred condition initiated by drives, needs, or desires.

Need An aroused physiological condition involving an imbalance.

Emotion is an *aroused* state within an organism that may occur in response to internal and external stimuli.

Drive An aroused condition within the organism that initiates behavior to satisfy physiological needs. Drives are inferred from behavior.

When an organism develops a physiological need, it usually shows this need in behavior. When an organism develops a need and becomes motivated, psychologists say that the organism is in a drive state. A **drive** is an aroused condition within the organism which directs it to satisfy physiological needs and thus regain an internal state of balance. Under conditions of drive, both animals and humans show goal-directed behavior; for example, when a physiological need develops for food, a person seeks it out.

Of course, physiologically aroused drives are not the only initiators of behavior. People want to feel safe and confident. They want to feel that they have achieved something in life or perhaps that they are loved by their families and friends. These goals, too, direct behavior. As you study motivation, you will see that in addition to biological drives there can also be learned or acquired drives.

When a person, particularly a psychologist, asks why, he or she is asking about the fundamental *causes* of a person's behavior. Many theories have developed. As we will see in chapter 11, Freud's theory concentrates on unconscious motivations; learning theory concentrates on past experiences and the consequences of previous behaviors; cognitive theories focus on decision making; and humanistic theories focus on "inner forces" within individuals that propel them toward some goal or fulfillment. Each of the theories is guided by certain common assumptions about people's behavior. These commonalities will guide our exploration of the "whys" of behavior.

Drive theory The approach to behavior that emphasizes the internal capabilities energizing organisms to attain, maintain, or seek some goal. The goal is often to reestablish a state of physiological balance.

Some of the most influential and well-researched theories of motivation fall under the title of **drive theory.** These theories assume that, for a variety of reasons, people are driven to attain, maintain, or seek some goal. These theories use the concept that drive is an internal condition that directs the organism to satisfy some need and regain a state of balance. Perhaps the most influential drive theory is the one originated by Hull (1943, 1952). This drive theory, which has been expanded upon and refined (Mowrer, 1960; Spence, 1956), basically postulates that a person's drive is the energizer of behavior and that a person's previous experiences and tendencies are cou-

In studying motivation we examine the conditions within an organism that direct it toward a goal because of drives or needs.

pled with a drive to determine present behavior. Thus, a person who is in a high drive state to achieve a goal *and* who has sufficient experience and knowledge will work hard and achieve the goal. By contrast, a high drive state alone is not sufficient—a very hungry rat (high drive) that does not know how to find its way around a maze will make many errors and spend a great deal of time seeking out its goal (at least compared to a rat that knows its way around the maze). Drive theories have been put forth often to explain many behaviors; the basic assumption, however, remains that a person is impelled to action, is energized, because of a need to reestablish a balance or attain some goal.

Another major grouping of motivation theories is **expectancy theory.** These theories suggest that a person's behavior is caused by expectancy of success and the value of the success. Among the expectancy theories, particularly notable have been those focused on achievement. An achievement theorist would suggest that a person engages in behaviors that fulfill certain needs for success, mastery, and fulfillment. Tasks not oriented toward those goals would not be motivating for an individual and would not be engaged in; if they were engaged in, they would be underrated and be undertaken with a lack of energy and commitment. Achievement-oriented theories generated a great deal of research in the 1950s and 1960s.

Cognitive theories of motivation move further away from physiology than do expectancy theories. They assume that people have choices to make in life about their goals and how those goals will be achieved. Rather than assuming that behavior is energized because of internal physiological needs or acquired learned motives, cognitive theory asserts that people are actively and regularly involved in deciding their current motivating forces and how their goals will be achieved. One particularly important cognitive theory explains why certain behaviors are engaged in when there are no direct observable rewards associated with them; this is the study of intrinsic motivation.

Expectancy theory The approach to behavior that emphasizes a person's expectancy of success and need for achievement as the energizing factor in human behavior.

Cognitive theory The approach to behavior that emphasizes that people have choices to make in life about their goals and how those goals will be achieved.

Mastery of a subject through extensive research can be rewarding.

Finally, a group of theories of value in helping to understand the whys of behavior is **humanistic theory.** As seen by a humanistic psychologist, a person's behavior is caused by desires for creativity, choice, and **self-actualization.** Humanistic psychologists have focused on the dignity of individual choice and freedom as well as the individual's feelings of worth. Rather than looking at components of behavior, they have focused on "the entirety of life"; thus, the person must be seen within the framework of his or her environment and values.

Our examination of the whys of behavior will begin with physiological drives that arise because of internal conditions within organisms. Because physiological drives determine behavior in very direct ways, we say that they are mechanistic; a mechanistic analysis of behavior views the organism as being pushed, pulled, and energized almost like a machine. Stimuli like hunger pangs create, energize, and initiate behavior. A hungry organism deprived of food for 24 hours spends most of its time looking for food; it is driven to seek food.

Expectancy theories that focus on acquired or learned social drives are considered cognitive theories because they focus on an individual's choices among various alternative forms of behavior; success and/or achievement is thought to help determine how and when individuals will respond. However, expectancy theories maintain certain mechanistic ideas and concepts and they try to predict a limited range of behaviors. Expectancy theories might thus be considered limited cognitive theories because they are partially mechanistic and partially cognitive.

Full cognitive theories and, to a greater extent, humanistic theories move away from mechanism and focus on human choice and expression. Humanistic theory acknowledges physiological drives but concerns itself largely with human qualities of fullfillment and actualization.

In many ways, our study of motivation will move from the mechanistic views of behavior to the cognitive views. The views to be presented do not stand alone and in isolation; however, they each account for different aspects of the whys of behavior. These four orienting theories (drive, expectancy, cognitive, and humanistic) have generated research on different topics. While each seeks to provide the whys of behavior, they have focused on different components of behavior. In studying motivation, we must remember that behavior is not initiated by any one single cause but rather for many reasons—people have needs for food, but they also have needs for love, affection, and self-esteem. Let us begin with the most mechanistic theories, the drive theories.

PHYSIOLOGICAL NEEDS: DRIVE REDUCTION

A physiological drive is an aroused bodily condition that activates and directs a person's behavior. When a person is in a physiological state of need, this activates a drive to reduce this need. While several physiological drives will direct behavior (oxygen, temperature balance, avoidance, and so on) the three primary ones that have been studied in depth are hunger, thirst, and sex.

Let us return to the story of Jose, the obese adult who was beginning to realize that both physiological and emotional factors are involved in eating behavior. Jose always knew that the way to decrease hunger pangs was to eat, but he also came to realize that eating itself had taken on some pleasurable feelings for him. Food tastes good, it can smell delightful, and the act of eating keeps us busy. So, sometimes people eat because they are hungry and sometimes because they have emotional feelings about food.

One of the principal physiological reasons for feeling hungry is food deprivation and the low blood sugar level that accompanies it. When a person has been deprived of food, it appears that a chemical imbalance is created by the low level of sugar substances in the blood. Since sugar is critical in the maintenance of cellular activity, signals are sent to the brain indicating the low blood sugar level. The immediate consequence of food deprivation is hunger pangs in the stomach, yet research has shown that these pangs are controlled by the brain. Experiments have been done with animals in which the nerves leading from the stomach to the brain have been severed so activity in the stomach cannot signal the brain as to food intake. These animals eat at appropriate times: when their blood sugar level is low.

It is easy to demonstrate that the amount of food people eat does not determine how hungry they feel. Let a hungry adult eat for 5 minutes and ask her how she feels 5 minutes later; she will report hunger. Yet 30 minutes later when her food has been metabolized and its sugar contents are being used by the body's tissues, she will report that she no longer feels hungry. How long it takes to lose the feelings of hunger depends upon the type of food eaten. A candy bar loaded with easily converted sugar will take away hunger quickly. Foods high in protein, such as meat, cheese, and milk, take a longer time to be digested and converted into sugar. Thus, it will take a longer time to feel satisfied after a meal of protein than after a meal of quickly converted energy sources such as candy bars and carbohydrates.

Much of our understanding of hunger and eating behavior has come from studies of the brain, particularly the region of the forebrain called the hypothalamus (see p. 51). Studies of the hypothalamus have shown that it may play a critical role in eating behavior. The hypothalamus has been shown in complex experiments to have two distinct areas which are involved in eating behavior. The ventromedial hypothalamus (VH) is called a "stop eating" center. When the stomach becomes full and/or when blood sugar level is high, the VH is active and the animal stops eating. The other part of the hypothalamus involved in eating is the lateral hypothalamus (LH). When the LH is stimulated an animal starts eating, so the LH is sometimes called a "start eating" center (Kent & Peters, 1973; Powley, 1977).

Researchers have stimulated the start and stop centers of animals with weak electric currents. When the LH was stimulated animals started eating, and when the VH was stimulated animals stopped eating. When stimulated, the animals started or stopped eating *regardless* of their blood sugar level or extent of deprivation (for example, Miller, 1963). An animal which had just finished eating, if stimulated in the LH, would start eating. A food-deprived animal which would normally eat voraciously would stop eating when its VH was stimulated. We see, therefore, that the hypothalamus has great control over whether or not an organism eats (see Ball, 1972; Peters et al., 1978).

In the 1950s and 1960s when the early experiments on feeding centers were conducted, their control over food intake seemed straightforward. However, more recent investigations have shown that other areas of the brain may also be involved. Furthermore, the VH may be influencing feeding by exerting control over hormonal systems and metabolic systems. The LH is probably involved in feeding, but so are other regions of the brain closely associated with it. The control of feeding is thus not so simple as we once thought. Data continue to unfold; it is likely that the LH and VH play important if not central roles in food intake, but we must recognize that other processes continue to be discovered (see Alheid et al., 1977; Grossman & Grossman, 1977).

Control over food intake is really quite extraordinary. People take in just about the right amount of food each day to maintain their weight. Most people vary the amounts and types of food they eat. That most people maintain a stable weight over time is amazing. As little food as an extra candy bar per day would, at the end of a year, produce approximately 18 pounds of fat!

OBESITY—A PHYSIOLOGICAL EXPLANATION. Too many people in contemporary society are significantly overweight. Many are 10 or 20 pounds overweight, and an increasing percentage of people are 30, 50, and 100 pounds overweight. At 327 pounds, Jose, whom we introduced earlier in this chapter, is one of those people. The simple cause of obesity is obvious; people eat too much relative to the amount of energy they expend. Excess food is stored as fat, and over a period of months and years fat tissue builds up. Thus, it would at first seem that the causes of obesity are simple, but we know that obese people eat too much because of physiological *and* psychological reasons.

An interesting theory has been presented by University of Michigan psychologist Richard Nisbett. Nisbett (1972) argues that some people have no choice but to be fat because every person has a different amount of fat that is natural for his or her body. So, some people are genetically programmed to be fat. The theory revolves around the notion of the fat cell. Body fat is stored in fat cells; if a person is born with many fat cells, he or she is more likely to be fat. Some studies have found that obese subjects had three times as many fat cells as normal-weight subjects. So, while obese adults might diet, they will decrease only the size, but not the number, of their fat cells. While the number of fat cells is genetically determined, it is also affected by nutritional experience early in life.

According to the fat-cell theory, weight is determined by the number of fat cells. Since the body tends to keep the size of fat cells at a constant level, people who have dieted and shrunk the normal size of their fat cells will be in a constant state of food deprivation. This theory assumes that the "normal" weight may not be the same for two people of equal height and body frame, but is actually determined by the number of fat cells in each person's body. It follows from this theory that the person born with many fat cells who has fought becoming fat by society's standards is in a never-ending battle against weight. Nisbett argues that many *"over*weight" people can actually be *"under*weight" relative to what their bodies' ideal weights should be. This physiological explanation of eating behavior and obesity is compelling because many formerly obese people readily admit that they are in constant battle to maintain their weight.

OBESITY—A PSYCHOLOGICAL EXPLANATION. According to Stanley Schachter of Columbia University (1971), obese humans eat too often and too much for reasons other than hunger. In a series of clever experiments, Schachter has shown that obese adults tend to eat not when they are hungry, but whenever food is presented. They also tend to eat if time has passed, regardless of whether they are hungry or not. While subjects of normal weight might eat 50% of the time that food is offered, obese subjects nearly always eat (see also Herman & Polivy, 1975).

Schachter reports a study in which he asked both obese and normal-weight subjects to sit at a desk and fill out some personality tests. Beside the subjects was a bag of almonds, which they were invited to munch on as they filled out the questionnaire. Schachter set up two conditions. In one condition, the almonds were covered with shells; in the other, the almonds had no shells. He assumed that eating nuts with shells was more work than nuts without shells. When subjects of normal weight were placed in this situation, about half ate nuts regardless of whether the nuts had shells or not. But when the obese subjects were placed in the same situation, 19 out of 20 ate the nuts without shells. When the nuts did have shells, only 1 out of 20 obese subjects ate nuts. Schachter concluded that when food is easy to get, obese subjects eat more than subjects of normal weight; likewise, when food is hard to get, obese subjects eat less food than normal-weight persons.

Schachter has also shown that obese adults will eat more from a brightly illuminated bowl of nuts than from a dimly illuminated bowl; adults of normal weight are unaffected by the degree of illumination. Further, when presented with a bowl of ice cream, obese adults eat more rapidly than normal-weight subjects. This type of evidence leads Schachter to believe that the *sight* of food serves to strongly motivate overweight people to eat.

Schachter argues that the availability of food, its prominence, and other *external* cues tell obese subjects when to eat. This is in contrast to normal-weight individuals, who eat not because of external signs, but because some *internal* physiological mechanism creating an imbalance initiates eating behavior (for example Tom & Rucker, 1975). Thus, Schachter believes that the eating behavior of the obese is under external rather than internal control. When food-relevant cues are presented to the obese, even obese children, they are more likely than those of normal weight to eat the food (Costanzo & Woody, 1979; Leon & Roth, 1977; Schachter, 1971; Schachter & Rodin, 1974). Not only do they eat more, they do so faster and with fewer bites (Lebow, Goldberg, & Collins, 1977; Marston et al., 1977). It must be pointed out, how-

Table 4.1 The effect of work on eating behavior. Note how the obese are dramatically affected by the variable of shells on the nuts provided to them.

	NUMBER OF NORMAL SUBJECTS WHO:		NUMBER OF OBESE SUBJECTS WHO:	
	EAT	DON'T EAT	EAT	DON'T EAT
Shells	10	10	1	19
No shells	11	9	19	1

Everything Tastes Good

Researchers who study obesity are aware that the people they study often distort their behavior when told they are being watched by a scientist. In order to investigate the eating patterns of obese people without this distortion, Stanley Schachter had to disguise the true purpose of his obesity studies. Recognizing that experimental controls are critical in doing research, he first decided to control how much people had eaten before an experiment began. When subjects arrived in a laboratory, they were given roast-beef sandwiches; then they were placed in an experiment which was supposedly to investigate taste. Subjects were seated in front of bowls of crackers and were presented with a set of rating scales. They were told to judge whether each cracker was salty, cheesy, or garlicky to the taste. They were further told that accuracy was very important and that they should taste as many or as few of the crackers of each type as they wanted in making the judgments. Like most of Schachter's experiments, there were two types of subjects, obese and normal-weight adults. The real experiment, of course, was not to see how well the subjects rated the crackers, but rather to see how many crackers they ate to make their judgments. As can be seen in Figure 4.1, the normal subjects ate considerably fewer crackers when their stomachs were full from the roast-

beef sandwiches. By contrast, the obese subjects ate even more when their stomachs were full. Schachter and his colleagues concluded that the actual state of the stomach had nothing to do with the eating behavior of the obese but rather was principally determined by external factors (Schachter, Goldman, & Gordon, 1968).

Many of Schachter's ideas have been supported by other lines of research. For example, anxiety plays an important role for people who are obese. Dieters tend to eat more when they are anxious (Herman & Polivy, 1975); furthermore, other research has shown that thought patterns—more than the numbers of calories consumed—determine what dieters eat (Polivy, 1976). In one recent study (Herman, Polivy, & Silver, 1979), subjects who generally tended to watch their caloric intake were compared to others who generally did not watch caloric intake. In the study, the subjects were either in a group that was overtly observed by the experimenter or in a group that was not. The normal nondieting subjects were not affected by the presence of an observer; however, the calorie watchers were very much affected—when there was no one present, the calorie watchers ate significantly more. Furthermore, the amount that they ate had little to do with how many calories they had consumed earlier (see also Polivy et al., 1979). The results are complicated and no clear, easy statement can be made about all dieters or about obese people. However, it could be concluded that people who tend to watch their calories are not particularly sensible in their eating patterns; they are affected by the presence of an observer some of the time, but not all of the time. This study did not use obese subjects; however, the calorie watchers and the obese share some common traits (Herman & Polivy, 1975; Hibscher & Herman, 1977). When Spencer and Fremouw (1979) used obese subjects who were accustomed to dieting all the time and told them that they had just consumed a high-calorie beverage, they were more likely to binge by eating more ice cream; by contrast, obese subjects who were nondieters ate less. Sometimes obese subjects respond to internal cues; more often they don't. External cues like clocks on the wall and the attractiveness of food are clearly involved in eating behavior, particularly the eating behavior of the obese. Furthermore, even obese children as young as 7 years of age show an external responsiveness to food cues (Costanzo & Woody, 1979). However, there is no simple relationship among these variables.

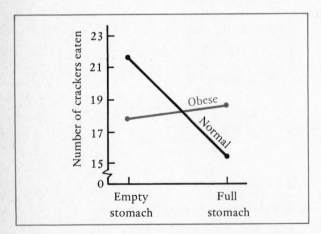

Figure 4.1 Schachter (1971) had normal-weight and obese subjects taste crackers. The normal-weight persons ate fewer crackers when their stomachs were full; by contrast, the obese persons ate more when their stomachs were full

ever, that the obese may not be any more externally responsive than normal-weight people; it may be that they have physiological responses that may be triggered more quickly than normal-weight people. While these possibilities are being explored, it does not change the finding that the obese seem to respond differently to food than do normal-weight people (Rodin, 1979). Differences between the obese and normal-weight people are under active study. While it is generally believed that the obese have a special eating style (too much, too fast, and too often), this view has been challenged. For example, Stunkard has suggested that there is no "obese eating style" and that differences between the obese and nonobese are small and inconsistent (Rodin, 1981; Stunkard et al., 1980).

OBESITY—A SUMMARY. The physiological evidence presented by Nisbett suggests that a person's base weight is biologically dictated and that every person's base weight is different. If a person has a large number of fat cells, he or she should be expected to be "fatter" than others. Although dieting will reduce the size of fat cells, these people will be in a constant state of need for food. Moreover, Schachter and his colleagues have demonstrated that obese people are more likely to eat than people of normal weight because of learned external cues to which the subjects respond. It is most likely that both of these explanations of obesity are true. Obese people probably have a predisposition toward weighing more than thin people. But at the same time, our society is food-oriented, and people learn to associate food with pleasurable events. Many obese people report that even after thoroughly satisfying meals they would be willing to eat if presented with something that looks tempting. So, because obese persons eat in response to external cues, they cannot blame all their obesity on fat cells.

There is little doubt that internal physiological cues act as a strong motivating force for people to seek out food. Similarly, it is also correct to suggest that external learned cues act to direct a person into behaviors that involve seeking out food. Thus, both physiological *and* learned factors are involved in satisfying the hunger drive. It is important to remember that hunger is an inferred motivational state that is sometimes physiologically based and sometimes cued by external events. Clearly, hunger rests not in stomachs but in the hypothalamus or in other areas of the brain that might activate it (see Table 4.3, p. 161.)

Thirst and Sex

People become hungry when there is an imbalance in their bodies requiring food; in the same way, they become thirsty when there is an imbalance requiring fluid. Thirst is an important physiological mechanism which serves as a strong drive for both animals and humans. While humans can live for weeks without replenishing food supplies, they can only live for days without adjusting a fluid imbalance.

In many ways, the phenomenon of thirst is much like hunger. When there is a fluid imbalance in their bodies, people's mouths and throats become dry, which is one kind of cue for them to drink. After drinking, their mouths and throats feel satisfied, and they go back to their normal activity. This is much like when they have hunger pangs. While the immediate intake of fluids or food does not act upon their imbalances, it does act as a cue indicating that appropriate substances have been consumed. Of course, receptors in the mouth and throat act only as the initiators to fluid regulation. If fluid never reaches their stomachs, people remain thirsty and are motivated within a few minutes to seek out more fluid.

The hypothalamus largely regulates fluid intake so there is an appropriate amount of fluid both within and around the cells. A general loss of fluid establishes an imbalance in the amount of fluids within and next to a cell. This imbalance triggers the hypothalamus to increase a drive for fluid. Fluid regulation is also controlled in part by the excretion of urine. When people's bodies contain too much fluid, they begin to excrete large volumes of clear fluid to establish a proper fluid balance. When the body is lacking fluid, urine output is diminished. When people wake after 8 hours of sleep, their bodies are in a mild state of fluid deprivation, so their urine tends to be concentrated, deep in color, and more pungent.

Water and food intake are controlled in much the same way. When food is consumed, signals indicating that the food has been ingested are sent to the hypothalamus. While their blood sugar level has not yet increased, people stop eating almost automatically. In the same way, receptors in the mouth and throat signal that fluid has been consumed, and thus fluid intake is decreased. The actual control of fluid intake lies not in the receptors of the mouth and throat, but in the cells of the hypothalamus. A delicate balance of fluid intake is necessary for proper functioning, so any imbalance is reflected by a physiological drive to restore the balance. Life depends on food and water; deprivation of one often leads to an increased drive for both (Corey, Walton, & Wiener, 1978). As Maslow has suggested, a person's physiological needs for food and water are the first and most important drives that must be satisfied (Maslow, 1962, 1969).

Although both eating and drinking have a physiological basis, we recognize that social and emotional factors also affect the way people might eat and drink. Basically, however, we consider these aspects of behavior to be under physiological control for most people. In any examination of sexual behavior, the contributions of emotional and social factors take on an even greater role. A large number of factors control behavior, particularly when the behavior involves other people.

Human sexual drives as initiators of behavior are no longer considered to be primarily or solely physiological. Sex is usually considered a biological drive, to some extent under physiological control but to a much greater extent under voluntary control. Sexual behavior of lower organisms, however, is largely under physiological and hormonal control.

An important difference between sex drive and other drives is that sexual behavior is not initiated solely because of physiological imbalances. Sexual behavior in animals is under hormonal control. If we remove the hormone-generating testes of male rats, they will show a marked decrease in sexual activity, but not total abstinence. In humans (depending on the age at removal), removal of hormone-generating organs may not affect sexual behavior at all. The sexual responsiveness of females of lower organisms dramatically displays the effects of hormonal control. Consider how a female dog responds sexually: she has distinct periods during which hormones are released into the bloodstream, and she becomes particularly responsive to sex-

THE WIZARD OF ID by permission of Johnny Hart and Field Enterprises, Inc.

ual encounters. Female human beings, however, are not nearly so much under hormonal control sexually and can choose to respond or not to sexual encounters at any time.

There is an important difference between lower organisms and human beings. Sex drives are controlled to a large extent by physiological mechanisms in a lower organism; by contrast, the role of experience and learning plays a much greater role with human beings. Previous experience in sexual behavior in rats is unnecessary, yet with dogs, cats, and monkeys, early experience becomes more important. If isolated from sexual experiences in the early part of their lives, these animals show a lack of sexual responsivity. The contrast between humans and animals is particularly striking; about 12 years pass before human beings become pubescent and show sexual responsivity.

Humans learn sexual behavior from peers and parents. The young are slowly initiated into knowledge and experience of sex. The sexual experiences of mature humans vary dramatically with culture. Some cultures approve of the initiation of sexual activity at adolescence and encourage it throughout life. Other societies are more restrictive and inhibit sexual activities until marriage. It is important, however, to note that sexual behavior is changing in Western society. Many formerly taboo topics, attitudes, and behaviors are now widely accepted. As attitudes change, behavior changes; this is something we don't have to worry about in rats. Their sexual behavior is relatively rigid and is not very dependent upon the culture in which they grow.

Sensory Stimulation

A desire for sensory stimulation is another human motive with little physiological basis but which does not seem to be learned. When deprived of a normal amount of visual, auditory, or tactile stimulation, human adults may become irritable and consider the situation or environment intolerable. Although a lack of sensory experience does not create any physiological imbalance, humans have a desire for sensory experiences. Similarly, studies of animals have shown that they too seek out sensory stimulation. Kittens like to explore their environment, and young monkeys will investigate mechanical devices and play with puzzles. Indeed, studies have shown that monkeys will work in order to play with puzzles and manipulate locks. Thus, it seems that animals and humans have a desire to explore, manipulate, and experience their world. Sensory stimulation will be discussed again in chapter 5 on Perception and later in this chapter when looking at arousal (p. 151).

The causes of behavior are extremely complex. There are clearly some physiologically initiated behaviors like hunger and thirst. There is sexual behavior with aspects of hormonal control, will, and learned behavior. Making behavior still more complex are the needs that people develop for sensory stimulation and for love and affection. Some researchers are now suggesting that such behaviors have their basis in the first minutes of life. They argue that future ability to feel warmth and affection may be determined by early learning experiences. So, in studying motivation, psychologists always look at the balance between the foundations of behavior—human physiology—and the learned aspects of behavior. As we learned in chapter 2 on biology, there is a complex interplay between our inherited nature and our continually changing nurturing.

It must be recognized that other kinds of biological drives direct human beings and animals into action. All organisms have biologically based needs for sleeping, maintaining body temperature, and breathing. Organisms also have drives to avoid pain and tissue damage. Organisms deprived of sleep or exposed to extreme cold or to a painful stimulation will seek relief from the discomfort. Typically, however, these needs are satisfied with little difficulty and are thus not studied as extensively.

IMPACT

Maternal-Infant Bonding

According to Marshall Klaus and John Kennell, the first few minutes and hours of your life may be critical for optimal personality development. The professors of pediatrics at Case Western Reserve University School of Medicine argue that there is a sensitive period in the first minutes and hours of an infant's life during which it is necessary for the mother and father to have close contact with the infant. There appears to be a specific kind of parental response to the infant and a special process of attachment occurs between mother and baby. During the attachment process the infant responds to the mother through body or eye movements. While it is unclear what physiological mechanisms might influence maternal attachment to the newborns, Klaus and Kennell present considerable evidence of innate maternal behavior patterns in all organisms. Lower animals show regular sterotyped patterns of attachment in caring for newborns. The behavior of a human mother is affected not only by hormonal changes, but also by many experiences, culture, and by the baby itself.

On the practical side, the researchers claim that the relatively small amount of time that modern mothers have with their children after birth in the hospital does not give them adequate exposure to the child. They point out that "the first days after discharge (from the hospital) are described by many mothers as hellish or as the most difficult days of their lives." As practicing physicians, Klaus and Kennell believe that medical facilities in the United States should be adapted to provide optimal conditions for the development of parent-infant attachment in the first days of life (Klaus & Kennell, 1976; see also Ainsworth, 1979).

Parents develop unique and special moments with their children.

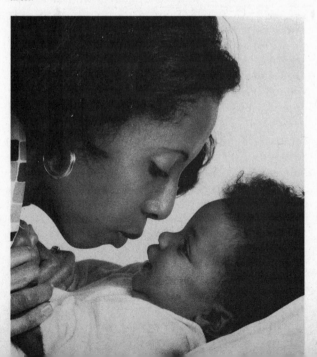

Instincts

When psychologists first looked at the whys of behavior, they considered **instincts** prime motivators. These early researchers believed that instincts were inborn behavior patterns that directed and controlled an organism's actions. This approach stressed heredity, genetics, and predetermined behavior patterns. However, by the early part of the 1900s, the instinct explanation of behavior was abandoned in favor of learning theories. Today, most psychologists do not think that humans have many—if any—instincts.

Instincts Inherited, inborn, unlearned, and predetermined behavior patterns.

The concept of instinctual motivation did not die completely. Other behavioral scientists (particularly ethologists) continued to consider the role of instincts in motivation. An **ethologist** is a person who studies animal behavior, usually in natural settings. Several prominent ethologists have used the concept of instinct to explain both animal and human behavior. They use the research done on imprinting to support their contention that some behavior patterns are inbred.

Ethologist A behavioral scientist who studies animals, usually in their natural setting rather than in a laboratory.

Imprinting is the process through which a particular behavior pattern specific to one species is established in a member of that species by exposing it to appropriate stimuli during a critical period early in its life. Early work in the area showed that ducks (and other species) imprinted on any moving object during its critical period would follow that object, human or nonhuman, as if it were its mother. The process of imprinting does show that some animals have instincts that direct behavior; clearly these are biologically determined. To date, however, no such process has been conclusively shown to exist in humans. The closest behavioral evidence to suggest imprinting with humans has been put forth by Klaus and Kennel. They suggest that there is a sensitive period in the first minutes of an infant's life during which it is necessary to have close contact with an adult for proper maternal-infant attachment to take place.

Imprinting The process by which animals form species-specific behaviors during a critical period early in life. These behaviors are not easily modified.

Competing Needs

The many desires, needs, and goals of human beings are diverse. We have discussed biologically based needs that energize and motivate people. But what happens if a person has two goals that are in conflict? What happens when there are two equally desirable desserts to choose from, or two equally difficult courses from which to choose? In situations where people are placed in conflict, they are driven to make a choice, but the choice is difficult. Over the years psychologists have tried to describe and quantify such conflict situations. One of the first psychologists to do this was Miller (1944, 1959). Miller developed a series of ideas about how animals and humans behave in situations where there are both positive and negative aspects. For example, if a hungry rat is placed in a runway where it must run down the alley to get food, the rat shows a definite tendency to approach the food; *but,* if the rat has to run down the alley and the alley is electrified, the animal is placed in a situation which it would prefer to avoid—being shocked. Running down the alley has both positive and negative components—it will satisfy the animal's hunger, but it will also shock its feet. Hungry adults may seek out junk food, but may want to avoid its calories—again seeking and avoiding behavior at the same time. Let us explore the three types of situations in which competing goals are established: approach-approach, avoidance-avoidance, and approach-avoidance.

Approach-approach conflicts are situations in which a person must decide on one of two equally pleasant goals. When choosing between two dates or between two movies, we often have a difficult time. Both movies are reportedly excellent and our goal is to see both. Yet only one choice is possible. The result is conflict, a minor conflict. Sometimes we have two equally attractive alternatives and the choice is important, perhaps between two equally prestigious universities. Again, conflict results, this time in a major form.

The conflict that arises from approach-approach situations is uncomfortable, but it is usually a choice people can live with. In **avoidance-avoidance** situations, there are two equally distasteful goals. For example, teenagers often have a number of household chores to perform. On any one Saturday, they may be given a choice of mowing the lawn or helping paint the garage. Most people would rather avoid both situations, yet they must choose one. Again, conflict results.

Perhaps the most difficult of the three situations which produces conflict is the **approach-avoidance** situation. Here people must deal with a situation that has both appealing and repelling aspects to it; thus, the goal is both approached and avoided. Studying for an exam is an approach-avoidance situation. We want to study to get good grades—approach; yet, we find studying both boring and difficult—avoidance. The goal, studying, has both approach and avoidance components. Miller was to develop a series of ideas about approach and avoidance behaviors. For example, one idea was that the tendency to approach a goal (such as candy) is stronger the closer the subject is to the goal. Further, when two incompatible responses are both evident, the stronger one will be expressed. Another is that the strength of the tendency to approach or avoid a goal is correlated with the strength of the drive on which they are based; thus, a child who is both hungry and thirsty will seek the food if he or she is more hungry than thirsty. Miller's aim was to develop a model which would predict how organisms would respond in conflict situations, particularly situations that have both positive and negative aspects.

Choosing among equally attractive alternatives can be difficult.

Approach-approach conflict

Avoidance-avoidance conflict

Approach-avoidance conflict

Double approach-avoidance conflict

Decisions, decisions, decisions . . .

The study of approach-avoidance conflicts has yielded data to support the ideas that Miller suggested (for example Mehrabian, 1980; Murray & Berkun, 1955). Miller's formulations have been successful in predicting animal behavior. With human beings, there is much evidence to suggest that people are placed in such situations regularly; Miller's formulations can account for many human behaviors. Of course, coping with competing goals can produce serious conflicts. People become anxious and upset, and their behavior is affected. When people's conflicts about choices affect their day-to-day behavior, they may be exhibiting symptoms of maladjustment. In chapter 12 on Abnormal Psychology we will discuss how anxiety can affect a person's ability to cope with the world.

Arousal Theory

Anxiety is a technical term that clinical psychologists use to describe the symptoms of some psychological disorders. Yet, we are all aware of that feeling of being anxious and of the vague discomfort that accompanies fear of the unknown. In relation to mastery and achievement needs, anxiety refers to a fear of failure. People who don't care about what they are doing have little anxiety but usually show poor performance in both work and play. But people who show a moderate degree of anxiety, and its accompanying arousal, often produce and do best. This relationship between motivation and task performance was described more than 70 years ago by R. M. Yerkes and J. D. Dodson. Now called the *Yerkes-Dodson law,* this principle states that when a person's anxiety and level of arousal are too high or too low, performance is usually not particularly good. When anxiety is at a moderate level, performance is significantly better. For easy tasks optimum performance occurs with a high level of arousal, but with increasing task difficulty the optimum level of performance is achieved at lower levels of arousal. When teaching someone a very difficult subject we don't push them as hard as when teaching them easy ones. You will see later in this chapter that we might expect that people with high needs for achievement have a relatively high level of anxiety and arousal. What would you suppose would happen if a person with a high need for achievement and success had too great an

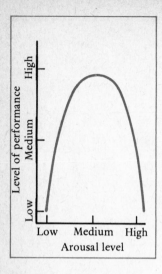

Figure 4.2 The basic Yerkes-Dodson law. This principle states that as arousal reaches some moderate level, performance is at its best

arousal level? From Figure 4.2 we see that the chances of high performance would be poor. A person who has a high need for achievement and a moderate level of arousal would be most likely to succeed. A person with a high need for achievement with very low motivation levels is relatively rare; more often, high-need achievers are anxious, and this may impair their performance.

THE CONCEPT OF OPTIMAL LEVEL OF AROUSAL.   Those researchers who have used the optimal-level arousal notion in formulating ideas about the whys of behavior make two fundamental assumptions about behavior that many traditional theorists do not make: *first,* individuals seek an "optimal level" of stimulation; *second,* arousal theories assume that behavior varies from disorganized, to effective, to optimal depending on the person's level of arousal. As is shown in Figure 4.2, there is an inverted U-shaped function relating effectiveness of behavior and arousal. Many traditional motivation and learning theorists have assumed that as a person's drive increases (and associated arousal level) there will be an increase in behavior. For example, a traditional learning theorist like Hull (1943, 1951; Perin, 1942) suggested that drive and ability will predict behavior. In this simple formulation of Hull's theory, as one increases an organism's drive level (by depriving it of food or water, for example), the resulting speed to run down an alley will increase. While there are clearly substantial differences among various traditional learning theorists, most all focus on links between stimuli and responses, behavior being determined by these factors.

As researchers began to explore the nature of arousal, they came to suggest that arousal itself may be the *cause* of behavior. For example, Hebb (1955) has suggested that human functioning is most efficient when people are at an optimal level of arousal. Fiske and Maddi (1961), using a similar idea, suggested that people try to maintain an optimal level of arousal which will vary with the time of day and their sleep-wakefulness cycle. Fundamental to such ideas was the newly introduced notion that it is not the stimulus that determines how an organism behaves, but rather the organism's internal response to the stimulus. Hull (1943) and other drive theorists mechanistically tied the motivation of behavior to physiological needs in the body; newer formulations of learning theory allowed for other stimuli to create needs (Dollard & Miller, 1950). But Hebb's idea shifted the focus away from stimuli and internal needs to a person's response-determining behavior. For Hebb, it was arousal that would energize behavior (Dember, 1974).

Yerkes and Dodson had recognized many years before Hebb that arousal was not always beneficial. When people are suffering from high anxiety, high arousal *usually* accompanies it. For example, researchers have found that when college students are particularly anxious they generally obtain lower grades. Some anxiety may be helpful, but often the accompanying arousal is so overpowering it decreases performance for many students. An important aspect of this finding is that we can identify college students who may not be able to function well and refer these students to counseling and psychological therapy to help them overcome their anxiety and thus do better academically (Spielberger, 1962). Of course, people who are driven toward success and achievement may be particularly susceptible to the problems of high anxiety and arousal levels.

With the development of optimal arousal theories, there was a distinct change in focus in the study of motivation. The shift was, of course, to place the causes of behavior on the internal responses of an organism. Optimal arousal theory is still a mechanistic drive theory, because arousal only energizes behavior, it does not direct it. However, since a human's response to situations is in part determined by thought processes, optimal arousal theories anticipated the development of more cognitive theories because they placed the cause of behavior within the organism. Optimal arousal theories represented a shift from solely mechanistic to cognitive theory (Dember, 1974). Optimal arousal theory has been most influential; you will see it again later in this chapter. (See Table 4.3, p. 161.)

A Summary

Imbalance and drive have been the organizing themes around which we have discussed hunger and thirst. Whenever an organism is placed in a situation in which there is a physiological imbalance, the organism is impelled toward action. Human beings can only survive for a few days without water, and even within a few hours they begin to seek out fluids to correct the imbalance in their bodies. Corrections of the imbalances involved can be under direct physiological control so that certain specific parts of the brain are involved. For example, the hypothalamus plays a very important role in eating and drinking behavior. Similarly, the sex hormones of male and female organisms exert some control in sexual behavior.

When psychologists examine the why of behavior, they see that hunger and thirst are controlled not only by people's learned experiences with eating and drinking, but also to a great extent by physiology. Why do people eat and drink? Initially and most importantly, they eat and drink to live. Secondarily, they learn that eating and drinking are pleasurable; this sometimes creates problems of obesity. While biological drives are to a great extent under physiological control, many kinds of motives are learned or acquired. You will see later that Maslow argued that once people satisfy their physiological needs, they will then seek to satisfy motives more complex and cognitive.

When psychologists look at the causes of behavior and examine the different types of mechanisms that might influence an individual's actions, they turn first to physiology. Yet, they have to acknowledge that these physiological mechanisms are not the sole causes of behavior. Human beings are complex organisms and many factors influence their actions. When examining sexual behavior, we noted that hormones influence a person's sexual drives, but his or her social and emotional situations are also influential. If physiological drives alone could account for behavior, then all humans would behave in exactly the same way; indeed, there would be no obese people! With the development of optimal arousal theories, psychologists recognized that a human's responses to various situations are determined in part by the organism itself, not solely by the stimuli that it encounters. With this shift, a subtle but important step was made—the transition from solely mechanistic drive-reduction theory toward learning and cognitive theory. As the next section will show, many motives are learned and many of a person's behaviors are a direct result of this learning process. Biology provides the framework for human behavior and learning experiences shape it further.

Motive A specific internal condition directing an organism's behavior toward a goal.

Everyone recognizes that people have to eat to live, so a dieter has a special problem: a dieter must eat, but only limited quantities. The obese have typically attached a very high value to eating and food; as a result, they eat too much, too often. The obese have motives for eating. It is important to realize that a **motive** does not have to have a physiological explanation. There are many times when people eat just because it is fun or to celebrate a social occasion. Similarly, an athlete practices for many hours not because of any physiological imbalance; rather, physical activity and practicing have taken on a positive value. The desire to excel directs behavior; it is motivating. In chapter 3 on Learning this type of behavior was called intrinsically motivated. It is performed not for overt external reinforcement, but for the sheer pleasure of doing it.

Social motive A condition directing humans toward maintaining or establishing feelings about themselves, others, and relationships.

Since many of our daily activities and interactions are social ones, we can consider a special group of motives that are distinctly not physiological. A **social motive** is a condition which directs us in maintaining or establishing feelings about ourselves, others, or relationships among people. Consider the way teenagers behave on a first date. They are concerned about the way they dress, their manners, and the type of place they are going to. They are trying to establish a certain kind of image or rapport, so their behavior is motivated toward establishing a relationship. The way a student behaves when meeting a United States senator is likely to be very different from the way she behaves when meeting her next-door neighbor. She may wish to impress on her senator the importance of some impending legislation on human rights. Her next-door neighbor, by contrast, may be her tennis partner, and she may confine those discussions to their mutual interest in tennis.

Social motives are determined by events and experiences that take place as early as the day of birth. Earlier in this chapter, we reported on the observations of Marshall Klaus and John Kennell; they argue that early attachments of a mother to her baby can affect that newborn's behavior for the rest of his or her life. Klaus cited data on the failure of newborns to thrive both physiologically and socially when they were separated from their mothers at birth. These data suggest that patterns of behavior, including social motives, are established in the first minutes of life as well as throughout childhood.

Need An aroused physiological condition involving an imbalance.

Social need An aroused condition within organisms involving feelings about themselves, others, and relationships.

Social motives do not emerge suddenly. Feelings and situations eventually converge to create situations that generate a social need. Earlier a **need** was defined as an aroused physiological condition involving an imbalance; but social needs do not involve any physiological imbalance. A **social need** is an aroused condition within an organism involving feelings about self, others, and relationships. There is a variety of social needs, including a human need for affiliation—establishing and maintaining friendly relationships with other people. Motives for affiliation create situations in which people seek friends, desire approval, do favors for others, and participate in other activities that will create friendly relations. People have social needs for order, achievement, cleanliness, and arrangement. Some researchers have argued that people have social needs for aggression and that these needs are fulfilled when they fight, belittle, or curse. Of course, having needs for achievement, affiliation, and good feelings about one's self are affected by many factors, even including one's socioeconomic status and race (Littig & Williams, 1978).

Table 4.2 Illustrative list of needs that Murray suggests initiate behavior

NEED FOR	BRIEF DEFINITION
Achievement	To overcome obstacles, to exercise power, to strive to do something difficult as well and as quickly as possible.
Affiliation	To form friendships and associations. To greet, join, and live with others. To cooperate and converse sociably with others. To love. To join groups.
Aggression	To assault or injure another. To murder. To belittle, harm, blame, accuse or maliciously ridicule a person. To punish severely. Sadism.
Autonomy	To resist influence or coercion. To defy an authority or seek freedom in a new place. To strive for independence.
Avoidance	To avoid blame, ostracism or punishment by inhibiting asocial or unconventional impulses. To be well behaved and obey the law.
Dominance	To influence or control others. To persuade, prohibit, dictate. To lead and direct. To restrain. To organize the behavior of a group.
Exhibition	To attract attention to one's person. To excite, amuse or entice others.
Nurturance	To nourish, aid or protect a helpless other. To express sympathy. To "mother" a child.
Order	To arrange, organize, put away objects. To be tidy and clean. To be scrupulously precise.
Rejection	To snub, ignore or exclude another. To remain aloof and indifferent. To be discriminating.
Sentience	To seek and enjoy sensuous impressions.
Sex	To form and further an erotic relationship. To have sexual intercourse.
Understanding	To analyze experience, to abstract, to discriminate among concepts, to define relations, to synthesize ideas.

Being the best can be an uplifting experience.

Need for Mastery and Achievement

A person's social motives for control and a sense of mastery often govern his or her life and create great needs for achievement. This need to feel in control not only motivates and energizes people but can cause unhappiness as well.

When peoples' goals, ideas, and beliefs are inconsistent with their actual behavior, this causes an uncomfortable feeling of anxiety. When placed in an anxiety-producing situation, people either usually work harder to achieve their goals, or sometimes change their goals so as not to feel nervous. In chapter 10 on Social Psychology, we will be discussing an influential theory of cognitive dissonance proposed by Leon Festinger. Essentially, Festinger argues that when placed in situations in which our beliefs are inconsistent with our behavior, either we change our beliefs or change our behavior. Imagine a person who has strong motives for mastery and control of his environment (e.g., Steele, 1977). However, this person's success at his job and other interactions do not meet his own expectations, and a situation of cogni-

Need for achievement A social need that directs a person to succeed and to strive constantly for excellence and success.

tive dissonance develops. Either the person has to reorganize his desires for success and establish new priorities or he must work harder at succeeding.

Most psychologists will agree that a person's need for achievement is one of the strongest social motives directing behavior. The **need for achievement** is a social motive that causes people to strive for bigger and better accomplishments. Since achievement is generally considered to be a significant social goal, people who have strong needs for achievement continue to strive for higher standards and levels of performance.

Even casual observation of behavior shows us that some people are driven with ambition and the need to get ahead and succeed in life. Usually these people were expected very early in life to be independent and to achieve in both the home and school settings. Adults who have high needs for achievement generally walked early, talked early, and had needs for achievement even upon entering grammar school. The home environment is very important in establishing these needs. The parents, and particularly the mothers, of need-achieving people generally lavish praise on their children for accomplishments by giving them physical and emotional rewards. You will see that carefully controlled research has supported these observations.

In early efforts to study achievement needs, researchers first had people describe pictures which had no captions. The themes of these pictures were vague and, therefore, open to several interpretations. Subjects were asked to imagine what is happening and what led up to this situation. You can see that there are many ways in which such a picture might be interpreted. The use of vague pictures is the basic procedure in the Thematic Apperception Test or, as it is usually called, the TAT. In the TAT, subjects are shown pictures and asked to be as creative as possible in describing them. They are instructed not to think in terms of right or wrong answers, but to answer four basic questions:

1. What is happening?
2. What has led up to this situation?
3. What is being thought?
4. What will happen?

Figure 4.3 A photograph from the Thematic Apperception Test

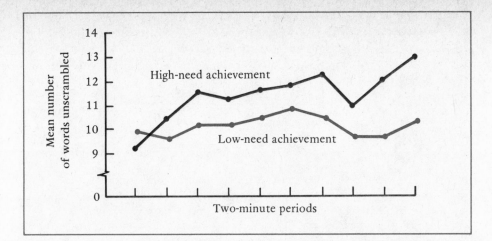

Figure 4.4 Performance of high- and low-need achievement groups (Lowell, 1952) on scrambled word tasks shows that while low-need achievers improve overall, high-need achievers improve even more

By using a complex scoring system, the researchers analyzed the answers to see the ways that subjects described the scene. Is competition with the standards stressed? Is someone in the story trying to do better than someone else? Are themes of getting ahead in the world stressed? Initially, researchers hoped to uncover a subject's feelings, thinking, and planning. The TAT revealed that some people are strongly motivated toward achievement, while others are not. These achievement needs were reflected in the subjects' interpretations of the TAT pictures. For example, high-need achievers told stories that stressed success, getting ahead, and competition.

High-achievement and low-achievement subjects perform differently in many ways. In one learning experiment, subjects were required to rearrange groups of scrambled letters (for example, WTSE) until they constructed a meaningful word (for example, WEST). Subjects with low need for achievement did not improve much over successive periods of testing. By contrast, subjects who scored high in need for achievement showed regular increases in performance from the first to the fifth period of testing. Motivational researchers like David McClelland interpret such results in terms of need for achievement. In a complex task, subjects with high needs for achievement find new and better ways of performing the task as they practice it, whereas subjects with low needs for achievement try no new methods. Again, high-need achievers are constantly striving toward excellence and better performance (Atkinson, 1964; McClelland, 1961, 1975; McClelland et al., 1953).

One way to think about motivation and the need for achievement is that subjects who have high needs for achievement would be willing to engage in tasks that low-need achievers would not be willing to engage in. When college students were asked to take part in a ring-toss game and were allowed to stand wherever they wished, subjects with high needs for achievement were most likely to shoot from intermediate distances. Few high-need achievers stood so close to the ring toss that they would always win; few stood so far away that they would always lose. They chose distances that were challenging. Subjects with low need for achievement distributed their choice of distances across the full range from very close to very far away. If you have a high need to achieve, the likelihood is good that you will adopt a task in which you have a reasonable, but not certain, probability of succeeding (Schneider, 1978). People who are achievement motivated rarely undertake

Pride in achievement is nurtured early in life.

Individuals with a high need
for achievement are likely to
take calculated risks.

tasks with a low probability of success (Atkinson & Feather, 1966; Atkinson
& Litwin, 1960); high-need achievers undertake tasks that will provide them
information about their own abilities (Trope, 1975). One possible reason that
high-need achievers pick tasks that are not easy is that performance on those
tasks is likely to yield information about a person's capabilities; tasks that are
particularly easy tell a person little or nothing about his or her ability—remember, high-need achievers want to succeed. This notion has been supported (Meyer, Folkes, & Weiner, 1976), but other interpretations have been
presented (Kuhl & Blankenship, 1979).

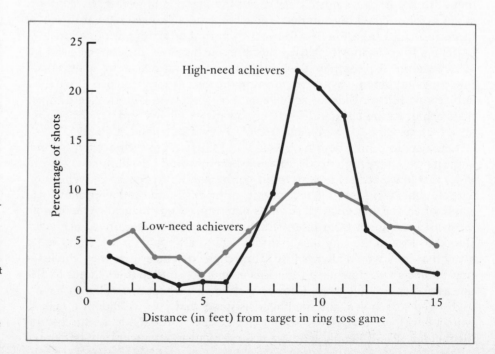

Figure 4.5 Percentage of
ring-toss shots taken from different distances is shown for
high- and low-need achievement subjects. The solid line
shows high-need achievers
who stand most often at about
8 to 12 feet from the target;
the low-need achievers stand
at all of the distances generally perceived as a challenge
(Atkinson & Litwin, 1960)

Achievement motivation is not inborn; it is learned. Children who grow up to be high in achievement need lived in homes in which a great deal of stress was placed upon excellence (e.g., Teevan & McGhee, 1972). This effect is even more pronounced in the firstborn child of a family. Parents typically give their first child more direction and help. As the first child learns the alphabet and does a puzzle, he or she is praised extensively. By the time parents have three children, they have less time to offer such lavish praise. We might therefore expect that firstborn children would have a higher achievement motive. This is precisely the case: a disproportionate number of eminent politicians, scholars, and business people are firstborn children. Furthermore, a disproportionate number of firstborns show a tendency toward affiliation and cooperativeness (Capra & Dittes, 1962) as well as a greater desire for attention than second- or third-born children (Suedfeld, 1964).

It is not surprising to find that the way parents interact with children is likely to affect their children's achievement motivation; parents are in the unique position of being able to deliver praise and criticism for various behaviors. When achievement behaviors are reinforced, learning theory predicts that they will likely occur again. To test the idea that children who are exposed to praise will likely be more achievement oriented and thus probably take higher levels of risk, Canavan-Gumpert (1977) presented fifth- and sixth-grade girls from a New York suburban school with math problems and either praised them or criticized them for correct or incorrect answers. After a practice task in which they were praised or criticized, the girls chose problems to do at one of eight difficulty levels. The major hypothesis of the study involved comparisons of the praise-success vs. criticism-failure treatments. The praise-success subjects were found to have more optimistic expectations, higher standards, and greater confidence about their future performance. Praise-success subjects were more optimistic about future performance and were willing to choose the problems of the highest difficulty level. Subjects in the criticism-failure group were dissatisfied with their performance

Parents often give more attention to the child with whom they can communicate most easily.

and chose the lowest difficulty level problems. In choosing the level of difficulty of new problems, the success-oriented subjects were willing to take the risk of tough problems and failure. The most important part of the Canavan-Gumpert study is the general finding that children can be affected very directly by praise and criticism and this affects their risk-taking behavior and ultimately their need for achievement. This becomes particularly evident when we consider personality variables. (See Table 4.3.)

PERSONALITY FACTORS.   Psychologists have long recognized that a person's unique value system and ways of dealing with the world affect motives. The study of personality (chapter 11) has provided a wealth of information about how individuals approach people, problems, and life in general. The role of personality in motivation is complex and no single theory or idea will suffice in explaining it.

We can see the important role of personality in motivation by examining an interesting approach that is closely tied to motivational theory. Two physicians, Friedman and Rosenman, introduced the idea that people can be classified into two distinct categories of personality styles and that these categories can predict their likelihood of having a heart attack. They suggest that people should be classified as Type A individuals if they: have a great sense of urgency about all things in life, are impatient, are aggressive, are easily aroused to anger, and are extremely achievement-oriented. They suggest it is these Type A individuals who are at risk for heart attacks. All other people are classified as Type B because they do not fit the Type A category (Friedman & Rosenman, 1974).

The Type A/Type B classification system was originally devised to help physicians and the public learn more about the behavior patterns associated with individuals who had a greater likelihood of heart attacks. Friedman and Rosenman wanted to help Type A people become Type B people. There is a correlation between individuals who exhibit Type A behavior and the incidence of heart attacks—for example, more men who exhibited Type A behavior had heart attacks than men who had Type B behavior.

Research has confirmed findings about differences between Type A and Type B individuals (for example, Glass, 1977; Lovallo & Pishkin, 1980). Type A individuals become even more competitive and achieve more in the presence of others; Type B individuals show only small changes in performance

We live in a society that teaches competition in all areas of life.

Table 4.3 Theories of motivation: Drive, Expectancy, Cognitive, and Humanistic.

THEORY	WELL KNOWN THEORIST	PRINCIPALLY EXPLAINS	KEY IDEA	VIEW OF BEHAVIOR IS:
Drive Theory	Nisbett	Obesity	Number of fat cells determine obesity	That it is mechanistic; obesity is biologically determined.
	Schachter	Hunger and obesity	External cues energize eating behavior	That it is partially mechanistic but recognizes the role of learning.
	Hebb	Optimal arousal	Performance is dependent upon level of arousal	That the efficiency of behavior is determined by one level of physiological arousal; a mostly mechanistic view.
Expectancy Theory	Atkinson	Achievement motivation	Humans learn the need to achieve	That achievement is a learned behavior but once established it energizes humans in many areas of their lives; thus, while clearly a learned behavior (which is cognitive), it is still somewhat mechanistic in its orientation.
	Friedman & Rosenman	The behavior of type A coronary heart attack-prone people	Time urgency leads to a competitive unending search for mastery, success, and heart disease	That Type A behavior is initiated early in a child's life through reinforcement and punishment; once established it is hard but not impossible to change; like achievement motivation theory, this view is still somewhat mechanistic in orientation.
Cognitive Theory	Deci	Intrinsic motivation	Intrinsic motivation is self-rewarding by making people feel competent	That intrinsic motivation is inborn; people seek out intrinsic motivation, but extrinsic rewards often decrease intrinsic motivation; decision making is crucial; a cognitive view.
Humanistic Theory	Maslow	Learned needs for fulfillment and feelings of self-actualization	Self-actualization	That humans seek to self-actualize after they have fulfilled basic needs for food and security; a totally cognitive, decision-oriented view.

in the presence of others (Gastorf, Suls, & Sanders, 1980). When challenged, Type A individuals show more physiological arousal than do Type B individuals (Dembroski, McDougall, & Shields, 1977). Further, Type A individuals are more likely to compare themselves to others (Dembroski & McDougall, 1978) and exhibit an exaggerated sense of need for achievement (Burnam, Pennebaker, & Glass, 1975). This heightened need for achievement is an important aspect of people who exhibit Type A coronary-prone behavior. It is possible that an early need to achieve may develop into a general behavior pattern that may be putting these people at risk for serious heart disease.

The development of a need to achieve has been studied to find some of the early sources of its development. One study found that children with a high need to achieve had mothers who fostered independence and rewarded accomplishment (Winterbottom, 1958). Closely associated with a person's need to achieve success are a person's attempts to avoid failure (Birney, Burdick, & Teevan, 1969). Teevan and McGhee (1972) have looked at how and why children may develop fear of failure. They administered the Thematic Apperception Test (TAT) to high school students to assess the extent to which they showed a fear of failure; a questionnaire was also administered to the subjects' mothers to investigate if the mothers fostered independence in their children when they were young. They further asked the mother how and when they rewarded their children when they exhibited desired or undesired behaviors. The questionnaires were kept anonymous but coded in a way that the high school students' scores on fear of failure and each mother's score on the various measures could be matched up and compared. The results showed that the students with a high degree of fear of failure had mothers who: (1) had early expectations for independence in their children; (2) provided neutral responses rather than positive ones when their children showed achieving behaviors; and (3) provided punishment for unsatisfactory behaviors in achievement situations. Thus, if a mother is neutral toward achieving behaviors and punishes unsatisfactory ones, a child is likely to develop a negative attitude toward achievement and become more motivated by a fear of the consequences of failure.

Type A individuals have been shown to have a distinct fear of failure (Gastorf & Teevan, 1980). Given their generally acknowledged high need for achievement, it is not surprising that such people, even as elementary school children, already exhibit Type A or Type B behaviors. Matthews and Angulo (1980) assessed children's competitiveness, impatience, and aggression. Competitiveness was assessed by having children compete with the experimenter in play car races; impatience was measured by watching for signs of frustrations, restlessness, sighs, and squirming; aggression was assessed by watching if and when children were violent with an inflatable doll after they were told that it was fun to punch the doll. The results were as one might expect: children who might be classified as Type A on Friedman and Rosenman's scale exhibited more behavior that was competitive, impatient, and aggressive than Type B children. The researchers were careful to state that the children who exhibit Type A behavior are not necessarily coronary-prone; they appropriately suggest that we need to know much more about Type A behavior and coronary disease before we could begin to make such a dramatic inferential leap. However, we know that, even as children, people are developing a sense of fear of failure and Type A behavior characteristics.

Being classified as a Type A person does not cause the incredible sense of time urgency, competitiveness, and achievement need; however, Type A people have developed an intense desire to control their environment (Carver & Glass, 1978) and become irritated when others slow down their rapid pace (Glass, Snyder, & Hollis, 1974). The actual causes of the development of a Type A behavior pattern probably can be traced to childhood relationships with parents and peers; however, that such behavior patterns exist can tell us much about people's motivations and how they respond to various situations. You will see later in this chapter and when we study aggression (chapter 10, Social Psychology) that blocking of goal-directed behavior often results in strong emotional responses—this should be particularly true for Type A individuals (see also DeGregorio & Carver, 1980).

Psychiatrist Warns of Overwork Syndrome

In popular reports about research, important details are often mentioned only briefly; for example, in this news article the results and conclusions are based on a very limited number of individuals.

WASHINGTON (UPI) If you find it hard to balance your work with rest and relaxation, you may wind up with symptoms of what a psychiatrist calls the overwork syndrome.

The signs vary but commonly include fatigue, irritability, sleep disturbances, concentration difficulties, memory lapses, episodes of confusion, gastrointestinal problems, or neuromuscular complaints.

Dr. John M. Rhoads of the Duke University Medical Center said the symptoms of overwork may mimic heart attack or even brain disorders. The problems can lead to alcoholism or drug dependency.

Rhoads discussed the syndrome in the *Journal of the American Medical Association* and said most people who have open-ended jobs without specific work hours are able to pace themselves even if they work long hours.

People who become ill are those who ignore the body's signals for rest, recuperation, and recreation.

"Cursed with a compulsive need to work, they deny the existence of fatigue and push themselves beyond reason," Rhoads said.

"They attempt to cope with diminished ability to concentrate, ease of distractibility, and drowsiness (early signs of fatigue) by forcing themselves to stay at the appointed task. In fact, they usually lengthen the work day to compensate for their lessened ability to produce efficiently."

Rhoads said the people most likely to fall victim to overwork syndrome are those in executive positions with no set work times and self-employers such as lawyers, doctors, accountants, clergymen and occasionally housewives.

Those who work too much do not complain about it, Rhoads said. Instead they go to the doctor complaining about one of the overwork symptoms.

In severe cases, Rhoads said it may be necessary to hospitalize the patient and give him specialized treatment. In mild cases, all that may be required are a vacation and advice on the need to balance work with rest and recreation.

Why do people work too hard and too long?

Rhoads said little research has been done on the problems of overwork, but from ten cases he described, he said it appeared the patients were attempting to solve their life problems by working excessively in a compulsive manner.

Of course, people do not have to spend the rest of their lives behaving the way a Type A personality does. People can develop new motives which energize them and maintain new behaviors. This process is not easy, but behavior and thought processes can be modified so as to adopt a new, more worthwhile life-style—a life-style that is not associated with heart attacks. We will be studying more about changing maladaptive behavior in Chapter 13 on Psychotherapy.

A Summary

There is no question that many individuals learn motives that foster a need for achievement. Achievement-related behavior has been clearly documented and been shown to be affected by important variables, among which are: (1) the hope of success and the fear of failure, (2) achievement needs which determine whether one will approach success and avoid failure, (3) the expectancy and value of success or failure, as well as (4) the likelihood of success. One of the main findings of this research is that people who are high in achievement motivation seek tasks of intermediate difficulty. Because of other variables that may be involved, researchers have modified original achievement theories to show that even people with low needs for achievement sometimes seek tasks of intermediate difficulty. For example, both will seek certain tasks at an intermediate level of difficulty, but if a task is also high in information value, then a high-need achiever will seek it out more than a low-need achiever. Furthermore, individuals with certain personality characteristics like Type A behavior are far more likely to develop a high cognitive need for achievement.

As researchers move from mechanistic to cognitive theory they become increasingly less precise in their predictions about behavior. One strength of achievement motivation theory is that it is rather precise; knowing certain characteristics about an individual allows a psychologist to predict with fair accuracy how much need achievement the subject will show. Conversely, knowledge of a person's need for achievement will allow one to predict his or her behavior in achievement-related activities.

COGNITIVE THEORY

We have all felt the pangs of hunger at one time or another; we know how they can energize our behavior toward food seeking. At the same time, we recognize that certain food-seeking behaviors are learned; people respond to cues such as television ads and billboards that encourage eating. So, food intake is clearly under mechanistic physiological control and it is also under cognitive or thought control. Cognitive theory assumes that individuals make decisions about how and when they will behave. According to the cognitive view, humans make decisions about what their goals are and how they should achieve these goals. The emphasis is on active decision making and the unique human qualities of abstract thought processes.

Achievement theories are cognitive in nature because they rely on a person's expectancy for success or failure; choices are made. Yet achievement theory does not make the full leap into contemporary cognitive psychology because it retains certain mechanistic details and descriptions. For example, need for achievement is established early in life and once established is easily maintained, somewhat difficult to change, and few day-to-day decisions are necessary. Further, contemporary cognitive theory places a much greater emphasis on the causal role of thoughts in behavior.

Cognitive Controls

Earlier, in presenting optimal arousal theory, we noted that arousal energizes behavior and that, depending on its level, behavior would vary from disorganized to effective. Cognitive psychologists have shown that arousal (which had been equated with drive by researchers like Hebb) is under active voluntary control, i.e., cognitive control. We all know people who "work themselves up" over minor events in their lives. These people become anxious, tense, and can even begin to exhibit symptoms evident even to a casual observer. The research literature has supported the idea that one's arousal level can be under voluntary control. A now classic study was done in 1964 by Lazarus and Alfert. In this study, a subject's level of arousal was monitored under conditions that could induce a great amount of stress. In their study, subjects watched a film dealing with a primitive ritual called subincision. Subincision is the ritual of deeply cutting the penises of adolescent boys. When subjects viewed this film different measures of arousal were taken, such as the electrodermal response (EDR). The EDR usually shows increases during periods of stress. During the film which showed five operations, some of the subjects heard a commentary that denied the pain and harm of the operation; presented in a detached way, the *denial commentary* allowed the subjects to build up psychological defenses against the content of the film. Another group of subjects, the *denial orientation* group, heard the same commentary but before the film was shown. A third group of subjects saw the film without the commentary; this *silent* group also had their electrodermal responses recorded. Figure 4.6 shows the results of the study. The EDR is plotted as a function of time; the time during which the five operations are done is also shown. Without any commentary, in the silent condition, the EDR increased compared to the control period before the film began; this is not surprising since the operations shown are quite stressful to watch. More important, the EDR was smaller for the group of subjects who heard a commentary denying the pain of the operation. The group that heard the denial before the film began, the denial orientation group, showed the lowest overall EDR. The results of this study are important because they show that subjects have some control over physiological reactions by insertion of denial instructions; those subjects who heard the commentary in advance of the film showed less arousal to the film when it was presented.

That human beings can control their emotional reactions to stressful situations is important. It suggests that, by using their own thoughts, people can

Figure 4.6 In a study by Lazarus and Alfert (1964), the electrodermal response (EDR) increased when stress-inducing operations were viewed. The extent of the increase in the EDR was greater for a group that received no commentary (silent) compared to groups which heard a denial of pain during (denial commentary) or before the film was shown (denial orientation). The baseline is the level of the EDR before the film was shown (left-hand portion of the figure). With the start of the film and the first operation, the EDR in all groups increased. The extent of the increase was greatest for the group of subjects who did not hear a commentary denying the pain.

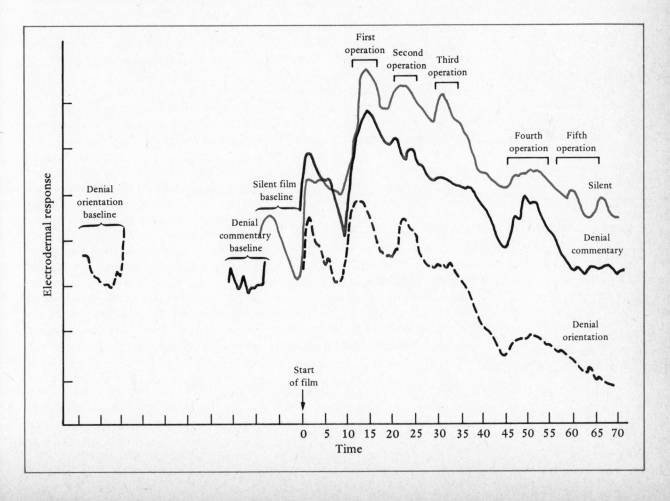

alter their emotional responses. In a study conducted by Koriat (Koriat et al., 1972), subjects were exposed to a stress-inducing film and were given instructions to enhance or reduce their emotional involvement with the content of the film. For example, subjects were told to "let yourself go to the fullest extent that you are able, to be upset in respect to events in the film that move you . . ." or they were told to "try to maintain as total detachment from it as you are capable of, and to be as unemotional as possible while watching the disturbing scenes in the movie . . ." (p. 606). The results of the study showed that the mere introduction of these enhancement or detachment instructions could alter a subject's emotional involvement. This study is important for researchers and practitioners of psychotherapy, because it shows that subjects can control their emotional involvement with a stressful situation by using cognitive or thought methods. The study also has impact on motivation researchers, because we know that increased emotions are usually accompanied by physiological arousal and that arousal affects performance in a complicated way.

Returning to optimal arousal theory for a moment, let's look again at how it suggests that a person's arousal will determine his or her performance on certain tasks. The theory also suggests that a person's arousal in some situations can be voluntarily controlled by thought processes. Subjects in the Lazarus and Alfert study were able to reduce their electrodermal response. Similarly, in the Koriat study the use of cognitive controls by the subjects altered their physiological responses. These studies showed that, through thought processes, people can adjust their level of arousal so as to optimize their performance. People who are too anxious can tell themselves to relax; people who are too relaxed can tell themselves to get up the energy to do the task. Each person tries to maximize his or her level of arousal when trying to achieve optimal performance.

Each of us has suffered from anxiety and its accompanying arousal from time to time. Before a test, before a first date, before a job interview, it is natural that people will be nervous. This anxiety usually shows itself in restlessness, sometimes in an inability to sleep, and even in sexual problems. In studying the causes of behavior, we have learned that emotional reactions to various situations can be modified through our thoughts. This means that many behaviors that are under both physiological and emotional control can be modified through our thought processes. So, when an overweight person has a dieting problem, psychologists recognize that the emotional response to food must be modified to change an obese person's reactions to it. Similarly, a man may be physiologically attracted to women, but he may suffer from an erectile dysfunction at a sexual encounter. Again, fear is often the problem, and through instruction and self-help techniques people can change their thoughts and thus change their resulting behavior. You will see later in this chapter that when researcher Stanley Schachter increased subjects' level of arousal, it was their thoughts rather than their physiological reactions that determined resulting emotional behavior.

Cognitive Motivation: Intrinsic and Extrinsic Motivation

In chapter 3 on Learning (p. 91), the idea that certain behaviors are performed because they are self-rewarding was introduced. Human beings engage in a wide range of activities for the sheer pleasure of doing them. We do crossword puzzles and jigsaw puzzles; we play solitaire. We paint pictures, we build cities with erector sets—only to take them down once they are built. We engage in many activities that have no apparent reward except the fun of doing the activity itself. We are motivated to do the activity because the activity itself is rewarding; we would say that the behavior is intrinsically motivated.

In trying to explain the whys of such behaviors, the notion that people seek an optimal level of arousal has often been suggested. Thus, when people's tissue needs for food have been met but they are still underaroused, they seek out some activity, like a puzzle, that will increase their arousal level to some optimal level. Puzzles that are too difficult will be avoided—people don't seek frustration. Fiske and Maddi (1961) suggested that optimal arousal level will vary with time of day and sleep-wakefulness; this suggests that optimal arousal at bedtime may merely be the quiet lull of music on a radio.

Optimal arousal theories have focused largely on physiological rather than psychological levels of arousal. Other optimal level of arousal theories (e.g., Berlyne, 1971, 1973) have been more comprehensive. For example, Berlyne (1973) has suggested that both increases *and* decreases in arousal level must be considered in studying intrinsic motivation. A far more cognitive theory of intrinsic motivation has been put forth by a University of Rochester psychologist, Edward Deci (1975), and much of what follows summarizes his work.

According to Deci (1975), **intrinsically motivated behaviors** are behaviors that a person engages in to feel competent and self-determining. People need to feel that they can effectively cope with their surroundings; furthermore, they want to feel that they are (at least somewhat) in control of their own fate. So as to feel competent and in control of their environment, people engage in behaviors that develop those feelings. There are two broad kinds of intrinsically motivated behaviors: *first,* there are challenges that are sought to achieve stimulation so that feelings of competence might occur (a person who is bored can hardly feel competent). *Second,* there are challenges that are undertaken that can be met, conquered, and that give a person a sense of real accomplishment, competency, and mastery.

> **Intrinsically motivated behaviors** Behaviors in which a person engages to feel more competent and self-determined.

Intrinsic motivation is inborn; we recognize that even young infants have been observed to be "bored" and seek out stimulation. Certainly, children ask an endless stream of questions; they seek to increase their sense of competency and control of their environment. Many children initially undertake puzzle solving for fun; often they are then reinforced or scolded by parents upon completion or lack of completion of the puzzle. It is this delivery of an extrinsic overt reward that may develop eventual needs for achievement and a potential fear of failure.

We know from learning theory that the delivery of rewards (obvious direct reinforcements) establishes and maintains many behaviors. However, none of these could be classified as intrinsically rewarding. Intrinsically motivated behaviors are engaged in for feelings of competence and self-determination; often these behaviors are interfered with by extrinsic rewards—money, food, or praise, for example.

The delivery of a reward (for example, money or praise) can decrease intrinsically motivated behavior. The intrusion of extrinsic rewards on intrin-

Children ask a never-ending stream of questions about the "whys" of the world.

sically motivated behaviors happens frequently to young children. While a well-meaning parent may reward a child for practicing the piano, it is this reward which makes practicing the piano a behavior which is dependent upon rewards. Playing had been a mere pleasure because it provided feelings of self-competence; now, playing the piano is done for rewards.

In a series of studies, Deci (1971, 1972; Deci et al., 1975) compared subjects who were engaged in puzzle solving with no reward (intrinsic group) to a similar group of subjects who were given rewards for puzzle solving (extrinsic group). The extrinsic group was compared to the intrinsic group on the number of minutes spent in puzzle solving when rewards were no. longer provided. Generally, subjects who were once rewarded for puzzle solving no longer spent as much time solving puzzles compared to the group that was never rewarded. In a different situation, similar results with young children have been found (Lepper, Greene, & Nisbett, 1973); further, if the rewards are expected before doing the activity, the effect on decreasing intrinsically motivated behavior is greater. Deci (1975) cites a fable presented by Ausubel (1948) which presents in a different context the effect of providing extrinsic rewards on a formerly intrinsically motivated behavior:

> In a little Southern town where the Klan was riding again, a Jewish tailor had the temerity to open his little shop on the main street. To drive him out of the town the Kleagle of the Klan set a gang of little ragamuffins to annoy him. Day after day they stood at the entrance of his shop. "Jew! Jew!", they hooted at him. The situation looked serious for the tailor. He took the matter so much to heart that he began to brood and spent sleepless nights over it. Finally out of desperation he evolved a plan.
>
> The following day, when the little hoodlums came to jeer at him, he came to the door and said to them, "From today on any boy who calls me "Jew" will get a dime from me." Then he put his hand in his pocket and gave each boy a dime.
>
> Delighted with their booty, the boys came back the following day and began to shrill, "Jew! Jew!" The tailor came out smiling. He put his hand in his pocket and gave each of the boys a nickel, saying, "A dime is too much—I can only afford a nickel today." The boys went away satisfied because, after all, a nickel was money, too.
>
> However, when they returned the next day to hoot at him, the tailor gave them only a penny each.

"Why do we get only a penny today?" they yelled.

"That's all I can afford."

"But two days ago you gave us a dime, and yesterday we got a nickel. It's not fair, mister."

"Take it or leave it. That's all you're going to get!"

"Do you think we're going to call you "Jew" for one lousy penny?"

"So don't!"

And they didn't. (Ausubel, 1948)

When an external reward is given to a person, the reward can do two things: first, it can strengthen an already existing behavior; second, it can provide information to a person about his or her performance. If the information is positive, it will likely increase a person's feelings of self-worth and competence. If the information is negative (for example, poor feedback on an exam), then self-worth is decreased and it is likely that the intrinsically motivated behavior will cease to be exhibited.

It must be stressed that the delivery of an extrinsic reward does not *always* decrease intrinsically motivated behavior (Condry, 1977). An athlete who is rewarded for a sport she loves to play will likely continue to play. Further, verbal extrinsic rewards are less likely to interfere with intrinsic motivation (Anderson, Manoogian, & Renwick, 1976; see also Fisher, 1978).

If people are given a feeling that they have control over themselves and their environment, they are more likely to perform work in a job setting because they enjoy it. As noted in the research of Fisher (1978), people want to feel that they are in control over their lives and work. Thus, workers may perform their jobs well, but their jobs are not meaningful to them unless they feel that their successful performance was brought about by their own efforts and choices. The practical implications for employers and work managers is clear: the more employees and workers feel that they are choosing their work and they are making positive contributions toward their product or service, the more likely they are to perform the work willingly and with the enthusiasm of intrinsically motivated work behavior.

MAKING CHOICES. Perhaps the most important aspect of the work on intrinsic motivation is that it shows that human beings make choices and use their thought processes in deciding the behaviors in which they want to engage. People engage in intrinsically motivated behaviors by choice—because they decide to. From a cognitive theorist's point of view, drive theories cannot adequately explain intrinsic motivation; they do not allow people to express their unique human qualities of thought and individuality. Learning theories (which are sometimes mechanistic) allow for more choice, but cognitive theories insist on choices—choices are made about goals and how to achieve them.

Cognitive theories account for intrinsically motivated behaviors, and they also allow for individuals to determine how they will respond to arousal or anxiety. A person who is aroused and anxious because of an impending examination can respond with fear, and even flight. Or, she can respond by thinking about her fear and arousal, do some studying, reduce her fear, and achieve a satisfactory grade. Whether people adjust their optimal level of arousal in line with one theory or another is not yet answered. Hebb (1955) has provided an important notion, Fiske and Maddi (1961) have developed it further, and Berlyne (1973) has made important contributions toward broadening the notion. A theorist has yet to combine these more physiological theories with the more cognitive approach put forth by researchers on intrinsic motivation like Deci (1975). Let us now look at the ideas of a humanistic theorist who has in some real ways combined some of the best ideas from all approaches—drive, expectancy, and cognitive. While Maslow's ideas are clearly within the humanistic framework, he did not discount the other approaches—his theory incorporated them all. (See Table 4.3, p. 161.)

HUMANISTIC THEORY

A first look at the causes of behavior shows us that physiological imbalances can initiate behavior; hunger clearly makes people seek out food. However, behavior is not just food seeking or merely fulfilling physiological needs. Behavior is complex and many, if not most, aspects of a person's daily activities are not initiated because of some physiological imbalance. People develop desires for love, safety, and achievement. Some develop desires for power, fame, or recognition. These desires are not physiological mechanisms triggered by a tissue imbalance, but rather are desires acquired as individuals mature and their basic inherited characteristics unfold in the environment.

Psychologists are of course aware of these different kinds of initiators of behavior, but it is not easy to study them in combination. In order to test the components of motivation reliably, most psychologists choose either to study physiological mechanisms and the imbalances that initiate behavior, or else they study the learned or acquired conditions that initiate behavior. As students of psychology, however, we have to keep in mind that both the physiological and learned aspects of behavior usually work in combination as the ultimate controllers of a person's behavior. No single desire or physiological mechanism can account for all behavior. Certainly, food and water needs must be satisfied before needs for power or glory, yet all of these aspects must be considered. One of the appealing aspects of Maslow's humanistic theory is that it incorporates both physiological and learned components of behavior.

Abraham Maslow (1908–1970) was a personality theorist who achieved considerable recognition through his conception of the causes of behavior. As a humanistic psychologist, Maslow assumed that people's behavior is motivated toward self-fulfillment so that they might be everything their potential allows them to become. According to **humanistic psychologists,** people are basically good; once they have certain basic needs fulfilled, they make attempts toward **self-actualization.** When people self-actualize they have achieved their true natures and have fulfilled their potential to the greatest degree possible. Maslow assumed that humans have inborn or innate motives to seek self-actualization. A **motive** is of course a specific internal condition that directs a person toward a goal.

Maslow, unlike many of the personality theorists we will discuss in chapter 11, was sensitive to the many different kinds of motives that direct behavior. He realized that unless a person's physiological needs of hunger and thirst are satisfied it is unlikely that he or she can feel self-actualized. Once these physiological needs have been met, Maslow argued, people have social motives of desires for safety, belongingness, and love. If these other levels of

Abraham Maslow (1908–1970) was one of the founders of humanistic psychology.

Humanistic psychology The approach to behavior that emphasizes human qualities, especially dignity, individual choice, self-concepts, and self-achievement.

Self-actualization The process of moving toward realizing one's potential to the greatest degree possible; the process of achieving everything that one is capable of doing.

Motive A specific internal condition directing an organism's behavior toward a goal.

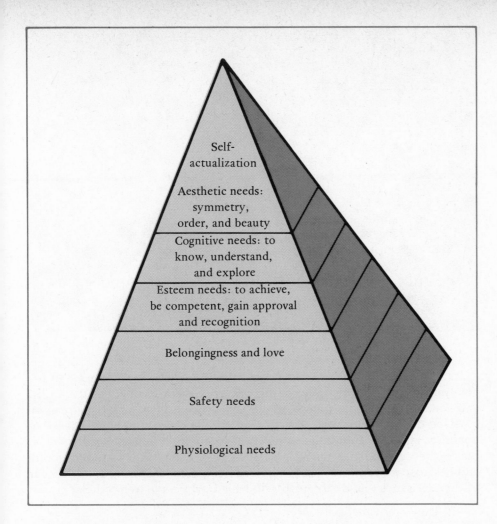

Figure 4.7 Maslow's pyramid of needs. Physiological needs are at the base of the pyramid. Each successive layer becomes more social in structure and to a greater extent is a learned social need rather than a need expressing physiological imbalance

motivation are satisfied, then people can truly self-actualize; they can then reach their fullest possible development and feel they have become everything they might within their unique potential for perfection and creativity.

Maslow conceived of the different types of motives as being in a pyramid-shaped structure with physiological motives and drives at the base of the pyramid. As we satisfy a low level need in the pyramid, then we can strive for the next higher level. We can never achieve feelings of self-respect or success unless we have our love, safety, and our physiological needs met. Certainly, we can never self-actualize unless the base aspects of the pyramid have been realized.

Maslow's theory of motivation and personality not only considers humanistic, aesthetic, growth, and enhancement motives, but it also considers physiological needs and the resulting drives that direct behavior on an hour-to-hour basis. Maslow never really claimed that all the physiological needs have to be met in full for an individual to achieve a higher level of fulfillment. Once the most basic physiological needs are met, then a person is better prepared for emotional needs to be met. Satisfying physiological needs and social desires is not an all-or-nothing situation; even a malnourished and starving child has emotional requirements that need attention.

Achieving our ambitions
often takes years of dedicated
hard work.

As a humanistic psychologist, Maslow assumed that people have an innate inclination to develop all of their potential and to seek beauty, truth, and goodness. While he recognized that basic needs must be satisfied before a person can self-actualize, Maslow argued that people can have a sense of openness and can capture the world and experience it in truly healthy ways. Maslow recognized that there is a wide range of personalities among people, and he chose to study only self-actualized people. Listed below are a number of characteristics that distinguish self-actualized people from others:

1. They are realistically oriented.
2. They accept themselves for what they are.
3. Their thought is unconventional, spontaneous.
4. They are problem centered.
5. They have a need for privacy.
6. They are independent.
7. Their appreciation of people is fresh.
8. They have spiritual experiences.
9. They identify with people.
10. They have intimate relationships.
11. They are democratic.
12. They do not confuse means with end.
13. They have a good sense of humor.
14. They are creative and nonconformist.
15. They appreciate the environment.

About how many people in life can we say all these things? While many of us have some of these traits, few of us have all of them. Yet according to Maslow we all strive and are directed toward becoming self-actualized.

As you will see in subsequent chapters, many of Maslow's ideas are interresting ways to organize our thinking, but they are often very difficult to submit to experimental investigation. While Maslow's theory may not be testable, it does point out that we must consider physiological drives first. Unless our most basic physiological needs are reasonably met, it seems unlikely that we will be able to grow and develop physically, let alone develop or acquire other new motives that might direct behavior. A disadvantaged migrant worker must first maintain physiological and safety needs; only after those are met can he or she seriously worry about developing a missing sense of self-respect or an undiscovered sense of beauty in the world.

As we examine the whys of behavior, we see that there are both physiological drives and learned motives that direct an organism toward certain goals. The goals may be food or water, or achievement and self-actualization; regardless of the target, drive and motives are goal-directed and behavior is purposeful. When goal-directed behavior is blocked and people are unable to achieve their desires or fulfill their needs, they are placed in stressful situations. In such situations, there are typical increases in arousal and great ranges of emotion that may vary from a willingness to kill to the depths of fatigue, anger, or despair. Usually these strong emotions are adjusted by cognitive controls—however, not always. We thus see that motivation and a person's resulting emotions are closely tied together.

A good sense of humor is a characteristic of a self-actualized person.

EMOTION

When placed in a similar situation, each of us has different feelings. Some of us become emotionally charged at an important football game, while others find football a bore. While most people become deeply saddened at the loss of a loved one, some people seem cold and lacking in feelings. Almost everyone would agree that crying is a strong emotional reaction; but people cry when they are happy *and* when they are sad. A woman may cry at the birth of her child *and* at the loss of a close friend. When researchers first began to study emotional behavior like crying, they realized that there was a wide range of emotions that needed to be evaluated: love, joy, fear, disgust, anger. These emotions had motivating properties because they would impel and direct a person's behavior toward action. Feelings of dependency might direct a person's behavior toward seeking help. Anger might cause feelings of hostility or revenge. Emotion is, therefore, directly involved in motivation.

When people are experiencing strong feelings about a situation, these feelings may be accompanied by a physiological response. If the feeling that a person experiences is fear, the fear is often associated with an increase in breathing rate, sweating, a dryness in the mouth, and sometimes nausea. We can see people perspiring when they are afraid, crying when they are sad, or finding increased energy when they are excited. The obvious physiological changes that take place when a person is in a emotional state have been the focus of much research. It becomes easy to see that an **emotion** is a feeling, usually accompanied by a physiological change, and is usually associated with a change in behavior. Emotions have a subjective or internal component that is private to each individual; these feelings are usually shared by many people, but one person's sense of joy and another person's feeling of joy may be qualitatively different. At least part of emotion is private, personal, unique, and thus psychologists refer to it as subjective.

Part of emotion is physiological; people often do not show physiological changes until *after* an event. A person can be angered or humiliated, only to

Emotion A subjective feeling generally accompanied by a physiological change that is usually associated with a change in behavior.

begin to show physiological signs after the angering situation has passed. Sometimes people's emotional responses are *preceded* by a physiological change. People often report that their bodies knew they had been through a difficult ordeal even before they recognized it. In automobile accidents, people's bodies will respond with increased physiological arousal, muscle tension, and avoidance responses—it is after the accident that people start to shake with fear, disbelief, even rage. So, physiological responses sometimes accompany our subjective feelings, sometimes they occur before, and sometimes occur after.

Because emotions involve feelings and physiological changes, people often respond to these changes by altering their behavior. Upon feeling afraid, people may scream. Upon recognizing a tragedy, people may make themselves unable to work. When angered, people often respond by seeking revenge or retribution. While experiencing love, human beings may respond with tender gestures of affection. Of course, such behavior does not have to be directly acted out; people may think about screaming, retribution, or tender words, but they often do not express these behaviors in directly observable, overt ways.

Over the years, psychologists have focused on the different aspects of emotional behavior. Some researchers focused on basic emotions and the cataloging of them (Bridges, 1932; Wundt, 1896); other researchers have focused on how people perceive the emotions of others (Tagruri, 1968). Still other researchers have directed their research toward the physiological bases of emotion (Bard, 1934). Others have recently focused on the control of emotional responses (Lazarus, 1974). Most recently, psychologists have been studying how we convey emotions to other people through non-verbal mechanisms such as gestures or eye contact (Zaidel & Mehrabian, 1969).

While psychologists have long recognized and acknowledged the three-part definition of emotion including feelings, physiological responses, and behavior, they have focused most of their research energy and theories on the latter two aspects. Because the behavioral view has so permeated experimental investigation, most researchers who have studied emotion have considered subjective feelings far too esoteric and unmeasurable. Researchers have not denied that people have such subjective experiences nor do they discount their importance—however, they have chosen to study aspects of emotion that are measurable and observable, aspects that can be observed in behavior.

The Development of Emotion

Emotional expression develops over time and, while certain aspects seem learned, other aspects seem to be inborn. Harry Harlow, a psychologist at the University of Wisconsin, has studied the development of emotion in rhesus monkeys. Initial studies were on the nature of early interactions of monkeys; Harlow found that monkeys who were raised from birth without their mothers were not surviving although they were well fed. Other monkeys raised in these conditions but who were given scraps of terrycloth were surviving. Terrycloth is hardly a critical developmental variable in the growth and development of monkeys; yet, its introduction into a wire cage made the difference between life and death for a number of monkeys. Harlow came to guess that the terrycloth was providing some measure of security or warmth for the

Figure 4.8 Photograph of one of Harry Harlow's monkeys

monkeys. This led to an experiment to see if infant monkeys had any inborn or natural desire for "love" or warmth that might be delivered from soft warm objects like terrycloth. The experiment, now a classic, had infant monkeys in cages with two wirecovered shapes that resembled monkeys. One of the wire monkeys was covered with terrycloth, one was bare. The wire monkeys were able to be fitted with bottles which provided milk. In some conditions, the wire mother was fitted with a bottle to feed the infants, in other conditions the terrycloth mother was fitted with the bottle. Regardless of the source of milk, the monkeys clung to the mothers covered with terrycloth. Further, these infant monkeys would cling to the terrycloth mother in new fearful situations; the wire mother, even with a bottle of milk, could not provide the comfort that a terrycloth-covered monkey could (Harlow, 1959; Harlow & Zimmerman, 1958).

While Harlow's infant monkeys sought the love of a terrycloth mother, these infants were also more aggressive and fearful than normally raised monkeys. They were not able to engage in normal sexual relations, and some of the wire-mother infants were engaged in self-destructive behaviors (Harlow, 1962). Harlow was to suggest that the emotions of fear, curiosity, and aggression are inborn and that the brain mechanisms underlying them develop over time and in a specific sequence. To test this idea he isolated monkeys for various periods during their lives. As Harlow expected, some behaviors were more affected by early isolation, other behaviors affected more by later isolation. When monkeys were only deprived of social contacts with other monkeys during the period from 18 to 24 months of age, later social behaviors were essentially normal. Harlow's results led him to conclude that the development of certain emotions follow a fixed time path; further, the interaction of nature and nurture must take place for proper social development. So, if social experiences are denied during the critical time period (during which brain mechanisms are ready to mature), the behavior will not develop properly. It was the *early* isolation of Harlow's wire and terrycloth monkeys that caused their eventual fearful, aggressive, and destructive behaviors (Deets & Harlow, 1971). We will be examining this idea of critical stages in development in chapter 6, Development.

HUMANS. The studies with animals do not stand alone; we know from human studies of sensory deprivation that they find such situations at a minimum boring and at a maximum intolerable. Humans need and seek stimulation; they are motivated to find it. When denied such stimulation, there are definite changes in behavior. It is, of course, unethical for researchers to isolate humans for extended periods of time, and totally out of the question to perform such experiments with infants. Yet, we know from naturalistic studies of infants that they come into the world with a pattern of development that seems relatively fixed. They smile at 6 weeks, they coo, babble, and gurgle at about the same time. In the same way, they develop a fear of strangers at 6 to 9 months and are all born with a startle (Moro) reflex. Studies of infant bonding (p. 249) have shown that there are critical periods in an infant's life where emotional relationships between parent and child are formed. While it is a broad inferential leap from Harlow's monkeys to human infants, it is reasonable to assume that infants, like monkeys, have an inborn need for social stimulation. According to Klaus and Kennel (1976) without such periods, infants will not develop emotions as well as infants who go through social bonding.

The Expression of Emotion

There are many different behavioral responses that a person might show when he or she becomes emotional. There are obvious expressions of emotion such as crying, fist shaking, and the clenching of teeth. There are less obvious behavior changes such as weeping, going limp, and a loss of energy. Psychologists have studied the smiling responses of infants, children, and adults. They have also observed the activity levels of animals and humans when they have been placed in situations that might induce stress and emotional reactions. Humans have excellent skills in interpreting the emotions of other people through different channels of expression, including voice, body, and facial expressions (Cunningham, 1977). One particularly interesting response that people use to convey and receive information about their emotional states is their facial expressions. A person's facial expression conveys a great deal and has been studied extensively over the last 50 years (Ekman & Oster, 1979).

Let us look more closely at what a behavioral response like facial expressions can tell us about emotion. In an excellent review of the role of facial expressions, Ekman and Oster (1979) pointed out that observers label facial expressions of emotion in the same way regardless of culture, and further, that members of different cultures use the same facial expressions when experiencing the same emotion.

You will see in chapter 6, Development, that facial expressions of emotion are present early in infancy; even 3- and 4-month-old infants respond differently to happy faces than they do to sad faces (Young-Browne, Rosenfeld, & Horowitz, 1977). Newborns have even been known to imitate the facial expressions of adults (Kaye & Marcus, 1978; Meltzoff & Moore, 1977). Certainly, children know exactly what the common facial expressions are and what they mean by the time they enter school (e.g., Greenspan, Barenboym, & Chandler, 1976). Perhaps most important is that facial expressions can provide an important vehicle of communication between a mother and her child (Ainsworth, 1979) and between children and adults.

While there are large individual differences, most people can tell fairly accurately how a person is feeling from his or her expressions (Ekman, Friesen, & Ellsworth, 1972). Some theorists have even gone so far as to suggest that we know what emotions we are experiencing from our facial expressions (Tomkins, 1962, 1963). Since the early 1920s when research on facial expressions first began, researchers have recognized that the face and its expressions provide a cue to how other people feel. It is a behavioral measure that is easily seen, can be captured on film, and can be interpreted by others. Most important, the research has shown that it can be an accurate index to a person's emotional state. Cartoonists and political satirists take facial expressions and blow them up bigger than life; they exaggerate facial expressions to convey meaning. Actors, opera stars, and children have been known to exaggerate facial expressions for the same reasons (see Buck, 1980).

Let us now examine more closely the kinds of *physiological* changes on which researchers have been able to focus. Early in the century, the first psychologists recognized that there were changes that took place physiologically when a person experienced an emotion. Generally, the changes that take place are noticeable and are often due to an increase in autonomic nervous system activity (p. 56). If a person were crossing the street and were to see a speeding car coming directly at him, we expect certain physiological changes. Similarly if a person feels that her disagreement with a friend is going to explode into a violent argument, we expect certain physiological reactions. In both cases, people are afraid and we can record changes in their heartbeat. Digestion slows or stops; there is an increase in blood pressure and heart rate, and breathing becomes deeper. Pupils dilate, salivation decreases (thus causing a dry mouth), and muscles often feel tense. All or some of these autonomic changes can occur. One widely studied measure of autonomic nervous system activation is the electrodermal response. The electrodermal response (EDR), which is still often referred to as the galvanic skin response, has been studied extensively; for decades, researchers have known that it is easy to measure and that it correlates well with other measures of the nervous system. The EDR is recorded by placing a small electrode on the skin and measuring the skin's conductance; skin conductance increases dramatically as a person becomes more aroused. When recording EDR, the electrode is often placed on the palm of the hand, an area that rapidly changes skin conductance as autonomic nervous system activity increases (see e. g., Duffy & Lacey, 1946). While the EDR is often used it must be pointed out that there are other autonomic nervous system indices that can be used; blood pressure was recognized early as a good index (Darrow, 1936) as was respiration rate (Brower, 1946) and the pupilary response (Lowenstein & Friedman, 1942).

Perhaps the most widely recognized measurer of emotion is the lie detector. The lie detector is not really a detector of lies but rather is a device that records changes in autonomic nervous system activity. Typically, a psychologist measures the EDR, heart rate, and blood pressure of subjects who are attached to a lie detector. Since lying is usually associated with an increase in autonomic nervous system activity, a trained researcher can monitor the autonomic nervous system responses of a person during a series of questions

The pain of a life crisis can be devastating.

that could be considered relatively neutral and compare those responses with responses to "critical" questions. Autonomic nervous system activity would remain at what might be considered a baseline level when a person is asked his or her name, address, age, social security number, occupation, and so forth. However, when asked if the person used a knife as a holdup weapon, a person who has something to hide usually shows a dramatic increase in autonomic nervous system activity. It is important to remember that most autonomic nervous system activity is involuntary; people generally cannot control their EDR in such a situation.

There are problems with lie detectors. First, not all people show marked autonomic nervous system changes when they become emotionally aroused. Second, habitual liars, by definition, do not show changes (or show very small changes) in autonomic nervous system activity when they lie. Third, recent research has shown that a person can bring some autonomic responses under voluntary control (biofeedback). Fourth, people can alter the baseline conditions. Taken together, the features of the lie detector can be useful to weed out a person who is lying; *however*, it is subject to significant error, particularly with the habitual liar or person who purposely wants to confuse the results, like a crook (see Szucko and Kleinmuntz, 1981).

When studying emotion researchers have recognized that autonomic nervous system responses are direct, observable, and measurable responses which they could quantify in a systematic manner; sometimes more than one such response measure is used in a single study (for example, Furchtgott & Busemeyer, 1979). In any case, much of our theorizing about emotions is based on known physiological responses.

The Control of Emotion

We live in a complicated world where many events can bring about a wide range of emotions; there are happy, jubilant periods in our lives; there are also times of despair, sadness, and depression. Earlier, when we examined the control of arousal, we learned that subjects' arousal level could be controlled through cognitive means. Subjects in the Lazarus and Alfert (1964) study were able to manipulate their EDRs when told in advance the nature of the pain that they would see in a film; even more convincing were the results of the study by Koriat et al. (1972) in which subjects were told to enhance their emotional involvement with a film or to take a detached attitude from the film's content. These studies showed that people can control their level of arousal; arousal level is, of course, one of the components of emotion.

The self-regulation view of emotional expression is cognitive. It stresses that the individuals manage or determine their emotional state in a willful way. People are not passive, nor do they respond to environmental or internal stimuli automatically. Rather, they are in a regular and constant state of cognitively evaluating the environment. So, rather than assuming that the obese eat because they merely see food, a researcher like Lazarus would suggest that people have determined how they will respond long before food is presented. Obese people often prepare themselves for a food-oriented vacation and respond appropriately whenever food is presented. People may diet and try to control their environment by eliminating candy bars around the home, but their general response to food is cognitively determined in advance (Lazarus, 1974). There is no question that environmental stimuli can determine emotions, but from a cognitive psychologist's view, they tell only part of the picture. Human beings as evaluators can exert a great deal of cognitive or thought control over emotional states.

An audition can be a frightening experience.

Theories of Emotion

Over the years there have been three major approaches to the study of emotion. The first two theories focused on the physiology of emotion and what comes first, physiological changes or emotional feelings. Only in the last 20 years have researchers acknowledged a third view, the cognitive view, which involves interpretation as well as physiology.

JAMES-LANGE THEORY. Although James was its principal proponent, William James and Carl Lange developed a theory of emotion which has since been named for both of them. According to the James-Lange theory of emotion, people experience physiological changes, *then* they interpret the causes of these physical changes and thus experience an emotion. So, a person does not cry because he feels sad; rather, he feels sad because he cries. People do not perspire because they feel afraid; they feel afraid after they have perspired. Simply stated, the James-Lange theory says people don't experience an emotion until after their bodies become aroused and respond with physiological changes. It is feedback from the body that produces feelings or emotions (James, 1884; Lange, 1885).

CANNON. Physiologists like Walter Cannon were very critical of the James-Lange theory. Cannon showed that physiological changes in many emotional states were identical. If blood pressure and heart rate increase in response to anger *and* to joy, how would a person know what his or her emotion should be? Cannon argues that when a person is showing emotional be-

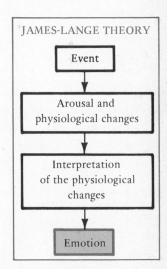

Figure 4.9 The basics of the James-Lange theory are shown in this flowchart. Note that arousal precedes interpretation, which precedes the eventual emotion

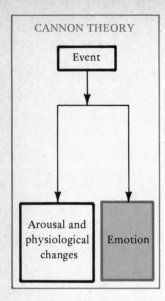

Figure 4.10 The basics of the Cannon theory. Note that arousal and emotional feelings occur simultaneously

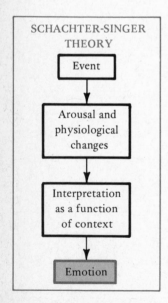

Figure 4.11 The basics of the Schachter-Singer theory. Note that the interpretation is of the context within which the subjects find themselves

havior two areas of the brain are stimulated, the thalamus and the cortex. The cerebral cortex is stimulated and produces an experience of emotion; the thalamus stimulates the sympathetic nervous system, which is responsible for physiological changes. According to Cannon, emotional feelings *accompany* physiological changes. This is in direct contrast to James and Lange, who place heavy emphasis on the interpretation of bodily changes (Cannon, 1927).

SCHACHTER-SINGER THEORY.   This relatively new cognitive theory of emotion draws on elements of both the James-Lange and Cannon theories. Stanley Schachter and Jerome Singer observed that emotions were interpreted, but not solely from bodily changes. People cry in situations which produce feelings of either joy or sadness and these situations are very clear. While a person may interpret his or her bodily sensations, they must be interpreted within a specific context. Observers cannot interpret what a person's crying means unless they know the situation that surrounds that behavior. If a man is crying at a funeral, we know that he is sad, but if he is crying at his daughter's wedding, we expect that he is joyful.

To prove their contention, Schachter and Singer (1962) injected volunteer subjects with adrenalin, a powerful stimulant. Injections of adrenalin will produce increased heart rate, excitement, energy, and even feelings of butterflies in the stomach. A group of subjects was told that they were being given an injection of adrenalin and the physiological response that they would most likely feel. A second group was given the drug but no information. A third group was given incorrect information. All of the subjects showed aroused behavior, but the object of the experiment was to see how this arousal would be interpreted.

To see if they could affect how the subjects interpreted their arousal, Schachter and Singer arranged a situation in which volunteer subjects were tricked. They hired some undergraduates and paid them either to act happy and relaxed or to act sad, depressed, and angry. These hired subjects—called stooges—pretended that they were volunteers in the drug study. The happy stooges shot wads of paper into a wastepaper basket and flew airplanes around the room. The unhappy stooges complained about the questionnaire they had to fill out and voiced their general dissatisfaction with the experiment. They were given shots just like the volunteer subjects; however, their shots were salt water. Their emotional behavior was strictly an act. Remember, the aim of the experiment was to see how the naive volunteer subjects interpreted the physiological changes that accompanied the shot of adrenalin. Would the volunteer subjects' emotions be affected by the act of the stooges?

All of the experimental subjects showed increased physiological arousal, but the subjects who were among happy stooges reported feeling that the drug made them feel good. Subjects who were with the angry stooges reported feelings of anger. Schachter and Singer reasoned that when people have no immediate explanation for their physiological arousal, they will label feelings in terms of the thoughts that are available to them. The physiological feelings that accompany both joy and anger are the same, but the emotion is determined by the situation. The adrenalin caused arousal in the volunteer subjects, but their emotions were determined by the situation they found themselves in. This cognitive theory of emotion suggests that physiological changes within a person are not enough to cause emotional reaction; rather, physiological changes must be interpreted within a context (see also Manstead, 1979).

The Schachter and Singer conception of emotion has modified the way psychologists think about emotional behavior. Not only were their experiments very convincing, but other kinds of anecdotal data also support the cognitive theory of emotion. When people first smoke marijuana or take other psychoactive drugs, they often approach the situation with definite expectancies. If told that the drug will produce feelings of hunger, new users of drugs will report a feeling of hunger. Similarly, when a particular drug is described as a "downer" users often interpret the bodily sensations that accompany the drug as being depressive. Expectancies affect our behavior as well. In chapter 9 we will discuss hypnosis and will show that many hypnotic behaviors can only be explained by the situation and the subject's expectancies (see also Bower, 1981; Leventhal, 1974; Plutchik & Ax, 1967).

From Schachter's view, emotion arises because of the following sequence: *first*, there is arousal; *second*, the person becomes aware of the arousal; *third*, an explanation for the arousal is sought; and *fourth*, and external cue is identified and so the internal reaction is labeled. It is this labeling that determines the kind of emotional feeling (Weiner, 1980). This view clearly states that arousal must precede emotional feelings, but this view has been challenged by Valins (1966).

Valins has shown that thoughts alone are sufficient to produce emotional behavior without arousal. In the Schachter studies, arousal was increased and then cues were introduced to help the subjects label their physical feeling. In Valins's study (1966), cues were provided and arousal was not increased. Male subjects viewed pictures of nude women; at the same time they heard heartbeats that had been previously recorded. The subjects were told that the heartbeats were their own but to ignore them; the heartbeats were speeded up or slowed down when nude slides were shown to the subjects. Thus, these subjects were being given a cue to their arousal, while they may not have been aroused. A control group saw the same slides, heard the same

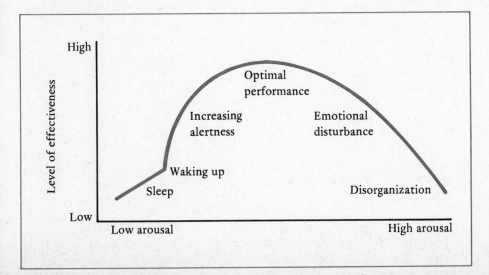

Figure 4.12 As motivation and arousal increase, emotional feelings often increase. Behavior is affected differently by these changes. This expresses the Yerkes-Dodson law

sounds, but were told that the sounds were meaningless and to ignore them. The experimental and control groups next judged the attractiveness of the nudes. The experimental group judged the pictures as more attractive than the control group; they were also more likely than the control group to want to take the picture home with them. By giving the experimental group a cue that they were aroused, it caused them to rate the pictures in a more positive way. The experimental group was no more aroused than the control group—they only *thought* they were. From Valins's view, these data show that arousal was not a prerequisite for labeling of emotion to happen; cognitive processes alone were important (see Harris & Katkin, 1975).

A Summary

One major source of emotion is anxiety and its accompanying arousal. It was suggested that aroused subjects will do better at a task than subjects who have little motivation. This point has been emphasized by Hebb (1972), who argued that the efficiency of a person's performance is dependent upon level of arousal. When a person is deeply asleep, there will be little performance. Similarly, when a person is at incredibly high levels of arousal, performance will be poor. There is an optimal level of performance in this curve.

We generally think of arousal as a motivator of behavior, yet we all know that a person can be "paralyzed" by fear (Hebb, 1972). As arousal increases, so do emotional feelings; emotion is accompanied by changes in arousal. Further, our thoughts can alter our emotions. So, there is a direct link between arousal, emotion, thoughts, and motivation. When there is increased arousal, people will show emotional responses that may motivate their behavior. When the arousal is too high, the emotional responses become too strong and behavior becomes disorganized. Arousal has positive effects because it energizes people, and only when the optimal level of arousal has been passed will behavior become disorganized. The effects of arousal, emotion, and thought become increasingly more important in the behavior of disturbed individuals. Many people classified as maladjusted are so fearful that they cannot organize their thinking and behavior. Their level of

arousal is often so high and out of control that a lack of coherent organized
behavior is often predictable.

183

Motivation and Emotion

SUMMARY

A person's motives are those conditions directing him or her to a certain behavior. There are different motives, including physiological ones based upon an imbalance such as needs for food and water and learned social motives such as needs for achievement, affiliation, or power. We study motivation because it helps explain many of the causes of behavior.

If you think back to our fat man, Jose, you can now see that his behavior—eating binges—was most likely brought about by a variety of circumstances. Jose had physiological needs which had to be satisfied, thus, part of his eating was physiologically based. Jose had also acquired social motives for eating, so part of his eating was based on pleasure: eating helped calm his nerves and sooth him emotionally. While many behaviors can be explained by a drive-reduction approach (for example, reducing hunger), we must remember that learned social motives play an active role in shaping behavior.

Part of Jose's eating was in response to emotional situations. Indeed, many obese people indicate that whenever they feel aroused they wish to eat. For example, seeing himself in a mirror may have aroused Jose; the arousal may cause anxiety and the emotional response may be interpreted as a need to eat. Schachter and Singer have shown that a person's interpretation of his or her physiological arousal and subsequent emotions will depend on environment. Thus, a person's behavior is going to be affected by motives (both physiological and learned), state of arousal, and environment.

A person's motives cannot be considered without looking at other factors, including ability. When discussing motivation and emotion, we have generally assumed that people are able to perform the task at hand. An athlete may have strong motives to run the race, may be appropriately aroused, and, assuming that he or she has the ability, will perform well. A person who never even jogs around the block will be unlikely to run the mile in 4 minutes regardless of motivation. This situation works both ways. A person may have the ability to run the mile in 4 minutes, but if he is not motivated to do so we won't see performance.

Let's step back. A person's behavior or performance is going to be affected by (1) motivation, (2) emotional state (including arousal), (3) ability, and (4) thought processes. Behavior is not a simple phenomenon that occurs solely because of motive or ability. Clearly, high motivation without ability will not yield high performance; nor will high ability with no motivation. For a person's performance to be maximal he or she needs strong motives, high ability, optimal arousal, and organized thought processes. A person's biological endowments, motives, abilities, and thoughts are all involved in behavior.

Physiological explanations of behavior are very useful. Indeed, an important part of our understanding of the causes of behavior has a physiological basis. Yet, psychologists are acknowledging more and more that our biology only provides the groundwork for our behavior. As Maslow has suggested, our physiological needs must be satisfied (at least to some extent) before our emotional needs are to be satisfied. Clearly, our biological framework and its accompanying mechanisms that initiate behavior are involved with, and interact with, our learned social motives. Human behavior is far too complex to be explained by just one of these factors. Both physiology and learned behaviors ultimately shape everything people feel, think, and do.

CHAPTER REVIEW

1. Motivation is a general condition within an organism that produces goal-directed behavior. It is an inferred condition initiated by drives, needs, or desires.
2. A need is an aroused physiological condition involving an imbalance.
3. A drive is an aroused condition within the organism that initiates behavior so as to satisfy physiological needs. Drives are inferred from behavior.
4. A motive is a specific internal condition directing an organism's behavior toward a goal.
5. A mechanistic analysis of behavior views the organism as being pushed, pulled, and energized almost like a machine.
6. The principal physiological reason for feeling hungry is food deprivation and the low blood sugar level that accompanies it.
7. The hypothalamus is important in eating behavior. The ventromedial hypothalamus (VH) is a "stop" eating center; the lateral hypothalamus (LH) is a "start" eating center.
8. According to the fat-cell theory, each person is born with a certain number of fat cells that may increase or decrease in size with food intake.
9. According to the fat cell theory, a person's normal weight is determined by the *number* of fat cells he or she possesses.
10. Schachter has shown that obese adults eat not only when they are hungry, but also whenever food is presented.
11. Schachter has argued that the availability of food and other external cues stimulate obese subjects to eat. Schachter believes that in the obese, eating behavior is under *external* rather than internal control.
12. Both internal physiological mechanisms and external cues act to direct a person into behaviors that involve seeking out food.
13. Thirst, like hunger, is both physiologically and externally controlled.
14. While an organism can do without food for a couple of weeks, life is dependent upon replenishment of fluid within a few days.
15. Sexual responsiveness of lower organisms is primarily under hormonal control, whereas in humans, learning plays a greater role.
16. Organisms seem to have inborn drives toward sensory stimulation that do not seem to be learned.
17. A special process of attachment occurs between a mother and baby during the first few moments of life.
18. Approach-approach conflicts are situations in which a person must decide on one of two equally pleasant goals.
19. Approach-avoidance conflicts are situations in which a person must deal with a situation that has both appealing and repelling aspects to it.
20. The Yerkes-Dodson law is a principle stating that when a person's anxiety and level of arousal are too high or too low, performance is usually not particularly good.
21. According to optimal arousal theories, individuals seek an optimal level of stimulation. Behavior varies from disorganized, to effective, to optimal depending on the person's level of arousal.
22. A social motive is a condition that directs humans toward maintaining or establishing feelings about ourselves, others, and relationships.
23. A social need is an aroused condition within an organism involving feelings about ourselves, others, and relationships.

24. There are many social motives, including needs for affiliation, achievement, arrangement, and organization.
25. A need for achievement is a social need that directs a person to succeed and to strive constantly for excellence and success.
26. In the Thematic Apperception Test (TAT), subjects respond to vague pictures and describe what is happening.
27. Anxiety is the vague, uncomfortable feeling that accompanies the fear of the unknown. In relation to need for achievement, anxiety refers to fear of failure.
28. Need for achievement is a learned motive taught by parents, friends, school setting, and culture.
29. Each person's need for achievement will vary. It is possible to have high needs for achievement in some areas of life and low needs in other areas.
30. Many behaviors that are under both physiological and emotional control can be modified through thought processes.
31. Intrinsically motivated behaviors are behaviors which a person engages in to feel competent and self-determining.
32. Extrinsic rewards generally decrease intrinsically motivated behavior.
33. Maslow, a humanistic psychologist, developed a theory of motivation that assumes that all people are basically good and that they strive for self-actualization.
34. Self-actualization is the process of moving toward realizing one's potential to the greatest degree possible; it is the process of achieving everything that one is capable of.
35. Harry Harlow's monkeys, deprived of their natural mothers, sought the love of terrycloth-covered wire mothers rather than plain wire ones.
36. Facial expressions of emotion are present early in infancy; even 3- and 4-month-old infants respond differently to happy faces than they do to sad faces.
37. The self-regulation view of emotional expression is cognitive; it stresses that the individuals manage or determine their emotional state in a willful way.
38. Emotions are aroused states within an organism that may occur in response to internal and external stimuli; they are usually accompanied by marked physiological changes.
39. The James-Lange theory of emotion argues that people experience physiological changes and then interpret the causes of these changes.
40. The Cannon theory of emotion argues that two areas of the brain are stimulated simultaneously, one creating emotional response, the other creating physiological changes.
41. The Schachter-Singer theory of emotion suggests that people interpret physiological changes within the context of a situation; context provides the cue to what the physiological changes mean.
42. Arousal is directly related to emotional feelings; we see little emotion unless there is arousal. A person's behavior is going to be affected by his motivation, his emotional state including arousal, and by his ability.
43. High motivation without ability will not yield optimal performance; similarly, high ability with little motivation shows inadequate performance.

SUGGESTIONS FOR FURTHER READING

BOLES, R. C. *Theory of motivation.* New York: Harper & Row, 1975.

SCHACHTER, S. *Emotion, obesity, and crime.* New York: Academic Press, 1971.

SCHACHTER, S., AND RODIN, T. J. *Obese humans and rats.* Potomac, MD: L. Erlbaum Associates, 1974.

STUART, R. B., AND DAVIS, B. *Slim chance in a fat world.* Champaign, IL: Research Press Company, 1972.

WEINER, B. *Human motivation.* New York: Holt, Rinehart and Winston, 1980.

SEEING AND HEARING are important dimensions of life because they allow us to experience the environment fully; they provide depth to our experience by allowing us to distinguish among objects and sounds. Our senses allow us to adapt effectively to the environment. Animals use their senses to find shelter and food; similarly, humans would not be able to cope without their senses. Our senses do not act alone but are part of a perceptual system that allows us to receive and interpret events in the environment. So, perception is not only seeing and hearing, but also interpreting events in the world into meaningful patterns of information.

MECHANISMS
    Structure of the Visual System
    Electrical Activity in the Visual System
EYE MOVEMENTS
    Saccades
COLOR VISION
    Color Coding
    Color Blindness
SENSORY EXPERIENCE
    Interacting Systems
    Sensory Deprivation
FORM PERCEPTION
    Perceptual Constancy
    Depth
    Illusions
    Gestalt Laws of Organization
COMPLEX PERCEPTUAL PROCESSES
    Reading
    Visual Search
    Attention
    Imagery
    Subliminal Perception
OTHER PERCEPTUAL SYSTEMS
    Hearing
    Hearing Impairment
    Taste and Smell
    Kinesthesis and Vestibular Sensitivity
    Pain
    Extrasensory Perception

SPECIAL FEATURES:

IMPACT: *Seeing with the Skin*
RESEARCH PROFILE 5: *Imagine That*
IN THE NEWS: *The New War on Pain*

CHAPTER 5

Perception

The most important day I remember in all my life is the one on which my teacher, Anne Mansfield Sullivan, came to me. I am filled with wonder when I consider the immeasurable contrasts between the two lives which it connects. It was the third of March, 1887, three months before I was seven years old.

On the afternoon of that eventful day, I stood on the porch, dumb, expectant. I guessed vaguely from my mother's signs and from the hurrying to and fro in the house that something unusual was about to happen, so I went to the door and waited on the steps. The afternoon sun penetrated the mass of honeysuckle that covered the porch, and fell on my upturned face. My fingers lingered almost unconsciously on the familiar leaves and blossoms which had just come forth to greet the sweet southern spring. I did not know what the future held of marvel or surprise for me. Anger and bitterness had preyed upon me continually for weeks and a deep languor had succeeded this passionate struggle.

Have you ever been at sea in a dense fog, when it seemed as if a tangible white darkness shut you in, and the great ship, tense and anxious, groped her way toward the shore with plummet and sounding-line, and you waited with beating heart for something to happen? I was like that ship before my education began, only I was without compass or sound-line, and had no way of knowing how near the harbour was. "Light! give me light!" was the wordless cry of my soul, and the light of love shone on me that very hour. . . .

HELEN KELLER
The Story of My Life

The blind and the deaf have disabilities that impair their ability to function. Yet Helen Keller, an incredible person, overcame her disabilities and coped with life and all of its challenges. Her challenge was enormous, but so were her abilities. With the inability to see or hear, even the simplest task was not easy for her. Helen Keller's perceptual systems slowed her perceptual growth but did not limit it. Her experiences make us appreciate our own rich and varied perceptual systems.

Consider the task of looking for a friend in a darkened theater. Even if you know your friend is a male, has blond hair, brown eyes, and is about six feet tall, finding him is usually difficult. Within a few minutes he is easier to find because the dark theater doesn't seem so dark. We all know that within a few minutes our eyes adapt to darkness; in fact, our visual system becomes more sensitive in the dark. In a lighted room, there are hundreds of objects in front of us; when we search for an object in a complex scene, we must be able to sort out part of that scene which includes faces, shirts, eyes, hair, screens, seats, lights, signs, and paintings. Each object is made up of many subparts of a variety of colors; to find our blond friend we have to choose the relevant features.

The task for our visual system is enormous. In a dark theater, many available cues are gone; for example, color information is no longer available; fine detail is difficult to see; objects may not stand out from the background. Even when these cues are available, how do we find one person among thousands? In many ways, this question represents the task of perception. The individual is presented with a wide visual array composed of many parts and must then make a meaningful interpretation.

The problem becomes more complex when you consider that there are other perceptual systems. The auditory system has many of the same challenges as the visual. Listening to a symphony orchestra we must learn to dis-

Our perceptual systems can pick the important stimulus out of the confusion of various stimuli in the environment.

tinguish among the different instruments. Standing at a crowded party, we can hear many conversations taking place and have to decide to listen to one conversation and block out other speakers. In the same way, it is impossible to listen to two lectures at the same time; while we can shift attention between lectures, we can't give full attention to both.

We all realize, of course, that in both humans and animals the perceptual systems are *not* independent of one another; they act together. Consider what happens when we read subtitles at a foreign movie. If we understand the audible language we move our eyes along the subtitles *and* listen; we are able to distinguish discrepancies because our visual and auditory systems are working together. When we ride a bike, our visual, auditory, and motor systems work together—all three work to coordinate successive actions. The analysis of stimuli and the use of this analysis is the task of perception. **Perception** is the process by which we attach meaning to stimuli by interpreting sensory input; this process is complicated and involves several levels of analysis within the nervous system. We will attempt to analyze perception mainly through the visual system and through the use of examples from other senses wherever appropriate.

Without our perceptual systems, we would be like vegetables. Perceptual systems allow us to interact with the environment; they allow us to receive stimuli, to gain understanding from stimuli, and then to act. What happens when part of this process breaks down? The blind and deaf are perfect examples of people who have experienced a breakdown in the perceptual apparatus. The blind cannot see and this certainly hampers their ability to get about, read, and learn. The deaf not only cannot hear, but, because hearing is used so much in speech, those who are born deaf rarely learn to talk. Again, we can see that our perceptual systems affect one another. Now, let's look at our visual system in some detail.

Perception The process by which people attach meaning to stimuli by interpreting their sensory input through complex processing mechanisms.

Our brains have an amazing ability to process information from many sensory inputs.

MECHANISMS

Perceptual systems respond to many types of stimuli. For example, one can stimulate the visual system by applying pressure to the eye. A more effective way to create a visual experience is to use the appropriate stimulus for vision—light or **electromagnetic radiation.** Electromagnetic radiation includes light, cosmic rays, x-rays, ultraviolet, infrared, and radar waves. **Light** represents only a small portion of those possible wavelengths, from 400 to 750 nanometers (a nanometer is 1 billionth of a meter). Light strikes the photoreceptors in the eye after coming directly from a source, or after being reflected from some other object. This is the first step in the perceptual process and really represents the first stage in the analysis of stimuli—the first stage of perception. Of course, to understand how this first stage of analysis takes place, you need to understand something about the structure or mechanics of the visual system.

Structure of the Visual System

In some ways, the eye can be thought of as a camera with a lens at the front and film at the back. The film, which is trying to record the visual world, is the retina. Let's take a closer look.

There are many important structures in the eye; while all are important, the most significant are presented in Figure 5.1. Light is transmitted through the *cornea* at the front of the eye. The cornea is the small transparent bulge that covers the pigmented *iris*. The iris constricts or dilates to make the *pupil* smaller or larger. Light passes through the pupil to the *crystalline lens.* Both the cornea and the lens help form images in much the same way a lens in a camera forms images. When the iris constricts and the pupil is made smaller, the quality of the image on the photoreceptors is improved; there is increased depth of focus; and the light level on the photoreceptors is decreased.

Electromagnetic radiation The entire spectrum of waves initiated by charged particles, including gamma rays, x-rays, ultraviolet, visual, infrared, and radar waves.

Light The portion of the electromagnetic spectrum (wavelengths from 400 to 750 nanometers) that is visible to the eye.

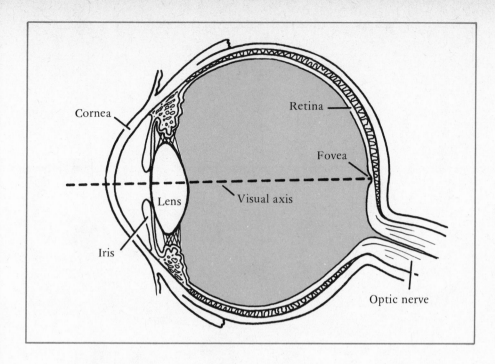

Figure 5.1 The main structures of the eye. Notice that the fovea is the central portion of the receptor layer called the retina. The photoreceptors connect to higher brain pathways through the optic nerve

The **photoreceptors,** which are responsive to light, line the back part of the eye and make up the tissue that is called the *retina*.

RETINA.   Without a retina, we would not be able to see—it contains the photoreceptors that are responsive to light. The impact stemming from automobile accidents sometimes causes the retina to detach. A detached retina is one that is no longer held in place at the back of the eye; people with detached retinas are unable to form clear visual images.

The thin tissue that makes up the retina is really made up of ten layers of cells. It provides the first analysis of visual information (see Figure 5.2). Of the 10 layers, 3 layers are especially important. The first is the layer of the photoreceptors themselves, the *rods* and the *cones*. Light causes an electrochemical change in the rods and cones, and electrical energy from them is transferred to the next major layer, the *bipolar layer*. Impulses from the bipo-

Photoreceptor   The two types of light-sensitive cells in the retina—rods and cones.

THE WIZARD OF ID by permission of Johnny Hart and Field Enterprises, Inc.

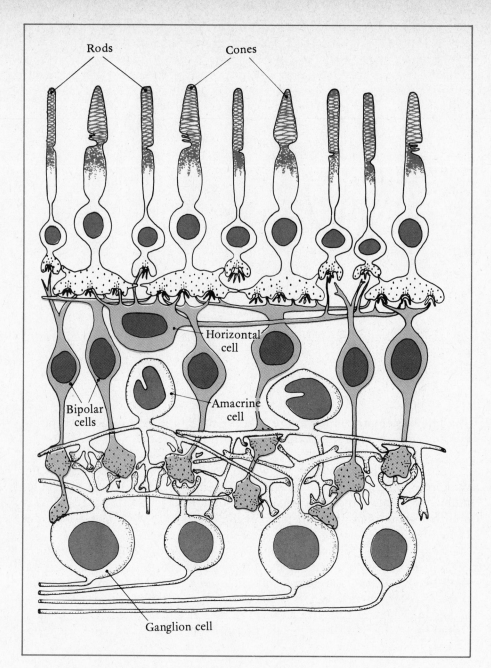

Rods

Cones

Horizontal
cell

Bipolar
cells

Amacrine
cell

Ganglion cell

Figure 5.2 Diagram of the neural interconnections in the three layers of a primate retina. Rods and cones comprise the first layer. The second major layer has three types of bipolar cells; connecting cells called amacrine and horizontal are also in this layer. The third major layer of cells are ganglion cells. Note the optic nerve fiber leaving the ganglion cells at the bottom of the figure (Dowling and Boycott, 1966)

lar layer are then transmitted to the *ganglion cells,* which make up the nuclei of the cells forming the *optic* nerve. So, even this very first stage of processing is complicated. The retina, composed of three basic layers (photoreceptors, bipolar, and ganglion), uses light to trigger electrical impulses which, in turn, are eventually conveyed to the optic nerve.

In each eye, there are 120 million rods and 6 million cones. These 126 million photoreceptors do not have separate pathways toward higher visual centers; rather, many of them converge and synapse on bipolar cells, and many bipolar cells converge on ganglion cells. This is the process by which several cells come to stimulate the dendrites of one other cell. So, many rods and cones come to stimulate just one bipolar cell; similarly, many bipolar cells converge on one ganglion cell. There are only 1 million optic nerve fibers; the 126 million photoreceptors eventually converge on these 1 million optic nerve fibers.

By now you have begun to see that the visual system, even at the level of the eye itself, analyzes stimuli and converts them into electrical impulses in complex ways. This is the process of coding. As electrical information proceeds through the nervous system, more and more convergence takes place and even more complex analysis continues.

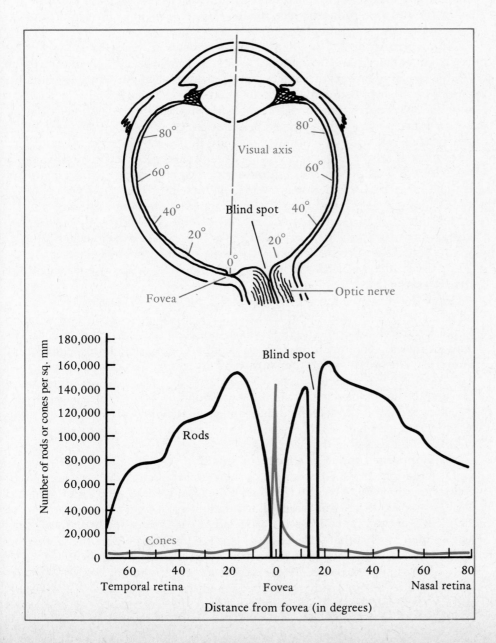

Figure 5.3 Top view of the left eye, and the corresponding densities of rods and cones across the retina

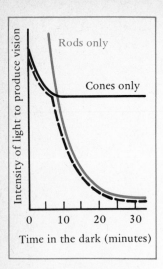

Figure 5.4 The dashed line represents a typical overall dark adaptation curve. The two solid lines represent separate dark adaptation for rods and cones. The process of light and dark adaptation is continually taking place a people's eyes are exposed to different light intensities. Notice that after 10 minutes the majority of dark adaptation has taken place

Dark adaptation The process by which chemicals in the photoreceptors regenerate and return to their inactive pre-light-adapted state, (this results in an increase in sensitivity).

DUPLICITY THEORY.   Researchers have had an idea of how the visual system operates for a long time. Well over a century ago, scientists suggested the existence of different types of photoreceptors like rods and cones. Even without fancy microscopes and advanced technology, the *duplicity theory* of vision was established. The duplicity theory suggests that vision is controlled by two classes of receptors whose functions are different.

Consider some of the differences between rods and cones. First, rods and cones are not evenly distributed across the retina. The fovea in the center of the retina contains only tightly packed cones. As can be seen from Figure 5.3, in other portions of the retina there are mainly rods with a relatively small number of cones. The distribution of receptors over the retina is important because rods and cones are responsible for different tasks. Cones are responsible for day vision, color vision, and judgments that involve fine discrimination. By contrast, rods are predominantly used for night vision and do not allow fine visual discrimination.

Other support for the duplicity theory has been provided by studies of dark adaptation. When we walk into a darkened theater and have difficulty looking for another person, it is because our eyes have not adapted to the dark. When this adjustment does occur, there is an increase in our ability to discern other objects in the dark. If people are brought into a darkened room and are then shown a spot light for a brief period, their sensitivity to the light is very low; yet, within 30 minutes they are fully adapted to the dark and much more sensitive to the light. As the eye becomes more sensitive, chemicals within the rods and cones return to their original inactivated pre-light-adapted state. **Dark adaptation** is the process by which chemicals in the photoreceptors regenerate and return to their inactive pre-light-adapted state. This results in an increase in sensitivity. When you closely examine the dark adaptation curve (see Figure 5.4), you see that there are two branches. The first section of the curve is determined by cones, whereas the second section of the curve is determined by rods. The speed at which rods and cones regenerate determines the shape of these two branches.

Obtaining data like those in Figure 5.4 is done in an experiment where subjects are asked to indicate if they can see a small and very dim patch of light. A typical experiment might be conducted like this: subjects are brought into a laboratory where they are shown a bright adapting light for 2 minutes. The bright light is then turned off and the subjects wait in a totally dark room. After 30 seconds in the dark, a very dim test spot is turned on for $\frac{1}{2}$ second. If the subjects see the light they respond by saying, "yes, I see it." It is likely that after a couple of minutes and several more presentations of the test spot, subjects will see the light. Just as when you enter a movie theater, the likelihood of seeing the test patch increases as time passes.

Many important variables affect your sensitivity to light and the resulting dark adaptation curve. For example, if the adapting light was *very* intense, your adaptation would be different than if the light were relatively dim. Similarly, if the adapting light were yellow, dark adaptation would take longer than if it were red (your receptors are relatively less sensitive to red wavelengths than to any other wavelengths—see Figure 5.12, p. 203). Many other variables have been documented over the years (Alpern, Rushton, & Torii, 1970; Barlow, 1972; Rushton, 1965). Studies of dark adaptation and the variables that affect it have taught us much about the visual system in general, and the duplicity theory specifically.

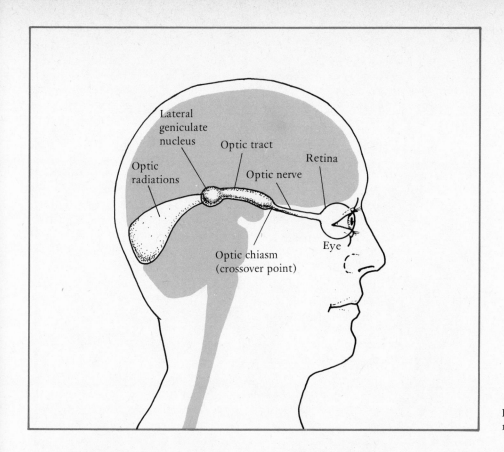

Lateral
geniculate
nucleus

Optic tract

Retina

Optic
radiations

Optic nerve

Optic chiasm
(crossover point)

Eye

Figure 5.5 The major components of the visual system

You should be able to see that both the structure and the function of the eye, and particularly the retina, are very complex and involve a fair degree of specialization and coding. At this stage the visual input has not even left the eye for more complex analysis!

HIGHER PATHWAYS.   As impulses leave the retina through the optic tract, they proceed via some complicated routes to higher centers of analysis. Both of our eyes have connections to both sides of our brain. Some impulses go directly from the eye to the same side of the brain that the eye is on, while other impulses cross over to the other side of the brain. This crossing over of impulses from the two eyes to the different sides of the brain helps us to have form perception. The point at which the impulses cross from the two eyes is called the *optic chiasm.* You can imagine that if the optic nerves were severed at the optic chiasm a strange type of vision would occur. Normally, however, impulses proceed to higher brain structures which process visual information, such as the *lateral geniculate nucleus,* and still further on to the *striate cortex.*

Electrical Activity in the Visual System

Stimulation of the photoreceptors brings about changes in the electrical activity of the visual system. This change in activity is shown at all levels of the visual system and is fairly easy to examine with the use of single-unit recording.

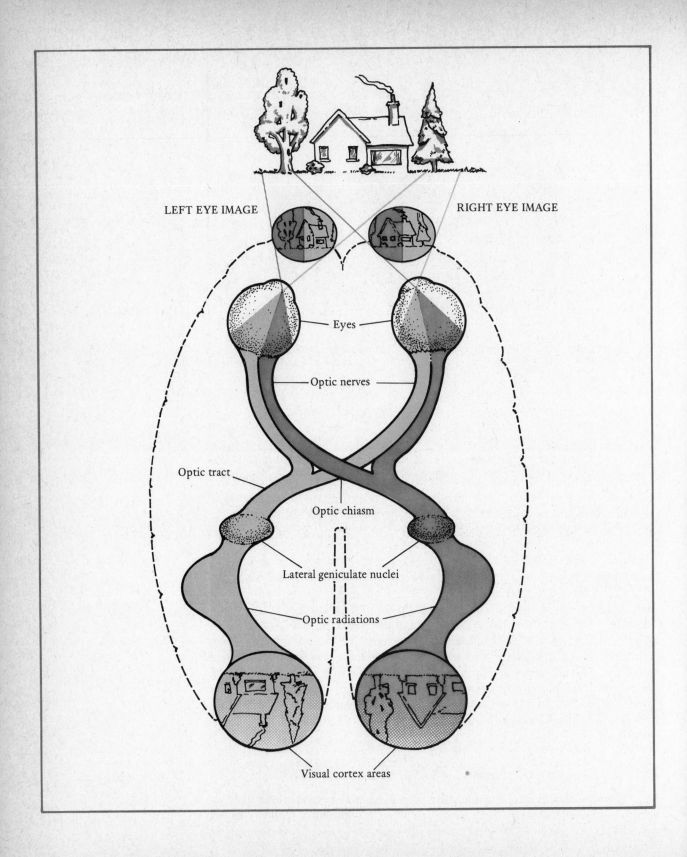

LEFT EYE IMAGE

RIGHT EYE IMAGE

Eyes

Optic nerves

Optic tract

Optic chiasm

Lateral geniculate nuclei

Optic radiations

Visual cortex areas

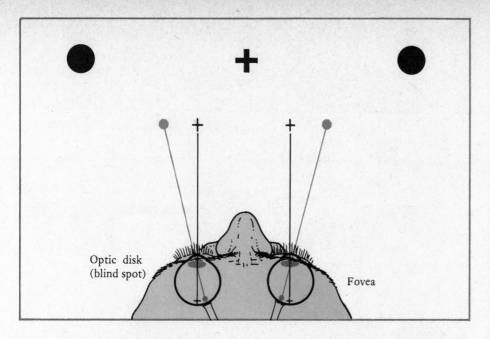

Figure 5.7 As is shown in Figure 5.3, the distribution of rods and cones on the retina is not even. At the center of the retina (the fovea) there are no rods, only cones. At about 18° of visual angle (a measure of size of images on the retina) there are no receptors at all—this is the place where the optic nerve leaves the eye, called the blind spot. Because the blind spot for each eye is on the nasal side of the eyeball there is no loss of vision—the two blindspots do not overlap. To demonstrate that you have a blindspot, close one eye and stare at the fixation spot and move the page in and out while staring at the spot. The black spot will disappear. If you switch eyes, the blind spot for the other eye will be apparent. Once you have located the correct distance, you might move the tip of a pencil along the book until it reaches the blind spot and watch the tip disappear. (Carlson, 1981)

Optic disk (blind spot)

Fovea

Receptive field The area of the retina that, when stimulated, produces a change in the firing of a single cell in the visual system.

As we saw in chapter 2, the electrical activity of a single cell can be examined by placing an electrode within or next to the cell. This type of single-unit recording has been done extensively with the visual system to see if it might provide any hints as to how people see form, shape, and color. In these studies, stimuli of different sizes and shapes have been shown to organisms; at the same time the activity levels of single cells in the visual system are recorded. In doing this, psychologists have identified certain receptive fields; a **receptive field** is an area on the retina that, when stimulated, produces changes in the firing of cells in the visual system. For example, if a vertical line is shown, certain cells will fire; but if a horizontal line is presented, they will not. As shown in Figure 5.8, Hubel and Weisel (1962) found cells in the visual system that are sensitive to the position of a line, its length, its movement, its color, and its intensity; their work earned them a Nobel prize in 1981. Of particular importance is their discovery that coding becomes more complex as we proceed through the visual system; so the visual cortex analyzes information that the retinal ganglion cells do not.

The analysis of single cells in the visual system not only tells us how the visual system operates, but also allows us to speculate how the visual system may be involved in perceiving form. Single cells respond differently to stimuli, so they must code stimuli in this way for a reason. We have said that some cells respond to vertical lines and other cells respond to horizontal lines. When two vertical lines are placed perpendicular to a horizontal line, one can perceive the letter H. Cells in the visual system respond simultaneously, and so input from both the cells responding to the horizontal line and input from the cells responding to the vertical line may have been analyzed together. Although the combined input idea of form perception is speculative, it might be the kind of analysis that enables individuals to rec-

Figure 5.6 As seen from above, this view of the basic components of the visual system clearly shows that information from each eye crosses at the optic chiasm.

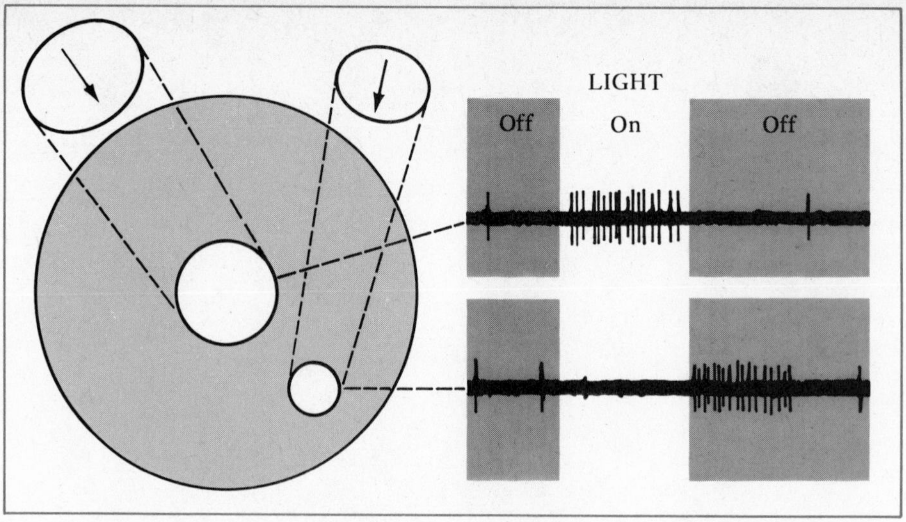

Figure 5.8 Hubel and Wiesel (1962) have found cells that will fire when stimulated in the center of the field to which they respond, but will not fire—and instead produce suppression—when stimulated on the outside of that center area

ognize form. However, many psychologists would argue that single cells form the basis for all of form perception. The idea is intriguing.

While ideas about how patterns are perceived are still being explained, we recognize that data about the electrical activity in the nervous system provides a great deal of information about how the visual system is organized, and particularly about how it develops. Consider a study reported by Hirsch and Spinelli (1971). They raised newborn kittens under conditions where the kittens' visual experiences were controlled. The kittens wore goggles that allowed only vertical lines to be exposed to one eye and horizontal lines to the other eye. After a few weeks, Hirsch and Spinelli found that the kittens' receptive fields were oriented either horizontally or vertically. They found that the vertically oriented cells were almost exclusively made to fire by the eye which had been exposed to vertical lines. Similarly, the eye that was exposed to horizontal lines stimulated cells that were horizontally activated. In a normal cat 80 to 90% of the cells in the cortex are activated by both eyes. Kittens in such studies also showed some interesting behaviors: kittens raised with horizontal experiences bumped into chair legs but could leap into the seat, while the kittens raised with vertical experiences had opposite problems (e.g., Blakemore & Cooper, 1970). These data are important because they show that the organization of the visual system is sensitive to experience. Most normal organisms experience many different (vertical, horizontal, and oblique) orientations in their environment. Although the visual system is largely built-in and has most of its connections available to the newborn, it is clearly affected by experience (see also Muir & Mitchell, 1973).

Understanding how electrical activity in the nervous system is transmitted and coded provides an enormous wealth of data. These data help psychologists to understand some of the basics about electrical coding, form perception, and coding development. Breakthroughs in the understanding of electrical coding are continuing to allow psychologists to make a careful analysis of how our visual system operates.

Neither humans nor animals are passive, but are active in constantly seeking out new types of stimulation. Our electrical coding system records these changes, and one of the principal ways that it gathers new information is through a complex system of eye movements.

Your eyes are constantly in motion; perhaps they are searching for a familiar face in a crowded auditorium or moving across a page of printed text. They follow ping-pong balls and tennis balls, as well as moving automobiles. An examination of eye movements can tell observers what people are looking at, how long they look at it, and perhaps where they will look next.

Making eye movements in the correct direction can be a problem for children who have difficulty reading. Consider a case study reported by Zangwill and Blakemore (1972). They found a male adult subject who was having difficulty reading. He would traditionally be diagnosed as reading disabled. By studying his eye movements, Zangwill and Blakemore found that the man was moving his eyes from right-to-left across a page, rather than in the normal left-to-right direction. They were forced to conclude that this subject's inappropriate eye movements were causing his reading disability. Some more recent studies of eye movements have shown that poor readers' eye movements are erratic and chaotic (Lefton et al., 1979).

Saccades

When our eyes move rapidly from one position to another, they are making a type of eye movement called **saccades,** jumping from one fixed position to another. Generally, saccadic eye movements are voluntary. They take about 20 to 50 milliseconds to execute, and little information is available during them (Matin, 1974, 1976; Volkmann, 1962, 1976). An interesting aspect of saccades is that it takes 250 milliseconds (one-quarter of a second) before an eye movement can be made. Once an eye movement command has been made, there is a delay of 250 milliseconds—this means that the eye can only make five saccades a second, at most!

Complicated devices have been invented that allow an experimenter to examine where a subject's eyes are fixating, how long they are fixating, and where the eyes moved from (Anliker, 1976; Young, 1976). In a study of eye movements and perception by Noton and Stark (1971), subjects were asked to look at a series of pictures. They were told that they would have to remember these pictures and choose them from another group somewhat later. During the learning phase of this experiment, the subject's eye movements were recorded. In subsequent testing, they were shown these same pictures in a group of other pictures; eye movement recordings were made again. Noton and Stark found that subjects tended to fixate on certain areas of each picture. They found fixed scan paths specific to both the subject and picture in both the learning and recognition phases of the experiment. The researchers suggest that this fixed pattern of eye movements is used in the perception and recognition of form with the subjects following a fixed path from feature to feature.

Noton and Stark suggest that eye movements are an integral part of our memory. In their view, we not only remember the picture because of some complex perceptual process, but also because of the nature of our eye movements. As shown in Figure 5.9, our eyes generally tend to fixate on important aspects of a visual array. Rarely does a subject look at blank space; he or she usually fixates upon important features such as eyes, nose, hand, or mouth. In any case, there are strong individual differences among scan paths. Perhaps there are personality correlates that might allow us to distinguish types

Saccades Rapid movements of the eyes from one position to another. The minimum fixation period between saccades is $\frac{1}{4}$ of a second.

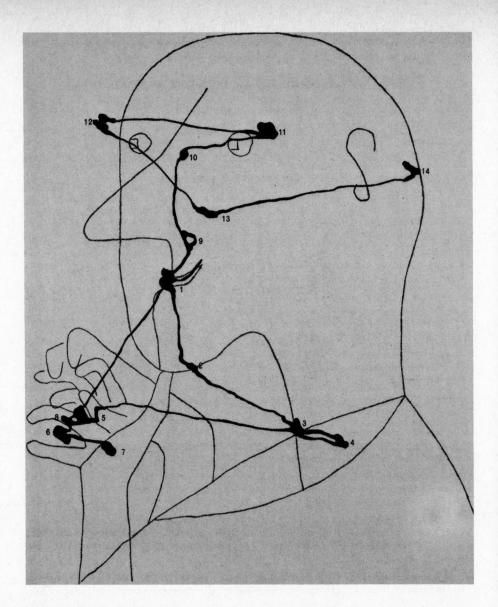

Figure 5.9 Eye movements made by a subject viewing a drawing adapted from Paul Klee's *Old Man Figuring*. The numbers show the order of the subject's visual fixations. Lines between the numbers represent saccades, which occupied about 10% of viewing time. The remainder of the time was spent fixating

of individuals based on their eye movements! This possibility remains unexplored.

COLOR VISION

Humans are able to discriminate color, which provides another dimension to our experience. The color of an object is determined by the wavelength of light that is reflected from it. As is shown in the endpaper figures, the visible spectrum has different hues associated with different wavelenghts; a light of 400 nanometers looks blue, and a light of 700 nanometers looks red. Also, different surfaces reflect different wavelengths; so, surfaces that reflect primarily blue light will appear blue in color because the reflected light is limited to blue wavelengths (see Nassau, 1980).

Seeing with the Skin

If you were to become blind, all would not be lost; modern science is in the process of developing a device that can help you "see" the world. An experiment has been reported at the Pacific Medical Center in which an apparatus was used to help the blind "see" (White et al., 1970). These researchers took a TV-like camera and focused it on an object. This image was sent to a matrix of 400 vibrators placed close to one another in an area of about 10 square inches. There was a close correspondence between the TV image and the bank of vibrators. Each vibrator was designed to move when its position was within an illuminated region of the camera field. Both blind and normal subjects had this vibrating attachment placed against their backs (see Figure 5.10).

Blind subjects were able to make spatial discrimination and line orientation judgments comparable to sighted subjects. Blind subjects were also able to experience change in the size of an image as an object was brought closer to or further away from the TV camera. The apparatus described by these researchers is cumbersome, crude, and inappropriate for anything but laboratory research at the present time. However, the possibilities of developing a miniaturized system that would help blind people to move about and perhaps "see" their world is most intriguing. The miniaturization of computer technology may make such artificial vision a possibility in the near future.

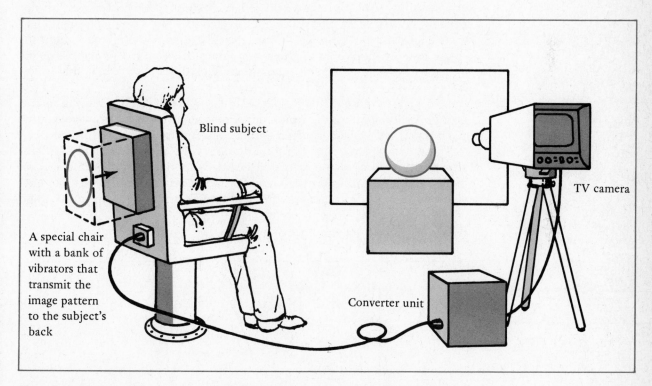

Figure 5.10 Blind individuals can have artificial vision through devices such as vibrators that can stimulate portions of their skin and convey picturelike information

There are three main properties of color: hue, brightness, and saturation. These are psychological terms that describe, respectively, the wavelength, intensity, and purity of light. Since these three properties are independent of each other, each will be discussed separately.

Hue The psychological property of light referred to as color and determined by its wavelength.

What is the relationship of hue to wavelength? When people speak of color they are referring to its hue—that is, whether the light looks red, blue, or orange. The **hue** of an object is determined by the wavelengths of the light it reflects. Light of short wavelengths looks blue; light of long wavelengths looks red. Hue is a psychological term; wavelength is a physical term. This is an important distinction, because objects do not possess color; rather, color is a psychological term attributed to the wavelengths reflected by an object. Our perception of color is determined by the wavelengths that reach our eyes. Look at what happens when we wear rose-colored glasses. The object that we look at is really not reflecting long (red) wavelengths; rather, our glasses have changed the wavelength mixture that falls on our retina. Remember, the color of an object is determined by the wavelengths of light that fall on the retina.

Brightness The lightness or darkness of reflected light.

The second major aspect of the color experience is brightness; the **brightness** of a patch of light refers to its lightness or darkness. Brightness is affected by three variables. First, the reflected light may have more energy than a less bright light. Second, long wavelengths have less energy than short wavelengths. Third, as shown in Figure 5.11, the photoreceptors are not equally sensitive or responsive to all wavelengths; they are most sensitive to wavelengths in the 500 to 600 nanometer range. So, although one might increase the energy of a light, the brightness of the object will also be determined by its reflected wavelength and the sensitivity of the eye to that wavelength.

Saturation The "depth" of hue of reflected light as determined by the purity (homogeneity) of the different wavelengths comprising the light.

A third way to describe the nature of color is through its saturation and purity. A **saturated** light is a pure one; it has a narrow band of wavelengths. A saturated red looks very deep and becomes pink when desaturated.

These two sets of terms—hue, saturation, brightness, wavelength, intensity, purity—describe the nature of the color experience from both a psychological and a physical point of view. It is appropriate to use terms like hue, saturation, and brightness together and terms like wavelength, purity, and

Figure 5.11 Spectral sensitivity of the average observer. Peak sensitivity at 555 nanometers has been set at a value of 1. The eye is therefore more sensitive to yellow wavelengths than to reds or blues

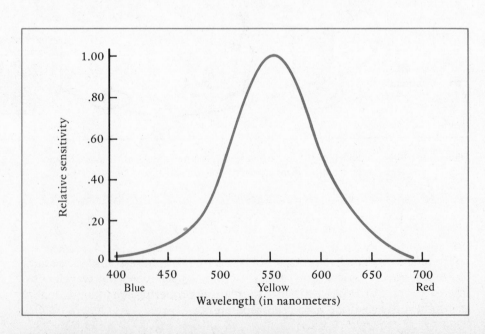

intensity together; psychological terms and physical terms should not be used interchangeably. Psychological experiences are related to, but not directly determined by, the physical characteristics of an object. A woman may wear rose-colored glasses and her perception—her psychological experience—of the world becomes tinged with pink.

Color Coding

We already know that the stimulus for color vision is light of various wavelengths. Light proceeds through the optics of the eye and stimulates photoreceptors—rods and cones. But we must remember that the rods and cones are not equally sensitive to different wavelengths. There are three classes of cones, each of which is maximally sensitive to different wavelengths. As shown in Figure 5.12, there are cones that are maximally sensitive to the short wavelength range, to the midwavelength range, and to the long wavelength range. When a cone is stimulated by a light to which it is not maximally sensitive, it will fire, but not as often.

We can see that these different types of cones, each with a different maximum sensitivity, may provide a basis for the coding of color in the nervous system. This is precisely what was proposed during the nineteenth century by two scientists, Young and Helmholtz, who developed similar theories of how people experience color. After their deaths, their theories were combined and named for them; the Young-Helmholtz theory of color vision is also sometimes called the **trichromatic theory.** According to this theory, all colors can be made by mixing the three basic colors (trichromatic, *three colors*). The combination of the neural output of the three types of cone receptors provides information to distinguish color. If the neural output of one type of cone is sufficiently great, then the color experience will be determined mainly by that cone color receptor. Combinations of neural output will provide us with different experiences of color.

Trichromatic theory Theory of Young and Helmholtz stating that all colors can be made by mixing basic colors of red, blue, and green.

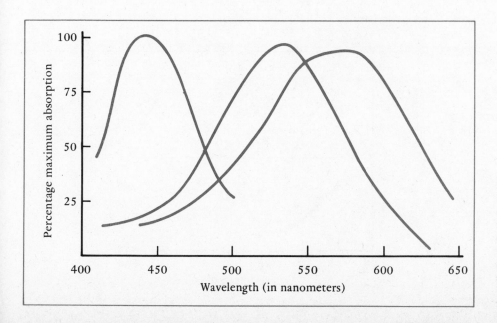

Figure 5.12 Sensitivity distributions for three types of cones in the eye of the primate. Notice that each of the distributions has a peak sensitivity in a different area of the electromagnetic spectrum; this suggests that certain cells may be more responsive to these wavelengths than to others

Hering proposed another theory of color coding around 1887. This **opponent process theory** suggests that color is coded by a series of receptors that respond either positively or negatively to different wavelengths. Thus, a red-green receptor would respond positively to a red light and negatively to a green light. There is a fundamental difference between these two theories; the trichromatic theory assumes three types of receptors, each maximally sensitive to one group of wavelengths. By contrast, the opponent process theory assumes that receptors respond positively or negatively to different wavelengths.

The trichromatic theory and the opponent process theory have both received research support. Support for the trichromatic theory has come from studies of the chemistry and absorption properties of the retina, which show three different classes of cones (see Figure 5.12) (see Marks, Doble, & MacNichol, 1964). Support for the opponent process theory has come from microelectrode studies of the lateral geniculate nucleus in monkeys. These studies show that cells at the lateral geniculate nucleus respond differently to input from different wavelengths. As shown in Figure 5.13, when a cell is stimulated with a light of 400 to 500 nanometers, it produces decreases in the response rate of the cell. When this same cell is stimulated with lights of longer wavelengths, its frequency of firing increases. These data suggest an opponent process system (Devalois & Jacobs, 1968).

These two major theories of color vision are not incompatible. The trichromatic theory best describes how information is coded at the retina. The opponent process theory best describes how information is coded at the lateral geniculate nucleus (e.g., Hurvich & Jameson, 1974). The way information is transferred from the retina to the lateral geniculate nucleus, and how this transfer takes place, is still unclear. Yet, psychologists' best description of the nature of color coding is that both theories are partially correct. Much of the original data collected in support of these theories came from people who were not experiencing color in a normal way. In fact, people who were color blind helped form the original theories of color vision.

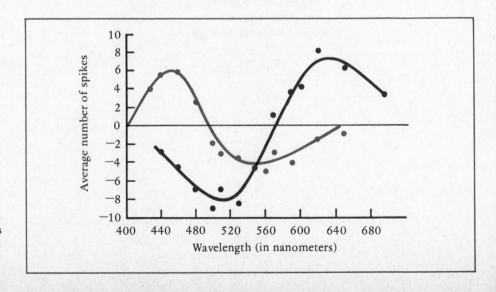

Figure 5.13 These data show two cells in the visual system. Each responds differently to different wavelengths with increases in activity or decreases in activity that depend on the wavelength of the stimulating light

Color Blindness

There are people known as **monochromats** who have only rods in their eyes and cannot distinguish among different hues. These individuals are very rare and are truly **color blind.** More often, individuals who are considered color blind are really people who are color deficient; these individuals, called **anomalous trichromats,** make up about 6% of men and .5% of women (Wyszecki & Stiles, 1967). The extent of the weakness varies, as do the wavelengths affected. Some **dichromats** have deficiencies in the red areas and some in the blue areas. In each case, a lack of a specific color-absorbing pigment in the cone system makes accurate color discriminations impossible. About 2% of males are dichromats and have an inability to discriminate between reds and greens (Wyszecki & Stiles, 1967). This not only affects the way they choose their clothes, it also has more important implications. Consider traffic lights, for example: they are red, yellow, and green. A person with a red-green deficiency not only has trouble distinguishing red and green, but both colors look yellow—the third traffic light! Red-green deficiencies are sex-linked traits transmitted through a female (who is not likely to be afflicted with it) to the next generation. An exact understanding of the genetics of color blindness is not yet available, but we do know that, like hemophilia, color blindness is a sex-linked characteristic. A breakdown of the different types of color-blind individuals is given in Table 5.1.

One of the most interesting and important results of studies of color-blind people has been the support provided for a color theory. If a person lacks a cone-color pigment and is unable to make certain color matches, then this would be reasonable evidence to suggest that the cone pigments are the first stage of color vision. Over the years, a number of individuals who have had color deficiencies have been examined in psychological laboratories to explore fully the nature of their color blindness. Individuals with red-green deficiencies are not exactly alike; some have peak sensitivities in different regions of the visible spectrum than do other people with red-green deficiencies. Furthermore, there are data that suggest that when one cone pigment is missing, it might be substituted with one of the other two cone pigments. Such a substitution would change the ways that a subject responds to various wavelengths; this is precisely what happens with color-blind individuals. Such persons often have a distorted response in some

Monochromats Persons with only rods in their retinas and who, therefore, cannot perceive hue.

Color blindness The inability to perceive different hues.

Anomolous trichromats Color-deficient individuals with weakness at various wavelengths. The extent of the color weakness varies.

Dichromats Persons who can distinguish only two of the three basic hues.

Table 5.1 Types of color blindness. Not everyone who exhibits some kind of color blindness has the same type of problem. Only monochromats are truly color blind—others have color weaknesses.

Monochromats	Total color blindness
Anomalous trichromats	
Protanomalous	Red weakness
Deuteranomalous	Green weakness
Dichromats	
Protanopes	Red blind
Deuteranopes	Green blind
Tritanopes	Blue blind

areas of the visible spectrum (e.g., Graham et al., 1961). Taken together, the data from color-blind individuals along with our knowledge of the physiology of rods and cones allows us to support further the trichromatic theory of color vision at the retinal level of processing.

SENSORY EXPERIENCE

Interacting Systems

Perceptual systems do not develop by themselves. The study by Hirsch and Spinelli (1971) showed that cells in the visual cortex of kittens were sensitive to experience. We argued from these data that the early experiences of kittens would partially determine how their visual systems would respond electrically. To develop fully, perceptual systems need more than just varied experience; they need to interact with each other. Look at eye-hand coordination: when a child reaches out to grasp an object, he or she has to coordinate the visual and touch systems. So, these two systems must learn to interact properly.

Let's examine a study of eye-hand coordination performed with monkeys by Held and Bauer (1967). Infant monkeys were raised in an apparatus that did not allow them to see all of their body parts (this was accomplished by placing a wide collar around each monkey's neck). After the monkeys were brought up in this manner, it was discovered that when they were allowed to see one of their hands, the monkeys looked at it for long periods of time. Furthermore, the monkeys' motor coordination in visually guided reaching was poor. According to Held and Bauer, the early experience of watching moving limbs provides necessary information for a monkey to direct arm reaching. They argued that both visual *and* motor information is coordinated by the two systems; if the two systems develop separately, there will be deficiencies in coordination. These data, therefore, strongly suggest that perceptual systems do not act independently of each other and that the systems must be coordinated.

We learn as children to experience the textures of our world.

Figure 5.14 Kittens were raised in a circular environment that allowed for either active or passive movement. Both kittens saw the same view of the world, yet showed dramatically different types of responses when tested in sensory-motor coordination

Further support for the necessity of coordination of perceptual systems was shown in another study conducted by Held (Held & Hein, 1963). Some kittens were placed in an environment that allowed active movements of their bodies as they explored the visual environment, while other kittens saw the same visual environment, but as a result of the first kitten's movements, not their own. As is shown in Figure 5.14, an active movement by the first kitten caused the identical, but not voluntary, movement of the second. As in the study reported by Held and Bauer, only kittens who were allowed to initiate voluntary movements were able to make good visually guided motor movements in later testing (see also, Melamed, Halay, & Gildow, 1973). More recent research by Held has shown that eye movements themselves, particularly in initial visual experiences, play an important role in subsequent visual behavior. In this study Held reported that when eye movements in cats were prevented, visual-motor development in the cat was retarded (Hein et al., 1979).

These studies by Richard Held show us that perceptual systems are interactive and work together. When a sensory or perceptual system is developing, varied experience is necessary as well as interaction among the systems. This type of finding is not limited to animal studies. Von Senden (1932) reported case histories of patients who had had cataracts from birth and, as adults, had had their lenses removed. A cataract is a lens clouding that essentially prevents patterned vision and can be corrected only with the removal of the lens. After surgery for cataracts, these adults saw for the first time. Von Senden reported that these patients had deficits in several skills. They had difficulty recognizing simple forms when they were in a different color or presented in a different situation. Here again human data show that the experience of our perceptual systems is critical to their efficient functioning.

Experience is important in the proper development and use of sensory systems. What would happen if a person were denied sensory experience? The Von Senden data suggest that perceptual development would be inadequate. Let's look at some experimental findings.

Sensory Deprivation

In studies of sensory deprivation, animals are deprived of sensory stimulation, such as light. These studies provide data about early experience and also deal with the general issue of nature versus nurture. For example, an animal is deprived of a particular sensory stimulation from birth to 6 months; then it is tested on skills involving that sense. If it performs at the same level as normal animals, experimenters conclude that the equipment for the sensory experience is inborn. By contrast, if the animal is denied sensory experience and is not able to perform as well as normal animals, they conclude that experience is an important aspect of the development of a normal sensory system.

Experiments of sensory deprivation have been done with kittens and other animals (Blakemore, 1978; Ganz, 1978). The data show that organisms pass through a period of susceptibility during which environmental influences are critical. According to Ganz, an animal's experience changes—and in many ways determines—how inborn structures will develop. If an animal is deprived of light or patterned vision, its visual apparatus does not develop properly. So, varied and active stimulation has been shown to be necessary for the animals to achieve a normally functioning sensory system.

Heron (1957) conducted an experiment in which he assessed the effects of the sensory environment on humans. The purpose of the study was to examine how humans react when nothing at all happens. The subjects weren't newborns but college students who were paid $20 a day to participate in the experiment. Their task was to be confined in a room that was warm and comfortable, but dull. As shown in Figure 5.15, they were to wear translucent plastic visors and gloves lined with cotton, and were to listen to the continuous hum of an air conditioner.

The experimenters saw dramatic results. Within just a few hours the subjects' performance on tests of mental ability was impaired. The students became bored, irritable, and after long isolation many of them began to see "images." The images were sometimes in simple forms, like animated movie cartoons, and were generally not under their active control. As described by the researchers:

> Later they slept less, became bored, and appeared eager for stimulation. They would sing, whistle, talk to themselves, tap the cuffs together, or explore the cubicle with them. This boredom seemed to be partly due to deterioration in the capacity to think systematically and productively. . . . The subjects also became very restless, displaying constant random movement, and they described the restlessness as unpleasant. Hence it was difficult to keep subjects for more than two or three days. . . . (Bexton, Heron, & Scott, 1954, p. 71)

In addition to all of these changes, brain-wave patterns were also changed. These data must be interpreted cautiously, because if you put subjects in

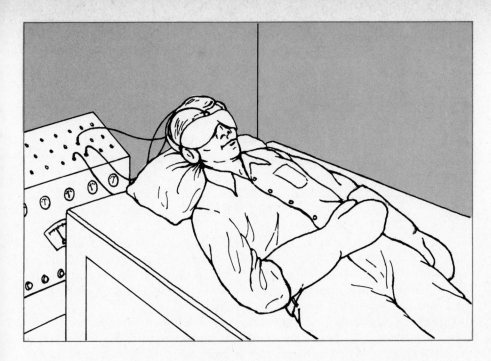

Figure 5.15 In a study by Heron (1957), subjects were enclosed in a room where their sensory experiences were deprived and there was nothing to do. The results were dramatic; within a few hours students who had volunteered became agitated and asked to end the experiment

identical conditions but tell them that the deprivation is an aid to meditation, they don't get irritable or hallucinate, and their mental ability improves (see Lilly, 1956; Zuckerman, 1969).

It seems clear that without regular and active sensory stimulation there are changes in the behavior patterns of humans. As Hebb (1972) has indicated, for humans "boredom" is too mild a word for the effects elicited by a lack of sensory stimulation. Hebb argues that the need for normal and varied stimulation is fundamental. College students are rarely placed in situations where they are deprived of sensory stimulation, but even after a couple of hours of studying, most will report that they need to talk to a roommate, listen to the radio, or generally seek out some kind of stimulation. People's need for affiliation may not be only social in nature; it may also have some physiological basis.

FORM PERCEPTION

Seeing is more than just cells in the cortex firing to vertical lines! We know that varied experiences are important and that perceptual systems are interactive, but let's say we have a normally developed perceptual system. How do we see form then? Form is not just a collection of lines or shapes. There is unity to form in that it exists in size, shape, and depth. We might also wonder how we recognize forms at a distance or forms that have changed size or shape.

Perceptual Constancy

People are fairly accurate at judging the size of an object. If we observe a man at a distance of 5 feet, we may judge his height to be about 6 feet. His image on our retina is fairly large. If we take the same man and move him to a dis-

Size constancy is the ability of our perceptual systems to know that an object remains constant in size regardless of its distance from us or the size of its image on our retinas

tance of 50 feet, the size of the image cast on our retina is very small, but, in judging the height of this individual at both distances, we still respond that he looks about 6 feet tall. *Size constancy* is the ability of our perceptual systems to know that an object remains constant in size regardless of its distance from us or the size of its image on our retinas.

Three variables determine size estimation. The first is the actual size of the object, the second is its distance from the observer, and the third is surrounding objects. When a man is moved from 5 to 50 feet away, the size of the image cast on the observer's retina is decreased because he is ten times farther away. But, due to size constancy, even with changes in the size of retinal image an observer is able to estimate size accurately (see Day & McKenzie, 1977).

One of the critical variables in maintaining size constancy seems to be an individual's experience with the actual sizes of an object. As an object moves from close to far away, its retinal size decreases. However, at the same time, its perceived distance from the observer also increases; these two systems work together. When retinal size decreases and perceived distance increases, estimation of the size of an object remains constant. Furthermore, the things that surround an observed object provide cues as to distance. When a person who is being observed moves farther away, his or her perceived size in relation to other stationary objects changes. Knowing the size of the surrounding objects helps us determine the distance of the person and that person's actual size.

Since experience with the world around us is important in helping establish and maintain size constancy, researchers have examined the extent of size constancy in infants and people with little experience with the world around them. Professor T. G. R. Bower (1966) devised a clever experiment. He took infants who were 50 to 60 days old and trained them to look toward an object. Every time they looked at the object they would be reinforced with a ''peek-a-boo.'' For a 2-month-old child a ''peek-a-boo'' is reinforcing, and it makes the looking behavior happen again. Bower then took objects that were either the same size or of a different size from the training object and placed them at the same distance, closer, or farther away from the infant. As an object is moved farther away from a person, the image cast on the retina decreases in size. Thus, the size of the image cast on the retina of the infant was varied. The sizes and distances were arranged so that small objects close to the infant and large objects at a great distance produced the same size retinal image. Size constancy would be shown if the infants only turned their heads to the original object, not to one of the same retinal size. The results showed that the infants turned their heads when the original object was displayed, not when objects of the same retinal size were displayed; thus, they showed size constancy.

McKenzie and Day (1972) failed to find the effect reported by Bower (1966). However, when a different procedure was used, McKenzie, Tootell, and Day (1980) showed that infants definitely have size constancy by 6 months of age and that it is probably present at 4 months.

Shape constancy is the maintenance of the apparent shape of an object despite changes in its tilt or orientation. People normally view a tree standing erect, yet when the tree is at an angle of 45° from the horizon, they still recognize it as a tree. This is because they recognize that it is tilted, so its orientation is different; its shape is essentially the same, although the retinal image may be somewhat distorted. Think about doorways—they always appear rectangular in shape regardless of the orientation of our heads or the angle from which we view them. When we tilt our heads, the rectangular shape of a door becomes trapezoidal; similarly, a round clock when viewed from an angle casts a retinal image that is oval. Our perceptual systems develop in a way that allows for discrepant and varied experiences. The development of size and shape constancy allows a uniform perceptual experience for observers; without them, the visual world would be in constant turmoil.

Depth

Seeing in the three dimensions of height, width, and depth is generally taken for granted; however, when people are faced with having to draw a picture showing depth, the problem becomes obvious. A drawing, like the retina, has only two dimensions, yet we perceive three. People perceive depth visually; our eyes are positioned in the head so that each sees a similar view of the world. These similar, but not exactly the same, views provide important cues for depth. Although the principal way people see depth is through the use of two eyes, people can have impressions of depth with only one eye. We can also experience depth when we look at a two-dimensional painting. When looking with one eye or at a painting, we are using monocular depth cues associated with depth that have little to do with the visual system itself.

MONOCULAR DEPTH CUES.   Depth cues that do not depend on two eyes are called *monocular depth cues*. One monocular depth cue is *linear* perspective. When objects appear to be close together, they are generally considered to be far away. Railroad tracks that go off in the distance appear very close together, whereas the same tracks near the viewer are seen as farther apart (see Figure 5.16). Another cue for depth is *interposition*; when one object blocks out part of another object, the first appears closer to the observer. A third monocular depth cue is *texture*. Surfaces that have a fine grain and are relatively smooth give the impression of being at great distances; by contrast, rough surfaces and textures give the impression of closeness. Two other cues that are often used to present depth (particularly by artists) are the *clearness* of an object and *shadowing*. Clear objects appear closer and shadowed; dark objects appear farther away. There are other monocular cues, particularly cues that convey information about distance. For example, mountains seen at

Figure 5.16 In a common illusion, railroad tracks that are actually parallel appear close together when they are far away

When one object blocks out part of another object, the first appears closer to the observer

a distance generally look blue—this is because long (red) wavelengths are more easily scattered as they pass through air, leaving a bluish tinge. Leonardo da Vinci recognized this phenomenon and used it in his paintings; he even developed an equation of how much blue pigment should be mixed with the normal color of an object depending on how far away he wanted the object to appear!

An important monocular depth cue not derived from the stimulus itself is accommodation. **Accommodation** is the changing of the shape of the eye lens when an object is moved closer to or farther from the observer. The lens accommodates to keep an object in focus on the retina. Accommodation is achieved by a series of muscles attached to the lens. These muscles provide active and regular feedback about the shape of the lens to higher processing systems. If people look from one object to another which is at a different distance, there will be changes in the accommodation of the lenses of their eyes; accommodation takes place even in young infants (Aslin & Jackson, 1979). This could also provide a cue for depth perception. While there are at least six different monocular depth cues available to observers, most people have two eyes and use binocular cues as well as the monocular ones.

Accommodation The change in shape of the lens of the eye when an object moves closer to or farther away from the observer.

BINOCULAR DEPTH CUES. Our two eyes are separated by approximately two inches, and each eye sees a slightly different view of the world. This is easily seen by holding up a finger in front of some distant object; first, examine the object with one eye; then, keeping your finger in the same place, examine the object with your other eye. The finger will appear displaced relative to the object. This difference (disparity) in the image projected upon the retina provides a strong and important binocular depth cue. **Retinal disparity** provides a cue to depth because the closer objects are to the eyes, the farther apart the images are on the retina. An object at a great distance will produce little retinal disparity.

Retinal disparity The slight difference in the visual images perceived by each eye.

Our eyes move toward each other, or converge, as an object moves closer to us; this *convergence* provides another binocular depth cue. The eyes are moved in their sockets by a series of muscles, and these muscles convey information to the brain about the amount of convergence that has taken place. Convergence can act as a binocular cue in the same way as accommodation.

Binocular depth cues are even evident in infants. While little conclusive evidence had been presented previously, one group of researchers (Fox et al., 1980) have shown that infants as young as 3½ months have the ability to perceive depth.

The perception of depth adds a third dimension to width and height, and provides a unique experience. It is achieved by the working together of both monocular and binocular cues. Two-dimensional surfaces such as paintings often give the appearance of depth. We can experience this depth without two eyes. When depth is perceived in this manner, it is usually through the monocular cues of linear perspective, shading, and interposition. While monocular and binocular cues both figure into the perception of depth, the binocular cues predominate, with the monocular cues used mainly when binocular cues are not available.

Illusions

There are times when depth cues and normal perceptual processes seem to break down and produce illusions. An **illusion** is a perception of a stimulus that differs from the way the physical stimulus would normally lead us to expect it to appear. A common example is the Müller-Lyer illusion, in which two lines of the same length appear to be of different lengths because of some attachments to the ends of the lines. Another common illusion is the moon illusion—the moon appears larger over the horizon than it does overhead. The actual size of the moon does not change, nor does the size of the image on the retina when the moon is overhead or at the horizon, yet the illusion is quite powerful. A third illusion is the Ponzo illusion. In this illusion, two

Illusion A perception of a stimulus that differs from the way the physical stimulus would normally lead us to expect it to appear.

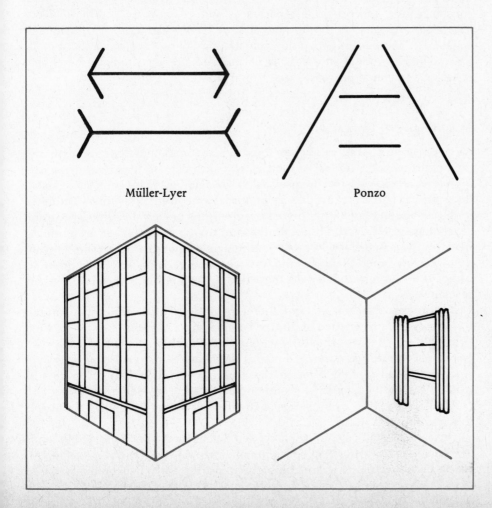

Müller-Lyer

Ponzo

Figure 5.17 Lines of the same size appear to be different in length in the Müller-Lyer and Ponzo illusions. The lower portion of the figure shows how the arrows in the Müller-Lyer usually represent "near corner" and "far corner"

horizontal lines of the same length are perceived as different in length. Such illusions have been apparent for a long time, yet explanations of them have been shaky at best.

Recently, however, theories interpreting these illusions have been brought forth. Generally these have accounted for the illusions by referring to the backgrounds against which the illusions are seen. The moon illusion is accounted for by considering that the moon seen overhead has a background of only sky, whereas the moon seen at the horizon has a background of sky and land. The land provides cues as to the distance of the moon from the observer and these distance cues change the observer's perception of the size of the moon (Restle, 1970). To illustrate how the moon illusion is dependent upon these cues, bend over and look at the moon on the horizon between your legs—it will reduce the magnitude of the illusion. The Ponzo illusion is accounted for by the linear perspective provided by the background lines in the figure. The Müller-Lyer illusion is explained by the angle and shape of the arrows that are attached to the lines being judged; that is, inward-facing lines are often interpreted as far corners, whereas outward-facing lines are interpreted as corners nearer to the observer. Near corners are generally seen as bigger or closer than far corners.

Most explanations of illusions are based on an observer's previous experiences and well-developed perceptual constancies. Some psychologists explain both the moon and the Müller-Lyer illusions by referring to perceptual constancy cues and previous experiences with distance and corners. Needless to say, researchers don't know all they would like to about illusions or constancy. These form perceptions are among the most complex that people have to make and will only be fully understood after continued research into complex perceptual processes (see Coren & Girgus, 1978).

Gestalt Laws of Organization

No description of how people see form can be complete without recognizing the important contribution of the Gestalt psychologists. Today, few perception researchers classify themselves as Gestalt psychologists; yet, Gestalt thinking has had a great influence on form perception. New formulations of form perception have incorporated the strengths of Gestalt thinking. Gestalt psychologists like Wertheimer, Koffka, and Köhler studied *form;* by studying how form was perceived, Gestalt psychologists attempted to explain perception. They assumed that since the way we perceive actually reflects brain organization, we can understand the workings of the brain by studying perception.

In studying perception (and therefore underlying brain organization), Gestaltists were concerned about the completeness of form, and one of their guiding principles was that "the whole is greater than the sum of its parts." The visual world is complex and made up of many parts; accordingly, people place order and organization on those parts by seeing them in groups or wholes. Rather than seeing a group of parts, a series of elements is seen as a whole. Figure 5.18 shows a series of 16 dots, yet humans organize these dots into a group, a square.

The early Gestalt psychologists argued that since the perceptual field tends to be made up by wholes rather than parts, people will try to impose organization on any units that are complete or, as the early psychologists called

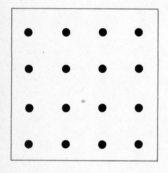

Figure 5.18

Form has unity in that it exists in size, shape, and depth

them, "good." Their organizing theme was the **Law of Prägnanz;** according to this law, items or stimuli that can be grouped together and seen as a whole will be seen that way. Thus, if prevailing stimulus conditions are appropriate, items that are simple in organization and can be grouped together will be seen in a group as a form. Using Prägnanz, the Gestalt psychologists showed that people segregate background from foreground and try to figure out ambiguous drawings and pictures.

With the idea of Prägnanz and the notion of wholes rather than parts, Gestalt psychologists developed laws of organization for figures including proximity, similarity, continuity, common fate, and closure. These "laws" are essentially only rules that predict which alternative areas of an ambiguous pattern will be seen as the figure and which will be seen as background (Hochberg, 1974, 1979). The *law of proximity* states that groups are formed by elements close to one another in space or time. The *law of similarity* says that similar items tend to be perceived in groups. The *law of continuity* states that a string of items projects where the next item will be found. The *common fate* principle says that items that move or change together are seen as a whole. Last, the *law of closure* states that parts of a figure not presented will be filled in by the perceptual system (see Figure 5.19).

One of the best known modern attempts to examine Gestalt principles has been that of Beck (1966). Beck asked subjects to divide patterns such as those shown in Figure 5.20 into regions along the most likely boundary. While

Law of Prägnanz The principle that items or stimuli that can be grouped together and seen as a whole will be seen that way.

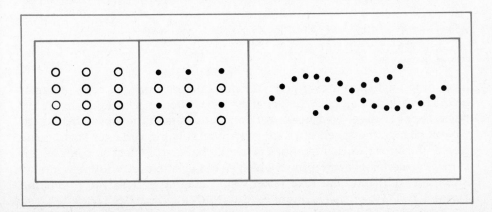

Figure 5.19 The law of proximity is shown in the far left portion of the figure. Here the circles appear to be in vertical columns, suggesting that items that are close together tend to be perceived as a unit. In the middle portion of the figure the filled circles, all similar to one another, appear to be arranged in horizontal rows, thus exhibiting the principle of similarity. A third Gestalt law, continuity, is shown in the right portion. This law suggests that an observer can predict where the next item should occur when a group of items projects into space

Figure 5.20 When people are asked to divide these lines into two groups, subjects generally draw the dividing line between the upright and tilted *T*s rather than between the backward *L*s and *T*s. Beck has argued that this supports the Prägnanz principles

there are *two* places that such a boundary might be placed in the figure, subjects were more likely to place the boundary between regions that differed in orientation rather than shape. So, subjects were more likely to place a boundary between the *T*s that differed in orientation rather than between the backward *L*s and the *T*s. The backward *L*s and the *T*s tended to form a group, a whole, a unit. The *L*s and the *T*s had a similar shape, and this shape took precedence over the tilted *T*s. Beck's work is important because it shows that people group together those elements that they see as alike. The *T*s and *L*s in Figure 5.20 share orientation, they are similar, and they are close. According to the law of Prägnanz, it would be appropriate for the *L*s and the *T*s to be seen together and they were.

Each of these Gestalt laws of organization suggests that perception is the process of seeing items together in an organized, meaningful unity. Many of these ideas have been used to explain perceptual phenomenon; however, it must be recognized that Gestalt ideas left untouched several major aspects of perception including certain constancies and illusions (Hochberg, 1974, p. 189). To illustrate, Gestalt laws do not explain why orientation predominated over shape in Beck's study. Both orientation or shape could have been used to break up the figure. Thus, while Beck's study supports Gestalt principles generally, it also shows how difficult it is to make predictions based on those principles. These basic Gestalt principles, recognized over 50 years ago, continue to exert an influence on current perceptual theorists, but they do not hold all of the answers.

COMPLEX PERCEPTUAL PROCESSES

Reading

In reading English, our eyes generally move across a printed page or chalkboard from left to right. Whether they are written in Old English, script, boldface, or cursive, we can identify and understand the words. Although we can change the speed of reading by manipulating variables such as the case of the letters, such alterations generally have little effect on comprehension. For example, paragraphs in which all of the letters are written in normal lowercase (difficulty) are read faster than paragraphs typed in alternating case (DiFfIcUlTy) (Fisher, Lefton, & Moss, 1978).

Of the many variables that affect reading speed, the most important is the number of visual fixations made. As we learned earlier the minimum duration of a fixation is 250 milliseconds, or $\frac{1}{4}$ of a second, although you might fixate on a specific word for longer than this. If you were to read a 1,000-word essay and fixate on each word for 250 milliseconds, the total time required to read the essay would be 250 seconds (250,000 milliseconds).

One way to decrease this 250-second reading time would be to look at every other word rather than at every single word. The 250-second reading time was calculated with the subject fixating on each word; if the subject fixates on every other word, this reading time is decreased by one-half—125 seconds. If subjects fixate on only every third word, the reading time is decreased to 83 seconds. If the subject fixates only once per line (assuming there are 10 words per line) the time to read could be decreased to 25 seconds. To increase reading speed, fixate fewer times! This is easily accomplished by examining more words in a single glance. When reading feature articles in a magazine, our reading rate is considerably faster than when reading a chemistry textbook because we look at more words in a single glance. There are more details in a chemistry text, and specific words and terms must be carefully examined; this generally means that more eye movements are necessary as the material becomes more complicated. It also means that it is fairly easy to increase reading speed when reading novels or material that is fairly predictable (see Just & Carpenter, 1980; O'Regan, 1979).

If reading speed is determined by frequency of fixation, then children should not only read more slowly but they should be fixating more often. This is exactly the case. In a study of eye movements of children (Spragins, Lefton, & Fisher, 1976), it was found that children examine fewer letter spaces in each fixation and fixate more often. In accordance with their slower fixation patterns, the reading speed for third-graders is approximately one-half that of adults.

Reading cannot be considered without looking at other types of perceptual processes. A person must be able to make fine visual discriminations to be able to read. Eye movements must be appropriate in terms of duration, frequency, and direction of scan. Reading, however, is not a special process that necessarily differs from other perceptual processes. For example, when you are looking through a telephone book to find an individual's name, there are two types of perceptual processes taking place. One is reading. You may want the phone number for Joseph Smith, not John Smith. The second process is search. You cannot be reading each name in the phone book; otherwise it would take you many hours to find a phone number. When looking for a number you search the page until you find approximately where the target "Joseph Smith" might be. Then proceed to read a series of names until you find the name of Joseph Smith.

Visual Search

Each time you look for the price of grapes in a newspaper or try to find the phone number of Joseph Smith, you are really performing a visual-search task. A number of researchers have conducted experimental studies of visual-search. One such series has been conducted by Calvin Nodine at Temple University in Philadelphia. Nodine and his colleagues have taken drawings by the noted artist Al Hirschfeld and asked subjects to find the target word NINA in the drawings. Hirschfeld has embedded his daughter's name, NINA, somewhere in each drawing. Finding NINAs is a regular activity for

Figure 5.21 This is a Hirschfeld drawing with NINA in three different places. In the study by Nodine, Carmody, and Herman (1979) subjects saw NINA embedded in a background that was complex or simple. In the original Hirschfeld, NINA is embedded in the gown of the woman in the left background. Another condition has NINA embedded in the skirt of the woman reading the newspaper. In another condition (not shown), a nonembedded NINA was on the blade of Burt Lancaster's axe. Subjects saw only one NINA target per page.

people who read the newspapers that carry Hirschfeld's drawings; finding them has also become a laboratory task. Not surprisingly, the extent to which the NINA is embedded in the background directly influences the ability and speed with which subjects can find the target (Kundel & Nodine, 1978; Nodine, Carmody, & Kundel, 1978).

Eye movements have been measured while subjects have searched for NINAs (Nodine, Carmody, & Herman, 1979). Nodine and his colleagues took some of the Hirschfeld drawings and photographically eliminated some of the detail; they then asked subjects to search for NINAs. Making NINA targets more or less evident by changing the surrounding affected search performance. The less detail in the background, the fewer times subjects missed the target; this is not surprising because the NINAs were easier to discriminate. The results also showed that when subjects fixated or dwelled on the general area of the target for more than 400 milliseconds (0.4 second) they were far more likely to find the target than when they spent less time fixating.

The results from a study that deals with searching for the word NINA are important because they can be related in very direct ways to real-world situations. Targets in the real world are often camouflaged or hidden in backgrounds. Animals hide from predators by remaining still and blending into the background; in the same way, army tanks are painted to blend in with the scenery so that they will not be easily detected. Targets in other kinds of scenes are often difficult to detect. A radiologist, for example, scans X-rays looking for small changes in density that might reflect a tumor or change in growth rate of an existing malady. So, search tasks in which targets are detected can tell basic researchers a great deal about how human subjects extract information; these kinds of data can have direct applicability for reading theorists, military strategists, and clinical practitioners like radiologists (Carmody, Nodine, & Kundel, 1980).

Attention

Attention is a term frequently used by experimental psychologists, clinical psychologists, and nonpsychologists. Teachers are concerned that students pay attention; football players must concentrate their attention on oncoming runners. Students believe that if they pay close attention to their studying, they will probably perform better. While people often speak about attention in terms of activation or arousal, those studying perception are concerned with selective attention and extracting information from the environment.

The perceptual process is one in which we are constantly attempting to extract signals from the world around us. As we listen to an instructor, we hear a lecture on a specific topic; as we listen to music, we hear words and melodies. Very often we are not just listening to an event. A person can be receiving many different messages at once (as at a cocktail party); yet, we know he can only listen to one of them at a time. While he may wish to listen to a variety of different conversations, this task is impossible. For these reasons the use of selective attention is often called the "cocktail party problem."

Since the cocktail party problem is a matter of selective attention, which stimuli do we decide to listen to? This question has been the focus of a number of research efforts. In selective listening experiments, subjects wear a pair of headphones and different messages are delivered to each ear. Typical subjects report that they are able to listen either to the left or the right ear, and they are able to provide information about the content and quality of the speaker's voice. If the voice in one ear is male and the voice in the other ear is female, the task of following one message and not the other is made easier. If the pitch of two male voices is different, the task is also easy. Furthermore, if the content of the voices coming from the two separate ears is different, subjects are better able to follow one message and not the other. However, if the voice, pitch, intensity, quality, and content are similar in both ears, subjects often shift their attention from one ear to the other and lose track of both messages.

Theories have been put forth to explain how people are able to attend selectively. One theorist suggests that since our memories have a limited capacity, there must be some type of mechanism or filter that chooses between the left ear and the right ear. An alternative explanation to this filter theory is an attenuation theory. Attenuation theorists argue that although all information proceeds toward higher processing centers, the information is not filtered but rather is tuned and selected. All information is analyzed, but only selected information may pass to higher centers without being attenuated.

In efforts to understand the nature of auditory attention, many selective-listening studies have examined the filter versus attenuation question. There are hundreds of these studies (Cherry, 1953; Lewis et al., 1975; Moore & Massaro, 1973; Norman, 1969; Treisman, 1969). One such study supported the attenuation model by using reaction time as a dependent variable; Lewis (1970) had his subjects shadow or repeat words that were presented in one ear while different words were presented at the same time to the other ear. Lewis recorded how long it took subjects to shadow words in the attended ear and he manipulated the kinds of words presented to the subjects in the nonattended ear. He found that responses were relatively slow (reaction time increased) if words in the nonattended ear were synonyms to the words in the attended ear. By contrast, when words in the nonattended ear were antonyms of the attended or shadowed word, response time decreased. Words in the nonattended ear were affecting response times to words in the attended ear—this shows that the messages to the nonattended ear are not

We can attend to only one message at a time, although we may try to manage more than one.

219

blocked or filtered out. For reaction time to be affected by the meanings of the words heard by the nonattended ear, subjects must have analyzed their messages for meaning.

For us, the importance of selective-attention studies is not whether people have a filter or an attenuator, but rather that information must be selected from available stimuli and that people have a limited capacity system. You cannot listen to four lectures at once. You are forced to extract information from only one of the speakers at a time, and only if you stop listening to this speaker can you extract information from another.

The process of selective attention is not confined to hearing. When a person searches through a list of letters for a target, she is also performing a visual selective attention task. In reading, a subject is asked to extract meaning from a paragraph. In casting our gaze about the world, we are attempting to extract critical features; then we selectively attend to the features that will provide useful information. Psychologists know that there are single cells in the visual system that are selectively attentive to features of the visual environment. There is a limited capacity within each of these systems, auditory and visual, and also a limited capacity to divide attention between them. (Massaro & Warner, 1977). Thus, there are both psychological and physiological data suggesting that feature extraction or selective attention is one of the tasks that people are all constantly involved in.

Imagery

It is easy to imagine what one has just seen, read, or remembered. People imagine; that is, they invoke a visual image of some past event or some event that they would like to see happen in the future. Our imagery systems can be called up by visual stimuli, auditory stimuli, and by other images. As shown earlier, one can even have vivid imagery from a lack of sensory stimulation.

Imagery has not always been considered an appropriate topic to study in psychology. In the early part of the twentieth century, psychologists felt that imagery had no real significance and could not adequately be experimentally examined. However, the past two decades have seen a revival of the study of imagery. Imagery is a difficult concept to do away with, because people use imagery.

Figure 5.22 In exploring the nature of imagery, researchers like Roger Shepard have drawn pairs of visual stimuli like those shown on the left so that one member of each pair appears to have been rotated in space. Shepard and Metzler (1971) asked subjects to respond as quickly as possible on whether such stimuli were the same or not. Sometimes the stimuli were drawn rotated in space only slightly; other times the rotations were as much as 180°. The subject's reaction times needed to respond correctly varied depending on how much rotation was involved. Shown in the figure is reaction time for "same" pairs plotted as a function of degrees of rotation. This is one of the first of a number of studies in the 1970s that began to explore visual image ability in very systematic and carefully controlled ways

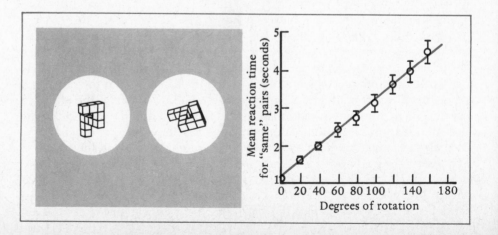

Although visual imagery might be considered apart from perception, there is a growing body of evidence to suggest that imagery may be a means of preserving perceptual information that might otherwise decay. This evidence suggests that people may be able to store glimpses of the world as a visual image for relatively long periods (Paivio, 1971). Although the role of imagery and perceptual and cognitive processes is still being clarified, it is impossible to deny that imagery exists. Gestalt psychologists, whose main area of interest was in form perception, recognized over 60 years ago the importance of imagery in perception; this importance is being awakened again. The difficulty for psychologists is that they have to devise techniques and experimental manipulations allowing its assessment (Cooper & Shepard, 1973; Kosslyn, 1973, 1975, 1978; Pinker, 1980; Plyshyn, 1973; Shepard & Metzler, 1971).

One such technique has been used extensively by Stephen Kosslyn of Harvard University. Kosslyn told subjects to imagine an animal like a rabbit and asked them to imagine it next to an appropriately scaled elephant or fly. The subjects reported that when imagining a fly there was plenty of room for an appropriately scaled rabbit, but when imagining an elephant, the elephant took up most of the room. Particularly interesting was that the subjects required more time to "see" the nose of the rabbit when it was next to the elephant than when it was next to the fly; further, when the rabbit was next

Figure 5.23 Kosslyn had subjects imagine elephants and flies; when they did, a rabbit that was subsequently imagined appeared small in size next to the elephant and large in size in relation to a fly (Kosslyn [1975] after Solso [1979])

Imagine That

Throughout the history of psychology, some researchers have had trouble imagining that psychologists should consider the study of imagery. To study imagery has been considered foolish and laughable at times, while it has been a major focus of research at other times. There are two sources of research that show us that imagery is important to study. First, decades of work on imagery have shown that imagery is an important perceptual memory aid. Second, research on imagery has shown that a special kind of imagery exists, eidetic imagery. Let us look more closely at how these two kinds of imagery systems work.

According to imagery researcher Alan Paivio (1971), if a person is presented with two words to remember, it is very likely that he or she will form an image of those words. So, if a person is told to remember the words *house* and *hamburger,* the person might form an image of a house made of hamburgers or a hamburger on top of a house. Later presented with the word *house,* the word hamburger is quickly evoked. Paivio suggests that there is a conceptual link between words that are paired together like this and that the mediating factor is the image. If Paivio is correct, then words that evoke high imagery should serve as better links between pairs of words to be learned than words that evoke little imagery. To study this hypothesis, Paivio and his colleagues have presented subjects with pairs of words to learn. After a study phase of the experiment, the subjects are then presented with just one of the words and the sub-

ject has to respond with its paired associate. Each pair of words has two parts, the stimulus word and the subject's response word; Paivio has manipulated the extent to which the stimulus words and the response words evoke imagery. For example, if the stimulus word is *telephone*, the imagery is clear; however, if the stimulus is *love, beauty,* or *truth,* there is little imagery that might be evoked. Concrete nouns evoke imagery, while abstract nouns do not. In a long series of studies, Paivio manipulated whether the stimulus or response member of a pair of words is concrete or abstract. His results were dramatic: when the words in a paired association were concrete nouns, they were remembered with significantly better accuracy than when they were abstract nouns. Nouns generally have better imagery than adjectives and so when words in another study were nouns or adjectives, those with nouns were more likely to be recalled than those with adjectives.

The results from the studies reported by Paivio with adjectives (Paivio, 1963), nouns (1965), pictures (Paivio & Yarmey, 1966), and even developmental studies with children (Paivio & Yuille, 1966) show that imagery is an important part of people's ability to remember pairs of unrelated events or objects. The studies are particularly important in showing researchers how people remember things. Perhaps even more importantly, the early research by Paivio opened the study of imagery to investigation after decades of neglect (see Paivio, 1971).

In the 1960s, while Paivio was trying to make the

to the elephant, its nose was harder to see compared to when it was next to the fly (see Figure 5.23).

Carrying his experiments a step further, Kosslyn (1978) has tried to measure the nature of images that humans develop. In a series of experiments, he asked subjects to imagine objects at a distance; the subjects were then requested to imagine that they were moving toward the object. Next, the subjects were asked if it seemed larger to them and if the object seemed to "overflow" so that they could not see all of it. Subjects were also asked to stop "mentally walking" at just the point where the object seemed to overflow. By having the subjects estimate the size of the object and the distance at which the images seemed to overflow, Kosslyn was able to estimate the size of the visual image that human beings can imagine. Using this "mental walk" technique, Kosslyn found that there is a limited "image space"; larger objects tended to overflow at imagined longer distances. In addition, visual images overflow in all directions at about the same size. Perhaps the most important finding from Kosslyn's work is that images have spatial properties. While images are a mental rather than physical phenomenon, they have edges—

study of imagery acceptable again, a different kind of imagery was being investigated, photographlike imagery. If one could maintain a photographlike image of each glimpse of the world, how easy learning would be! If this were possible, everyone would have large memory banks that would include each page of text that he or she had read, as well as glances at an object that may have been only casually seen. While many individuals report that they have photographlike memories, none report that they maintain a visual image of every glance. Most images that people report can be considered normal vivid imagery. However, Ralph Haber (1969, 1979) of the University of Illinois, Chicago Circle, has shown that some children have a special type of imagery called eidetic imagery.

Eidetic imagery is vivid, long-lasting, and complete, and it is so rare that fewer than 4% of school-age children can be called eidetic. After some initial cross-screening for normal imagery, Haber's basic procedure was to place a picture on an easel for about 30 seconds. The subjects were instructed to move their eyes around so that they would see all of the details. The picture was then removed. The subjects continued to look at the blank white easel and were probed as to the nature of their imagery. Subjects who were eventually to be termed eidetic reported that their images lasted from a half minute to a full minute in duration. Their imagery was so vivid that even minute details of pictures could be reported. If the picture showed a cat with a striped tail, the subjects would be able to report how many stripes there were. If eidetic children could not remember parts of a picture, they reported that they did not look at those parts long enough. When asked to move their images from the easel to another surface, they reported that when the image was moved, it fell off the edge of the easel. A few eidetic children were even able to develop three-dimensional images.

Both adults and children use imagery daily as a memory aid, in fantasy, and in spatial problems. Because only a small portion of the sample group tested showed eidetic imagery, it is clear that eidetic imagery is special. Further investigation of eidetic imagery is crucial, for we may be able to further develop and utilize our memory and imagery systems (see Haber, 1979).

The research has shown that there are at least two kinds of imagery, normal imagery and eidetic imagery. Both serve different functions and operate differently. A child with normal vivid imagery might know the number of stripes on the cat's tail, but his or her eyes would wander. The eidetic child's eyes would go to the point where the cat's tail had been, *as if it could still be seen*. From a historical view, an important aspect of this work is that it would not have been considered legitimate to investigate these topics for much of the history of modern psychology. Today researchers not only recognize the importance of imagery in our perceptions and recollections of the world, but they are making imagery a focus of their research efforts.

points beyond which visual information ceases to be represented. Kosslyn has made one of the first real attempts at measuring the size of the mind's eye and has further legitimized the study of mental phenomena like imagery.

Subliminal Perception

From time to time in the popular press, there will be a report of experiments done on subliminal perception in which people were influenced to do something without being aware of it. A typical report will talk of how researchers from a well-known university presented messages without the subjects being aware of it; further, these messages affected the subjects' subsequent behavior. The early work on subliminal perception was done in the 1950s by nonpsychologists who tried to show that one could influence moviegoers to buy popcorn without their being aware of the advertising message flashed on the screen. The prospects of such ideas sent the hearts of advertising executives into overdrive. But when nonpsychologists try to do psychological experiments, there are often gaping flaws in the studies. Many of these early

Subliminal Perception Perception of a stimulus presented below some duration or luminance level at which subjects are not aware of the presentation 50% of the time.

"studies" had no control groups and early reports did not specify the exact variables in the study and who the subjects were.

When psychologists began to seriously study the phenomena, there were some early reports of subliminal perception. These researchers spoke of **subliminal perception** because "subliminal" means "below the threshold"; a stimulus presented below the threshold was one that subjects were not aware of or could not see (half of the time). Again, later research showed that many of the studies were flawed. Some presented the stimuli for durations so long that several words might be easily seen. Yet, some of the subjects were unable to see even single words. Some of these studies presented "dirty" or taboo words to subjects; the studies attempted to see if presenting these dirty words affected the response of the subjects on the words compared to other neutral or nonemotionally charged words. The problem was that saying the dirty words to the experimenter (often of the opposite sex) was embarrassing to many of the subjects. Since it was embarrassing, part of the time some of the subjects said that they did not see the words when they were presented. The problem thus became one of an unwillingness of the subjects to say out loud the words that they actually saw; the subjects were thus defending themselves against potential embarrassment.

Some well-conducted, controlled studies have been done that avoided some of the methodological problems. A typical experiment involves the presentation of threatening stimuli and neutral, nonthreatening stimuli for a very brief duration or at a very low intensity in a tachistoscope. The subjects might have to respond by indicating if they saw the word or by pressing a button as soon as they saw the word (no verbalizing of nasty words). In these experiments, threatening stimuli are usually more difficult to see; typically, this means that they have to be presented for a longer time or at a greater intensity level. Since the threatening words raise the threshold (more time or greater intensity level is necessary), it has been concluded that subliminal perception actually exists. However, this presents a curious situation: if the threatening stimuli actually raise the threshold, then they must have been analyzed sufficiently for subjects to realize that they are threatening. For this to happen, the threshold is being raised not at a sensory or perceptual level, but probably at some higher cognitive level. Some researchers have suggested that perhaps the unconscious or some other personality variable is acting as a censor of information; this view has the subject react by taking longer to respond or by requiring more time or intensity before he or she will admit to seeing the stimulus. Accordingly, this view suggests that there is a stage beyond sensory or perceptual stages that affects the perceptual process. When variables like motivation, previous experience, and unconscious censoring devices enter into our explanation of subliminal perception, the topic becomes far more complicated. With these variables included, we recognize that increased thresholds may be reflecting nonperceptual variables.

Psychologists have come to agree that an intensity threshold is an inappropriate measure of a potential unconscious censoring device and so when taken together, the data on subliminal *perception* are weak at best and nonexistent at worst. But, this does not mean that it cannot or does not exist. Erdelyi (1974) has suggested that some of our new information about processing allows for a potential censoring device. For example, if a dirty or taboo word is contained in iconic storage (p. 111) then a decision at a cognitive level might be made to withhold transfering it from iconic storage to short-term memory. This is a kind of perceptual defense against taboo material and suggests that subliminal perceptions *might* exist (see also Williams & Evans, 1980). Most researchers presently maintain a very healthy skepticism about subliminal perception and perceptual defense; they do not rule it out completely, but the data suggesting its existence are still weak.

OTHER PERCEPTUAL SYSTEMS

Perception is not just a single process that involves independent action by the eyes, ears, or motor systems. It represents a coordination of many different processes acting together. Until now, the focus of this chapter has been on visual perception for several reasons. The first is that there are more data and theories on vision than on any of the other senses. A second reason is that the visual sense often takes precedence over the other senses. And last, vision is typical of the other senses and perceptual systems. In discussing perception, more than visual perception must be considered; therefore, hearing and the other senses will be briefly examined.

Hearing

Listening to a symphony by Beethoven is delightful, as well as intriguing and difficult. Listening can be captivating and difficult because there is so much going on at once. With upwards of 20 instruments playing, the listener is forced to process many sounds, rhythms, and intensities simultaneously. A music enthusiast will state that this is precisely what makes Beethoven delightful.

Hearing is an important dimension of our perceptual experience. But, like seeing, the process of converting physical stimuli to psychological experiences like sound is a complex one. Let's examine the way we hear more closely and begin with the stimulus for hearing.

The physical stimulus for hearing is a pressure change through a medium, usually a change in air pressure. The medium may be gaseous, liquid, or solid; we experience this pressure change as **sound.** Obviously, the air we breathe is clearly a medium through which changes in air pressure can be delivered. When a tuning fork is struck, the prongs of the fork move; as these prongs move, they displace air; with the changes in air pressure, we perceive sound.

In studying sound, two psychological terms—pitch and loudness—appear. These two qualities of sound are psychological attributes; their physical determinants are frequency and amplitude.

The pitch of a tone or sound is determined by its frequency. **Frequency** is the number of times there is a complete change in air pressure in any unit of time. Thus, within 1 second there might be 50 complete changes (50 cycles per second) or there might be 10,000 changes (10,000 cycles per second). High-pitched tones have high frequencies and low-pitched tones have low frequencies.

The **amplitude** or intensity of a sound wave determines its loudness. A low-frequency tone can be very loud or very soft; it is either of high ampli-

Sound A psychological term describing changes in pressure through a medium; the medium may be gaseous, liquid, or solid.

Frequency A measure of the number of complete pressure waves per unit of time; it is measured in Hertz (Hz) or cycles per second.

Amplitude The intensity of a sound wave or its total energy; it determines the loudness of a sound and is usually measured in decibels.

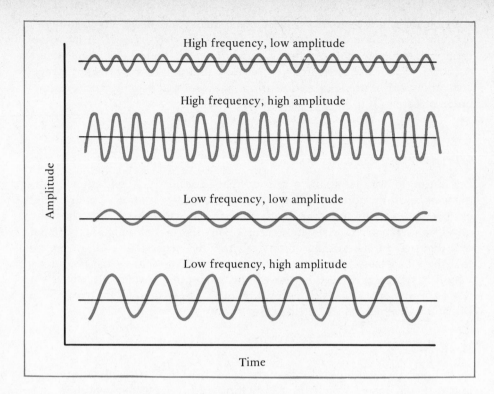

Figure 5.24 Frequency and amplitude are independent. High-frequency waves can have high amplitude (loud) and low amplitude (soft)

Table 5.2 The intensities of various kind of sounds produce different psychological experiences.

DECIBEL SCALE

HUMAN RESPONSE		ILLUSTRATIVE EXAMPLES
Painfully loud	140	Threshold of severe pain
		Rock band at 15 ft
	120	Jet takeoff at 200 ft
		Riveting machine
Very annoying	100	Subway train at 15 ft
Prolonged exposure produces damage to hearing		Water at foot of Niagara Falls
	80	Inside automobile at 55 mph
		Freeway traffic at 50 ft
	60	Normal conversation at 3 ft
Quiet		Quiet restaurant
	40	Quiet office
Very quiet		Library
	20	Whisper at 3 ft
Just audible		Normal breathing
	0	Threshold of hearing

tude or low amplitude. As shown in Figure 5.24 high-amplitude waves have more energy in them; there is a greater force of pressure applied to the ear or other medium which is undergoing a change in pressure. The intensity of sound, or sound pressure, is usually measured in terms of decibels. For every increase of 20 decibels there is a tenfold increase in intensity. As shown in Table 5.2, normal speech is at about 60 decibels; painful sound is at about 120 decibels. Thus, a sound which is 60 decibels higher than normal speech will be painful.

The ear acts as the receptive organ for audition. Like the eye, the ear is fairly complex, with many important structural features. All of these structures are not critical for our understanding of the process of hearing. Thus, only the major ones will be mentioned. The ear is divided into three major parts: external ear, middle ear, and internal ear. The tissue on the outside of our heads that we generally refer to as the ear is part of the external ear. The middle ear consists of tissue and bone that help begin the process of converting changes in air pressure into electrical energy. An important part of the internal ear is known as the *cochlea.* It is in this snaillike tube that changes in air pressure produce pressure against hair cells. The stimulation of hair cells brings about electrical activity in the nervous system.

When sound waves enter the ear, they produce pressure changes on the eardrum. This starts a sequence of events that includes the movements of some tiny bones within the ear. These bones eventually stimulate the basilar membrane in the cochlea. Different frequency sound waves stimulate different areas of the basilar membrane, and these different locations stimulate different hair cells that, in turn, provide the initial electrical coding of sound waves.

Electrical impulses make their way through the auditory nervous system in much the same way that visual information does. Psychologists have studied this electrical activity in much the same way—through single-cell record-

Secrets are often shared in a whisper.

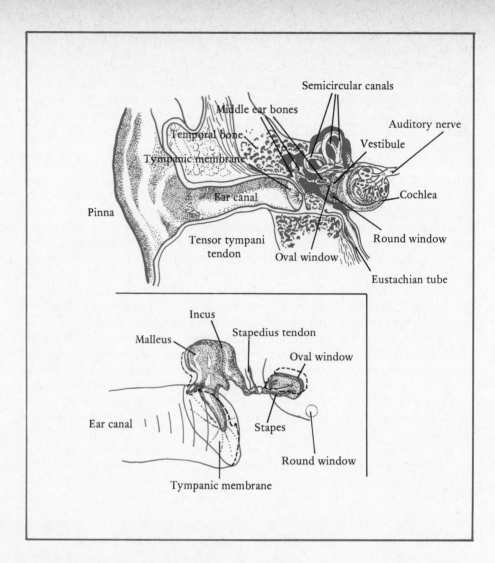

Figure 5.25 Diagram of the human ear showing its major structural components. (Redrawn from Carlson, 1981, p. 188.)

ing. Studies of single cells in the auditory areas of the brain have shown that there are cells which are responsive to certain frequencies and less responsive to others. For example, Katsuki (1961) has found cells that are maximally sensitive to certain narrow ranges of frequencies. If a sound of somewhat higher or lower frequency is sounded, the cells will fire, but not as vigorously. If a sound is made which is considerably different in frequency, the cells might not fire at all. The results are analogous with those reported by Hubel and Wiesel. As was discussed earlier, they found receptive fields in which proper stimulation brought about dramatic changes in the firing of a cell. Thus, there are many similarities between vision and audition.

Hearing Impairment

There are two main causes of hearing impairment: conduction deafness and nerve deafness. In **conduction deafness,** there is some interference with the conduction of sound to the neural mechanism of the inner ear. In **nerve deaf-**

Conduction deafness Deafness resulting from interference with the conduction of sound to the neural mechanism of the inner ear.

Nerve deafness Impairment in hearing due to damage to the cochlea or the auditory nerve.

ness, there is some damage to the cochlea or the auditory nerve.

CONDUCTION DEAFNESS. In conduction deafness, air waves are not able to reach the mechanism of the inner ear. This situation can be the result of a variety of causes, some as simple as a buildup of wax in the external ear canal. Other causes for conduction deafness include the hardening of the tympanic membrane and the destruction of the tiny bones within the ear which eventually stimulate the basilar membrane in the cochlea. Diseases that can create middle-ear pressure can also damage portions of the hearing mechanism.

NERVE DEAFNESS. In nerve deafness, there is damage to the cochlea or the auditory nerve; the most common cause is exposure to high levels of sound intensities. If a loud noise is presented to a subject for a long period of time or repeatedly, a person's sound threshold may increase permanently. An increase in threshold means that a higher amplitude (louder) sound will be necessary to achieve the same effect. We consider this a hearing impairment. Hearing impairments often come about just with an increase of age, particularly for sounds in the high-frequency range. Since speech depends primarily on low frequencies between 1,000 or 5,000 hertz, this causes a minimum of difficulties in most circumstances. However, when listening to a flute concerto, the loss of high frequencies significantly reduces an older person's ability to enjoy the music.

Far too often children in a classroom have been diagnosed as having low intelligence levels and have been labeled "stupid" by their classmates because they suffer from hearing losses. Sometimes children with partial hearing do not realize that they may be missing out on much of what is said to them. Of course, having a hearing impairment is not a behavior problem, but the unhappiness that may result from the labeling by misguided family and friends can clearly create behavior problems. In chapter 10 on Social Psychology, it will be pointed out that other people tend to attribute negative characteristics about individuals to the individuals themselves rather than to the circumstances in which people find themselves.

MEASUREMENT AND DIAGNOSIS. When a person is suspected of having a hearing impairment, the standard clinical tool for measuring hearing capacity is an audiometer. An audiometer produces different sound frequencies that can be presented to a patient through a headphone. The theory behind an audiometer is to find how much air pressure is necessary for subjects to hear a sound. For example, if an older person has lost the ability to hear high frequencies because of nerve deafness, the air pressure level at which these high frequencies would have to be presented to be heard would be significantly higher than for a normal person. The results of testing with an audiometer are presented on an audiogram. An audiogram is a graph showing hearing sensitivity at each of the selected frequencies in terms of the necessary air pressure required for a subject to just hear a specific frequency. This graph is then compared to the normal audiogram for adult subjects with no known hearing loss.

After it has been established that there is a hearing loss, a number of different tests can be used to assess where and why the hearing impairment came about. For example, there are bone conduction tests to measure hearing impairment, and tests to measure any pathology involved with the tiny bones within the middle ear. While a number of very sophisticated techniques have been devised to assess and diagnose hearing impairment, one of the simplest is the recognition of spoken words. If people cannot hear speech, it is very clear that they have a hearing impairment. Speech sounds are usually presented over a tape recording and are standardized in terms of loudness and voice pitch. A subject's performance is based on the number of words that can be repeated correctly at various intensity levels. This simple test of hearing can be used to assess hearing impairment and can be operated by nonmedical individuals who can then refer potential patients to physicians.

Many theories of hearing have been put forth over the past century, but most fall into two major classes. *Place theories* argue that the analysis of sound occurs at the inner ear. *Frequency theories* argue that the analysis of pitch and intensity occurs at higher levels of processing, perhaps at the auditory area of the cortex. There are problems with a strict interpretation of both theories; modern researchers have, therefore, put together complex theories of auditory information processing that account for the way humans hear. These theories include specific action in parts of the cochlea as well as complex frequency analyses at higher levels. The data are still unfolding; as in studies of visual information processing, the advent of electrophysiological techniques and single-cell recording have provided a wealth of new information. This much is certain: the intricacies of Beethoven can only be understood through a complex processing system of the type with which humans are endowed.

Taste and Smell

One of the great delights of life for many people is eating. While many eat only to fill their stomachs, the true gourmet eats for the pleasure of tasting and smelling. Food provides a perfect stimulus for the palate and the nose, for it contains many different substances that act as stimuli for both tasting and smelling.

When a person places a food substance in his or her mouth, the food is partially dissolved in saliva and stimulates the primary receptors for taste stimuli, the taste buds. On the tongue are a series of thousands of little papillae; looking like little bumps, each of these papillae is separated from the next by a "moat" and on the walls of these moats are the taste buds. The taste buds are actually made up of a number of taste cells. The individual taste cells have a relatively short life and are consequently always being renewed.

While the examination of basic tastes is continuing, most researchers accept the idea that there are four basic tastes: sweet, sour, salty, and bitter. Of course, most food that people eat is not made up of just one of these primary taste experiences. Veal parmigiana is obviously a complicated stimulus to the tongue! However, if we isolate stimuli that initiate only one taste sensation, we find that there are certain regions of the tongue that seem to be more sensitive than others. For example, the tip of the tongue is more sensitive to sweet tastes than the back of the tongue; by contrast, the back of the tongue is more sensitive to bitter tastes than the tip. It is important to remember that the taste cells are sensitive to all taste stimuli, but a given cell is more sensi-

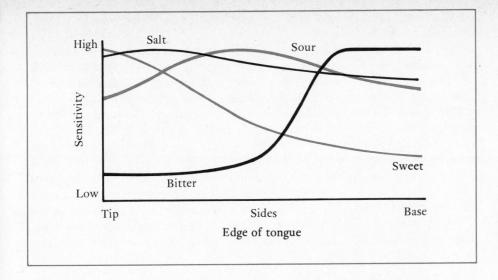

Figure 5.26 Variations in gustatory sensitivity along the edge of the tongue. Some portions of the tongue are more sensitive to certain tastes than others

tive to some stimuli than to others. In the visual sense, cones are sensitive to all wavelengths but are most sensitive to certain wavelengths. Shown in Figure 5.26 is the relative sensitivity of different portions of the tongue to the four basic stimuli for taste.

Like the sense of taste, smell (or, as it is technically called, olfaction) is a chemical sense, but here the stimulus is a chemical in the air. It is not as easy to classify basic smells as it is to classify basic tastes, but typical classes include flowery, foul, fruity, resinous, spicy, and burnt. It is not totally clear how odors affect the receptor cells of the olfactory epithelium. The *olfactory epithelium* contains the olfactory rods that are the true olfactory or smell nerve fibers. For different reasons, the electrophysiology of taste and smell are difficult to examine. The nerves of taste are not easily separated, whereas the nerves of smell are difficult to reach.

The olfactory rods of the olfactory epithelium may number as many as 30 million in each nostril. When a chemical substance in the air moves past the receptor cells, it must be partially absorbed into the mucus that covers the cells. When absorbed, it initiates the processes of smell. The number of molecules of chemical needed to initiate and recognize a new smell is amazingly small. Only 40 to 50 molecules are necessary for us to smell certain substances! This means that the olfactory system is *very* sensitive. In fact, it is thousands of times more sensitive than the taste system. Little research (compared to vision or audition) has been done on the olfactory system. This may be because of the inaccessible location; another reason may be because of the thousands of possible types of smell. Perhaps the most likely reason is because we do not rely on olfaction the way we do on vision or hearing.

Kinesthesis and Vestibular Sensitivity

Kinesthesis refers to feelings aroused by movements of the muscles, tendons, and joints; the study of kinesthesis provides information about bodily movements and internal sensations. In a previous section, we discussed how the movements of the muscles around the eye provide information concerning distance of objects through cues associated with accommodation and convergence. Similar coordination systems are constantly at work throughout the body.

The vestibular sense is the sense of bodily orientation and postural adjustment. Associated with the body wall of the cochlea of the ear are vestibular sacs and semicircular canals. These canals and sacs act together to provide information about the orientation of the head and body to both the eye-movement system and the posture system (Parker, 1980). Rapid movements of the head bring about changes in the semicircular canals. These changes bring about compensatory eye movements and sometimes changes in body orientation. Studies of the vestibular sense have become important in recent years because of the new role of space travel in science. Humans now move at enormous speeds through weightless space. The workings of the system that brings about dizziness when a person is spun about are therefore important. Psychological studies of the vestibular sense have become an important concern of the National Aeronautics and Space Administration.

Pain

People generally look forward to sensory experiences. We look forward to new smells, sights, tastes, sounds. However, we generally do not look forward to pain. Palpitating, penetrating, piercing, or pinching pain is not a delight. Yet, we all know that pain is adaptive. Without pain, we would not know when our bodies or sensory systems have been hurt or damaged.

One of the great problems in the study of pain is that it can be aroused in so many different ways. Stomach pains are easily raised by hunger, while the pain of toothaches is often initiated by an abscess. There are many kinds of headaches and each can be described differently. There are other kinds of pain, including postoperative pain, pain from terminal cancer, abdominal pain, chest pains, labor pains, frostbite, and even pain in a nonexisting limb

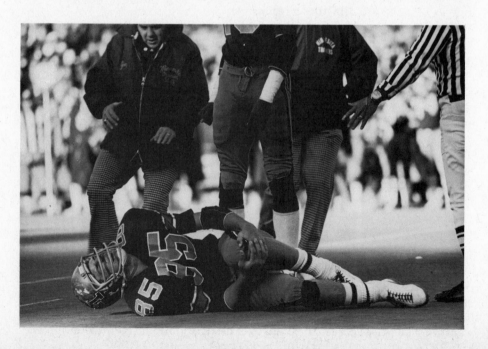

Pain is a signal to *stop* and take care of ourselves.

lost by trauma or surgery (see Melzack & Loeser, 1978; Omura, 1977). To explore pain more fully, psychologists have attempted to find stimuli that will allow them to study pain effectively. Chemical stimuli have been used to induce and measure pain (Smith et al., 1974). Another technique has been to use heat or cold stimulation (for example, Scott & Barber, 1977) and still another has been to use electrical shocks (for example, Smith et al., 1970; Tursky, 1977). It has been argued that the best method has been the use of electrical stimulation (Omura, 1977). Certain areas of the body are more sensitive to pain than others; the sole of the foot and the ball of the thumb are relatively insensitive compared to the back of the knee and the neck region. Furthermore, individuals have different sensitivities to pain. Some people have a low threshold for pain—that is, a comparatively low-level stimulus is responded to as painful—while others have fairly high thresholds (Sternbach, 1968, 1975; Woodrow et al., 1972). A person's threshold remains fairly constant and does not seem to vary with psychological state, but this idea has been challenged (Burke, 1973).

The receptors for pain are generally thought to be the free nerve endings appearing throughout the body. While there are a variety of different arrangements of free nerve endings, they are widely and frequently distributed. One commonly held belief about pain is that it results from overstimulation of skin or free nerve endings; however, this belief is wrong. One does not need to stimulate the skin very hard with a sharp knife to bring about pain. A great deal of pressure can be brought to bear with the back of the same skin-cutting knife and it will be felt as pressure, not pain. So, the mechanisms that account for pain are not so simple that they can be described by mere overstimulation ideas.

The most widely accepted explanation for how pain is processed by the human body is the Melzack-Wall gate control theory. Ronald Melzack and Patrick Wall have developed a theory of how pain is processed based on certain well-established principles of the nervous system (Melzack & Wall, 1965, 1970). The basic idea of the gate control theory is that the pattern of nervous system activity established in the body determines the extent to which one will feel pain. When a signal is sent toward the brain that might normally indicate a painful stimulus, it goes through a series of "gates." These gates can be opened or closed or even partially opened or closed. The extent to which these gates are open determines how much of the original pain signal gets through. A chemical called substance-P released by the sensory nerve fiber transmits pain impulses across the gate; this pain signal can be blocked by an innate brain opiate called *enkephalin* (Snyder, 1980). Certain drugs, electrical stimulation, and even acupuncture needles (Omura, 1976) have been thought to close the gates, partially or fully, so as to make the original painful stimulus less potent. The actual theory is more complicated and depends on sizes of nerve fibers as well as their level of development. It is for this reason that the Melzack-Wall theory is based on patterns of activity in the nervous system; certain patterns can be set up that can diminish (or even eliminate) feelings of pain. It has long been known that some synapses in the body are excitatory in nature and others are inhibitory; the Melzack-Wall theory relies heavily on this interplay of excitatory and inhibitory cells so as to establish patterns of activity that diminish (inhibit) excitatory or painlike feelings. In balance, it must be pointed out that gate control theory is by no means universally accepted; a number of researchers have argued that the

The New War on Pain

While somewhat controversial among scientific researchers, the notion of "gate control" to eliminate or diminish pain has been gaining supporters.

NEWSWEEK Pulsing, rasping, grating, pinching, throbbing, gnawing, wrenching, burning: no medical symptom is more ubiquitous—or more variously described—than pain. To most people, pain is a mercifully brief interlude. It may be nothing more than a tension headache or a pulled muscle. Or it may, in such forms as the crushing sensation in the chest that signals a heart attack, serve a vital function by indicating that something has gone wrong in the body. But for millions of people, pain is neither a minor nor a major symptom. It is a disease in itself, a debilitating and seemingly interminable affliction that may have begun as an acute warning sign but remained to take over its victim's body. For its sufferers, chronic pain becomes a way of life. Seeking relief, they hobble and limp from doctor to doctor and surgeon to surgeon. Americans with back pain—the most common chronic syndrome—account for more than 18 million physician office visits a year, while those with migraine and other headaches take up more than 12 million hours of doctors' time. . . .

New discoveries about the complex nature of pain have caused much of the excitement. First, psychologist Ronald Melzack of Montreal's McGill University and neuroanatomist Patrick D. Wall of the University of London announced a "gate-control" theory of pain which has illuminated how pain impulses are transmitted and how they may be blocked. The theory may explain how acupuncture and electrical stimulation stop pain. More recently, researchers in the U.S. and Great Britain discovered that the body produces its own natural narcotics, called enkephalins, that may lead to the production of nonaddictive painkillers.

Innovative ways of treating chronic pain also have developed rapidly. At least fifteen centers have sprung up across the U.S. devoted exclusively to chronic-pain problems. The clinics bring to bear the skills of a wide range of medical disciplines, from anesthesiology to psychiatry, to search out the cause of a patient's problems and prescribe the best treatment. The philosophy that guides the clinics in their treatments is the recognition that chronic pain is a complex malady in which physical, psychological and social factors play a part.

evidence does not exist to support it (Dyck, Lambert, & O'Brien, 1976; Vylicky et al., 1969), but other research is supportive (Dennis & Melzack, 1977; Melzack & Loeser, 1978).

A number of individuals are afflicted with chronic, unceasing pain. Many of these individuals have sought the help of acupuncturists. Initially developed in China, acupuncture is a technique of inserting long, fine needles into various sites in the body to relieve pain. Needle insertions are often far from the site of pain, and one practitioner may use different sites than another practitioner. Controlled studies of acupuncture have shown varying results; some have provided support (Gaw, Chang, & Shaw, 1975; Lee et al., 1975; Mann et al., 1973), while other studies have found weak or nonexistent effects (Clark & Yang, 1974; Day et al., 1975; Li et al., 1975).

Investigation of pain receptors and the nature of pain has been relatively meager when compared to work on vision and audition (see Weisenberg, 1977). But pain is an adaptive and important aspect of our sensory and perceptual lives; while it is a difficult one to investigate, it is no less interesting.

Extrasensory Perception

Many people are fascinated with the possibility that extrasensory perception really exists. Extrasensory perception, or ESP, as it is sometimes called, is really a term used to describe several different phenomena, including telepathy, clairvoyance, and precognition. *Telepathy* is the process by which thought processes are transferred from one person to the next. *Clairvoyance* is the ability to recognize objects or events that are not impinging on the normal sensory receptors. The ability of a person to recognize the content of a message in a sealed envelope is an example of clairvoyance. Many people who make no claim to having extrasensory perception have experienced forms of precognition. *Precognition* is the perception of future events. Many individuals have studied the nature of ESP; indeed, the British Society for the Study of Psychic Phenomena has existed since the 1800s (with Nobel laureates serving as presidents).

Until recently, ESP had never been taken very seriously by the psychological community. The phenomena reported by people who have claimed to have ESP have generally been tricks and the products of clever showpeople. However, in recent years there has been some evidence to suggest that ESP may exist. The evidence is not strong, nor has it been repeated on many occasions. Furthermore, when visible, the phenomena are not affected by certain characteristics of experiments the way normal perceptual events are. None of these criticisms yield a devastating rejection of ESP, but they do make most perceptual psychologists somewhat wary.

The recent resurgence of scientific interest in ESP was to a great extent the result of two journal articles on the subject. The first, published in the respected scientific journal *Nature,* reported on the results of some ESP experiments at the Stanford Research Institute with Israeli magician Uri Geller. The article reported some seemingly incredible findings suggesting that Geller indeed possessed ESP. In the same week another article published in the British magazine *New Scientist* dramatically undermined many of the findings presented in the Stanford Research Institute report.

With the original research paper in disrepute, the scientific community placed little weight on the potential of ESP. There is not enough evidence that it exists. There are too many reasons to believe that its purporters, like Geller, are mere showpeople. And last, there is too little careful research in the field. Whatever the outcome of the final research on ESP, the entire process shows how psychologists use scientific methods to investigate such problems. Most scientists maintain a healthy skepticism about ESP; however, some would argue that psychologists refuse to accept data that do not agree with their preconceptions. The active consideration of the possibilities of ESP continues.

SUMMARY

Our perceptual systems are arranged so that we can take a large amount of information and process it in meaningful and complex ways in order to experience the world fully. Our perceptual systems are adaptive, for without them we would be unable to cope with even the simple demands of life. Think of the handicaps a blind or deaf person is faced with; certainly these difficulties make us more aware of the wealth of complex analyses that our perceptual systems are involved in.

Each of our perceptual systems has developed a complex processing system to handle its sensory domain. Each of these systems can act independently of the other; our visual system doesn't have to have the auditory system to work, nor does the auditory system have to have a working smell or taste system. However, it is important to remember that though some senses predominate over others, our perceptual systems work together to achieve an integrated knowledge of the world.

The interaction of our senses through our varied experiences seems to be a critical variable. Remember the study by Held and Hein (1963)? It showed that early experience in receiving visual and tactile information simultaneously was necessary for the development of good motor coordination in newborn kittens. Although perceptual processing begins at the moment of birth, early experiences in the life of a newborn will determine how well his or her perceptual system will develop.

Our perceptual systems provide us with a wealth of information. Our senses make our lives more varied and complete. Without our senses and our integrated perceptual system our adaptive abilities would be limited and the dimensions of our lives would be narrower. Actual perception involves many processing strategies and all of the senses. A complete and accurate definition of perception must be sufficiently vague to account for all of the senses and all of the variables involved. The definition of perception presented at the beginning of this chapter allows for all of the senses, the variables, and the processing strategies. Perception is the process by which people attach meaning to stimuli by interpreting their sensory input, clearly a complicated process.

CHAPTER REVIEW

1. Perception is the process by which people attach meaning to stimuli by interpreting their sensory input through complex processing mechanisms.
2. The main structures of the eye are the cornea, iris, pupil, crystalline lens, and retina.
3. The retina is made up of ten layers, the most important of which are, (1) the rods and cones, (2) the bipolar layers, and (3) the ganglion cell layer.
4. The ganglion cells make up the nuclei of long axons that form the optic nerve.
5. The duplicity theory of vision suggests that vision is controlled by two classes of receptors with different functions. After information leaves the retina, it proceeds to higher centers of analysis through the optic chiasm, the lateral geniculate nucleus, and on to the striate cortex.
6. Visual receptive fields are areas on the retina that, when stimulated, produce changes in the firing of cells in the visual system.
7. Saccadic eye movements have a latency of 250 milliseconds.
8. The three main characteristics of color—hue, brightness, and saturation—are also described by the physical terms, wavelengths, intensity, and purity.
9. The trichromatic theory of color vision put forth by Young and Helmholtz argues that all colors can be made by mixing three basic ones and that the retina has three basic types of cones.
10. The opponent processing theory put forth by Hering suggests that color is coded by a series of receptors that either respond positively or negatively to different wavelengths.
11. Studies of sensory deprivation have shown that early experience in the life of an organism is important if perceptual systems are to function properly.
12. The monocular cues for depth perception include linear perspective, texture, and accommodation. The primary binocular cue is retinal disparity.
13. Size constancy is the ability of the perceptual system to know that an object remains constant in size regardless of its distance or the size of the retinal image.

14. An illusion is a perception of a stimulus that differs from the way the physical stimulus would normally lead us to expect it to appear.
15. Reading speed is determined in large part by the number of fixations a person makes per minute; to change reading speed we change the number of fixations per minute.
16. In studies of visual search, the speed with which subjects search for a specific target is measured.
17. Studies of attention have shown that there seems to be a filter that allows us to attend to some stimuli but not to others.
18. While images are a mental rather than physical phenomenon, they have edges—points beyond which visual information ceases to be represented.
19. The data on subliminal perception are weak at best and nonexistent at worst, but this does not mean that it cannot or does not exist.
20. Sound is a psychological term describing changes in pressure through a medium; the medium may be gaseous, liquid, or solid.
21. The frequency and amplitude of a sound wave determine how it will be heard.
22. The ear, the receptive organ for audition, can be divided into three major parts: the external, middle, and internal ear.
23. In nerve deafness, there is damage to the cochlea mechanism or the auditory nerve and the most common cause is exposure to high levels of sound intensities.
24. Both place theories and frequency theories have been used to account for hearing.
25. On the tongue are a series of thousands of little papillae, looking like little bumps. Each of these papillae is separated from the next by a "moat," and on the walls of these moats are the taste buds.
26. The olfactory epithelium contains the olfactory rods, which are the true olfactory (smell) nerve fibers.
27. Taste, smell, pain, kinesthetic, and vestibular systems are much like the visual systems in that they all receive, code, and process information in meaningful and complex ways.
28. The receptors for pain are generally thought to be the free nerve endings that appear throughout the body.
29. The most widely accepted explanation for how pain is processed by the human body is the Melzack-Wall gate control theory.
30. Extrasensory perception, or ESP, includes such phenomena as telepathy, clairvoyance, and precognition. While not widely accepted, the phenomena are under active research.

SUGGESTIONS FOR FURTHER READING

COREN, S., AND GIRGUS, J. S. *Seeing is deceiving: The psychology of visual illusions.* Hillsdale, NJ: Lawrence Erlbaum Associates, 1978.

COREN, S., PORAC, C., AND WARD, L. M. *Sensation and perception.* New York: Academic Press, 1979.

DEMBER, W. N., AND WARM, J. S. *Psychology of perception* (2nd ed.). New York: Holt, Rinehart and Winston, 1970.

GELDARD, R. F. *The human senses* (2nd ed.). New York: John Wiley & Sons, 1972.

HABER, R. N., AND HERSHENSON, M. *The psychology of visual perception* (2nd ed.). New York: Holt, Rinehart and Winston, 1980.

HOCHBERG, J. E. *Perception* (2nd ed.). Englewood Cliffs, NJ: Prentice-Hall, 1977.

LUDEL, J. *Introduction to sensory processes.* San Francisco, CA: W. H. Freeman Company, 1978.

WHEN PSYCHOLOGISTS STUDY how an organism develops, they gain insight into the nature of biological, social, and psychological processes underlying growth. With this information, developmental psychologists may predict the behavior of an organism as well as determine how they can best help it develop its potential. Development is a lifelong process beginning with conception and continuing until death. It touches all spheres in which an organism or individual interacts. This chapter provides an overview of physical, intellectual, and social development and portrays behavior as a constantly changing process that occurs in a systematic manner. By understanding child development, psychologists can help children cope with the demands of life and help parents and educators cope with the demands of ever-changing children. By understanding adult development, psychologists can help adults cope with the unique demands of their lives and help educators, health care providers, and other service personnel meet the demands of their constantly changing needs.

CHAPTER 6

Development

The loving mother teaches her child to walk alone. She is far enough from him so that she cannot actually support him, but she holds out her arms to him. She imitates his movements, and if he totters, she swiftly bends as if to seize him, so that the child might believe that he is not walking alone . . . And yet, she does more. Her face beckons like a reward, an encouragement. Thus, the child walks alone with his eyes fixed on his mother's face, *not* on the difficulties in his way. He supports himself by the arms that do not hold him and constantly strives towards the refuge in his mother's embrace, little suspecting *that in the very same moment that he is emphasizing his need for her, he is proving that he can do without her,* because he is walking alone.

KIERKEGAARD
1846

For each individual, their development is their history.

There are vast individual differences among children; while some are slow to develop a sense of independence, others develop rapidly. This phenomenon is often noted by parents and psychologists who see the great differences among children. Activity levels, native abilities, and growth rates differ. Of course, each of these factors contributes to the overall personality of children and how they view themselves. We will examine later how personality and self-concepts are formed, but now let us look more closely at how development proceeds and how each individual's basic characteristics interact with the environment to produce people who are unique not only in heredity, but also in experiences. Each of us goes through infancy, childhood, adolescence, adulthood, and ultimately death. Our changing abilities and varied interactions during life stages have some common characteristics.

Psychologists are interested in how people develop and mature. They are not alone in this curiosity; most people are interested in their own development and the kinds of things they did when they were children and the interactions they had when they were young. Humans spend significant portions of their lives looking back at the past and remembering growing up. The reasons for this looking back are obvious; much of our present behavior is determined by events that happened in the past. We look at the way we grew up to gain some insight into why we are the way we are. As adults with children of our own, we bring them up in much the same way that our parents brought us up and tell them stories about the times when we were their size. Usually, however, our stories don't begin early enough because development begins long before we can remember.

THE FIRST NINE MONTHS OF LIFE

Zygote A fertilized egg.

Embryo Human organism from the fourth day after conception through the fortieth day.

A person's growth starts with the moment of conception. As an ovum and sperm join to form a **zygote,** or fertilized egg, life has begun. Fertilization actually takes place in the fallopian tubes, and the newly formed zygote slowly descends to the uterus over a period of 3 to 5 days. The zygote then implants itself in the blood-lined walls of the uterus. In human beings, from the fourth day or so after conception through about the eighth week, the developing organism planted in the uterus wall is no longer called a zygote but rather an **embryo.** The embryonic stage of development is a particularly important one because during these early weeks, critical growth processes are taking place that will affect the organism for the rest of its life. At around the fortieth day after conception or during the eighth week of pregnancy, the embryo reaches a new stage of development at which it receives a new name; the unborn baby is called a **fetus** from this eighth week until it is born.

Since the process of maturation and development begins, on the average, a full 266 days before birth, let's take a closer look at the first 266 days or the first 9 months of life. The first 9 months are divided into trimesters, three periods of 3 months each. In an excellent book entitled *The First Nine Months of Life* (New York: Simon & Schuster, 1962) Geraldine Flanagan describes the growth process in some detail.

Fetus The unborn organism from the fortieth day after conception until birth.

The First Trimester

THE FIRST DAY.   When the sperm and the egg combine to form the zygote, within minutes the basic characteristics of the individual are established. The sex of the child and its hair, skin, and eye color are determined. The likelihood that it will be tall or short, fat or lean, and its basic intellectual gifts are also established. During the first day the fertilized egg begins to divide; within 10 hours division has already produced four cells.

THE FIRST WEEK.   Within a few days, about a dozen cells make their way down the fallopian tubes to the inner linings of the uterus. There these cells become implanted and begin the process of differentiation that will allow different organs and parts of the body to be formed. Some of the cells will form the **placenta.** This is a group of blood vessels and tissues connecting the unborn child's umbilical cord to the uterus. The placenta serves as a mechanism for exchange of nutrients and waste products. By the end of the first week as many as one hundred cells are clearly attached to the wall of the uterus. The zygote is now officially an embryo.

Placenta A group of blood vessels and membranes connecting a human fetus's umbilical cord to the uterus. It serves as a mechanism for the exchange of nutrients and waste products.

THE FIRST MONTH.   During the first month, the embryo really begins to develop and take shape. The initial hundred cells are now thousands. By the end of the month, microscopic examination can show the beginnings of arms and legs. While only a half-inch long, the body has the rudiments of eyes, ears, mouth, and brain. By the twenty-fifth day after conception, a primitive version of the heart is usually beating. By the end of its first month the embryo is 10,000 times larger than the fertilized egg was, and soon during its second month it will begin to resemble a human.

THE SECOND MONTH.   During the fourth and fifth week, though the embryo is still not complete, it is constantly changing; by the seventh or eighth week, the embryo is considered complete. Even though it is less than an inch long, weighing only $\frac{1}{30}$ of an ounce, it begins to resemble a human being. The embryo is growing approximately a millimeter a day, with each day bringing great changes in development. From one day to the next new parts of the human form are taking shape. On day 33 what will be the nose takes shape; on day 37 the nose seems fully formed. Around day 47 the first true bone cells appear, thus bringing to a close the embryonic period. At this point the growing organism is considered a fetus.

THE THIRD MONTH.   While weighing only an ounce, at the end of the third month the fetus is about 3 inches long, can kick its legs, turn its feet, and swallow, although the mother cannot yet feel the baby. Growth continues during the third month so that features become more defined and sex characteristics begin to show. The digestive, breathing, and motion systems become stronger as it grows.

The Second Trimester

During this middle part of the pregnancy, the fetus develops significantly. In the fourth month, it grows considerably and increases in length to as much as 10 inches. The fetus puts on weight, increases in strength, and consumes a good deal of food, oxygen, and water through the placenta. Its heartbeat is stronger and can be heard with a stethoscope. Its muscles become significantly stronger—the mother can feel movement in the early part of the fifth month. The fetus will gain 2 inches in height in the fifth and sixth months and will be about 14 inches tall at the end of the sixth month. Most important, during the sixth month the fetus can maintain regular breathing. This is significant because if the baby is born prematurely, it must be able to breathe. When a baby is born prematurely during the sixth month with an immature respiratory system, sufficient oxygen will not be carried to the baby's tissues to allow for continued life. At the end of the second trimester, after about 28 weeks, maintaining life outside of the uterus becomes a real possibility. Fetuses born before 28 weeks have serious problems sustaining life.

The Third Trimester

Pregnant women gain a considerable amount of weight in this last third of their pregnancy. The fetus has grown significantly. In the seventh month it may gain a pound, in the eighth month 2 pounds, and in the ninth month it may gain a pound a week. During this trimester, the fetus becomes increasingly stronger. Its respiratory system continues to develop, as do its internal organs. The musculature has grown and matured significantly; mothers will report strong kicking and movement during this time. While the basic structure of the fetus has been determined long before the third trimester, development is still proceeding. If the fetus is born too much ahead of its approximate due date, its lungs and other organs are not sufficiently developed to sustain life without help from advanced medical technology. For example, an infant that is born weighing under 5 pounds often has trouble breathing and may need the help of mechanical instruments to facilitate breathing until its lungs have sufficiently matured. While medical technology has made some startling advances with premature babies, a full-term baby is still the ideal for its health and development (see Table 6.1).

PREGNANCY AND BIRTH

The first 9 months of life begin at the moment of conception. Incredibly, an ovum and a sperm join and create a multicellular wonder called a human baby. The maturation of this fetus is indeed remarkable as it develops from

Table 6.1 The first 9 months of life: Major developments

AGE	SIZE	CHARACTERISTICS
1 week	150 cells	Ovum attaches to uterine lining.
2 weeks	Several thousand cells	Placental circulation established.
3 weeks	$\frac{1}{10}$ inch	Heart and blood vessels begin to develop; basics of brain and central nervous system form.
4 weeks	$\frac{1}{4}$ inch	Kidneys and digestive tract begun. Rudiments of ears, nose, eyes.
6 weeks	$\frac{1}{2}$ inch	Arms and legs, jaws forming around mouth.
8 weeks	1 inch, $\frac{1}{30}$ oz	Bones begin to develop in limbs; now referred to as fetus. Sex organs forming.
12 weeks	3 inches, 1 oz	Sex distinguished. Kidneys functioning, liver manufacturing red blood cells. Fetal movements.
16 weeks	$6\frac{1}{2}$ inches, 4 oz	Heartbeat may be detected by physician, beginning of calcification of bones.
20 weeks	10 inches, 8 oz	Mother feels movements.
24 weeks	12 inches, $1\frac{1}{2}$ lb	Vernix (white waxy substance) protects body. Eyes open, eyebrows and eyelashes form, skin wrinkled and red, respiratory system not mature enough to support life.
28 weeks	15 inches, $2\frac{1}{2}$ lb	Fully developed. Needs to gain in size, strength, and maturity of systems.
32 weeks	17 inches, 4 lb	Fat layer beneath skin to regulate body temperature.
36 weeks	19 inches, 6 lb	Settles into position for birth.
38 weeks	21 inches, 8 lb	Full term—266 days from conception

single cells to hundreds of cells, first during the embryonic stage and then during the fetal stages. There are many important events to consider during pregnancy and many events that will bear on the development of the unborn child. As an unborn child grows, its future life is affected by the internal environment and life-support systems as provided by its mother. Environmental factors affecting the mother, such as diet, infection, radiation, or drugs, also affect the infant she carries. Physicians are quick to indicate that prenatal nutrition affects not only the mother's health but the child's health as well. Throughout pregnancy, a mother's nutrition is important to the child, because oxygen and nutrients, if they are available, can only be effectively delivered to the child through the bloodstream. For example, the absence of vitamin E in the diet can create an oxygen deficiency. While the mother may never be aware of these deficiencies, they can harm the growing baby. Furthermore, babies born to women who are on a low protein diet are more vulnerable to serious diseases and are more likely to have difficult births.

The life of a fetus is now under more active investigation than ever before. It is difficult to read a newspaper without finding an article about how drugs affect pregnant women. Increasingly, scientific studies have been showing that drugs of any kind affect the growth of an unborn organism. Such damage is especially likely if the drug were taken during the early weeks and months of pregnancy, particularly during the embryonic stage.

We see that the development of a new person proceeds with little active involvement of a mother; but, at the same time, we recognize that her nurturing of the growing organism within her is extremely important, especially during certain critical stages. We conclude therefore that *nurture* is affecting *nature*. These processes of nurture and nature are dependent upon each other and act together to affect the development and growth of human beings.

Maternal Emotions

Since a baby receives its oxygen supply and nutrients through the placenta, changes in the blood composition of a pregnant woman can affect her unborn child. Obviously many things, particularly drugs, can change blood composition. Whenever hormones are released into the bloodstream, they cross the placenta to the baby. Hormones are released for a variety of reasons including strong emotions, such as anxiety and fear.

Many researchers believe that a woman's emotional state during pregnancy affects the fetus in significant ways; however, the scientific literature in support of this idea is minimal at best. It is very hard to decide what causes an infant to behave the way it does—genetics, a difficult birth, maternal emotions, or even nutrition. Often, more than one of these events occur together. A woman who has been very upset about her pregnancy may not have received adequate nourishment and may have undergone great hormonal changes due to the emotional stress she may have been under. The infant she carries is potentially subject to the same hormonal imbalance during critical developmental periods. Once born, that child may be easily upset, not easily soothed, and prone to periods of distractibility. It must be emphasized, however, that such ideas are still considered speculative by most serious scientists.

There is little evidence to suggest that maternal emotions directly affect the subsequent physical development of a newborn. However, there are data to suggest that a woman's disposition during pregnancy and her attitude toward her unborn will affect how she will treat the child and how warmly it will be received. Furthermore, studies have shown that a mother's attitude toward her child will influence her ability to nurse the baby and provide the warmth and love that will foster emotional growth and development.

The Birth Process

No more fascinating event can happen in the life of a man and a woman than to experience the birth of a child. For an average of 266 days they await the final moment at which an organism, part of each of them, will enter the world. In many societies, the birth process is a taboo subject, a difficult experience, and one that is considered shameful. Contemporary American society has kept the birth process one from which men are excluded and one which women have been taught to dread. However, in some societies and increasingly in ours the birth of a baby is an exciting, shared experience.

For centuries in many cultures women have delivered babies without the aid of physicians, and the event has been attended by friends and been considered a joyous one. While attitudes about the birth process are changing in Western society, many women still fear this most natural of all functions.

When a baby is to be born, a woman goes into labor. **Labor** is the process

Labor The process whereby the uterus contracts to open and allow the baby to descend through the birth canal to the outside world.

through which the uterus contracts to open and allow the baby to descend through the birth canal to the outside world. Every woman's labor is different, but there are certain characteristics of labor that all women experience. Labor can be divided into three stages: early labor, active labor, and the transition period.

Women go through all three stages of labor; yet the extent to which they are in each stage varies dramatically. For example, women who have never had a child before typically have a 9- to 12-hour labor, whereas second- and third-time mothers have labors that may be as short as 3 or 4 hours. Labor is not particularly comfortable, but it does not have to be particularly painful.

Early labor is characterized by infrequent contractions of the uterus. In the past, people have called these contractions labor pains. The sensations that a woman feels are the muscles of her uterus contracting to dilate, or open, the cervix to allow the baby to descend through the birth canal. The cervix has to open to about 10 centimeters to allow the baby's head to pass through. In early labor, the cervix dilates from being totally closed to about 3 centimeters. In this stage of labor a woman's contractions may be anywhere from 5 to 30 minutes apart. Rhythmically, every 20 minutes or so, she will have a contraction that lasts approximately 30 seconds. As time passes, her contractions come closer together, perhaps 5 minutes apart.

In the second stage of labor or, as it is sometimes called, *active labor,* the woman's cervix dilates from 3 to 7 centimeters. Contractions now come approximately every 3 to 5 minutes, are somewhat more intense, and it is during this stage that the woman is usually hospitalized. The third stage of labor is called *transition.* Transition is the period in labor during which the cervix dilates to a full 10 centimeters. Contractions become stronger, last longer,

Preparing for childbirth means practice in both selected physical exercises and breathing techniques.

and are the least comfortable. If a woman is to experience pain in labor, her major discomfort will occur during this transitional stage before the baby is born.

When the cervix has dilated a full 10 centimeters and the mother has passed from early labor through transition, the baby is now ready to descend the birth canal and be born. In a period of anywhere from 5 minutes to 2 hours the woman bears down with her abdominal muscles to push the baby from the uterus through the birth canal. It is this slow process of descent through the birth canal that people typically think of when they speak about a baby being born. As the baby emerges from the birth canal, its head becomes visible, followed by its shoulders, stomach, and feet. The baby is still attached to its mother by the umbilical cord. Within a few minutes the placenta at the other end of the umbilical cord detaches from the walls of the woman's uterus and is also delivered.

A woman's behavior in labor is not easy to characterize. Her feelings and overt behaviors in early labor are very different from those she experiences in active labor or transition. For example, in early labor a woman is very much aware of her surroundings and basically feels good emotionally and physically. In active labor and in transition she usually feels tired, less comfortable, and less tolerant of intrusions on her birth experience. In recent years, psychologists and physicians have been studying how these physical changes in labor affect a woman's emotions and her relationship with her child. Increasingly, they are finding that the birth experience, including the discomfort, is an important part of the relationship between mother and child. The relationship that a mother forms with her child, even in its first hours of life, can have long-lasting behavioral consequences (de Chateau, 1977).

The process of labor and delivery of a child can be summarized and described; however, each woman's birth experience is unique. Perhaps the best way to characterize it is to read excerpts from one woman's diary. Linda tells the story of her birth experience:

Getting contractions all night, but nothing strong enough to keep me awake. Got up at 11, they were still coming—kept up all day but were very easy to ignore. About 7 P.M. friends came over and I began to notice that the contractions were getting stronger. It's weird to think that we're probably going to have a baby tonight! I'm not admitting it to myself, I keep expecting the contractions to go away!

We got to the hospital, were taken to an examining room and a nurse from Labor & Delivery checked me to verify that I was in labor. At 12:30 A.M. I was admitted, at 2 to 3 cm dilation; only $\frac{1}{3}$ of the way, but the slowest part (to 3 cm) behind us.

Into the labor room and Alan had to wait outside while I was prepped, piles of information recorded. Funny how you lose all modesty and inhibitions. Finally, I got settled in bed, Alan came back in and we got down to work. By 3:30 A.M. we were both falling asleep. Alan looked so tired I felt so sorry for him. I dozed between contractions and he woke me when one was due. Every time the nurse checked me, it was another disappointment—dilation was progressing so very slowly. At about 7:30 A.M., still only 4 cm dilated, the contractions suddenly picked up. They got very strong and much harder to manage. All our training came together now. Alan got to his feet and didn't sit down again until after the birth. In 45 minutes I dilated from 4 to 6 cm and everything began to get hazy. I was having trouble concentrating, my eyes kept closing, my hands were tensing and tingling. Alan was massaging my abdomen, talking to me, counting the seconds, encouraging me. He was fantastic. Suddenly I felt like I *had* to push! I had no control over this overwhelming urge, it was as if some internal hand was pushing so hard I couldn't stop it. The nurse raced in, checked me, "complete" and all hell broke loose. No leisurely buildup to delivery, no rational progression of techniques. One nurse was sent to call the doctor and the bed began rolling down the hall.

I was no longer having those intense contractions, but it was so unreal, so hard to believe labor was over and we were about to welcome our first child. Into the Delivery Room, onto the table. There seemed to be so much time for everything. Alan came in, mask and all, and just looked so silly. We adjusted everything, mirrors, lights, took a couple of pictures. When I felt the contractions, which were quite mild now, I pushed, in between I just babbled—how fantastic, super, I can't believe it! With the third push, the head was really showing and didn't recede when the contraction ended. With the next contraction I could see the head and then felt a pop—the head was born and the rest of the body just slid out! Dr. Brent said it's a girl and we just were so excited, crying, laughing. I just couldn't believe it. I knew she was mine and I was so thrilled. She was so beautiful—we were prepared for a newborn molded head, pushed in face, bluish body—not our Sarah! They cleaned her off and gave her to me (Alan continually photographing). There we were only 5 minutes after she was born, 9 A.M., and I felt great!

THE NEWBORN

With 9 months of development behind them, newborns enter the world nearly fully functional. They smell, hear, see, touch, and can experience pain. While their taste system is not fully developed, this too will become functional within a short time. However, it is important to remember that the nervous systems of newborns are not completely developed and are sensitive to experience. An infant's nervous system is still undergoing great changes; there is a proliferation of new dendrites and an increased capacity to use the sensory system to experience the world. Yet, the newborn comes into the world well equipped. Many have considered the newborn to have few abilities to perceive the world the way adults do; however, this is not true. The perceptual systems of newborns are amazingly good. They will follow moving lights with their eyes, and their pupils will dilate and constrict with changes in the light levels in a room.

The development of perceptual systems in human newborns has been examined in a series of studies reported by Fantz (1961). In such studies, newborns are placed inside an experimental apparatus on their backs and are allowed to view various kinds of picturelike material. Sometimes the pictures are faces; sometimes they are patterns. In either case, the experimenter records how long the infant fixates or looks at each picture and how often each kind of picture is viewed (see Figure 6.1). This technique allows the psychologist to assess the nature of an infant's perceptual abilities. For example, if the infant spends no more time looking at a picture of a face than a series of random squiggles, the observer infers that faces have no more meaning to the child than squiggles. Researchers can assess the extent to which the child's perceptual abilities present either a homogeneous blank field or a field that has thin lines very close together. By comparing how far apart these lines have to be for the infant to attend to them, they can assess visual ability to make fine discrimination. If visual acuity is not good, lines that are very close together are seen as homogeneous fields and are not examined very often.

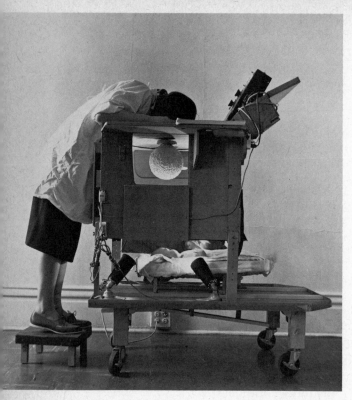

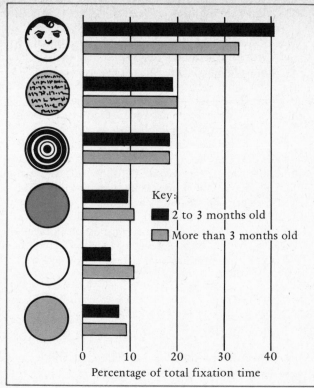

Figure 6.1 A child is placed at the bottom of a viewing box in which either the experimenter can observe the nature of the child's eye movements or a camera can be placed there to record where the child is looking. When the total time spent looking at patterns is broken down into the kinds of patterns the infant looked at, it is very clear that infants looked at faces or patterned material much more often than at homogeneous fields

Rooting reflex Reflex in the infant that causes it to turn its head toward the direction of stimulation of the lips or cheek.

Sucking reflex Reflex in which an infant makes sucking motions when presented with a stimulus to the lips, such as a nipple or object.

Results from studies like this one have shown that newborns have amazingly good perceptual systems and prefer complex fields to simple ones. They prefer curved patterns rather than straight ones (Fantz & Miranda, 1975). They prefer to look at human faces rather than random patterns or mixed-up faces. Ready to experience the world, newborns enter it with an amazing ability to experience the world through the senses and to perceive the environment (Lewis & Maurer, 1980). They know the difference between warmth and cold and between light and darkness. They arrive ready to begin to have the outside world shape them.

Reflexes

At birth, the infant comes equipped with certain reflexes that are innate. A primary reflex is the rooting reflex. In **rooting,** babies turn their heads toward the direction of stimulation, so if the lips or cheeks are touched by the breast, nipple, or hand, infants will turn their heads toward the stimulation. In addition, babies will suck when provided a nipple; sucking has adaptive value, for without **sucking** an infant would not be able to obtain needed nourishment. Infants also have a **grasping reflex;** when an object touches or is placed in their hands, they will grasp it vigorously. When the soles of their feet are touched or scratched, infants project their toes outward and up—the **Babinski reflex.** Still another reaction is the **Moro reflex,** an outstretching of arms and legs and crying when there is an intense noise or change in the environment. Often these reflexes are used to assess neurological damage and an infant's rate of development.

248

Figure 6.2 The visual cliff is a method used by Walk and Gibson (1961) to determine the extent of infants' depth perception. Infants are placed on a glass surface, half of which is covered with a checkerboard pattern. The same pattern is placed several feet below the transparent half of the glass surface. The infants are allowed to crawl from the patterned area onto the transparent area. If the infants have no depth perception, they should be willing to crawl onto the transparent side as often as the patterned side. However, if the infants do have depth perception, they will refuse to crawl onto the transparent side, even with a mother's inducement and suggestion to come to her. These findings have recently been confirmed and extended to show that as long as they have the ability to crawl, infants will show the avoidance behaviors (Rader, Bausano, & Richards, 1980)

We see that newborns are equipped to experience the world. As each day passes, they are exposed to new experiences that will modify their impressions of what the world is like. Infant abilities and reflexes have been laid down in advance through genetics and the transmission of genes. While biological variables will continue to change and affect development, nurturing and experiences with the environment will be more critical in determining how infants respond from this point on.

Grasping reflex Reflex in the infant that causes it to grasp vigorously any object that touches or is placed in its hand.

The environment, however, will not be the exclusive determinant of behavior. We know that biological and environmental influences continue to interact. It is true that many biological factors are already determined; it is also true that biological development seems "prewired" to initiate certain behaviors at certain points in life. However, biological variables are influenced by the environment. In the same way, the environment is influenced by biological variables. Nature and nurture interact in a complex manner and a lifelong process. We will see later that this lifelong interaction between nature and nurture plays an especially important role in the development of language and intelligence and in maladjustment.

Babinski reflex Reflex in the infant that causes it to project its toes outward and up when the soles of its feet are touched.

Moro reflex Reflex in the infant that causes it to outstretch its arms and legs and cry when there is a loud noise or change in the environment.

Bonding

Although psychologists have always argued that a person's environment is important to development, the case has never been made as strongly with newborns as in the last decade. Psychologists and physicians are realizing that the first few minutes and hours of a child's life are crucial for the development of certain behaviors. In particular, these researchers are becoming acutely aware that a special emotional attachment process, which seems to be inborn, takes place between parent and child. This attachment has often been called **bonding** (see p. 148).

Early research into the relationships of parents to infants showed that pro-

Bonding A special emotional attachment process that takes place between parent and child.

longed sensory deprivation is not good for children (Bowlby, 1958; Freud, 1965; Spitz, 1945); the newer research shows that it is disastrous (Kennell, Voos, & Klaus, 1979). Researchers like Marshall Klaus and his colleagues are presenting evidence to suggest that immediately after delivery of a baby there is a period of heightened sensitivity for the mother; during this period she can interact with her newborn and begin to form a specific attachment to the child. They argue that during these first moments a series of mutual interactions takes place between mother and child that binds them together in a unique relationship. Mothers have always been known to be particularly sensitive to the needs of a newborn. Klaus and his colleagues are arguing that it is the early attachment process that allows for this sensitivity between mother and child; furthermore, children separated from their mother at birth and kept isolated do not develop this attachment and do not develop as well as infants who have formed such bonds. Lacking such bonding does not mean that the infant will be lacking in intelligence or be maladjusted. Klaus's argument is that children who are allowed to form such attachments tend to have easier infancies—easier on the parent and the infant. Infants who have good bonding are calmer, quieter, eat better, and sleep better. While it is possible to make speculations of how infant attachment might affect adult development, such ideas must be tentative. Regardless, the data are growing to be quite compelling, so we can conclude that babies should have as much physical and emotional contact with their mothers (and fathers) as possible. This, of course, means changes in most hospital routines. These changes are often slow to take place. As Klaus and colleagues suggest, "In every hospital, keeping parents and infant together should be the rule, not the exception" (Kennell, Voos, & Klaus, 1979; see also Svejda, Campos, & Emde, 1980).

In chapter 4 on motivation, we saw the process of bonding in monkeys (p. 175). When newborn monkeys were taken away from their real mothers and provided a replacement or surrogate mother, they clung to them, as if seeking love. These results suggest strongly that infant monkeys have a desire for warmth and affection and choose it even if they have to work harder to get nourishment. This seemingly inborn need for love and affection is important for psychologists' understanding of the relationship of newborns' instincts and their need for love and affection.

Klaus and Kennell (1976) assert that the important process of attachment begins very early in life. Once acquired, this attachment seems to be fairly permanent. You will see later in this chapter that when children are separated from their mothers or fathers for brief periods (for example, in day-care centers), the attachment to the mother or father is not broken. Thus, once established, attachment is relatively permanent unless the child is separated from the parents for a long period of time. Like any interaction between two individuals, attachment once formed is subject to change. Any changes that take place depend on the individuals involved and the nature of their interaction (Vaughn, Egeland, & Sroufe, 1979).

INFANCY AND CHILDHOOD

During the first year and a half of life, the $7\frac{1}{2}$ pound newborn will put on considerable weight. Indeed, an infant may weigh as much as 20 to 25 pounds at the end of a year. When children can represent the world in abstract ways

How to Stop Crib Deaths

The unexplained death of infants in the early months of life is referred to as sudden infant death syndrome. *Babies between 2 and 5 months of age simply stop breathing, for no apparent reason. The following news article explains this topic:*

NEWSWEEK The mother gently places her baby in his crib, gives him a tender pat and tiptoes out of the room. For the rest of the night, not a sound comes from the infant's room. But when the mother returns to waken the child for his 6 o'clock feeding, she makes a shattering, tragic discovery. Her baby lies curled, silent and lifeless, in the corner of the bed, a blood-tinged froth around his nose and mouth.

The child is yet another victim of SIDS, the "sudden infant death syndrome," a baffling disorder that claims the lives of some 10,000 babies in the U.S. each year. There have been many theories about SIDS, but the cause still eludes researchers. Now, however, two Brown University investigators have proposed a new explanation and, perhaps, found a way of preventing SIDS.

In general, doctors are better prepared to say what does not cause SIDS than what does. The old notion that the victims suffocated in their bedclothes has long since been put to rest. Severe allergic reactions to milk, defective immune reactions, bacterial infection and adrenal deficiency have also been ruled out as possible causes of SIDS. Deaths are most common in the late fall and win-

ter, and many SIDS victims have a history of previous colds. But the disorder can't be blamed on specific viral infections, either. The findings of the Brown researchers are consistent with a new theory that SIDS is the result of a deficiency in the nerve responses concerned with breathing, possibly triggered by a respiratory infection.

Froth

In sleep, respiration is at a low level. A stuffy nose would require that the baby open its mouth to breathe. But with impaired neurologic controls over respiration, this normal reflex response fails, and the baby clamps his mouth shut. As oxygen levels in the blood continue to fall, the child goes into the early stages of a seizure, as shown by the bloody froth on the lips of SIDS victims, and dies.

Even if this sequence of events doesn't prove entirely correct, the two researchers think that their observations can prevent SIDS. They believe that children of low birth weight or who require oxygen therapy should be given tactile stimulation tests. Those who score poorly should be closely watched and, when they catch colds, perhaps even hospitalized so that their breathing can be monitored around the clock. If respiration should stop, nurses could quickly resuscitate the infant. "It might mean overburdening hospitals," Anderson-Huntington admits, "but what are hospitals for except to save lives?"

---

through language, they have left the stage of infancy and moved into childhood. As you will see in a moment, at 18 months a child is often walking and beginning to talk. Childhood represents those years from about $1\frac{1}{2}$ to age 12 or 13.

When psychologists look at infancy, they see intellectual growth as an important and overriding part of the child's development. Many prominent psychologists and educators consider this first year and a half to be the most critical stage in the development of intelligence. Jean Piaget, the noted Swiss psychologist, suggested that the fundamentals of all intellectual development take place during the first 2 years of life. This is important for parents, educators, and psychologists; in the past, most people considered the infant little more than an organism that reacted to stimuli and had little understanding of the world. However, infants have a remarkable grasp of their surroundings, and it is through their interactions with their surroundings that later intellectual development will be based.

As the rooting, grasping, and Babinski reflexes drop out of the early weeks and months of life, new behaviors appear. At about 4 to 8 weeks the infant begins to sleep for longer periods of time. An infant smiles at the sight of

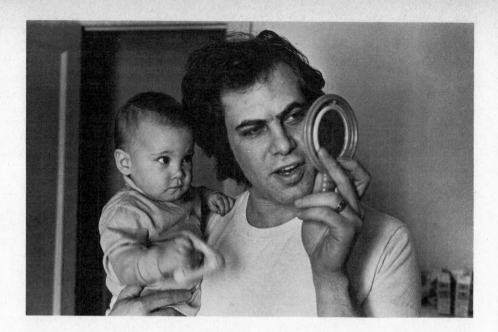

Seeing yourself in a mirror is puzzling at first.

mother and is enchanted with human speech. The infant begins to reach out for objects, and, if provided with a mobile above the crib, the infant stares at it for long periods of time, often reaching out to touch it. Moving objects are intriguing to an infant of 2 or 3 months and the infant will stare at them for long periods.

There is a distinct progression in communication between mothers and their infants. As infants grow older, the amount of time that they will focus on a mother and pay attention to her increases significantly. Initially the dialogue between infant and mother has no words, but as they come to know each other and develop a sense of attachment, gestures, smiles, and vocalizations are more common (Kaplan, 1978).

A 4-month-old girl will have much greater control over her head movements and posture than she did formerly; now she is able to sit with support. The 4- and 5-month-old girl is fascinated by toys and can play with them for longer periods of time. She recognizes her parents and is soothed by their voices; indeed, she is soothed much more easily now than in her early months of life. By the fourth or fifth month, most babies have been introduced to a solid food and they are no longer fed only milk.

A great developmental change takes place at about 6 or 7 months (see Figure 6.3). Children learn to sit without the support of their parents' hands. They can grasp objects in both hands and will manipulate them and usually jam them into their mouths. They can be left in a playpen or crib for much longer periods of time, and they are able to turn themselves from front to back or vice versa. During this period, they generally become much more independent, and in the next months they may learn to crawl.

As children reach the seventh month of development, the physical changes that have taken place are clearly enormous. Now, social changes begin to become obvious. Infants' newfound ability to crawl and explore the environment gives them freedom. They can seek out favorite objects and people and avoid situations that seem potentially threatening. This ability to

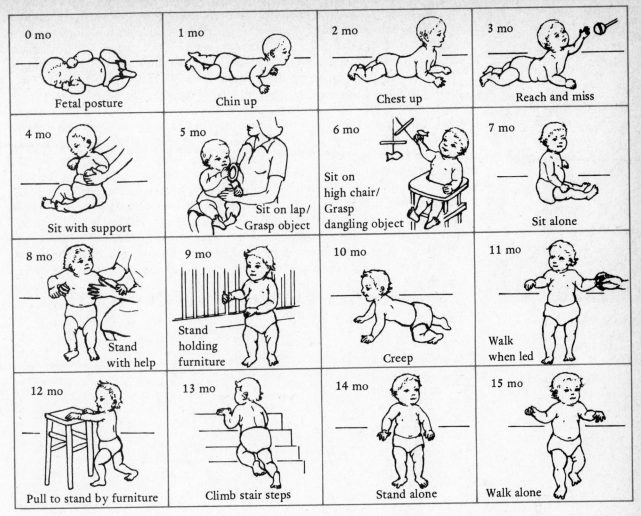

0 mo Fetal posture	**1 mo** Chin up	**2 mo** Chest up	**3 mo** Reach and miss
4 mo Sit with support	**5 mo** Sit on lap/ Grasp object	**6 mo** Sit on high chair/ Grasp dangling object	**7 mo** Sit alone
8 mo Stand with help	**9 mo** Stand holding furniture	**10 mo** Creep	**11 mo** Walk when led
12 mo Pull to stand by furniture	**13 mo** Climb stair steps	**14 mo** Stand alone	**15 mo** Walk alone

Figure 6.3 With each passing month, the infant's motor abilities increase dramatically, so that walking is possible within about one year

approach or avoid situations through increased motor ability is most easily seen in the strong emotional attachments that infants have for their care-taker, usually their mother. It has been shown that a strong attachment between a mother and a one-year-old is particularly good. Infants who show such strong attachments later tend to be more curious, self-directed, and independent; strong attachment fosters the growth of self-reliance (Ainsworth, 1979; Bowlby, 1973). However, these attachments to the mother may become so strong that the sight of strangers brings anxiety and fear responses. For the period of 8 to 15 months, infants often exhibit an intense fear of people other than the mother; this intense fear of others is called **stranger anxiety**. Related to, but different from, stranger anxiety is the fear that children have when mother is absent. A 9-month-old baby may become very fearful when mother leaves the room; this situation is referred to as *separation anxiety*.

From somewhere around 9 to 15 months the mother's world is never the same again, because during this period infants begin to stand and eventually walk. They are allowed to investigate a whole new world because they can actively explore places that they have never been able to get to before.

The second year of life brings about further increases in infants' ability to

Stranger anxiety A syndrome in children from 8 to 15 months old wherein the presence of strangers makes them fearful.

Children begin to utter sounds early in life, much to the delight of their parents.

move around in the environment. Children are now able to walk and climb, as well as manipulate the environment. Furthermore, their body proportions are changing dramatically. They become wider, taller, and add increased length to their legs and body. While their body continues to develop through the adolescent years, major brain growth occurs in these early years. In fact, brain growth will be essentially complete by age 13 (Lenneberg, 1967).

The developmental changes that take place in childhood are particularly interesting to the psychologist. These changes include such major developments as increased body proportions and motor abilities, as well as new hormones released as the child develops the appearance of secondary sex characteristics. As we have seen, brain development continues as does intellectual development, but for most developmental psychologists, the period of childhood is more interesting from the standpoint of intellectual growth. Psychologists are very concerned about how 3-, 4-, and 5-year-olds learn language and how they come to understand concepts, solve problems, and reason. Childhood is also important to psychologists who study personality and abnormal psychology because adults' personal problems often stem from their childhood experiences.

A basic difference between the infancy years and the childhood years is that major changes in growth and development are not as easily seen in

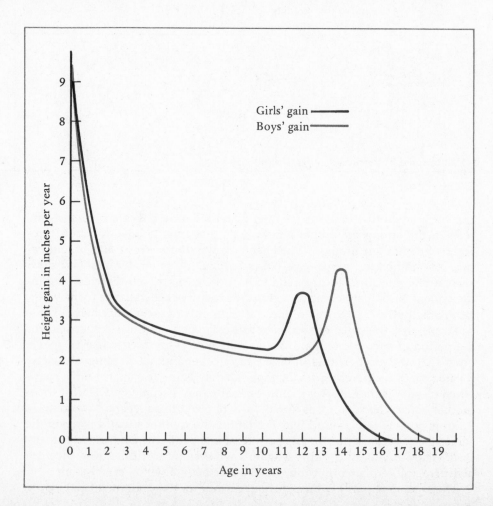

Figure 6.4 Average growth curves for boys and girls. Shown is the height gain each year from age 1 to 18 (data from Tanner et al., 1966)

Child-Rearing Techniques

All parents face the dilemma of how to raise their children. Most parents, and usually their in-laws, have a theory about the best way to do it. Hundreds of articles and books have been written on how to discipline children, how not to spoil them, how they should be fed, and how they should be reared. Should they be breast fed? Should they be bottle fed? When should they be weaned? When should solid foods be introduced? Very often issues centering around breast versus the bottle and schedules of feeding are blown out of proportion. Although each of these issues cannot be discussed here, certain basic principles should be considered.

Breast feeding is a more natural way of providing nourishment to infants. There are certain substances found in breast milk that are not in cow's milk or in specially prepared formula, although formula contains most of the nutrients and vitamins necessary for children's healthy growth. Infants do thrive on both breast and bottle. But it is understandable that parents are often anxious about the nature of the feeding process. A mother who is concerned about providing warmth, love, and closeness for her child can do so by either breast feeding or by bottle feeding. However, a woman who is anxious about breast feeding does her child a disservice by feeding at the breast, because if she is tense and anxious, she will convey this feeling to her child. For this child, feeding will not be a pleasurable, relaxed experience. Thus, feeding by breast or bottle is less important than the emotional climate established by the feeding process.

Schedules of feeding are also of great concern to parents. One school of thought suggests that babies should be provided stability by being put on schedules that are relatively rigid so that they learn a routine of eating, sleeping, and play. In contrast, self-demand feeding suggests that babies should be fed when they are hungry, as often as they are hungry. Babies who are on a self-demand schedule generally eat as often or perhaps somewhat more often than babies who are on a strict schedule. Today, more mothers are allowing self-demand feeding and have become somewhat more relaxed about the quantity of food provided and the frequency of infant feeding. This more relaxed attitude and willingness to work around the baby produces a warm, satisfying emotional climate for the child.

Nevertheless, self-demand feeding and breast feeding are often considered the first step toward spoiling the child. Too often we hear parents speaking of spoiling infants. Children are spoiled when they insist upon their own way, demand attention, and have little frustration tolerance. But it is unfair to speak of spoiling when referring to infants. Infants have no frustration tolerance; they demand attention; and they are largely self-centered. Parents cannot spoil a young infant. In contrast, children of one year or older should be developing certain social interactions that allow them to be children, but require somewhat less self-concern and greater frustration tolerance of them. Socialization involves decentration and an increased possibility for spoiling. The 5-year-old who makes demands upon parents with little tolerance for their feelings not only shows a lack of socialization skills and an inability to decenter, but is also spoiled.

Many of the concerns new parents have about child rearing and infant care deal not so much with the development of the infant as with socialization and personality formation. These personality issues will therefore be examined more closely in subsequent chapters on personality development.

childhood years. At birth, the newborn responds only with reflexes and random movements. The newborn seems to have few capabilities, but with each passing day, the infant changes dramatically. However, the day-to-day changes in the older child are not as obvious because generally these are intellectual changes that improve the child's ability to cope with the world more effectively.

INTELLECTUAL DEVELOPMENT

Intellectual development becomes of increasing concern with the growing emphasis placed on education in Western society. Educators are introducing foreign languages at the elementary school level, and we might ask if second-

Young children experience a
diverse array of sights and
sounds.

or third-graders can learn French, why can't they learn calculus? Why not
start children in school when they learn to talk and have them through with
high school at age 10 to 13 and finishing college at age 17? The answer becomes obvious when this example is carried to extremes.

In earlier chapters, we considered the nature versus nurture controversy
and the respective contributions of each day-to-day behavior. While numerous theories abound and provide support for both biological and environmental viewpoints, one approach stands out more than any other when considering intellectual growth. The theory of intellectual development put forth
by Swiss psychologist Jean Piaget (1896–1980) combines notions of nature
and nurture. This theory shows how people's inherited capacities interact
with their environment to yield an intellectually functioning child and adult.
One of Piaget's greatest strengths as a theorist was that he recognized that
people's inherited abilities do not determine their behavior, but rather set
the foundation for their interaction with the world. Piaget emphasized that
these interactions of the developing person with the environment eventually
determine the ability of the person to behave adaptively.

Piaget's theories are very elaborate and cover a wide range of human activities; for our purposes, however, a brief outline must suffice. Piaget was a
very sensitive and careful observer of children. In fact, his stages of development were outlined over the years as he watched his own children grow. By
observing his three children, he was able to note small changes in their behavior.

Piaget divides the course of intellectual development into a series of
stages, with each stage to be successfully experienced before the next stage
begins. As standing precedes walking, so certain stages of development
must precede others if the fulfillment of human potential is to be achieved.
This stage concept is the structure around which Piaget builds his theory.
Piaget argues that if a parent presents a very young child with concepts that
are far too advanced for his particular stage of development, the child will not

be able to come to understand the new concept and no real learning can take place. Thus, each stage must be passed through before the next stage begins. These stages are not fixed to certain ages but are flexible and represent approximate ages. For example, Piaget's first stage lasts from birth until approximately age 2. It might last until age $1\frac{1}{2}$, or perhaps until age $2\frac{1}{2}$; the specific age is not important. Piaget stresses that the kind of intellectual achievement possible is dependent upon the stage of the child. There are fairly large individual differences between children as to when they will enter the next stage of development.

From childhood to adulthood each person is faced with new concepts and new experiences. There are two processes whereby people deal with new concepts and thus move on from one stage to another. These processes are called accommodation and assimilation. According to Piaget, when a person is confronted with a new concept or experience, previously developed cognitive structures and behavior must be modified in order for the person to adapt to the unfamiliar situation. Piaget calls this process **accommodation.** As the accommodation process is taking place, the new concepts and experiences are absorbed and incorporated into existing cognitive structures and behaviors and can then be used in all similar situations. Piaget calls this process **assimilation.** Thus, an individual accommodates to new information and assimilates it, only to be confronted with more new information requiring further accommodation and assimilation. The processes of assimilation and accommodation are complementary in that they interact, mutually supporting the never-ending growth of intellectual and behavioral patterns.

When first presented with the characters of Chinese script, an individual who has assimilated our alphabet must discriminate the unfamiliar lines, visualize the new angles, and discern differences among the characters. Then, meaning must be attached to each of the characters. These tasks require a modification of the individual's way of thinking; therefore, accommodation is taking place. As the person begins to recognize and understand Chinese script, the new concepts will be categorized, absorbed, and incorporated into the person's existing cognitive structures and the person will be able to use this new knowledge whenever similar Chinese characters are presented. We can be sure that the individual has accommodated and assimilated Chinese script when it is used in a meaningful way.

Accommodation A process described by Jean Piaget whereby existing cognitive structures and behaviors are modified by new concepts and experiences.

Assimilation A process described by Jean Piaget whereby new concepts and experiences are incorporated into existing ones and are then used in a meaningful way.

New concepts modify an individual's existing cognitive structures and framework of knowledge, a process Piaget calls accommodation. This new information is then incorporated and used in a meaningful manner; this is the process of assimilation

Assimilation and accommodation are constantly used as a child grows intellectually and behaviorally. Consider this example. A child has learned to grasp an object, say a spoon. The child has also grasped similar objects such as forks, crayons, and sticks, demonstrating that he has assimilated the responses necessary for grasping long, slim objects. When the child first tries to grasp a differently shaped object such as a ball, he must modify the response by widening his grasp in order to pick it up. Here the child must accommodate in order to grasp the spherical object. So, the child has assimilated the behavior pattern of grasping slim objects; this serves as a building block for learning the new, more complex behavior of grasping spheres.

Piaget's Four Stages

This complementary process of assimilation and accommodation is continually taking place. As new behaviors and ways of functioning are accommodated and assimilated, still newer ones become the focus of a developing child's world. This process happens at each of Piaget's four stages of development. Let us take a closer look at the development of each stage.

The first and most important stage is the **sensory-motor period** that lasts from birth to about age 2. Piaget considers it the time during which the basis of all intellectual development is established. The child is born as an uncoordinated reflexlike organism. During the months of the sensory-motor period,

Sensory-motor stage The first of the four major stages in Piaget's theory of intellectual development. It is the period roughly covering the first 2 years of life, during which the child begins to interact with the environment and during which the rudiments of intelligence are established.

Figure 6.5 Piaget's stages of development

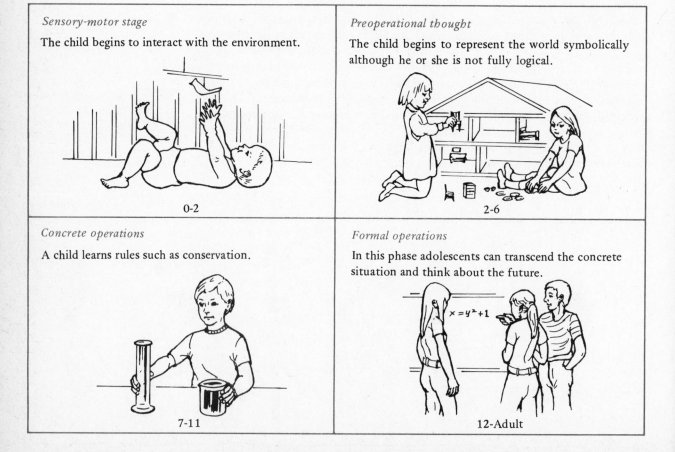

Sensory-motor stage

The child begins to interact with the environment.

0-2

Preoperational thought

The child begins to represent the world symbolically although he or she is not fully logical.

2-6

Concrete operations

A child learns rules such as conservation.

7-11

Formal operations

In this phase adolescents can transcend the concrete situation and think about the future.

$x = y^2 + 1$

12-Adult

the rudiments of intellectual behavior are formed. Consider the changes that take place during these first 2 years of life. A child is born unable to respond to the demand of a complex world. Yet within a few weeks she has learned some simple habits. She is able to smile at the sight of her mother; she has learned to seek out the stimulation of a mobile hanging over her head; she has learned to reach out; she has learned to anticipate events in her environment. When the child sees her mother's breast or a bottle, she knows that food is coming. She has learned some basic, simple facts of life.

During the sensory-motor stage, this child begins to interact with her environment. She reaches out for her mobile and tries to touch it repeatedly. By the time the child is 6 or 8 months old, she is not only sitting up and crawling, but she is also seeking out new and more interesting kinds of stimulation. She is no longer willing to just watch a mobile spin, rather she is concerned with manipulating her environment and what Piaget calls "making interesting sights last." At about 8 months, the child begins to develop intentionality. She begins to manipulate the environment rather than letting the environment manipulate her. The child now sets aside obstacles to reach a goal. She crawls to the other side of a room to reach objects. In future months, the child will not only begin to manipulate her environment by walking but also by talking.

In the second half of the sensory-motor stage (the period from 12 to 24 months) the child no longer remembers events just with visual images, but also begins to use logic. Language is developing. Through language, the infant is freed from the concrete world of visual imagery and can represent the world symbolically. The 2-year-old can talk of grandma, parents, friends, TV programs, or other events. The 2-year-old is no longer an uncoordinated, reflex-oriented organism, but rather a thinking, walking, talking human being.

Once children have reached this point in development, they have been catered to and most of life's demands have been minimal. The infant is usually self-centered; this self-centeredness is called egocentrism. **Egocentrism** is an individual's failure to be able to perceive a situation or event in more than one way. For an infant, egocentrism refers to the inability to see that the world does not exist solely for the infant's interests and needs. There are different kinds of egocentrism, including the inability to see, feel (experience), or think in the ways others might. Infants are thus limited to seeing, feeling, and thinking from their own viewpoint, not others. At the end of Piaget's Stage 1, the children are going through the process of changing from being totally egocentric to realizing that there is a difference between themselves and the world. This process is called decentration. **Decentration** begins at the end of the sensory-motor period, continues as the child grows older, and is pretty much completed during the stage of concrete operations from around 7 to 11 years of age (see Ford, 1979).

The changes that take place during these first 2 years of life are momentous not only for the child but also for the parents. Once dependent upon its mother and father for everything, the newborn is now a 2-year-old who may not only have developed language and reasonable thought processes, but may also have become manipulative, difficult to deal with, and often belligerent. Although these new habits may be annoying, they are signs of continued development and they further indicate that the child is about to enter the stage of preoperational thought.

Egocentrism An individual's failure to be able to perceive a situation or event in more than one way; in infancy, it is the attitude that directs all concerns and behaviors to personal interests and needs.

Decentration The process that begins in children at about age 2 of changing from a totally self-oriented viewpoint to one that recognizes other people's feelings, ideas, and viewpoints.

Piaget described the process of egocentrism as the child developed (match the numbered description to each box): 1. "Egocentrism . . . directs all concerns and behaviors to personal interests and needs." 2. ". . . one who realizes that there is a difference between himself and the world." 3. ". . . ones who represent the world symbolically." 4. ". . . children discover certain facts about the environment which remain constant. Rules are established." 5. "They can conceive of different ways to represent situations." 6. "The adolescent goes through a phase in which he attributes an unlimited power to his own thoughts so that the dream of a glorious future or of transforming the world through ideas . . . seems to be not only fantasy, but also effective action which in itself modifies the empirical world."

Preoperational stage Piaget's second major stage of intellectual development. This stage lasts from about 2 to 7 years and is the time when preoperational (symbolic) thought is developed.

Concrete-operational stage Piaget's third major stage of development, which occurs from approximately ages 7 to 11 years. During this stage, the child develops thought processes enabling him or her to understand constant factors in the environment, rules, and higher-order symbolism (such as arithmetic, geography).

Conservation The ability to recognize that something that has changed in some way (such as the "shape" of liquid in a container) is still the same thing, of the same weight, substance, or volume.

In the stage of **preoperational thought,** children are no longer tied to the immediate here-and-now. They are no longer sensory-motor organisms, but rather ones who represent the world symbolically. This period starts at about 2 years and continues until children are 6 or 7 years of age. However, the children still cannot totally "decenter"; they still remain somewhat egocentric. They cannot think about the world the way older persons do or consider how others might feel. Children at this stage make little attempt to adapt their speech to that of others. Furthermore, children of 3 to 5 years of age make little or no attempt to justify their reasoning. During this stage, adults try to teach the child to interact with others (Flavell, 1963).

Preoperational children are no longer infants. They are in a trying period for parents, because they are not fully logical, they do not justify their reasoning, and they often are behavior problems. People sometimes speak of the "terrible 2s," for during this stage children have learned to manipulate their world enough so that parents often consider them a terror. Although the logical thought processes of the children are developing and they are becoming more socialized, social and intellectual changes will not become apparent until the next stage of development.

The stage of **concrete operations** is the period from approximately 7 to 11 years. Children are now actively involved in school, are able to take care of themselves, have friends, and have often assumed many responsibilities. During this stage, the children discover certain important facts about the environment that remain constant. Rules are established. During the period of concrete operations, children learn **conservation,** the ability to recognize that an object that has been transformed is still the same object and represents the same amount of weight, substance, and/or volume.

In a typical conservation task, a child is shown two beakers: one is short, squat, and half full of liquid; the other is tall, thin, and empty (see Figure 6.6). The experimenter then pours the water from the short, squat beaker into

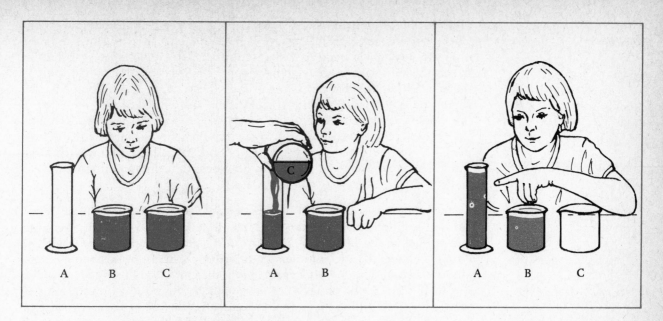

the tall, narrow beaker and asks the child, "Which had more, the first beaker or the second?" If the child is unable to conserve volume, he will respond by indicating that the taller beaker has more volume. He might respond, "This one, it's taller." But if he is able to conserve volume, he will suggest that it's the same water; therefore, the amount in both beakers is equal (see, for example, Perret-Clermont, 1980).

The final stage of development, starting at age 12, is the stage of **formal operations.** Unlike concrete-operational children whose thought is still somewhat concrete and tied to immediate situations, adolescents can transcend the concrete situation and think about the future. They can conceive of different ways to represent situations. They organize their world and try to deal with it in terms of the future. Formal-operational children are developing the ability to consider all possible relations. The style of their logic is no longer concrete but one in which they form hypotheses and deduce reality. The adolescent's intellectual world is no longer tied to concrete things; it is full of informal theories of logic, and ideas about themselves and life (Flavell, 1963). The egocentrism of the sensory-motor child and of the preoperational child is largely gone. However, according to Piaget, a new kind of egocentrism, based on a naive realization of the world, has developed. Piaget says, "The adolescent goes through a phase in which he attributes an unlimited power to his own thoughts so that the dream of a glorious future or of transforming the world through ideas (even if this idealism takes a materialistic form) seems to be not only fantasy, but also an effective action which in itself modifies the empirical world" (Inhelder & Piaget, 1958, pp. 345–346). Many adolescents form grand ideas of reforming the world. They decide that they will become social reformers and will bring the world to an understanding of peace. Their egocentrism and naive hopes will eventually disappear as they come to grips with the challenges of life.

Piaget's theory is highly complex and could be discussed in much greater detail. Let us review some of the most important points. Piaget suggests that cognitive development is a process in which each new stage builds upon the

Figure 6.6 Conservation is the process by which individuals know that an object that has been transformed is still the same object regardless of its shape. When the contents of C are poured into A, young children will indicate that there is more water in A than in B. When children make such responses, they are showing that they do not yet have the ability to conserve

Formal-operational stage Piaget's fourth and final stage of intellectual development. This stage begins at about age 12 years; the individual can think hypothetically so that all possibilities are considered. The individual is now capable of deductive logic.

previous one and has at its base a complex sensory-motor period. Piaget considers egocentrism a critical aspect of development, an aspect that must be changed through the process of decentration. The exact stages or ages at which these aspects of development appear is less important than the fact that all children in all societies go through these stages of development. The actual content of the thoughts of children in the United States compared to the thought content of the children in France or India is less important than the nature of the thought. This is to say that Piaget was concerned with how people think, not what they think. Through knowledge of the way children think, psychologists can understand how best to facilitate thinking.

PIAGET: IMPLICATIONS.   Let us come back to our original question, "Why not start a child in school when she learns to talk and have her through with high school at age 13?" Why shouldn't our 2-year-old understand calculus? When you consider the arguments put forth by Piaget, the answers to these questions seem obvious. At 2 years of age, the child is not ready for calculus. Her intellectual abilities have not developed to the point where calculus is understandable. Although you might train a 2-year-old to do many complex tasks and to respond in many specific ways, she cannot learn to do many other things that her physical structures (her brain) cannot grasp. Certain properties of intellectual development are acquired at different stages, and to ask a child to perform tasks that are beyond her stage of development is a waste of time. Parents will best serve their children by understanding their developmental level and capabilities. It is helpful for a mother to know that her 2-year-old does not understand logic and the concept of time sufficiently enough to understand that 3 weeks from Monday she will receive a toy in the mail.

With knowledge of the way children's abilities grow, educators and psychologists facilitate children's intellectual development. Piaget points out that adults must try to optimize the stimuli in the child's environment. Thus, the sensory-motor child, the infant, should be provided with great amounts of stimulation, both physical and intellectual. He should be provided with moving stimuli, stimuli that change colors, shape, and form. This suggestion is supported by a variety of research showing that children and animals who are provided with sensory stimulation from birth through the early months develop better, intellectually and socially, than groups deprived of the same stimulation.

Parental love and interaction with the child are essential in the formative years of development. When the child is young and is asking questions, trying to find out about the world, learning relationships, and dealing with conservation tasks, her ability to change can only develop if she is provided with appropriate stimulation. Parents must provide situations that will foster intellectual development. Although it may be foolish to try to teach a 2-year-old calculus, it is equally foolish to not provide her with stimulation appropriate for her age level. In Piaget's terms, adults must try to teach the 3-year-old how to accommodate new information and to assimilate it into the ever-changing world.

One of the child's greatest accomplishments during the maturational processes is the ability to communicate with other individuals. Although young children have methods of communicating certain desires and needs, effective communication is best achieved through the development of language.

Learning to use language represents a dramatic change in a child's life and deserves special consideration.

Language Development

Language opens up new worlds for children. They are now able to express themselves and to indicate their desires and needs. They are able to express love and fear, and they are capable of interacting on a more mature level with the people who surround them. Language allows children to represent the world in more meaningful and complex ways. Language development allows them to interact effectively and to cope with a demanding world.

Language development proceeds at a rapid rate once it is under way. By age 6, most children have a vocabulary of thousands of words. But at what point does language development begin, and how does it develop? At birth, a child has no language. In the first few months of life, parents may hear their baby cooing and babbling; by 6 months this babbling may become differentiated, and the child is clearly making different sounds. Very often babies of 6 and 8 months repeat the same sounds for hours or days. At the end of a year a child often has learned a few simple words, perhaps, "mama," or dada," or some other combination of sounds that represent some other object. From this naming stage of attaching labels to objects and events, the child begins developing simple two- and three-word sentences.

It is amazing how a young child using two-word sentences has a relatively complex vocabulary and can convey a large number of thoughts. This system is unique to the child and his or her parents; for many others, this system would not be meaningful. More important than the individual utterances themselves is the way they grow to become larger and more complex sentences—the way the child learns grammar.

Grammar, the rules for language, is learned at an early age. Although 5- and 6-year-old children have not learned all of the rules of language, their speech is correct and consists of nouns, verbs, and adjectives in a relatively proper order. We will be exploring how children develop language in chapter 8; there we will examine closely the relative contribution of nature and nurture in language development. You will see that language has a strong biological basis, but the language one learns is determined by one's experiences in the environment.

Two-year-olds practice naming animals by pointing and vocalizing.

The Development of Morality

As children grow older, there are vast changes in their behaviors. Many of these changes are directly apparent to an observer. As children's speech matures, their ability to express new ideas is expanded. Similarly, as children develop conservation of weight and volume, they have new abilities to conceive of the world in realistic ways. While all of these changes are taking place, children are also internalizing a set of values as to what is right or wrong. Human beings have the ability to make decisions about right or wrong, about good or bad. They make decisions about morality. **Morality** is a person's attitude about a situation used to evaluate it and decide if it is right or wrong; moral judgments determine if a situation or event conforms to proper standards of conduct. These attitudes about morality are not inborn; they develop over time and throughout a person's life. From a very early age, parents teach behavior, attitudes, and values that are considered appropriate and correct. Through the process of learning such values, children develop a conscience. (Later, in chapter 11, we will discuss the conscience in terms of Freud's concept of the superego.) When children are constantly told to be quiet and respectful in a church, they learn and eventually internalize the idea that churches are for quiet, reverent behaviors. Such internalizing of ideas does not happen overnight; rather, it is a slow process of learning the values, ideals, and standards of a family and society.

In his study of children, Piaget asked many questions of both young and older children to examine their reasoning ability and their ability to analyze questions of conscience. He found that young children have ideas about morality that are rigid and rule bound. In playing a game, a young child knows the rules and doesn't allow the rules to be broken for a younger sister who does not understand them. This child sees rules as rigid barriers and boundaries. By contrast, older children recognize that rules are established by people and sometimes need to be bent, depending on the situation. Piaget came to conceptualize children's cognitive inflexibility formally. Young children's inflexibility binds them to a rule so that they see it as demanding and rigid. By contrast, older children have developed a sense of relativity. They have recognized both that certain rules and values are set up because of agreed upon standards and respect for others and that these rules and values sometimes change over time (Piaget, 1932). When Piaget asked 4- and 5-year-old children why they shouldn't cheat in a game of marbles, the young children responded that it was because there are rules and it is wrong to break the rules. In the same way, children responding to questions about lying

Morality Human attitudes about social practices, institutions, and individual behavior used to evaluate events to decide if the events are right or wrong.

would indicate that lying is bad today, will be bad tomorrow, and, under any and all circumstances, one should never lie. Between the ages of 5 to 12, children move from this inflexibility to a sense of relativity in which they recognize, for example, that the rules of a game of marbles are based on circumstances. To sum up, Piaget's view is that a child moves from inflexibility to a sense of relativity. This is possible because a child has developed new cognitive structures and has assimilated and accommodated new ideas.

Piaget's conceptualizations of the development of rules were to a very great extent qualitative; he described how children respond to certain kinds of questions and when they change to other forms of answers. Growing out of Piaget's work was the research of Harvard psychologist Lawrence Kohlberg (1969). According to Kohlberg, there is a distinct development of morality that proceeds through a series of stages. Kohlberg's research and his stage theory were developed after presenting different types of stories to people and then asking them questions about the meaning of the story and how they felt about it. For example, in one story a poor man stole a drug for his wife who would have died without the drug. Having no money, he stole that his wife might live. As adults, our interpretation of the poor man's plight is different from that of a 5-year-old who has trouble seeing the circumstances of morality and the difficult position in which the poor man is placed.

Kohlberg's research shows that young children make decisions about right or wrong based upon avoiding punishment and obtaining rewards. This is level 1 morality. So, a preschool 5-year-old argues that people should not steal because they will be punished if they do; furthermore, such a child argues that good people are rewarded for good behavior.

School-age children are at a second level of moral development, and they adopt conventional ideas about morality. They conform to avoid disapproval by others and censure by authorities. Level 2 morality is governed by a more thoughtful process that considers the implications of a person's behavior and how it might affect others.

The third level of morality is composed of two major parts. The first most

In their second year of life, children develop special abilities!

Kohlberg suggests a three-stage model of moral development.

Stage Two: Conventional role conformity

I don't steal because my parents wouldn't think much of me if I did.

Obedience to avoid disapproval

I don't steal because it's against the law and I'd feel guilty if I broke the law.

Obedience to authority

Stage Three: Morality of conscience

I want people to respect my property and, in turn, I respect theirs. Therefore, I don't steal.

Obedience to laws that meet the needs of society

Normally I wouldn't steal because if I did I'd really look down upon myself. But, if a life depended upon my stealing something, I'd do it.

Obedience to one's own conscience

people eventually reach as adults; the second part is often not reached. Level 3 is the morality of contracts and laws. In this stage, people make judgments of good or bad based upon the needs of society and maintaining community welfare and order. The second part of level 3 is the morality of conscience, where people make judgments based more on their own internal values rather than on those of society.

When a man steals a drug he cannot afford in order to help his dying wife, his behavior is judged differently depending on the level of the observer's moral development. At each level of moral development, his behavior can be justified *and* condemned. However, the reasons behind the justification or condemnation vary significantly with a person's stage of moral development. Level 1 children see punishment and reward: the man should be punished because he stole the drug; or, because the man tried to save his wife's life, he was good. Level 2 individuals judge behavior in terms of rules and law: the man broke the law; it's wrong to steal; he should go to jail. Only at level 3 can an adult make moral judgments based on the needs of others and especially his own conscience: a person's life was saved; this is more important than the law; the man is justified. Morality, like intelligence, develops in a specific order where one stage of morality must precede the next. It must also be recognized that Kohlberg and Piaget have studied the development of moral thoughts and reasoning, as opposed to moral or immoral behavior. They have focused on how people make moral decisions rather than studying the actual overt behavior that might result from those decisions (Rothman, 1980).

This thumbnail sketch of Kohlberg's views shows that his ideas are very much like Piaget's view of morality. However, there are some important differences. For example, Piaget saw each stage largely independent from the next; Kohlberg saw the stages overlapping. Thus, a child who was entering the higher stages of development of morality might still use earlier reasoning from time to time. Kohlberg went further than Piaget in systematizing the development of morality and developed ideas about how a child's interaction with parents and friends can affect their conceptions of morality. Thus, when children realize that working within or around rules affects other family members, this alters their view of the rules. So, an older girl will spare her mother embarrassment by responding positively to a question about Mom's carefully chosen "beautiful" new dress. A younger child won't break the rules of lying and will tell Mom how ugly the dress really seems to her.

It is important to remember that morality develops slowly over time and is largely affected by what the people say and how they interact with children. Children often internalize the values that parents teach. So, if morality is observed in the home, it may be internalized; however, when such moral values do not exist in the home, they are less likely to develop in the child. From this stage's view of moral development, people must pass through the earlier stages of morality before they can advance to the next higher level; the order of the stages thus remains constant (see, for example, Kurtinas & Greif, 1974).

The implications of the theories of morality put forth by Piaget and later by Kohlberg are important for educators and parents. Kohlberg has suggested specific methods that can aid in the development of morality and conscience. Teachers and parents should discuss moral issues with children. Kohlberg asserts that parents need to explore difficult problems like war, death, education, and even issues like cheating on taxes. In doing so, children not only can internalize the values of society but also learn to think on their own. When adolescents are on a higher level of moral reasoning, they are more likely to think about the morality of issues. The self-image that adolescents develop is often based upon how they view themselves in relationship to others and others' morality; it is not surprising, therefore, that adolescents who are on a higher level of moral reasoning are more likely to take on less sex-typed role characteristics. In a study of 13-, 17-, and 20-year-olds it was found that the higher the level of moral reasoning, the more likely were both males and females to adopt characteristics of the opposite sex into their own self-image (Leahy & Eiter, 1980).

From Kohlberg's view, children learn morals when they are provided with opportunities for role taking (Kohlberg, 1971). Role taking is the process of adopting other perspectives that are different from one's own. Thus, children

What Determines Intelligence: Nature Versus Nurture

We study development so as to understand the conditions and variables that might help maximize the potential of developing children. Uppermost on many people's minds is the development of intelligence. All parents want their children to be bright and to be able to get ahead in the world. People who have high IQs generally make more money, have a better quality of life, and are often healthier than those with lower IQ scores. Knowing this, people spend an inordinate amount of time trying to maximize the intellectual development of their children (Kagan, Kearsley, & Zelazo, 1980). While we will examine the meaning and development of intelligence more closely in the next chapter, let us look at two research studies that have pointed out different variables that affect intelligence as measured by IQ tests. One study supports biological causes for IQ; the other study supports environmental causes. Most psychologists argue that it is neither solely environment nor heredity that affects IQ scores and it is their combination that will eventually determine a person's future adjustment. Let's look first at the study that suggests biological influences are important.

Until recently, researchers only made assumptions about prenatal influences on behavior and intelligence. However, some studies have shown lately that children who were born prematurely have lower IQ test scores than children who were not premature. Prematurity refers not only to when a baby is born, but also to its weight. Regardless of its birth date, any baby weighing less than 5 or 5½ pounds is considered premature.

An educational psychologist, Rosalyn Rubin, conducted a serious study of birth weight and its relation to intelligence and achievement. Rubin examined whether babies of lower birth weight achieved differently than babies of higher birth weight when both were tested at school age. To rule out any possible sociological variables including race and income, Rubin chose mainly babies of white, urban middle-class families. She classified them into groups as being born prematurely or not. Testing these children years later, the results showed that the premature babies were less successful academically than the other babies. On IQ tests, there was a 10 point difference between the two groups, with the premature babies scoring lower (Rubin, Rosenblatt & Balow, 1973).

This study was a correlational one. It showed that, when tested on academic-type tasks, children born premature have a greater likelihood of scoring low than babies who are not premature. The relationship, or correlation, was not a perfect one; not all premature babies will have lower IQ test scores, nor will all normal weight or heavy babies develop into geniuses. Rubin's study showed that the correlation was greater in males. Furthermore, this study looked at only one segment of society, using a small sample of subjects. This, of course, limits the generality of its findings. For the group tested, however, the findings were significant.

The causes of low birth weight are not clear. Many women who eat normal diets and experience otherwise normal pregnancies deliver premature babies. Eating excessively and putting on weight in pregnancy seem unrelated to birth weight. Still, birth weight seems re-

who have opportunities to consider moral dilemmas from another person's point of view are more likely to develop a more mature sense of morality. Role taking is a process that parents can provide, but one that is also provided by the school, church, and even the local politicians. Parents can be a direct source of moral values, but many others are also important (Haan, Langer, & Kohlberg, 1976). It is important that parents are not the only source of moral value development. Parents may fail at providing moral education; they might not provide role-taking opportunities. However, all is not lost, because parental failures do not logically require a lack of moral development—parents are only one source of many sources of moral development (Windmiller, 1980).

By teaching children to evaluate the world and their own values, they learn the difference between a routine behavior established to maintain order and a moral rule. Lying to a friend is violating morality; staying out too late after a date is violating a rule; distinctions between situations like these

lated to academic achievement. This may indicate that prematurity and/or birth weight could be dependent on some third factor, one that is genetic, that determines birth weight, academic achievement, and possibly personality or other aspects of behavior.

The studies of birth weight and prematurity show that these variables are important in determining IQ, but other studies lean more heavily on the environment side of the issue, particularly the family or home environment. One such important variable is family size. Studies have shown that the larger a family, the greater the possibility that its members will have low IQs. Children who have many siblings tend to perform less well on standardized tests of intelligence than children from smaller families. When examining which child of a family does better on standardized tests, it has generally been found that firstborns do better than second- or third-born children.

There are some conflicting results about birth order; a study by Belmont and Marolla (1973) examined birth order and family size in a population of almost 400,000 19-year-old men born in the Netherlands. These men were required by law to report for a physical examination upon their nineteenth birthday and, at that time, they presented data about the number of children in their families and their birth order. They were then given tests on measures of language, arithmetic, and nonverbal intelligence. The results of this study showed that on tests of intelligence, firstborns scored better than their siblings. In addition, second-borns scored higher than third-borns and third-borns higher than fourth-

borns, and so on. Birth order, therefore, was closely related to intelligence in this study.

When Belmont and Marolla examined the effect of family size, they found that as the family size increased, there was a decrease in intelligence scores no matter what the order of birth position. The results were interpreted to show that birth order and family size had separate effects on tests of intelligence. It is possible to speculate on a number of reasons why birth order and family size might produce changes in tests of intelligence. One might suggest that with a larger family less attention is given to individual children. In the case of birth order, perhaps less attention is given to each successive child. Belmont and Marolla suggest that education should be examined very closely, since intelligence varies with education level and social class.

The potent influences of family size are undeniable; at the same time, however, a woman's diet and the resulting health of her newborn baby clearly affect development. It was shown earlier that drugs taken during pregnancy and even during delivery affect a child's development. Perhaps it is impossible to assess accurately how much a person's behavior is due to nature and how much is due to nurture; however, more and more research is focusing on such concerns and is showing an increasingly complex variety of influences. Researchers are recognizing that issues which once seemed simple now seem complex. Psychologists are acutely aware that both nature and nurture are sources of influence and will produce effects that are directly observable on tests like the IQ test.

are often not made by parents (Craig, 1974). When parents offer the same punishment for breaking a routine rule as they do for breaking a moral rule, the development of the child's morality is hindered. By being aware of moral development (Damon, 1980) and by talking about moral issues, parents and teachers can initiate and stimulate the development of mature internalized moral values (Sullivan, 1980).

SOCIAL DEVELOPMENT

As children grow, the influence of the family and especially parents takes on a lesser role than it did in the early months and years. When children are still newborns, they may have the benefit of extended family interactions that can be facilitative (Willerman, 1979) or they may spend a great deal of their time staring out into space (White, 1978). While parents do not teach children

We learn to act like women or men by acting out the roles we see around us.

everything that they come to know, they have an important role in helping children develop social interactions (Willerman, 1979). Knowing this, parents watch the physical development of children and marvel at it. It is amazing to watch a young child grow, seeing changes from day-to-day. Parents know that they are acting as models for their children, and as such that their children reflect many of their behaviors, attitudes, and ideas. Recognizing this, one type of development of great concern to parents and teachers is social development. Social development determines how well children will interact with the world, and the nature of their interactions with the world determines how well they will get along with others. We will explore the process of socialization again when we study social psychology (chapter 10). Let us now examine a number of social behaviors that are closely tied to a child's development.

SOCIALIZATION.   Social development begins at birth. Throughout the formative stages of life, a child's pattern of social activities begins to develop. The nature of early interactions with parents is a crucial part of personality development. One need not be a psychologist to recognize that children need lots of love and attention. Lining the shelves of bookstores are self-help books that tell people how to be better parents and how to love their children. It is hard for a parent to offer too much love to a newborn; in fact, the argument is often made that a newborn cannot receive too much love and cannot be spoiled. They have a need to be hugged and cuddled. They have a need to be nurtured and made to feel good. A cranky infant becomes easily soothed when picked up by a parent and hugged and cuddled. Even 3-year-olds need to have constant reassurance that they are loved. Of course, as the famous psychoanalyst Bruno Bettelheim once said, "Love is not enough."

Parenting involves more than giving love, but providing that love is very important. As we saw earlier, the special relationship of bonding between parent and child (whether human or monkey) helps set up the formation of the socialization process. Although the child needs constant love and affection in the early months, eventually parents have to teach children to become independent.

As Piaget noted, social interactions in the first year are rather limited in that children are *egocentric* and almost totally self-centered. They have not learned to differentiate their needs and desires from those of the world. In the early weeks, they spend most of their time sleeping. They learn to interact with their parents, yet they have not learned to consider themselves apart from their parents, to consider their feelings, or to place themselves in their position. At the end of the first year, children may exhibit a fear of strangers and a strong attachment to their mother. With each month they learn new skills. For example, 2-year-olds have learned the word "no" and have begun to learn to manipulate their environment, so that they can tell their parents, "No, this," or "no go," or "no play," or "no peas." Children have learned strong emotions, how to differentiate themselves from others, to manipulate their world, and interact with other people.

In the "terrible twos" children quickly learn the word "NO!"

Although children remain largely egocentric in the first years of life, during the next stage, the preoperational stage, their egocentrism gives way to social interactions. They learn how to interact effectively with other people. Two-year-olds generally play alone, or, if they are playing with other children, play along with them side by side, having relatively little interaction with them. This changes as children move through the preoperational stage, at which time they are often sent to nursery school or kindergarten and are made to interact with their peers. They are forced to socialize and accept the demands of society for social interaction, responsibility, and sharing. These newfound responsibilities and freedoms bring about a variety of new behaviors. They teach children social skills and enable them to place themselves in another person's place. Piaget suggests that this socialization process delivers a telling blow to egocentrism.

The process of breaking down egocentrism is not a quick one, nor does it happen in isolation from all of the events that happen in a child's life. Even the kind of toys a child plays with affects egocentrism. Quilitch and Risley (1973) reported a study in which different kinds of toys were provided for children to play with. Some toys were isolate toys, which are generally played with by one child at a time. A second group of toys designed for competition are played with by two or more children at a time. The experimental situation allowed the children to use both social and isolate toys. Two groups of children received social toys first; two other groups of children received isolate toys first. The number of children playing with each other was used as an index of social play. The results of the experiment showed that differences in social play were dependent upon the type of toys provided the child.

Quilitch and Risley concluded that the type of toys given to the children produces dramatic effects on the amount of time they spend playing with each other. The children in the study were about 7 years of age and, therefore, had gone through the Piagetian preoperational stage. They should have been appropriately socialized and able to interact with other children. The results reported could not be the result of a lack of socialization or decentration; rather, the researchers concluded that the kind of toys the children

Learning to cooperate is an important part of growing up.

played with affected their social behavior. These results have strong implications not only for toy makers, but for the buyers of toys—parents.

What are the characteristics of children who have gone through the preoperational stage? What kinds of behavior can they be expected to show? Seven-year-olds can dress themselves, have many social interactions, have friends, are beginning school, and have a thirst for knowledge. Although they seem to be maturing very rapidly socially, they are still attached to their mother and father and suffer conflicts between their adult and baby characteristics. Seven-year-olds often prefer reverting to babylike behavior to accepting adult responsibilities. However, school gives children little choice. There they are required to socialize and to interact with peers and teachers.

Each year children become more efficient at developing their skills, more efficient learners, and more efficient socializers. In addition, the preadolescent is learning sex-role stereotypes, learning how to act as a boy or a girl. They often assume strong roles in their life and family. They are preparing themselves for adolescence, the stage of formal operations.

Social Behavior: The Role of Diet

In the 1970s, parents, educators, psychologists, and physicians were talking about a common problem in children, hyperactivity. **Hyperactivity** is an *At-*

Hyperactivity A group of symptoms that include overactivity, distractability, restlessness, and short attention span (see Attention Deficit Disorders).

tention Deficit Disorder that we will examine in more detail in chapter 12. Usually Attention Deficit Disorders include symptoms of overactivity, distractability, restlessness, and short attention span. Hyperactivity in children has been estimated to vary from 3 to 15% of school-age children. While originally thought of as being caused by brain damage, many people (particularly in the late 1970s) began thinking that one cause of hyperactivity was food substances that children were consuming (Williams & Cram, 1978).

Attention Deficit Disorders are important to developmental psychologists because they directly affect a child's social development. A child who is restless, inattentive, and easily distracted from work and play often has trouble adjusting. Hyperactivity is an area of investigation that shows an overlap among the cognitive, social, emotional, and biological influences on behavior. Children who have trouble concentrating often do not do well in school (cognitive); they often have trouble establishing and maintaining friendships (social). They sometimes develop other forms of adjustment problems (emotional) and are often treated with changes in diet and drugs (biological). Thus, we can easily see the complex role of both nature and nurture in the development, maintenance, and treatment of this fairly common disorder (Lahey, Green, & Forehand, 1980; Zenthall, 1980).

The growing concern about hyperactivity was brought about in part because of the method of treatment for the problem. Children were being placed on stimulants to control their hyperactivity. While it is a paradoxical finding, stimulants seem to calm hyperactive children and help them control their classroom behavior and performance (see, for example, Weingartner et al., 1980). Stimulants are potentially dangerous, potent, and addictive. So as to move away from stimulants, parents and physicians sought other treatment. In the mid 1970s, Benjamin Feingold, a physician, developed a diet in which he removed certain food substances from the diets of children who were diagnosed as hyperactive; he claimed that between 30 and 50% of the children showed marked improvement. The diet was free of salicylates, artificial food colors, and artificial food flavors. Feingold's (1975, 1976) basic idea was that certain children are born with a predisposition to hyperactivity and that these food substances trigger the symptoms. According to Feingold, if you remove the substance from a child with this kind of predisposition, then you will remove the hyperactive behaviors.

The response from the public was amazing. Large numbers of people placed their children on the diet and there were many successes. However, much of the scientific community has been skeptical because the diet was based more on clinical observation of Dr. Feingold's patients than on any theory or formal understanding of biochemistry. The Feingold supporters don't care about formal theory; they say that the diet works.

There has been a large amount of research done to investigate the adequacy of diet as an explanatory concept for hyperactivity. Some studies found some modest support for the Feingold diet; other studies found none. No study has given unqualified support for the diet. But certain findings do suggest that in about 10 to 25% of younger hyperactive children, a diet free of artificial additives is beneficial. The jury is still out on the Feingold diet and other research is being conducted (see also Pelham et al., 1980).

A study done at the University of South Carolina with hyperactive children has shown that sugar and sugar products were involved in destructive-aggressive and restless behaviors observed in the free play of hyperactive children. According to Prinz, Roberts, and Hantman (1980) sugar consumption is a very important component in the diet of hyperactive children, and when hyperactive children are on a diet low in these substances, hyperactive behaviors are less apparent. Prinz and his colleagues were cautious; they made no sweeping claims that removing all sugar would decrease all hyperactivity, but they did claim that sugar plays a potentially important role in the hyperactive child's behavior.

There are certain problems in all of the studies investigating diet and behavior. It is hard, if not impossible, to control totally what a child is eating and what it contains. Furthermore, assessing a child's behavior has certain difficulties associated with it. Parents observe different behaviors from teachers. It is difficult to know *exactly* what a child consumes during an entire 3- or 8-week period of testing. And furthermore, some children may be more affected by dietary restriction than other children. While researchers are developing methodologies for the examination of these different variables, the research is continuing and the role of diet in the management of hyperactivity continues to be investigated. It seems very likely that, given our knowledge of how our bodies affect our behavior, the control of diet may be a potent and perhaps critical variable in helping shape the behavior of many children afflicted with problems like hyperactivity.

Who Cares for the Children: The Effects of Day-Care Centers

With more than 42% of mothers of preschool children in the work force, it is not surprising that psychologists and parents are considering very carefully the role of early childhood interactions and later development.

Over the years, American men and women have adopted the widely held view that the mother is *the* principal care giver for an infant and any and all care should be given by her. American society has taught that when a child is reared by others, less than optimal development will take place. The underlying idea that many parents have held is that care given to an infant affects its future development in profound ways. Parents, and especially mothers, have been reluctant to allow day-care centers to take care of their children; as Kagan has suggested, "She is reluctant to let that responsibility slip into the hands of others" (Kagan, Kearsley, & Zelazo, 1980, p. 173).

The fears of American women are not without foundation. For years they have been taught that the mother is the only effective provider of infant care. Early psychological studies supported this idea and suggested that the effects of nonmaternal care could be devastating (Bowlby, 1958; Freud, 1965; Spitz, 1945). However, in the last decade there has been intensive research on the effect of nonmaternal care on infants and their subsequent development. These studies have focused especially on the role of group day-care centers. They have attempted to assess in what ways group day care affects future development.

The study of group day-care centers and their effects on children is a problem of considerable magnitude. There are huge individual differences between day-care centers. In a given center, the number of students and teachers may vary. The frequency of staff changes is important, as are staff experience and qualifications. The child's age of entry into such a program, as well as the extent of the child's day-care experience, must also be considered. No less important than any of these variables is the child's family back-

Quality care is the key to successful development.

ground. Etaugh (1980) and Kagan et al. (1980) have summarized these methodological problems.

Controlled research on the effects of group day-care centers on childhood development has focused on three major areas: mother-child attachment, intellectual development, and social development. Psychologists have focused on attachment between the mother and child because they have long believed that such attachments help secure and form the long-term basis of security and trust (for a review see Bowlby, 1973 and Klaus and Kennell, 1976). It is generally believed that the child's future emotional security depends upon a strong, loving bond between infant and mother or primary caretaker (Kagan et al., 1980). If this relationship is broken, such security and emotional health are weakened; thus, maintenance of an attachment or bond is crucial. Psychologists have found that nonmaternal care does not detract from the infant's emotional bond or attachment to the mother (Etaugh, 1980; Portnoy & Simmons, 1978). Furthermore, there is no firm evidence that brief separations, such as day-care, create later psychological trauma.

From the intellectual side, parents are concerned that nonmaternal care will detract from a child's cognitive growth. There is considerable literature to suggest that a stimulating, varied early environment is necessary and appropriate for optimal intellectual development. However, the data show that good-quality group day-care centers provide a sufficient environment so that no differences in intellectual functioning can be found between middle-class children with day-care training and those reared exclusively at home (Belsky & Steinberg, 1978). Further, good-quality group day-care programs can help prevent a decline in intellectual functioning that is sometimes apparent in some lower income families (see, for example, Golden et al., 1978).

Socially, children who are reared at home and who are given care in quality group day-care programs are remarkably alike. While some studies have reported more aggression in children of day-care centers (Largeman, 1976), other studies have found opposite or nonsignificant effects (Macrae & Herbert-Jackson, 1976). Overall, day-care centers increase both positive and negative interactions with peers (Belsky & Steinberg, 1978).

In examining the literature on day-care centers, researchers have been *very* careful to qualify their evaluations. Children to be compared must be within the same social class (Kagan, 1979). The effects of group day-care centers are not the same as home rearing *unless* the day-care center is particularly well staffed and has a low faculty-student ratio. Both home-reared and day-care center children must come from intact and psychologically supportive families for no difference to be apparent. The day-care program must be nurturing and cognitively challenging (Kagan et al., 1980). Admittedly, few day-care centers meet all of these criteria; when they do, the home backgrounds of the children involved do not always meet optimal situations.

Under optimal situations, group day-care centers and home rearing result in children with similar psychological profiles. However, long-term studies of the effects of day care on children's later development have yet to take place. Perhaps even more important are the goals that parents have for themselves and their children. Good day care may produce fine children; however, parents may have special goals that a day-care center cannot meet. Regardless of the quality of the day-care center, a parent cannot achieve the pleasure of watching a child mature while the child is in a day-care center. We must remember that children are different, as are their parents; the parents have goals, needs, and desires that are unique and must also be respected.

What does a modern parent do with respect to day care? First, parents must establish goals for themselves and their child. Second, if those goals—by necessity or design—require day-care centers, a *high quality* nurturing day-care center should be found. Third, the home must provide a psychologically supportive environment. Fourth, parents must use common sense and do what feels right for them. If they feel that day care is harmful and they desire to be home with their child, then they should stay home. If by necessity or design they choose the services of a day-care center, good judgment should be used to optimize the day-care setting and home environment.

And Father Makes Three: The Father's Role in Child Rearing

In past years, mothers and fathers have not shared equally in the day-to-day caring of infants and children. Traditionally, the wife as mother and housekeeper undertook the responsibilities of child care. However, with changes in modern society and especially with the increased number of women in the work force, men have increasingly become involved with their children. This involvement sometimes begins in the first moments of life.

There are many reasons why fathers have not often been involved in child rearing. Among these are the biological and culturally defined roles. For example, breast feeding limits the father's role with a newborn. Because of the close association of feeding with the mother, fathers have often been excluded (at least in this society) from caretaking generally. However, recent research has shown that fathers are engrossed with their newborns (Greenberg & Morris, 1974) and also are as affectionate and responsive as mothers are (Parke & O'Leary, 1976).

Research on the way parents interact with children is complicated. Fathers and children do not exist in a social vacuum. For example, a father's interaction with his child is affected by his wife being present; thus, a father's play with his child changes when his wife enters the room (Clarke-Stewart, 1978). While it was once generally assumed that fathers affected their children in only indirect ways through the mother (Lewis & Weinraub, 1976), more recent evidence suggests that fathers influence their children directly (Parke, 1979).

The role of parent interactions with children has been studied intensively. One of the principal findings of such studies is that the mother-child or father-child interaction is affected markedly by the presence of the other parent. For example, Parke and O'Leary (1976) observed mothers interacting with their infants both alone and in the presence of the father. When they are alone with their infants, mothers smile more at their newborns and interact with them more. Overall, the quality of mother-child interactions decreased when fathers were around.

Fathers can have direct influences on their children, but few are involved enough to make a large impact, especially during the early months. There is no question that fathers spend less time than mothers with their children. Researchers find that fathers are perceived by children as playmates; mothers are perceived as caretakers. If children want to play, they choose their fathers; if they want to be consoled, they seek out their mothers (Clarke-Stewart, 1978). In a middle-class sample of parents, only 7.5% of fathers shared infant caretaking responsibilities equally with their wives and only 25% had a regular caretaking responsibility. In fact, in this same study 43% of all the fathers reported that they had never changed diapers at all (Kotelchuck, 1976). While the amount of time fathers spend with their infants is rather limited, the quality of their time is as high as that of mothers (Booth & Edwards, 1980; Parke, 1979). Fathers understand their infants; they know how to respond to them and are effective caretakers and givers of affection—when they take charge of such activities.

Rough and tumble has been a traditional role for fathers, and research shows that the father has a very important place in a child's development.

There is no question that even today fathers have less contact with their children than do mothers. However, the quality of a parent's time with a child is as important as is the quantity. Fathers can have quality time with their children and have a direct impact on their children's social and intellectual development (Parke, 1979). The role of the father is very important. It has been shown that the father's absence produces a variety of detrimental effects, although many of them may be deterred by an aware mother (Lamb, 1979).

The marked increase in the number of women in the work force has brought about significant changes in the role of fathers in child care. Increasingly, men are required to spend more time with their children. In general, roles of men and women are changing in the United States. Among younger couples, men and women are becoming somewhat more androgynous; that is, they are taking on similar characteristics. Thus it is now common to find men involved in traditionally defined "women's work" and especially in infant and child caretaking responsibilities. These newly defined roles and responsibilities are changing the texture of American society. While these changes are slow to take place and are often limited to certain socioeconomic groups, they are taking place nonetheless. Both mothers and fathers can provide care to a child. As in day-care centers, quality care must be the focus for optimal development.

THE SINGLE PARENT. In the 1980s, more and more parents of children are single parents. Men and women are divorcing at a faster rate than ever before. In addition, there is an increasing number of never married parents. To these, add parents who are widowed, and we see millions of single parents rearing children without the aid of a spouse. Many of the support systems traditionally provided for single parents are no longer available; families often do not live together in the same community. With their increasing number and our mobile society, single parents are bearing the burden of parenthood alone. Psychologists are increasingly devoting efforts toward helping such parents; they have special needs and represent a significant minority of the population. Psychologist Leroy Baruth has written a book entitled *A Single Parent's Survival Guide: How to Raise the Children* (Dubuque, Iowa: Kendall/Hunt Publishing Company, 1979). In the book he addresses some of the problems of being a single parent. The following is a summary of his 10 specific techniques for child care:

1. Be honest with your children about the situation that caused you to become a single parent.
2. If the situation involves a separation or divorce, assure the children that they are not responsible for the decision to discontinue the relationship.
3. Be honest about your own feelings. This will demonstrate to the children that it is all right for them to express how they feel.
4. Try to maintain as much of the same routine and surroundings as possible. This will provide the children with a feeling of security that not everything has changed.
5. Do not try to be both mother and father to your children. Establish a family atmosphere of team work where responsibilities are shared.
6. In the case of separation or divorce, realize that the relationship is over and do not encourage the children to hope for a reconciliation.
7. The children must be reassured that they will continue to be loved, cared for,

and supported. This should be done not only by words but also by your attitude and behavior.

8. You should not use the children in an effort to gain bargaining power with your separated or divorced spouse.
9. Make use of grandparents and other relatives so the children maintain a sense of belonging to a continuing family.
10. Try to seek the companionship and counsel of other single parents. They can be a source of advice and support that will help immeasurably in child rearing. (pp. 6 and 7)

Sexual Attitudes

While contemporary American society may be pushing sexuality on many unwilling men and women, the instruction of young boys and girls regarding sexual attitudes is still primarily the parent's responsibility. We noted that children learn attitudes, as well as how to interact with other people, by many means, including instrumental conditioning, observational learning, and classical conditioning. With sexuality, parents teach a child his or her sexual identity, and parents direct a child's initial sexual responses.

Much sexual behavior is tied to intimate relationships with another person. The intimacy of relationships is taught, at least initially, in the home. Children watch their parents interact; they notice if the parents hug, if they kiss, and whether or not they touch. Do they seem ashamed of their naked bodies? Do they talk about sex in the household? Or do they stiffen at open references to sexual matters and act embarrassed, nervous, or repressive?

A person's relationship with his or her parents plays a crucial role in the development of sexual ideas. For example, the closer one's relationship to one's parents, the less permissive are one's ideas about sexual behavior. Furthermore, in general terms, the more liberal or permissive the parents, the more liberal or permissive the children. As in so many other areas of human behavior, parents try to socialize their children in a way that is consistent with their own beliefs and behaviors (DeLamater & MacCorquodale, 1979).

ADOLESCENCE

In adolescence, social interactions differ markedly from those of earlier years. The adolescent is a human being who is physically an adult and whose mental capabilities are reaching or have reached maturity. One of the conflicts that arises in adolescence, at least in the United States, is a result of the gap between the physical size of adolescents and their emotional maturity. Very often adolescents' emotional capabilities don't keep pace with their physical development. On one hand, adults tell the adolescent it is time to behave as an adult; on the other hand, they restrict the adolescent from becoming a full adult. Their sexual freedom and incomes are restricted, and how they spend their money is often dictated. Although they may be intellectually capable of dealing with formal operations, emotionally they remain egocentric and at a much earlier stage of development. The conflicts that adolescents experience may, in large part, come about because of a lack of correspondence among physical, intellectual, social, and emotional development. We must also realize that adolescence as a "problem" period is partially an effect of modern industrial social conditions. Adolescence as a problem period was *not* seen in the eighteenth century's apprentice system, nor is it visible in the form we know it in the nonindustrial societies today. So, the problems of adolescence must be considered within a cultural context.

The changes that take place from the moment of conception all the way to age 13 are dramatic ones. A sperm and an ovum have combined and have eventually created a multicellular differentiated organism. After 9 months of development a newborn comes into the world fully equipped. The first 2 years show incredible physical and mental growth; during the next 10, further intellectual growth and socialization accompany rapid physical development. However, it is not until adolescence that many of the mature adult qualities of our species become obvious. At 13 years of age, plus or minus a year or two, boys and girls experience significant growth spurts. Their hormonal systems put gonadotrophins into their bloodstreams that produce secondary sex characteristics, including increased genital size and body hair. Adolescent boys and girls can grow as much as 4 to 5 inches in a single year; very often they grow out of clothes even before they've worn them. This newfound growth is exciting, but sometimes difficult to deal with because the adolescent is forced into a new situation in life.

Adolescents have reached the Piagetian stage of formal operations, and adult society knows that they are able to think logically and conceive ideas. Adult society expects adolescents to think rationally and behave as adults. This is a rational and reasonable demand of adult society; yet, the ability to cope with the complexities and restrictions of a high-technology society does not come all at once. The stage of formal operations, like Piaget's other stages, matures slowly. Some adolescents have reached the stage of formal operations at age 13; others take a few more years. So, adolescents have changing intellectual abilities, changing body proportions, and new sexual urges. Coupled with parental expectations for more mature adult behavior, these situations taking place simultaneously create the classic adolescent identity crisis of Western society.

The Identity Crisis

The process of forming a self-concept, an image of who one is and what one wants in life, is a difficult one. In contemporary Western society, adolescents are expected to behave like adults; yet, only a few months or years before, they were allowed to behave as children. Wanting the freedom and responsibilities of adulthood but clinging to childlike ways for security creates a frustrating situation for the growing adolescent. Our society is increasingly placing demands upon youth to make career decisions earlier and earlier in adolescence. In the eighth-grade, at only 13 or 14 years of age, students must make a decision about their choice of curriculum in high school. Should they go on toward a college curriculum, a business curriculum, or perhaps technical training? This decision is an important one, requiring motivation. Often, the decision is such a confusing one that it is made for the adolescent by his or her parents.

Perhaps no single individual has been more closely associated with the problems of the adolescent than the noted developmental psychologist Erik H. Erikson. All of the growth and turmoil of adolescence creates what Erikson has called "the identity crisis." Indeed, Erikson has suggested that the major task adolescents have to complete is forming an identity and deciding who they are and what they want in life. You will see in chapter 11, Personality, that the process of forming an identity and a self-concept is a complex one. For example, self-concepts are not only formed from what one believes oneself to be, but also from what others believe one to be. In addition, people often attribute characteristics to themselves based upon the situation they find themselves in. For these reasons, adolescents are very impressionable and often find themselves caught up in political, religious, or ideological groups. These groups allow adolescents to find out what they believe in and what satisfies their own needs to feel competent. The adolescent years represent years of growth—not so much intellectual or physical, but toward a personal sense of becoming a mature, stable adult. As Erikson suggests, successful completion of these identity crisis years allows young adults to develop mature relations with members of the opposite sex so that they might convey love and emotional security to them. If the identity crisis is not successfully resolved, the adolescent is faced with a sense of role confusion and an inability to cope with the demands of adulthood (see Erikson, 1963, 1968). Erikson believes the search for identity grows logically from the sociocultural pressures and the tasks they impose on development. Unlike Freud, Erikson does not believe that adolescence is a time of inevitable upheaval.

Erik H. Erikson developed one of the most influential of psychosocial theories.

Erikson has provided a social-stage theory of development that has achieved wide prominence in the psychological world. Like Freud, Erikson suggests that the child goes through a series of stages and that each stage must be successfully completed to create a healthy adult. Problems at any particular stage will bring about conflict at that stage; each stage is centered around two alternatives representing possible outcomes of that stage.

Stage 1 is the stage of *basic trust vs. mistrust*. During the first months of life, a child makes distinctions about the world and decides whether or not it is a comfortable, loving place in which he can place his basic trust. As the child proceeds to Stage 2 and becomes a toddler and faces toilet training, he passes through the stage of *autonomy vs. shame and doubt*. If the child is successful in his toilet training and other control tasks, he gains autonomy and begins to behave as a more mature individual. If, however, this stage is not easily passed through, he will develop fears, shame, and doubt.

The third stage is that of *initiative vs. guilt*. At ages 4 and 5, the child develops the ability to take initiatives and to identify with parents. During this stage, he can develop independence and good feelings about himself; in contrast, he can feel guilty, unacceptable, and have poor feelings about his own sexuality. As a child proceeds to Stage 4, the stage of *industry vs. inferiority*, he should develop feelings of confidence in his own abilities. From ages 7 to 11, either he develops this confidence or he experiences failure, inferiority, and feelings of incompetence.

Stage 5 is the beginning of adolescence. It is Erikson's stage of *identity vs. role confusion*. An adolescent must decide who he is and what he wants to do in life. Either he will begin to develop a sense of his identity, or he will become confused and often rebellious. Stage 6, *intimacy vs. isolation*, is the time of young adulthood when people begin to choose others with whom they can love, identify, and become intimate. During this stage, people learn to relate on a warm social basis with a member of the opposite sex, or they become isolated and separate from the crowd. In Stage 7, *generativity vs. stagnation*, a person seeks out more than just intimacy; he or she also hopes to convey information, love, and warmth to others, particularly his or her children. In adulthood, a person hopes that he is influencing either his own family or the world at large. The opposite pole of this stage is stagnation, where a person feels that his life has not been dynamic but rather boring and unexciting. The final stage in Erikson's eight stages is *ego integrity vs. despair*. This stage of development is the one in which a person, later in life, decides whether his or her existence has been meaningful, happy, and cohesive or whether it has been one of waste, or lacking in productivity. Many individuals never reach Stage 8 or ego integrity vs. despair; they are often fixated in Stages 5, 6, or 7. However, when a person reaches Stage 8, he or she has begun to understand what life is about.

Erikson's psychosocial stages of development parallel Freud's stages, particularly as they pertain to the early years. Although Freud is instinctually oriented and Erikson is socially oriented, they share the view that a problem at a particular stage leads to conflict and an inability to pass through future stages easily. A crucial difference between them is that Erikson sees personality development as proceeding throughout the life span, whereas Freud sees it as relatively complete in childhood. Erikson is thus one of the true life cycle theorists.

ADULTHOOD

Until the last decade, developmental psychologists focused most of their attention on the development of children. In fact, researchers were usually most interested in early infant or early childhood development. Their aim was to understand how an infant or child learns to cope with the world. Coping with the world is not solely a function of children, however. Adults need to cope as well. Indeed, therapists' offices are filled with adults who have trouble coping. As a result of researchers beginning to realize that adulthood brings with it its own unique complexities and problems, the study of life processes in adulthood has been undertaken.

Adults are presented with a special set of circumstances. They not only have to cope with themselves, but with their job, family, children, relatives, and the constantly changing demands of society. Researchers are now realizing that they cannot just look at the early stages of development; they have to look at the full life cycle.

Daniel Levinson of Yale University has developed a stage theory of male adult development (Levinson, 1978). Although Levinson's ideas and research have focused on men, they are generally applicable to women as well. Levinson argues that adults have four basic eras in their life cycle: adolescence and early, middle, and late adulthood. Within each of these eras different types of problems and situations present themselves. Levinson's four eras and the ages they approximately span are

- Ages 11–17 Adolescence
- Ages 18–45 Early adulthood
- Ages 46–65 Middle adulthood
- Ages 65– Late adulthood

In *adolescence*, a young person is moving toward becoming an adult; he or she is trying out new roles and responsibilities. He is still immature and vul-

Returning to college is challenging but rewarding.

nerable but is making his entry into the adult world. The second area of the adult life span begins with *early adulthood,* starting at about age 18 and continuing until about 45. With great physical vigor, people in early adult ages seek education, careers, family, and friends. The first major choices in life are made: family, occupation, style of living. Through these years, the novice adult moves toward greater independence and into a more "senior" position in work, family, and community. Over this span of 20 years a man raises his children, rises to a position at work, and begins to see his offspring grow and leave home. The era of early adulthood is one of striving, gaining, and accepting responsibility. By the end of the era, at age 45 or so, a man is a full generation removed from his children and is often taking on the responsibility of caring for his parents.

The era of early adulthood has the much discussed mid-life crisis. During the ages 30 to 35 many men experience one of several crisis periods in their lives during which they evaluate their positions in life and often try to change those positions. During this period, people realize that their lives are half over and that if they are to change their lives, they must do so now. This can be a difficult time during which people resign themselves to their lives, or decide to change, become better, and renew efforts toward excellence. When Erik Erikson talked about this stage he called it "generativity vs. stagnation."

The third era of the adult life cycle, *middle adulthood,* spans the years from 46 to 65. The era begins with an adult who has gone through a mid-life crisis and is living with decisions made during his early adulthood. Career and families are usually well established, and people are either achieving a sense of satisfaction and feelings of self-worth or they feel much of their life has been wasted. In the middle of this era, some men go through a crisis similar to that of the early adulthood era. Sometimes this crisis is a continuation of the one of the late thirties; other times it can be a new one. As a man approaches his sixties, he begins to prepare himself for the era to come. This age and the years of preparation for late adulthood are the days when people's final orders of business are taken care of. Retirement is approaching and people are really coming to terms with who they are. At this point in his life there are few major decisions to be made. These years prepare a man for a decade of great fulfillment or one of despair.

The years after 50 are the years of perspective and mellowing. In these years, particularly in their early sixties, people learn to make decisions about the quality of their lives not in terms of money or day-to-day success, but according to whether their lives have been meaningful, happy, and cohesive. Erikson would call these years the age of "ego-integrity," when people stop blaming others for their problems and there is less concern about disputes with others. At this point people try to achieve everything that they can from life because they know that two-thirds of life have passed and they wish to make the most of their remaining years. Ambitions for glory, fame, and fortune are put aside, and people either learn to live with who they are or despair and become bitter.

Levinson's fourth and final era, *late adulthood,* typically covers the years of retirement. From age 65 on, people can relax and enjoy the fruits of their lives. Children, grandchildren, and even great-grandchildren can be the focus of an older person's mature life. While less studied than early eras, the stage of late adulthood is the one during which people develop true perspective on the meaning of their lives. As you will see in the next section, there are a number of misconceptions about the capabilities of the aged.

While Erikson presented an important stage theory of the development that occurs during early stages of life, Levinson's life cycle approach focuses not on the early stages of development but on adulthood. Piaget was concerned with intellectual development in youth, Erikson with social development, and as you will see in subsequent chapters, Freud focused on sexual development. It is likely that in the future more and more research will be done on the process of becoming an adult and the stages through which adults pass.

AGING

In studying development, researchers have focused closely on the early years; today, we know much about infant and early childhood development. At the same time, our knowledge about older people is growing at a rapid rate. There are just as many people over the age of 65 as there are under age 6, but programs, funding, and research with older people is limited. Parents and psychologists alike are fascinated by the growth and development of children. The maturing of the human newborn and its subsequent development during infancy and childhood are truly marvelous, but even changes during adolescence and adulthood have unique characteristics. People do not live forever and their life spans are marked not only by periods of growth, but sometimes by periods of diminished capabilities, losses in memory, and increased likelihood of disease. We often mistakenly think of development in terms of the years from birth through adolescence, but development also continues through adulthood.

Who Are the Aged?

Of the 230 million people who live in the United States, more than 23 million (10% of the population) are considered old. This percentage is likely to grow, for as medical science continues its technological advances, more people are living longer. By the year 2030, it is expected that 15 to 20 % of the population will be over the age of 65 (see Figure 6.7). Today, a man's life expectancy is about 72 years and a woman's about 77 years. But, while more and more people are living their full life expectancy, they are being beset by social, cultural, and medical problems. They have increasing medical costs, few resources, and, in many cases, few friends and interested family members.

Theories of Aging

Throughout the ages, people have questioned why they must get old and die. The basic question is, "Why do people grow old?" Three basic theories have been put forth to account for the aging process, each one stressing a different component of the likely causes of aging (Kimmel, 1974).

Figure 6.7 The percentage of the population that will be over age 65 in the future is shown. As can easily be seen, the average age of U.S. citizens is increasing; some call it the graying of America (data from Usdin & Hofling, 1978)

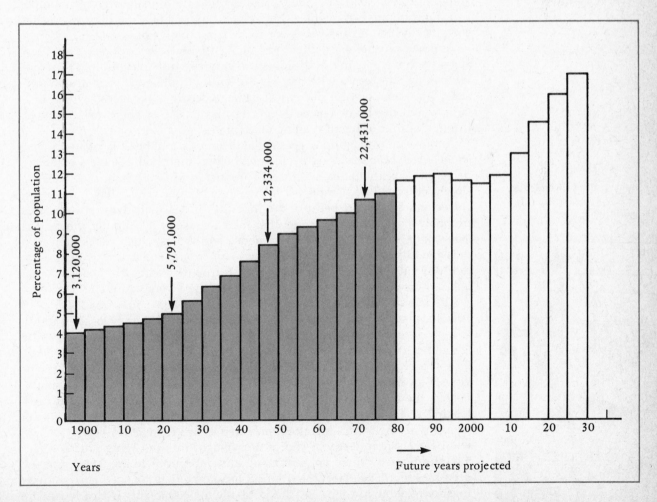

Years

Future years projected

HEREDITY. Intuitively, you might expect that heredity determines how long a person will live. This notion suggests that a person's genes contain the characteristics that will determine longevity, and thus one's years are numbered by nature.

EXTERNAL FACTORS. Kimmel (1974) has suggested that external factors also affect how long a person lives. For example, people who live on a farm instead of in the city will live longer. Similarly, overweight people live fewer years than people of normal weight. People who smoke cigarettes die sooner, as do people who continually are under great tension or who expose themselves to disease or radiation. So, it's easy to see how factors external to the organism can affect life span.

PHYSIOLOGICAL APPROACHES. It seems clear that heredity and external factors determine—at least to some extent—how long people will live. Perhaps more important, however, are changes in people's biological abilities and in their life-maintaining processes. These changes may determine to a greater extent the nature of the aging process and the length of a person's life. There are several explanations of the aging process involving physiology. For example, the *wear-and-tear* theory suggests that the human organism simply wears out because of overuse. Much like the parts of a machine which has seen its day, the organs necessary to sustain life give out.

Another physiological theory of aging involves *homeostasis*. This view suggests that a person's body adjusts to varying situations but that this ability to adjust decreases with age. As the ability of the body to maintain constant body temperature decreases, damage occurs and causes aging. Similarly, when the body can no longer bring the use of sugar under control through output of insulin, aging takes place.

Another view of aging suggests that it comes about because of an *accumulation of metabolic waste*. As people grow older, their bodies have a gradually decreasing ability to deal with waste products and, as a result, their cells are slowly poisoned or hampered in their functioning. This view has not received much support because the inability to deal with waste products is probably a symptom of aging rather than a cause of it. Another theory, *autoimmunity*, suggests that people generate antibodies which attack their own cells and ultimately destroy the life-cycle functions. This theory, too, has not received much scientific support, but it is true that with age, people cannot fight off disease as well as they could when they were younger.

The last of the basic physiological theories of aging involves the idea of *cellular aging*. This notion suggests that as cells grow old, they lose the ability to reproduce themselves. In fact, some data do suggest that cells have a finite life and can produce only a certain number of times.

As you can see, it is not easy to explain why people age. There are obviously a variety of ways through which people grow old, but surprisingly, only in the last couple of decades have psychologists and physicians been looking at the behavioral and physiological changes that take place with aging. With the increasing attention given to this field, it is likely that there will be even more research and greater insight into the aging process.

Unfortunately, there are still many misconceptions about aging and the processes that take place therein. People assume that the aged have no feelings, are unable to cope, and are generally deficient. This is clearly not the

Humans have a wonderful capacity for developing new skills throughout life.

case, although physiological and intellectual changes do take place with the process of growing old.

Physiological Changes in Aging

There are many physiological changes that the elderly have to face. For example, alterations in calcium metabolism cause bones to become more brittle, and there is also a greater likelihood of disease of the joints such as arthritis. Teeth fall out because of gum diseases, and skin looses some of its elasticity. More folds and wrinkles appear than ever before. Because of a lack of companionship and the loneliness that results, many old people become less concerned with eating and suffer vitamin deficiencies as a result.

There are also some distinct changes in the sensory abilities of older people. They are far more likely than younger people to show decrements in the senses. It has generally been shown that the vision, hearing, taste, and the sense of smell of older people require a higher level of stimulation if they are to respond in the same way that a young person's sense receptors respond. For example, as a rule visual acuity decreases in the aged to such an extent that they are unable to make fine visual discriminations without the aid of glasses. Their eyes also adapt to the dark much less effectively. There are frequently marked losses in hearing—particularly in the high frequency ranges—and the senses of taste and smell are much less acute than in the past.

The greatest changes that take place in the central nervous system are shown in tests of reaction time. Much of the slowness of the aged is really a result of changes in the ability to respond quickly. While there have been many explanations for the decreasing ability of the central nervous system to respond to the demands of an individual's environment, the important point to remember is that these changes bring about a characteristic slowing of activity with advancing age.

The slowing and changing of a person's responses with age become particularly apparent in the aged's sensory-motor abilities, the ability of the body to respond to the senses. For example, should an emergency occur, an elderly driver of an automobile may not be able to stop the car as quickly as a younger driver could under similar circumstances. While often their sensory abilities are not impaired, their ability to respond to the changes in the environment is often not as good as that of younger people.

Intellectual Changes with Aging

Perhaps more distressing than any other change that comes with aging is the *assumed* decrements in intellectual ability. However, there has been considerable debate as to what changes do take place. On one side are researchers who argue that intelligence and cognitive processes are stable over the life of an individual. Other research has shown that there are definite declines in certain intellectual functions with advances in age. For example, memory decreases with advances in age (Arenberg, 1978). Even those who have maintained that general intellectual functioning remains stable over a life span are recognizing now that certain aspects of intellectual functioning do deteriorate with age (Craik, 1977). One real problem is defining what intellectual functioning is. If a standardized intelligence test is to be given to aged persons they are likely to do poorly, not because of reasons of intelligence but because intelligence tests often require manipulations of objects in a timed fashion. This means that a person's slowed reaction time or decreased manual dexterity (often due to arthritis) may effect the IQ score. While there are some definite aspects of thought that do deteriorate, many researchers (perhaps the more liberal and optimistic) still argue that changes due to the aging processes, including the slowing of reaction time, an increased likelihood of disease, and psychological problems, such as loneliness, can affect a person's performance. As Kimmel (1974) has suggested,

> Comfortable rehearsed skills may be more attractive than learning a new set of skills; but, if retraining and continuing education occurred during the early and middle adult years, there is little reason an elderly person could not learn as well as a young person. Certainly, up to the age of sixty-five there is little decline in learning or memory ability; factors of motivation, interest, and lack of recent educational experience are probably more important in learning complex knowledge than age per se. Learning may just take a bit longer for the elderly and occur more at the individual's own speed instead of at an external and fast pace. (p. 381)

To sum up, the current view is that older individuals' intelligence increases or stays the same until just before death.

DYING: THE FINAL STAGE

Death is generally a difficult topic for most people—even scientists—to discuss and think about, so the processes of dying have received little study. However, in recent years there has been a growing interest in discussing death. Researchers are beginning to try to understand some of the psychological and physiological complexities of death. Elisabeth Kübler-Ross has been at the forefront of the "natural dying" revolution. Kübler-Ross argues that it is far more humane for people to die at home among those that they love than in hospitals where they are attached to machines and tubes.

Kübler-Ross has written several books on death and dying. In her 1969 book called *On Death and Dying* (New York: Macmillan Publishing Company, 1969), she analyzes the processes of death and discusses the patient's and the family's fears and hopes. This work on death and dying began when Kübler-Ross was asked to write a paper on "Crisis in Human Life"; since she had decided that her paper was to be on dying, she chose to interview a dying patient. Eventually she interviewed hundreds of dying individuals and established seminars on the process of death and dying.

Kübler-Ross's ideas about death and dying are not accepted fully by the entire scientific community. Recently, some of her ideas have relied more on intuition than on scientific discovery and fact. Regardless, her initial ideas and conceptualizations of the stages preparing a person for death have generated a great deal of discussion and debate. It is clear that further scientific inquiry is necessary to systematize these ideas (see, for example, Rodabough, 1980).

Kübler-Ross described five stages through which dying individuals proceed upon learning that they are terminally ill: (1) denial, (2) anger, (3) bargaining, (4) depression, and (5) acceptance. As we briefly outline each of these stages, it is important to note that Kübler-Ross suggests that hope usually persists throughout all stages of the dying process. As Kübler-Ross has indicated, "We were always impressed that even the most accepting, the most realistic patients left the possibility open for some cure, or the discovery of a new drug, or the 'last minute success' in a research project" (1969, p. 139).

The Five Stages of Dying

DENIAL.   When patients are first told that they are going to die, they typically respond with disbelief. They feel that mistakes have been made, that the tests have been wrong, or perhaps that the doctor is incompetent. As Kübler-Ross indicates, denial serves as a buffer against the shocking news. Although such denial is usually a temporary defense, it will eventually be replaced by partial acceptance.

ANGER.   Feelings of anger, rage, envy, and resentment follow denial. Once people realize that they are going to die and stop denying it, they logically ask, "Why me?" Anger is directed toward family, doctors, and hospitals. In fact, their rage is directed toward anyone and everyone with whom they come in contact. Often the family may come to react angrily to the patient because they are tired of being abused. This only makes the situation worse, though, because they often avoid the patient or shorten their visits, forgetting the reasons for the patient's anger.

BARGAINING.   The stage of bargaining helps the patient cope, if only for a brief time. In bargaining he or she makes deals, perhaps with God, perhaps with her- or himself or maybe even with doctors. The bargaining usually takes the form of "I'll be good if you'll provide me some more time or special services, and most importantly an extension of life." Like the opera star who wants to "perform just one more time," the terminally ill bargain to postpone the inevitable. Kübler-Ross notes, however, that most bargains are made with God and are usually kept a secret.

DEPRESSION.   Not surprisingly, depression soon sets in. Tests and medication are often painful, and treatments and hospitalization are often financial burdens. The terminally ill often lose their jobs once they have lost the ability to function as they have in the past. Feeling guilty for the inconvenience they cause their families only adds to their sadness. All of these reasons create depression for the terminally ill. Depression often occurs because the patient cannot accept giving up and losing everything and everybody that he loves, but Kübler-Ross tells us that "if he is allowed to express his sorrow he will find the final acceptance much easier, and he will be grateful to those who can sit with him during this stage of depression without constantly telling him not to be sad" (1969, p. 87).

ACCEPTANCE.   If the patient has had enough time to work through the previous stages, he can approach the stage of acceptance where he is neither angry about his fate, nor depressed. Often tired and weak, patients at this point have usually resigned themselves to death. This is the time that the dying patient can find some peace of mind at having accepted his fate. He often wishes to be left alone without visitors. Sometimes he may make a gesture or hold someone's hand while sitting in silence.

While some patients fight to the end, most will one day finally admit that they are tired of fighting. This is not a happy time but a time of resignation and surrender.

DEATH: THE FINAL STAGE OF DEVELOPMENT.   As indicated earlier, death is the final stage of the life cycle and can be approached maturely by dying individuals and their families. Kübler-Ross goes to great lengths to discuss not only the dying patient but his family as well. She is keenly aware of the needs of patients and their families. As a physician herself, she is particularly sensitive to the relationships between doctors, hospitals, the terminally ill, and their families, and she understands such problems as the family's need to deal with the patient's memory. In the past few years, hospitals for terminally ill patients have been well received. These special facilities called *hospices* provide care to terminally ill patients and their families. Like the renowned St. Christopher's in London, many have as their main purpose efficient loving care for their patients in all aspects of the patient care—not only physical, but also emotional, social, and spiritual. In writing about care at St. Christopher's, Thelma Ingles (1980) wrote

> Most of the staff treated patients as individual mature human beings. Only a few nurses occasionally lapsed into the paternalistic technique so common in hospitals where firm discipline is sometimes seen as essential to the success of a therapeutic regime. (p. 50)

Increasingly, more research reports are being presented on the nature of death and dying. Much like the natural childbirth revolution it is likely that

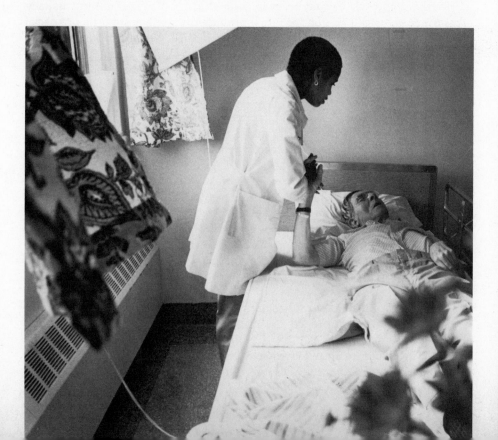

The process of dying is difficult; however, good communication with loved ones can make the process easier for everyone.

there will be a death and dying revolution. Death and dying can be seen as part of the life process, or they can be viewed as a dramatic, painful, and tortured experience both for the patient and the family. Research on exactly when death occurs, how the dying should be treated, and how their families might better cope will continue for many years.

SUMMARY

Development is not just the process of growth. At birth, a person is reflexlike and totally dependent upon the world; but, during the first 16 years of life, there is enormous physical, intellectual, and social growth. At birth, each person is unique and has only those potentialities that his or her parents have provided through genetics; however, from birth on, development will depend upon not only genetics but also on the environment. Intellectually and socially a child's early interactions with the world will determine when and how she will develop.

Piaget has shown that all children develop in the same series of stages, even though there can be dramatic differences in the age of onset of each stage. The extent to which a child develops and grows will be determined by the types of social and intellectual interactions she has. Children who are presented with a varied, rich, and colorful world have the greatest chance of maximizing their potential. Children who are denied social, visual, and intellectual stimulation are deprived children because this deficit will limit the extent to which they can develop. It is incumbent upon educators and parents to maximize the potential of each person. We can maximize anyone's potential by providing opportunities for them to grow in a stimulating, varied environment that encourages growth.

People are born with different potentialities and all have different experiences. The probability that any two people will be genetically alike is infinitesimal; in addition, a person's interaction with the environment over a period of years makes being like someone else an even greater unlikelihood. Psychologists not only wish to know about the genetic contributions provided at birth, but also about the developmental process of physical, intellectual, and social growth. Clearly, Piaget's theory of intellectual development provides a different way to look at the teaching process and how educators might go about providing education. Memorization and drillings of facts are totally against a Piagetian conception of intellectual development, growth, and discovery. The evidence suggests that Piaget's theory is correct, and educators, therefore, have clear directions for change in our educational systems and methods of teaching.

Social interactions must be considered in the same way as intellectual ones. Children are ready for certain types of social interactions at different ages. The consequences of play materials for children or play groups are determined by a child's age and stage of development. A 4-year-old will be markedly dependent upon his parents, whereas a 14-year-old will be increasingly dependent upon his peer group. Again, interactions with the environment become increasingly important as a child grows older and his behavior is determined more by outside influences than just by the genetic contributions of his parents.

While parents are the critical determinants of children's social development, other people may have significant impact on their development of morality. Kohlberg's research has shown a distinct developmental progression of morality beginning with avoiding punishment and obtaining rewards. As children grow older they adopt conventional ideas about morality. As adults, people may develop a high level of morality that is based on both societal needs and on conscience.

Development does not end at age 18. People continue to develop, mature, and even have life crises as they reach adulthood and old age. The process of aging is now being carefully investigated, and the process of dying itself has recently been subjected to careful scrutiny. Development is the process of maturation from conception to the last stage, death.

CHAPTER REVIEW

1. A person's growth starts at the moment of conception.
2. A zygote is a fertilized egg.
3. An embryo is a human organism from the fourth day after conception through the fortieth day.
4. The fetus is the unborn organism from the fortieth day after conception until birth.
5. The placenta is a group of blood vessels and membranes connecting a human fetus's umbilical cord to the uterus. It serves as a mechanism for the exchange of nutrients and waste products.
6. Labor is a process through which the uterus contracts so as to open and allow the baby to descend through the birth canal to the outside world.
7. At birth, the sensory, motor, respiratory, and circulatory systems of a person are fully functional.
8. At birth, the child is a reflexlike organism, spending most of the day sleeping, crying, and eating.
9. Humans are born with innate reflexes, including rooting, sucking, Babinsky, and Moro reflexes.
10. Between 9 and 15 months an infant begins to stand and, eventually, walk.
11. Drugs have been used to treat Attention Deficit Disorders (hyperactivity). These disorders are characterized by restlessness, disruptive classroom behavior, and an inability to concentrate.
12. Piaget has divided intellectual development into a series of stages, each of which must be successfully mastered before the next stage begins.
13. Accommodation is the process of modifying a person's existing structures and framework of knowledge. Information is then absorbed, incorporated, and utilized in a meaningful manner, which is the process of assimilation.
14. The sensory-motor period is Piaget's first and most important stage. During this stage, the rudiments of intellectual behavior are formed and the child begins to interact with the environment and tries to bring some of it under control. This stage is from birth to age 2.
15. Toward the end of the sensory-motor period, the child begins to go through the process of decentration, of moving from a totally self-oriented person to one who realizes that there is a difference between self and the world.
16. Piaget's second stage is preoperational thought, in which the child tries to represent the world in symbolic ways, particularly through language. This stage is from age 2 to 6.
17. During the stage of concrete operations (from ages 7 to 11) children are actively involved in school and in learning rules about the world, including conservation.
18. Conservation is the ability to recognize that something that has changed in some way (such as the "shape" of liquid in a container) is still the same thing, of the same weight, substance, or volume.

19. The final stage in Piaget's theory of development occurs from age 12 through adulthood and is the stage of formal operation. During this stage, the child tries to organize her world, to think about it logically, and to deal in terms of the future and in terms of hypothetical situations.
20. Morality is defined as human attitudes about social practices, institutions, and individual behavior used to evaluate events so as to decide if the events are right or wrong and conform to the ideals of proper human conduct.
21. Kohlberg's research shows that young children make decisions about right or wrong based upon avoiding punishment and obtaining rewards.
22. School-age children adopt conventional ideas of morality; adults adopt more mature views, opting for contracts, laws, and ultimately decisions made by the conscience.
23. By being aware of moral development and by talking about moral issues, parents and teachers can initiate and stimulate the development of mature, internalized moral values in children.
24. Social development begins at birth with a thoroughly egocentric infant.
25. Egocentrism eventually gives way to social interactions; the process of socialization ends a child's egocentrism. An adolescent's self-concept will in many ways determine his social interactions, and his self-concept is something that is learned early in life.
26. Under optimal situations, group day-care centers and home rearing result in children with similar psychological profiles.
27. The effects of group day-care centers are not the same as home rearing *unless* the day-care center is particularly well staffed and has a low faculty-student ratio. For no difference to be apparent, both home-reared and day-care center children must come from intact and psychologically supportive families.
28. Fathers are engrossed with their newborns and can also be as affectionate and responsive as mothers are.
29. While it was once generally assumed that fathers affected their children in only indirect ways through the mother, more recent evidence suggests that fathers influence their children directly.
30. With the marked increase in the number of women in the work force, there are significant changes in the role of fathers in child care. As in day-care centers, high quality care must be the focus for optimal development.
31. Adolescents and adults pass through stages as well as children. A stage theory of social development has been put forth by Erik Erikson.
32. Ten percent of the population is older than 65 years of age.
33. Heredity, external factors, and physiological approaches have been used to explain aging.
34. Intelligence increases or stays the same until just before death.
35. Death and dying are under active study and have been the focus for the development of a five-stage theory by Elisabeth Kübler-Ross.

SUGGESTIONS FOR FURTHER READING

ERIKSON, E. H. *Childhood and society.* New York: Norton Co., 1950.

FLAVELL, J. H. *Cognitive development.* Englewood Cliffs, NJ: Prentice-Hall, 1977.

GINSBURG, H., AND OPPER, S. *Piaget's theory of intellectual development: An introduction* (2nd ed.). Englewood Cliffs, NJ: Prentice-Hall, 1978.

HAMILTON, M., and REID, H. *A hospice handbook: A new way to care for the dying.* Grand Rapids, MI: William B. Eerdmans Publishing Company, 1980.

HELMS, D. B., and TURNER, J. S. *Exploring child behavior: Basic principles.* Philadephia, PA: W. B. Saunders, 1978.

KIMMEL, D. C. *Adulthood and aging.* New York: John Wiley & Sons, 1974.

KÜBLER-ROSS, E. *Death. The final stage of growth.* Englewood Cliffs, NJ: Prentice-Hall, 1975.

OVER THE CENTURIES human beings have developed remarkable civilizations characterized by advancements in ideas, technology, and communication. Being intelligent, humans have used their unique abilities to develop sophisticated concepts about the world. Modern people have used their intelligence to discriminate against minorities, build nuclear bombs, and wage war; but they have also used their intelligence to solve problems of housing, food, and pollution. Because few behaviors are reflexive, most human behavior, whether constructive or destructive, is determined by thought; people make decisions to act the way they do. The study of intelligence is the study of mental abilities and how they may determine thought patterns and behavior. One focus of this chapter is to show how difficult it is to examine the nature of intelligence or even define what intelligence is. Another is to show that the role of intelligence is crucial in the placement of special groups of people, particularly the gifted and the retarded.

CHAPTER 7

Intelligence

THE BOOKWORM AND THE BOATMAN

Although the weather was fine and the sun was shining, it was not too hot to be comfortable. The birds were singing in the branches of the trees which grew along the margin of the river, and beneath them might be seen walking a learned scholar, book in hand.

Taking his eyes for a moment from the pages, he glanced at the cool river. It has been very hot lately, but it was better today, and as he looked he thought how inviting the river appeared. He could not swim in it, for it was infested with crocodiles, but what about a boat? "I will find a steady boatman," he said aloud, "and engage him to row me about on the broad stream for an hour or two."

After a little searching, he found the sort of boat and boatman he desired, and they were soon floating lazily upon the broad bosom of the river. After a long silence the bookworm asked, "Have you read the scriptures?"

"No, sir," was the reply.

"Then half of your life is wasted," said the scholar. "It is required of every man to know something of the teaching of the great ones, and to meditate daily upon their sayings. It is a great pity, a very great pity indeed."

There followed a long silence, which was at last broken once more by the learned man. "Have you any knowledge of the stars, by studying which men may understand the times and seasons and the ebb and flow of the tides? Can you read them, and by their aid foretell future events?"

"No, sir," replied the boatman again.

"Then three-quarters of your life has been wasted," exclaimed the scholar.

Now the boatman, happening to glance down at this moment, caught sight of a small trickle of water, which as everyone knows is often to be seen in the bottom of a boat, and is in no way a sign of danger. They were now at a great distance from the bank, and he determined to ask his passenger a question.

"Sir," said he, looking fearfully at the small pool in the boat's bottom. "I fear we are about to sink. Have you learned to swim?"

"No," said the scholarly one, "I have always relied upon the good God to preserve my poor life from danger."

"Then," said the boatman with a grin, "I am afraid the whole of your life may be wasted."

The wise one saw at once that he was being mocked, and when he had paid the oarsman he departed in silence, thinking that perhaps the fellow was right. There were other things of importance besides books and study. At any rate swimming might on occasion be more useful than reading.

As for the boatman, he too was deep in thought, for he remembered how calmly the scholar had received his statement that the boat was about to sink. "There must be something good in quiet study," thought he, "if it prepares a man to keep calm in the face of sudden dangers."

WILFRED E. DEXTER
Marathi Folk Tales

Recognizing a person's intellectual capabilities isn't as easy as you might think. Sometimes quiet people are not assumed to be particularly bright; similarly, people who talk extensively are often seen as being extremely intelligent. The extent to which people talk and communicate ideas, their effectiveness in coping with life, and their ability to show intelligent behavior often have nothing to do with one another. There are many ways in which people can show effective and intelligent behavior; both the bookworm and the boatman came to acknowledge this idea. There is no easy way to define what intelligent behavior is; so often, intelligence has to be defined in terms of the situation in which people find themselves. Intelligent behavior for the scientist is very different from intelligent behavior for the hunter. Yet, both can show their special intelligence and effective behavior. The problem of defining intelligence and intelligent behavior becomes very complex and often becomes confused with how verbal people are. Look at the scenario about Rob presented in the next paragraph. How many times have you felt the same way and wished you were more intelligent, or at least more articulate?

The time is a week before Christmas. It is 9:30 in the morning. The place is a classroom with 20 students writing hurriedly in blue books. The situation: the final exam in English literature. We hear Rob saying to himself, "I can't write this answer. If only I were as smart as the other people in this class. If only I were as creative as my friends are. Why can't I take an oral examination; I'm so much better verbally than I am on paper."

Rob is questioning his basic intelligence as well as his ability to communicate with other people, in this case, with his instructor. Rob is confusing intelligence with achievement. He is really questioning his thought processes, but there is nothing wrong with the way he thinks. Rob is really a very clever fellow; ask him about any event in the world of sports, past or present, and he can give you every fact associated with it. Names, dates, batting averages, number of touchdowns, and even birth dates are all part of Rob's working fund of knowledge. Sports are only part of Rob's talents; the ability to program computers is another one of this young man's special abilities.

Part of the problem psychologists face is that intelligent behavior in one situation often doesn't tell much about intelligent behavior in other situations. Sports-minded Rob is a whiz with sports and computers, but he has incredible difficulty with English literature. While many people who are particularly verbal also have good mathematical skills, there are mathematicians who can't learn Spanish and streetwise drug dealers who can't read a paragraph. Thus, the problem of measuring and defining intelligence is a difficult one. The problem becomes more complex when we realize that much of our intellectual capability is expressed through what we say and how we say it. Even though he is very bright, Rob's high intelligence does not necessarily create excellent scores on a test of English literature.

Whatever Rob's problem, psychologists have ways of assessing it and determining if some remediation is available to him. One of the first steps that a psychologist might take is to do an assessment. In a psychological assessment, an individual is given a battery of tests with the aim of evaluating the individual's strengths and weaknesses, with suggestions for remediation if they are necessary. In Rob's case, one of the first things that the psychologist might do would be to conduct an intelligence test. Since Rob seems like a bright young man and is quite capable in some areas of his life, an intelligence test might provide some important information.

From an intelligence test a psychologist would be able to decide if Rob had basic intellectual abilities that would allow him to achieve academically. An intelligence test is precisely designed to make such predictions; if intelligence tests do anything well, they predict academic achievement. However, an intelligence test alone would not be enough for an adequate assessment of Rob's potential problems. Intelligence tests do not thoroughly measure a person's ability in nonacademic skills. For example, some intelligence tests subtract points if a person responds with a nonconventional answer to a ques-

Intelligence can be shown in many forms.

tion; the nonconventional answer might be highly creative and novel, yet it is considered unacceptable on some standardized tests. For these reasons, among others, psychologists do not consider the intelligence test a real measure of innate ability. In Rob's case, an intelligence test would only confirm something that is fairly obvious—Rob is intelligent.

To better understand Rob, a psychologist would measure some specific achievement levels that Rob has acquired over the years. Achievement tests have been designed to measure how much information a person knows about a specific topic or how well a specific skill has been learned. There are a wide range of achievement tests including tests of French, science, mathematics, and psychology. Rob would likely take a personality test that would characterize the way he responds to situations to see if he has any psychological abnormalities. A test like the MMPI (Minnesota Multiphasic Personality Inventory) contains a long series of items that are answered with "yes" or "no" and asks about attitudes, feelings, motor disturbances, and physical symptoms. When scored carefully, it has been shown to predict well if there are psychological disturbances that might interfere with a person's day-to-day functioning. The MMPI will be considered in more detail in chapter 11 on Personality (see p. 510).

Using a variety of tests allows a psychologist to evaluate an individual's current situation so as to make predictions about the future; it also allows for suggestions for remedial work or potential therapy. In Rob's case, a good course in writing might do the trick; in fact, it might be discovered that Rob is a normal, well-adjusted sophomore who suffers from nothing more than a high level of anxiety and a resulting inability to concentrate and study effectively. Rob will probably do well in life; we know this because we are able to compare his performance on a series of tests with the performance of other individuals.

After years of development, a good test allows a knowledgeable examiner to make inferences about future performance. A psychologist's prediction may not always come true; many events in a person's life can adversely affect development. Yet, based on a sample of behavior, psychologists have examined the performances of thousands of other similar people and have found strong predictive abilities of tests. For example, intelligence tests predict academic achievement very well. Similarly, certain tests of special abilities (music, mechanical ability, creativity) are able to predict well whether an individual will profit from further training in a specific area. This predictive ability of tests is due to their careful construction and standardization on samples of people with whom single individuals can be compared. We are able to make predictions about Rob because we know how others of the same age, sex, socioeconomic status, and academic achievement levels have performed. The study of psychological testing began in the early part of this century when Alfred Binet was commissioned in Paris to separate those students who would profit academically from further schooling from those who probably would not. Binet was, of course, one of the founders of the intelligence testing movement. So as to better understand the nature of intelligence, we must first have a background in how any test is constructed and developed; let us begin there.

TESTING

When teachers, psychologists, or researchers wish to compare an individual against others, they often turn to a test. A test is a standardized device for looking at the responses of a person to certain specific stimuli, usually questions or problems. We all are familiar with tests; we take them in course work; we have been administered intelligence tests and achievement tests; one must even be tested to determine ability for serving in the U.S. Armed Forces. Perhaps the place where tests are used more than any other place is in a school setting; teachers regularly give tests to assess their students' performance. Schools often give achievement and intelligence tests as well. The test results that are administered in a school setting are often used by psychologists to help make decisions about the future of those recently tested students. For example, a 7-year-old who is unable to read is often assessed by a school psychologist. The psychologist runs a battery of tests on the individual; intelligence tests are run, achievement tests are administered, and, if the case warrants, personality tests as well. By interpreting these tests meaningfully, a psychologist can be fairly sure about an individual's abilities, strengths, and weaknesses. Based on these results, a psychologist might suggest remedial work or might diagnose the student as learning disabled, mentally retarded, or emotionally handicapped. The future of this child's subsequent education in the school and home will be a direct consequence of the suggestions of the school psychologist.

Psychologists need to have a large battery of tests to help in diagnosis. Consequently, over the years a large number of psychological tests have been developed and evaluated. When well constructed, tests diagnose certain problems and have good predictive value in determining the individual's future performance, perhaps in a job setting.

The first step in test development is deciding what kind of test is to be constructed. Next, specific items have to be constructed; these items then

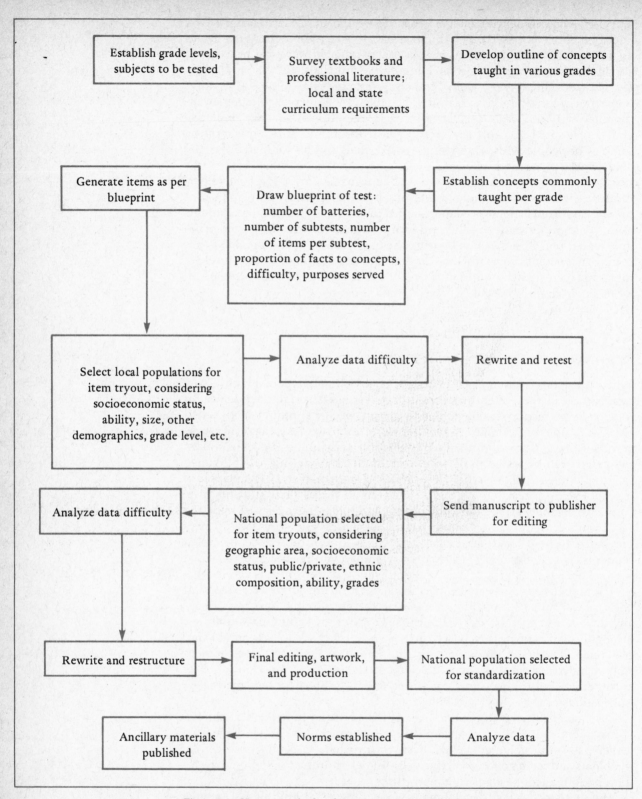

Figure 7.1 How a standardized test is constructed (after Rudman, 1977, with modifications)

have to be evaluated. Finally, there is the process of providing a uniform procedure in the administration and scoring of a test. Without uniform procedures, comparisons of different test results cannot be made. If a particular intelligence test is given to one individual and the same test is given to another individual, but the time they had to complete the test was different, comparing the results is not legitimate. Careful development involves setting controlled time limits and instructions, and also specific materials, demonstrations, and responses to questions. If test scores are to be compared, uniformity on the part of the administrator of the test is crucial (see Figure 7.1).

After a test has been constructed and procedures established, **standardization** with a large group of subjects must be done for the purpose of establishing norms. The test is given to a large sample of people who are matched with respect to age, sex, socioeconomic variables, and other potentially important characteristics. With this process completed, a comparison of a single person's test score with the **norms** allows for reasonable, interpretable comparisons. For example, if you were told that you achieved a score of 176 on a test of psychology, you would need to know how others did to compare yourself with them. If you found that you scored higher than most other people, you would feel good about your score. However, if you found that most people who took the psychology test did better than you did, you might be disappointed. Thus, before a test score can be interpreted adequately, a certain norm has to be established; the psychologist needs to know how most people do on a test of psychology so that they can be used as a reference group. In the process of establishing norms, the test is typically given to a large and representative sample of subjects for whom the tests have been designed. If the test is designed only for college freshmen, it might be given to 2,000 freshmen. These freshmen would be chosen such that they were representative of different kinds of students; there might be an equal number of men and women; there would be freshmen from large schools and small schools. Your sample would likely include students from different geographical areas of the country. Furthermore, you would want to be sure that the ages of your students were representative. A **representative sample** is a sample of individuals who match the population with whom they are to be compared; they are to match with respect to important variables, for example, socioeconomic status and age. It is very likely that in a large enough representative sample, some students would do very well, others very poorly, and still others about average. Imagine if your norms were established with a sample of students who were women, aged 40 to 50, returning to college after their children had grown, and who had experienced 30 years of adult interactions. Their success might be quite different from a group of naive 16-year-old boys.

On most tests some people do very well, some people do very poorly, but most people do about average; when test scores distribute themselves in such a way, psychologists say that the data are normally distributed or that the data fall on a normal curve. A **normal curve** is a bell-shaped curve that is based on a mathematical formula; it is arranged so that a certain percentage of the population falls under each part of the curve. The higher the curve, the more people are represented by a specific score. So, in Figure 7.2, p. 302, we see that many people score in the middle ranges, while very few achieve very high or very low scores.

Standardization The process of developing a uniform procedure in the administration and scoring of a test; the process also includes developing norms for the test from a large, representative sample of subjects.

Norms A list of scores and the corresponding percentile ranks or standard scores of a group of examinees on whom a test was standardized.

Representative sample A sample of individuals who match the population with whom they are to be compared; they are to match with respect to important variables, for example, socioeconomic status and age.

Normal curve A bell-shaped curve that is based on a mathematical formula; it is arranged so that a certain percentage of the population falls under each part of the curve.

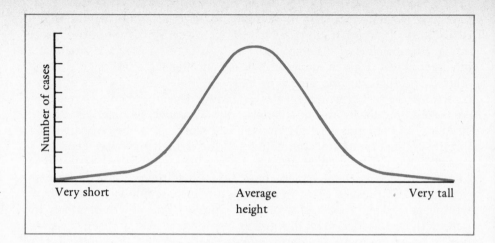

Figure 7.2 With characteristics like height, weight, or even intelligence, most people are about average. In this bell-shaped curve, or normal distribution, very few people are represented at the extremes

Figure 7.3 A normal curve can be divided into standard deviations such that each standard deviation above or below the mean or average score accounts for a different percentage of the population. The first standard deviation either above or below the mean accounts for 34.13% of all individuals who might be measured. The second standard deviation above or below the mean accounts for 13.59%. The next two standard deviations taken together account for only 2.27%. Notice that only .13% of all people who take a test score higher than three standard deviations above the mean

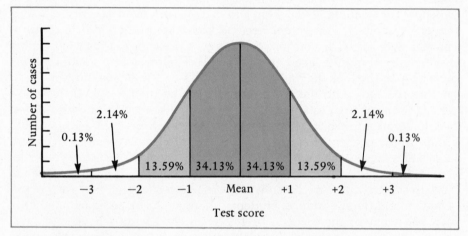

The normal curve is divided into standard deviations (Figure 7.3). Standard deviations are discussed more fully in the appendix (p. 683); but for our purpose, each standard deviation accounts for a different percentage of the population. So, 68.26% of all people who take the test achieve scores within one standard deviation of the mean or midpoint of the distribution.

The normal curve with its division into standard deviations is important because many tests are devised so that comparisons of an individual can be made against a normal curve. For example, intelligence tests are often arranged so that the mean score, the average score, is 100; the standard deviation is often 15 or 16 points. If we go back to our normal curve, we see that with a mean of 100 and a standard deviation of 15 points, 34.13% of the population will have an intelligence score of between 100 and 115. In the same way, .13% of the population will have an intelligence score greater than three standard deviations above the mean. If the mean is 100 and a standard deviation is 15 points, three standard deviations above the mean is 45 points or a score of 145. Only .13% of the population has an intelligence score of greater than 145 points (Figure 7.4).

Most tests contain a large number of items, sometimes hundreds. Some tests have a series of subtests, each subtest examining a different aspect of the person's knowledge or, in intelligence tests, their intellectual function-

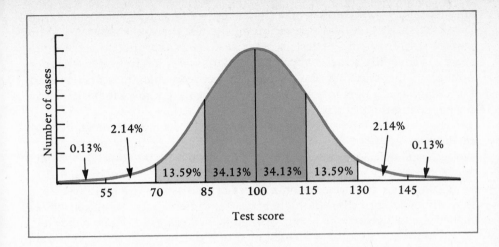

Figure 7.4 When intelligence is measured through a standardized IQ test, we compare an individual's score against a normal distribution with a mean of 100 and a standard deviation equal to 15 points. As before, 68.26% of the population will score between one standard deviation below and one standard deviation above the mean. With a mean of 100, one standard deviation below the mean is 85 points (100 − 15 = 85) and one standard deviation above is 115 points (100 + 15 = 115). Notice that only 2.27% (2.14 + .13 = 2.27) of the population will have a score greater than 130 and only .13% of those people who take the test will have a score greater than 145 points

ing. In order to make the raw score of a specific test interpretable, scores have to be converted into a meaningful, comparable framework. Knowing your raw score on a subtest usually does not tell you how well you did. In fact, on many tests, particularly intelligence tests, **raw scores** are converted into a new score by taking a subtest and adjusting that score for a person's age, sex, or grade level. After making such adjustments, raw scores can be made meaningful.

Many test scores are usually expressed in terms of some kind of standard score or percentile. The raw score of a test is often first converted into a score that is interpretable based upon an individual's age, grade, or sex; then, a standard score is derived. A **standard score** is a score that expresses an individual's relative position compared to others. Assume that we have a 100-item intelligence test. We administer this test to students in the third grade and students in the eleventh grade, and we expect students in the eleventh grade to answer more items correctly than students in the third grade. We compare an individual's score to the score typically achieved by other students at this grade level. Eleventh-graders usually score 70 questions correctly. If an individual scores 90 questions correctly, we know she has done better than most students at her grade level. Similarly, third-graders usually

Raw score An examinee's unconverted score on a test; for example, the number of correct answers.

Standard score A score that expresses an individual's relative position to the mean based on the standard deviation; it is often derived by converting a raw test score to one interpretable on the basis of a population variable such as age or grade.

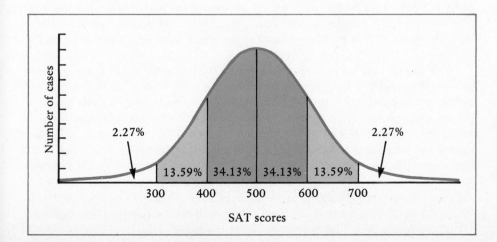

Figure 7.5 Like many standardized tests, the Scholastic Achievement Test (SAT) has been organized so that scores fall in a normal distribution. The mean SAT score for the verbal or the quantitative section is 500. The standard deviation of the SAT is 100. Using this information, 34.13% of the students taking the test will achieve an SAT of 400 to 500

Percentile score A score indicating what percentage of the population under consideration would obtain a lower score.

answer 25 questions correctly; if a student answers 15 questions correctly, we know that he has done a poorer job on the test than most students at his grade level. This kind of test is often evaluated according to a percentile score. A **percentile score** is a type of standard score that indicates what percentage of other students would obtain a lower score than the score obtained. For example, if a person's percentile score is 84, he knows that 84% of the people taking the test have a lower score than he has.

In the early 1900s intelligence was measured by a simple formula. People's intelligence quotient (IQ) was calculated by dividing their mental age by their chronological age, then multiplying the result by 100 (IQ = mental age ÷ chronological age × 100). Children's mental ages were calculated by examining their performance on a series of test items. The more test items they achieved correctly, the higher was their mental age. Children with a mental age of 8 years who also happened to be 8 years old would have an IQ of 100 (IQ = 8 ÷ 8 × 100 = 100). Similarly, if the mental age was 18 and the chronological age was 15, and IQ would be 120 (IQ = 18 ÷ 15 × 100 = 120).

IQ testing at different ages can show different amounts of variability. This means that at each age there is a different standard deviation. To help simplify measures of IQ, the traditional "mental age ÷ chronological age" formula was replaced by a score called the deviation IQ. A **deviation IQ** is a standard score that has a mean and a standard deviation that stays constant at all ages. Thus, a child of 9 and a child of 16 who both have an IQ of 115 fall in the same relative position compared to other individuals who might have taken the same IQ test. For example, our 9- and 16-years-olds both are in the 84th percentile; they both scored better than 84% of all other individuals their age who have taken the same IQ test.

Deviation IQ A standard IQ test score that has the same mean and standard deviation at all ages.

Of all things that psychologists have done to help make tests useful, perhaps the most important has been to make sure that the tests are reliable and valid.

Reliability and Validity

Reliability The ability of a test to give the same score for a single individual through repeated testings.

A test is reliable if it will yield the same score on the same individual through repeated tests or if it will yield the same score on the same individual with a different form of the test; **reliability** is the consistency or stability of test scores. If you were to give two versions or forms of the same test to a student and she were to do better on one than on the other, which test score do you believe? If a test's results are not consistent from one testing session to another or from two comparable groups of people, meaningful comparisons are impossible.

Test-retest reliability A method of assessing the reliability of a test by administering it to the same group of examinees on two different occasions and computing the similarity between their scores.

There are several ways of checking to see if a test is reliable. The simplest, **test-retest reliability,** is to administer the same test to the same individual on two or more occasions. If the individual achieves a score of 90 on one day and 135 on another day, then the test is not reliable. Since the individual being tested might remember some of the items from one day to another, a different way of checking reliability is to use **alternate forms** of the same test. Many tests are written with two or more forms of the same test. If the two forms are virtually identical in their aims but have different items, administration of these two different forms should also yield the same result. Another way to check a test's reliability, called **split-half reliability,** is to split or divide the test in half; the two scores from the two halves should again yield

Alternate-form reliability Estimating the reliability of a test by correlating scores on two forms of a test.

Split-half reliability Estimating the reliability of a test by splitting it into comparable halves and correlating the scores from the halves.

Table 7.1 Types of validity frequently used to assess the meaningfulness of a test

Content validity	Measures the extent to which a test reflects a sample of the actual behavior to be measured.
Face validity	Measures the extent to which a test "looks" appropriate just from reading the items.
Predictive validity	Measures the extent to which a test can predict a person's behavior in some other kind of setting.
Construct validity	Measures the extent to which a test actually measures a certain trait like intelligence, anxiety, or musical ability.

similar if not identical results. These three procedures (test-retest, alternative forms, and split-half) all have certain problems. But taken together and with some sophistication on the part of the test constructors, good estimates of the reliability of tests can be generated.

A test's reliability can be calculated; in this way, a test developer can report how reliable a test score is. Based on statistical formulas, the **standard error of measurement** is the number of points that a score may vary because of the imperfect reliability of a test. For example, in an IQ test an individual may score 115 with a standard error of measurement equal to 3 points; a test developer can claim with about 68% confidence that the individual's real score is from 112 to 118. This range is plus or minus 3 points of the obtained score of 115. So, a test is reliable if it consistently gives the same results and if it has a relatively small standard error of measurement.

While a test's reliability is crucial, if the test does not measure what it is supposed to measure, then it is virtually useless. A test's **validity** tells a test developer whether a test measures what it is supposed to measure; without validity, inferences cannot be made from a test. If a test is supposed to measure mechanical aptitude, then it must measure it, not musical ability or personality characteristics. In the same way, if an intelligence test is to measure intelligence, it should not reflect musical training (see Table 7.1).

Standard error of measurement Based on statistical formulas, the standard error of measurement is the number of points that a score may vary because of the imperfect reliability of a test.

Validity A property of tests which means that a test measures only what it is supposed to measure.

Intelligent Testing: Interpretation

Thousands of dollars and hundreds of hours go into the preparation of a standardized test. Thousands of individuals are tested to make sure that the sample of subjects accurately reflects the population. Well-devised and carefully constructed tests must be administered carefully; perhaps even more important, the people who provide information to parents and teachers must interpret the test scores accurately. A test provides a single score or perhaps a series of scores on different subscales; without a knowledgeable interpretation of what these scores mean, a teacher or parent is done a disservice. Scores on a test must be placed within a context that is meaningful for a parent or teacher. Without such a context a test score in isolation is little more than a number.

Typical intelligence test scores are relatively easy to interpret. Many of the popular IQ tests provide a single IQ score; however, there is far more information in these tests than this single score. For example, the most popular IQ test for children is the Wechsler Intelligence Scale for Children—Revised or, as it is usually called, the WISC-R. This test will yield an overall IQ score, a score for verbal IQ, for performance IQ, and for 12 subtests. Researcher Alan Kaufman has made the argument (1979) that the global or overall IQ score should be de-emphasized and the test examiner must explore the components of the IQ score to provide an accurate picture of an individual. Kaufman suggests that the burden of psychologists is to be smarter than the test they use; that is, interpretation of test scores is the key to our understanding of IQs. He argues that without such interpretation a single IQ score can be biased, inaccurate, and misleading. However, he claims that if we are intelligent testers, then we have much to learn about an individual from an IQ test like the WISC-R.

INTELLIGENCE TESTING

The Origins of Intelligence Testing

Intelligence tests were hardly the aim of the first psychologists. In the late 1800s some of the founders of psychology began looking at individual differences; they were interested in why some people responded to light, sound, and temperature differently than others. Eventually, some of the researchers began to look at differences between individuals in terms of cognitive or thought functions.

The persons most often associated with the beginnings of IQ testing were Binet and Simon. In 1904 Alfred Binet was chosen to study and develop procedures for the education of retarded children in Paris. Binet in collaboration with Simon developed the Binet-Simon Scale in 1905. This test was a 30-item set of problems arranged in order of difficulty from the easiest to the most difficult. The test was standardized in a rough sort of way on a small number of children; it represented the first crude test of intellectual functioning. In 1916 L. M. Terman in the United States revised the Binet-Simon Scales and developed an intelligence test that is known as the Stanford-Binet (Terman, 1916).

The term IQ was first used by Stern (1914). In the early IQ tests a child's mental age or ability was estimated by the number of correctly answered items. The mental age was then divided by the chronological age, and the resultant ratio was then multiplied by 100 to yield an intelligence quotient, IQ. The development of the Stanford-Binet launched IQ tests into the twentieth century. Of course, it must be emphasized that the 1916 Stanford-Binet was still a relatively crude instrument or test.

The greatest changes in IQ testing came about in the late 1930s and 1940s. David Wechsler, a psychologist at the Bellevue Psychiatric Hospital in New York City, developed the Wechsler-Bellevue Intelligence Scale. This IQ test was standardized on a large sample of adults with a fair degree of attention paid to the representativeness of the sample. This scale was fundamentally different from that developed by Binet and Terman. Before further discussing intelligence tests, we must examine the meaning of the concept called intelligence.

Your Sister Determines Your Intelligence

The number of brothers or sisters you have may be the critical factor in deciding your intelligence level. Evidence has been accumulated to show that a person's family size will determine his or her intelligence level: children of large families have lower intelligence levels.

University of Michigan psychologists Robert Zajonc and Gregory Marcus have proposed an explanation of the factors that determine intelligence and achievement levels. They found that when family size increases, scores on intelligence tests and achievement tests decrease. Furthermore, they argue that when you are the third or fourth child in a family, your abilities are less than if you were the first or second child.

The basic idea that the researchers present is that within a family the intellectual growth of every member is dependent upon all the other members of the family. For example, when two mature adults have a child, the intellectual climate in the home is that of two mature adults and a child. We might assign an arbitrary value to this intellectual level. Let us give each of the adults 30 units and the child 0 units. If each of the adults has 30 units and the child 0, the average intellectual ability in the home is 20 ($30 + 30 + 0 = 60 \div 3 = 20$). In the same way, when a second child joins the family configuration, the average intellectual performance in the family decreases still further. Each of the parents still has 30 units. Perhaps the first child is increased to 4 units so that the average intellectual functioning in the family is only 16 ($30 + 30 + 4 + 0 = 64 \div 4 = 16$). We see that the number of units of intellectual stimulation has decreased from 20 to 16. If we add a third child, the intellectual climate in the family decreases still further to 14.4 ($30 + 30 + 8 + 4 + 0 = 72 \div 5 = 14.4$).

The researchers suggest that overall intellectual performance of each of the members of the family will decrease as the family size increases. The model also suggests that children born early in a family perform better than children who are born later. These data have some serious implications because they suggest that large families have lower overall intellectual performance than smaller ones. This is not always the case, however; Zajonc and Marcus point out that the effects of larger families can be canceled out by other important factors. For example, they indicate that longer spacing between the birth of children cancels out the negative effects of birth order and in some extreme cases even reverses them. Thus, when children are spaced farther apart, the negative effects of birth order on intellectual performance are minimized.

The researchers also point out that intelligence isn't everything and that large families may contribute to the growth of individual members of the families in attributes other than intelligence. Large families can create feelings of social competence, moral responsibility, and ego strength. The researchers are also quick to note that their model of intelligence, birth order, and family size is a statistical one and that their findings do not hold true for all individuals and all families.

Zajonc and Marcus do make a prediction. They argue that performance on intelligence tests and achievement tests will increase in the 1980s. The data show that the number of births and family size have decreased in the last two decades. Furthermore, the spacing of these children has increased. Their model of birth order and family size suggests that smaller families will have higher overall intellectual functioning. Thus, Zajonc and Marcus predict that the declining scholastic aptitude test (SAT) scores of the 1970s will be reversed. They predict that in the late 1980s the overall intellectual functioning of maturing adults will show gains compared to adults a decade before them. We won't be able to judge their predictions until 1985 or so, but this will be the real test of their model (Zajonc, 1976; Zajonc & Marcus, 1975).

Toward a Definition of Intelligence

Rob, near the beginning of this chapter, questioned his abilities and blamed his poor test performance on his intelligence. Rob was really asking some basic questions about people's abilities: "Why do two individuals who study an equal amount of time for an examination achieve different scores?" or "Why do some succeed in medical school while others have difficulty finishing high school?" A fairly typical response to these questions is that high intelligence produces success. Intelligence is one of the most debated, questioned, and widely used concepts in scientific circles and in everyday life.

Intelligence ratings are often used to determine an individual's fate. School teachers divide classrooms into groups based on their intelligence scores. Colleges and graduate schools use tests to evaluate and accept or reject potential students. Social scientists have used the concept of intelligence in examining racial and socioeconomic groups.

Of course, how people behave is determined by many important factors, including their inherited abilities as well as the environment in which they grow. In studying the factors that affect intelligence and intelligence test scores we must recognize that the relative contributions of these two factors, nature and nurture, vary from person to person and from one culture to the next. This means that a person's environment can be enriched with stimulation, culture, and knowledge; without such enrichment a person's heredity will weigh more heavily in the development of intelligence. Rob showed many intelligent behaviors when working through his computer programming or in recalling important sports statistics. Yet he was unable to express clearly his ideas and knowledge about English literature in an examination. Expressing ideas in writing and remembering sports statistics are tasks involving different kinds of intelligence. Rob's abilities in one task were at a very high level; in the other they were only average. So, intelligence does not refer to one special or unique ability but probably refers to a group of different kinds of abilities.

Intelligence means different things to different people. McNemar (1964) has suggested that no definition of intelligence is required, "all intelligent people know what intelligence is—it is the thing that the other guy lacks!" While intelligence may be a difficult term to define, intelligence tests have been devised and the abilities of different people can be described. The definitions of intelligence that have been offered vary, but all of the definitions have certain concepts in common. First, the concept of intelligence in psychology has to be defined in terms of observable, objective behavior. This objectivity has led many psychologists to suggest that "intelligence is what intelligence tests measure." Second, most definitions of intelligence refer to an individual's capacity to learn. In the same way, most definitions also include some idea about knowledge already acquired. Last, many definitions of intelligence suggest that the ability to adjust and adapt to the environment is a sign of intelligence (Robinson & Robinson, 1976).

Woodrow suggested that "intelligence . . . is the acquiring capacity" (1921, p. 207). Binet argued that intelligence was a collection of faculties (Binet & Simon, 1905). Intelligence has been defined as making "good responses from the point of view of truth and fact" (Thorndike, 1926); "innate, general, cognitive ability" (Burt, 1955); and "the ability to carry on abstract thinking" (Terman, 1921). Perhaps the most widely cited definition of intelligence is the one put forth by the well-known test constructor, David Wechsler. Wechsler suggests that for a person to be considered intelligent, the person must cope with the world (1975); so Wechsler maintains that "**intelligence** is the aggregate or global capacity of the individual to act purposefully, to think rationally, and to deal effectively with the environment" (1958, p. 7). For Wechsler, an IQ test is effective only to the extent that it measures an individual's ability to act purposefully.

Wechsler's definition of intelligence contains the basic components of most definitions of intelligence outlined above. The definition is expressed behaviorally—intelligence is the way people act. The definition involves people's ability to learn and consider previous knowledge. Most important

Intelligence According to Wechsler, the aggregate global capacity of the individual to act purposefully, to think rationally, and to deal effectively with the environment.

According to Wechsler, "intelligence is the aggregate ability or global capacity of the individual to act purposefully, to think rationally, and to deal effectively with the environment"

from Wechsler's view is that intelligence deals with people's ability to adapt to the environment. So, while other definitions are acceptable and perhaps just as correct, Wechsler's has stood the test of time. The definition of intelligence is important because it has helped determine how test developers have gone about devising IQ tests and how they have sought to understand the nature of intelligence. In order to understand some of the reasons why intelligence has become a debated topic and why the intelligence testing movement has come under fire, let us examine some of the approaches that have been used to discover the nature of intelligence.

Approaches to Intelligence

With the growth of intelligence testing since the early 1900s, a large body of data has developed describing characteristics that may be involved in intelligence. These data have included information on age, race, sex, socioeconomic status, and environmental factors. In addition, theories have developed to describe the nature of intelligence and how it is formed. We will describe four approaches that have been very influential.

PIAGET.   In chapter 6, Development, we encountered Jean Piaget's theory of development which is largely centered around the intellectual growth of a child. Piaget suggested that (1) intelligence is the process of adaptation to the environment and (2) intellectual development consists of changes in the way this adaptation is accomplished. According to Piaget a child goes through a series of invariant stages of intellectual development, and in each of these stages different types of cognitive processes are available to the child. According to this theory, it would be foolhardy to teach a 3-year-old calculus, because a 3-year-old biologically does not have the mental operations available that will allow him or her to grasp the concepts of calculus.

WECHSLER.   One of the pioneering researchers in the intelligence testing movement was David Wechsler. Wechsler argued that IQ tests do not directly measure an individual's capacity to deal with the world. The problem is that tests involving spatial relations and verbal comprehension tell a psychologist little about an individual's overall capacity to deal with the world about him or her. Rather, each subtest helps provide a picture of aspects of a person's resourcefulness. In other words, the specific abilities measured on a subtest are less adequately measured than the general ability of the individual to deal with problems and face the challenge of those problems. Specific subtest scores are not identical with intelligence; it is their combination in unique ways that allows for intelligent behavior. Remember Wechsler's definition of intelligence: it is the aggregate or *global* capacity of the individual to act purposefully, think rationally, and deal effectively with the environment.

Wechsler tried to take test scores and place them in a meaningful context. Rather than looking solely at a score, Wechsler suggested that psychologists must remember that intelligence is more than just doing mathematics or problem solving. Intelligence is a broader concept. Earlier it was suggested that intelligence test scores need to be interpreted and placed in a meaningful context. Wechsler did precisely this. He recognized that the test scores themselves did not directly measure intelligence, but rather provided information to a psychologist about some aspects of a person's functioning and resourcefulness.

FACTOR THEORIES.   Factor theories use the correlation technique known as factor analysis, in which a large number of tasks are given to a subject. Scores are made on each task, and then correlations are computed between the different tasks. By correlating the scores, researchers hope to see which tasks are related to one another; tasks with high correlations probably test similar aspects of intellectual functioning. For example, verbal comprehension, spelling, and reading speed usually correlate; this suggests that some underlying attributes of verbal abilities determine an individual's score on all three of these tests. The aim of **factor analysis** is to discover what the factors of intelligence really are.

Early in this century C. E. Spearman (1904) used factor analysis to maintain that there were two components of intelligence; Spearman argued that there was a general factor and a number of specific factors that were unique to separate tasks. According to Spearman, a certain amount of the general and the specific factor was necessary in any task. This general approach to intelligence is called the two-factor theory of intelligence.

Spearman's work was to be carried a step further by L. L. Thurstone (1941). Thurstone postulated seven factors of intelligence and a general factor somewhat analogous to Spearman's general factor. The **factor-theory approach to intelligence** reached its peak with the theory put forth by J. P. Guilford (1967). According to Guilford, human intellectual abilities and activities can be described in terms of three major factors: operations, products, and contents. As is shown in Figure 7.6 Guilford's three-dimensional model postulates 120 separate factors, 80 of which Guilford says have already been demonstrated.

The advantage of the theories put forth by Spearman and Thurstone is that a single score can be given which specifies an individual's intelligence. The Guilford approach suggests that intelligence must be evaluated according to many different dimensions and that a number of scores must be provided to assess an individual's abilities. Presently, more research and support have been provided for the multifactor approach to intelligence testing; a single

Factor analysis A statistical procedure designed to determine the mutually independent elements (factors) in any set of skills.

Factor-theory approach to intelligence Theories of intelligence based on factor analysis. Among the best known are those of Spearman and Thurstone.

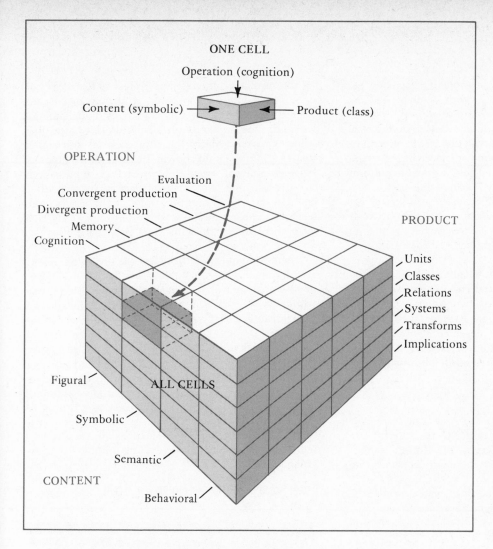

ONE CELL

Operation (cognition)

Content (symbolic) ⟶ ⟵ Product (class)

OPERATION

Evaluation
Convergent production
Divergent production
Memory
Cognition

PRODUCT

Units
Classes
Relations
Systems
Transforms
Implications

Figural

ALL CELLS

Symbolic

Semantic

CONTENT

Behavioral

Figure 7.6 Guilford (1959) suggested three dimensions of intellectual abilities: operations, products, and content. Each of these dimensions has many attributes. The combination of all of these dimensions produces 120 separate factors

and unified answer to the problem of intelligence testing is not yet available (see also, Guilford, 1980).

JENSEN'S TWO-LEVEL THEORY.   Arthur Jensen, whom we will discuss in more detail later, has suggested that intellectual functioning is made up of two factors, associative abilities and cognitive abilities. Jensen argues that these two abilities, both formed largely by heredity, account for different kinds of intellectual functioning. Associative abilities are those where certain stimuli and events are associated with one another; for example, in IQ tests, memory tasks and knowledge of information are associative in nature. By contrast, cognitive abilities are those that deal with more abstract thinking and conceptualizations. The task involved in solving a word problem or defining a new word or concept is that of cognitive ability. This idea is not new, even the founders of the testing movement suggested different kinds of intellectual functioning. Some suggested one level, others two, and some like Thurstone, many.

Jensen's theory leads researchers squarely into the debate of the principal

Cultural Testing Biases

As soon as psychologists began giving IQ tests, they realized that a person's experience with language was important. If a person could not understand test instructions, he or she certainly could not do well on the test. Most subtle differences were also thought to affect performance on tests; if someone had never heard of the concept of addition, how could she be asked to perform a mathematical computation? Recognizing that a person's experiences in life might affect test scores, researchers began to investigate the relationship between life experiences and test results. Researchers were particularly concerned with the biases that IQ tests might have built into them.

Myra Shimberg (1929) conducted a study of possible test biases on urban and rural children in New York State. Shimberg standardized two different tests on urban and rural school children. Each test had 25 questions, examples of which are presented below. Reading over the different groups of questions makes it obvious that they test for a different kind of information.

Information Test A

1. What are the colors in the American flag?
2. Who is the president of the United States?
3. What is the largest river in the United States?
4. How can banks afford to pay interest on the money you deposit?
5. What is the freezing point of water?
6. What is a referendum in government?

Information Test B

1. Of what is butter made?
2. Name a vegetable that grows above ground.
3. Why does seasoned wood burn more easily than green wood?
4. About how often do we have a full moon?
5. Who was president of the U.S. during the World War?
6. How can you locate the pole star?

The results are interesting. In Test A the rural children in elementary school had significantly lower scores than urban children. In contrast, on Test B the situation was quite the opposite; rural children did better than urban children. Many IQ tests include information items such as the kind shown. The differences obtained between rural and urban children on these IQ tests were in part a function of the tests rather than any real differences in intellectual capacity. Cultural differences on IQ tests can appear, and those who interpret IQ tests must be particularly sensitive to these potential biases (see Loehlin, Lindzey, & Spuhler, 1975).

There is no question that a test can be specifically biased in one direction or another. Williams (1970) developed a test in which items would favor blacks over whites. A black person taking this test would have a clear advantage; if it were called an IQ test, it would also be biased. Because such biases can be created and because of a lack of understanding on the part of nonpsychologists, many people have suggested that testing, especially IQ testing, be banned. They argue that minority groups have not been exposed to the same education and experiences as white middle-class individuals for whom such tests were designed. Another frequent criticism is that minorities have not had as much experience with standard English as have white middle-class individuals.

Creativity and intelligence can be expressed in many ways.

Much debate and research have been conducted on issues such as these. The focus has been to assess if IQ differences between racial groups or minorities actually exist, and if they exist, to find the reasons for the differences. Obvious variables to be investigated are cultural differences like language. The verbal languages of a ghetto black and a middle-class white are different: they use different words, different idioms, and their day-to-day language patterns are affected by their neighbors and neighborhoods. Shimberg clearly showed this; Williams was also able to demonstrate it. Yet research has shown that differences in language alone do not account for IQ differences. For example, Hall and Turner (1974) found that blacks and whites have very similar verbal comprehension; Hall and Turner have argued that even the culturally disadvantaged hear so much standard English on television and at school, that they can automatically understand spoken English. Labov (1970) suggested that ghetto children are "bathed in verbal stimulation from morning to night" (p. 136). But we also recognize that the quality of their stimulation is probably more important than its quantity (Schoggen & Schoggen, 1976). Thus, one's dialect or language in the home has little effect (by itself) on school performance (Schachter, 1979).

The relative contribution of cultural testing biases in reported differences in IQ scores is very important and very complicated; the research over the last few years has become very sophisticated. Jensen (1976) examined the WISC-R scores from a sample of 600 whites and 600 blacks which formed a random sample of California schoolchildren from grades 5–12. Between the races, there was a 12-point IQ score difference favoring whites; *however*, the average difference between siblings within the same family was also 12 points. Jensen argued, "If the Wechsler IQ test is so culturally biased . . . what kind of bias is it that produces as large a difference between siblings as between blacks and whites . . . the notion that IQ tests discriminate largely in terms of race or social class is a myth" (p. 340). After examining a number of important variables in several widely used standardized tests of intelligence, Jensen concluded that they show practically no evidence of a culture bias for blacks vs. whites. Jensen does not claim that these biases cannot exist; they clearly can. However, he claims that on tests like the WISC-R, they don't. Other psychologists support his view (Sattler, 1981; Vernon, 1979).

The study of cultural testing biases is not complete. When psychologists first recognized that these biases might exist, they immediately began to investigate the potential biases in tests like the WISC-R. The psychological journals have hundreds of research papers that continue to validate and closely examine IQ tests. The tests are *very* closely examined for potential biases, inaccuracies, and poor questions. Of course, no test is perfect and no test will predict future performance exactly. However, through continued research into test construction, test validation, and the causes of differences between scores, psychologists come to better understand the nature and meaning of intelligence and intelligence testing. In 1929 Shimberg recognized that testing biases can be evident, and through the years psychologists have specifically tried to eliminate such biases by creating better tests with better norms for comparison. Intelligence testing, like other areas of psychology, continues to evolve and become more sophisticated.

IQ differences between groups can exist; at the same time, a test can be culturally biased or inexpertly normed. However, just because a test yields differences in IQ between two racial groups does not mean that it is culturally biased and unfair. Far more important is the predictive ability of a test and whether it will allow accurate estimates of performance on some external criterion, for example, college grades (Vernon, 1979). It is important to remember that IQ tests have been developed to allow us to make predictions about performance, not to measure some innate ability. While tests like Shimberg's can be biased in one direction, Williams's can be biased in another direction, and neither will make accurate predictions about intelligent functioning. Tests like the WISC-R, however, are excellent predictors of academic success. We will be examining this issue again later in this chapter.

© King Features Syndicate, Inc., 1972.

components of intellectual development, that of the relative contributions of nature and nurture. Jensen's theory is weighted heavily toward the genetic side of the nature vs. nurture argument (Jensen, 1969, 1970). Before considering this important issue, let us look somewhat more closely at what constitutes an intelligence test.

The Stanford-Binet Intelligence Scale

The Stanford-Binet is still one of the most widely used intelligence tests. It has a long history of development beginning in 1905. Binet and Simon's original intelligence test consisted of 30 short tests that were arranged in order of difficulty. So the first tests involved recognizing food from nonfood or pointing to objects and naming them. Early IQ tests, including the Binet, were not well standardized and the norms were not based on representative samples. In the same way, early IQ tests had a particularly heavy bias toward verbal test questions. As will be shown later, IQ scores can be separately examined to show verbal and nonverbal types of intelligence.

Let us look more closely at the administration of a Stanford-Binet. An examiner first establishes a basal age; a basal age is typically a year or so below the expected mental age of the student. The **basal age** is the age level on the test at which a student can pass all of the tests, but the tests are not so easy that the student feels the test ridiculous. The administration of the test items generally begins at the basal age level and continues until a ceiling age is established. A **ceiling age** is the first test age level at which all tests administered are failed; at this level testing is discontinued. The basal age plus the number of tests passed above the basal age determine a person's eventual score.

Tests in the Stanford-Binet vary greatly in the nature of their content. Some tests require perceptual discrimination while others require following directions. Some tests require practical considerations and the use of judgment. Memory tests are used often and require the recall of pictures, digits, or designs. Maze tracing, paper folding, and rearranging geometric figures are also included. At the upper levels of the test, verbal skills are required and include arithmetic, vocabulary, and analogies. Comprehension is an important skill that is tested.

Does the Stanford-Binet actually measure intelligence? The answer is a qualified *yes*. The Stanford-Binet yields an overall IQ score and is a measure of intellectual functioning; as such, it has been shown to be a good predictor of academic performance. Many of its tests correlate very highly with one another, and furthermore, the same components on the test seem to be evident

Basal age The test age level at which a student can pass all of the parts of the test, but the tests are not so easy that the student feels the test ridiculous.

Ceiling age The test age level at which all tests administered are failed.

at different age levels. The single most common factor that underlies the Stanford-Binet is verbal fluency and verbal reasoning ability; in fact, verbal abilities become increasingly more important in determining a Stanford-Binet IQ score at older ages.

In many ways the Stanford-Binet has been considered *the* standard intelligence test. It has a long history of development and has been standardized and renormed. However, reliability and validity of the latest Stanford-Binet are based on earlier versions of this test. Some researchers are placing less confidence in this test than they have in previous years.

The Wechsler Scales

All IQ tests are not alike. Over a period of 35 years, David Wechsler devised a series of IQ tests that differ substantially in form and interpretation from that of the Stanford-Binet. Early editions of the Stanford-Binet were never quite adequate at testing the IQ of adults; Wechsler also argued that validity was lacking in some of the Stanford-Binet items. In 1939 Wechsler first developed the Wechsler-Bellevue Intelligence Scale and his main objective was to be able to test the IQ of adults. In 1955 Wechsler subsequently published the Wechsler Adult Intelligence Scale (WAIS), which was basically a better standardized test without some of the technical difficulties of the Wechsler-Bellevue. In 1981, a revision of the WAIS was published called WAIS-R (R stands for Revised).

In 1949, Wechsler developed a scale for children, the Wechsler Intelligence Scale for Children, the WISC; revised in 1974, the WISC-R is an IQ test for children aged 6 through 16 years. The Wechsler Preschool and Primary Scale of Intelligence (WPPSI) was developed in 1967 for children aged 4 to $6\frac{1}{2}$ years.

The administration of the three Wechsler Scales is very similar, but the content for the adults is obviously different from that of the preschoolers. There are certain distinct commonalities among the three tests. The verbal tasks determine the verbal IQ, and the performance (nonverbal) tasks, the performance IQ. As shown in Table 7.2, p. 316, verbal subtests involve the use of language; the tests involve responding to questions that require specific information as well as telling how things are alike. The performance tests involve the manipulation in logical ways of pictures, blocks, and objects; overt verbal responses are not necessary.

Unlike the Stanford-Binet, which groups the test items by age level, the Wechsler Scales group the test items by content. So, a person is tested on the information subtest all at once; similarly all of the arithmetic problems are presented at once. A subject's score on each subtest is calculated and converted to a standard or scaled score. These scaled scores take the subject's age into account and make possible comparisons of scores across different ages of individuals. So, on the subtest *Digit Span* an 8-year-old's scaled score of 7 is comparable to an 11-year-old's scaled score of 7. By referring to appropriate tables, verbal, performance, and full-scale IQ scores are obtained; they are deviation IQs with a mean of 100 and a standard deviation of 15 points.

The Wechsler tests point sharply to the need for evaluating the data from IQ tests rather than just accepting some single overall score of intellectual functioning. The Wechsler tests provide 3 different IQ scores and 12 different subtest scores. By carefully evaluating all of these data a psychologist can

Many tests involve spatial nonverbal tasks.

Table 7.2 Some subtests on the WISC-R

TESTS	SUBTESTS	TYPE OF ITEMS
VERBAL	Information	Given a question, recall a general fact that has been acquired in formal and informal school settings.
	Similarities	Given two ideas, use another concept in describing how both are alike.
	Arithmetic	Given a word problem, solve it without pencil and paper.
	Digit Span	Given an orally presented string of digits, recall them.
	Vocabulary	Given a vocabulary word, define it.
	Comprehension	Given a question requiring practical judgment and common sense, answer it.
PERFORMANCE	Picture Completion	Given an incomplete picture, point out the part that is missing.
	Picture Arrangement	Given a series of pictures that tell a story, put them in the right sequence.
	Block Design	Given a picture of a block design, use real blocks to reproduce it.
	Object Assembly	Given a jigsaw-type puzzle, put the pieces together to form a complete object.
	Coding	Given a key that matches numbers to geometric shapes, fill in a blank form with the shapes that go with the numbers.

gain a great deal of information about an individual. Evaluation of the data from IQ tests has been stressed as the key to understanding an individual's cognitive abilities.

TESTS AND TESTING: CONTROVERSY

In the 1970s there was an outcry from segments of society which called into sharp criticism testing, in general, and especially intelligence testing. The controversy has focused around two major issues. The first is the validity and meaning of intelligence tests. Some researchers have argued that IQ tests are not valid; these psychologists and educators claim that we do not know what intelligence tests actually measure, and that whatever they measure is not really intelligence but some other property of human beings. The second argument against testing, and specifically IQ testing, focuses around testing biases. In the psychological journals, the popular press, and in courtrooms around the country, some minority groups are claiming that tests have been used to discriminate against them. They argue that tests can be biased against individuals who have not experienced certain living standards. They argue that the tests are racially biased because some minorities live in geographic locations that, because of the school setting or other cultural reasons, necessitate a different kind of education—an education that does not prepare them for standardized tests of intelligence.

In the last two decades the public, educators, and psychologists have begun to examine testing very carefully and to focus on some of its weaknesses (Kamin, 1974). Not everyone has criticized testing; however, some have been vocal, loud, and persuasive in their arguments (see, for example, Williams, 1970). Their arguments have some merit and cannot be discounted. For example, we observed the possibility of cultural bias in testing in Research Profile 7 when we examined Shimberg's 1929 test of intelligence with urban and rural children. Psychologists, educators, and, lately, the courts have acknowledged fully the complexity of tests and testing. The issue and problems are complex; to avoid oversimplified conclusions, we should explore them at length. Here is a summary of five of the major criticisms of tests and testing. Following the criticisms of some researchers are responses to these criticisms by other researchers.

CRITICISM 1: *There is no unified, clear, agreed upon definition of intelligence; therefore, how can we measure it?*

RESPONSE: Although different IQ tests seem to measure different abilities, as a whole, the major ones have face validity. They generally contain items of problem solving and rational thinking. In Anglo-American society such a standard is considered appropriate (Mercer, 1977).

CRITICISM 2: *IQ test items usually consist of learned information and so reflect the school and quality of a child's schooling rather than the child's true intelligence.*

RESPONSE: Most vocabulary items on IQ tests are learned from the environment, not through schooling. In addition, vocabulary and the learning of facts seem to be mediated by the ability of verbal reasoning.

CRITICISM 3: *When given in school settings, IQ and other tests are often administered inexpertly. Included in this criticism are the* **halo effects** *of evaluating certain students more positively because of preconceived attitudes* (see Crowl & MacGinitie, 1974).

Halo effect The tendency to let one of an individual's characteristics influence the evaluation of other characteristics.

RESPONSE: It is true that incorrectly administered tests given in large groups are likely to bring about illegitimate IQ test scores. In addition, biased teachers and uncooperative students affect IQ test scores. However, these effects are often exaggerated by opponents of the testing movement.

CRITICISM 4: *For some people, practice in test taking helps their performance; this creates individuals who are "testwise" and who can make good use of their time, guess the tester's intentions, and find clues in the test* (Millman et al., 1965).

RESPONSE: The items on IQ tests are hardly items to which experienced test takers

Intelligent boxing requires strength, skill, and knowledge.

are used to. While some students are testwise, such effects are not very large, if evident at all, especially when IQ tests are considered.

CRITICISM 5: *Motivation is part of the process of test taking, and often an individual's score may depend on his or her motivation to succeed rather than actual intelligence.*

RESPONSE: There is no question that an examinee's attitude toward a test situation is important. For this reason experienced test givers maintain an especially neutral attitude. The IQ tests themselves cannot be faulted.

These criticisms and arguments clearly show that the interpretation of IQ test scores is crucial. Critics of IQ testing have noted that without relevant information, IQ test scores can lead to serious negative consequences for the examinee. When test scores are provided without interpretation, they can foster narrow conceptions of the student's ability. This might come in the form of teacher attitudes or by neglecting talents and abilities that go untapped by IQ tests. Because they are used in isolation, some have claimed that IQ test scores have often determined future careers inappropriately (see Rudman, 1977). When provided with uninterpreted information, parents and children often accept such results without question.

Cultural Biases on Tests

That IQ tests are culturally biased against minority groups has been the other major claim of critics of intelligence testing. The basic argument has been that because of a lack of certain *specific* life experiences, certain minority groups cannot do well on an IQ test. Vernon (1979) and Jensen (1974) have argued that two aspects of test difficulty are often confused. One is rarity or unusualness of the concepts or items appearing on the IQ test. The other aspect of difficulty is the complexity of the task involved, that is, the extent to which the tasks require difficult mental manipulations. There is no question that a test can be constructed so as to bias it toward a specific ethnic group or geographical location. Shimberg's Test A versus Test B reported earlier in Research Profile 7 (p. 312) clearly showed that a test constructor can bias test results. However, when the complexity of a manipulation is the focus of a test item, such differences are less apparent. Minority groups often make the claim that the verbal items on IQ tests are aimed at white middle-class society and are not contained in the life experiences of their groups and that this is unfair (see Baratz, 1970). Vernon (1979) has summarized much of this literature and asserts that these differences do not account for differences between blacks and whites (see also, Jensen, 1976; Miele, 1979). Sattler (1981) has also concluded that

> The evidence, gathered from many studies and with a variety of intelligence and ethnic minority groups, points to one conclusion: Intelligence tests are not culturally biased. They have the same properties for ethnic minorities as they do for white children. While there are some limited exceptions to this conclusion, it appears to be warranted from an impartial assessment of the data.

Many of the criticisms of IQ tests have been based more on arguments than on facts (Rudman, 1977). The most vocal critics of IQ tests are most often not informed educators and school psychologists, but rather free-lance writers and professionals from other disciplines. There is no question that there are still problems with IQ tests; however, many of the arguments put forth against IQ testing do not hold up against scientific scrutiny; many are based on emotional readings of the tests by biased, uninformed individuals. If the

Table 7.3 Some misconceptions about intelligence tests and testing

MISCONCEPTION	REALITY
Intelligence tests measure innate intelligence.	IQs always are based on the individual's interactions with the environment; they never solely measure innate intelligence.
IQs are fixed and never change.	IQs change in the course of development, especially from birth through 6 years of age. Even after 6 years of age, significant changes can occur.
Intelligence tests provide perfectly reliable scores.	Test scores are only estimates. Every test score should be reported as a statement of probability (or odds): "There is a 90% chance that the child's IQ falls between X and Y."
Intelligence tests measure all we need to know about a person's intelligence.	Most intelligence tests do not measure the entire spectrum of abilities that are related to intellectual behavior. Some stress verbal and nonverbal intelligence but do not adequately measure other areas, such as mechanical skills, creativity, and social intelligence.
A battery of tests can tell us everything that we need to know in making judgments about a person's competence.	No battery of tests can give us a complete picture of any person. A battery can only illuminate various areas of functioning.

Source: Adapted from Sattler, 1981, with modifications.

data can be produced to show that IQ tests are truly biased or invalid, then responsible psychologists will be the first to purge them from the shelves of diagnostic devices.

In isolation, IQ scores mean little. In addition to these scores, information about the individual's home, personality, socioeconomic status, and specific abilities is crucial in understanding an individual's intellectual functioning. The interpreter of the IQ score must be a knowledgeable researcher into the total dynamics that make up an individual. IQ tests have a meaningful place in the psychological assessment of people; however, to be meaningful, they must be evaluated by people who know how to deal with the scores.

It must be emphasized that IQ cannot predict or explain all types of behavior. It is a measure of intellectual ability that is derived from a small sample of a restricted range of activities. As Sattler has noted (1981), intelligence can be seen in many forms, and an IQ test tells little about the ability of a human being to be flexible in new situations so as to function in mature responsible ways. Although an IQ test score measures abilities, it "reflects experience as well as potential, education as well as aptitude" (Tyler, 1971, p. 48). (See Table 7.3.)

INTELLIGENCE: NATURE VS. NURTURE

Each person's life experiences are different from every other person's. Even cultures vary from one another; people who are raised in the south have a different set of experiences and values from people who live in the northeast. While biological capacities are established even before birth, people's life experiences differ quite dramatically. Both of these factors, biological and environmental, play an important role in our understanding of intelligence.

Both factors determine how much and what kind of intelligent behavior an organism will exhibit. Psychologists can manipulate organisms' environments and observe the changes that take place in their behavior; there are even ways of changing a single organism's biology, for example, through drugs. The question of the relative contribution of heredity and environment to the development of intelligence is still under active consideration and all of the answers are not yet in. However, one fact remains clear: psychologists are easily able to manipulate such factors and the changes that take place because of these manipulations are dramatic. Isolated mountain children have abilities and environments that differ from urban childrens', and twins have life experiences that differ from nontwins'. In the same way, the kinds of tests psychologists use to measure specific abilities can alter the nature of the results obtained. Myra Shimberg's intelligence tests (described in Research Profile 7 on p. 312) will yield different results depending on who takes them.

Let us first look at the nature side of this argument. If we take a large number of animals and test their ability to find their way through a complicated maze, we can divide them into two groups, dull ones and bright ones. If we take the dullest ones and breed them together, and the brightest ones and breed them, we tend to produce second generations that are a little brighter and a little bit duller. It is easy to breed animals selectively. Some results of a study of **selective breeding** are shown in Figure 7.7. After only six generations of selective breeding, Thompson (1954) was able to show that dull animals made twice as many errors as bright ones in maze learning. Similar experiments have shown that selective breeding is relatively easily achieved by using simple tasks to differentiate the bright from the dull. To what extent can intelligence be selectively bred?

In 1969 an article by Arthur Jensen appeared in the *Harvard Educational Review*. In this article Jensen was concerned about how much one can boost a human's IQ and scholastic achievement. One of the issues Jensen addressed was the differences that had been obtained in IQ scores between blacks and whites. On the average blacks scored 16 points lower on IQ tests than whites. Jensen stated that "Genetic factors are strongly implicated in the average negro-white intelligence difference" (p. 82). This statement caused an enormous amount of debate, concern, and scientific inquiry on the subject.

Blacks do generally score lower than whites on IQ tests; for Jensen (1969, 1977) the determining factor in IQ is genetics. Jensen (1976, 1980) adopted a viewpoint that the genetic heritage from one's parents contributes significantly more than the environment in which one is raised. In the nature-nurture controversy, Jensen opted for nature, suggesting that the difference in the IQs of black and whites is due to the "inferior" heredity of blacks. The negative response of the scientific community was immediate and strong. Other psychologists criticized Jensen's logic and raised questions concerning the accuracy of the studies that he cited and the validity of IQ tests in general. Jensen and others who adopted similar positions became the targets of political and personal abuse (see also Jensen & Inouye, 1980).

Serious studies of the potential effect of heredity and environment on intelligence have been under scrutiny for many years. Each of these studies has attempted to examine the general question, "To what extent does the environment or heredity determine IQ"? Many of these studies use twins as subjects. Identical twins (monozygotic) share the same genetic heritage. Thus, any differences in the IQs of identical twins must come about because

Selective breeding Breeding controlled in order to produce the expression of specific genetic traits.

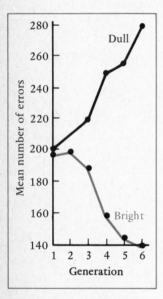

Figure 7.7 When rats were selectively bred and then tested in maze learning (Thompson, 1954), dull rats made more errors than rats who were from the brighter strains

of variables other than their heredity. Similarly, fraternal twins generally share a similar home environment, but each has a distinct and different genetic makeup. In an analysis of the twin studies, Loehlin, Lindzey, and Spuhler (1975) have concluded that the data do not provide decisive evidence on the issue of the genetic or environmental components of IQ in blacks and whites. While some of the studies have found evidence in support of genetic differences, more have found evidence supporting the influence of environmental factors (see, for example, Plomin & DeFries, 1980). The issue has become even more complicated because some of the early studies on the role of genetics in IQ have been shown to have serious scientific flaws; furthermore, some of the data were actually faked (see Hearnshaw, 1979; Kamin, 1974).

There are no systematic and convincing data to show that genetics affects the IQ of blacks or whites more than environment. This does not mean that blacks as a group do not score lower on IQ tests. This fact still remains. However, the interpretation of these results remains critical. Why do blacks score lower than whites on these tests? What does this difference mean? Blacks may score lower on IQ tests than whites for a number of reasons. First, there may be a genetic component. Second, blacks in the United States are disproportionately represented among those who live in culturally impoverished slums. Third, there may be a built-in bias in IQ tests against blacks; IQ tests may have a cultural bias; many blacks, especially in poverty areas, may not have been exposed to relevant words or concepts on IQ tests. A number of studies have been done to demonstrate that one's socioeconomic status or schooling can affect IQ scores. The relative weight of these three factors (genetics, environment, and test biases) has yet to be firmly established. Perhaps even more important is the recognition that within a racial or ethnic group the differences among individuals are greater than the differences between racial or ethnic groups.

If the environment and lack of cultural opportunities or experiences affects IQ scores in such significant ways, the specific town or geographic location within which one lives should have an impact on IQ. Studies have been done to show that this is precisely the case. Such studies have been done on the IQs of children who were isolated in the Blue Ridge Mountains 100 miles

People develop special abilities, skills, and interests by which they can show intelligent behavior.

Table 7.4 Median correlation coefficients between IQs of persons of different degrees of relationship*

RELATIONSHIP	MEDIAN CORRELATION
Identical twins (monozygotic), reared together	.88
Identical twins (monozygotic), reared apart	.75
Fraternal twins (dizygotic), reared together	.53
Siblings, reared together	.49
Siblings, reared apart	.46
Unrelated children, reared together	.17

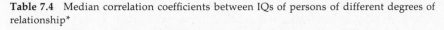

* Were genetics the sole factor in determining IQ, identical twins reared together or apart should have the same IQ and thus a correlation of 1.0. However, the correlation coefficient is not 1.0. Furthermore, the degree of the relationship in IQs decreases when any two siblings (twins or not) are brought up apart from one another. These two findings lend strong support to the idea that environment must play a role, if not the more important role, in determining IQ scores.

Source: Adapted from Loehlin, Lindzey, & Spuhler, 1975, with modifications.

west of Washington, D.C. Each of the communities investigated was made up of a small number of families living in scattered, mud-plastered log huts. Generally, the adults were illiterate and communication with the outside world was somewhat limited. In testing the IQs of these children, testers were quick to note that their lack of language and school training decreased their scores on standardized tests. This particularly was true in tests of calculation and problem solving. Very often it was noted that it was unclear whether the children understood the directions; the terms used to describe the directions often seemed foreign to them. One study (Sherman & Key, 1932) concluded that IQ depends upon the opportunities available to gather information. The researchers decided that the IQs of these children developed only as their environment demanded development. Since the different communities each required different degrees of social and intellectual adjustment, the IQs of the children were highest in the communities with the fullest social development and lowest in the communities where there was the least social development. We can conclude, of course, that if an IQ test is to measure differences in intellectual ability, it should do so regardless of social development.

Social development and biological factors in determining intelligence are related in complex ways. Studies that compare nature and nurture have to separate social and biological influences within socioeconomic groups as well as between them. As Fischbein (1980) has suggested, this has often been overlooked.

How must all of these data be interpreted? It has not been shown that blacks have an inferior genetic heritage to whites in regard to IQ. The role of genetics vs. environment in intelligence has not yet been resolved. On a social level a more important issue arises. What if there were a significant overall difference between ethnic groups? What if this difference were attributable to heredity rather than to environment? Like the color of one's skin and the name one has been given, an individual's birthright, heredity, and individuality are something to be proud of. No person's brilliance, good looks, or parents give them more rights, more equality, or a special place in the sun. Differences between racial or ethnic groups—whether significant or not—do not change their rights before the law and should not be denied to anyone regardless of heredity, environment, or IQ (see Loehlin et al., 1975). Rather than innate intellectual capacity, IQ tests measure, to a great extent, the degree to which people have adapted to the culture in which they live. It should be pointed out that all individuals have some sort of special capability. Whatever that capability is, it is also socially dependent; for example, you may be a genius if you are a good hunter in Africa, a good snowball thrower in the Arctic, or a tremendously astute and successful sales person in the U.S. Too often the concept of genius is attached to academic achievement. This position is a misrepresentation of the concept of IQ and one of the reasons it is being discarded in many educational settings.

THE GIFTED

Usually in the first weeks of the first-grade some kind of reading readiness test is given. Achievement tests are usually given at the end of each academic year. Sometime along the way, at least one, usually two, or even three group-

Twins: Nazi and Jew

The unique genetic background of identical twins allows for fascinating psychological investigations. Most "twin studies" have tried to establish the relative contribution of heredity vs. environment. Usually the studies involve pairs of twins raised together in the same household. Some studies have compared twins who have been raised apart so that their environments have been totally different. The following news article shows how dramatically different one's environment can be from one's brother.

NEWSWEEK Oscar Stohr learned as a little boy to be a strict Catholic and a good Nazi. He could thrust up his arm and shout "Heil Hitler" on cue. He learned to hate capitalists and Jews. He was ready to join the Hitler Youth corps when World War II ended.

Jack Yufe studied Hebrew as a little boy at the synagogue in Port of Spain, Trinidad. He learned to shout "God Save the King" and fear U-boat raids, and he feasted on war movies in which Germans were portrayed as "the scum of the earth."

Oscar and Jack, now 47, are identical twins. As babies they were separated by their parents' bitter divorce. Oscar lived with his maternal grandmother in the Sudetenland of Czechoslovakia and grew up "loyal to the thoughts of the Führer." Jack lived with his Jewish merchant father in the Caribbean, then joined an Israeli kibbutz at 17. When he returned from Israel in 1954, he passed through Germany to meet the brother his father had told him about. The reunion was a near disaster. Jack was appalled when the translator warned him not to tell Oscar he was Jewish. But when Jack heard that psychologist Thomas Bouchard of the University of Minnesota was studying long-separated twins, he contacted Bouchard, who paid Oscar's way to the U.S. The twins have now completed tests aimed at helping to resolve one of scientists' favorite questions: does environment or heredity shape human behavior and thoughts?

Idiosyncrasies:

Because identical twins possess the same genes, any differences between them must come from how they were raised. Bouchard is already struck by the twins' "similarity in temperament, tempo, the way they do things." Both have a taste for sweet liqueur and spicy food. They share idiosyncrasies, too, flushing the toilet before and after using it. Both starred in sports and struggled at math. During his brother's visit to his home in Chula Vista, Calif., Jack made notes when Oscar mirrored his own behavior: ". . . expects wife to take care of all needs without question . . . enjoys sneezing loud and scaring people."

Although heredity may have made Oscar and Jack look and act alike, it could not make them think the same thoughts. Jack, the Californian, is rather liberal, and he regards his twin as "very traditionalistic, typically German." Jack is also tolerant of feminism. "Oscar is still very domineering as far as women go," Jack says. Retorts Oscar: "In your dealings with women you are too dominated by them."

Workaholic:

The brothers' attitudes toward work differ, too. Oscar, a factory supervisor and staunch union man in Germany, enjoys vacations in Italy and Yugoslavia and skis the Alps. Jack, who owns a clothing and appliance store, is a workaholic: "His business seems to dominate his life," Oscar says, but he tells Jack, "You are too soft and warmhearted to your employees."

The Star of David that Jack wears around his neck still stands between them. In Germany, Oscar never mentions his Jewish heritage and says that he did not realize how religious Jack was. "I thought that was the way he was forced to be," Oscar says wistfully. The twins are nevertheless relaxed with each other, united by regret over their separation. Although psychologist Bouchard has yet to analyze the brothers' answers to his 15,000 test questions, some conclusions already seem apparent: while heredity seems to have an edge in shaping idiosyncratic behavior and taste, environment still sculpts thought and outlook.

---

administered IQ tests are given. Anyone going on to college takes the Scholastic Achievement Test (SAT). All of these are standardized tests, each supposedly measuring different aspects of performance or ability (although it has been argued that they all measure the exact same thing). In addition to all of these standardized tests, a student is given daily, weekly, and semester tests on information that was to have been learned. Even first-graders take

Gifted children are often streetwise.

"major exams" on the alphabet, phonics, and word recognition before they can go onto the next level in their reading book. We are an educated society and we are also a highly tested society. By the end of the first-grade our teachers know a great deal about our abilities; by the end of the fourth-grade we can be labeled and classified as to our projected future development.

A parent doesn't need a standardized test to tell a great deal about a child's intellectual performance. Most aware parents can tell you how their children are doing. For example, when a child has learned to read at age 3, parents know that they have an exceptionally bright child. Similarly, when a child has not learned to differentiate colors or simple shapes upon entering the first-grade, most parents recognize that their child is slower than other children. Children's language abilities often reflect their level of intellectual advancement; for example, when a 3-year-old is speaking in coherent paragraphs and using sentence constructions that have the word *because*, it is fair to assume that the child is trying to make causal statements. Using causal statements is an ability that most children do not develop for another year or two at the earliest.

Intellectually, most children are average. As was shown earlier, if one measures intelligence through an IQ test on a large enough sample of children, a normal distribution will be evident. There will be a mean IQ of 100, a standard deviation of about 15 points, and 68.26% of the students will score within one standard deviation of the mean. Out of the total population a small number of people will be truly exceptional—these people will show an incredibly high IQ. Out of 10,000 people only 227 will have an IQ greater than 130. In the same way, few parents or kindergarten teachers will see a child who can read at age 3 or who can do multiplication at age 4. Children with such superior cognitive abilities are rare. (See Figure 7.8.)

Exceptional children and adults are evident not only in the sphere of superior reasoning abilities, but there are also children who are exceptional artists and dancers. When watching a group of twelve 6-year-olds who are enrolled in a ballet class, it is very likely that most of them will have limited abilities. Dance teachers report that only an occasional child has the "gift," a natural ability for dance. Many children and adults learn to play the piano; in the same way, few excel. However, from time to time a music teacher will come

Figure 7.8 When intelligence is measured through a standardized IQ test, we compare an individual's score against a normal distribution with a mean of 100 and a standard deviation equal to 15 points. As before, 68.26% of the population will score between one standard deviation below and one standard deviation above the mean. With a mean of 100, one standard deviation below the mean is 85 points (100 − 15 = 85) and one standard deviation above the mean is 115 points (100 + 15 = 115). Notice that only 2.27% (2.14 + .13 = 2.27) of the population will have a score greater than 130 and only .13% of those people who take the test will have a score greater than 145 points

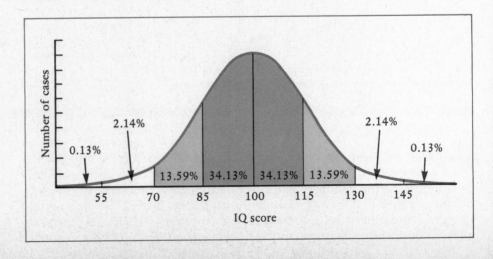

Creative individuals develop ways of making difficult or boring tasks more fun.

upon a youngster who has got it; the teacher will report to the parent that the child is "musically gifted." Over a wide range of behavior some people have the special talent to excel far beyond normal expectations. Many gifted artists, pianists, or dancers are rather average in other areas of their lives; they do not necessarily possess superior cognitive abilities. That children can be gifted in certain areas of their lives has been recognized for centuries. Mozart was a "boy genius." Similarly, many great scientists made some of their most important theoretical discoveries at early ages. All are recognized for their special "gifts." Let us look more closely at the concept of giftedness.

Like the concept of intelligence, the concept of giftedness has meant many different things to many people. Every parent likes to think of his or her child as special in some way. But over the years giftedness has taken on certain distinct properties and attributes. While there is no universally accepted definition of giftedness (as there is no firm definition of intelligence), there is a definition that is fairly widely accepted. This definition was given in 1972 by then commissioner of education S. P. Marland in a report to the U.S. Congress; it encompasses most of the attributes that have just been hinted at. It is important to note that this definition has superior cognitive abilities as only one of its components.

> Gifted and talented children are those identified by professionally qualified persons and who by virtue of their outstanding abilities are capable of high performance. These are children who require educational programs and services beyond those normally provided by the regular school program. . . .
>
> Children capable of high performance include those with demonstrated achievements and/or potential in any of the following areas: (a) general intellectual ability, (b) specific academic aptitude, (c) creative or productive thinking, (d) leadership ability, (e) visual and performing arts, or (f) psychomotor ability.

The gifted child has a unique set of abilities. These may be superior cognitive abilities, leadership abilities, or the abilities may be in the performing arts. The gifted are defined as needing special education, education that goes beyond normal classroom activities. Of course, if such special schooling does not take place, it is likely that the gifted will not realize their full potential. How many Mozarts have gone unrecognized or untaught because of a lack of special education programs is unknown. As Gallagher (1979) has pointed out, the United States has a special love-hate relationship with the gifted. We all want the gifted to succeed; they are the future and they make the great breakthroughs in medicine, science, and art. Yet, at the same time, we design our public school systems for the average child. So, while we praise, honor, and revere the success of the talented and gifted, we design education systems for the average and put little emphasis on special students. Indeed, in many school systems, the *special student,* often the gifted one, is relegated to the back of the room. Kept apart from the other children because he or she is different, the gifted's uniqueness is not fostered and is sometimes ridiculed.

Programs for the Gifted

Exceptional children not only comprise the gifted but also the learning disabled, the handicapped, and the retarded. Extra funds are appropriated in school districts to establish special programs; however, such funding is rather miniscule relative to the number of students who need such special education. Of all the children who need special classes, the gifted's classes would cost the least; however, more often than not, such classes and special teachers do not exist.

Within the educational systems in the United States and Canada is a wide diversity of how the gifted are given treatment. In some school systems treatment is nonexistent; in others, treatment is limited to brief periods or to special groups. In larger cities, the likelihood of finding special programs is greater. When they are not in gifted classes, the gifted are usually excellent students who develop special interests. Good teachers usually allow them to work on enrichment materials within the classroom. An even better system is to have children grouped together who are gifted so that they might work together and learn from one another. School systems with more funds have special programs that allow children to leave their regular classrooms for a certain period of each day, each week, or each month. These systems have a regular and systematic method for dealing with children who are gifted. Some larger school systems have schools that are specifically for children with superior cognitive abilities; other school systems have schools of the performing arts or schools of science. The key is special educational grouping; without such groupings the gifted may be left behind.

While the federal government has acknowledged the need for special education for the gifted, it has not done much to help. Some of the states have been making an attempt to educate the gifted. More money was being spent in 1980 than ever before, and some states have hired psychologists and educators solely for the purpose of programming for the gifted. It must be remembered that states and local communities bear the major portion of the financial burden for education (about 92%). In any given year, states like California, Pennsylvania, and Illinois spend more on gifted and talented education than does the federal government (Jackson, 1979). Equally important, states have been recognizing that the gifted represent more than just children with high IQs and superior cognitive abilities, and that the definition of gifted goes far beyond that. So, while funds, progress, and programs have been slow in developing, they have been making headway.

The gifted's behavior represents one end of a continuum of behavior, in-

Providing nontraditional ways of learning has been a focus of many educators.

telligent and talented behavior. They should not be set apart and cloistered from society, but rather society has an obligation to itself, and to them, to nurture and foster their intellectual and talented gifts. Every person is talented in some way. Everyone is not gifted or of exceptionally high IQ, because people fall on a continuum with some children scoring higher than others. The intelligence measured on an IQ test is indicative of a child's reasoning powers; such reasoning powers can be expanded and enriched rather than left lying dormant. When a child expresses a desire to play a musical instrument, most parents encourage that interest; when a child has athletic abilities, parents encourage sports involvement. When a child shows through a measured score of intelligence that he or she has the capacity to be brilliant and to shine, then that capacity should be fostered in every way possible. Children who are gifted need special programs that will accelerate their development and enrich their already existing skills. To a very great extent, the formal education of children takes place in the school; it is for psychologists and educators to use their tests, their programs, and their energy to foster the potential of these students.

MENTAL RETARDATION

If intelligence involves the ability to act purposefully and to cope effectively with the environment, then about 5 million people in the United States lack this ability. Indeed, a special term has been developed to describe these people who lack intellectual gifts; they are called mentally retarded. Mental retardation in Western society brings with it a number of problems and the necessity for certain special considerations. People who are profoundly retarded are unable to take care of themselves, and they are usually hospitalized and given custodial care. In contrast, people who border on mental retardation are often classified only as slow learners; sometimes they are not included in special classes for the retarded and can be a behavior problem in the classroom and the community. A wide range of behavior is associated with mental retardation, which covers the span from a slow learner to the inactivity of a person who is little more than an alive body. It remains one of society's tasks to understand the special problems of the mentally retarded and to understand the cause of the condition that they and their families have to bear.

The mentally retarded do cope with their environment and they do act purposefully. Most of them learn to walk; many can feed themselves; some are even working with employers such as the United States Postal Service. The mentally retarded hug those they love, ask for their parents, and get angry when things are not going well for them. We may change their environment, but they can learn to cope with a new environment. In fact, many get along well and act purposefully in almost any environment. They simply are deficient in intelligence, and because of this they frequently cope less effectively with the normal environment.

What Is Mental Retardation?

Mental retardation Below average intellectual functioning as measured on an IQ test with impairment in adaptive behavior which originates during the developmental period.

Solving even simple puzzles requires intelligence.

Mental retardation is more than just a lack of intelligent behavior. An individual is classified as mentally retarded according to three specific criteria: (1) intellectual functioning, as assessed by an individually administered IQ test, must be far below normal; (2) the person must be unable to meet the social demands of adjustment to the environment; and (3) both intellectual and social problems must be present relatively early, particularly during the developmental years before age 18. Thus, a person who is classified as mentally retarded must not only have a lower IQ but must also have trouble adapting to the environment and must exhibit these problems in childhood.

When psychologists speak of below normal IQ, they are typically referring to some score on a standardized test, such as the WISC-R and the WAIS-R. This would mean that a person with an IQ of less than 70 would be considered retarded, a figure that represents only 2.2% of the population. With a population in the United States of over 225 million people, this would mean that approximately 5 million people are potentially retarded (.022 × 225,000,000). Of course, not everyone who falls within this segment of the population is retarded to the same extent; there are marked degrees of retardation.

Levels of Retardation

Not all of the mentally retarded are affected in equal degrees. As noted earlier, some people show only minimal retardation and are often classified as slow learners. There are, on the other hand, mentally retarded people who have extreme trouble coping with the demands of life. There are basically four types of mental retardation, each corresponding to a different score on a standardized test of intelligence. As is shown in Table 7.5 anyone who is classified as re-

Table 7.5 Types and distribution of mental retardation when IQ is measured on the Stanford-Binet and Wechsler tests

CLASSIFICATION	STANFORD-BINET IQ	WECHSLER IQ	PERCENTAGE OF THE MENTALLY RETARDED
Mild	52–68	55–69	90
Moderate	36–51	40–54	6
Severe	20–35	25–39	3
Profound	Below 20	Below 25	1

tarded has to have an IQ lower than 70. People with IQs greater than 70 are of normal intelligence

MILD RETARDATION. The mildly mentally retarded (IQs of 55 to 69) includes the largest number (approximately 90%) of those who are generally classified as retarded. Most of these people can get along in life with some help from family and friends. They usually require some degree of supervision in their work but they can acquire certain academic and occupational skills (e.g. Allington, 1981). As adults, intellectually they are on the level of a 10-year-old. There are many special programs in which the mentally retarded are trained to work and taught how to get along in the community. Generally these people do not need institutionalization, are not severe behavior problems, and cope with the environment with a marked degree of success.

MODERATE RETARDATION. Moderate mental retardation (IQs of 40 to 54) accounts for approximately 6% of those who are classified as retarded. Most moderate mental retardates are in need of special classes and special jobs if they are not institutionalized. Although few people in this group are employed, these people can hold simple jobs. Often the moderately retarded live in an institution or as a dependent of their families. While they are able to speak, write, and interact among friends, they appear somewhat clumsy in motor coordination, posture, and social skills. Their intellectual level is closer to that of a 5- or 6-year-old, but they are able to take care of themselves and adapt to the environment, at least to a minimal degree.

SEVERE RETARDATION. Only about 3% of all those classified as retarded (IQs of 25 to 39) may be placed within the category of severe mental retardation. People in this group show severe motor, speech, and intellectual retardation, and most of them are unable to develop personal hygiene skills and are dependent upon the staff of the institutions in which they live. The severely retarded engage in very little verbal activity; they can perform even simple tasks only with training. Many of the severely retarded have become so because of birth disorders and traumatic injury to the brain.

PROFOUND RETARDATION. A relatively small number of the mentally retarded, only 1%, fall into the category of profound mental retardation (IQ below 25). These people require total supervision and constant care in an institution, and they are unable to master even simple tasks. They are often physically underdeveloped and both their motor and intellectual develop-

Mild retardation (IQ of 55 to 69) A category that includes persons with a fair degree of independence but who require some supervision and guidance in intellectual tasks and on their jobs.

Moderate retardation (IQ of 40 to 54) A category that includes persons who are semi-independent and are able to take care of themselves hygienically, but who are partially dependent upon families and friends for intellectual and financial support.

Severe retardation (IQ of 25 to 39) A category that includes people who are capable of some self-help when provided supervision. Intellectual performance is severely impaired. Some physical symptoms are apparent, including changes in posture and movement.

Profound retardation (IQ below 25) A category that includes people who require total custodial care. Physical, motor, and intellectual development are severely impaired.

ment are minimal. Physical deformities and other congenital defects (such as deafness, blindness, and seizures) often accompany profound mental retardation.

What Causes Mental Retardation?

As in any area of intellectual functioning components of both nature and nurture are operating in mental retardation. These two approaches to retardation, biological and environmental, are a good way to organize the causes of retardation conceptually. The first approach suggests that mental retardation has an organic cause; this means that there is a physiological basis to the lack of intellectual and social adaptability. Included under these organic causes of mental retardation are defective genes, chromosomal aberrations, and birth defects. The alternative approach to studying mental retardation suggests that the cause is an environmental one stressing cultural-family factors. The cultural-familial approach assumes that there is no brain pathology and there is evidence for retardation in at least one of the parents or siblings.

BIOLOGICAL CAUSES. Mental retardation can be caused by physiological problems. For example, a child may be born with a certain type of disease or aberration, or in early childhood a disease or injury may damage the brain. Regardless of the way the brain is damaged, organic causes of mental retardation can typically bring about severe and often profound retardation.

Before birth, a child may suffer from three different types of disease: systemic, infectious, and traumatic. *Systemic diseases* include chromosomal aberrations, such as Down's syndrome, and defective genes, such as phenylketonuria (PKU). *Infectious diseases* can be severely damaging to an unborn child; for example, when a mother contracts rubella, or German measles, during pregnancy, her unborn child may be severely damaged. Similarly, syphilis can cause severe brain damage even before birth. The brain and other parts of the nervous system of an unborn child can be damaged because of physical agents. The brain may be damaged by poisoning, hormonal deficiency, malnutrition, or a lack of oxygen in the bloodstream. Some studies have shown that pregnant women who smoke a great deal reduce the level of oxygen in their bloodstream and thus deprive their unborn children of needed oxygen. Whether this deprivation of oxygen can create mental retardation is still undetermined. However, a developing organism needs oxy-

Table 7.6 Diseases that cause mental retardation

TYPE OF DISEASE	EXAMPLE
Systemic	Down's syndrome (Mongolism)
	Phenylketonuria (PKU)
Infectious	Rubella (German measles)
	Encephalitis
	Syphilis
Physical agents (trauma)	Malnutrition
	Poisoning
	Hypoxia (oxygen deprivation)

gen and by cutting down the supply, a mother who smokes certainly does not facilitate the growth and development of her unborn child.

CULTURAL-FAMILIAL RETARDATION. The cultural-familial mentally retarded are those for whom no physiological basis for their condition can be identified, and yet, they remain mentally retarded, often having at least one relative, parent, or sibling who is also retarded.

Persons who are mildly retarded often do not show signs of retardation until early school years when intellectual performance is required. Remember, the mildly retarded can get along with others, are able to speak, and do not show severe motor disturbances. Many people who are classified as mildly retarded come from lower socioeconomic classes. This has certain important implications. First, children of lower socioeconomic classes are generally not reinforced for intellectual activities. In addition, they are sometimes provided with a poor diet and poor models. This means that a lower-class family often expects less from a child than a middle-class family does. These people generally have been brought up in environments that do not foster intellectual stimulation, encourage growth, or require mental activity. While the environment does not directly determine whether such a person will be retarded or not, it certainly does not provide an atmosphere for growth and maximum development. As Davison and Neale (1978) have suggested, the overwhelming majority of retarded children would probably achieve higher levels of intellectual and social functioning if they were provided with appropriate training at home. With care, education, and encouragement, mentally retarded people can make far more adjustments than many give them credit for; without this special care they will not prosper. In slum settings where people are too depressed economically and emotionally to give extra help, retarded people can make very few of the gains that they might in special extra care settings. Of course, this contributes to the increased number of more severely retarded people found in economically and culturally depressed areas.

The two classification approaches to mental retardation, organic and cultural-familial, may be a reasonable way of distinguishing between two broad types of mental retardation. Generally people who are classified as organically mentally retarded have a poorer chance for development and growth than those who come from cultural-familial categories. Since the large majority of the retarded can be classified as culturally-familially retarded, their maximum potential has probably not been reached.

The Law and the Mentally Handicapped

The mentally retarded are only one group of individuals who are handicapped; others also suffer from various diseases and impairments. In the last decade individuals have gone to the courts to try to ensure proper education for such people. They have argued that the constitutional rights of the handicapped are actively violated when they are tested and evaluated in inappropriate ways. The courts have agreed, and with the passage of Public Law 94–142 (the Education for All Handicapped Children's Act), the constitutional rights of minorities and the handicapped have been given special protection. The law is complicated and is still being tested in the courts; however, Sattler (1981) has summarized it concisely as follows:

It mandates, for example, (a) that consideration be given to the child's native language, (b) that only valid tests be used for the assessment, (c) that more than one assessment technique be used, (d) that the child's physical handicaps be considered, (e) that all relevant factors be considered in the evaluation, (f) that a team approach be used, (g) that the assessment procedures not be racially or culturally discriminatory, (h) that an individualized educational program be designed, (i) that parents have the right to an independent evaluation, (j) that re-evaluations be performed at least every three years, (k) that parents have the right to examine their child's records, and (l) that the child be placed in the least restrictive educational environment.

It is likely that in the next decade we will see further changes in the law which will place the role of psychologists in ever more important situations in determining the educational placement of the mentally retarded.

Mainstreaming

Regardless of how people are classified as mentally retarded—whether their retardation is considered mild, moderate, severe, or profound, or whether they were classified by the dual classification of organic or cultural-familial— they are still individuals whose intellectual functioning is below that of most people. Is it appropriate to call these people mentally retarded? Intelligence and ability to adapt to the environmental and social demands of life are two of the main criteria for determining whether a person is mentally retarded. Both intelligence and adaptation to the environment are normally distributed. This means that there is a wide range of intelligence scores and degrees of ability to adapt to the environment. Most people adapt to a moderate extent; some people adapt very well; and some less well. Similarly, most people have average intelligence while some have markedly high intelligence and others have markedly low intelligence.

Except for those few who have organic causes for their retardation, the retarded should not be considered a special segment of the population. Admittedly, the retarded have more difficulty adapting to the environment and more difficulty getting along in an intellectually aware world. Yet the mildly retarded are able to conduct a normal life, bear children, and share the similar feelings of all people. The behavior of the retarded is often considered abnormal, yet their behavior only represents one end of a continuum. The environment of the retarded makes a vast difference in how they respond to the demands of a complex society. It is society's job to try to optimize their potential with special care settings and extra help.

The type of special care that the retarded are given has undergone considerable debate over the last 20 years. Traditionally children diagnosed as mildly retarded have been sent to special schools within schools. The idea of "special education" is to provide a special education to make significant gains through extra help and specially trained educators. However, there has been a shift in thinking among educators, psychologists, and specialists in mental retardation; the shift has been toward mainstreaming. **Mainstreaming** is the integration of mentally retarded children into a regular classroom setting. The focus of mainstreaming is to help "normalize" life for the retarded child.

Special education programs were originally devised to provide specialized instruction with special programs and specially trained teachers. However,

Mainstreaming The administrative practice of placing handicapped children in regular classroom settings with the support of special education services.

more often than anyone would desire, funding for these special programs has been limited and the quality of instruction poor. Furthermore, important criticisms of the concept of special education have developed. *First,* it has not been considered optimally effective. *Second,* placement in special classes has often produced negative social effects because of the labels attached to the children. *Third,* segregating the children in special classes has slowed down their ability to meet the normal demands of socialization. *Fourth,* a disproportionate number of minorities were in special education classes. *Finally,* the courts upheld the idea that special education has deprived these children and their parents of their constitutional rights to equal educational opportunities.

As a consequence of these basic objections, programs that normalize or mainstream children have developed. In mainstreaming, children are assigned to a regular class and regular procedures are modified for the retarded only when necessary. While special instruction for a part of the day is often necessary, at least half of a day is usually spent with the regular classroom. Special classes are not done away with; both these classes and support from teachers with special skills are necessary and appropriate to help with the regular mainstreaming instruction procedure. Most important, within mainstreaming the educational needs of the child are first; these needs are based upon performance rather than on some often arbitrarily assigned label (see Birch, 1974).

Mainstreaming is not simple or easy to achieve. Various research studies done over the past 20 years have found conflicting results. Ziegler and Hambleton (1976) found no differences for the mildly retarded between special education programs and regular classroom settings; one cannot expect these same effects for the profoundly retarded (Smith & Arkans, 1977). The research literature is extensive and professionals in the field support mainstreaming; schools are rapidly changing and placing children in new environments. Old methods are being replaced, and educators are developing new ways of helping the retarded.

It is likely that over the next decade there will be further changes in the education of the retarded. The most important element to consider is the retarded person as an individual. Each child, teenager, and adult must be allowed to develop to the maximum that he or she can. School systems and society as a whole have the obligation to optimize the social and intellectual capacities of the retarded. Increasingly, parents and educators are working to facilitate the lives and education of the retarded; the legal system of the United States is being supportive, so we should continue to see less labeling, less segregation, less indifference, and far more positive and productive programs to help normalize and mainstream the person who has been diagnosed as mentally retarded.

The special needs of the mentally retarded are shared by other people with congenital handicaps. Perhaps one of the best ways that we can understand some of their needs is to read the following excerpts from a speech given by Aileen Weiss, a mother of a mentally retarded young woman and a former member of the President's Commission on Mental Retardation (1978):

I am the mother of a 20-year-old mentally retarded daughter. Twenty years ago I had no training for raising a developmentally disabled child, but it didn't take long before I realized that raising her would take courage, persistence, ingenuity, good

Special people need special attention.

humor, commitment, and fight—just to get her the very things every human being took for granted.

Vicki was diagnosed as severely and profoundly retarded, and you would have thought that she had a dread disease. For some reason everything she needed was called "special"—special schools, special medical treatment, special job training, special work.

Vicki lives in an institution . . . and I recall many years ago when we drove through those big black gates—I died just a little! I'm pleased that those gates are no longer there. When Vicki was admitted to [the village], there were 30 in a bedroom. As a parent, I was so happy to have someone to share this enormous responsibility with us that it never dawned on me to question the fact that institutions were like this. When I realized that perhaps it did not have to be like this, I was too scared to question it for fear that I would be told, "If it doesn't suit you—you may take Vicki home!" . . .

One Christmas my husband and I asked several of the children at [the village] what they would like for a present, and one little fellow said, "Mrs. Weiss, please could I have a pair of private shorts?"—meaning one that was brand new and belonged only to him and didn't come out of a barrel of clothes that each child was given on a daily basis. Needless to say, he got them, wrapped in a beautiful Christmas box. I don't think he opened the box until Easter. He just kept it, asking, "Does it really belong just to me?" . . . One day a mongoloid child in the bed next to Vicki died. Although the dormitory matrons felt a deep loss, they carried on their daily activities so as not to upset the other children in the building. The matrons were shocked when one of the children in the building asked to see the chaplain. When he arrived, the child asked the chaplain for permission to cry because her friend had died!

My daughter Vicki will be 21-years-old in July, and there is no way her mother and father will outlive her; therefore Vicki now has another need. I am asking all of *you* to be Vicki's advocate. Advocacy is a tough business, but you must not back down from your commitment to fulfill her basic human needs and rights. . . . The law is a great promise; but the fact is that the passage of new legislation will not bring about easy or quick changes. Due process, legal provisions won't add up to instant solutions to problems that have been around a long time. Change is going to take a lot of work, but when that change comes, we will realize that the *needs* of the developmentally disabled persons were never *special* needs at all. They are just the needs of other human beings.

SUMMARY

Whenever psychologists wish to examine an individual's intellectual capabilities or his or her achievement in some specific area, they administer a standard test. A test is a device that allows a psychologist to assess a person's responses to very specific stimuli and to compare one individual to others. The others to whom an individual is compared are a representative sample of people who are comparable to the population for whom the test was constructed. By comparing an individual with the norms, a psychologist can assess where any individual stands relative to other people who take the test as well as being able to make predictions about his or her future performance. A good test allows for accurate predictions.

For a test to be an accurate predictor of future performance it needs to be reliable as well as valid. Reliable tests are consistent. They have a small standard error of measurement; this means that the number of points that a person scores will vary only a little because of the imperfect reliability of the test.

A test's validity represents the extent to which the test actually measures what it is supposed to measure. So an intelligence test should measure intelligent functioning, not musical ability. Similarly, an achievement test in world history should not measure mechanical ability.

Particularly important in interpreting tests is considering the individual within a larger context. While an intelligence test may provide an IQ score, this score alone does not tell the whole story. A clinician in assessing an individual's intelligence must look at family background, motivation, socioeconomic status, and the subtest scores on the intelligence test itself.

Intelligence testing has a long history starting with Alfred Binet in France. Through the years intelligence tests have become more sophisticated, reliable, and valid. Intelligence tests like the Stanford-Binet and the WAIS-R have undergone a great deal of development so as to assess intelligence accurately. One of the problems in assessing intelligence has been defining it; over the years a number of definitions have been provided. Perhaps the most widely accepted one is that of Wechsler: intelligence is the aggregate or global capacity of the individual to act purposefully, to think rationally, and to deal effectively with the environment. While intelligence tests have been subject to a great deal of criticism regarding potential cultural or racial testing biases, solid scientific research has shown that differences in measured IQ between racial groups are the same as differences found between siblings. Thus, researchers assert that such biases do not exist in tests like the WISC-R. This does not mean that they could not exist in other tests, but the most widely used tests of intelligence are not biased against any one racial group.

All tests, IQ tests in particular, have been vocally criticized in the last two decades. Many nonpsychologists have suggested that they are biased and inadequate measures of intelligent behavior. However, many of the criticisms of testing have been based more on arguments than on facts and most do not stand up against scientific scrutiny. Sophisticated interpreters of test scores are able to make very accurate predictions about future performance. With intelligence, they are able to make very accurate predictions about success in academic settings.

There is no question that genetics determines part of a person's measured intelligence, but at the same time, there is no question that a person's environment is also critically important. In earlier chapters we saw that children's social and intellectual interactions determine the extent to which they will grow socially and intellectually. Psychologists are therefore forced to conclude that intelligence is not determined solely through genetics or the environment. Our genetic background is determined by our parents; there is no way to change our genes. However, our environment is easily changed and varies from person to person and from decade to decade. Parents can maximize their children's intelligence by maximizing the stimulation in their environments. Society can maximize its overall growth by providing increased educational and cultural opportunities for its young.

Perhaps the group that could be most helped through increased educational opportunities are the gifted and the mentally retarded. Gifted children are children who show outstanding abilities for high performance. They may show potential in intellectual ability, leadership, or the visual and performing arts. Usually the gifted are those of superior cognitive abilities; while only about 3% of the population can be considered gifted, few of these children will be given any special training. The problem for society is clear; superior abilities of the gifted and talented which are not nurtured will not develop. Early intervention with the gifted is crucial if their talents are to be fostered.

While the gifted are at one extreme, often showing particularly high intellectual abilities, at the other extreme are the mentally retarded. These are people who exhibit behaviors unlike the behavior of most others because they have trouble coping with day-to-day problems. A person who is mentally retarded not only has a low IQ but also has trouble adjusting to a shifting environment. There is no question that the mentally retarded have trouble coping with life, but their problems in coping are largely caused by factors outside of themselves. The mentally retarded have difficulty growing beyond their own intellectual and social deficits. This does not mean that the mentally retarded are not trainable and cannot learn to cope with the demands of life. Quite the contrary, increasingly the mentally retarded are being mainstreamed into regular classroom settings where there is an attempt to normalize their lives and provide a maximum education and social adjustment.

Clearly there are dramatic individual differences in IQs, thinking strategies, and rates of language acquisition among individuals; these differences are often reflected in economic success. These differences between people may reflect true intellectual differences, but they do not make any person more worthwhile. These differences usually reflect educational levels, motivation, environment, and previous experience. Psychologists do not claim that individual differences between people do not exist; clearly some people have greater basic mental abilities than others. People cannot and should not minimize these differences; more important, however, these differences should not be exaggerated. Differences in basic mental abilities do not make some people less worthy, less sensitive, or less happy. The differences between people are what make each of us unique. So, while all people are created different in terms of abilities, in terms of being human, all people are created equal.

CHAPTER REVIEW

1. When well constructed, tests diagnose certain problems and they have good predictive value in determining the individual's future performance, perhaps in a job setting.
2. Standardization is the process of developing a uniform procedure in the administration and scoring of a test; the process also includes developing norms for the test from a large representative sample of subjects.
3. Norms are a list of scores and the corresponding percentile ranks or standard scores of a group of examinees on whom a test was standardized.
4. A representative sample is a sample of individuals who match the population with whom they are to be compared; they are to match with respect to important variables, for example, socioeconomic status and age.
5. A normal curve is a bell-shaped curve that is based on a mathematical formula; it is arranged so that a certain percentage of the population falls under each part of the curve.
6. Of all people who take IQ tests, 68.26% achieve scores within one standard deviation of the mean or midpoint of the distribution.

7. A raw score is an examinee's unconverted score on a test, for example, the number of correct answers.

8. A standard score is a score that expresses an individual's relative position to the mean based on the standard deviation; it is often derived by converting a raw test score to one interpretable on the basis of some population variable such as age or grade.

9. A percentile score is a score indicating what percentage of the population under consideration would obtain a lower score.

10. A deviation IQ is a standard score on an IQ test that has the same mean and standard deviation at all ages.

11. Reliability is the ability of a test to give the same score for a single individual through repeated testings.

12. Based on statistical formulas, the standard error of measurement is the number of points that a score may vary because of the imperfect reliability of a test. This imperfect reliability is to be expected.

13. A test's validity tells a test developer whether a test measures what it is supposed to measure; without validity, inferences cannot be made from a test.

14. Individual intelligence tests provide an opportunity for a clinician to observe an examinee's personality, attitudes, language performance, and visual-motor abilities; taken together with IQ scores, this information allows for an important diagnostic ability.

15. The persons most often associated with the beginnings of IQ testing are Binet and Simon.

16. According to Wechsler, intelligence is the aggregate or global capacity of an individual to act purposefully, to think rationally, and to deal effectively with the environment.

17. Wechsler has argued that to be intelligent people need to be aware, goal-directed, rational, and that their behavior must be worthwhile; he argues that intelligence tests measure the capacity of people to understand the world about them and their resourcefulness in coping with its challenges.

18. A factor analysis approach to intelligence uses correlational techniques to determine which tasks are involved in determining intelligence; usually several factors are found, each accounting for a different aspect of a person's mental abilities.

19. The Stanford-Binet tests vary greatly in the nature of their content. Some tests require perceptual discrimination while others require following directions.

20. The Wechsler Intelligence Scales provide a verbal IQ, a performance IQ, and a full-scale IQ score.

21. Unlike the Stanford-Binet, which groups the test items by age level, the Wechsler Scales group test items by content.

22. According to Sattler the evidence gathered from many studies and with a variety of intelligence and ethnic minority groups points to one conclusion: intelligence tests are not culturally biased.

23. Most intelligence tests do not measure the entire spectrum of abilities related to intellectual behavior. Some stress verbal and nonverbal intelligence but do not adequately measure other areas, such as mechanical skills, creativity, and social intelligence.

24. IQs are always based on the individual's interactions with the environment; they never solely measure innate intelligence.

25. Arthur Jensen is the leading proponent of the nature point of view on differences in intelligence for different races. The data suggest that there is no decisive evidence on the issue of genetics or environmental components of IQ in blacks and whites.

26. The gifted child has a unique set of abilities, which may be superior cognitive abilities, leadership abilities, or abilities in the performing arts.

27. By choosing a criterion of the top 3% of the population as having the potential for

giftedness, almost 2 million children in the public schools could be classified as gifted.

28. The most outstanding characteristic of the gifted has generally been conceded to be their superior cognitive abilities.

29. Mental retardation is below average intellectual functioning with impairment in adaptive behavior, which originates during the developmental period, generally before the age of 18.

30. There are four basic types of mental retardation, each corresponding to a different score on a standardized test of intelligence. The range of behaviors associated with these classifications varies from people who are slow learners to those who are unable to master self-care techniques and whose physical, motor, and intellectual development are severely impaired.

31. There are both biological and cultural causes for mental retardation. Regardless of cause, the retarded have difficulty adapting and coping with the demands of the environment and modern life. The behavior of the retarded can vary dramatically, yet all retarded individuals are at one end of a continuum of intellectual functioning.

32. Mainstreaming is the integration of mentally retarded children into a regular classroom setting. The focus of mainstreaming is to help normalize life for the mentally retarded child.

33. The research literature is extensive and professionals in the field support mainstreaming; old methods are being replaced, and educators are developing a new way of helping the retarded.

SUGGESTIONS FOR FURTHER READING

AIKEN, L. R. *Psychological testing and assessment* (3rd ed.). Boston, MA: Allyn & Bacon, Inc., 1979.

ANASTASI, A. *Psychological testing* (4th ed.). New York: Macmillan Publishing Company, Inc., 1976.

LOEHLIN, J. C., LINDZEY, G., AND SPUHLER, J. F. *Race differences in intelligence*. San Francisco, CA: W. H. Freeman Company, 1975.

ROBINSON, N. M., AND ROBINSON, H. B. *The mentally retarded child* (2nd ed.). New York: McGraw-Hill Book Company, 1976.

VERNON, P. E. *Intelligence: Heredity and environment*. San Francisco, CA: W. H. Freeman Company, 1979.

ZAJONC, R. B. Birth order and intelligence. *Psychology Today*, 1975, *8*, 43–87.

THE STUDY OF LANGUAGE is the study of how people go about communicating; closely associated with these abilities are their thought processes. We know that the human ability to communicate and think about the world is something no other species has; yet our knowledge about *how* humans think has only recently been studied. By examining how and under what circumstances humans learn language many researchers have attempted to understand the nature of language *and* the nature of human thought. By turning to the laboratory, thought processes have been extensively studied; we have learned that our language, and especially our thoughts, makes humans unique. This chapter presents the basic principles of the study of language and thought and attempts to show their complex relationship.

CHAPTER 8

Language and Thought

Washington churns out its usual nonsense. The chief of the United States Capitol Police posts a notice: "Vehicles will be parked chronologically as they enter the lot" (1975 models in this corner and 1973 models over there). The Undersecretary of the Treasury, Edwin H. Yeo III, is asked about additional loans to New York City: "If we find the reasonable probability of repayment is slipping away from us, then we'll have to respond in terms of extension of future credit." If they don't pay what they owe, we won't lend them any more. . . .

Nelson Rockefeller, when asked whether he would be nominated at the 1976 Republican convention, foreswore the oral fragment. "I cannot conceive of any scenario in which that could eventuate," he said. Won't things improve when the younger generation of politicians takes over? No. Edmund Brown, Jr., asked whether his 1976 candidacy was really aimed at 1980, replied, "My equation is sufficiently complex to admit of various outcomes." Declining to ride to a money-raising dinner in a chauffeur-driven Mercedes, he explained, "I cannot relate to that material possessory consciousness," and used an unwashed Ford instead. Conspicuous inconspicuous consumption. . . .

American English, drawing on so many regional differences, so many immigrant groups, and such a range of business, farming, industrial, athletic, and artistic experiences, can have an incomparable richness. Instead, high crimes and misdemeanors are visited upon it, and those who commit them do not understand that they are crimes against themselves. The language belongs to all of us. We have no more valuable possession.

EDWIN NEWMAN
A Civil Tongue

When people begin to speak with so much jargon, with so much puffed up false dignity, and with so many trick phrases, their language begins to lose its meaning. According to Edwin Newman, people who speak in this way have lost a civil tongue. Maintaining a civil tongue sometimes means being silent, other times speaking up, but always speaking clearly. Too often in the 1980s we hear people speaking with so many initials and acronyms that they no longer make sense to others. Newman's point is simple: we convey information through speech and language; unless we do it with simplicity and clarity, we will soon convey little more than gibberish.

Long before Edwin Newman had thought of writing his first book, psychologists were trying to grapple with the same issue in another guise. From a psychologist's view, the way people use language can affect their subsequent behavior. When a man who has always had trouble expressing himself is faced with resolving a conflict at his job, he finds that he often garbles his words. In such an instance it is easy to see how important the use of language is in effective communication of our ideas.

From Edwin Newman's view, people who do not communicate effectively through proper language must be thinking in a way that is not effective. But for a psychologist, such an analysis is not so simple. Psychologists have recognized that language and thought are related, but that they are also separate processes. Language *and* thought increase in maturity and complexity with increases in age and experience; however, a mature vocabulary does not necessarily mean mature thoughts. Because thought is usually expressed through language, psychologists have closely examined these two topics with the aim of understanding them as separate processes and aspects of behavior which work together.

The ability to use language is one of the most important of human skills.

The relationship of language to thought is not simple. Experience and the environment affect both language and thought. Similarly, one's genetic and inherited abilities also affect both language and thought. Psychologists have spent a great deal of effort trying to unravel the genetic vs. environmental factors that might be responsible for language and/or thought. As we study these two topics, you will see that the processes are difficult, interesting, but not yet totally resolved. The nature vs. nurture issue is a central one in the study of language behavior; you will see that it has dominated the study of language. One of the principal techniques used to study language has been to study the developing infant. Accordingly, let us begin with an examination of how a developing infant acquires language.

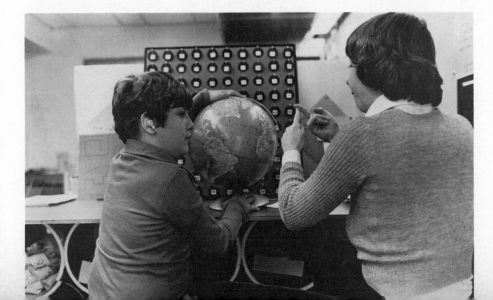

For the deaf, learning language requires extra time and energy, as well as special teachers.

INFANTS AND WORDS

Adults learn to express themselves as children and this process of communication begins very early in life. A newborn child has few ways to communicate with a caregiver. Hungry infants cry when experiencing hunger pains; this is their only way to indicate their need for nourishment. You will see there are slight variations in newborns' vocal utterances, but these differences are small.

Language develops during the first years of life; Piaget says that thought processes develop simultaneously with language. We learned earlier (p. 258) that Piaget suggests that the basis of all intellectual growth begins in the first 2 years. According to Piaget, a child's interactions in these years allow the development of cognitive structures that shape thought processes. Of course, language and thought are only two of the many processes undergoing change. Social interactions develop. Children learn to eat by themselves; in some cases children learn to control their bowel and bladder functions. It is a busy time of life.

Nature vs. Nurture

Language develops so naturally that it seems as if certain aspects of language are inborn. But at the same time, we know that the environment of a newborn will affect language development. Psychologists have focused closely on the relationship of language to one's biological heritage and to the environment in which one is reared. They have tried to separate in a meaningful manner the nature and nurture components of language behavior. Let us briefly review some of these biological and environmental influences that might affect language development.

When care givers are especially attentive and provide a great deal of verbal stimulation, this is likely to increase a child's cognitive skills later in life

Infants often imitate each other, especially if they are twins.

(Bradley & Caldwell, 1976); in fact, White found that well developing 1- and 2-year-olds had considerably more talk directed at them (White et al., 1973). While the quantity of verbal stimulation may affect language development, Schachter (1979) has suggested that the quality of verbal stimulation is far more important. Certainly some language exchange between care giver and child is necessary for normal language development (Curtiss, 1977).

Biological influences on language and thought are also important. Intelligence and basic adaptive thinking are determined in part by the genetics of one's biological parents. You will see later in this chapter that certain aspects of language are biologically based; for example, the emergence of words and of sentences begins at different ages, but once it begins it proceeds at a relatively smooth pace. Similarly, early speech often incorporates physical gestures such as a hand wave.

Both environmental and biological influences affect the development of language and thought. By studying these processes psychologists attempt to better understand language and thought and their relationship with the environment and biology. Before examining those issues any further, let us examine the development of language more closely.

LANGUAGE

The continuing and developing emergence of language is amazing. Consider 4-year-olds and their developing language system and knowledge of the world. Children at the age of 4 ask an endless stream of questions. Unlike their younger brothers and sisters, who are unable to speak effectively, 4-year-olds communicate remarkably well. Unlike their older brothers or sisters, who go to school and read, 4-year-olds are dependent on their parents for much of their knowledge about the world. The ability to communicate has opened new worlds; the vehicle for this communication is language.

Much of people's behavior is seen through language. Our day-to-day interactions with people are largely verbal. We exchange information in the classroom and on the phone; we talk to sales people and to parents and friends. From the moment we awake in the morning, we use language to communicate ideas. Of course, behavior cannot be measured only through language skills. It is quite difficult to deal with the effectiveness of behavior without first seeing how language operates and how it represents what people may or may not be thinking.

Until recently, the study of language has largely been left to linguists. Linguists studied the structure of language, how people produce speech, and the development of words and sentences. But in the past two decades psychologists too have undertaken the task of trying to understand language. Clearly language is a behavior, and psychology is the study of behavior. There has thus been a marriage between psychology and linguistics; this marriage created specialists who call themselves psycholinguists. **Psycholinguists** are concerned with how language is acquired, perceived, comprehended, and produced.

The "miracle" of language acquisition in children has long puzzled linguists and psycholinguists; how could an infant with rudimentary thinking skills acquire a mature language like English? In studying language, psycholinguists have often begun with the study of grammar. For most of us the

Psycholinguistics The study of how language is acquired, perceived, comprehended, and produced.

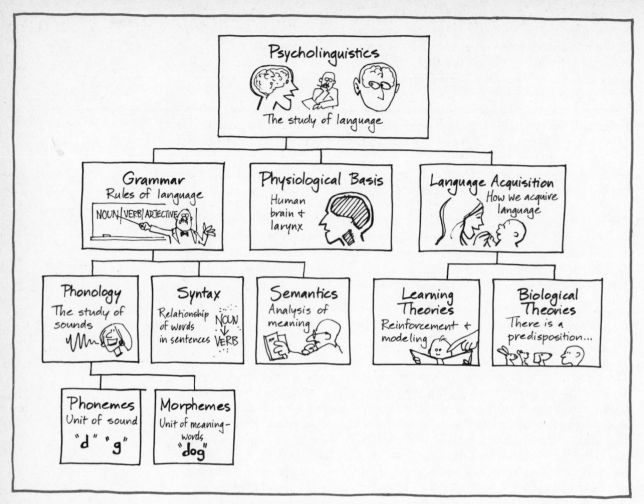

Like other areas of psychology, psycholinguistics has been shown to be complex and multifaceted.

Grammar The linguistic description and rules for how a language functions.

study of grammar evokes images of seventh-grade teachers telling us about a noun being a name for a person, place, or thing. However, grammar represents more than parts of speech. **Grammar** is the linguistic description of a language; a grammar contains the rules of how a language works. By studying such aspects of language and especially by seeking how it develops in young children, psycholinguists attempt to understand the nature of language.

In studying language we examine three major components: *phonology,* the study of the sounds of language; *syntax,* the study of the relationship between words and how they combine to form sentences; and *semantics,* the study of meanings of words and sentences.

Psycholinguists study a child's grammar in hopes of learning how and why it may have developed in a particular way. With the developmental approach, they try to assess the relative contributions of nature and nurture. If language has a strong biological basis, then many aspects of language should be evident early in a child's life. Furthermore, all children, regardless of their culture or language, should develop a grammar in a similar way. The relative contribution of the environmental side would be strengthened if the role of learning in language development were found to be more prominent.

Phonology

Early in life children make speechlike sounds. At 6 weeks of age (to the delight of their parents) they begin to coo. During the first 12 months the frequency of making sounds increases with many changes in the types of sounds made; older infants combine sounds into pronounceable units.

The basic units of sound that infants make and that compose the words in a language are called its **phonemes.** Examples of phonemes in English are the sounds of the letter *b* and *p*; other phonemes are *f* and *v*. Still other phonemes in English are a combination of more than one sound to make a more complex basic sound unit, for example, the *w* and *h* sounds that are combined in the single *wh* phoneme in *wh*eeze. Depending on how they are combined, there are 45 different phonemes in English. All the words of English are composed of these 45 basic sounds.

Words consist of **morphemes,** the basic unit of meaning in a language. A morpheme is one or more phonemes strung together to make a meaningful unit. A morpheme like *do* is made up of two phonemes, the sounds of the letters *d* and *o*. Words can easily be put together by adding prefixes and suffixes to existing morphemes. The morpheme *do* can have *ing* or *er* added to it to make *doing* or *doer*. At the beginning level, an infant may take the sound of the letters *m* and *a* and string them together to make the morpheme *ma*; this simple morpheme serves an infant very well and is often one of the first utterances that parents can distinguish as a meaningful unit. Morphemes like *ma* often refer to a specific object or person. These initial utterances are clearly words. Frequently heard words are *bye-bye, mama,* and *bebe*.

At about 1 year, children utter the first sounds that we classify as real speech. They may have one, two, or even four or five words that refer to objects or people. In the next year of life, vocabulary will increase to about 50 words and by the age of 3 to as many as 1,000 words (Figure 8.1, p. 348). When Nelson (1973) conducted an intensive investigation into children's language, she found that their first words referred to food, toys, and animals. So it is likely that a child's first words might be *juice, milk, cookie, block, truck,* or *dog*. The number of words a child may have by 18 months varies dramatically. At 18 months some children have only three or four words; others have as many as a few dozen.

Syntax

Syntax is the study of the relationship between words and how they combine to form sentences. Once children have a vocabulary of words that have distinct meanings for them, they can begin to string these words together. Basic two-word sentences are really quite amazing. When children say, *milk allgone, daddy allgone, doggie allgone,* or *apple allgone,* they show that they know how to string words together into a meaningful basic sentence. As is shown in Figure 8.2, p. 349, the mean length of sentences increases at a fairly regular rate as the child grows older. Brown (1970) has pointed out that the emergence of the use of sentences appears at different ages. However, once the use of sentences begins, its rate of development is fairly steady.

When pairs of words are uttered together, a child can convey much more to a listening adult. The 18-month-old may make assertions like *mama look* or *bye-bye mama*. Initial attempts to study such utterances suggested that the

Phonology The study of the sounds of language termed phonemes.

Phonemes The basic units of sound in a language.

Morpheme The basic unit of meaning in a language.

Syntax The relationships of groups of words and how words are arranged into phrases and sentences.

347

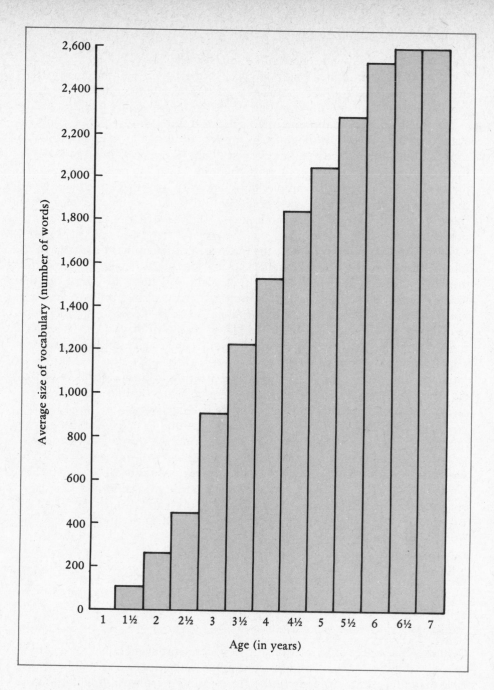

Figure 8.1 Children's average vocabulary size increases rapidly between the ages of 1½ and 6½ (data adapted from Moskowitz, 1978, on work done by Smith)

order or position of the words and their type could describe early speech (Braine, 1963); later analysis showed these descriptions were inadequate (Bowerman, 1973). Other investigations have suggested that young children have an innate grammar and that they use grammatical relationships in a way similar to adults (McNeill, 1970a). But again, children's speech at this stage does not seem to follow a simple, orderly pattern—sometimes children seem to use words in the wrong order. In fact, there is not enough evidence to conclude firmly that children use the structures of subjects and verbs in a meaningful way; the two-word utterances of the 2-year-old are not systematic and grammatical.

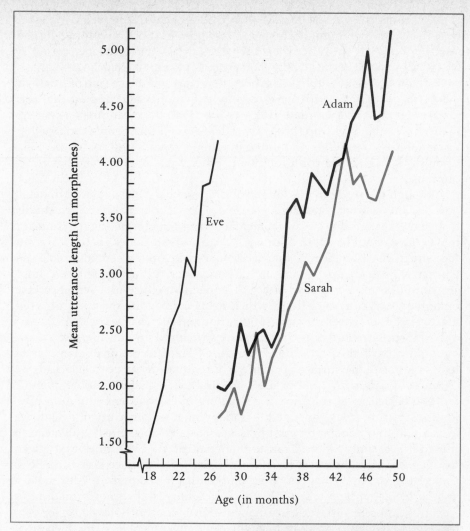

Figure 8.2 The length of children's utterances increases as they get older. Children start to develop language at different ages, but they tend to develop language at a similar rate

"This is mommy's nose." Children's early speech is simple and concrete.

TRANSFORMATIONAL GRAMMAR. Do children have language acquisition built in or preprogrammed? This was the major question underlying the concerns of linguists in 1957 when they considered the problems raised by Noam Chomsky. The study of grammar came into sharp focus in 1957; in that year Noam Chomsky published a book that changed the course of linguistic theory. In it he described transformational grammar and argued that each person is born with the innate ability to transform the meaning of a sentence to the words that make up the sentence. He argued that people can use their inborn ability to generate an infinite number of meaningful sentences. Since Chomsky's original contribution, many other types of grammars have been put forth.

Although the study of the sounds of language has been explored in detail, how and under what conditions people develop a grammar has been studied to a much greater extent. A fundamental idea of **transformational grammar** is that each sentence has both a surface structure and a deep structure. The **surface structure** is the form of the words that make up the sentence; so a sentence may be made up of a noun phrase and a verb phrase and have a simple structure like *Alex gave Mary a dog*. The **deep structure** of a sentence is an underlying structure or pattern which helps convey the meaning of a sentence. So the sentences *Alex gave Mary a dog* and *Alex gave a dog to Mary* have different surface structures, but they are structured around the same meaning—they have the same deep structure. Transformational grammar attempts to relate the surface structure of a sentence to its deep structure.

Since a grammar is a set of rules, we find that transformational grammar has two basic sets of rules, phrase structure rules and transformation rules. Phrase structure rules generate the underlying deep structure of a sentence, breaking it into noun and verb phrases; associated rules break down each of these phrases still further. Transformational rules are the rules that govern the changes from the deep structure to a particular surface structure. So an underlying structure may be based on the idea that a person, Alex, gave to another person, Mary, a dog. This deep structure can be transformed into at least two different surface structures, including *Alex gave Mary a dog* or *Mary was given a dog by Alex*. Both have the same meaning *and* same deep structure.

At present, the evidence suggests that 2-year-olds do not have a system of rules that relate surface to deep structure. Five- and 6-year-olds have limited ability to make complex transformations. The development of the major transformations of grammar, which include embedding sentences within one another, takes place from ages 6 through 12 (Ingram, 1975).

Chomsky's transformational grammar has generated a great deal of psychological research into the way people code and retrieve complex sentences. According to transformational grammar, the more complex a sentence or idea, the more levels of analysis will be necessary to code and remember it. Thus a sentence like

The ants in the kitchen ate the sweet jelly which was on the table.

contains four basic ideas.

There are ants in the kitchen.
There was jelly on the table.
The jelly was sweet.
The ants ate the jelly.

Transformational grammar The approach to studying the structure of a language, originally developed by Chomsky, which asserts that each *surface structure* of a sentence has associated with it a *deep structure*. This grammar has transformational rules associated with it to generate surface structures from deep structures.

Surface structure The organization of a sentence which is closest to its written or spoken form.

Deep structure The organization of a sentence which is closest to its underlying meaning.

Bransford and Franks (1971) investigated whether complex sentences are coded in some meaningful way that does not depend on word order. They presented subjects with sentences that were made up of the different basic ideas like the ones above; each sentence contained one, two, or three ideas, but never four. Afterward, they were shown longer sentences, including several with up to four ideas, that they had not heard before. The subjects reported with highest confidence levels that they had previously heard these four-idea sentences even though these sentences had *never* been presented to them. To think this, they must have combined the information from the two- or three-idea sentences to generate one complex idea. Bransford and Franks interpreted this result to mean that subjects had extracted a complex idea from the shorter sentences and stored the overall idea rather than the specific words or sentences. Thus, the meaning of sentences and the level of analysis seem far more important than the specific words or word structure (James & Hillinger, 1977; Sachs, 1967).

Transformational grammar as presented by Chomsky (1957, 1972, 1975) is not the only linguistic description of a language. However, it has been so widely used, tested, and written about that it clearly is the principal way many linguists and psychologists think about grammar.

Semantics

As infants, children do not understand fully the meaning of their parents' utterances. However, as time passes, they come to understand more; as each month passes, still more words take on meaning. **Semantics** is the analysis of meaning. Consider the sentence, *Now, this guy is fast!* What are the potential meanings of this sentence? It is really quite impossible to tell out of context; it might mean that the man is smart; this would be the slang usage of the word *fast*. It might also mean that he is sneaky, using the word *fast* to refer to his "pulling a fast one." The word *fast* might even mean that the man is slow

Semantics The study of the meaning of components of language.

Play provides an opportunity to be creative and to practice newly acquired skills of language and thought.

or stupid, if the sentence were said in an ironic context. Of course, the word *fast* might really mean that the man is moving quickly.

Thus, single words can convey a variety of meanings, and in trying to understand the meaning of language, the psycholinguist is faced with having to understand not only the meaning of single words, but their relationship to other words. Meaning is more than just referring to or imagining an object or event. When strung together, individual words are not the mere addition of their individual definitions; therefore, in studying meaning, we study both word meaning and sentence meaning.

To study meaning (semantics) adequately, psychologists have recognized that they have to understand word meaning, the relationship among words, and how words are placed together in a context that allows for thought to be generated. Studies of semantics are complicated because they involve so many elements. It is not surprising then that this is the least understood aspect of language.

How We Learn Language: Nature vs. Nurture

We can examine environmental effects on language development by studying the case reports of sensory-deprived infants. Case reports have been provided of infants who have been left in situations in which they have been deprived of stimulation by being locked in rooms apart from the world. One such report was presented by Davis (1947) who described a child named Anna. From $5\frac{1}{2}$ months of age until 6 years of age, the child was kept in an atticlike room on the second floor of a house by an emotionally unstable, frightened adult. During this time Anna received only enough care to keep her alive; her diet consisted almost solely of milk. Anna's contact with the outside world was nonexistent. She could not walk, talk, or do anything that showed normal intelligence.

Two years after being discovered Anna was able to walk, understand some simple commands, feed herself, and remember some people. But she was unable to speak. By the time Anna was $10\frac{1}{2}$-years-old, just before her death from an unrelated ailment, she had begun to develop simple speech. She talked mainly in phrases, would repeat words, and would try to carry on a conversation.

A similar, even sadder report has been presented by Curtiss (1977) who described a child called Genie who was confined to a small back bedroom, harnessed to an infant's potty seat, and left unable to move. Restrained either in a harness or in a straitjacket, Genie heard no sounds, nor saw the light of day for years. Force-fed and deprived of all types of stimulation, Genie grew into a malnourished, underdeveloped child. At 13 years of age when she was discovered, Genie's language development consisted of understanding a few words (rattle, bunny, red, blue, green, and brown) to which she always responded in the same way. Genie was faced with learning her first language at age 13. She has never developed *normal* language. Today, she has language and can develop new sentences of her own design, but her language is constrained and rule governed. She has been taught the rules of language in specific and precise ways. They were not acquired naturally within the usual time period.

By studying the processes of language acquisition in a deprived child like Genie, psycholinguists can gain a great deal of information about the course of language acquisition. In the case of Genie they have focused on the extent of her language learning *after* the period during which most people's language development is complete. Of course, psycholinguists already have a great deal of data about how children learn language. They know the types of sounds that children make, and they know the length of sentences at different ages. They can also analyze how words are strung together into meaningful sentences. With all of these data psychologists and linguists have tried to place language acquisition within a meaningful context. Approaches that have been developed to explain language acquisition have generally revolved around an issue that rears its head so often in psychology, nature versus nurture. Some of the theories are biologically based and some are based on environmental factors. Few serious researchers adhere to a strictly biological approach, and most do not favor a purely environmental one either. The real issue is to determine what the relative contribution of nature is compared with nurture.

Nurture: Learning Theories

On the environment side of the language-acquisition debates are the learning theorists who argue that language is learned. However, there are two groups of these theorists. Those who favor a *conditioning approach* argue that language is learned through traditional learning principles. Using this approach Staats (Staats & Staats, 1963) argued that the specific reinforcement of infants leads to words being produced. Similarly, reinforcement of words in combination leads to the production of sentences.

Parents provide reinforcement by becoming excited, poking, touching, patting, and feeding children upon hearing vocalization. A mother's glee upon hearing her child's first real word is exciting. Thus, Staats argues that acquiring language becomes reinforcing in itself. Once a child is able to ask questions and communicate, the reinforcement of using words and sentences grows even greater. A mother says to her child, *Is daddy going outside?* The child responds, *Allgone daddy.* The mother responds by reinforcing the child, *That's right, daddy is allgone, daddy allgone.* There are even data from studies with chimps which show that through instrumental training procedures, chimps can be taught to communicate.

A serious weakness of conditioning explanations of language is that parents pay little attention to the grammatical structure of a child's speech and often reinforce children for improper forms—yet children still learn language (Slobin, 1975). From Slobin's view, "A mother is too engaged in interacting with a child to pay attention to the linguistic form of his utterances" (p. 290). Thus, while parents will approve of true statements and criticize false ones, the parent does so without regard to its grammatical correctness.

In summary, the conditioning approach to learning language argues that the reinforcement of parental approval and the self-reinforcement of speech increases the probability that children will emit words and sentences. For those who believe in a conditioning approach to language acquisition, the experience that a child has in the formative years is critical.

A second learning theory of language acquisition is that of *imitation*, or copying adult speech. Children copy the speech of adults and often repeat it over and over again. By imitating the speech of an adult, a child copies the use of proper forms of language. The child sometimes is reinforced for copy-

Learning Language

If we knew how people learned language, then we would have the key to education; this is an idea that has been expressed repeatedly through the years by English teachers and especially elementary school teachers. Educators place heavy emphasis on the ability of individuals to communicate their ideas effectively; this is certainly not an unreasonable idea. Without a knowledge of a language, how can a person affect other people in even the simplest ways? The deaf, who do not have a natural spoken language, develop a language to communicate with the world. Sometimes the deaf learn to communicate with sign language; at other times they learn natural spoken English. In any case, they learn to communicate their ideas so as to make themselves understood. The research on how people learn language is mixed with varying views of how a child learns language. Some researchers adopt a strictly biological approach; others, a strictly learning approach; still others suggest both approaches. Let us examine three simple but elegant approaches that have examined language development.

If learning a language is a result of conditioning procedures, is it possible to increase the use of language by young children? Can the frequency of infant vocalizing be increased if the adult makes a social response after the child has vocalized? Three-month-old children living in an institution served as subjects in a study designed to answer this question (Rheingold, Gewirtz, & Ross, 1959). An experimenter would lean over an infant with an expressionless face; the number of vocalizations that the infant made were counted. During the next couple of days the experimenter reinforced vocalizations by smiling, making noises, and touching the infant's stomach. In the last days of the study, the experimenter returned to the initial situation in which he did not reinforce vocalization.

The results of the study showed that reinforcing vocalization by touching, smiling, and making noises increased the amount of infant vocalizing. When the experimenter returned to the no-reinforcement conditions, the frequency of vocalizing decreased. The experimenters concluded that adult responses affect the vocalizing of a young infant. They suggested, "mothers might be able to increase or decrease the vocal output of their children by responses they make when the children vocalize." Vocalizing can be conditioned.

Vocalizations in infancy may have nothing to do with language development; there is considerable debate whether the babbling of an 8-month-old has anything to do with the language of a 4-year-old child. Clark (1973) has proposed that as children learn language, their initial knowledge of word meaning is very superficial and that through experience the child will develop a finer meaning of a word. From Clark's view, a child initially overextends the use of a word to include many other objects that are similar in appearance. Clark refers to this extended use of a single word as *overgeneralization;* children overgeneralize and call similar objects by the same name. For example, initially the name for all four-legged animals is dog. Of course, the child has the perceptual abilities to distinguish between dogs, cats, and sheep. However, the child has not yet refined the use of the word *dog* only to dogs. Through experience and narrowing down the finer meaning, a child learns the adult meaning of a word. Clark does not rely on reinforcement principles, and her ideas are applicable only to learning the meaning of words.

Much of the evidence for overgeneralization comes from studies of language acquisition in which researchers have listened to the speech of infants and toddlers. By recording their vocalizations, investigators can track how and under what situations children use cer-

ing the adult speech, but the imitation model does not require that reinforcement exist.

Although children imitate adult speech, this is probably not the only way children go about learning language. If this were the way language was learned, children's speech would be grammatical all the time, because adults generally speak grammatically. A child can be told to correct her grammar and say, *I don't have any more,* rather than, *I don't have no more,* and she can repeat it several times. Still, when asked to say that sentence again later, she will very likely say, *I don't have no more.* However, children *do* imitate and learn certain rules and speech patterns from parents. For example, the dialects of different areas of the country are learned from imitation; children from Brooklyn are rarely heard saying, *Y'all come back now.*

tain words. With older children investigators have been able to ask questions. For example, a 5-year-old might be involved in a study in which the following dialogue takes place between a researcher (R) and a child (C):

R: What's a brother?

C: It's a boy.

R: Are all boys brothers?

C: Yes.

R: Is your father a brother?

C: No, because he's a man.

Notice that from this dialogue the researcher is able to infer that the child has excluded adult men from being brothers; the child has defined *brother* in a way that *boy* and *brother* become synonyms (Clark, 1973; Piaget, 1928). Six- and seven-year-olds do not make such errors but rather limit the generality of the word *brother*.

From Clark's view, such data show that the addition of new ideas refines the word *brother*. Once the child has defined *brother* as a male, the child also needs to add that age is irrelevant, that a brother is a sibling, and that if a boy has a brother that means he also is a brother. Clark suggests that each of these four aspects of the word *brother* are added; once added, children stop overgeneralizing and limit the word *brother* only to true examples.

Clark's (1973) view of how children learn word meanings has been expanded upon by other researchers. For example, Anglin (1977) has shown that children undergeneralize as well. So, word meaning is not acquired in a simple way, rather children learn to limit their overgeneralizations (and undergeneralizations) in order to bring their use of words in closer agreement with accepted adult usage.

To investigate how children develop other language abilities, Brown and Berko (1960) examined the ability of adults and children to use new words grammatically. Adults and children were presented a sentence containing real words and nonsense words. For example, they were shown the sentence, *Let's wug some fish*. The children were then asked to use the word *wug* correctly in another sentence. A typical response was something like, *The fish were wugged yesterday*. This response shows that the child had used *wug* as a verb, perhaps referring to the words *catch* or *feed*. Whatever the word was referring to, the children and adults used the word in accordance with its part of speech as established in the original sentence. Brown and Berko found that scores on this type of test improved regularly with age. They concluded that formal changes in word association and skill in placing words in their proper grammatical context are part of a child's developing ability to use English syntax.

The three research programs used different approaches to the study of language, and they used different age children in their studies; in some ways, this makes these studies difficult to compare. However, the studies lend support to the idea that language is learned. All three studies argue that specific sounds, meanings, or constructions are learned. These studies, taken together with other studies, lend strong support to the idea that language acquisition is a learned phenomenon, at least in part. The studies do not rule out the biological component to language; at the same time, they require that learning is an important part of language acquisition. As has often been shown in psychology, the nature vs. nurture issue is not a simple one, both nature and nurture account for many behaviors, including language acquisition.

While both the conditioning and imitation approaches have utility in explaining how some of language is learned, there are two serious weaknesses with learning approaches in general. First, learning theories do not explain why speakers can generate an infinite number of sentences. The rules for generating language, grammar, allow for an indefinite number of possible sentences—neither conditioning approaches nor imitation approaches fully account for the ability of speakers to generate not only new sentences, but also a wide variety of syntactic combinations which they may never have previously encountered or used. This ability to generate new sentences is a serious problem for these two learning approaches. As you will see in a moment, this is not true for biological approaches.

The second serious weakness of learning approaches is that these theories do not take into account some kind of a biological or maturational readiness factor. For example, reading written language is initiated at about age 6. However, all children do not and cannot read at the same time; some children show reading readiness earlier than others. Readiness implies that appropriate development must have taken place before children can learn. This reading readiness must be to a great extent biologically determined; if it were not, parents should theoretically be able to teach a young infant to read soon after birth.

These two problems with the use of learning approaches imply that learning is not the sole mechanism by which language is acquired, even though learning is used to a great extent; it is important that we examine the alternative approach.

Nature: Biological Theories of Language

Some linguists maintain that language is learned in part through a child's experiences and in greater part because of innate linguistic capacities. This approach to language admits that environmental variables of hearing speech and being reinforced are important. However, this approach asserts that part of language is innate and that most children learn the rules of grammar at a very early age. Researchers like Eric Lenneberg (1967) have argued that people are born with a predisposition toward grammar. Language, then, unfolds as people interact with their environment.

Lenneberg (1967) argued that there is an innate *biological determinant* of language behavior. This notion suggests that organisms are born with a capacity for language and have an innate readiness to produce language. This view argues that language is not wholly learned, but that some portions of it are inborn. Certain aspects of language seem to be universal to all people. For example, transformational grammar is acquired in some form by all humans, regardless of their culture. Furthermore, all cultures use some structures that function as nouns and verbs. Lenneberg argued that children's capacity to learn language is a consequence of maturation, and he speaks of a critical period for language acquisition. He argued that at birth and in the early months, maturation limits the infant's ability to speak. In contrast, however, by about 18 months to 2 years, children have developed the ability to speak and use language; their neurological capabilities have matured so that language acquisition is possible. Additional support for the biological approach is provided in studies of language in chimps; you will see later that these studies show that chimps can develop some language abilities. Researchers argue that part of this ability is inborn. Thus, the biological approach suggests that organisms are born with a capacity for language, almost as if they were prewired, with experience being the trigger that activates the already existing framework.

According to Lenneberg, the brain continues to develop from birth until about age 13, and during this period the children can continue to develop a grammar and the rules for learning language. After age 13 there is little room for improvement or change in the neurological structures. Lenneberg argued that brain-damaged children who lose speech and language can relearn some speech and language, whereas adults or adolescents who lose language and speech are unable to reacquire the same language ability because their brains are no longer developing.

Serious criticisms of some of Lenneberg's original claims have been made, especially of the idea that there is a critical period of language development. Lenneberg asserted that language acquisition continues until puberty and that the optimal period of language development is at age 2. He further suggested that lateralization of brain function is not complete until puberty. (We will examine lateralization more fully later in this chapter, p. 379.) Krashen (1973) and Kinsbourne (1975) have attacked these conclusions and Lenneberg's original data. For example, certain data suggest that lateralization of function is present at birth (see, for example, Entus, 1977; Witelson & Pallie, 1973). In addition, the case of Genie presented earlier (Curtiss, 1977) shows that language can develop after puberty when brain development is supposed to be complete. Lenneberg's specifics have been challenged, but even his strongest critics do not rule out his basic ideas about the biological base of language.

Overall, the biological approach suggests that there is an interaction between children's native predisposition for language and their environment. This approach does not rule out the necessity for interacting with language; it assumes that language acquisition is the acquiring of a series of rules that allow children to generate sentences.

Language and the Chimp: Nature vs. Nurture, Continued

The brains of humans have been analyzed in detail to learn if they are specialized for language in any way. The literature shows that the brain is not symmetrical in function and that certain areas seem specialized for language development. In attempting to analyze the potential contribution of nature and nurture in language, psychologists have analyzed extensively the psychology of human language. The focus has generally been on human language because language has always been thought to be a unique quality of human beings. There was never any thought to examining the nature vs. nurture issue with nonhumans because nonhumans have never been thought to have language abilities. Historically, attempts to teach animals to speak and use language have been failures (Kellogg, 1968). These attempts led most psycholinguists to conclude that there was no evidence that any nonhuman has the capacity to acquire language.

Recently major research projects have shown that chimpanzees can develop certain aspects of language. The chimps cannot talk; they do not have the necessary vocal apparatus. However, they have been taught to use different methods of communication. Deaf individuals do not talk, so they use a different language system to communicate. Chimpanzees do not talk; can chimpanzees have language (Rumbaugh & Savage-Rumbaugh, 1978)?

By studying chimps, researchers have hoped to learn more about language, its development, and particularly the relative contribution of heredity vs. environment. With chimps, psychologists can control and shape the environment, which of course cannot be done with humans.

WASHOE. Washoe is a chimpanzee that was raised like a human child. At 1 year of age she was brought into the home of Allen and Beatrice Gardner (1969). During the day Washoe spent her time in the Gardner's home or in their large fenced yard; at night she slept in a trailer. The Gardners and their research assistants who worked with Washoe did not talk. Instead, anyone

Nonhumans communicate with one another and with humans.

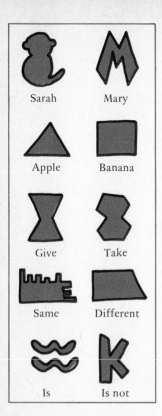

Figure 8.3 Plastic pieces that varied in color, size, and shape were used to write sentences for Sarah

Figure 8.4 Sarah was shown pieces that stood for word sentences. This picture shows the sentences *"Apple" is the name of apple* and *"Banana" is not the name of apple*

who interacted with Washoe did so through Ameslan, an American Sign Language of the deaf. Instead of being taught to speak words, Washoe was taught signs that stood for words, simple commands, and concepts. For example, Washoe learned the signs for the words *more, come, gimme, flower, tickle,* and *open.* Within 7 months Washoe learned four signs; at the end of about a year she had 12. Within 22 months she had 34 signs, and at 4 years she had 85 different signs. Eventually, by the end of her fifth year, Washoe had accumulated a total of 160 different signs (Fleming, 1974).

Washoe has learned a large number of signs that refer to specific objects or events. She has been able to generalize these signs so that she can combine them in sentences in a meaningful order. The one weakness in the experiments with Washoe has been the lack of proof that Washoe has grammar built into her language system. This weakness makes Washoe's accomplishments less exciting and convincing, but certainly no less fascinating.

SARAH. The chimp Sarah was raised in a cage; her contact with human beings was far more limited than Washoe's. Psychologist David Premack (1971) worked with Sarah and taught her words and sentences through instrumental training methods. In Sarah's training the words she dealt with were plastic symbols that were magnetized and placed on a board in front of her (Figure 8.3). In training Sarah, Premack might place several symbols before her and put a banana slightly out of her reach. As Sarah chose the appropriate symbol, he would give her a banana as a reward. Thus, Sarah came to associate a specific symbol with a banana because if she chose one of the other symbols, she would not be given reinforcement. Sarah was required to make a specific response; she was required to place the banana token on the board before being allowed to have the banana.

Gradually, Sarah developed a small but impressive vocabulary. She learned how to make compound sentences and to answer simple questions (Figure 8.4). The limitation of the studies with Sarah is that she was unable to generate new sentences on her own. For example, Sarah was able to say, *Place banana dish, Place apple dish,* and *Place orange dish* by learning to substitute different words within the same sentence construction. However, it was never shown that Sarah could generate the sentence, *Is the apple in the dish?,* or *There are apples in the dish, aren't there?*

LANA. Lana is a chimp who learned to interact with a computer at the Yerkes Primate Research Center. Rumbaugh, Gill, and Von Glaserfeld (1973) provided Lana with 6 months of computer-controlled language training. Lana was shown a series of keys that might be depressed. Symbols were displayed on each of the keys; the symbol, the color of the key, and brightness of the key were controlled by a computer. The symbols used to teach Lana were in Yerkish, a made-up language of distinctive geometric symbols. The location of each Yerkish word was varied from position to position.

Using an instrumental training procedure with a computer, Lana's trainers demonstrated some of the rudiments of language acquisition. Nevertheless, as in the studies with Washoe and Sarah, this study has not yet shown that the chimpanzee can manipulate grammatical relations in meaningful and regular ways.

LANGUAGE IN APES? These studies of the acquisition of language in chimpanzees have shown that apes are able to acquire certain specific language-

Some psychologists maintain that chimps may be able to transmit language-like abilities to their offspring.

like abilities. They are able to learn to attach meaning to symbols, and they are able to string these symbols together into meaningful patterns. Also, the chimps can use these symbols in novel and meaningful ways. It has not yet been demonstrated that chimps have a grammar which allows them to generate alternative ways of saying the same sentence. Their language is usually tied to specific word order.

A Columbia University psychologist, H. S. Terrace (1979, 1980), has suggested that the years of work done by psychologists with apes have been overestimated. Not only does he suggest that apes do not have language abilities, but that most if not all of the data reported so far only show that apes are mirroring their teachers' signs. If Terrace's analysis is correct, this is a devastating criticism.

Terrace has reported some significant differences between chimp language and that of young children. For example, in raising his chimp, Nim, he found that Nim's utterances did not increase in length as young children's do. While Nim acquired many words, she did not use them in longer and longer sentences as time passed. In addition, only 12% of Nim's utterances were spontaneous; the remaining 88% were in response to her teachers. Terrace points out that a significantly greater percentage of children's utterances are spontaneous. Terrace found there were important differences between Nim's language and that of children; he has further asserted that he could find no evidence of grammatical competence in his data or in his analysis of his predecessors. Needless to say, the researchers who have been working with apes feel differently and are hotly debating Terrace's view (see, for example, Woodruff & Premack, 1979).

Do apes have language? Yes and no. The language of chimpanzees is very much like the language of young children. It is concrete, specific, and limited. These chimps have not yet shown the ability to generate the infinite number of grammatically correct sentences. Lacking this ability places skeptics like Terrace among the majority of psychologists (see Seidenberg & Petitto, 1979). Whether further work with chimpanzees will ever provide clear evidence of a grammatical structure may be determined in the future. Train-

Idioglossia

When twins develop a private language that no other person seems to understand, psychologists refer to that speech as idioglossia. The fascinating work done with a pair of children considered to have such speech shows that it may be less remarkable than we thought. This language development may be following some of the same rules of normal language development.

TIME   For more than two years the chirpy little girls discussing potato salad so incomprehensibly in a language clinic at San Diego's Children's Hospital have been among the world's most celebrated twins. They have been tested and video-taped, charted phonetically, featured on television and offered contracts for the film rights to their curious story. Grace and Virginia Kennedy are now nine. The excitable, blue-eyed sisters called each other Poto and Cabengo, and sometimes Madame and Milady. For a while they were thought to be retarded. But at the same time they seemed to be speaking an original language. At the very least their exchanges were thought to represent the most developed form of idioglossia ever recorded in medical history.

Idioglossia is a phenomenon, badly documented at best, in which two individuals, often twins, develop a unique and private language with highly original vocabulary and syntax. It is commonly confused with a subcategory, "twin speech," a private collection of distorted words and idioms used by 40% of twins because they feel lonely or playful or both. Twins usually give it up at age three. But Gracie and Ginny were discovered at six, still unable to speak English. They had an apparent vocabulary of hundreds of exotic words stuck together in Rube Goldberg sentence structures and salted with strange half-English and half-German phrases. The preposition out became an active verb: "I out the puda-too-ta" (I throw out the potato salad). *Potato* could be said in 30 different ways. Linguists, speech pathologists and educators hoped the twins' private communication would offer a rare window into the mysteries of developing language: How is it balanced between genetically programmed neurological functions and environmental stimuli?

The twins arrived at the San Diego hospital in 1977 after proving too bright for schooling designed for the mentally retarded. Shy and uncommunicative when first tested at the language clinic, the two little girls would rush into the hallway to compare notes after each session. Their talk, Clinic Director Chris Hagen told TIME Correspondent James Willwerth, sounded "as if a tape recorder were turned on fast forward with an occasional understandable word jumping out."

Ginny and Gracie blossomed with therapy. "It was obvious these kids hadn't had much exposure to anything," recalls Speech-Language Pathologist Alexa Ro-

ing an animal to use language in ways similar to human beings still remains a possibility. In fact, it has been reported (Fleming, 1974) that chimpanzees may be teaching other chimpanzees to sign. Will these same chimps teach their offspring to sign?

NATURE VS. NURTURE: A SUMMARY.   Like many other areas of psychology, the acquisition of language is not fully understood. Psychologists know that reinforcement is used to help children learn language and that children imitate the language of their peers and parents. Furthermore, certain aspects of language behavior clearly must be innate. However, which learning or biological theory will predominate as the data unfold is less clear; at the present time the best bet is that psychologists will come to see language acquisition as a result of an interaction among the differing theories.

In any case, language acquisition remains an important aspect of development; without language, children have difficulty interacting with others and with learning. The acquisition of speech and language, therefore, is a landmark for children in their developmental process and facilitates cognitive development.

The nature-nurture controversy is by no means settled. Every couple of

main, who was assigned to Gracie. "They wanted attention." . . .

It was all but unintelligible. The hospital decided to video-tape therapy sessions so linguists and speech pathologists could first slow it down, then analyze at leisure the relationship between obvious garbles like "pintu" (pencil), "nieps" (knife) and "ho-anks" (orange) and real-life objects they apparently represented. Meier and Newport began laborious phonetic transcriptions to break the twins' dialogue down to traceable parts. . . .

Whether it was developed from loneliness or as a rebellious game or was simply a neurological accident, the twins' private communication has turned out to be something less than a true invented language. Linguists Meier and Newport now call Gracie and Ginny's speech "deformed English." What had seemed to be a vocabulary of hundreds of new words, when slowed down and analyzed on tape recordings proved to be about 50 complex mispronounced words and phrases jammed together and said at high speed.

. . . One initial mystery, "toolaymeia" (for spaghetti), turned out to be a corruption of *o sole mio*, the family way of referring to Italian pasta. . . .

But if the dominant linguistic view is that a private communication must be mostly original to be called a "language," anything spoken fluently is considered language or a "linguistic exercise." Clinic Chairman Hagen is convinced that the Kennedy case suggests there is a large psychological input in language development. Says Hagen: "They were in somewhat sensory-deprived environment, but they didn't stop at a signal system. To me their private language represents strong evidence that man has a basic drive to communicate beyond minimal needs. Language evolves to do just that."

Gracie and Ginny now attend separate severe language disorder classes in the San Diego public school system. Put in different schools so they will not fall back to their private communication, they speak jerky, passable English. But they are woefully behind in social and emotional development. . . . Both girls have motor-coordination problems. One of Ginny's teachers discovered that she lacks what Jean Piaget defines as "object permanence," the developmental stage in which a normal child, at about age two, learns to retain images he or she does not see. But for Ginny, out of sight is out of mind. . . . The twins now register IQ scores of 80 (up from 50) and have mastered simple reading and mathematical skills. The question of whether their remarkable private communication might hide a superior intelligence short-circuited by emotional problems is still unanswered.

years researchers find that the relative contributions of each major factor seem to shift slightly. New types of psychological studies are devised to investigate different components of the phenomenon and another side of the issue emerges. We see this type of evolution of theory when we examine Lenneberg's (1967) assertions about brain lateralization. In recent years new data have shown that brain asymmetry is evident even at birth. These findings have modified our evaluation of the biological foundations of language and further shaped theoreticians' ideas. Perhaps the most recent major attempt at examining how language is learned has come from the controversial experiments with chimps.

LANGUAGE AND THOUGHT

Having a large vocabulary in itself does not give a chimp language nor does it make a person an effective communicator; understanding words and their meanings is only one part of being able to communicate. At the same time, however, knowledge of language, vocabulary, and meaning is necessary and has been shown to be closely related to measured intelligence. We know that as children grow and mature, we can easily observe their changing ability to communicate through language; we also observe their increased ability to think in more logical ways. Thought and language both make rapid headway during the developmental years. When they are studied, it is often hard to separate language from thought. One's thoughts are often expressed through language and one's language might even help shape one's thoughts. This complicated relationship between language and thought began to elicit a great deal of interest when a provocative hypothesis was put forth by B. L. Whorf.

An anthropologist and linguist, Benjamin Lee Whorf asserted that verbal and language abilities affect thought in a direct way. Whorf's view was that a person's language structure determines thought and perception (Whorf, 1956). To investigate if language actually determines thought, Eleanor Rosch Heider (1972) examined if people's thoughts about colors are determined by their language. She studied the language structure and color-naming processes of two cultures that have two very different languages (Heider, 1971, 1972; Heider & Olivier, 1972; Rosch, 1973).

Heider examined the language and color naming of English-speaking and Dani-speaking subjects. The Dani are a primitive Stone Age tribe in Indonesian New Guinea. If language determines thought, then two different language structures (English and Dani) should produce different thoughts. Every language has ways of classifying colors, although no language includes more than 11 basic colors (Berlin & Kay, 1969). In Dani, there are only two basic color names: *Mola* for bright colors and *mili* for dark colors. All colors are classified by the Dani as being either *mola* or *mili.* In English there are many more than two classifications of color; for example, we easily distinguish red, blue, yellow, green. When presented with color chips, Dani subjects predictably named them either *mola* or *mili,* English-speaking subjects named these same chips according to several color groups.

English and Dani are quite different in their language structure of naming colors. If Whorf were correct, then they should have different thoughts and perceptions of color as well—language structure would determine thought. One of Heider's experiments proceeded in this fashion: the Dani subjects were shown single-color chips for 5 seconds. Heider waited for 30 seconds and then asked the subjects to pick the same color from a group of 40 color chips. Heider recorded which chip was chosen as a match.

Whorf's hypothesis would have predicted that a subject's language would determine thought and perception. Thus, since the Dani have only two basic color-naming words, they should confuse colors *within* a group. If color chip X and color chip Y are both from *mola,* then they should be confused—they are thought about as the same basic color, *mola.*

The Dani subjects did not confuse colors within a single category, *mola* or *mili;* English-speaking subjects did not confuse colors either. So, while the Dani had only two names for colors, their ability to remember (think) about the colors was not limited to two classifications. Their language did not determine their thoughts.

Whorf's basic idea was wrong; one's language does not determine one's thought. There is no question that various languages have developed specific modes of grammar and thought processes; however, this is probably because of their specific environment and culture. It has been adaptive for Eskimos to worry about many kinds of snow. The language of the Eskimos did not deter-

A person's language doesn't determine thought, but it does help organize the world.

mine their thoughts, but rather their thoughts about snow helped shape their language and the words in it.

Thought processes are very complex and a simple variable like language structure is unlikely to account for the way people think. A person's thoughts can be reflected in language. Indeed, as we ask people to describe their thought processes, they do so through a verbal exchange. Yet psychologists have found that they have been able to discover much about thought by using nonverbal methods. So, when we watch a child solve a puzzle and see the child turn a piece around and upside down, we infer the nature of the child's thought. We can see the child mentally rotating the object by watching the child's manipulations of it. In the same way, adults who are asked to solve complicated problems may make characteristic errors that can be observed; when a breakthrough occurs and the problem is solved, we can also observe the manipulations that have been made just previous to the solution. Let us explore thought processes and their relationship to language. You will see that language and perception together may sometimes shape the way people can approach problems.

THOUGHT PROCESS

Building better mousetraps is still the order of the day in a free-enterprise, capitalistic society. When people decide to solve a problem like inventing an adding machine, an alarm clock, or a fountain pen, they are calling on the highest levels of their ability. The thinking person looks for creative ways to conceptualize a problem and solves it accordingly. Researchers aim to isolate thought processes without confusing them with language-specific situations or abilities. It is difficult to study thought processes without placing people in situations where prior experiences are kept to a minimum. To this end, researchers have devised experimental situations that minimize helpful cues and previous experience. Studies of this kind try to look solely at the process of thought, not at a person's specific ability to respond with a correct solution.

Many barroom psychologists have suggested that life is a string of endless problems. Their philosophy is based on the notion that all of us must work through situations that are often difficult and are not handled with pat responses. In problem-solving situations people are faced with a task where the answer or solution is not readily evident. Everyone is faced with having to solve problems daily. People confront simple problems, such as which brand of peanut butter to buy, as well as more complex problems involving careers and marriage. Psychologists are interested in problem solving because it allows them to examine the nature of thought. Psychologists are interested in how people go about sifting out all of the alternatives that are available to them. What do people think about when they make decisions about peanut butter purchases? How do people work out all of the possible moves when they play chess or backgammon?

When people are being taught a new board game, they are usually instructed as to the object of the game. For example, in chess the object is to capture your opponent's king. As soon as people learn the object of the game, they develop strategies for solving the problem at hand—king capturing. Such strategy planning is an attempt to solve a problem. Researchers have studied chess playing to analyze how people play the game and why they chose certain moves over others; these studies have focused on the chess players' decision making in order to examine the process of thought. Understanding and identifying the steps in thought processes help researchers predict problem-solving strategies for problems not yet encountered. Psychologists also study thought to facilitate it in the classroom or teach problem-solving strategies to a new problem solver, such as a child.

A Problem to Be Solved: Functional Fixedness

When a child insists that raincoats are for rain, it is hard to argue with her. When four-year-old Sarah sees that her father is taking her raincoat down from the closet for a trip to the zoo, Sarah insists that it is not raining outside. Patiently, father explains that it need not be raining for her to wear this coat; he explains that it can be used as a wind breaker, a light spring jacket, and as a raincoat. Reluctantly, Sarah wears her non-raincoat raincoat. Sarah has exhibited a basic characteristic of most people, functional fixedness. Still too young to see it any other way, she sees a raincoat as having only one purpose, for rain. **Functional fixedness** is a person's inability to see how an object can function with more than its stated or usual purpose. Typically, in studies of functional fixedness a subject is presented with a task and provided with tools that can be used in various ways. The results of these studies show that the function of the tool is often concealed by its name. For example, Duncker (1945) asked two groups of subjects to put three candles on a door at eye level for an experiment in vision. Each subject was presented with a variety of objects including tacks, three small boxes of different shapes and colors, and other implements. The correct solution for the problem was to tack the boxes onto the door (at eye level) and use them as platforms for the candles. One group's boxes were filled with tacks, candles, and matches; the control group was given empty boxes with the items alongside in a separate part. Duncker's hypothesis was that the boxes would be seen as containers for the tacks and candles and that this assumption would interfere with the subjects' abilities to think of them as potential platforms. All of the subjects in the second group (those given empty boxes) solved the problem while

Functional fixedness The inability to see in an object a function other than one normally associated with it.

Problem solving takes many forms.

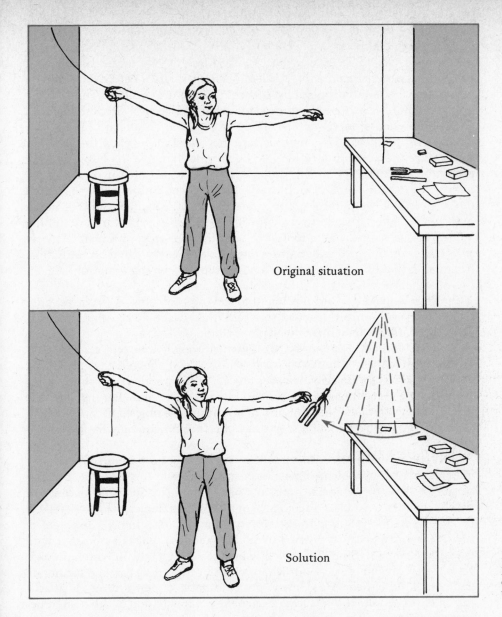

Original situation

Solution

Figure 8.5 In the two-string problem the subject must set one string in motion to tie both strings together

only 43% of the subjects in the first group (those given boxes used as containers) solved the problem. According to Duncker, when an object is used for a specific function, the probability of its being considered for use in another function decreases; its function is fixed because the observer associates only one use with the object and fails to perceive others.

Another example of functional fixedness is the two-string problem. Here the researcher leads an individual into a room in which there are two strings hanging from the ceiling. The subject's task is to tie the two strings together. However, he is unable to reach one string while holding the other. The only way to solve this problem is to set one string in motion. Once the first string is swinging the subject simply picks up the other one. Finally, as the original string approaches he grabs it and attaches it to the second string.

In the two-string problem the subject must realize that he should attach an object to the string and use it as a weight so that the string may be set in motion. Birch and Rabinowitz (1951) placed subjects in a situation in which the string could be set in motion by using one of two pieces of electrical equipment, a switch and a relay, which were on a table. Before entering the experimental situation the subjects were divided into groups. The "switch group" had previously been required to install an electrical circuit by using a switch. A second group of subjects, the "relay group," was required to place a relay within an electrical circuit before they entered the experiment. After completing the pretesting tasks (i.e., solving the circuit) the subjects were presented with the two-string problem and asked to solve it by using the items (a switch and a relay) on the table before them. Subjects who had used the relay in the pretraining group tended to use the switch as a tool in the experiment. Similarly, subjects who had used the switch in pretraining tended to use the relay as a tool in solving the two-string problem. The results indicate that prior experience with an object can prevent an individual from using that object as a tool in a new problem-solving situation. Again, this study shows the effect of functional fixedness.

Functional fixedness is a detriment to solving problems. A fixed response to an object will inhibit problem solving. Thus, if people are unable to perceive the world from many vantage points, their ability to solve problems can be severely limited. Studies have shown, however, that one can decrease functional fixedness. Glucksberg and Danks (1968) showed that providing nonsense names for objects increases the availability of their novel use. They argue that an object's use is determined in part by its name. For instance, the description *gadget* has been applied to multipurpose objects because attaching a nonsense syllable name to an item does not functionally fix it to a specific task.

Verbal labels can affect the extent to which objects become functionally fixed. How many problems have not been solved over the centuries because of labels? How many social problems have remained unsolved because of names attached to groups, ideologies, or political strategies? The verbal label of "poor person" might prevent society from approaching the problem of solving poverty because of the functional fixedness that is associated with being labeled poor. Similarly, labeling people as "mentally ill" often invokes certain stereotyped ideas about what kinds of things they can and cannot do and what kind of behaviors they might be capable of performing. By attaching labels to people, things, and ideas, people's conception of them often become functionally fixed and too often they limit the ways they can conceive alternative possibilities.

When is a horn not a horn?

Functional fixedness is a person's inability to see how an object can function in more ways than its stated or usual purpose

IMPACT

Thinking in Other Categories

You are programmed to think the way you do. Creative thinking requires you to break out of this confining program and restructure your thinking. You have a *set* to respond in a particular way, just as the starter's words "Get ready . . . get set . . ." before the gun goes off to start a race prepare you to make only one response when you hear the gun fire. This *set* is a predisposition, a limitation, a narrowing of the possibilities. Previous experience sets you for a continuation of the past, a repetition of previous modes of response. Set is the opposite of creativity. The notion of set is illustrated by the claim, "We've always done it that way—why change?" When you are set, you are in a rut.

A demonstration of the effect of set can be seen in the following example. Let us suppose you have three water jars—A, B, and C—each with a different capacity, and you must somehow obtain precisely D quarts of water. For example:

A	B	C	To Get D
20 qts.	30 qts.	2 qts.	8 qts.

How can you use jars A, B, and C to obtain exactly 8 quarts of water? In the above case, you would solve the problem by taking B (30 quarts) and subtracting A (20 quarts) and also subtracting C (2 quarts) to yield D (8 quarts): $B - A - C = D$. Now try the following problems:

	A	B	C	To Get D
1.	43	89	2	42
2.	25	59	2	30
3.	32	69	3	31
4.	52	78	3	20
5.	43	93	4	42
6.	31	61	4	22
7.	17	37	3	14
8.	41	86	4	37

When you have finished solving the problems, you may note that all of these problems can be solved by the solution $B - A - 2C = D$. However, problems 7 and 8 have a much simpler solution: namely, $A - C = D$. If you failed to perceive the simpler solution to the last two problems, you have been affected by *set*. Your experience on problems 1 through 6 predisposed you to a particular way of solving the problems, even though a simpler solution was possible.

According to *the principle of psychological set, prior experience influences the readiness to make a particular response*. Most of the time this predisposition or readiness is useful and adaptive; for the most part, what worked in the past will work in the future, so it is appropriate to continue a reaction successful at an earlier point in time. Sometimes, however, the biasing effect of set is not productive: it limits innovation and may block the solution of new and complex problems.

In a standardized, stable world, set is efficient; in a rapidly changing world suffering from "future shock," set is often limiting and rigidifying. In such a world—this world, in fact—breaking set is an urgent task (M. K. Holland, 1975; see also Luchins, 1942).

Forming Concepts

People have ideas about themselves and the way they see themselves. These self-perceptions or self-concepts often include words like sensitive, shy, quiet, likable, and private. Each of these terms describes a way people think about themselves and classify certain characteristics. When people say that they are shy, this usually refers to a number of behaviors; they may act shy in groups, they may be afraid to approach friends about borrowing things; they may even be timid about telling people close to them how they feel. When people classify a group of behaviors, events, or objects together, they are developing a concept about them. By the time they are adults, people have developed a wide number of concepts. For example, in the concept of classical music they place the music of Bach, Mozart, and Beethoven. In the concept of popular music they place the works of the Beatles, the Eagles, and the Rolling Stones. **Concepts** are ways of classifying events and objects that helps bring order to people's lives and helps them organize their thinking. People start to develop concepts at early ages, particularly in a school setting. One of the most common tasks that first- or second-grade children are asked to do is to group or classify objects. Typically, children are shown a picture and six alternatives; they are then asked to choose which of the alternatives is most like the original picture. In one such test, the sample might be a picture of a woman; the alternatives from which the children choose may be five pictures of men and one picture of a woman. The children's correct response is to select the picture of the woman. A significant portion of primary school children's day is spent in classification. They are taught letters, numbers, and sounds. They are taught about people, holidays, and historical events. On a sophisticated level we say that the teacher is trying to teach them concepts.

When forming concepts people classify objects together and set them apart from others on the basis of some common feature. There are, for example, two classifications, "women" and "men." Clearly, all women are not alike, but they do have common features that make them different from men.

Concept A classification of objects or ideas that sets them apart from others on the basis of some common feature.

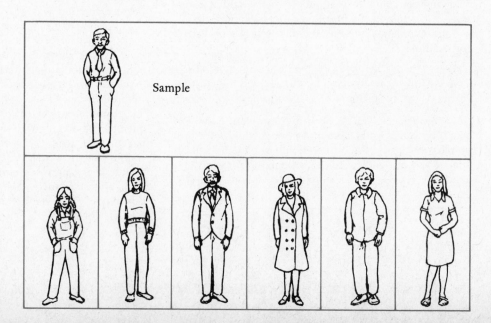

Figure 8.6 A typical classification task used in a child's formative years. The child's task is to circle the picture that is most like the sample

People classify certain groups of things as animals. Not all animals are alike, but they clearly are different from houses or humans. The ability to form categories and concepts helps people think about the world. If people were unable to distinguish between groups of things, their thought processes would be quite jumbled.

The ability to form concepts is important and basic to people's existence as thinking beings. Even in the earliest stages of children's lives, they are forming concepts. Children know parents from strangers within the first few months of life. Within a year they are able to discriminate objects, colors, and people. They can verbalize these differences by the age of 2. Admittedly, these early concepts are simple ones; however, they form the rudiments of a more complex conceptual behavior that will develop over time.

People's ability to form concepts about the world provides a framework by which they can classify events and make them meaningful. Simple concepts like "animals" and "flowers" are mastered early, but as people mature and become educated, they develop more complex and sophisticated concepts. People's concepts of good and bad, developed early in life, are constantly being changed. Similarly, their ideas about sophisticated versus unsophisticated behavior are constantly changing. While such concepts are constantly being reconsidered and reconceptualized, there are certain basic ways that people go about forming these concepts. This is the focus of researchers who study concept formation. By understanding the process of how concepts are formed, psychologists try to understand the entire thought process. Of course, concept building is only one part of the thought process, but it is a very important part. In order to eliminate outside variables and to study the phenomenon in a carefully controlled and unemotional manner, psychologists have turned to the laboratory to study simple concept formation. Let us look closely at the task these researchers use.

THE BASIC TASK. In order to examine conceptual behavior psychologists have done laboratory studies in which the subject's task is to form a concept. In a typical task, a subject is presented a series of figures. As is shown in Figure 8.7, a variety of differently shaped, sized, and colored objects is presented to the subject. The experimenter tells the subject that there is something about some of these objects that relates them. The subject's task is to identify what it is about some of the objects that makes them similar. The subject looks at the first stimulus and asks the experimenter, "Does this first stimulus have the property that I'm looking for?" The experimenter responds, "yes" or "no." The first stimulus is a large red triangle. If the experimenter responds that this is an instance of the concept, the subject knows that the concept may be largeness, it may be redness, or it may be triangularity. On the second trial the subject sees a small red triangle. If the experimenter responds that this too is an instance of the concept, then the subject knows that size is not important. On a third trial a large blue triangle is presented. If this, too, is a positive instance, then the subject might begin to think that perhaps the relevant dimension is triangularity. In all three trials the object was a triangle and in all three trials it was a positive instance of the concept to be learned. On the fourth trial the instance to be examined is a large blue circle. If the concept is triangularity, then the experimenter has to respond that this is not an instance of the concept to be discovered. The subject is convinced triangularity is the relevant dimension and announces, "I've discovered the concept!"

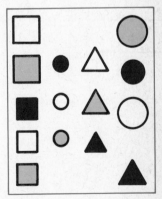

Figure 8.7 In a concept-learning task, a variety of shapes, sizes, and color objects are presented to a subject, whose task is to classify them

Dimension A conceptual feature that sets an object or phenomenon apart from others lacking that feature.

Positive instance A term applied when a stimulus falls within a category that is an example of the concept under study.

Negative instance A term applied when a stimulus does not fall in any category exemplary of the concept under study.

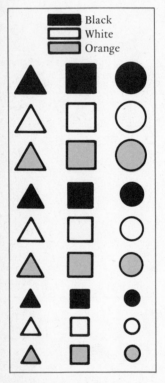

Figure 8.8 In the selection paradigm, all possible combinations of the dimensions are shown to a subject. The subject chooses which instance to examine next

Mediation A process which provides a connection between previously unconnected things.

Consider some elements of concept-learning tasks. Stimuli vary along dimensions. A **dimension** of an object is some feature of that object that sets it apart from others. For example, a large red triangle has three dimensions: size, color, and shape. Within each of these dimensions there are different *values* or *attributes.* The dimension color may have red, blue, and green instances. The dimension size may have large, medium, and small instances. The dimension shape may have triangles, circles, and squares. In the example provided above we required that the subject learn only that the relevant dimension was shape. When a stimulus falls within a category that is an example of a concept, we refer to it as a **positive instance.** A **negative instance** is an example of a stimulus that does not fall within the concept being examined.

There are two basic ways of conducting concept-learning tasks. In the *reception method* subjects are presented with a series of different instances, and their task is to classify each as a positive or a negative instance. After each trial they are told if their responses have been correct or incorrect. For example, in Figure 8.8, the subject is shown each of the 27 objects presented. The objects are introduced one at a time, and the subject's task is to classify each object as a positive or negative instance. The presentation of stimuli continues until it is clear that the subject knows the concept. After 10 or 20 trials of a subject's responding correctly to new stimuli, a researcher can be certain that the subject has learned the concept.

Another way of investigating concept learning is through the *selection method.* In the selection method the subject is shown all of the possible instances. The experimenter generally designates one of the stimuli as a positive instance. The subject then guesses what the concept is and chooses a second stimulus. Next, the subject asks the experimenter, "Is this a positive instance?" Upon learning whether the next stimulus is positive or negative, she picks up a third, fourth, and fifth instance. Through this procedure it is possible for the experimenter to determine which stimuli the subject wants to look at. In this way researchers can attempt to examine the hypothesis or strategies that the subject is using to form a concept.

Formation of Concepts

It is possible that people are able to form concepts about situations without much effort at all, almost like absorbing new ideas passively. If this is the case, as one group of theorists suggests, formation of conceptions is really just the association of certain stimuli and responses. Alternative ways of thinking about concept formation suggest that in doing it people are very active hypothesis testers and concept formation is an active doing process. These passive and active interpretations of concept formation have taken on formal theories in the literature.

TWO THEORIES. *Mediation* theorists argue that upon presentation of a stimulus, internal processes take place within the subject to produce an understanding of the concept. Thus, when we see several different dogs, **mediation** processes take place within us to elicit the concept "dog." These internal processes called mediators act as a bridge between a variety of dogs and the single response—the concept of dogs. Mediation theory provides the internal connection. This type of theory was very popular in the 1950s

Mediation is a process that provides a connection between things

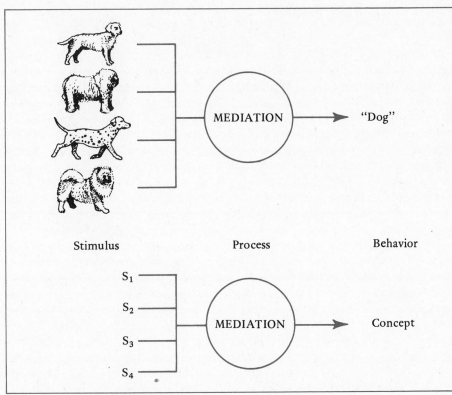

Figure 8.9 Mediation theory argues that a mediation process allows the response "dog" to all of the stimuli that are instances of dogs

and 1960s, but has since been replaced with a more sophisticated theory called hypothesis-testing theory. Psychological theory continues to evolve.

Hypothesis-testing theory approaches forming concepts with the individuals being actively involved. The hypothesis-testing model is based on the learner's active testing behavior. The subject does not have automatic reactions to connections between stimuli and responses. Rather, the subject generates certain hypotheses about stimuli, tests those hypotheses, and makes a decision. Concept formation involves the acquisition of new information by testing, eliminating old hypotheses, and testing new ones. Levine's (1975) hypothesis-testing theory predicts that on every trial, regardless of the hypothesis tested, a subject learns something that will help form a concept. In general, hypothesis-testing theories assume that concept learning is a very active process.

Young children are able to form concepts but have great difficulty in articulating their potential hypothesis-testing strategies. Clearly, an 18-month-old child cannot form a complicated strategy of color naming. By contrast, a college student attempting to learn basic calculus uses a complicated strategy of concept formation. The college student is more likely to be an active and assertive learner than a young child. Involvement of the learner may be the critical variable that differentiates between adults and children and between those who learn and those who have difficulty learning.

Conservative focusing A strategy for problem solving where the individual tries to arrive at a solution by eliminating alternative possibilities.

HYPOTHESIS TESTING EVOLVES.   When researchers first began to investigate the nature of concept formation, they identified two basic ways that subjects might go about forming concepts. According to Bruner, Goodnow, and Austin (1956) subjects either adopt focusing strategies or hypothesis-testing strategies. A *strategy* is a procedure for discovering a concept. One easy-to-use strategy that is efficient, but limited in the types of concepts that it may be used to form, is conservative focusing. In **conservative focusing** the subject tries to eliminate possibilities. If, for example, you are told that a number you have to guess is between 1 and 10, the best way of finding the number is to ask if the number is greater than 5. If the answer is yes, you have eliminated half the numbers. The next efficient question is, "Is the number greater than 8?" If the answer is yes, only one further question is necessary, "Is the number 9?" The subject need not have been so conservative; he might have guessed the number by first asking, "Is the number 6? Is the number 5? Is the number 2? Is the number 7?" It is obvious that the odds are against the subject when he gambles by choosing one number, then another number, then a third. Conservative focusing is a typical strategy; when people talk about using the processes of elimination, they are often referring to this strategy. Many times, however, subjects use conservative focusing strategies and then, at some point, shift their strategy toward a gambling strategy.

Initially, investigators attempted to examine concept formation by asking subjects to describe their strategies. Very often these studies use a selection method. As indicated earlier, in the selection method all of the stimuli are put forth before the subject; the subject can then choose any single stimulus as a possible positive or negative instance. Subjects are asked for a hypothesis as they choose an instance to be tested. If the subject picks a large red triangle, the experimenter will ask, "Why?" The subject might respond, "I think the concept that I'm trying to learn is 'large triangles.' This is an instance of a large triangle." By having the subject respond with a hypothesis on each trial, the experimenter can gain information about the subject's hypothesis-testing behavior.

Levine has developed an alternative approach to examine the hypothesis-testing behavior (Levine, 1966). A subject is presented with a trial and then given feedback. For the next four trials, feedback is not given; subjects indicate to the experimenter the stimuli they think illustrate the concept to be learned. The experimenter is able to infer the hypotheses that the subjects are using by observing which stimuli the subjects choose. The subjects' responses reflect their hypothesis testing. This technique has the advantage that there is less interaction between the subject and the experimenter and the experimenter can still observe the subject's behavior and infer the nature of the subject's hypothesis.

Using this knowledge, Levine (1975) has been able to identify three different types of hypothesis-testing strategies in adults. In *hypothesis checking* subjects test out one hypothesis at a time; this is an unsophisticated strategy and resembles gambling. In *dimension checking*, subjects test the hypothesis of a single dimension. In *global focusing*, subjects keep all possible hypotheses in mind but focus in on one at a time, ruling out alternatives as they are given feedback. Global focusing is the most efficient strategy that a subject can use and is the one adopted by most college students. To be an efficient user of global focusing one has to be very actively involved in seeking solutions and forming the concept.

People's ability to form concepts, by whatever method, is an important part of their ability to solve problems in their day-to-day lives. If people have not formed adequate concepts of themselves and other people, this interferes with their effective communication skills. If parents have an inadequate and incomplete concept of child rearing, then there is a fair likelihood that children with behavior problems will result. For example, people can form concepts revolving around ideas of permissiveness or perhaps around discipline. They group different ways of behaving toward children within these two polar opposites. Usually, parents adopt one or the other of these two conceptual ways of dealing with children. Sometimes they alternate between them; but, basically, one way of behaving becomes characteristic for the parent. Therefore, concepts can be used to organize ideas and behavior so as to put those ideas and behavior into action. Some people have more flexible conceptual frameworks than others, which usually helps them to be better problem solvers and parents. Certainly, creative people are better at solving problems and forming flexible conceptions of the world than noncreative people.

Expanding Our Thoughts: Brainstorming

When a special committee is formed to evaluate a situation and recommend solutions to a community, there are usually several people who all have differing viewpoints as to how to handle the problem. After defining their problem, committees often decide to consider all possible alternatives, forgetting their value, at least at first. They ask members of the committee to write down any and all ideas they have ever had as to how to solve the problem. Then, after making a comprehensive list, the committee starts to rank-order the items and evaluate the possibilities. Without knowing it, committees like this are using an effective psychological problem-solving tool called brainstorming. **Brainstorming** is a process by which individuals solve problems by indicating all possible solutions that occur to them; people are instructed to make no judgments as to the worth of those solutions. Thus, in brainstorming, a person or group of people is told to try to solve a problem by coming up with as many solutions to the problem as possible within a certain amount of time. If some groups of subjects are given instructions using brainstorming and others are not given such instructions, dramatically

Brainstorming A technique in which subjects are asked to solve problems by indicating all possible solutions that occur to them without making evaluative judgments on those solutions.

In brainstorming, people solve problems without regard to the quality of those judgments by indicating all possible solutions that occur to them

different results occur. For example, in a study by Meadow, Parnes, and Reese (1959) one group of subjects was told to brainstorm. A second group was told to solve the problems with good-quality solutions. The nonbrainstorming subjects were told that their score would be reduced if they produced poor solutions. The results of the study showed that more good solutions were produced by brainstorming than under nonbrainstorming. In another study which showed similar effects (Parnes & Meadow, 1959), subjects *trained* in creative problem solving produced a greater number of high-quality ideas when using brainstorming than untrained subjects. In the same way, brainstorming can be used to help individuals in writing essays or term papers.

Generally speaking, the results of the studies of brainstorming show that there is a positive correlation between the quantity and the quality of ideas produced in a brainstorming session. The governing idea behind the brainstorming technique is that subjects will produce more ideas of higher quality if they feel unconstrained by not having to evaluate the ideas immediately. If subjects make a long list of solutions to a problem and know these solutions will be evaluated at a later time, then their performance will be better. By removing the immediate evaluation, subjects are more willing to invent potentially creative solutions to solve problems. Using brainstorming to solve problems both for individuals and for groups clearly has potential. How often have people refrained from offering a solution to a problem because they thought it might be considered silly? Their idea might have been the best solution. Brainstorming is a way to help break away from thinking in categories. It is a way to decrease functional fixedness and open up new avenues by which people can express their creativity.

Through examining problem solving and concept formation researchers gain insight into how individuals think. By studying brainstorming they can gain insight into how alternative methods of thinking might become available. We recognize that forming concepts and solving problems are only two aspects of a person's thought processes. People are faced with new supermarkets, reading textbooks, and new games; but in addition many are faced with real and important challenges in coping with their lives. When they are unable to meet these challenges, they often seek out some type of psychotherapy. However, most people face life's day-to-day challenges quite well. They take their past experiences and their present problem-solving strategies and use these tools in helping them cope with the business of the job or family. When faced with some problematic situation such as how to discipline children, how to divide up the working day, or even how to confront a boss for a raise, people usually sit down and decide what the problem is and how it can best be attacked. Alternatives are eliminated, best solutions chosen, and then a planned strategy is employed. Problem solving is by no means confined to the laboratory; yet it is in the laboratory that researchers gain insight into how people think and sift through alternatives. It is in the laboratory that researchers learn the important variables in the process of solving life's problems in creative ways.

THOUGHT AND CREATIVITY

When people are asked to solve a problem or to form a concept, they are in a situation which demands that they make evaluations. They must form a potential hypothesis about how tasks might be solved and then perhaps test a hypothesis and evaluate potential solutions. When faced with a difficult problem, the creative solution is often the best method. Creative solutions are not obvious; they are novel. A creative individual often produces the solution to a problem which might not have been conceived by anyone else. Consider the problem, "How much is 4 plus 4?" There is only one answer. By contrast, if asked to design a new museum, an architect might produce a variety of different designs. It is not easy to determine what a creative solution is. Similarly, it is not easy to determine who a creative individual is. Creativity has a high value attached to it in Western society. Creative people often advance quickly in their jobs. They are often sought out by their employers, community, and friends. Creative people are valued because of their different perspective on the world. Yet, when asked to define creativity, most people have few creative responses.

What Is Creativity?

Creativity is not a thing or a commodity; rather, it is a process. Creativity is the process of developing original, novel, and appropriate responses to a problem, artistic work, or scientific discovery. There have been many attempts to define **creativity.** Three factors seem most important: originality, novelty, and appropriateness. An *original* response to a situation is rare or unusual. Responses to stimuli that are not usually given are often considered original responses. *Novel* responses are new and often have no precedent; these responses are often considered strange and unusual. Solutions to situations can be original and novel, but unless they are *appropriate,* they cannot be termed creative. A mentally disturbed individual may produce bizarre hallucinations that are original and novel solutions, but they cannot be considered creative because they are inappropriate. An appropriate solution is one that is deemed a reasonable response to the situation. Building a home of toothpicks is probably an original and novel way to build a house, but it is

Creativity A characteristic that in general is considered to include originality, novelty, and appropriateness.

B.C. by permission of Johnny Hart and Field Enterprises, Inc.

clearly not an appropriate way since houses built of toothpicks would tend to be structurally weak. A variety of dimensions of creativity can be invoked; however, these three are more reliable than any others (Johnson, 1972; Vinacke, 1974).

Researchers like Morris Stein (1974) have examined the processes of being creative and have defined a series of three stages: *hypothesis formation, hypothesis testing,* and *communication of results.* In the first stage, hypothesis formation, people try to form an idea, a solution, or a new response to a problem. However, in formulating a truly creative idea, people cannot pluck the idea from thin air on demand. Rather, people have to have certain skills and background in that field which lay the groundwork for tentative ideas. Only then can a person constructively try to study, think, be original—be creative.

Forming a creative response is no easy feat; people have to confront situations and try to think in nonstereotyped manners. They have to explore avenues that have not been explored before and think in new ways. While sometimes creative individuals experience an "ah-ha," lightbulb feeling, more often creative people's new ideas come about through a slow intuitive understanding of the field of endeavor.

New ideas or hypotheses need to be tested. The creative person may be a scientist, writer, plumber, or electrician; regardless, creative ideas must be tested against reality. At this stage the criterion of appropriateness is crucial. Novel and original responses that are not appropriate will be useless. As Stein has suggested, a person has to ask, "Is this idea crazy?" An artist takes brush in hand and transposes mental visualizations to canvas; a composer sits at a piano and transcribes inner whisperings to audible music; a writer pushes out ideas onto paper to see if the "reasonable" idea really does have rhythm, flow, and meaning. If the sight, sound, and meaning of a work make sense and are reasonably novel, original, and appropriate, then a person feels that his or her idea has real potential. At this point, the person moves toward the third stage, that of the communication of results.

Many times creative ideas are so elegant, and even simple, that people respond by indicating that they wonder why they never thought of the idea themselves. Communicating the idea is sometimes a relatively straightforward process like uncovering a painting. Sometimes the process is more difficult and requires explanations such as when Einstein had to explain his theory of relativity.

There are huge differences in the creative process and in the characteristics of people who are involved in creative endeavors. In order to achieve a better understanding of the nature of creative processes and how people go about being creative, let us look more closely at some of the characteristics of creative people.

What Makes a Creative Person?

What is the creative individual like? Are the thought processes of the creative individual different from those of the merely normal person? Perhaps the personalities of creative individuals are different from those of people who are not classified as creative. If we understand the nature of the thought processes of the creative individual, we may be able to teach others how to become creative. Furthermore, an understanding of the personality characteristics of the creative individual might allow us to spot these gifted individuals early in life and facilitate their creative thought.

COGNITIVE CHARACTERISTICS. Are the thought processes of the creative individual different from those of a noncreative one? Guilford (1967) has defined creative thinking as a form of thought process that is divergent. **Divergent thinking** occurs in response to a problem that has yet to be defined, discovered, and solved, and when there is no set way of solving a problem. According to Guilford, the divergent mode of thinking is the essence of creative performance. With this definition psychologists conclude that any solution to a problem which can be worked out through time and practice is not a creative solution.

Divergent thinking A term defined by Guilford to mean the production of new information from known information or the generation of logical possibilities. To Guilford, also the basis of creativity.

Do creative individuals perform better on IQ tests than noncreative individuals? This question would be easy if it could be answered by saying that creative individuals are more intelligent. Similarly, this could be easily explained if it could be shown that creative individuals were not more intelligent. Some studies have found a distinction between creativity and intelligence test scores; these studies argue that they are unrelated. By contrast, other studies have shown a positive correlation between IQ tests and creativity. The data on IQ tests and creativity are still inconclusive. Of course, the lack of relationships between IQ tests and creativity probably reflects the nature of IQ tests. As was presented in chapter 7, IQ tests measure specific abilities and do not tell researchers about a person's abilities in all areas of life. The lack of conclusive relationships of IQ tests and creativity may only reflect the inability of IQ tests to tap this aspect of thinking.

Creative individuals are flexible in their thought processes. The creative are not rigid in an approach to a problem; they desire a complex array of thoughts, ideas, and data which might aid them in creative solutions (Dellas & Gaier, 1970). Thus, the creative artist may wish to work not only in oils but in charcoal, pastels, and latex all at once. The final painting may combine one, all, some, or none of the materials at hand. The creative solution to a scientific problem may involve technology that exists, which needs to be developed, or technology beyond the realm of modern science. Creative people are not functionally fixed to specific ideas or ways of working; rather, they approach problem solving and creativity in unique and divergent ways.

All children need to learn basic skills, yet creative children often need unstructured opportunities so that their creativity can unfold in natural ways. Since most educational programs are made for the average student, many bright and creative youngsters are held back by our often inflexible school system. Teachers provide standard courses from traditional books with customary outcome measures such as tests. Even in more progressive schools children are expected to learn certain basic materials by fairly traditional ways. All children, but especially creative children, should be allowed to *discover* knowledge, using their own techniques and abilities unencumbered by current educational methods.

Creativity is expressed in many ways, including a safer, more efficient bicycle.

You don't have to be far out to be creative.

MacKinnon (1962) has noted that teachers of creative students may be somewhat frustrated. Creative students are independent nonconformists, and their work may be disruptive to others. Creative students often experience great tension and strong opposites in their personality characteristics. This turbulence can be disruptive in the classroom. As MacKinnon has suggested, educators must recognize the source of creative individuals' disturbances so that they may be in a better position to support and encourage them in their creative endeavors.

Creativity, Computers, and Thought

Computers are not human; they will not cry if someone insults them, nor will they respond to nonverbal gestures such as a frown from an angry parent. But, computers are like human beings in certain respects, especially when we consider the thought processes of human beings. For example, a computer stores information, it accepts new information, and it processes and retrieves data as well. Over the years a number of attempts have been made to make the computer act as a human acts. Those researchers who have focused on *artificial intelligence* have tried to program computers to carry out some human activity in the best possible way that it might be done. By analyzing how a specific activity *might* be done, researchers have hoped to gain insight into how the human brain actually operates. Some research attempts try programming a computer to act the way a human brain actually does, not the way the brain might act; these research attempts have been called *computer simulation.*

Those who have written computer programs to study artificial intelligence and computer simulation have focused on three major areas. The first is perception. We have a great deal of knowledge of how the visual system processes information. So, many programs have been written to have the computer respond to patterns the way a human does. These attempts have tried to make the computer respond to letters or forms in the same manner that line element detectors of the perceptual system respond (see p. 197).

Another focus of the computer analogy has been in the area of memory research. The human brain stores a great deal of information and is able to retrieve it quickly and efficiently. The information-processing approach to perception and memory has been a direct outgrowth of those who have drawn computer analogies (see p. 110). When a researcher attempts to draw a flow diagram of information from the sensory register to short-term and long-term memory, the researcher is relying on a computer approach. Those who study memory extend the computer analogy still further by referring to storage areas called buffers and to central processors and memory elements. In addition, computers have also been programmed to understand and produce language; these programs have stored in memory information about the rules of generating English sentences.

The most widely investigated aspect of computer simulation and artifical intelligence has been problem solving. Computers have been taught to play checkers, chess, and backgammon. They have been taught to solve simple number completion tasks as well as complicated problems involving large chunks of memory. The most sophisticated studies of problem solving and the computer have attempted to incorporate aspects of human memory systems into the computer program.

An aspect of computer simulation that has not yet been adequately explored is creativity. Computers have been programmed to think the way humans do. They can play chess and generate sentences that are grammatical. But the computer lacks the spark of human essence; it lacks the ingenuity to provide original, novel, and appropriate responses to problems that it is presented. A computer learns and can process huge amounts of information. In seconds a computer can process mathematical problems that would take a human weeks to figure out even with the aid of calculators. But the computer has not yet been taught to respond with appropriate creative responses. It can generate novel and even original responses, but far too often these responses are not appropriate; furthermore, computers cannot yet evaluate their own ideas. Creativity remains a human quality. Perhaps someday our understanding of creativity will increase to the level that a computer can be programmed to be creative in a human sense.

The impact of the computer on psychology has been significant. It has shaped theoretical development, for example, in information-processing analysis. It has aided researchers in the discovery of how people solve problems. Furthermore, the computer allows psychologists to take their models of how aspects of behavior like memory occur and test them out. If a researcher thinks that a specific theory accounts for pattern perception or memory loss, this theory can be put to the computer test; a computer can be simulated to act in the way that the theory predicts and the theory can be tested. While the computer does not act exactly the way the human brain does, it can be programmed to act as if it were the brain. In this way, the computer aids psychologists in their understanding of thought processes.

BRAIN FUNCTIONING: NATURE VERSUS NURTURE

When watching the creative genius of a musician, playwright, or dancer, many people stop and wonder if there is some special thing about their brain or its organization that allows for creativity, intelligence, or unique capabilities. Over the years psychologists have examined brain organization and have learned much about how the brain is organized (see Walker, 1980). In chapter 2, the Biological Bases of Behavior (p. 50), it was noted that the brain is functionally divided into two major lobes or hemispheres and that these hemispheres are connected by a major trunk line called the corpus callosum. There is considerable evidence that distinctly different functions are handled by the left and right sides of the brain. The left side of the brain is especially organized for speech and language activities, while the right side is organized for processing music and spatial tasks. As we saw earlier in the chapter, biological theories of language rely heavily on the idea of brain specialization.

The evidence for certain brain functions being lateralized to one side of the brain is impressive. For example, Geschwind (1970) has found that when there is language impairment due to a head injury, 97% of the time it comes from a left-hemisphere injury. Other evidence has been marshalled to support the **lateralization** of function idea, particularly studies of split brains. These studies showed that when a person's corpus callosum has been surgically severed for medical reasons, the person has two independently functioning hemispheres. Thus, if information is transmitted to only one hemi-

Lateralization The concentration of a particular brain function in one hemisphere.

sphere (admittedly a very unlikely occurrence), the other hemisphere is not aware of it. So, if a person's language functions are lateralized to the left hemisphere, then any new language information conveyed to the right hemisphere alone will not be appropriately processed. For example, the data show that if a person is exposed to a poem through the left hemisphere, the poem is easily learned; but if the poem is exposed to the right hemisphere, such learning is impossible. An interesting study with Morse code was conducted by Papcun and his colleagues in 1971. The study showed that Morse code was processed primarily in the left language-processing hemisphere by experienced users of the code; by contrast, there was little or no lateralization of processing with inexperienced users. Palermo (1978) has suggested that not until Morse code is processed as a meaningful language medium is it lateralized to the left hemisphere; until then, it is treated as a series of relatively meaningless dots and dashes and is processed by both hemispheres equivalently.

It is clear that there is a definite lateralization of function of the brain with respect to speech and language. The evidence is overwhelming. However, it is unclear if the brain is organized in some special way for especially intelligent or creative individuals. To date, there have been many hypotheses put forth to suggest special brain organization and functions. However, most of our knowledge about such lateralization and development comes from studies of language, language impairment, and from studies of diseased brains. Currently researchers are doing electroencephalographic studies of the brain to see if there are any differences in the brain waves of special populations like the gifted and talented. However, such research is very complicated. The subject population is not clearly defined (see Young & Ellis, 1981). The tasks that one might give to these subjects are unclear. Furthermore, the exact meaning of a difference in brain waves of some special group is still unclear. The individual differences between people are sufficiently great that finding a different brain wave pattern does not necessarily mean anything important.

Studies of brain localization are not without importance. On the contrary, our knowledge about language and language-mediated behaviors has grown immensely because of studies of lateralization and brain waves. It is likely that in the future we will learn more about problem solving and concept formation through brain studies of creative individuals, gifted children, or even the exceptionally intelligent.

At the present, most psychologists recognize that such thought processes must have a biological base. In analyzing the nature vs. nurture issue, researchers must concede that certain components of behavior, particularly language behavior, must be mediated more by genetics than by environment. For example, we know that our language abilities have a genetic basis. This does not deny possibilities for enrichment and expansion by experience; however, it is our biological predisposition to language that allows our experiences to let nature unfold. In the same way, it may be that some of our problem-solving and concept-forming abilities may be biologically predetermined.

Any biological predisposition that a person may hold does not fix that person unalterably. As was noted in studying intelligence and as will be noted later when studying abnormal behavior, a biological predisposition only allows a behavior to unfold if a person is exposed to the appropriate environ-

A biological predisposition allows a behavior to be exhibited if a person is exposed to appropriate environmental influences.

mental experiences. When people enrich or expand their environments, they can maximize their potential. But, if they let their opportunities for growth and development pass by, then such inborn abilities are not readily evident. As has been stressed before, nature or nurture can take precedence; however, it is most likely that a combination of nature and nurture accounts for most behavior.

SUMMARY

One of the most complex cognitive processes is language. The study of language is useful because it provides an understanding of how people begin to think and communicate. For example, you have seen that children develop language in a relatively orderly and meaningful way. Although certain word patterns develop before others, once language development has begun, its growth is systematic. How language is learned is particularly important. It seems that there must be some biological component to language because all people develop language and have some kind of universal grammar. At the same time, there is no question that children learn language by imitating their parents and peers; parents reinforce their children's language and bring about its increased use.

No one theory can account for all of language behavior—children do imitate and parents do reinforce; furthermore, some aspects of language seem to be innately determined. A comprehensive theory of language development —a theory yet to be developed—will have to account for all of these factors. A comprehensive theory of language will probably also account for chimps learning language in a way similar to humans, at least at the early stages of language acquisition. The study of chimps and their use of language is an important and largely unexplained frontier for psychologists because it allows psychologists to study nonhuman thought and to manipulate conditions in which animals live. It is very difficult to manipulate the environment of human beings, but it is very easy to manipulate the environment of a chimp. Studies of chimps learning language are proving to be an interesting and potentially important way of studying thought.

Studies of concept formation have been used to examine how people think. Yet psychologists have not made as much headway in understanding this type of thought as we would like. We have learned that subjects adopt specific hypothesis-testing strategies; we know that they use conservative focusing and memory. But the basic nature of concept formation has yet to be firmly established. This type of research area is a particularly difficult one for psychologists. It is easy to examine people's basic mental abilities or how well they have developed language; however, the examination and evaluation of how they think are still a major challenge—processes that have not yet been mastered.

One aspect of thought processes that seems most distinctive is the creative responses an individual uses to solve problems and form conceptualizations. Creative solutions are original, novel, and appropriate. Using divergent thinking, some people can solve problems better than others who do not use it. For example, some people become functionally fixed on the use of an object, and consequently they are limited in their creativity and ability to cope with problem solving.

Overall, problem solving, concept formation, and creativity are tied closely together. All three are complex cognitive activities that are sometimes linked to intelligence and too often linked to verbal labels. Functional fixedness has been shown to a great extent to be closely associated with verbal labels. It is difficult to study thought *processes* independent of verbal levels, but psychologists are making progress. Through the study of *how* people think we can gain insight into the best methods of teaching them to think, particularly in the developmental years before age 16.

Underlying thought processes in general and language in particular is the organization of the brain. Over the years psychologists have been discovering the nature of the brain and how it is organized. Recent studies have shown that there is a distinct lateralization of functions and some of this lateralization is evident even at birth. How this specialization of function aids the developing organism is not yet fully understood; however, with new and sophisticated techniques, researchers are learning more about our biological predisposition to language and thought each year.

CHAPTER REVIEW

1. Psycholinguistics is the study of how language is acquired, perceived, comprehended, and produced.
2. Grammar is the linguistic description and rules for how a language functions.
3. Syntax is the relationships of groups of words and how words are arranged into phrases and sentences.
4. The basic sounds of language are phonemes; the basic unit of meaning is the morpheme.
5. Transformational grammar is the approach to studying the structure of a language, originally developed by Chomsky, which asserts that each surface structure of a sentence has associated with it a deep structure. This grammar has rules associated with it to generate surface structures from deep structures.
6. Semantics is the study of the meaning of the components of language.

7. There are three possible ways in which children learn language; one way is through conditioning; another is through imitation. They may also learn language because it is biologically or innately determined.

8. Washoe, Sarah, and Lana are chimpanzees who have shown that they can acquire some kind of languagelike abilities and that they are able to learn to attach meaning to symbols and string these symbols together into meaningful patterns. Yet it has not been demonstrated that chimps have a grammar that allows them to generate alternative ways of stating the same ideas. Language in chimps is concrete, specific, and limited, much as it is in young children.

9. Thought processes are very complex and a simple variable like language structure is unlikely to account for the way people think.

10. Functional fixedness is an individual's inability to see how an object's functions can serve two purposes; functional fixedness has been shown to be a detriment in problem solving and is closely associated with verbal labels.

11. In concept formation people try to classify objects together and set them apart from others on the basis of a common feature.

12. In concept-learning studies, stimuli vary along dimensions, which are features of an object that set it apart from others. Within each of these dimensions are different values or attributes.

13. In the reception method of concept-learning studies, a subject is presented with a series of different instances and the task is to classify them. By contrast, the selection method uses a subject who sees all of the possible instances and who chooses each instance to ask if it is positive.

14. In conservative focusing the subject tries to eliminate possibilities.

15. In brainstorming people solve problems without regard to the quality of judgments by indicating all possible solutions which occur to them.

16. Creative responses are original, novel, and appropriate. Creative people have divergent thinking capacities and discover knowledge using these techniques; with regard to personality dimensions, they differ very little from others.

17. The three stages of being creative are hypothesis formation, hypothesis testing, and communication of results.

18. Those researchers who have focused on artificial intelligence have tried to program computers to carry out some human activity in the best possible way that it might be done.

19. While the computer does not act exactly the way the human brain does, it can be programmed to act as if it were the brain.

20. Biological theories of language rely heavily on the idea of brain specialization.

21. Lateralization is the concentration of a particular brain function in one hemisphere.

SUGGESTIONS FOR FURTHER READING

BRANSFORD, J. D. *Human cognition.* Belmont, CA: Wadsworth Publishing Company, Inc., 1979.

CLARK, H. H., AND CLARK, E. V. *Psychology and language.* New York: Harcourt Brace Jovanovich, Inc., 1977.

DESMOND, A. J. *The ape's reflexion.* New York: Dial Press/James Wade, 1979.

DE VILLIERS, J. G., AND DE VILLIERS, P. A. *Language acquisition.* Cambridge, MA: Harvard University Press, 1978.

FOSS, D. J., AND HAKES, D. T. *Psycholinguistics.* Englewood Cliffs, NJ: Prentice-Hall, Inc., 1978.

GLASS, A. L., HOLYOAK, K. J., AND SANTA, J. L. *Cognition.* Reading, MA: Addison-Wesley Publishing Company, 1978.

SCHACHTER, F. F. *Everyday mother talk to toddlers.* New York: Academic Press, 1979.

SLOBIN, D. A. *Psycholinguistics* (2nd ed.). Glenview, IL: Scott, Foresman and Company, 1979.

NORMAL THOUGHT PROCESSES have been the focus of psychological investigation since the development of modern psychology. The study of the contents and processes of consciousness was the main activity of some of the first psychologists. The study of consciousness, like other areas of scientific investigation, has gone through periods of both popularity and unpopularity; today, altered states of consciousness are actively being studied. In hypnosis, sleep, and drug states, people's normal states of consciousness and thought are altered; they no longer behave as they usually do. These altered states of consciousness, thought, and behavior are important because they not only present different forms of behavior but may also help us understand how behavior can be changed through simple techniques. Behavior change is of great concern to therapists who treat emotionally disturbed patients. A key question for our consideration is, then, to what extent should these altered states be encouraged? This chapter examines the nature of consciousness and the effects of hypnosis, sleep, and drugs on conscious behavior.

Altered States of Consciousness

It woke me up in the middle of the night. The cat in my guts. Clawing at my belly. Digging deeper every minute. I pulled the covers over my head and curled into a tight ball of pain. My watch glared at me in the dark. Only ten hours since my last fix. No, dammit! I'm off shit for good. I ain't gonna be no junkie no more. My head was on fire. My body was soaked with sweat. My legs shook with a life of their own. My skin hurt. I groaned and pushed my knees into my chest. It wasn't even a day since my last fix!

I stumbled to the john in the dark and threw up until there wasn't nothing left to throw up. Except bitter green stuff. Then the dry heaves shook me. I crumpled on the floor, with my head hanging over the toilet. There was a brown ring around the bowl, where the water stopped, that smelled of old piss. It made me retch again and shake so hard I grabbed the bowl to hold me up. I wanted to die. I thought about sticking my head down the toilet to drown, but the stink made me pull back. My stomach twisted into a knot and exploded into retching, gurgling heaves that ripped through my guts and knocked the wind out of me. My throat was raw. My back was breaking. When my breath hit my arm, it burned into the flesh and made me shiver. I hung over the toilet. I couldn't move.

When it finally got light, I pulled myself up on the sink. My face stared at me from the mirror. It was ashy. The eyes was dead. Sunk into two deep holes. Pieces of gray skin flaked off my cheek. Vomit hung on my hair. The face scared me.

I smashed my fist into the mirror. There wasn't no other way. One fix, just to keep me from looking so bad. I slipped into my shoes and grabbed a sweater. One fix. Just to get me through this hell. And then no more. Ever again in life. I hauled ass up the stairs and banged on Bill's door. We was old friends. From back home, when we was kids. We started doing dope together. And got a habit together, too. Many a time we'd shared our last stuff and hit the street together to scare up the bread for our next fix. Bill knew I was quitting.

"You hurting, man?" he asked when he let me in. I could tell right away he was hanging.

"I can't make it this way, Bill. Gimme some stuff. I'll pay you back later."

He didn't say nothing. Just reached into his closet and held out his tools. "Here, man. I know how it is. You're in luck. I grabbed an old lady's pocketbook with 180 bucks in it, last night. So I got a good stash for today. We'll share today and cop tomorrow."

"No, man." I shook my head at him. "I'm off stuff for good. I only need to get me over the hump. This is my last fix."

Bill grinned, watching me make my vein pop up hard. He was my best friend, but for a minute I hated him for that grin. I took aim and pushed the plunger down and then up again, jacking off slowly to make the feeling last. A small fountain of blood squirted into the barrel. I pushed it down and up again. Each time a little more blood came up and danced with the heroin, until the blood and heroin were one and slid slowly into my arm. I pulled the needle out. The spot got warm, and the warmth spread. It oozed into my fingers and across my chest. Over my belly, past my knees, and into my toes. The pain melted away. I felt good. I sank into the feeling, like into a tub of warm water. It cradled me. But it wasn't like it used to be. Once it was floating on clouds and soaking in music. Now it just took the pain away and let me breathe.

Later some of the other guys came by and they was all glad to see me again. Nobody said nothing about how I was gonna quit. I didn't either. We shot up again. One more day wasn't gonna make no difference one way or the other, and everybody knew winter wasn't a good time to quit. I was gonna quit for sure. Very soon. But not right now. This wasn't a good time.

INGRID FRANK AND GEORGE RICHARDSON
"Epidemic!" Penthouse
Excerpts from a junkie's diary.

Both the behavior and thoughts of junkies are altered. Their conceptions of life, themselves, and their immediate surroundings are being determined by a potent drug, heroin. The problems connected with heroin addiction have altered, controlled, and probably ruined this junkie's life.

When people's abilities to deal with life effectively are impaired because of a drug substance like heroin, it is fair to say that their normal thought processes are also impaired. When not in some hypnotic state, awake and aware adults are conscious; their thought faculties are normally logical and reasonable. But there are many people who attempt in one way or another to alter their ordinary functioning. The junkie with a physiological dependence on heroin is an extreme example. The housewife who is in the process of developing a dependence on alcohol is a frequent occurrence. Even more common are youths who drink beer on Friday night to get high. All are attempting to change their normal state of being; whether to achieve a high, escape reality, or satisfy their dependence, these people are allowing their brains and behavior to be affected by drugs.

One need not use drugs to alter normal states of thinking. In hypnosis most people put their behavior and thought processes under the control of a hypnotist. People are willing to think, say, and do things that they might otherwise never do. In the same way, when sleeping, people's dreams and thoughts are often bizarre. Hypnosis, sleep, and drug states represent altered states of thought processes. In other words, subjects are not awake, aware, and alert; rather, they are hypnotized, asleep, or drugged. Is the behavior of an individual who is in an altered state the same as that of a normal, awake adult? Decidedly not.

By studying altered states of consciousness, psychologists have tried to better understand normal consciousness. One of the biggest problems that psychologists have in this regard is to define consciousness. Over the years, psychological inquiry has moved away from studying consciousness as a topic; only recently have psychologists begun to focus again on consciousness as an area of inquiry. The study of consciousness has been undertaken from two points of view, normal consciousness and altered states of consciousness. You will see later that some researchers see these two views as not very far from one another; they argue that they are two sides of the same coin. By contrast, others will argue that normal consciousness is a complete and significantly different state from altered states of consciousness.

Since psychologists study behavior, they have focused on observable and measurable phenomena. Researchers who study consciousness have all recognized that consciousness and its altered states are affected by both biological and environmental influences. Consider eating and sleeping. Biology dictates that as human beings, people have physiological needs for eating and sleeping; similarly, social interactions affect the way people eat and to some extent even the way they sleep. These two behaviors, eating and sleeping, affect each other. When people drink coffee it stimulates them and often does not let them get the rest they need at night. Subsequently, in the morning, due to a lack of sleep, people often drink more coffee to help keep them awake. In this case, coffee gives people more energy, but it also affects their sleep patterns. Later in this chapter we will see that the state of consciousness called sleep and its various patterns directly affect behavior. There is a complex interplay between biology and environment and both are important in normal and altered states of behavior.

So, to better understand the biological and environmental components of consciousness, researchers have examined behavior when normal conscious states have been altered. Just studying altered states does not provide all the answers to how and why people think and behave the way they do; however, by examining both normal and altered states scientists have hoped to gain some insight. While the task is by no means complete, progress has been made. Let us explore the nature of consciousness before examining some of its altered states. You will see that conscious behavior is easier to talk about than it is to measure, describe, or even define.

CONSCIOUSNESS

Each evening as people drift off into sleep they experience a few moments in which they are neither awake or asleep, nor are they aware or unaware. Sometimes this period is very brief, lasting only a few seconds, other times it lasts many minutes. A similar state of being may be experienced during a boring lecture to which an individual has stopped listening; in these instances, people feel neither aware of their immediate surroundings nor thoroughly lost in daydreams and fantasy. One can argue that there exists a range of states of being from alert and aware to the extreme of being unaware and unresponsive. This working idea has guided many practitioners: physicians speak of people as lacking consciousness when they are no longer responsive to sensory stimuli like light and sound. Some psychologists have referred to conscious processes as guiding behavior. In popular terms, when people are so drugged that they are no longer responsive, we say that they are "out of it," the "it" referring to a normal, alert, and aware state of consciousness.

While most nonpsychologists readily accept the idea that there exists a state of consciousness, psychologists are more hesitant. Over the years they have debated the meaning of consciousness. With changing approaches to the study of behavior came changes in the willingness of psychologists to consider consciousness as a topic. The problem has often been one of definition; psychologists have never been sure what they are studying. Natsoulas (1978) had distinguished seven distinct definitions, some of which satisfy many behavioral scientists; but for some, a complete and accurate definition of consciousness is not so simple (e.g., Ornstein, 1977; see also Shapiro, 1977).

Consciousness The general state of being aware and responsive to stimuli and events in the environment.

Altered state of consciousness A pattern of functioning that is dramatically different from ordinary awareness and responsiveness.

Consciousness is the general state of being aware and responsive to stimuli and events in the environment. An **altered state of consciousness** is a pattern of functioning that is dramatically different from ordinary awareness and responsiveness. These definitions place the focus of consciousness on awareness of the environment and responsiveness to it. As we arise in the morning some of us are far from fully aware and responsive. In the same way, as the day wears on, many people find their awareness decreasing so that in the evening hours they may drift off into a short nap. As people move from one state of awareness to another, their responsiveness, thought processes, and physiological responses change. A napping father may barely hear the play of his 2-year-old child after the evening meal. Yet, that same play may seem extremely loud and annoying when he is concentrating keenly on the details of his checkbook. The same stimulus produces two different responses depending on dad's state of consciousness.

When face-to-face with a counselor, it is hard to "tune out".

Everyone recognizes that different situations require different levels of consciousness. A calculus test requires extreme attention; so does playing racketball. Listening to a lecture requires alertness and attention; however, a lecturer who strays from the point is often "tuned out" for a few moments at a time. Some researchers suggest that there are different levels of consciousness, but others suggest that there are discrete differences in consciousness rather than levels (Tart, 1972, 1975, 1977). For example, suppose a person consumes 10 ounces of alcohol and we compare his intoxicated behavior to his own normal state of consciousness. Those who favor a "levels" interpretation of consciousness suggest that when a person is heavily drinking he is in a lower or deeper *level* of his range of conscious levels; those who favor a "states" interpretation suggest that the heavy drinker has achieved a type of consciousness different from normal consciousness and unique to his present inebriated condition. The mere ingestion of a drug like alcohol, regardless of the amount, changes a person's consciousness—some suggest to a different level and others suggest to a different state. Thus a distinction has evolved between levels and states of consciousness.

Theories of Consciousness

As in other areas of psychology, theory has guided research. Investigators have used theory to make predictions about behavior under various states or levels of consciousness. For example, a biologically based theory of consciousness has been proposed by Jaynes (1976). The theory suggests that the evolution of the human brain holds the key to altered states and that consciousness is based on the differences in the function and physiology of the two hemispheres of the brain. Weil's (1972, 1977) theory suggests that humans have an inborn drive to experience altered states of consciousness. For Weil, consciousness can be altered through techniques varying from drugs to meditation, but it is psychological ideas and concentration that change one's functioning. In a different and somewhat more systematic approach, Tart (1972, 1977) makes a similar argument and draws a distinction between normal and altered states. He suggests that altered states show a radically different pattern of functioning from normal states. Diverse in ideas and approaches, these theories are very controversial.

Ornstein (1977) has suggested a theory of consciousness which has received some widespread support. Ornstein's theory is based upon the physiological organization of the brain. His basic idea is that there are two modes of consciousness that are controlled by the two sides of the brain. The two modes of consciousness are the active-verbal-rational-analytic mode and the receptive-spatial-intuitive-holistic mode; these two modes are sometimes called the *active* and *receptive* modes of consciousness (see also Deikman, 1976).

From Ornstein's view, human beings, in their search for survival, have developed an active mode of consciousness that is automatic; people have learned to automatically shut out experiences, events, and stimuli that do not directly relate to their ability to survive. Humans automatically limit their awareness; to recognize the receptive mode of their consciousness, people need to expand their normal awareness. Through techniques like meditation, biofeedback, hypnosis, and even certain drugs, people can learn to expand their awareness and consciousness.

Ornstein and his collaborator, David Galin, support many of their ideas with data from laboratories of physiological psychologists who have shown that the brain is divided in significant ways and that the left and right hemispheres of the brain operate differently (Galin, 1974; Ornstein, 1976). As we saw in several chapters (pp. 53, 57, and 379), brain organization is divided into two major hemispheres that are connected by the corpus callosum (Figure 9.1). Studies of individuals who have had their corpus callosum severed surgically have provided a great deal of data on the operation of these hemispheres. One of the principal findings of these studies is that the hemispheres operate differently and may be specialized for different functions. In most humans, the left side of the brain seems to be specialized for language processing and verbal reasoning; damage to the left side of the brain creates serious speech and language problems. In addition, Sperry and others have shown that learning and memory seem to operate independently in each hemisphere, each with its own conscious sphere of activities (Sperry, 1968).

There are interesting data to support the idea that the left and right sides of the brain are specialized for different functions. Remember, the left side of the body is controlled to a great extent by the right hemisphere, while the right side of the body is controlled by the left hemisphere. Some of the important studies of brain specialization were done with patients whose hemispheres had been disconnected surgically. These patients were presented with objects in either of their hands. For example, if you present a pencil to the right hand (left hemisphere) of a blindfolded patient whose hemispheres have been surgically disconnected, the patient is able to describe it and name it easily; the same pencil, if grasped by the left hand (right hemisphere), cannot be described, and subjects only guess as to what it is. By contrast, if the patient's task is to match the object to others of the same shape, the right side of the brain and its corresponding left hand show better performance than the left side of the brain and the right hand (Gazzaniga, 1967). From such data researchers have suggested that the left side of the brain is specialized for analytic verbal functions and the right side for spatial holistic functions. These two physiological modes of operation lend support to Ornstein's

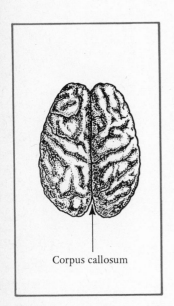

Corpus callosum

Figure 9.1 Looking from above, the brain is divided into two hemispheres that are connected by the corpus callosum

ideas and Galin (1974) has even concluded "there appear to be two separate, conscious minds in one head" (p. 31).

Ornstein and Galin suggest that our two modes of consciousness operate in a complementary fashion with one working while the other is inhibited. With intellectual activities in the active mode and intuitive activities in the receptive mode, Ornstein (1977) argues that the integration of these two modes underlies human beings' highest accomplishment.

Theories of consciousness like Ornstein's are difficult to subject to scientific scrutiny. You will see later in this chapter that when individuals enter altered states by meditation and drugs there are distinct changes in their conscious behavior. However, the relationship of altered states to ordinary consciousness and brain physiology is yet to be discovered.

Many researchers who conduct investigations that are directly relevant to the study of consciousness never mention the word. Uncomfortable with the concept, they examine the relationship of brain structure and behavior or the relationship of drugs and behavior, but avoid the topic of consciousness. Even though they are hesitant, consciousness researchers have used such data to explain consciousness and its altered states. For example, a great deal of research has been conducted on drugs and how they affect behavior. In the same way, hypnosis and sleep are situations where one's behavior is altered, and they have been studied extensively.

In this chapter we explore behavior and consciousness. We attempt to understand behavior by comparing normal or ordinary consciousness to situations that might be considered altered states. There is not a clear agreement among psychologists whether discrete and different states actually exist. Well-known psychologists like Ornstein (1977) argue that since our consciousness is constantly changing, the idea of discrete states may be misleading (Ornstein, 1977, p. 81); at the same time, others like Tart draw fundamental distinctions between normal and altered states (Tart, 1977, p. 215). These arguments about the nature of consciousness will continue for many years because understanding consciousness is one of the fundamental problems of psychology. Without providing the definitive answer to the discrete versus nondiscrete debate, psychologists have investigated how behavior is affected in these special circumstances. Let us begin with an explanation of hypnosis—clearly, a state of consciousness that seems different from the normal state.

HYPNOSIS

"You are falling asleep. Your eyelids are becoming heavy. They are as heavy as lead. The strain on your eyes is becoming greater and greater. Your muscles are relaxing. You are feeling sleepy. You are feeling sleepier and sleepier. You are feeling very relaxed."

These instructions are typical of the hypnotic induction procedure. Most of us are familiar with this procedure; we have seen it in the movies, nightclubs, or, perhaps, even in our dentist's office. **Hypnosis** has special status in Western culture. It is thought of as a mystical, special state in which individuals no longer have control over their behavior. Psychologists are particularly interested in hypnosis because of its use as a therapeutic tool, and especially because it is considered an altered or at least a different level of conscious-

Hypnosis A state of consciousness that has been altered from the normal waking state through trance-induction procedures. Subjects' responsiveness to suggestions increases as they become more deeply hypnotized.

ness. Hypnotized subjects are aware of their surroundings and the hypnotist; they are clearly conscious, yet their level of awareness and their willingness to follow instructions are altered. That hypnotized individuals are in a changed or altered state of consciousness is the traditional and widely accepted view.

The traditional view of hypnosis held by many psychologists includes the following assumptions: (1) it is a special state of consciousness that is very different from the waking state, (2) it is generally brought about through "trance induction," (3) when people have been placed in hypnosis they remain in that state until they are brought out of it by a command from the hypnotist, such as "Wake up!", (4) hypnosis can vary from light to very deep, and (5) as people become more deeply hypnotized they become increasingly responsive to a wide variety of suggestions, including anesthesia, age regression, hallucination, and amnesia (Barber, Spanos, & Chaves, 1974).

Hypnotic susceptibility The willingness to follow unconventional instructions while under hypnotic influence.

This willingness to follow unconventional instructions is called **hypnotic susceptibility** or suggestibility. Not all individuals are equally susceptible to hypnosis. Children between the ages of 7 and 14 seem to be the most susceptible. Children can be hypnotized more easily and more deeply than adults, but most of us can be hypnotized to some extent (Cooper & London, 1966; Hilgard, 1965). People who have been hypnotized report that they know they have been hypnotized and that they are aware of their surroundings; in addition, some report that they feel in a special, almost mystical trance. Furthermore, they typically report a sense of time distortion (Bowers, 1979).

While hypnosis is widely recognized and has been used for over 100 years, some researchers question its validity and reliability. Some of these researchers have shown that simply indicating to subjects that they will be in a hypnosis experiment affects their behavior (Barber & Calverley, 1965; Hilgard, 1965). These skeptics have remained in the minority, and the procedure of hypnosis is still widely used, particularly in therapy (see, for example Porter, 1978; Sanders, 1978). There are many ways to assess whether, and to what extent, an individual can be hypnotized. One way is through a suggestibility scale which tells the experimenter the degree to which an individual exhibits hypnotic behavior. Suggestibility scales can be filled out objectively by observing the subject's behavior, and they can be filled out subjectively

Tests of hypnotic susceptibility often involve tasks like arm raising.

by examining the subject's responses to questions that ask whether or not the subject actually experienced each suggested effect.

Special Effects of Hypnosis

AGE REGRESSION.   **Age regression** describes a state in which an individual is able to remember an earlier time and report events about it. For example, a hypnotized individual might relive and provide details about an experience that took place many years earlier. When subjects are given suggestions for age regression they might act like 4-month-old infants, for example, or they might even recall the exact day of the week on which they were born. Many subjects experience particularly vivid age regressions when they are hypnotized, although evidence shows some blurring of facts and details. As with many of the studies that examine hypnosis, studies that report age regression have not always been carefully controlled or checked for accuracy of recall (see also, Nash, Johnson, & Tipton, 1979).

Age regression An individual's ability to return to an earlier time in life and report events about that time in detail. Age regression may be induced through hypnosis.

HYPERMNESIA.   **Hypermnesia** is heightened memory. It is a hypnotic state in which subjects are able to remember events or information more easily and more accurately than when they are not hypnotized. The evidence suggests that hypnosis is useful in facilitating the recall of information from memory (e.g., Popkin & Small, 1979). However, techniques not involving hypnosis may work just as well for this purpose (Hilgard, 1965; see also Brabender & Dickhaus, 1978; Hoppe & Dahl, 1978).

Hypermnesia Heightened memory. Hypermnesia may sometimes be induced through hypnosis, and evidence suggests that hypnosis may be useful in facilitating the recall of information from memory.

When asked to recall information in a situation where subjects were to recall events that they had seen on a videotape, subjects who were hypnotized made more errors answering leading questions than nonhypnotized subjects (Putnam, 1979). Putnam has suggested that hypnotic subjects will not only make more errors but will believe that they have been quite accurate. This kind of result has led other researchers to question seriously the use of hypnosis in courtroom settings (see Worthington, 1979), although some are of the opinion that hypnosis can be an important aid in crime detection. For example, hypnosis has been used as an aid in various ways to help solve crimes. The FBI has been sufficiently impressed with the use of hypnosis in helping to solve crimes that it is training selected agents in techniques of interviewing hypnotized subjects. It must be recognized, however, that all states and courts do not allow testimony of hypnotized subjects to be admitted as evidence because of the suggestibility of subjects under hypnosis (Doucé, 1979).

SURGERY AND PAIN.   A number of studies have been reported in which individuals undergo surgical incisions and removal of tumors without drugs. These subjects are hypnotized and told that surgery will not be painful. Some patients are able to tolerate surgery without drugs; however, many of the studies have not been conducted with adequate experimental rigor. In addition, the effectiveness of hypnotism in reducing surgical pain has been exaggerated. In many of the cases in which hypnotism is used, analgesic drugs (pain relievers) are often used along with hypnotism. Furthermore, most patients commonly show signs of pain even when they are hypnotized. The skin is particularly sensitive to the surgeon's scalpel, so consequently, many of these hypnotized individuals have some kind of local anesthetic to dull the skin for the initial surgical incision (Barber, Spanos, & Chaves, 1974).

Control of pain has been successfully reported. In a case study presented by Siegel (1979) a woman who had undergone an above-the-knee amputation was suffering from lower-leg pain *after* her operation. Because she was tense and relaxation alone was insufficient to help her relieve her anxiety and pain, hypnosis was used and was effective. When subjects are relaxed and have a positive attitude toward the situation, they report a reduction in pain. Thus, owing either to hypnosis or the subject's positive attitude and low level of anxiety, there is a reduction in pain in a wide variety of situations including heat, pressure, and childbirth. While hypnosis has been used as a primary method to relieve pain in some clinical settings, it is used rarely compared to standard pain-reduction procedures, and its ability to reduce pain actively has regularly been challenged (Hilgard & Hilgard, 1975; Spanos et al., 1979). Perhaps the most effective use of hypnosis in reducing pain is its combination with standard analgesic drugs.

CLINICAL USES OF HYPNOSIS. There is a fair amount of evidence to suggest that a subject's hypnotic susceptibility can affect the outcome of some intervention techniques (Mott, 1979). Hypnosis is sometimes used by therapists as an aid to help patients relax, remember, or reduce anxiety. For example, some evidence suggests that hypnosis can help individuals to lose weight. In one study, a group of obese patients was hypnotized during several therapy sessions in order to facilitate weight loss. Subjects were given posthypnotic suggestions to decrease their desire to eat. These patients were taught to convert the craving for large quantities of food into an appreciation for the subtle flavors of small portions of nonfattening foods. The patients also received suggestions that emphasized feelings of confidence in their ability to achieve physical well-being and attractiveness by losing weight. These studies report positive effects of hypnosis (Hershman, 1955; Mann, 1959). Similar kinds of studies have shown that hypnosis can clearly help relieve test anxiety (Boutin, 1978), but other research shows that it does not increase academic skill learning (Cole, 1979) or verbal comprehension (Brabender & Dickhaus, 1978).

Other kinds of medical problems such as psoriasis have been affected through hypnotic techniques (Frankel & Misch, 1973). Warts have been treated by hypnosis (Johnson & Barber, 1978); even vaginismus (involuntary spasms of the vaginal muscles) has been treated through hypnosis (Gottesfeld, 1978). Many clinical reports suggest that hypnosis aids in reduction of smoking; however, there is little sound *research* to suggest that hypnosis can eliminate smoking (Johnston & Donoghue, 1971; see also, MacHovec & Man, 1978). The research on the elimination of smoking is controversial. One recent study used hypnosis and treated smokers in a single session. The study found that 60% of the subjects stopped smoking and that a follow-up 6 months later, 45% were still nonsmokers (Stanton, 1978); this study takes an optimistic approach to the treatment of smoking by hypnosis, a view not held by all psychologists (see also, Athanasou, 1974; Hunt & Bespalec, 1974).

STAGE HYPNOSIS. Hypnosis is often used in show business. Typically, a volunteer subject from the audience is brought up on stage, is hypnotized, and performs an age regression or shows an insensitivity to pain. Hypnotists instruct their subjects to perform certain amazing feats. One such feat is the "plank" routine. A subject lies between two chairs. The subject's calves rest on one chair and his or her head and shoulders rest upon another. The individual's body remains rigid and straight for many minutes. The hypnotist even may instruct an assistant to stand on the subject's chest or stomach. While this feat seems amazing to the audience, it is not amazing to a hypnotist or a knowledgeable observer. One need not undergo a hypnotic trance in order to remain relatively rigid for a few minutes between two chairs. When placed in such a position, the human body can endure weights of up to 300 pounds with little difficulty (Barber, Spanos, & Chaves, 1974).

An Alternative View

Theodore Xenophon Barber is one of the major skeptics of traditional theories of hypnosis. Barber has postulated a totally different approach to hypnosis which he calls the *cognitive-behavioral viewpoint*. Barber does not believe in the "hypnotic trance," and he argues that such concepts are unnecessary and misleading. He suggests that subjects "carry out so-called hypnotic behavior when they have positive attitudes, motivations, and expectations toward the test situation which leads to a willingness to think and imagine with the themes that are suggested" (Barber, Spanos, & Chaves, 1974, p. 5). For Barber, hypnotic behaviors are no different from the behaviors of subjects who are willing to think about and imagine themes that are suggested. If subjects' attitudes toward the situation are ones in which they expect effects, then the effects have a greater tendency to occur.

Barber has compared subjects who have been induced into the hypnotic trance with those who are told to imagine, concentrate deeply, and have positive attitudes. He typically tests three groups of subjects in his experiments. The first group is a control group; its members are given neutral instructions to concentrate or simply to close their eyes. A second group of subjects is presented with a series of "task-motivating" instructions. These subjects are told to imagine vividly, to concentrate, and to try very hard to experience those things that are described to them. The third group, the hypnotic group, is induced into hypnosis as traditionally defined.

Only 16% of the control subjects showed a responsiveness to task suggestions. By contrast, over 50% of both the hypnotic-induction group and the task-motivating-instruction group generally showed responses to task instructions. Barber concluded that task-motivation instructions are almost as effective as hypnotic-induction procedures in raising responsiveness to test suggestions (Barber et al., 1974).

Typically, Barber's studies show that groups of subjects given task-motivating instructions performed similarly to subjects who were given hypnotic-induction procedures (see also, O'Brien, 1977). For Barber, the concept of hypnotism, as well as the hypnotic trance, is meaningless; hypnotism is simply giving a conscious subject task-motivating instructions. Hypnotism is neither a special state nor a special trance; it involves no special art. Subjects who are hypnotized are willing and able to accept task-motivating instructions in order to perform specific tasks (Goldstein, 1981). Many of the spectacular feats that are performed by subjects under hypnosis can be shown to be an artifact of a hypnotic showman.

Barber's studies have received support from other laboratories. For example, in examining task-motivating instructions vs. hypnotic procedures,

Salzberg and DePiano (1980) found that hypnosis did not facilitate performance more than task-motivating instructions; they argued that task-motivating instruction was more effective in cognitive tasks than hypnosis. They concluded "when attention is paid to necessary controls, hypnosis has not been shown to facilitate performance" (p. 268).

Clearly, Barber's arguments have some credibility because the data show that hypnosis-like effects can be achieved in other ways (e.g., Holmes & Delprato, 1978; Salzberg & DePiano, 1980). Hypnosis and its techniques have been used with a fair degree of success for decades. We do not have to discard the concept of hypnosis; we have to reconsider what it is. Hypnosis probably should be rethought, not ignored. It is highly likely that it will continue to be used for decades to come.

MEDITATION

Meditation The state of consciousness characterized by intense concentration, restriction of sensory stimuli, and deep relaxation. Meditative states are brought about through a number of techniques.

Not exactly hypnosis, not exactly sleep, not exactly an ordinary state of thinking and awareness—this is meditation. While only recently studied by psychologists, **meditation** is the experience of detachment from the world due to intense concentration, a restriction of incoming stimuli, and deep relaxation. With somewhat magical overtones and claims to calmness and peace, meditators assert that the process helps calm their nerves and brings about an inner peace. While several forms of meditation exist, all try to get meditators to bring their focus of attention away from the outside world through intense concentration.

Meditation is not hypnosis, nor is it biofeedback or other forms of self-regulation or control. It is also not the ordinary or normal conscious state. Meditation is often considered a kind of hypnosis-like activity because it seems to be fairly easy to induce, and individuals seem to enter a trancelike state. In meditation individuals focus their attention inward and try to exclude all outside stimuli; in this sense it is a form of intense concentration very much like hypnosis. Also, like hypnosis, people can learn to bring about meditative states through practice. Because meditation can alter the physiological responses that individuals show (Wallace & Benson, 1972), its ability to help relieve tension, anxiety, and accompanying arousal cannot be discounted.

Meditation has its roots in the Eastern religions of Buddhism and Hinduism, and its popular forms, Zen, yoga, and transcendental meditation, have only recently been actively pursued in the Western world. For traditional meditators, the change in one's level of conscious awareness is not just to an altered or different state but to one of several levels of awareness. Meditation, according to the Eastern tradition, can bring about one of eight levels of awareness.

Each of the different forms of meditation has associated with it special techniques that help induce an altered state of awareness. For example, in Zen Buddhism people concentrate on their breathing and count their breaths; advanced Zen meditators sit in special positions. Also popular in the Western world is yoga, in which individuals focus their attention by gazing at a fixed stimulus while performing special exercises in particular body positions.

Those who practice meditative techniques enjoy their benefits and claim to find an inner peace and calmness. While the scientific community has been slow and reluctant to believe these claims, research into meditation has been conducted and theories have developed to help explain the nature of meditation. Most of these theories stray from traditional psychological ones and rely on concepts that are far from measurable and observable. It is for these reasons that psychologists have generally been unwilling to consider meditation very seriously. However, there are data to support some of the claims of meditators. Meditators have been shown to be able to alter their oxygen consumption during meditation. Brain-wave activity of meditators can be altered, and sleep patterns of meditators change. It must be recognized that this type of result has not always been found (Akers et al., 1977; Pagano et al., 1976).

Meditation is one of several techniques that can be used to help individuals achieve a state of calmness that allows information to enter their receptive modes of functioning; this is a view held by Deikman (1976). Like Ornstein (1977), Deikman suggests that there are two modes of consciousness, one that is an action mode and one that is a receptive mode. Deikman's idea is that through meditation the receptive mode is allowed to function. By switching to the receptive mode people allow themselves to permit "the operation of capacities that are nonfunctional in the action mode" (p. 83).

Experimental investigations of meditators show that they achieve bodily states similar to individuals who have been trained to relax and concentrate deeply. Meditation has been compared to hypnosis because of the deep concentration its practitioners achieve; it has similarly been compared with biofeedback, because with biofeedback, subjects are also taught to relax deeply and concentrate to bring their bodies under voluntary control (see Wallace & Benson, 1972). Serious controlled research on meditation is limited, but new studies are being conducted and breakthroughs in our understanding of this phenomenon are forthcoming (see Smith, 1975, 1976). Meditative techniques have not always been found to be beneficial for reducing anxiety (Goldman et al., 1979; Zuroff & Schwarz, 1978). One recent study has shown that in comparing meditators to hypnotized subjects, physiological responses of the two groups were nearly identical (Bärmark & Gaunitz, 1979). The researchers concluded that "meditation is a . . . state of consciousness which resembles the hypnotically altered state" (p. 237). This view is challenged by supporters of meditation as a unique altered state capable of creating profound changes in a person's physiological and psychological state (Ferguson, 1975).

Meditation is an altered state of consciousness, and by studying it researchers are learning more about human physiological responses. By studying meditation, hypnosis, and biofeedback, psychologists are gaining insights into the extent to which human beings can alter their states of consciousness at will. You will see later in this chapter that altered states are easily achieved with drugs; however, the study of self-regulation is relatively new. Far more controlled research is done on biofeedback than is done on meditation; too often the research of potentially important topics like meditation is done by followers of a movement rather than by dispassionate scientists.

SLEEP

Most people have commented at one time or another that sleep is a waste of time. Some argued that they waste approximately 8 hours a day. On the other hand, during vacations, weekends, and holidays, these same people spend a considerable amount of time sleeping. We know that everyone needs different amounts of sleep and that people sleep at various times during the day or night (Östberg, 1973). Since sleep is such a common activity, one might think that psychologists have a great understanding of it. However, this is not the case. Psychologists know a great deal about sleep and what happens physiologically when one is sleeping, yet they do not fully understand why people sleep or how sleep might help people recuperate and revitalize.

Although each of us requires a different amount of sleep, we all sleep; we consider sleep a normal part of each day. We do not think of it as an altered state of consciousness, but it is certainly a changed state of our normal levels of awareness. By studying sleep, psychologists not only gain information about this interesting daily behavior but they also learn more about levels of consciousness and whether sleep is merely a lower level or a truly different type of consciousness.

People require varying amounts of sleep. Although most individuals require about 8 hours, some people can function with only 4 or 5 hours (Meddis et al., 1973; Tune, 1969). Others, however, need 9 or 10 hours. Teenagers tend to sleep longer than college students; old people tend to sleep less than young people. Most young adults sleep between $6\frac{1}{2}$ to $8\frac{1}{2}$ hours per night (Tune, 1969). People who are active and expend a lot of energy would *logically* require more sleep, it would seem, than those who are less active; however, this is not the case. People who are in bed 24 hours a day in a hospital sleep about the same amount of time as people who are construction workers.

Everyone needs a different amount of sleep.

In the late 1950s, sleep researchers discovered the existence of two kinds of sleeping, REM and NREM. They found that subjects' eyes moved very rapidly during **sleep** and that sometimes these movements occurred in a systematic manner. These periods are called **REM sleep,** an acronym for rapid eye movements. All other periods of sleep are called **NREM sleep** periods, for no rapid eye movements.

If an experimenter records the electrical activity of the brain during sleep, distinct sleep stages are revealed. Electrodes are attached to different places on the subject's scalp and forehead. These electrodes are attached to a recorder that allows the experimenter to monitor the subject's electroencephalogram, EEG, throughout the night. As was presented in chapter 2, the electroencephalogram is a record of an organism's brain-wave pattern. Long wires are attached to these electrodes to allow the subject full mobility; thus, the subject can sleep easily and comfortably. In addition to the EEG, measures of eye movement activity can be made by measuring the electrooculogram, and measures of facial muscle tension can be made through the electromyogram.

If one examines the EEGs of subjects throughout the night, five distinct patterns of electrical activity are apparent. The first four stages are NREM sleep stages; the fifth is REM sleep. The first four stages of NREM sleep show dramatically different EEGs, as well as different behavioral patterns. When we first fall asleep (Stage I), our sleep is rather light, and we can easily be awakened. After about 30 to 40 minutes, we enter into Stages II, III, and IV. Stage IV is the deepest sleep; it is most difficult to wake people from Stage IV sleep (Langford et al., 1974; Levere et al., 1974). In the early part of the night, there is considerably more Stage IV sleep than in later parts of the night. Subjects leave Stage IV sleep and reenter Stage III and Stage II again. Subjects then enter the stage of REM sleep. In REM sleep, the subjects exhibit a characteristic EEG pattern and eye movements; they also show dream activity. There is more REM sleep later in the night. REM sleep is really a fifth stage of sleep; however, it is not referred to as such. Researchers refer to Stages I through IV separately from REM sleep (Agnew & Webb, 1973) (Figure 9.3).

Sleep Nonwaking state of consciousness characterized generally by unresponsiveness to the environment and general body immobility. Sleep proceeds in a cyclic pattern over five stages.

REM sleep (rapid eye movement) A sleep stage characterized by high-frequency, low-voltage brain activity similar to that exhibited by the awake, alert individual. During rapid eye movement sleep individuals often move their eyes rapidly and, if awakened, report dream activity.

NREM sleep (no rapid eye movement) All periods of sleep that are not rapid eye movement. There are four distinct stages of no rapid eye movement sleep.

Figure 9.2 In sleep labs subjects are connected electrically to equipment that monitors their brain waves

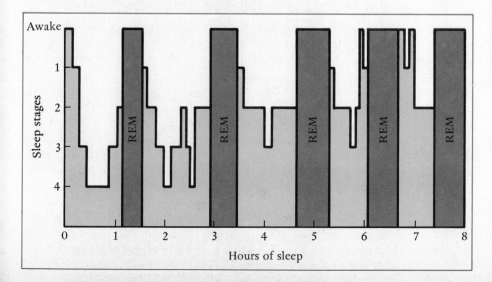

Figure 9.3 Normal sleepers experience about five complete sleep cycles per night. This figure shows the amount of time individuals spend in each sleep stage

REM Sleep   Stage 2   Stage 1

Dream activity occurs principally in REM sleep.

When the electrical activity of the brain is recorded, a number of distinct sleep stages are noticeable. Figure 9.4 shows six brain-wave tracings. The first tracing shows the EEG of the normal, awake adult; it represents a fast, regular rhythm of brain-wave activity. In Stage I sleep, the pattern of EEG activity is somewhat different; the brain waves are of lower amplitude (height) and are relatively fast with mixed frequencies. In Stage II sleep, there is also low-amplitude, nonrhythmic brain-wave activity; in addition, there are special patterns of EEG activity called sleep spindles and K complexes. A sleep spindle is a rhythmic burst of waves that wax and wane over a period of 1 or 2 seconds; a K complex is the higher amplitude burst of activity that appears in the last third of the Stage II tracing. Sleep spindles and K complexes appear only during NREM sleep. Stage III sleep is a transitional stage between II and IV; here brain-wave activity is slow and of higher amplitude. Stage IV sleep, the deepest sleep possible, has even higher amplitude brain-wave traces; these high-amplitude waves are called delta waves.

The last tracing in Figure 9.4 shows an EEG transition from NREM Stage II to REM sleep. In the first part of the tracing there is a clear K complex. This K complex indicates that it is Stage II sleep. The last part shows that it is REM sleep. REM sleep is characterized by its unique "sawtooth" waves. During periods in which sawtooth waves are apparent, rapid eye movements can be seen and subjects typically dream.

By watching the electrical activity of the brain, a researcher can tell exactly what sleep stage an individual is in. If delta waves are clearly apparent, the subject is in Stage IV sleep. To confirm this finding, a researcher may try to wake the subject and ask if he or she was dreaming. Two behavioral indices are readily evident. First, subjects are very difficult to awaken in Stage IV sleep; this is deep sleep, and, upon awakening, subjects will often appear confused, disturbed, and may take several seconds to rouse fully from their sleep. Second, when subjects are in Stage IV sleep they generally will not dream. While subjects may have some vague notion of mental activity, the typical vivid imagery of their dreams is not apparent. By contrast, during REM sleep subjects are more easily aroused and will report with great detail the imagery and activity of a dream state.

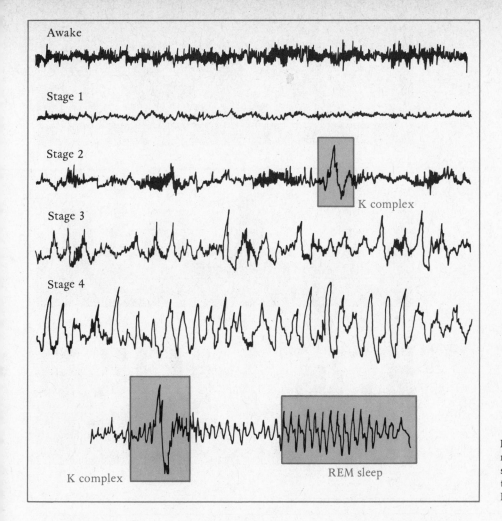

Awake

Stage 1

Stage 2

K complex

Stage 3

Stage 4

K complex

REM sleep

Figure 9.4 EEG measurements show the differences in sleep cycles; note the distinctive patterns of K complex and REM sleep

REM sleep is often called paradoxical sleep because of the somewhat contradictory processes which appear during it. In REM sleep the deep breathing, slowed heart rate, and lower blood pressure of Stage IV sleep are gone. Instead of appearing rested, subjects seem agitated with eyes moving and heart rate and breathing much more variable. You will see in the next section that when people are deprived of this "active" REM sleep there are serious alterations in sleep patterns and behavior. Since REM sleep is considered necessary for restorative functions and normal waking and sleeping behaviors, you might think that it would be a deep sleep. However, it is just the opposite—it is an active, variable sleep. We therefore say that REM sleep is paradoxical in nature.

A full sleep cycle takes approximately 90 minutes. Since the average subject's sleep is approximately 8 hours and a sleep cycle takes 90 minutes, there are generally five sleep cycles per night. Consequently, there are generally five REM periods during the night. The duration of sleep has a major influence on the amount of REM sleep; longer sleep times produce more REM sleep (Agnew & Webb, 1973). It is interesting to note that there is a distinct development of sleep cycles from before birth to adulthood. For example, before birth, humans initially show no eye movements. Later, this is followed by a period of eye movement and of facial and body movements. By the time

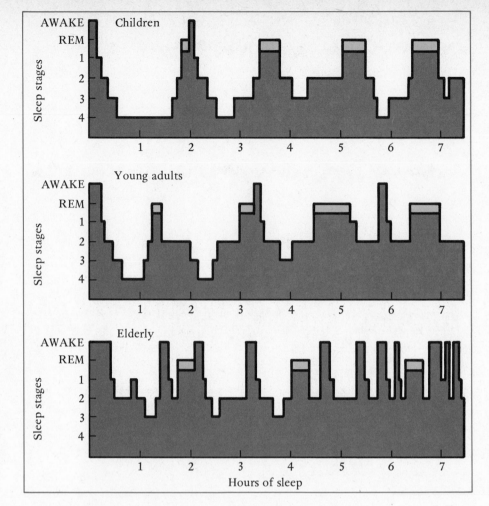

Figure 9.5 REM sleep (lighter area) occurs cyclically throughout the night at intervals of approximately 90 minutes in all age groups. REM sleep shows little variation across different age groups, whereas Stage IV sleep decreases with age. In addition, elderly people have frequent awakenings and a marked increase in total waking time

Table 9.1 Minutes of REM sleep for children ages 3 to 15

REM PERIOD	3–5 YRS.	6–9 YRS.	10–12 YRS.	13–15 YRS.
1	18	18	18	20
2	24	26	29	29
3	27	32	35	30
4	35	35	37	35
5	31	34	32	27
6	29	34	32	27
7	28	58		
8	25			
9	38			

Source: William, Karacan, and Hursch, 1974.

a baby is born about 50% of its sleep time is in the REM sleep. The proportion of REM sleep to Stage IV sleep decreases dramatically from the first year of life to adulthood (Ellingson, 1975; Kleitman & Englemann, 1953; Parmelee & Stern, 1972).

Sleep Deprivation

Everyone needs sleep, a fact that becomes painfully obvious to people when they are deprived of it. When people who normally sleep 8 hours are deprived of a couple of hours on a particular night, the effects are not dramatic. They may be tired during the following day, but they can function in a relatively normal manner. But when you lose a couple of hours of sleep for several nights in a row, the effects of sleep deprivation begin to catch up with you. You might then take on a tired appearance and be short-tempered; sometimes you might become lethargic and irritable.

A number of researchers have examined subjects who were totally or partially deprived of sleep for various amounts of time (for example, Webb & Agnew, 1974). The general procedure is to have subjects come into the sleep laboratory for several nights; their EEGs and eye movements are recorded while they sleep. The recordings taken over the first three or four nights are considered baseline data; they are the norm and suggest what subjects normally do. The subjects are then deprived of sleep. They may be deprived of only REM sleep; this is accomplished by waking the subject every time the EEG and eye movement pattern indicate REM sleep. Subjects may be partially deprived of REM sleep by being awakened after a certain amount of time based on an estimation of how much REM sleep they normally have each night.

Studies of total sleep deprivation are those in which subjects are not allowed to sleep at all. What happens to the EEG patterns and periods of REM and NREM *after* the sleep deprivation has taken place? In one study, subjects were partially deprived of REM sleep (Dement, Greenberg, & Klein, 1966). First and most important, when deprived of REM sleep people reported feeling sleepy. These subjects also slept for longer periods in a REM state on a subsequent night. Thus, partial REM sleep deprivation has a cumulative effect. Assume that we deprive ourselves of 30 minutes of REM sleep a night for five nights in a row. This would be roughly the same as depriving ourselves of a typical night's sleep in which we are in REM periods for 150 minutes.

REM sleep deprivation can be reversed by gaining extra amounts of REM sleep. One study was conducted in which subjects were totally deprived of sleep for 205 hours ($8\frac{1}{2}$ days). On nights immediately following the experiment, marked changes in sleep patterns occurred. First, there was a greater amount of REM sleep. Second, there were increases in Stage IV sleep. Stage I and Stage II sleep—the lightest stages of sleep—represented the smallest portion of time that the subjects were asleep (Kales et al., 1970; see also Webb & Agnew, 1975).

The effects of sleep deprivation on sleep patterns are clear: people catch up on their REM sleep. When subjects are deprived of REM sleep on a regular basis, they become anxious and irritable. These subjects report difficulty in concentrating. As soon as subjects are allowed to have REM sleep again, psy-

Sleep and Memory

Is it possible that while sleeping one can learn to speak a foreign language? This idea has been expressed often in the popular literature. Magazines have often run advertisements for such "learn while you sleep" programs; *however*, the research literature shows that despite the claims of a few investigations, such claims for real, long-lasting learning during sleep are false at worst and exaggerated at best (Aarons, 1976). However, sleep can be an aid in memory and learning in a different way.

Research done in the 1920s has shown that it is better to sleep before a test than to be involved in other kinds of activities. In a now classic study, Jenkins and Dallenbach (1924) had subjects learn lists of nonsense syllables which they would have to recall at a later time (Figure

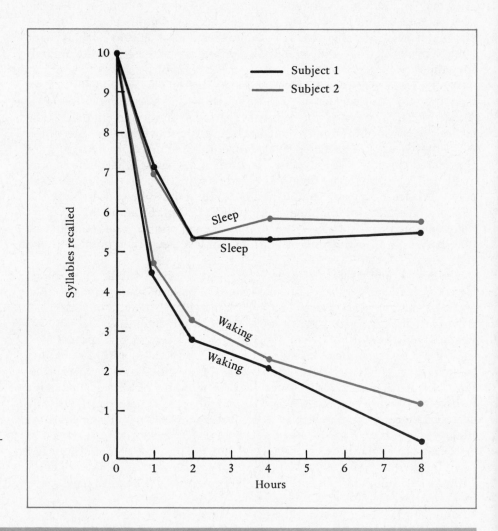

Figure 9.6 In the study by Jenkins and Dallenbach (1924) two subjects recalled items that they had previously learned. Their recall was delayed and they either slept during this time *or* they engaged in normal waking activities. The results showed that the intervening activity interfered with the subjects' recall performance more than sleeping

9.6). The subjects recalled the list immediately after the lists were presented or after as many as 8 hours later. During the time period intervening between learning and recall, the subjects either slept or were engaged in normal waking activity. The purpose of the study was to see if the intervening activity interfered with memory. When the sleep data were compared with the waking data, the waking subjects showed poorer performance. The intervening activity had deleterious effects on recall performance. There was a loss of memory during sleep; *but,* the loss was greater if the person was engaged in normal waking activities that might interfere with memory. The old maxim of going to sleep before an exam rather than engaging in other activities has some truth to it.

This 1924 study by Jenkins and Dallenbach was conducted with two subjects, but its basic findings have been repeated over the years. For example, Lovatt and Warr (1968), using 40 subjects, tested paired associate learning after an 8-hour retention interval and showed that learning followed by sleep is superior to learning followed by waking activity. Even more interesting, however, are the results of a study by Benson and Feinberg (1977), who investigated the phenomenon in a unique way. Benson and Feinberg had subjects learn lists of paired associates either in the morning or at night, just before sleep. After 8, 16, or 24 hours, subjects were tested on their recall. When sleep immediately followed learning, recall was better than when a waking period immediately followed learning. Thus, those subjects who learned the lists in the morning and were tested at night did worse than those subjects who learned the material at night and tested in the morning. This is not surprising; it repeats the finding of Jenkins and Dallenbach. What is surprising is that after 24 hours in which all subjects had both slept and had been awake, those subjects who learned the paired associates just before sleeping showed better recall. In other words, after 24 hours, when the amount of sleep and waking activity were equated, those who learned the material just prior to sleep showed superior performance. Benson and Feinberg have argued that sleep not only "insulates" subjects from interfering activity, but

when it follows learning it allows for a period during which information can be consolidated. Their data suggest that sleep following learning enhances learning. This is an exciting and potentially very important result.

The effect of sleep before situations like examinations has been studied by other researchers using other techniques. Fowler, Sullivan, and Ekstrand (1973) conducted a study to examine whether different parts of the sleep cycle were more important in sleep. Early research has shown that the first half of a normal night of sleep contains little REM sleep, and the second half contains a great deal. So to assess the role of the different parts of a night, subjects were brought into the sleep laboratory. They were given a task to perform, allowed to go to sleep, and then after 3 hours of sleep were required to take a test calling for the use of memory. Another group of subjects was allowed to sleep for 3 hours. They then were awakened, taught the same material, sent back to sleep, and awakened again 3 hours later to take the post-test.

By providing the subject with a learning situation just before the first part of sleep instead of prior to the second part of sleep, these researchers were able to assess how REM sleep affects memory. The study showed that after an interval with a high amount of REM sleep, a subject's memory does not perform as well as it does after a relatively high amount of Stage IV sleep. On scoring the subjects' ability to recall items from previously learned material, it was found that the subjects with higher amounts of REM sleep did not do as well as those with more Stage IV sleep. The authors concluded that REM sleep does not facilitate memory and that Stage IV sleep may be more beneficial.

The research literature shows that sleep is an important aid to memory; Benson and Feinberg suggest that it could improve it. In addition, we know that Stage IV sleep is more important than REM sleep for the recall of information. We do not know all of the answers about sleep and how it affects memory, but our knowledge of how sleep operates on our behavior is constantly growing through such studies. A night's sleep will not guarantee learning or excellent memory, but lack of it will surely impair performance.

Sleep deprivation has serious side effects on people's ability to perform their day-to-day functions.

chological changes disappear (see McGrath & Cohen, 1978). Dement (1960) concludes that a certain amount of dreaming each night is necessary. He suggests that it is possible for serious disruptions of personality to occur as a result of prolonged REM suppression. It must be pointed out, however, that there are some researchers who argue strongly that REM sleep deprivation does not produce serious psychological changes (Albert, 1975; Vogel, 1975; also, Bonnet, 1980; Cohen, 1979).

A frequently asked question about sleep and sleep deprivation is the extent to which humans can alter normal sleep patterns and maintain normal sleep and wakefulness. For example, can a person adapt to a non-normal sleep schedule such as 3 hours of sleep followed by 6 hours of wakefulness? When Webb and Agnew (1977) maintained subjects on different sleep-wakefulness regimens, they found that after an initial adaptation period the basic structure of sleep persisted regardless of the regimen. They used five different regimens of sleep: 3 hours of sleep and 6 hours of wakefulness; 4 hours of sleep and 8 hours of wakefulness; 6 hours of sleep and 12 hours of wakefulness; 10 hours of sleep and 20 hours of wakefulness; and 12 hours of sleep and 24 hours of wakefulness. Regardless of the regimen, the basic pattern of sleep was not altered. This does not mean that sleep is not altered; there were some changes in the proportion of Stage IV sleep in the short regimens; in addition, REM sleep was more likely in some of the sleep stages than in others. But taken together, the results suggest that human beings are remarkably adaptable in their sleep patterns and maintain a basic overall pattern of sleep stages regardless of the regimen of sleep-wakefulness.

REM normal   REM deprivation   Following REM deprivation

I Can't Sleep

Insomnia is the prolonged inability to obtain sleep. There are many people who spend large portions of the night unable to sleep. These same individuals spend most of the daytime tired, listless, and seeking sleep. A number of these different sleep disturbances can be treated medically. Very often, sleep disturbances are caused by anxiety and depression (Kales et al., 1976). People have trouble sleeping because they are tense, anxious, and unable to relax. These insomniacs may seek the help of drugs.

There are many drugs that can be used to induce sleep; those used most often are hypnotics. **Hypnotic drugs,** or as they are sometimes called, sleeping pills (such as Miltown and Equanil) easily induce sleep. But in examining the sleep patterns of subjects who have taken hypnotic drugs, researchers find that these drugs do not induce natural sleep. Hypnotic drugs, in fact, *reduce* the proportion of REM sleep in a night. Since the lack of REM sleep may alter normal behavior, the use of hypnotics to obtain sleep is probably a mistake. When a person has difficulty sleeping for a few nights as a result of anxiety or tension, the use of drugs to achieve sleep is not totally unwarranted. However, when chronic insomnia is the problem, hypnotics should not be taken (Kales et al., 1974; Oswald, 1968).

Barbiturates and alcohol produce effects similar to those of hypnotics. Both of these drugs reduce the amount of REM sleep and, in some cases, alter the number of eye movements within REM sleep. Sleep after one has ingested alcohol is often tumultuous; when drinkers awaken in the morning they generally do not feel rested.

The results of studies of drugs and sleep show that most drugs that are currently used to achieve sleep alter the normal sleep cycle. These alterations in sleep cycles are not beneficial to the insomniac because they disrupt normal REM sleep, and a persistent inability to achieve REM sleep can lead to temporary behavior problems.

Insomnia Prolonged inability to obtain sleep due to physiological or psychological factors.

Hypnotic drugs Drugs used to induce sleep. Common hypnotics are Miltown and Equanil. The sleep induced by them is not normal sleep, as the rapid eye movement stage has been reduced or prevented.

407

Perchance to Dream

Most people dream. In fact, most of us dream four or five times each night. Often you may not recall your dreams; if you do, you may only recall one of them. As will be presented in chapters to follow on personality and psychotherapy, Freud used dreams extensively in analyzing personality and in treating emotional disturbances. Thus, psychologists' interests in dreams have a long history. It is only in the last 30 years, however, that active research on sleep and dreams has taken place. It was during the initial studies of sleep and dreams that researchers found that dreaming took place during REM sleep. Dement and Kleitman (1957) monitored the eye movements of subjects during sleep; they were able to assess when subjects were in REM sleep. Every time subjects reached REM sleep, they woke them up and asked them if they were dreaming. Similarly, they woke subjects during NREM sleep and asked them if they were dreaming. The results of the studies were dramatic. Of the subjects in REM sleep, 79% reported dreams. By contrast, only 7% of those subjects who were in NREM sleep reported them. The researchers were forced to conclude that dreaming is accompanied by rapid eye movements and a characteristic EEG and that this cycle occurs approximately five times a night.

Dement and Kleitman also noted that the pattern of rapid eye movements is related to the visual imagery of the dream. When a subject dreams about climbing a series of ladders, eye movements are vertical; when a subject dreams about two people throwing tomatoes at each other, eye movements are horizontal.

Dreaming Altered consciousness that seems to occur largely during rapid eye movement sleep and during which an individual may have visual, tactile, and auditory experiences.

Dreaming is not the only kind of mental activity that takes place during sleep. It has been shown that other kinds of cognitive activity take place even during NREM sleep. However, there is a qualitative difference in the type of material that is thought of during NREM sleep and REM sleep. Reports of cognitive activity during NREM sleep are vague; by contrast, reports of thought during REM sleep are often vivid in visual and auditory imagery, have a great deal of detail, and are very long (Foulkes, 1962).

Most people do not recall their dreams. If they remember them, they usually do so because they awoke in the middle of one (Webb & Kersey, 1967). One study estimates the probability of remembering a dream upon awakening in the morning at 37%. When 762 subjects were asked the question, "Do you recall having dreamed this morning or last night?" the percentage of reported dreams was in fact 37%.

Dreams have long occupied an important place in psychology; for example, they often have been used in the treatment of emotional disturbances. Freudian psychoanalysts have long used dream analysis as a therapeutic aid. Many contemporary therapists have used dreams to varying extents to understand a patient's current or past problems. The assumption of these therapists is that dreams express a person's true desires or they might act as "censors" for unacceptable thought. Such a function of dreams is not yet clearly established. However, two researchers from Harvard Medical School, Allan Hobson and Robert McCarley, have claimed that there is a physiological explanation for dreams (1977). Essentially they argue that during periods of REM sleep the parts of the brain responsible for memory, vision, audition, and perhaps even emotion are stimulated. Of course, since the parts of the brain that are stimulated are not organized into a meaningful or coherent whole, the resulting dream may be fragmented images, with some coming from a person's long-term memory stores. There are physiological data suggesting that all memories are held in a long-term memory store. By stimulating random areas of the brain during sleep, the dreams that one experiences may be, and often are, fragmented and incoherent. They may even present strange and bizarre scenes, as in nightmares.

DRUGS: AN INTRODUCTION

Physicians wrote over 2 billion prescriptions for drugs last year. During the 1970s, almost 50 million prescriptions were written each year for the tranquilizer diazepam (Valium). It has been reported that one-third of all Americans between the ages of 18 and 74 have used some kind of drug that alters both brain activity and daily behavior (Bernstein & Lennard, 1973; Blackwell, 1973).

Each day, most Americans consume substances that have drugs in them. Cola drinks and coffee contain caffeine. Cigarettes contain nicotine, and beer and wine contain alcohol. Millions of people are alcoholics; a half million people are heroin addicts; millions smoke marijuana; cocaine is evident among the rich and well known. American culture is saturated with drugs. Many of these drugs are not considered dangerous, yet they are far more potent than suspected. Cigarette smoking is dangerous to your health. Caffeine can be an addicting drug. It is easy to demonstrate the addictive nature of these drugs; for instance, if you asked regular smokers or coffee drinkers to stop, they would probably tell you that they have tried before but cannot do it.

Drugs are part of the American way of life. In order to help get over a hangover from drinking too much alcohol last night, you might have a cup of coffee; it helps you to wake up in the morning. Then you might take aspirin to relieve your headache. Each time we take a drug we attempt to change our ability to function. Sometimes these changes are an attempt to increase alertness and performance; other times, drugs are taken to relax us and relieve us of high levels of arousal and tension. As we place a drug in our bodies it alters physiology and behavior. In doing so, it changes normal consciousness to some other level or state. Certainly, when we take a tranquilizer our ordinary level of consciousness is changed—we become relaxed. After three beers our ordinary responses and alertness are also changed. After many beers, however, it is reasonable to argue that we have not only changed our physiology and behavior but also have qualitatively changed our consciousness. Drugs, in whatever doses, affect consciousness; they change behavior. Some drugs are more potent than others and their effects more long lasting. The remainder of this chapter explores the nature of several potent, widely used, and consciousness-changing drugs.

Because drugs are so widely used and because they alter behavior so dramatically, a close examination of their effects is warranted. The ingestion of a small pill can have long-lasting effects; it may change one's consciousness permanently. For these reasons, let us begin with a widely recognized drug which most all people recognize as addictive and against the law, heroin.

Drug abuse is a problem for all segments of society.

HEROIN

Narcotic A drug that dulls the senses, relieves pain, tranquilizes, and can cause elation. Many narcotics such as heroin and morphine are derivatives of opium. Narcotics are generally addictive.

Addictive Any drug which produces physiological symptoms when the drug is no longer administered and thus causes both physical and psychological dependence. Addictive drugs usually produce tolerance.

Withdrawal symptoms A series of physical states, varying in intensity, that occur when a drug is no longer administered to a person who has developed a physiological dependence on it.

Tolerance A progressive insusceptibility to the effects of a specific drug when the drug is administered repeatedly. Tolerance usually accompanies addiction although it can also be developed to many nonaddictive drugs.

To be a heroin addict is to be caught in a never-ending spiral of addiction. Heroin is a **narcotic** drug that dulls the senses, relieves pain, tranquilizes, and causes elation. It is manufactured from morphine, a derivative of opium. Opium has been used to prevent children from crying excessively and for the reduction of pain from headaches, surgery, childbirth, and menstruation. Heroin can be smoked, eaten, and, most typically, injected into a vein.

Narcotic drugs such as heroin are addictive. An **addictive** drug produces a physiological reaction when the drug is no longer administered. Furthermore, an addicting drug produces physical dependence—without the drug, its user suffers from **withdrawal symptoms.** These withdrawal symptoms typically include headaches, nausea, dizziness, sneezing, stomach pains, and an intense craving for the drug. Addicting drugs usually produce tolerance. **Tolerance** means that consistent, day-to-day use of the same amount of the drug will lead to reduced effects. In other words, after repeated use, a particular amount of that drug can no longer give the user the same desired effect. Consequently, an addict has to use greater and greater amounts of the drug in order to achieve the "high" desired. As a rule, addictive drugs generally produce both withdrawal symptoms *and* tolerance.

The most serious effect of heroin is that it causes a decreased ability of the respiratory, or breathing, system. While it causes a few changes in the heart, arteries, and veins, it has no major effect on blood pressure or heart rate. In addition, heroin can bring about constipation and loss of appetite (Drug Abuse Council, 1974). Heroin users are often using other drugs in addition to heroin; furthermore, they often do not eat properly and are sometimes engaged in activities that do not lend themselves to proper nutrition and sleep habits. Taken together, an "average" addict is usually not in great physical shape, although this is not a direct cause of the heroin itself.

Surprisingly, long-term use of heroin, in and of itself, does not seem to be related to any major physiological damage. In fact, there is "general agreement throughout the medical and psychiatric literature that the overall effects

Addiction   Withdrawal   Tolerance

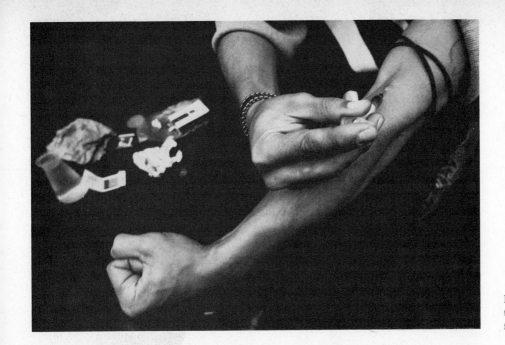

Nonsterile conditions can be the cause of disease and death for junkies.

of heroin on the addict's mind and body under conditions of low price and ready availability are on the whole amazingly bland'' (Brecher, 1972, p. 27). There are many eminent professionals who have been heroin addicts for over 20 years. To most people's surprise, it has generally been conceded that long-term addiction to narcotics does not cause marked physical deterioration. Similarly, there is doubt that deaths among addicts are caused by overdoses. It takes a considerable amount of heroin to kill an adult, and lethal doses are much more substantial than those taken by even heavy users of heroin. More often than not, heroin addicts die from taking a mixture of drugs such as heroin and alcohol. Disease is also a chief cause of death among heroin addicts. Since heroin is typically injected directly into the bloodstream with a hypodermic syringe, nonsterile needles and other paraphernalia used in this process often causes infection and disease (Brecher, 1972; Huber, 1974). Heroin addicts do have a higher suicide rate than the population generally (Miles, 1977); often when other causes are not determinable, coroners assume a person with needle marks must have died of heroin (see also Emery, Steer, & Beck, 1979).

On the one hand, medical science tells us that heroin as a drug, in and of itself, is not dangerous. It is an addicting drug that may be used safely and effectively for some medicinal purposes. But heroin addiction has become rampant. Heroin is consistently misused by some to achieve a high and escape from reality. Heroin addicts have a series of problems. They are often culturally disadvantaged youths, often poor, and generally uneducated. They usually become addicted to heroin as a result of peer pressure and a desire for upward mobility within their groups. Of course, since heroin is illegal, it maintains the status of a forbidden fruit. Many psychologists and others argue that the laws that control heroin sale actually contribute to its widespread use. Since the possession and sale of narcotic drugs in the United States is against the law, the individual who wishes to use heroin must obtain it illegally. About 5 million heroin addicts in the United States obtain their drugs in this manner. Estimates of the number of heroin addicts vary dramatically. A "ball-park" figure of a half million is often used, but estimates vary up to 13 million active users (Hunt, 1977; O'Donnell, 1977).

It would be convenient for psychologists and physicians if heroin addiction were easy to define, categorize, and treat. However, there is considerable disagreement about who is a heroin addict. How much heroin has to be consumed and how often are the principle questions that are not agreed on. It has generally been thought that the mere use of heroin once or twice will almost guarantee addiction. However, such notions have recently been challenged, and it has been shown that the average time for a user to become hooked varies dramatically from as little as 3 weeks to as much as 6 years (Robins, 1979; Waldorf, 1973). Clouding the definition to a greater extent is the fact that heroin addicts use other drugs as well. Multiple use of drugs is very common; most heroin addicts have tried and sometimes regularly use other drugs, including alcohol, amphetamines, barbiturates, and cocaine. When people consume more than one drug, it is hard to classify them into categories, and even if this is possible, their treatment becomes more complicated by the medical, psychological, and social problems that are associated with using many drugs simultaneously.

Environmental factors and social influences often have a great effect on heroin consumption. A sophisticated drug culture has developed and the individuals involved in it, many of them addicts themselves, are organized and shrewd. Many heroin addicts support their habit by selling drugs to other addicts. A typical addict might need about $25 worth of heroin per day. Addicts often have habits that cost as much as $50 or $75 per day. Excluding housing expenses, meals, and entertainment, a heroin habit of $50 per day—a habit that is maintained 7 days a week, 52 weeks a year—costs more than $18,000 a year to support. Most heroin addicts spend a substantial portion of their time in activities to obtain money to support their habit. Approximately 40% of the money used to purchase heroin is obtained through illegal channels such as burglary, robbery, shoplifting, and prostitution. Almost half of all heroin consumed is financed by the funds generated through heroin dealing. It has been shown that the price of heroin and the extent of crime in the community vary together (Silverman & Spruill, 1977), and that even upperclass users have sold drugs in order to support their own habits (Levengood et al., 1973). The chain linking the opium field and the heroin addict is a profitable one. Each of the individuals involved in this chain sells heroin to someone in another group; each makes a profit, supports his or her own habit, and turns other people on (Drug Abuse Council, 1974).

Laws do not create heroin addiction; people do. Even the most liberal advocates of drug reform do not advocate heroin use. However, they do advocate more humane treatment of the heroin addict and the reform of current laws in order to lessen the status of heroin as a forbidden fruit. Heroin addicts are physiologically addicted to a potent drug; they are usually in poor physical condition and generally need psychological or medical help. Heroin, a scourge on our society, must be dealt with from legal, medical, and psychological standpoints. Only through the combined efforts of the legal system, the medical profession, the improvement of social conditions, and existing laws can serious drug addiction be checked.

How does the professional treat heroin addiction? Throughout the nine-teenth and twentieth centuries, users have tried to kick the habit of heroin addiction. "Cold turkey" is the slang term for total abstinence from the drug. Another method, slow detoxification, is a reduction in the amount of the drug from day to day until total abstinence is achieved (Newman, 1979). Still another technique substitutes other kinds of drugs into the addict's system before total abstinence is achieved. The results of studies that examine the success of the wide variety of such programs show that they have failed dis-mally. Of heroin addicts who have achieved abstinence through one pro-gram or another, 80 to 90% become addicts again in a relatively short period of time. This generally has been the status of most treatment programs in-cluding halfway houses, therapeutic communities, church organizations, and social service agencies (Brecher, 1972; Kleber & Slobetz, 1979; Vaillant, 1970).

The only major successful heroin treatment program has been methadone maintenance. Methadone is an addicting drug. Like heroin, methadone must be consumed on a daily basis or else withdrawal symptoms will occur; unlike heroin, methadone does not develop tolerance in the user. Individuals can function on a regular daily dosage of methadone which does not need to be escalated. Methadone maintenance programs have been established around the country. In these programs heroin addicts voluntarily come to a clinic each day where they are given doses of methadone. Approximately 75,000 former heroin addicts are on some kind of methadone maintenance program (Dole, 1980; Lowinson & Millman, 1979).

There are six important differences between heroin and methadone use: (1) methadone is legal when dispensed by a physician, (2) it is medically safe with minimal side effects, (3) tolerance does not develop, (4) most individu-als who are on methadone maintenance programs tend to adjust to society very well, (5) methadone blocks the heroin effect, and (6) because it is a pre-scription drug rather than an illegal one, it is not especially expensive. (See Table 9.4, p. 423.) A normal injection of heroin will have no effect on individ-uals who are on the methadone maintenance program. Thus, methadone treatment patients who might be tempted to use heroin to achieve a high do not do so since the methadone blocks it. Furthermore, since methadone is legal, many of the individuals who come to methadone clinics are able to as-sume normal jobs and earn money to support themselves instead of the habit (Brecher, 1972; Kreek, 1973, 1979).

Methadone maintenance programs are not without critics or problems. Many patients abuse methadone by selling it to other drug addicts. Since methadone clinics have been set up, there has been an alarmingly high rate of accidental methadone poisoning in children (Smialek et al., 1977). In addi-tion, there are some moral questions regarding the appropriateness of shift-ing individuals from one addicting drug to another. But despite problems, corruption, and political controversies, methadone maintenance programs remain a reasonable method for addicts to quit the heroin habit and join in a lawful life-style. Some researchers have argued that there are few reasons why an individual who is on a methadone maintenance program cannot overcome a methadone habit as well (Soloway, 1974).

PCP: A Terror of a Drug

While heroin has always been recognized as a problem drug, only in the last 20 years have certain other drugs achieved wide popularity. Marijuana was used by a small number of youth in the 1950s and LSD was a drug largely confined to the laboratory. Today, a drug intended for veterinarians has achieved an alarming popularity—this drug, PCP, is very dangerous. As this news article shows, PCP is cheap to make, profitable to sell, and devastating to both mind and body.

TIME   Angel dust is the most common name. It is also known as goon, busy bee, crystal, hog, elephant tranquilizer and superjoint. By any name, phencyclidine (PCP) is the most dangerous drug to hit the streets since LSD became widely available a decade ago. Its use is growing rapidly; a National Institute on Drug Abuse (NIDA) study found that nearly a third of the young patients reporting to drug-treatment centers have tried PCP and one-fifth used it regularly. Angel dust has been linked to hundreds of murders, suicides and accidental deaths—214 last year in the Detroit area alone. Says a Boston drug hotline worker about new PCP users: "They don't know what they're getting into. They think it's just some easy high. Man, are they surprised!"

A user in California walked into a house that he had picked at random, killed a baby and stabbed a pregnant woman in the stomach. Under influence of the drug, a man in San Jose, Calif., tore out both his eyes with his bare hands. In the Chicago area, more than a dozen cases of drownings have been attributed to PCP use: victims lose a sense of direction and space and cannot fight their way out of the water.

The effects of the drug are so unpredictable that users call it "heaven and hell." Irrational or violent action is typical of chronic users, but even dabblers are not immune to sudden rages. A small dosage of PCP can produce a high that resembles drunkenness and can lead to anything from euphoria and a sense of bouncing to depression and hallucinations. Larger doses can bring convulsions, psychosis, uncontrollable rage, coma and death. "It's a real terror of a drug," says NIDA Director Robert DuPont. "Everything people used to say about marijuana is true about angel dust."

Developed in the 1950s as an anesthetic, PCP was banned for human use after tests showed erratic side effects, and it is now legal only as a tranquilizer for monkeys and apes. It can be snorted as a powder, injected as a fluid or swallowed as a pill. But usually the drug is dusted or sprayed over parsley, mint leaves or marijuana and smoked. Some dealers doctor low-quality marijuana with it. Others simply sell it to naive youngsters as LSD, THC (the active ingredient in marijuana), mescaline or even cocaine.

One reason for the rapid proliferation of PCP is that the drug is cheap and available. For $100, a handy amateur can manufacture PCP worth $100,000 on the street. "It's a terribly easy thing to do," says Hugh Shanahan, a federal Drug Enforcement Agency official in Los Angeles. "It requires no sophisticated equipment. Even someone without a chemistry background can do it." Thus PCP is churned out in hundreds, possibly thousands of makeshift labs around the country, often in remote areas, where there is less chance that its telltale ether odor will be detected.

Though police often track down these producers through tips from shocked and disgruntled PCP users, they have another way of finding the labs. Some solvents used in turning out PCP are so volatile that L.A. police have zeroed in on several labs simply by following up fire-department reports of suspicious explosions.

PCP may require an entirely different enforcement program. Officials who were trained to cope with limited imports of natural drugs are now facing an array of new synthetics that can be easily concocted at home. Some 20 variations of PCP are probably already on the streets, most of them perfectly legal because authorities have not got around to banning them. "We're heading into a new, dangerous era," says Dr. Mitchell Rosenthal, head of Phoenix House, a drug-free program in New York City. "The natural substances—opiates and so forth—are not going to be the problem of the future."

Government planners are belatedly mapping a campaign to educate the public about the dangers of angel dust. But one official is frankly puzzled about how to approach PCP users. Says he: "It's hard to understand why people are taking PCP. They don't take it to get high. They don't take it to make sex better. They take it to zonk themselves out. In a way, it's a disguised death wish."

In Great Britain, heroin addiction has been treated as a medical and non-criminal problem. Doctors are allowed to prescribe maintenance doses of narcotics. The number of heroin addicts remains quite low, although it increased in recent years to 3,000. (In contrast, there are about 50 times as many addicts in the United States, after adjusting for population differences.) While the English experience is not without problems, the number of heroin addicts in Britain is dramatically less than the number in the United States (Drug Abuse Council, 1974).

MARIJUANA

Marijuana is one of the most widely used and most misunderstood drugs. Marijuana is the popular name for the plant *Cannabis sativa*. It is prepared by drying the leaves and flowering tops of the cannabis plant. Reports regarding the behavior of individuals who have consumed marijuana vary from one extreme to another. Some reports suggest that marijuana simply has a small elation effect, while others report that marijuana induces psychoses. Many of these reports have been exaggerated; however, unlike a decade ago, the dosage or potency level of a single joint of marijuana now varies widely.

The use of marijuana has a long history. In the 1800s, marijuana was often used as a remedy for everything from toothaches to childbirth. It was not until the early part of the twentieth century that people became aware of marijuana and its potential hazards and had it outlawed. The very strict marijuana laws issued in this country in the 1930s were the result of belated prohibition efforts and general scare tactics on the part of puritanical "reformers."

There are many ways that one can consume marijuana. It can be added to drinks and food, or, as is most common in the United States, it can be smoked. Smoking marijuana is one of the most inefficient ways to consume it; much of the active ingredient in marijuana, **THC** (tetrahydrocannabinol), is lost in the smoke that escapes into the air. It has been estimated that anywhere from 20 to 80% of the active dose of a marijuana cigarette is lost this way. Within a minute or so after smoking marijuana, one begins to feel its effects. The maximum intensity of its effects occur within one-half hour after it is smoked. The effects of the drug begin to diminish within 1 hour and are nearly completely gone after 3 to 5 hours. Individuals who have smoked marijuana report feeling high. They report a sense of elation and a feeling of well-being; they become less task-oriented (Babor et al., 1978). There are reports of adverse reactions to marijuana (Ganz & Volkmar, 1976). Individuals under the influence of marijuana demonstrate impaired performance on simple intellectual and psychomotor tasks (e.g., Bourassa, 1977). After using marijuana, heart rate increases and a dilatation of some blood vessels occurs. There is no change in respiration, pupil size, or blood sugar level (Hollister, 1971; Rossi et al., 1978; Weil, Zinberg, & Nelson, 1968).

Marijuana is a consciousness-altering drug, and it is used specifically for that purpose. Psychologists study marijuana because it is used widely and because of its consciousness-altering capabilities. The extent of marijuana usage has only recently been recognized. It is not restricted to deviants or the young. Rather, a large portion of the population has smoked marijuana on at least one occasion. One study states that there is no significant difference in

THC (tetrahydrocannabinol) The active ingredient in marijuana. Although tetrahydrocannabinol exists in many forms, those not in the Δ^9 ("delta-nine") configuration are generally physiologically inactive.

Marijuana is widely used by many elements in society.

the number of students versus nonstudents who use marijuana. Furthermore, this study shows that the majority of marijuana users appear to be reasonably conventional in both attitudes and behavior. Similarly, subjects who have smoked marijuana differ only slightly in personality from those who have not indulged (see also Weller & Halikas, 1980).

Not only is marijuana widely used but it is increasingly being used by younger and younger people. For example, in 1980, the Secretary of Health reported that of people aged 18 to 25, 60% had used marijuana; 47% of 16-year-olds have used the drug; and 8% of 12-year-olds have used marijuana. The secretary reported that in 1977, 43 million Americans had tried marijuana and about 16 million Americans were currently using the drug. One in ten high school seniors smoke marijuana daily (Burns & Sharma, 1976; Petersen, 1980).

Marijuana has its adverse effects; it slows down reaction time, it interferes with the retrieval of information from memory, and it produces a relaxed state and a false sense of elation. There have rarely been serious suggestions that marijuana does not have deleterious effects. These effects have been clearly documented (Ginsberg & Greenley, 1978; Manheimer, Mellinger, & Balter, 1969; Melges et al., 1971; Nahas, 1977; Petersen, 1977; Rafaelsen et al., 1973; Weil & Zinberg, 1969; Zinberg & Weil, 1970).

The critical question regarding marijuana is not linked to its psychological and psychomotor aspects. Scientists know that marijuana impairs performance and many of those who smoke marijuana do so specifically to impair their performance, as do those who use alcohol and other drugs. More important is the question, "To what extent is marijuana damaging to an individual's psychological and physical health?" If it can be shown that marijuana is dangerous to one's health, we must consider to what extent it should be controlled or eliminated. Should the possession of marijuana and its use be criminal offenses?

An excellent review of the history of marijuana, its social and political consequences, was provided by Edward Brecher and the editors of *Consumer Reports* (1972, 1975a, 1975b). Brecher has outlined some central issues around which debate continues concerning marijuana and health. For each of these issues there is conflicting evidence. Debate continues around these central areas but the equivocation that was evident in the mid-1970s is today tilting toward showing that marijuana is not only potent but potentially dangerous for long-term users (Petersen, 1980). Let us review the evidence.

- *Does smoking marijuana damage the brain irreversibly and age it prematurely?* Some studies have shown that marijuana smokers exhibit evidence of brain damage (Campbell et al., 1971). First, it is unclear whether or not these patients had brain damage before they started smoking marijuana. Second, studies showing brain damage have not been repeated owing to the difficult and potentially hazardous technique used to gain this information. In a highly publicized study by Kolansky and Moore (1971), it was reported that marijuana smokers exhibited adverse psychological as well as neurological effects. These researchers report that among 20 males and 18 females studied in this experiment, 8 developed psychoses, 4 attempted suicides, and 13 unmarried female patients became sexually promiscuous and 7 of them became pregnant. These were clinical reports of patients of Dr. Kolansky and Dr. Moore and did not include important experimental controls. In a *controlled* experiment where marijuana smokers and nonmarijuana smokers were compared neurologically and in tests designed to reveal brain damage, no differences were found between the two groups. The data do not show evidence in humans for brain damage due to marijuana at the dosage level tested in the laboratory.

• *Does smoking marijuana lower the body's resistance to infectious disease and cancer?* A study reported in 1974 argues that the body's ability to maintain immunities is impaired by smoking marijuana. This study concluded that marijuana smokers lack the means of defense to combat infectious disease and cancer. By contrast, other studies compare the immunity response of smokers and nonsmokers, and they conclude that chronic marijuana smoking does not produce a gross cellular immunity defect. Again, conflicting evidence abounds (Cushman & Khurana, 1977; Nahas et al., 1974; Petersen et al., 1976).

• *Does smoking marijuana increase the likelihood of birth defects and hereditary diseases?* It has been reported that marijuana damages chromosomes, the carriers of heredity. Once more, the results are contradictory. Some studies have shown that there is a damage of chromosomes in chronic marijuana smokers; by contrast, using carefully controlled techniques, other researchers have not detected any changes in chromosomes. And so, we have still more conflicting viewpoints (Nichols et al., 1974; Stenchever et al., 1974).

• *Does smoking marijuana cause precancerous changes in the lungs and other lung damage?* Smoking either cigarettes or marijuana causes lung damage. The Brecher report agrees that inhaling smoke causes lung damage. There is no reason to doubt that marijuana smoke is any different from tobacco smoke in this respect. The degree of lung damage that it can cause is an unanswered question. As Brecher indicates, it is somewhat unreasonable to worry about a person who smokes 2 or 3 marijuana cigarettes a week when he or she may also be smoking a pack of 20 tobacco cigarettes per day. The potency of some marijuana has increased over the last decade and thus the potential effect of the marijuana on the lungs has also increased. Thus far there is no direct and conclusive evidence to show that marijuana causes lung cancer; *but,* aspects of lung-cancer-producing agents are found in marijuana and are found in significanctly greater percentages than in cigarettes (Novotny et al., 1976). It is likely that daily and/or regular usage of marijuana has effects similar to daily and heavy usage of tobacco.

• *Can smoking marijuana lead to sterility, impotence, or both among men?* Some evidence suggests that marijuana smokers have relatively low sperm counts and often report impotence. These studies have shown that the level of testosterone (a male sex hormone) in the bloodstream is lower in marijuana smokers than in nonsmokers. Low sperm counts and impotence may be related to lower testosterone levels. Again, by contrast, other studies state that testosterone levels of casual smokers and heavy smokers are not significantly lower than those of control subjects who are nonsmokers (Hembree et al., 1979).

• *Does smoking marijuana impair intellectual functioning?* The effects of marijuana on intellectual functioning during the period immediately following its being smoked are clear. There is a loss of immediate memory, attention span is altered, driving skills are impaired (e.g., Miller et al., 1977). When marijuana is combined with other drugs like alcohol its effects are likely to be exaggerated. Because of methodological problems in conducting such studies, the effects of long-term use of marijuana on human populations are unclear, though there is some evidence to suggest its deleterious effects (Wig & Varma, 1977).

• *Does a tolerance to marijuana develop and will its users continue to seek more drugs?* People who use marijuana regularly find that with repeated dosages there is a diminished response; it takes more of the drug to achieve the same high (Karler, 1977). A dependence on marijuana has been reported by some researchers; however, the term dependence has come to take on so many meanings that it is often used imprecisely. Jones (1977) has suggested that the research shows that there are some withdrawal symptoms for heavy users (particularly in countries where drug use is much heavier than in North America). However, the literature does not support the idea that marijuana users when denied the drug will begin drug seeking.

Taken together, many of the results of these studies are equivocal. After one research report is presented, others follow and provide conflicting information. One study reports damage; another study reports no damage. Some studies are difficult to repeat; other studies are not repeated at all. Some of the most important studies are yet to be done. As Brecher argues, marijuana is not harmless: "No drug is safe or harmless to all people at all dosage levels or under all conditions of use" (1975a, p. 149).

How hazardous is marijuana compared with other drugs? It has been suggested (Petersen, 1980) that this is a misleading question because to compare marijuana with other drugs is inappropriate. For example, alcohol is a recreational drug like marijuana, but we as a society allow alcohol to be legal while marijuana remains illegal. Second, we know the problems associated with alcohol, both medical and psychological—these facts have been well documented for decades. Again, by contrast, marijuana is a relatively new drug, used secretively, not habitually, and has been studied little compared with alcohol. At its *current* level of usage, estimates of marijuana's damage to a user's body and psychological health would suggest minimal damage. However, because of changes in society's use of the drug, because of changes of its availability, its potency, and its frequency of usage, predictions about the future effects of marijuana on today's youth and future generations are speculative. (See Table 9.4, p. 423).

Researchers like Petersen (1980) are quick to point out that we know little about the effects of marijuana in many areas. We know little about how marijuana might affect a woman's offspring. Further, we know little about its long-term effects on people who use the drug from early adolescence through the middle portions of life. Its long-term effects on users have not been well documented.

The legal implications of marijuana studies are another issue. Like any other drug, marijuana is probably harmful to some people, at some time, at some dosage level. To what extent then should it be legalized? At the present time marijuana possession is a criminal offense in the majority of the states. The notion behind imprisonment for marijuana possession and use is that it is a dangerous drug and a threat to our society. Alcohol and nicotine are also

Drug sales are not carefully monitored by the Bureau of Weights and Measures, but are usually put together hastily by a drug subculture.

dangerous drugs; however, our society does not provide laws against their possession.

When considering the potential problems of marijuana usage, the environmental factors that are involved must be carefully considered. As has been recognized with other drugs like heroin, both people's biology and their environment contribute to day-to-day behavior. While the social situation in the United States is changing, the sale or possession of marijuana is still against the law in most states. Yet it must be recognized that marijuana laws have been wholly ineffective. Arrest and imprisonment have not curbed marijuana use; marijuana use has grown greater with each year. At the same time, the number of arrests has increased. Brecher, however, argues that "marijuana is here to stay. No conceivable law enforcement program can curb its availability" (1975b, p. 266).

Several states have decriminalized marijuana. **Decriminalization** means that possession of marijuana is a civil violation rather than a crime. There are no arrests in such cases, nor are there jail sentences, bail, or involved trials. For example, the state of Oregon presents a citation similar to a traffic ticket to those who possess marijuana. Decriminalization in Oregon has not produced a tremendous increase in marijuana usage. Furthermore, police work has been efficient because police officers now specialize in areas of violent crime and crime against property rather than spending valuable resources attempting to catch marijuana smokers. The relationship between young people and the police has consequently improved. Oregon's experience with decriminalization shows that there has not been a dramatic increase in marijuana use, crime, or social decay (Brecher, 1975b).

Decriminalization Reducing a legal offense to a civil violation (such as a traffic ticket) rather than a crime.

The medical community is beginning to expand its use of marijuana for relief from the side effects of chemotherapy. The question continues as to whether or not marijuana is safe and acceptable. The question also continues as to the extent to which society wishes to concern itself with this drug.

ALCOHOL

Since 1971 alcohol consumption in the United States has been at an all-time high. People consume alcoholic beverages before dinner, during dinner, and after dinner. Weddings, birthdays, and parties are considered incomplete without alcohol; those who do not drink are often ridiculed. Most people consider alcohol appropriate; many consider it chic; some consider it a necessity. The drinking age in many states has been lowered. There has also been an increase in the number of retail outlets for alcohol.

Alcohol is absorbed into the bloodstream rapidly from the stomach and small intestines. When alcohol is consumed on an empty stomach it is absorbed very rapidly. By contrast, the absorption of alcohol consumed on a full stomach is a slower process. Mixing alcohol with water slows the process, and adding soda water to alcohol speeds it up (Ray, 1972).

Alcohol is not a stimulant; it is a central nervous system depressant. Alcohol may seem to be a stimulant because it decreases inhibitions and thus brings about increases in some kinds of behavior normally inhibited or tightly controlled. In the 1700s, alcohol was used as an anesthetic because it decreased pain and rendered patients immobile. With increasing amounts of alcohol in the bloodstream, an individual exhibits behavior that typically be-

Table 9.2 Blood alcohol level and behavioral effects

PERCENT BLOOD ALCOHOL LEVEL	BEHAVIORAL EFFECTS
.05	Lowered alertness, usually good feeling, release of inhibitions, impaired judgment
.10	Slowed reaction times and impaired motor function, less caution
.15	Large, consistent increases in reaction time
.20	Marked depression in sensory and motor capability, decidedly intoxicated
.25	Severe motor disturbance, staggering, sensory perceptions greatly impaired, smashed!
.30	Stuporous but conscious—no comprehension of the world around them
.35	Surgical anesthesia; about LD 1 [the lethal dose for 1% of the population], minimal level causing death
.40	About LD 50

comes increasingly slower and often shows severe motor disturbances. An example of this type of behavior is the staggering walk of a drunk person.

Alcohol does not affect everyone in the same way. A 250-pound man is not affected the same way that a 100-pound man is affected. The reason for this difference is obvious. A single one-ounce drink will only raise the blood alcohol level in a large person to a low level of intoxication; by contrast, the same drink in a small person will likely bring about intoxication.

The conscious waking behavior of individuals who have consumed alcohol is highly correlated to blood alcohol levels. Table 9.2 shows different blood alcohol levels and behaviors associated with them. A blood alcohol level below about .10% may cause a person to be mildly intoxicated, showing no dramatic behavioral effects. By contrast, blood alcohol levels greater than .10% usually indicate that the subject has consumed too much alcohol to function responsibly. Table 9.2 is designed for the typical person; however, everyone's blood alcohol level is determined by weight and sex. Table 9.3 shows the approximate blood alcohol level for various males and females of different weights for the amounts of alcohol consumed. While 5 ounces of alcohol may bring about decided intoxication for a heavy person, it may stupefy a small person. In most states in the United States a minimum point of .10% blood alcohol level is used to determine intoxication. Individuals who have a .10% blood alcohol level or greater are generally arrested and taken off the road if they have been driving. In no state is this criterion greater than .15% blood alcohol (Ray, 1972).

It has been estimated that there are about 9 or 10 million people in the United States who are problem drinkers if not alcoholics; this is about 7% of the total adult (over 18) population (see Chafetz, 1979). About 80% of urban American adults report having used alcohol at some time. One survey showed that 53% of adults questioned had consumed some alcoholic beverages during the week prior to the survey (Brecher, 1972). A survey done in 1976 showed that the average per capita number of gallons of alcoholic beverages consumed in the United States was 2.68 gallons (Noble, 1978).

People drink alcoholic beverages for a variety of reasons, but most preva-

Table 9.3 Relationships among sex, weight, oral alcohol consumption, and blood, alcohol level

ABSOLUTE ALCOHOL (OZ)	BEVERAGE INTAKE*	BLOOD ALCOHOL LEVELS (mg/100 ml)					
		FEMALE (100 LB)	MALE (100 LB)	FEMALE (150 LB)	MALE (150 LB)	FEMALE (200 LB)	MALE (200 LB)
½	1 oz spirits† 1 glass wine 1 can beer	.045	.037	.03	.025	.022	.019
1	2 oz spirits 2 glasses wine 2 cans beer	.090	.075	.06	.050	.045	.037
2	4 oz spirits 4 glasses wine 4 cans beer	.180	.150	.12	.100	.090	.070
3	6 oz spirits 6 glasses wine 6 cans beer	.270	.220	.18	.150	.130	.110
4	8 oz spirits 8 glasses wine 8 cans beer	.360	.300	.24	.200	.180	.150
5	10 oz spirits 10 glasses wine 10 cans beer	.450	.370	.30	.250	.220	.180

* In 1 hour
† 100 proof spirits

lent is their desire to relax. Alcohol, as a depressant, helps people rid themselves of tension and anxiety. In doing so people move from a state of consciousness that is very active and tense to an altered state. Sometimes this altered state is mild, wherein tension is relieved; other times, after multiple drinks, the state is problematic. When people become drunk, they have left their ordinary consciousness behind and often behave in erratic, irrational ways. These new states of consciousness are hardly those sought by psychologists who suggest that we should open ourselves to the receptive mode of functioning. Too often the altered state is dangerous for the individuals and those around them.

The use of alcohol is so prevalent in our society that a number of different terms have been developed over the years to describe its abuse. Both scientists and the public speak of alcohol abuse, problem drinkers, alcoholics, and physiological and psychological dependence. Whenever people show some kind of problem related to alcohol one can say that they are involved in **alcohol abuse.** We refer to people who have medical, social, or psychological problems with alcohol as having **alcohol-related problems.** A **problem drinker** is a person who shows some alcohol-related problem, which may include alcoholism. **Alcoholism** is a physiological addiction to alcohol. While alcoholics are problem drinkers, not all problem drinkers are alcoholics.

Of adults who drink, as many as 36% can be classified as problem drinkers or people with a potential for problem drinking. The percentage is higher for men (44%) than for women (27%) and it is higher for people age 18 to 20 than for any other age group. Problem drinkers may have trouble functioning socially, or there may be health or marital problems because of drinking, but this is not alcoholism. Alcoholism is *physiological* addiction to alcohol. There

Alcohol abuse Any situation in which a person shows problems related to alcohol.

Alcohol-related problems Medical, social, or psychological problems associated with alcohol.

Problem drinker A person who shows alcohol-related problems; these may include alcoholism.

Alcoholism Physiological addiction to alcohol; psychological dependence usually develops in alcoholism.

421

Anxiety lessens

Disinhibition

Sedation

Stupor and sleep

Loss of consciousness

Anesthesia

Death

Figure 9.7 The initial effects of alcohol are to reduce anxiety. This eventually leads to sedation, a total loss of consciousness, and, potentially, death (Ornstein, 1977)

is both a physiological and psychological need to consume alcoholic products and to experience their effects. Tolerance is generally, but not always, apparent.

Unlike heroin, alcohol can be consumed regularly throughout life without causing addiction. Many people are called social drinkers and consume alco-

Table 9.4 Some major drugs: heroin, methadone, marijuana, and alcohol

DRUG	SOURCE	DURATION OF EFFECT (IN HOURS)	BEHAVIORAL EFFECTS
Heroin	Morphine derivative	3–6	Relief of pain; relaxation; sleep
Methadone	Synthetic	4–6	Relief of pain; treatment of heroin addiction
Marijuana	*Cannabis sativa* plant	2–5	Elation; changes in mood; relaxation; decreased motor ability; judgment impaired
Alcohol	Various plants	1–5	Tension reduction; sense of well-being

hol on a regular or semiregular basis. They have no trouble controlling the amount of alcohol they consume, and they do not report cravings for alcohol. By contrast, alcoholics do become addicted. True alcoholics crave alcohol; without alcohol they will develop physiological withdrawal symptoms. Often true alcoholics develop tolerance; a single drink or even a few will not satisfy their cravings. Closely related to alcoholism are alcohol-related problems where people develop a psychological dependence upon alcohol. Problem drinkers often begin drinking in order to escape from reality. Slowly, almost imperceptibly, alcohol becomes an addictive drug. Alcoholics are unable to face the world without alcohol. Eventually it becomes a psychologically addicting drug.

Alcoholism can be effectively treated in some cases through psychological and medical help. The most widely known program of this type is Alcoholics

IMPACT

Teenagers and Drinking

The number one killer of teenage Americans ages 15 to 19 is the motor vehicle. Drinking, drugs, and reckless driving combine to kill these youths, and most teenagers recognize the problem. One study done by a national survey agency found that 44% of the teenagers they surveyed would like to see the requirements for obtaining a driver's license made stricter.

About half of all car deaths that occur in the United States involve drinking. Teenagers who are relatively inexperienced drivers are also relatively inexperienced drinkers. Learning to drive well takes hundreds of hours of experience; similarly, learning how alcohol affects you also takes repeated experiences.

The consequences of drinking and driving are devastating. Not only are thousands of lives lost, but insurance premiums are high. In many states the insurance rates for teenagers are three or four times the rate for adults, even with similar driving records.

Driving is a complicated behavior that involves both sensory and motor alertness; alcohol and many drugs are central nervous system depressants and make sensory and motor discriminations more difficult. Perceptual processes are impaired, reaction time is slowed, and overall mental abilities are diminished while drinking.

Of course, not all teenagers drink when they drive, and adults can be faulted with the same charges. Yet, from a statistical standpoint, more teenagers drink when they drive than do older people. Teenagers and authorities are aware of the dilemma; still, the effect on people's lives is devastating.

Saturday evening or Wednesday morning—it makes little difference to an alcoholic.

Anonymous. This organization helps individuals to abstain from alcohol within a therapeutic and emotionally warm climate. While Alcoholics Anonymous is not always successful, its rate of success is considerably better than treatment programs with heroin addicts. The alcoholic must be given medical and psychological help. Alcoholics need to understand that the world is not necessarily a hostile place and that they can live in it without alcohol.

Within the psychological and medical community there is a major difference of opinion as to how the alcoholic should be treated. The traditional approach, that taken by Alcoholics Anonymous, is that the goal of treatment should be abstinence. The fundamental assumption is that one is an alcoholic forever and that one can treat the disease by arresting it through total abstinence. This view is adopted by most treatment programs. An alternative view that is being presented by a large number of practitioners is that *some* nonproblematic drinking should be the goal of a treatment program. The view is based on the idea that alcohol abuse is learned, can be unlearned, and that total abstinence is an unreasonable, unachievable goal for many people.

Those who favor the abstinence view argue from clinical experience that efforts to control drinking have been futile in the past. Those who opt for the controlled view argue that those who are successfully treated for alcohol abuse often exhibit symptoms in other areas of their life and that alcohol abuse is a symptom of some other underlying more basic problem.

The National Institute of Alcohol Abuse and Alcoholism endorses the concept of total abstinence (Noble, 1978). The issue is far from resolved. Research into different treatment programs is continuing (Lloyd & Salzberg, 1975). For example, treatments with drugs are being pursued. Behavioral therapies involving controlled drinking are being studied (for example, Miller, 1978). Detoxification centers and halfway houses are being considered. There have been few systematic, carefully controlled studies of alcoholism and its treatment. Practitioners who treat alcoholics are quick to point out that there are many overt and covert blocks to treatment in our society and that most alcoholics go untreated. Even knowing this, the resources, treatments, and procedures to help alcoholics have been relatively limited (Noble, 1978).

From a medical and a psychological standpoint, excessive alcohol consumption represents one of the greatest social problems in the United States. The Department of Transportation has estimated that alcohol is involved in more than 28,000 automobile accident deaths and more than 80,000 automobile accidents each year. In addition, violent crimes and suicides are committed far more often by people who have consumed alcohol than by those who maintain sobriety (Hindman, 1979). Increased risk of heart disease and cancer are also associated with heavy drinking (Hennekens et al., 1979; Yano et al., 1977), as is increased risk to newborn infants of alcoholic mothers (Little, 1979; Warren, 1978).

Alcohol was outlawed in the early part of this century; the constitutional amendment that outlawed alcohol was then repealed. Prohibition did not work because people continued to drink and black market bootlegging of alcohol thrived. More crime, death, and sadness were created by black market bootleg alcohol than by legal alcohol. The United States learned a lesson regarding alcohol fairly quickly in the early part of the century. Still, alcohol is the biggest law enforcement problem in the United States today. Millions of arrests are made each year for drunkenness. One study shows that 43% of those who have committed homicide have been drinking prior to the crime. Alcohol has been shown to be involved in both child beating and suicide. It may cause chronic sexual impotence (Lemere & Smith, 1973). Alcohol is a dangerous, potentially addictive drug. It alters a person's state of consciousness in dramatic ways; its effects on the central nervous system and on psychological stability, and its contribution to the loss of life, are far greater than any potential hazards of marijuana or heroin. Since cultural values largely determine what drugs are legal, resources should be directed at education and a reevaluation of society's role in drug control.

CIGARETTE SMOKING

"The Surgeon General has determined that cigarette smoking is dangerous to your health." This warning is written (by law) on each of the millions of packs of cigarettes sold in the United States each year. Cigarette smoking is not a minor habit or vice; physicians join the Surgeon General in describing it as a major cause of lung cancer and heart disease. Even those smokers who know these facts continue their habit because they cannot stop. Unlike the use of alcohol and marijuana, occasional smoking is a rarity. Only about 2% of all smokers do so intermittently and occasionally; most people who smoke become regular users sooner or later. Three or four casual cigarettes smoked during adolescence are signs that the person will become a regular smoker as an adult (Russell, 1971). One study has shown that women under the age of 40 who smoked more than 35 cigarettes per day were 20 times more likely than women who didn't smoke to have heart attacks (Slone et al., 1978; see also Richmond, 1981a, 1981b).

The active ingredient in cigarettes that creates dependence is nicotine. Although there are many reasons for a smoker's habit, dependence upon nicotine is the most critical. The definition of addiction offered earlier generally involves both withdrawal symptoms and tolerance. When people who smoke regularly are denied nicotine, they exhibit physiological withdrawal symptoms. When smokers are deprived of their drug they become nervous, drowsy, anxious, and light-headed, develop headaches, and exhibit a loss of energy and fatigue. For most people cigarette smoking is an addictive behavior; it produces physiological dependence and tolerance (Brecher, 1972; Jarvick, 1973; Schachter et al., 1977).

Smoking behavior is determined, at least in part, by the levels of nicotine in the bloodstream. Smoking is a behavior that is determined by particular chemicals that condition the body. Experiments that have manipulated the amount of nicotine content in cigarettes have shown that the larger the content of nicotine in the cigarette, the fewer the number of cigarettes smoked. Furthermore, cigarettes with low nicotine content were smoked more rapidly than cigarettes with high nicotine content (Frith, 1971; Schachter, 1977).

Excess smoke from a cigarette that is not being puffed upon has almost twice the tar and nicotine of the smoke inhaled by the smoker. On the average, the smoke inhaled by the person smoking a cigarette contains 11.8 milligrams of tar and .8 milligrams of nicotine compared to 22.1 milligrams of tar and 1.4 miligrams of nicotine from idle smoke. Smoke from a cigarette in an ashtray may be twice as toxic as that inhaled by a smoker. Although the con-

Table 9.5 Life expectancy of males in the United States as a function of age and number of cigarettes smoked.

AGE	NEVER SMOKED REGULARLY	CIGARETTES SMOKED (DAILY AMOUNT)			
		1–9	10–19	20–39	40+
25	48.6	44.0	43.1	42.4	40.3
30	43.9	39.3	38.4	37.8	35.8
35	39.2	34.7	33.8	33.2	31.3
40	34.5	30.2	29.3	28.7	26.9
45	30.0	25.9	25.0	24.4	23.0
50	25.6	21.8	21.0	20.5	19.3
55	21.4	17.9	17.4	17.0	16.0
60	17.6	14.5	14.1	13.7	13.2
65	14.1	11.3	11.2	11.0	10.7

centration of the substance inhaled by the nonsmoker is less than the concentration inhaled by the smoker, the nonsmoker's exposure will last for longer periods of time. Consider what happens to a nonsmoker who sits in an airplane next to two individuals who smoke. Generally, air circulation is poor, and the nonsmoker is subjected to a significant hazard (White & Froeb, 1980).

Cigarette smoking is addictive. As is the case with heroin addicts, the number of smokers who quit their habit and remain ex-smokers is very small. Only 18% of smokers who stop smoking continue to abstain. Among ex-smokers of less than a year, as many as 80% relapse. Cigarette smoking is clearly a habit that is easily acquired but difficult to break (Bernstein & McAllister, 1976; Russell, 1971). It is estimated that today there are 30 million nonsmoking Americans who once were smokers (Jaffe & Kanzler, 1979). Roughly 1 million Americans quit smoking each year. Some find the process *extremely* difficult, others do not find it as torturous as has been suggested in the popular press (Horn, 1979; Shiffman, 1979). In any case, a wide number of techniques have developed to help people stop smoking (Conway, 1977).

It is hardly frivolous to repeat that cigarette smoking is dangerous to your health. The Surgeon General's report of 1964 establishes this fact. In addition to the dependence described above, cigarette smoking produces changes in electroencephalographic activity. It also affects one's memory. Further, high school students who have as little as 1 to 5 year's smoking experience have exhibited lung damage. Last, mothers who smoke are significantly more likely to encounter difficulties when giving birth and to have babies that weigh less than those of nonsmoking mothers (Brown, 1968; Fielding, 1978; Houston, Schneider, & Jarvick, 1978; Kline et al., 1977; Mulcahy & Knaggs, 1968; Seely, Zuskin, & Brouhuys, 1971).

Why don't cigarette smokers stop smoking? Cigarette smokers have difficulty quitting because the habit is addictive in nature. The withdrawal symptoms associated with abstaintance from cigarette smoking are often painful and difficult (see also Schachter, 1977). There is dramatic evidence to show that cigarette smoking is dangerous to one's health; yet, the per capita

"How good is it?" The answer to that question is clearly documented by the Surgeon General of the United States.

cigarette consumption has only slightly decreased during the past decade and this decrease is especially small among adolescents (Murray & Cracknell, 1980; Richmond, 1981a, 1981b).

SUMMARY

Students of psychology study altered states of consciousness for two reasons. First, many people experience altered states, and psychologists want to understand and describe their behavior. Second, and more important, psychologists may be able to gain greater insight into normal consciousness if they can understand altered states. By comparing normal and altered states, researchers hope to gain some insight into the way these different modes of operating occur. Contrasts such as this have been useful in describing normal compared with abnormal behavior; researchers hope that the same types of contrasts will provide insight into thought processes. Consider hypnosis —subjects show susceptibility to hypnotists' suggestions and will do tasks in this state that they normally might not do. They may even show rather spectacular effects. Hypnosis-like effects, however, have been obtained without trance-induction procedures. The studies by Barber and his colleagues demonstrate that some of the altered states achieved through hyp-

nosis can also be brought about without hypnosis. Many psychologists conclude that hypnosis is not a special state of mental activity since we can
produce its effects through other techniques. This is not to say that hypnosis
is not an altered state. Psychologists are simply stating that they now know
that hypnotic effects can be obtained through other techniques as well.

The mental activity of sleep is certainly very different from normal processes. One of the most interesting aspects of sleep is that although we may
not remember all of our dreams, we continue to have them throughout the
night. The content of our dreams is often bizarre in imagery, characteriza-
tion, and content. Psychologists also know that dreams normally take place
during REM sleep. They are not totally certain why REM sleep is important;
however, they do know that without REM sleep, behavior becomes disturbed. Furthermore, after people have been deprived of REM sleep, they
have compensatory nights in which they have extra REM sleep. There is no
question that a lack of sleep will alter behavior and subsequent sleep patterns.

Hypnosis and a lack of sleep will alter behavior but drugs will alter it in
even more dramatic ways. Some drugs are addictive. Addictive drugs such
as heroin and to a lesser extent even nicotine alter people's normal behavior.
People often want to quit their habit but are unable to do so because they are
addicted to the drug. They would suffer from withdrawal symptoms if they
were denied the drug. Conversely, other drugs, such as marijuana, are not
addictive; however, like heroin, they are illegal.

The tough drug laws in the United States have helped to make heroin and
marijuana popular forbidden fruit. It seems that without the sensational coverage by the press and the antidrug laws that have come about in the twentieth century, these drugs would never have achieved the popularity that
they have today. Some drugs have therapeutic value. Marijuana has been
used for medicinal problems. Still, these drugs have been abused. Since they
are psychologically and physiologically addicting, these drugs deserve serious attention.

Drugs are dangerous and addicting. Should people stop consuming them?
To what extent should the government allow the use of drugs? Nicotine and
heroin are addicting drugs and they produce withdrawal symptoms and tolerance. Of these drugs, only heroin has been outlawed. It is obvious that the
social, political, and economic effects of a drug culture have some severe effects on how people deal with the behavior-altering aspects of drugs. It is
difficult for psychologists to assess the effect of drugs in a vacuum; it is hard
to know how Americans would behave if drugs were not outlawed. This is
not to suggest that nicotine should be outlawed or that heroin should be
made legal. However, what is necessary is a reappraisal of our current position in regard to possession of criminal drugs and the sentences that our
court system imposes on those who possess them. By keeping some drugs
illegal, the government allows black market sales of them to increase. This
situation was made quite apparent when alcohol was made illegal during
Prohibition.

Heroin addicts can be treated with methadone and alcoholics can be
treated through Alcoholics Anonymous and other programs. These programs
must be supported. In addition, a national decriminalization of the less dangerous drugs like marijuana should and probably will be implemented in the
near future. The critical variables in all of these drugs need to be examined

uncontaminated by emotional and historical precedents. Our current laws are not effectively impeding the illegal use of drugs or discouraging their unwise or dangerous use.

Psychologists are involved in the study, treatment, and control of consciousness-altering drugs like alcohol and marijuana. These substances can be therapeutically effective in certain situations. They can open people's consciousnesses to new levels that may have gone untapped. However, drug substances are abused; many are against the law. Few people use drugs in ways that help them achieve new and higher planes of thinking. Most use them just to achieve a high; so, we have a serious drug problem in the United States and Canada.

CHAPTER REVIEW

1. Consciousness is the general state of being aware and responsive to stimuli and events in the environment.
2. An altered state of consciousness is a pattern of functioning that is dramatically different from ordinary awareness and responsiveness.
3. One of the more widely supported theories of consciousness is the one put forth by Ornstein; his basic idea is that there are two modes of consciousness in humans that function in a complementary manner.
4. Ornstein and his collaborator David Galin have characterized differences between the active and receptive modes of consciousness as differences between analytic and holistic styles of operating.
5. There is not a clear agreement among psychologists whether discrete and different states of consciousness actually exist.
6. The traditional view of hypnosis argues that a special state of consciousness exists that is different from the waking state and is induced through trance induction.
7. Special effects such as age regression, hypermnesia, and a lack of pain in surgery have been gained through the use of hypnosis.
8. The cognitive-behavioral viewpoint suggests that subjects carry out hypnotic behaviors when they have positive attitudes, motivations, and expectations toward the test situation; this atmosphere leads to a willingness on the part of the subject to think and imagine according to themes that are suggested.
9. Meditation has its roots in the Eastern religions of Buddhism and Hinduism. Its popular forms, Zen, yoga, and transcendental meditation, have only recently been actively pursued in the Western world.
10. In anecdotal reports, meditators claim inner peace and tranquility; experimental investigations of meditators show that they achieve bodily states similar to individuals who have been trained to relax and concentrate deeply.
11. Serious controlled research on meditation is limited. Meditative techniques have been reported to be effective in reducing anxiety, but laboratory investigations have not provided corroborating evidence.
12. REM sleep patterns are periods during sleep when a subject's eyes move about rapidly in a systematic manner. REM is one of the five sleep stages.
13. A full sleep cycle takes approximately 90 minutes, and there are approximately five sleep cycles per night. Therefore, five REM periods occur during an average night's sleep.
14. When subjects are deprived of sleep, they must catch up on REM sleep during subsequent nights.
15. As a rule, addictive drugs produce withdrawal symptoms and tolerance.
16. Heroin is a narcotic and addicting drug; as such, it is illegal.
17. Although it is addicting, heroin, in and of itself, is not dangerous. It has, in part,

become a scourge on society as a result of the laws that have been invoked to control its use and the subsequent crime that is generated.

18. One successful treatment of heroin addiction has been through the methadone program. Methadone is an addictive drug, but it is legal and medically safe; tolerance does not develop from methadone use, and it blocks the heroin effect.

19. People who smoke marijuana report feeling high, and they exhibit an increase in heart rate and a dilatation of some small blood vessels. Used widely in the United States, marijuana is not harmless under all conditions; however, scientific evidence does not show any effects of serious damage in those who smoke marijuana occasionally. The long-term effects are as yet unassessed.

20. Blood alcohol levels determine how alcohol will affect behavior. People who have a .10% blood alcohol level or greater are generally considered intoxicated, and they are arrested and taken from the road when caught driving. Alcohol can become physiologically addictive and there are many people who are alcoholics.

21. Cigarette smoking is dangerous to one's health because cigarettes contain tar and nicotine; nicotine adversely affects the circulatory system and tar affects the respiratory system. Cigarette smoking is an addictive behavior and only 18% of smokers who have stopped smoking are able to continue their abstinence.

22. Certain drugs are dangerous because they are addicting and produce withdrawal symptoms and tolerance. However, heroin addiction, for example, can be treated through methadone programs; other civic and health groups offer various therapeutic treatment programs.

SUGGESTIONS FOR FURTHER READING

BARBER, T. X. *LSD, marijuana, yoga, and hypnosis.* Chicago, IL: Aldine-Atherton, 1970.

BARBER, T. X., SPANOS, N. P., AND CHAVES, J. F. *Hypnotism, imagination, and human potentialities.* New York: Pergamon Press, 1974.

BARBER, T. X. ET AL., Eds. *Biofeedback and self-control: 1975.* Chicago, IL: Aldine-Atherton, 1976.

BRECHER, E. M. ET AL., Eds. *Licit and illicit drugs: The Consumer's Union report on narcotics, stimulants, depressants, inhalants, hallucinogens, and marijuana—Including caffeine, nicotine, and alcohol.* Boston, MA: Little, Brown and Company, 1972.

DEMENT, W. C. *Some must watch while some must sleep.* San Francisco, CA: W. H. Freeman, 1974.

HILGARD, E. R. *The experience of hypnosis.* New York: Harcourt Brace Jovanovich, 1968.

JAYNES, J. *The origin of consciousness in the breakdown of the bicameral mind.* Boston, MA: Houghton Mifflin, 1976.

LEAVITT, F. *Drugs and Behavior.* Philadelphia, PA: W. B. Saunders Company, 1974.

ORNSTEIN, R. *The psychology of consciousness.* New York: Harcourt Brace Jovanovich, 1977.

ZINBERG, N. E. *Alternate states of consciousness.* New York: Free Press, 1977.

IN THE COURSE of a normal day people see many others with whom they interact. These interactions are very important; social psychologists have realized that the way others behave seems to affect an individual's behavior in significant ways. Social psychologists have studied the effects of how other people's characteristics and behavior can change the way human beings respond. We all recognize that in a group situation people act differently than when they are alone. Similarly, most people are influenced easily by someone whom they think is in a position of authority. In efforts to maintain a sense of balance in their lives many people learn to set up boundaries, both physical and psychological, to minimize the effects of other people. Social psychologists therefore study how other people influence our individual behavior.

CHAPTER 10

Social Psychology

. . . Time for you and time for me,
And time yet for a hundred indecisions,
And for a hundred visions and revisions,
Before the taking of a toast and tea.
. . . .
And indeed there will be time
To wonder, "Do I dare?" and, "Do I dare?"
Time to turn back and descend the stair,
With a bald spot in the middle of my hair—
(They will say: "How his hair is growing thin!")
My morning coat, my collar mounting firmly to the chin,
My necktie rich and modest, but asserted by a simple pin—
(They will say: "But how his arms and legs are thin!")
Do I dare
Disturb the universe?
In a minute there is time
For decisions and revisions which a minute will reverse.

For I have known them all already, known them all:
Have known the evenings, mornings, afternoons,
I have measured out my life with coffee spoons;
I know the voices dying with a dying fall
Beneath the music from a farther room.
   So how should I presume?
. . . .
I grow old . . . I grow old . . .
I shall wear the bottoms of my trousers rolled.

Shall I part my hair behind? Do I dare to eat a peach?
I shall wear white flannel trousers, and walk upon the beach.
I have heard the mermaids singing, each to each.

I do not think that they will sing to me.
. . . .

T. S. ELIOT
The Love Song of J. Alfred Prufrock

Throughout our lives come times when we step aside and evaluate our personal situation. We ask ourselves if we are being true to lifelong goals in careers, in love, or in parenthood. Often we may have doubts whether our lives today are really consistent with the religious, political, or personal values that we built up and defined for ourselves when younger. Reflecting on these things, we may find our doubts becoming fears that life is moving on in a stagnant pattern, with too little time, courage, or energy left to make the big effort to deal with a long-cherished ideal. We may ask, "Shall I change my life to reach my aim, or shall I change my ideals?" Like J. Alfred Prufrock we may ask, "Do I dare?"

For many, the prospect of such change is too upsetting. Maintaining old attitudes and ideas seems more reassuring, especially if these ideas have been held for decades through life's changing situations. Consider a politician of the Democratic party who formed his liberal political values in the early 1960s. Twenty years later he may be beginning to recognize that these old liberal ideas are not as sound as they once appeared. Wishing to be reelected, his more flexible cronies (attempting to keep pace with the country) may have transformed themselves into conservative Republicans. For his flexible friends, maintaining old ideas for a lifetime is for those who have lost touch. They might argue that a politician who maintains the same ideas over a 20-year period may have isolated himself from his constituency.

Certainly, the process of change can be hard. Ideas established early in life become part of our self-image and are difficult to modify. Rather than change, some people cope with life in other ways. They may try to reinterpret their own behavior. They may surround themselves with others who hold similar beliefs by joining clubs of like-minded individuals. In some cases people's attitudes about life and how it should be lived are so distant from the current values of society that maladjustment eventually occurs.

Some people have trouble keeping their values straight. In some cases, we may use others' standards to measure our own behavior and self-worth. Attitudes in general, especially about ourselves, are determined not only by how we see ourselves, but also by how we think others see us. The way our behavior is influenced by the behavior and attitudes of others is the special concern of social psychologists. They examine how individual behavior is influenced by other people and how we as adults in turn affect others.

Many of a person's basic attitudes about life are established through socialization. **Socialization** is the process by which people learn the behaviors, attitudes, and beliefs that allow them to function appropriately in society. Socialization begins early in life and has a great impact during the developmental years. However, the process of socialization and learning new ways of living does not stop at age 18; socialization is a lifelong process. Parents are the first and most important agents of socialization. They teach children their basic beliefs about the world; they teach values and religious concepts. Parents thus shape greatly how children view the world. Other people and world events help shape the behavior of individuals; relatives, friends, clergy, teachers, politicians, and society itself all help modify and change a person's attitudes about the world.

Socialization The process by which individuals learn the rules of their society and establish their own values, attitudes, and long-lasting personal characteristics.

Consider this example: a traditional attitude established early in life is the role of men and women in society. In many families, from infancy on, girls wear pink and boys wear blue; later on, girls wear dresses and frilly clothes and boys wear pants. In these families, girls must be neat while boys are allowed to be messy. Thus, even in the first 2 years of life, girls and boys of these families are treated differently. By the time children are 3 years old, strong sex roles are established. The girls will play with doll houses and the boys will play with racing cars.

Society has done such a good job that by the time children are 6 years of age, they have firm attitudes about the roles of women and men. These roles are taught by parents, television, books, and movies. In past years, women were generally portrayed as nurses, housewives, and teachers, while men were seen as doctors, policemen, firemen, and attorneys (see Cordua, McGraw & Drabman, 1979). These attitudes are changing rapidly; this is a difficult task, however, as attitudes established early in life are difficult to change.

The development of attitudes is a lifelong process. A child born in the 1960s may have learned an attitude about women that seems to be out of place in the 1980s; others have influenced this individual's attitudes. Throughout our development we establish attitudes about ourselves as well as the world. We acquire certain needs, desires, and values. Through the

Social psychology The study of how individual behavior is affected by the behaviors or characteristics of others.

process of socialization we may become shy or perhaps develop a strong need for privacy. Thus we see that other people's ideas and behaviors help shape our ideas.

Social psychology is the study of how individual behavior is affected by the behavior or characteristics of others. The purpose of social psychology is, therefore, to examine behavior—everything *we* do to express how we feel and think; social psychology focuses on how our behavior is affected by what *others* do and how they feel and think. This chapter will begin with the study of the effects of social stimuli on the individual, then progress through how people perceive others, how they interact with others, how people behave while in groups, and finally how people respond to environmental stimuli.

ATTITUDES

Attitudes A pattern of relatively enduring feelings, beliefs, and behavior tendencies toward other people, ideas, or objects.

Much of our day-to-day behavior is determined by attitudes that we generally have held for a long time. An **attitude** is a pattern of feelings, beliefs, and behavior tendencies toward other people, ideas, or objects which lasts for a relatively long period of time. Attitudes are, therefore, a person's feelings, beliefs, and behavior tendencies or dispositions toward people, political candidates, or religions.

An attitude has three basic components. The *cognitive component* is the belief. For example, we may believe in the democratic system of government. We believe that democracy is the best system of government that has been devised because it has provided freedom, liberty, and justice to millions of people. Attached to our cognitive component is an *emotional component* which involves feelings of liking or disliking. As citizens of the United States, we generally feel that our government is the best one. We feel pride in the flag and are joyous when singing the national anthem. This emotional component brings excitement, deep feelings, and firm commitment. Often linked with the cognitive and emotional components is a *behavioral compo-*

Attached to our cognitive component is an emotional component which involves feelings of liking or disliking

Who we are and what we should do is taught to us very early in our lives.

nent. People may display their beliefs and feelings about the United States through acts of patriotism or service. When a family hangs the flag on a national holiday, it is expressing a belief in a system and an emotional feeling of patriotism. This is the behavioral component of an attitude; the family is displaying its attitude publicly. However, the behavioral component of an attitude is not always public. Many people hold beliefs and feelings that are shown openly only to a limited extent. Many believe strongly in democracy, yet do little to support it. In the same way, many feel strongly that certain minority groups are inferior; yet their attitude toward these minority groups does not always show in their overt behavior.

A person's behavior is usually determined by attitudes and how strongly the attitudes are believed. If someone holds an attitude, it will usually show up in what that person does. However, when an attitude is not firmly established, overt behavior is not always seen. For example, an employer may hold an attitude that race has no bearing on job performance, yet this belief may not be firmly established. When interviewing a prospective employee, a decision to hire may be determined by the employer's emotional experiences with just a few individuals. Thus, attitudes, experience, and current behavior are intertwined. People's attitudes are determined by their experiences; their attitudes, along with their other personal characteristics and perceptions of the environment, determine behavior.

Attitude Formation

In psychology there are many controversies about the whys of behavior. Often these controversies revolve around heredity vs. environment. Yet when people raise the topic of how attitudes are formed, nearly all agree that attitudes are established by the laws of learning. People learn to have feelings and beliefs about other people, and they often develop these attitudes early in life. The three basic learning approaches to the formation of attitudes are classical conditioning, operant conditioning, and social or observational learning.

CLASSICAL CONDITIONING.   In classical conditioning a formerly neutral stimulus elicits a response. So for Pavlov's dogs, bells evoked salivation; and in humans, eye blinks can be elicited by lights. When a neutral stimulus is paired with an unconditioned stimulus often enough, the neutral stimulus alone will eventually evoke a conditioned response. A person may develop respect for a certain politician because of classical conditioning. Each time a certain local political candidate is seen, she is surrounded by high-ranking, well-respected federal officials and senators. By associating with such people, a local official can also come to evoke a response of respect or admiration. By being paired with other stimuli, a formerly neutral local politician evokes a response or attitude of respect. This is a principal method used in advertising—associating a known admired person, situation, or product with an unknown one.

Each time a parent makes a negative comment about a political figure, neighbor, or relative, the process of classical conditioning is potentially in operation; a formerly neutral stimulus is paired with a negative attitude for a child. Eventually, upon seeing the formerly neutral stimulus, the child takes on the behavior of producing negative comments. The pairing of attitudes with people, events, and ideologies is done quite effectively, without effort, and works efficiently to help shape a child's views of the world.

INSTRUMENTAL CONDITIONING.   One of the basic principles of operant conditioning is that a behavior which is emitted and then reinforced is likely to occur again. In attitude formation when a child or an adult utters something about an idea and another person agrees with him, the likelihood increases that the idea will be expressed again. When an instructor tells a joke, and her students smile, laugh, and acknowledge her humor, the likelihood that she will emit jokes in the future increases. So her attitudes and demeanor in her class are thus shaped by her students.

You may develop regular voting behavior in local elections because of operant conditioning. Suppose all the candidates you voted for in your first election were successful. More important, the candidates you voted for brought about a needed highway into the location in which you live. The result was very dramatic to business and to property values. Your vote for these individuals and their subsequent behavior brought you positive reinforcement through tangible rewards. No doubt you will vote again—your voting behavior was reinforced. Your attitude about voting was established and will probably be maintained because it was reinforced.

In socializing a child, parents help the child to develop "right" or "proper" attitudes by selectively reinforcing ideas and behaviors consistent with their "correct" view of the world. So parents with strong prejudices against Southerners will reinforce their child when they hear the child using the term "Georgia cracker." Teachers choose to shape their students' attitudes about theories by reinforcing them with grades for the "correct" responses. In the same way therapists will reinforce a client's thoughts when they are leading the client toward a clinical breakthrough. For example, when the client suggests that perhaps many of his problems stem from his own feelings of inferiority, the therapist might respond with "That is certainly worth exploring in more detail. How do you feel when . . ."

SOCIAL LEARNING.   According to the social or observational learning approach we learn by watching others and then imitating their behavior. When a little girl watches someone like a mother interacting with a day-care worker or next-door neighbor, she is usually carefully observing her mother's behavior. It is very likely that when she has to speak with a teacher, her attitudes will reflect those expressed by her model, her mother. Many of our attitudes are established by watching the behavior of significant people in our lives and imitating it; these people include parents, relatives, teachers, and friends. It may seem amazing that fifth-grade students wear political buttons expressing liberal or conservative ideologies. The children are only expressing the views of their parents; yet, as years pass, children of Republicans, for example, often continue to hold attitudes similar to those of their parents.

If you are an aspiring politician, one of the ways you can best get votes is to behave the way other successful politicians behave. By observing their behavior and imitating them, you develop (you hope) similar positive characteristics. Of course, some of your most important behaviors as a politician include your attitudes about legislation, workers' rights, and housing. Crafty politicians often observe and imitate the attitudes and behaviors of successful politicians who have preceded them. Thus, these politicians' attitudes have been formed and shaped by observational learning.

Children learn to imitate their parents' attitudes about politics, religion, and the economy. Clients learn to resist guilt, loneliness, and despair by imitating and practicing their therapist's views toward guilt or loneliness. By watching and imitating the behavior of significant others, people learn new attitudes that eventually become their own.

ATTITUDES ARE LEARNED.   Three different approaches have been presented, each suggesting that attitudes are learned. Regardless of how they are learned, an important point to remember is that they *are* learned; they are not inborn or innate. Many people can influence attitude formation. Clearly parents have the most direct effect in terms of time and influence on a young

According to social learning theory, we learn by observing the behavior of others and then by imitating it.

Peer influence is very great among teenagers.

child's early attitudes. However, as a child becomes educated and interacts with other people, there are new influences on attitudes and behaviors.

A person's peer group helps shape behavior. Classmates expressing their views affect attitudes, as do discussions on politics, religion, sex, and marriage. Friends often discuss opinions so that they might clarify issues and ideas. Religious philosophy often affects a person's attitudes about politics and the way people should live. One's school system affects attitudes by being either conservative, liberal, or moderate in approach. The mass media affect attitudes by presenting what many Americans feel about issues.

People infer their emotional states and the causes of behavior from situations they find themselves in

The study of attitude formation is of particular importance to psychologists, for much of day-to-day behavior is determined by our attitudes. Let's return to the example provided at the beginning of the chapter about the role of women in today's society. Modern American society is changing its attitudes about women. Fifteen years ago the prevalent attitude was that a woman was a dependent housewife and mother; for many, today's conception of women is dramatically different. Women are now viewed as people who can choose a role in life with equal status, standing, and privileges. Yet this attitude is not universal, nor is it necessarily accepted by the majority of people.

Attitude Change

Since attitudes are learned, they can be modified. Like attitudes, learned behaviors are not permanent, but are subject to new experiences. How did attitudes about women, blacks, American Indians, or any other groups of people change? Many factors are involved in changing attitudes. Who tries to change attitudes? Is it the president of the United States, a local labor leader, a parent, or a next-door neighbor? Is an attitude one that has been held for 30 or 40 years, or is it a newly formed attitude?

Perhaps the most common example of people trying to change others' attitudes can be found in the media, particularly in television commercials. The premise of a television commercial is to convey to the listener the idea that the product in question is not only good but also that it is better than the product being used by the viewer. Use brand X rather than Y; X has more widgets per square inch, and so on. Television has become the medium of attitude change in the Western world; private enterprise uses it, political candidates use it, as do health groups, fund-raising groups, and presidents.

Several important factors determine the extent to which an attitude can be changed, and one of these is the characteristics of the person who is trying to change your attitudes.

THE COMMUNICATOR.   To change your attitudes you must believe in the integrity and value of the person trying to change your attitude. If you listen to a local politician speaking about the energy crisis, you might not walk away as convinced as you would be if the speaker were the president of the United States. Similarly, when told by your mother that you need to lose 10 pounds, your attitudes about your weight are not as affected as they would be if you were told the same thing by your family doctor.

It becomes obvious that the power, prestige, and degree of attractiveness of the person trying to change your attitude are very important. The individual needs to be trusted, respected, and liked, or it is likely that you will not trust his or her motives or intentions. If you don't trust the speaker who is attempting to influence your attitudes, it is unlikely that your attitudes will be changed (Anderson, 1971; Horai et al., 1974).

The effects of the communicator and his or her credibility are not simple and may vary in many ways. If, for example, the communicator is generally seen as a knowledgeable and important person but he or she is speaking too quickly, inexpertly, or with a too high-level vocabulary, this can and will likely affect the listener's judgments and thus the communicator's ability to change an attitude (Carbone, 1975; Cronkhite & Liska, 1976; Miller et al., 1976).

THE COMMUNICATION.   Attitudes are most effectively changed through powerful arguments. Even if we trust, respect, and admire the source of an argument that attempts to change attitudes, the actual content of a communication presented by a speaker is important. If an approach is presented forcefully with conviction and logic, attitude change is more likely. When the attitude being sought is not too different from an existing attitude, then attitude change is more likely (Nemeth & Endicott, 1976). Furthermore, if the consequences of a lack of change are unpleasant, attitude change is far more likely (Evans et al., 1975). For example, a study was done on attitudes about the energy crisis. A major finding was that when people perceived the consequences of the energy crisis as very serious, their attitudes about energy consumption changed. When the negative consequences were presented as being minimal, attitudes about energy consumption had changed only to a limited extent (Hass, Bagley, & Rogers, 1975).

Rogers (1975) has suggested that when trying to change people's attitude through fear, there are three basic determinants of whether attitudes will be changed. *First,* the magnitude of the fear-producing event or consequence must be great enough. *Second,* the likelihood that the event or consequence will happen if no adaptive behavior is performed must be great enough. *Third,* to avoid the danger, the behavior that is suggested must be reasonable in averting the danger (Hass et al., 1975; Rogers & Mewborn, 1976). So, if one wishes to change a person's mind by appealing to fear, it is important that the new behavior you are suggesting is reasonable, that the consequences of not adopting the behavior are likely, and that the consequences of nonadoption will be relatively severe. Politicians take heed!

Regardless of who is trying to change your attitudes and regardless of what they say in the attempt, other variables will still affect your willingness to change your mind. In some situations, we are not receptive to convincing speeches. Yet, some of us are more easily persuaded. In addition, if we hear an argument, commercial, or politician often enough, we begin to believe them. It has been shown that repeated exposure to situations can change attitudes and that repeated exposure to ideas presented on television can be an effective method to change stereotypes (Flerx, Fidler, & Rogers, 1976).

Let us consider a specific change in attitudes—those of racial integration. The United States has shown dramatic changes in attitudes about racial integration over the last three decades. These changes are the results of many factors and have affected different groups of people in a variety of ways. For example, individuals of different religions respond differently toward integration, as do people in divergent income groups and residents of various areas of the country. According to Greeley and Sheatsley (1971), in 1942, 2% of whites in the South were in favor of school integration. In 1956 the proportions increased to 14% and in 1971 to over 50%. Age has been shown to be a critical variable and this has often interacted with regions of the country in which the individual lives. For example, in 1970, Southerners who were under 25 years of age were as likely to be integrationists as Northerners aged 45 to 60 years of age. Generally, people under 25 years of age were considerably pro-integration. Greeley and Sheatsley suggest that changing attitudes in the South will entail an influx of a new generation and general change in attitude by many older Southerners (see also Katz & Zalk, 1978).

For the social psychologist, the key finding is that age, sex, ethnic background, and location have major effects on attitudes. Even more important, it is clear that these variables work together so that attitudes cannot merely be changed through attempting to manipulate only one variable.

Attitude Change: The Search for Consistency

Let us review for a moment. We have established that people's behavior and especially their attitudes are established early in life. We also know that attitude development and change is a lifelong process which is affected by many important factors. Yet individuals respond to various circumstances differently. Some people seek change throughout their lives. Others may have tried to be consistent for three decades only to find that to do so they have to go to extreme lengths. While some people change beliefs and others stay set in their ways, most people seek some type of consistency and balance in their lives; they want to feel that they have adopted reasonable ways of living. J. Alfred Prufrock asked if he should dare to change. When he walked along the beach with his trousers rolled, he knew that the mermaids would not sing to him. Most important, however, were his own feelings about his choices. Some psychologists have argued that people seek to maintain a consistency between their attitudes and behavior so that they feel comfortable with themselves. Let us look at four approaches to attitude and behavior change; in a different way, each suggests that people need to seek consistency in their lives.

COGNITIVE DISSONANCE. Trying to change other people's attitudes about an idea is difficult, but sometimes changing our own attitude is even more trying. People are in a constant state of change and regularly need to evaluate their attitudes and situations. As we develop knowledge about ourselves and others, we see if we are happy with our attitudes and situations and what steps are necessary to make life more fulfilling.

When people are placed in the position of knowing things about situations that are in conflict with one another, they experience an uncomfortable feeling. People desire consistency in their lives; so, if you have very strong feelings against the use of drugs and find that your sister is heavily dependent upon them, you might become quite upset. Most likely, you will try to change your sister's drug-taking behavior; if you cannot change her behav-

Sometimes there are no good solutions or answers to a difficult problem.

Cognitive dissonance A state in which individuals feel uncomfortable because they are involved in two or more thoughts, attitudes, or behaviors that are inconsistent with one another.

ior, you may have to change some of your attitudes in order to maintain some level of consistency. The uncomfortable feeling that you might feel is what psychologists call dissonance. In situations where people feel dissonance, they are motivated to try to reduce it. An influential theory of **cognitive dissonance** has been proposed by Leon Festinger (1957) and has generated a great deal of research (Wicklund & Brehm, 1976).

Festinger has suggested that whenever people are placed in a situation in which their attitudes are not consistent with their behavior or other attitudes, something has to change to reduce the uncomfortable feeling that exists. Festinger suggests that we consider what happens when someone has had to form an attitude or make a choice between two competing objects or viewpoints. If the two objects or viewpoints are equally attractive, people usually try to persuade themselves that the attitude which they chose is more attractive. This might be done by claiming that their choice is more attractive than originally thought. Some exaggerate the negative features of one choice and inflate the positive features of the other choice. People are faced with these types of decisions every day. Should I purchase this book or that one? This one has a good story line, but that one is well illustrated. Since both are due on Wednesday, shall I work on chemistry homework or the math assignment? The choice is made and then people justify that choice; they have tried to reduce cognitive dissonance. People try to reduce cognitive dissonance to seek consistency in their lives; sometimes this search can produce highly irrational attitudes that are nevertheless needed to reduce discomfort from competing consequences.

The theory of cognitive dissonance has critics (see, for example, Bem, 1967; Chapanis & Chapanis, 1964), but even so it can be used to explain many social phenomena. For example, you might be attracted to an individual who is not dressed properly for an occasion or who is physically unattractive; you might then remark that her intelligence supersedes her physical characteristics. You have made an excuse to reduce cognitive dissonance which, as we have seen, is generally an adaptive procedure for helping people feel comfortable with their attitudes and behavior.

When people experience cognitive dissonance, they often change their ideas or they change their behavior.

The uncomfortable feeling of dissonance is not always easy to deal with. For example, a smoker may know that his habit is ruining the lining of his lungs and, therefore, he should stop. Yet, he still enjoys smoking and wants to continue to smoke. These are two competing thoughts, both of which have unpleasant consequences; so a person may rationalize and minimize the scientific evidence of lung cancer. Festinger's original claim was that if people are to change attitudes (and behaviors), some negative consequences (dissonance) must be associated with keeping present attitudes. So a person who changed his attitudes and stopped smoking did so because the dissonance associated with continued smoking was too great. Some research supports this idea (Goethals & Cooper, 1975; Sogin & Pallack, 1976), but other studies have found that people often engage in activities that help reduce the uncomfortable feeling but do not change the inconsistent set of beliefs (see Steele, 1975).

Cognitive dissonance arises in all areas of life. An actress who has trained for years perfecting her craft feels that she is an excellent performer. Yet she may find that she has no reliable employment. While out of work she is placed in a situation of inconsistent ideas; she is an excellent actress, but she is not recognized or employed. She is in a state of cognitive dissonance.

An important component of Festinger's theory of cognitive dissonance is that people are often motivated to reduce dissonance through attitude change. Since motives stimulate behavior, we see that cognitive dissonance reduction can be an explanatory concept for why people behave the way they do. Assume that a woman has two competing attitudes about political candidates for the office of the president of the United States. Dissonance theory leads us to expect the voter to find a persuasive argument for one candidate. The feeling of being pulled in two directions is sufficiently uncomfortable so that it will motivate her to seek information that will change her attitudes one way or the other. When people become energized and motivated, they often show physiological arousal. If cognitive dissonance is motivational, then we might expect physiological arousal to be associated with it. The literature supports this view and has found that when people are placed in situations that produce dissonance, they report physiological arousal (Drachman & Worchel, 1976; Zanna, Higgins, & Taves, 1976).

BALANCE THEORY.   An even more general theory of cognitive consistency has been introduced under the term balance theory. In determining our attitudes and how we feel about others, we often ask those close to us how they feel about a judgment. If you and your roommate both like a third person, we call this a balanced relationship. In **balance theory,** balance occurs when there is a satisfying relationship between two people who hold similar views. Pioneering studies on friendship and balance theory show that, in part, friendships are formed on the extent of agreement about which friends are acceptable and which are not. Again, we see that people are seeking to maintain some consistency in their lives.

What happens when a relationship is in imbalance? Assume that you like Mary and Jeff. What happens if Mary does not like Jeff? Psychologists speak of this relationship as being imbalanced. In such relationships people try to change others' attitudes. If you can change Mary's attitude about Jeff, then an imbalance no longer occurs. A second alternative is for you to change your mind about Jeff and decide that you do not like him either. Balance theory

Balance theory An attitude theory in which people prefer to hold consistent beliefs with others and try to avoid incompatible beliefs.

suggests that for people to maintain stable, balanced relationships they need to agree so that unpleasant situations do not occur.

EQUITY THEORY.   People are frequently involved in verbal interchanges with others in which a relationship is sometimes thrown out of balance; balance theory suggests that people try to keep relationships in balance. However, there are times when the maintenance of a consistent, evenly balanced relationship is difficult—sometimes even impossible. Place someone in a situation where she feels that she has been hurt, slandered, or generally treated unfairly, and she usually tries to get restitution. When a person has been the object of aggression, she often exaggerates the extent of the aggression so as to force the aggressor to make amends. How many times have you been in an argument with someone and told her how hurt you were by her behavior? The more we talk about the hurt, the bigger the hurt grows, and usually, our aim is to get the person who hurt us to apologize or to make up for the offending behavior. This situation describes the basics of equity theory. Equity theory holds that people attempt to maintain stable, consistent, interpersonal relationships in which the proportion of each member's contributions is equal to that of the other members of the group so that all members are treated fairly. So, according to equity theory, people need to maintain a balanced relationship through a process of "tit for tat." If you harm me, then I need deep apologies. Those apologies help "even the score" and thus restore a sense of autonomy.

Equity theory works on the positive side of behavior as well; it is probably best summed up in the notion, "You scratch my back, and I'll scratch yours." People who do favors expect favors in return. When a politician responds to his constituents' pleas and has a road paved, he expects their votes on election day. Similarly, when a husband brings his wife flowers on their anniversary, he often expects lavish praises for his thoughtfulness. Without knowing a thing about equity theory, most people use its principles in day-to-day life. We may do a favor for a friend because we know we will need to request one sometime in the near future. We can thus predict from equity theory that an aggressive act will most likely produce a response of an aggressive act in order to maintain an equal balance in the relationship.

REACTANCE THEORY.   A person's attitudes about others or situations change when someone or something tries to restrict freedom of choice. According to social psychologist Jack W. Brehm (1966), whenever people's freedom of choice is threatened, they will be motivated to reestablish the freedom that has been lost. Brehm has shown that people display what he calls "reactance," a form of negative influence that results when people feel that their freedom of choice is threatened. So, if an adolescent is told that he cannot date members of a minority group (and thus his freedom of choice is limited), his attitudes toward the group might change and he might seek them out more often than ever. Reactance theory is derived from the notion of forbidden fruit; whenever a person is told that he may not do one thing, he finds that that choice becomes more attractive. Choosing the forbidden fruit provides a sense of autonomy.

When a subject is placed in a situation where she is told how she *must* respond, her behavior is significantly different than if it is suggested how she *might* respond or if she is given free choice in responding. Think of TV

commercials and how announcers often leave the choice up to you. Instead of telling you that you must choose brand X or brand Y, they present compelling evidence for their product but leave the "choice" to you and your logical thought processes. If they told you how you had to respond, it is likely that you would show some reactance and thus not buy their brand. Thus the advertiser appeals directly to your need for balance and autonomy and avoids setting you up for *reactance* by setting you up for "independent" judgment—often on the basis of lopsided information. When convincing a friend of a certain way to behave or how to handle a difficult situation, we usually do not tell her how she has to do it, but rather suggest alternatives; we leave the logical (and, of course, correct) choice up to her. Clever advertisers and friends know that telling people how to behave is restricting their freedom; this might result in no change or in even opposite behavior.

MAINTAINING CONSISTENCY: A SUMMARY. Attitudes are established throughout our lives but particularly in the early years. If people seek to change their attitudes and behavior, the process is often difficult; in this process people often try to maintain some type of balance and consistency in their thoughts and behavior. Sometimes maintaining this consistency or balance is a task of maintaining a balance in relationships between people (such as in balance and equity theory); other times, it is an attempt to reduce inconsistency between ideas and choices (cognitive dissonance theory). Still other times, people are responding so as to avoid negative attitudes (reactance theory). An underlying idea in each of these four approaches is that people seek to maintain attitudes and behavior that they can live with. Attitude change is sometimes necessary, but behavior change is often equally necessary. Whether the goal is to maintain an existing idea or to change to a new one, people seek order in their lives. Because others affect our behavior, this often requires adjustments in our attitudes and behavior.

SOCIAL PERCEPTION

Groucho Marx enters through a doorway; with cigar in hand, eyebrows raised, and knees bent, he says nothing and the audience roars with laughter. Groucho has a way of communicating humor without saying a word; we infer a great deal about Groucho by observing his posture, cigar, and eyebrows. We feel we understand this master comedian. As Groucho has communicated with us, we communicate with others and try to come to know and understand the persons around us. Through our understanding of them we can come to know ourselves better, to communicate more effectively, and in some ways lead happier lives.

People are complex, and no single rule, theory, or situation is going to describe them completely. Yet, if we are going to get along with others and try to understand them, there must be certain ways in which we pick up information about how and why they behave the way they do. Sometimes people provide us with information directly; they tell us about themselves. At other times they provide information nonverbally through gazes, gestures, and other subtle means of expression. After watching a person communicate nonverbally in a particular set of circumstances, we are usually able to attribute certain characteristics to him. Let us take a closer look at **social perception,** the process by which we perceive people through nonverbal communication and through the process of inference called attribution.

Social perception The process through which we come to know and understand the people around us.

Person Perception: Nonverbal Communication

Many of the conclusions that we draw about what people are trying to communicate to us are made based upon their facial expressions. When people are smiling, we know that it usually expresses happiness. When a person's brow is furrowed and eyes are twitching, this suggests anger, disgust, or perhaps fear. A nonverbal communication allows us to infer the feelings and emotions of others and especially their feelings toward us. A number of researchers have made studies of different emotions that are represented by facial expressions and have generally shown that there are six: happiness, sadness, surprise, fear, anger, and disgust. Most people are able to distinguish these different emotions through facial expressions, although some people can do it better than others.

Facial expressions are excellent indicators of a person's feelings and attitudes. Children as well as adults have been shown to be good interpreters of facial expressions (see p. 176). One of the critical features that conveys this information is the eyes. Studies have been done with pictures of people in which their eyes have been retouched. In one of these studies a photograph is used in which a man is looking off into space and the pupils of his eyes are small. In another photograph the pupils of his eyes have been retouched and are slightly larger. Subjects in the experiments are dramatically affected by such manipulations. They will report distinctly different emotions when asked about the person in the two pictures, even though all other aspects of the photographs remained the same except the size of the pupils.

Eye contact is an easily observable measure of nonverbal communication. The eyes convey a great deal; for example, Ellsworth and Ross (1975) showed that eye contact promoted communication among females but was avoided among pairs of males. Eye contact has been used as a reinforcer in the classroom (Finuf, 1980) and it has generally been shown to be an important nonverbal method of communication (Mehrabian, 1972).

In examining the nature of nonverbal communication, Argyle (1972) has distinguished a series of ways individuals convey information to others. One way is through bodily contact, such as hitting, striking, embracing, kissing, and any other kind of touch. Another way to convey information is through proximity, the distance a person maintains when interacting with others. You will see later in this chapter that in a given culture the amount of space between two individuals in conversation varies depending on the nature of the conversation taking place. Other methods that convey information nonverbally are orientation and posture. This refers to the angle at which a person sits or stands, for example, leaning forward or being relaxed. Head nods and facial expressions also convey information. Personnel officers often will evaluate prospective applicants by examining the nature of their eye contact. Does the applicant always look down to the floor or is she willing to have regular and direct eye contact?

Body language is the communication of information through positions and gestures which can convey mood and attitude even without words or facial expression. In both experimental studies and in clinical reports it has been found that there is a dramatic correlation between body movements and the emotional character of verbal content. For example, when a person's body is relaxed, it is unlikely that there will be much aggressive content in conversation. Similarly, when the pitch of a person's voice is high, the aggressive content in conversation is also likely to be high. Simple changes in the body, such as a tilt of the head, a nod, or eye contact, can communicate positive attitudes to others (Chaiken, Sigler, & Derlega, 1974). While the reasons are not fully clear, research shows that women are better at communicating and interpreting nonverbal messages than men are; this is especially true about visual facial expressions (Hall, 1979). Women are also more likely to send nonverbal facial messages than men; however, women are more cautious in their interpretation of the nonverbal messages that are sent to them by men (Rosenthal & DePaulo, 1979).

Body language The communication of information through body positions and gestures.

There are huge individual differences among people in their ability to convey information through nonverbal mechanisms (Buck, 1979; Buck et al., 1980); thus, body language cannot tell us everything about a person. If body language is our only vehicle for obtaining information about a person, we may be in trouble because it is not always an accurate measure of a person's emotions.

Person Perception: Attribution

In getting to know others, we often infer the causes of different aspects of their behavior. **Attribution** is the process through which we infer or decide about other people's motives and intentions from observing their behavior. The process of attribution allows us to infer a person's behavioral intentions toward others. So, if we see another person as hostile, we might be prepared to deal with his hostility so as to avoid him. People make attributions for the

Attribution The process through which we infer other people's motives and intentions from observing their overt behavior.

purpose of guiding their own behavior toward others. Attribution seems like a simple enough process; we watch someone's behavior and then infer the causes of it. If it is noon time and we watch a person eating a hamburger and french fries, we are usually fairly certain that the person is eating because it is lunch time and the person is hungry. Similarly, a college student working crossword puzzles creates no special problem because we can infer that the student enjoys doing crossword puzzles and that this is a way of passing time.

We can usually make judgments about someone's behavior quite accurately. However, there are times when this behavior is externally caused rather than internally caused. Our crossword puzzle player may have been involved in an experiment for her psychology laboratory. She may really despise doing crossword puzzles but this is part of a laboratory assignment. However, if we want to know something about the internal characteristics that motivate a person's normal day-to-day behavior, we cannot be concerned about behavior that is caused by external factors such as psychology laboratories. This distinction becomes clearer when we look at the following example. When a woman is raped, she is forced to have sexual intercourse against her will. We assume that this union takes place under difficult circumstances in which she is fighting off her male attacker. Yet this might not always be obvious; a rapist may hold a knife to the woman's throat, indicating that her throat will be slit unless she submits to intercourse with him. If we were to pass by moments after the rapist had put aside his knife, we might see few overt signs of violence. If we had watched the behavior of the woman, we would have seen few overt signs that her behavior was externally motivated and was not performed willingly. As is obvious in this example, in attributing traits and causes to a person, we must be sure that the observed behavior is determined by the person in question, not by some outside force.

Figure 10.1 The attribution process: three basic questions

Observed?   Intended?   Coerced?

We can see that the attribution process really involves three basic stages. Kelley Shaver (1977) has outlined these concisely (Figure 10.1). Stage 1 involves the question, "Was the action observed?" Stage 2 asks, "Was the action intended?" Stage 3 asks, "Was the action coerced?" Let's take a concrete example: John Smith is accused of shooting someone, and we are to make a judgment of who and what caused the shooting. Our first question: "Was the action observed?" Yes, the action was observed, John Smith did the shooting. The second question is: "Was the action intended?" and our answer is also yes, it was very clear that John Smith intended to shoot his victim. When making such a decision there are no value judgments being made. Stage 3 provides the critical component; it asks "Was the action coerced?" If the action was coerced (if Smith was forced to shoot his victim), then we cannot attribute the behavior to Smith's enduring personal characteristics. If the action was not coerced, was intended, and was observed, then we can make the decision that the behavior observed was a result of John Smith's personal disposition. We can attribute the behavior to John Smith's personality.

When a person's behavior is shaped by external causes, we cannot infer characteristics about the individual; thus, it is important to be able to judge whether the causes of someone's behavior can be attributed to internal characteristics of the individual or because of external causes. Kelley (1967) has devised three criteria to help determine whether the causes of a behavior are due to internal characteristics of an individual or to external factors. These criteria are: *consensus, consistency*, and *distinctiveness*. As is shown in Table 10.1, to be able to say that a behavior is due to normal internal characteristics of a person, we typically have to believe that: (1) few other people act in the same manner (low consensus), (2) the person acts in this same general way in other similar situations (high consistency), and (3) the person would act in the way he or she just has on other occasions (low distinctiveness). If the person's behavior meets these three criteria, then we typically say that the behavior performed is due to the internal characteristics of the individual. If, by contrast, (1) other people act the same way as the person (high consensus), (2) the person might act in the same manner in a similar situation on other occasions (high consistency), and (3) the person acts differently in other situations (high distinctiveness), then we say his or her behavior is caused by an external force or situation (Jackson & Larrance, 1979; Kelley, 1972, 1973).

Table 10.1 Kelley's criteria for internal vs. external attributions are based on consensus, consistency, and distinctiveness.

INTERNAL	EXTERNAL
Low consensus: Few others act the same way	High consensus: Others act the same way
High consistency: Person acts in the same way in other similar situations	High consistency: Person acts in the same way in other similar situations
Low distinctiveness: Person acts in the same way on other occasions	High distinctiveness: Person acts differently in other situations

Let us look at a case where one makes a judgment about why a person took a specific action. Assume you know a person at school who is often rude to members of the opposite sex. Since other people usually don't act this way (low consensus), since the person acts this way on other occasions with the opposite sex (high consistency), and since the person acts this way most of the time (low distinctiveness), you would attribute her rudeness to *internal* characteristics of her personality; you might think her a jerk! By contrast, you would be far more likely to say that the person's rudeness was because of the situation she found herself in if most people would have acted rudely in this situation (high consensus), the person would only act rudely in other similar situations (high consistency), and the person is known to act differently in other situations (high distinctiveness). In this case you might say that her rudeness is caused by the high temperatures, failing a test, or perhaps something that the person of the opposite sex might have said.

PERSONAL BIASES.   An interesting aspect of attribution theory is that we tend to perceive our own behavior as being caused by various situational factors; however, we generally perceive the behavior of others as stemming primarily from an individual's internal characteristics (Jones & Nisbett, 1972; Nisbett et al., 1973). In other words, when people are asked to judge whether personal characteristics or situational factors determine behavior, when referring to other people they generally respond that personal characteristics determine behavior, but when describing themselves, they attribute their own actions to situational factors. Young children are often heard to say, "You made me hurt myself." But, when a friend hurts himself, the same youngster will proclaim, "You're clumsy." The causes of other people's behavior are often obscured by a person's general orientation about the world; furthermore, it is often hard to be accurate about the causes of one's own actions, as we shall see when we consider self-perception. This effect becomes even more pronounced in achievement-oriented situations (Medway, 1979).

One way of formally conceptualizing the idea of internal vs. situational characteristics determining behavior has been developed by Rotter. Julian Rotter (1966) developed an idea of "internal vs. external locus of control," and he conceptualized this on a rating scale. The I-E scale, as it is sometimes called, quantifies the extent to which people attribute the causes of behavior to internal factors or situational factors. Consider how you might respond to the following items and where you would place the locus of control:

1. "The idea that teachers are unfair to students is nonsense" vs. "Most students don't realize the extent to which their grades are influenced by accidental happenings."
2. "Heredity plays the major role in determining one's personality" vs. "It is one's experiences in life that determine what they're like."
3. "People are lonely because they don't try to be friendly" vs. "There's not much use in trying too hard to please people because if they like you, they like you."

Locus of control has many direct applications, which might include attribution theory, personality, and, particularly, psychotherapy. In therapy, individuals often place the blame for their problems on others. We will be examining locus of control further in chapter 11, Personality (p. 526).

A JUST WORLD.   The just world belief is the belief that the world is a just one in which people get what they deserve. According to Melvin Lerner (1970), most people believe that there is an appropriate link between what they do and what happens to them. In other words, people get what they deserve, so those who work hard in life find some ultimate reward.

A just world belief is related to a person's locus of control; people who are internal in their locus of control tend to believe in a just world (Zuckerman & Gerbasi, 1977). A consequence of the just world belief is that people who are victims of crime or of unfortunate experiences are blamed by the onlookers for these unfortunate experiences. People who suffer through no fault of their own tend to be valued less and blamed more by noninvolved observers. Lerner accounts for this phenomenon by noting that the suffering of an innocent victim threatens an observer's belief in a just world.

Even if you are not personally responsible for someone else being injured, seeing someone injured can sometimes increase the likelihood that you will help. Seeing someone else injured is upsetting because it disturbs your belief in a just world and sometimes motivates you to eliminate the unjust suffering.

According to the just world belief, people get what they deserve.

ATTRIBUTION: SOME IMPLICATIONS.   Recognizing that people have orientations that are external or internal and that some people have a view of a just world, we can see some key aspects of attribution theory in general. The attributional process involves observing an action and deciding that it was intentionally produced, while being sure that it was not coerced. This process becomes very important in making judgments about defendants in court cases. A jury has several important decisions to make. They have to decide whether the behavior was observed and whether it was coerced or the result of enduring personal characteristics of the accused. For example, did the accused kill because of threats of a third person or because of the orders of a commanding officer? War criminals have used the defense of following orders. This type of defense was common in the Nuremburg trials of Nazi war crimes; it was also used by those defending Lt. William Calley's involvement in the Mai Lai massacre during the Vietnam War. Attorneys defending these accused individuals argued that they were coerced into their behavior by their superior officers. For a jury, however, the question of the accused's guilt is called into question as soon as environmental, or outside, coercion is invoked by the defense. We will look at the willingness of people to comply with the orders of people in positions of authority later in this chapter.

Self-Perception

People's perceptions of themselves are sometimes called self-concepts. A self-concept is the sum of a number of characteristics. A woman's self-concept may be determined by her physical appearance, her work habits, or her athletic abilities. Another woman's self-concept may be more narrowly defined; she may focus more closely on her abilities as a mother or as a wife. People develop a sense of self by combining aspects of their marital, occupational, family, recreational, and sexual roles.

Self-concepts or **self-perceptions** develop over time and through experience. Your attitudes about yourself will determine to a great extent how you evaluate the behavior of others. As we have seen, how you view yourself also

Self-perception One's attitude toward and beliefs about oneself. Self-perception is often a reflection of others' attitudes toward oneself and is largely formed during childhood and adolescence.

453

Switching roles in family life is becoming increasingly common; this is especially true in homes where both partners in a marriage have full-time jobs.

determines the extent to which others may be able to influence your behavior. Attitudes about one's self are established early in life, but they are re-evaluated often and can have dramatic effects on behavior. Children ask, "Mommy, am I pretty?" or "Mommy, do you like me?" Similarly, in adolescence there is a new definition of roles and a constant self-evaluation taking place. Upon entering the mainstream of life, young people question their identity. Self-concepts are questioned as one tries to establish a firm identity that is consistent with previous attitudes and new values. A successful completion of this identity questioning, or, as it is sometimes called, an identity crisis, brings about relatively stable individuals who can adapt to new situations with a firm understanding of themselves and their values.

A person's self-perception is clearly influenced by how he or she is perceived by others

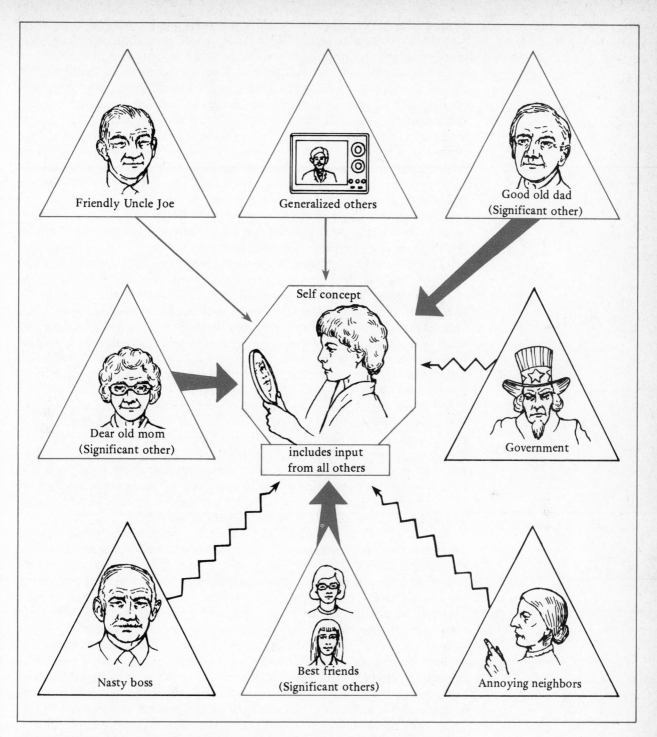

Figure 10.2 People's self-concepts are determined by many other people. Sometimes these individuals provide positive experiences; other times they provide experiences that take away from people's positive feelings about themselves. The development of a self-concept can thus be seen as the sum of both the positive and the negative influences provided by others (data from Albrecht, Thomas & Chadwick, 1980)

An understanding of self is an understanding of one's beliefs, what brought about these beliefs, and why they should be maintained. An understanding of self also implies that an individual has examined his or her own behavior and realizes its consequences. Take, for example, prejudice against minority groups. If a person has a belief that all people are created equal but his behavior is inconsistent with his belief, his self-concept is challenged. The cognitive dissonance he experiences often requires a reexamination of his beliefs. Many beliefs are established early in life through parent-child interactions, so people have to decide if their current values are their own, or beliefs that were imposed on them. An understanding of your own values is an important aspect of growing up, for only if you have a firm self-concept will you be able to accept challenges to your values.

Like Maslow (whose theories were explained on p. 170), a number of personality theorists have suggested that happiness is only achieved when an individual has a complete and actualized self-concept. The noted theorist Eric H. Erikson (1963), whose theories were presented in chapter 6, Development, has argued that happiness is only achieved when one reaches a stage of ego integrity, a stage of self-actualization. Ego integrity is reached only after a period of many years when value systems and conceptions of self are firm, have withstood challenge, and are consistent with behavior. Other personality theorists have presented the concept of self as a central part of a person's personality. For example, psychologist Alfred Adler has argued that feelings of inferiority play the central role in anxiety and that people try to compensate for these feelings (see p. 516).

Studies of social perception show that conceptions of self are important in determining both an individual's psychological health and perceptions of other people. If in a particular situation a person feels that conservative behavior is appropriate and then finds others behaving in nonconservative ways, he may consider these behaviors inappropriate. Person perception is usually a result of comparing others to ourselves. When a person has a strong self-concept, he generally knows the type of behavior, people, politicians, and religious ideologies that he feels comfortable with.

We know that self-perception and the perception of others are not separate processes. We perceive others in reference to our own value system of ideas (Webster & Driskell, 1978). If we are very assertive in our behavior, we see others who are assertive as expressing normal, appropriate behavior. Yet, if we are relatively quiet, shy, and passive, we may see others who are assertive as being inappropriate, loud, and even aggressive. You will see later in the chapter that people often try to limit and control their interactions with other people by maintaining a sense of privacy and personal space.

People's attitudes about themselves are determined by a wide number of important variables throughout their lives. Certainly early parental attitudes are important, and social interactions with friends play a role. Furthermore, biological predispositions to certain personalities affect self-perception. An impressive body of literature has developed to suggest that your physical attractiveness affects other's attitudes toward you and thus how you will subsequently perceive yourself (Phillips & Zigler, 1980). Attractive schoolchildren are thought to get higher marks, misbehave less, and are predicted to have more successful careers than unattractive schoolchildren (Clifford & Walster, 1973; Dion et al., 1972; Lerner & Lerner, 1977). In general, attractive adults are seen more positively and are granted more freedom and liberties

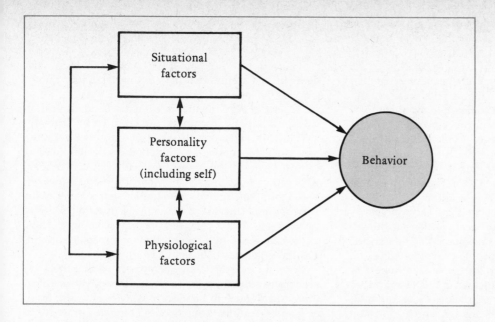

Figure 10.3 It is not surprising to find that spatial, personality, and psychological factors all have effects on each other and ultimately on behavior (adapted from Albrecht et al., 1980)

than unattractive adults (Cash & Kehr, 1978; Kleinke et al., 1975), which is bound to affect their feelings about themselves and their abilities (Reis, Nezlek, & Wheeler, 1980). For example, when people rate themselves as physically less attractive, they are more likely to have problems with anxiety about members of the opposite sex (Mitchell & Orr, 1976). Physically unattractive people tend to be ignored by members of both sexes, are attributed with negative traits, and are often isolated (Krebs & Adinolfi, 1975). Taken together, we see that a child's conception of self is in great part determined by a superficial characteristic like physical attractiveness (see, for example, Zweigenhaft, Hayes, & Haagen, 1980).

Social psychologist Daryl Bem (1972) has proposed a theory of self-perception in which he suggests that people perceive themselves by observing their own behavior and the circumstances in which it occurs. Bem suggests that people often do not understand the causes of their own behavior; thus they are only able to look at it after the fact and in the context of the external situation where their behavior occurred. Support for Bem's notion comes from several areas of research, one of which is the work of Schachter, which was discussed in chapter 4, Motivation and Emotion (see p. 180). Schachter showed that subjects interpret aspects of their emotional states; this interpretation is based upon their bodily states and on situations in which they find themselves. A subject whose bodily state was excited and who was surrounded by happy individuals reported feeling happy. Subjects who found themselves excited but in a tense situation behaved angrily. Schachter's work on emotion supports Bem's idea that people need to interpret their behavior in the context of the situation they find themselves in. If people believe that the causes of their own behavior are situationally determined, then both Bem and Schachter are correct. People infer their emotional states and they infer the causes of behavior from the situations in which they find themselves. If people are in a satisfying situation, one they consider appropriate to their self-images, then they develop what psychologists call a "belief in a just world" as was previously discussed.

Eyewitness Testimony

We all depend on reports from others about events we did not see or hear personally. Sometimes these reports are accurate and detailed, but sometimes important misrepresentations occur. Can we believe people's eyewitness reports? Can we believe people's memories of events in the past?

Perhaps one of the most important situations in which people are called upon to remember previous events is in the courtroom. There people are relied upon to recall accurately events in the past. The problem is that eyewitnesses often report seeing different things. For example, Langman and Cockburn (1975) described the eyewitness testimony of people who reported seeing Sirhan Sirhan shoot United States Senator Robert F. Kennedy. Each of the eyewitnesses to this event, many of them standing next to each other, saw different things. Similarly, a study was done in which an assault on a professor was staged in a classroom of students. Seven weeks later more than 60% of the eyewitness stu-

dents picked an innocent man from a set of four photographs (Buckhour, Figueroa, & Hoff, 1974).

An early experiment on eyewitness identification was conducted at Dartmouth and reported by Brown in 1935 in which students observed an individual and then saw him again among a group of others. When asked to indicate who in the group they had seen earlier, only 83% picked the correct man. More surprising, however, was a group of students who had never seen any of the men before. When asked to identify a man that they had never seen, 29% "recalled" having seen him. Thus, people were willing to report they had seen an individual they had never actually seen.

Several researchers have demonstrated that there are numerous errors in eyewitness testimony, yet such testimony continues to be used to convict both the innocent and the guilty (Loftus, 1974; Loftus & Loftus, 1976; Loftus & Palmer, 1974).

In balance, it must be pointed out that not all researchers support Bem's position. Some have found that people have very good conceptions of their own views of themselves and other people and that external cues play less than maximal roles. It is most likely that internal dispositions, attitudes, feelings, and past beliefs together with external cues shape people's attitudes about themselves and their situations (Brown et al., 1975; Hendrick & Gieson, 1976; Kruglanski, 1975; Taylor, 1975).

AGGRESSION

Under certain circumstances, many people are aggressive. We speak of aggressive salespersons, an aggressive painting, and sometimes of an act of physical aggression. Aggression is an emotionally charged topic; people have strong feelings about the extent to which people are aggressive. Among nonpsychologists there are many vague and conflicting ideas about aggression. For a social psychologist, **aggression** is any behavior that has as its goal harming or injuring another person or thing. Most aggressive acts are not physical. For example, we may attempt to harm someone verbally, or through a gesture, or in writing. We may hire someone else to do the harmful act; we might injure or harm through gossip, rumor, or innuendo. Aggression abounds in everyday life. We see it on an international level through acts of war. Politicians slur and harm (reduce votes given to) other politicians. One friend will slander another. Why should individuals, groups, and governments attempt to injure or harm others? The purpose of the study of aggression is to determine the behaviors that people are capable of and why

Aggression Any behavior that has as its goal harming or injuring another person or thing.

A simple comment or response can evoke strong emotional responses; for some people, small frustrations can bring about a great deal of aggression.

they occur. There are three major approaches to explain why people are aggressive: *instincts, acquired drives,* and *social learning.* In the nature vs. nurture controversy, the instinctual view favors the nature side; the acquired drives and social learning views favor the learned, nurture side. Let us examine these divergent views of aggression.

Approaches

INSTINCTS.   Some psychologists believe that many aspects of behavior are inborn; these psychologists are called *nativists.* A nativistic view argues that aggression is innate. This view holds that people are "preprogrammed" to be aggressive, and thus human beings are genetically predisposed toward aggression. Freud, for example, suggested that aggression is inborn in everybody and that people have a death instinct that is a destructive release of aggression against themselves. This concept is not widely accepted; as Freudian theory developed, it concentrated more on the notion that people need to develop ways to cope with their sexual urges.

Another nativistic view has been put forth by the ethologists. The Nobel Prize–winning ethologist Konrad Lorenz has investigated aggressive behavior through the technique of naturalistic observation. He has noted that most animals do not attack members of their own species. Unlike most animals, humans not only attack their own species through war, but, in addition, develop new technology to attack their own species with greater ferocity. According to Lorenz, people's aggression is instinctive and spontaneous and will constantly be expressed, often as a fighting instinct (Lorenz, 1964). Thus, instinct serves to maximize the utilization of food, space, and resources in general. From Lorenz's view people will always be looking to further express their aggressive (fighting) instincts. From Lorenz's view aggression in humans is inevitable; he then goes on to stress the possible social implications of people's aggressive fighting instincts. Lorenz has been sharply criticized (Bandura, 1973), and the validity of many of his speculative claims has been called into question (Zillman, 1979).

ACQUIRED DRIVES.   Aggression need not be considered an innate component of behavior. Indeed, most psychologists discount innate components of behavior when speaking about aggression. Psychologists consider that most aggressive behaviors are learned. They favor the nurture side of the nature vs. nurture argument. That aggression is acquired or learned has been the focus of a theory that has been under development for over 40 years. This theory was initially put forth by Dollard, Doob, Miller, Mowrer, and Sears (1939) in the **frustration-aggression hypothesis.** This view suggests that frustration of any goal-directed behavior leads to aggression. This means that people who are frustrated in attempting to reach goals will have an aggressive response aroused within them.

This simple and elegant idea has undergone a great deal of research and evaluation. As a theory of aggression it has seen many modifications and changes, but overall this view has been widely accepted (Bandura, 1973). From anecdotal evidence we know that people involved in goal-oriented tasks often do become aggressive or angry when they are frustrated. The evidence for the frustration-aggression hypothesis was examined and reevaluated by Berkowitz (1964). He suggested that frustration creates a tendency toward, or a readiness for, aggressive acts rather than actual aggression. When frustration occurs, certain stimulus cues must be available for aggression to occur also. Berkowitz has completed a series of studies showing that different stimuli have cue value. If a frustrated subject sees a gun or a knife, the subject tends to be more aggressive than if the only available stimulus were a rubber duck. So, contemporary formulations of this theory have refined it to suggest that frustration may cause a number of responses, among which might be aggression. Aggression is certainly more likely to occur given the right circumstances and proper cues (Donnerstein, 1980).

Frustration-aggression hypothesis A view that suggests that frustration of any goal-directed behavior leads to aggression.

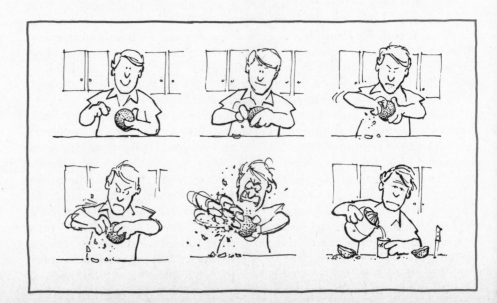

When people involved in goal-oriented tasks are frustrated, they often become aggressive or angry

To show that his notions have validity Berkowitz conducted an experiment to see if items generally associated with aggression can bring about aggressive responses from people who are already angry and ready to act aggressively. In Berkowitz's own words:

> One hundred male university students received either 1 or 7 shocks, supposedly from a peer, and were then given an opportunity to shock this person. In some cases a rifle and revolver were on the table near the shock key. These weapons were said to belong, or not to belong, to the available target person. In other instances there was nothing on the table near the shock key, while for a control group 2 badminton racquets were on a table near the key. The greatest number of shocks was given by the strongly aroused subjects (who had received 7 shocks) when they were in the presence of the weapons. The guns had evidently elicited strong aggressive responses from the aroused men. (Berkowitz & LePage, 1967, p. 202)

Berkowitz's results and ideas have achieved a great deal of attention; experiments have been done to repeat or extend the basic findings of Berkowitz and Lepage (1967), but the results were not always in the direction that Berkowitz would predict (see Halderman & Jackson, 1979; Tannenbaum & Zillman, 1975). In many ways we find that the frustration-aggression hypothesis is too simple. It is far too sweeping in its assumptions and does not account for all of the data. People do not *always* become aggressive when frustrated. However, in many ways the frustration-aggression hypothesis is an example of good psychology. It led to research and other formulations which are more useful in describing behavior. Berkowitz's experiments grew out of earlier work on frustration-aggression, and it is now generating other kinds of research and insights. No theory is perfect and will account for all people's behavior at all times, but a good theory will generate new insights and more experimentation so that we might come closer to the real causes of behavior.

In some situations, there is no question that frustration can produce aggression.

SOCIAL LEARNING.   Children imitate adults and other children. A child who is confronted with a new toy will often learn to use the toy by imitating an adult or another child's use of it. Children are constantly being thrust into new situations to which standard responses are not yet firmly established. So, if parents or teachers are aggressive, children learn to be aggressive by imitating their behavior. In contrast, if children watch someone being punished for aggressive behavior, they learn that aggressive behavior is something that should not be imitated.

According to Bandura, aggressive behavior can be established or eliminated through observational learning. This technique of imitation has been used by child psychologists for many years in child-rearing practices, but it has rarely been considered applicable in curbing aggression. According to Bandura and his colleagues, aggression is a learned imitated behavior. They argue that children are not born with aggressive instincts, but see others (including parents and people they admire) showing aggression and thus become aggressive themselves. A model who is rewarded for aggression promotes aggression in a viewer; conversely, a model who is punished for it decreases aggression in a viewer (Bandura, 1971). Bandura further asserts that human beings exert a strong sense of "cognitive control" over their aggressive behavior. Humans are aware of the consequences of their actions and this awareness guides their actions (Bandura, 1973). (For a review of cognitive controls see chapter 4, Motivation and Emotion, p. 164.)

461

While Bandura sees aggression as a socially learned behavior, he does not rule out other types of learning in the establishment of aggression. Clearly, reinforcement and punishment are viable mechanisms for the direct teaching of aggressive acts (Bandura & Walters, 1963); but in Bandura's view, aggression can be established, maintained, or eliminated through the process of viewing others involved in aggressive acts.

Aggressive Stimuli: Television

The three perspectives presented suggest different reasons why individuals are aggressive. The first suggests that individuals are innately aggressive; the second that aggression is learned and provoked by frustration; and the third that people learn to be aggressive by observing others. There are certain stimuli that generally bring about aggression. When people feel that they have been slandered, they are often aggressive. When people are morose or unhappy, they are often aggressive. When people are threatened or feel that through aggression they might feel better, they often behave aggressively. Most acts of violence are triggered by a stimulus; they do not just occur randomly. Since most people realize that there is usually an antecedent stimulus to aggression, one of the more interesting aspects of social psychology has been the study of aggression and the mass media.

Does TV violence affect the nature and amount of aggressive behavior in adults and/or children? Research on this question is important, for it has serious social implications, and the results are startling. A number of laboratory studies have indicated that watching violence and aggressive action on television increases the amount of aggressive behavior by its viewers (McCarthy et al., 1975). Admittedly, some studies have shown that watching TV depicting violence did not bring about an increase in violence, but rather a decrease (see Gorney et al., 1977; Kaplan & Singer, 1976). The implications of these studies are very important, since the mass media dominates much of a child's and many adults' waking hours (see also Liebert et al., 1977; Quisenberry et al., 1978).

Children do learn from TV, and it does occupy them much of their time. Recent studies have shown that children who see large doses of TV violence

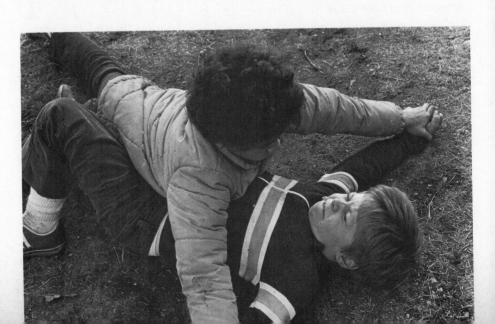

Children learn to be aggressive, at least in part, through media influences.

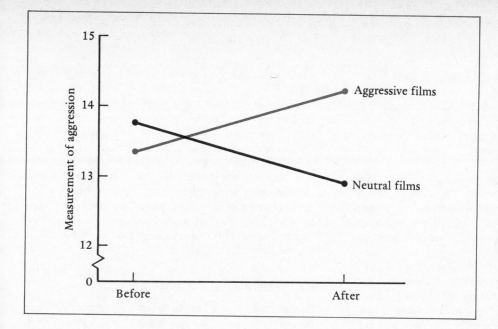

Figure 10.4 A film with aggressive content (*Clockwork Orange*) or neutral content (*Fiddler on the Roof*) was shown to adult subjects. A measure of aggressiveness was made before and after viewing the films. After viewing an aggressive film the subjects were more hostile than before viewing the film; those who saw the neutral film became less aggressive. These results support the general finding that viewing violence leads to an increase in aggressive behavior (data adapted from Goldstein, Rosnow, Raday, Silverman, & Gaskell, 1975)

are more likely to be passive observers of real life violence and less likely to intervene to help a victim of violence (Drabman & Thomas, 1975). Furthermore, children under the age of 5 believe that what they see on TV is the truth; in addition, as much as 85% of their viewing time is during adult program hours. Their innocence, combined with the effects of adult programs, makes children particularly vulnerable to the negative aspects of TV (Jones, 1977).

Television is saturated with violence, which alters people's attitudes toward violence. For example, according to Gerbner and Gross (1976), one-half of all prime-time TV characters are involved in some violence, and about one-tenth in killing. To control the lawlessness on the screen, about 20% of TV males are engaged in law performance duties, while in the real world, the figure is less than 1%. As a result, viewers of violence on TV become fearful and are more likely to feel that they might be the victims of violent acts. Gerbner and Gross point out that TV violence may not necessarily produce violence in overt behavior, but psychologists must be concerned about how it changes people's overall views of life (see Doob & MacDonald, 1979).

When discussing attitude change earlier in this chapter, I pointed out that repeated exposure to a theme or attitude on television can alter a person's own attitudes. If this is the case, then TV violence or any TV theme can alter and shape the attitudes of children and adults alike.

Research in TV programming has indicated some positive effects. An analysis of the influence of "Sesame Street" and "Mr. Roger's Neighborhood" has demonstrated that children who were exposed to these shows were more likely to show good social behaviors and better personal behavior with other children. TV does have some good programming (Coates, Pusser, & Goodman, 1976).

In the last decade a dramatic amount of interest in the effects of television on human behavior has been shown. Much of this work has focused on how television affects people and their aggressive behavior. It is likely that in the

What TV Does to Kids

Scientific research has shown that children and adults imitate the behavior of people they see as important and influential. Since children are spending so much time watching television, the potential influence of television on their behavior is most dramatic. The following article outlines some potential hazards of TV watching.

NEWSWEEK It is only in recent years—with the first TV generation already well into its 20s—that social scientists, child psychologists, pediatricians and educators have begun a serious study of the impact of television on the young. "The American public has been preoccupied with governing our children's schooling," says Stanford University psychologist Alberta Siegel. "We have been astonishingly unconcerned about the medium that reaches into our homes. Yet we may expect television to alter our social arrangements just as profoundly as printing has done over the past five centuries."

The statistics are at least alarming. Educators like Dr. Benjamin Bloom, of the University of Chicago, maintain that by the time a child reaches the age of five, he has undergone as much intellectual growth as will occur over the next thirteen years. According to A. C. Nielsen, children under five watch an average of 23.5 hours of TV a week. That may be less than the weekly video diet of adults (about 44 hours), but its effects are potentially enormous. Multiplied out over seventeen years, that rate of viewing means that by his high-school graduation today's typical teenager will have logged at least 15,000 hours before the small screen—more time than

he will have spent on any other activity except sleep. And at present levels of advertising and mayhem, he will have been exposed to 350,000 commercials and vicariously participated in 18,000 murders.

The conclusion is inescapable: after parents, television has become perhaps the most potent influence on the beliefs, attitudes, values, and behavior of those who are being raised in its all-pervasive glow. George Gerbner, dean of the University of Pennsylvania's Annenberg School of Communications is almost understating when he says: "Television has profoundly affected the way in which members of the human race learn to become human beings." . . .

Violence: Paranoia and Propaganda

The debate over the link between TV violence and aggressive behavior in society has had a longer run than "Gunsmoke." Today, however, even the most chauvinist network apologists concede that some children, under certain conditions, will imitate antisocial acts that they witness on the tube. Indeed, a study of 100 juvenile offenders commissioned by ABC found that no fewer than twenty-two confessed to having copied criminal techniques from TV. Last year, a Los Angeles judge sentenced two teenage boys to long jail terms after they held up a bank and kept twenty-five persons hostage for seven hours. In pronouncing the sentence, the judge noted disgustedly . . . the entire episode the boys had seen two weeks earlier. . . .

next decade continued research will show the long-term effects of television on people's behavior and attitudes about violence. While television was available in the mid 1940s, full and active programming did not take place until the 1950s and the two-TV family did not emerge until the 1960s. Today's adults are a product of the media blitz; they might even be called the media generation. Long-term studies on the effects of *years* of television on individuals' behavior will be particularly telling. Does the television affect us in enduring and particularly long-lasting ways? If it can and does, how might we better program television and the viewing audience so as to help optimize our human potential through television. While there are and will be many advocacy groups supporting different kinds of viewing—for example, against violence, sex, sugar, religion—a stable national policy is likely to emerge from the research conducted in universities today on many subjects, including introductory psychology students! All of the data are not yet in, but certainly our initial view suggests that TV's potential for education—either positive or negative—is *very* great.

Can Aggression Be Produced in Children?

Social learning theorist Albert Bandura conducted an important research study to investigate whether aggression can be produced in children after they observed it in other people. Children were exposed to aggression portrayed by actors, by films of real people showing aggression, and in cartoons. The study showed that subjects who viewed the aggression were nearly twice as aggressive as subjects in a control group who were not exposed to it.

In this classic study by Bandura, Ross, and Ross (1963), 4-year-old children were brought to a laboratory in which they saw adults exhibiting aggressive behavior in which they kicked, hit, and generally made aggressive actions toward a large inflated doll. A second group of subjects was shown a film in which the same actors were filmed while exhibiting similar aggressive behavior. A third group of subjects saw a film depicting an aggressive cartoon character. After they were shown the aggressive sequences, the subjects were observed for the amount of imitative aggression in a different setting. The results showed that children became more aggressive after having seen live adults or a film that had aggressive content, and they imitated the aggressive behavior.

Many observers have been quick to point out that certain aspects of this experimental setting are inappropriate for drawing conclusions about the effect of TV violence on children. For example, the object of aggression in these studies was generally an inflated plastic toy, not a real person. As such, these scenes are dramatically different from the type portrayed on TV in which one human being aggresses against another, usually within the context of a plot. Although there are problems with studies of this nature, they present some initial evidence to suggest that when children are provided with aggressive stimuli, they imitate it in subsequent play. This notion is also supported by the study reported by Quilitch and Risley (1973), discussed in chapter 6, Development. This study showed that the type of toys children played with affected subsequent play.

Research on the effects of TV violence on children's behavior comes from other types of studies. In a correlational study conducted by McCarthy and her colleagues (1975), different kinds of television watching were compared with the amount of violent behavior children showed in their day-to-day living. Numbers of hours of TV watching, kinds of programs watched, as well as behaviors like conflict with parents, fighting, and delinquency were measured. The data support the previous contention that when children watch a great deal of violence on television, they are more likely to be found in violent, aggressive activities than children who watch less violence on TV. Of course, the study also found that the children who spent most of the time in front of the TV were from disadvantaged backgrounds and whose mothers reported that positive events occurred rarely for these children (see also Hartnagel et al., 1975).

A great deal of research has supported the Bandura studies. For example, in a study reported by Worchel, Hardy, and Hurley (1976), subjects who viewed violent films were compared with subjects who viewed nonviolent ones on a measure of aggressiveness. They interacted with a series of research assistants, one of whom was directed to act in a bumbling, blundering, and inadequate manner. This assistant was of course working for the experimenter. On three occasions the assistant committed serious blunders. After the subjects viewed the films and interacted with the assistant, the experimenters asked them to rate the research assistant. They informed the subjects that their rating of the assistant would determine which of the three assistants would be rehired. Both the violent and nonviolent viewers saw the bumbling assistant. If the violent viewers rated the bumbling, blundering assistant lower than the nonviolent viewers, then the lower rating could be attributed to the violence watching. This was precisely the case. The subjects who viewed the violent films rated the bumbling assistant lower and did not recommend the assistant for rehiring. The subjects were thus more aggressive following violent film watching than following nonviolent film watching.

The impact of studies like Bandura's has been significant. Newer studies have confirmed many of Bandura's early findings (see Drabman & Thomas, 1977), and research on social learning theory and the extent to which people imitate others continues. Television programmers, sponsors, and parents continue to worry about violence and sex portrayed on TV. Since the social consequences of this research have been profound, it is particularly important that all aspects of this research be confirmed, repeated, and fully explored.

CONFORMITY

Social psychologists have shown that our behavior is determined by still another complex phenomenon. Most people are amazingly willing to go along with the wishes of others; this is especially true if the person sees the others as important in some way. The extent to which an individual goes along with a significant person tells us a great deal about how compliant individuals are to people in positions of authority. It also may tell us something about a person's self-perception and his or her own values.

Studies of Obedience

Parents often work hard at making children obedient; they ask that children comply with their rules. Obedience toward parents is an appropriate behavior, but should people obey everyone in a position of power? The military demands obedience, and any job that requires a team effort, particularly athletics, requires it. Obedience has its place; however, a distinction must be drawn between an appropriate authority and one who assumes a position of authority.

From a classic experiment Milgram (1963) presented data that he had collected about obedience. Two subjects were brought into a laboratory and were told that they were in a learning experiment. One of the subjects was a confederate of the experimenter and was collaborating with him in the study. The two subjects were told that one was to be a teacher and one was to be a learner. They drew lots as to who would adopt which role, but the drawing was rigged. The naive subject was always chosen as the teacher and the confederate was always the learner. They were told that the purpose of the experiment was to investigate paired-associate learning. The learner was to indicate which of four words was associated with a pair of words presented earlier.

The learner was placed in a booth in which electrodes were attached to his arms. The naive subject was shown a shock generator box that consisted of 30 switches, each of which was labeled with a different shock intensity. The level of shock intensity was labeled by indicating low shock, moderate shock, very strong shock, extreme intensity, and danger—severe shock. In reality, the shock generator was not attached to the confederate learner.

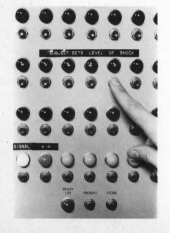

The confederate made many wrong responses and the experimental subject was told to punish him every time he made an error. A social psychologist and a lab assistant who was wearing a white lab coat encouraged the subject to increase the shock voltage by one level each time the learner made a mistake. As the shock level was increased, the learner produced sounds appropriate with increasing levels of pain. As the shock intensity reached the point of severe shock, the learner pounded on the walls of the experimental booth and no longer made vocal responses to the paired-associate stimulus. The psychologist told the subject that the learner's lack of response should be treated as an error and that he should be shocked. As seen in Figure 10.5, the results of the experiment showed that 65% of the subjects continued to shock the learner until the end of the shock series. No subjects stopped before the point of intense shock.

Milgram (1965a) has indicated that there may indeed be some problems with his study. He suggests that it is possible that his experiment at Yale

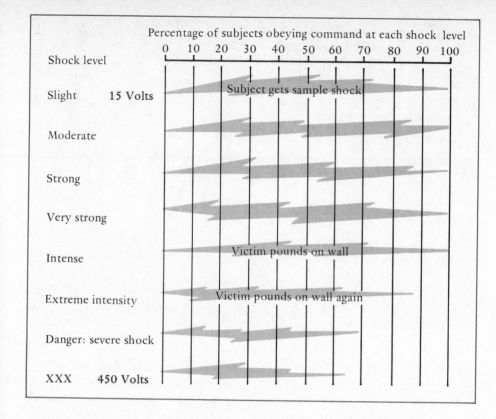

Percentage of subjects obeying command at each shock level

0 10 20 30 40 50 60 70 80 90 100

Shock level

Slight   15 Volts   Subject gets sample shock

Moderate

Strong

Very strong

Intense   Victim pounds on wall

Extreme intensity   Victim pounds on wall again

Danger: severe shock

XXX   450 Volts

Figure 10.5 At different levels of shock intensity, subjects were willing to shock other subjects in the study by Milgram (1963). Sixty-five percent of the subjects were willing to use the highest levels of shock intensity. Virtually all of the subjects were willing to provide shocks of moderate and even strong intensity

University invoked a particular type of experiment bias. In referring to his studies, Milgram noted that the experiments were conducted at Yale University, an organization that most subjects regard with respect and sometimes awe. In postexperimental interviews several participants remarked that the locale and sponsorship of the study gave them confidence in the integrity, competence, and benign purposes of the personnel; many indicated that they would not have shocked the learner if the experiments had been done elsewhere.

This issue of background authority in Milgram's experiment is important for an interpretation of the results that had been obtained thus far; moreover, it is highly relevant to any comprehensive theory of human obedience. Consider, for example, how closely our compliance with the imperatives of others is tied to particular institutions and locales in our day-to-day activities. On request we expose our throats to a man with a razor blade in the barber shop, but we would not do so in a shoe store; in the latter setting we willingly follow the clerk's request to stand in our stocking feet, but we would resist the command in a bank. In the laboratory of a great university, subjects may comply with a set of commands that would be resisted if given elsewhere. "One must always question the relationship of obedience to a person's sense of the context in which he is operating . . ." (Milgram, 1965a, p. 69).

To further investigate this problem, Milgram completed another study in an office building in Bridgeport, Connecticut. Here subjects were invited to the experiment through a circular in the mail and were paid, as the Yale subjects were, although they had no knowledge that Milgram or his associates

"By order of the commanding officer we are here to . . ."

were from Yale. The results showed that 48% of the subjects from Bridgeport delivered the maximum shock. This compares reasonably with the 65% under similar conditions at Yale. Milgram suggests that the type of institution is judged according to its supposed function and brings about compliance on the part of the subjects. Milgram argues that an institution's qualitative position within a category may be less important than the type of institution it is.

The Milgram work on obedience has been repeated many times. One recent study examined obedience in a cross-cultural study. Jordanian students who were enrolled in psychology classes at the University of Jordan were told to deliver shocks. As in the original Milgram study, about 65% of the students were willing to give shocks to other students. Obedience to authority has thus been shown not to be culture-specific to the Western hemisphere (Shanab & Yahya, 1978).

Of course, not all of Milgram's subjects were obedient; some refused to participate in the experiment. Furthermore, when the subjects were in the presence of other subjects who refused to participate, the probability that a subject would not obey was increased (Milgram, 1965b; Powers & Geen, 1972). The effect was dramatic in that the percentage of subjects who defied the experimenter and refused to participate in the experiment increased to as much as 90%. These data suggest that individuals are dramatically influenced by sources of authority and by their peers. As will be shown in the next section, the effect of other people on an individual's behavior is remarkable.

Milgram's experiments show that subjects in an experimental situation who think that they are delivering painful shocks to another person will do so if told to by a person in authority. Among the problems with the studies initiated by Milgram, the most important is the ethics of the experiment. Deception is often used in social psychology research. Although the technique is in itself questionable, more important is the problem of possible psychological harm that could be done to the subjects. Subjects thought they were inflicting pain on another person. The subjects were debriefed. **Debriefing** is the procedure of explaining to subjects after completion of an experiment in which they have served, the true nature or purpose of the experiment. Since it is often necessary in psychological testing to use naive subjects (that is, subjects who don't know what the experiment is about) in order to obtain unbiased responses from them, debriefing *after* completion of the experiment both preserves the validity of a subject's responses and is consistent with the ethical considerations of using human subjects. Milgram's subjects were fully debriefed, told the purpose of the experiment, and shown that the learner was not shocked. Even so, the subjects now realize that they were capable of inflicting severe pain on others. Research that involves this kind of experimentation is under active and constant scrutiny by the Ethics Committee of the American Psychological Association.

Psychologists are not insensitive and callous. Milgram had a psychiatrist interview a sample of his obedient subjects one year after their participation in the study and absolutely no evidence was found of any psychological trauma or injury. Furthermore, another study has found that people reported that their participation in an obedience experiment was a positive experience, they did *not* regret having been in it, nor were there even any short-term negative psychological effects (Ring, Wallston, & Corey, 1970).

There are other problems with this research. One of the most critical is that the subjects were volunteers, and volunteers often bring certain biases to any experimental situation. What is the possibility that the subjects are not behaving normally because they are in an experiment? Perhaps the subjects were willing to administer the shocks only because they were in an experiment: they might not do this in a real-life situation. In addition to being in an experiment, they were also instructed by the experimenter to give the shocks.

Learned Helplessness

Most people feel that they can control their environment to a reasonable extent. Many of Milgram's subjects took control in the experiment in which they found themselves and refused to shock the learners. But what happens when we find ourselves in situations in which we seem to have little control over what is happening? Assume that you are a subject in an experiment and you have to solve puzzles. The puzzles are relatively simple and there are only a few ways to solve them. Yet no matter what you do, you seem unable to find the correct sequence to put the puzzles together. This is an experimental situation, but other situations can and do create such frustration. Many things happen to us that are beyond our immediate control. For example, you may be a university instructor who is trying to increase educational effectiveness through audiovisual presentations. Yet the bureaucracy of the university is such that you are not able to obtain even $5 for a replacement bulb for a projector. Similarly, individuals are confronted by such global problems as a polluted environment, warring nations, a shrinking food supply, and an increasing population. In situations like these most of us feel that we have little or no control over what is happening. While we would like to control some of these problems, we realize that we have little influence over events.

Debriefing The procedure of explaining to subjects after completion of an experiment in which they have served, the true nature or purpose of the experiment.

Learned helplessness The behavior of giving up or not responding; it is exhibited by subjects who are exposed to negative consequences or punishment and who have no control of when or whether it will be delivered.

When placed in situations where organisms have no control over the negative things that are happening to them, they often stop responding. Martin Seligman and his colleagues have shown that when exposed to a series of inescapable shocks, dogs who are subsequently given a chance to escape further punishment fail to learn the escape response. Seligman (1975) termed this behavior **learned helplessness.**

The phenomenon of learned helplessness was first explored with animals but has subsequently been studied with human beings. A typical experiment that is conducted involves presenting different groups of subjects with a task. The first group receives reinforcement for correct responses; the second group receives reinforcement, but it is not dependent upon performance; and the third group is a control group that is never provided reinforcement. We say that learned helplessness has occurred whenever the group that receives noncontingent consequences shows deficits in learning compared to the other groups. The same type of experiment can be conducted with punishment so that subjects are punished for a behavior, punished without regard to their behavior (noncontingent), or not punished (a control group).

A large number of research studies have been done to investigate the generality of learned helplessness in different areas of human and animal behavior. It has been shown to be evident in human problem solving (Eisenberger et al., 1976), emotions (Gatchel & Proctor, 1976), and especially depression (Seligman, 1975; McCarron, 1973). From Seligman's view the major reason for learned helplessness is that the organism believes or expects that its responses will not affect or influence the future. When people feel that their responses do not change what will happen tomorrow, then, Seligman suggests, anxiety, depression, and particularly nonresponsiveness result.

Seligman's research shows that people learn the response of helplessness or giving up when they are exposed to negative consequences or punishment and have no control over when this punishment will be delivered or whether it will be delivered. Seligman points out that when people learn that they cannot control their environment, they develop a sense of sadness and hopelessness. The individuals with neurotic disorders and even more disabling disorders described in the next few chapters often feel that they have little or no control over the consequences of their behavior. They become sad and often depressed. You will see that the differences between various types of depression depend on the extent to which people believe that they have control over their behavior and the world. People who have lost touch with reality feel that they have no control, whereas the mildly maladjusted realize that they still have some control.

Seligman's original view has generated a great deal of new research and new ideas about how people develop learned helplessness. Many researchers have expressed the idea that Seligman's earlier views are inadequate to explain human helplessness fully (see Roth, 1980). Accordingly, Miller and Norman (1979) have proposed an attribution model of learned helplessness which takes into account variables such as the person's locus of control (internal vs. external) and a number of other individual differences (for example, the person's sex and prior expectancies). They argue that a person's attributions and judgments of causality will predict the extent of learned helplessness in humans. For example, a person who has a strong external locus of control and believes that things other than himself control his destiny and success is more likely to develop a sense of learned helplessness than a person with a strong internal locus of control (Cohen et al., 1976; Hiroto, 1974). Research on helplessness is growing at a rapid rate. For example, Klee and Meyer (1979) have attempted to use biofeedback to help prevent learned helplessness in humans. Goetz and Dweck (1980) have focused on children's sense of learned helplessness; Zuroff (1980) and Pittman and Pittman (1980) have attempted to further expand upon the locus of control and its relationship to learned helplessness. Differences between men's and women's susceptibility to learned helplessness has also been explored (Wilson, Seybert & Craft, 1980). As in many other areas of psychology, it is likely that as the next few years unfold, some important and definitive answers will become apparent (see Abramson et al., 1978; Brown & Inouye, 1978; Hanusa & Schulz, 1977; Skinner, 1979).

Conforming by Inactivity: Bystander Intervention

When people are placed in situations in which the alternative ways of behaving produce aversive consequences, it is not surprising that they choose not to act. This is the conclusion of a long series of studies conducted by Latané and Darley. Bibb Latané from Ohio State University and John Darley from Princeton described a series of experiments that have been termed studies in bystander intervention (Latané & Darley, 1970). They asked the general question of when and under what conditions will a stranger provide help to someone. When you are walking down the street with a bag of groceries and you drop them, what is the likelihood that someone will help you pick up your things? If you approached someone for change to make a call, would he give it to you? What happens when a person observes a serious accident or crime? Will she do something to help? Will she intervene?

In large cities there are many kinds of emergencies: there are accidents, thefts, even stabbings and killings. It has been observed that in such situations, people stand and watch these emergencies and do nothing about them. Latané and Darley point out that it is suprising that when so many people watch a serious emergency, no one acts to help. They have suggested that with many bystanders we would expect one person of several might provide help—"the *number* of people who stand and watch is what shocks us . . ." (Latané and Darley, 1970, p. 38).

People often choose to watch or to listen rather than to help someone in trouble. In one of their studies, Latané and Darley (1970) brought college students to a laboratory and told them that they were going to be involved in a study of persons who had personal problems in college life. They were brought into individual rooms and told that to maintain anonymity, a discussion would be held over an intercom system rather than face to face. During the course of the discussion, one of the other subjects in the discussion was to undergo a very serious nervous seizure, almost like epilepsy. In reality, of course, no one underwent a seizure and, in fact, the only real subject in the experiment was our one naive subject. All of the discussions our naive subject heard were tape recorded in advance. After listening to much discussion about college problems, one of the tape recordings included one of the other students having a nervous seizure. The dependent variable in the study was the speed with which the naive subject reported the emergency to the experimenter. The major independent variable was the number of people the subject *thought* to be in the discussion group.

On arriving for the experiment, the naive subject found himself in a long corridor with doors opening off of it to several small rooms. A laboratory researcher met him and took him to one of the rooms and seated him at a table. The subject was given head phones with an attached microphone and was told to listen for instructions. He was informed that they would be discussing personal problems in a high-pressure, urban environment, and so as to avoid embarrassment and to maintain anonymity, they were placed in these private rooms rather than face to face. Furthermore, they were also told that since their discussion might be inhibited by the presence of an outside listener, the experimenter would not listen to the initial discussion but would get the subject's reactions later by questionnaire.

Of course, the whole situation was contrived and the subject was being set up. The subject was told that each person in his group would talk in turn presenting his problems to the group. A mechanical switching device would regulate the discussion sequence with each subject's microphone being turned on for about 2 minutes. Only one subject could be heard at a time. In the series of people who were to talk, the future victim (who was to have a nervous seizure) spoke first. He talked about his difficulties getting adjusted to New York City and mentioned that he was prone to seizures, particularly when he was studying hard. The other people in the experiment supposedly took their turns and the naive subject talked last in the series. Then, it was the victim's turn to talk again. After he made a few relatively calm comments, he started growing increasingly loud and incoherent, stuttering and indicating that he needed help because he was having "a-a-a real problem-er-right now and I-er-if somebody could help me out it would-it would-er-er s-s-sure be good . . ." At this point the experimenter began timing the speed of the real subject's response. The victim's speech about seeking help was abruptly cut off after 125 seconds.

The major independent variable in the study was the number of people that the subject believed also heard the seizure. The naive subject was led to believe that the discussion group was one of three sizes: either a two-person group (the naive subject and the person who would later have the seizure, that is, the victim), a three-person group (the victim, the naive subject, and one confederate voice), or a six-person group (the victim, the naive subject, and four confederate voices). The dependent variable was the time elapsed from the start of the victim's seizure until the naive subject left his experimental cubicle to get help from the experimenter.

When there were only two subjects in a group, (the subject and the victim), 85% of the naive subjects responded by helping before the end of the seizure. When three subjects were in a group (the subject, the victim, and one other), 62% of the naive subjects responded by the end of the seizure. When our naive subject thought that there were five others beside himself (the subject, the victim, and four others) only 31% of the naive subjects responded by the end of the seizure. Eventually, all of the subjects in the two-person group reported the emergency, but only 62% of the subjects in the six-person group did.

Bystanders, the real subjects, were less likely to respond if they thought other people were present. In a debriefing at the end of the experiment, subjects were interrogated as to what they thought when they heard the victim calling for help. Some of the subjects responded that they did not know what to do (28%); others responded that they did not know exactly what was happening (40%).

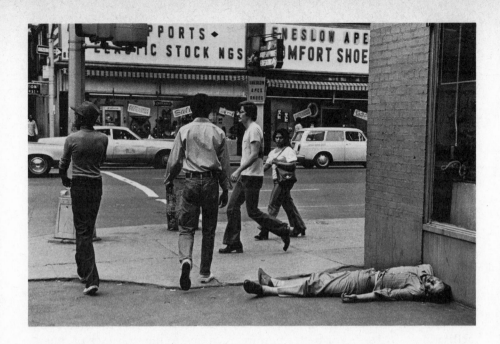

According to studies on bystander intervention, people are afraid of the consequences of helping.

Despite their failure to respond, the subjects were in reality not indifferent, according to Latané and Darley. They suggested that the subjects were still in a state of indecision and conflict concerning whether to respond or not. They argued that the subjects were worried about the guilt and shame that they would feel if they did not help the person in distress; in addition, they were concerned about making fools of themselves by overreacting. Latané and Darley suggested that the subjects were caught between two negative choices: the first is letting the victim continue to suffer; the second is the potential cost of rushing in to help and then not knowing how to help. Because both of these choices were negative in nature, the victims continued to suffer because the bystander vacillated rather than choosing to help.

Latané and Darley eventually argued that it is actually the number of people observing that acts to inhibit an individual's impulse to help. A bystander recognizes the cost of her intervention; intervening may mean she may suffer embarrassment or even punishment; in reality, the bystander recognizes that she does not know the costs to herself for intervening. People are not inhuman, but, rather, their failure to act is determined because of social norms. The other bystanders are strangers; helping someone may involve some personal risk, and not being familiar with a specific situation or place decreases a person's willingness to act. Latané and Darley concluded that bystander apathy is more a function of people and their relationship to other bystanders rather than because of apathy and alienation.

GROUPS

We know that people affect individual behavior in direct ways; people will be obedient to others who are seen as important. People try to maintain a strong self-concept by not making fools of themselves. We have also seen that groups of people inhibit the responses of a bystander. When groups of people are organized, their effect on individual behavior is even greater. Application forms for colleges or jobs often contain a question that asks what organized groups you belong to. You might respond by indicating that you are a member of the Democratic party, Boy Scouts of America, the National Organization for Women, American Association of University Students, or perhaps a member of a local Rotary Club. Group membership helps satisfy our desire to belong and gives us a sense of purpose we can share with other people. Groups have influences on individual behavior, and the nature of groups themselves is important in examining social interactions.

Influences on the Individual

By joining a group, people make a decision that they agree with the purposes of the group. If a major function of the group is to raise money for the Cancer Society, a person's membership indicates a willingness to raise money.

A person's behavior is not only affected by joining a group, but also by the presence of the group. When practicing a new game, sport, or other activity, one may proceed with a certain degree of success. When others enter the area, one may do even better than before. This kind of effect is called **social facilitation**—increased or better performance due to the presence of others. It has generally been found (Zajonc, 1965) that the influence of other individuals produces a general increase in anxiety and motivation level in the learner or performer. With heightened attention and motivation, subjects who are performing well perform better; those subjects performing poorly do worse. Obviously many factors could enter into social facilitation, including the number of individuals who are observing the subject, their sex, their relationship to the subject, and whether they are evaluating the subject or just watching. Indeed, it has been shown that the fear of being evaluated creates social facilitation rather than just the mere presence of people (see Innes & Young, 1975; Martens & Landers, 1972). But what happens when individuals are asked to perform together within a group? A number of theories have been developed to explain the results of group association.

BEHAVIOR OF GROUPS: "THE RISKY SHIFT." Groups are willing to take chances that individuals might not take. They are willing to make decisions that are risky or even daring. An example of a risky shift is a situation in which a person who, by himself, is unwilling to invest money in a venture but who will change his mind and do so upon hearing that his group is investing. Early formulations of the risky shift dealt mainly with the willingness of a person to behave in formerly unacceptable ways when other members of the group did so. More recent formulations suggest that people will not only take risks but also that they will become more polarized in their attitudes. If an individual holds a conservative belief, when she is placed in a group of conservatives, she is likely to become even more conservative. Members of a group become more extreme in the initial direction of orientation, and this, too, is considered part of the risky shift. So the **risky shift** is the phenomenon that following group discussions, individuals are willing to take risks or more daring actions than prior to their discussion. As is shown in Figure 10.6, such new decisions may not necessarily be in the one direction; if a person with a formerly conservative attitude is involved in a group discussion, she might become more conservative; in the same way a person

Social facilitation The phenomenon that people often do better at a task when they are, or believe they are, being observed by others.

Risky shift The phenomenon that following group discussions, individuals take risks or more daring actions than prior to their discussions.

Very liberal   Mildly liberal   Mildly conservative   Very conservative

Figure 10.6 After group discussions people who hold mildly liberal or mildly conservative views tend to become even more liberal or more conservative. This demonstrates part of the risky shift, that is, people become willing to take risks or make decisions that they would not have made as individuals before a group discussion

who may have been liberal on an issue might become even more liberal after being involved in a group discussion. Both of these individuals will have taken the risky shift. These shifts happen in a wide number of settings, not only the social psychology laboratory. One situation where these effects become particularly evident is the jury room of a court. Juries have been shown to take their initially mild view toward someone being tried and to become more extreme in this view; thus it has been shown that the *initial* view held by a jury becomes its verdict. So, in general after a group discussion, a group is likely to take its initial view and argue for it more strongly (Kalven & Zeisel, 1966; Meyers & Kaplan, 1976).

There are a number of reasons why the risky shift might occur. One is that there is a **diffusion of responsibility.** If a group makes a decision to invest money, no one individual is responsible for the decision. Take the classic TV story of the lynching of the innocent man. The individuals in the group all admit that alone they would never have strung him up, yet as a group they did. The diffusion of responsibility allows for a riskier decision than any individual alone would be willing to make.

Irrational group behavior has often been interpreted in terms of deindividuation. **Deindividuation** suggests that group behavior results when individuals lose their distinctive personalities and become willing to emit behaviors that they might never have shown before. Individuals lost in a group where they cannot be singled out and evaluated are willing to do things previously considered inappropriate (Diener et al., 1980). To people in a group the consequences of their individual behaviors are less clear. In the early 1970s a campus phenomenon called "streaking" was prevalent. In streaking, a naked person is supposed to dart out from a bush, run across a campus or through a crowded lobby, and disappear. Streaking groups soon began to

Diffusion of responsibility Feelings of individuals in a group that they cannot be held individually responsible for the group's actions.

Deindividuation Group behavior due to the individuals within the group losing their distinctive personalities and becoming less concerned about proper evaluation of a course of action.

form in which hundreds of students would streak through the campus. Think about streaking in terms of social facilitation, diffusion of responsibility, and deindividuation. Groups of streakers attract people who encourage them—social facilitation. With a large group no single individual can be held accountable for the formation of the group—a diffusion of responsibility. Last, with a group of 500 naked undergraduates running across campus, there is deindividuation. No single individual is held responsible, so the nature of their behavior is not considered a matter of individual responsibility, but a group decision. While deindividuation may account for some individuals' behavior, this idea has been challenged (Propst, 1979).

Although some aspects of the risky shift might occur because of a diffusion of responsibility and deindividuation, other explanations can account for it and particularly the polarization effects that happen within groups. One such account is through *social comparison.* In a group, most individuals initially think that their view is more extreme than the other members of the group; they feel that they are more fair, right-minded, tougher, liberal, or whatever. After finding that they are not far from where others are in the group, they become more polarized to show that they are even more tough, right-minded, fair, or liberal. By comparing themselves with other people, individuals eventually shift or become more polarized in their initial view. Thus, this kind of social comparison is a major way of accounting for group polarization and for part of the risky shift (Brown, 1974; Jellison & Davis, 1973; see also Kerr et al., 1975; Pruitt, 1971).

A different view of group polarization and the risky shift comes from those who favor the idea of *persuasive arguments.* This idea suggests that after hearing others' views that are in the same direction, people become even more extreme in their views. So, after hearing another persuasive, mildly liberal view, a person who is mildly liberal on an issue will become even more liberal, more polarized. Furthermore, the more arguments favoring a particular view in a group discussion, the more likely an individual is to shift her view toward that direction and become more extreme in that view (Ebbesen & Bowers, 1974; Morgan & Aram, 1975).

It is likely that social comparison *and* persuasive arguments can account for group polarization. Within a group many important decisions are made, and yet the data suggest that instead of becoming more reasoned, people within a group only retreat to their *own* view, do so with greater frequency,

Mildly held views often become more extreme after discussion in a group.

and to a greater extent. If others in a group hold similar views, this acts to reinforce and polarize an individual to an even greater extent. Many important decisions in our families, churches, communities, country, and even the international community are made in groups. From what we know from the social psychology laboratory, it causes wonder as to the value of group discussion when individuals wind up maintaining their own view most of the time.

While a group discussion often creates polarization, it also allows for the risky shift to be made. The risky shift and the polarization that usually accompanies it can account for behaviors that have severe consequences. The Mai Lai massacre and Nazi Germany might be partially accounted for because of diffusion, deindividuation, and generally a lack of responsible individual behavior. Groups have an important purpose, for individuals acting as a group can accomplish more than single individuals. However, when we join a group, we must still maintain our own individuality and conscience. People often conform to a group rather than act responsibly.

Conformity to a Group

We know that individuals conform to the wishes of others whom they think are important; we see this in studies of obedience; we see that this effect is

Groups put a great deal of pressure on individuals to conform; in this case, a person's attire is dictated clearly by group behavior.

even greater when organized groups of people attempt to influence an individual. Studies of conformity have shown that individuals often conform to a group even when not pressured to do so. Let us take a couple of examples. In a classroom of 250 students an instructor asks the class to answer a relatively simple question, but no hands are raised. If asked, most students will report that they will not raise their hands because no one else did. At formal dinners there are rarely individuals who are not dressed appropriately. At weddings brides wear white; at funerals people generally wear dark colors. There are no firm rules of social behavior and of dress, but people do conform.

The classic experiment in studies of conformity was performed by Solomon Asch (1951). Although many versions of this study have been conducted, for our purposes the following simple one will suffice. A group of subjects is brought into a room. They are told that they are going to be involved in a line discrimination task. The study uses deception; only one member of the group is a naive subject. The other group members are cohorts of the investigator and know the purpose of the study. The group is told that they will be shown two different lines and asked to make comparisons indicating which line is longer. The group is then shown the lines and asked to indicate the longer one, the top or the bottom one. Generally the discriminations are easy to make, but the cohorts of the experimenter consistently make the wrong decision. When there are 10 cohorts and 1 experimental subject, the subject generally goes along with the group. Even though it is clear which line is longer, the subject responds as the group does rather than use his own judgment—he conforms. Of course, in experiments of this kind, not all of the subjects conformed; however, enough did so that psychologists became concerned and investigated the phenomenon at greater length.

One of the critical variables in conformity studies is the number of individuals used as confederates. When 1 or 2 individuals are confederates, the effect of the pressure to conform is considerably less than if 20 individuals are agreeing that one line is longer than the other. Another important variable is the number of disagreeing votes. If 1 of those 20 confederates agrees with the subject, the subject will choose the appropriate line.

What allows a group to exert such a strong influence over individual behavior? The first variable is how much information is provided when one is making a decision. When a situation is ambiguous and people are not sure what to do, they seek out the advice of others. In a political race where the candidates are not well known, very often friends will seek out the opinions of others they trust. As indicated earlier, when the self-concept is not well formed or is ambiguous, an individual's self-evaluation or opinion about other people or things is often determined by others; so people with poorly defined self-concepts often try to ingratiate themselves with others of whom they think highly (Jones, 1964, 1965).

Another important variable that determines whether an individual will conform is the relative competency of the group. If a student feels that she is not well versed in a specific task, she is more likely to conform to the group way of performing. This pressure becomes even stronger when the group is large. A student in a large class may not answer a simple question if she assumes that her classmates are more competent. A person's position within a group also affects her behavior. A person held in high regard by a group will either feel that her position is so strong that she will naturally respond appropriately, or she will respond as the group does in fear of losing her status. The extent to which a person's behavior is public often determines her responses. If behavior is not public, individuals are more willing to make decisions that are inconsistent with their group. Voting in a free democracy is a private decision made behind closed doors; in this way there can be no group pressure on individual behavior.

That people conform to others in a group is a well-established fact. What is not totally clear is why they do so. Several different theories have developed that provide some hints as to why people conform. One approach, that of social conformity, suggests that people conform to avoid the stigma of being wrong, deviant, out of line, or very different from others. Since many opinions and ideas cannot be directly observed or judged, people rely on others to help them evaluate their own positions. When people find that their position is dramatically different from those in a group, then they begin to question their own views. From the social conformity view, people want to do the "right" thing, and they define "right" as whatever is generally accepted (Festinger, 1954).

Attribution theory has been used to explain conformity or lack of conformity. When a subject in a typical Asch experiment finds that he can explain the behavior of the confederates, he is less likely to conform. This means that when a person is able to find causes for other people's behavior in a group, then the typical experimental finding of conformity will disappear (Ross, Bierbrauer, & Hoffman, 1976).

Other explanations for conformity and lack of it comes from ideas about independence. While people in a group would like to be independent, they have to face the consequences of independence. If they choose not to go along with the group, they will be seen as deviant, often less powerful, and certainly they risk serious disapproval and peer pressure to conform and thus create a sense of unanimity. People choose to conform because being independent in the face of "everyone else" is so difficult.

It is likely that social conformity, attribution, and the risks of independence all create part of the conformity effect. People are complicated, and no simple rule, theory, or idea is going to account for all people under all circumstances or conditions. At times men will be more susceptible to conformity than women. At times the same person will not conform, but in the presence of certain other people he might conform. As psychologists try to sort out all of the variables and work through different theories, they approach understanding how a group exerts as much power as it does in manipulating individual behavior.

ENVIRONMENTAL INFLUENCES ON BEHAVIOR

We have seen that people's ideas about themselves are determined by factors as diverse as their names, how their friends act toward them, their locus of control, and how they perceive others in positions of authority. We have seen that the effect of other people on individual behavior is very great and that this effect can be exaggerated still further when others are in groups. People become more polarized in their views; they are more compliant, and, in some important ways, give up their sense of identity. While people may know their identity and what their values are, in group situations they may gain some anonymity and often feel less responsible for their own individual behavior.

Crowding

Perhaps the ultimate group influence is seen in situations of crowds. People are often placed in situations where they are surrounded by dozens, hundreds, and sometimes even thousands of other people. A single individual becomes one of a multitude. Sometimes these situations may make a person feel closed in; other times the excitement of a crowd is exhilarating. Consider a large, empty theater. If you were alone in the eleventh row, you might experience a sense of loneliness. As the theater fills up, however, some people begin to have feelings of being crowded. In the same way, early arrivers at a party often feel awkward and socially ill at ease; yet, within an hour, that originally empty space may be teeming with people, noise, and heat. Two different size spaces—a large movie theater and a small apartment—can seem both empty or crowded. In one case, it may take 400 or 500 other people to make you feel crowded. In the other case as few as 20 people may make you begin to have feelings of being crowded.

It is not the exact size of a space or room, nor is it only the number of people contained in a space that gives people feelings of being crowded. Crowding is a psychological state; crowding is a feeling that people have when there are "too many" people within a given space. A formal distinction must be made between density and crowding. Density refers to the number of people in a specific space; **crowding** is the feeling people have that their space has been restricted or limited too much. Although a specific area may have many people in it, a person may not feel crowded; for example, a football stadium at homecoming may be dense with people, but you do not feel crowded. Place the same spectators in a coliseum or a concert hall and change the context to one of waiting their turn to be processed for registration and people's feelings change. So density refers to numbers of people per unit

Crowding The feeling people have when their space has been restricted or limited to too great an extent.

The crush of daily crowding can have serious deleterious effects on people's day-to-day behavior.

space; crowding refers to how individuals feel about their density and how they respond to that density (Stokols, 1972, 1976).

A further distinction must be made between spatial density and social density. When doing psychological research on crowding and density, researchers were quick to realize that one can vary *social density*, the number of people in the same size space, or one can vary *spatial density*, the size of the space with the same number of people. If both of these important variables are varying at the same time, the actual effects of density are difficult or impossible to determine (see Figure 10.7, p. 482).

Let us examine some of the data on the effects of high density on human behavior. One of the early and interesting studies on the effects of crowding was done in 1973 by two researchers, Stuart Valins and Andrew Baum, at the State University of New York at Stony Brook. Valins and Baum asked freshmen students a series of questions about their life in their dorms. The dormitories at Stony Brook are arranged in two different and regularly used designs: the corridor design and the suite design. The corridor design involves long hallways that house 2 people per room with a total of 34 people per floor; the students share common bathroom and lounge facilities. Suite-designed dormitories generally require four or six students to share common bath and lounge facilities with several suites per floor. At Stony Brook, actual space per student was very much the same in corridor and suite dormitories. For example, the number of square feet per student for bedrooms was 88 and 79, respectively, for corridor and suite arrangements. So the real difference between the two kinds of dormitories is in terms of arrangement of the available space. Responding to the questionnaire, corridor residents reported too many residents on their floor and too many unwanted interactions. Of the corridor residents, 67% found their living space crowded, whereas only 25% of the suite residents responded in this way. Valins and Baum concluded that

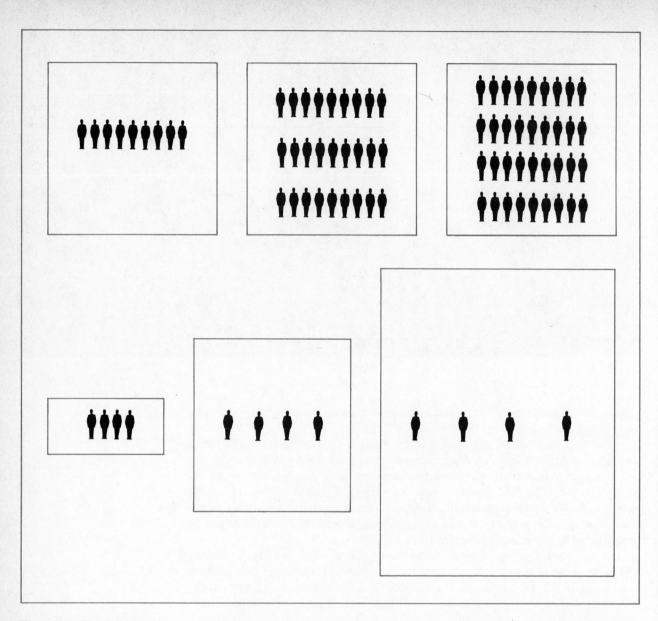

Figure 10.7 Manipulations of *social density* are manipulations of the number of people in the same size space. Manipulations of *spatial density* are manipulations of the size of the space with the number of people held constant

corridor designs promote "excessive social interaction and that such inter-action is associated with the experience of crowding" (p. 249).

If high-density dormitories produced feelings of crowding as Valins and Baum suggested, then these feelings should be evident in people's behavior. One group of researchers (Bickman et al., 1973) investigated the extent to which students who lived in high-density housing would show helping be-havior compared with those in low-density housing. They used an interest-ing measure of helping called the *lost-letter technique*. In this technique stamped, addressed letters are purposely dropped on the floors of dormitory corridors; it is reasoned that someone coming across the letter would assume that someone else in the dormitory lost the letter. The dependent variable in these studies is a measure of helping behavior—how many of the letters that were "lost" were mailed.

In the Bickman study, the independent variable was the kind of housing students lived in—high-density, medium-density, or low-density. Bickman conducted two separate studies; the first study took place at the University of Massachusetts and at Smith College. The dormitories at the University of Massachusetts were of two kinds: high-rise, 22-story towers, each housing over 500 students; and medium-density dormitories with 4 to 7 stories per building averaging about 165 students per dormitory. The low-density dormitories were at Smith College and had 2 to 4 stories and averaged about 58 students per dorm. Thus, there were dormitories with around 500 students, 165 students, or 58 students.

Letters were dropped in an unobtrusive way with no more than one letter per corridor and were generally placed in areas leading toward stairwells and elevators. The letters each contained a short thank you note that was addressed, sealed, and stamped, but bore no return address. The results were straightforward: as measured by the mailing of letters, helping behavior was 63% in high-density dormitories, 87% in medium-density dormitories, and 100% in low-density dormitories. The same techniques were employed in the second study at the University of Pennsylvania, where similar results were found: 64%, 77%, and 91% of the letters were mailed from high-, medium-, and low-density housing complexes, respectively.

When questionnaires were distributed to the students in these housing complexes, the students generally reflected attitudes that referred to the kind of housing they lived in. For example, students in the higher density dormitories reported less trust, cooperativeness, and responsibility. The researchers concluded that students in the higher density dormitories behaved in a less socially responsible manner toward other dormitory residents.

The literature on high density and crowding presents a mixed picture of human behavior. The effects of crowding are not consistent over all kinds of situations or people, but certain general effects are found. In situations of high social density, people tend to feel alone or anonymous; they feel stressed, overloaded, and sometimes overaroused. This causes them to react by withdrawing, becoming apathetic, and sometimes by becoming hostile. When density, either spatial or social, is low, its effects are minimal. However, as density increases, people begin to show adverse behavioral effects; they withdraw, feel stressed, task performance is impaired, and, in a general sense, they are adversely affected. When there is sufficiently high density, people withdraw into themselves. Almost as a protective mechanism, in high-density situations people tend to stand alone as if others did not exist.

Adding a few people to the same sized room will not make us withdraw; similarly, shrinking our living and working spaces by a few square feet will not produce dramatic behavioral responses. But shrink our space, add a few people, and place us in a context of stress and the ingredients for negative behavior effects are established. Altman (1975) would explain this kind of reaction in a context of privacy. He would suggest that in situations of high density, people are feeling a lack of boundary controls and, thus, a loss of privacy. To control or regain control over their lack of privacy, Altman might argue that a turning inward will accomplish the same effect.

Personal Space

A person's sense of self and individuality is often intruded upon in public places, classrooms, and on the street. So as to maintain a sense of individuality and personal control, each of us erects invisible barriers; if others step over these barriers, they are intruding. In an empty movie theater, if a person sits closer than five seats away, you might feel that he or she is intruding. On a sofa in a physician's waiting room, a comfortable distance might be two seats away. Most people want more space between themselves and strangers than between themselves and family or friends. You might walk arm in arm with a brother or sister but would avoid physical contact with a stranger. You might whisper in the ear of your girlfriend but maintain at least a foot distance from an elevator operator.

Personal space The area around an individual that is considered private by the individual; an invisible boundary around a person.

People try to maintain an appropriate personal space. **Personal space** is that area around an individual which is considered private by the individual; if someone encroaches upon that space, it causes displeasure and often withdrawal. Personal space is an invisible boundary around a person; the size of this space can change and depends upon a person's situation and who she finds herself with. So, arm in arm with a familiar date feels comfortable; that same distance from a new date feels awkward. Of course, there is no electrified grid that holds people apart; but, in most cultures, there are established norms of personal space that most people adhere to and that are learned while a child is still fairly young.

Altman (1975) considers personal space a privacy-regulating mechanism by which one excludes others. Clearly, people use personal space to regulate whom they will allow to approach them; if strangers approach, people withdraw. But some of the first views of personal space came not from a psychologist but rather from an anthropologist, Edward Hall. Hall (1966) suggested that personal space was a mechanism by which people communicated with others. He argued that like other customs that varied from culture to culture, the use of personal space also varies. For example, Western cultures insist on a fair amount of space between strangers, whereas close distances are reserved for intimacy and close friends. By contrast, the Arab world allows for much closer distances; an acceptable distance for strangers in Saudi Arabia might offend a suburbanite of San Diego (Watson & Graves, 1966).

Hall classified a series of four spatial zones or spatial distances that one uses in social interactions with others: *intimate, personal, social,* and *public.* At the distances associated with each zone, certain characteristics of interaction are acceptable for Western cultures and certain kinds of sensory events are associated with them.

An *intimate distance* from 0 to 18 inches is acceptable for comforting one who is hurt, for lovers, and for physical sports. The closeness of intimate distance allows one to hear another's breathing, smell the other's unique scents, and examine every detail of the person's skin, hair, and eyes. This is a distance reserved for people who know each other well and have a great familiarity with one another.

A generally more acceptable distance for close friends and everyday interactions is *personal distance* from $1\frac{1}{2}$ to 4 feet. Within personal distances, one can have close interaction at $1\frac{1}{2}$ to 2 feet, where you might tell a spicy story to a close friend. One might walk through the city streets and maintain a conversation at 2 or 3 feet; and, at 2 to 4 feet, it is easy to maintain good contact with someone with whom one works but not seem impersonal. Personal distances are those that we use for most social interactions.

In *social distances,* from 4 to 12 feet, business and interactions with strangers take place. In business, intimate contact is not necessary or desirous;

The open spaces of public
buildings can help give
people a sense of personal
space and privacy.

bank tellers, receptionists, co-workers, and strangers are often positioned so
that close personal contact is held to a minimum. At 4 to 6 feet, people are
close enough to communicate their ideas effectively while maintaining a
clear space that keeps them apart. Sometimes the personal space is controlled
in the social zone by using physical barriers like a desk to separate a clerk,
receptionist, or teacher from the people with whom one has to interact.

In *public distances*, from 12 to 25 feet, personal contact is minimized. When
politicians speak to lunch clubs, when teachers stand behind desks, when
actors or musicians perform from a stage, the distance is sufficiently great

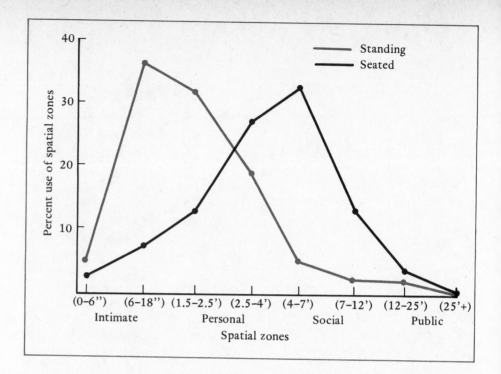

Figure 10.8 The use of the different spatial zones is shown. The percentage of time spent in each spatial zone by people who are standing is shown by the color curve; people who stand primarily use the personal zone and intimate zone. People who are seated primarily use the personal and social zones (data from Altman and Vinsel, 1977)

that any personal communication between the individuals is eliminated. (See Figure 10.8.)

Research studies are supportive of the ideas of the maintenance of personal space. For example, Willis (1966) recorded the initial speaking distances of people as a function of their sex, age, and race. He found significant differences among these variables, but the actual data were in close agreement with Hall's (1966) formulation of distance zones. It has been shown that pairs of males maintained farther distances from one another than pairs of females did (Aiello & Jones, 1971). Horowitz, Duff, and Stratton (1964) found that the people with Schizophrenic Disorders require more personal space. Even children as young as 4 years old exhibit personal space needs (Eberts & Lepper, 1975).

People try to maintain physical distances between themselves and others so as to maintain a personal space. Over the years many research studies have been done to investigate personal space; often these have involved an experiment of violating an individual's personal space. In a research study performed by Barefoot, Hoople, and McClay (1972), personal space was investigated without an invasion by an experimenter. The researchers devised a situation in which they sat in a hall of an administration building near a water fountain which was placed prominently in a hallway. The experimenters, pretending to read a book, observed the number of people who passed by the fountain and the number of people who stopped to drink. The experimenters avoided looking at the subjects, except for a brief glance. For half of the subjects, the experimenters were placed in a chair that was only one foot away from the drinking fountain; for the other half of the subjects, the experimenters were five feet from the drinking fountain. Data were also gathered in a control condition in which the experimenter was seated on a bench opposite the fountain and approximately 10 feet from it. There were

Table 10.2 The mean percentage of subjects drinking is presented as a function of the distance of a male or female experimenter.

	MALE EXPERIMENTER	FEMALE EXPERIMENTER
Near	12.2	7.2
Far	19.2	16.9
Control	23.3	19.6

both male and female experimenters and only data from males were analyzed (data from female subjects were not included because there were not enough female passersby).

The experiment was a simple one. People were placed either near to or far from the drinking fountain and the percentage of people who stopped to drink was recorded. If subjects really did not like to have their personal space violated, then they would avoid drinking from the fountain in both near and far conditions compared to a control group. The results of the study were straightforward. As shown in Table 10.2, a smaller percentage of the subjects drank from the fountain in the near condition than in the far and control conditions.

As predicted, the subjects tended to avoid a situation if it would cause them to come into close physical proximity with another person. This finding supports the general idea that an invasion of personal space is aversive and individuals will avoid the situation if they can.

Regardless of their orientation, most researchers agree that people's personal space needs change and that people are adaptable and can shift their demands for personal space as their overall and specific situations change (see Altman & Vinsel, 1977). As Altman has suggested, personal space is a privacy-regulating mechanism, and people make appropriate changes in their immediate environment so as to maintain that sense of privacy.

Privacy

After being away for many weeks or months you may begin to feel lonely for the comforts of home. You may yearn for the privacy of your own room, the familiarity of old books, and a sense of ownership of what is yours. Most people grow up in homes that provide them with a certain amount of privacy; we have a place at the table that is ours, a shelf in the bathroom that is reserved for us, and more generally, certain territories that "belong" to us. There is a consistency in our environment.

When we speak about the comforts of home, we are often referring to the special sense of privacy, ownership, and space that is afforded to us. In contrast, in dormitories, libraries, dining halls, and communal bathrooms, such feelings of comfort and personalization are minimal, if not totally absent. Since the environment can shape behavior, it also can change people's sense of well being.

To a very great extent, people try to control how the environment affects them. If you are interrupted too many times when trying to study in a dorm room, you might go to the library, lock your door, or perhaps put a "Do Not Disturb" sign on your door. If you find dormitory life too crowded under any circumstances, then you might move into an apartment. Sometimes feelings of being crowded and lack of privacy can be alleviated when certain territories are staked out as your own. If you know that certain portions of a room, closet, and shelf space are yours to do with as you see fit, this sometimes can give you the feeling of control that is necessary for you to feel comfortable in an environment. Irwin Altman postulated that privacy is the central element in understanding the behavior of humans in their environment. He argued that privacy is the key to understanding feelings of crowding and personal space. Using this idea, let us explore the nature of privacy.

Privacy is a process of controlling boundaries between people so that access to them is limited. When a woman goes into a room and closes the door behind her, she literally closes herself off from other people—she limits her access. She has set up a boundary—a closed door—and can do what she wants as she wants to do it. Two people might enter a room and close a door to control access. Indeed, groups of people who desire a sense of privacy, perhaps a therapy group or a family, might seek being alone to engage themselves in a particular activity.

Privacy The process of controlling boundaries between people so that access to them is limited.

Everyone needs a few private minutes for themselves in a space that they can call their own.

Each person seeks some privacy from time to time; we want to be alone and away from other people. At other times we seek out others and desire to chat, play games together, or, perhaps, just be in someone else's company. We each have a desired level of privacy that can vary from day to day or minute to minute; what we desire is not always what we achieve, however. Sometimes when we desire privacy the most, we are least able to achieve it. Other times when we would like other people's company, we are unable to find it.

MECHANISMS OF CONTROL. There are various ways to control other people's access to you. You can tell them that you want to be alone. Indeed, you can insist on being alone, and to some extent we all use this device. The use of nonverbal mechanisms, which we discussed earlier, is an even more common way to tell people that you wish not to be disturbed. Body position, head tilt, and duration of a gaze at an intruder are quick ways to tell someone to "stay away." After living with parents for most of our lives, we know their nonverbal ways of telling us that they need some privacy; it might be a hand gesture, a nod of the head to the left, or perhaps it is a stare over the top of a pair of bifocals. In each case children learn at an early age what their parents are trying to convey, which very often is "not now."

There are other ways to guard your privacy and to ward off intruders. The way you dress tells others something about you. People who are dressed in business suits are trying to convey an image. Most people are far more willing to approach people who are dressed casually than the more formally attired person.

People tell you how much privacy they desire by the shape and layout of their office spaces and homes. Are the spaces open and airy or are the spaces compartmentalized with doors, corridors, locks, and barriers. Highly placed executives who are seeking to avoid salespeople and the general public have their privacy safeguarded by secretaries. The secretaries in outer offices act to guard the privacy of these executives by warding off intruders on their time and space. So the person who acts as the appointment secretary to the president of the United States not only guards his privacy but also holds a responsible and important position.

Each of us has a need for privacy. At times we need the solitude and quiet of being alone to gather ourselves together, to reflect, to study, or just to relax. Privacy, from Altman's view (1975), allows people to develop and nurture a sense of *self*. Without privacy, people feel that they have no control over who and what can intrude upon them, which can lead to feelings of worthlessness and poor functioning. Altman's idea that the *self* requires privacy is the organizing theme of his view of the relationship of the environment to individuals' behavior. While this view is not necessarily widely accepted, we all seek privacy, and it is in private moments that people often determine the course of their lives.

While most people seek out privacy, it is difficult for many people to find. A young household with many children often affords little privacy for parents. A busy corporation with many high-level executives seeking the time of its chief executive affords him little time to reflect. Even the president of the United States has Camp David as a retreat where he can go to seek privacy. For a president, Camp David provides acres of space. For a parent, the space may be a hotel room for a weekend while grandma visits and takes care of the kids. Even a shower stall provides a few minutes and a few inches of space and time that people can call their own.

TERRITORIALITY.   Maintaining a sense of privacy often becomes such an important goal in people's lives that in suburbia the notion that "good fences make good neighbors" is an axiom of living. People buy homes, furnish them, decorate them, and spend hours of back-breaking work weeding, trimming, and cutting lawns. Often they then begin to exhibit clear signs of territorial behavior. **Territorial behavior** is behavior involved in establishing, maintaining, personalizing, and defending a delimited space. People who own a home and land consider it their exclusive space. It is not to be intruded upon, encroached upon, and, for some people, it is not even acceptable for others to step upon it. Territoriality refers to the exclusive use of a specific area by a person or group of people. Of course, certain territories like a person's home are exclusive by actual ownership. However, other territories are public in ownership but take on territorial characteristics. The cafeteria of a high school is often divided up by students into territories of girls or boys, seniors or freshmen, or perhaps the rough types or the jocks. Neighborhood streets, particularly in cities, are often associated with territoriality. Gangs divide up neighborhoods and declare certain areas as "their turf." Whether a territory is exclusively private or public can vary over time. Private homes, golf clubs, or fraternities can change their character and become more open (or more exclusive and territorial) and public territories like streets also change in character over time. Usually, private places have a tendency to stay the same with respect to territoriality, whereas public places are likely to change their nature and kind of territoriality over time.

In territorial behavior, one marks space as a personal, private area where intruders are not welcome. Street gangs have been known to defend their turf with gang wars for years, and organized crime has violently defended its demarcated areas of space. Most of us are more subtle in defining, marking, and defending our territories. We build a fence around our house. We plant bushes. We put up a sign that says, "Stay Off the Grass." We might go so far as to buy a big dog with a very vigorous bark and bite. Most often, we defend our territories with a disapproving stare, a sidelong glance, a physical marker that indicates our degrees of feeling about territoriality. Teenagers often mark their doors with signs that say "Keep Out" or "Private Property." Closed chainlink fences around a house tell a passerby something about the sense of territoriality of its owner.

Of course, extremes in territoriality are not always apparent. Most people have a private bedroom which is their territory. Even when this room is shared with another, they divide up certain areas of spaces that they call their own. When these areas and spaces are encroached upon, anxiety often results and defensive actions which vary from mild comments to aggressive and potentially violent acts can and do occur.

Like personal space, one's territory is a privacy-regulating mechanism. Altman's view is that territories which are fixed in space and personal space which surrounds the person act to provide an individual with a sense of *self*. Many experts agree with Altman's view that a well-developed sense of self, including feelings of self-worth, status, and well-being are tied in to having a defined sense of privacy, personal space, and territory.

Territorial behavior Behavior involved in establishing, maintaining, personalizing, and defending a delimited space.

We have learned that people affect how others behave. Social psychologists have gone to great lengths to show us that behavior on a one-to-one basis as well as within large groups is dramatically affected by the pressure of others. For example, a person's attitudes about the world are formed and changed by single individuals and by groups. Both parents and peer groups can change the attitudes that a teenager might have and as his attitudes change, his behavior may change. People may have attitudes that are not reflected in their behavior, but it is unlikely that these attitudes will not be conveyed to others through small, subtle gestures.

Behavior is certainly affected by many variables, but one of the most critical seems to be a person's self-concept. A self-concept seems to be one of the critical underlying factors in determining a person's social interactions. When we have a strong self-concept, our attitudes and beliefs are firm. We know who we are and what we want to do; however, when our self-concept is weak, our behavior is too often directed by other people, other groups, and not by our own convictions.

It becomes easy to see that early social interactions of a child with her parents, peers, and institutions strongly affect her self-concept and social behavior later in life. If the child's home environment has nurtured independence and a strong self-concept, it is likely that the child will successfully withstand an identity crisis. If the child is able to resist pressures to perform behavior she considers antisocial or unethical, she will have conquered a major stumbling block in life.

Social psychology is important because behavior is affected by our interactions with other people. Think about the role of the mass media in influencing behavior. Television has certainly affected the way people behave and has become an important issue within social psychology. Television can affect people's behavior, at least for short periods of time. The studies on aggression, obedience, and group behavior are important when we think of the role of mass media. Can the mass media affect our attitudes about the Mai Lai massacre, Nazi Germany, and the assassinations of important political figures? As students of psychology, we must be critically aware of what affects behavior and how we might change behavior.

Psychologists are making advances in the control of behavior through research technology, but the issue of manipulation and control of behavior is bound up with ethical questions. To what extent do social psychologists or a government have the right to manipulate social change by deception, mass media, or statute? These questions are very serious, and the psychology profession is trying to determine what their effects are and what limits should be placed on the control of behavior.

Throughout our lives we try to maintain a sense of consistency of attitudes, beliefs, and behavior. We have learned that one often has to go to extreme lengths to do so and in some cases behavior is not consistent with attitudes. Part of one's behavior is a search to maintain a consistent sense of self, of knowing who one is and what behaviors are appropriate for oneself. But we do not exist alone on this planet; we know that others affect us and affect us in dramatic ways. Very often the number of people who intrude upon one's life is more than just a neighbor or a family member; sometimes people are placed in situations that can be characterized as crowded. When personal space or territory becomes dense with people, we begin to experience feelings of crowding. From Altman's view (1975), people begin to experience a lack of privacy and a lack of control. When we experience these feelings, we feel crowded and unable to manage effectively.

Privacy is an overriding theme within the study of how other people and the environment affect individuals. We establish a bubble around ourselves, an invisible bubble, in which we try to control our personal space. People do not like to have their personal space invaded, so we go to some lengths to maintain some space. While we carry our personal space around with us all the time, the space that is staked off, marked, and stable is typically called our territory and we show specific territorial behavior.

We see that social psychology is the study of how others affect individual behavior; yet we recognize that the effect of other people is determined by many complex factors. We need to consider not only the number of people involved but also the personal characteristics of these other people and the individuals being studied. When placed in a crowd, a person who has great needs for privacy reacts differently from a person who is less affected by the presence of others. Similarly, some people are more compliant than others and are more likely to be affected by others in a group. Many of the differences we see between people and how they are affected by others are determined by their self-concepts and the mechanisms they invoke to try to maintain consistency.

CHAPTER REVIEW

1. Social psychology is the study of the behavior of individuals and how it is affected by the behaviors or characteristics of others.
2. An attitude is a pattern of relatively enduring feelings, beliefs, and behavior tendencies toward other people, ideas, or objects.
3. An attitude has three components: cognitive, emotional, and behavioral.
4. While many attitudes are taught by parents, a person's peer group can affect his or her attitudes, as can the mass media.
5. Cognitive dissonance is a state in which individuals feel uncomfortable because they are involved in two or more thoughts, attitudes, or behaviors that are inconsistent with one another.
6. Attribution is the process through which we infer other people's motives and intentions from observing their overt behavior.
7. Balance theory is an attitude theory which states that people prefer to hold consistent beliefs with others and to try to avoid incompatible beliefs.
8. Attitudes about one's self are established early in life, and one's role in society is constantly being evaluated.
9. First impressions are lasting ones, and they are conveyed through what people say and what they don't say. For example, body language is the communication of information through body positions and gestures.
10. Aggressive behavior is any behavior which has as its goal harming or injuring another person or thing. Not all aggressive acts are physical.
11. Aggression can be viewed from a nativistic point of view, from an acquired drive point of view, as learned social behavior, or as a response to aggressive stimuli.
12. A classic experiment by Milgram showed that people will be obedient to an authority figure even though this obedience goes against their personal ethical standards.

13. Group behavior shows that people are affected by having a group around them, for example, through social facilitation.
14. Groups are willing to take chances that single people might not take, often because there is a diffusion of responsibility and deindividuation.
15. Studies of conformity have shown that people often conform to a group even when not pressured to do so.
16. Crowding is the feeling a person has when his or her space has been restricted or limited to too great an extent.
17. There is a distinction between social and spatial density. Social density refers to the number of people in the same size space. Spatial density refers to the size of the space varying with the same number of people.
18. In the lost-letter technique, stamped addressed letters are purposely dropped with the idea of measuring how many of the letters that were "lost" would eventually be mailed.
19. Personal space refers to the area around an individual; territorial behavior refers to a very specific place.
20. One carries one's personal space wherever one goes; by contrast, one's territory remains relatively fixed in space.
21. Density refers to the number of people in a specific sized space.
22. Personal space is that area around an individual that is considered private by the individual; if someone encroaches upon that space, it causes displeasure and often withdrawal.
23. Hall classified a series of four spatial zones or distances that one uses in social interactions: intimate, personal, social, public.
24. Privacy is the process of controlling boundaries between people, which limits access to them.
25. There are many ways in which people may control their privacy, including nonverbal mechanisms.
26. Territorial behavior is behavior involved in establishing, maintaining, personalizing, and defending a delimited space.

SUGGESTIONS FOR FURTHER READING

BARON, R. A., AND BYRNE, D. *Social psychology: Understanding human interactions* (3rd ed.). Boston: Allyn & Bacon, 1981.

BELL, T. A., FISHER, J. D., AND LOOMIS, R. J. *Environmental psychology*. Philadephia, PA: W. B. Saunders, 1978.

FESTINGER, L. *A theory of cognitive dissonance*. Stanford, CA: Stanford University Press, 1957.

LEATHERS, D. G. *Nonverbal communication systems*. Boston: Allyn & Bacon, 1976.

MIDDLEBROOK, P. N. *Social psychology and modern life* (2nd ed.). New York: Harper & Row, 1980.

MILGRAM, S. *Obedience to authority*. New York: Harper & Row, 1974.

SHAVER, K. G. *An introduction to attribution processes*. Cambridge, MA: Winthrop Publishers, 1975.

WEBSTER, M. *Actions and actors*. Cambridge, MA: Winthrop Publishers, 1975.

WRIGHTSMAN, L. S. *Social psychology*. Monterey, CA: Brooks Cole Publishing Company, 1977.

EACH OF US has a personality and a characteristic way of responding to others. If we were to ask a friend about a new person in the neighborhood one of the first comments made would probably refer to her personality. You are talking about how that person behaves and reacts to people and events. Many variables affect how our personalities develop and what events help shape our behavior. This chapter describes three different ways of looking at personality, each presenting a different perspective. These theories of personality help show how psychologists might look at a person's behavior and see different things. No one theory is a more accurate method of studying personality than others, but each theory has strengths that the others lack.

CHAPTER 11

Personality

"Don't smoke," "don't eat animal fats," "eat whatever you please," "don't drink soft water," "drink any kind of bacteria-free water you want," "watch your weight," "obesity bears no relation to heart disease," "jog," "don't jog," "avoid cholesterol," "avoid sugar and starches," "avoid whiskey," "avoid sexual intercourse"—all these statements have been made at one time or another by physicians and researchers. Is it any wonder that some people figure none of us knows precisely what he is talking about?

Consider the problem this way. Coronary artery and heart disease is obviously the result of a variety of factors working together . . . but . . . At least half the people who get heart attacks can be linked to *none* of the known and suspected causative factors—smoking, diet, exercise habits, other contributing diseases, and so forth. . . .

Plainly, another factor is at work here, and this is the one we have discovered and dubbed Type A Behavior Pattern. It is a particular complex of personality traits, including excessive competitive drive, aggressiveness, impatience, and a harrying sense of time urgency. Individuals displaying this pattern seem to be engaged in a chronic, ceaseless, and often fruitless struggle—with themselves, with others, with circumstances, with time, sometimes with life itself. . . .

M. FRIEDMAN AND R. H. ROSENMAN
Type A Behavior and Your Heart

Change your personality and you may be able to prolong your life—this is the idea being promoted by two California physicians. According to Meyer Friedman and Ray Rosenman (1974) certain characteristic behavior patterns are associated with heart disease. They argue that if you are a Type A person you are far more likely to have a heart attack than if you are a Type B person. The difference between Type A and Type B people lies in their personal approaches to life, the way they perceive the world, and the way they respond to it. Friedman and Rosenman claim that people classified as Type A are in a constant struggle with time, always trying to achieve more and more in less and less time. This personal style predisposes the person to heart disease. Of course, this is somewhat different from traditional medical thinking. That people's hearts can be affected so dramatically by the way they respond to life does not seem very scientific. Yet, this is precisely their claim. Most people can determine if they are more like Type A or Type B individuals.

People can describe the way they respond to the world; they have fairly realistic impressions about themselves and could probably describe their personalities with certain catchwords—shy, sensitive, quiet, concerned—all of which are components of personality. **Personality** refers to a set of relatively enduring behavioral characteristics which describe how a person reacts to the environment. Personality is the way someone behaves over a long period of time under a variety of situations. We all have variations in our personalities and we are not *always* cautious or impulsive, shy or friendly; thus, personality labels characterize individuals as they appear in most circumstances. In discussing personality, psychologists are referring to enduring and stable characteristics: youngsters who are athletic generally remain athletically oriented throughout their lives.

Knowledge of people's personalities allows psychologists to predict their future behavior in a wide range of circumstances. Once we are able to characterize personality, we are then able to predict to some extent how an individ-

Personality A set of relatively enduring behavioral characteristics that describe how a person reacts to the environment.

496

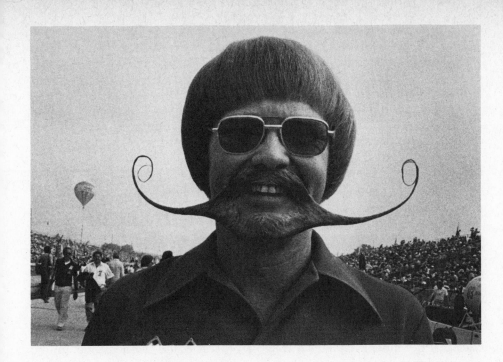

Personality plus.

ual will behave. An understanding of personality characteristics allows us to deal with individuals in a realistic and accepting manner. For example, if a psychologist knows a child has difficulty in responding to orders, he or she can deal most effectively with the child, not by giving orders, but by giving the child alternatives. Similarly, a child who has feelings of inferiority needs to be treated differently from a child who is self-confident.

Many parents use learning principles, child-guidance textbooks, and common sense in their attempts to make their children into what they think they should be. However, each child's personality development is unique, and very often two children within the same family will show dramatically different personalities. Personality theorists try to understand how personality develops and the many influences that make a person unique.

APPROACHES

Three different approaches to the study of personality will be discussed. In their own way, each deals with the development of stable and consistent patterns of behavior. The separate theories use different terms and concepts to describe personality; furthermore, they try to explain personality development by using different psychological mechanisms. We must recognize that there are far more than just three approaches. For example, there are psychologists who argue that the trauma of being born shapes personality, and others who argue that the symbolism of one's dreams is handed down from generation to generation. Personality theories are diverse and dissimilar. However, Maddi (1976) has grouped together different personality approaches. As we follow his guidelines, we shall consider the ideas of one or two theorists within each of these three approaches.

Conflict approach A theoretical approach to personality that assumes that there are opposing forces within the individual that are constantly clashing. Freud was its major proponent.

Fulfillment approach A theoretical approach to personality that assumes that each individual is constantly striving to become everything that he or she might. Carl Rogers is a major proponent of this approach; Alfred Adler, another major proponent, presents a slightly more extreme view.

Behaviorism An approach to personality that assumes that persons respond to the environment as they have learned to respond.

In the **conflict approach** it is assumed that there are constantly clashing forces within a person. According to this approach, life is a compromise at best. The conflict approach is very popular, and Freud's theory of personality emerged from this set of ideas.

In contrast, the **fulfillment approach** to personality suggests that there is one force within each person. According to this approach, people are constantly striving toward fulfillment and an understanding of their environment. Life is not seen as a compromise, but as a continual struggle for fulfillment and/or perfection.

The third approach to personality is a radical departure from the others. **Behaviorism** is the personality approach that suggests that behavior, and therefore personality, is determined by learning principles, including classical conditioning, instrumental conditioning, and observational learning. Behaviorists attempt to account for personality by using behavioral principles such as those discussed in chapter 3 (see p. 67).

Regardless of the approach, a theory of personality usually has a set of basic ideas or *core* elements that describe its general nature (Maddi, 1976). We shall describe these core elements, as well as peripheral characteristics, with details from day-to-day behavior. For example, a core tendency might be that people seek to fulfill themselves; along with this core tendency is the idea that fulfillment happens through a process called self-actualization. So we see that core tendencies are basic driving forces within the individual that determine one's overall direction of living; associated with these basic or core tendencies are characteristics that are typical goals or ideas (like self-actualization).

As people grow and mature, they go through a process of *development*; for a personality theorist, development is the combining of a person's core tendencies with the realities of the outside world, parents, friends, and church. Through development people learn about aspects of the world which may or may not fit in with their own core tendencies. We will look at how each theorist views development so that we can explore specific day-to-day details of personality; we call these details the *peripheral* characteristics of personality.

Day-to-day behavior is complex, and any specific act or behavior may be caused by a person's core tendency and approach to life; alternatively, it may be a response to a number of different variables. People learn to respond in a variety of ways to different circumstances; therefore, we recognize that a specific behavior may be attributed to personality, but it also may depend solely on a specific situation. For example, a person who has as a basic tendency a fulfillment approach to life may show some behavior that is less than optimal. This behavior does not nullify the core tendency; rather, we recognize that it may be one of a number of specific behaviors affected by learning, faulty development, estranged parents, or society as a whole.

In examining each of the personality theories in this chapter we will consider their *core tendencies,* how they view the *development* of personality, as well as the specifics of *peripheral* characteristics of personality. It is important to remember that this framework assumes that core tendencies are inherent and basic to personality, while peripheral characteristics are learned through the process of development and are modifiable through therapy or new learning and new development.

As the material in this chapter is presented, you will note some similarities between the approaches, but the differences in the way these psychologists see the development of personality and how people go about coping with the demands of life will be even more apparent. No single approach to personality is right or wrong. There are many who believe Freud's theory or who have modified his position to make it acceptable. Furthermore, there are many who find the fulfillment approach more reasonable. Except for some strict behaviorists or for some Freudian psychoanalysts, most therapists use parts of each of these theories to help people with personality disorders. The conflict theory of Sigmund Freud has been the most influential and far-reaching theory of personality, so we shall examine it first.

CONFLICT APPROACH: SIGMUND FREUD

Freud's name has become a household word. Freud is part of American life because his work has shaped the way educated people think about behavior. Regardless of whether Freud's theories are right or wrong, his influence upon the psychological world exceeds that of any other individual both present and past.

Sigmund Freud (1856–1939) was born in Austria where he became a physician and did research in neurology. Early in his career he used hypnosis to help treat people with both physical and emotional problems. Freud noticed that many of his patients needed to talk about their problems and, upon talking about them, they often felt better. Freud's medical practice was mainly among the middle and upper classes of Austrian society; many were society matrons who, because they lived in a repressive society, had limited opportunities for the release of sexual tensions. It is from these patients that Freud began to conceptualize behavior.

Freud saw people as expressors of energy. He argued that people have two basic instincts, sexual and aggressive, and that these instincts are not always socially acceptable. When unacceptable behaviors are exhibited, the result is often punishment, guilt, and anxiety. Thus, Freud's theory describes the *conflict* between a person's instinctual needs and the demands of society. *For Freud, a person's core tendency is to maximize instinctual gratification while minimizing punishment and guilt* (Maddi, 1976). Freud's approach to personality is called psychoanalytic theory, and psychoanalysis is the method of therapy based upon it.

Core of Personality

Freud's theory is complex; it considers the sources and consequences of conflict, and how people deal with it. For Freud, a person's source of energy lies within the structure of consciousness.

CORE SOURCES OF CONFLICT. Freud argued that there are three levels of consciousness. The first level is **conscious behavior.** Conscious behavior consists of the thoughts, feelings, and actions we are aware of. **Preconscious behavior** is mental activity that we can be aware of if we attend to it. We have to stop, think, examine, and discover the causes of preconscious behavior.

Conscious behavior Freud's first level of consciousness. It includes what a person thinks, feels, and does that the person is aware of.

Preconscious behavior Freud's second level of consciousness, including mental activity that a person can be aware of if he or she attends to it.

Unconscious behavior
Freud's third level of consciousness, including mental activity that is beyond a person's awareness (unless brought out through psychoanalysis).

Id In Freud's theory, the source of instinctual energy which works on the pleasure principle.

Pleasure principle The guiding principle of the id, which seeks complete and immediate gratification of all needs and desires.

Ego In Freud's theory, the part of the personality that seeks to satisfy the id and superego in accordance with reality.

Superego In Freud's theory, the moral branch of mental functioning.

Thus, preconscious mental activity is available for scrutiny and understanding only if we examine it closely. For example, sometimes we are short with our parents if they correct our behavior. After examining the situation we may realize that we were abrupt because they corrected us.

Freud's third level of consciousness is the **unconscious.** Unconscious mental activity is mental activity that we are unaware of and cannot become aware of except through certain techniques. We can think of the levels of consciousness in terms of layers of sand. The top layer is very easy to mold, change, and sift through. The next layer, preconsciousness, takes a bit more work to dig through to understand. The deepest level of consciousness, the unconscious, is buried within a person's core.

As Freud developed his theory it became more complex. The primary structural elements of his theory are the id, ego, and superego. Each component accounts for a different aspect of a person's functioning. It is easy to think of these components as being real aspects of the human brain; however, we must remember that the id, ego, and superego are concepts, not real structures. The **id** is the source of a person's instinctual energy; it works on the **pleasure principle,** which assumes that people try to maximize gratification. Freud considered much of the instinctual energy to be sexual in nature, although he saw some of it as aggressive. The id is demanding, irrational, selfish, and pleasure-loving. Deep within the unconscious, the id seeks to maximize pleasure and does not care about other individuals, society, or morals.

The second major structural component of a person's functioning is the **ego.** Whereas the id seeks to maximize pleasure and obtain gratification, the ego seeks to satisfy the person's needs in accordance with reality. A child seeks an ice-cream cone and wants it. Her id tells her to grab the ice-cream cone and eat it: the pleasure principle. However, her ego tells her that this is not the best way to get an ice-cream cone. The child knows the reality of the situation. If she takes the ice-cream cone, she may be punished. Working on the reality principle, the child knows that the best way to achieve gratification is to ask for permission. Sometimes the ego stops the id from functioning, but more often it directs the id toward appropriate ways of behaving. While the id is demanding, unrealistic, and works on the pleasure principle, the ego is patient, reasonable, and works on the reality principle.

The third component of the structure of personality is the **superego.** The best way to characterize the superego is to think of it in terms of the moral branch of mental functioning. The superego acts to tell the id and the ego whether an approach toward gratification is moral and ethical. If a child seeks her ice-cream cone and asks her mother for it, her superego will indicate that this is morally correct. This approach toward obtaining ice cream will not invoke guilt, fear, or anxiety in a child. In contrast, a child may see candy on the table and know her mother is out of the room. Her ego knows that taking the candy would be very simple, and this would satisfy her id. However, the superego holds the child back from taking the candy; it has taken over the role of conscience and parental authority. So, we see that the superego helps to control the id by internalizing parental authority through the process of socialization.

If we think of functioning in the terms of id, ego, and superego, we see how Freud conceptualized the unconscious as three competing forces. In some people the id is stronger than the superego; perhaps these people turn

out to be sexual deviants or criminals—their needs for gratification are greater than conscience. Perhaps those people who become involved in antismut campaigns have overly strong superegos and do not have chances to express their ids. The relative strengths of the id, ego, and superego determine the degree of stability of each person.

Maintaining a balance among the id, ego, and superego is crucial to normal personality development, according to Freud.

CORE SOURCES OF ENERGY.   Freud assumed that the id works through two instinctual forces, the life instinct and the aggressive instinct. (The aggressive instinct was only slightly discussed by Freud.) The life (or sexual) instincts make up the **libido;** the libido works on the pleasure principle, and seeks immediate gratification. The ways that the libido expresses itself are usually determined not only by the id but by the ego and superego as well. An overly strong superego may try to overcontrol the id by producing guilt and shame. Similarly, an overly strong ego may try to overtake the id by controlling this sexual energy and allowing for little pleasure.

Libido   Freud's "life force," and the source of energy for the id, ego, and superego. Seeking immediate gratification, the libido works on the pleasure principle.

Anxiety develops when there is a lack of balance between the id, ego, and superego. **Anxiety** is a feeling of emotional discomfort; it is a state of tension, fear, and uneasiness. Anxiety can be mild (such as before a quiz or a date) but it can be so powerful that a person becomes immobile and unable to perform even the simplest tasks. Anxiety does not need to be connected to a specific event, and it is often accompanied by an increased physiological arousal. Most of the fear and apprehension that characterize anxiety are unrealistic. Many of Freud's patients were so gripped by anxiety that they were unable to move their legs and were essentially paralyzed. Freud found that once they were able to discover the source of their anxiety and deal with it, their paralysis disappeared.

Anxiety   A generalized feeling of fear and apprehension that may or may not be connected to a particular event or object and that is often accompanied by increased physiological arousal. Generally, these fears and apprehensions are attributed to unrealistic sources.

CORE CONSEQUENCES OF CONFLICT.   Anxiety is not a pleasant state. The uncomfortable feeling that students have before an examination is not something that they would like to endure all the time. Freud argued that the way people deal with anxiety is, to a great extent, the determinant of how they will behave. Thus, anxiety becomes one of the central and organizing themes of Freud's conception of personality. Since anxiety is one of the initiators of behavior and since it determines to a great extent how people will behave, Freud tried to characterize the way people deal with anxiety. He argued that

A defense mechanism is a way people reduce anxiety by distorting reality.

Defense mechanism A way of reducing anxiety by distorting reality.

Projection A defense mechanism in which a person attributes to others those undesirable traits in himself or herself.

Denial A defense mechanism in which a person *denies* the reality of the source of anxiety.

Reaction formation A defense mechanism in which a person acts out the *opposite* of his or her anxiety-producing feelings.

Rationalization A defense mechanism in which a person reinterprets behavior in terms that are acceptable.

Repression A defense mechanism in which anxiety-producing feelings are blocked from conscious awareness and pushed into the unconscious.

one of the principal ways that people avoid anxiety is to develop defense mechanisms. Defense mechanisms try to defend the ego against the awareness of instinctual needs. A **defense mechanism** is a way that people reduce anxiety by distorting reality. Anxiety is often so painful that we push feelings into our unconscious. Freud argued that rather than deal with our feelings and fears, we forget them or examine them in some other way. In fact, Freud contended that much of behavior is an attempt to deal with anxiety. Of course, all behavior is not maladjusted and people do not spend all of their lives trying to avoid life's challenges. Freud's point is that in trying to maximize pleasure and avoid pain, we sometimes use techniques like defense mechanisms to make our behavior acceptable. Well-adjusted, normal adults sometimes have to justify some potentially unacceptable feeling or behavior. Sometimes the anxiety is quite appropriate, such as anxiety before a job interview or a track meet. Thus, defending against anxiety is a normal and adaptive response. Only people with a neurotic disorder will use these mechanisms to such a great extent that reality is truly distorted.

There are many kinds of unconscious defense mechanisms. In **projection,** people attribute to others their own undesirable traits. Thus, an individual who recognizes that he has strong aggressive tendencies sees other people as being aggressive toward him. In **denial,** the person totally denies reality. Thus, the girl who has strong sexual feelings may totally deny her interest in the opposite sex rather than deal with those feelings. In **reaction formation** a person defends against anxiety by adopting an opposite feeling. The classic example of a reaction formation can be seen in the behavior of the person with strong sexual urges who claims religious fervor. Another is the censor of pornographic literature who has strong needs to view such literature; thus, while denouncing pornography he can view it avidly.

Most of us have used the defense mechanism of **rationalization.** By rationalizing we try to reinterpret undesirable behavior so that it appears acceptable. As we buy an extravagant fur coat, we rationalize our spending of an exorbitant amount of money by saying, "It will last a long time; it's always fashionable; and besides, I need a present for myself." When we rationalize, we try to make unreasonable behavior seem reasonable.

Freud's most important defense mechanism is **repression.** When behavior or thoughts are repressed, they are totally dismissed to the unconscious. So

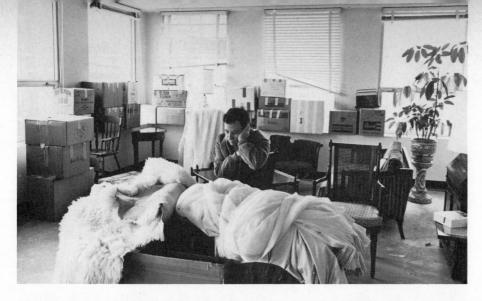

When tasks seem overwhelming, anxiety often results.

Denial

Projection

Reaction formation

Rationalization

when we repress a feeling or desire, we are totally unaware of that wish or desire. A young boy who has great sexual urges may repress them because he was taught that sexuality is sinful. Such urges are so anxiety producing that they are totally forgotten and are outside of consciousness. Freud argued that repressed feelings are expressed in different ways and that many behavioral abnormalities and personality quirks can be attributed to them. Whenever a person responds to a situation by indicating, ''I don't know why I did that,'' Freud would argue that some repressed feeling or desire is expressing itself—the id overcame the ego and superego.

Each of these defense mechanisms is a way of dealing with the uncomfortable feelings that anxiety produces. Anxiety before an examination is good, because it motivates us to study. However, if anxiety is so painful that it weakens the ability to function normally, some people drop out of school. For these people, the fear of failure is just too great. Freud's conception of anxiety and how it is dealt with represents a central theme throughout his theory of personality. It must be noted that ideas about defense mechanisms have not gone unchallenged. For example, Holmes (1978) has closely examined projection. Contrary to Freud's predictions about how projection reduces anxiety and stress, Holmes argues that there is no reliable evidence to suggest that attributing one's own undesirable traits to others results in a reduction of stress. After examining the limited research on the use of projection to reduce stress, Holmes questioned whether projection actually is a defense mechanism. His analysis places at least a part of Freud's theory in an embarrassing position.

Development of Personality

As children grow and experience many of life's events, they have an opportunity to experience both positive and negative things that will affect subsequent development. While the core tendency and the characteristics of personality are central throughout life, as children develop, new learning is inevitable and will shape day-to-day behavior.

Freud held that the core aspects of personality are laid down very early in life; therefore, they are stable and can be changed only with the greatest difficulty. He asserted that the instinctive energy of the id is biologically determined. At birth, the instincts of the baby are focused around the mouth; this is the infant's primary pleasure-seeking center. It is through the mouth that the infant obtains food, thereby reducing hunger. So, naturally, the first stage of development is called the **oral stage.** The infant achieves oral gratification in feeding, thumb sucking, and in babbling. During these early months of development an infant's basic feelings about the world are established. An adult who is sour on the world and who considers the world a bitter place to be often has had difficulty during the oral stage of development.

The second major stage of development is the **anal stage.** Around the ages of 2 and 3 the child learns to respond to some of the demands of society. One of the principal demands made by parents is that the child learn to control the bodily functions of urination and defecation. Most 2- and 3-year-olds find pleasure in defecating; there is a pleasant feeling in moving their bowels. Thus, the anal area of the body is the focal point for certain pleasures. Here lies a conflict between the id and the ego, between babylike be-

Oral stage Freud's first stage of personality development. From birth until about 1½ to 2, it is the stage during which gratification is obtained primarily through the mouth.

Anal stage Freud's second stage of personality development. From 1½ until age 3, it is the stage during which gratification is obtained through defecation and a child learns to respond to the outside demands of society.

havior and adultlike behavior. During the anal stage, Freud argued, children develop certain lasting personality characteristics which reflect their toilet training.

Freud's third stage is the **phallic stage,** around ages 4 and 5; this stage centers around the genitals. The child begins to realize the difference between males and females and becomes aware of sexuality. Males experience erections, and both male and female children may masturbate. During this period of life, children want to know the origins of babies. They are also becoming aware of sexual relationship between their parents. Many of the feelings of children during this stage are repressed. Freud argued that the Oedipus complex, which shall be discussed next, is in the most remote portions of the unconscious and is unavailable for scrutiny. So, neither children nor adults are aware of many of their sexual or Oedipal urges. However, it is through the Oedipus complex that the basis of sex-role development takes place. Table 11.1, p. 506 shows Freud's psychosexual stages of development.

In the phallic stage, males develop the Oedipus complex, fear of punishment, and castration anxiety. The Oedipus complex is a love for the mother, hostility toward the father, and fear of castration and/or punishment by the father. A major developmental achievement is the resolution of the Oedipus complex. A young boy realizes his father's close relationship with his mother, but rather than oppose (and fear) his father, he chooses to identify with him. In this way a young boy begins to model his behavior after that of his father. A boy passes through the **Oedipus complex** by identifying with his father so that he feels that he can gain more of his mother's attention. The Oedipus complex is most aptly expressed in the old song's words, "I want a girl, just like the girl, that married dear old Dad."

For the female, the Oedipus complex (sometimes called the Electra complex) is somewhat different. When a young girl realizes that she lacks a penis she first undergoes what Freud called penis envy. Then the female child attaches her love to the father and thereby symbolically acquires a penis. A young girl will ask her father to marry her so that they can raise a family together. Realizing that this probably is unlikely, she still wishes to have her father's affections. To gain this attention, she identifies with her mother and behaves the way her mother does. As with a young male, the young female identifies with the parent of the same sex and hopes to achieve the affection of the parent of the opposite sex. The critical component in the Oedipus complex is the development of identification with the parent of the same sex. During this stage the child learns to behave the way a man or a woman does. The entire notion of the Oedipus and Electra complex has been widely argued. At a minimum these ideas have always been controversial, and many psychologists do not consider them valid. Feminists have rejected these ideas totally. Regardless, Freud argued that it is through the phallic stage that children learn to identify with the same sex parent and adopt parental values.

Freud's fourth stage of development is the **latency stage.** From the age of 7 until puberty, the child continues to develop physically, but any sexual urges are relatively quiet. According to Freud, no major changes occur during the latency period. However, upon reaching the last stage of development, the **genital stage,** all of the old sexuality, fears, and repressed feelings are exhibited again. The turmoil of adolescence takes place during the genital stage, when the adolescent has to shake off old dependencies on parents and learn to deal with members of the opposite sex in a sexual and social manner.

Phallic stage Freud's third stage of personality development. From ages 3 to 7 it is the stage during which gratification is obtained primarily from the genitals. During this stage children pass through the Oedipus complex.

Oedipus complex During the phallic stage, feelings of rivalry with the parent of the same sex for love of the parent of the opposite sex. Through identification with the parent of the same sex, the Oedipus complex is mastered.

Latency stage Freud's fourth stage of personality development. From age 7 until puberty, it is the interim stage between the phallic and genital stages.

Genital stage Freud's last stage of personality development. From puberty through adulthood, it is the stage during which sexual conflicts of childhood surface again in the adolescents as they develop their sexuality.

The Oedipus complex often begins without a parent being aware that it is happening.

Table 11.1 Freud's psychosexual stages of development

STAGE	AGE	
Oral Infant achieves oral gratification in feeding, thumb sucking, and babbling.	0-2	
Anal The child learns to respond to some of the demands of society (learning to control bodily functions).	2-3	
Phallic The child begins to realize the differences between males and females and becomes aware of sexuality.	3-7	
Latency The child continues his or her development but sexual urges are relatively quiet ones.	7-11	
Genital Period of adolescence when the growing child shakes off old dependencies and learns to deal maturely with the opposite sex.	11-Adult	

Many of the adolescent's repressed feelings of sexuality toward his or her mother or father again arise. This becomes obvious during the dialogue of a therapy session:

THERAPIST: Tell me, Maria, how have you been doing the past week?

MARIA: I've had some really strange dreams lately, doctor.

THERAPIST: Oh?

MARIA: I dreamed that my mother told me that she didn't want me to live at home anymore. I don't know why I would think such a thing, even in a dream.

THERAPIST: What makes you so sure your mother would or could never say such things?

MARIA: But, I just know my mother never would . . . at least I think she wouldn't . . .

THERAPIST: Hmmmmmmmmmm.

When it was first developed around 1900, Freud's psychosexual theory of development received great attention, both favorable and unfavorable. The notion that young children had sexual feelings toward their parents was considered absurd. Yet, as we watch young children and the way they identify with parents, we can see that there are some elements of truth to his conception of how development proceeds. Freud, however, was not nearly as interested in the normal development of the individual as he was in the type of behavior pathology or disorder that appeared because of imperfect development.

Peripheral Characteristics

A person's core tendencies are going to shape the overall direction of his or her life. Through the course of development these core tendencies are going to be guideposts and will interact with a child's learning experiences. Sometimes these learning experiences will be positive in nature; they will be productive, worthwhile growth experiences. Other times, however, children will have negative or bad experiences that can affect them profoundly. For example, if a child has a rough time with his Oedipal stage of development because of an absent parent or a permissive father, the proper sex-role stereotyping will be unlikely to develop. With this in mind, Freud recognized that many of a person's day-to-day characteristics, their peripheral characteristics, are going to be shaped by their development. Many of the peripheral characteristics which Freud described could be called character types.

Freud's theory of personality development is not a simple one. When something goes wrong with personality development, the disorder cannot be traced to one single component of personality. A personality disorder does not come about because of a faulty ego or because of a poor experience at some developmental stage. Personality disorders appear because of many interconnected factors.

In development children proceed from one stage to the next and make adjustments to their views of the world. If a child has not successfully passed through a stage, then he or she becomes fixated at that stage. A fixation occurs as a result of overindulgence or frustration, and when it occurs it means that there are unresolved conflicts. For example, children who have not successfully passed through the phallic stage have probably not resolved their Oedipus complexes. They may still have hostility toward the parent of the same sex and have an overbearing and unrealistic attachment to the parent of the opposite sex. Throughout life these children may suffer the consequences of these overreactions. A boy may generally consider men hostile and wish to attach himself to females in a dependent kind of relationship (the kind he might have had with his mother).

The idea of a fixation and people having a difficult time coping with some of life's situations is not unique to Freud. In discussing social development of children in chapter 6, we discussed Erikson's use of the idea of fixation. In

Table 11.2 Approaches to personality: conflict

APPROACH	MAJOR PROPONENT	CORE OF PERSONALITY	STRUCTURE OF PERSONALITY	DEVELOPMENT	PERIPHERAL CHARACTERISTICS: BEHAVIOR PATHOLOGY RESULTS
Conflict	Sigmund Freud	Maximizes gratification while minimizing punishment or guilt; instinctual urges direct behavior	Id, ego, superego	5 Stages: Oral, anal, phallic, latency, genital	Because of imbalance in id, ego, superego, and due to fixations.

analyzing the life cycle of adults, Levinson uses a similar notion. Freud was one of the first *psychologists* to use such a concept, and we can see that it is a useful one. If people are having a difficult time at a certain stage in their lives, then it is unlikely that they will be able to cope with more complex demands effectively. Neither Freud nor any other theorist really argued that a fixation at some stage means that a person stops developing. Rather, stage theories which use the idea argue that unless an earlier stage is mastered as successfully as possible, subsequent stages cannot be fully dealt with (see Table 11.3).

This idea is much like the one Maslow suggested when we considered motivation in chapter 4. Maslow argued that unless a person's physiological needs are met it will be difficult for him or her to worry about satisfying needs for love and belonging. Yet, as long as minimum hunger and thirst needs are satisfied, people can go on to satisfy emotional needs. The same concept is being used with the idea of a fixation at a particular stage of development. If someone is stuck with an unresolved conflict, severe behavior maladjustment *might* emerge. It is more likely, however, that a partially unresolved conflict will make the successful and full completion of new stages more difficult to complete.

According to Freud, good personality adjustment generally refers to a balance among competing forces. In this way a child is not too self-centered but at the same time not too moralistic. Freud would argue that restrictive, punitive, and overbearing parents produce children who are emotionally disturbed and who have a difficult time coping with life. Much of the popular literature of the last decade deals specifically with this problem. For example, in *Portnoy's Complaint*, Philip Roth writes of an overly strict mother who tries to emasculate her son through overcontrol; she tries to keep the id out of her kid. Much of the women's liberation movement has attempted to allow women to express their ids without the control of a male-dominated society.

Table 11.3 Psychologists are fond of stage theories. A stage theory is a way of conceptualizing the development of a person or a process over time to see how the individual changes and grows. I have presented four major stage theories of development in this text: The theories of Piaget (p. 258), Erikson (p. 280), Levinson (p. 281) and, in this chapter, Freud. Each of these theorists has examined the development of personality characteristics and found some striking commonalities. Each suggests that previous stages must be mastered successfully before an individual proceeds to the next stage. Fixation at any stage means arrested development and an incomplete mastery of future stages. Further, each sees growth and development as a continuing process. Notice the similarities between their theories.

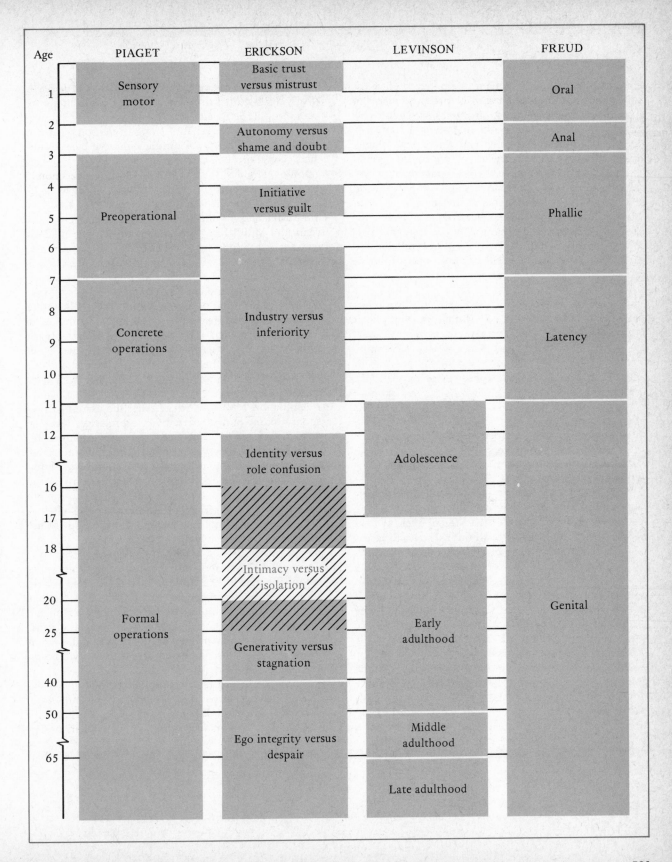

Personality Inventories

A number of psychologists have attempted to place together known facts about behavior patterns; many of them have gathered information about their clients and subject populations by the administration of standardized tests. While an IQ test will provide a psychologist an indication of people's intellectual functioning, it only gives some indication about their general behavior patterns. To better assess and predict how people respond to a variety of situations, personality inventories with many scales have been developed. Even as early as 1931, psychologists were developing ways of assessing personality precisely (Bernreuter, 1931). With a reliable and valid personality test a psychologist can begin to make some reasonable predictions about how a person responds to a variety of situations.

One of the most widely used and well-researched personality inventories is the Minnesota Multiphasic Personality Inventory, or, as it is more commonly called, the MMPI. The MMPI consists of a series of 550 statements to which the examinee responds either true or false. The items in the test consist of statements like these:

I tire easily.
I become very anxious before examinations.
I worry about sex matters.
I become bored easily.

The items in the test focus around attitudes and feelings, motor disturbances, and bodily complaints. The test consists of ten subscales that describe various aspects of functioning and three additional scales to assess whether the examinee has been responding truthfully. Administered individually or in a group format, the MMPI results in a profile of scores that allows a psychologist to make an assessment of an individual's current level of functioning, an individual's characteristic way of dealing with the world, as well as some reasonable predictions of the person's ability to function in specific situations. The norms for the MMPI were developed by examining the profiles of a group of psychiatric patients and over 700 normal people. A mean on each scale tells how most normal individuals score; if a person is significantly above the mean (more than two standard deviations), this is considered evidence of maladjustment.

The MMPI is the most researched test ever devised. Nearly 5,000 studies have been reported in the literature examining it. Some studies have been validity studies; others have assessed reliability (e.g., Swenson, Pearson, & Osborne, 1973). Racial differences have been examined (Gynther, 1972), as have age and other demographic variables like education and socioeconomic groups (Lanyon, 1968). The psychological journals regularly contain studies examining the predictive ability of the MMPI and a wide number of variables. Over the years the MMPI has been shown to be a useful test; when it is carefully interpreted by a skilled examiner, the MMPI has good predictive ability. It is a test that is often used by psychologists and psychotherapists.

The MMPI depends upon examinees' reports of their own behavior; it can be administered very easily. Other personality tests differ in their aims and are much more complicated in their administration. The list of such tests is lengthy. We shall consider briefly two other widely used tests, the Rorschach Ink Blot Test and the Thematic Apperception Test (TAT); both of these tests are projective tests.

Unlike the MMPI, which restricts the examinee's response to one of two alternatives, a projective test permits a wide variety of responses; each examinee responds in a unique way. An assumption of projective tests is that the responses obtained reflect underlying personality dynamics which the examinee may not be aware of. It is for this reason that projective tests are used, especially if it is important to determine whether the examinee is faking responses or trying to hide something from the psychologist. A basic assumption of any projective test is that a person's unconscious motivations will direct current verbal responses and future behavior. Because the test offers fewer guidelines for responding, examinees project their ideas and feelings into their responses; this supposedly allows a clinician to better assess the "deeper" levels of personality structure; these tests rely heavily on the idea that the examinees' true motivations, feelings, and needs will be reflected in their verbal responses.

In the Rorschach test an inkblot is shown to the examinee; ten are shown in total, five in black and white, two with some red ink in them, and the remaining with various pastel colors. They are symmetrical in design

Figure 11.1 In a Rorschach test, an ink blot like this one is shown to examinees; they are to respond in an open-ended way telling the psychologist what the ink blots look like. From their descriptions, psychologists make inferences about a person's underlying drives, motivations, and unconscious conflicts

with a specific shape or form; the examinees are asked to tell the clinician what they see in the design. A detailed report of the examinee's response is made for later interpretation. Specific questions are asked of the examinee after the ten inkblots have been shown. Here is a typical response to a Rorschach inkblot:

> My first impression was a big bug, a fly maybe. I see in the background two facelike figures pointing toward each other as if they're talking. It also has a resemblance to a skeleton—the pelvis area. I see a cute little bat right in the middle. The upper half looks like a mouse. (Aiken, 1979, p. 261).

Good clinical judgment is necessary to place all of a subject's responses within a meaningful context. While norms are available (Goldfried et al., 1971), even for children (Levitt & Truumaa, 1972), a skilled interpretation of this test is particularly crucial. Many researchers find the test useful, but they also recognize that its validity is not fully established and accepted (Goldfried et al., 1971).

Far more structured than the Rorschach is the Thematic Apperception Test or the TAT. The TAT was introduced in studying motivation and need for achievement (p. 156). The TAT consists of black-and-white pictures which depict one or more persons in a variety of situations. Examinees are asked to tell a story about a picture indicating what situation is presented in the picture, what led up to the situation, what will happen in the future, and what the people are thinking and feeling. A standardized procedure for scoring of TAT responses is available with norms and the most frequent responses to each card (Atkinson, 1958). The test has been modified for children (Bellak, 1975) and for the aged (Wolk & Wolk, 1971). As part of a battery of personality tests, the TAT has been shown to be particularly useful in examining a person's characteristic way of dealing with others and the needs which govern a person's interactions with the world.

As a theorist develops a personality theory or as a clinician develops a diagnosis of a client's problem, no single test will provide all of the information. In order to obtain an overall description of psychological functioning, many psychologists administer a battery of tests which often includes an intelligence test like the WAIS-R (Wechsler Adult Intelligence Scale-Revised), the MMPI, and projectives like the TAT or Rorschach. A wide number of other tests are used to assess more specific aspects of a person's functioning; these include tests of vocational interests, special abilities, brain dysfunction, motor coordination, anxiety, and sexual functioning. From a number of tests, more confidence can be placed in the data, and current levels of functioning are more easily characterized. Personality tests thus are useful in predicting future behavior while only requiring a relatively small sample of behavior—responding to a test.

Men have traditionally been allowed to express their sexuality and aggressive tendencies, but women have been told to be feminine, demure, and pure. In her popular novel, *Fear of Flying*, Erica Jong presents the story of Isadora Wing trying to find her identity. Isadora's id has overcome her ego and superego. The id, ego, and superego have each had their heyday in her life, but through analysis and some bizarre circumstances, the antihero of *Fear of Flying* finds her identity.

Thus, for Freud, fixations, or even partial fixations, would usually occur because of frustration or overindulgence which hinders the expression of sexual or aggressive energy at a particular psychological stage. This in turn leads to the development of defense mechanisms and sometimes maladjustment. Personality, therefore, reflects an ongoing conflict between a person's need for immediate gratification and the demands of society—two irrevocably opposed forces.

FULFILLMENT APPROACH: CARL ROGERS

Carl R. Rogers (1902–   ) presents a fulfillment approach to personality development in which people try to express their capabilities, potentialities, and talents to the fullest degree possible. Rogers suggests that there is an inborn tendency in people which directs them toward becoming whatever their inherited nature is. Instead of seeing personality development as an ongoing conflict between forces, Rogers sees personality development as a fulfillment of one's potential.

Rogers makes two basic assumptions about behavior. First, he assumes that behavior is goal-directed and worthwhile. He also assumes that since people are innately good they will almost always choose adaptive self-actualizing behaviors. These assumptions are the cornerstone of his theory of personality and lay the foundation of his approach to treatment of abnormal behavior (to be discussed in chapter 12).

Core of Personality

Like Freud, Rogers's theory developed from therapeutic interests and experiences. As a practicing clinical psychologist, Rogers listened to thousands of patients talk about their problems. In fact, Rogers was one of the first to tape-record and transcribe the interactions of the client and therapist. He found that when patients were given the opportunity to talk in their own terms, they talked about their experiences and thoughts of who they were; it became apparent "that the self was an important element in the experience of the client and that in some odd sense his goal was to become his 'real self'" (Rogers, 1959, p. 201). Rogers's theory of personality has as its main structure the concept of **self;** the self is composed of a group of characteristics and perceptions of an individual, his or her relationship to others, and to other aspects of life. Thus, the self is how persons see their behavior and internal characteristics. In Rogers's theory of personality persons are assumed to be in the process of fulfilling their potentials or becoming everything that they can be.

Rogers suggests that there is not only a concept of self but also one of the ideal self. An **ideal self** is what a person would like to be. Thus, while each of

Understanding of self and personal desires is a key to Rogerian therapy.

Self A group of characteristics and perceptions of an individual, and his or her relationship with others and to other aspects of life. The self is the main structural component of Rogers's theory of personality.

Ideal self What a person would like to be.

us has a self-concept, we also have a concept of what we would like to be. When there is a reasonable degree of correspondence between the real self and the ideal self, we are generally happy. However, if there is a great discrepancy between our self-image and our ideal self, we are often dissatisfied and unhappy.

Rogers's approach to personality is unidirectional; it always moves in the direction of fulfillment. Of course, people are not always fulfilling their potential and moving in positive directions. Sometimes they have periods where there is no growth, and this may go on for long periods. Yet, regardless of an individual's rate of growth toward fulfillment, there is no assumption about internal conflict. People are not seen as at war with themselves, and different aspects of the self are not seen to oppose one another. Rogers is not so naive as to suggest that all people at all times are undergoing growth; however, his view is clearly an optimistic and hopeful one.

While Freud spoke of a minimum of three conflicting levels of structure, the id, ego, and superego, Rogers had one structural component to personality, the concept of self. While Freud saw human beings' energy in conflict, to Rogers, *the core tendency is to actualize, maintain, and enhance the experiencing organism.* Rogers's basic principle is that people have a tendency toward maximizing their self-concepts through **self-actualization.** When the self becomes actualized, it has grown, expanded, and become more social. People become self-actualized when they have expanded their self-concepts and have developed their potentialities so as to approximate their ideal selves. Self-actualization is not a process that takes place at any one point in life, but is one that is continuous. According to Rogers, when people are experiencing anxiety because their self-concepts are not what they would like them to be, they try to self-actualize and develop into their ideal selves. Again, Rogers recognizes that people are not always experiencing growth; he understands that anxiety can develop. But still, anxiety is useful because it motivates people to become everything of which they might be capable.

Self-actualization For Rogers, the ongoing expansion of the self toward the ideal self.

Development of Personality

Freud characterized development as a series of stages during which certain activities were principally involved. Rogers posits no such discrete stages. He suggests that through cumulative development people learn to self-actualize effectively and to achieve a greater understanding of themselves.

Rogers was particularly aware that early in life children develop basic feelings about themselves and that social influences affect the development of self-concepts. When children are constantly told that they are beautiful, intelligent, and clever, their ideas about themselves are very different from those of children who are told that they are bad, dirty, shameful, and general nuisances.

Rogers does not argue that negative feelings toward children should not be expressed. Quite the contrary, he suggests that children must grow up in an atmosphere where they can experience life fully. This involves seeing the good sides of their behavior as well as the bad sides. They need to grow in an environment in which they can explore all different aspects of their personalities.

The process of development is learning to evaluate one's self and the process of self-actualizing. When children have been allowed to develop firm self-concepts, they respect themselves and others. They are aware of themselves and how others see them. People with positive self-concepts and high self-esteem are generally flexible and open to new experiences so that they can continue to expand themselves and thus continue the process of self-actualization. The development of a positive self-concept is a cornerstone of Rogerian views of personality.

Peripheral Characteristics

When people are fully functioning and are moving in a positive direction their lives have meaning and they feel that they are moving toward self-actualization. A person who has a positive view about the world in which she lives is likely to be willing to experience new ideas and events and thereby fulfill herself to a greater extent. With each new experience, her self-concept becomes stronger and more defined, and again, the eventual goal of self-actualization is brought still closer. This becomes particularly evident in therapy, as is seen in the following exchange:

THERAPIST: Good morning, Edith.

EDITH: Good morning, doctor. (Long pause) I've had a really good week this past week. I was able to cope with my anxieties. I did much better with my husband. I had a tough time with the children though. They were awfully rebellious. I tried my hardest to understand them.

THERAPIST: Oh?

EDITH: They kept attacking me and saying that I was unfair and selfish. I tried to evaluate what they said, always remembering that I was the parent, they were the children.

THERAPIST: How did their attacks make you feel?

EDITH: A little shaky—still I tried to keep *my* image of myself intact. They might have been able to attack specific things that I did or said—but I know who I am.

Rogers suggests that the reason people become unhappy is because they are unable to fit new types of behavior within their self-concepts. For example, there are persons who have a self-concept which includes high moral principles, strict religious observances, and strict self-control. How does this person react when viewing pornographic material and becoming sexually aroused by it? The person becomes anxious because the feelings experienced are inconsistent with his or her self-concept. To avoid anxiety the person denies or distorts these experiences. A healthy self-concept allows for new experiences and allows for acceptance or rejection of the new experience. Persons with rigid self-concepts will guard their self-concepts against potential threatening feelings and experiences. Rogers argues that people distort their perceptions of their behavior to make it acceptable to their self-concepts. Thus, a married man who is experiencing hostility toward his wife may reinterpret or distort that hostility because his concept of a happily married man does not allow for it. People need to have positive self-images and thus will do whatever is necessary to achieve such feelings about themselves. Rogers argues that people who are not moving in such positive directions develop conflicts and anxiety because they deny and distort reality.

The greatest cause of anxiety and behavior disorder results when there is a large discrepancy between self-concept and ideal self. If a person realizes that

Rogers suggests that people become unhappy because they are unable to fit new types of behavior into their self-concepts

his ideal self is significantly different from the way he actually is, he can self-actualize and try to change his behavior, or if he does not, he will likely become anxious and a generally unhappy person. The healthy person will try to self-actualize and become the best person possible. Even if the person is never able to achieve his ideal self, he is able to deal with this inability; he has a knowledge of what his capabilities are. The unhealthy person, instead of trying to grow, will distort reality, remain anxious, and be unhappy with himself and others. Behavior pathology can thus be seen as an inability of a person to self-actualize to the fullest extent possible.

There are many ways by which healthy people can seek to enhance their self-concepts. In the last two decades different approaches toward personal growth have developed; one of the most popular has been the encounter group. The encounter group, or T group as it is sometimes called (T stands for training), is a group of individuals who seek to expand their awareness and fulfill themselves to a greater extent. Encounter groups have taken many forms, but all have as their goal personal growth, fulfillment, self-actualization, and a strengthening of the concept of unconditional positive regard for others and for the individuals themselves. Sometimes encounter groups

Encounter groups help people expand their awareness of themselves so that they might better understand and appreciate their situations.

Table 11.4 Approaches to personality: conflict and fulfillment

APPROACH	MAJOR PROPONENT	CORE OF PERSONALITY	STRUCTURE OF PERSONALITY	DEVELOPMENT	PERIPHERAL CHARACTERISTICS: BEHAVIOR PATHOLOGY RESULTS
Conflict	Sigmund Freud	Maximizes gratification while minimizing punishment or guilt; instinctual urges direct behavior	Id, ego, superego	5 Stages: oral, anal, phallic, latency, genital	Because of imbalance in id, ego, superego, and due to fixations.
Fulfillment	Carl Rogers	Actualize, maintain and enhance the experiences of life through the process of self-actualization	Self	Process of cumulative self-actualization	Because of wide discrepancy between self and ideal self.
Fulfillment	Alfred Adler	Striving for superiority and perfection	None stated	Process of striving for superiority by overcoming feelings of inferiority	Because of inability to succeed and overwhelming feelings of inferiority.

meet for a weekend and, with the help of a leader or facilitator, they talk, do exercises, and try to provide a warm accepting situation wherein their members can explore new kinds of growth experiences. While the research on encounter groups has shown mixed results, people who attend them usually feel good about their experience and have an enhanced self-concept (Kilmann & Sotile, 1976).

Rogers's conceptions of personality show his abiding concern with each individual's personal development, a development of self. Rogers strongly argues that each person's evaluation of his or her situation must be evaluated from a personal, internal frame of reference, not that of others. Thus each person's happiness and stability lies within his or her conception of self; unhappiness comes about when there is too great a discrepancy between real self and ideal self. Rogers argues that people choose their own behavior patterns and that behavior is generally goal-directed and worthwhile, and so people are bound to try to self-actualize and fulfill their potential.

FULFILLMENT APPROACH: ALFRED ADLER

Alfred Adler (1870–1937) also presents another form of the fulfillment approach to personality. Unlike Carl Rogers's approach, Adler's position is that people are striving toward perfection and superiority. Superiority and perfection are not just processes of fulfillment but are an ultimate aim toward which a single individual strives. The focus is not only on the self but on the individual as a member of society as well. Adler's thinking was influenced very heavily by Freud, and many think of his theory as an extension of Freud's. However, as you will see, there are some fundamental differences.

Does Your Name Fit Your Personality?

People's ideas about themselves are often constructed by how others see them. If your self-image is in part determined by how others see you, then your name may play an important role in shaping personality. The following news article shows that names do play a significant role in people's lives.

NEWSWEEK School children with funny or unusual names are often picked on by their classmates. Now a psychologist at San Diego State University has found evidence that teachers also discriminate against oddly named pupils.

In an experiment conducted by Prof. Hubert Harari, eighty elementary-school teachers and student teachers were asked to grade four different compositions written by fourth- and fifth-grade students. Some of the papers were attributed to students named Michael and David; the others were supposedly written by Elmer and Hubert, which Harari describes as "losers' names." The student teachers were not influenced by the choice of names, but on the papers graded by experienced teach-

ers, Elmer and Hubert consistently received nearly a full grade lower than Michael and David, no matter which paper their names appeared on.

Loser: A similar study of girls' names was inconclusive. One "loser," Bertha, got lower grades than "winners" Karen and Lisa, but the other supposedly undesirable name, Adele, scored a little higher. Harari theorizes that boys with odd names are more likely than girls to have chips on their shoulders; knowing this, veteran teachers view the Elmers and Huberts with a jaundiced eye.

In the wake of his study, Harari has been flooded with inquiries from name-conscious parents. His advice is to avoid panic. "I don't think it's necessary for every parent to give his child an ordinary name," he says. "Just stay away from the really strange ones. For instance, Sonny and Cher named their daughter Chastity. Can you imagine what that child is going to have to face?"

Core of Personality

As a personality theorist who believed that people are basically good, Adler's *core tendency is that people strive toward superiority or perfection.* Whereas Rogers stressed the idea of fulfilling one's potentiality through self-actualization, Adler stressed that people strive toward reaching a very specific end or goal—that end or goal is perfection. In some ways the goals that people set up for themselves are fictional; it is likely that these goals will never be reached, but for Adler it was these goals that energize behavior. Adler even spoke of a *fictional finalism;* a goal state that is impossible to realize but acts as one of the energizers of behavior (Adler, 1920, 1933a).

People strive for superiority in order that they might reach perfection; they are motivated or energized to do so because of feelings of inferiority. From Adler's viewpoint when people feel a sense of imperfection they seek to improve themselves. So, when people feel less than perfect, they will strive to better themselves. Feelings of inferiority are not negative; quite the opposite, feelings of inferiority impel people to strive for superiority and express their core tendencies.

A crucial aspect of Adler's view is that people are social beings; as individuals they might seek to strive for superiority, but, as a group, people are inherently social in nature. Adler recognized that people interact with parents, family, and society from their first day of birth and he therefore stressed the social nature of human beings. This is an important point: most other theorists assume that people are social because they are forced to be; Adler said that being social was innate, inherent in being human.

Fulfillment approaches to personality assume that people want to become everything that they might. Meditation is one technqiue used to help people expand their awareness.

One of the ways that people express their social approach to life is by adopting a unique *style of life*. An individual's style of life allows an expression of characteristics which can reflect his or her own personality, feelings, and strivings. A person's style of life allows her to express needs for superiority; Adler recognized that people are not all the same, nor will they all approach achieving superiority in the same way. People have to live within a social framework, but they all have different social goals and may seek to express their feelings and goals for superiority in different areas of life. Some people may seek to be superior architects, while others may seek to be superior social advocates.

Adler felt that each person developed her own *unique* style of life in which attitudes and behaviors expressed a specific approach to achieving superiority. These views of superiority are in part going to be determined by society; human beings are social and they will seek goals and values that are basically social in nature (Adler, 1920, 1929, 1933a, 1933b).

Development of Personality

Similar to Rogers's position, Adler felt that a child's social interactions were going to be particularly important in determining eventual personality attributes. While Rogers stressed social interactions in the development of self-concepts, Adler suggested that people are innately social. This means that a child's relationships with other people, particularly parents, will determine to a great extent the nature of his or her personality. Adler argued that the *family atmosphere* in a child's early years leads to very specific kinds of life-styles. A child's relationship with her parents as well as her position in the family will be very important. For example, a child who is the firstborn is likely to have a different relationship with people from a child who is third in birth order. The child responds to her birth order and parents by choosing life-styles which will be consistent with those social interactions. For example, firstborns tend to be people who have a high need for achievement (see p. 159). They are pushed by their parents toward success, leadership, and independence. According to Adler it is likely that a firstborn would develop a life-style that reflects high needs for achievement and a very strong striving toward superiority and perfection. Through the process of development and by interacting with others, individuals choose life-styles which develop the specifics of personality, peripheral characteristics.

Peripheral Characteristics

Adler and his followers have relied heavily on the idea that persons' relationships with their siblings and their family atmosphere will determine their styles of life. It therefore follows that birth order is also going to be important to Adlerian theory. Birth order will play a central role in determining the range of feelings that a child might have about himself and his family. For example, older children tend to have stronger needs for superiority than younger children. But, a younger child may feel competitive with an older sibling and thus develop strong needs for success, mastery, and achievement.

Closely associated with birth order are feelings of inferiority. As each child enters the family situation, the child will bring to it new talents, strengths, and weaknesses. This is going to affect others within the family by creating feelings of potential inferiority or lack of worth. It is, of course, these feelings of inferiority which will create greater strivings for superiority and mastery. From Adler's view, these inferiorities and the resulting expressions of needs for perfection will determine the specific aspects (the peripheral characteristics) of a person's behavior. If the family atmosphere is one which stresses cooperation, respect, and love, then it is likely that a child will express her needs for superiority in positive, fulfilling, socially acceptable ways. By contrast, if the family atmosphere is not a positive one, one that contains a lack of love, distrust, or even neglect, then it is likely that the antisocial, negative, and potentially destructive peripheral characteristics of behavior will develop. Adlerians developed a series of ideas about constructive versus destructive behavior and how these might be actively or passively pursued.

Adlerian psychology stresses social interactions; normal behavior follows a course of socially acceptable strivings and an interesting and usually unique life-style. When a person shows abnormal behavior, the Alderian typically assumes that it probably began in childhood. Adlerians assume that poor social interactions, particularly with parents, lead to a misguided or faulty style of life. In therapy, maladjusted behavior is treated by helping a client to achieve positive social interactions with other human beings. Feelings of inferiority are channeled into ways of achieving feelings of accomplishment.

While Adler's theory differs from Rogers's in many ways, they both make a fundamental assumption about human behavior. They both assume that humans can and will fulfill themselves whenever possible. While Rogers stressed self-actualization in becoming what one might become, Adler's model is more extreme. For Adler, an individual strives toward perfection, toward superiority, and the motivation for this striving for superiority comes about through feelings of inferiority and a fictional finalism. Adler's ideas of the *inferiority complex* and *life-styles* have made their way into other popular theories of psychology and are perhaps his most notable contribution.

BEHAVIORAL APPROACH

Few concepts could be more abstract than the id, ego, and superego; even the term self-actualization is somewhat mysterious. Behaviorists have rejected all of these concepts in favor of stimuli and responses, which are definable, observable, and measurable.

Learning theory is an alternative to traditional personality theories. It is unlike most personality theories both in the types of events that it discusses and in its approach. Learning theorists are largely concerned with the learning process and see behavior as fluctuating in response to changes in environmental situations and in schedules of reinforcement. By contrast, personality typically refers to behavior that remains the same over a long period of time. Thus, there are some immediate conflicts between the behavioral approach and typical personality approaches.

Core of Personality

For behaviorists, the structural unit of personality is the response. Any behavior that is exhibited, regardless of the situation, is seen as a response to stimuli or as a response awaiting reinforcement. Of course, people are motivated to emit responses. For example, people are energized to eat because of hunger. A child may be motivated to eat all of his vegetables and to expect a response from his parents. The child is waiting for reinforcement for his behavior. Eventually children learn to eat vegetables because they taste good and because parents are pleased with them if they eat the vegetables. Continuous reinforcements eventually become unnecessary; the child won't need to be reinforced each time he eats his vegetables. Usually, behaviors (responses) are not randomly emitted; rather, they are emitted to satisfy some need. Thus, for a behaviorist the basic organizing theme of life, the *core tendency, is to reduce or satisfy the social or biological needs that energize behavior;* this is accomplished through responses (behaviors) that are reinforced.

In studying stimuli and responses it is important to remember that a reinforcer is any event which is going to make a response occur with a greater frequency. Children who are reinforced for good behavior tend to exhibit good behavior more often than children who are not reinforced. The use of stimuli, responses, and reinforcement can be considered from dramatically different points of view. I have shown this earlier in considering the work of Pavlov and Skinner (classical versus instrumental conditioning). Personality can be viewed from equally diverse points of view. There is a classical conditioning approach to personality, an instrumental conditioning approach, and, in addition, an observational learning approach.

CLASSICAL CONDITIONING. In classical conditioning, an initially neutral stimulus is paired with another stimulus which elicits some response. A neutral stimulus might be a bell which, when paired with food, will elicit the response of salivation. Through careful pairing of the bell with the food, the bell alone will elicit salivation.

Classical conditioning can account for a variety of behaviors, for initially neutral events may bring about new responses. For example, upon seeing a rat, many people become frightened. Rodents are often seen within dark cellars; in this way, dark cellars also often become a fearful stimulus. Upon entering a dark cellar, an individual experiences fear because he or she associates dark cellars with rodents, and rodents elicit fear.

Many studies have been done to try to classically condition behavior. For example, bed wetting is often a problem with children. A bed-wetting child has not learned to waken before emptying his or her bladder. The problem is that a full bladder does not awaken the child. In a study conducted by Mowrer and Mowrer (1938), subjects slept on a special bed. This bed was arranged so that when urination occurred a bell was forced to sound which easily awoke the child. By pairing the bell with the increase in bladder tension, children stopped bed wetting. The initially neutral stimulus, the ringing of the bell, became paired with bladder tension so that upon an increase in bladder tension, the children would wake up and then empty their bladders in the toilet rather than the bed.

INSTRUMENTAL CONDITIONING.   Instrumental behaviors are responses that a person emits. As each behavior is emitted, there is some consequence, such as reinforcement or punishment. When the child eats her vegetables, she expects the reinforcement of praise or, perhaps, dessert. Instrumental conditioning considers that these consequences are an absolute essential.

For personality development the basic assumption of instrumental conditioning is simple: behavior that is reinforced tends to occur again. When people find that a certain behavior that they emit is reinforced, they tend to emit a similar behavior in a similar situation. Responses that are reinforced shape personality. People who emit consideration or affectionate behavior are often highly reinforced and will continue to be considerate and affectionate. In contrast, if people are not reinforced for this type of behavior, they will usually be hostile. If we look at the entire range of behaviors that people emit, we can begin to assess personality.

Using a simple behavioral analysis, we can begin to see how people develop behavior patterns and how behavior is in constant flux. Remember, a behavioral tradition suggests that learning is the process which shapes personality and that learning takes place because of experience. New experiences happen all the time; thus, a person is constantly learning about the world and changing accordingly. Personality can thus be seen from a behavioral viewpoint as something that is always changing and modifiable.

Many names can be closely tied with the instrumental conditioning approach to learning and personality. However, B. F. Skinner, a Harvard psychologist for whom the Skinner box was named, is one of the most visible. Skinner has written volumes on the nature of learning and the role of reinforcement. Skinner's visibility to the public comes not from his scientific accomplishments, but from his personal views of life and his political-social statements, as shown in his book *Walden II.* Basically, Skinner, as a behaviorist, sees that all behavior can be shaped and managed so as to achieve a potentially ideal individual in a potentially ideal society. People and society are modifiable; as a behavioral psychologist Skinner feels that any behavior (including personality) can be shaped and molded so that it is considered appropriate and worthwhile.

OBSERVATIONAL LEARNING.   In observational learning it is assumed that people can learn new behaviors by watching others perform those behaviors. When a child watches his parents use proper table manners, the child learns those proper table manners. Similarly, a novice tennis player will learn certain techniques and strategies while watching a tennis pro. It is assumed that the observer will imitate the behavior of someone else, the model. Most parents will tell their older children to be good models for their younger siblings; they ask them to behave properly so that the younger children will do the same.

A behavior that is the result of observational learning need not be exhibited to be considered learned behavior. In many situations behaviors are exhibited that have not been shown for many weeks, months, or, perhaps, ever! Many parents have noted the excellent table manners of their children in the presence of company, yet on a daily basis these same table manners are never exhibited. Obviously, the children have learned the appropriate responses but choose to show them according to whim.

One of the major differences between observational learning theory and classical ideas about learning is that learning may be independent of reinforcement. This means that an individual's learning of a new response has nothing to do with reinforcement; a person can learn the behavior merely by watching it. Thus, unlike instrumental techniques in which reinforcement is considered central, the observational learning approach points out that when a model performs a behavior, the observer becomes able to imitate it. Therefore, personality develops as a function of imitating behaviors of others. All of us have observed aggressive, hostile behavior in others. Although we know how to behave with a hostile attitude, most of us choose other ways of expressing our emotions. Behaviors we learn through observation and imitation are usually reinforced; this, of course, increases the likelihood that they will be repeated. Observational learning can take place without reinforcement, but even the most staunch advocates of this position recognize that reinforcement acts to maintain such behaviors once they are learned.

Observational learning theory differs dramatically from other learning approaches in another important way; it not only allows, but emphasizes, the role of thought processes in learning. Humans are not seen as passive organisms who respond to stimuli with a particular response in all situations. Rather, they are seen as establishing plans and ways of coping with situations based upon their thought processes. People who have observed and experienced a behavior pattern may show the behavior in their day-to-day lives; or, they may choose not to show such a behavior pattern. Observational learning theorists recognize the role of various needs that a person may develop; they suggest that these needs help shape the way a person views some learned behavior. For example, Rotter (1964) has classified a series of needs which are very common among people and are learned; it follows that these needs help shape attitudes about specific situations. Assume a woman has developed a need for recognition and status; if she later observes a technique that lends itself toward gaining status, she might not only observe and learn the technique but might also place great value on it. Other situations where little recognition is attained may also be learned, but then be discounted as ineffective.

Rotter's view is only one among many observational learning theorists;

others have focused on different aspects of cognitive or thought processes in shaping behavior patterns. Bandura (1974, 1977) focused heavily on the ability and need for humans to regulate their own behavior through thought processes rather than externally delivered reinforcements. Similarly Mischel (1973) has argued that people are engaged in two-way interactions with their environment; thus, people influence the world as much as the world (stimuli) influences people. From Mischel's view, a stimulus may produce a number of different responses from a person depending on how the person evaluates the context in which he finds himself (Mischel, 1979). In Mischel's analysis a person's response will be determined by one of several processes or variables: *competencies,* what people know and can do; *encoding strategies,* the way people process, attend to, and select information; *expectancies,* people's anticipation of outcomes; *personal values,* the importance people attach to situations; and *self-regulatory systems,* the system of rules people have set up for themselves to guide behavior.

As observational or social learning theory has developed, it has increasingly suggested the active cognitive role of the human being in shaping behavior. Unlike radical behaviorists like Skinner, these theorists are adding a new dimension to learning theory. They suggest that thought processes must be added to learning theory to fully explain the uniqueness of human interactions. Human personalities are so different from one another because each of us has different thoughts, ideas, and expectancies about the world. These thoughts vary over time, affect our plans, and our evaluations of the world, as well as how we react to it. Social learning theorists argue that by adding cognitive processes to traditional learning theory, unique human abilities and characteristics are better explained.

One of the most important ways that young men and women learn new personality characteristics and behaviors is by observing other people who they feel are important, powerful, or influential.

523

A Child with an Obscene Personality

If you are a parent, school counselor, or teacher, one of the biggest problems you face is how to handle discipline. All parents and teachers are confronted with discipline problems at one time or another. Psychology can't provide all of the answers, but it can provide some. Here is what one group of psychologists did with a rather unique behavior problem. A case history was reported of a 10-year-old child in the Florida Public Schools who had a high rate of obscene talk. Within an hour's period he would often utter as many as 150 obscene words and phrases.

Lahey, McNees, and McNees (1973) took this child out of the classroom for a minimum of 5 minutes every time he uttered an obscene word. During this "time-out" procedure, he was taken out of the classroom and placed within a well-lit, empty room. The child was told he would be placed in a time-out room every time he made an obscene statement. The study showed that within a few days, placing this child within the time-out room reduced the number of obscenities he spouted dramatically. Initially he was uttering about two obscenities per minute; after initiation of the time-out periods, he was uttering fewer than five obscenities per hour.

The time-out procedure is often used in learning situations both in the classroom and the laboratory. As with any kind of reinforcement or punishment procedure, the subject learns that the time-out procedure is contingent upon behavior; if he emits an obscenity, he will be placed in the time-out room. So, to avoid the time-out room, he does not emit the obscenities. Just as reinforcement is used to shape behavior, there are other techniques, such as the time-out procedure, which are also used.

Development of Personality

Behavioral theories do not suggest specific stages of development; rather, they describe learning as a gradual growth process. From an instrumental conditioning point of view, behaviors which are reinforced when a child is young become established as proper behaviors. As a child becomes older, he or she may need to be reinforced fewer times for the same behaviors to continue to occur. Whereas a very young child may need continuous reinforcement, an adult may need to be reinforced only once every few weeks or every few years. Thus, from a conditioning point of view, the main change that occurs with development is the schedule of reinforcement or how often a person needs to be reinforced to maintain the behavior.

Observational learning approaches to personality suggest that the relationship of the model to the imitator is often important. For example, when a child views the behavior of a parent or some other important authority figure, her imitative behavior will be significantly more extensive than if she views the actions of an acquaintance or a stranger. Clearly, as a child grows, her relationships with parents and other models change. In addition, the relationship between the acquisition of a skill and the performance of that skill will change. We have already noted that although many behaviors may be acquired by watching the behaviors of others, we may not exhibit them. Thus, as children grow older, they may choose to exhibit certain behaviors while inhibiting others. Again, table manners are a perfect example; while a child may have learned all of the niceties of proper table manners, she may choose to exhibit them infrequently. One of the primary areas of therapy is to teach people new responses to old ideas. This becomes one of the principal areas of therapy as is seen in the following exchange:

THERAPIST: Tell me Lois, how are you controlling your 2-year-old's tantrums?

Table 11.5 Approaches to personality: conflict, fulfillment, and behavioral

APPROACH	MAJOR PROPONENT	CORE OF PERSONALITY	STRUCTURE OF PERSONALITY	DEVELOPMENT	PERIPHERAL CHARACTERISTICS: BEHAVIOR PATHOLOGY RESULTS
Conflict	Sigmund Freud	Maximizes gratification while minimizing punishment or guilt; instinctual urges direct behavior	Id, ego, superego	5 Stages: oral, anal, phallic, latency, genital	Because of imbalance in id, ego, superego, and due to fixations.
Fulfillment	Carl Rogers	Actualize, maintain and enhance the experiences of life through the process of self-actualization	Self	Process of cumulative self-actualization	Because of wide discrepancy between self and ideal self.
Fulfillment	Alfred Adler	Striving for superiority and perfection	None stated	Process of striving for superiority by overcoming feelings of inferiority	Because of inability to succeed and overwhelming feelings of inferiority.
Behaviorism	B. F. Skinner	Reduction of social and biological needs that energize behavior through the emitting of responses; responses are learned	Response	Process of learning new responses	Because of learning faulty or inappropriate behaviors.

LOIS: At first I was having trouble. Becky would sit down in a supermarket and cry and scream. I tried to calm her down by offering her food, toys, or just about anything. Then I remembered what you said.

THERAPIST: What's that?

LOIS: I tried not to reinforce her tantrums. Becky would throw a tantrum every time she didn't get her way. I was making the situation worse. If she wanted an ice cream and I said no, she would throw a tantrum. I would give her the ice cream. I realize now I was creating her tantrums—I was giving her reinforcement every time she threw one. She learned that the way to get what she wanted was to throw a tantrum.

THERAPIST: So what have you done?

LOIS: I no longer reinforce her tantrums. Every time she throws a tantrum I just let her cry, scream, or yell. It didn't work very well at first. I thought I was going nuts. Becky screamed and cried one time for 45 minutes. Another time she screamed for 20 minutes. However, after about 3 days, this difficult behavior began to cease. By the fifth day she wasn't throwing tantrums at all. Now I reinforce her for behavior that I consider correct and never, under any circumstances, reinforce her for tantrums. You were right, Doctor, I can change my child's behavior through reinforcement.

Peripheral Characteristics

Most theories of personality have elaborate schemes for describing behavior; learning theory is not faced with such abstractions. Behavior for learning theorists is easy to describe and explain: it is a response pattern, like any response pattern, learned through the same basic learning principles. Normal behavior is behavior that is reinforced by society and is adaptive. Abnormal behavior and personality disorders are behaviors that diverge from the norm, are not adaptive, and are generally not reinforced by society. Of course, abnormal behavior may develop; if a person sees that his hostile, aggressive behavior is reinforced he may be hostile and aggressive. A person who finds that washing his hands 20 or 30 times a day helps relieve his anxiety about dirt will continue to wash his hands frequently.

Behavior that is learned through imitation can also be abnormal. Children can observe violent, aggressive, hostile people and imitate this behavior rather than more socially desirable behaviors. Observational learning can thus account for many abnormal behaviors. If we combine the imitation aspects of observational learning theory with the reinforcement properties of conditioned learning, we can easily account for most behaviors.

GLOBAL THEORIES VS. MICROTHEORIES

This chapter presents several of the important theories of personality; there is no question that Freud's theory, Rogers's formulations, and the others presented are very important landmarks in understanding normal behavior development. They form the foundation for many treatment programs for the maladjusted. Unfortunately, many of these theories have gone untested. This has come about, in part, because some of the concepts used are vague and difficult to test. For example, the ego is a concept and not some physiological state that can easily be manipulated by depriving it of food. In the same way, the concepts of self and maximizing one's potential are difficult to measure, define, and manipulate. Thus, over the years many of the classic global theories that have attempted to explain large portions of behavior have been criticized because they are less subject to critical scrutiny than other theories.

The laboratory is never too far from most psychologists, and they have sought to define behavior patterns in systematic ways. Unfortunately, the data that have emerged have been narrow in focus and explain only certain aspects of psychological functioning. A global theory like Freud's is all encompassing; these smaller well-researched theories account for specific behaviors in specific situations. For example, the frustration-aggression hypothesis put forth many years ago suggests that frustration produces aggression; as a smaller theory, or microtheory, this idea has been widely tested, significantly modified, and rejected in its earlier simple form. Today we know much more about the causes of aggressive behavior than we ever did and recognize its multiple causes (see for example, Edmunds & Kendrick, 1980).

A Microtheory: Locus of Control

A microtheory that has been widely studied in the last 15 years has been one examining the extent to which individuals believe that they have control over their environment. People often attribute the cause of their own behavior to some internal characteristics of the individual. Julian Rotter (1966) developed an idea of internal vs. external locus of control, and he conceptualized this on a rating scale. Rotter's scale contains statements about oneself and people in general. Consider how you might respond to items listed below and where you would place the locus of control.

1. People's misfortunes result from the mistakes they make. vs.
   Many of the unhappy things in people's lives are partly due to bad luck.
2. With enough effort we can wipe out political corruption. vs.
   It is difficult for people to have much control over the things politicians do in office.
3. There is a direct connection between how hard I study and the grades I get. vs.
   Sometimes I can't understand how teachers arrive at the grades they give.
4. What happens to me is my own doing. vs.
   Sometimes I feel that I don't have enough control over the direction my life is taking.

Perlmuter and Monty (1977) have written on the notion of locus of control and have argued that it has many direct applications which might, of course, include attribution theory, social psychology, and particularly psychotherapy. In therapy individuals often place the blame for their problems on others. A study of an individual's ideas about locus of control can be an effective therapy aid.

Research on locus of control has been extensive; it has been examined in relation to various types of therapy, need for achievement, and frustration. The aim of some of these studies has been to quantify behavior patterns. The internal vs. external dimension has been useful. For example, people classified as internal are more likely to react negatively if their freedom to choose is restricted (Moyer, 1978); they are also more likely to illegitimately report success on an impossible task if it has been rated as being a skilled and difficult one (Karabenick & Srull, 1978). Internal individuals feeling that they have control over their environment, are more likely to engage in preventive health measures. Internal individuals are better than external persons at losing weight (Balch & Ross, 1975), and college students characterized as internal are more likely to profit from psychotherapy (Kilmann, Albert & Sotile, 1975). Because people develop expectancies based on their beliefs about the sources of reinforcement in their environments, it follows that specific behaviors associated with those beliefs are likely to follow. As shown in Figure 11.2, p. 528, specific expectancies lead to specific behaviors; if reinforced, this strengthens the expectancy and leads to a further belief in internal or external controls (see for example, Perlmuter, Scharff, Karsh, & Monty, 1980).

Internality vs. externality is conceived of as a single dimension, yet other researchers have shown that locus of control is more complicated; some researchers have even found that there are as many as four or five factors that underlie it (Garza & Widlak, 1977; Zuckerman & Gerbasi, 1977). The internality-externality dimension has been used in conceptions of intrinsically motivated behavior (Deci, 1975). From Deci's view, for intrinsically motivated behavior to occur people must believe that reinforcements (intrinsic or

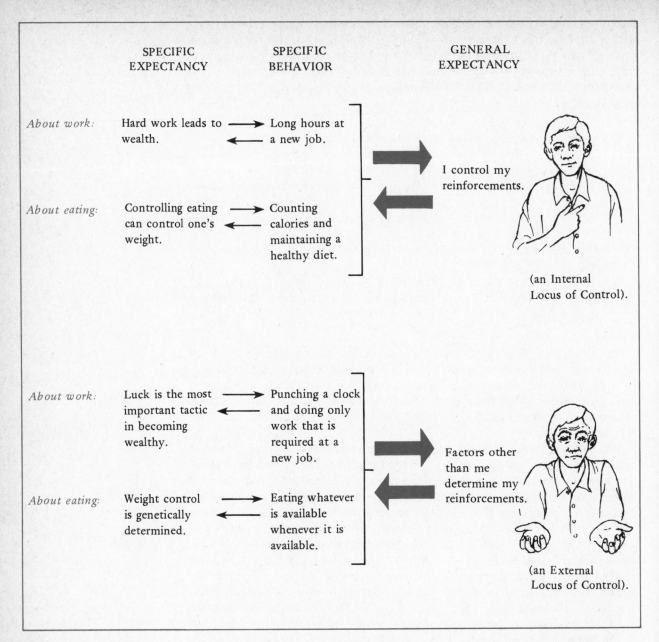

	SPECIFIC EXPECTANCY	SPECIFIC BEHAVIOR	GENERAL EXPECTANCY

About work: Hard work leads to wealth. ⟶ ⟵ Long hours at a new job.

About eating: Controlling eating can control one's weight. ⟶ ⟵ Counting calories and maintaining a healthy diet.

I control my reinforcements.

(an Internal Locus of Control).

About work: Luck is the most important tactic in becoming wealthy. ⟶ ⟵ Punching a clock and doing only work that is required at a new job.

About eating: Weight control is genetically determined. ⟶ ⟵ Eating whatever is available whenever it is available.

Factors other than me determine my reinforcements.

(an External Locus of Control).

Figure 11.2 General expectancies about life are determined in a three-stage process. Specific expectancies lead to behaviors; they are in turn reinforced. This eventually leads to a general expectancy about life and it is either internal or external in locus of control

extrinsic) are determined by their behavior—they must feel that they have control over the environment (see p. 166 for a discussion of intrinsic motivation). Deci argues, therefore, that a person who receives negative feedback and failure information will move away from a locus of control that is internal to one of externality. As we saw in studying attribution theory (p. 449), a person's locus of control, internal or external, will play an important role in helping to decide the causes of various behaviors.

Locus of control is a concept that is continuing to undergo development and refinement. Introduced in 1966, further developed in 1971, and elaborated upon in the late 1970s, we now recognize that the simple dimension of internal vs. external locus of control needs expansion; yet, it has generated many experiments and has helped explain phenomena like intrinsic motivation and causal attribution. Like many other psychological theories, locus of control will continue to undergo development and evolve so as to explain well a limited range of behaviors. Locus of control cannot be conceived of as a global theory; it describes a number of specific behaviors but is not comprehensive enough by itself to explain all or even most of an individual's behavior.

SUMMARY

Three different approaches that I have presented have shown distinctly different ways of thinking about personality. The conflict approach of Freud is dramatically different from the fulfillment approaches of Rogers and Adler;

Most personality theories recognize the critical role of early environmental influences on children's behavior.

the theories emphasize different core tendencies. Most theories of personality have some abstract components, such as the id, although the behavioral approach stresses only stimuli and responses.

As students of psychology, you can evaluate the approach that you feel has the most merit. Some psychologists feel that a Freudian approach to personality is the most reasonable one; others are more comfortable with Rogers's fulfillment model. Most modern American psychologists are eclectic. Rather than choose one specific personality approach, they consider personality development from many approaches. This means that for each patient that they see in therapy, the type of approach that they use to help the patient will depend upon the patient's problem. If a person is having a problem with self-image, the therapist may use a fulfillment approach. If the client has feelings of guilt about sexuality, a more Freudian approach may seem appropriate.

Regardless of the specific approach used, it seems clear that a combination of all of the different theories is very often advantageous. Because most personality theories cannot stand on their own, most therapists and students of personality use the best of each of these approaches. The number of strict Freudian therapists is declining. This is probably because a strict interpretation of Freud usually narrows the view of the interpreter. Likewise, the behaviorism of the present decade is certainly not the behaviorism that early behaviorists envisioned; today's behaviorism reflects scientific growth and sophistication. Personality theorists and therapists also can no longer adhere to a strict dogma of one theory, but must recognize the strengths and weaknesses of their theory as well as the strengths and weaknesses of other theories.

CHAPTER REVIEW

1. Personality is a set of relatively enduring behavioral characteristics that describe how a person reacts to the environment.
2. The conflict approach assumes that there are forces within a person which are constantly clashing; life is a compromise at best.
3. The fulfillment approach argues that one force within each person strives toward fulfillment and understanding of the person's self and environment; life is a constant struggle for perfection.
4. Behavioral views of personality assert that personality is determined by the laws of learning, including classical conditioning, instrumental conditioning, and observational learning.
5. Core tendencies are the basic driving forces within an individual that determine a human being's overall direction of living.
6. Core tendencies are shown by typical goals or ideas that help compose them. Peripheral characteristics are the specific details of personality—they are the day-to-day facts that describe individuals.
7. The conflict approach as discussed by Freud suggests that a person's basic tendency is to maximize instinctual gratification while minimizing punishment and guilt.
8. Freud's structure of personality includes the id, ego, and superego.
9. The id, working on the pleasure principle, is the source of human instinctual energy. The ego tries to satisfy the id in accordance with reality and works on the reality principle. The superego acts as the moral branch of mental functioning.
10. The source of life instincts for Freud is the libido, which works on the pleasure principle and seeks immediate gratification.

11. Defense mechanisms are ways people reduce anxiety by distorting reality. Examples of defense mechanisms are projection, denial, reaction formation, and rationalization.
12. Freud's most important defense mechanism is repression.
13. Freud divided the development of personality into a series of stages: oral, anal, phallic, latency, and genital. Fixation at any single stage is a major source of conflict and anxiety.
14. The fulfillment approach of Carl Rogers argues that there is an inborn tendency in people which directs them toward becoming whatever their inherited nature is; personality development is the fulfillment of one's inherited abilities.
15. The structure of personality for Rogers is the self. An ideal self is what a person would like to be.
16. Rogers's core tendency is to actualize, maintain, and enhance the experiencing organism; he does this through the process of self-actualization.
17. Rogers does not suggest stages of development, but rather, argues that through development, a person learns to self-actualize effectively and achieve greater understanding of self.
18. Rogers argues that people become unhappy because they are unable to fit new behaviors into their self-concepts; persons with rigid self-concepts will invoke defense mechanisms to guard against potential threatening feelings and experiences.
19. For Adler, a person's core tendency is to strive for superiority or perfection; a person is often driven towards superiority because of feelings of inferiority.
20. According to Adler, individuals, through the process of development, develop a style of life that allows them to reflect their own uniqueness. Adler assumed that people are inherently social in nature and seek close, warm social relations with others.
21. The structural unit of personality for behaviorists is the response; all behaviors are seen as responses to stimuli or as responses waiting for reinforcement.
22. The core tendency for behaviorists is to reduce or satisfy the social or biological needs that energize behavior.
23. Both classical and instrumental conditioning and the central notion of reinforcement have been used to account for a variety of behaviors.
24. Behavioral theories argue that the development of personality is a gradual growth process in which certain behaviors are reinforced and others are not. Disturbed behavior comes about because of faulty learning patterns.
25. In observational learning it is assumed that people can learn new behaviors by watching others perform those behaviors.
26. Two major differences between observational learning and classical ideas about learning are: first, learning may be independent of reinforcement; and second, observational learning not only allows, but emphasizes, the role of thought processes.

SUGGESTIONS FOR ADDITIONAL READING

EWEN, R. B. *An introduction to theories of personality*. New York: Academic Press, 1980.

FREUD, S. *The problem of anxiety*. New York: W. W. Norton Company, 1936.

FROMM, E. *The art of loving*. New York: Harper & Row, 1956.

HALL, C. S., AND LINDZEY, G. *Theories of personality* (3rd ed.). New York: John Wiley and Sons, 1978.

MADDI, S. R. *Personality theories: A comparative analysis* (3rd ed.) Homewood, IL: Dorsey Press, 1976.

SKINNER, B. F. *Beyond freedom and dignity*. New York: Knopf, 1971.

EVERYONE HAS to learn how to cope with life's problems. We all face challenges from day to day; sometimes these challenges are minor, but at other times they are serious and deserve considerable thought. The task of coping with the demands of life can overwhelm some people, and as a result, they begin to exhibit abnormal behavior. These individuals become maladjusted and do not respond to life's demands the way people normally do. Malajustment means faulty adjustment—it refers to people who have trouble coping. One of the central elements in measuring abnormal behavior is examining the extent to which people are aware of their behavior. Even more important is the extent to which they are incapable of distinguishing between what is real and what is fantasy. Some are so gripped by anxiety or so lost in fantasy that they no longer are able to cope with even the simple demands of life. This inability to deal with reality and cope with the environment marks the dividing line between maladjustment and psychosis.

CHAPTER 12

Abnormal Psychology

There were 117 psychoanalysts on the Pan Am flight to Vienna and I'd been treated by at least six of them. And married a seventh. God knows it was a tribute either to the shrinks' ineptitude or my own glorious unanalyzability that I was now, if anything, more scared of flying than when I began my analytic adventures some thirteen years earlier.

My husband grabbed my hand therapeutically at the moment of take-off.

"Christ—it's like ice," he said. He ought to know the symptoms by now since he's held my hand on lots of other flights. My fingers (and toes) turn to ice, my stomach leaps upward into my rib cage, the temperature in the tip of my nose drops to the same level as the temperature in my fingers, . . . and for one screaming minute my heart and the engines correspond as we attempt to prove again that the laws of aerodynamics are not the flimsy superstitions which, in my heart of hearts, I *know* they are. Never mind the diabolical INFORMATION TO PASSENGERS, I happen to be convinced that only my own concentration (and that of my mother—who always seems to *expect* her children to die in a plane crash) keeps this bird aloft. I congratulate myself on every successful takeoff, but not too enthusiastically because it's also part of my personal religion that the minute you grow overconfident and really *relax* about the flight, the plane crashes instantly. Constant vigilance, that's my motto. A mood of cautious optimism should prevail. But actually my mood is better described as cautious pessimism. OK, I tell myself, *we seem* to be off the ground and into the clouds but the danger isn't past. This is, in fact, the most perilous patch of air. Right here over Jamaica Bay where the plane banks and turns and the "No Smoking" sign goes off. This may well be where we go screaming down in thousands of flaming pieces. So I keep concentrating very hard, helping the pilot (a reassuringly midwestern voice named Donnelly) fly. . . . Thank God for his crew cut and middle-American diction. New Yorker that I am, I would never trust a pilot with a New York accent.

ERICA JONG
Fear of Flying

A fear of flying is only one of Isadora Wing's phobias. Erica Jong's heroine in *Fear of Flying* is afraid of life and spends most of her time hiding from it. Like most of us, Isadora Wing has some normal fears. However, she also has fears that are intense, irrational, and that include avoidance. Psychologists classify as abnormal those people who choose to avoid life rather than try to cope with it. Most people have some fear of flying—particularly the takeoffs—but only a few allow their fears to prevent them from flying. In a more general sense, most people have some anxiety about what the future holds for them, but only a few try to live totally in the past. Practical experience and research tell us that coping with life and dealing with reality are the cornerstones of normal behavior. This chapter examines abnormal behavior: behavior characterized by fear, maladjustment, the failure to cope, and the inability to deal with reality.

Let us consider the case of Evan, who is thinking of dropping out of school. It has been a difficult semester for him. He had an emergency appendectomy that took him out of classes for 2 weeks. Four days after returning to school he learned that his grandfather died. And, to top the whole thing off, lurking constantly in the background is the spectre of calculus, which has haunted him throughout the semester. Evan has become anxious; he is afraid of what might happen to his health. He feels that the best thing to do is to drop out of school for the remainder of the semester.

From time to time each of us is faced with decisions that have serious consequences. If you were placed in Evan's situation, would you drop out or would you try to cope with the demands of the semester by staying in school? Some of us would try to cope and do the best we could; we would argue that it would be difficult but worth the extra effort. Others might argue that the strain is not worth the credits; they would say that they would ultimately learn more and be healthier physically and emotionally if they were to drop out for the semester and go to summer school. Both of these alternatives, dropping out and staying in, are reasonable. There is a logical reason for both. Neither choice would classify the student as abnormal.

A student might be under a considerable amount of strain during the period of making such a decision. There might be considerable pressure applied by pending examinations. In addition, parents may be applying pressure and close friends may be trying to help by counseling. When the pressures become too great, people's behavior is often affected. Sometimes they may do and say strange things. In such situations, should you consider this behavior abnormal? Or should you consider that this response to these difficult circumstances is quite normal? What is the range of normal and abnormal behavior?

WHAT IS ABNORMAL BEHAVIOR?

As already noted, people make decisions every day of their lives. Sometimes these decisions are trivial, but at other times they have serious consequences. Perhaps you might decide to be friendly toward some people or indifferent toward others. Past experiences, present feelings, and others' actions might have contributed to how you feel now. How do others perceive your behavior? Can they understand your friendliness or your indifference? Do they see your behavior as reasonable?

Psychologists have tried to determine what is normal behavior and what is abnormal behavior. As in other areas of psychology, the field of abnormal psychology acknowledges many differing views. Some psychologists consider abnormal behavior to be that which is different from what most people do; others see abnormal behavior as the expression of inner hostility. Before we can describe abnormal behavior, we must come to a common understanding of what behavior is abnormal. We shall describe four different orientations, or models; each suggests a fundamental reason for an individual's manifesting abnormal behavior. A **model** is an analogy that helps scientists find order and relationships among data; a model uses a structure from one field to help describe data in another (in this case, abnormal psychology). These models of behavior comprise four categories: statistical, medical, behavioral, and legal.

Model A perspective or approach derived from one field and set of data to help describe data from another field.

The Statistical Model

When we watch movies from the 1930s and 1940s, we often comment on how different the people look—their clothes were so baggy, long, and dowdy. Of course, we all realize that the reason why the clothes look so funny is that the fashions have changed. In the 1940s, the clothes that the stars wore were not only appropriate but were the trend-setting fashions of the time. Many other

Table 12.1 Table of abnormal behaviors

VIEW OF BEHAVIOR	APPROACH	
Behavior that differs from most people's is considered abnormal.	Statistical	
Abnormal behavior is "disease-like" and can be diagnosed and treated.	Medical	
Abnormal behavior is a set of faulty behaviors learned through traditional learning techniques or reinforcement and extinction.	Behavioral	
A criminal is not responsible for abnormal behavior if it is the product of some mental abnormality or defect.	Legal	

things—political and religious beliefs, hair length, dance styles—also change with time.

A statistical approach to behavior suggests that normal behavior is behavior that does not deviate too much from the average. A man who is extremely tall is often said to be abnormally tall. His height is considered abnormal because he is significantly different from average people. Similarly, a woman whose behavior differs significantly from the average person's is said to en-

The statistical model suggests that behavior is abnormal if it is different from the way most people go about doing things

gage in abnormal behavior. For example, a woman who spends all of her time alone is considered to be abnormal when she is compared to other people who are socially inclined. The statistical approach to behavior suggests that all behavior is on a continuum. This means that although most people function in the middle of the behavioral spectrum, there are a few people at both ends of the scale.

The **statistical model** is straightforward: behavior is abnormal if it is different from the way average people go about doing things. The statistical model makes no assumptions about the causes of a behavior or its origins; rather, its focus is solely on how a single individual compares to how most other people act in similar situations. In some cases, the statistical model is used because evaluations about individuals need to be made. For example, children who exhibit symptoms of hyperactivity are only considered true cases if they are well above the mean in terms of activity as rated by their teachers. In such a case, psychologists infer that the individual is exhibiting a behavior pattern which a large portion of the population does not exhibit; using this criterion, such a behavior pattern is sometimes called a maladjustment.

A focus of the statistical approach is to compare a specific behavior with current values and standards. People are maladjusted if they differ significantly from their contemporaries. The statistical model has proved to be useful, but it has a particular weakness because values change over time. Behaviors judged abnormal today may be judged quite differently a decade from now. The statistical model is influenced easily by social and political changes. As a new social movement occurs, new definitions of maladjustment come about; these then become the standards for the statistical model. The creative genius of Picasso was considered abnormal when he first manifested it through his paintings. The statistical approach toward abnormal behavior is thus relative; it cannot specify the details of any behavior that will be considered abnormal over a period of time. This approach always considers behavior relative to current norms and standards. Furthermore, some of society's most highly admired abilities (like Picasso's) are not distributed normally, and everyone has certain features or abilities that are unique or unusual. This is a sociological or "social norm" method based on averages, and it can only establish the extent or frequency of behavior that deviates from the norm. It offers no route to improving disorders.

Statistical model An approach toward behavior in which behavior that deviates from the average range of behavior is considered to be abnormal.

It is Halloween. Is this behavior abnormal?

Medical model An approach
to abnormal behavior in
which behavior is seen as a
result of, or as caused by, an
internal condition or motivation.

The Medical Model

In contrast with the statistical model, many psychologists have adopted the **medical model;** this approach suggests that abnormal behaviors are caused by some type of internal problem. Initially, the medical model focused on biological and physiological conditions that initiated abnormal behaviors. Over time, however, the strict medical approach gave way to a medical model analogy that served as the foundation for traditional psychology and psychiatry. Psychologists and psychiatrists treat psychologically troubled individuals as though they were sick; hence the term "mental illness." Many of the terms and concepts of psychology and psychiatry are borrowed from medicine: treatment, case, symptom, syndrome. The medical model of abnormal behavior suggests that there is some kind of internal motivation or cause for abnormal behavior and that the cause can be treated. Proponents of the medical model assume that the reason for abnormal behavior is this underlying motivation that causes certain behavioral symptoms. This is often a matter of very subjective "professional judgment," and the medical profession is not that well equipped to judge the causes of many behavior disorders.

There are several advantages to the medical model. The primary advantage is that it assumes that abnormal behavior can be treated and cured. People should not be locked up in a cage or considered bizarre because their behavior is different from that of other people. In the early part of this century, the use of the medical model led to humane treatment of patients with mental health problems by replacing the cage with the hospital. In some ways, this has been a disadvantage because the medical model categorizes and treats people in very specific ways. In doing so, it has placed the therapist in the role of a person who "cures." Furthermore, it has brought about an emphasis on hospitalization and drug treatment, while promoting the concept that abnormal behavior is a symptom of a larger underlying problem. The medical model has also created a tendency on the part of the public to believe superstitiously that associating with people who have behavior problems could bring about behavior problems in others. By this process of analogy, many people may become fearful of those who have mental health problems. This fear of behavior abnormalities has often hampered effective treatment programs.

Behavioral Models

Behaviorists object strongly to the medical model with its focus on underlying causes and, instead, suggest that abnormal behavior is the result of faulty learning. Rather than emphasize underlying thoughts and processes, behaviorists focus on how people have learned different behaviors. Behaviorists support the environmental side of the nature vs. nurture controversy. When a woman has learned to avoid certain people because they produce feelings of anxiety in her, she may generalize to such a degree that she may be afraid of all people. In the same way, a boy may learn that the world is an unhappy place if reinforcements are few and far between; he may become pessimistic, introverted, and anxious. The behaviorists represent an important force in the field of abnormal psychology. They feel that abnormal behaviors—however they are defined—are caused by patterns of conditioning and learning. They

According to the behavioral approach, behaviors are caused by patterns of conditioning and learning

believe that just as the abnormal behavior was learned, so in some way an alternative, and more successful, pattern of behavior can also be learned. Thus, behaviorally oriented psychologists try to help people modify their maladjustments by using specific learning techniques. Behaviorists select a behavior to change not because others label it as "abnormal," but because the behavior causes distress for a person. They try to eliminate maladjustment and teach people to learn new and adaptive life-styles. Behaviorists recognize how a particular disorder came about, but they are far more interested in the process of changing it.

Legal Definitions

There is a wide range of abnormal behaviors that vary from acts that are only mildly maladaptive to those in which serious harm is done to other people. Attorneys often argue that a person's behavior is abnormal when he or she is unable to evaluate right and wrong. The legal approach essentially comes down to a series of political judgments: what people or basic political values are harmed by certain kinds of behavior? Who is entitled to coerce others in society? Who shall be held responsible and punished for the force or harm done to others by certain behaviors? A focus of the legal model of abnormality is maintaining social norms. As long as individuals comply with society's demands for "normality," the individual is seen as well adjusted.

Legally, there are three ways that persons can be judged insane. (1) If people are judged mentally incompetent of understanding responsibilities, they may be judged insane. (2) Similarly, if people are judged capable of harming either themselves or others, they may be committed to an institution for medical and psychological care instead of being placed in a prison. (3) Most important, people are not considered responsible for their crimes if the crime is a consequence of their mental abnormality. Those who are judged to be abnormal and thought to have been compelled to act in abnormal ways are not held responsible for their acts. If, however, their behavior is not a direct consequence of their behavioral problems, then they are held responsible. Most psychologists try to avoid the legal definition of abnormal behavior because it is such a narrow one. Like the complications in the medical model, problems arise for psychologists as soon as they try to categorize people into discrete groups; many misdiagnoses are made. At present, our diagnostic abilities to determine competence are still imperfect.

Abnormal Behavior?

Does abnormal behavior actually exist? The answer to this question depends on your approach. Most psychologists are fairly eclectic; they work with a mix of definitions and have no "absolutes." Practitioners are, however, guided by the four basic models discussed.

Beyond these varied approaches, there are some commonsense standards in every society. People whose behavior can be classified as abnormal have sometimes lost touch with reality. Those who do not know what is right or wrong clearly exhibit abnormal behavior. Few would doubt that a self-confessed rapist exhibits abnormal behavior; rapists themselves often acknowledge the abnormality of their actions. Regardless of their approach, psychologists are faced with classifying people's behavior into systematic categories. The categories are useful in helping people describe abnormal behavior and in aiding the psychologist to show differences in types of behavior.

"Abnormal" often depends on how each society defines "normal" ways of coping; for example, in the Soviet Union, people are placed in mental institutions for a variety of reasons that often include political dissent (Wing, 1978). Within Western societies, the four approaches that were just discussed have been considered reasonable ones, and many practitioners work with a mix of the four. Still, as we have seen, none of these is able to maintain a hard and fast definition of abnormal behavior that will satisfy all theoreticians or practitioners.

In recent years, many psychologists have preferred to speak about *maladjustment* rather than *abnormality*. The shift is important because it suggests that the problem behaviors are ones which can be treated and that while a person's behavior may be maladaptive today, the person can be treated so that future behavior can be adaptive and worthwhile.

In assessing abnormality, projective tests like the Rorschach help

Daily Handwashing:

Is this abnormal behavior?

HOW DO WE DIAGNOSE ABNORMAL BEHAVIOR? *DSM-III*

Over the years psychologists and psychiatrists have shared great difficulty in diagnosing and describing abnormality. Many psychiatrists have adopted a medical model toward the study of abnormal behavior. Being physicians, many consider abnormal behavior to be diseaselike in nature. It follows then that they would classify behaviors in a systematic and diseaselike fashion. Over the years, various systems have been developed to help classify and label different kinds of maladjustment. The most recent one has undergone a great deal of study and development. Called *DSM-III*, the third *Diagnostic and Statistical Manual of Mental Disorders* is a 494-page manual that is issued by psychiatrists with the help of many mental-health practitioners including psychologists and social workers.

The classification of abnormality is an evolving scheme. Classifications have always been available, but they have undergone significant changes over the years as psychologists have developed new knowledge and sophistication. It has been shown that before *DSM-III*, diagnostic categories were very loose and lacking in precision. Before *DSM-III*, if you were to ask 100 psychiatrists to diagnose a patient's problems, you would get a marked degree of variability; psychiatrists could not come to the same conclusion regarding the condition of a particular person. For example, in a 1962 study, Beck and his colleagues found that agreement on specific diagnoses among psychiatrists was only 54%. When the psychiatrists were allowed to give a preferred diagnosis as well as an alternative, the rate of agreement increased only to 82%.

Part of the reason that psychiatrists may not have been able to agree about diagnoses was that the symptoms that patients were revealing did not correspond very consistently with psychiatric classifications. Zigler and Phillips (1961) showed a relationship between symptoms and diagnoses; however, this relationship was so small that membership in a particular diagnostic group generally showed only a minimal amount of information about how

Table 12.2 Major classifications within *DSM-III*, each of which is further broken down into subtypes (with some minor modifications)

MAJOR DISORDERS LISTED IN *DSM-III*	
Disorders of Infancy, Childhood, and Adolescence	Personality Disorders
Organic Mental Disorders	Anxiety Disorders
Substance Use Disorders	Somatoform Disorders
Schizophrenic Disorders	Dissociative Disorders
Paranoid Disorders	Psychosexual Disorders
Psychotic Disorders	Factitious Disorders
Affective Disorders	Disorders of Impulse Control
	Adjustment Disorders

the patients behaved. This meant that symptoms did not necessarily reflect diagnostic categories. With the loose and poorly defined categories of abnormality, it was no wonder that psychiatrists had an agreement rate of only 54%.

Because of the remarkable lack of precision that previous diagnostic categories provided, *DSM-III* was prepared. A major breakthrough in helping provide precision in diagnostic categories, *DSM-III* takes a different approach to abnormal behavior than most psychologists and psychiatrists are used to. It has thus met with some resistance, some controversy, and, at a minimum, much interest. For example, psychologists have found the increased recognition of social and environmental influences on behavior to be favorable. On the negative side, however, many psychologists are unhappy with the continued use of many psychiatric terms that may perpetuate the use of a medical rather than behavioral model. With 19 major categories of maladjustment and over 200 subtypes, *DSM-III* has made great strides toward providing explicit criteria. Table 12.2 shows the major classifications; within each of these categories are many subtypes.

In the past, psychologists and psychiatrists have had great difficulty classifying and agreeing as to the diagnostic categories that adequately describe behavior. Because *DSM-III* was introduced just a short time ago, it is unclear as to whether it will bring precision and clarity to the field. Some have argued that it is too precise, others that it is too complicated, and still others have disagreed with the grouping of behavior patterns. There are some fairly dramatic changes in the classification system compared to what many therapists are used to using. It is very likely that the detail, time, and effort that went into this system of classification will help the study of abnormal behavior. It is also likely that better and more precise diagnoses will focus research and clinical opinions so that patients with the same problems will be compared and analyzed against other patients with the same problems, not different ones. Of course, it does not change the fact that many disturbed patients are seeking help and having a new label attached to them does not help relieve their suffering or extend therapy to the disadvantaged and poor.

METHODS. To classify, diagnose, and treat patients, one must observe their behavior in some way. One obvious way is to use naturalistic observations. People confined within a mental institution or in some other controlled setting may be observed objectively by professional personnel. More often, however, abnormal behavior is assessed through clinical interviews in which an individual comes to a professional for help. A patient will describe to a therapist the nature of the behavior and discuss past history and current symptoms.

The therapist has a variety of different ways to gain information. The client can be interviewed and asked to complete questionnaires, personality inventories, and clinical tests. We examined two of the more popular projective tests in chapter 11 (p. 510). One of these is the Rorschach, or Ink Blot, Test. Similarly, the Thematic Apperception Test is one in which people are asked to create stories about pictures they have been shown. By interpreting the contents of these stories, psychologists are able to understand better the types of behavior that a client may exhibit. A number of tests have also been devised to diagnose organic problems of the brain. Many people have experienced either traumatic injury to the head or birth abnormalities that have rendered them incapable of making certain decisions or experiencing certain types of behavior. Children who are diagnosed as learning disabled, for example, can be tested by a neurologist to assess whether this problem has a neurological basis. Thus, clinical psychologists often use tests of organic brain dysfunctions as well as neurological tests to assess the extent to which any behavioral abnormality may be a function of biological inadequacies or trauma to the brain.

ANXIETY DISORDERS

Almost everyone experiences anxiety. While some people only feel anxious before an unusual situation such as an examination, others find anxiety to be something they have to live with from minute to minute. The anxiety that one experiences before an examination is not quite the same as that of a person who is gripped with anxiety all of the time; in other words, anxiety is not a specific symptom. In speaking of **anxiety,** we must consider a range of symptoms. The most significant of these are fear, apprehension, inattention, palpitations, respiratory distress, dizziness, faintness, sweating, irritability, chest pains, feelings of impending disaster, and, at times, fear of death (Marks & Lader, 1973). Of course, there are large individual differences from person to person and from occasion to occasion.

Anxiety can be examined in many ways. People can tell you when and how they feel when they are anxious. Psychologists can watch an anxious person's behavior and see how it differs from that of a nonanxious person's; they can also take physiological measures of a person who is anxious. Being anxious is not like having a broken leg; anxiety cannot be quickly diagnosed and easily treated. Anxious people may or may not show their anxiety, and it may or may not affect their day-to-day behavior. Like most abnormal behavior, anxiety can be relatively mild or fairly debilitating; severe anxiety must be dealt with or else it may eventually lead to hospitalization.

Anxiety is at the core of many theories of abnormal behavior, notably Freud's. According to Freud, anxiety is the central problem with which people have to cope. In Freud's biologically based conflict approach (as discussed in chapter 11), he suggested that people are always in a state of con-

Anxiety A generalized feeling of fear and apprehension that may or may not be connected to a particular event or object and that is often accompanied by increased physiological arousal. Generally, these fears and apprehensions are unrealistic. Symptoms include fear, apprehension, inattention, palpitations, dizziness, sweating, and chest pains.

Table 12.3 The 10 most common symptoms of patients with an Anxiety Disorder are shown in the table. The numbers indicate the percentage who showed symptoms as compared with a group of control subjects.

| SYMPTOMS OF ANXIETY DISORDERS | | |
SYMPTOM	PATIENTS	CONTROLS
Palpitations	97	9
Tires easily	95	19
Breathlessness	90	13
Nervousness	88	27
Chest pain	85	10
Sighing	79	16
Dizziness	78	16
Faintness	70	12
Apprehension	61	3
Headache	58	26

Source: Marks and Lader, 1973, p. 13.

flict, and this conflict brings about anxiety. In Freud's view, anxiety is the result of the id trying to express some form of deep-seated sexuality or hostility while the superego is trying to control it. Anxiety manifests itself, for example, when a boy feels hostility toward his father in the midst of his Oedipus complex.

Behaviorists, as well as Freudians, have used the term anxiety. Many behaviorists see anxiety as a group of internal responses that are learned through traditional learning methods. When a boy sees his father's hand being raised to give him a spanking, he knows that pain will follow and he is fearful. By successive learning experiences with the hand-raising, pain-following sequence, he eventually comes to fear the hand raising as such. A troubled child will show fear, anxiety, and avoidance behaviors whenever he sees his father raise his hand, even if his father has no intention of striking him. This is a common sign of a psychological disorder that the behaviorists claim as proof of their theory that anxiety is learned behavior.

It is important to remember that anxiety can be short-lived or chronic; a person may have a brief period of anxiety or the anxiety may be long-lasting. Anxiety is generally considered one of the central symptoms of maladjustment.

About 2 to 4% of the population has at some time had a disorder that *DSM-III* would characterize as an Anxiety Disorder. One study found that as many as one-third of all adults have suffered from anxiety at one time or another (Lader, 1975). Of course, anxiety is often present in many disorders. Persons with Substance Use Disorders and Psychosexual Disorders also experience anxiety. However, merely experiencing anxiety does not allow for the classification of Anxiety Disorder. It is important to recognize that, while people may experience various degrees of anxiety, the different models of abnormality that were presented earlier do not all agree on the extent to which anxiety should be considered "normal." The extent of people's anxiety varies on a continuum from little anxiety to paralyzing, debilitating anxiety.

The pain and maladjustment of people who experience crushing anxiety allows them to be categorized as exhibiting a type of Anxiety Disorder. So, while many people may experience anxiety, its extent—and particularly how it affects day-to-day behavior—becomes a key issue in determining maladjustment.

NEUROTIC DISORDERS.   In today's fast-paced and hectic society, people experience many pressures that cause them to have feelings of anxiety, panic, and even depression. Articles in the popular press and many self-help books have been written to help people cope with some of these pressures and the processes and causes that underlie them. People who experience symptoms like those associated with anxiety are often suffering from what Freud called neurotic disorders. Freud characterized as a neurosis a large group of disorders that really fall within several diagnostic categories of *DSM-III*. Freud assumed that anxiety underlies all neurotic disorders, but today only those disorders in which anxiety is a prominent feature are called Anxiety Disorders. People have **neurotic disorders** when they experience a group of symptoms that are distressing and are unacceptable. People who exhibit neurotic disorders do not violate social norms and they are in touch with reality; their disorder is not physical in origin, and it is relatively long-lasting.

Neurotic disorder A disorder characterized by a group of symptoms that are distressing and unacceptable to an individual. Individuals with the disorder do not violate social norms and they are in touch with reality.

Because people with neurotic disorders can be markedly different in their problems and their symptoms, *DSM-III* classifies them in five different diagnostic categories. You will see that the neurotic disorders described have few common and directly comparable features. Each clearly represents a different pattern of behavior and maladjustment. While Freud may have categorized them all together under the grab bag of neurosis, today we classify them more precisely because of our diagnostic categories, diagnostic criteria, and our understanding of the causes of these disorders. It is important to note that in each of the three Anxiety Disorders to be discussed next (all neurotic disorders), anxiety is a chief and central problem to the patient.

Generalized Anxiety Disorders

A person who exhibits the symptoms of a **Generalized Anxiety Disorder** shows persistent anxiety of at least one month's duration. Chronic anxiety does not necessarily correspond to any specific incident; rather, this anxiety is often said to be "free-floating." **Free-floating anxiety** has no obvious source; it is simply felt. Sometimes the source is obvious enough, but the person with a Generalized Anxiety Disorder is simply avoiding the problem of finding or facing it. In extreme cases some symptoms of a Generalized Anxiety Disorder come about because of specific types of stress environments, such as among those in prisoner of war camps, where specific anxieties that are uncontrollable become generalized. People who are diagnosed as having Generalized Anxiety Disorder are anxious almost constantly. They are tense and irritable, and they often report an especially intense sort of anxiety. They are unable to concentrate and have difficulty making decisions. Other symptoms include sleep disturbances, excessive sweating, muscle tension, headaches, and insomnia.

Generalized Anxiety Disorder A disorder characterized by persistent anxiety of at least one month's duration and that includes problems in motor tension, autonomic hyperactivity, apprehension, and concentration.

Free-floating anxiety Anxiety that is not clearly attached to any particular object or situation. Patients feel a sense of impending doom, and their anxiety remains with them most of the time.

Generally, psychologists say that there are four areas of functioning in which the person suffering from a Generalized Anxiety Disorder shows problems:

1. *Motor tension.* The person is unable to relax and exhibits jumpiness, restlessness, and tension.
2. *Autonomic hyperactivity.* The person sweats, has a dry mouth, and urinates frequently. Also exhibited are a lump in the throat and a high resting pulse rate.
3. *Apprehensive.* The person worries constantly and anticipates misfortune to self and others.
4. *Vigilance.* The person has difficulty concentrating, is irritable, and impatient.

The following case of a person exhibiting symptoms of a Generalized Anxiety Disorder is presented by Coleman, Butcher, and Carson (1980, p. 209):

> After ten years of very successful practice, a 34-year old dentist noted that his practice had declined slightly during the closing months of the year. Shortly after this he began to experience mild anxiety attacks and complained of continual worry, difficulty in sleeping, and a vague dread that he was "failing." As a result, he increased his hours of practice during the evenings from one to five nights and began driving himself beyond all reason in a desperate effort to "insure the success of his practice." Although his dental practice now increased beyond what it had been previously, he found himself still haunted by the vague fears and apprehensions of failure. These, in turn, became further augmented by frequent heart palpitations and pains that he erroneously diagnosed as at least an incapacitating if not a fatal heart ailment. At this point his anxiety became so great that he voluntarily came to a clinic for assistance.

While most normal people feel anxiety from time to time and are occasionally irritable and apprehensive, they differ from the people who have a Generalized Anxiety Disorder and who manifest these characteristics most of the time. People who suffer from a Generalized Anxiety Disorder live in a world that is filled with tension. They are overly concerned, on edge, overly tense, and easily irritated; they consider the world a tense, difficult place.

Phobic Disorders

Phobic Disorder A disorder characterized by the fear and consequent attempted avoidance of specific objects or situations; the fear is recognized as unreasonable.

A person who exhibits a phobia fears a given situation and tends to avoid that situation even though it presents no real danger. A **Phobic Disorder** is the fear and consequent attempted avoidance of specific objects or situations; the fear is recognized as unreasonable. People who exhibit phobias show them in three ways: behaviorally, physiologically, and cognitively. Behaviorally, they exhibit avoidance and escape behaviors; physiologically, they show increased heart rate and breathing patterns; cognitively, they report thoughts of disasters and embarrassment.

Agoraphobia A disorder characterized by a fear of being alone in public places from which escape might be difficult.

There are three basic kinds of phobias: Agoraphobia, Social Phobia, and Simple Phobia. **Agoraphobia** is a marked fear of being alone in public places from which escape might be difficult. Furthermore, there are avoidance behaviors that eventually interfere with a person's normal life activities. This fear of going into situations where escape might be difficult is quite debilitating. Some individuals avoid going into open spaces, traveling in airplanes, or being in crowds. In a severe case of Agoraphobia people may choose not to leave home because of a lack of security. Agoraphobia is often brought on by stress, particularly interpersonal stress; it is more common in women than men, and often, but not always, is seen in addition to other disorders (Goldstein & Chambless, 1978; Marks, 1969). One housewife who had Agoraphobia for 8 years said,

> It causes terrible problems. The children miss out on lots of things, as I can't take them around to parties and so on; and my husband has to take time off to take them to dentists, doctors and so on. He does all the shopping, and this makes life hard for him. I am in the house all day on my own, with only the dog to talk to, and feel that I am really going mad. The house is like a prison: all I do all day is housework, to keep myself busy. Having agoraphobia makes one very, very lonely as you can't go out to see anyone. If only I had someone to talk to, it wouldn't be so bad. (Melville, 1977, p. 22)

A **Social Phobia** is an irrational fear and desire to avoid situations where the person is exposed to the scrutiny of others; the person fears that he or she might behave in an embarrassing or humiliating way. A person who exhibits a Social Phobia experiences significant distress, recognizing that his or her fear is unreasonable. A Social Phobia is understandable because most of us have been in situations where we think we are being evaluated and these thoughts create some anxiety. The person with a Social Phobia not only fears the evaluation, but avoids evaluations by not dealing with people or situations in which they might occur. People who suffer from a Social Phobia often fear eating in public, speaking before others, and would, for example, have great difficulty entering the education field. One person who suffered from a Social Phobia reported,

Social Phobia A disorder characterized by a fear of, and desire to avoid, situations where the person is exposed to scrutiny by others and where that person might behave in an embarrassing or humiliating way.

> At secondary school I changed, especially when I became more aware that there was an opposite sex. I developed a fear of people in general, was frightened of making a fool of myself, always imagined everyone was talking about me behind my back, and worried what they thought of me. I became very self-conscious, with no confidence. I developed round shoulders, walked everywhere with my head bowed, and seldom looked at people when I talked to them. . . .
>
> When I left college, I went to work as a shorthand typist in a small insurance broker's. I got the job through a friend's mother who recommended me, which saved me struggling through endless interviews. . . .
>
> Gradually the firm began to expand, employing younger staff. My problems got worse—I wouldn't enter a room full of men, still hesitated at answering the phone. Then someone at the office held a party, and although I worried all week beforehand, and lost my appetite, I plucked up the courage to go. (Melville, 1977, pp. 72–73)

A person who exhibits a **Simple Phobia** shows an irrational and persistent fear of an object or situation along with a compelling desire to avoid it; all specific phobias other than Agoraphobia and Social Phobia are classified as Simple Phobias. Most people are familiar with a variety of specific phobias that would be classified as Simple Phobia. There are those who have *claustrophobia* and are afraid of closed spaces. Those who are afraid of the sight of blood are called *hematrophobics*. There is *acrophobia*, the fear of heights—many people fear heights, although they would not avoid going up to the top of a tall building. By contrast, the fear of acrophobics becomes so great that they would, under no circumstances, view the skyline of New York City from the top of one of its major buildings.

Simple Phobia A disorder characterized by an irrational and persistent fear of an object or situation along with a compelling desire to avoid it; all specific phobias other than Agoraphobia and Social Phobia are classified as Simple Phobia.

To be considered a person who has a true Phobic Disorder, a fear must be disproportionate to the situation. While mild Phobic Disorders are relatively common, disabling Phobic Disorders are relatively rare. Mild phobias are

People who have phobias of dogs often have unrealistic ideas of their size and ferocity

People with claustrophobia would avoid a situation like this

found in roughly 7.5% of the population, whereas severe disabling phobias are found in less than one-half of 1% of the population (Agras, Sylvester, & Oliveau, 1969). Phobias are more frequent between the ages of 30 and 60 than at any other point in life. While mild Phobic Disorders are relatively common in normal people, they occur even more commonly in patients who have other disorders (Seif & Atkins, 1979). Men and women develop phobias about equally often (Marks, 1977). It is important to realize that, once established, phobias are maintained by the relief derived from the escape or avoidance that accompanies them; the behavior is maintained by the process of negative reinforcement (see p. 86 for a review of negative reinforcement).

A man who washes his hands 100 times a day in order to avoid germs has an Obsessive-Compulsive Disorder. A person with an **Obsessive-Compulsive Disorder** is characterized by persistent unwanted thoughts, urges, and actions. The patient has certain obsessions or unavoidable preoccupations with thoughts or ideas. Thus, a woman may be obsessed with the notion that germs are invading her immediate surrounding environment; to avoid contamination from these imagined germs, she often has the compulsion to perform certain complex ritualistic cleaning acts. Such compulsions often are strict routines; the patient, in this instance, cleans her house in a certain way a specific amount of time. If the patient does not perform these compulsive desires, she often develops severe anxiety. The person with an Obsessive-Compulsive Disorder combats anxiety by carrying out such rituals (see Pollak, 1979).

A person who suffers from a severe Obsessive-Compulsive Disorder may show behavior that is quite maladaptive. For example, a person who displays orderliness may be over-orderly; he may live by routine and become easily upset by changes in routine. Such a person is overly meticulous and perfectionistic. He becomes overly fond of indexing, tabulating, and organizing (Ingram, 1961). Being orderly is not a disorder; however, when orderliness becomes the prime concern of one's life, then symptoms of Obsessive-Compulsive Disorder are apparent. Consider the following report of a person who feared dire consequences of a lack of certain compulsive rituals:

> I used to write notes to remind myself to do a particular job, so in my mind there was a real risk that one of these notes might go out of the window or door; so after locking up, I would look all round to see there was nothing lying around. I used to worry about how far these documents might have blown. My fear was that if one of these papers blew away, this would cause a fatality to the person carrying out my design project. I felt I was only doing my job properly if I kept my documents. I found it difficult to walk along the street, as every time I saw paper I wondered if it was some of mine. I had to pick it all up, unless it was brown chocolate paper, or lined paper, which I didn't use. And before I got on my bike, I checked that nothing was sticking out of my pocket and got my wife to recheck. She was very patient. I would have to sit in a certain seat on the bus so that, when I walked downstairs, I could look back up and check no papers were on the seat. I couldn't smoke a cigarette without taking it to bits and checking there was no document between the paper and tobacco. I couldn't even have sex because I thought a piece of paper might get intertwined into the mattress. I could do nothing that would cause the loss or destruction of a document, and in the hottest summer the windows had to be made absolutely airtight in case a document blew out. I was only working on the project part-time at one point, and when I arrived at my office job I used to go into the gents and check through my entire pockets, so that I knew that everything on my desk was the firm's property only and there was no chance of getting the two muddled up. (Melville, 1977, pp. 66–67)

Compared to people with a Generalized Anxiety Disorder, the number of individuals with Obsessive-Compulsive Disorders is relatively small. Yet aspects of this classification are evident in many Anxiety Disorders. Many people have small obsessions and compulsions that help them to cope with anxiety. Even people without Anxiety Disorders often exhibit regular ritualistic behaviors to help cope with anxiety and adapt to their jobs or environ-

Obsessive-Compulsive Disorder A disorder characterized by persistent and uncontrollable thoughts and irrational beliefs. These persistent thoughts make individuals feel compelled to perform compulsive rituals that interfere with their daily lives.

ments (Gottheil & Stone, 1974). Sometimes this takes the form of supercleanliness, or sometimes it may involve job competitiveness.

Anxiety Disorders: A Summary

In contemporary society, many people have been diagnosed as having Anxiety Disorders. These diagnoses, however, come from friends and relatives more often than they come from psychologists or psychiatrists. Is there a specific behavior pattern common to all people with Anxiety Disorders? Nearly all are anxious and have irrational fears about coping with life. Rather than cope with their fears, these people make their condition worse by avoiding their problems. Whether people have a Simple Phobic Disorder or obsessive-compulsive traits, they usually exhibit anxiety and usually have trouble handling the business of life.

An individual who exhibits certain symptoms should not immediately be assumed to have an Anxiety Disorder; only anxiety as a symptom is common to all people who exhibit Anxiety Disorders. Clearly the behavior of the person who exhibits obsessive-compulsive symptoms is very different from that of the person who exhibits symptoms of Agoraphobia. Anxiety Disorders share the common property of anxiety, but they are different disorders.

Freud's impact on psychology and psychiatry is so great that terms like *neurosis* are part of the jargon of psychology. They have made their way into everyday language, and nonpsychologists call anyone with a behavioral quirk neurotic. However, being precise and consistent requires a proper diagnosis, one that is consistent with modern knowledge about maladjustment. In the 1980s, using the term neurosis as a catchall term can no longer be considered efficient or appropriate. You will see in chapter 13 that the treatment for various Anxiety Disorders takes on a wide variety of forms and depends on the type of disorder involved.

SOMATOFORM AND DISSOCIATIVE DISORDERS

Somatoform Disorders

Somatoform Disorder A disorder characterized by physical symptoms for which there are no evident physical causes and for which there is evidence that the causes are psychological conflicts; the symptoms, often pain, are real and are not under voluntary control.

Somatization Disorder A disorder characterized by recurrent and multiple complaints of several years duration for which medical attention has been ineffective.

Several kinds of maladjustment that used to be grouped together and called neuroses are today diagnosed within the major categories of Somatoform and Dissociative Disorders. **Somatoform Disorders** are those that involve physical symptoms for which there are no evident physical causes and for which there is evidence that the causes are psychological factors or conflicts. The symptoms, often pain, are real and are not under voluntary control. We will briefly examine two Somatoform Disorders: Somatization and Conversion Disorders.

In a **Somatization Disorder,** there are recurrent and multiple complaints of several years duration for which medical attention has not been effective. The disorder begins before the age of 30 and is rarely seen in males; a year seldom passes without some medical attention. Such a patient will report feeling sickly for a good part of her life. Patients may sometimes report muscle weakness, double vision, memory loss, or deafness. Gastrointestinal problems like vomiting and diarrhea are common. Painful menstrual periods with excessive bleeding, as well as sexual indifference, are common. Frequent complaints are made about pains in the back, chest, and genitals. Women who are experiencing some of these symptoms are often beset by anxiety as well as a depressed mood; sometimes even hallucinations are apparent. This is not a very common disorder; only about 1% of females have this diagnosis and even fewer males are so diagnosed.

A **Conversion Disorder** is the loss or alteration of physical functioning that is not due to a physiological disorder and seems to be due to some internal (psychological) conflict. Those suffering from a Conversion Disorder often report a loss of the use of arms, legs, or hands. A person who complains of a loss of vision or pain may be exhibiting a Conversion Disorder. A patient may develop multifaceted ailments; in addition to being blind, he or she may become deaf, mute, or totally paralyzed. Patients may be able to get a great deal of attention and support because of this kind of disorder—support that might otherwise not be forthcoming. Men and women are equally likely to develop a Conversion Disorder; however, Conversion Disorders are not common—especially when compared to the frequency of Anxiety Disorders.

Dissociative Disorders

In the past, the disorders today called Conversion Disorders and Psychogenic Amnesia were both called hysterical neurosis. While it is true that both disorders share some commonalities and have certain similar processes, today we recognize that they are fundamentally different disorders and cannot be grouped together. As our knowledge of these disorders has increased, our classification system has grown more sophisticated.

As part of the new classification system, in **Dissociative Disorders** there is a sudden but temporary alteration in consciousness, identity, or motor behavior. One Dissociative Disorder, **Psychogenic Amnesia,** is a sudden inability to recall important personal information that is too extensive to be explained by ordinary forgetfulness. Often the amnesia is brought on by traumatic incidents involving a threat of physical injury or death. While the condition is relatively rare and more common in wartime or natural disasters, recovery is usually complete.

Often associated with Psychogenic Amnesia, but presenting a dramatically different kind of behavior, is Multiple Personality. A remarkable disorder, the diagnosis of **Multiple Personality** is appropriate when existing within a person are two or more distinct personalities, each of which is dominant at a particular time. Each personality is complete with its own unique styles, memories, and behavioral patterns; each personality is evident when it is considered dominant. Switching from one personality to the other is usually caused by stress.

Cases of Multiple Personality are extremely rare and are usually not diagnosed until adolescence; furthermore, the distinct personalities are often opposites in behavior patterns. While the different personalities are usually unaware of one another, sometimes one of the personalities may "listen in" on the lives of the others. When a person is in one personality, the other personalities (when active) will generally acknowledge that some unaccounted for time has passed. Different-sex personalities are allowed, and one personality may be very adaptive and efficient in coping with life while the other personality may exhibit maladaptive behavior (see Greaves, 1980).

Conversion Disorder A disorder characterized by the loss or alteration of physical functioning that is not due to a physiological disorder and that seems to be due to some internal psychological conflict.

Dissociative Disorder A disorder characterized by a sudden, but temporary, alteration in consciousness, identity, or motor behavior.

Psychogenic Amnesia A disorder characterized by a sudden inability to recall important personal information that is too extensive to be explained by ordinary forgetfulness.

Multiple Personality A disorder characterized by the existence within an individual of two or more different personalities, each of which is dominant at a particular time.

It must be emphasized that Multiple Personality as a diagnosed disorder is *very* rare. Few cases are known and we have little data and understanding of its causes. The media and public often confuse Multiple Personality with Schizophrenia, which is far more common. Somatoform and Dissociative Disorders have been studied rather little compared to many other disorders; this is probably due to their relative infrequency in the population. Nevertheless, these disorders do occur, and those beset by the problems need attention and some form of psychotherapy (see chapter 13).

DEPRESSION: AN AFFECTIVE DISORDER

Affect A feeling or mood that is easily seen by others; an emotional response.

Major Depression A disorder characterized by loss of interest in almost all usual activities as evidenced by a sad, hopeless, or discouraged mood. Other symptoms include sleep disturbances, loss of energy, and feelings of unworthiness and guilt.

Most people feel fatigue now and then. Sometimes they have sleepless nights, and there have been times when people have said, "What's the use," or "Things seem so futile." When people's mood or **affect** becomes so depressed or sad that there is a change in their outlook on life and their overt behavior, they may be suffering from depression. Sadness, irritability, or moroseness are symptoms of **Major Depression.** While everyone has felt depressed from time to time, a range of behaviors exists that are classified as a Major Depression, and they are more extreme than just a "blue" mood. The person who exhibits symptoms of a Major Depression is not merely experiencing a fleeting anxiety but shows a relatively extreme reaction.

A person who exhibits a Major Depression generally has had the depression triggered by a specific incident. A depression is often an excessive or prolonged reaction to the loss of a loved one or a failure within one's life. The death of a wife or a child, for example, often leads the husband or the parent to become deeply depressed. The loss of a job or a home can cause a similar kind of depression. A person who exhibits the symptoms of depression is often slow in movement and speech. Every task seems to require a great effort; few acts seem worthwhile. While most people who exhibit symptoms of Major Depression are able to express their reason for feeling sad and dejected, they are unable to explain why their reaction is so deep and so prolonged. While the reaction of such a person is often appropriate at the time of the loss or failure, its continuation for an extended period of time leads to maladjustment. Thus, while the loss of a loved one may bring about appropriate, immediate grief, its continuation for an extended period of time causes the person to fail to continue to cope with life's challenges and demands.

The essential characteristics of Major Depression are a depressed, sad, hopeless mood and a loss of interest in all or almost all usual activities and pastimes. The behavior of depressed patients is not necessarily overtly bizarre, but they experience symptoms like poor appetite, insomnia, loss of energy, feelings of worthlessness, inability to concentrate, sleep difficulties, and even thoughts of death and suicide. People who experience Major Depression hide and withdraw from other people.

A major depressive episode can begin at any age. Symptoms are usually rapidly apparent and last for a few days, weeks, or months. The episode may be a single one or it may recur a second or third time. Sometimes episodes are separated by years of normal functioning, then are followed by a series of two or three brief episodes of depression with but a few weeks between them. In as many as 35% of cases the depressive symptoms become chronic.

Depression is not confined to the old

Patients who are diagnosed as having a Major Depression Disorder have a gloomy outlook on life, an especially slow thought process, and an extremely exaggerated view of present problems with a tendency to blame themselves. Also important, they may have delusions or false beliefs that induce guilt and feelings of shame. Sometimes these distortions of reality are consistent with their basic ideas about their own guilt and unworthiness, or sometimes they seem to have little to do with their reasons for depression. In these cases, people who are in states of depression often report delusions of persecution.

The degree of impairment will vary, but in virtually all people diagnosed as having a Major Depression, there is interference in social and occupational functioning. Females are more likely to be depressed than males (Kaplan, 1977) and are more likely to express those feelings openly (Blumenthall, 1975). For example, in the United States between 19 to 23% of females and 8 to 11% of males have experienced a major depressive episode at some time. Furthermore, about 6% of females and 3% of males have experienced sufficiently severe episodes that they have required hospitalization.

Like other kinds of maladjustment, people who exhibit symptoms of Major Depression show a variety of behaviors. So as to better understand how such a person might behave, consider the following brief case study:

Mrs. Thomas, in her middle 70s, had been depressed off and on for five years, since her husband, who had had an operation for cancer, insisted on taking his dis-

553

Table 12.4 Depression can vary in its depth from mild to moderate to severe depression. Beck (1972) examined a percentage of subjects in a large sample which showed different clinical depressed features.

	DEPTH OF DEPRESSION			
CLINICAL FEATURE	NONE (%)	MILD (%)	MODERATE (%)	SEVERE (%)
Sad faces	18	72	94	98
Stooped posture	6	32	70	87
Crying in interview	3	11	29	28
Speech: slow, etc.	25	53	72	75
Low mood	16	72	94	94
Diurnal variation of mood	6	13	37	37
Suicidal wishes	13	47	73	94
Indecisiveness	18	42	68	83
Hopelessness	14	58	85	86
Feeling inadequate	25	56	75	90
Conscious guilt	27	46	64	60
Loss of interest	14	56	83	92
Loss of motivation	23	54	88	88
Fatigability	39	62	89	84
Sleep disturbance	31	55	73	88
Loss of appetite	17	33	61	88
Constipation	19	26	38	52

Source: Beck, 1972, p. 40.

charge from the hospital. During the next year, until his death, "I never had a wink of sleep." Until he died he was very difficult, but she denied that previously the marriage had been unhappy. "Of course, he used to drink, and he'd had malaria, which made him violent sometimes, but we got on." Since his death she had lived alone, often visiting her nine children, all married, none living more than a few miles away. "They're very good children. They've got their own lives to live. I feel a burden to them. If I could live nearer to them I'd be all right." "They give me every material thing that I could want—but it's not what I need." She remained unable to sleep, which she attributed to the fear of break-ins, as she had suffered two minor burglaries in successive years. Before retiring she barricaded her front door with all the furniture she could move, and she would get up very early and pace the landing in her dressing gown for hours. Several times in the course of the interview she exclaimed, "If things don't get better I'll kill myself. I've nothing to live for really, have I?" Lately she had been so preoccupied by her misery that she had not noticed things, like whom she met in the street; yet she was highly sensitive to what was going on around her, and worried that she was being commented on and gossiped about. "Not that they'd have anything to say—I've always led a good life." (Pitt, 1974, pp. 75–76)

Because there can be so many different circumstances that can bring about a reaction of depression and because the extent of the depression can vary so dramatically from individual to individual, *DSM-III* distinguishes four completely different categories of maladjustment that represent depression. One of the characteristics that distinguishes between categories is whether the depressed reaction stems from a single episode or whether the depression is recurrent.

Another important characteristic that may or may not be evident when a person suffers from an affective disorder like depression is the presence of psychotic symptoms. The principal characteristic of behavior classified as **psychotic** is that the person is out of touch with reality. People with psychotic symptoms are no longer able to compare their personal views of the world with physical and social cues to see how closely they correspond; we say that people with psychotic symptoms cannot *test reality*. Such individuals are not able to cope with the demands of life in rational and reasonable ways, as their reasoning ability is often grossly impaired. They generally need hospitalization and constant, regular therapy. You will see that psychotic symptoms are especially evident in an even more severe disorder, schizophrenia.

Psychotic Gross impairment of reality testing within an individual; this impairment usually interferes with an individual's ability to meet the ordinary demands of life.

A person who is diagnosed as having a Major Depression will exhibit the symptoms of most feeling or mood disorders. A man who is experiencing a period in which he feels sad and depressed cannot be characterized as having a Major Depression; in the same way, a woman who finds her work boring, tedious, and depressing is not experiencing a Major Depression. Those who experience serious depressive episodes show relatively extreme reactions. Patients who are in an episode of depression show a slowing of activities and a loss of enthusiasm. These patients may sit for long periods of time, showing no interest in the world about them; this includes abstinence from eating and sex. These patients report feelings of unworthiness, failure, and guilt. Many times they consider suicide (Pokorny, 1977). They might say,

> I am feeling very depressed. I feel as though I'm dragging myself down as well as my family. I have caused my parents no end of aggravation. The best thing would be if I dug a hole and buried myself in it. If I would get rid of myself, everybody would be upset for a time but then they would get over it. They would be better off without me. (Beck, 1972, p. 81)

Patients who are more seriously disturbed show motor and thought processes that are disrupted to an even greater extent. Any spontaneity that might have been shown is no longer evident. Feelings of guilt and sin become more pronounced. These patients report that they are responsible for severe problems of the world such as depression, disease, or hunger. These patients also report that their body may be disintegrating or that their brain is being eaten from the inside out. These patients then often report all sorts of strange diseases. They will typically report that they have no hope for themselves or for the world; nothing seems interesting to them.

A typical person with a serious depressive disorder might be heard to say in a therapy session,

> There seems no way out of my dreadful situation . . . just dreadful . . . I've lost any hope I once had and now know the truth . . . everything is lost, hopeless. I'm the cause of misfortune for me and my family. They wouldn't be in such difficult straits if it weren't for my utter uselessness. All is lost; there's no hope left for me. If I died the world would be a better place. I'm beyond hope; my life has been a useless wasted catastrophe. Nothing is important anymore . . . nothing . . . I really don't deserve to live; if I had any guts I'd do myself in. My life has been such a waste . . . It's hopeless.

In some cases, people become dramatically and profoundly depressed; these patients essentially become nonresponsive. They must be confined to their beds, washed, fed, and bathed. Patients in this kind of depressive stupor have completely lost touch with reality and hallucinate regularly. They may believe that the world is a strange place containing many strange animals. These patients are totally confused, isolated, and withdrawn. They accept all of the guilt for the wrongdoings of the world and see themselves as total failures, unworthy, and full of sadness and despair.

Causes of Depression

As in so many other areas of psychology, both biological and learning theories have developed to help explain why people become depressed. The biological theories suggest that certain chemical processes account for depression; the learning theories suggest that people develop a set of faulty ideas and learn to be depressed.

NATURE: BIOLOGICAL THEORIES. There is evidence to suggest that depression may be genetic in origin (Allen, 1976; Depue & Monroe, 1978). You will see later that genetics and heredity play an even greater role in disorders such as schizophrenia.

Significant attention and support have been given to the idea that neurotransmitters in the brain are involved in depression. Neurotransmitters are the chemicals released across the synapse when a neuron fires. While there are many different neurotransmitters, one that seems particularly important (at least in regard to depression) is norepinephrine. The *norepinephrine hypothesis* suggests that there is an insufficient amount of norepinephrine at the receptor sites; this view argues that depression is caused by a lack of the substance and that if the substance level is increased, depression will be alleviated. Aversive stimuli are known to *decrease* norepinephrine levels; thus, being in a stress situation may decrease a person's level of norepinephrine and bring about depression. There is some support for this idea, although there is considerable disagreement as to the specific chemicals and how they work (Akiskal & McKinney, 1975; Depue & Evans, 1976; see also, Davis, 1977 for a review).

A great deal of medical research is taking place to assess whether norepinephrine levels are indeed associated with the depth of depressions (see Buchsbaum et al., 1976, 1978). Other lines of research are combining long-standing treatments like psychotherapy with drug treatments. In one such study (DiMascio et al., 1979), severely depressed patients were given either psychotherapy alone, an antidepressant drug alone, or a combination of psychotherapy and drug therapy. The results of the study were dramatic; compared to a group of subjects who were not depressed, the effect of psychotherapy or drug therapy was about equal. They both reduced depressive symptoms. However, the *combination* of psychotherapy and drug therapy helped these patients the most.

At present, most practicing psychologists know that certain drugs seem to help depressed patients. How these drugs work and how they affect neurotransmitters in the brain is still under active investigation. Brain mechanisms and neurochemical substances are difficult to investigate. However, the research is promising, and it is likely that people suffering from a biologically caused depression may have significant help available in the near future.

557
Abnormal Psychology

NURTURE: LEARNING THEORIES. In contrast to biological theories, those who favor a learning view argue that people who are depressed have learned to become depressed; furthermore, if they change their views and behavior, they will lessen their depression. One particularly influential view is that of Peter Lewinsohn. Lewinsohn believes that depressed individuals have few positive reinforcements in their lives; being around a depressed patient rarely makes one happy and one is unable to make the depressed patient more optimistic about his or her situation. From Lewinsohn's view, once a person becomes depressed, the depression will be maintained because people find that person unpleasant to be with. A depressed person may live in a nonreinforcing environment; he or she may be old, sickly, or unhealthy, which will certainly not lead to reinforcements. Furthermore, a person with poor social skills never learns to express prosocial behaviors, is often punished for the behaviors that he or she does emit, and finds that the world is an aversive and depressing place to be. Thus, Lewinsohn's idea of a lack of reinforcement in a person's life is certainly one way that a person may develop and maintain a depression (Lewinsohn, 1974; Lewinsohn & Talkington, 1979; Lewinsohn, Youngren, & Grosscup, 1979).

Another influential learning theory has been proposed by psychiatrist Aaron Beck. This view suggests that people learn to be depressed because they have negative views of the world, themselves, and their future. In Beck's view, people have negative views of themselves that cause them to magnify their errors; they compare themselves, usually unfairly, with others; when they come up short, they see the difference as disastrous. They not only view themselves poorly, but they see the human condition as being in very bad shape; they view the world as a place that will help defeat positive behavior. Thus, a poor self-concept along with negative hope for the world certainly will produce a negative future. These negative feelings *produce* depression. It is important to point out that from Beck's view depression does not cause the negative feelings; rather, it is the other way around (Beck, 1967, 1972, 1976) (see Table 12.5, p. 558).

According to Beck, people who are depressed are likely to hold such views and have less optimistic views about the world and themselves. The research supports this idea. People who rate themselves as depressed also select depressed ideas about the world when given choices; they are harsher on themselves than nondepressed individuals, and they have particularly low levels of self-expectation (Hammen & Krantz, 1976; Lobitz & Post, 1979; Nelson, 1977; Space & Cromwell, 1980). Beck's theory has been influential among psychologists because its view is consistent with the idea that people *learn* to be depressed because of a lack of appropriate reinforcements. Given the strong learning bias of many practicing psychologists, this view has great appeal; the view is in need of further experimental support, but it has been very influential.

Another learning approach to depression that is still undergoing development is the view of *learned helplessness*. As was presented in our study of social psychology (p. 469), learned helplessness is the situation in which a person learns that reinforcements and punishments are noncontingent; this means that people's rewards and punishments seem to have little to do with

Table 12.5 To assess the extent of a person's depression accurately, Beck (1972) has developed an inventory or scale that can be given to an individual. Shown are some of the items from the scale in which people have to choose which statement best describes how they feel at the time they complete the inventory.

BECK'S DEPRESSION INVENTORY

A. (Sadness)

    I do not feel sad

    I feel blue or sad

    I am blue or sad all the time and I can't snap out of it

    I am so sad or unhappy that it is quite painful

    I am so sad or unhappy that I can't stand it

B. (Sense of Failure)

    I do not feel like a failure

    I feel I have failed more than the average person

    I feel I have accomplished very little that is worthwhile or that means anything

    As I look back on my life all I can see is a lot of failures

    I feel I am a complete failure as a person (parent, husband, wife)

C. (Guilt)

    I don't feel particularly guilty

    I feel bad or unworthy a good part of the time

    I feel quite guilty

    I feel bad or unworthy practically all of the time now

    I feel as though I am very bad or worthless

D. (Self-Dislike)

    I don't feel disappointed in myself

    I am disappointed in myself

    I don't like myself

    I am disgusted with myself

    I hate myself

Source: Beck, 1972, pp. 333–334.

their behavior. When people feel that this is the case, they may choose to stop responding. Seligman's ideas of learned helplessness (Abramson, Seligman, & Teasdale, 1978; Seligman, 1976) are similar to Beck's view in that thought patterns determine depression. In a recent version of the idea, Seligman suggests that people's attributions as to the causes of their successes or failures will determine if they will become depressed. When people attribute the causes of their mistakes or failures to internal conditions about themselves, they come to view themselves with low self-esteem. When they also feel that eventual outcomes are uncontrollable, then they will develop a sense of learned helplessness. They will choose not to respond because they feel that responding makes no difference (see also Garber, Miller, & Seamen, 1979).

    These three views, Lewinsohn's, Beck's, and Seligman's, all suggest that reinforcement and where, how, and when it is delivered will determine the course and nature of depression. Each takes a different view, with the latter

Study: Depression Affects Mothering

Reports about research like the following news article suggest that you can "catch" depressions almost like a cold or the flu. While people are influenced by those with whom they live, such emotional problems as those described are not transferable like a cold; the relative contributions of the environment and heredity are not fully established.

UPI—WASHINGTON Young mothers going through mental depression sometimes cease to care about their children, says a Yale University researcher.

A study in New Haven, Conn., found some women had difficulty discharging motherly functions for as long as two years after their depression symptoms disappeared.

"These mothers experienced a particularly devastating impairment of their ability to care for children," Myrna Weissman, director of the Yale University depression research unit, told a National Conference of Depressive Disorders Thursday.

"They showed loss of affection, disinterest in the children, difficulty in communicating with the children and considerable hostility toward them," she said.

Many of the children develop symptoms associated with the mother's illness such as increased school problems, hyperactivity, fighting and accidents and intense conflict with the mother.

Depression affects one in ten persons seriously enough to require treatment, according to statistics from the National Institute of Mental Health.

Ms. Weissman, a specialist in rates and incidence of disease, said that studies show more women are affected than men.

Based on 1970 hospital admissions for all depressive disorders, 175 women were admitted for every 100 men, she said. Women treated on an outpatient basis outnumbered men by a 238–100 ratio. Community surveys in New York City, Baltimore, Md., northern Florida, Carroll County, Md., and New Haven all show more women with depression symptoms than men.

two being more cognitive and thought-oriented than the former. However, all make the same basic assumption that depression is learned.

NATURE AND NURTURE.   As you probably suspect by now, there is no direct, straightforward, and clearcut cause of depression. Through their efforts in treating depression with drugs, medical researchers have shown that neurotransmitters are probably involved in depression. Furthermore, there is reasonable evidence to suggest that the level of neurotransmitters in the brain determines or causes depression, rather than depression causing a low level of neurotransmitter. At the same time, however, there is compelling evidence and intuitive appeal for learning theories. People who are depressed develop very negative views about the world; often they held similar negative views before their depression. Depressed behavior clearly suggests that reinforcements no longer have value; depressed patients choose lethargy rather than responsiveness, regardless of the reinforcement (see Akiskal, 1979).

Depression is a major and problematic maladjustment. It affects millions of individuals and their families. As our knowledge of the neurochemistry of the brain and the behavior of the depressed person becomes more complete, we hope the number of depressed people will diminish.

SCHIZOPHRENIC DISORDERS

Cary does not have many friends. He has trouble relating to his peers, and they have difficulty understanding him. One of the reasons Cary is not well liked is that he is very moody. Sometimes he is outgoing and friendly, yet at other times he is quite depressed and withdrawn; this behavior makes lasting relationships difficult. Sometimes Cary's behavior is bizarre; he will do and say strange things, almost as if to attract attention. Sometimes his conversations do not seem reasonable or logical; he appears to be lost in a dream world. While Cary has not yet been hospitalized, his behavior presents many of the characteristics of a person diagnosed as having a Schizophrenic Disorder, commonly called schizophrenia.

Unlike many psychological disorders, schizophrenia often incapacitates a person and makes hospitalization necessary. The behavior of patients with schizophrenia includes sudden changes in mood, thought, perception, and behavior. These changes often accompany distortions of reality and an inability to respond appropriately in both thought and feeling. The term schizophrenia has been used as a catchall for a number of different types of disorders. However, certain distinct and essential features are necessary for a person to be characterized as having a **Schizophrenic Disorder.** (1) There must be a lack of reality testing. (2) More than one area of a person's psychological functioning must be involved. (3) There is virtually always a deterioration of social and intellectual functioning. (4) The onset of the illness is usually before age 45, and (5) duration of the illness must be at least 6 months. With these criteria a diagnosis of some type of Schizophrenic Disorder can be made; however, it must be emphasized that Schizophrenic Disorders represent a group of disorders, each of which may have been brought about for dramatically different reasons. For example, a Disorganized Type and a Paranoid Type of Schizophrenic Disorder show very different symptoms; they have different diagnostic criteria; and they are brought about by different reasons. Yet both kinds of Schizophrenic Disorders must, at a minimum, meet the five criteria presented earlier.

About 1% of the population is diagnosed as having some kind of Schizophrenic Disorder, and almost one-fourth of the patients who are admitted to mental hospitals each year are diagnosed with it (Rubenstein & Coelho, 1970). A person who is diagnosed as having a Schizophrenic Disorder is unable to meet the ordinary and reasonable demands of life. While there are hundreds of thousands of hospitalized patients who are diagnosed as such in the United States, many other hundreds of thousands of potential patients are not being treated or, even more likely, are undiagnosed. There are approximately 100,000 to 200,000 new cases of schizophrenia diagnosed per year; the diagnosis is more frequent in lower socioeconomic groups and in nonwhites. The total cost of schizophrenia to our country's human resources is inestimable; the cost in economic terms alone is at least $12 billion per year (Gunderson & Mosher, 1978). It is interesting to note that European psychiatrists assign the diagnosis much less frequently than American professionals. For example, in the United States the number of new cases each year is 10 times as great as in Great Britain (after allowing for population differences) (Wing, 1978).

Essential Characteristics

Patients diagnosed as having some form of schizophrenia have problems with various aspects of their behavior, particularly with attention, emotions, and perception, as well as motor behavior. Some patients exhibit all of these

Schizophrenic Disorder A group of disorders characterized by a lack of reality testing and deterioration of social and intellectual functioning, which begins before age 45 and lasts for at least 6 months. Individuals with this diagnosis often show serious personality disintegration with significant changes in thought, mood, perception, and behavior.

characteristics; others have problems with only one. The most common schizophrenic behaviors appear as severe disturbances in thought, perception, and emotion (affect).

THOUGHT DISORDERS.   One of the first signs that a person may be suffering from a Schizophrenic Disorder is that he or she has problems conducting a logical and coherent conversation. A patient with schizophrenia randomly changes topics of conversation with little or no apparent reason. His conversations are incoherent and lacking in meaning and order. In referring to his own thoughts, one patient indicated,

> My thoughts get all jumbled up. I start thinking or talking about something but I never get there. Instead I wander off in the wrong direction and get caught up with all sorts of different things that may be connected with the things I want to say but in a way I can't explain. People listening to me get more lost than I do. (McGhie & Chapman, 1961, p. 108)

Patients with schizophrenia often have delusions. A **delusion** is a false belief that a person holds even when contrary facts are presented. Thus, a patient with schizophrenia may have the false belief that her food has been poisoned; when her doctor or other patients are served from the same supplies, the patient continues to believe that her food is contaminated. Even in the face of contradictory evidence, the patient with schizophrenia maintains false beliefs. Many such patients have delusions of persecution and believe that the world is a hostile place; they believe that they are victims of plots and conspiracies. These delusions of persecution are often accompanied by delusions of grandeur. The patient feels that he is a particularly important person, and that this is the reason for his persecution. His delusions may be complicated by his taking on the role of an important character in history; for example, a patient may think that he is General Douglas MacArthur. He deludes himself into believing that he is truly MacArthur and that there is a conspiracy of people who wish to do harm to him; he has both delusions of grandeur and delusions of persecution. Clearly, this patient has lost contact with reality.

Delusion A false belief that is inconsistent with reality and is held in spite of contradictory evidence.

PERCEPTUAL DISORDERS.   Another sign that a person may be experiencing a Schizophrenic Disorder is the appearance of hallucinations. Voices are often heard that speak directly to the individual. Often the voices comment on the patient's own behavior and even command the patient to behave in certain ways. The voices that a patient might hear are typically seen as coming from outside of the patient's head. While hallucinations of a visual, tactile, and olfactory nature can be present, the most common hallucinations are auditory.

EMOTIONAL DISORDERS.   One of the most striking characteristics of a patient diagnosed as having a Schizophrenic Disorder is that he or she seems to display inappropriate emotional responses. For example, a patient with schizophrenia might become depressed and cry when her favorite food falls on the floor; yet, upon hearing of the death of a close friend or relative, she may laugh and think the event hysterically funny. Other patients with schizophrenia show no emotion. They seem to be incapable of experiencing a normal range of emotions, and their emotional range is said to be flat; they

Figure 12.1 The *Schizophrenia Bulletin* features art done by current and former mental hospital patients. This drawing was by Carol, a 19-year-old girl whose progress was followed by Dr. James Harris at the Phipps Clinic. Carol drew the picture in June 1975 while she was in occupational therapy. At the time, she felt estranged from other patients. While the picture was being drawn, Carol was unaware of its significance, and it was almost a year before she could make any association to the faces. Since this time, Carol has drawn several hundred pictures. In the later drawings, the mask has come off and the feelings that the faces represent are becoming more acceptable to her. The faces depicted on the cover are numbered in the diagram above; Carol's description of each face is as follows:

I. Mask.

II. This face represented the part of me that was envious of the way other patients were able to converse; they looked comfortable with each other.

III. Maternal figure; this part of me tried to mother people (a way to keep them at a distance?).

IV. Evil person. She felt angry at everyone she saw; she wanted to kill them all.

V. The Egyptian face referred to my interest in ancient history—my tendency to withdraw into the past.

VI. The only sane person; she can see what's going on and is worried.

VII. She couldn't endure what she was feeling, so she decided to die.

display a flattening of affect. *Affect* is a person's emotional response. Virtually no event can bring about an emotional response, either appropriate or inappropriate, in these patients. They show blank, expressionless faces even when presented with a remark or situation that would evoke a response in normal individuals.

Some patients with schizophrenia display inappropriate affect and very often their emotions are extreme or ambivalent. An *ambivalent affect* means that a person experiences both positive and negative feelings toward the same person or object simultaneously. Thus, a patient may love and hate her doctor at the same time. A patient's ambivalent emotions are usually caused by her experiencing simultaneous conflicting feelings. Such a patient may seem happy at one moment, but she may seem dejected and totally sad the very next moment. She may experience a wide range of emotional behaviors within a brief period of time.

The thoughts, perceptions, and emotions of the patient with schizophrenia are seriously disturbed; yet, it is interesting to note that even the mentally ill can sometimes distinguish "sick" from normal roles. Chesno and Kilmann (1975) told subjects that they were not insane and that they were to view themselves as normal; these patients subsequently showed a higher release rate than patients who did not receive this information. The patients were responding to the label that the researchers put on them. The way patients see themselves and their subsequent behavior may be determined by the label society places on them. If patients are told that they are sick, they may act sick; by contrast, if they are told that they are really normal and not insane, they may have a better chance of modifying their behavior toward normalcy.

Types of Schizophrenic Disorders

Patients diagnosed as having a Schizophrenic Disorder exhibit a large cluster of symptoms that characterize their behavior. Ninety-seven percent show a lack of insight, and over 70% report verbal and auditory hallucinations. More than 65% hear voices, are suspicious, and show a flattening of affect (Santorious, Shapiro, & Jablewsky, 1974). It is often difficult at times to determine in which specific category a patient should most aptly be categorized (Gift et al., 1980). Yet categorization does take place; there are five basic types of schizophrenia, which are shown in Table 12.6. As can be seen from the table, patients with schizophrenia manifest a wide variety of symptoms.

Table 12.6 Types of Schizophrenic Disorders as presented in *DSM-III* (with minor modifications)

CLASSIFICATION	SYMPTOMS
Disorganized Type	Frequent incoherence, absence of systematized delusions, and blunted, inappropriate, or silly affect
Catatonic Type	Stupor in which there is a marked decrease in reactivity to environment; or an excited phase in which there is excited motor activity, apparently purposeless and not influenced by external stimuli
Paranoid Type	Delusions and hallucinations of persecution or grandeur, and/or unfounded jealousy
Undifferentiated Type	Prominent delusions, hallucinations, incoherence, or grossly disorganized behavior *and* does not meet the criteria for any of the other types, or meets the criteria for more than one type
Residual Type	History of at least one previous episode of schizophrenia with prominent psychotic symptoms but has at present a clinical picture without any prominent psychotic symptoms, and there is continuing evidence of the illness such as inappropriate affect, illogical thinking, social withdrawal, or eccentric behavior

Disorganized Type One of five major subtypes of schizophrenia, characterized by frequent incoherence, absence of systematized delusions, and blunted, inappropriate, or silly affect.

DISORGANIZED TYPE. The Disorganized Type of schizophrenia seems to have many of the traditional symptoms. Thought processes seem severely disturbed; these patients have hallucinations, delusions, and are frequently incoherent. The **Disorganized Type's** affect and emotional behavior are also quite bizarre. Their behavior is often silly, inappropriate, and sometimes obscene; they often experience periods of giggling, crying, and/or irritability. The Disorganized Type's mood does not seem to be linked to the immediate situation, and they may smile, giggle, or cry at any given point in time. Patients diagnosed with Disorganized Type often lack good personal hygiene and exhibit a rather severe disintegration of a normal personality system. Disorganized Type schizophrenia is a relatively severe change in personality that shows marked loss of reality testing. While possibly due to a change in diagnostic practices, the number of cases of Disorganized Type schizophrenia has decreased rather dramatically in the twentieth century (Morrison, 1974), accounting for as few as 5% of diagnosed cases (Guggenheim & Babigian, 1974).

Paranoid Type One of five major subtypes of schizophrenia, characterized by delusions and hallucinations of persecution and/or grandeur; irrational jealousy is sometimes evident.

A seriously disturbed person often exhibits a great deal of fear. Often this extreme fear of others is seen in schizophrenia

PARANOID TYPE. Patients diagnosed as Paranoid Type are among the most difficult to study because their outward behavior often seems appropriate to situations. They account for as many as 45% of diagnosed cases of schizophrenia (Guggenheim & Babigian, 1974; Nathan et al., 1969). They are able to take care of their own body functions and can get along well with people. Yet they show a lack of reality testing. **Paranoid Type** patients have extreme delusions of persecution and, occasionally, of their own self-concept (i.e., grandeur). While often particularly religious, such patients hold the false belief that people are making a concerted effort to destroy them. They feel that events in the world have particular significance to them. Thus, if the president of the United States makes a speech about crime, the Paranoid Type patient will feel that the president is referring specifically to his or her crimes. A patient diagnosed as a Paranoid Type may see strange and bizarre images; she may feel she is being chased by ghosts or intruders from another planet. She is very likely to have auditory hallucinations.

A patient with a Paranoid Type schizophrenia might have an intense conversation with a therapist that is really quite involved, yet really lacking in reality testing, as in the following exchange:

THERAPIST: How are you?

PATIENT: How is he?

THERAPIST: No, how are you today?

PATIENT: I'm OK except for the Russians.

THERAPIST: The Russians?

PATIENT: They've been here all week trying to thwart my plan. You see, the CIA has been working with me to halt communist aggression. And, well, don't tell anybody . . . but, the word has leaked out to the Russian high command and they want me killed. It's really quite an elaborate plot. They have hired some moon men to fly back to Earth with those Russian astronauts to poison my food. In that way, I'll die quietly. But, I'm going to fool them—I'll only eat fresh fruit which they can't poison. By the way, I'm not sure if I explained it to you, the Chinese are in on this caper as well.

While the Paranoid Type has strange delusions, hallucinations, and bizarre thought processes, his or her behavior is not as fragmented and incoherent as the Disorganized Type's. He often seeks out other people and does not show extreme withdrawal from social interaction. The Paranoid Type's behavior is often unpredictable, and sometimes hostile. Patients can be alert, intelligent, and responsive, but those who deal with them must remember that their delusions and hallucinations impair their ability to deal with reality. The degree of their disturbance varies over time.

CATATONIC TYPE.   Catatonic Type schizophrenia is often shown in films because it presents extreme types of overt behavior. There are two major subtypes of **Catatonic Type** schizophrenia, the excited and the withdrawn. The *excited* catatonic patient shows excessive and sometimes violent motor activity; the *withdrawn* catatonic patient often seems stuporous, mute, and very negative. Withdrawn patients show a relatively high degree of muscular rigidity; they are not immobile but show a rather decreased level of activity, speaking, moving, and responding. Such patients are usually totally aware of the things that are going on around them even though they may remain mute and unresponsive.

In an excited state, the patient diagnosed as a Catatonic Type may talk and shout continuously and engage in seemingly uninhibited, frenzied, agitated, and aggressive motor activity. A withdrawn type can exhibit occasional signs of the excited phase. Usually these excited episodes appear and disappear suddenly. After relatively long periods of showing withdrawal symptoms, the patient may suddenly become excited and run around, shout, and exhaust herself totally. The Catatonic Type patient may use immobility and unresponsiveness to maintain control over her environment by not responding to outside sources. Five percent of first admissions to mental hospitals are diagnosed with Catatonic Type schizophrenia (Guggenheim & Babigian, 1974).

Catatonic Type   One of the five major subtypes of schizophrenia, characterized by stupor in which individuals are mute, negative, and basically unresponsive. Characteristics can also include displays of excited or violent motor activity. Individuals can switch from the withdrawn to the excited state.

Table 12.7   Four alternative dimensions of schizophrenia have been used to gain further perspective on this debilitating disorder. Used in addition to or in place of *DSM-III* categories, many practitioners find these dimensions useful.

DIMENSION	DESCRIPTION
Process-Reactive	Process schizophrenia develops slowly, while reactive schizophrenia has a sudden onset. Prognosis better for reactive type.
Chronic-Acute	Chronic schizophrenics show a slow development of symptoms and require long-term hospitalization. Acute schizophrenics may show no previous symptoms, have one psychotic episode, and return to non-psychotic behavior. Prognosis better for acute types.
Paranoid-Nonparanoid	Patients who have delusions of persecution are classified as paranoid and have a better prognosis than nonparanoid patients.
Premorbid Adjustment	Patients who adjusted to life in relatively normal ways before hospitalization have a better prognosis than those with poor premorbid adjustments.

Table 12.8 Likelihood of recovery in schizophrenia

	PERCENTAGE RECOVERED	PERCENTAGE IMPROVED	PERCENTAGE UNIMPROVED
DSM-III Categories:			
Disorganized Type	9	36	55
Paranoid Type	16	48	36
Catatonic Type	28	44	28
Alternative Dimensions:			
Acute	39	57	4
Chronic	18	38	44

Source: From Stephens, 1978, p. 38.

UNDIFFERENTIATED TYPE. Some patients exhibit all of the essential features of a Schizophrenic Disorder but do not fall into the Disorganized, Catatonic, or Paranoid Types. In such cases when individuals exhibit prominent delusions, hallucinations, incoherence, and grossly disorganized behavior, they are characterized as having a Schizophrenic Disorder of the Undifferentiated Type.

RESIDUAL TYPE. Those people who are showing symptoms attributable to a Schizophrenic Disorder but who are presently in touch with reality are characterized as Residual Type. To be classified as such, patients must show evidence of a Schizophrenic Disorder such as inappropriate affect, illogical thinking, or eccentric behavior and they must have a history of at least one previous episode of schizophrenia. The Residual Type of schizophrenia may have subclasses that indicate the duration of the illness and whether or not there is a reemergence of psychotic episodes.

The Causes of Schizophrenia: Two Theoretical Approaches

The behavior of a person with a Schizophrenic Disorder is often so disorganized that at first it seems exceedingly difficult to determine what causes such behavior. When a Disorganized Type patient sits giggling over nothing for hours on end, or a Catatonic Type remains in a stuporous state for weeks at a time, it seems that it may be impossible to trace the beginnings of schizophrenia. Let us begin our examination of the causes of schizophrenia by looking at the theoretical approaches of psychoanalysis and behaviorism.

PSYCHOANALYSIS. Freud argued that when a person exhibits a problem behavior, the person is, in fact, fixated at a particular stage of development. A person with schizophrenia, according to Freud, is fixated or stalled at the first stage of development, the oral stage. Such a person seeks intense gratification and is unable to cope with the demands of the outside world. At the oral stage of development a person is still all id; the person has not developed an ego yet and is still working on the pleasure principle. In Freud's scheme, the ego works on a "reality principle," and a person who is fixated at the oral stage has not developed an ego; thus, the person is not effectively dealing with reality.

This view of schizophrenia is consistent with other knowledge. For example, patients with schizophrenia are withdrawn and have few close social contacts, and in addition, much of their language is self-centered. These symptoms show evidence of egocentrism and self-centeredness; they are precisely the characteristics that Freud attributes to the function of the id. Freud would argue that a person who has developed a strong ego is more likely to develop a neurotic disorder rather than a Schizophrenic Disorder. Thus, the difference between a person with a neurotic disorder and a person with schizophrenia may be that the former is fixated or stalled in the advanced anal or genital stage of development, whereas the latter is fixated in the most primitive stage, the oral stage.

BEHAVIORISM.   Behaviorism accounts for schizophrenia through traditional learning principles. This approach argues that reinforcement and extinction (discussed in chapter 3) can account for many behavior patterns of patients with schizophrenia. For example, a woman may be punished for pleasurable events during her childhood such as relaxing or talking with others; she may find herself emotionally disturbed later in life when she seeks these same pleasures.

Early childhood experiences affect our later views of the world.

The process of extinction can explain much of the behavior of a person diagnosed as having Schizophrenic Disorder. In behavioral terms, continued inattention to relevant cues in the environment can bring about schizophrenic-like behavior. Consider a man who does not become involved in important events, people, and objects in the real world; he is withdrawn, is not responding to normal reinforcements, and exhibits schizophrenic-like behavior. When such behavior is exhibited, others very often reinforce it by catering to the inattentive patient. With the extinction of normal responses and the reinforcement of schizophrenic-like behavior by family and society, we have the ingredients for the learning theory explanation of schizophrenia.

Neither the psychoanalytic nor the behavioral approach seems capable of thoroughly accounting for the behavior of a person with schizophrenia. There is no vast body of literature to suggest that either theory is correct. Psychologists have spent an even greater amount of their time determining whether schizophrenia is a biologically determined or learned disorder. If schizophrenia is environmentally determined, it is important to know what factors bring it about. By knowing the extent of environmental versus biological contributions, psychologists will be better equipped to prevent and treat schizophrenia.

Nature vs. Nurture

BIOLOGICAL FACTORS: NATURE.   If biological makeup were the determining factor, the children of people diagnosed as having a Schizophrenic Disorder would likely have schizophrenia. This would mean that researchers would be able to identify some chemical or gene that a person with schizophrenia has which normal people do not have. To some extent, both of these possibilities have proved to be true: (1) high levels of certain chemicals have been found in the bloodstreams of patients with schizophrenia, and (2) the children and brothers and sisters of patients having schizophrenia are more likely to exhibit symptoms of schizophrenia than relatives of normal people.

Patients with schizophrenia constitute about 1% of the total population. If one parent has schizophrenia, the probability that an offspring will also have schizophrenia varies between 3 and 14%—significantly greater than 1%. Some studies have shown that the children of two parents with schizophrenia have about a 35% probability of developing schizophrenia (Rosenthal, 1970). Overall, studies of the families of patients with schizophrenia show that there is an increased likelihood of new occurrences if there is schizophrenia already in the family. However, families of patients with schizophrenia do not provide a conclusive case. Family members do not all have exactly the same genes; they only share a genetic heritage.

In order to find people who share exactly the same genetic heritage, researchers have to seek out identical twins. Identical twins are monozygotic, which means they come from exactly the same fertilized egg. If schizophrenia were totally genetically determined, both members of a pair of identical twins would exhibit schizophrenia. This is not the case. If one twin has schizophrenia, the probability that the other twin will also have schizophrenia varies between 0 and 86%. The probability that there will be a similarity of traits shared by the two twins is called the **concordance rate.** Thus, identical twins have concordance rates for schizophrenia of between 0 and 86%. If schizophrenia were totally genetically determined, the concordance rate would always be 100% since identical twins share exactly the same genetic heritage.

Concordance rate The percentage of occasions when two close relatives will show the same particular trait.

Schizophrenia may have nothing to do with genes, but researchers have speculated that it may be caused by the environment in which the twins are raised. Since twins are usually brought up together in the same environment, the best way to examine schizophrenia in identical twins is to have them raised by different sets of parents. A number of studies have been conducted that have attempted to examine concordance rates of twins reared separately in different adoptive homes (Heston, 1966; Rosenthal, 1970). The identical twins still share the same genetic heritage, of course, but what is the concordance rate when they are brought up in separate environments? If the concordance rate for identical twins is greater than that for fraternal twins, or brothers and sisters, then the role of genetics is important in schizophrenia. This is precisely the case. Even though brought up apart from their natural mothers and apart from each other, identical twins have a higher concordance rate than fraternal twins or control subjects (Kety et al., 1975; Rosenthal et al., 1968; Stone, 1980; Wender et al., 1974).

We cannot conclude that genetics determines schizophrenia. If genetics were the sole contributor to schizophrenia, then the concordance rate of identical twins would always be 100%. Yet these results cannot be discounted. Viewed together, the adoptive twin and family studies suggest that there must be some genetic component to schizophrenia (Kessler, 1980).

In addition to these genetic studies, other researchers have shown that there are chemicals in the bloodstream that may also contribute to the development of schizophrenia. Theories based on these studies argue that there is usually too much or too little of some type of brain substance or that there is a presence or absence of a particular type of chemical in the brain. Many different researchers have presented evidence that sites in the brain exist where there are biochemical disturbances. For example, dopamine pathways in the brain have been considered among the main sites of biochemical disturbances (Kety, 1979).

The Biological Causes of Schizophrenia

The cause or causes of schizophrenia have been researched for years; mountains of data have accumulated supporting both environmental and biological determinants of this profound emotional illness. All of the answers are not yet in, but three recent areas of research have presented some exciting and potentially important results.

To investigate whether some substance in the blood might be the cause of schizophrenia, physicians Herbert Wagemaker and Robert Cade used dialysis on patients who had schizophrenia. In this procedure, the patient's blood is purified on a kidney machine. Using dialysis, different chemicals can be removed from the blood selectively.

Wagemaker and Cade selected a group of patients who were young and showed classic symptoms of schizophrenia. All of the subjects had marked personality deterioration and frequent hospitalizations; all had been diagnosed as having schizophrenia for at least 4 years. The subjects were in dialysis once a week for a minimum of 16 weeks. The results were quite dramatic. Eighty-three percent of the subjects on dialysis no longer showed behaviors associated with schizophrenia; they no longer had hallucinations or delusions. Once socially withdrawn patients were now able to work, go to school, and have friends (Wagemaker & Cade, 1977).

The results from this study are exciting. But the researchers were cautious and recognized that their study was just a first step in analyzing the biological causes of schizophrenia. They speculated, however, that the cause of schizophrenia might be a buildup of a specific substance in a patient's bloodstream; when the substance is removed, as in dialysis, the symptoms of schizophrenia disappear. Other recent theories have suggested that dialysis removes a particular endorphin (pain killer) from the blood (Watson et al., 1979).

The subjects treated with dialysis remained normal in behavior after the study was completed. Wagemaker and Cade suggested that research using large numbers of patients and better control procedures would be important. Dialysis may not provide the ultimate answer to the cause of schizophrenia; however, carefully controlled scientific research continues into the large number of potential causes of this devastating emotional illness.

From a very different vantage point, other researchers claim that brain chemistry and the way information is transferred at the synapse holds the key to schizophrenia. For example, there is considerable evidence that the level of dopamine, a neurotransmitter in the brain, may determine schizophrenic symptoms. When people diagnosed as having a Schizophrenic Disorder are given antipsychotic drugs that decrease dopamine levels, schizophrenic symptoms are alleviated (at least to some extent). It is unlikely that dopamine alone causes schizophrenia; we know, for example, that various other neurotransmitters affect behavior directly and some, like serotonin, affect other neurotransmitters, like dopamine.

It is important to remember that just because a drug reduces symptoms of a Schizophrenic Disorder does not conclusively demonstrate that the disorder itself is primarily biological in origin (Kety, 1979). The best evidence for a biological basis to schizophrenia comes from studies of genetics. We know that there is considerable evidence to suggest genetic factors play a significant role in the development of schizophrenia. For example, the concordance rate in monozygotic (identical) twins is about five times greater than the rate in dizygotic (fraternal) twins. Furthermore, adoptive studies where children have been raised by nonbiological parents still show a higher rate of concordance (Karlsson, 1966; Kety, 1979; Kety et al., 1968, 1975; Rosenthal et al., 1968). Thus, Kety (1979) has shown that those who are genetically related to individuals with schizophrenia—even though they have been adopted—show a significantly higher rate of schizophrenia than in the population at large. These data forced Kety and his co-worker to conclude that genetics must be the fundamental cause of schizophrenia.

The studies done on genetics, particularly with adopted individuals, provide some strong support for a genetic base to schizophrenia. These data do not supersede the biochemical data on dopamine and serotonin; nor does the genetic work supersede the data presented by Wagemaker and Cade on dialysis. People diagnosed as having a Schizophrenic Disorder may pass on to their offspring problems in brain chemistry, blood chemistry, and other genetically determined traits. These three groups of studies, blood chemistry, brain chemistry, and genetics, support each other. They all argue that heredity more than environment determines schizophrenia. They do not say that environment is not important in schizophrenia. All agree that certain home environments, certain stresses, and certain family situations can facilitate the development of schizophrenia; however, they conclude that nature plays a greater role than nurture.

That the neurotransmitter *dopamine* is very important has been supported by several lines of evidence. For example, a group of drugs called *phenothiazines* seem to block the receptor sites in the dopamine pathways; when patients with schizophrenia take phenothiazines, many of their disturbed thought processes and hallucinations disappear. Conversely, drugs that stimulate the dopamine system (like amphetamines) aggravate existing Schizophrenic Disorders. Taken together, there is a fair amount of evidence to suggest that dopamine may have a particularly important role in schizophrenia, although this evidence is controversial (Griffith et al., 1972; Meltzer & Stahl, 1976; Snyder, 1974).

It is hard to deny the role of biology and chemistry in schizophrenia; the evidence is strong that there must be some kind of biological determinant or at least predisposition (Bowers, 1980). In this case, "predisposition" means that a person may be born with a tendency toward developing schizophrenia, which would increase the possibility that a problem would develop (Kety, 1979; Stone, 1980). The possible role of biological factors in schizophrenia is explained further in the Research Profile on p. 569.

ENVIRONMENTAL FACTORS: NURTURE. Many psychologists who favor an environmental view accept the idea that people with schizophrenia have difficulty maintaining attention; whether due to distractibility, anxiety, or restlessness, patients with schizophrenia have trouble concentrating and focusing attention. Of course, a person who stops attending to appropriate cues may act in strange ways, which may begin a pattern of behavior that eventually could be diagnosed as schizophrenia (Nuechterlein, 1977; Shakow, 1977).

Another learning view suggests that people diagnosed as having a Schizophrenic Disorder are likely to develop and maintain that disorder because of faulty reinforcement patterns. Thus, a person who receives a great deal of attention for behavior that others see as bizarre is likely to continue to emit those behaviors. Other reinforcement theories suggest that bizarre behavior and thoughts are reinforcing because they take patients who are suffering from acute anxiety and an overactive autonomic nervous system away from their anxiety. From this view, bizarre behavior is reinforcing because it distracts the person from pain.

An environmental point of view argues that a person's interactions with the environment determine whether or not schizophrenia will develop. Freudian psychologists argue that early childhood relationships determine whether or not a person will become fixated at the oral stage; similarly, behaviorists argue that faulty reinforcement and extinction schedules cause schizophrenia. Both theories suggest that the relationships a person has with the environment may bring about schizophrenia.

Sometimes parents say things that have two meanings. They play games with their children by saying, "No, you may not have this," while at the same time, smiling and suggesting that the child in fact may have it. A normally adjusted child realizes these differences and knows that the parent is kidding when she says no because the parent is wearing a big grin. Many parents place children in situations that offer two competing messages, and the child does not know what to do; this is called a **double bind.** In a double bind situation, the person has an intense relationship with the communicator of information. The speaker gives two competing messages at the same time, and the child does not know how to respond. Double bind situations

Double bind A situation in which a person has been given two different and inconsistent messages.

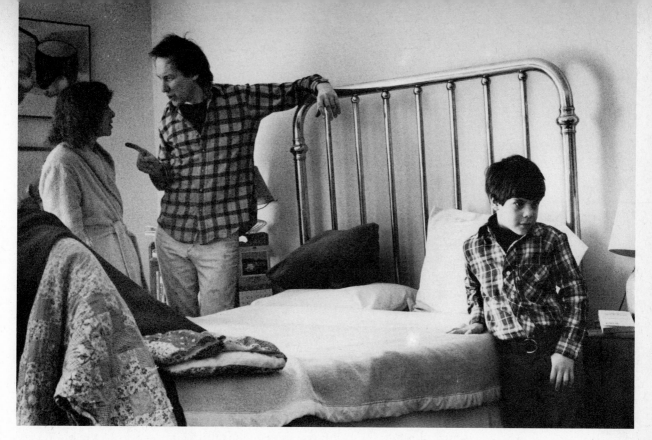

Family discord is one of the contributing factors to schizophrenia

can take place with parents and family members (Mishler & Waxler, 1968) and may thus further lead to an environment conducive to the development of schizophrenia.

One possible reason that children and adults develop schizophrenia is that the homes from which they emerge are not conducive to normal emotional growth. People who develop schizophrenia tend to grow up in families in which there is a considerable degree of conflict. Parents of patients generally show considerable strife, are often alcoholics, and have insecure emotional relationships themselves. Their homes often minimize closeness and warmth (Grant, 1975). One noted researcher, Theodore Lidz (1973), has suggested that parents of a person diagnosed as having schizophrenia may show marital schism or marital skew. *Marital schism* is characterized by continuing overt conflict between the spouses with each undercutting the worth of the other to their children; there is often competition for the loyalty of the children. In *marital skew* one parent shows abnormal (even schizophrenic-like) behavior that the other parent accepts without question. Lidz's argument is that children who grow up in homes with marital schism or skew adopt faulty views of the world and of interpersonal relationships. A child who grows up in such a home is likely to expect reinforcements for rather abnormal behaviors. In addition to parental emotional difficulty, communication between parents and their children is generally not adequate. Such families tend to show emotional immaturity and an inability to face up to difficult problems. Thus, the children of these parents have a tendency to withdraw and to grow in an emotionally fragmented environment; this environment would clearly lead these children toward emotional disorders and eventually schizophrenia.

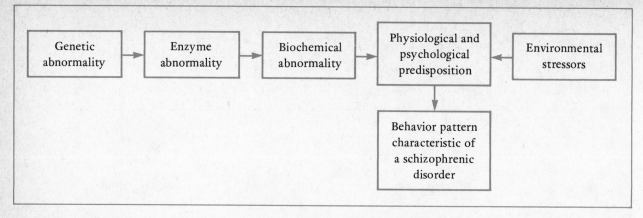

Figure 12.2 From a biological view, the environment does not create schizophrenia; rather, it triggers behaviors in persons who are predisposed to it. Thus, for those who opt for the combined view of nature and nurture, genetic abnormalities lead to situations in which environmental stressors trigger the behavioral pattern of schizophrenia

NATURE PLUS NURTURE.   Whether any single individual will develop schizophrenia is determined by many variables. Some people, either because of family, genetics, or brain chemistry, are going to be more vulnerable to developing a Schizophrenic Disorder than others. The more vulnerable one is, the less environmental stress, disorder, or anxiety might be necessary to initiate an episode of schizophrenia (Zubin & Spring, 1977).

While causes of schizophrenia are still unclear, certain facts cannot be dismissed: (1) there does seem to be a connection between genetics and schizophrenia; (2) genetics alone, however, cannot account for the development of schizophrenia; (3) specific types of chemical substances within the brain may account for the development of schizophrenia; (4) environmental factors, including double bind situations and emotionally immature families, clearly contribute to the development of schizophrenia; (5) early childhood relationships seem to weigh heavily on the environmental side of schizophrenia; and (6) the most likely cause of schizophrenia is a biological predisposition that is aggravated by a climate of emotional immaturity that does not offer communication and stability. The treatment for these disorders is complex, involving both medical and psychological components. We shall consider the psychological aspects in more detail in the next chapter.

PSYCHOSEXUAL DISORDERS

All adults have some sexual feelings or sexual relationships during their lifetime. No other single behavior seems to involve more anxiety, fear, and superstition than a person's own sexuality. Many of Freud's notions of how the personality develops revolve around sexuality. Much of modern American society is involved in the youth culture and its sexuality. Differences between people and their desires for sex and problems with impotence, frigidity, or other types of sexual inadequacies cannot be considered abnormal behavior; these are usually temporary symptoms of some other type of problem.

Sexual Deviations

When psychologists refer to sexual deviations or *Paraphilias* they are describing sexual practices directed toward objects other than people, involving real or simulated suffering or humiliation, or toward sexual activities with non-consenting partners. These categories of events represent significant sexual deviations. Many of the people who exhibit such behavior find it distasteful; still, they are unable to involve themselves in normal sexual behavior. A person faced with these unconventional choices of objects, activities, and circumstances is considered to have a **sexual deviation.** A sexual deviation is characterized as a Psychosexual Disorder when psychological problems rather than physical problems are the cause.

Some people, usually males, have the Paraphilia or sexual deviation of Fetishism. **Fetishism** is the disorder in which sexual arousal and gratification are brought about from objects rather than people. Very often the objects of gratification are shoes, underwear, or toilet articles. Instead of receiving total gratification from a woman, a man may have a fetish toward her shoes. Instead of being aroused by a woman's sexuality, he may be aroused only by her gloves or underwear. Some men have leather fetishes; leather is sexually arousing for them. While fetishism is potentially found in both men and women, males seem far more prone to fetishes than females.

A person suffers from the disorder of **Transvestism** if he or she becomes sexually aroused or receives sexual gratification from wearing the clothes and adopting the life-styles of the opposite sex. This is sometimes called *cross-dressing*. Transvestites consider themselves to be members of their own sex, and they are not necessarily homosexual in orientation. They receive sexual gratification by dressing in the clothing of the opposite sex and feel frustrated if their cross-dressing is interfered with.

Most normal people have a fairly wide range of sexual activities that bring about gratification. When a person chooses an unusual sexual activity that involves nonconsenting individuals, he or she is characterized as having a sexual deviation. For example, a person who is diagnosed as having the disorder of **Voyeurism** is a person who achieves sexual satisfaction by watching people in different states of undress or sexual activity. When a person can achieve sexual pleasure only through looking at others in some sexual state, that person is considered a voyeur with an unconventional choice of sexual activity. Voyeurs, often men, generally do not want to be seen; some researchers suggest that voyeurs enjoy the element of risk that is involved in watching a person undress or engage in sexual activity. The voyeur or "Peeping Tom" is frustrated in his normal sexual outlets and can achieve gratification only through this rather unconventional sexual behavior.

Another unconventional choice of sexual activity is the Paraphilia of Exhibitionism. **Exhibitionism** is the disorder in which adult males obtain sexual gratification primarily from exposing their genitals to involuntary observers, usually strangers. The exhibitionist achieves sexual gratification by surprising both women and children with his genitals. Often exhibitionists enjoy observing the reactions of fear, disgust, and surprise expressed by their victims. Most exhibitionists masturbate soon after a recent exhibitionistic scene because they find their exhibitionism exciting.

Some men derive sexual satisfaction through sexual contact with children. These people are diagnosed as having the sexual disorder of **Pedophilia.** A pedophile is a man who molests, fondles, or has sexual relations with a child. The personality profile of a pedophile is that of a calm, quiet person who is well acquainted with the child and is a relative. Many are married and seemingly well adjusted sexually and socially. The personality profiles of pedo-

Sexual deviations Sexual practices directed toward objects rather than people, involving real or simulated suffering or humiliation, or directed toward sexual activities with nonconsenting partners.

Fetishism The Psychosexual Disorder in which sexual arousal and gratification are brought about from objects. Very often the objects of gratification are shoes, underwear, or toilet articles.

Transvestism A Psychosexual Disorder characterized by recurrent and persistent cross-dressing for the purpose of achieving sexual excitement.

Voyeurism A Psychosexual Disorder characterized by repetitive acts of looking at people in different states of undress or sexual activity as the preferred method of achieving sexual gratification.

Exhibitionism A Psychosexual Disorder characterized by repetitive acts of exposure of the genitals to strangers as the preferred method of achieving sexual stimulation and gratification.

Pedophilia A Psychosexual Disorder characterized by repetitive acts of engaging in sexual activity with children as a preferred method of achieving sexual stimulation and gratification.

philes vary as a function of their age group. Younger pedophiles tend to have less sexual experiences; older ones generally suffer from loneliness and may even have schizophrenia (see Regestein & Reich, 1978).

Sexual Sadism A Psychosexual Disorder characterized by the infliction of physical or psychological pain in order to achieve sexual excitement.

Sexual Masochism A Psychosexual Disorder characterized by receiving the infliction of physical or psychological pain in order to achieve sexual excitement; this often includes being humiliated, bound, or beaten.

SUFFERING.   Two other major types of Paraphilias that cause bizarre behavior are **Sexual Sadism** and **Sexual Masochism.** A sexual sadist is a person who achieves sexual gratification from inflicting pain upon a sexual partner; a sexual masochist is a person who achieves sexual gratification from experiencing pain that someone else is inflicting. Sadists and masochists often experience sex together because the sadist provides pain for the masochist; thus, both are sexually satisfied. While there are some sadists who inflict pain and mutilate their partners, most sadists fantasize and achieve sexual satisfaction through their fantasies. Many normal males and females have some sadomasochistic behavior in sexual relationships. Sometimes these sadomasochistic tendencies are only fantasies; at other times, however, they are exhibited. Only when a person's sexual gratification comes *solely* or *primarily* from either sadism or masochism is he or she considered sexually deviant.

Gender Identity Disorders

Transsexualism A Gender Identity Disorder characterized by a sense of discomfort and inappropriateness about one's biological sex. This is accompanied by a wish to be rid of one's own genitals and to be a member of the opposite sex.

Another kind of Psychosexual Disorder is Transsexualism. Transsexualism is a Gender Identity Disorder rather than a sexual deviation. The essential characteristic of **Transsexualism** is a persistent discomfort about one's biological sex and a wish to live as a member of the opposite sex. The diagnosis of Transsexualism is only appropriate if the disturbance has been of more than 2 continuous years and is not due to some other maladjustment. Personality profiles of transsexuals are unclear, but transsexuals usually are not sexually experienced compared to normals (Derogatis et al., 1978). Transsexuals are persons who believe that nature has played an unfair trick on them and they are truly a member of the opposite sex. A male transsexual believes that he is a woman in a man's body. Many male transsexuals dress as women and try to adopt the life-styles of women. Increasingly many transsexuals are electing to have gender operations, usually after long periods of counseling and preparation (Lothstein, 1978). For example, a male may wish to have his penis removed, and he may take silicone injections in order to increase the size of his breasts. At the same time, this male has female hormone injections to soften many of the features of his body. Both transvestites and transsexuals wear clothes of the opposite sex. Transvestites wear these clothes because they achieve sexual gratification. Transsexuals wear the clothes because they believe that they are truly a person of the opposite sex caught in the wrong body.

THE ANTISOCIAL PERSONALITY

Some people show severe types of personality disorders and cannot be classified as clearly as those having a Psychotic Disorder or Schizophrenic Disorder, yet they have deeply ingrained, serious behavior problems. As we saw in studying personality in chapter 11, personality refers to long-standing, enduring behavioral characteristics. The Antisocial Personality is an adult person who is relatively unsocialized and whose behavior brings him or her into conflict with society. These people are incapable of loyalty to others and are selfish, callous, and irresponsible. Very often they are unable to feel guilt or learn from experience or punishment; they blame others for their behavior. People who are classified as an **Antisocial Personality** come into conflict with society because they are unwilling to conform to and live with society's rules. Rather than feel guilt or shame about not conforming with society, they do whatever they please. They are cool; they brag about their sexual exploits; and they have trouble maintaining steady employment. These persons are not psychotic; rather, they are antisocial and are characterized as smooth operators who have shallow relationships with other people (see also Schalling, 1978).

The Antisocial Personality has become an important diagnostic category because his or her behavior is likely to affect other people adversely. Unlike the person with an Anxiety Disorder or the depressed person, he is not gripped with anxiety or despair, but instead is unconcerned with both his behavior and/or society at large. Cleckley (1964, 1976) has outlined some characteristics of the Antisocial Personality that essentially portray him as a person who lacks social responsibility, insight, shame, and feelings for other people; yet, at the same time he may be sociable, engaging, and have a glossy but superficial charm (Grant, 1977).

Antisocial Personality Disorder A disorder characterized by a history of continuous and chronic behavior in which others' rights are violated. Beginning before age 15, such individuals exhibit lying, thefts, delinquency, and a general violation of rules. Such individuals come into conflict with society because of a lack of guilt and because they cannot understand others; they behave irresponsibly, do not fear punishment, and are often egocentric.

Causes of Antisocial Personality: Nature vs. Nurture

Nature-nurture is again a helpful way of describing and explaining Antisocial Personality. As in so many areas of psychology, there are those who are convinced that genetics and hereditary components determine the behavior of a person diagnosed as an Antisocial Personality; and, by contrast, others argue that the environment produces this behavior.

NATURE. Adopted children separated at birth from antisocial parents are likely to show antisocial behavior later in life (Cadoret, 1978; Schulsinger, 1972). This is hardly conclusive genetic evidence, but it is suggestive. It has also been discovered that the brain waves of people diagnosed as Antisocial Personalities show abnormal activity. This leads some researchers to suggest that the person diagnosed as an Antisocial Personality may have faulty brain mechanisms. One of the areas that shows abnormal activity is the limbic system, and psychologists know that it plays an important role in the regulation of fear-motivated behavior, including the avoidance of punishment. If the limbic system is somewhat different in the person diagnosed as having Antisocial Personality, then perhaps his or her behavior is due to some inherent or faulty physiological mechanism.

It is also possible that the nervous system of people with an Antisocial Personality is different from that of the normal. Perhaps such individuals fail to learn from experience because their autonomic nervous systems are defective (see chapter 2). Assume that the autonomic nervous system always functions at a very low level; if this were true, then few acts that such a person might commit would raise the autonomic nervous system to a higher level. When a normal person does something wrong, she exhibits the symptoms of anxiety—fear, palpitations, sweating. If a person's autonomic nervous system functions at low levels, then she will not experience anxiety. Therefore, she will not learn to associate these symptoms with antisocial behavior. There is evidence for decreased autonomic arousal in people with this disorder (Waid, 1976).

Those diagnosed as an Antisocial Personality *can* learn to avoid certain painful situations (Lykken, 1957; Schachter & Latané, 1964; Schmauk, 1970). Schachter and Latané alternately injected people diagnosed as antisocial personalities with adrenaline or a placebo. The subjects were not told what drug they were injected with. The adrenaline was administered to raise the autonomic nervous system activity and thus increase autonomic activity. When placed in a situation in which they could avoid receiving a shock, the subjects given adrenaline were able to avoid it significantly more times than when they were given the placebo. The work of Schachter and Latané lends support to the idea that people with an Antisocial Personality are relatively anxiety free and underaroused. Schachter and Latané's work shows that such patients can learn to avoid punishment.

NURTURE. A child's early life experiences may significantly affect later personality development. This is not only true from a Freudian point of view, but also from a strictly behavioral standpoint. Can the Antisocial Personality be learned? Greer (1964) found that 60% of the subjects diagnosed as Antisocial Personality he examined had lost one parent during childhood and at an earlier age than control subjects had. Many other studies have shown that the early childhood experiences of these people have been significantly different from those of normal control subjects. For example, people diagnosed as having an Antisocial Personality recall many more deviant events in their early years than others. The recollections of such individuals are quite accurate. Robins (1966) conducted a long-term study of the lives of a large number of children who were involved with a child guidance clinic during a certain period. She found that people diagnosed as having an Antisocial Personality came from unstable family environments where the father had often been so diagnosed himself and the home had been unstable. Robins's study has received considerable support (Stott & Wilson, 1977).

Both Robins (1966) and Stott and Wilson (1977) found a strong relationship between antisocial behavior in childhood and adolescence and later criminal behavior as an adult. In considering the data presented by Robins and others, psychologists conclude that child-rearing practices and unstable family situations may lead to the person with an Antisocial Personality's inability to learn fear, guilt, and punishment. While many children grow up in various family situations, the person diagnosed as having an Antisocial Personality seems to have learned faulty and maladaptive behaviors from the family situation; consequently, he or she develops inappropriate behaviors. If the environmental viewpoint is correct, the Antisocial Personality may be a learned behavior that is the result of poor experiences early in life.

DISORDERS OF INFANCY, CHILDHOOD, AND ADOLESCENCE

In infancy, childhood, and adolescence, the number of years in which a person can have experienced the environment is limited. This period of life therefore is particularly useful to psychologists in explaining the contributions of nature and nurture in various disorders. Imagine a 5-year-old who is showing symptoms of disruptive behavior and maladjustment in the classroom. Psychologists recognize that the child may have come from a home in which emotions are not easily expressed or where there are other problems of communication. At the same time, they recognize that the possible contribution of biological factors may play a particularly heavy role. A 2-year-old child who is exhibiting signs of extreme restlessness may have some type of neurological disorder. While the specific causes of a single person's disorders are difficult to determine, psychologists have studied in detail the development and course of a number of disorders that are evident in the developmental years. They are categorized separately from adult disorders; they are assigned only when the symptoms arise in the developmental years before age 19. We will examine some of the disorders with the aim of characterizing important symptoms and causes. We study these disorders to examine more closely the relative contributions of nature and nurture, recognizing that young children have had less time to have learned faulty behaviors or to have experienced maladaptive environments. Let us examine first a widely discussed disorder known by most people as hyperactivity, but more appropriately called an Attention Deficit Disorder.

Attention Deficit Disorder (Hyperactive Child Syndrome)

When a 5-year-old child fails to finish things, is easily distracted, needs lots of supervision, has difficulty staying seated, and acts before he thinks, he may be exhibiting symptoms of Attention Deficit Disorder. Often called *hyperkinetic syndrome*, a child with an **Attention Deficit Disorder** shows inappropriate inattention, impulsivity, and often hyperactivity. These children rarely seem to be able to stay seated and pay attention in a classroom setting. They make careless, impulsive errors on schoolwork and tests. They have limited attention for schoolwork and even for play activity.

Attention Deficit Disorders are often evident before the age of 3 and may disappear at puberty or continue through adolescence and adult life. The disorder appears in about 3% of children and is 10 times more common in boys than in girls. Teachers often detect Attention Deficit Disorders quickly because the school environment requires that a child exhibit attention and focusing of energy.

There are many reports in the media about the nature and causes of "hyperactivity." In some school districts, as many as 25% of the students have been classified as hyperactive, which suggests overdiagnosis. Yet, to be diagnosed by a clinician as having an Attention Deficit Disorder, a child must meet the diagnostic criteria in Table 12.9 on the next page.

Researchers have speculated on the causes of Attention Deficit Disorder for years, and many feel the influence of biology is most significant. They support their claims with the following findings: (1) children who exhibit these symptoms are more likely to have another family member with the disorder; (2) the disorder is usually evident early in a child's life; (3) parents of these children report that they were very active babies; (4) many of these children were born prematurely; (5) many exhibit certain perceptual and motor deficits; and (6) some children with the disorder exhibit more abnormalities in their electroencephalographic records (EEGs) than do normal children (Satterfield et al., 1974).

In chapter 6, Development, the treatment of this disorder was examined

Attention Deficit Disorder A Disorder of Infancy, Childhood, and Adolescence characterized by restlessness, inattention, distractibility, and overactivity that begins in children before the age of 7; also known as hyperactive syndrome or hyperkinetic syndrome.

Table 12.9 Diagnostic criteria for Attention Deficit Disorder with Hyperactivity as presented in *DSM-III* for children aged 8 to 10. The disorder must have begun before the age of 7, have a duration of at least 6 months, and not be due to schizophrenia, Affective Disorder, or severe or profound mental retardation (with minor modifications)

CHARACTERISTICS	AS EVIDENCED BY
Inattention	(At least three of the following)
	1. Often fails to finish things he or she starts
	2. Often doesn't seem to listen
	3. Easily distracted
	4. Has difficulty concentrating on tasks requiring sustained attention, such as schoolwork
	5. Has difficulty sticking to a play activity
Impulsivity	(At least three of the following)
	1. Often acts before thinking
	2. Shifts excessively from one activity to another
	3. Has difficulty organizing work (this is not due to cognitive dysfunction)
	4. Needs a lot of supervision
	5. Frequently calls out in class
	6. Has difficulty awaiting turn in games or group situations
Hyperactivity	(At least two of the following)
	1. Runs about or climbs on things excessively
	2. Has difficulty sitting still (fidgets excessively)
	3. Has difficulty staying seated
	4. Moves about excessively during sleep
	5. Is always "on the go" or acts as if "driven by a motor"

in detail (p. 272). As you probably remember, some of the treatments have focused on drugs, others on diet, and some even on drinking substances like coffee. We see that the focus of treatment is often on relieving symptoms by physical agents—again, this may suggest that the causes of the disorder are physical in origin. The most effective treatment has proved to be behavior modification programming in school and home plus medication. All the answers are not in, but the research literature is actively pursuing the question.

Particularly important for parents and educators is recognizing that labeling a child as having hyperactivity or as being "minimally brain damaged" may in itself be damaging. Even more than adults, children are susceptible to taking on behavior characteristics that others say they have. When a child is told that she is hyperactive, she is more likely to emit those behaviors; so, if she is expected to emit inattention, a child will likely be inattentive. Furthermore, once children are so labeled, we often react to them in ways that lead them to further inattention or even other types of disorders (Jones, 1977).

Conduct Disorders

Conduct Disorder A Disorder of Infancy, Childhood and Adolescence characterized by the persistent violation of others rights or violation of major age-appropriate norms. Can be classified as aggressive or nonaggressive, socialized or undersocialized. Onset is usually before the age of 13.

More serious than ordinary mischief and pranks, the acts of a child who is diagnosed as having a **Conduct Disorder** violate the basic rights of others or the norms of society. Sometimes these children are aggressive and violent;

older children with a Conduct Disorder of the aggressive type are involved in physical assault, mugging, and even rape (Stewart et al., 1980). While those diagnosed as having a Conduct Disorder of the nonaggressive type do not commit acts of aggression against people, they persist in rule breaking, truancy, or running away from home.

Children with Conduct Disorders may also be classified as socialized or undersocialized. Socialized children show attachment to other people, but may be callous and manipulative. Undersocialized children are characterized by an inability to establish a normal degree of affection with others. Undersocialized children have few friends and maintain very superficial relationships; they have few feelings about the well-being of others, and guilt and remorse are absent. So children with Conduct Disorders may be aggressive or nonaggressive, and in addition they may be characterized as socialized or undersocialized. Consider this short case history of an undersocialized aggressive Conduct Disorder presented by Coleman, Butcher, and Carson (1980):

> Craig, an eight-year-old-boy, had already established himself as a social outcast by the time he entered first grade. He had been expelled from kindergarten two times in two years for being unmanageable. His mother brought him to a mental health center at the insistence of the school when she attempted to enroll him in the first grade. Within the first week of school, Craig's quarrelsome and defiant behavior had tried the special education teacher, who was reputedly "excellent" with problem children like him, to the point that she recommended his suspension from school. His classmates likewise were completely unsympathetic to Craig, whom they viewed as a bully. At even the slightest sign or movement on his part the other children would tell the teacher that Craig was "being bad again."
>
> At home, Craig was uncontrollable. His mother and six other children lived with his domineering grandmother. Craig's mother was ineffective at disciplining or managing her children. She worked long hours as a domestic maid and "did not feel like hassling with those kids" when she got home. Her present husband, the father of the three youngest children (including Craig), had deserted the family. (p. 496)

Generally more common among boys, children who are diagnosed as having a Conduct Disorder often have school problems. For teenagers, associated problems often include unwanted pregnancies, fights, legal difficulties, and drug abuse. Extreme antisocial behavior sometimes results in institutionalization.

In contrast to children having Attention Deficit Disorder, the family background of those who exhibit symptoms of a Conduct Disorder is less stable. The family is often one of strife and discord. There are frequently separations, divorces, and stepparents. The parents themselves may exhibit symptoms of an Antisocial Personality, and they often provide harsh and inconsistent discipline. The aggressive types of Conduct Disorders are often found among children who have been institutionalized at an early age (Wolkind, 1974). Indeed, Robins (1970) suggests that, later in life, these children are likely to develop the symptoms of the Antisocial Personality described earlier in the chapter. While biological influences on Conduct Disorders are probably part of the story, there is sufficient evidence that most practitioners place the weight of the evidence for Conduct Disorder on a child's experiences at home—the environment.

Self-Starvation

Many people worry about being overweight, but some might worry too much. Perhaps you know someone who seems on the point of allowing this to develop into an unrealistic obsession. Consider the case of Marina. Like many other girls her age, Marina was concerned with her weight because she planned to make the cheerleading team. Like many of the other girls she went on a diet. This is the point at which the similarity between Marina and her friends ends. When Marina reached her weight loss goal she looked terrific; however, she continued to bring her weight down until she weighed only 74 pounds. Her eyes looked sunken; her arms and legs began to resemble sticks.

Marina believed that she was still too fat, and she continued to diet, exercise, and maintain a regimen that would bring about further weight loss. Marina was a victim of anorexia nervosa or "starvation disease." Anorexia nervosa is considered an Eating Disorder and is characterized by an obstinate and willful refusal by patients to stop losing weight. The patient's refusal to eat eventually brings about emaciation and sometimes malnutrition. This psychological disorder usually strikes young high school girls from well-educated families. As many as 40 out of every 10,000 young women may develop the disorder.

These young people maintain a distorted picture of how they look regardless of their emaciated appearance. While many researchers continue to delve into the physiological and psychological origins of anorexia nervosa, many therapists believe that the disease has strictly psychological origins. Typically, anorexia nervosa patients are hospitalized. Placed in situations where they are forced to eat, the patients are rewarded by gaining privileges at such times, for instance, as when they consume certain quantities of food. They usually undergo simultaneous psychotherapy and may need to be force-fed a liquid diet.

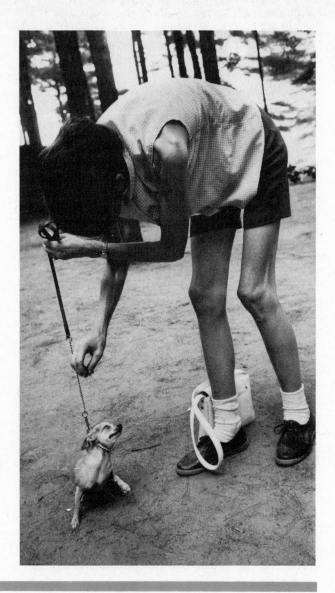

Infantile Autism A Pervasive Developmental Disorder of Infancy, Childhood, and Adolescence characterized by a lack of responsiveness to other people, gross impairment in language skills, bizarre responses to the environment, and an onset before the age of 2½; also known as early infantile autism or autism.

A Pervasive Developmental Disorder: Infantile Autism

Children diagnosed as having **Infantile Autism** show a lack of responsiveness to other people; they communicate little, if at all. They show bizarre responses to certain aspects of their world, often including a peculiar interest in, and attachment to, objects. While fairly rare, with only 2 to 4 cases per 10,000 people, Infantile Autism begins before a child is 2½.

Because Infantile Autism appears early in a child's life, it has sometimes been called Early Infantile Autism or sometimes merely Autism. Children diagnosed as autistic show a coolness and unresponsiveness to the environment. As babies they rarely if ever smile; they are not cuddly and rarely speak. In general, we say that as infants they lack a responsiveness that other normal babies show. As these infants mature physically, they do not make adequate progress in speech or in social interactions. Such children show a lack of eye contact, play, and social skills. Repetitive motions that are characterized as bizarre are apparent. Gajzago and Prior (1974) report,

> A was described as a screaming, severely disturbed child who ran around in circles making highpitched sounds for hours. He also liked to sit in boxes, under mats, and [under] blankets. He habitually piled up all furniture and bedding in the center of the room. At times he was thought deaf though he also showed extreme fear of loud noises. He refused all food except in a bottle, refused to wear clothes, chewed stones and paper, whirled himself, and spun objects. . . . He played repetitively with the same toys for months, lining things in rows, collected objects such as bottle tops, and insisted on having two of everything, one in each hand. He became extremely upset if interrupted and if the order or arrangement of things were altered. (p. 264)

Three times more common in boys than girls, Infantile Autism leaves two-thirds of its children severely handicapped and unable to lead independent lives. Only 17% eventually make adequate social adjustments and are able to do some type of work as adults. Children diagnosed as having Infantile Autism have low measured IQs; only 30% have an IQ greater than 70.

In the past, many children diagnosed as having a Pervasive Developmental Disorder were diagnosed as having childhood schizophrenia. The relationship of childhood schizophrenia to Infantile Autism is still unclear; some suggest that Infantile Autism is a precursor to schizophrenia, but others suggest that the two disorders are completely different syndromes (see Wing, 1976; 1978). *DSM-III* classifies them separately.

The causes of Infantile Autism are not well understood. Since the first clinical description of it in the 1940s, the evidence has not shown that nature or nurture is especially responsible. Initially, researchers thought that cold and unresponsive mothers were the cause (Kanner, 1943), but recent research shows that the parents of these children are quite normal (McAdoo & De-Meyer, 1978). Kanner's early research suggested that autistic children come from high socioeconomic classes; more recent research shows this is not the case (Keith et al., 1976; Ornitz & Ritvo, 1976). This issue is still not fully resolved (Cantwell, Baker, & Rutter, 1978). Some researchers have suggested that the children with Infantile Autism are not really withdrawn, but rather are choosing in an active way to manipulate their environment on their own terms—terms excluding others (Clancy & McBride, 1969; Tinbergen, 1974). The causes of Infantile Autism are not known; while there may be some biological predisposition to Infantile Autism, genetic studies have not shown this. In addition, environmental studies are equivocal. While the strongest evidence is for a physiological basis, we must unfortunately admit to knowing little about the causes of Infantile Autism (see Wing, 1976).

Unlike those with Attention Deficit Disorders or Conduct Disorders, children with Pervasive Developmental Disorders show gross distortions in development, language, perception, motor movement, and reality testing. Infantile Autism is characterized as a Pervasive Developmental Disorder because these children are affected in many areas of their psychological development at the same time and to a severe degree. Children characterized as having a Pervasive Developmental Disorder are not *late* in development;

they show a *distortion* in development. As Bettelheim (1969) has suggested, "while the schizophrenic child withdraws from the world, the autistic child fails to ever enter it" (p. 21). Treatment of these children can take place; behavioral techniques that emphasize reinforcement of positive prosocial behaviors have been effective in some cases (see Bartak, 1978; Lovaas, 1977; Ward, 1978). However, only some cases can be helped, and even then an intensive therapeutic environment is necessary.

SUMMARY

The first purpose of this chapter has been to demonstrate that a wide range of behaviors exists, from normality to abnormality. When we consider any specific behavior, we have to think of where that behavior falls relative to other behaviors. Indeed, there are many ways to look at behavior; we have examined the statistical, medical, behavioral, and legal approaches. Regardless of the specific approach used to examine a behavior, certain classes of behavior are considered abnormal by virtually every examiner.

Anxiety is the chief characteristic of Anxiety Disorders and is a generalized and unrealistic fear or apprehension. For example, people with an Obsessive-Compulsive Disorder involve themselves in many ritualistic behaviors that help them cope with their obsessions. Regardless of the specific disorder, they exhibit anxiety and fear in getting on with the business of life. Coping with life seems to be one of the principal components of normal and intelligent behavior. People with serious disorders, however, do not cope with life in an efficient manner. They are, therefore, maladjusted people.

Most people, even the maladjusted, cope with the demands of life, each to a different extent. Most are not so helpless that they have lost touch with reality. The problems of the maladjusted come with their attempts to cope with the changing environment and their own anxiety about the environment. While these people do not always maximize their potential outputs as individuals, they struggle to overcome their difficulties.

Those who suffer only from minor maladjustments have problems; however, they manage to cope. People who are psychotic are unable to deal with reality, and they fail to function adaptively. The person diagnosed as having a Schizophrenic Disorder lives in a fantasy world of strange images, delusions, and hallucinations and is certainly unable to deal effectively with even simple demands of life. A person diagnosed as having Paranoid Type schizophrenia can carry on a reasonable conversation for periods of time, yet in other periods may become totally confused. The critical difference between maladjustment and psychotic behavior, then, lies within the realm of reality testing.

People who are diagnosed as having schizophrenia have lost touch with reality; they may be unable to differentiate between behavior that is considered adaptive, purposeful, and worthwhile and that which is maladaptive, unconstructive, and often dangerous. The fantasies of the person with Paranoid Type schizophrenia hurt no one; it is only when his or her thoughts are translated into overt behavior that he may hurt himself and others. It is for precisely these reasons that the person with schizophrenia is often not hospitalized; many people who exhibit psychotic behavior never put their fantasies into action. It seems clear that thousands of people whose thought processes are severely disturbed live "normal" lives. Luckily for society, these people rarely carry their thoughts and feelings into actions.

To diagnose behavior as abnormal is not enough. As students of psychology, we must consider where each person's behavior falls relative to reality testing and abnormality. We must remember that a "significant deviation" must be a deviation not only from the norm but also from a constantly changing criterion of normality. What is considered normal behavior today would certainly have been abnormal 100 years ago. The diagnostic categories of the American Psychiatric Association that have been used in describing abnormal behavior are descriptive and clearly subject to change over time. While reality does not change over time, people's conception of normal behavior does change.

CHAPTER REVIEW

1. The statistical model argues that behavior that deviates from the average is considered abnormal.
2. The medical model states that abnormal behavior is a result of an underlying condition that causes specific symptoms.
3. The behavioral model of maladjustment assumes that all maladjusted behavior is learned.
4. The legal definition of abnormal behavior argues that a person is not considered responsible for his or her crime if it is a consequence of mental abnormality.
5. Anxiety is a generalized feeling of fear and apprehension that may or may not be connected to a particular event or object and that is often accompanied by increased physiological arousal. Generally, these fears and apprehensions are unrealistic. Symptoms include fear, apprehension, inattention, palpitations, dizziness, sweating, and chest pains.
6. Free-floating anxiety is not clearly attached to any particular object or situation; it is a form of anxiety that gives a patient a feeling of impending doom. Free-floating anxiety remains with a person almost constantly.
7. A neurotic disorder is a disorder characterized by a group of symptoms that are distressing and unacceptable to an individual. Individuals with the disorder do not violate social norms, and they are in touch with reality.
8. Major Depression is defined as a disorder characterized by loss of interest in almost all usual activities and a sad, hopeless, discouraged mood. Other symptoms include sleep disturbances, loss of energy, and feelings of unworthiness and guilt.
9. Patients who are diagnosed as having a Major Depression Disorder have a gloomy outlook on life, an especially slow thought process, and an extremely exaggerated view of present problems with a tendency to blame themselves.
10. Psychotic behavior shows a gross impairment in reality testing within an individual; this impairment usually interferes with an individual's ability to meet the ordinary demands of life.
11. The norepinephrine hypothesis suggests that there is an insufficient amount of norepinephrine at the receptor sites; this view argues that depression is caused by a lack of the substance and that if the substance level is increased, depression will be alleviated.
12. Peter Lewinsohn's view of depressed individuals is that they have few positive reinforcements in their lives; being around a depressed patient rarely makes people happy and they are unable to make the depressed patient more optimistic about his situation.
13. According to Beck, people learn to be depressed because they have negative views of the world, themselves, and their future.

14. The learned helplessness view of depression suggests that when people attribute the causes of their mistakes or failures to internal conditions about themselves and when they come to view themselves with low self-esteem and when they feel that eventual outcomes are uncontrollable, then they will develop a sense of learned helplessness.

15. A Schizophrenic Disorder is a group of disorders characterized by a lack of reality testing and by deterioration of social and intellectual functioning. It begins before age 45 and lasts for at least 6 months. Individuals with this diagnosis often show serious personality disintegration with significant changes in thought, mood, perception, and behavior.

16. Patients diagnosed as having some form of schizophrenia have problems in various aspects of their behavior, particularly with attention, emotions, and perception, as well as motor behavior.

17. The thought disorders of individuals with schizophrenia are relatively severe because the patients have delusions and hallucinations.

18. A delusion is a false belief that is inconsistent with reality and is maintained in spite of contradictory evidence.

19. People with schizophrenia exhibit inappropriate emotional responses to various situations.

20. Some patients with schizophrenia display inappropriate affect and very often their emotions are extreme or ambivalent.

21. Disorganized Type schizophrenia is a disorder characterized by hallucinations, delusions, and incoherent thought processes. The emotional behavior of people with Disorganized Type schizophrenia is often bizarre and even obscene; they often experience periods of giggling, crying, and irritability.

22. Paranoid Type schizophrenia is a disorder characterized by severe delusions of persecution and sometimes delusions of grandeur. While often coherent, people with Paranoid Type schizophrenia have strange thought processes even though their behavior is not as fragmented and incoherent as that of a person with Disorganized Type schizophrenia.

23. Catatonic Type schizophrenia is a disorder characterized by either excited or withdrawn states of behavior. The behavior may either be excessively violent motor activity or a stuporous, mute, negative state involving no interaction with the environment.

24. Both psychoanalysis and behavioral approaches have attempted to account for schizophrenia.

25. Biological studies of schizophrenia have suggested that it must be inborn, at least to some extent. This theory is supported by the concordance rate of identical twins compared with fraternal twins.

26. Many different researchers have presented evidence that sites exist in the brain where there are biochemical disturbances; for example, dopamine pathways in the brain have been considered among the main sites of biochemical disturbance.

27. It is important to remember that the fact that a drug reduces symptoms of a Schizophrenic Disorder does not conclusively demonstrate that the disorder itself is primarily biological in origin. Environmental factors (including the double bind situation) suggest that a person's home environment and early interactions in life will determine whether or not he or she will develop schizophrenia.

28. Overall, it seems that there is some genetic contribution to schizophrenia, but environmental factors seem to be important as well.

29. Sexual Deviations are sexual practices directed toward objects rather than people, involving real or simulated suffering or humiliation, or toward sexual activities with nonconsenting partners.

30. Fetishism is a disorder in which sexual arousal and gratification are brought about from objects.

31. Transvestism is a disorder in which sexual arousal and gratification are brought about from wearing the clothes and adopting the life-style of the opposite sex.

32. Exhibitionism is a disorder in which adult males obtain sexual gratification primarily from exposing their genitals to involuntary observers, usually strangers.
33. Pedophilia is a disorder in which a man molests, fondles, or has sexual relations with a child.
34. Sexual Sadism is a disorder in which sexual gratification is achieved by inflicting pain upon a sexual partner. Sexual Masochism is a disorder in which sexual gratification is achieved by receiving pain from a sexual partner.
35. Transsexualism is a Gender Identity Disorder characterized by a sense of discomfort and inappropriateness about one's biological sex. This is accompanied by a wish to be rid of one's own genitals and become a member of the opposite sex.
36. Antisocial Personality Disorder is a disorder characterized by a history of continuous and chronic behavior in violation of the rights of others. Beginning before the age 15, such individuals exhibit lying, thefts, delinquency, and a general violation of rules. Such individuals come into conflict with society because of their lack of guilt and because they cannot understand others; they behave irresponsibly, do not fear punishment, and are often egocentric.
37. The chief characteristics of individuals with an Antisocial Personality suggest that they are incorrigible and cannot learn to avoid punishment or to fear society. Yet psychological studies have shown that in some situations such individuals can be taught to fear the consequences of antisocial behavior.
38. Disorders of Infancy, Childhood, and Adolescence are categorized separately from adult disorders; they are assigned only when the symptoms arise in the developmental years before age 19.
39. A child who fails to finish things, is easily distracted, needs lots of supervision, has difficulty staying seated, and acts before he thinks may be exhibiting symptoms of Attention Deficit Disorder.
40. A Conduct Disorder is characterized by the persistent violation of the rights of others or by the violation of major age-appropriate norms. Conduct disorders are classified as aggressive or nonaggressive, socialized or undersocialized; onset is usually before the age of 13.
41. Infantile Autism is a Pervasive Developmental Disorder of Infancy, Childhood, and Adolescence characterized by a lack of responsiveness to other people, gross impairment in language skills, bizarre responses to the environment, and an onset before the age of $2\frac{1}{2}$ years. It is also known as early infantile autism or autism.

SUGGESTIONS FOR FURTHER READING

BECK, A. T. *Depression: Causes and treatment*. Philadelphia: University of Pennsylvania Press, 1967.

COLEMAN, J., BUTCHER, J. W., AND CARSON, R. C. *Abnormal psychology and modern life* (6th ed.). Glenview, IL: Scott, Foresman, 1980.

DAVISON, G. C., AND NEALE, J. M. *Abnormal psychology: An experimental clinical approach* (2nd ed.). New York: John Wiley & Sons, 1978.

Diagnostic and statistical manual of mental disorders (3rd ed.). Washington, D.C.: American Psychiatric Association, 1980.

GREEN, H. *I never promised you a rose garden*. New York: New American Library, 1971.

LAHEY, B. B., AND CIMINERO, A. R. *Maladaptive behavior: An introduction to abnormal psychology*. Glenview, IL: Scott, Foresman, 1980.

ROBINSON, N. M., AND ROBINSON, H. B. *The mentally retarded child* (2nd ed.). New York: McGraw-Hill, 1976.

SCHREIBER, F. R. *Sybil*. Chicago, IL: H. Regenery Company, 1973.

SZASZ, T. S. *The myth of mental illness: Foundations of a theory of personal conduct*. New York: Harper & Row, 1961.

WHEN PEOPLE EXHIBIT the symptoms of problem behavior discussed in chapter 12, they often seek help. The mildly maladjusted are aware of their anxiety and struggle to cope with it; the seriously disturbed and maladjusted have a more difficult time coming to grips with reality, but they are generally aware that something is wrong. Even the normal crises of life sometimes are too difficult for some people to cope with. When people reach a point where they know they need help, they may try to find it in therapy. Many types of therapy are available, but in this chapter we shall only consider therapy in which emotional disorders are treated by psychological means. The wide diversity of psychotherapies should help show that psychologists' views of people's problems determine how they will treat that problem.

CHAPTER 13

Psychotherapy

TWENTY QUESTIONS

1. Can a person who used to wear a Ban the Bomb button
   And a Free Angela Davis button
   And an Uppity Women Unite button
   And a Get Out of Viet Nam button
   Find happiness being a person with a
   Set of fondue forks, a fish poacher, and a wok?

2. Is there an economic rule that says
   No matter how much we earn and how little we spend,
   There's no such thing as getting out of hock?

3. How do I know if the time has come to
   Accept my limitations,
   Or whether I still ought to try to
   Fulfill my promise?

4. How come I'm reading articles
   With names like a Woman's Guide to Cosmetic Surgery
   More than I'm reading the poems of Dylan Thomas?

5. If I had an either/or choice
   Would I prefer to be deservedly respected,
   Or would I prefer to be mindlessly adored?

6. If we totally take the blame when our children
   Stutter and wet their beds,
   And are busted and maladjusted and drop out of school,
   Do we get to take the credit if our children
   Grow up to be brilliant, plus very nice people,
   Plus mentally healthy and chairmen of the board?

7. When, instead of vice versa,
   Did I start to pick investments over adventure,
   And clean over scenic, and comfortable over intense?

8. Why does a relationship
   Between an older woman and younger man
   Suddenly seem to make a lot of sense?

9. Why am I always buying the clothes which,
   When they first come out,
   Nothing on earth (I swear) could make me buy?

10. What are the things which,
    Even though people won't be upset (they swear)
    If I'll only admit,
    I should always deny?

11. Are some human beings
    Intellectually and emotionally incapable
    Of ever reading a road map,
    Or could I still learn to?

12. If six days a week I'm responsible
    And self-sufficient and competent and mature,
    On the seventh could I go find a womb to return to?

13. Couldn't a person who isn't expecting
    Praise for what she's doing
    At least expect some praise for not expecting it?

14. If I think that the fellow next door
    Is attempting to give me a kiss in the kitchen,
    Am I first allowed to be kissed before rejecting it?

15. How can I learn to relate to marijuana
    And bisexuality
    When I'm more at home with The Anniversary Waltz?

16. How come I've got these incredible insights
    Into all of my faults,
    And I've still got my faults?
17. Why couldn't somebody tell me
    That I haven't changed since college
    Without being practically blind or
    A terrible liar?
18. Why, since I've never had any intention
    Of going out on the streets and selling my body,
    Is it hard to be reaching an age where
    I won't find a buyer?
19. How come a charter member of NOW
    Is afraid to confess to her husband
    That the first day she drove their new car
    She dented the fender?
20. How will I ever be able to tell
    If what I achieve in life
    Ought to be called serenity—not surrender?

> *Judith Viorst*
> *How Did I Get to be 40 . . . and Other Atrocities*

People face crises in their lives at fairly predictable times. During these times, they ask themselves why they do what they do and if their lives have been meaningful. The questioning and self-doubt that Judith Viorst expresses are part of her midlife crisis. The author is questioning her ability to cope with life's situations and challenges. Her questions and self-doubts are normal. Most people have such crises at one time or another; most do not become overwhelmed by their self-doubts but sort out the important points, evaluate their situations, and go on meeting life's challenges. They cope quite well. Sometimes the self-doubt and the process of evaluation does not lead to adaptive coping behavior—instead, it leads to maladjustment, anxiety, and unhappiness. When this is the situation, many people make the very adaptive response of seeking professional help.

Consider the case of Steve, who faced a special kind of life crisis. When Steve returned home from his tour of duty in Vietnam, everyone knew that he was going to need a period of adjustment. The Vietnam war was unlike other wars, and many soldiers had had serious emotional problems adjusting to society when they came home. Steve's family was well aware of the potential problems. After 2 months of rest and rehabilitation, Steve returned home, and it seemed as if he were emotionally quite stable and making a good adjustment to civilian life.

Steve had been a good child, well behaved, polite, and liked by his peers. His grades had been good, and he had dated frequently in high school. When he was drafted into the armed services, he went somewhat reluctantly, but knowing his duty. It has always seemed that Steve was a stable young man.

Upon his return from Vietnam he was in a constant search to "get his head together." The war experience did not make Steve fall apart, but it did shake him up and remind him of some childhood emotional problems he was now unable to forget.

Steve became very anxious. He was never able to decide what he was afraid of, or why; yet, he was constantly in a state of anxiety. After being home for 4 months, Steve accepted a job with a local insurance firm. He was making a decent salary and moved out of his parents' house. On moving into his own apartment and beginning an independent life, he realized that he could no longer live with constant anxiety. He found himself becoming too concerned about small things and not worrying about important ones. He began to realize that he was spending most of his time being apprehensive and fearful. He realized that unlike his friends, or himself a few years before, he was fraught with anxiety and had few peaceful moments. This awareness of maladjustment moved Steve to the decision to seek help through psychotherapy.

Steve's goal was to get rid of his anxiety. He no longer wanted to be fearful —he wanted to be happy. He hoped that the help of a psychologist would allow him to achieve a more fulfilling life. He had never seen a psychologist and the idea of a "shrink" was somewhat frightening for him. Given the severe strain of war and the abrupt transition, Steve's reaction was not severely abnormal. He was facing problems of adjustment after a difficult experience and years away from home. Recognizing that a professional might provide the help he needed to restore himself to normal functioning in society, he made an appropriate move. Now, years later, married and with one child, Steve seems to have it all together. Well-adjusted seems a better term to describe Steve than maladjusted. He has discontinued psychotherapy, and his therapist is convinced that they have had their last visit. Steve knows that he can always go back and see his therapist, but he speaks with confidence about his ability to cope with his feelings and the world about him. Psychotherapy made the difference.

There are many types of treatment methods available to those who seek it. Severely depressed individuals often need tranquilizers, and sometimes even electroconvulsive shock therapy is warranted. People who are diagnosed as having a Schizophrenic Disorder may be in need of antipsychotic drugs; those whose disorders are less severe may seek treatments that include manipulations of their diet. Some mental health practitioners are even including physical exercise like jogging as part of a treatment program. Psychologists are most likely to focus their programs of treatment around psychotherapy. Psychologists do not rule out alternate forms of treatment for the maladjusted, because in many situations such programs are the preferred method of treatment. However, psychotherapy is the way most psychologists go about treating emotional disorders. **Psychotherapy** is the treatment of emotional disorders by any of a wide variety of psychological means. Steve sought out psychotherapy because he was unhappy with himself and hoped the therapist would help straighten him out. In general, the aim of a therapist is to help people like Steve cope with life and to achieve a more fulfilling, emotionally rewarding life-style. Each person's life situation is always changing and all of us are faced with new challenges and responsibilities. Psychotherapy often helps us to adapt to new situations and challenges we are having trouble coping with.

We learned in chapter 12 that maladjustment may occur in many people's lives for a number of reasons. Young children may suffer from Attention Deficit Disorders like hyperactivity; adolescents may be diagnosed as having a Conduct Disorder. Adults may be inflicted with any of a long list of potential

Psychotherapy The treatment of emotional disorders by psychological methods.

disorders—limited in scope, like a Simple Phobia, or profound in impact, like a Schizophrenic Disorder. When people realize that they are in need of psychological help, they or their families seek the services of a therapist or some other type of mental health practitioner. Part of the purpose of this chapter is to show the factors that are involved in choosing an appropriate psychotherapy, one that is suited to a specific individual's particular problem. The specific techniques in psychotherapy vary, depending upon the therapist's orientation to psychology. Therapists' orientations to treatment will depend on their approach to personality. As we saw in chapter 11 on personality, a psychologist can conceptualize the normal personality many different ways. These ideas shape psychologists' conceptions of abnormal behavior and its subsequent treatment through psychotherapy. Were Steve to have gone to a Freudian psychoanalyst, he surely would have been treated differently than if he had gone to a behavior therapist. A Freudian would have assumed that Steve's problems were hidden within his unconscious and have felt that these unconscious motivations must be uncovered if Steve were to understand his behavior. In contrast, a behavior therapist would have been more concerned with Steve's immediate situation and emotional problems; his goal would have been to teach Steve ways to eliminate the discomfort. When a person goes to a therapist, he or she often feels that the choices are limited and that there are few alternative ways of living. Regardless of the therapist's orientation, one of the goals of therapy will be to show the person that a choice does exist and that maladjusted ideas and behavior can be alleviated.

In general, there are two classifications of psychological treatment procedures—insight therapies and behavioral therapies. An **insight therapy** is one that tries to help patients see why they behave the way they do. Insight therapists assume that maladjustment and abnormal behavior occur because people do not adequately understand themselves, their needs, and their motivations. The goal of insight therapy, therefore, is to help a person discover these needs and motivations. A basic assumption of insight therapy is that once people are aware of their motivations, their behavior will almost automatically change and become more adaptive. Insight therapists have strong commitments to helping individuals see relationships between underlying motivation and current behavior. The focus of insight therapy is to treat the cause of the behavior, not the specific abnormal symptom.

Behavior therapy is dramatically different from insight therapy in its approach to treatment. Sometimes called behavior modification, **behavior therapy** is a treatment approach by which therapists try to change maladjusted and abnormal behavior using methods studied by experimental psychologists in their study of normal behavior. These therapists have examined closely the nature of learning (see chapter 3). Behavior therapists assume that most behavior is learned; therefore, abnormal behavior and maladjustment are seen as a set of faulty behaviors that have been learned. Insight is not necessary for behavior change, and concepts such as unconscious motivation are ignored. Current behavior is the focus of treatment. Behavior therapists treat people by having them first unlearn old, faulty behaviors and then learn new behaviors.

Whether insight therapy or behavior therapy is used, changes in a person's behavior do not just happen. There are some important basic ingredients to therapeutic change, regardless of the procedure employed. *First,* therapists must demonstrate respect, interest, understanding, tact, maturity,

Insight therapy A therapy which attempts to show a patient a meaningful relationship between possibly unconscious motivation and current maladjustments or abnormal behavior. Insight therapy assumes that abnormal behavior is caused by an individual's failure to understand motivations and needs. Once insight is achieved, behavior should change almost automatically.

Behavior therapy A therapy based on the application of learning principles, such as classical and instrumental conditioning, which changes people's overt behavior rather than their subjective feelings, unconscious processes, or motivations; synonymous with behavior modification.

Behavior therapy

Insight therapy

Both behavior and insight therapy use different techniques to help people function more effectively

Placebo effect A nonspecific therapeutic change that comes about primarily because a person expects change rather than because of any specified treatment given by a therapist.

and an ability to help. *Second,* by maintaining a helping relationship, a therapist can influence a patient through suggestion, encouragement, interpretation, and by setting examples and manipulating rewards. *Third,* a patient must have the capacity and willingness to profit from treatment. Behavior change does not come about just because a person wants to be happy. A person needs to want to change and be willing to go through some alterations in life-style and ideas. A therapist who is knowledgeable, accepting, and objective will facilitate behavior change, but the patient must always make the changes himself (Garfield, 1973; Strupp, 1973).

A factor common to both insight therapy and behavior therapy is that each has placebo effects. **Placebo effects** are changes in behavior during psychotherapy that take place because of a person's expectations of change, rather than as a result of any specific treatment given by a therapist. Physicians have found that giving people sugar pills and telling them that the pills are strong medicine will help relieve many problems. In much the same way, people show relief of symptoms just because they have sought out psychotherapy. Of course, the placebo effects in psychotherapy are usually transient, and any long-lasting therapeutic effects are due to the therapy itself. Still, we must recognize that for some people, the attention of a therapist and the chance to express their feelings to another person can be therapeutic; these therapeutic effects may have nothing to do with the therapist's treatment program. Let us now consider the actual effectiveness of treatment programs.

EFFECTIVENESS OF PSYCHOTHERAPY

Psychotherapists bear the brunt of many jokes in which people suggest that their therapy is only costing them money and has brought about no changes. People who make jokes are implying that they would probably show a relief from their symptoms on their own without psychotherapy. Ever since 1952, the effectiveness of psychotherapy has been carefully scrutinized. In that year, an important study was published by Eysenck which challenged the effectiveness of psychotherapy and claimed that psychotherapy produced no greater changes in maladjusted individuals than did naturally occurring life experiences. Over the last 30 years, an enormous amount of effort has been expended in responding to Eysenck's claim (Bergin & Lambert, 1978; Erwin, 1980).

While hundreds of studies have been done to evaluate the effectiveness of psychotherapy, perhaps the most important to date was a fairly recent one by Smith and Glass (1977). Using sophisticated techniques, they analyzed data and presented convincing evidence for the effectiveness of psychotherapy. This study examined volumes of data on the outcome of different kinds of therapy and argued strongly that a client in therapy is far better off than an untreated individual. Other studies have made similar claims, and all support the general notion that psychotherapy is very effective (Emrick, 1975; Luborsky, Singer & Luborsky, 1975). Psychotherapeutic effectiveness varies greatly and depends upon the disorder being treated. For example, treatment of specific phobias may have a high success rate, but psychotherapy is less successful for Schizophrenic Disorders. There are, of course, many variables that will affect the outcome of psychotherapy. Perhaps one of the most important is the characteristics that the therapist brings to the therapy setting, such as the therapist's personality, sex, level of experience, or empathy (e.g., Gurman & Razin, 1977); it is also well known that client variables, such as social class, age, education, therapeutic expectations, and level of anxiety are also very important (e.g., Berzins et al., 1975; Luborsky et al., 1980).

The data and techniques used by Smith and Glass (1977) have not gone unnoticed and many have challenged their results. However, taken together, most psychologists are convinced of the effectiveness of psychotherapy. Comedians may continue to tease the "shrink," but patients are functioning more effectively because of therapy.

INSIGHT THERAPY

There is a wide range of insight therapies, yet each has as its goal helping people understand their behavior and motivation. We noted before how insight therapy assumes that abnormal behavior is caused by individuals' lack of understanding of their motivations. Underlying all insight therapies is the assumption that specific abnormal behaviors are symptoms of underlying problems. It is through understanding underlying motivations, goals, and conflicts that the abnormal behavior is treated. Insight therapies often help people restructure their personalities, reshaping them to a more adaptive personal life-style.

Psychoanalysis

Classical Freudian **psychoanalysis** is an insight therapy that teaches patients to discover the true motivation for their behavior. The focus is an uncovering of unconscious motivations that can lead to conflict and maladaptive behavior. Psychoanalysis, as a Freudian method of treatment, is practiced by a psychoanalyst. A psychoanalyst is an individual who is specifically trained in psychoanalysis (usually at an institute). In fact, most clinical psychologists

Psychoanalysis The therapeutic system developed by Freud by which insight into a person's true motivation is obtained via certain special techniques, including free association, dream analysis, and transference. A lengthy insight therapy, it assumes human beings are basically in conflict.

who are insight-oriented are *not* psychoanalysts. However, many therapists use a *psychodynamically* based therapy which is loosely connected or rooted in Freudian theory. A person must be financially secure to go through psychoanalysis. Typically, psychoanalysis involves meeting with the therapist 5 days a week for an hour per day for approximately 5 years. A therapist charges by the hour; so a 5-year psychoanalysis might easily cost as much as $50,000!

Not everyone should go through psychoanalysis. Psychoanalysis is a difficult process, and people must intensely desire to find their true motivations. In psychoanalysis one works through many problems and, therefore, needs to be intelligent and highly motivated. Many people who seek therapy are not motivated enough to work through psychoanalysis; others who might find help through other therapies lack the ability to achieve insight into complicated relationships. Because there must be compatibility between the patient and the therapist, in the first sessions of psychoanalysis a patient and therapist should decide if they feel comfortable with each other. This compatibility is important because psychoanalysis is built upon a relationship between the therapist and the patient.

GOALS OF THERAPY. When a patient comes to a psychoanalyst for help, she is asking the therapist to help her discover her conflicts and to help her cope with them. According to Freud, the troubled patient has symptoms because of unconscious conflicting thoughts and feelings directing behavior. When a person shows an imbalance among id, ego, and superego (see p. 501) then conflict and maladjustment are likely to develop. Of course, a person is not directly aware of these conflicts—they are unconscious. These unconscious feelings direct behavior; only when a person becomes aware of these forces, these unconscious motivations, can behavior change. The goal of psychoanalysis is to help a patient understand her unconscious motivations and, thereby, her behavior. This is done by restoring a balance among competitive forces. The methods of psychoanalysis allow a person to be aware of her own motivation so that she can evaluate reality and choose an effective, logical, and reasonable plan for living. Psychoanalysis tries to make people aware of their feelings rather than letting them live in a repressed emotional world.

TECHNIQUES. When a person comes to a psychoanalyst for help, he must be prepared to talk about his feelings and ideas with the therapist. Many of the techniques used in psychoanalysis involve having the patient report previous events in his life or remember painful, difficult experiences in childhood. Since Freud believed that current behaviors are initiated because of unconscious urges or instincts, the therapist tries to uncover those urges. By helping the patient see how these urges and the conflicts initiate abnormal behavior, insight is achieved and the process of reeducating the patient begins. Each psychoanalyst has a favorite technique to help a patient reach an awareness of unconscious motivation, but there are some traditional ones that are frequently used. For example, in traditional psychoanalysis a patient lies down on a couch with the therapist out of view. Through this arrangement a patient can be more relaxed and less threatened by the authority figure presented by the therapist. The couch is used in psychoanalytic therapy, but rarely in other kinds of therapy.

Goals of therapy—Freudian approach: The troubled patient has thoughts and feelings which he is unaware of that direct his behavior. The therapist helps him discover and cope with them

One of the major techniques of psychoanalysis is free association. In **free association** the patient is told to speak out loud any and all thoughts that come to him. Regardless of how trivial or meaningless any thought might be, the patient is told to tell the therapist whatever comes to mind. A therapist might say to a patient,

> I can help you best if you say whatever thoughts and feelings come to your mind, even if they seem irrelevant, immaterial, foolish, embarrassing, upsetting, or even if they're about me, even very personally, just as they come, without censoring or editing. (Lewin, 1970, p. 67)

The idea is for the patient to recognize connections among his thought patterns. One of the most difficult aspects of free association is that patients tend to delete thoughts, memories, or images that they feel might be shameful, embarrassing, or difficult to talk about. However, a patient who is working hard at psychoanalysis will try not to delete any feelings.

Free association A technique of psychoanalysis in which persons speak out loud all those thoughts and feelings that occur to them, however illogical their order or content.

In traditional Freudian therapy, the psychoanalyst often sits out of view of the relaxed patient

Dream analysis — interpretation

Client-centered — nondirective

Dream analysis is often a part of psychoanalysis; it is not considered typical of nondirective client-centered therapy

Dream analysis A psychoanalytic technique of interpreting a patient's dreams to gain insight into the patient's motivation.

Resistance In psychoanalysis, the uncooperativeness by which a patient shows unwillingness to understand situations, interpret them, provide information about them to the therapist, or use other traditional techniques.

Another technique of psychoanalysis is dream analysis, which is based on Freud's assumption that dreams represent the unconscious trying to burst into reality. In **dream analysis** a patient is asked to tell the therapist about his dreams in detail. The patient is encouraged to dream, to remember his dreams, and to report them to the therapist. The goal of the technique is for the patient to realize the meaning of his dreams with the help of a therapist.

Both free association and dream analysis involve an important component of psychoanalysis, and this is the aspect of *interpretation*. An analyst tries to interpret a patient's thoughts, feelings, and behavior. The analyst tries to find a common thread in a patient's behavior that shows motivation. Assume that a patient becomes nervous and jittery every time he speaks about women. The therapist may conclude that early in life the patient may have had trouble with women, perhaps his mother. He may, therefore, wish to explore the patient's attitudes and feelings about his mother more fully. The analyst hopes that this may provide a clue to the patient's unconscious motivation.

Very often patients exhibit **resistance** or unwillingness to interpret situations, understand them, or cooperate with the therapist. Sometimes patients become belligerent and difficult. This usually means that a highly emotional topic or turning point is being approached. To help minimize resistance, therapists try to be very accepting of the patient's behavior. When a therapist is thoroughly accepting of a patient's feelings and behavior, the patient is more likely to explain, describe, and be thorough in the accounts of his or her feelings. An objective and knowledgeable therapist can then provide the most effective treatment for the patient. Consider this interaction where a patient who is a married woman is aware of her resistance but unaware of why she is being resistant:

THERAPIST: I wonder what the long silences mean.

PATIENT: Nothing comes to my mind, that's all. I kind of wish the time was up.

THERAPIST: Perhaps you are afraid to bring up certain things today.

PATIENT: Like what?

THERAPIST: Well, is there any event that happened since I saw you that you have not mentioned to me?

PATIENT: (silence) Yes, there was. I met a man last Wednesday who sent me. I made a big play for him and am going to see him Sunday.

THERAPIST: I see.

PATIENT: I have wondered why I did this. I realized you wouldn't tell me not to, but I feel guilty about it.

THERAPIST: Was that the reason why you were silent?

PATIENT: (laughing) Honestly, I thought there wasn't much to talk about. I minimized the importance of this thing. But I realize now that I didn't want to tell you about it.

THERAPIST: What did you think my reaction would be?

PATIENT: (laughs) I guess I thought you'd think I was hopeless or that you'd scold me. (Wohlberg, 1977, p. 618)

One of the traditional aspects of psychoanalysis begins to appear when a patient realizes that the therapist is thoroughly accepting of his or her behavior; by accepting the patient's behavior, the psychoanalyst facilitates transference. In **transference** patients act toward the therapist in an emotionally charged, often unrealistic manner; patients transfer previous feelings about others (especially their parents) to the therapist. When the therapist allows the patient to transfer these feelings, he or she is allowing the patient to work through these feelings. The patient may act toward the therapist the way he might have acted toward his father. The opportunity to explore his feelings often dramatically helps the patient because the therapist does not allow the process of transference to take place unguided. The psychoanalyst is in a position to direct or guide the patient to allow certain potentially repressed feelings to emerge. Later, the therapist has the chance to call the patient's attention to these expressions of hostility or love so as to help the patient gain some insight into his behavior and underlying problems.

Transference A psychoanalytic procedure during which a therapist becomes the object of a patient's emotional attitudes about others. The patient often develops love or hate feelings toward the therapist that he or she might have for a parent.

EGO-PSYCHOLOGISTS.   A group of psychoanalysts who are often referred to as **ego-analysts** or ego-psychologists have attempted to change some of Freud's basic ideas about psychoanalysis. As they have become more sophisticated, they have tried to modify psychoanalysis to the greater benefit of their patients. These ego-psychologists assume that psychoanalysis is the appropriate way to bring the patient to emotional health; however, they place more emphasis on the patient's ability to control the environment and to determine the time and the way that certain instinctual drives will be satisfied. Rather than assuming that people are pushed and pulled by unconscious and competing urges, ego-psychologists assume that people have control over when they will allow their biological urges to erupt. Because ego-psychologists pay attention to adaptive behavior, they have adopted a therapy style that tries to enhance a person's ego control. The goal of the ego-psychologist is to help patients develop a stronger and more organized control of their egos. As noted in chapter 11 on personality, the ego in Freud's theory is that part of the structure of personality which works on the reality principle and tries to control behavior by responding to the demands of the environment.
Ego-psychologists still work within a psychoanalytic framework. The dif-

Ego-analysts Followers of Freud who argue that the ego has greater control over behavior than Freud suggested. This therapy technique is more concerned with reality testing and control over the environment.

ference between the ego-psychologist and the traditional Freudian therapist is that the ego-psychologist tries to stress adaptive control by the ego over the id and demands of the superego. Traditional psychoanalysis has a similar goal, but focuses more upon *understanding* the unconscious material in the id and superego and, through therapy, increasing the amount of ego control.

EFFECTIVENESS.   Because psychoanalytic treatment is so costly and time consuming, one of the most frequently asked questions is the extent to which it is effective. While there are only a limited number of research studies done which make appropriate comparisons (in fact only about five) results show that psychoanalysis is as effective as other therapies (Luborsky & Spence, 1978). However, psychoanalysis has not been shown to be more effective than other types of therapy (Fisher & Greenberg, 1977). One important finding about patients who entered psychoanalysis was that those who entered with a higher level of anxiety showed greater overall improvement at the end of their therapy (Burstein et al., 1972; Kernberg et al., 1972; Luborsky et al., 1971) and that younger patients improved more than older ones (Hamburg et al., 1967). Taken together, we see that psychoanalysis is an effective therapy; however, it is more effective for some patients than others.

Client-Centered Therapy

Client-centered therapy An insight therapy developed by Carl Rogers which seeks to help persons evaluate the world and themselves from their own vantage points so that they can become everything that they are capable of. The principal therapeutic technique uses a nondirective emotionally therapeutic environment in which a therapist provides unconditional positive regard.

If Steve, our Vietnam veteran, had sought therapy in psychoanalysis, his treatment would have been lengthy, expensive, and might have focused on painful early childhood experiences. Had he sought out Carl Rogers or another client-centered therapist, he would have been exposed to a very different treatment procedure. The **client-centered therapy** of Carl Rogers is also an insight therapy, but it is based on different assumptions from those of psychoanalysis. Client-centered therapy is not focused on resolving inner conflicts that result from inborn competing forces; rather, it assumes that people have a considerable amount of choice and free will in determining their behavior. To understand client-centered therapy, one has to realize that Rogers makes some basic assumptions about people that have helped shape his treatment approach. These assumptions differ significantly from a Freudian view (Ford & Urban, 1963; Rogers, 1951, 1959, 1961):

1. A client's behavior can only be understood from the client's vantage point. Very often clients have misconstrued events in the world, and we, as therapists, have to understand how the client sees these events.
2. A healthy person is aware of all of his behavior and he chooses his behavior patterns.
3. People are innately good and effective in dealing with the environment.
4. Behavior is purposeful and goal directed.
5. Effective therapy only takes place when a client manipulates his own behavior, not when the therapist manipulates it.

GOALS OF THERAPY.   It is important to recall that Rogers's basic theme is that people have an innate tendency to actualize themselves and realize their potential. As noted in chapter 11, Rogers conceived the structure of personality as being the *self*, with each person always trying to move toward a more

Goals of therapy—Client-centered approach: The client has the potential to achieve and actualize. The purpose of therapy is to release an already existing capacity in a potentially competent individual

ideal self. It is through the process of self-actualization that a person develops and matures into a fulfilled self-actualized individual. When a person comes to a therapist for help, she is asking the therapist to help her achieve self-actualization and form a strong self-concept. The understanding of her self will be one focus of therapy, because a person needs to be able to evaluate herself and the world around her. One of the primary goals of client-centered therapy is self-understanding; this is set in sharp contrast to Freudian goals of understanding unconscious motivations and gaining control over competing forces within the unconscious.

When a person comes for therapy, the therapist does not provide a cure; rather, the therapist helps the person gain perspective. Therapy never cures, but rather it helps the person learn to adapt to an ever-changing world. Rogers assumes that the client has the potential to achieve and to actualize; he says that the purpose of psychotherapy is to "release an already existing capacity in a potentially competent individual." Rogers's view of people assumes that we are always changing and adapting; the goal of his therapy is to help people make these constant changes.

There is a sharp division between the insight therapies of Freud and Rogers. Freud saw humans as inherently selfish and hedonistic beings who must learn to rechannel aggressive and sexual urges. Rogers, on the other hand, saw human nature as basically good, competent, and potentially compatible with society. So for Rogerian therapists, problem behaviors occur when there is insufficient warmth in the environment to allow the person's natural potential to actualize.

TECHNIQUES. According to Rogers, a person who comes for therapy is a client who is seeking to find himself, not a patient who is sick, needing medicine or a cure. Client-centered therapy is nondirective. A **nondirective therapy** is one in which the therapist does not direct the client but rather facilitates the client's search for growth. In client-centered therapy the therapist is not seen as an omniscient source of authority; it is not the therapist's values,

Nondirective therapy A form of therapy in which the client plays the active role and determines the direction of therapy. The therapist is permissive, almost passive, and totally accepting of feelings and behavior.

opinions, and feelings that count—it is the client's feelings. Remember, Rogers feels that the therapist must consider a client and his or her emotional health from the client's vantage point. Even the choice of the word "client" rather than "patient" is critical in Rogers's approach to therapy.

One of the key points of client-centered therapy is that it is nondirective; in contrast, psychoanalytic therapy is much more directive. In client-centered therapy a person learns to evaluate himself and the world around him with little interpretation by the therapist; it is the client who has to evaluate the world from his own vantage point. In psychoanalytic treatment, however, the therapist interprets the behavior and feelings of the patient. The therapist directs the patient's "cure" and helps him understand his behavior.

One of the basic techniques of client-centered therapy is that the therapist be a warm accepting person who projects unconditional positive feelings toward the client. The therapist fully accepts and recognizes the emotional feelings of the client and encourages her to discuss her feelings. Many people in the life of the client have been negative and unaccepting; many people have taught her that she is bad or unlikable. This is not true of the therapist. The client-centered therapist is always trying to show unconditional respect and positive regard for the client. Regardless of what the client might have said or done in the past or present, the therapist tries to convey the attitude that the client is genuinely a warm human being whose actions and attitudes will not be condemned by the therapist. She must communicate to the client that she understands what the client is saying and feeling. To this end she often reflects back to the client the client's own thoughts. This not only allows the client to rehear what he or she has just said, but allows the therapist to show the client that she heard and understood the client's feelings and needs. For Rogers, this quality of *empathic understanding* is an important part of the therapeutic relationship. In Carl Rogers's own words:

> The more the client perceives the therapist as real or genuine, as empathic, as having an unconditional regard for him, the more the client will move away from a static, unfeeling, fixed, impersonal type of functioning and the more he will move toward a way of functioning which is marked by a fluid, changing, acceptant experiencing of differential personal feelings. (Rogers, 1961)

In client-centered therapy a person learns to reevaluate the world within a new frame of reference: toward an understanding of himself. If a therapist were to provide advice or information, then a client might take on the therapist's point of view, but in Rogerian therapy the client must adopt his own point of view. Although client-centered therapists are nondirective in approach, they must be highly trained to help guide a client. Such guidance may be achieved by a bodily movement as slight as a nod or small gesture that may help the client stay on the right track. It is usually quite obvious to a therapist where a patient's faulty set of behaviors or attitudes lies. For example, a man may have developed a low self-esteem and undervalue his life's achievements. So, by asking the right questions, or responding with an exclamation of "Oh" or "Ah, hum," a therapist can subtly and importantly guide the areas a client explores.

Both the therapist and the client are at work; they face each other and generally sit in chairs or at a desk. A concentrated atmosphere, rather than a relaxed one, is maintained and questions are kept to a minimum because the client does most of the talking. The therapist pays close attention to everything the client says and does.

Rogerian therapy involves a forthright exchange between client and therapist with both members actively working on a specific situation or problem

According to Rogers, as weeks pass, the clients come to express themselves more clearly, and can understand where they learned faulty sets of behaviors. Initially, it is likely that clients will express attitudes and ideas adopted from others. Thus, a woman who feels pressure to conform might say, "I should be successful in my courses"; she implies because my parents count on my success. She might say, "I should always be a loving mother"; again, implied is that any other attitude is unacceptable in her middle-class group. As therapy progresses and the person begins to evaluate the world from her frame of reference, she tries to behave as she wants to, rather than how she thinks others want her to. Later, her statements may be "I should be successful in my courses only if they have long-range meaning to me" or "I should be a loving mother when I feel that way, but I need not be fearful of other attitudes when they exist." As therapy progresses and the client feels an empathic understanding from the therapist, it is usual for her to move from using other people's ideas toward using her own (Rogers, 1951, p. 149). She begins to talk about herself in a more positive way, and, as a result of this new attitude, more positive actions occur. The client will thus feel better about herself and eventually will suggest to the therapist that she knows how to deal with the world. Both the therapist and the client realize that therapy has helped the client develop positive regard and has allowed her to cope with and understand her own behavior.

Research in client-centered therapy has been very active. Researchers have been especially concerned about the best responses a therapist can make to a client's statements. Client-centered therapists' remarks can be broadly classified into three types: those that *reflect* the client's feelings, those that *restate* the client's feelings, and remarks that question or *probe* for more information. These techniques are widely used by psychoanalytically oriented psychologists, Gestalt therapists, and by behavioral therapists. To investigate which of these verbal remarks work best, Clara Hill and James Gormally at the University of Maryland examined reflections, restatements, and probes with a group of 24 male and 24 female subjects (Hill & Gormally, 1977).

Volunteer subjects who requested counseling were each seen by the therapist for half-hour sessions. During this time, the counselors used one of the three verbalizations. In *reflection*, the counselor reflected the subjects' overt feelings by saying, for example, "You feel angry because your father does not support you anymore." In *probe* conditions, the counselor might say "How do you feel about your father not supporting you anymore?" In the *restatement* condition the counselor might just restate the client's remark by saying "Your father doesn't support you anymore."

The dependent variable in this study was the number of times the clients talked about their feelings. The researchers had hypothesized that perhaps *probes* would be more effective than *restatements* or *reflections* in eliciting feelings. The results showed that *probes* resulted in more discussion of feelings than either *reflections* or *restatements*. This does not mean that therapy should consist entirely of *probe* type statements. However, Hill and Gormally do suggest that it may be a better or more effective technique in an initial therapy session.

Studies like this one are particularly important because they help isolate the important characteristics of therapy and therapists. While this specific study was limited because of the small number of subjects used, the limited

Table 13.1 Summary table of insight therapies

TYPE OF THERAPY	GOAL	TECHNIQUES
Psychoanalysis	To discover conflicts; to uncover instinctual repressed urges; to show how instinctual urges control current behavior.	A directive therapy in which the analyst takes an active role in interpreting the dreams and free associations of patients; transference is a critical component.
Client-centered	To help people gain perspective so as to adapt and to self-actualize and fulfill their potential as individuals.	A nondirective therapy in which the client analyzes his own behavior from the client's own vantage point; therapeutic environment is totally accepting, with therapist providing unconditional positive regard.
Gestalt therapy	To expand awareness of the here and now so as to resume natural functioning.	Patient is asked to see the world from a different perspective; patient uses different language and focuses on current situations rather than past ones.

time each subject was seen in therapy, and the number of dependent variables, this research is a serious attempt at isolating important characteristics of the client-centered therapeutic situation.

Gestalt Therapy

Gestalt therapy An insight therapy founded by F. S. Perls which emphasizes the "how" and "what" of behavior, stressing the importance of a person's getting in touch with his or her feelings in the present. Therapy is the process of becoming aware.

Gestalt therapy is an insight therapy, but it is dramatically different from both psychoanalysis and client-centered therapy. Frederick S. Perls (1893–1970) was the founder and principal proponent of Gestalt therapy. Perls was a physician and psychoanalyst who was trained in Europe; he later came to the United States but was generally considered an outcast by the psychoanalytic community. Perls adopted a different approach to the treatment of patients in his form of analysis; instead of stressing the "why" of behavior, Perls stressed the "how" and the "what."

The fundamental concept of Gestalt therapy centers on a patient's understanding and awareness of the world. According to Perls, if a patient understood and was fully aware of the immediate here and now, he or she would cope better. The immediate here and now is composed of all aspects of a person's situation (Latner, 1973). So while seeking insight into his or her behavior, a patient should be concerned with the immediate situation and immediate problems, not those of the past.

GOALS OF THERAPY. The goal of Gestalt therapy is to expand the patient's awareness so that natural functioning can resume; by understanding the present, a person enlarges himself and comes closer to reality, thereby shunning delusions or unrealistic expectations. Only when a client is aware of the here and now can he become sensitive to previous tensions and repressions that have made his behavior maladaptive. Having become aware of the

Goals of therapy—Gestalt approach: The therapist hopes to expand the patient's awareness so that natural functioning can resume; by understanding the present, a person enlarges himself and comes closer to reality

present and having accepted himself, the patient can explain earlier behavior and plan future appropriate behaviors. But when a person is not fully aware of the events taking place around him, of the here and now, he feels weak and divided, fraught with tension, and consumed by defenses and unrealities. Fears and anxiety cloud perceptions of reality. It is through an understanding of the total situation within which a person finds himself a legitimate part that he can come to grips with potential problems.

TECHNIQUES.   As with other therapies, Gestalt therapy is conducted in many ways. Since the aim of Gestalt therapy is to make people aware of their present feelings and activities, many techniques have been devised to help a patient become aware of the here and now. For example, one technique is to have a patient change the way she talks about the world. A patient may be asked to talk about feelings or emotions as if the feelings belonged to another person. Alternatively, a patient may be asked to behave in the opposite way to the way she feels. A person who feels hostile or aggressive toward her boss might be asked to play act as if she were warm and affectionate in her relationship with her employer. The aim of having a patient use different types of language and deal with different situations in different ways is to have her come in touch with her feelings.

The techniques a Gestalt therapist uses are designed to help a patient develop appropriate emotional expressions to *current* situations. When a person has experienced a difficult situation in the past, she is asked to concentrate on her feelings about it now. Feelings expressed in the present can be dealt with. Thus, a therapist might ask a patient to relive a situation and discuss it as if it were happening at the present time; when a patient does this, she often can deal with her emotions and understand why she feels the way she does.

From Perls's point of view, many people with maladjustments and anxiety have become very adept at avoiding anxiety and other unpleasant experiences. By forcing the patient to deal with unpleasant experiences in a therapy

T.A.: Doing OK

One of the most widely read selfhelp books in the last two decades has been an appealing book called I'm OK—You're OK. *While the scientific community is still researching the approach and waiting to pass judgment, people are flocking to lectures, workshops, and seminars where the fundamentals are taught. The approach stresses the positive side of human behavior and has wide appeal. There is no emphasis on aggressiveness, sex, or deep mystical insight, but a focus on common sense positive feelings.*

TIME In the 1960s it was encounter groups. In the 1970s it is transactional analysis, or T.A., the pop-psychological path to happiness charted by Sacramento Psychiatrist Thomas A. Harris in his bestseller *I'm OK—You're OK.* T.A., or close facsimiles of it, is now practiced by some 3,000 psychiatrists, psychologists, social workers and ministers in the U.S. and fourteen foreign countries. In fact, it may be the most widely used and fastest-growing form of treatment for emotional distress in the world. . . .

The central thesis of T.A., as Harris teaches it, stems from Psychiatrist Alfred Adler's concept of a universal "inferiority feeling." Most people, Harris says, never stop thinking of themselves as helpless children overwhelmed by the power of adults. For that reason they go through life believing that they are inferior, or "not OK," while they view everyone else as superior, or "OK." The aim of T.A. Therapy is to instill the conviction that "I'm OK—you're OK," meaning that no one is really a threat to anyone else and that in the end everything comes up roses.

More specifically, transactional analysts believe that what makes a person unhappy is an unbalanced relationship between the three parts that constitute every human personality: Parent, Adult, and Child. Harris rejects any suggestions that these are the equivalent of Freud's superego, ego, and id. "The Parent, Adult and Child are real things that can be validated," he insists. "We're talking about real people, real times and real events, as recorded in the brain." Be that as it may, the theory is that unless the mature, rational Adult dominates the personality, or, in the language of T.A., is "plugged in," the overly restrictive Parent and the primitive, self-deprecating Child will foul up most "transactions," or relationships with others.

To put his Adult in charge, Harris says, the troubled person must "learn the language of transactional analysis and use it in examining his everyday transactions." He must also learn to diagram these transactions, using three circles to represent the personality components of each person and drawing arrows to show how two people interact. Parallel lines depict "complementary transactions," which occur, for instance, when a husband's Adult speaks to his wife's Adult and gets a response in kind. In that type of exchange, the husband might ask, "Where are my cuff links?" and his wife might reply, "In your top left dresser drawer"—or, perhaps, "I'm not sure, but I'll help you find them."

Crossed lines like this denote uncomplementary transactions, and bode trouble. For example, the Adult-to-Adult question about the cuff links might be answered with a sharp, "Where you left them," a reproof that comes from the wife's Parent and is addressed to what she sees as the inept Child in her husband's personality.

T.A. therapy sessions usually involve eight to fifteen participants and often begin with one member trying to describe why "I'm not OK." The group responds by giving him all the reasons that he should be OK. Therapist and group members alike try to help each member ana-

setting, the patient can learn to come to terms with his problems. To this end, therapists try to urge patients into dealing with their current feelings and thoughts, rather than pushing them down. They might tell a patient who is obviously distressed when talking about her mother to continue to explore her feelings, even if it means experiencing discomfort, rather than suppressing them. Patients are reassured that having angry, hostile, or otherwise unpleasant feelings is okay and that these feelings should be explored.

BEHAVIOR MODIFICATION

The behavioral approach to therapy operates on the principle that people can learn a new behavior better suited to their needs. This means that if people

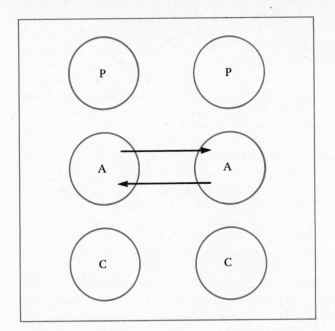

Figure 13.1

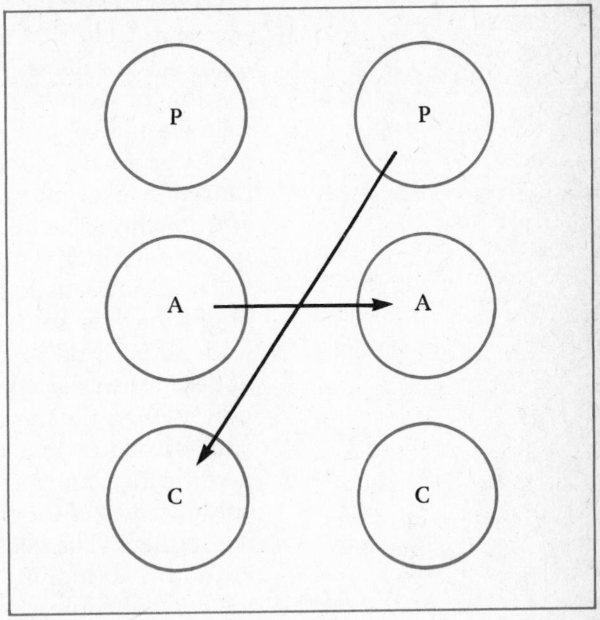

Figure 13.2

lyze, and change, his "life script"—the blueprint that, according to T.A., a child unconsciously draws up to shape his whole life. . . .

All Adults. As a way of inspiring groups' members, T.A. therapists usually make "contracts" with them to achieve specific goals like giving up alcohol or such amorphous ones as "to get more OK," "to be able to give myself to others" or "to exercise more control over my Parent." One far-out leader shouts, "You're OK!" to his groups, and another asks members to clasp hands in a circle dance while singing Ding, Dong, the Witch is

Dead. Harris, who now does more teaching and training than therapy, usually begins his lectures with a few jokes to loosen things up. Sometimes he asks a listener to come forward and stand at the foot of the speaker's platform, thus demonstrating what it is like to have to look up at a parent and feel like a "not OK" child. Often, members of Harris' staff surprise the audience by interrupting him with comments of their own. The purpose is to suggest that Harris and his listeners are all adults together, and that he is no parent proclaiming infallible truths to obedient children. . . .

are exhibiting some behavior that is not adaptive they can learn a new one to replace it. The key words deal with the concept of learning. **Behavior modification,** or behavior therapy, as it is sometimes called, is the systematic application of learning principles to alter human behavior so as to alleviate suffering and enhance functioning.

How does behavior therapy differ from insight therapy? When a therapist adopts a behavioral approach toward treatment, she assumes that the most efficient path to change maladjustment is through changing overt behavior. If a person has a nervous tic, eliminate the nervous tic; if a person has a fear of heights, eliminate the fear of heights; if being in crowds makes a person fearful, eliminate the fear response to being in crowds. In each of these examples the therapist tries to eliminate a behavior or establish a new one; she

Behavior modification A therapy based on the application of learning principles, such as classical and instrumental conditioning, which changes people's overt behavior rather than their subjective feelings, unconscious processes, or motivations; synonymous with behavior therapy.

does not seek to find the origins of a behavior, and if she does find them, her discovery is not likely to affect her method of treatment.

If in the course of examining a client's problems the cause of the problem is some *other* situation, the behavior therapist may focus on the originating problem. Goldfried and Davison (1976) provide a good example: a client's marriage is faltering due to excessive arguments with his spouse. In assessing the client's problem the therapist learns that these arguments usually follow a period of heavy drinking; the drinking in turn has been brought about by a hard day at work. It may turn out that the hard days at work are caused by excessive pressure that the client places upon himself for his own performance. The behavior therapist would not focus on the fighting behavior; it is far more likely that he or she might focus on helping the client develop some realistic standards for self-evaluation. The behavioral approach might uncover some events that led to a specific behavior (self-evaluation leads to hard days, drinking, and family arguments). The therapist would not examine closely this client's early experiences as a child with self-evaluation. Rather, the therapist might focus on helping the client develop realistic adult standards that are consistent with the client's known capabilities, past performance, and *realistic* future performance. The client is not taught to take on the values of the therapist nor is he to interpret past events to find meaning in them. The goal of therapy is not to restructure or reshape personality but rather to modify an existing maladaptive behavior and create effective methods of coping. Many behavior therapists consider the unnecessary exploration of a person's internal experiences an invasion of privacy.

Why have psychologists turned to behavior modification, and how does this differ from insight therapy? Insight therapy is often oriented around a medical model. The medical model assumes that abnormal behavior is the product of some underlying cause, and insight therapy is aimed at eliminating these underlying causes. There are three basic reasons why many psychologists have become unhappy with insight therapy and the medical model approach. The *first* reason is that many of the theories which describe behavior use concepts that are almost impossible to define. Words like id, ego, and superego are difficult to define and represent concepts that are difficult to measure. The *second* major problem with insight therapy deals with its effectiveness; some studies have shown that patients *not* given insight therapy improved as much as those given therapy. A *third* major problem with the insight-oriented, medical model is that once a person is labeled as being "abnormal," it is assumed by many that the abnormality creates maladaptive behavior. If asked why the maladaptive behavior occurred, those favoring a medical model approach answer that the behavior occurred because the person is abnormal. So people are abnormal because they exhibit maladaptive behavior; they are maladaptive because they are abnormal—this is, of course, circular reasoning. By contrast, behavioral approaches assume that abnormal behavior occurs because of problems in living and adjustment; if the client is taught new ways of coping, the maladjustment will disappear (see Eysenck, 1952; Kazdin & Wilson, 1978; O'Leary & Wilson, 1975).

The behaviorist is concerned only with behavior. If people's behavior is seen to be distorted, the therapist can help them change their behavior. As noted earlier, behaviorists assume that most behavior is learned; this is a fundamental difference between behaviorists and those who follow other approaches. Therapists who use insight therapy generally assume that if one treats only overt behavior, there may be symptom substitution. **Symptom substitution** is the occurrence of another behavior resulting from the same basic cause. An insight therapist might argue that if we eliminate a nervous tic the person might develop a speech impediment. The point of such an argument is that one cannot just eliminate symptoms; one must eliminate the underlying cause of the symptoms as well.

Insight therapists predict symptom substitution from behavior modification; behaviorists predict no symptom substitution. The issue between the two approaches, insight vs. behavior, is resolved by a simple question: Does symptom substitution follow treatment through behavior therapy? The data generally show that the answer to this question is *no*. A number of studies have shown that if the treatment of behavior is properly carried out through the use of behavioral principles, then nothing that generally resembles symptom substitution follows (see, for example, Kazdin, 1975).

Goals of Therapy

The goal of behavior modification is to influence a person's behavior so that he will have improved self-control through expanded skills, abilities, and independence. The aim is to use basic learning principles to help alleviate a person's suffering and enhance his functioning. Behavior modification tries to change a person's current behavior and restructure his responses to different situations. Behavior therapists assume that a person's current situation is far more relevant to his behavior than childhood experiences, intrapsychic conflicts, and personality structure. We see that behavioral therapy works on an educational rather than medical model. The therapist *teaches* skills rather than *treats* an illness. Behavior is generally influenced by changing a person's environment, the way he responds to the environment, and the way he interacts with others (Stolz, Wienckowski, & Brown, 1975). Once a person's behavior has changed, many attitudes, fears, and intrapsychic conflicts may become much easier to modify. Furthermore, when people enter into a thera-

Symptom substitution When a symptom is eliminated and another symptom resulting from the same basic cause occurs.

Goals of therapy—Behavior modification approach: The therapist tries to change a person's current behavior and restructure his responses to different situations

peutic relationship many aspects of their behavior change; these include the behaviors which are specifically being treated, as well as other areas of a person's life; for example, a person being treated for a nervous tic might find that the frequency of emitting tics has decreased *and* he now is more easily able to engage in discussions about emotional topics. The person might also find that his job performance is better, even though it is not directly related to verbal expressions.

Technique: The First Steps

All of the important variables that were emphasized when we explored insight therapy are important in behavior therapy; a therapist must be warm and accepting. The client must desire a behavior change. There must be a mutual respect between client and therapist. The way the therapist and client interact, often called the therapeutic relationship, is equally important in behavior therapy as it is in insight therapy. The atmosphere of a behavior therapy session and an insight therapy session may appear no different to a client or an observer; yet, the techniques and goals of the therapist may differ greatly.

We know from our study of maladjusted individuals that people seek therapy for a wide number of reasons. But, when they see a therapist, certain basic procedures are followed; consider the problem of a child who has been referred to a behavior therapist because of an inability to learn to read. Children who cannot learn to read effectively often have other disorders, for example Attention Deficit Disorders (hyperactivity). In one experiment Lahey asked reading disabled children to read a passage orally and then to answer questions about the passage. When praise and pennies were given for correct answers, accuracy of comprehension increased in children whose reading comprehension was 2 years below grade level (Lahey, McNees, & Brown, 1973).

This study by Lahey and his colleagues is typical of many behavior modification studies. People are referred for treatment for some type of behavior problem. The problem may be reading comprehension, anxiety, nervous tics, depression, or a lack of self-confidence. Three basic procedures usually follow. *First,* some definition of the problem must be made, and an evaluation of how often the behavior occurs. In the case of the person with nervous tics, we might find that the person's problem is that he exhibits nervous tics on the average of seven times an hour. During the first phase, the therapist would also be interested in the range of situations in which the tic occurred, what effects it might have on the person's environment, and what alternative behaviors are available to the person. The *second* phase of behavior modification is to provide the treatment itself. In the Lahey study the subjects were provided pennies and praise. The behavior of the subjects was monitored; in the reading study the behavior being monitored was comprehension. *Third,* we assess whether there has been a behavior change during the treatment phase; we withdraw the reinforcement and observe the behavior again. In the Lahey study the withdrawal of treatment would be the withdrawal of pennies and praise (see Figure 13.3, Baseline II). When pennies and praise were withdrawn, the subjects returned to previously poor accuracy. When pennies and praise were reintroduced accuracy again improved. Of course, the ultimate aim of any therapy is to produce lasting behavior change. When

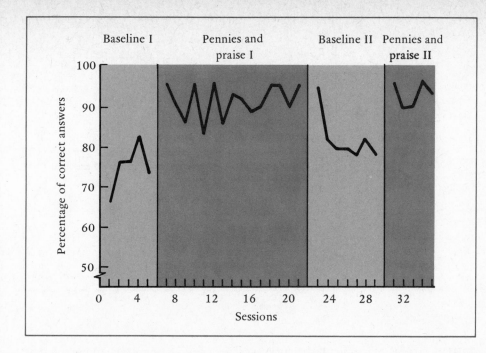

Figure 13.3 Some data from a study of modification techniques by Lahey, McNees, and Brown (1973). Note how accuracy of comprehension varies depending on whether pennies and praise were given. Baseline I are data before pennies and praise were given; Baseline II, data after pennies and praise have been given and withdrawn. After Baseline II pennies and praise were reintroduced and accuracy increased again

reinforcements are withdrawn and subjects still exhibit modified behavior, then we know that treatment has been effective.

The Lahey study on the modification of deficits in reading for comprehension is one of many types of behavior modification therapies that has been conducted. As suggested earlier, behavior modification is not a specific technique but represents a group of different techniques to help people change their behavior. There are four separate trends in the development of behavior therapy: instrumental conditioning, counter conditioning, modeling, and cognitive restructuring.

Technique: Instrumental (Operant) Conditioning

Instrumental conditioning techniques were used in the Lahey study which has just been described; a positive reinforcer or reward was given to subjects for correct responses. The positive reinforcer was pennies and praise. For each correct answer the children were told that they were correct, and a penny was given to them. Following an incorrect answer, the experimenter said nothing and did not give the subject a penny. As we saw in chapter 3, a positive reinforcer is any event which increases the probability of a previous response occurring again. Positive reinforcement can be used to develop and maintain useful behaviors; in addition, the removal of positive reinforcement can be used to decrease the frequency of antisocial behavior. Positive reinforcement techniques have been used in such places as the classroom, mental institutions, and prisons and have been used to help people who want to lose weight, stop smoking, and make new friends. (For a review of reinforcement principles, see pp. 85 to 89.)

TOKEN ECONOMY. The goal of instrumental conditioning is to change people's behavior, usually by rewarding them for adaptive behavior. This ap-

Token economy

Tokens are very effective as reinforcers

proach has been particularly successful in mental hospitals, where it has been used as a basis of a token economy. In a **token economy** participants receive tokens when they engage in appropriate behavior. At some later time they are able to exchange these tokens for other positively reinforcing items or activities, such as candy, new clothes, and games. A token is used in much the same way as money is used in society; a certain number of tokens are necessary to obtain certain pleasures. The more tokens patients earn, the more reinforcing events they can exchange them for.

In a token economy participants are paid tokens for different behaviors. For example, a patient in a hospital might clean tables after meals or help in a hospital laundry to earn tokens. On a simpler level, a patient might be given tokens for maintaining personal appearance and being clean with combed hair and brushed teeth.

The number of tokens given to a patient is determined by the level of difficulty of the job and how long the person has performed it. For brushing her teeth, a patient might receive 3 tokens, but for working in the laundry folding sheets for 3 hours, she might receive 40 tokens. At the end of a week, tokens might be redeemed for special toilet articles, reading and writing material, or special passes to walk around the grounds of the hospital. The aim of the token economy is to strengthen the behaviors that are compatible with social norms. One of the advantages of a token economy is that it can be run by a paraprofessional like a ward nurse, or by anyone else who can provide tokens to a patient. So, parents, aides, correctional officers, and friends can be involved in a token economy that is being used to help modify the behavior of an individual (Ayllon & Azrin, 1965, 1968; Stoltz, Wienckowski, & Brown, 1975). Not only do token economies help the patients with specific tasks like housekeeping and self-care (Gershone et al., 1977), but when these behaviors change there is often a decrease in depression and hallucinations (Anderson & Alpert, 1974; O'Brien & Azrin, 1972).

Operant procedures are not only used in token economies. One of the most effective uses has been with children who are either antisocial, slow

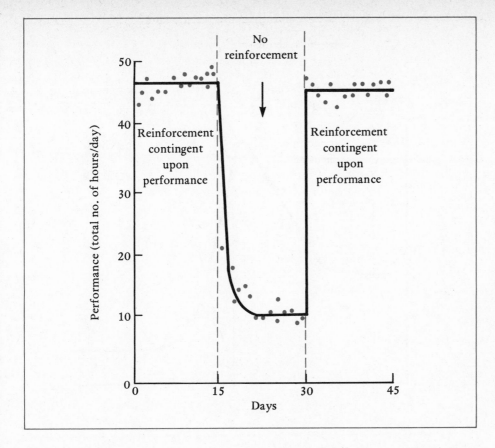

Figure 13.4 In a token economy when patients were delivered tokens for performing desired activities, their performance increased compared to when tokens were not delivered. In a study by Aylon and Azrin (1965) total performance of a group of patients was monitored over a 45-day period. As is shown in the figure, when tokens (reinforcement) were contingent upon performance the group of patients produced about 46 hours of work per day; yet, when the tokens were removed performance dropped to about 10 hours per day (Ayllon & Azrin, 1965, p. 377)

learners, or in some way maladjusted. Operant procedures have been used to bring about a wide range of desirable behaviors, including increased reading speed, improved classroom behaviors, proper toilet use, and the maintenance of personal hygiene. Regardless of the desired behaviors, the general approach is the same. A behavior that is reinforced tends to occur again; therefore, therapists only reinforce desirable behaviors. A large number of studies have been conducted to show that reinforced behaviors, for example, good classroom behavior, dramatically alter children's behavior (Drabman, 1976; Kazdin, 1975). With hospitalized patients, Ayllon and Haughton (1964) instructed staff members to reinforce them for psychotic verbalizations during one time period, and to reinforce neutral verbalizations during another time period. As we expect, the frequency of psychotic verbalizations increased when reinforced and decreased when not reinforced. As shown in Figure 13.5 the verbal responses of the patients were directly dependent upon whether the reinforcement being delivered was for psychotic output or neutral output.

EXTINCTION AND PUNISHMENT. The same basic instrumental techniques can be used to *decrease* the frequency of an undesired behavior through extinction and/or punishment. In extinction the subject is no longer reinforced for a behavior. As was shown in chapter 3, in the process of extinction, when we remove reinforcers the likelihood decreases that a person will exhibit the

Figure 13.5 The frequency of psychotic verbal behavior can be increased or decreased depending on whether or not reinforcement is provided by others around hospitalized patients. During a baseline time, psychotic and neutral verbal behavior occurred approximately equally; however, during a time when psychotic utterances were reinforced the number of verbal responses that were psychotic in nature increased and neutral verbal output decreased. By contrast, when neutral verbal responses were reinforced they increased in frequency while psychotic verbalizations decreased. The verbal output of hospitalized mental patients can clearly be shaped by instrumental conditioning procedures (Ayllon & Haughton, 1964, p. 91)

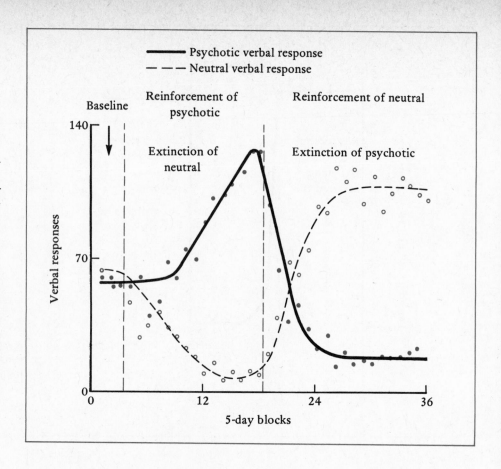

same behavior again. Let's consider an example. A 3-year-old child is raising havoc in his household by demanding an extraordinary number of stories be read to him. If no one reads the stories to him, he screams violently until he gets what he wants. By reading the stories to their child, the parents are reinforcing his behavior. He cries; they read. The behavior that we might try to attempt to train is a lack of crying, and one way to eliminate this crying behavior is to no longer reinforce it. Since the reinforcement for the child is reading, the reading must be discontinued. So, when the child cries, the parents do not read him a story. The chances are strong that he will cry loudly and violently. This may continue for two or three nights; however, it has been found that if we fail to reinforce the child's behavior, the behavior will be extinguished (see Williams, 1959).

A second way to decrease the frequency of some undesired behavior is to punish it. This often involves the presentation of some aversive stimulus. When a child continues to play with valuable objects on a table, we might say "No!" and slap his hands (Koegel & Covert, 1972); with adults in the laboratory we might provide a stronger type of aversive stimulus, perhaps an electric shock. Usually, such a punishment technique is combined with positive reinforcement. For example, a person who has a sexual fetish for women's shoes might receive an electric shock when he becomes sexually aroused (Hallam & Rachman, 1972, 1976; Marks & Gelder, 1967; Marks et al., 1970). At the same time, he may be positively reinforced for becoming aroused when he sees a normal sexual stimulus. As noted in chapter 3, punishment can be

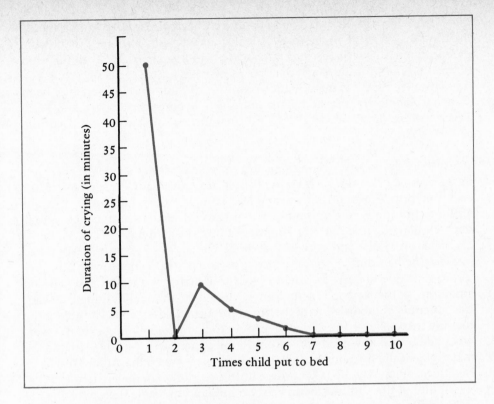

Figure 13.6 When a child cries upon being put to bed, the duration of crying can be decreased dramatically if parents ignore and do not reinforce the child with attention. Shown in the figure is the duration of crying when the crying is ignored on a series of times a child is put to bed (Williams, 1959, p. 296)

used to suppress behavior; however, it most effectively controls behavior when combined with positive reinforcement.

TIME-OUT. A widely used technique that involves many of the basic principles of learning theory is the **time-out** from reinforcement procedure. Time-out, as it is usually called, is the procedure of removing a person from a desired situation; it thus acts as a punishment because it decreases a specific undesired behavior. Imagine a child who regularly throws temper tantrums; each time she wants a piece of candy, an ice-cream cone, or even her little brother's toys, she throws a screaming, yelling, kicking tantrum. This is a frustrating, annoying, and difficult situation for parents; they often become agitated, and out of their own frustration and embarrassment, give in. In time-out the child is removed from her present situation and is placed in a room without toys, TV, or music. Alternately, she might be placed in a "thinking chair," away from the rest of the family; a back hallway, bathroom, or washroom is often used for the time-out room or the thinking chair. Not only did the child not get her desired candy, but she was removed from her potential source of reinforcement (attention from her parents). The child is kept in the chair or in the time-out room for 5 minutes. If she refuses to stay, more time is added to the initial 5 minutes.

Not only is the time-out procedure a very effective tool in helping eliminate behaviors like tantrums, but when combined with positive reinforcers for appropriate behavior, children who have been having behavior problems can make dramatic gains. The positive reinforcers and the chair are delivered for very specific behaviors. So, a child might be given an extra dessert if he cleans his room, brushes his teeth, and avoids fights with his brother. If all

Time-out The procedure of removing a person from a desired or reinforcing situation; acting as a punishment it decreases the likelihood of an undesired behavior. It is most appropriately called a time-out from reinforcement procedure.

three behaviors are exhibited he not only gets his extra dessert, but he avoids the thinking chair. If an argument breaks out with the younger brother, the parent immediately places the child in the thinking chair. This combination of the time-out procedure and positive reinforcers for prosocial behaviors is a dramatically effective therapeutic technique (Wahler, 1976) and has been shown to be effective for reducing aggressive behaviors (Pendergrass, 1972) and delusions (Davis et al., 1976), and even for treating alcoholism (Griffiths et al., 1977).

IMPLOSIVE THERAPY. Using imagery to raise a patient's anxiety has been the technique of implosive therapy. People are continually exposed to certain cues that induce fear and anxiety and lead to maladaptive behaviors. The aim of the technique is to eliminate the avoidance of anxiety and anxiety situations by using extinction. The founder of implosive therapy, T. G. Stampfl, has taken this idea and argued that since we teach a person to respond to fear-producing stimuli, we can teach a person *not* to respond with fear.

Implosive therapy An extinction procedure in which a patient is brought to a very high level of anxiety by imagining fearful situations. The aim is to reduce (extinguish) the fear and avoidance responses; this is accomplished by showing the patients that they will survive the anxiety and can now start to produce responses other than fear and avoidance.

In **implosive therapy** a patient is told to imagine the feared and avoided situations in their most difficult forms; there is no gradual buildup; instead, the patient is bombarded with the worst forms of anxiety first. The aim of the therapy is to *increase* the patient's anxiety to an overwhelming extent. Overwhelmed by anxiety-producing stimuli, the patient will quickly learn that he is not physically hurt nor has his life fallen apart. When the patient reaches a high level of anxiety, he is kept there until a reduction in the anxiety-producing ability of the stimulus occurs. At no time in implosive therapy is the patient told to suppress whatever symptoms he has; it is assumed that anxiety and avoidance of anxiety is *learned* and can be *unlearned*. Implosive therapy attempts to treat the learning process. Storms (1976) provides the following implosive story that a therapist told a client with Agoraphobia, the fear of leaving home and being caught in dangerous situations from which one might not be able to leave:

> She is walking down the street and noting the color of the lamp poles and the green leaves on the trees. As she steps out into the street, a car runs over her toe. Then she steps back and starts out again and gets knocked down by a bus. This bruises her, and she is feeling some pain and is struggling to get up when her hand is run over by a motorcycle, severing her fingers. A truck crushes her ribs. Her lungs fill with blood. She is dying and people gather around and do not help in any way. They just scoff at her and laugh at the ugly sight. This is one of the things that bothers her—people not helping and criticizing her by saying, That's no loss to the world anyhow. The ambulance comes. People cover her with a white sheet. She dies. (p. 141)

When improperly used, implosive therapy can have bad effects. Imagine a situation in which a patient has been treated through implosive therapy but has not totally unlearned her responses to fear-producing stimuli; in this case, rather than having helped the patient, we may have made her problems worse by making her even more fearful. While implosive therapy is used by many therapists, it is still undergoing considerable validation and research (Hekmat, 1973; Morganstern, 1973; Orenstein & Carr, 1975).

Counterconditioning The learning of a new response to a familiar stimulus through a process of reconditioning. The two major types of counterconditioning procedures are systematic desensitization and aversive counterconditioning.

Technique: Counterconditioning

The second major approach to behavior therapy comes in the form of **counterconditioning.** One of the aims of any behavior therapy is to change a per-

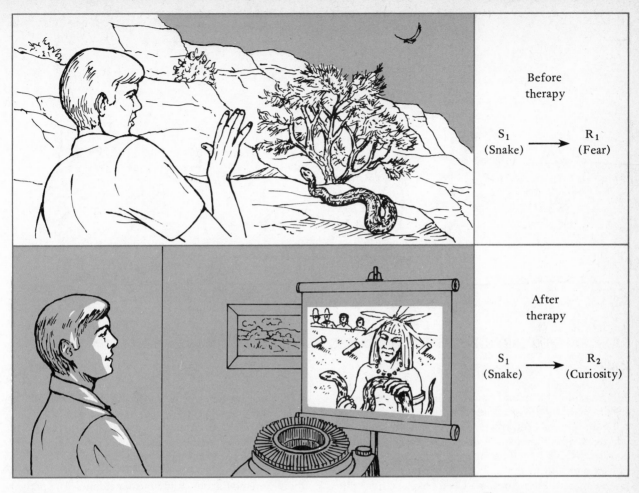

Before
therapy

S_1 $\longrightarrow$ R_1
(Snake) (Fear)

After
therapy

S_1 $\longrightarrow$ R_2
(Snake) (Curiosity)

son's response to old stimuli. If a particular stimulus brings about a particular response and that response is either inappropriate or maladaptive, we have to teach a person to adopt new responses. As shown in Figure 13.7, a specific stimulus (S_1) brings about a specific response (R_1). It is hoped that after an individual has undergone therapy that the same stimulus (S_1) will bring about a new response (R_2). This general method of reconditioning is called counterconditioning. There are two basic approaches to counterconditioning; systematic desensitization and aversive counterconditioning.

SYSTEMATIC DESENSITIZATION. In **systematic desensitization** people are taught to relax when presented with stimuli that elicit anxiety. Assume that driving alone in an automobile is a stimulus situation (S_1) which brings about the response of fear (R_1); this fear is often overly dramatic and inappropriate. Eventually, we would like to have the idea of driving alone (S_1) bring about a less fearful and more reasonable response (R_2); perhaps the response would be curiosity or relaxation.

The basic technique in systematic desensitization is to gradually expose people to the source of anxiety while they participate in behavior that decreases anxiety. The stimulus that the psychologist uses can thus be imagined or real. For example, we might have a patient imagine a car rather than see a real one. Initially the car might be imagined at a great distance, a dis-

Figure 13.7 In counterconditioning people try to learn a new response to a familiar stimulus; it is essentially the process of reconditioning

Systematic desensitization A counterconditioning procedure in which a patient, while deeply relaxed, imagines a series of increasingly fearful situations. With successive trials, the patient learns relaxation rather than fear as a new response to a former fearful stimulus.

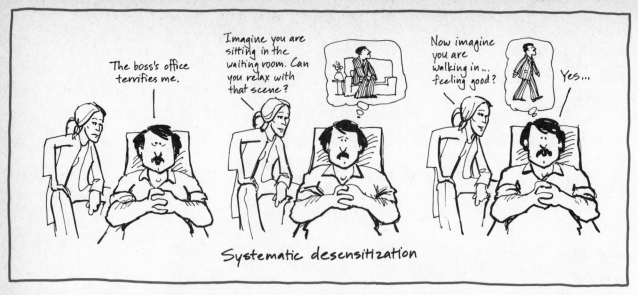

Systematic desensitization involves the development and use of imagery

RESEARCH PROFILE 13

Systematic Desensitization

Being a child abuser and having a dread fear of snakes are dramatically different problems that come about for different reasons. Yet, recent research has shown that a relatively new therapeutic technique works for problems as diverse as child abuse and snake phobias. The powerful technique that so many practitioners are using is systematic desensitization. Let us explore how this therapy technique is used to treat these two problems.

What is the best way to treat people who come to therapy because they are child abusers? Research on the treatment of these people has generally focused on group therapy, self-help programs, and individual case work. Therapist Wyman Sanders, a researcher at UCLA School of Medicine, has reported the successful treatment of a child abuser with the technique of systematic desensitization (Sanders, 1978).

Sanders began to use the procedure while treating a 27-year-old man who was referred because of child abuse. First, Sanders had his patient learn to relax the muscles of his body. Then the patient made a list of anxiety-producing situations and rated them on a scale of 0 to 100. For example, his baby lying on the floor laughing received a rating of 10; a rating of 60 was given to the situation where the baby was fussing, crying, and would not play. A rating of 100 was given to the situation where the baby was crying and the patient had done everything that he could to get the baby to stop, but the baby continued to scream loudly.

For a series of twelve sessions the patient was told to relax totally. While in this state he was instructed to listen to each of his anxiety-producing items as many times as necessary until he was able to maintain his relaxed state for three successive presentations. The treatment was effective. For over one year after treatment there were no further child abuse incidents. The patient reported feeling better and handling his emotions in constructive ways.

In his case report, Sanders noted that systematic desensitization was used along with other kinds of therapy; however, it was his opinion that the desensitization process was the major factor in the elimination of the abusive behavior.

Further research needs to be conducted in the treatment of child abuse. Yet systematic desensitization has been effective in this situation. Like most practicing therapists, Sanders used a combination of systematic desensitization, a behavioral technique, with traditional insight therapy. It is most likely that such combinations of divergent methods will produce the best therapeutic effects with problems like child abuse. However, it has been shown repeatedly that with problems like phobias, the mere use of behavioral techniques like systematic desensitization is very effective.

Let's explore another use of systematic desensitization. In our culture a fear of snakes is common. While many people do not like snakes, some develop a phobia

tance that would not make the patient fearful. Further imagining might involve the car coming closer. Next, the patient would slowly begin to imagine getting in the car. As the patient comes to realize that she will not be hurt or isolated by this imagined scene, she can eventually tolerate more stressful imagery or actually involve herself in the behavior.

Systematic desensitization procedures such as the one just described have three components. First, the subject must be taught to relax. Then the subject has to describe situations that bring anxiety. The third step is to have the subject imagine the scenes that elicit anxiety while she is deeply relaxed. As the subject thinks about these anxiety-producing scenes while relaxed, she learns new responses to old stimuli. Typically, the client and therapist develop a hierarchy of fearful or anxiety-producing events. For example, if a client were so fearful of examinations that she could not even show up for an exam, the therapist might have her rate a series of imagined scenes dealing with examinations in terms of their ability to evoke anxiety. A high-anxiety scene might be seeing the test paper being given to her in the classroom. A scene with a moderate ability to evoke anxiety might be picturing the class-

that really involves an intense irrational fear of snakes and inappropriate avoidance behaviors. Many therapeutic techniques have been developed to help people with snake phobia (for example, Bandura, Blanchard, & Ritter, 1969), but particularly effective has been systematic desensitization. When people with snake phobia were treated with systematic desensitization, Lang and Lazovik (1963) found significant improvement compared to a control group that was not treated. Furthermore, in a 6-month followup, not only was the difference between the treated and nontreated groups still there, but the difference was slightly greater. These findings were subsequently confirmed in another study (Lang, Lazovik, & Reynolds, 1965), and Davison (1968) also provided additional support. Using variants of systematic desensitization, Bandura (Bandura et al., 1975) and Ritter (1968) have also argued for the effectiveness of systematic desensitization.

Systematic desensitization is not the therapeutic cure for all conditions. Quite the contrary, it probably should not be used with people who are exhibiting serious psychotic symptoms (Cowden & Ford, 1962; Wolpe, 1973), but it has been shown to be especially effective in helping people who are fearful and anxious. There has been a fair degree of controversy as to *how* systematic desensitization actually works. For example, one view suggests a patient's expectancy for success in treatment is the real reason that systematic desensitization works.

This view argues that the specific procedures of systematic desensitization are not crucial at all, but merely being in therapy creates an expectancy and positive attitude which creates therapeutic success. Some researchers have argued that systematic desensitization is not really a counterconditioning procedure at all, but rather it is really the process of extinction (Wilson & Davidson, 1971).

Active research continues on systematic desensitization as a therapeutic tool and on the process itself. Regardless of how it works, thousands of clients have been treated with systematic desensitization for a wide range of problems; generally helped most are those with problems in which anxiety plays a large role, like phobias. Systematic desensitization is likely to continue to be actively investigated; since it was first introduced it has undergone modifications which have increased its effectiveness. The next decade will probably see more experiments which will refine and limit the use of systematic desensitization only to certain types of behavior disorders, perhaps Anxiety Disorders. We see this limiting and refinement process regularly in psychology; through research, psychologists continue to let their theories and practices become more refined and evolve in a meaningful way.

room building; a low-anxiety scene might be imagining her automobile 2 days before the exam is to be given. Often starting off with the lowest anxiety-producing scenes, a subject is taught to relax rather than become fearful as each new scene is introduced. There are many ways in which to construct hierarchies of anxiety-producing events, but the general idea is to make each level somewhat more anxiety producing than the next.

One of the reasons that phobias are effectively treated with systematic desensitization is that people can easily imagine the object or event that they are afraid of. Imagining ability is *very* important if a traditional form of systematic desensitization is to be used. Good imagery is necessary if a good hierarchy is to be developed. Presented below is a hierarchy that has a good deal of imagery that might be used for a person with a fear of flying. Notice how imagery plays an important role:

1. Your boss tells you that, in 6 months, you'll have to fly out to the coast for a new account.
2. You're sitting in your living room, watching a football game on TV, and you hear a plane overhead.
3. A colleague at work tells you of the great plane trip he had to Florida.
4. Your wife asks you, a week before your trip, whether you'll be needing any formal clothes to take along.
5. You're up in the attic, looking for your two-suiter to take along on your trip to the coast.
6. As you look through your desk diary, you're reminded that the coast plane trip is coming up in two weeks.
7. The evening before the trip, you're folding socks and underwear into your suitcase.
8. The taxi is pulling off the expressway at the exit marked "Airport," on the way to your trip.
9. There are five people ahead of you in line at the Pan Am ticket counter, having their baggage checked and tickets validated.
10. You're walking down the ramp onto the plane, and the flight attendant asks for your boarding pass.
11. As you look out the window, you observe the plane just getting airborne, and you can see the Bay Bridge in the distance.
12. You've been flying for a couple of hours, the air gets choppy, and the captain has just put on the fasten-seat-belt sign.
13. The ride is quite bumpy, and you check to see that your seat belt is fastened.
14. You wake up the morning of your trip to the coast and say to yourself, "Today's the day I leave for the coast." (Goldfried & Davison, 1976, pp. 121–122)

Aversive counterconditioning
A counterconditioning technique by which aversive or noxious stimuli are paired and associated with desirable stimuli or stimuli that need to be avoided. Eventually, to avoid the noxious stimulus the patient adopts a new response to the undesirable stimulus.

AVERSIVE COUNTERCONDITIONING.   The second major type of counterconditioning is aversive counterconditioning. In **aversive counterconditioning** a person who has had a particular response toward a stimulus is taught a different one. Consider an alcoholic. An alcoholic is a person who generally considers alcohol as rewarding. Nevertheless, he realizes that alcohol is destructive, so he comes to a therapist to be treated for alcoholism. A behavior therapist might try to elicit a new, that is, negative or aversive, response toward alcohol. The technique is simple: alcohol must be made unpleasant for the subject. An alcoholic might be taught that alcohol brings about nausea. To accomplish this he might be given a drug which causes nausea whenever alcohol is consumed. Eventually, under such treatment just the thought of alcohol would produce nausea in the patient (Davidson, 1974).

Aversive counterconditioning has been used successfully with homosexuals who wish to change their sexual orientation. Feldman and MacCulloch (1971) devised aversive counterconditioning techniques to discourage homosexuals from looking at sexually arousing stimuli. In a study done by these researchers, a male homosexual who desired to alter his behavior was asked to rate a series of pictures of naked males according to the degree of sexual arousal they evoked. He was then presented with one of the pictures he had rated as least arousing; following presentation of the picture he was given an electric shock. Then he was told that he could avoid future electric shocks by pressing a button in front of him. Upon pressing the button the picture of the naked male disappeared, a picture of an attractive female took its place, and the shock was avoided. Slowly, over a period of trials, in each new picture the attractiveness of the naked male pictures increased; still, to avoid the shock, the patient had to press the button.

The aim of this aversive counterconditioning is to teach the subject to avoid the shock by not staring at the most appealing male nudes. These successful results have been quite controversial, but they do show that aversive counterconditioning can be effective in the treatment of behavioral disorders (Birk et al., 1971; Colson, 1972; Mandel, 1970). Aversive counterconditioning has been used not only with homosexuals and alcoholics, but also with people whose problems are obesity, smoking, exhibitionism, and fetishes (Koenig & Masters, 1965; Morganstern, 1974; Whitman, 1969; Yates, 1975).

In many situations aversive counterconditioning is combined with positive reinforcement for proper prosocial behaviors. In general, the effectiveness of counterconditioning techniques is better if it is set in combination with other contingencies that promote adaptive, effective behavior patterns. Overall, although involving different procedures, both systematic desensitization and aversive counterconditioning aim to replace old responses with new responses that are adaptive and effective.

Technique: Modeling

Imitation is the highest form of flattery. This means that if someone copies your behavior, he or she obviously thinks it is worthwhile. In the fashionable world of the twentieth century, people are always imitating the behavior of others; they imitate dress styles, musical tastes, and commitment to social causes. People in the fashion industry are particularly concerned with how Hollywood stars dress. Similarly, they are concerned with how important political figures, such as the president, dress; if the president wears a sweater, the sweater industry assumes that more men are likely to wear them.

While adults are often caught up in imitating others, children imitate even more often; they are always in the process of imitating and are particularly sensitive to the behavior of other people, especially their parents. Even at the age of 1 or 2, children imitate their parents. It would not be surprising to find a 2-year-old doing exercises on the floor if he had observed his mother doing exercises on the floor. Much of toilet training behavior is also learned by watching parents. In the same way, table manners and responses to animals are learned by observation and imitation.

Albert Bandura (1969) has suggested that these basic principles of observational learning may be useful in therapy. Bandura and his colleagues have

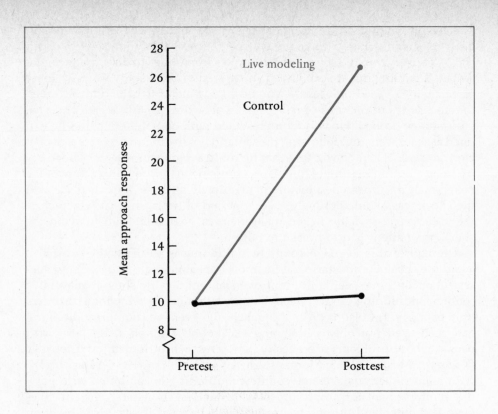

Figure 13.8 Subjects who had snake phobias were tested as to how many approach responses they would make toward a snake. A control group who went untreated changed little from pretest to posttest; however, a group of subjects who underwent treatment which consisted of watching a live model with a snake made many more approach responses in a posttest (Bandura, Blanchard, & Ritter, 1968, p. 183)

Modeling Learning by observing and imitating the behavior of other people.

argued that both children and adults learn new responses by watching and observing models, and they have shown that people benefit from therapy in which modeling is the principal therapeutic technique. Bandura (1977) argues that **modeling** is a very effective treatment procedure often more effective than many other therapeutic techniques. For example, Bandura, Blanchard, and Ritter (1968) asked people who had snake phobias to watch both live and filmed displays of other people handling snakes (Figure 13.8). The result was that the observer had a reduction of fear just by watching others with snakes. This same kind of result has been effective in treating children's fear of dogs (Hill, Liebert, & Mott, 1968), adults' fear of snakes and animals (Bandura & Barab, 1973), test anxiety (Jaffe & Carlson, 1972), and sexual problems (Wincze & Caird, 1976).

Bandura believes that three areas of behavior are most strongly influenced by modeling: (1) learning new behavior, (2) eliminating phobias, and (3) the increased ease of expression of already existing behavior. In each of these areas people can be helped to express behavior which is more adaptive than the old behavior and more consistent with their own life-style by watching the behavior of others. A therapist might point out to a client which behaviors he or she should observe. The therapist may also have a client act out certain behaviors, or, as Lazarus (1971) does, a therapist can show a client how to handle a personal problem and then tell the client to attempt to imitate it.

One of the problems with modeling is that patients often watch the behavior of "inappropriate" models. This approach assumes that the client exhibiting abnormal behavior has been exposed to inappropriate behaviors. For ex-

Table 13.2 Forms of behavior therapy

TYPE OF THERAPY	GOALS	TECHNIQUES
Operant conditioning	To learn new responses to old stimuli.	Reinforcement and punishment are used to establish new behaviors and eliminate old "faulty" undesirable ones.
Counterconditioning		
1. Systematic desensitization	To teach patients new adaptive responses.	Patients are taught to relax when presented with a fearful stimulus or situation; the technique involves teaching a new response like relaxation to an old fearful stimulus.
2. Aversive counterconditioning	To teach patients new responses.	Patient learns a new response to a previous stimulus; noxious stimuli are often used.
Modeling	To teach the patient to observe useful worthwhile behaviors of a model and imitate them.	The patient observes a model and then tries to imitate this same behavior rather than use old maladaptive ones.
Cognitive methods: Rational-emotive therapy	To change the way that a client thinks about himself and the world.	Clients are taught to think through situations, logically; they are asked to reconsider many of the irrational assumptions which have guided their lives.

ample, though parents are appropriate role models for children, they may, by example, teach maladaptive behaviors. It is precisely for this reason that people want TV violence to be discontinued; anti-TV violence proponents argue that people imitate the behaviors they see on the screen. If people actually model their behavior after TV heroes or TV villains, then should not violence on TV be removed? We have already seen in chapter 10 that the studies of the effects of TV violence are clear. People imitate the behaviors of others and particularly those whom they consider to be important people (Beutler et al., 1975; Brown et al., 1975; Thelen & Kirkland, 1976). As parents, friends, teachers, older brothers and sisters, we must realize that others are not only observing our behavior, but are often imitating it. A therapist is critically aware of this property of human behavior and tries to teach a client to observe the behavior of purposeful, worthwhile, goal-directed people.

Technique: Cognitive Restructuring

Most behavior therapies deal only with overt behavior. Yet a growing branch of behavior therapy is concerned with modifying a person's thought processes. These cognitive therapists attempt to modify the set maladaptive or faulty thought processes of a disturbed person (Mahoney, 1977). Unlike insight therapy, but like other forms of behavior therapy, cognitive restructuring therapy focuses on current behavior and is unconcerned with childhood experiences. The most widely known cognitive therapy is the rational-emotive therapy of Albert Ellis.

Albert Ellis, founder of rational-emotive therapy.

RATIONAL-EMOTIVE THERAPY. **Rational-emotive therapy** is a cognitive restructuring therapy. The basic assumption of rational-emotive therapy is that
people can live the most self-fulfilling, creative, and emotionally satisfying
lives by intelligently organizing and disciplining their thinking. Most behavior therapies have assumed that abnormal behavior is caused by faulty or
irrational behavior patterns, but Ellis and his colleagues assume that abnormal behavior arises from faulty and irrational patterns of *thinking* (Ellis &
Harper, 1961; Ellis, 1962, 1970). Thus for Ellis, maladaptive feelings and behavior are caused by maladaptive thoughts.

Ellis argues that the following sequence typifies psychological disturbance; an event occurs in a person's life, and this event gives rise to some
irrational ideas. These irrational ideas, in turn, often lead to negative emotions and behaviors. The first goal of therapy is to help the person examine
the events that have occurred and the irrational conclusions drawn from
them. The ultimate aim of therapy is the elimination of the irrational thought
processes; this should bring about a decrease in anxiety, a decrease in maladaptive behavior, and a happier, more fulfilled person.

Ellis has provided a series of basic irrational assumptions which he feels
are the cause of many emotional problems and maladaptive behaviors. Consider the irrational idea that "it is a dire necessity for an adult to be loved or
approved by virtually every person whom he comes in contact with." Ellis
points out that this is a nonsensical idea because it is easy for a person to live
happily without the approval of others. Ellis goes on to say that if you really
care about yourself and are not overly concerned with what others think
about you, you'll have little time to spend worrying or being self-centered. A
person should not blame or punish himself for being imperfect, for everyone
has foolish thoughts and feelings. Here is a list of Ellis's (Ellis & Harper,
1961) basic irrational assumptions:

- *Irrational Idea 1:* The idea that it is a dire necessity for an adult to be
  loved and approved by almost everyone for virtually everything he does.
- *Irrational Idea 2:* The idea that one should be thoroughly competent, adequate, and achieving in all possible respects.
- *Irrational Idea 3:* The idea that certain people are bad, wicked, or villainous and that they should be severely blamed and punished for their
  sins.
- *Irrational Idea 4:* The idea that it is terrible, horrible, and catastrophic
  when things are not going the way one would like them to go.
- *Irrational Idea 5:* The idea that human unhappiness is externally caused
  and that people have little or no ability to control their sorrows or rid
  themselves of negative feelings.
- *Irrational Idea 6:* The idea that if something is or may be dangerous or
  fearsome one should be terribly occupied with it and upset about it.
- *Irrational Idea 7:* The idea that it is easier to avoid facing many of life's
  difficulties and self-responsibilities than to undertake more rewarding
  forms of self-discipline.
- *Irrational Idea 8:* The idea that the past is all important and that because
  something once strongly affected one's life, it should indefinitely do so.
- *Irrational Idea 9:* The idea that people and things should be different from
  the way they are and that it is catastrophic if perfect solutions to the grim
  realities of life are not immediately found.

• *Irrational Idea 10:* The idea that maximum human happiness can be achieved by inertia and inaction or by passively and uncommittingly "enjoying oneself."

In rational-emotive therapy the therapist tries to alter the irrational beliefs and thought processes of a client. The therapist's task is to determine the client's internalized thought processes and to help the client realize that his or her thought processes are irrational and untrue. If rational-emotive therapy is successful, then the client will adopt new behaviors based upon new rational thought processes. Again, a basic assumption of rational-emotive therapy is that human behavior is determined by what a person thinks. If faulty thought processes can be eradicated and replaced with rational ideas about the world, then maladjustment and abnormal behavior can be eliminated.

The irrational assumptions that Ellis puts forth are not without some foundation. People have needs to be liked, they have needs to be competent, and they have the human needs to be loved and feel secure. Only when people place irrational values on these needs do they become maladaptive and lead to emotional disturbance, anxiety, and abnormal behavior. Rational-emotive therapy focuses on placing cognitive assumptions within a reasonable framework with a balance among each individual's needs, society's demands, and a complex, constantly changing environment.

OTHER COGNITIVE METHODS. With these fundamental ideas of cognitive changes, researchers like Donald Meichenbaum (1977) have developed self-help techniques by which individuals are taught to think about their behavior so as to facilitate problem areas. These self-help techniques have helped people with problems as diverse as shyness, speech impediments, impulsivity, and even schizophrenia (Glass et al., 1976; Meichenbaum, 1974; Meichenbaum & Cameron, 1973). Self-instructional techniques like the kinds that Meichenbaum employs use *adaptive* thinking and training procedures. Thus, Meichenbaum might have his subjects conduct private monologues in which they work through adaptive ways of thinking and coping with situations.

In self-instructional training a client is taught to help himself whenever he feels stress coming on. Rather than focusing on a client's irrational beliefs, clients are taught a repertoire of things that they might do or say that will help make their behavior more adaptive. Using such statements in combination with relaxation training and being reinforced for more adaptive behavior makes this kind of self-help, self-instructional procedure a very effective one.

Another cognitive restructuring therapy that focuses on irrational ideas has been put forth by Beck (1963). Beck calls his method "cognitive therapy." As was presented earlier in studying depression (see chapter 12, Abnormal Psychology), Beck has suggested that depression is caused by a patient's negative views of the world, himself, and the future. So, Beck claims that a successful client must pass through four stages in correcting faulty views:

First, he has to become aware of what he is thinking. Second, he needs to recognize what thoughts are awry. Then he has to substitute accurate for inaccurate judgements. Finally, he needs feedback to inform him whether his changes are correct. (Beck, 1976, p. 217)

Table 13.3 Comparison of psychoanalytic, client-centered & Gestalt, and behavioral approaches to psychotherapy

ISSUE	PSYCHOANALYSIS	CLIENT-CENTERED & GESTALT	BEHAVIOR THERAPY
Nature of psychopathology	Pathology reflects inadequate conflict resolutions and fixations in early development, which leave overly weak controls or strong impulses or both.	Incongruence exists between the depreciated self and the potential, desired self. The person is overly dependent on others for gratification and self-esteem.	Symptomatic behavior derives from faulty learning of mal-adaptive behaviors. The symptom is the problem; there is no "underlying disease."
Goal of therapy	Attainment of psychosexual maturity, strengthened ego functions, and reduced control by unconscious and repressed impulses.	Fostering self-determination, authenticity, and integration by releasing human potential and expanding awareness.	Relieving symptomatic behavior by suppressing or replacing maladaptive behaviors.
Role of therapist	An *investigator*, searching out root conflicts and resistances.	An *authentic* person in true encounter with patient, sharing experience. Facilitates patient's growth potential.	A *trainer*, helping patient unlearn old behaviors and learn new ones.
Role of unconscious material	Primary in classical psycho-analysis, less emphasized by ego-analysis.	Though recognized by some, emphasis is on conscious experience.	No concern with unconscious processes.
Role of insight	Central, though conceived not just as coming from intellectual understanding but also as emerging in "corrective emotional experiences."	While insight is used by many, others place more emphasis on awareness, the "how" and "what" questions rather than the "why."	Irrelevant and unnecessary.

Source: Adapted from Korchin, 1976, Table 14-2.

There are some very significant differences among the procedures used by Beck, Meichenbaum, and Ellis. As Mahoney & Arnkoff (1978) have suggested, the differences in the therapies are more in procedure than in their ultimate goal. The aim of rational-emotive therapy, self-instruction, and cognitive therapy are all the same: changing people's thought patterns. Increasingly, data are accumulating which suggest that these cognitive methods of therapy are very successful with adults (Reeves, 1976; Rush et al., 1975), although their successful use with children is more limited (Hobbs, Morguin, Tyroler, & Lahey, 1980). It is likely that as these methods are refined and studied further they will be used along with other behavior and insight therapies on a more regular basis.

GROUP THERAPY

Fat people of the world—unite! One of the serious problems that plague people in the United States is obesity. Many Americans tend to be fat; they eat too much and don't get enough exercise. A number of different organizations have begun to help overweight people overcome their problems; one of the most successful organizations is Weight Watchers. The Weight Watchers organization attempts to use a sensible program of eating combined with weekly group meetings to help overweight people lose weight. By teaching people new eating techniques, Weight Watchers tries to change people's eating behavior. Three basic services are provided: (1) a diet or program of eat-

Turning Brainpower into Action

It is possible for you to turn your brain into a mechanism to control your body. Earlier (on pp. 62–63) we saw the concept of biofeedback in which a person monitors the electrical activity of different parts of his or her body. The idea behind biofeedback is that by monitoring electrical activity a person can learn to change that activity. For example, the person with migraine headaches who monitors the muscle tension in her neck can reduce muscle tension by relaxing, and thus eliminate or reduce migraine headaches. We suggested earlier that biofeedback can go beyond the simple migraine headache. Think about the person with a phobia, perhaps of snakes. In the technique of systematic desensitization an individual is taught to relax while he is being presented images of snakes, or even really sees a snake at a distance. Of course, the aim of systematic desensitization is to teach people new responses (relaxation) to old fearful stimuli (snakes). Biofeedback may hold the key for the treatment of snake phobia and other disorders. A person can learn to monitor her own fearful responses by monitoring electrical brain activity. When people become fearful normal brain-wave activity becomes very active and a characteristic pattern of electrical activity develops. By contrast, when a person is deeply relaxed,

a different pattern of brain-wave activity is generated. A psychologist can use biofeedback to help teach patients to relax by having them monitor and then alter their brain waves.

You can see how the psychologist can use the biological bases of behavior and an understanding of biofeedback to help patients who are anxious or upset. Indeed, biofeedback machines are now being developed which a person can take home at a modest cost. The application is clear. Every time a person starts to feel tense and fearful she can attach an electrode and monitor her brain-wave activity so as to reduce fear and tension. Eventually, of course, the aim will be to reduce fear and anxiety without the use of the machine to monitor electrical activity. However, a person learns to be fearful over a number of years, and it may take a number of months to unlearn such fear responses.

You can see that biofeedback holds great potential for a variety of specific ailments. It also has potential for the person with an Anxiety Disorder because such a person is fraught with anxiety and tension. Tension and fear can be reduced through biofeedback and systematic desensitization and can be an effective method of treatment procedure for a person's emotional disorders.

---

ing which helps people lose weight and keep it off; (2) weekly meetings to provide inspiration and information; and (3) a group of people all meeting together for the same purpose and thus achieving some therapeutic aims.

Groups like Weight Watchers have been successful not only in weight reduction, but also in helping people with problems of alcohol addiction, smoking, and gambling. Some of these therapy groups are formal; others just consider themselves helping organizations. Each group's methods form a therapeutic technique, and each group has its own technique.

A number of people coming together for the purpose of receiving some type of psychological treatment is called **group therapy.** While group therapy is very popular today, the concept is not a new one. Group therapy was introduced around the turn of the century, became formalized as a technique in the 1930s, and has become increasingly popular since World War II.

One reason for the popularity of group therapy is that it is less expensive than individual therapy because more people are being treated. A single therapist only has so much time; if she only sees clients in individual therapy, the most she can see is 40 clients per week, or one client per hour. Also, there are far more people who need therapy than there are therapists to accommodate them. But in a single hour with a group, a therapist might help 8 to 10 clients. So, in 5 hours of group therapy a psychologist can help as many as 40 clients, the same number that she can see in individual therapy during an entire week.

Group therapy A method of treating emotional and behavioral problems in which several people are seen simultaneously.

Although not the norm, some group therapies can take on unusual formats to help clients become more aware of their feelings

By the same measure group therapy is less expensive than individual therapy because a therapist is able to see 10 clients within an hour and does not need to charge each client the individual therapy fee. So the combination of decreased costs and increased case loads alone certainly justifies group therapy.

Group therapy has been shown to be particularly useful in treating certain types of problems—even more useful than individual therapy. The social pressure of a group can be very powerful, and watching other people in a group can be a useful therapeutic tool. Thus, group therapy is an important technique not only because more patients can be treated and it is less expensive, but also because it is an effective, useful, and important technique for many clients' problems.

Group therapy is not a specific technique. Each group has its own types of clients, therapist, and approaches. The way a group handles certain problems is largely determined by the type of group and its therapist. There are psychoanalytic groups, client-centered groups, Gestalt groups, as well as behavior therapy groups. Each group confronts its members and their problems in a different way. No two groups are the same and no two groups would deal with an individual member in the same way. In some ways it is impossible to classify all of the different types of groups because each therapist shapes his or her own group. Yet, there are still certain major traditional approaches to group therapy.

In a traditional group therapy a number of clients, usually fewer than 10, meet on a regular basis with a therapist at a clinic, hospital, or the therapist's office. The makeup of the group is usually controlled by the therapist, who examines the members' ages and needs, problems and potentialities. A therapist selects group members in terms of what they can gain from and offer to the group. Thus, the goal is to construct a group with compatible ages, needs, and problems; a carefully selected group makes greater therapeutic gains.

The format of traditional group psychotherapy varies from group to group, but generally each member tells the group his or her problems. The other members of the group generally relate to the group how they have experienced similar problems and how they have coped with them. An individual member is helped in a number of ways. *First,* he or she has a chance to express his or her fears and anxieties to a group of people who are warm and accepting, each member realizing that every person has emotional problems. *Second,* the members of the group can help another member by giving advice about a particular problem. *Third,* a group member can watch others in the group cope with difficult problems. By watching others, he can learn how to handle his own anxieties and problems. *Fourth,* a group member can role-play or otherwise "try out" new behaviors in a safe, nonpunitive yet evaluative environment. *Fifth,* the group may exert certain pressures upon a member to perform more adequately or appropriately. A group may pressure a member into confronting his wife or mother, and they may require him to report back the next week about being more assertive.

Groups are not necessarily sedate and quiet. There are often fairly intense expressions of emotion because members interact on an emotional as well as an intellectual level. As a group develops a cohesiveness and the members learn to understand themselves and each other, members are able to provide mutual help when difficult problems arise during therapy. Sometimes a single member of a group does not contribute; this member may resist telling the truth or helping herself. A group can apply pressure to this person to "shape up." They can pressure her into exposing her fears, confronting her boss, or dealing with the rest of the members of the group. Throughout all of these activities the therapist may take a directive role. Sometimes he may deem it necessary to be directive in helping the group cope with a specific problem or member; other times the therapist may allow the group to work through its problems independently.

In traditional group therapy the therapist or therapists (sometimes there may be two therapists) allow the group to shape its own structure and mode of functioning. As a member feels that he is better able to cope with life and his problems, he may eventually leave the group. He is replaced with a new member who in some sense becomes an initiate. He has to learn to establish new relations with the other members of the group and to fit into the group's social structure. The member's task of orienting to a new group and the group's job to develop a relationship with a new member is often therapeutically good both for the new member and the group. A group meeting a new member is much like many situations in life. Each of us must continually deal with new situations and people; a group has the same problems. A therapist may help the group to understand the way they deal with their own problems in meeting and coping with others by analyzing the way the group and the new members interact.

Psychodrama

Psychodrama is a group therapy technique in which clients act out or dramatize various situations, feelings, and roles in an attempt to gain insight from them. A client in psychodrama might be asked to play the principal role or to react to the way another client is behaving. By watching a psychodrama other members of the group see how people respond to different emotions and feelings. By participating in the group, members have a chance to act out and express their feelings as well as an opportunity to react to the way others feel.

Much of modern group therapy psychodrama stems from the work of J. L. Moreno, a Viennese psychiatrist who first used the technique in the 1930s. While Moreno had his patients actually use a stage, many modern therapists use forms of psychodrama without such elaborate techniques. For example, Gestalt therapists often have clients work through feelings by having them assume the roles of others. Psychodrama, therefore, is not limited to group therapy, but it is used in individual therapy as well.

The therapist can play a variety of roles in the psychodrama. She can be essentially nondirective and allow the drama to take its own shape, or she can be very directive. As in most group psychotherapies, the role of the therapist is usually determined by how the group is proceeding and whether it is achieving its therapeutic aims. While very little research has been done on psychodrama, those who have used it attest to its beneficial therapeutic effects.

In psychodrama, clients express their feelings in a nonthreatening situation—often for the first time in their lives

A special type of group therapy, called **encounter group therapy,** has developed over recent years as an outgrowth of the sensitivity training movement. Encounter and sensitivity groups are generally designed to help people realize their feelings by helping them to achieve self-actualization and to better develop interpersonal relationships. Self-actualization is the process by which people move toward realizing their potential to the greatest degree possible and by doing so achieve everything they are capable of doing. This process is at the pinnacle of Abraham Maslow's pyramid of needs (chapter 4). In general, encounter groups have been used to improve personal and social functioning by bringing together groups of people who wish to increase their awareness and effectiveness as individuals. After attending an encounter group one woman said,

> The immediate impact on my children was of interest to both me and my husband. I feel that having been so accepted and loved by a group of strangers was so supportive that when I returned home my love for the people closest to me was much more spontaneous. Also, the practice I had in accepting and loving others during the workshop was evident in my relationships with my close friends. (Rogers, 1970, p. 318)

It is common for people who have been through encounter groups to make statements like the following:

> It helped clarify my feelings about my work, gave me more enthusiasm for it, and made me more honest and cheerful with my coworkers and also more open when I was hostile. It made my relationship with my wife more open, deeper. We felt freer to talk about anything, and we felt confident that anything we talked about we could work through. (Rogers, 1970, p. 318)

Each encounter group is unique. Some groups are very much like regular therapy groups in terms of format and goals; other groups are specialized. There have been encounter groups for blacks, women, athletes, drug addicts, alcoholics, homosexuals, and singles. There have been encounter groups with minimal leader participation as well as groups that follow formal procedures. Some encounter groups have been held in the nude, in swimming pools, and at mountain retreats. The marathon encounter group has been an outgrowth of the encounter group movement. In a marathon encounter group, a group meets for a prolonged period of time, generally 24 hours, to interact and grow emotionally. Usually the purpose of a marathon group is to deal with immediate feelings. Participants have reported that these extended experiences bring about changes in self-understanding and self-actualization which lasts for long periods of time. Some have said that marathon groups enable the participants to become aware of social pretenses and to begin to question whether or not such social roles are necessary.

Although marathon groups are supposed to heighten the intensity of feelings, lower defenses, and thereby facilitate therapeutic change (Harper, 1975), research on the marathon encounter group does not provide support for these supposed positive effects. The beneficial effects that are obtained in a marathon group seem to be temporary at best (Kilmann & Sotile, 1976). Nevertheless, proponents of the marathon encounter group movement argue that a "one shot" marathon encounter has highly facilitative effects for the members of the group (Yalom et al., 1977). At present there is no evidence to suggest that the marathon encounter group is better than traditional therapy spaced out in one-hour sessions over many days or weeks (see also Bare & Mitchell, 1972).

COMMUNITY PSYCHOLOGY

A new branch of psychology—community psychology—was born in the 1960s. In 1963 President John F. Kennedy sent a message to the Congress calling for "a bold new approach" to mental illness. His message was followed by legislation and funding for community mental health centers. As the concept of community mental health developed, so did a new branch of psychology.

Community psychology An approach to the treatment of mental health problems that provides local services to the community on a continuous basis. Treatment programs are extended to reach people who might not seek them out.

The community approach to psychology provides mental health services to the community before the community needs them. Ordinarily, most types of therapy centers provide psychologists and psychiatrists when a person seeks them out, but the concept of **community psychology** is to provide mental health services with continuous care for people requiring short-term hospitalization and outpatient care for those clients who live at home while receiving therapy. Many community mental health centers offer partial hospitalization for patients who require hospitalization during the day but who return home to their families at night. Community mental health centers also provide a major service in their consultation and education programs. Mental health centers can provide lectures, forums, and literature for the community on a variety of topics that might include therapy, family planning, and drug rehabilitation.

Special Programs: The Neighborhood Clinic

Communities at large have become aware of mental health problems, and a special kind of service agency—the neighborhood clinic—has developed on a small scale in different regions of the nation. Since some of these service agencies have been established by members of the community and supported by donations and benefactors, they offer free help to local citizens. In many of the larger communities, special anonymous treatment facilities for drug addicts, alcoholics, and people in need of psychotherapy have been created. These treatment facilities do not charge for treatment, and information is not authorized to be given out to the authorities, parents, or friends. Anonymity is often totally maintained, and both youth and adults are treated for a variety of problems.

Many community psychologists work with mental health institutions in establishing neighborhood service centers. A neighborhood service center is an attempt to cope with problems of mental health, unemployment, lack of education, as well as all the other problems that neighborhoods have. With partial government support, many of these neighborhood service centers are able to facilitate neighborhood rehabilitation and provide mental health services for members of the community, many of whom are drug addicts, antisocial personalities, and people who are seriously disturbed.

Crisis Intervention

Among the key aims of community psychology is to have people in the community act as paraprofessionals and become involved in local therapy and intervention programs. **Paraprofessionals** are not untrained workers; rather, they are people with specific mental health skills that allow them to undertake many important and necessary tasks professional psychologists do not have the time to handle. Many of these paraprofessionals are housewives, high school teachers, and college students. Although paraprofessionals can never take the place of highly trained psychologists or psychiatrists, they can help improve mental health in the community.

One of the areas in which paraprofessionals have been particularly successful is crisis intervention. Many times during a person's life therapeutic assistance is needed. Sometimes these stressful situations need immediate attention. *Crisis intervention* is an attempt to deal with those short-term, but immediate, situations when people need help. A community health center often provides a unique and appropriate place for such short-term therapy. In such crisis situations the paraprofessional, psychologist, or psychiatrist provides direct, immediate, and supportive therapy to help the person in crisis cope with the situation. The focus is on present circumstances, not on childhood experiences. Very often crisis intervention revolves around a specific event in a person's life. A client has lost his job and feels desperate. A child has become deathly ill, and the family needs emotional support. A woman has been raped, and she needs emotional help and therapy to overcome the trauma of her situation.

Crisis intervention is not a specific set of techniques or procedures, yet it is clearly different from traditional psychotherapy. The goal of crisis intervention is the resolution of immediate problems and emotional conflicts. There is generally only brief contact between the crisis worker and the person needing help, but there is still a high level of activity by the crisis worker in order to help the client. Any therapeutic technique or activity that is deemed feasible is employed, including telephone contacts and working with entire families. Crisis intervention covers a wide range of crises such as those resulting from rape, delinquency, drug use, illness, marital problems, poverty, and growing old (Auerbach & Kilmann, 1977).

The development of crisis intervention has brought the use of hotlines. A *hotline* is a telephone that is staffed 24 hours a day to help people who need direct and immediate help. For example, a person who needs emotional help because he is contemplating suicide might call a therapist on a hotline. The therapist would then try to help the person with immediate directive therapy. Hotline therapy does not take the place of systematic psychotherapy; however, it can be an important mode of crisis intervention for a person who has become panicky or dramatically disturbed.

Is crisis therapy effective? Some studies show that crisis intervention therapy is even better than traditional therapy; others show no difference; still others indicate minimal effects compared with traditional therapy. One of the problems in evaluating crisis therapy is that the techniques used in crisis intervention vary from one therapist to the next and from one study to the next. Indeed, this is a key factor of crisis therapy: to deal with problems as they arise according to the specifics of the situation. In this way crisis intervention therapy is situation-specific; therefore, it is difficult to compare it with traditional therapeutic techniques. Controlled research into crisis intervention can take place and its most important variables can be identified (see Slaikeu, 1979). Because crisis intervention therapy has saved many lives and has been a great help to many people, it is likely that it will continue to

Paraprofessional A person who works alongside professional psychologists and aids them in providing psychological services.

Community psychologists often staff hotlines for people who are in a crisis and need immediate help

thrive, particularly in community mental health settings (Auerbach & Kilmann, 1977).

Psychology as a Community Activity

One of the central aims of community psychology is to provide services to the community. Preventive programs are established to identify high-risk individuals and provide services before there is a need for crisis intervention and/or hospitalization. While there will always be a need for psychotherapists to see patients on a private basis and in groups, there is a growing need for psychological services within the community. Again, the aim of the community psychologist is to seek out mental health problems before they arise. Because the community psychologist is action oriented, she tries to deliver psychological services to the community through a variety of different methods; she helps provide staffing at mental health centers; she helps set up 24-hour-a-day hotlines; she may work toward setting up a suicide prevention center; and she may provide psychological services to groups of alcoholics or drug addicts. Rather than have the community seek out the psychologist to find help, the community psychologist tries to provide a program that reaches out to the community to provide mental health services. Community psychologists advocate changes in community institutions and organizations. It is the belief of many community psychologists that some social conditions and organizational procedures often make existing maladjustment worse and sometimes create new maladjustment. Community psychologists are thus action and change oriented.

SUMMARY

Psychotherapy has been defined as the treatment of abnormal behavior and maladjustment by psychological means. The purpose of this chapter has been to show that treatment procedures can vary widely, from insight therapies, which attempt to discover a person's internal and perhaps unconscious motivations, to behavior therapy, which is concerned only with a person's symptoms and immediate problems. Treatment procedures also differ widely, from one-to-one psychoanalytic procedures through group therapies which may be conducted on a once-a-week basis or on a marathon basis. In every case, regardless of the treatment procedures used, the aim is to change people's behavior.

The choice of a specific therapist and treatment procedure is largely up to the client. It is the client's responsibility to determine whether he or she wishes to seek out a behavior therapist or a psychoanalyst. But very often patients make the wrong choice, and because this is usually evident to the therapist, most therapists will refer a patient to someone who offers a more appropriate therapeutic method. The client and therapist must feel compatible, particularly in traditional psychotherapy and psychoanalysis.

Insight therapies are clearly different from behavior therapies. In insight therapies, the therapist's goal is to help a patient discover conflicts so that he might cope with them. Clearly, the goals of psychoanalysis are different from the goals of Rogerian therapy; certainly the techniques that are used in psychoanalysis and in client-centered therapy are dramatically different.

Insight therapies assume that knowledge and understanding of the present *and* the past are necessary so that people can discover why they behave the way they do, whereas behavior therapies concern themselves largely with a person's immediate situation. Behavior therapists argue that symptom substitution does not exist and that if we can change a person's behavior, we will alleviate suffering and enhance appropriate functioning. The goal of behavior modification is to change a person's behavior in the present because people live in the present.

It is most likely that insight therapies and behavior modification procedures are appropriate under certain conditions and with certain types of problems. When a person has a nervous tic, a behavior modification procedure may be the best approach. So, while transactional analysis may be the right type of therapy for some people, group therapy or an encounter group may be the best for others.

We must remember that the goal of psychotherapy, regardless of the treatment procedure, is the same: to treat people's emotional problems by psychological means. Different psychologists with different approaches to the study of behavior have adopted markedly different theoretical positions which have guided their research programs and treatment procedures. No one specific approach is better, more adequate, or more true than others. Different procedures will bring about different types of behavior changes. In addition, because no two people have the same problem, personalities, and backgrounds, they can best be treated by a procedure that meets their needs appropriately.

CHAPTER REVIEW

1. Psychotherapy is the treatment of emotional disorders by psychological means.
2. Insight therapy attempts to show a patient meaningful relationships between unconscious or underlying causes and current maladjustments or abnormal behavior. Insight therapy assumes that abnormal behavior is caused by a person's lack of understanding of his or her motivation and needs. Once insight is achieved, behavior should almost change automatically.
3. Behavior therapy is based on the application of learning principles, such as classical and instrumental conditioning, which change people's overt behavior rather than their subjective feelings, unconscious processes, or motivations.
4. A placebo effect is a nonspecific therapeutic change that comes about primarily from a person's expectation for change rather than because of any specified treatment by a therapist.
5. In psychoanalysis, insight into a person's true motivations is obtained by special techniques, including free association, dream analysis, and transference. Psychoanalysis, a lengthy, expensive insight therapy, assumes that human beings are basically in conflict.
6. One of the major techniques of psychoanalysis is free association, in which patients speak aloud all thoughts and feelings that occur to them, however illogical their order or content.
7. Dream analysis is another psychoanalytic technique in which a therapist provides patients insight into their dreams.
8. Resistance is a lack of cooperation by a patient in psychoanalysis through which he or she shows an unwillingness to help the therapist understand or interpret information.

9. One of the major techniques of psychoanalysis begins when a patient undergoes transference. This takes place when a patient transfers emotional attitudes to a therapist who becomes the object of the patient's emotions. The patient often shows the therapist the love and hate that he or she might feel for a parent.

10. Ego-analysts are followers of Freud who argue that the ego has a greater control over behavior than Freud suggested.

11. Client-centered therapy, developed by Carl Rogers, seeks to help a person evaluate the world and herself from her own vantage point so that she can become everything that she might; in this nondirective therapeutic procedure, the therapist provides unconditional positive regard toward the client.

12. Client-centered therapy is nondirective. While the client plays the active role, the therapist remains permissive and passive, allowing the direction of therapy to be determined by the client.

13. Gestalt therapy is an insight therapy founded by Perls which encourages individuals to get in touch with their feelings in the present and to enter into the process of becoming aware.

14. Behavior modification procedures assume that symptom substitution does not occur. Symptom substitution is the occurrence of another symptom resulting from the same basic cause as the previous symptom which has been eliminated.

15. A token economy is an instrumental conditioning procedure by which patients are reinforced with tokens for socially acceptable behavior. These tokens are later exchanged for desirable items or privileges. This procedure can be used very effectively in hospitals.

16. One of the major techniques of behavior modification is systematic desensitization, in which a person is taught to relax while imagining scenes of increasingly fearful situations. The aim is to teach the patient relaxation rather than fear, as well as new responses to a formerly fearful stimulus.

17. Another major type of counterconditioning is aversive counterconditioning. This is a technique by which aversive stimuli are paired and associated with stimuli that are undesirable or need to be avoided. Ideally, to avoid the painful stimulus, the patient adopts a new response to the old stimulus.

18. Modeling is learning by observing and imitating the behavior of other people. It is a particularly useful technique in learning new behaviors, eliminating phobias, and increasing the ease of expression of already existing behavior.

19. Rational-emotive therapy is a cognitive therapy that emphasizes logical, rational thought processes. Founded by Ellis, the therapy assumes that patients are led into maladjustments by basic irrational assumptions.

20. Group therapy is a particularly useful method of treating several people simultaneously for emotional and behavioral problems.

21. Group therapy has become popular because many people can be treated in a group, thereby expanding the help a psychologist can provide. Group therapy is relatively less expensive than individual therapy and is particularly useful for certain types of problems.

22. Psychodrama is a group therapy technique in which a client acts out or dramatizes various situations and feelings in an attempt to gain insight from their dramatization.

23. An encounter group is a group of people who meet together to become more aware of their feelings, to better understand and improve their behavior, and to facilitate their social interactions. The focus is on increased awareness. Encounter groups that last for extended sessions are called marathon encounter groups.

24. Community psychology's approach to the treatment of mental health problems is one in which services are provided to the community on a continuous basis. Such treatment programs are designed to reach people who might not seek them out. The locations of treatment centers vary so that more people can reach them, and they include a variety of programs, such as clinics and drug crisis intervention centers.

AYLLON, T., AND AZRIN, N. *The token economy: A motivational system for therapy and rehabilitation.* New York: Appleton-Century-Crofts, 1968.

BANDURA, A. *Principles of behavior modification.* New York: Holt, Rinehart, & Winston, 1969.

BARTON, A. *Three worlds of therapy.* Palo Alto, CA: National Press Books, 1974.

MIKULAS, W. L. *Behavior modification.* New York: Harper & Row, 1978.

ROGERS, C. R. *Client-centered therapy.* Boston, MA: Houghton Mifflin, 1951.

SCHAEFER, H, H., AND MARTIN, P. L. *Behavioral therapy.* New York: McGraw-Hill, 1975.

APPLIED PSYCHOLOGISTS take basic psychological principles and use them in practical ways to better the human condition. As an area of investigation, applied psychology consists of many often overlapping subfields. In applying basic psychological principles, psychologists use data and theory in an interdisciplinary manner. By merging various fields, psychologists make pragmatic decisions which affect people's day-to-day lives. This chapter considers three areas of psychology which have emerged as applied disciplines, each to a varying extent. They each have developed their own theories, but have all borrowed heavily from the discipline from which they grew—the study of behavior.

CHAPTER 14

Psychology as an Applied Science

I really must describe that closet in a German peasant house which served as a temporary punishment cell. It was the length of one human body and wide enough for three to lie packed tightly, four at a pinch. As it happened, I was the fourth, shoved in after midnight. The three lying there blinked sleepily at me in the light of the smoky kerosene lantern and moved over, giving me enough space to lie on my side, half between them, half on top of them, until, by sheer weight, I could wedge my way in. And so four overcoats lay on the crushed-straw-covered floor, with eight boots pointing at the door. They slept and I burned. The more self-assured I had been as a captain half a day before, the more painful it was to crowd onto the floor of that closet. Once or twice the other fellows woke up numb on one side, and we all turned over at the same time.

ALEKSANDER SOLZHENITSYN
The Gulag Archipelago

The first night of Aleksander Solzhenitsyn's journey into the prison system of the Soviet Union was pleasant compared to the tortures that he would eventually endure. We all know that prisons were never meant to be grand or luxurious. While prisons in this country are designed to be more humane than those experienced by Solzhenitsyn, fact finders have found abominable conditions. There has been overcrowding, malnutrition, poor health, and far too few efforts at rehabilitation. Wherever they are located, prisons are an intense environment; by definition, they restrict a person's freedom by controlling every aspect of a prisoner's life. Too often, this controlled, restricted environment is one of squalor, overcrowding, and brutality.

Many people would argue that prisoners get what they deserve; from a psychologist's view, such living conditions are hardly conducive to establishing prosocial behaviors. Today, most everyone (and especially psychologists) recognizes that the environment in which people live helps shape their day-to-day behavior as well as the way they will act in the future. When people are forced to live in overcrowded, poorly ventilated, poorly staffed, and poorly funded prisons, we are not surprised when they emerge worse than when they entered. Acutely aware of environmental variables, psychologists have sought to develop prison systems into more humane living and working quarters.

Psychologists study what people feel, think, and do, and so it is not hard to see that psychologists are involved in almost every area of human behavior—including those of criminals.

Some see psychology as too much of a rigorous and detached science. They see psychology as a rigorous discipline, filled with laws and theories of behavior; they view psychology as a strictly research discipline. Others see psychology differently. For others, psychology is an applied discipline; it takes basic knowledge about human functioning and applies it to better the human condition. Those who favor this view try to use psychology in direct ways.

In some ways, we can see a conflict between the two sides of psychological study. On one side are psychological researchers who study behavior (often in laboratory settings) so as to build theories and make predictions about behavior. Many times these researchers limit themselves to a small aspect of behavior hoping to explain in full the conditions under which it occurs. On the other side are the applied psychologists and science writers who take information from the basic researcher and attempt to apply it to everyday problems in meaningful ways. These psychologists focus on people's desire to know about themselves and to manage their own behavior. We regularly see popular magazines devising "tests" to help us measure everything from our intelligence to our ability to sexually please a person of the opposite sex.

Even a casual reader of popular magazines recognizes that the 20-question "quiz" on a person's sexuality is not scientifically valid. Yet, such quizzes and often inexpertly written magazine articles influence many people and their future behavior. Psychologists are faced with a problem. They have a large body of knowledge about human behavior; they also know that people are eager to learn how to manage their own behavior. However, presenting psychological theory within a meaningful applied context is not always easy to do. One of the aims of this textbook has been to present psychological theory and principles and their applications. Many of these day-to-day uses have been seen in *IMPACT* panels throughout the text.

Psychology is a rigorous science, and much of the research conducted in psychological laboratories can be used in practical problem solving. For example, many psychologists are especially concerned with helping people solve emotional problems. Accordingly, they have developed treatment programs to help people make adjustments and eventually live happier lives.

Today, many psychologists are working in applied fields, seeking to bring the full weight of research and theory to bear on practical problems. In doing so, they have sometimes developed whole new fields of study. In other cases, a smaller number of psychologists from different fields have joined together to investigate some specialty area; they have then applied their knowledge to small but practical real-life problems.

THE APPROACH

Psychologists specializing in an applied area have had to develop an interdisciplinary approach. They have generally taken information, theory, and applications from several subareas of psychology and combined them in meaningful ways. Often this includes a mix of learning theory, biology, motivation, personality, or social psychology. Consider the specialty area of psychology and law enforcement: to study how police officers conduct themselves under stress, researchers have gathered information about learning, motivation, and personality. Another area closely associated has been the examination of the sequence of events and behaviors that occur in the courtroom.

Many clinical psychologists have directed their efforts in a totally different area, for example, at developing programs which allow people to use techniques like biofeedback to treat migraine headaches. Stress management is another frequent application of psychological principles. Hardly a day goes by without some psychologist appearing on television or radio speaking on how to communicate more effectively with your spouse; in this case, psychologists bring basic ideas about social psychology, personality, and marriage together.

Several of the applied areas of psychology no longer need to borrow and mix; they have matured as disciplines and have developed theories and their own research literature. These new fields have emerged as full-fledged applied research areas. Throughout this text we have been examining the impact of psychology on our everyday lives; we will now focus on three particular areas of applied psychology that have emerged on their own as virtually separate new applied disciplines. First we will see that industrial/organizational psychology has a long history and has developed its own theories, data, and applications. Next we will look at environmental psychology, a relatively new field that borrows heavily from other psychological disciplines. Finally we will see that while the study of criminal behavior is less well researched and has borrowed heavily from various disciplines, it is equally important. Psychologists within these fields have tried to use basic psychological facts to better individual lives so as to ultimately better society. Let us begin with the field that has the longest history of research and is the most well-developed of these three areas, industrial/organizational psychology.

INDUSTRIAL AND ORGANIZATIONAL PSYCHOLOGY

As an applied science, industrial/organizational psychology attempts to take psychological principles, many of which were derived in laboratory settings, and apply them in the work place. The focus of industrial/organizational psychology is on how people behave in organizations; these organizations are usually in industry, government, or education. Researchers have focused on gathering information about how people are best characterized in these settings so as to use this knowledge in practical ways. Psychologists who work in industry have focused on individual behavior and how it is affected by others and the environment within which a person works. As you will see shortly, psychologists have tried to use basic psychological principles to help people effectively manage their own behavior.

Personnel Selection

The decision of whom to hire is one of the key choices that an employer makes. There are many industrial/organizational psychologists who focus on developing systems that allow for the best match between employers and prospective employees. In helping make these decisions psychologists try to find people who are best suited to a particular position. This means finding people who will enjoy their work and feel satisfied; it also means finding people who are best suited to an individual company's needs and will be productive employees.

When an industrial/organizational psychologist helps develop selection procedures, the psychologist will usually use a series of steps or processes. Among these steps will be:

1. A standardized application
2. A standardized interview
3. A standardized work sample
4. A standardized series of tests

When an individual applies for a position in a large or a small company there are a number of ways that an employer can make decisions as to a candidate's suitability. Obviously, an interview can tell an employer a great deal. A person's previous experience in a job is usually good evidence of suitability. Another criterion which might be used is a work sample; perhaps the most familiar work sample is the standardized typing test. All of these measures can be standardized by psychologists in important ways. Interview questions can be standardized. Experience scales can be devised. In the same way, work samples can be evaluated against some standard.

A key component of the process is that the criteria used are *standardized;* comparisons among applicants must be made and they all must be compared to a standard criterion. This is no easy task. Cutoffs need to be established so as to determine minimum performance levels; however, individual differences also need to be taken into account. An individual's maturity, sense of humor, and even the difficult-to-define "twinkle in the eye" are often indicators of certain unique skills or abilities that an employer may wish to take into consideration.

While many different measures and criteria might be used, increasingly standardized tests have been involved in making selection decisions. From the early part of this century psychologists have been studying testing procedures and have developed sophisticated techniques to measure human abilities and potential. As presented in chapter 7, a standardized test is a test that has a uniform procedure for its administration, scoring, and interpretation as well as a list of norms. There are a huge number of standardized tests; indeed, there are over 300 publishers of tests. Tests have been devised to measure intelligence, aptitude, achievement, personality, interests, special abilities, humor, and mechanical abilities. In addition, projective tests have been developed to help examine a person's underlying motivations, and tests like the MMPI have been developed to measure potential maladjustment.

We know from our examination of tests like the MMPI that many tests have been very well researched (see p. 510). An intelligence test like the WAIS-R is a fine predictor of academic achievement; similarly, the MMPI is an excellent predictor of maladjustment. Of course, skilled administration and interpretation of these tests is necessary. Psychologists are particularly sensitive to the idea that tests are a measure of behavior but that they are only *one* small sample.

The use of tests to help make predictions about future work performance has become an important part of industrial/organizational psychology. However, psychologists have been especially careful in examining test results. They have examined closely how well tests can be used to predict future performance; they are concerned that their tests are valid measures (see Guion, 1976). Work performance is a complicated set of behaviors; industrial/organizational psychologists have therefore been particularly aware of the strengths *and* limitations of tests as predictors of future behavior.

While tests can predict future success or failure, they are not perfect. A test cannot take into consideration changing personal and motivational factors. A man who becomes depressed after a death in his family may become less effective in the work place. Similarly, but in the opposite direction, a woman who has taken on new responsibilities may find that her self-esteem has increased and her efficiency at her job may increase because of her newly found self-confidence.

The process of personnel selection is complicated and no single measure can be used to hire an employee. Human beings are complex and employers have to sort through a great deal of information if they are to choose their new employees wisely. In addition to the already difficult process of personnel selection are other complicating factors. Federal guidelines for affirmative action must be considered; minorities must be given equal opportunities;

women must not be discriminated against; age is irrelevant. In past years, employers often would exclude many qualified applicants because of their marital status, their age, or their race. Today, it is against the law. Indeed, affirmative action programs have attempted to balance the inequities that exist in many large (and small) companies where minorities and women are dramatically underrepresented.

In large companies that employ hundreds or thousands of individuals, personnel selection is a complicated process. Companies seek the best-qualified applicants; however, they also seek applicants who will be efficient, productive, and happy. While a specific candidate for a position may be well qualified, the candidate may not "fit in" with a growth attitude that a company has developed. A man who is a skilled draftsman may be well qualified for a position; however, he may not be desirous of opportunities which a company may have in mind for such a person. Companies and individuals have unique needs; these needs may change. Because needs change, psychologists have recognized that selection is a continuous, constantly evolving process. Sometimes, a well-matched employer-employee relationship becomes imbalanced after a few months or years. A situation which at one time was well suited for an aspiring woman may become dull and stagnant. In the continuing process of selection, such a woman may opt to find a new situation in her company or seek a new company. Thus, as Gilmer (1977) has suggested, selection is a two-way street—companies select people and people select companies.

The process of selection, while constantly becoming more rigorous and scientific, still remains partially subjective; Guion (1976) suggested that it is an art that is used each time an administrator needs to make a personnel decision. In many ways, industrial/organizational psychologists try to provide as much science as possible to the "art" of selection.

Motivation and the Worker

Once an employee is selected and begins work for a company, both are faced with a new challenge. Companies exist to provide goods and services to people, usually in exchange for money. To be competitive in a free enterprise system employers need workers who will produce their product for as little as possible and in as great a volume as possible. By being productive, a worker allows a company to be successful and make a profit. However, people do not work solely for monetary rewards.

We all know that money is important; people have monetary needs to buy food and shelter. They have also developed social needs for certain "creature comforts" like expensive stereo systems and sports cars. In addition, people have social needs for affiliation, love, respect, and feelings of self-worth. In many important ways, an employer and the work situation must fulfill each of these needs to a different extent. An extremely well-paid plumber may find work tedious and unfulfilling; by contrast, a clerical worker who finds his job important and challenging may stay in that position even though his monetary requirements are not met fully.

Human beings are complex and no single motivation will guide and direct all of their behaviors. We learned in chapter 4 that people have physiological needs that direct their behavior, but they also have learned, social needs.

Human beings think about their situations and evaluate carefully how and under what conditions they are willing to involve themselves in various behaviors. For example, behaviors that are engaged in strictly because they bring pleasure to the person and have no external reward associated with them are said to be intrinsically motivated (see p. 166). We know that when intrinsically motivated behaviors are reinforced with some direct external reward they often cease to be emitted as frequently. We therefore see that an employer-employee relationship must consider not only economic factors. American industry has learned that economic rewards are only one aspect of motivation and sometimes are not even the most important ones.

DETERMINANTS OF JOB PERFORMANCE.   Through the years employers have sought various ways to motivate their employees to be productive (and hence profitable). Let us consider a theory that has developed to help explain under what conditions workers seem most motivated, the Vroom expectancy theory.

Vroom's basic idea was that performance on a job is determined by both *motivation* and *ability* (Vroom, 1964). A person has to have the ability to do the job or task. We call it expectancy theory because from this view, motivation is determined by what people expect to get by their performance. The theory also suggests that motivation is determined by how people value the task. For example, if a person finds completing a certain task highly rewarding, offering no negative elements, then it is highly motivating. By contrast, a specific task may be rewarding to complete, *but* it may have associated with it various tedious time-consuming and boring tasks. In such a situation the probability of completing the task decreases; Vroom therefore suggests that the task is not as motivating.

While motivation and ability are the key elements to Vroom's theory, Lawler and Porter (1967) have modified and extended it. They assert that performance is determined by *motivation, ability*, and *role perceptions*. Role perceptions are the ways people see themselves and their jobs; this requires that

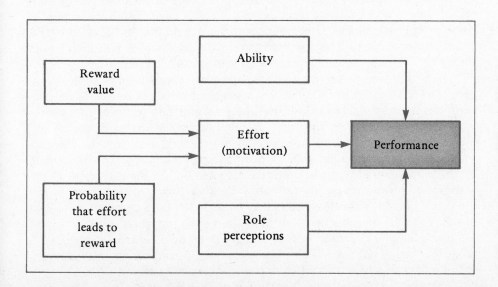

Figure 14.1 The managerial model put forth by Lawler and Porter (1967) suggests that ability, motivation, *and* role perceptions determine work performance. They also note that the values of a reward and the probability that an effort will be successful affect motivation level. The Lawler and Porter modification of the Vroom expectancy model is widely accepted, but probably not the final word on the variables that affect work performance.

they understand fully the nature of their positions and all that is required of them. Too often people do not understand the requirements of the job—not because of a lack of effort (motivation) or ability (see also Lawler, 1973).

The expectancy model has not met with universal agreement. Its critics argue that it is too limited in scope and cannot account for all of the data (Campbell & Pritchard, 1976). However, until a more powerful model replaces it, it is likely to continue to exert a strong influence on industrial/organizational psychology.

CAN MOTIVATION BE MANAGED? Employers and psychologists have long recognized that people are motivated for various reasons. We all know that rewards are important, but we have learned the likelihood that the person will be successful at a task is also important (Vroom, 1964). Companies have attempted to manage employee motivation in order to increase it. Sometimes these motivation management techniques fly in the face of common sense and sometimes even of common decency. There are three basic approaches to the management of motivation: paternalistic, behavioral, and participatory management.

Dating back hundreds of years, and common in the United States during the 1800s, was a system of *paternalistic management.* The basic idea was that a company should act in a paternal or "fatherly" manner taking care of its employees' needs and desires—happy employees would be productive. The mining towns of Appalachia were common scenes of paternalism where the mining company provided housing, schools, recreation, and even churches for its employees. These aspects of living were provided to employees not based on performance, but rather because they were employees.

The paternalistic system is contrary to most psychologists' views of behavior. When people are provided with rewards not contingent on their behavior, they often stop responding. We have a large literature in the study of learning that shows that reinforced behavior tends to occur again. Instrumental conditioning teaches us that for a behavior (work) to be established and maintained rewards must be contingent upon performance. In the laboratory we reinforce a rat *only* if it presses the bar a certain number of times. In paternal systems all the employees, both hard working and lazy, are provided reinforcements. This hardly creates a situation which will increase an individual's desire to work hard—there are no contingencies.

Totally opposite in orientation are *behavioral* approaches to motivation. This view sees a worker solely in terms of performance. As we learned in studying instrumental conditioning, humans and rats will work to get rewards; consequently, this approach asserts that people will work *only* if tangible rewards are provided for specific work performance. In this view, rewards are contingent upon work performance; a factory worker who is paid by the piece is an example of motivation by behavioral management. Hardworking employees make more money because they produce more work; they are productive. Their rewards may come in the form of commissions, or in salary raises, bonuses, stock options, and even job titles.

The behavioral approach has advantages over the paternalistic system because it is based upon learning theory. However, people who are reinforced solely for work performance (for example, the pieceworker) often band together and keep productivity low so that no one has to work too hard. In a factory, someone who "overworks" makes everyone else look bad and is called a "rate buster."

We have stressed that human beings are motivated to work for a wide range of reasons. Recognizing this, the process of *participative management* has evolved. The basic idea is that if individuals participate in the decisions that affect their lives, they will be more likely to be motivated to work. When individuals feel competent and self-determining, this is likely to increase their level of motivation (Deci, 1975). With participative management people can feel self-determining because they are involved in the decision-making process.

Participatory management has been analyzed in great detail and is widely used in many companies. Locke and Schweiger (1979) have asserted that participatory management can vary in *degree, content,* and *scope.* Degree is the extent of participation from little to full. Content refers to the activities involved—work schedules, task assignments, or major policy decisions. Scope refers to the range of activities in which individuals are engaged. As is shown in Figure 14.2, participatory management affects various aspects of people's lives. It leads to situations which help motivate workers and thus results in greater productivity and ultimately job satisfaction.

Figure 14.2 Participatory management leads to increased work effectiveness and job satisfaction for a variety of reasons. It also leads to many psychological changes; according to Locke and Schweiger (1979) it affects one's *values, thoughts,* and *motivations.* This in turn leads to behaviors which are more effective in producing productive *and* happy workers (Locke & Schweiger, 1979).

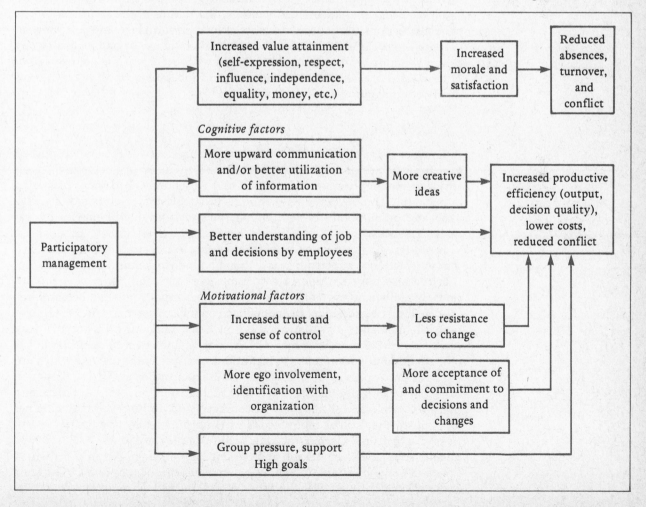

Like most forms of behavior, there is a complex array of variables that enters into the effectiveness of participatory management. Its success depends upon the work setting, the individuals involved, and the nature of the decisions to be made (Locke & Schweiger, 1979). Having individuals involved in decision making usually increases job satisfaction and rarely decreases it. Like the paternalistic and the behavioral systems, participatory management remuneration does not offer all of the answers to increasing either productivity or job satisfaction.

Industrial/organizational psychologists have recognized that the mere delivery of rewards by themselves will not create productive or satisfied workers. Similarly, the involvement of workers in decision making may increase job satisfaction or productivity, but again, this technique alone is insufficient.

While participatory management may be effective in one company, it may not be effective in another. Sometimes this may be due to hiring policies. For example, if a company hires ambitious young individuals, the employees may be more likely to take risks or disregard the feelings of other employees; this might eventually lead to a lack of cooperation. Other companies who stress team and participatory management in the interview situation may hire employees who are cooperative in their personal disposition. Thus, we see that work performance is determined by a person's motivation, the job situation itself, the person's co-workers, the nature of the company, and a person's responsibility characteristics. Work performance and job satisfaction are often closely related; unhappy workers may not be productive. By contrast, happy workers who are satisfied with their jobs are not *necessarily* productive. Let us explore the dimension of job satisfaction the way an industrial/organizational psychologist would.

Job Satisfaction

A person's satisfaction with a job reflects attitudes toward it. As we studied in chapter 10, Social Psychology, an attitude is made up of a belief that has an affective (feeling) component attached to it which may or may not be shown in behavior. Thus, when a worker holds the belief that a job is tedious, it is likely that anger about the tedium may be shown in overt behavior by frequent absences.

In studying happiness or satisfaction with a job, researchers have realized that satisfaction is affected by more than just the work being performed. Satisfaction also depends upon co-workers, working conditions, pay, promotions, benefits, and even others outside of the company like family members.

A clear distinction must be made between job satisfaction and job motivation. On one hand, job satisfaction is how one *feels* about work and the work place (remember, attitudes may or may not be shown in behavior). On the other hand, motivation refers to conditions or states within people which energize them. A person has many reasons to work or not work, and these reasons may or may not be associated with job satisfaction. A tired, bored, and overworked electrician may *feel* discouraged and angry—she may hate her job, but she may still be motivated to work hard. She may find the pay incentives so great that she puts in long hard hours (even though she may hold hostile feelings toward her job and her hourly work). So, we make a distinction between job satisfaction and job performance; the former is determined and reflected in attitudes, the latter is determined by motivation and reflected in actual work.

Recognizing that job satisfaction can be shown in changing work performance as well as through absenteeism and turnovers, industrial/organizational psychologists have sought to quantify job satisfaction so as to help employers and workers. Over the years reliable and valid standardized scales have been developed to measure a person's job satisfaction. Typically, these tests yield an attitude score. For example, a scale might have an item like this one:

My supervisor is consistently fair in dealing with his subordinates.
    Strongly agree
    Agree
    Undecided (neither agree nor disagree)
    Disagree
    Strongly disagree.

Or an employee might answer yes or no to statements on a survey like this:

Do you feel you would rather be doing some other type of work?
Does your supervisor know his or her job well?
Are you interested in company community activities and projects?
Do you feel that you have a good future with this company?

The aim of such scales is to provide employers with an index of employee job satisfaction. An underlying assumption that industrial/organizational psychologists make is that job satisfaction is related to work performance. There is, of course, truth to this idea. However, work performance is also related to the extent of the reward given, the frequency of rewards, working conditions, benefits, co-workers, and, especially, the individual worker's internal set of values and desires for growth and development (see, for example, Weaver, 1980).

An industrial/organizational psychologist helps employers select well-trained, qualified employees for a position. If the employers then provide a context in which to work that will help meet the employers' needs for profit and productivity *and* the workers' needs for monetary rewards and self-esteem, then, a happy employer-employee relationship is found. The industrial/organizational psychologist can help make this happen by providing advice, consultation, and by applying basic learning and motivational theory.

Leadership

In every organization there are people who emerge as leaders; a leader is a person who influences other people's behavior. In some organizations leaders emerge spontaneously, in others the role of leader is dictated by some governing body. In a small club a leader may emerge because of hard work and obvious abilities; in a large company, the president may be defined as the leader and the presidency may be inherited. In the first situation a leader has emerged because of leadership abilities. In the second situation, the leader is *given* a position of authority; we see that a leader's abilities may or may not be consistent with the demands of the job.

One of the key tasks of leaders is motivating group members to perform their respective tasks. Organizations have purposes; a fraternal organization may have as its goal community service. Its leader must motivate members to be involved, work hard, and raise money for community activities. In industry, a leader may be required to set goals for the company and make policy decisions. In industry leaders are usually also required to encourage, promote, and develop motivated employees. You will see later that being a leader is not so easy and the variables that allow for effective leadership are not related in a simple manner.

The study of leadership has gone through three major phases of development, each with a characteristic focus. These phases may be considered the study of leadership *traits, behaviors,* and *situations.* Each of these topics has generated a great deal of research; you will see that it is the combination of all of these characteristics that ultimately describes leadership and effective leaders.

The study of the characteristics of individual leaders and their specific personality *traits* was carried on intensively until the early 1950s. The focus of this research was to isolate those characteristics of individuals that made them good or poor leaders. For example, these studies sought to see if all good leaders were assertive, directive, or perhaps authoritarian. The research on the traits of leaders was almost doomed to failure. A leader is not characterized easily by traits like assertiveness or passivity. Many leaders were shown to be assertive; but many others were characterized as nonassertive. In fact, the individual differences between leaders were extreme. One of the reasons that these early studies were unable to find a common denominator among leaders was because leaders have different goals and are involved in different organizations. The president of General Motors Corporation has extremely different responsibilities from the president of a local garden club. While an individual's personality traits may tell us something about leadership, the differences among leaders may be greater than their similarities.

The focus of research moved quickly to leaders' *behaviors.* These studies examined closely the behavior in which leaders engaged; they sought to find if there was a characteristic way that leaders acted with members of their organizations. Some of the pioneering work on leadership was done at the University of Michigan's Institute for Social Research. The Michigan studies, as they are sometimes called, led to the finding that leaders are often employee-oriented or task-oriented. The difference between employee- or task-orientation centers around how leaders influence behavior. With an employee orientation, a leader acts to maintain and enhance individual employees' feelings of self-worth and esteem; such leaders attempt to make employees and co-workers feel valued and important. A task-oriented leader focuses energy on getting the job done efficiently, quickly, and with as little effort as possible.

The study of leaders' behaviors soon became more complex and ideas began to develop and were expanded and qualified. Some researchers extended the dimensions of leaders' behaviors from two to four (see, for example, Bowers & Seashore, 1966); others suggested further refinements and blurring of once simpler categories (Hammer & Dachler, 1975). As with *trait* approaches, research showed that individual differences among leaders were great and that sometimes a leader's behavior was determined by personal traits, sometimes by the leader's overall orientation (employee or task), and sometimes by the group of people being influenced or led.

Some groups of individuals have characteristics which demand an employee orientation more than a task orientation. Consider an underpaid, overworked, but dedicated social worker; such a man might have a great need to have his self-esteem bolstered. He may feel that his work is worth-

while, but know that he is drastically underpaid. A supervisor must motivate him not with authoritarian task-oriented orders but with concerns for his needs for self-worth and feelings of competence. We recognize that everyone has needs for self-esteem; however, highly paid executives may be willing to be led in a more task-oriented way because they recognize that their high salary is because of their productivity. We see that the relationships between job performance, job satisfaction, and the way a worker is treated are closely related. Leaders must consider their own traits, various possible behaviors they might use to influence others, as well as the situation in which the leader and co-workers are placed.

In the 1970s, research shifted from leaders' behavior to the *situations* in which behaviors were performed. Certainly, our garden club president has a different task *and* situation than the president of a major profit-motivated corporation. Some situations lend themselves to leadership and influence over others' behaviors; others place a leader in a situation where control and influence are minimal. Imagine the situation where a leader or supervisor is warm and friendly, employee-oriented, and in a service position where such an approach is useful. However, imagine also that the organization is in financial trouble; workers are being laid off regularly and our supervisor has no control over who is let go. This climate of unrest may not lend itself to a spirit of such a leader. A better leader (at this time) might be directive, task-oriented, and one who can keep the organization functioning. Thus, we again see a complex interplay of factors; sometimes, one of the variables weighs more heavily in effective leadership, and at other times the web of factors seems nearly impossible to untangle. Research evaluating these potential variables continues to explore leader/worker relationships.

Researchers have become keenly aware of how environmental design can affect human behavior. People have needs for personal space, privacy, and even a sense of territoriality; designing environments to fit these needs is especially helpful. Yet, while designers may be aware of human needs and behavior patterns, these considerations are often left behind. Sometimes it seems as if designers have architectural concepts in mind rather than pleasant and appropriate environments for living and working.

The users of space and its designers are usually different people; city planners, town councils, and mayors often design, approve, and fund urban housing projects. They usually have little concept of how an urban living space should be designed for maximum efficiency and comfort of its inhabitants.

Environmental psychology is the study of how physical settings affect human behavior and how people change the environment to make it comfortable and acceptable to them. Environmental psychology is an applied science and much of its focus is on solving applied problems through research. One of the early environmental studies dealt with the influence of the design of a ward on the behavior of patients in mental hospitals. You might think that the organization and layout of a hospital ward should be easy to figure out, yet the research that was conducted in the 1960s led to some important discoveries. One discovery was that the design of a hospital can change the outcome of a patient's treatment; some of this early work thus led to new designs of mental hospital wards (Proshansky & O'Hanlon, 1977).

If physical settings shape behavior, then think of how city life compared with rural farm settings might change the way a person responds to joyful events, loved ones, economic pressures, or stress. Cities offer opportunities for work, culture, and leisure that are not available in rural settings; it is for this reason they are so attractive to many individuals. At the same time, however, descriptive profiles of cities often include terms like huge, monumental, noisy, fast, teeming, cold, and rude (Milgram, 1970). When people live in such environments, it is likely that their responses to new events will be shaped, or at least modified, by the fast-paced, teeming life in which they are accustomed to living. Of course, a city is complex and is made up of buildings, events, culture, noise, entertainment, and myriad other characteristics. All of these variables can change from place-to-place and from day-to-day within a city, and the effects on any single individual will vary. A city can be so quiet that it can be considered lonely; it can be so noisy that it can be considered teeming. Cities must be viewed as offering a wide range of situations that can affect behavior in both positive and negative ways. Recognizing the diversity of city life, some environmental psychologists have focused on how people live in cities.

The study of the city as a living place is only one component of environmental psychology. Some argue that it is too global, too large, too complex, with far too many variables to assess its effects on human behavior. These psychologists, therefore, often focus on smaller units, perhaps neighborhoods, or specific urban housing developments. Some environmental psychologists have gone a step further and looked at only individuals, or, at most, small groups of people.

In summary, environmental psychologists study the relationship between human behavior and the environment. They have realized that human be-

Environmental Psychology
The study of how physical settings affect human behavior and how human behavior affects the environment.

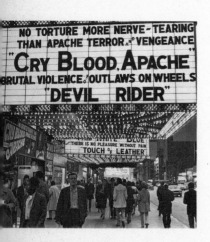

Cities provide all types of stimulation.

City living is often crowded *and* enthralling.

havior cannot be evaluated without considering where and how people live; they have, therefore, studied the components of the physical environments and how these components affect behavior.

Directions

Trying to explain behavior as a response to the environment is not as straightforward as it might seem. Environmental psychology is a young discipline and has not yet developed a comprehensive and unified theory which can account for human behavior. Compare the task of the environmental psychologist with the task of a memory researcher. Memory researchers often provide subjects with a long list of numbers to learn. Human subjects are fairly predictable, remembering the beginnings and endings of lists quite well. Investigating this phenomenon, researchers have manipulated the length of the list, the words contained in the list, how many times the list is presented, as well as other characteristics of the situation that could affect memory. Much of this psychological inquiry has tried to explore the wide number of variables that affect memory.

While environmental psychology accepts the basic assumption of scientific inquiry, environmental researchers have realized that the environment represents more than just the shape of a building, the layout of a dormitory, or the arrangement of buildings in a housing project.

Noise Creates Aggression

As applied psychologists, many researchers have been concerned about the potential of stress-producing environmental stimuli.

Consider noise. Noise is a serious stressor. Researchers have suggested that stressors like noise can elicit aggression in humans. A great deal of basic research has been conducted to learn about how noise affects human beings; the ultimate aim of this research is to apply this knowledge to practical situations where noise is constant and at high level—perhaps in cities or factories. The following is a review of three such research studies where noise was manipulated (independent variable) to assess its effect on aggressive behaviors (the dependent variable).

In an interesting study done by Geen and O'Neal (1969), subjects were aroused with loud bursts of noise while they were asked to deliver electric shocks to another person. Of course, they were really not delivering shocks to the other individual, but they thought they were. The study was designed so that the subjects saw either an aggressive film or a control neutral film before the opportunity to aggress was made available. The results of the study were fairly straightforward, showing that the greatest number of shocks was given by subjects who received both the arousing noise and the aggressive film cues before their opportunity to deliver the electric shocks. Not only did the noise-aroused group who saw the aggressive film deliver more shocks, but they delivered shocks of a higher intensity. These results are consistent with other data on the effects of loud noises on subjects' behavior as well as with previously reported data on the effect of watching aggressive stimuli on subsequent behavior.

The effects of noise on aggressive behaviors were studied further by two researchers from Iowa State University, Donnerstein and Wilson (1976). Using deception, they conducted a clever laboratory experiment on the effects of noise. Subjects were placed in situations where they were to give electric shocks to another student; these students were actually confederates of the experimenter and received no electric shocks. During the session, brief bursts of noise of moderate or high intensity were delivered. Furthermore, just before the experiment began, in half the cases the confederate either angered the unsuspecting subject, and in the other half of the cases did not anger the subject. The results of this study are shown in Figure 14.3. Not surprisingly, the angered subjects delivered shocks of greater intensity than the nonangered ones. Furthermore, among the angered subjects, those who received high noise bursts gave shocks of greater intensity than those exposed to noise of lower levels.

Confirming their expectations, Donnerstein and Wilson (1976) concluded that bursts of loud noises act as stressors and facilitate aggression. They decided to examine the effects of noise one step further. In a 1972 review of the effects of noise on behavior, Glass and Singer argued that when subjects feel that they have control over the noise so that it is predictable, the disruptive effect of noise on behavior is not as great. Donnerstein and Wilson decided to test this prediction. Again, using deception, they conducted a study where students were to give shocks to a confederate of the experimenter. While working on a set of math problems (before the shock phase of the study), the subjects were either exposed to no noise or high noise. Of the subjects exposed to high noise, half of them were told that they could terminate the noise whenever they wanted; the other half were told nothing and, presumably, thought they had no control over the noise. Thus, there were three groups of subjects: no noise, noise without control, and noise with control. As in their previous study, half of the subjects were angered by the confederate before the experiment began and half were not angered.

If Glass and Singer (1972) were correct about feelings of control, then subjects who perceived that they had control over the noise should produce shocks of less intensity than those with no perceived control. This prediction was confirmed. As shown in Figure 14.3, angry subjects delivered shocks of greater intensity than nonangry ones. Those subjects who were exposed to high levels of noise *and* did not perceive control over the noise were also more aggressive in the shock delivery.

Let us look at one additional study on how noise affects behavior. In a laboratory study of the effects of noise on helping behavior, Mathews and Canon (1975) showed that noise had deleterious effects. Subjects reported to a laboratory for an experiment where they found another subject who was actually a confederate of the experimenter seated in one of the two available chairs reading an article. Upon being called in to take his turn in the experiment, the confederate rose awkwardly and, as he rose, dropped some of his papers and they scattered on the floor. The confederate moved without hesitation to recover the dropped materials. The dependent variable in this study was the presence or absence of helping behavior on the part of the subject in front of whom the materials had been dropped. A helping response was recorded if the subject rose and assisted the confederate in retrieving the dropped materials.

The independent variable in the study was the noise

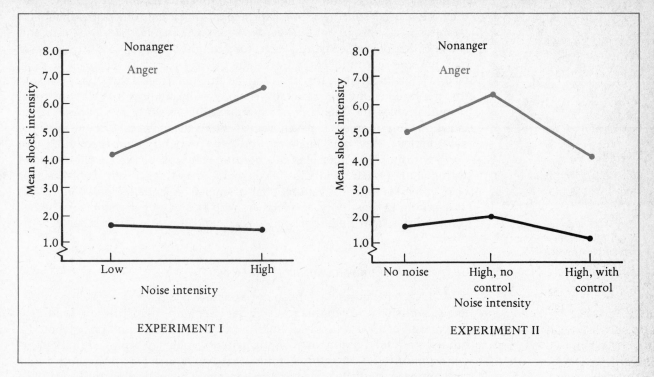

Figure 14.3 On the left side are the results from Experiment I of Donnerstein and Wilson. Notice that the angered subject gave shocks of higher intensity than nonangered ones; also, if a subject was exposed to high intensity noise, he gave the highest level of shock intensity.

In Donnerstein and Wilson's Experiment II, mean shock intensity is presented as a function of noise level. Again, angered subjects gave higher levels of shock than nonangered subjects; those subjects who perceived that they had no control over the noise gave the highest level shocks of all (Donnerstein & Wilson, 1976).

level in the room. There were three conditions: no artificially induced noise, a low level of noise, and a high level of noise. The results of this study were fairly straightforward. The percentage of students helping with no noise was 72%. In the condition of low levels of noise, the percentage of students helping was 67%, and with the high level of noise, the percentage of students helping was 37%. The researchers concluded that high levels of noise produced a reduction of attention to peripheral events, that is, those events not related to central ongoing activities and concerns of the subjects.

Noise can clearly be a stressor. But the relationship between noise and behavior is not a simple one. Like the Yerkes-Dodson law, the effects are dependent on the type of task involved as well as the level of noise achieved. Furthermore, personal characteristics must be considered, including such characteristics as a person's sex, previous experience with noise, and a person's attention span. Like other aspects of behavior, there is no simple rule that will relate a person's behavior with level of noise.

The number of ways that a relatively simple variable like noise can influence a person's day-to-day behavior points out how complex an issue the environmental psychologist faces. When considering a large-scale environment like a city, the number of variables becomes particularly large and their interaction and involvement with each other becomes enormous. Accordingly, laboratory experiments studying individuals in the city *may* begin to lose some of their effectiveness. Laboratory experiments usually isolate one, two, or perhaps, three variables and manipulate them in order to see how these specific variables affect specific behaviors. In a large-scale environment like a street, neighborhood, or city, dozens of variables are entering into the situation and all of them can change in different directions.

The stress of noise can be overwhelming unless you take preventive actions.

Single variables like size, shape, and number of people per square foot are all potent variables—they will all affect human behavior (see p. 480). But they are *interrelated;* the number of people in a room determines whether people perceive the room as crowded—but this is affected by the size and shape of the room, the layout of furniture, height of ceilings, lighting, time of day, number of windows, and even the color of the walls. Since all of these factors affect the perception of a room as crowded, researchers have realized that the study of environmental psychology is the study of the relationship of many variables and that it is nearly impossible to study single variables in isolation. Environmental psychologists study the physical attributes of the environment, the social aspects, and even the individual behaviors that occur within it. The floor plan of a hospital ward can be seen as pleasing and warm when its staff members are congenial and caring; it can also be seen as cold, impersonal, and dysfunctional when staff members are distant, aloof, and lacking in sensitivity. Researchers who look at global systems like cities, communities, and neighborhoods, must consider a wide number of variables.

Changing the Environment as It Changes Us

Many research studies have been done on how to design space so as to maximize its efficiency; often this research has been done in institutional settings. The design of a ward in a hospital is a frequent research endeavor; should a nurses' station be central to all of the patients' rooms or arranged in a columnar fashion? In investigations of the density of housing environments, high-rise compared with low-rise apartments have been studied intensely. The study of the open and closed classroom concept has been frequently assessed. Libraries, museums, and living rooms have been studied. In each of these studies the aim has been to assess how living and working spaces determine behavior. Eventually, these spaces are changed to reflect new findings in environmental psychology.

Let's consider the design of a nurses' station in a hospital. The aim of a hospital is to provide for the care of patients. Admittedly, hundreds of people work in hospitals and considerations of design are important not only for the patients' well-being but also for the well-being of the hospital workers. In large hospitals, dozens of patients are on a floor; this means that on a hospital floor there are many nurses, doctors, aides, and janitorial and other support people. The traditional floor plan for a hospital is a long corridor or, perhaps, two corridors headed by a nurses' station. This nurses' station acts as a center of all activity on the hospital floor. All communications, medications, visitors, doctors, and flowers flow through the nurses' station.

As an alternative to this traditional design, hospital designers have provided floor plans that are radial in nature; these floor plans have a nurses' station that is at the hub of a wheellike arrangement of rooms. Given this arrangement, most patients' rooms are close to the nurses' station. This means less walking for the nurses and a potentially more efficient design for all involved. When Trites and his co-workers (1970) investigated worker satisfaction with different hospital designs, they found a distinct preference for the radial compared with the long corridor design; however, other research has not found beneficial effects of the radial design (Lippert, 1971). For our purposes, it is important to see that such research into the nature of environment-behavior interaction can and does take place.

Two New Approaches to the Open Classroom

Architects have long been aware of how space can be effectively used; in the last two decades psychologists and educators have also been making suggestions as to how to use space, particularly in the classroom. Based on some of Piaget's ideas, open classrooms in which children can move from project to project are increasingly being used in elementary school settings. In the following article, it is easy to see that architects are profiting from the advice of environmental psychologists and educators.

ARCHITECTURE AUSTRALIA   Two State primary schools recently completed in Victoria have been designed around the open classroom concept. This allows teachers, working alone or in teams, considerable freedom in the way class activities are planned and provides pupils with a variety of spaces according to their specific needs. The basic unit requires a central teachers' station which can be used for preparation, storage and correction of class material, and permits supervision of up to four teaching areas.

Each teaching area accommodates a full class (around 30), and can be opened up to adjacent areas when necessary for larger classes. They usually have, or share, wet areas for science and art projects, and withdrawal rooms for quiet activities, student counseling, and individual tutorials. Teaching units share a resource centre which pupils are encouraged to use for individual study and project work. Larger schools include an art/craft room, canteen and multi-purpose hall.

The schools at Queenscliff and Oakleigh illustrate radically different approaches to this educational idea.

Queenscliff, with its small resident population, is a holiday resort. The new school is located on a hilltop, with extensive views of the bay on the same site as the original building which was destroyed by fire. The learning areas are wrapped around three sides of a glasshouse containing central staff workspace. The fourth side is adjacent to administration offices and toilets. The shape and size of learning areas appears to be arbitrary: walls, floors and ceilings change direction, level, and slope, without reference to each other, resulting in a riot of awkward junctions, inaccessible clerestory lighting and unnecessary roof plumbing.

Although the users profess to be quite satisfied with their new school there are occasions when the lack of privacy can be keenly felt: as when the whole school turns its attention to the teacher who vents his spleen on some poor misguided pupil. It will be interesting to visit this school again in ten years time and see what changes have had to be made to suit new teaching methods and learning programs.

Oakleigh Primary is much larger than its Queenscliff sister. Located on a busy main road in an industrial and residential suburb, Oakleigh Primary turns its face from the world, and looks inward to intimate courtyard/open air teaching spaces. The original school still stands and is a model of the old style: with its prim classrooms surrounding a lofty timber-ceilinged hall complete with stained glass windows, it has been restored to its former glory. Externally the bits that used to be painted cream and green have been painted canary yellow and signal red (what else but primary colors for a primary school?) to match the new building.

The new building is planned along a central circulation spine which kinks slightly and ramps up, gently following the ground slope. In a couple of places there are intimate spaces where one can sit quietly or hold a reasonably private conversation away from the bustle of the main traffic. Ranged along one side of the spine are the art and craft room, canteen, multi-purpose room, administrative offices, resource centre, and toilets. On the other side are two sets of open classroom suites each containing four learning areas, and looking at semi-private open spaces.

The classroom suites are so arranged that it is possible to run either open learning/team teaching or the traditional style classes side by side: or to switch from one to the other as occasion demands, whilst still maintaining a reasonable level of visual and acoustic privacy. Visually and functionally this is straightforward building. On the whole the detailing is as simple and direct as might be expected in a standard factory building. And like a factory building there are the occasional bits of *ad hoc* detailing around awkward junctions. The adoption of the open classroom concept into the Victorian State School system has been slow and may herald further innovations both for educational and economic reasons. The schools at Queenscliff and Oakleigh illustrate different approaches to planning. Both are examples of an easy-going friendly architectural character: they are welcoming buildings in which education might be an enjoyable creative experience.

Some office spaces are designed to maximize privacy; other office spaces are designed to maximize communications among workers. Factories have special design considerations; museums need specific design features due to their often awesome size and complexity. The design of each of these spaces has changed over the years to reflect people's attitudes and ideas about work, leisure, and architecture itself.

No single place receives more attention than the home as a living and working space. Dozens of magazines are published each month on how to personalize, decorate, change, modify, and build living spaces. People spend more time in their homes than any place else and want their homes to reflect their attitudes and living styles. As we saw in chapter 10, Social Psychology, the home provides a place in which people can manipulate their own sense of territoriality, personal space, and privacy. When a woman wants to be alone in her home, she goes into her room to gain some privacy. Some homes are designed to maximize privacy by having many rooms with doors and locks. Other homes have more open spaces with high ceilings that allow sound and light to travel unabated by walls.

When a young couple buys a home they might have specific needs to get away from the children. As children get older and family social interactions become more important, such special places may become less needed. As children leave the home and develop families of their own, people find that they have a home with many rooms and dividers that they no longer need. At this point many adults move from their family homes into smaller apartments with more appropriate space, room design, and design utility.

The environment affects a person's behavior, and people in turn affect the environment and shape it so as to maximize their well being, both physiological and psychological. Increasingly, research is leading the way to appropriate functional and aesthetically pleasing environments which can maximize space and people's needs. Environmental psychology needs the expertise of researchers in various areas, including sociologists, architects, city planners, artists, and pollution experts. These individuals with the knowledge of how humans behave in various settings can make intelligent, well-planned decisions about the future of both the natural and the built environment.

The City: Four Conceptual Frameworks

The city might be called the ultimate arouser. No other place can provide so much sight and sound, excitement and entertainment, as well as despondency and despair. A city is not a twentieth-century phenomenon with new and unique problems; cities have been the focus of debate for centuries, and the center of economic and cultural opportunities as long as humans have recorded history. Interest in cities is not new; sociologists have studied the make-up and characteristics of cities for decades. Similarly, architects and city planners have focused on the structure of living and working spaces in cities. Environmental psychologists have tried to describe and explain the behavior of individuals in cities and how this behavior is different from rural dwellers. Through environmental research they have also attempted to improve living conditions for urban residents.

Improving psychological conditions within a city is no simple task; the point was made earlier that even such a simple variable as noise has many

Over the years, people have attempted to create all types of special and unique environments in which to live and play.

factors that enter into the equation. By definition, a city is a complex place with thousands or millions of people spread out over acres of land. The inhabitants usually work and play within the confines of the city; furthermore, even suburbanites come to the city to shop and use its cultural facilities. The characteristics of a city, including its climate, physical layout, and especially its people, lend to each city a unique flavor or character. New York City is unique and very different from San Francisco, and both of these cities differ from New Orleans, Montreal, or Houston.

From a psychologist's view, there are certain aspects of all cities that are alike. There is a special excitement as well as certain stresses and pressures that affect city dwellers. There are huge numbers of people; there is little space; there is noise pollution, air pollution, and water pollution. Movement within a city is often difficult. Feelings of community and involvement are sometimes missing. Involving all of these variables is the perception process itself; people's perceptions of cities and their place within a city is altered because of dozens of variables. Thus, because of their different ways of perceiving space, a husband and wife who share similar values, ideals, and aspirations may evaluate the city in different ways.

Environmental psychologists have tried to conceptualize the city, its strengths, and its problems by studying it from various views. These conceptual frameworks summarize research and explain certain environment-behavior interactions. Perhaps one of the most intuitive conceptual frameworks is that of the city as an arouser, a stimulus which brings about excitement and sustains stress.

FRAMEWORK: AROUSAL AND STRESS.   If noise, heat, pollution, and crime are stressors, it is easy to assume that the behavior of people who are exposed to such stressors will be affected, at least to some extent. Consider noise; as we have suggested earlier, noise (unwanted sounds that are intermittent, loud, annoying, and generally unpredictable) can influence behavior. Cities have high levels of noise—horns, construction noises, jack hammers, traffic, police whistles, sirens, air conditioners, as well as people talking, arguing, and screaming. While people adapt to noise relatively easily, it must be remembered that noise is only one of many of the potential stimuli in a city.

Cities are teeming with people; some people perceive cities as crowded places with little personal space for living. It is recognized that in a place that is crowded, people tend to feel stressed, overloaded, and sometimes aggressive. Of course, a large population in and of itself does not create aggression or antisocial behavior; yet, it must be recognized that in cities with large populations, the number of violent crimes like murder, rape, and assault is considerably greater (even after adjusting for population differences). For example, the number of violent crimes in cities with over 1 million people is seven times greater than in cities with only 100,000 people. Knowing that high crime rates exist creates stress, fear, and arousal.

FRAMEWORK: OVERLOAD.   The overload concept of the environment suggests that when stimulation exceeds normal limits, people's behavior is less effective. Some researchers believe that behavior in cities is determined by excesses of everything. There is too much noise and pollution, too many people and events, and, generally, too many stimuli for a single person to process at once. These researchers make a fundamental assumption about human beings: they assume that people have a limited capacity to process information and that they will process as much as they can, but when the environment overloads them with too much, too many, and too fast, people will want out.

Noise could help overload individuals, yet most people adapt to the "hum of the city." Pollution can be annoying, but again, most people adapt. There are thousands of people in a city, and in spite of feeling crowded, most people adapt. With so many sounds, scents, and events, there must be some discrimination of what is important and what is unimportant. Milgram suggested that the overload of the city causes people to be selective about which stimuli they will attend to (Milgram, 1970). He suggested that different inputs and stimuli are valued differently; so, when bombarded with a day's events, people will ignore, disregard, and be apathetic to some people and some situations. In a more recent formulation of the overload notion, Cohen (1977) has made similar arguments and points out that the demands for attention in city life are so great that at the end of a day, people's ability to concentrate on new events is limited.

We all recognize that there are strengths to the overload notion; it is hard to do two things at once. In fact, when visiting a large city like New York, most people, at least for the first few days, feel overwhelmed; but soon they become goal-oriented in their behaviors. People develop ideas of where they are going, how to get there, and what they shall do. In many ways, visitors learn to become city inhabitants very quickly. The overload explanation of the city behavior helps us understand the important experiments done on bystander intervention, which were presented in chapter 10.

FRAMEWORK: ADAPTATION LEVEL.   Adaptation level theory suggests that people adapt to certain levels of environmental stimulation; the level at which they feel comfortable is determined by their previous experiences, their experiences just prior to the present moment, and can vary dramatically from individual to individual. Adaptation level theory has been put forth by Wohlwill (1974) using an older idea introduced by Helson (1964).

According to adaptation level theory, a person's environment can vary in its *diversity*, *intensity*, and also in its *pattern*. Thus, people's situations may be very diverse, intense, and patterned or, by contrast, they can be much the same, lacking in intensity, and generally unstructured. To some extent, these three dimensions are independent and each can vary. For some people, an environment may be highly structured but it may lack intensity; by contrast, a new city may seem to have no structure to its street pattern, but may seem very intense because of the urban press of sound and sight.

In some important ways the idea that people can adapt their responses to the particular pattern to which they are exposed is compelling. It allows for adaptive change in individuals. Of course, some people find a change from one environment to another an easy one to make; we say that they are adaptive and flexible. Others find change tedious and difficult; for them change produces stress and anxiety.

The strength of adaptation level theory is that it allows for both stress notions and overload notions to be used, in addition to the idea of adaptation. While some researchers have refined and adapted this theory (Altman, 1975; Sonnenfeld, 1966), the basic idea of the individual changing as the environment changes is consistent with current data about behavior and the environment. Adaptation level theory suggests that people wish to attain an optimum level of stimulation, structure, and diversity. What determines an optimum level for any given individual and how and why this varies from person to person is still an unanswered question.

FRAMEWORK: THE ECOLOGICAL PERSPECTIVE. It has 50 pews, an altar, an organ, and stained glass windows. From these clues we all recognize the description of a church. Classrooms can similarly be described with just a few clues. Hospitals, parks, and bathrooms all have specific functions which are defined by the size, shape, structure, and function of their contents. In trying to describe how the behavior of people is influenced by the environment, Barker (1968) developed an approach to environment-behavior relations which has been called the ecological approach. The ecological approach to psychology looks at behavior settings. A **behavior setting** is a place like a church, park, or hospital that has a regular and specific pattern of activity that takes place in it. The activities within the behavior setting are usually specific and determined by the objects and furniture found inside; furthermore, behaviors outside the behavior setting are different from those within it. **Ecological psychology** examines the interdependent relationship between a person's behaviors and the behavior settings in which they occur.

Barker's ecological psychology led to a theory in which he postulates that in a behavior setting there is an optimum number of individuals who should occupy it. If more than this optimum is found in the setting or if there are too few people in the behavior setting, then maximal use of the setting is not being made. In situations where there are too few or too many people, Barker refers to them as being undermanned or overmanned. Most people have been to a high school dance when there are too few people there to make it work; for example, when the high school gym has but 12 dancers amid thousands of streamers. Similarly, when a church social hall has tables set for 200 but there are only 9 diners, there is a sense of an insufficient number of

Behavior Settings Places like a church, a park, or a hospital that have a regular and specific pattern of activity that takes place in them.

Ecological Psychology The study of interdependent relationships between a person's behaviors and the behavior settings in which they occur.

People are better able to develop a sense of who they are when they can explore their feelings without the stress of a city.

people to begin dinner. In both of these settings, within an hour the situation may have changed drastically. A dance floor may soon be too crowded to dance and when a few extra people show up there may be too few seats for the church supper.

If we consider the city as a large behavior setting, we see that certain characteristics of city life rapidly become evident. For those in a city to lead a varied, diverse, and active social and cultural life, there must be a minimum number of participants. When a city's opera, ballet, and symphony are underattended, they cannot operate on the revenues generated; such activities, when undermanned, eventually risk extinction. When a city is overmanned, these same institutions can produce frustration if there are not enough cultural outlets to satisfy all of its inhabitants. Sprawling cities like Los Angeles, New York, and Chicago have huge cultural lives with many kinds and levels of entertainment to appeal to their inhabitants.

The consequences of undermanning are more likely to be seen in smaller scale settings like the church. For example, Wicker (1979) reported on comparisons of differences between a large church in Milwaukee with small ones. On a variety of measures, Wicker showed that with the small church, members participated in a wider range of activities and assumed more responsibility and leadership roles. They also contributed more money to the church each year. Wicker interpreted these findings in terms of Barker's theory: when there are many behavior settings and things to be done but relatively few people to do them, members experience strong pressures on their time and talents. Thus, members of the smaller church tended to take on more positions of leadership in more settings than individuals within the larger churches.

The ecological approach, whether used to describe large numbers of individuals in cities or small numbers in church settings, is a theory of group behavior, not individual behavior. Furthermore, the Barker approach speaks to how the environment influences behavior *and* how behavior influences the environment.

Toward a Theory of Environmental Psychology: Perception and Adaptation

Social psychologists have long histories of research which guide their current investigations. They may be researchers investigating the role of instincts in aggression, or perhaps, how learning affects the social development of young children. Personality theorists have a long history of theory and research— researchers are Freudians, or perhaps, behaviorists. When studying history and systems of psychology, we see that theory and research, each guiding the other, have determined the eventual direction of a field. Environmental psychology is young and is still seeking a unified theory to account for the relationship of environment and behavior. Stress notions account for some behaviors, overload notions account for others. Adaptation level theory, while difficult to test, takes into account people's changing as the environment changes. Barker's theoretical ideas of overmanning and undermanning allow for an account of how groups are affected and how they affect their environment. Each of the frameworks involve two major and important steps. The first involves a perception of the environment. Individuals and groups make certain assumptions about the environment based on how they perceive it. Sometimes these ideas are accurate, sometimes they are misleading. In any case, individuals' actions are determined by how they feel within a situation; their feelings are determined by how they see themselves in relation to others.

After determining what the environment is and how they feel about it, people then make adaptation decisions. If the environment is one within which people feel uncomfortable, stressed, or anxious, they attempt to try to reduce their stress or anxiety. People sometimes try to change their behavior setting or leave it. If your apartment is too crowded and noisy, you might try to shield some of the sound with heavy drapes and accoustical ceiling tiles. Or, you might feel that the environment is sufficiently bad that you should totally withdraw, perhaps by moving to another apartment or even to another section of town. In extreme cases, adaptation is ineffective and behavior breaks down, resulting in maladjustment. Of course, if the environment is one where a person feels well situated, then no adaptation is necessary.

Because the environments are so complicated, particularly large scale environments, a single unified theory of the city is yet to evolve. Researchers are still specifying issues, delineating problems, and exploring the scope of the city. Environmental psychology as an applied focus continues to evolve.

PSYCHOLOGY AND CRIMINAL BEHAVIOR

Being 15 can be difficult; being 15 in a correction center for juvenile delinquents makes it harder. The environment in which people develop helps shape their personalities and behavior. Few people in the 1980s think that behavior, whether purposeful or destructive, is determined solely by biological mechanisms. A 15-year-old girl who is reared in a loving, warm home is far more likely to develop into a woman who is happy and well-adjusted than the same girl, born of the same parents, reared for 10 years of her life in a juvenile correctional center.

Recognizing the role of biology and environment in the development of behavior patterns has been a focus of psychologists who try to understand and modify criminal behavior. A certain segment of society is engaged in activities which, as defined by society, are against the law. As we are all too well aware, the rate of crime in the United States is dramatic. People are afraid to live in cities because of the excessive crime and violence; major centers like Atlanta, New York, Chicago, and Los Angeles are plagued with urban problems. Cities are not the sole repositories of crime, however. Crime is seen in the suburbs; white-collar crime is seen in businesses and industry. Crime is seen in the local, state, and federal governments. The study of criminal behavior is a discipline unto itself and for many psychologists understanding it becomes a special focus.

A criminal is a person who performs a criminal behavior. This may seem like a simple enough definition, but criminologists have been arguing about the nature of it for years (Bottomley, 1979). Psychologists are especially interested in trying to understand the potential psychological causes of criminal behavior. However, merely understanding the causes of behavior is not enough; psychologists interested in criminal behavior also are involved in the *treatment* of criminals through therapy. They are active in assessing the development of the prison system; they also are involved in *assessment* of prisoners and in making predictions about their future behavior. They help set up programs for *training* prisoners in new careers and are regularly involved as *consultants* to correctional institutions. For many, these varied roles (assessment, treatment, training, and consultation) help them build more comprehensive theories which can predict and explain criminal behavior (Twain, McGee, & Bennett, 1973).

To be a psychologist whose special focus is crime and behavior requires a detailed knowledge of basic psychological principles which underlie many different aspects of human behavior. Laboratory research is not the focus of such psychologists; rather, it is the use of psychological principles to help in making day-to-day decisions which affect an increasing number of people—criminals.

Some Basic Terms and Statistics

To understand fully the problems of criminal behavior, it is necessary that certain basic terms be clarified. First, crime is not a psychological term, but rather a legal one. Laws define crime. From a psychologist's view, any behavior that is involved in crime is a criminal behavior; so, psychologists study criminal behavior, not crime. Second, there are two basic types of criminal behaviors which broadly refer to serious crimes and less serious ones. Specifically, felonies and misdemeanors are types of crimes which encompass specific violations of the law. Felonies are serious crimes and there are significant differences as to which crimes are felonies and which are misdemeanors. These differences, however, vary dramatically from state to state. Murder is a felony in all states, but robbery may not be, depending upon whether or not the robber was armed and the value of the goods stolen.

Crime in the cities is a stark reality.

The incidence of serious crime in the United States is alarming. For example, at the beginning of the 1980s there were approximately 20,000 murders taking place each year. Each year there were more than 1 million motor vehicle thefts and 3 million burglaries. Of course, there are huge differences in the frequency of certain types of crime for various parts of the country and for certain cities. In general, large cities have more crime than smaller ones, and cities are plagued with more crime than rural areas. In general, men are more likely to commit serious crimes than women. Nearly 45% of all murderers are under the age of 25; in 40% of murder cases, the offender is a relative or friend of the victim.

It is relatively easy to see that the extent of crime in the United States is enormous. It has been estimated that the annual economic cost is over $85 billion. Even this estimate may be an underestimate because many crimes are not reported. People often do not wish to get involved with the criminal justice system. With this overview as a background, let us now examine some of the causes of criminal behavior by exploring three diverging views. Each has as its focus psychological implications.

The Causes of Criminal Behavior: Three Views

As applied psychologists, those who evaluate and treat criminals must have a basic knowledge of what causes criminal behavior. While many behavioral psychologists are not particularly concerned with the causes of a specific criminal's problem, as a group, psychologists have studied intensely the potentially important elements in identifying criminals and criminal behavior. As in so many other areas of psychology, nature and nurture have been orienting themselves. We shall examine three views of criminal behavior; the first focuses on biology and unique personal experiences, the second on cultural and situational influences, and the third offers a combination of the first two.

THE PERSON-CENTERED MODEL. Everyone recognizes that people differ from one another in important ways. The person-centered model recognizes this and asserts that it may occur for two reasons. The first is because of biology and genetics. People are different from one another from birth on, and these differences are hereditary. This view held initially that instincts were the sole cause of behavior; however, this radical approach was replaced and modified with a medical model. Those who favor the medical model suggest that criminals behave the way they do because something has malfunctioned; there is an underlying cause for a set of behaviors. The medical model sees criminal behavior as a symptom of some underlying problem. This approach has been seriously criticized because it takes the view that people have become criminals because they have criminal minds due to faulty biological processes. Often circular in reasoning, people are said to perform criminal behaviors because they are criminals; further, they are criminals because they perform criminal behaviors.

A second person-centered approach focuses on the person and the person's *past* experiences. Using learning theory as its basis, this approach asserts that people learn faulty behavior patterns through the processes of observation and reinforcement. This idea suggests that criminals do not learn appropriate behavior control mechanisms that guide prosocial behavior. The focus of this form of person-centered approach is clearly on learning; people (including criminals) learn to behave the way they do.

While both the medical model and the learning model put the emphasis on the person, the former asserts that criminal behavior is a symptom of some underlying cause. The latter suggests that criminal behaviors are learned. As you will soon see, treatment by those who favor the medical model is very different from those who favor the learning model. It is important to recognize that the person-centered model accounts for biological and learning factors in criminal behavior. Often called a commonsense approach, it suggests that *people* and their internal characteristics are the causes of behavior.

THE SITUATION-CENTERED MODEL. In contrast to the person-centered approach, the situation-centered model suggests that the causes of criminal behavior are due to the context and the environment in which a person commits a crime. A radical form of this approach suggests that the environment alone determines the way a person will respond. A milder and more easily accepted version of this model suggests that criminal behavior is affected greatly by the context in which people find themselves.

Even the mild version of the situation-centered approach is unacceptable to many psychologists. It is not favored because it sees people as having little personal cognitive control over their behavior; rather, behavior is seen to be determined by external factors.

The strongest evidence and support for the situation-centered model comes from experiments by Zimbardo. Zimbardo (1975) had well-adjusted, carefully screened subjects participate in a simulation study of prisons; 24 college men played the roles of "prisoner" or "guard." The prison was part of a dormitory, but during the 2 weeks that comprised the study, the similarities between the mock prison and a real one became alarmingly similar. Picked up without warning on a Sunday morning, prisoners were stripped, searched, and sprayed with disinfectants. Guards were told to maintain order in the "prison." Within a few days, guards became rude, aggressive, and abusive. Prisoners became hostile, belligerent, and depressed. By the end of the 2 weeks, the subjects reported some serious psychological changes. The guards were abusing their powers; the prisoners were developing a sense of learned helplessness (see p. 469).

These well-adjusted normal Stanford University students were soon behaving in ways that might be classified as maladjusted. Nonhostile young men became hostile; assertive young men became helpless. The internal characteristics of these men did not guide their behavior; rather, the situation that they found themselves in did. This study showed that people allowed the situation to control and manipulate their behavior.

The situation-centered model cannot fully account for human behavior. It is not sensitive to individual differences. A strict version suggests that *all* people would respond in exactly the same way to the same situation. This is not the case. Furthermore, even a mild version does not allow for much cognitive control over behavior. Within a particular setting, individual differences among people are often significantly greater than similarities. This model thus disregards a factor which cannot be ruled out when we consider the complexity of human behavior.

THE INTERACTIONIST MODEL. The aim of the interactionist model is to combine the best elements of the person-centered model and the situation-centered model. This model does not place the emphasis solely on the person nor solely on the environment; rather, it suggests a combination. Thus, people have certain personality characteristics which generally guide their behavior, *but,* the situations they find themselves in facilitate or inhibit their behavior still further.

From this view, a specific situation provides information to a person which not only modifies existing behavior but also helps shape future behavior. So, behavior is not *determined* by the environment, but rather it is influenced by it (Endler & Magnusson, 1976). This view is supported in the psychological literature. In chapter 4, Motivation and Emotion, the study by Schachter was presented in which subjects were injected with adrenalin and their autonomic nervous systems became energized. In that study when subjects were around happy people they felt happy; when they were around unhappy people they felt angry. Schachter interpreted these results to suggest that the situation people find themselves in determines how they interpret their arousal (see p. 180).

Criminal behavior can clearly be viewed from the interactionist position. When Adams (1970) examined the effects of placing inmates in psychotherapy, he found that those who profited from it were those who were initially judged able to profit from it. The finding was that psychotherapy was not universally facilitative. Another way of saying this is that the environment (psychotherapy) did not always shape behavior in one direction; rather, person variables, past experiences, and current behaviors entered into the therapeutic ability of psychotherapy.

THE THREE VIEWS: NATURE AND NURTURE.   The *person-centered* view considers both nature and nurture; it places the causes of current criminal behavior on potential biological variables as well as on past experiences. The *situation-centered* view places the emphasis *solely* on the environment and especially on current experiences and situations—nature and biology are wholly excluded. The *interactionist* view allows for biology to play a role; it allows for past experiences to play a role, *and* it allows for current situations to help modify behavior.

If forced to pick one view, most psychologists would subscribe to the interactionist view. Certainly, current situations including poverty, unemployment, hunger, drug habits, and personal relationships directly affect some criminal behavior. A 25-year history of drug experiences, ghetto living, and learning experiences which have fostered working outside the mainstream of society cannot be disregarded. Biological variables are also acknowledged to be important; but, most psychologists recognize that at present it is hard to identify biological and genetic factors. It is especially hard to separate biological factors from early environmental ones. The interactionist view allows for nature, nurture, and past and current situations to be the causes of current criminal behavior—the interactionist view provides no easy answers.

Responses to Criminal Behavior: Three Views

As individuals, and collectively as society, people have responded to criminal behavior in various ways. Some people want retribution; they seek to get even and inflict some type of pain or punishment on a criminal. Others have responded to criminal behavior with attempts at correction; this approach takes the view that behavior can be changed through positive actions and the teaching of new, worthwhile behaviors. Still others have responded to criminal behavior with intervention approaches; these individuals seek to change society, criminal behavior, and even the system of laws. Let's examine these three views more closely; you will see that the views people have about the causes of criminal behavior help shape how they respond to criminals. As a society, we determine how criminals shall be treated; we often respond in characteristic and very human ways.

PUNISHMENT.   A society's response to criminals is usually in the form of punishment. Those who favor the concept of punishment do so for two basic reasons. First, people desire retribution. Depriving criminals of freedom causes them to suffer; for many people this is justice. The arguments for retribution are to a great extent moral judgments. From this point of view, punishment is the natural response to a criminal behavior.

A second reason for punishment is that people feel that through it criminals can be reformed. This argument is utilitarian; people should be punished so as to help make them better members of society. J. Edgar Hoover, former director of the FBI, stated that view succinctly in an address in 1936:

Adequate detection, swift apprehension, and certain, unrelenting punishment. That is what the criminal fears. That is what he understands, and nothing else, and that fear is the only thing which will force him into the ranks of the lawbiding. There is no royal road to law enforcement. If we wait upon the medical quacks, the parole panderers, and the misguided sympathizers with habitual criminals to protect our lives and property from the criminal horde, then we must also resign ourselves to increasing violence, robbery, and sudden death. (Hoover, 1936)

The utilitarian arguments for punishment are supported by three assertions; punishment serves (1) to provide incapacitation, (2) to act as a deterrent, and (3) to act as a rehabilitative stimulus. Clearly, a person who is dangerous and who commits crimes cannot harm others in society once behind bars. Punishment clearly *incapacitates* criminals. This protection from a criminal is generally short-lived, or at least only temporary because nearly half of all people who are sent to prison serve less than $2\frac{1}{2}$ years.

For some people punishment can act as a *deterrent*. This is probably the most commonly held reason for the delivery of punishment. There is no question that a prison can deter criminal acts for a short time (during the confinement in prison), but its ability to deter future crime is seriously questioned. Consider the rate of recidivism. Recidivism is the rearrest of a criminal following release from prison. The rate of recidivism nationwide is between 33% and 60% (Tittle, 1972). Today, most people who study the prison system have acknowledged that the primary reasons for its maintenance is retribution, not to deter future crimes. Citizens are angry with criminals and they want to get even (Fogel, 1975).

Society also delivers punishment to *rehabilitate* criminals; this view holds that through the delivery of punishment, criminals can receive retribution *and* learn to become more productive citizens. Some argue that retribution *and* rehabilitation can take place at the same time (Lion, 1974); however, you will see in the next section that psychologists seriously question this.

CORRECTIONS. Many modern criminal justice specialists have focused on the role of prisons in helping shape future behavior of criminals. Their goal has been to deliver the punishment that society has deemed necessary; but, at the same time, provide rehabilitation. From a psychologist's view, punishing people and trying to get them to emit new positive prosocial behaviors are goals which work in opposite directions.

We know from learning theory that punishment acts to suppress behaviors; reinforcement acts to establish, increase, or maintain them. A basic problem for correctional institutions is how to suppress negative antisocial behaviors while at the same time increasing positive prosocial behaviors. A man who has lost his freedom in jail is hardly in a frame of mind to be rehabilitated. Yet, that has been the overall goal of the criminal justice system.

Psychologists have helped criminal justice experts learn how the correctional system is not working. They have provided data, theory, and practical information on the negative social consequences of punishment. For example, we know that punishment often initiates aggression; prisoners seek to "get even" with the deliverers of punishment (society). We also know that prisoners often imitate the punishing behavior they are given, thus they become punitive (violent) in their behavior with others. We also know that punishment cannot help build a positive relationship between a correctional system and a prisoner. So, from a psychologist's view, imprisonment cannot really act to help people to build better lives and become rehabilitated.

Most psychologists argue that the delivery of punishment acts mainly as retributive justice. Everyone wants justice to be done; however, psychologists have learned that within a prison system there is only a small likelihood of a significant behavior change that is in a positive direction. Consider what happens when a prisoner does not conform to prison rules. In such cases the prisoner is placed in solitary confinement. The results of such confinements hardly cause behavior change in a positive direction. Read one prisoner's first hand account:

> I was recently released from "solitary confinement" after being held there for 37 months. A silent system was imposed on me and to even "whisper" to the man in the next cell resulted in being beaten by guards, sprayed with chemical mace, blackjacked, stomped, and thrown into a "strip-cell" naked to sleep on a concrete floor without bedding, covering, wash basin, or even a toilet. The floor served as toilet and bed, and even there the "silent system" was enforced. To let a "moan" escape from your lips because of the pain and discomfort . . . resulted in another beating. I spent not days, but months there during my 37 months in solitary. . . . Maybe I am incorrigible, but if true, it's because I would rather die than to accept being treated as less than a human being. . . . I know that thieves must be punished and I don't justify stealing, even though I am a thief myself. But now I don't think I will be a thief when I am released. No, I'm not rehabilitated. It's just that I no longer think of becoming wealthy by stealing. I now only think of "killing." Killing those who have beaten me and treated me as if I were a dog. I hope and pray for the sake of my own soul and future life of freedom, that I am able to overcome the bitterness and hatred which eats daily at my soul, but I know to overcome it will not be easy. (Zimbardo, 1971, p. 1)

Once a man or woman has been in prison the likelihood of returning (recidivism) is at least 30%. From a correctional perspective, recidivism is too global a measure of the effectiveness of prisons. A man who has been imprisoned may go through many types of rehabilitation. He may cure his drinking problems and he may learn to gain control over his impulsiveness. Still, he may wind up in prison again. With recidivism being an all or none measure, it is probably too global to measure the actual effectiveness of prisons. While this argument is acknowledged, recidivism is still the most frequently used measure of the effectiveness of rehabilitative programs (see, for example, Lipton, Martinson, & Wilks, 1975).

INTERVENTION. The third way by which society can respond to criminal behavior is with intervention techniques. These techniques work with criminals, society, the legal system, and especially individual communities. The aim (much like the aim of community psychology) is to reach out into the community to provide systems, programs, and methods which will stop criminal behavior before its start or soon after it has begun. A closely associated goal is to limit the extent of people's crimes before they become further involved in criminal behavior.

Applied psychologists who work with criminals find that the prison environment does not lend itself to rehabilitation. Therefore, intervention-oriented psychologists seek to place prisoners in community settings where they might watch and learn the behavior of people who are in the mainstream of life. The interventionist is faced with a dilemma: the community is the best place to reorient a criminal, but criminals are in prison. Even prisoners who work in the community during the day are brought back to the prison at night. Consequently, many of the prosocial behaviors learned during the day are often punished at night.

Recognizing these problems, the interventionist seeks not only to change criminal behavior, but also to change the mode in which society tries to punish, reform, and rehabilitate criminals. The interventionist approach goes far beyond the criminal and seeks to reform society's response to criminals. This is no easy task.

THREE VIEWS: WILL THEY COME TOGETHER? Punishment, correction, and intervention all have an element of punishment running through them. One of the key differences among these approaches is the extent to which they place the burden of blame or guilt on the individual. Those who favor retribution blame the person. Correctional officers focus on the person but acknowledge that change is possible and should be sought. Interventionists acknowledge individual control over behavior; they go further and suggest that rehabilitation is the problem for the individual *and* for society. From their view it is society's response to criminals which minimizes the likelihood of rehabilitation. The continuum from retribution to intervention is not clearly marked off; from year to year individuals and society change their views on how to deal with criminal behavior.

Applied psychologists bring a different vantage point to the field of criminal justice. They are less concerned with crime and social institutions and more concerned with the study of individuals and behavior. From this view, they develop theories and treatment programs to help people live more fulfilling lives. A problem for applied psychologists who work within the criminal justice system is that too often basic behavior principles are disregarded because of a lack of time, money, or interest. Prison life is abominable; retribution is generally the norm, not reform. Until society wishes to change the living and working conditions of those who have come to emit criminal behaviors, it is likely that recidivism will remain high. Psychologists can help reduce the extent of criminal behavior; however, they are only one component of a larger system of criminal justice.

SUMMARY

Psychologists face the dilemma of trying to take basic research and apply it in meaningful ways. This is really not hard to do because psychology studies behavior and nearly everything that people think, feel, and do is seen in behavior.

While there are many areas of applied psychology, several have achieved full status as applied disciplines. This chapter has reviewed three of these disciplines, each to a different extent. Industrial/organizational psychologists have examined a wide range of behaviors in the work place, educational institutions, and in organizations in general. In this chapter we have considered the complex relationships among motivation of workers, their job satisfaction, how they relate to their leaders, and how all of these factors subsequently affect personnel selection procedures. We saw that job satisfaction and motivation are often closely related and sometimes interdependent.

The environment in which one lives, plays, and works can have a direct and immediate impact on people's lives. Simple variables like temperature and noise can make people feel stressed and aggressive. Environmental psychologists study how the environment affects individual behavior and how individuals in turn change the environment in both positive and negative ways.

These environments can be on a large or small scale. Of course, in a large-scale environment like a city or neighborhood, there are many more variables that might affect how an individual behaves. By contrast, in a small-scale environment researchers are better able to predict how a single individual will respond.

Environmental psychologists have developed several theoretical ways of looking at environment-behavior interactions. Both the stress and overload models of behavior suggest that there will be deleterious effects on performance when an individual is bombarded with too many stimuli too quickly. The adaptation level view speaks to how we adapt when placed in environments that are different from what we are used to. Coming from a slightly different perspective, the ecological view speaks about the interaction of the human being and the environment. The ecological view focuses on behavior settings and how they determine behavior.

Environmental psychology is a young discipline. It has yet to find a unified theory to account for behavior, but it is rapidly making headway. Researchers who study the environment have realized its great role in affecting behavior. Today, city planners, architects, and environmental psychologists are working together to help plan living and working spaces so as to make them more effective, comfortable, and pleasing.

The study of criminal behavior is one in which applied psychologists try to use basic psychological principles in the testing, evaluation, and prediction of current and future behavior. Society has made clear its position about criminals; by its actions society seeks retribution rather than rehabilitation. Efforts to reform people by teaching them prosocial behaviors have been minimal and ineffective. Intervention-oriented psychologists have tried to change not only criminals and their behavior, but the response of society and the entire system of criminal justice. Unfortunately, their effect has been minimal; societal change is slow. Furthermore, our criminal justice system has a long history which resists change.

Applied psychologists take basic research and use this information to help people better themselves and the human condition. As scientists, they are careful in their use of knowledge; as applied scientists, they use their knowledge of research in nonlaboratory settings. We can thus see that research and application really go hand in hand. Psychologists often mix research and application in their professional lives by doing basic research (often in a university setting) and then acting as consultants and practitioners to industry and private groups.

CHAPTER REVIEW

1. Applied psychologists have sought to bring the full weight of research and theory on practical problems. In doing so, they have in some cases developed whole new fields of study.

2. Industrial/organizational psychology attempts to take psychological principles, many of which were derived in laboratory settings, and apply them in the work place.

3. When an industrial/organizational psychologist helps develop selection procedures, he or she will usually use a series of steps or processes. Among these steps will be a standardized application, a standardized interview, a standardized work sample, and a standardized series of tests.

4. Industrial/organizational psychologists have been particularly aware of the strengths and limitations of tests as predictors of future behavior.

5. In the selection process, federal guidelines for affirmative action must be considered. Minorities must be given equal opportunities; women must not be discriminated against; age is irrelevant.

6. Vroom's basic idea was that performance on a job is determined by both motivation and ability; Lawler and Porter have modified this theory and extended it to include role perceptions.

7. There are three basic approaches to the management of motivation: paternalistic, behavioral, and participatory.

8. In paternal systems all the employees, both hard-working and lazy, are provided reinforcements; from the behavioral view rewards are contingent solely on a worker's performance.

9. In participatory management the basic idea is that if individuals participate in the decisions that affect their lives, they will be more likely to be motivated to work.

10. A person's satisfaction with a job reflects his or her attitudes toward it.

11. A clear distinction must be made between job satisfaction and job motivation. One's job satisfaction is how one feels about work and the work place. One's motivation refers to states within people which energize them.

12. One of the key tasks for leaders becomes motivating group members to perform their respective tasks.

13. The study of leadership has gone through three major phases of development, each with a characteristic focus. These phases may be considered the study of leadership traits, behaviors, and situations.

14. Environmental psychology is the study of how physical settings affect human behavior and vice versa.

15. A stressor is a stimulus that brings about uncomfortable feelings of anxiety, tension, and especially physiological arousal.

16. At low levels of sound intensity, noise has only marginal effects on simple tasks.

17. When noise is of moderate intensity and is unpredictable and intermittent, there is impairment in tasks that require sustained attention or memory.

18. The stress framework suggests that when individuals are stressed, there is increased physiological arousal and behavior is affected.

19. The overload framework suggests that when there is too much noise, too many people and events, and generally too much for a person to process at once, people tune out and only process as much as they can.

20. The overload framework suggests that people are selective as to the stimuli they will pay attention to.

21. The adaptation level view of environmental psychology suggests that people adapt to certain levels of environmental stimulation, and the level at which they feel comfortable is determined by their previous experiences and varies from individual to individual.

22. The idea of overmanning and undermanning is a crucial component and outgrowth of the ecological view of behavior.

23. Psychologists are involved in the assessment and treatment of criminals; they also are involved in setting up training programs and consultation.

24. The person-centered model focuses on the person, his or her biology, and past experiences as causes of criminal behavior.

25. The situation-centered model suggests that the causes of criminal behavior are due to the context and the environment in which a person commits a crime.
26. The aim of the interactionist model is to combine the best elements of the person-centered model and the situation-centered model. This model does not place the emphasis solely on the person or solely on the environment; rather, it suggests a combination.
27. A society's response to criminals is usually in the form of punishment by sending them to prison.
28. The utilitarian arguments for punishment are supported by three assertions; punishment serves (1) to provide incapacitation, (2) to act as a deterrent, and (3) to act as a rehabilitative stimulus.
29. From a psychologist's view, punishing people and trying to get them to emit new positive, prosocial behaviors are goals which work in opposite directions.
30. Most psychologists argue that the delivery of punishment acts mainly as retribution.
31. The aim of intervention techniques is to reach out into the community to provide systems, programs, and methods that will stop criminal behavior before it starts or soon after it has begun.
32. Punishment, correction, and intervention all have an element of punishment running through them. One of the key differences among these approaches is the extent to which they place the burden of blame or guilt on the individual.

SUGGESTIONS FOR FURTHER READING

ALTMAN, I. *The environment and social behavior.* Monterey, CA: Brooks/Cole, 1975.

FISHER, J. D., BELL, P. A., & LOOMIS, R. J. *Environmental psychology.* Philadelphia, PA: W. B. Saunders, 1978.

GILMER, B. V. H., & DECI, E. L. *Industrial and organizational psychology* (4th ed.). New York: McGraw-Hill, 1977.

GLASS, D. C., & SINGER, J. E. *Urban stress.* New York: Academic Press, 1972.

HUSSEY, F. A., & DUFFEE, D. E. *Probation, parole, and community field services.* New York: Harper & Row, 1980.

LILLYQUIST, M. J. *Understanding and changing criminal behavior.* Englewood Cliffs, NJ: Prentice-Hall, 1980.

MCCORMICK, E. J., & ILGEN, D. R. *Industrial psychology* (7th ed.). Englewood Cliffs, NJ: Prentice-Hall, 1980.

PROSHANSKY, H. M., ITTELSON, W. H., & RIVLIN, L. G. (Eds.) *Environmental psychology* (2nd ed). New York: Holt, Rinehart & Winston, 1976.

WICKER, A. W. *An introduction to ecological psychology.* Belmont, CA: Wadsworth, 1979.

TOCH, H. (Ed.) *Psychology of crime and criminal justice.* New York: Holt, Rinehart & Winston, 1979.

PSYCHOLOGISTS WHO conduct experiments try to decide what factors control behavior and how these variable factors might be changed to create different behavior. When studying behavior, psychologists collect data by using carefully controlled procedures. After a study is completed, the psychologist is faced with thousands of numbers that must be summarized. Statistics summarize data so that they can be understood as a whole without examining many individual scores. Statistics let the experimenter see the meaning of data so that inferences can be drawn about large populations of people from small numbers of experimental subjects. This unit presents some basic information about the scientific method and statistics that help psychologists to describe, understand, and make inferences from experimental data.

Scientific and Statistical Methods

NINE RULES OF SUPERSTITIOUS ETIQUETTE

1. Do *not* take any risks or attempt any new enterprise on Friday the 13th.
2. *Do* hang a horseshoe with its prongs pointed upward—so the good luck does not "run out."
3. Do *not* light three cigarettes with one match.
4. *Do* wear clothing inside out. It is an excellent disguise to keep Death from recognizing you.
5. Do *not* get married in May.
6. *Do* knock on wood (three times) after mentioning good luck. To knock on wood insures that your good luck will continue.
7. Do *not* cross knives on the dinner table. It symbolizes the crossing of daggers and swords in dueling matches.
8. *Do* enter and exit from the same door when visiting a friend's house.
9. Do *not* trip before you start out a new day or before you begin a new adventure. It is a bad omen for you and your associates.

DAVID WALLENCHINSKY AND IRVING WALLACE
The People's Almanac

People are rule-oriented and often run their lives around rules that are nonsensical. The nine rules of superstitious etiquette have a basis in history. According to *The People's Almanac*, Friday the 13th is a day of calamity: Jesus died on Friday; Eve tempted Adam on Friday; the biblical Flood began on Friday. There were 13 men present at the Last Supper and Greek philosophers scorned 13 as an "imperfect" number. Both Friday and the number 13 are associated with unhappiness and evil. Yet, logically, we know that these were a series of coincidences.

Psychologists study behavior in systematic ways to rule out coincidences and to find the real causes of behavior. People will always generate superstitious rules that in reality are unlikely to hurt anyone. It is also likely that they won't help anyone either. Let's look at a guideline and warning put forth by the scientific community a number of years ago.

"Warning! The surgeon general has determined that cigarette smoking is dangerous to your health." In 1964 the surgeon general of the United States issued a report which showed that the frequency of heart disease and lung cancer was higher in people who smoked cigarettes than in people who did not smoke. Part of this report was based on questionnaires that investigated the relationship between cigarette smoking and health. Typically, questionnaires asked people if they smoked, how much they smoked, and about the condition of their health. Many studies asked the families of those dying of cancer and heart conditions to what extent these persons smoked cigarettes during their lifetimes. The results were dramatic: people who smoked had a shorter life expectancy than nonsmokers. For example, a 25-year-old man who smokes a pack of cigarettes a day has a life expectancy that is 6 years shorter than a nonsmoker of the same age.

The early smoking studies showed a correlation between smoking and a shorter life span. A *correlation* is a number that tells to what extent two or more factors are related. So, if one factor or variable changes, a correlation tells us how the other variable changes. These studies did not argue that cigarette smoking itself caused a shorter life span (a correlational study cannot argue cause and effect); however, they did claim that those who smoke more do die sooner.

EXPERIMENT I

After these early correlational studies, many experimental studies were conducted to assess the effects of cigarette smoking. In these experiments animals were given rewards for smoking cigarettes in a smoking machine that allows an experimenter to control the amount of cigarette smoke that the animal is inhaling. A typical experiment might take place like this: there are four groups of monkeys. The first group of monkeys does not smoke cigarettes at all. This group is a control group used to compare all of the other monkeys to see if smoking shows any effect. The second group of monkeys smokes the equivalent of 3 cigarettes a day; a third group smokes 10. The fourth and final group smokes the equivalent of 30 cigarettes per day. Each day for several months the monkeys smoke in the machine.

At the end of each week and at periodic intervals after the experiment is over, the health of all of the animals is assessed. Veterinarians examine the animals thoroughly; these checkups include blood analysis, blood pressure, and heart rate. The results indicate that animals who did not inhale smoke are as healthy as ever. However, monkeys who inhaled cigarette smoke show a variety of ailments, including increased blood pressure, increased heart rate, and a lessened ability to convey oxygen into the bloodstream.

In this experiment there were four groups of animals; one group had not smoked cigarettes, but the other three had. The nonsmoking groups remained healthy while the other three developed cardiovascular and lung disorders. Before the experiment began, the experimenter made sure that all the monkeys came from the same colony, that all were nearly the same age, and that there was a balance of sexes and other characteristics. Since these other health-affecting factors were held constant, researchers were compelled to conclude that cigarette smoking produced the difference in the animals' physical conditions.

EXPERIMENT II

Let us consider an experiment in which the effects of making rats go without food influences the speed with which they will run to a box that contains food pellets. We have four groups of rats: Group 1 rats are allowed to eat as much and as often as they want; Group 2 is denied food for 6 hours before testing; Group 3 is denied food for 12 hours before testing; and Group 4 is denied food for 24 hours before testing. The experimenter **hypothesizes** that food deprivation will make the rats run more quickly toward a box that contains food. The experimenter also thinks that compared with Group 1 (no food deprivation), the other groups will show increased speed when food has been withheld for a long time. In this experiment, Group 1 is the comparison or control group while Groups 2, 3, and 4 are the experimental groups.

Hypothesis A tentative idea adopted to account for some facts; more important, it guides the investigation of others.

The results of studies like this are usually straightforward, and we usually see that the experimental groups run toward the goal much faster than the control/comparison group. In fact, in a study like this, we usually see that Group 1 runs the slowest and Groups 2, 3, and 4 each run faster than the next.

As was presented in chapter 1, good experimentation requires careful assignment of the subjects to groups. Both the control group and the experimental groups should have come from essentially the same larger group of subjects before the experiment began. Any differences researchers find between the subjects are supposed to be due to the experimental manipulation rather than any real differences between the subjects themselves. Thus, the assignment of subjects to their respective groups often requires a matching of subjects based on important variables like age, weight, sex, and perhaps socioeconomic class.

Every good experiment will have a control group for comparison purposes. A control group allows the researchers to compare the experimental group against a standard for comparison. A control group provides this standard. Reliable, repeatable data can only be collected when experimenters are confident that the experimental situation is such that the control and experimental groups have been properly constituted and were essentially the same before the experiment began.

It is very important to control experiments properly so that psychologists can use statistics not only to describe the results, but also to draw inferences and reach conclusions from the results. Remember that the purpose of statistics is to summarize data and understand what the data mean. Many studies are reported in newspapers and TV in which inferences are made that cannot be drawn from the data. These studies may report a high incidence of disease in people who consume a drug. Yet, too often, the incidence of disease for the control group of people who didn't take the drug is left out. Similarly, educationally deprived children need to be compared with the normally educated, and retarded people need to be compared with a group of normal ability.

DESCRIPTIVE STATISTICS

Descriptive statistics A method of describing, summarizing, and condensing data.

Statistics is a branch of mathematics that allows its user to evaluate experimental situations. In **descriptive statistics** the aim is to summarize, condense, and describe data. Using statistics helps researchers organize the way they think about data.

Organizing Data

When psychologists conduct experiments, they often find they have large volumes of data. Suppose a social psychologist collected some survey data on the number of hours that children watch television. She might ask parents to monitor their children's TV watching behavior. The results might show that the 100 children being monitored watched between 0 and 20 hours per week. The following is the actual number of hours for each of the 100 children:

11	18	5	9	6	20	2	5
9	7	15	3	6	11	9	14
19	1	10	3	4	4	10	4
6	8	9	10	13	12	9	8
8	1	15	9	4	3	7	10
16	5	6	12	8	2	13	8
10	12	6	9	8	12	5	17
14	7	3	14	13	7	9	2

10	17	11	13	16	7	5	4
10	11	9	11	16	8	15	17
15	7	10	10	12	8	10	11
14	1	12	7	6	0	5	13
11	18	9	8				

For these data to be meaningful it is likely that they would first be organized into a frequency distribution. A **frequency distribution** tallies the number of times each score occurs. As is shown in Table A.1, more children watch 9 hours of TV weekly than any other number of hours.

Frequency polygons are typically constructed from such frequency distributions. A **frequency polygon** is a graph showing the different possible scores on the horizontal axis, known as the *abscissa*. The frequency of each score is plotted on the vertical axis, known as the *ordinate*. Figure A.1, p. 680, shows data from the frequency distribution with straight lines connecting the data points.

When a large number of scores is taken on some phenomenon, a frequency polygon often takes the shape of a bell, or what is more technically called a **normal distribution.** Normal distributions with their bell shapes usually occur when there are a few individuals at the extremes and many

Frequency distribution A chart or array, usually arranged from the highest to the lowest score, that shows the frequency of the occurrence of the different scores.

Frequency polygon A graph of a frequency distribution that shows the number of instances of obtained scores; data points are usually connected by straight lines.

Normal distribution A bell-shaped distribution of scores in which the tendency is for most scores to cluster around the mean with few scores much higher or lower. A normal distribution is usually obtained only in situations where a large number of measures are taken.

Table A.1 A frequency distribution tallies the number of times each score occurs. In this distribution, few individuals score with very high and low scores (number of hours of TV watching), while most individuals have scores in the middle range

NUMBER OF HOURS OF TV WATCHING	NUMBER OF INDIVIDUALS WATCHING	TOTAL NUMBER OF INDIVIDUALS
0	1	1
1	1 1 1	3
2	1 1 1	3
3	1 1 1 1	4
4	1 1 1 1 1	5
5	1 1 1 1 1 1	6
6	1 1 1 1 1 1 1	7
7	1 1 1 1 1 1 1	7
8	1 1 1 1 1 1 1 1 1	9
9	1 1 1 1 1 1 1 1 1 1	10
10	1 1 1 1 1 1 1 1 1	9
11	1 1 1 1 1 1 1	7
12	1 1 1 1 1 1	6
13	1 1 1 1 1	5
14	1 1 1 1	4
15	1 1 1 1	4
16	1 1 1	3
17	1 1 1	3
18	1 1	2
19	1	1
20	1	1

Figure A.1 When graphing results of a study, experimenters plot the frequency with which different scores occur. Frequency is shown on the ordinate or vertical axis; the actual scores occur on the abscissa or horizontal axis. In this graph the frequency of number of hours of TV watching are shown for 100 children. The data points are connected by straight lines, and the resulting graph is called a frequency polygraph

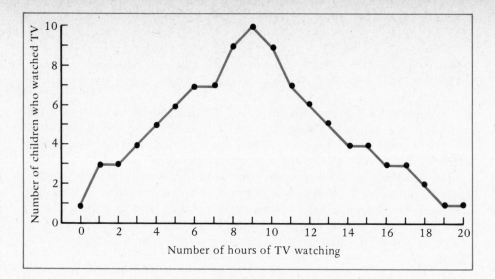

scores accumulating at the center. This usually happens with many naturally occurring phenomena such as height, weight, intelligence, or even TV watching.

Measures of Central Tendency

Consider the following three statements:

- Men are taller than women.
- Women live longer than men.
- Wealthy people are more educated.

As educated and aware adults we realize that these statements must be qualified because some women are taller than men and some educated people are poor. We assume that these statements mean, "*on the average* men are taller than women." This means that if you take all of the men in the world and compare their heights to all of the women in the world, *on the average* men will be taller. In trying to summarize and condense millions of pieces of data, we have condensed the data and made use of some descriptive statistics.

A measure of central tendency is a descriptive statistic that tells us what single score best represents the entire set of scores. A group of people, or rats for that matter, will almost always have a member who scores high or low. So, to describe the group *as a whole* we often use a measure of central tendency. The most frequently used measure of central tendency is the mean.

MEAN. "Men are taller than women." How might we go about studying this statement? One way would be to examine the height of a large number of men, some from each country, each race, and each age group; we would then do the same thing for women. After measuring the height of many thousands of men and women, we might then figure the average height and plot the results on a bar graph such as Figure A.2. It is obvious that on the average men are taller than women. The way these data were computed was to take the heights of each of the subjects, add them all together, and divide by the number of subjects in each group. As is shown in Table A.2, if we measure

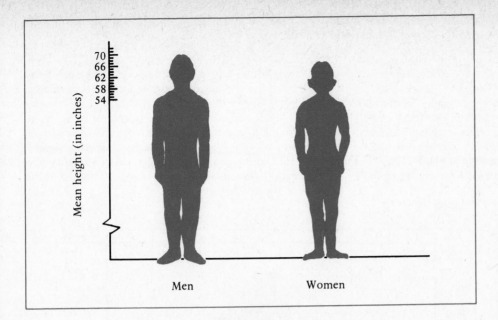

Figure A.2 Mean height for men and women. Heights are calculated by adding up the heights of thousands of men and women and dividing by the number of people added into the calculations

Table A.2 Height in inches. To calculate means, like height, add up the scores and divide by the number of entries

MEN		WOMEN	
Alfred	62	Lorraine	58
David	62	Golde	59
Benjamin	64	Marcy	61
Ross	67	Mickey	64
Paul	68	Sharon	64
Cary	68	Rozzy	66
Mark	69	Bonnie	66
Evan	70	Sue	66
Michael	70	Cheryl	66
Dave	70	Ruth	67
Steven	70	Iris	67
Morry	70	Nancy	67
Alan	70	Theresa	67
Bernie	70	Sylvia	67
Lester	70	Jay	68
Al	70	Linda	68
Mike	73	Elizabeth	71
Arnold	79	Jesse	75
Corey	79	Gabrielle	76
Stephen	79	Sarah	77
Total height for men	1400 in.	Total height for women	1340 in.

Mean for men: $\frac{\Sigma S}{N} = \frac{1400}{20} = 70$ in.

Mean for women: $\frac{\Sigma S}{N} = \frac{1340}{20} = 67$ in.

The Mean Sets the Pace

Our grade on an examination is often determined by how others in the class do on the exam. This is what instructors mean when they say that a grade "is on a sliding scale or curve." If the average student in a class only scores 50% of the questions correct, then someone who scores 70% of the questions correct has obviously done a good job. Similarly, if the average student in the class scores 85% correct, then someone who scores only 60% has done a poor job.

When grades are on a sliding scale, instructors generally plot their results on a graph. A mean is calculated and inspection of the scores generally allows an instructor to "slide the scale" to an appropriate level. As is shown in Figure A.3, the average score on a test of trigonometry was 65%. Since the average student achieved only 65% correct, he or she was given a C. Students who did better were given Bs, and those who ranked at the top of the class were given As.

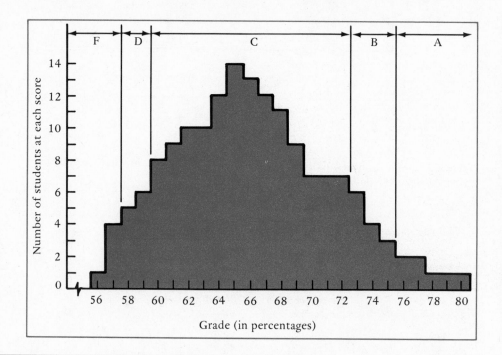

Figure A.3 When grades are on a sliding scale, instructors often draw a graph showing the number of individuals at each score. Then they draw cutoff points for As, Bs, Cs, Ds, and Fs

the heights of 20 men and 20 women, we can add up the total inches represented and divide by the number of people. This will give us the average height of a person in that group.

This average height of arithmetic average is called a **mean.** Mathematically this formula is written as

$$\text{Mean} = \frac{\Sigma S}{N}$$

The Σ means to add up; S stands for each individual score; and N stands for the number of scores that are available. The mean is a descriptive statistic because it describes some data.

Mean The arithmetic average, a measure of central tendency that is calculated by adding up all the scores and dividing by the number of scores.

Mode A measure of central tendency that is the most frequent observation.

MODE.   Another way of describing the central tendency of a set of data is to use the mode. The **mode** is the most frequent observation. Figure A.4

shows the same data that are in Table A.2; the frequency of the different scores is plotted. For example, there is only one person who is 58 inches tall and only three who are 79 inches tall. The mode, the most frequent data point, occurs at 70 inches because more people are 70 inches tall than any other height. Thus, the mode of this group of data is 70 inches.

MEDIAN. The **median** is the 50% point; half of the observations fall above the median and half fall below. Figure A.5 shows the same data on height. We can see that half of the data fall above 68; the median is therefore 68.

Very often the mean, mode, and median may turn out to be the same number. These three descriptive statistics are measures of a central tendency that tells the researcher something about the average or typical subject. If you had to guess the height of a person you had never met, your best guess would place a male at about 70 inches and a female at about 67 inches because these are the average heights for males and females.

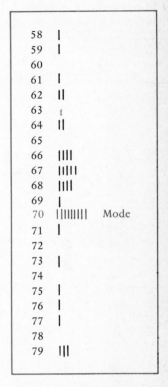

Measures of Variability: The Range and Standard Deviation

A measure of central tendency like a mean is a single number that indicates how a hypothetical "average" subject might be described. But we know that hypothetical average people do not really exist. Some people will score above the mean and others will score below it. Knowing how an average subject might score is useful, but if we know the full range of scores in a group, this provides us with even more information. A statistic that describes the extent to which scores differ from one another in a distribution is called a measure of **variability.** Among a group of 40 subjects taking an IQ test, it is likely that some will score high IQs and that some will score low IQs. If all of the subjects had scored the same IQ, we would say that there was no variability among the subjects. This is very unlikely. People are different and a wide number of personal and situational characteristics will affect their obtained scores. By knowing the extent of the variability, researchers have a way of estimating how much subjects differ from the mean or "average" subject. One such measure of variability is the range. The **range** indicates to a researcher the spread of scores in a distribution. To calculate the range you subtract the lowest from the highest score. So, if the lowest score on a test was 20 and the highest was 85, the range is 65 points. The mean of this group might be 45, 65, or 74 points; regardless, there was a 65 point spread from the lowest score to the highest one.

We see that the range provides a limited measure of how variable the subjects in a group are. Within a group of 100 students nearly all of them may have scored within 10 points of the average or mean score of 65 points. Still, one student scoring a 20 and one student scoring 95 creates a range of 75 points. We thus see that the range is a measure of how variable subjects might be, but it is a relatively crude one. There are better and more precise measures of the spread of scores within a group. Such statistics tell a researcher not just the mean and the spread of scores, but also how the scores are distributed.

Assume that we have a group of high school students who have been tested on the speed at which they press a button when a light is flashed on; this is a reaction time study. Thirty students were chosen at random from the tenth-grade. The time they took to press the button is shown in Table A.3.

Standard deviation A descriptive statistic that provides a measure of variability in a set of data.

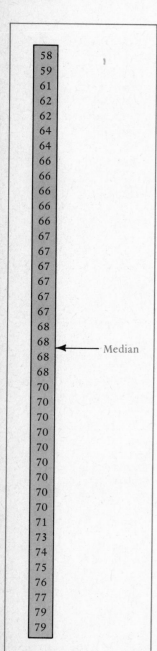

Figure A.5 The median is the 50% point

This table shows that the students' reaction times varied quite a bit; some students responded quickly, but others had slower reaction times. If you are only told the mean reaction time, you must assume that this is the best estimate of how long it takes a high school student to respond. However, if we want to know something about the relationship between the average time and the times that were above and below this average, we must have a measure of variability like a standard deviation.

A **standard deviation** is a descriptive statistic that tells the researcher about the variability of the data. Table A.4 shows the reaction times of two groups of subjects in responding to a light. The first group shows a large degree of variability. By contrast, the second group of subjects all took about the same amount of time, but there is not much variation from subject to subject—each subject's score was not very different from the next subject's. Therefore, the standard deviation (estimate of variability) for Group 1 subjects will be substantially higher than the standard deviation for Group 2 subjects.

It turns out that the mean reaction times for Groups 1 and 2 in Table A.4 were exactly the same. Both groups of subjects took an average of 555 milliseconds to respond (there are 1,000 milliseconds in a second.) However, if we know the variability associated with each mean, we know more about the persons who make up the group. If we were asked to guess how long it would take a person to respond to a light, we would be more confident in saying that a Group 2 subject would respond in 555 milliseconds; this is the case because all of the subjects in Group 2 took between 530 and 580 milliseconds, and the small amount of variability led to a small standard deviation. By contrast, the subjects in Group 1 all took dramatically different reaction times; the standard deviation of their group (the variability) was very high. Our best guess for both groups is exactly the same, 555 milliseconds, but, again, it is likely that we will be more confidant about Group 2 than Group 1.

A standard deviation tells us information about all of the people in a group, not just the average one. When we are told that cigarette smoking is dangerous to our health, we have to ask, "How dangerous?" Statistics might show that an individual who smokes 20 cigarettes per day will decrease his or her life span by 6 years. But we are compelled to ask how much variability exists and whether it decreases the life expectancy of all or just most smokers by 6 years. In other words, does it decrease some people's lives by 2 months and other people's lives by 10 years? How much variability exists around this mean of 6 years; what is the standard deviation?

Measures of variability such as standard deviation are very useful in helping us describe data. They provide the researcher and student with information about the way a *group* of subjects behave, not just the average subject.

The Normal Curve

There are many events that happen systematically. Certain findings occur far more frequently than others; some of these events follow the pattern of a normal curve. A **normal curve** is a graph of a distribution of scores in which the mean, mode, and median are generally assumed to be equal; the distribution of scores in a normal curve is symmetrical around this central point. In a normal curve average behavior occurs far more frequently than deviant behavior does. Height, for example, is normally distributed; there are more people of

Table A.3 Reaction time in milliseconds. When 30 students were involved in a reaction time study, their responses or reaction times varied dramatically from individual to individual

450	490	500
610	520	470
480	492	585
462	600	490
740	700	595
500	493	495
498	455	510
470	480	540
710	722	575
490	495	570

Mean = 540

Table A.4 Reaction time in milliseconds. When two groups are compared for estimates of variability, Group 1 shows a wide range of scores and thus much variability. Group 2, by contrast, shows a narrow range of scores and thus little variability

GROUP 1	GROUP 2
380	530
400	535
410	540
420	545
470	550
480	560
500	565
720	570
840	575
930	580
Mean = 555	Mean = 555
Standard deviation = 197	Standard deviation = 17

average height than there are people who are very tall or very short. As is shown in Figure A.6, there are far more people who are 69 inches tall than who are 78 inches tall. Height, weight, shoe size, intelligence, and very often scores on tests in introductory psychology are normally distributed.

Standard deviations describe characteristics of the normal curve. In a normal curve the bulk of the data occur within eight standard deviations, four on either side of the mean. As is shown in Figure A.7, p. 686, each standard deviation on either side of the mean accounts for a different proportion of all of the people.

In Figure A.8, the mean of the distribution is 50 and the standard deviation is 10. A single deviation is equal to 10 points; however, each increase of 10 points over the mean or each decrease of 10 points under the mean accounts for fewer and fewer people. Just over 34% (34.13%) of the individuals tested are accounted for with scores between 50 and 60. With scores of 60 to

Normal curve A graph of a distribution of scores in which the mean, mode, and median are assumed to be equal; such a graph is bell-shaped and symmetrical around the mean. Normal curves are evident only when a large sample of scores is taken.

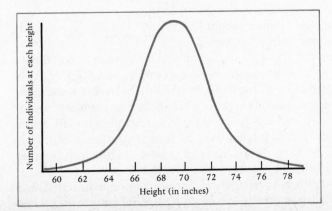

Figure A.6 In a normal distribution, or a normal curve, there are far more people who are of average height, weight, or intelligence than people who are at the extremes

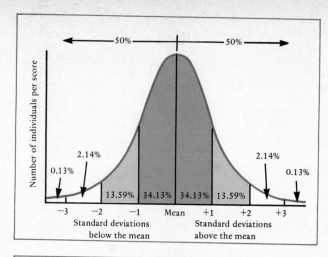

Figure A.7 In a normal curve, or a normal distribution, the bulk of the data occur within eight standard deviations, four on either side of the mean; each accounts for a different proportion of the population

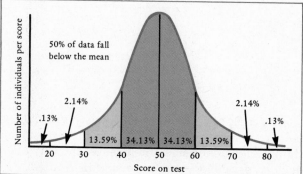

Figure A.8 In a normal distribution, each standard deviation accounts for a different percentage of the population. In this figure, every increase of 10 points on a test brings about fewer and fewer individuals

70 only 13.59% are accounted for. With a score greater than 70 only about 3% of individuals are accounted for. Of the people who took the test, 34.13 + 13.59 + 2.14 + .13 accounts for 50%. Thus, 50% of the people had test scores less than 50. The normal curve not only can represent test scores but can describe any activity involving a number of subjects in which the results are normally distributed.

Men's heights provides a further illustration of a normal curve. The mean height of men is 70 inches, and there is a standard deviation of 4 inches. Therefore, we can conclude that 34.13% of men have a height between 66 and 70 inches, 13.59% have a height between 62 and 66 inches, while only about 3% of all the men in the world have a height less than 62 inches. As is shown in Figure A.9, height is normally distributed.

By knowing the mean and standard deviation of data, we can also estimate where a person stands in relation to others. For example, assume Dennis is 74 inches tall; the mean height of individuals is 70 inches with a standard deviation of 4 inches. We know that Dennis's height is one standard deviation above the mean. If we add up the percentage of people who fall below this point, we find that Dennis is taller than 84% of the population (.13 + 2.14 + 13.59 + 34.13 + 34.13 = 84%). Similarly, at 66 inches Rob is taller than 16% of the population (.13 + 2.14 + 13.59 = 15.86).

Scores on tests such as the SAT are generally normally distributed. These tests are used to help colleges decide whom to accept into their programs.

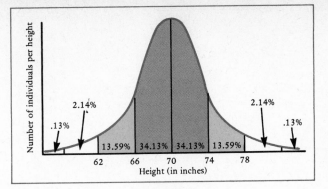

Figure A.9 When the mean of a distribution is 70 and the standard deviation is 4, an individual who has a score of 74 falls in a position such that his or her score is higher than 84% of the population (.13 + 2.14 + 13.59 + 34.13 + 34.13 = 84)

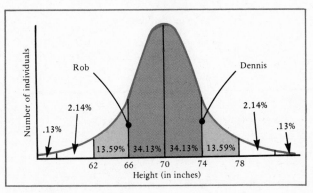

Figure A.10 Each individual falls in a different place relative to others in a normal distribution. Those who fall above the mean and below it are said to do better or worse, respectively. In the case of height they are said to be taller or shorter than average height

Correlation A measure of the degree of a relationship between two variables; it expresses how changes in one variable relate to changes in the other. A correlation is expressed in terms of the correlation coefficient that varies in extent from −1 to +1.

These tests are arranged so as to have a mean of 500 and a standard deviation of 100. Where do you fall relative to all the others who take the Scholastic Aptitude Test (SAT)?

Correlation

Other useful statistics to help describe behavior are the **correlations** found in comparisons made from the data gathered in surveys and questionnaires. A correlational study is one which shows that there is a relationship between two variables. The degree of relationship between two variables is expressed by a numerical value called the *correlation coefficient*, which ranges from −1 to +1.

When two variables are perfectly correlated, they have a correlation of 1. Also, two variables are perfectly correlated if knowing the value of one, you are able to predict *precisely* the value of the second variable. For example, in Figure A.11, knowing the speed at which a car is going can tell you precisely the distance it will go within one hour. There is a perfect relationship between speed of the automobile and distance traveled. But let's consider two variables that are not perfectly related: height and weight. Clearly, the relationship between height and weight is that tall people generally weigh more than short people. However, this relationship is not perfect because some tall people weigh less than some short people. This imperfect relationship is shown in Figure A.12, p. 688, which indicates that knowing a person's height does not tell us his or her weight exactly. These two variables, height and weight, show a relationship, or a correlation, of .65.

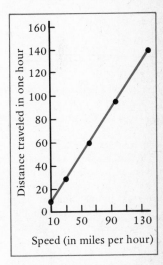

Figure A.11 When two variables are perfectly correlated, they have a correlation of 1. With a correlation of 1, knowing the value of one variable allows you to predict, precisely, the value of the second variable

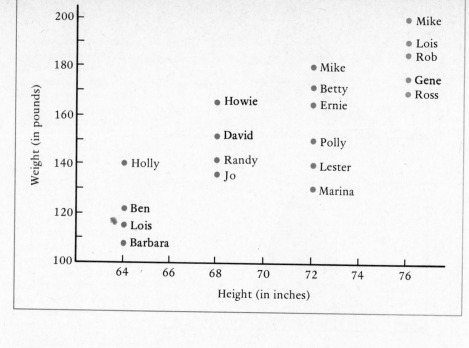

Figure A.12 When two variables are related, knowing the value of one helps you predict the value of the second. Knowing that a person is tall allows you to predict his or her weight in a general sense. A perfect prediction is not available unless the correlation is a correlation of 1

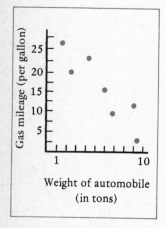

Figure A.13 An increase in one variable does not always mean an increase in the other. In a negative correlation an increase in one variable brings about a decrease in the other

When one variable shows an increase in value and the other variable also shows an increase, there is a positive relationship or correlation; height and weight are an example since as height increases so does weight. But all variables are not related in this manner. Consider the relationship between automobile weight and gas mileage. As automobile weight increases, gas mileage decreases. As is shown in Figure A.13, there is a relationship (although not a perfect one) between weight and gas mileage. Like the height and weight example, this relationship is probably a correlation of about .6 or .7. However, this is a negative relationship which shows that as one variable increases the other decreases. The strength of this relationship is just as strong; only its direction is changed. A relationship of + .7 is no stronger than a relationship of − .7; they both show a correlation of .7. Only the direction of the relationship is changed by the plus or minus sign.

Let us consider another example of a negative correlation. There is a strong negative correlation between the loudness of a sound and an observer's distance from the sound. People who live close to an airport report that airplanes are painfully loud, but the farther you live from an airfield the quieter the noise. Thus, the loudness of the airplane is directly related to the distance one lives from the airport. There is a negative correlation here between these two variables: as your distance from the airport increases, loudness decreases.

Some variables such as eye color and weight show no relationship at all. This lack of a relationship is expressed by a correlation of 0. Figure A.14 plots some data of height and IQ. The figure shows that neither tall nor short people have particularly higher IQs. IQ does not seem to be related to height in any systematic manner. Again, the absence of a relationship between two variables in one direction or another is suggested by a correlation of 0.

Thus, correlations can vary from − 1 through 0 to + 1. A 0 correlation suggests no relationship. A correlation of any number greater than 0 or less than

0, regardless of its sign (plus or minus), suggests the strength of a correlation. The larger the number, the greater the correlation. Some examples: a correlation of − .8 is greater than a correlation of + .7; a correlation of − .5 is greater than a correlation of + .3; a correlation of + .6 is greater than a correlation of − .5. The strength of the relationship is determined by the size of the number, not its sign (see Figure A.15).

INFERENTIAL STATISTICS

Let's go back to our reaction time study for a minute. What would happen if we give caffeine to students who were pressing a button for the onset of a light and compared their speed to a control group that is given an injection of salt water? The results might show that the caffeine students are able to respond faster by 20 milliseconds. Twenty milliseconds seems like it might be a significant and real difference. A significant difference means that the difference between the two groups of observations (experimental vs. control group) is probably due to the independent variable rather than to mere chance alone. In this case, 20 milliseconds difference in reaction seems like a significant difference and is, therefore, probably due to the injection of caffeine. What if the difference between the caffeine group and the control group were 5 milliseconds? Would we still argue that this is a significant difference? Perhaps. What if the difference were only 1 millisecond? (See Figure A.16, p. 690.)

When psychologists refer to a **significant difference,** they mean that the obtained difference is trustworthy and not likely to be due to chance variations among the scores. A significant difference means that there will be a persistent, similar pattern of scores if the test or task is given to another similar group of subjects. As a general rule, psychologists assume that a difference is statistically significant if its likelihood of occurrence by chance is less

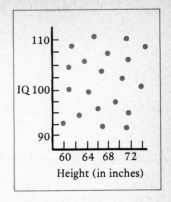

Figure A.14 When two variables show no relationship, they have a correlation of 0. Whereas weight and height are correlated, IQ and height have a correlation of 0—no relationship

Significant difference A difference that occurs between two or more groups in an experiment because of manipulations of the independent variable and not because of mere chance. A result is said to be significant or trustworthy if its probability of occurrence by chance alone is less than 5 times out of 100, or less than 5%.

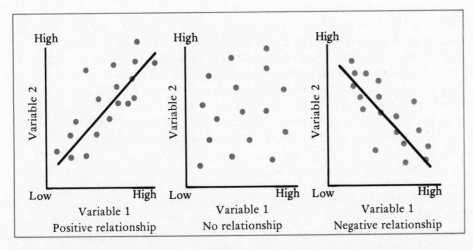

Figure A.15 The left panel shows a positive correlation where an increase in one variable brings about an increase in the other. The right panel shows a negative correlation; here an increase in one variable brings about a decrease in the other variable. The middle panel shows a 0 correlation, with one variable not predicting the other

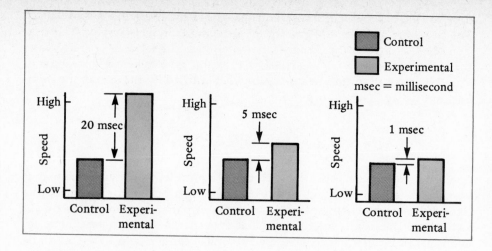

Figure A.16 Which difference is significant? When researchers are faced with having to determine if a difference between two groups is significant, they are trying to decide if the difference could be due to mere chance or is really due to the independent variable being manipulated

than 5 times out of 100. Many researchers accept a difference as significant only if its likelihood of occurrence by chance is less than 1 time out of 100 times. Even if such differences are obtained, to be thoroughly convinced, most researchers wish to see an experiment or test repeated showing the same results a second time. Repeating an experiment for the purpose of verifying a result is called *replicating* the experiment. If after replicating a study the same results are found and the probability that the results are due to chance is less than 5 out of 100 times, then a researcher can be confident in saying that there is a significant difference between one group and another.

Most experiments are done to prove or disprove hypotheses. For example, different groups of rats may be given doses of various drugs, after which their ability to tell the difference between shapes is assessed. The purpose of the study is to find out how the different drugs work and how they affect form perception. The experimenter may find that groups of drugged rats are no longer able to discriminate shapes as compared to a control group. But she may find that another dosage of the drug produces an increase in their ability to make decisions about shapes. Are these differences significant?

It is difficult to make decisions as to what is a significant difference. To help make decisions about data, a branch of statistics called inferential statistics has been developed. **Inferential statistics** are used to decide whether two or more groups are different from one another and whether or not this difference is a result of chance alone. If the difference in reaction time for our high school students is only 1 millisecond, it is unlikely that the two groups differ significantly. However, were this group to have a difference of 1,000 milliseconds, we would probably be willing to assume that this difference is not due to chance.

Typically, means and suitable measures of variability are used in inferential statistics to help make decisions. A mean tells what the average subject does; a measure of variability describes how a group's set of scores are distributed. Table A.5 contains the same data that were presented earlier. Here two groups of subjects responded to a light, and on the average they both took the same amount of time. Yet, it is obvious that there is greater variability in Group 1 than in Group 2. In Table A.6 are another two groups of subjects who responded to a light; however, their means are different. Group 1 took 10 milliseconds less time than Group 2. However, in examining the data

Inferential statistics Statistical methods used to reach and infer conclusions from a set of data with a minimal degree of error.

Table A.5 Reaction time in milliseconds. When two groups of subjects responded with a reaction time measure, they both took about the same amount of time, 555 milliseconds. Yet, Group 2 variability was significantly smaller than Group 1 and thus presents more reliable data

GROUP 1	GROUP 2
380	530
400	535
410	540
420	545
470	550
480	560
500	565
720	570
840	575
930	580
Mean = 555	Mean = 555
Standard Deviation = 197	Standard Deviation = 17

Table A.6 Reaction time in milliseconds. While the two groups of subjects show a 10 millisecond difference in reaction time, the wide degree of variability in each group decreases the likelihood that a researcher would accept this difference as a significant one

GROUP 1	GROUP 2
390	380
400	400
410	410
420	420
460	470
480	480
510	500
600	720
870	840
910	930
Mean = 545	Mean = 555
Standard Deviation = 192	Standard Deviation = 197

we notice that there is much variability within both groups of subjects. We would probably be unwilling to believe that these two groups *really* differ.

Inferential statistics uses formulas that consider means, individual subject scores, and overall variability. The smaller the variability, the greater the likelihood that the two groups differ significantly. If variability is very small, a difference of 5 milliseconds between the groups may be a real difference. However, if variability is very large, a difference of 30 milliseconds between two groups may not be considered significant.

SUMMARY

When psychologists study behavior, they want to be able to make firm statements; they want to be able to say that a behavior is directly affected by certain variables. To show cause-and-effect relationships, they conduct experiments to manipulate independent variables so that behavior can be examined through dependent variables. To be certain that a dependent variable is only affected by the experimenter's manipulation, psychologists go to great lengths to try to control experiments and experimental subjects. Once the data have been collected, statistical procedures are employed to help describe it. Included in these procedures are measures of central tendency as well as measures of variability, such as the standard deviation.

Measures of central tendency only tell us about average people. However, once we have information about the variability of a group, we can tell how most people behave as well as how the extremes within a group might behave. We have to consider that many sources of variability can be introduced into data. Some subjects may be performing slowly because they are ill, tired, or even bored, while other subjects may do particularly well because they have practiced the task before. There will almost always be variability within subjects, and we have to realize that this variability will affect our results.

Measures of central tendency in combination with measures of variability also allow us to make inferences from our data. These inferences allow us to generalize from our data and make statements about an entire population based upon a small sample of people. All of the experiments we have talked about have used limited numbers of subjects. Thirty or forty students from a high school class are barely enough by which to make inferences about all high school students. Yet, if the subjects are carefully chosen, we may be able to make fairly accurate statements, even when just a few subjects are tested. By contrast, if the differences within or among groups of students are great, then we are not able to draw firm conclusions, and our statistical technique will show that there is a lack of significance.

Unlike controlled experiments, surveys, questionnaires, and interviews present data that only show correlations. A correlation only suggests a relationship between two variables and does not show cause and effect. But correlations are not to be pushed aside; when strong correlations between variables exist, they can often be taken as evidence for support of an important argument. The important point to remember about correlations is that they only provide information about a relationship—either a positive relationship or a negative relationship.

Statistics and the scientific method are closely tied together and are both necessary for a scientist to study behavior. Once data are collected, statistics allow the psychologist to reduce the large volume of information into a reasonable arrangement. In addition, statistics allow the psychologist to examine data at a glance and make inferences from those data with a reasonable degree of certainty. As long as psychologists are collecting information on a limited number of subjects and are using this information to generalize to a larger population, statistics will be important. So that we can make our inferences with confidence, we must be sure that inferences are not based on chance alone and the degree of variability among members of a group is significantly small.

CHAPTER REVIEW

1. The mean is calculated by adding up all of the scores and dividing that sum by the number of scores; the formula is written

$$M = \frac{\Sigma S}{N}.$$

2. The mode, another measure of central tendency, is the most frequent observation.
3. The median is the 50% point.
4. Variability is a measure of the extent to which scores in a distribution differ from one another.
5. The range is a measure of variability that describes the spread of scores within a group; it is calculated by subtracting the lowest score from the highest score.
6. Standard deviations are measures of variability. When variability is low, we are more willing to accept a mean as representative of the average subject within a group.
7. Eight standard deviations account for virtually all of the data under the normal curve. The first standard deviation on either side of the mean accounts for 34.13%;

the second standard deviation, 13.59%; the third standard deviation, 2.14%; and the fourth standard deviation, .13%. In a normally distributed group of scores, 50% of the people have scores below the mean and 50% of the people above the mean.

8. A normal distribution is a bell-shaped distribution of scores in which the tendency is for most scores to cluster around the mean with few scores much higher or lower. A normal distribution is usually obtained only in situations where a large number of measures are taken.

9. A normal curve is a graph of a distribution of scores in which the mean, mode, and median are assumed to be equal; such a graph is bell-shaped and symmetrical around the mean. Normal curves are evident only when a large sample of scores is taken.

10. A correlation is a measure of the degree of a relationship between two variables; it expresses how changes in one variable relate to the changes in the other. A correlation is expressed in terms of the correlation coefficient, which varies in extent from -1 to $+1$.

11. When two variables are perfectly correlated, they have a correlation of 1. When two variables are totally unrelated, they have a correlation of 0.

12. A positive correlation means that an increase in one value is related to an increase in the other. A negative correlation means that an increase in one variable brings about a decrease in the other.

13. A significant difference is a difference that occurs between two or more groups in an experiment because of manipulations of the independent variable and not because of mere chance. A result is said to be significant or trustworthy if its probability of occurrence by chance alone is less than 5 times out of 100, or less than 5%.

14. Inferential statistics are used to help psychologists make decisions. The decisions that they have to make often refer to the question of whether one group is significantly different from another.

15. Using measures of central tendency in combination with measures of variability, psychologists can make inferences with a reasonable degree of certainty.

SUGGESTIONS FOR FURTHER READING

ANDERSON, B. F. *The psychology experiment: An introduction to the scientific method.* Belmont, CA.: Wadsworth, 1967.

BACHRACH, A. J. *Psychological research: An introduction* (2nd ed.). New York: Random House, 1966.

CAMPBELL, D. T., & STANLEY, J. C. *Experimental and quasi-experimental designs for research.* Chicago: Rand McNally, 1967.

EDWARDS, A. L. *Experimental design in psychological research* (3rd ed.). New York: Holt, Rinehart & Winston, 1968.

ROSENTHAL, R., & ROSNOW, R. L. *The volunteer subject.* New York: John Wiley & Sons, 1975.

Glossary

accommodation A process described by Jean Piaget whereby existing cognitive structures and behaviors are modified by new concepts and experiences; in perception, accommodation is the change in shape of the lens of the eye when an object moves closer to or farther away from the observer.

addictive Any drug that produces physiological symptoms when the drug is no longer administered and thus causes both physical and psychological dependence. Addictive drugs usually produce tolerance.

affect A feeling or mood that is easily seen by others; an emotional response.

afferent The term used to denote pathways and signals of the peripheral nervous system that run toward the central nervous system.

age regression An individual's ability to return to an earlier time in his or her life and report events about that time in detail. Age regression may be induced through hypnosis.

aggression Any behavior that has as its goal harming or injuring another person or thing.

agoraphobia A disorder characterized by a fear of being alone in public places from which escape might be difficult.

alcohol abuse Any situation in which a person shows problems related to alcohol.

alcohol-related problems Medical, social, or psychological problems associated with alcohol.

alcoholism Physiological addiction to alcohol; psychological dependence usually develops in alcoholism.

all-or-none The principle by which a neuron will either fire at full strength or not fire at all.

altered state of consciousness A pattern of functioning that is dramatically different from ordinary awareness and responsiveness.

alternate form reliability Estimating the reliability of a test by correlating scores on two forms of a test.

amnesia A loss of memory, usually due to traumatic unjury.

amplitude In audition, the intensity of a sound wave or its total energy; it determines the loudness of a sound and is usually measured in decibels.

anal stage Freud's second stage of personality development. From 1½ until age 3, it is the stage during which gratifica-

tion is obtained through defecation and a child learns to respond to the outside demands of society.

anomalous trichromats Color-deficient individuals with weakness at various wavelengths. The extent of the color weakness varies.

antisocial personality disorder A disorder characterized by a history of continuous and chronic behavior in which others' rights are violated. Beginning before age 15, such individuals exhibit lying, thefts, delinquency, and a general violation of rules. Such individuals come into conflict with society because they lack guilt and cannot understand others; they behave irresponsibly, do not fear punishment, and are often egocentric.

anxiety A generalized feeling of fear and apprehension that may or may not be connected to a particular event or object and that is often accompanied by increased physiological arousal. Generally, these fears and apprehensions are unrealistic. Symptoms include fear, apprehension, inattention, palpitations, dizziness, sweating, and chest pains.

approach-approach conflict An anxiety-producing situation where individuals must decide between two equally attractive alternatives or goals.

approach-avoidance conflict An anxiety-producing situation where an individual is both attracted to and repelled by an alternative or goal.

assimilation A process described by Jean Piaget whereby new concepts and experiences are incorporated into existing ones and are then used in a meaningful way.

attention deficit disorder A Disorder of Infancy, Childhood, and Adolescence characterized by restlessness, inattention, distractibility, and overactivity which begins in children before the age of 7; also known as hyperactive syndrome or hyperkinetic syndrome.

attitude A pattern of relatively enduring feelings, beliefs, and behavior tendencies toward other people, ideas, or objects.

attribution The process through which we infer other people's motives and intentions from observing their overt behavior.

autism See Infantile Autism.

autonomic nervous system The part of the peripheral nervous system that controls the vital processes of the body, such as heart rate, digestive processes, blood pressure, etc. Its two main divisions are the sympathetic and parasympathetic systems.

aversive counterconditioning A counterconditioning technique by which aversive or noxious stimuli are paired and associated with desirable stimuli or stimuli that need to be avoided. Eventually, to avoid the noxious stimulus the patient adopts a new response to the undesirable stimulus.

avoidance-avoidance conflicts An anxiety-producing situation where both alternatives or goals are equally distasteful or negative.

Babinski reflex Reflex in the infant which causes the infant to project its toes outward and up when the soles of its feet are touched.

balance theory An attitude theory in which people prefer to hold consistent beliefs with others and try to avoid incompatible beliefs.

basal age The test age level at which a student can pass all of the parts of the test but the test is not so easy that the student feels it is ridiculous.

behavior Every aspect of an organism's actions including thought, emotional, and physical activities; some of these actions may not be directly observable.

behaviorism School of psychology that rejects the notion that the proper subject of psychology is the contents of consciousness and argues instead that psychology can only describe and measure what is observable either directly or through the use of instruments. As an approach to personality, it assumes that each person responds to the environment as he or she has learned to respond.

behavior modification A therapy based on the application of learning principles, such as classical and instrumental conditioning, which changes people's overt behavior rather than their subjective feelings, unconscious processes, or motivations; synonymous with behavior therapy.

behavior settings Places such as a church, a park, or a hospital that have a regular and specific pattern of activity which takes place therein.

behavior therapy A therapy based on the application of learning principles, such as classical and instrumental conditioning, which changes people's overt behavior rather than their subjective feelings, unconscious processes, or motivations; synonymous with behavior modification.

biofeedback The general technique by which individuals can monitor the "involuntary" activity of certain organs and bodily functions and thereby learn to control them.

body language The communication of information through body positions and gestures.

bonding A special emotional attachment process that takes place between parent and child.

brainstorming A technique in which subjects are asked to solve problems by indicating all possible solutions that occur to them without making evaluative judgments on those solutions.

brightness The lightness or darkness of reflected light.

case study A method of interviewing subjects to gain information about their background, including data on such things as childhood, family, education, and social and sexual interactions.

catatonic type One of the five major subtypes of schizophrenia, characterized by stupor in which individuals are mute, negative, and basically unresponsive; characteristics can also include displays of excited or violent motor activity. Individuals can switch from the withdrawn to the excited state.

ceiling age The test age level at which all tests administered are failed.

central nervous system (CNS) The part of the nervous system consisting of the brain and spinal cord.

chromosomes Strands in the nuclei of cells that carry genes. They are composed of a DNA core and are responsible for hereditary transmission of traits. Found in pairs, they represent genes of both the mother and father.

classical conditioning A conditioning process where by being paired with a stimulus that naturally elicits a response, a neutral stimulus also comes to elicit a similar or even identical response; sometimes it is called *Pavlovian conditioning*.

client-centered therapy An insight therapy developed by Carl Rogers which seeks to help people evaluate the world and themselves from their own vantage point so that they can become everything that they might. The principal therapeutic technique uses a nondirective emotionally therapeutic environment in which a therapist provides unconditional positive regard.

cognitive dissonance A state in which individuals feel uncomfortable because they are involved in two or more thoughts, attitudes, or behaviors that are inconsistent with one another.

cognitive theory The approach to behavior which emphasizes that people have choices to make in life about their goals and how those goals can be achieved.

color blindness The inability to perceive different hues.

community psychology An approach to the treatment of mental health problems that provides local services to the community on a continuous basis. Treatment programs are extended to reach people who might not seek them out.

concept A classification of objects or ideas that sets them apart from others on the basis of a common feature.

concordance rate The percentage of occasions when two close relatives will show the same particular trait.

concrete-operational stage Piaget's third major stage of development, which occurs approximately from age 7 to 11 years. During this stage the child develops thought processes enabling him or her to understand constant factors in the environment, rules, and high-order symbolism (such as arithmetic, geography).

conditioned response The response brought about by a conditioned stimulus.

conditioned stimulus The stimulus, which through repeated association with an unconditioned stimulus, becomes capable of eliciting a response.

conditioning A systematic procedure through which conditioned responses are learned.

conduct disorder A Disorder of Infancy, Childhood, and Adolescence characterized by the persistent violation of others' rights or violation of major age-appropriate norms. Can be classified as aggressive or nonaggressive, socialized or undersocialized. Onset is usually before the age of 13.

conduction deafness Deafness resulting from interference with the conduction of sound to the neural mechanism of the inner ear.

conflict approach A theoretical approach to personality which assumes that opposing forces within the individual are constantly clashing. Freud was its major proponent.

conscious behavior Freud's first level of consciousness. It includes what a person thinks, feels, and does that the person is aware of.

consciousness The general state of being aware and responsive to stimuli and events in the environment.

conservation The ability to recognize that something which has changed in some way (such as the "shape" of a liquid in a container) is still the same thing, of the same weight, substance, or volume.

conservative focusing A strategy for problem solving where the individual tries to arrive at a solution by eliminating alternative possibilities.

consolidation The term used to describe the change from a temporary neural circuit to one that has evolved over time to a more permanent circuit.

construct validity The extent to which a test actually measures a certain trait like intelligence, anxiety, or musical ability.

content validity A property of test items which shows that the test reflects a sample of the actual behavior to be measured.

control group In an experiment the group of subjects that does not receive the treatment under investigation and that is used for purposes of comparison.

conversion disorder A disorder characterized by the loss or alteration of physical functioning that is not due to a physiological disorder and that seems to be due to some internal psychological conflict.

convolutions Folds in tissues which are a characteristic of the cerebral hemispheres and overlying cortex in humans.

correlation A measure of the degree of a relationship between two variables; it expresses how changes in one variable relate to changes in the other. A correlation is expressed in terms of the correlation coefficient which varies in extent from -1 to $+1$.

counterconditioning Learning a new response to a familiar stimulus through a process of reconditioning. The two major types of counterconditioning procedures are systematic desensitization and aversive counterconditioning.

creativity A characteristic that in general is considered to include originality, novelty, and appropriateness.

crowding The feelings people have when their space has been restricted or limited to too great an extent.

dark adaptation The process by which chemicals in the photoreceptors regenerate and return to their inactive, pre-light-adapted state, and this results in an increase in sensitivity.

debriefing The procedure of explaining to subjects after completion of an experiment in which they have served, the true nature or purpose of the experiment.

decentration The process that begins in children at about age 2 of changing from a totally self-oriented view to one that recognizes other people's feelings, ideas, and viewpoints.

decriminalization Reducing a legal offense to a civil violation (such as a traffic ticket) rather than a crime.

deep structure The organization of a sentence that is closest to its underlying meaning.

defense mechanism A way of reducing anxiety by distorting reality.

deindividuation Group behavior caused by the individuals within the group losing their distinctive personalities and becoming less concerned with proper evaluation of a course of action.

delusion A false belief that is inconsistent with reality and is held in spite of contradictory evidence.

denial A defense mechanism in which a person *denies* the reality of the source of anxiety.

dependent variable The behavior measured in an experiment to assess whether changes in the independent variable affect the behavior under study.

descriptive statistics A method of describing, summarizing, and condensing data.

deviation IQ A standard IQ test score that has the same mean and standard deviation at all ages.

diabetes mellitus A condition in which too little insulin is present in a person's blood to allow sufficient quantities of sugar to be transported into body cells. This can result in hyperglycemia.

dichromats Persons who can distinguish only two of the three basic hues.

diffusion of responsibility Feelings of individuals in a group that they cannot be held individually responsible for the group's actions.

dimension A conceptual feature that sets an object or phenomenon apart from others lacking that feature.

disorganized type One of five major subtypes of schizophrenia, characterized by frequent incoherence, absence of systematized delusions, and blunted, inappropriate, or silly affect.

dissociative disorder A disorder characterized by sudden but temporary alteration in consciousness, identity, or motor behavior.

divergent thinking A term defined by Guilford to mean the production of new information from known information or the generation of logical possibilities. To Guilford, also the basis of creativity.

double bind A situation in which a person has been given two different and inconsistent messages.

Down's syndrome Also known as mongolism, a genetic defect in humans in which there are three No. 21 chromosomes. Individuals with Down's syndrome are usually physically deformed and mentally retarded.

dream analysis A psychoanalytic technique of interpreting a patient's dreams to gain insight into the patient's motivation.

dreaming Altered consciousness that seems to occur largely during rapid eye movement sleep and during which an individual may have visual, tactile, and auditory experiences.

drive An aroused condition within the organism that initiates behavior to satisfy physiological needs. Drives are inferred from behavior.

drive theory The approach to behavior that emphasizes the internal capabilities which energize organisms to attain, maintain, or seek some goal. The goal is often to reestablish a state of physiological balance.

early infantile autism See Infantile Autism.

eclecticism The combining of theories, facts, or techniques. This term usually describes the practice in clinical psychology of using whatever therapy techniques are appropriate for an individual client rather than relying only on the techniques of a particular branch of psychology.

ecological psychology The study of the interdependent relationships between a person's behavior and the behavior settings in which the behavior occurs.

efferent The term used to denote neural pathways or signals that run away from the central nervous system to other structures of the body.

ego In Freud's theory, the part of the personality that seeks to satisfy the id and superego in accordance with reality.

ego-analysts Followers of Freud who argue that the ego has greater control over behavior than Freud suggested. This therapy technique is more concerned with reality testing and control over the environment.

egocentrism An individual's failure to be able to perceive a situation or event in more than one way; in infancy it is the attitude that directs all concerns and behaviors to personal interests and needs.

electroencephalogram (EEG) The record of an organism's electrical brain patterns. EEGs are recorded by placing electrodes on the scalp of a subject; they pick up the electrical activity of the brain beneath the skull.

electromagnetic radiation The entire spectrum of waves initiated by charged particles, including cosmic rays, x-rays, ultraviolet, visual, infrared, and radar waves.

embryo The human organism from the fourth day after conception through the fortieth day.

emotion A subjective feeling generally accompanied by a physiological change that is usually associated with a change in behavior.

encounter group A group of people who meet together to become more aware of their feelings, behaviors, and interactions. This increased awareness is their goal.

endocrine glands Ductless glands that secrete hormones directly into the bloodstream.

environmental psychology The study of how physical settings affect human behavior and how human behavior affects the environment.

ethologist A behavioral scientist who usually studies animals in their natural setting rather than in a laboratory.

exhibitionism A Psychosexual Disorder characterized by repetitive acts of exposure of the genitals to strangers as the preferred method of achieving sexual stimulation and gratification.

expectancy theory The approach to behavior that emphasizes a person's expectancy of success and need for achievement as the energizing factor in human behavior.

experiment A situation in which an observer systematically manipulates certain variables to describe objectively a relationship between the variable of concern and the resulting behavior. Inferences about causes and effects can be drawn from well-designed experiments.

experimental group The group of subjects in an experiment that receives the treatment under investigation.

extinction The process whereby the probability of an organism emitting a conditioned response is reduced when reinforcement is withheld.

face validity A property of a test in which the test "looks" appropriate just from reading the items.

factor analysis A statistical procedure designed to determine the mutually independent elements (factors) in any set of skills.

factor theory approach to intelligence Theories of intelligence based on factor analysis. Among the best known are those of Spearman and Thurstone.

fallopian tubes The tubes that link the ovaries and the uterus. The ovum descends through these tubes toward the uterus, and fertilization occurs in these tubes.

fetishism The Psychosexual Disorder in which sexual arousal and gratification are brought about from objects, such as shoes, underwear, or toilet articles.

fetus The unborn organism from the fortieth day after conception until birth.

fixed interval A schedule of reinforcement where a reinforcer occurs after a specified interval of time, providing the required response has occurred at least once.

fixed ratio A schedule of reinforcement in which a reinforcer occurs after a set number of responses.

formal-operational stage Piaget's fourth and final stage of intellectual development. This stage begins at about age 12; the individual can think hypothetically so that all possibilities are considered. The individual is now capable of deductive logic.

fraternal twins Double births resulting from the release of two ova in the female which are then fertilized by two sperm; their genetic makeups are not exactly the same.

free association A technique of psychoanalysis in which people speak out loud all those thoughts and feelings that occur to them, however illogical the order or content.

free-floating anxiety Anxiety that is not clearly attached to any particular object or situation. Patients feel a sense of impending doom, and their anxiety remains with them most of the time.

frequency A measure of the number of complete pressure waves per unit of time; it is measured in hertz (Hz) or cycles per second.

frequency distribution A chart or array, usually arranged from the highest to the lowest score, that shows the frequency of the occurrence of the different scores.

frequency polygon A graph of a frequency distribution that shows the number of instances of obtained scores; data points are usually connected by straight lines.

frustration-aggression hypothesis A view which suggests that frustration of any goal-directed behavior leads to aggression.

fulfillment approach A theoretical approach to personality which assumes that each individual is constantly striving to become everything that he or she might. Carl Rogers is a major proponent of this approach; Alfred Adler, another major proponent, presents a slightly more extreme view.

functional fixedness The inability to see in an object a function other than one normally associated with it.

functionalism The school of psychology that grew out of structuralism and was concerned with how and why the conscious mind works the way it does.

gene The unit of heredity transmission carried in chromosomes and made up of deoxyribonucleic acid (DNA) and protein.

generalized anxiety disorder A disorder characterized by persistent anxiety of at least one month's duration and which includes problems in motor tension, autonomic hyperactivity, apprehension, and concentration.

genetics The study of heredity.

genital stage Freud's last stage of personality development. From puberty through adulthood, it is the stage during which sexual conflicts of childhood surface again in adolescents as they develop their sexuality.

Gestalt psychology The school of psychology which argues that behavior cannot be studied in parts but must be viewed as an interdependent whole.

Gestalt therapy An insight therapy founded by F. S. Perl which emphasizes the "how" and "what" of behavior, stressing the importance of a person's getting in touch with his or her feelings in the present. Therapy is the process of becoming aware.

grammar The linguistic description and rules for how a language functions.

grasping reflex Reflex in the infant that causes it to grasp vigorously any object which touches or is placed in its hand.

group therapy A method of treating emotional and behavioral problems in which several people are seen simultaneously.

halo effect The tendency to let one of an individual's characteristics influence the evaluation of other characteristics.

heredity The potential transmitted from parents to offspring through genes.

higher order conditioning The process by which a neutral stimulus that is paired with a conditioned stimulus takes on conditioned stimulus properties.

hormone A chemical that regulates the activities of specific organs or cells. Hormones are produced by the endocrine glands and are transported to their site of action by the bloodstream.

hue The psychological property of light referred to as color and determined by its wavelength.

humanistic psychology The approach to behavior that emphasizes human qualities, especially dignity, individual choice, self-concepts, and self-achievement.

hyperactive syndrome See Attention Deficit Disorder.

hyperactivity A group of symptoms which include overactivity, distractability, restlessness, and short attention span (see Attention Deficit Disorders).

hyperglycemia A condition in which too much sugar is present in the blood.

hyperkinetic syndrome See Attention Deficit Disorder.

hypermnesia Heightened memory. Hypermnesia may sometimes be induced through hypnosis, and evidence suggests that hypnosis may be useful in facilitating the recall of information from memory.

hypnosis A state of consciousness that has been altered from the normal waking state through trance-induction procedures. Subjects' responsiveness to suggestions increases as they become more deeply hypnotized.

hypnotic drugs Drugs used to induce sleep. Common hypnotics are Miltown and Equanil. The sleep induced by these is not normal sleep because the rapid eye movement stage has been reduced or prevented.

hypnotic susceptibility The willingness to follow unconventional instructions while under hypnotic influence.

hypoglycemia A condition resulting from the overproduction of insulin, causing very low blood sugar levels. It is usually characterized by a lack of energy, and often faintness and dizziness.

hypothesis A tentative idea adopted to account for certain facts; more important, it guides the investigation of others.

id In Freud's theory, the source of instinctual energy which works on the pleasure principle.

ideal self What a person would like to be.

identical twins Double births resulting from the splitting of a zygote into two identical cells which then separate and develop independently. Identical twins have the same genetic makeup.

illusion A perception of a stimulus that differs from the way the physical stimulus would normally lead us to expect it to appear.

implosive therapy An extinction procedure in which a patient is brought to a very high level of anxiety by imagining fearful situations. The aim is to reduce (extinguish) the fear and avoidance responses; this is accomplished by showing the patients that they will survive the anxiety and can now start to produce responses other than fear and avoidance.

imprinting The process by which animals form species-specific behaviors during a critical period early in life. These behaviors are not easily modified.

independent variable The variable in an experiment that is directly and purposely manipulated by the experimenter.

infantile autism A Pervasive Developmental Disorder of Infancy, Childhood, and Adolescence characterized by a lack of responsiveness to other people, gross impairment in language skills, bizarre responses to the environment, and an onset before the age of $2\frac{1}{2}$; also known as early infantile autism or autism.

inferential statistics Statistical methods used to reach and infer conclusions from a set of data with a minimal degree of error.

insight therapy A therapy that attempts to show a patient a meaningful relationship between possibly unconscious motivation and current maladjustments or abnormal behavior. Insight therapy assumes that abnormal behavior is caused by an individual's failure to understand his or her motivations and needs. Once insight is achieved, behavior should change almost automatically.

insomnia Prolonged inability to obtain sleep due to physiological or psychological factors.

instincts Inherited, inborn, unlearned, and predetermined behavior patterns.

instrumental conditioning A conditioning procedure in which responses that organisms emit are increased or decreased in probability of reoccurring by delivery of a reinforcer or punisher. The process is sometimes called *operant conditioning*.

insulin A hormone produced by the pancreas that is necessary for the body to transport sugar from the blood into body cells to be metabolized.

intelligence According to Wechsler the aggregate global capacity of the individual to act purposefully, to think rationally, and to deal effectively with the environment.

interference The suppression or confusion of one bit of information with another received either later or earlier.

interview A series of open-ended questions used to gather basic and detailed information about a person. Although time consuming, this technique allows a psychologist to probe a potentially important issue or problem in depth.

intrinsically motivated behaviors Behaviors that a person engages in to feel more competent and self-determined.

introspection The technique of examining the contents of one's mind through self-report and careful examination of what one is thinking and feeling.

labor The process whereby the uterus contracts to open and allow the baby to descend through the birth canal to the outside world.

latency stage Freud's fourth stage of personality development. From age 7 until puberty, it is the interim stage between the phallic and genital stages.

lateralization The concentration of a particular brain function in one hemisphere.

law of Prägnanz Items or stimuli that can be grouped together and seen as a whole will be seen that way.

learned helplessness The behavior of giving up or not responding; it is exhibited by subjects who are exposed to negative consequences or punishment and who have no control of when or whether it will be delivered.

learning A relatively permanent change in behavior that occurs as a result of experience.

libido Freud's "life force," and the source of energy for the id, ego, and superego. Seeking immediate gratification, the libido works on the pleasure principle.

light The portion of the electromagnetic spectrum, with wavelengths from 400 to 700 nanometers, that is visible to the eye.

long-term memory The mechanism by which a relatively permanent record of information is kept; being relatively permanent, long-term memory resists the loss of information.

mainstreaming The administrative practice of placing handicapped children in regular classroom settings with the support of special education services.

major depression A disorder characterized by loss of interest in almost all usual activities as evidenced by a sad, hopeless, or discouraged mood. Other symptoms include sleep disturbances, loss of energy, and feelings of unworthiness and guilt.

mean The arithmetic average, a measure of central tendency that is calculated by adding up all the scores and dividing by the number of scores.

median A measure of central tendency that is the point above which 50% of all observations occur.

mediation A process that provides a connection between previously unconnected things.

medical model An approach to abnormal behavior in which behavior is seen as a result of, or as caused by, an internal condition or motivation.

meditation The state of consciousness characterized by intense concentration, restriction of sensory stimuli, and deep relaxation. Meditative states are brought about through a number of techniques.

memory The ability to recall or remember information, events, or skills learned in the past.

mental retardation Below average intellectual functioning as measured on an IQ test with impairment in adaptive behavior which originates during the developmental period, generally before the age of 16.

mild retardation (IQ of 55 to 69) A category that includes persons with a fair degree of independence but who require some supervision and guidance in intellectual tasks and on their jobs.

mode A measure of central tendency that is the most frequent observation.

model A perspective or approach derived from one field and set of data to help describe data from another field.

modeling Learning by observing and imitating the behavior of other people.

moderate retardation (IQ of 40 to 54) A category that includes persons who are semi-independent and are able to take care of themselves hygienically, but who are partially dependent upon families and friends for intellectual and financial support.

monochromats Persons who have only rods in their retinas and who, therefore, cannot perceive hue.

morality Human attitudes about social practices, institutions, and individual behavior used to evaluate events to decide if the events are right or wrong.

Moro reflex The reflex in the infant that causes the infant to outstretch its arms and legs and cry when there is a loud noise.

morpheme The basic unit of meaning in a language.

motivation A general condition within an organism that produces goal-directed behavior. It is an inferred condition initiated by drives, needs, or desires.

motive A specific internal condition directing an organism's behavior toward a goal.

multiple personality A disorder characterized by the existence within an individual of two or more different personalities, each of which is dominant at a particular time.

narcotic A drug that dulls the senses, relieves pain, tranquilizes, and can cause elation. Many narcotics such as heroin and morphine are derivatives of opium. Narcotics are generally addictive.

naturalistic observation Careful and objective observation of events as they occur in nature, without their experimental control or manipulation.

nature The inherited characteristics of an individual that are determined by genetics.

need An aroused physiological condition involving an imbalance.

need for achievement A social need that directs a person to succeed and to strive constantly for excellence and success.

negative instance A term applied when a stimulus does not fall in any category exemplary of the concept under study.

negative reinforcement Reinforcement that acts to increase the probability of a response due to the removal of an aversive event.

nerve deafness Impairment in hearing due to damage to the cochlea or the auditory nerve.

neuron The basic unit of the nervous system. Typically, a neuron is a single cell composed of *dendrites*, which receive information; a *cell body*, which generates electrical signals; and an *axon*, which transmits neural signals.

neurotic disorder A disorder characterized by a group of symptoms that are distressing and unacceptable to an individual. Individuals with the disorder do not violate social norms and they are in touch with reality.

nondirective therapy A form of therapy in which the client plays the active role and determines the direction of therapy. The therapist is permissive, almost passive, and totally accepting of feelings and behavior.

normal curve A graph of a distribution of scores in which the mean, mode, and median are assumed to be equal; such a graph is bell-shaped and symmetrical around the mean. Normal curves are evident only when a large sample of scores is taken.

normal distribution A bell-shaped distribution of scores in which the tendency is for most scores to cluster around the mean with few scores much higher or lower. A normal distribution is usually obtained only in situations where a large number of measures are taken.

norms A list of scores and the corresponding percentile ranks or standard scores of a group of examinees on whom a test was standardized.

NREM (no rapid eye movement) sleep All periods of sleep that are not rapid eye movement sleep. There are four distinct stages of no rapid eye movement sleep.

nurture The experiences of an individual in an environment.

observational learning The learning procedure by which organisms learn new responses by observing the behavior of a model and then imitating it; also called social learning theory.

obsessive-compulsive disorder A disorder characterized by persistent and uncontrollable thoughts and irrational beliefs. These persistent thoughts make individuals feel compelled to perform compulsive rituals that interfere with their daily lives.

Oedipus complex During the phallic stage, feelings of rivalry with the parent of the same sex for love of the parent of the opposite sex. Through identification with the parent of the same sex, the Oedipus complex is mastered.

opponent process theory The theory of Hering which states that color is coded in the visual system by a series of receptors that respond positively or negatively to different wavelengths of light.

oral stage Freud's first stage of personality development. From birth until about 1½ to 2, it is the stage during which gratification is obtained primarily through the mouth.

ovary The female sex gland in which eggs are produced.

ovum A female reproductive cell; an egg that after fertilization develops into a new member of the species.

paranoid type One of five major subtypes of schizophrenia, characterized by delusions and hallucinations of persecution and/or grandeur; irrational jealousy is sometimes evident.

paraprofessional A person who works alongside professional psychologists to aid them in providing psychological services.

parasympathetic nervous system The part of the autonomic nervous system that is generally conservatory, storing up bodily resources when they are not needed. Its activities are balanced by those of the sympathetic nervous system.

pedophilia A Psychosexual Disorder characterized by repetitive acts of engaging in sexual activity with children as a preferred method of achieving sexual stimulation and gratification.

percentile score A score indicating what percentage of the population under consideration would obtain a lower score.

perception The process by which people attach meaning to stimuli by interpreting their sensory input through complex processing mechanisms.

peripheral nervous system The parts of the nervous system that are not part of the central nervous system. The two main subdivisions are the somatic and autonomic nervous systems.

personal space The area around an individual considered private by the individual; an invisible boundary around a person.

personality A set of relatively enduring behavioral characteristics that describes how a person reacts to the environment.

phallic stage Freud's third stage of personality development. From ages 3 to 7, it is the stage during which gratification is obtained primarily from the genitals. During this stage children pass through the Oedipus complex.

phenylketonuria (PKU) A genetic defect that creates an inability to metabolize an amino acid, phenylalanine. This usually brings about mental retardation shortly after birth if the condition is not detected. It can be treated successfully by a diet low in phenylalanine (the amino acid present in milk).

phobic disorder A disorder characterized by the fear and consequent attempted avoidance of specific objects or situations; the fear is recognized as unreasonable.

phonemes The basic units of sound in a language.

phonology The study of the sounds of language termed phonemes.

photoreceptors The two types of cells in the retina that are light-sensitive, that is, rods and cones.

placebo effect A nonspecific therapeutic change that comes about primarily because a person expects change rather than because of any specified treatment given by a therapist.

placenta A group of blood vessels and membranes connecting a human fetus's umbilical cord to the uterus. It serves as a mechanism for the exchange of nutrients and waste products.

pleasure principle The guiding principle of the id, which seeks complete and immediate gratification of all needs and desires.

positive instance A term applied when a stimulus falls within a category that is an example of the concept under consideration.

positive reinforcement Reinforcement that acts to increase the probability of a response reoccurring by the introduction of a rewarding or pleasant stimulus.

preconscious behavior Freud's second level of consciousness, including mental activity, which people can be aware of if they attend to it.

predictive validity The extent to which a test can predict a person's behavior in some other kind of setting.

preoperational stage Piaget's second major stage of intellectual development. This stage lasts from about 2 to 7 years and is the time when preoperational (symbolic) thought is developed.

primacy effect The phenomenon in which items presented first in a list or series are more accurately recalled.

primary punisher Any stimulus or event that by its mere delivery or removal acts naturally (without learning) to decrease the likelihood of a response that has preceded it. For example, the delivery of electric shocks acts as a punishment to a rat; similarly, the removal of food acts naturally to decrease the likelihood of a behavior that preceded it.

primary reinforcer Any stimulus or event that by its mere delivery or removal acts naturally (without learning) to increase the likelihood of a response which precedes it. For example, food acts as a reward for a hungry organism; similarly, the removal of a painful stimulus acts naturally as a reward.

privacy The process of controlling boundaries between people so that access to them is limited.

problem drinker A person who shows alcohol-related problems; these may include alcoholism.

profound retardation (IQ below 25) A category that includes people who require total custodial care. Physical, motor, and intellectual development are severely impaired.

projection A defense mechanism in which people attribute to others those undesirable traits in themselves.

psychiatrist A medical doctor who has done a residency to study behavior and who treats patients with emotional and physical problems.

psychoanalysis The therapeutic system developed by Freud through which insight into a person's true motivation is obtained via certain special techniques, including free association, dream analysis, and transference. A lengthy insight therapy, it assumes human beings are basically in conflict.

psychoanalyst One who has studied the technique of psychoanalysis (usually a psychiatrist) and uses it as a primary method of treating emotional problems.

psychodrama A group therapy in which members act out their feelings.

psychogenic amnesia A disorder characterized by a sudden inability to recall important personal information that is too extensive to be explained by ordinary forgetfulness.

psycholinguistics The study of how language is acquired, perceived, comprehended, and produced.

psychologist One who studies behavior and uses behavior principles in scientific research or applied settings. Psychologists have advanced graduate training and usually hold Master's and Ph.D. degrees.

psychology The science of behavior.

psychotherapy The treatment of emotional disorders by psychological methods.

psychotic Gross impairment of reality testing within an individual; this impairment usually interferes with an individual's ability to meet the ordinary demands of life.

punishment The process by which a response that is followed by an undesirable or noxious stimulus decreases in probability of reoccurring.

questionnaire A printed form with questions. Usually given to a large group of people, a questionnaire can gather a substantial amount of data in a short amount of time.

range A measure of variability that describes the spread of scores within a group; it is calculated by subtracting the lowest from the highest score.

rational-emotive therapy A behavior-cognitive therapy that emphasizes logical, rational thought processes. Originated by Albert Ellis, the therapy assumes that emotional disorders are caused by patients' basic irrational assumptions.

rationalization A defense mechanism in which a person reinterprets behavior in terms that are acceptable.

raw score An examinee's unconverted score on a test, for example, the number of correct answers.

reaction formation A defense mechanism in which people act out the opposite of their anxiety-producing feelings.

recency effect Phenomenon in which items presented to the subject more recently are more accurately recalled.

receptive field The area of the retina that when stimulated produces a change in the firing of a single cell in the visual system.

reflex An involuntary behavior that occurs in response to stimuli without prior learning.

refractory period The recovery period of a neuron after it fires, during which time it cannot fire again. This period allows the neuron to reestablish its electrical balance with its surroundings.

reinforcer Any event that increases the probability of the reoccurrence of a response that precedes it.

reliability The ability of a test to give the same score for a single individual through repeated testings.

REM (rapid eye movement) sleep A sleep stage characterized by a deep sleep, muscle relaxation, and by high-frequency, low-voltage brain activity similar to that exhibited by the awake, alert individual. During rapid eye movement sleep individuals often move their eyes rapidly and, if awakened, report dream activity.

representative sample A sample of individuals who match the population with whom they are to be compared; they are to match with respect to important variables, for example, socioeconomic status and age.

repression A defense mechanism in which anxiety-producing feelings are blocked from conscious awareness and pushed into the unconscious.

resistance In psychoanalysis, the uncooperativeness by which a patient shows an unwillingness to understand situations, interpret them, provide information about them to the therapist, or use other traditional techniques.

retinal disparity The slight difference in the visual images perceived by each eye.

risky shift The phenomenon that following group discussions, individuals take risks or more daring actions than prior to their discussions.

rooting reflex The reflex in the infant that causes it to turn its head toward the direction of stimulation of the lips or cheek.

saccades Rapid movements of the eyes from one position to another that have a minimum fixation period of $\frac{1}{4}$ second.

saturation The "depth" of hue of reflected light as determined by the purity (homogeneity) of the different wavelengths comprising the light.

schizophrenic disorder A group of disorders characterized by a lack of reality testing and deterioration of social and intellectual functioning which begins before age 45 and lasts for at least 6 months. Individuals with this diagnosis often show serious personality disintegration with significant changes in thought, mood, perception, and behavior.

secondary punisher A neutral stimulus that has no value to the organism, which through repeated pairings with a punishing stimulus has taken on punishing qualities.

secondary reinforcer A neutral stimulus that has no value to the organism, which through pairings with a reinforcing stimulus has taken on reinforcement value.

selective breeding Breeding controlled in order to produce the expression of specific genetic traits.

self A group of characteristics and perceptions of an individual, and his or her relationship with others and to other aspects of life. The self is the main structural component of Roger's theory of personality.

self-actualization The process of moving toward realizing one's potential to the highest degree possible; the process of achieving everything that one is capable of doing.

self-perception One's attitude toward and beliefs about oneself. Self-perception is often a reflection of others' attitudes toward oneself and is largely formed during childhood and adolescence.

semantics The study of the meaning of components of language.

sensory-motor stage The first of four major stages in Piaget's theory of intellectual development. It is the period roughly covering the first 2 years of life during which the child begins to interact with his or her environment and during which the rudiments of intelligence are established.

sensory register The process and mechanism by which initial coding and brief storage of stimuli occur. The duration of the visual sensory register is $\frac{1}{4}$ second.

severe retardation (IQ of 25 to 39) A category that includes people who are capable of some self-help when provided supervision. Intellectual performance is severely impaired. Some physical symptoms are apparent, including changes in posture and movement.

sexual deviations Sexual practices directed toward objects rather than people, involving real or simulated suffering or humiliation, or directed toward sexual activities with nonconsenting partners.

sexual masochism A Psychosexual Disorder characterized by receiving the infliction of physical or psychological pain in order to achieve sexual excitement; this often includes being humilated, bound, or beaten.

shaping The process of gradually training an organism to give the proper responses. This is done by selectively reinforcing behaviors as they come closer and closer to the desired response.

short-term memory The memory process that temporarily stores information for immediate or short-term use. The duration of short-term memory is about 30 seconds and has a limited capacity of 5 to 9 items.

significant difference A difference that occurs between two or more groups in an experiment because of manipulations of the independent variable rather than due to mere chance. A result is said to be significant or trustworthy if its probability of occurrence by chance alone is less than 5 times out 100, or less than 5%.

simple phobia A disorder characterized by an irrational and persistent fear of an object or situation along with a compelling desire to avoid it; all specific phobias other than Agoraphobia and Social Phobia are classified as Simple Phobia.

Skinner box Named for its developer, B. F. Skinner, this hollow box contains a responding mechanism (usually a lever) capable of delivering a reinforcer (often food or water) to the organism.

sleep Nonwaking state of consciousness generally characterized by unresponsiveness to the environment and general body immobility. Sleep proceeds in a cyclic pattern over five stages.

social facilitation The phenomenon that people often do better at a task when they are, or believe they are, being observed by others.

social motive A condition directing humans toward maintaining or establishing feelings about themselves, others, and relationships.

social need An aroused condition within organisms involving feelings about themselves, others, and relationships.

social perception The process through which we come to know and understand the people around us.

social phobia A disorder characterized by a fear of, and desire to avoid, situations where the person is exposed to scrutiny by others and where that person might behave in an embarrassing or humiliating way.

social psychology The study of how individual behavior is affected by the behaviors or characteristics of others.

socialization The process by which individuals learn the rules of their society and establish their own values, attitudes, and long-lasting personal characteristics.

somatic nervous system The part of the peripheral nervous system that controls skeletal muscles and, in turn, bodily movement.

somatization disorder A disorder characterized by recurrent and multiple complaints of several years duration for which medical attention has brought no improvement.

somatoform disorder A disorder characterized by physical symptoms for which there are no evident physical causes and for which there is evidence that the causes are psychological conflicts; the symptoms, often pain, are real and are not under voluntary control.

sound A psychological term describing changes in pressure through a medium; the medium may be gaseous, liquid, or solid.

spike discharge An electrical current sent down the axon of a neuron.

split-brain patients Term applied to people whose corpus callosum, which normally connects the two cerebral hemispheres, has been surgically severed.

split-half reliability Estimating the reliability of a test by splitting it into comparable halves and correlating the scores from the halves.

spontaneous recovery The reoccurrence of a conditioned response following a rest period after extinction.

standard deviation A descriptive statistic that provides a measure of variability in a set of data.

standard error of measurement Based on statistical formulas, the standard error of measurement is the number of points that a score may vary because of the imperfect reliability of a test.

standard score A score that expresses an individual's relative position to the mean based on the standard deviation; it is often derived by converting a raw test score to one interpretable on the basis of a population variable such as age or grade.

standardization The process of developing a uniform procedure in the administration and scoring of a test; the process also includes developing norms for the test from a large representative sample of subjects.

statistical model An approach toward behavior in which behavior that deviates from the average range of behavior is considered to be abnormal.

stimulus discrimination The process by which an organism learns to respond to a specific stimulus and then to no other similar stimulus; the complementary process to stimulus generalization.

stimulus generalization Responding to stimuli similar to but not the same as the training stimulus.

stranger anxiety A syndrome in children from 8 to 15 months old where the presence of strangers makes them fearful.

stressor A stimulus that brings about uncomfortable feelings, anxiety, tension, and especially physiological arousal.

structuralism School of psychology founded by Wilhelm Wundt (1832–1920) who believed the proper subject matter of psychology was the study of the contents of consciousness. Structuralists developed and used the technique of introspection.

subject An individual who participates in an experiment and from whose behavior data are collected.

subliminal perception Perception of stimulus presented below some duration or luminance level at which subjects are not aware of the presentation 50% of the time.

sucking reflex Reflex in which an infant makes sucking motions when presented with a stimulus to the lips, such as a nipple or object.

superego In Freud's theory, the moral branch of mental functioning.

superstitious behavior Behavior learned through coincidental association with reinforcement.

surface structure The organization of a sentence that is closest to its written or spoken form.

sympathetic nervous system The part of the autonomic nervous system that responds to emergency situations. It is active only on occasion; sympathetic activity calls up bodily resources as needed.

symptom substitution When a symptom is eliminated and another symptom resulting from the same basic cause occurs.

synapse The small space between the end branches of the axon of one neuron and the receptive site (dendrite, cell body, or neural membrane) of another neuron.

syntax The relationships of groups of words and how words are arranged into phrases and sentences.

systematic desensitization A counterconditioning procedure in which a patient, while deeply relaxed, imagines a series of increasingly fearful situations. With successive trials, the patient learns relaxation rather than fear as a new response to a former fearful stimulus.

territorial behavior Behavior involved in establishing, maintaining, personalizing, and defending a delimited space.

test-retest reliability A method of assessing the reliability of a test by administering it to the same group of examinees on two different occasions and computing the similarity between their scores.

THC (tetrahydrocannabinol) The active ingredient in marijuana. Although tetrahydrocannabinol exists in many forms, those not in the Δ^9 ("delta nine") configuration are generally physiologically inactive.

time-out The procedure of removing a person from a desired or reinforcing situation; acting as a punishment, it decreases the likelihood of an undesired behavior. It is most appropriately called a time-out from reinforcement procedure.

token economy An instrumental conditioning procedure by which patients are reinforced with tokens for socially acceptable behavior. These tokens are later exchanged for desired items or privileges.

tolerance A progressive insusceptibility to the effects of a specific drug when the drug is administered repeatedly. Tolerance usually accompanies addiction although it can also be developed to many nonaddictive drugs.

transference A psychoanalytic procedure during which a therapist becomes the object of a patient's emotional attitudes about others. Patients often develop love or hate feelings toward the therapist that they might have for a parent.

transformational grammar The approach to studying the structure of a language, originally developed by Chomsky, which asserts that each *surface structure* of a sentence has a *deep structure* associated with it. This grammar has transformational rules associated with it to generate surface structures from deep structures.

transsexualism A Gender Identity Disorder characterized by a sense of discomfort and inappropriateness about one's biological sex. This is accompanied by a wish to be rid of one's own genitals and to be a member of the opposite sex.

transvestism A Psychosexual Disorder characterized by recurrent and persistent cross-dressing for the purpose of achieving sexual excitement.

trichromatic theory The theory of Young and Helmholtz which states that all colors can be made by mixing the basic colors of red, blue, and green.

unconditioned response The unlearned or involuntary response to an unconditioned stimulus.

unconditioned stimulus A stimulus that normally produces an involuntary measurable response.

unconscious behavior Freud's third level of consciousness, including mental activity that is beyond a person's awareness (unless brought out through psychoanalysis).

validity A property of tests which means that a test measures only what it is supposed to measure.

variability A measure of the extent to which scores in a distribution differ from one another.

variable interval A schedule of reinforcement in which a reinforcer occurs after intervals of different lengths of time, providing the required response has occurred at least once.

variable ratio A schedule of reinforcement in which a reinforcer occurs after a varying number of responses.

variables The potentially changeable conditions or characteristics of a situation or experiment.

voyeurism A Psychosexual Disorder characterized by repetitive acts of looking at people in different states of undress or sexual activity as the preferred method of achieving sexual stimulation and gratification.

withdrawal symptoms A series of physical states, varying in intensity, that occur when a drug is no longer administered to a person who has developed a physiological dependence on it.

zygote A fertilized egg.

Bibliography

AARONS, L. Sleep assisted instruction. *Psychological Bulletin;* 1976, *83,* 1–40.

ABRAMSON, L. Y., SELIGMAN, M. E. P., & TEASDALE, J. D. Learned helplessness in humans: Critique and reformulation. *Journal of Abnormal Psychology,* 1978, *87*(1), 49–74.

ADAMS, H. E., FEUERSTEIN, M., & FOWLER, J. L. Migraine headache: Review of parameters, etiology, and intervention. *Psychological Bulletin,* 1980, *87,* 217–237.

ADAMS, S. The PICO project. In N. Johnston, L. Savitz, and M. Wolfgang (Eds.), *The sociology of punishment and correction.* New York: John Wiley & Sons, 1970.

ADLER, A. *The practice and theory of individual psychology.* Original publication: 1920. Hardcover English edition: London: Routledge and Kegan Paul, 1925. Paperback reprint: Totowa, NJ: Littlefield, Adams, 1973.

ADLER, A. *The science of living.* Original publication: 1929. Paperback reprint: New York: Anchor Books, 1969.

ADLER, A. On the origin of striving for superiority and social interest. Original publication: 1933a. In H. L. Ansbacher and R. R. Ansbacher (Eds.), *Superiority in social interest: A collection of Alfred Adler's later writings.* New York: Viking Press, 1973.

ADLER, A. Advantages and disadvantages of the inferiority feeling. Original publication: 1933b. In H. L. Ansbacher and R. R. Ansbacher (Eds.), *Superiority in social interest: A collection of Alfred Adler's later writings.* New York: Viking Press, 1973.

AGNEW, H. W. JR., & WEBB, W. B. The influence of time course variable on REM sleep. *Bulletin of the Psychonomic Society,* 1973, *2,* 131–133.

AGRAS, S., SYLVESTER, D., & OLIVEAU, D. The epidemiology of common fears and phobias. Unpublished manuscript, 1969, as cited in G. C. Davison and J. M. Neale, *Abnormal psychology: An experimental clinical approach* (2nd ed.). New York: John Wiley & Sons, 1978.

AIELLO, J. R., & JONES, S. E. Field study of the proxemic behavior of young school children in three subculture groups. *Journal of Personality and Social Psychology,* 1971, *19,* 351–356.

AIELLO, J. R., EPSTEIN, Y. M., & KARLIN, R. A. Effects of crowding on electrodermal activity. *Sociological Symposium,* 1975, *14,* 43–57.

AIELLO, J. R., DERISI, D. T., EPSTEIN, Y. M., & KARLIN, R. A. Crowding and role of interpersonal distance preference. *Sociometry,* 1977, *40*(3), 271–282.

AIKEN, L. R. *Psychological testing and assessment* (3rd ed.). Boston, MA: Allyn & Bacon, 1979.

AINSWORTH, M. D. S. Infant-mother attachment. *American Psychologist,* 1979, *34*(10), 932–937.

AKERS, T. K., TUCKER, D. M., ROTH, R. S., & VIDILOFF, J. S. Personality correlates of EEG change during meditation. *Psychological Reports,* 1977, *40,* 439–442.

AKISKAL, H. S. The biobehavioral approach to depression. In R. A. DePue (Ed.), *Psychobiology of the depressive disorders.* New York: Academic Press, 1979.

AKISKAL, H. S., & MCKINNEY, W. T. Overview of recent research in depression. *Archives of General Psychiatry,* 1975, *32,* 285–305.

ALBERT, I. B. REM sleep deprivation. *Biological Psychiatry,* 1975, *10,* 341–351.

ALBERT, M. S., BUTTERS, N., & LEVIN, J. Temporal gradients in the retrograde amnesia of patients with alcoholic Korsakoff's disease. *Archives of Neurology,* 1979, *36,* 211–216.

ALBRECHT, S. L., THOMAS, D. L., & CHADWICK, B. A. *Social psychology.* Englewood Cliffs, NJ: Prentice-Hall, 1980.

ALHEID, G. F., MCDERMOTT, L. J., KELLY, J., HALARIS, A., & GROSSMAN, S. P. Deficits in food and water intake after knife cuts that deplete striatal DA or hypothalamic NE in rats. *Pharmacological Biochemistry of Behavior,* 1977, *6,* 273–287.

ALLEN, M. G. Twin studies of affective illness. *Archives of General Psychiatry,* 1976, *33,* 1476–1478.

ALLEN, K. E., TURNER, K. D., & EVERETT, P. M. A behavior modification classroom for head start children with problem behaviors. *Exceptional Children,* 1970, *37,* 119–127.

ALLINGTON, R. L. Sensitivity to orthographic structure in educable mentally retarded children. *Contemporary Educational Psychology,* 1981, in press.

ALPERN, M., RUSHTON, W. A. H., & TORII, S. The attenuation of rod signals by backgrounds. *Journal of Physiology,* 1970, *206,* 209–228.

ALTMAN, I. *The environment and social behavior.* Monterey, California: Brooks-Cole, 1975.

ALTMAN, I., & VINSEL, A. M. Personal space: An analysis of E. T. Hall's proxemics framework. In I. Altman & J. F. Wohlwill (Eds.), *Human behavior and environment: Advances in theory and research* (vol. 2). New York: Plenum Press, 1977.

ALTMAN, I., TAYLOR, D. A., & WHEELER, L. Ecological aspects of group behavior in social isolation. *Journal of Applied Social Psychology,* 1971, *1,* 76–100.

THE AMERICAN PSYCHIATRIC ASSOCIATION *Diagnostic and Statis-*

tical Manual of Mental Disorders (3rd ed.) Washington, D.C.: American Psychiatric Association, 1980.

ANDERSON, J. R., & BOWER, G. H. A propositional theory of recognition memory. Memory and Cognition, 1974, 2, 406–412.

ANDERSON, L. T., & ALPERT, M. Operant analysis of hallucination frequency in a hospitalized schizophrenic. Journal of Behavior Therapy and Experimental Psychiatry, 1974, 5, 13–18.

ANDERSON, N. H. Integration theory and attitude change. Psychological Review, 1971, 78, 171–206.

ANDERSON, R., MANOOGIAN, S., & REZNICK, J. Undermining and enhancing of intrinsic motivation in pre-school children. Journal of Personality and Social Psychology, 1976, 34, 915–922.

ANDERSON, J. R., & ROSS, B. H. Evidence against a semantic-episodic distinction. Journal of Experimental Psychology: Human Learning & Memory, 1980, 6, 441–466.

ANDISON, F. S. TV violence and viewer aggression: A cumulation of study results 1956–1976. Public Opinion Quarterly, 1977, 41, 314–331.

ANGLIN, J. M. Word, object, and conceptual development. New York: W. W. Norton, 1977.

ANLIKER, H. Eye movements: On-line measurement, analysis, and control. In R. A. Monty & J. W. Senders (Eds.), Eye movements and psychological processes. Hillsdale, NJ: Lawrence Erlbaum Associates, 1976.

APPEL, J. B., & PETERSON, N. J. What's wrong with punishment? Journal of Criminal Law, Criminology, and Police Science, 1965, 156, 450–453.

ARENBERG, D. Differences and changes with age in the Benton visual retention test. Journal of Gerontology, 1978, 33, 534–540.

ARGYLE, M. Nonverbal communication in human social interaction. In R. Hinte (Ed.), Nonverbal communication. New York: Cambridge University Press, 1972.

ASCH, S. E. Effects of group pressure upon the modification and distortion of judgements. In J. Guetzkow (Ed.), Groups, leadership, and men. Pittsburg, PA: Carnegie Press, 1951.

ASLIN, R. N., & JACKSON, R. W. Accomodative-convergence in young infants: Development of a synergistic sensory-motor system. Canadian Journal of Psychology, 1979, 33, 222–231.

ASTBURY, J. The crisis of childbirth: Can information and childbirth education help? Journal of Psychosomatic Research, 1980, 24, 9–13.

ATHANASOU, J. A. Smoking behavior and its modification through hypnosis: A review and evaluation. Terpnos Logos, 1974, 2(2), 4–15.

ATKINSON, J. W. (ED.) Motives in fantasy, action, and society. Princeton, NJ: Van Nostrand, 1958.

ATKINSON, J. W. An introduction to motivation. Princeton, NJ: Van Nostrand, 1964.

ATKINSON, J. W., & FEATHER, N. T. A theory of achievement motivation. Huntington, NY: Krieger, 1966.

ATKINSON, J. W., & LITWIN, G. H. Achievement motive and test anxiety conceived as motive to approach success and motive to avoid failure. Journal of Abnormal and Social Psychology, 1960, 60, 52–63.

AUERBACH, S. M., & KILMANN, P. R. Crisis intervention: A review of outcome research. Psychological Bulletin, 1977, 84(6), 1189–1217.

AUSUBEL, N. Applied psychology. In A treasury of Jewish folklore. New York: Crown, 1948 (as cited in E. L. Deci, Intrinsic motivation. New York: Plenum Press, 1975).

AYLLON, T., & AZRIN, N. H. The measurement and reinforcement of behavior of psychotics. Journal of the Experimental Analysis of Behavior, 1965, 8, 357–383.

AYLLON, T., & AZRIN, N. H. The token economy: A motivational system for therapy and rehabilitation. New York: Appleton-Century-Crofts, 1968.

AYLLON, T., & HAUGHTON, E. Modification of symptomatic verbal behavior of mental patients. Behavior Research and Therapy, 1964, 2, 87–97.

AZRIN, N. H., & HOLTZ, W. C. Punishment. In Werner K. Honig (Ed.), Operant behavior—Areas of research and application. New York: Appleton-Century-Crofts, 1966.

BABOR, T. F., MENDELSON, J. H., GALLANT, D., & KEUHNLE, J. C. Interpersonal behavior in group discussion during marijuana intoxication. The International Journal of the Addictions, 1978, 13(1), 89–102.

BADDELEY, A. D., & WARRINGTON, E. K. Amnesia and the distinction between long- and short-term memory. Journal of Verbal Learning and Verbal Behavior, 1970, 9, 176–189.

BALCH, P., & ROSS, A. W. Predicting success in weight reduction as a function of locus of control: A uni-dimensional and multi-dimensional approach. Journal of Consulting and Clinical Psychology, 1975, 43, 119.

BALL, G. G. Self-stimulation in the ventromedial hypothalamus. Science, 1972, 178, 72–73.

BANDURA, A. Principles of Behavior Modification. New York: Holt, Rinehart, & Winston, 1969.

BANDURA, A. Analysis of modeling processes. In A. Bandura (Ed.), Psychological modeling—Conflicting theories. Chicago: Aldine-Atherton, 1971.

BANDURA, A. Aggression: A social learning analysis. Englewood Cliffs, NJ: Prentice-Hall, 1973.

BANDURA, A. Behavior theory and the models of man. American Psychologist, 1974, 29, 859–869.

BANDURA, A. Self-efficacy: Towards a unifying theory of behavioral change. Psychological Review, 1977, 84, 191–215.

BANDURA, A. Social learning theory. Englewood Cliffs, NJ: Prentice-Hall, 1977.

BANDURA, A., & BARAB, P. G. Processes governing disinhibitory effects through symbolic modeling. Journal of Abnormal Psychology, 1973, 82, 1–9.

BANDURA, A., & MENLOVE, F. L. Factors determining vicarious extinction of avoidance through symbolic modeling. Journal of Personality and Social Psychology, 1968, 8, 99–108.

BANDURA, A., & WALTERS, R. Social learning and personality development. New York: Holt, Rinehart & Winston, 1963.

BANDURA, A., BLANCHARD, E. B., & RITTER, B. Relative efficacy of desensitization and modeling approaches for inducing behavioral, affective, and attitudinal changes. Journal of Personality and Social Psychology, 1969, 13, 173–199.

BANDURA, A., JEFFERY, R. W., & GAJDOS, E. Generalized change through participant modeling with self-directed mastery. Behavior Research and Therapy, 1975, 13, 141–152.

BANDURA, A., ROSS, D., & ROSS, S. A. Imitation of film-mediated agressive models. Journal of Abnormal and Social Psychology, 1963, 66, 3–11.

BANDURA, A., ROSS, D., & ROSS, S. A. Vicarious reinforcement and imitative learning. Journal of Abnormal and Social Psychology, 1963, 67, 601–607.

BARATZ, J. C. Teaching reading in an urban negro school system. In F. Williams (Ed.), Language and poverty. Chicago: Rand McNally, 1970.

BARBER, T. X., & CALVERLEY, D. S. Toward a theory of hypnotic behavior: Effects on suggestibility of defining the situation as hypnosis and defining response in suggestions, it's easy. Journal of Abnormal and Social Psychology, 1965, 29, 98–107.

BARBER, T. X., SPANOS, N. P., & CHAVES, J. F. Hypnosis, imagination, and human potentialities. New York: Pergamon Press, 1974.

BARD, P. Emotion. I. The neuro-humoral basis of emotional reactions. In C. Murchison (Ed.), *Handbook of general experimental psychology*. Worcester, MA: Clark University Press, 1934.

BARE, C. E., & MITCHELL, R. R. Experimental evaluation on sensitivity training. *Journal of Applied Behavioral Science*, 1972, 8, 263–276.

BAREFOOT, J. C., HOOPLE, H., & MCCLAY, D. Avoidance of an act which would violate personal space. *Psychonomic Science*, 1972, 28, 205–206.

BARKER, R. *Ecological psychology*. Stanford, CA: Stanford University Press, 1968.

BARLOW, H. B. Dark and light adaptation: Psychophysics. In D. Jameson & L. M. Hurvich (Eds.), Visual psychophysics. *Handbook of Sensory Physiology*. Berlin, W. Germany: Springer-Verlag, 1972.

BARMARK, S. M., & GAUNITZ, S. C. B. Transcendental meditation and heterohypnosis as altered states of consciousness. *The International Journal of Clinical and Experimental Hypnosis*, 1979, 27, 227–239.

BARON, R. A. Aggression as a function of ambient temperature and prior anger arousal. *Journal of Personality and Social Psychology*, 1972, 21, 183–189.

BARON, R. A., & LAWTON, S. F. Environmental influences on aggression: The facilitation of modeling effects by high ambient temperatures. *Psychonomic Science*, 1972, 26, 80–83.

BARTAK, L. Educational approaches. In M. Rutter & E. Schopler (Eds.), *Autism: A reappraisal of concepts and treatment*. New York: Plenum, 1978.

BARTLETT, F. C. *Remembering: A study in experimental and social psychology*. New York: Macmillan, 1932.

BARUTH, L. G. *A single parent's survival guide: How to raise the children*. Dubuque, IA: Kendall/Hunt, 1979.

BATESON, G., JACKSON, B. D., HALEY, J., & WEAKLAND, J. Toward a theory of schizophrenia. *Behavioral Science*, 1956, 1, 251–264.

BECK, A. T. Thinking and depression. I. Idiosyncratic content in cognitive distortions. *Archives of General Psychiatry*, 1963, 9, 324–333.

BECK, A. T. *Depression: Clinical, experimental, and the theoretical aspects*. New York: Hober, 1967.

BECK, A. T. *Depression: Causes and treatment*. Philadelphia: University of Pennsylvania Press, 1972.

BECK, A. T. *Cognitive therapy and emotional disorders*. New York: International University's Press, 1976.

BECK, J. Effects of orientation and of shape similarity on perceptual grouping. *Perception and Psychophysics*, 1966, 1, 300–302.

BEGG, I., & WICKELGREN, W. A. Retention functions for syntactic and lexical vs. semantic information in sentence recognition memory. *Memory & Cognition*, 1974, 2, 353–359.

BEIBER, I., DAIN, H. J., DINCE, P. R., DRELLICH, M. G., GRAND, H. C., GUNDLACH, R. R., KREMER, N. W., RISKIN, A. H., WILBUR, C. B., & BIEBER, T. B. *Homosexuality: A psychoanalytic study*. New York: Random House, 1962.

BELL, A. P., & WEINBERG, M. S. *Homosexualities: A study of human diversity*. New York: Simon & Schuster, 1978.

BELL, P. A., & BARON, R. A. Aggression and heat: The mediating role of negative affect. *Journal of Applied Social Psychology*, 1976, 6, 18–30.

BELLAK, L. *The TAT, CAT, and SAT in clinical use* (3rd ed.). New York: Grune & Stratton, 1975.

BELMONT, L., & MAROLLA, F. A. Birth order, family size, and intelligence. *Science*, 1973, 182, 1096–1101.

BELSKY, J., & STEINBERG, L. D. The effects of day care: A critical review. *Child Development*, 1978, 49, 929–949.

BEM, D. J. Self-perception: An alternative interpretation of cognitive dissonance phenomena. *Psychological Review*, 1967, 74, 183–200.

BEM, D. J. Self-perception theory. In L. Berkowitz (Ed.), *Advances in experimental social psychology*. New York: Academic Press, 1972.

BENEDETTI, G. Individual psychotherapy of schizophrenia. *Schizophrenia Bulletin*, 1980, 6, 623–638.

BENSON, K., & FEINBERG, I. The beneficial effect of sleep in an extended Jenkins and Dallenbach paradigm. *Psychophysiology*, 1977, 14, 375–384.

BERGIN, A. E., & LAMBERT, M. J. The evaluation of therapeutic outcomes. In S. L. Garfield & A. E. Bergin (Eds.), *Handbook of psychotherapy and behavior change: An empirical analysis* (2nd ed.). New York: John Wiley & Sons, 1978.

BERKOWITZ, L. The effects of observing violence. *Scientific American*, February 1964. San Francisco, CA: W. H. Freeman, 1964.

BERKOWITZ, L., & LEPAGE, A. Weapons as aggression-eliciting stimuli. *Journal of Personality and Social Psychology*, 1967, 7, 202–207.

BERLIN, B., & KAY, P. *Basic color terms: Their universality and evolution*. Berkeley, CA: University of California Press, 1969.

BERLYNE, D. E. What next? Concluding summary. In H. I. Day, D. E. Berlyne, & D. E. Hune (Eds.), *Intrinsic motivation: A new direction in education*. Toronto, Canada: Holt, Rinehart & Winston, 1971.

BERLYNE, D. E. The vicissitudes of aplopathematic and thelematoscopic pneumatology (or the hydrography of hedonism). In D. E. Berlyne & K. B. Madsen (Eds.), *Pleasure, reward, and preference*. New York: Academic Press, 1973.

BERNAL, G., & BERGER, S. M. Vicarious eyelid conditioning. *Journal of Personality and Social Psychology*, 1976, 34, 62–68.

BERNREUTER, R. G. *The personality inventory*. Stanford, CA: Stanford University Press, 1931.

BERNSTEIN, A., & LENNARD, H. L. The American way of drugging. *Society*, 1973, 10, 14–25.

BERNSTEIN, D. A., & MCALISTER, A. The modification of smoking behavior: Progress and problems. *Addictive Behavior*, 1976, 1, 89–102.

BERZINS, J. I., BEDNAR, R. L., & SEVERY, L. J. The problem of intersource consensus in measuring therapeutic outcomes: New data and multi-variate perspectives. *Journal of Abnormal Psychology*, 1975, 84, 10–19.

BETTELHEIM, B. Laurie. *Psychology Today*, 1969, 2(12), 24–25, 60.

BEUTLER, L. E., JOHNSON, D. T., NEVILLE, C. W., ELKINS, D., & JOBE, A. M. Attitude similarity and therapist credibility as predictors of attitude change and improvement in psychotherapy. *Journal of Consulting and Clinical Psychology*, 1975, 43, 90–91.

BEVER, T. G., GARRETT, M. F., & HURTIG, R. The interaction of perceptual processes and ambiguous sentences. *Memory and Cognition*, 1973, 1, 277–286.

BEXTON, W. H., HERON, W., & SCOTT, T. H. Effects of decreased variation in the sensory environment. *Canadian Journal of Psychology*, 1954, 8, 70–76.

BICKMAN, L., TEGER, A., GABRIELE, T., MCLAUGHLIN, C., BERGER, M., & SUNADAY, E. Dormitory density and helping behavior. *Environment & Behavior*, 1973, 5, 465–490.

BIGHAM, J. Memory: Studies from Harvard (II). *Psychological Review*, 1894, 1, 453–461.

BINÉT, A., & SIMON, T. Méthodes nouvelles pour le diagnostic du niveau intéllectual des anororaux. *L'Année Psychologique*, 1905, 11, 191–244.

BIRCH, H. G., & RABINOWITZ, H. S. The negative effect of previous experience on productive thinking. *Journal of Experimental Psychology*, 1951, *41*, 121–125.

BIRCH, J. W. *Mainstreaming*. Reston, VA: Council for Exceptional Children, 1974.

BIRK, L., HUDDLESTON, W., MILLER, E., & COHLER, B. Avoidance conditioning for homosexuality. *Archives of General Psychiatry*, 1971, *25*, 314–323.

BIRNEY, R. C., BURDICK, H., & TEEVAN, R. C. *Fear of failure*. New York: Van Nostrand Reinhold, 1969.

BLACKWELL, B. Psychotropic drugs in use today. The role of diazepam in medical practice. *Journal of the American Medical Association*, 1973, *225*, 1637–1641.

BLAKEMORE, C. Maturation and modification in the developing visual system. In R. Held, H. W. Leibowitz, & H.-L. Teuber (Eds.), *Perception* (*Handbook of sensory physiology*, Vol. 8). New York: Springer-Verlag, 1978.

BLAKEMORE, C., & CAMPBELL, F. W. On the existence of neurones in the human visual system selectively sensitive to the orientation and size of retinal images. *Journal of Physiology*, 1969, *203*, 237–260.

BLAKEMORE, C., & COOPER, G. F. Development of the brain depends on the visual environment. *Nature*, 1970, *228*, 477–478.

BLOOM, L. M., LIGHTBOWN, P., & HOOD, L. Structure and variation in child language. *Monographs of the Society for Research in Child Development*, 1975, *40* (Serial No. 160).

BLUMENTHALL, M. D. Measuring depressive symptomatology in a general population. *Archives of General Psychiatry*, 1975, *32*, 971–978.

BONEAU, C. A., & CUCA, J. M. An overview of psychology's human resources. *American Psychologist*, 1974, *29*, 821–840.

BONNET, M. H. Sleep, performance and mood after the energy-expenditure equivalent of 40 hours of sleep deprivation. *Psychophysiology*, 1980, *17*, 56–63.

BOOTH, A., & EDWARDS, J. N. Fathers: The invisible parent. *Sex Roles*, 1980, *6*, 445–456.

BOTTOMLEY, A. K. *Criminology in focus: Past trends and future prospects*. Oxford, England: Martin Robertson, 1979.

BOURASSA, M. The effect of marijuana on judgement and analogical reasoning. *International Review of Applied Psychology*, 1977, *26*, 21–29.

BOUTIN, G. E. Treatment of test anxiety by rational stage directed hypnotherapy: A case study. *The American Journal of Clinical Hypnosis*, 1978, *21*, 52–57.

BOWER, G. H. Mood and memory. *American Psychologist*, 1981, *36*, 129–148.

BOWER, T. G. R. The visual world of infants. *Scientific American*, 1966, *215*, 80–92.

BOWERMAN, M. F. Structural relationships in children's utterances: Syntactic or semantic? In T. E. Moore (Ed.), *Cognitive development and the acquisition of language*. New York: Academic Press, 1973.

BOWERS, D. G., & SEASHORE, S. E. Predicting organizational effectiveness with a four-factor theory of leadership. *Administrative Science Quarterly*, 1966, *11*, 238–263.

BOWERS, K. S. Time distortion and hypnotic ability: Underestimating the duration of hypnosis. *Journal of Abnormal Psychology*, 1979, *88*, 435–439.

BOWERS, M. B., JR. Biochemical processes in schizophrenia: An update. *Schizophrenia Bulletin*, 1980, *6*, 393–403.

BOWLBY, J. The nature of the child's tie to his mother. *International Journal of Psychoanalysis*, 1958, *39*, 350–373.

BOWLBY, J. *Attachment and loss*. Vol. II. *Separation: Anxiety and Anger*. New York: Basic Books, 1973.

BRABENDER, V., & DICKHAUS, R. C. Effect of hypnosis on comprehension of complex verbal material *Perceptual and Motor Skills*, 1978, *47*, 1322.

BRACKBILL, Y. Obstetrical medication and infant behavior. In J. D. Osofsky (Ed.), *Handbook of infant development*, New York: John Wiley & Sons, 1979.

BRADDICK, O., CAMPBELL, F. W., & ATKINSON, J. Channels in vision: Basic aspects. In R. Held, H. W. Leibowitz, & H.-L. Teuber (Eds.), *Perception* (*Handbook of sensory physiology*, Vol. 8). New York: Springer-Verlag, 1978.

BRADLEY, R. H., & CALDWELL, B. M. The relation of infants' home environments to mental test performance at fifty-four months: A follow-up study. *Child Development*, 1976, *47*, 1172–1174.

BRAINE, M. D. S. On learning the grammatical order of words. *Psychological Review*, 1963, *70*, 323–348.

BRANSFORD, J. D., & FRANKS, J. J. Abstraction of linguistic ideas. *Cognitive Psychology*, 1971, *2*, 331–350.

BRAUN, H. W., & GEISELHART, R. Age differences in the acquisition and extinction of conditioned eyelid response. *Journal of Experimental Psychology*, 1959, *57*, 386–388.

BRECHER, E. M., & THE EDITORS OF CONSUMER REPORTS. *Licit and illicit drugs*. Vernon, NY: Consumers Union, 1972.

BRECHER, E. M., & THE EDITORS OF CONSUMER REPORTS. Marijuana: The health question. Is marijuana as damaging as recent reports make it appear? *Consumer Reports*, 1975a, *40*, 143–149.

BRECHER, E. M., & THE EDITORS OF CONSUMER REPORTS. Marijuana: The legal question. *Consumer Reports*, 1975b, *40*, 265–266.

BREHM, J. W. *A theory of psychological reactance*. New York: Academic Press, 1966.

BRIDGES, K. M. B. Emotional development in early infancy. *Child Development*, 1932, *3*, 324–341.

BRODY, E. B. Can mother-infant interaction produce vulnerability to schizophrenia? *The Journal of Nervous and Mental Disease*, 1981, *169*, 72–81.

BROMET, E., HARROW, M., & TUCKER, G. J. Factors related in short-term prognosis in schizophrenia and depression. *Archives of General Psychiatry*, 1971, *25*, 148–154.

BROWER, D. Respiration and bloodpressure in sensory motor conflict. *Journal of General Psychology*, 1946, *34*, 47–58.

BROWN, B. B. Some characteristic EEG differences between heavy smoker and nonsmoker subjects. *Neuropsychologia*, 1968, *6*, 381–388.

BROWN, D., KLEMP, G., & LEVENTHAL, H. Are evaluations inferred directly from overt actions? *Journal of Experimental Social Psychology*, 1975, *11*, 112–126.

BROWN, H. B. An experience in identification testimony. *Journal of the American Institute of Criminal Law*, 1935, *25*, 621–622.

BROWN, I., JR., & INOUYE, D. K. Learned helplessness through modeling: The role of perceived similarity in competence. *Journal of Personality and Social Psychology*, 1978, *36*, 900–908.

BROWN, J. Some tests of the decay theory of immediate memory. *Quarterly Journal of Experimental Psychology*, 1958, *10*, 12–21.

BROWN, R. (ED.) *Psycholinguistics, selected papers* (chap. 8, The first sentences of child and chimpanzee). New York: The Free Press, 1970.

BROWN, R. *A first language: The early stages*. Cambridge, MA: Harvard University Press, 1973.

BROWN, R. Further comment on the risky shift. *American Psychologist*, 1974, *29*, 468–470.

BROWN, R., & BERKO, J. Word association and the acquisition of grammar. *Child Development*, 1960, *31*, 1–14.

BROWN, R. D., BROWN, L. A., DANIELSON, J. E. Instructional treatments, presenter types, and learner characteristics as significant variants in instructional television for adults.

Journal of Educational Psychology, 1975, *67*, 391–404.

BRUNER, J. S., GOODNOW, J. J., & AUSTIN, G. A. *A study of thinking.* New York: John Wiley & Sons, 1956.

BUCHSBAUM, M. S., COURSEY, R. D., & MURPHY, D. L. The biochemical high-risk paradigm: Behavioral and familial correlates of low platelet monoamine oxidase activity. *Science*, 1976, *194*, 339–341.

BUCHSBAUM, M. S., MURPHY, D. L., COURSEY, R. D., LAKE, C. R., & ZEIGLER, M. G. Platelet monoamine oxidase, plasma dopamine-beta-hydroxylase and attention in a "biochemical high risk" sample. *Journal of Psychiatric Research*, 1978, *14*, 215–224.

BUCK, R. *Human motivation and emotion.* New York: John Wiley & Sons, 1976.

BUCK, R. Individual differences in nonverbal sending accuracy and electrodermal responding: The externalizing-internalizing dimension. In R. Rosenthal (Ed.), *Skill in nonverbal communication.* Cambridge, MA: Oelgeschlager, Gunn & Hain, 1979.

BUCK, R. Nonverbal behavior and the theory of emotion: The facial feedback hypothesis. *Journal of Personality and Social Psychology*, 1980, *38*, 811–824.

BUCK, R., BARON, R., GOODMAN, N., & SHAPIRO, B. Unitization of spontaneous nonverbal behavior in the study of emotion communication. *Journal of Personality and Social Psychology*, 1980, *39*, 522–529.

BUCKHOUR, R., FIGUEROA, D., & HOFF, E. *Eyewitness identifications: Effects of suggestion and bias in identifications from photographs.* Brooklyn, NY: Brooklyn College Center for Responsive Psychology, 1974 (Report No. Cr-11).

BURKE, D. C. Pain in paraplegia. *Paraplegia*, 1973, *10*, 297–313.

BURNAM, M. A., PENNEBAKER, J. W., & GLASS, D. C. Time consciousness, achievement striving, and the Type A coronary-prone behavior pattern. *Journal of Abnormal Psychology*, 1975, *84*, 76–79.

BURNS, M., & SHARMA, S. Marijuana "high"—A first-time effect? *Psychological Reports*, 1976, *38*, 543–546.

BURSTEIN, E., COYNE, L., KERNBERG, O. F., & VOTH, H. The quantitative study of the psychotherapy research project: Psychotherapy outcome. *Bulletin of the Menninger Clinic*, 1972, *36*, 1–85.

BURT, C. L. The evidence for the concept of intelligence. *British Journal of Educational Psychology*, 1955, *25*, 158–177.

BUSCHKE, M. Two-dimensional recall: Immediate identification of clusters in episodic and semantic memory. *Journal of Verbal Learning and Verbal Behavior*, 1977, *16*, 201–215.

BUTLER, R. N. Overview on aging. In G. Usdin & C. K. Hofling (Eds.), *Aging: The process and the people.* New York: Brunner/Mazel, 1978.

BYCK, R., & VAN DYKE, C. What are the effects of cocaine in man? In R. C. Petersen & R. C. Stillman (Eds.), *Cocaine: 1977* (NIDA Research Monograph No. 13, DHEW Publication No. (ADM) 79-471). Washington, D.C.: U.S. Government Printing Office, 1977.

CADORET, R. J. Psychopathology in adopted-away offspring of biologic parents with antisocial behavior. *Archives of General Psychiatry*, 1978, *35*, 176–184.

CALIFORNIA STATE DEPARTMENT OF EDUCATION. *Moral and civic education and teaching about religion.* Sacramento, CA: California State Board of Education, 1973.

CAMPBELL, A. M. G., EVANS, M., THOMPSOM, J. L. G., & WILLIAMS, M. R. Cerebral atrophy in young cannabis smokers. *Lancet*, 1971, 1219.

CAMPBELL, F. W., & ROBSON, J. G. Application of Fourier analysis to the visibility of gratings. *Journal of Physiology*, 1968, *197*, 551–556.

CAMPBELL, J. P., & PRITCHARD, R. D. Motivation theory in industrial and organizational psychology. In M. D. Dunnette (Ed.), *Handbook of industrial and organizational psychology.* Chicago, IL: Rand McNally, 1976.

CANAVAN-GUMPERT, D. Generating reward and cost orientations through praise and criticism. *Journal of Personality and Social Psychology*, 1977, *35*, 501–513.

CANCRO, R. *Annual review of the schizophrenic syndrome (1976–7).* New York: Brunner/Mazel, 1978.

CANNON, W. B. The James-Lange theory of emotion; a critical examination and an alternative theory. *American Journal of Psychology*, 1927, *39*, 106–124.

CANTWELL, D. P., BAKER, L., & RUTTER, M. Family factors. In M. Rutter & E. Schopler (Eds.), *Autism: A reappraisal of concepts and treatment.* New York: Plenum Press, 1978.

CAPRA, P. C., & DITTES, J. E. Birth order as a selective factor among volunteer subjects. *Journal of Abnormal and Social Psychology*, 1962, *64*, 302.

CARBONE, T. Stylistic variables as related to source credibility: A content analysis approach. *Speech Monographs*, 1975, *42*, 99–106.

CARLSON, N. R. *Physiology of behavior* (2nd ed.). Boston, MA: Allyn & Bacon, Inc., 1981.

CARMODY, D. P., NODINE, C. F., & KUNDEL, H. L. An analysis of perceptual and cognitive factors in radiographic interpretation. *Perception*, 1980, *9*, 339–344.

CARVER, C. S., & GLASS, D. C. Coronary-prone behavior pattern and interpersonal aggression. *Journal of Personality and Social Psychology*, 1978, *36*, 361–366.

CASH, T. F., & KEHR, J. Influence of nonprofessional counselors' physical attractiveness and sex on perceptions of counselor behavior. *Journal of Counseling Psychology*, 1978, *25*, 336–342.

CATTELL, R. B., & DREVDAHL, J. E. A comparison of the personality profile (16PF) of eminent researchers with that of eminent teachers and administrators and the general population. *British Journal of Psychology*, 1955, *46*, 248–260.

CHAFETZ, M. E. Alcohol and alcoholism: The complexities of alcohol abuse require multiple research approaches toward effective treatment and prevention. *American Scientist*, 1979, *67*, 293–299.

CHAIKEN, A. L., SIGLER, E., & DERLEGA, V. J. Nonverbal mediators of teacher expectancy effects. *Journal of Personality and Social Psychology*, 1974, *30*, 144–149.

CHANCE, P. *Learning and behavior*, Belmont, CA: Wadsworth, 1979.

CHAPANIS, N. P., & CHAPANIS, A. C. Cognitive dissonance: Five years later. *Psychological Bulletin*, 1964, *61*, 1–22.

CHELOHA, R. S., & FARR, J. L. Absenteeism, job involvement, and job satisfaction in an organizational setting. *Journal of Applied Psychology*, 1980, *65*, 467–473.

CHERRY, E. C. Some experiments on the recognition of speech with one and with two ears. *Journal of the Acoustical Society of America*, 1953, *25*, 975–979.

CHESNO, F. A., & KILMANN, P. R. Societal labeling and mental illness. *Journal of Community Psychology*, 1975, *3*, 49–52.

CHOMSKY, N. *Syntactic structures.* The Hague, Netherlands: Mouton, 1957.

CHOMSKY, N. *Language and mind* (enlarged ed.). New York: Harcourt Brace Jovanovich, 1972.

CHOMSKY, N. *Reflections on language.* New York: Pantheon Books, 1975.

CLANCY, H., & MCBRIDE, G. The autistic process and its treatment. *Journal of Child Psychology and Psychiatry*, 1969, *10*, 233–244.

CLARK, E. V. Non-linguistic strategies and the acquisition of word meanings. *Cognition*, 1973, *2*, 161–182.

CLARK, W. C., & YANG, J. C. Acupunctural analgesia? Evaluation by signal detection theory. *Science,* 1974, *184,* 1096–1098.

CLARKE-STEWART, K. A. And Daddy makes three: The father's impact on mother and young child. *Child Development,* 1978, *49,* 466–478.

CLECKLEY, H. *The mask of sanity* (4th ed.). St. Louis, MO: Mosby, 1964.

CLECKLEY, H. *The mask of sanity* (5th ed.). St. Louis, MO: Mosby, 1976.

CLIFFORD, M. M., & WALSTER, E. Research note: The effect of physical attractiveness on teacher expectation. *Sociology of Education,* 1973, *46,* 248–258.

COATES, B., PUSSER, H. E., & GOODMAN, I. The influence of "Sesame Street" and "Mister Rogers' Neighborhood" on children's social behavior in the preschool. *Child Development,* 1976, *47,* 138–144.

COHEN, D. B. Dysphoric affect and REM sleep. *Journal of Abnormal Psychology,* 1979, *88,* 73–77.

COHEN, S. Environmental load and the allocation of attention. In A. Baum & S. Valins (Eds.). *Advances in environment research.* Hillsdale, NJ: Lawrence Erlbaum Associates, 1977.

COHEN, S., GLASS, D. C., & PHILLIPS, S. Environment and health. In H. E. Freeman, S. Levine, & L. G. Reeder (Eds.), *Handbook of medical sociology.* Englewood Cliffs, NJ: Prentice-Hall, 1977, as cited in P. A. Bell, J. D. Fisher, & R. J. Loomis, *Environmental psychology.* Philadelphia: W. B. Saunders, 1978.

COHEN, S., ROTHBART, M., & PHILLIPS, S. Locus of control and the generality of learned helplessness in humans. *Journal of Personality and Social Psychology,* 1976, *34,* 1049–1056.

COLE, R. D. The use of hypnosis in a course to increase academic and test-taking skills. *The International Journal of Clinical and Experimental Hypnosis,* 1979, *27,* 21–28.

COLEMAN, J. C., BUTCHER, J. N., & CARSON, R. C. *Abnormal psychology and modern life* (6th ed.). Glenview, IL: Scott, Foresman, 1980.

COLLINS, A. M., & QUILLIAN, M. R. Experiments on semantic memory and language comprehension. In L. W. Gregg (Ed.), *Cognition in learning and memory.* New York: John Wiley & Sons, 1972.

COLSON, C. E. Olfactory aversion therapy for homosexual behavior. *Journal of Behavior Therapy and Experimental Psychiatry,* 1972, *3,* 185–187.

CONDON, W. S., & SANDERS, L. W. Synchrony demonstrated between movements of the neonate and adult speech. *Child Development,* 1974, *45,* 456–462.

CONDRY, J. Enemies of exploration: Self-initiated versus other-initiated learning. *Journal of Personality and Social Psychology,* 1977, *35,* 459–477.

CONRAD, R., & HILLE, B. A. The decay theory of immediate memory and paced recall. *Canadian Journal of Psychology,* 1958, *12,* 1–6.

CONRAD, R., & HULL, A. J. Information, acoustic confusion, and memory span. *British Journal of Psychology,* 1964, *55,* 429–432.

CONWAY, J. B. Behavioral self-control of smoking through aversive conditioning and self-management. *Journal of Consulting and Clinical Psychology,* 1977, *45,* 348–357.

COOPER, L. A., & SHEPARD, R. N. The time required to prepare for a rotated stimulus. *Memory and Cognition,* 1973, *1,* 246–250.

COOPER, L. M., & LONDON, P. Sex and hypnotic susceptibility in children. *International Journal of Clinical and Experimental Hypnosis,* 1966, *3,* 13–19.

CORDUA, G. D., MCGRAW, K. O., & DRABMAN, R. S. Doctor or nurse: Children's perception of sex typed occupations. *Child Development,* 1979, *50,* 590–593.

COREN, S., & GIRGUS, J. S. *Seeing is deceiving: The psychology of visual illusions.* Hillsdale, NJ: Lawrence Erlbaum Associates, 1978.

COREY, D. T., WALTON, A., & WIENER, N. I. Development of carbohydrate preference during water rationing: A specific hunger? *Physiology and Behavior,* 1978, *20,* 547–552.

COSTANZO, P. R., & WOODY, E. Z. Externality as a function of obesity in children: Pervasive style or eating-specific attribute? *Journal of Personality and Social Psychology,* 1979, *37,* 2286–2296.

COWDEN, R. C., & FORD, L. I. Systematic desensitization with a phobic schizophrenic. *American Journal of Psychiatry,* 1962, *119,* 241–245.

CRAFT, J. L. Human learned helplessness as a function of sex and degree of control over aversive events. *Bulletin of the Psychonomic Society,* 1980, *16*(3), 209–212.

CRAIG, R. Lawrence Kohlberg and moral development: Some reflections. *Educational Theory,* 1974, *24,* 121–129.

CRAIK, F. I. M. Age differences in human memory. In J. E. Birren & K. W. Schaie (Eds.), *Handbook of the psychology of aging.* New York: Van Nostrand Reinhold, 1977.

CRAIK, F. I. M., & TULVING, E. Depth of processing and the retention of words in episodic memory. *Journal of Experimental Psychology: General,* 1975, *104,* 268–294.

CRONKHITE, G., & LISKA, J. A critique of factor analytic approaches to the study of credibility. *Communications Monographs,* 1976, *43,* 91–107.

CROWL, R. K., & MACGINITIE, W. H. The influence of students' speech characteristics on teachers' evaluations of oral answers. *Journal of Educational Psychology,* 1974, *66*(3), 304–308.

CSOKA, L. S., & BONS, P. M. Manipulating the situation to fit the leader's style: Two validation studies of leader match. *Journal of Applied Psychology,* 1978, *63,* 295–300.

CUNNINGHAM, M. R. Personality and the structure of the nonverbal communication of emotion. *Journal of Personality,* 1977, *45,* 564–584.

CURTISS, S. *Genie: A psycholinguistic study of a modern-day "wild child."* New York: Academic Press, 1977.

CUSHMAN, P., & KHURANA, R. A controlled cycle of tetrahydrocannabinol smoking: T and B cell rosette formation. *Life Sciences,* 1977, *20,* 971–980.

DAMON, W. Structural-development theory and the study of moral development. In M. Windmiller, N. Lambert, & E. Turiel (Eds.), *Moral development and socialization.* Boston, MA: Allyn & Bacon, 1980.

DANIEL, T. L., & ESSER, J. K. Intrinsic motivation as influenced by rewards, task interest, and task structure. *Journal of Applied Psychology,* 1980, *65,* 566–573.

DANIELS, N. IQ, intelligence, and educability. *Philosophical Forum,* 1976, *6,* 56–69.

DARROW, C. W. The galvanic skin reflex (sweating) and blood-pressure as preparatory and facilitative functions. *Psychological Bulletin,* 1936, *33,* 73–94.

DAVIDSON, W. S. Studies of aversive conditioning for alcoholics: A critical review of theory and research methodology. *Psychological Bulletin,* 1974, *81,* 571–581.

DAVIS, J. M. Central biogenic amines and theories of depression and mania. In W. E. Fann, I. Karacan, A. D. Pokorny, & R. L. Williams (Eds.), *Phenomenology and treatment of depression.* New York: Spectrum Publications, 1977.

DAVIS, J. R., WALLACE, C. J., LIEBERMAN, R. B., & FINCH, B. E. The use of brief isolation to suppress delusional and hallucinatory speech. *Journal of Behavior and Experimental Psychiatry,* 1976, *7,* 269–275.

DAVIS, K. Final note on a case of extreme isolation. *American Journal of Sociology,* 1947, *52,* 432–437.

DAVIS, S. M., & DRICHTA, C. E. Biofeedback theory and application in allied health speech pathology. *Biofeedback and Self-Regulation,* 1980, *5,* 159–174.

DAVISON, G. C. Systematic desensitization as a counter-conditioning process. *Journal of Abnormal Psychology*, 1968, 73, 91–99.

DAVISON, G. C., & NEALE, J. M. (EDS.) *Abnormal psychology: An experimental clinical approach* (2nd ed.). New York: John Wiley & Sons, 1978.

DAY, R. H., & MCKENZIE, B. E. Constancies in the perceptual world of the infant. In W. Epstein (Ed.), *Stability and constancy in visual perception*. New York: John Wiley & Sons, 1977.

DAY, R. L., KITAHATA, L. M., KAO, F. F., MOTOYAMA, E. K., & HARDY, J. D. Evaluation of acupuncture anesthesia: A psychophysical study. *Anesthesiology*, 1975, 43, 501–517.

DE CHATEAU, P. The importance of the neonatal period for the development of synchrony in the mother-infant dyad—A review. *Birth and the Family Journal*, 1977, 4(1), 10–24.

DECI, E. L. Effects of externally mediated rewards on intrinsic motivation. *Journal of Personality and Social Psychology*, 1971, 18, 105–115.

DECI, E. L. Effects of contingent and non-contingent rewards and controls on intrinsic motivation. *Organizational Behavior and Human Performance*, 1972, 8, 217–229.

DECI, E. L. *Intrinsic motivation*. New York: Plenum, 1975.

DECI, E. L., CASCIO, W. F., & KRUSELL, J. Cognitive evaluation theory and some comments on the Calder Staw critique. *Journal of Personality and Social Psychology*, 1975, 31, 81–85.

DEETS, A., & HARLOW, H. F. Early experience and the maturation of agonistic behavior. Paper presented at the convention of the American Association for the Advancement of Science, New York: Dec. 28, 1971 (as cited by R. Buck in *Human motivation and emotion*. New York: John Wiley & Sons, 1976.).

DEGREGORIO, E., & CARVER, C. S. Type A behavior pattern, sex role orientation, and psychological adjustment. *Journal of Personality and Social Psychology*, 1980, 39, 286–293.

DEIKMAN, A. Bimodal consciousness and the mystic experience. In P. R. Lee, R. E. Ornstein, D. Galin, A. Deikman, & C. T. Tart (Eds.), *Symposium on consciousness, San Francisco, 1974*. New York: Viking Press, 1976.

DELAMATER, J., & MACCORQUODALE, P. *Premarital sexuality*. Madison, WI: University of Wisconsin Press, 1979.

DELK, J. L. Use of EMG through biofeedback and behavioral treatment of an obsessive-phobic-depressive syndrome. *Disease of the Nervous System*, 1977, 38, 938–939.

DELLAS, M., & GAIER, E. L. Identification of creativity: The individual. *Psychological Bulletin*, 1970, 73, 55–73.

DEMBER, W. N. Motivation and the cognitive revolution. *American Psychologist*, 1974, 29, 161–168.

DEMBROSKI, T. M., & MCDOUGALL, J. M. Stress effects on affiliation preferences among subjects possessing the Type A coronary-prone behavior pattern. *Journal of Personality and Social Psychology*, 1978, 36, 23–33.

DEMBROSKI, T. M., MCDOUGALL, J. M., & SHIELDS, J. L. Physiologic reactions to social challenge in persons evidencing the Type A coronary-prone behavior pattern. *Journal of Human Stress*, 1977, 3, 2–9.

DEMENT, W. C. The effect of dream deprivation. *Science*, 1960, 131, 1705–1707.

DEMENT, W. C. *Some must watch while some must sleep*. San Francisco, CA: W. H. Freeman, 1972.

DEMENT, W. C., & KLEITMAN, N. The relation of eye movements during sleep to dream activity: An objective method for the study of dreaming. *Journal of Experimental Psychology*, 1957, 53, 339–346.

DEMENT, W. C., GREENBERG, S., & KLEIN, R. The effect of partial REM sleep deprivation and delayed recovery. *Journal of Psychiatric Research*, 1966, 4, 141–152.

DENNIS, S. G., & MELZACK, R. Pain-signalling systems in the dorsal and ventral spinal cord. *Pain*, 1977, 4, 97–132.

DEPUE, R. A., & EVANS, R. The psychobiology of depressive disorders. In B. H. Maher (Ed.), *Progress in experimental personality research* (Vol. 8). New York: Academic Press, 1976.

DEPUE, R. A., & MONROE, S. M. The unipolar-biploar distinction in the depressive disorders. *Psychological Bulletin*, 1978, 85, 1001–1029.

DEROGATIS, L. R., MEYER, J. K., & VAZQUEZ, N. A psychological profile of the transsexual. *The Journal of Nervous and Mental Disease*, 1978, 166, 234–254.

DEVALOIS, R. L., & JACOBS, G. H. Primate color vision. *Science*, 1968, 162, 533–540.

DE VILLIERS, J. G., & DE VILLIERS, P. A. *Language acquisition*. Cambridge, MA: Harvard University Press, 1978.

DICK, A. O. Iconic memory and its relation to perceptual processing and other memory mechanisms. *Perception and Psychophysics*, 1974, 16, 575–596.

DIENER, E., LUSK, R., DEFOUR, D., & FLAX, R. Deindividuation: Effects of group size, density, number of observers, and group member similarity on self-consciousness and disinhibited behavior. *Journal of Personality and Social Psychology*, 1980, 39, 449–459.

DIETVORST, T. F. Biofeedback assisted relaxation training with patients recovering from myocardial infarction. Unpublished doctoral dissertation, Purdue University, 1977. *Dissertation Abstracts International*, 1978, 38(7-B), 3389.

DILOLLO, V. Temporal integration in visual memory. *Journal of Experimental Psychology: General*, 1980, 109, 75–97.

DIMASCIO, A., WEISSMAN, M. M., PRUSOFF, B. A., NEU, C., ZWILLING, M., & KLERMAN, G. L. Differential symptom reduction by drugs and psychotherapy in acute depression. *Archives of General Psychiatry*, 1979, 36, 1450–1456.

DION, K., BERSCHEID, E., & WALSTER, E. What is beautiful is good. *Journal of Personality and Social Psychology*, 1972, 24, 285–290.

DOLE, V. P. Addictive behavior. *Scientific American*, 1980, 243(6), 138–158.

DOLLARD, J., & MILLER, N. E. *Personality and psychotherapy*. New York: McGraw-Hill, 1950.

DOLLARD, J., DOOB, L. W., MILLER, N. E., MOWRER, O. H., & SEARS, R. R. *Frustration and aggression*. New Haven: Yale University Press, 1939.

DONNERSTEIN, E. Pornography and violence against women: Experimental studies. *Annals of the New York Academy of Sciences*, 1980, 347, 277–288.

DONNERSTEIN, E., & WILSON, D. W. Effects of noise and perceived control on ongoing and subsequent aggressive behavior. *Journal of Personality and Social Psychology*, 1976, 34(5), 774–781.

DOOB, A. N., & MACDONALD, G. E. Television viewing and fear of victimization: Is the relationship causal? *Journal of Personality and Social Psychology*, 1979, 37(2), 170–179.

DOUCÉ, R. G. Hypnosis: A scientific aid in crime detection. *The Police Chief*, 1979, 46, 60–61, 80.

DOWLING, J. E., & BOYCOTT, B. B. Organization of the primate retina: Electron microscopy. *Proceedings of the Royal Society* (London), 1966, Series B, 166, 80–111.

DRABMAN, R. S. Behavior modification in the classroom. In W. E. Craighead, A. E. Kazdin, & M. H. Mahoney (Eds.), *Behavior modification: Principles, issues and applications*. Boston, MA: Houghton Mifflin, 1976.

DRABMAN, R. S., & THOMAS, M. H. The effects of television on children and adolescents: Does TV violence breed indifference? *Journal of Communication*, 1975, 25, 86–89.

DRABMAN, R. S., & THOMAS, M. H. Children's imitation of aggressive and prosocial behavior when viewing alone and in pairs. *Journal of Communication*, 1977, 27, 199–205.

DRACHMAN, D. A., & ARBIT, J. Memory and the hippocampal complex, II. *Archives of Neurology*, 1966, 15, 52–61.

DRACHMAN, D. A., & WORCHEL, S. Misattribution of arousal as a means of dissonance reduction. *Sociometry*, 1976, *39*, 53–59.

DREVDAH, J. E., & CATTELL, R. B. Personality and creativity in artists and writers. *Journal of Clinical Psychology*, 1958, *12*, 21–26.

DRUG ABUSE COUNCIL. Heroin maintenance: The issues. The effects of heroin. *Journal of Psychedelic Drugs*, 1974, *6*, 185–199.

DUFFY, E., & LACEY, O. L. Adaptation in energy mobilization: Changes in general level of palmer conductants. *Journal of Experimental Psychology*, 1946, *36*, 437–452.

DUNCKER, K. On problem solving. *Psychological Monographs*, 1945, *50*(270).

DYCK, P. J., LAMBERT, E. H., & O'BRIEN, P. Pain in peripheral neuropathy related to size and rate of fiber degeneration. In M. Weisenberg & B. Tursky (Eds.), *Pain: Therapeutic approaches and research frontiers.* New York: Plenum Press, 1976.

EBBESEN, E. B., & BOWERS, R. J. Proportion of risky to conservative arguments in a group discussion and choice shift. *Journal of Personality and Social Psychology*, 1974, *29*, 316–327.

EBBINGHAUS, H. *Über day gedächtnis.* Leipzig, Germany: Duncker & Humbolt, 1885.

EBERTS, E. H., & LEPPER, M. R. Individual consistency in the proxemic behavior of pre-school children. *Journal of Personality and Social Psychology*, 1975, *32*, 841–849.

EDMUNDS, G., & KENDRICK, D. C. *The measurement of human aggressiveness.* Chichester, England: Ellis Horwood Limited, 1980.

EDNEY, J. J. Property, possession, and permanence: A field study in human territoriality. *Journal of Applied Social Psychology*, 1972, *2*, 3, 275–282.

EISENBERGER, R., PARK, D. C., & FRANK, M. Learned industriousness and social reinforcement. *Journal of Personality and Social Psychology*, 1976, *33*, 327–232.

EKMAN, P., FRIESEN, W. V., & ELLSWORTH, P. *Emotion in the human face.* Elmsford, New York: Pergamon Press, 1972.

EKMAN, P., & OSTER, H. Facial expressions of emotion. *Annual Review of Psychology*, 1979, *30*, 527–554.

ELLINGSON, R. J. Ontogenesis of sleep in the human. In G. C. Lairy & P. Salzarulo (Eds.), *The experimental study of human sleep: Methodological problems.* Amsterdam: Elsevier Press, 1975.

ELLIS, A. *Reason and emotion in psychotherapy.* New York: Stuart Press, 1962.

ELLIS, A. *The essence of rational psychotherapy: A comprehensive approach to treatment.* New York: Institute for Rational Living, 1970.

ELLIS, A., & HARPER, R. A. *A guide to rational living.* North Hollywood, CA: Wilshire Book Company, 1961.

ELLSWORTH, P. C., & LANGER, E. J. Staring and approach: An interpretation of the stare as a nonspecific activator. *Journal of Personality and Social Psychology*, 1976, *33*, 117–122.

ELLSWORTH, P. C., & ROSS, L. Intimacy in response to direct gaze. *Journal of Experimental Social Psychology*, 1975, *11*, 592–613.

EMERY, G. D., STEER, R. A., & BECK, A. T. Suicidal behavior among heroin addicts: A brief report. *Psychological Reports*, 1979, *44*, 237–238.

EMRICK, D. C. A review of psychologically oriented treatment of alcoholism. *Journal of Studies on Alcohol*, 1975, *36*, 88–108.

ENDLER, N., & MAGNUSSON, D. *Interactional psychology and personality.* New York: John Wiley & Sons, 1976.

ENTUS, A. K. Hemispheric asymmetry in processing of dichotically presented speech and nonspeech stimuli by infants. In S. J. Segalowitz & F. A. Gruber (Eds.), *Language development and neurological theory.* New York: Academic Press, 1977, 64–73.

ERDELYI, M. H. A new look at the new look: Perceptual defense and vigilance. *Psychological Review*, 1974, *81*, 1–25.

ERIKSON, E. H. *Childhood and society* (2nd ed.). New York: W. W. Norton, 1963.

ERIKSON, E. H. *Identity: Youth and crisis.* New York: W. W. Norton, 1968.

ERWIN, E. Psychoanalytic therapy: The Eysenck argument. *American Psychologist*, 1980, *35*, 435–443.

ETAUGH, C. Effects of nonmaternal care on children. *American Psychologist*, 1980, *35*, 309–319.

EVANS, R. I., ROZELLE, R. M., NOBLITT, R., & WILLIAMS, D. L. Explicit and implicit persuasive communications over time to initiate and maintain behavior change: New perspectives utilizing a real-life dental hygiene situation. *Journal of Applied Social Psychology*, 1975, *5*, 150–156.

EYSENCK, H. J. The effects of psychotherapy: An evaluation. *Journal of Consulting & Clinical Psychology*, 1952, *16*, 319–324.

EYSENCK, H. J. Classification and the problems of diagnosis. In H. J. Eysenck (Ed.), *Handbook of abnormal psychology.* London: Pitman, 1960.

FANN, W. E., KARACAN, I., POKORNY, A. D., & WILLIAMS, R. L. (Eds.) *Phenomenology and treatment of depression.* New York: Spectrum Publications, 1977.

FANTZ, R. L. The origin of form perception. *Scientific American*, 1961, *204*, 66–72.

FANTZ, R. L., & MIRANDA, S. B. Newborn infant attention to form of contour. *Child Development*, 1975, *46*, 224–228.

FEINGOLD, B. F. Hyperkinesis and learning disabilities linked to artificial food flavors and colors. *American Journal of Nursing*, 1975, *75*(5), 797–803.

FEINGOLD, B. F. *Why is your child hyperactive?* New York: Random House, 1975.

FEINGOLD, B. F. Hyperkinesis and learning disabilities linked to the ingestion of artificial food colors and flavors. *Journal of Learning Disabilities*, 1976, *9*(9), 19–27.

FELDMAN, M. P., & MACCULLOCH, M. J. *Homosexual behavior: Therapy and assessment.* Oxford, England: Pergamon Press, 1971.

FERGUSON, C. A. Baby talk in six languages. *American Anthropologist*, 1964, *66*, 103–114.

FERGUSON, C. A. Baby talk as a simplified register. In C. A. Snow & Charles A. Ferguson (Eds.), *Talking to children: Language input and acquisition,* New York: Cambridge University Press, 1977.

FERGUSON, P. C. The psychobiology of transcendental meditation: A review. *Journal of Altered States of Consciousness*, 1975, *2*, 15–36.

FESTINGER, L. A theory of social comparison processes. *Human Relations*, 1954, *7*, 117–140.

FESTINGER, L. *A theory of cognitive dissonance.* Evanston, IL: Row, Petersen, 1957.

FIEDLER, F. E. A contingency model of leadership effectiveness. In L. Berkowitz (Ed.), *Advances in experimental social psychology* (Vol. 1). New York: Academic Press, 1964.

FIEDLER, F. E. Personality, motivational systems, and behavior of high and low LPC persons. *Human Relations*, 1972, *25*, 391–412.

FIEDLER, F. E. The contingency model—New direction for leadership utilization. *Journal of Contemporary Business*, 1974, *3*, 65–79.

FIEDLER, F. E., CHEMMERS, M. M., & MAHER, L. L. *Improving leadership effectiveness: The leader match concept.* New York: John Wiley & Sons, 1976.

FIELDING, J. E. Smoking and pregnancy. *New England Journal of Medicine*, 1978, *298*, 337–342.

FINUF, S. *Nonverbal communication: Effects of training sixth grade children in orienting behaviors on teacher and peer relations of social skills.* Unpublished doctoral dissertation, Columbia, SC: University of South Carolina Press, 1980.

FISCHBEIN, S. IQ and social class. *Intelligence,* 1980, *4,* 51–63.

FISCHER, J., & GOCHROS, H. L. *Planned behavior change: Behavior modification in social work.* New York: Free Press, 1975.

FISHER, C. D. The effects of personal control, competence, and extrinsic reward systems on intrinsic motivation. *Organizational Behavior and Human Performance,* 1978, *21,* 273–288.

FISHER, D. F., & KARSH, R. Modality effects and storage in sequential short-term memory. *Journal of Experimental Psychology,* 1971, *87,* 410–414.

FISHER, D. F., JAROMBEK, J. J., & KARSH, R. Short-term memory (1958-1973): An annotated bibliography. U.S. Army Human Engineering Laboratory, Aberdeen Proving Ground, Maryland, October, 1974.

FISHER, D. F., LEFTON, L. A., & MOSS, J. H. Reading geometrically transformed test: A developmental approach. *Bulletin of the Psychonomic Society,* 1978, *11,* 157–160.

FISHER, R. P., & CRAIK, F. I. M. The effects of elaboration on recognition memory. *Memory & Cognition,* 1980, *8*(5), 400–404.

FISHER, S., & GREENBERG, R. P. *Scientific credibility of Freud's theory and therapy.* New York: Basic Books, 1977.

FISKE, D. W., & MADDI, S. R. *Functions of varied experience.* Homewood, IL: Dorsey, 1961.

FLANAGAN, G. *The first nine months of life.* New York: Simon & Schuster, 1962.

FLAVELL, J. H. *The developmental psychology of Jean Piaget.* New York: Van Nostrand Reinhold, 1963.

FLEMING, J. D. Field report: The state of the apes. *Psychology Today,* 1974, *7,* 31–46.

FLERX, V. C., FIDLER, D. S., & ROGERS, R. W. Sex role stereotypes: Developmental aspects and early intervention. *Child Development,* 1976, *47,* 998–1007.

FLEXSER, A. J., & TULVING, E. Retrieval independence in recognition and recall. *Psychology Review,* 1978, *85,* 153–157.

FODOR, J. A. The mind-body problem. *Scientific American,* 1981, *244*(1), 114–124.

FODOR, J. A., BEVER, T. G., & GARRETT, M. F. *The psychology of language.* New York: McGraw-Hill, 1974.

FOGEL, D. ". . . We are the living proof . . ." The justice model for corrections. Cincinnati, OH: W. H. Anderson, 1975.

FORD, D. H., & URBAN, H. B. *Systems of psychotherapy: A comparative study.* New York: John Wiley & Sons, 1963.

FORD, M. E. The construct validity of egocentrism. *Psychological Bulletin,* 1979, *86,* 1169–1188.

FOSS, D. J., & HAKES, D. T. *Psycholinguistics: An introduction to the psychology of language.* Englewood Cliffs, NJ: Prentice-Hall, 1978.

FOULKES, W. D. Dream report from different stages of sleep. *Journal of Abnormal and Social Psychology,* 1962, *65,* 14–25.

FOWLER, M. J., SULLIVAN, M. J., & EKSTRAND, B. R. Sleep and memory. *Science,* 1973, *179,* 302–304.

FOX, R., ASLIN, R. N., SHEA, S. L., & DUMAIS, S. T. Stereopsis in human infants. *Science,* 1980, *207,* 323–324.

FRANKEL, F. H., & MISCH, R. C. Hypnosis in a case of long-standing psoriasis in a person with character problems. *International Journal of Clinical & Experimental Hypnosis,* 1973, *21,* 121–130.

FRENCH, S. N. Electromyographic biofeedback for tension control during fine motor skill acquisition. *Biofeedback and Self-Regulation,* 1980, *5,* 221–228.

FREUD, A. *Normality and pathology in childhood: Assessment of development.* New York: International Universities, 1965.

FREUD, S. *New introductory lectures on psycho-analysis.* New York: W. W. Norton, 1933.

FRIEDMAN, H., & TAUB, H. A. A six-month follow-up of the use of hypnosis and biofeedback procedures in essential hypertension. *The American Journal of Clinical Hypnosis,* 1978, *20,* 184–188.

FRIEDMAN, M., & ROSENMAN, R. H. *Type A Behavior and Your Heart.* Greenwich, CT: Fawcett Publications, 1974.

FRITH, C. D. The effect of varying the nicotine content of cigarettes on human smoking behavior. *Psychopharmacologia,* 1971, *19,* 188–192.

FURCHTGOTT, E., & BUSEMEYER, J. K. Heart rate and skin conductants during cognitive processes as a function of age. *Journal of Gerontology,* 1979, *34,* 182–190.

GAJZAGO, C., & PRIOR, M. Two cases of "recovery" in Kanner syndrome. *Archives of General Psychiatry,* 1974, *31,* 264–268.

GALIN, D. Implications for psychiatry of left and right cerebral specialization: A neurophysiological context for unconscious processes. *Archives of General Psychiatry,* 1974, *31,* 572–583.

GALLAGHER, J. J. Issues and education for the gifted. In A. H. Passow (Ed.), *The gifted and the talented: Their education and development.* The 78th Yearbook for the National Society for the Study of Education. Chicago: University of Chicago Press, 1979.

GANZ, L. Sensory deprivation and visual discrimination. In R. Held, H. W. Leibowitz, & H.-L. Teuber (Eds.), *Perception (Handbook of sensory physiology.* Vol. 8). New York: Springer-Verlag, 1978.

GANZ, V. P., & VOLKMAR, F. Adverse reactions to marihuana use among college students. *Journal of American College Health Association,* 1976, *25,* 93–96.

GARBER, J., MILLER, W. R., & SEAMAN, S. F. Learned helplessness, stress, and the depressive disorders. In R. A. DePue (Ed.), *The psychobiology of the depressive disorders.* New York: Academic Press, 1979.

GARDNER, R. A., & GARDNER, B. T. Teaching sign language to a chimp. *Science,* 1969, *165,* 664–672.

GARFIELD, S. L. Basic ingredients or common factors in psychotherapy? *Journal of Consulting and Clinical Psychology,* 1973, *41,* 9–12.

GARZA, R. T., & WIDLAK, F. W. The validity of locus of control dimensions for Chicano populations. *Journal of Personality Assessment,* 1977, *41,* 635–643.

GASTORF, J. W., & TEEVAN, R. C. Type A coronary-prone behavior pattern and fear of failure. *Motivation and Emotion,* 1980, *4,* 71–76.

GASTORF, J. W., SULS, J., & SANDERS, G. S. Type A coronary-prone behavior pattern and social facilitation. *Journal of Personality and Social Psychology,* 1980, *38,* 773–780.

GATCHEL, R. J., & PROCTOR, J. D. Physiological correlates of learned helplessness in man. *Journal of Abnormal Psychology,* 1976, *85,* 27–34.

GAW, A. C., CHANG, L. W., & SHAW, L.-C. Efficacy of acupuncture on osteoarthritic pain. *New England Journal of Medicine,* 1975, *293,* 375–378.

GAZZANIGA, M. S. The split brain in man. *Scientific American,* 1967, 24–29.

GEEN, R. G., & O'NEAL, E. C. Activation of cue-elicited aggression by general arousal. *Journal of Personality and Social Psychology,* 1969, *11,* 289–292.

GERBNER, G., & GROSS, L. The scary world of TV's heavy viewer. *Psychology Today,* 1976, *9,* 41–45.

GERSHONE, J. R., ERRICKSON, E. A., MITCHELL, J. E., & PAULSON, D. A. Behavioral comparison of a token economy and a standard psychiatric treatment ward. *Journal of Behavior Therapy and Experimental Psychiatry,* 1977, *8,* 381–385.

GESCHWIND, N. The organization of language in the brain. *Science,* 1970, *170,* 940–944.

GIFT, T. E., STRAUSS, J. S., RITZLER, B. A., KOKES, R. F., & HARDER, D. W. How diagnostic concepts of schizophrenia differ. *The Journal of Nervous and Mental Disease,* 1980, *168,* 3–8.

GILLUM, R., LEON, G. R., KAMP, J., & BECERRA-ALDAMA, J. Prediction of cardiovascular and other disease onset and mortality from 30-year longitudinal MMPI data. *Journal of Consulting and Clinical Psychology*, 1980, *48*, 405–406.

GILMER, B. V. H. Personnel selection. In B. V. H. Gilmer & E. L. Deci (Eds.), *Industrial and organizational psychology* (4th ed.). New York: McGraw-Hill, 1977.

GILMER, B. V. H., & DECI, E. L. *Industrial and organizational psychology* (4th ed.). New York: McGraw-Hill, 1977.

GINSBERG, I. J., & GREENLEY, J. R. Competing theories of marijuana use: A longitudinal study. *Journal of Health and Social Behavior*, 1978, *19*, 22–34.

GLANZER, M., & CUNITZ, A. R. Two storage mechanisms in free recall. *Journal of Verbal Learning and Verbal Behavior*, 1966, *5*, 351–360.

GLASS, C. R., GOTTMAN, J. M., & SHMURAK, S. H. Response-acquisition and cognitive self-statement modification approaches to dating-skills training. *Journal of Counseling Psychology*, 1976, *23*, 520–526.

GLASS, D. C. *Behavior patterns, stress and coronary disease.* Hillsdale, NJ: Lawrence Erlbaum Associates, 1977.

GLASS, D. C., & SINGER, J. E. *Urban stress.* New York: Academic Press, 1972.

GLASS, D. C., SNYDER, M. L., & HOLLIS, J. F. Time urgency and the Type A coronary-prone behavior pattern. *Journal of Applied Social Psychology*, 1974, *4*, 125–140.

GLUCKSBERG, S., & DANKS, J. H. Effects of discriminative labels and of nonsense labels upon availability of novel function. *Journal of Verbal Learning and Verbal Behavior*, 1968, *7*, 72–76.

GOETHALS, G. R., & COOPER, J. When dissonance is reduced: The timing of self-justificatory attitude change. *Journal of Personality and Social Psychology*, 1975, *32*, 361–367.

GOETZ, T. E., & DWECK, C. S. Learned helplessness in social situations. *Journal of Personality and Social Psychology*, 1980, *39*, 246–255.

GOLDEN, M., ROSENBLUTH, L., GROSSI, M., POLICARE, H., FREEMAN, H., & BROWNLEE, E. *The New York City infant day care study.* New York: Medical and Health Research Association of New York City, 1978.

GOLDFRIED, M. R., & DAVISON, G. C. *Clinical behavior therapy.* New York: Holt, Rinehart & Winston, 1976.

GOLDFRIED, M. R., STRICKER, G., & WEINER, I. R. *Rorschach handbook of clinical and research applications.* Englewood Cliffs, N.J.: Prentice-Hall, 1971.

GOLDMAN, B. L., DOMITOR, P. J., & MURRAY, E. J. Effects of Zen meditation on anxiety reduction and perceptual functioning. *Journal of Consulting and Clinical Psychology*, 1979, *47*, 551–556.

GOLDSTEIN, A. J., & CHAMBLESS, D. L. A reanalysis of agoraphobia. *Behavior Therapy*, 1978, *9*, 47–57.

GOLDSTEIN, J. H., ROSNOW, R. L., RADAY, T., SILVERMAN, I., & GASKELL, G. D. Punitiveness in response to films varying in content: A cross-national field study of aggression. *European Journal of Social Psychology*, 1975, *5*, 149–165.

GOLDSTEIN, Y. The effect of demonstrating to a subject that she is in a hypnotic trance as a variable in hypnotic interventions with obese women. *The International Journal of Clinical and Experimental Hypnosis*, 1981, *29*, 15–23.

GORANSON, R. E., & KING, D. Rioting and daily temperature: Analysis of the U.S. riots in 1967. Unpublished manuscript, York University, 1970, as cited in P. A. Bell, J. D. Fisher, & R. J. Loomis, *Environmental psychology.* Philadelphia, PA: W. B. Saunders, 1978.

GORNEY, R., LOYE, D., & STEELE, G. Impact of dramatized television entertainment on adult males. *American Journal of Psychiatry*, 1977, *134*, 170–174.

GOTTESFELD, M. L. Treatment of vaginismus by psychotherapy with adjunctive hypnosis. *The American Journal of Clinical Hypnosis*, 1978, *20*, 272–277.

GOTTFREDSON, G. D., & DYER, S. E. Health service providers in psychology. *American Psychologist*, 1978, *33*, 314–338.

GOTTHEIL, E., & STONE, G. C. Psychosomatic aspects of orality and anality. *The Journal of Nervous and Mental Disease*, 1974, *159*, 182–190.

GRAHAM, C., & LEIBOWITZ, H. W. The effect of suggestion on visual acuity. *The International Journal of Clinical and Experimental Hypnosis*, 1972, *20*, 169–186.

GRAHAM, C. H., SPERLING, H. G., HSIA, Y., & COULSON, A. H. The determination of some visual functions of a unilaterally color-blind subject: Methods and results. *Journal of Psychology*, 1961, *51*, 3–32.

GRANT, B. W. *Schizophrenia: A source of social insight.* Philadelphia, PA: Westminster Press, 1975.

GRANT, V. W. *The menacing stranger.* Oceanside, NY: Dabor Science Publications, 1977.

GREAVES, G. B. Multiple personality: 165 years after Mary Reynolds. *The Journal of Nervous and Mental Disease*, 1980, *168*, 577–596.

GREELEY, A. M., & SHEATSLEY, P. B. Attitudes toward racial integration. *Scientific American*, 1971, *225*, 13–19.

GREEN, D. E. Patterns of tobacco use in the United States. In N. A. Krasnegor (Ed.), *Cigarette smoking as a dependence process* (NIDA Research Monograph No. 23, DHEW Publication No. (ADM) 79-800). Washington, D.C.: U.S. Government Printing Office, 1979.

GREENBERG, M., & MORRIS, N. Engrossment: The newborn's impact upon the father. *American Journal of Orthopsychiatry*, 1974, *44*, 520–531.

GREENSPAN, S., BARENBOYM, C., & CHANDLER, M. J. Empathy and pseudo-empathy: The affective judgements of first- and third-graders. *Journal of Genetic Psychology*, 1976, *129*, 77–88.

GREER, S. Study of parental loss in neurotics and sociopaths. *Archives of General Psychiatry*, 1964, *11*, 177–180.

GRIFFITH, J. D., CAVANAUGH, J., HELD, J., & OATES, J. A. Dextroamphetamine: Evaluation of psychomimetic properties in man. *Archives of General Psychiatry*, 1972, *26*, 97–100.

GRIFFITHS, R. R., BIGELOW, G., & LIEBSON, I. Comparison or social time-out and activity time-out procedures in suppressing ethanol self-administration in alcoholics. *Behavior Research and Therapy*, 1977, *15*, 329–336.

GRIFFITT, W. Environmental effects on interpersonal affective behavior: Ambient effective temperature and attraction. *Journal of Personality and Social Psychology*, 1970, *15*(3), 240–244.

GROSSMAN, S. P., & GROSSMAN, L. Food and water intake in rats after transections of fibers en passage in the tegmentum. *Physiological Behavior*, 1977, *18*, 647–658.

GUGGENHEIM, F. G., & BABIGIAN, H. M. Catatonic schizophrenia: Epidemiology and clinical course. *Journal of Nervous and Mental Disease*, 1974, *158*, 291–305.

GUILFORD, J. P. Three faces of intellect. *American Psychologist*, 1959, *14*, 469–479.

GUILFORD, J. P. *The nature of human intelligence.* New York: McGraw-Hill, 1967.

GUILFORD, J. P. Fluid and crystallized intelligences: Two fanciful concepts. *Psychological Bulletin*, 1980, *88*, 406–412.

GUION, R. M. Recruiting, selection, and job placement. In M. D. Dunnette (Ed.), *Handbook of industrial and organizational psychology.* Chicago, IL: Rand McNally, 1976.

GUNDERSON, J. G., & MOSHER, L. R. The cost of schizophrenia. In R. Cancro (Ed.), *Annual review of the schizophrenic syndrome* (1976–7). New York: Brunner/Mazel, 1978.

GURMAN, A. S., & RAZIN, A. M. *Effective psychotherapy: A handbook of research.* New York: Pergamon Press, 1977.

GYNTHER, M. D. White norms and black MMPIs: A prescription for discrimination. *Psychological Bulletin*, 1972, *78*, 386–402.

HAAN, N., LANGER, J., & KOHLBERG, L. Family patterns of moral reasoning. *Child Development*, 1976, *47*, 1204–1206.

HABER, R. N. Eidetic images. *Scientific American*, 1969, *220*(4), 36–44.

HABER, R. N. Twenty years of haunting eidetic imagery: Where's the ghost? *The Behavioral and Brain Sciences*, 1979, *2*, 583–629.

HALDERMAN, B. I., & JACKSON, T. T. Naturalistic study of aggression: Aggressive stimuli and horn-honking: A replication. *Psychological Reports*, 1979, *45*, 880–882.

HALL, E. T. *The hidden dimension.* New York: Doubleday, 1966.

HALL, J. A. Gender, gender roles, and nonverbal communication skills. In R. Rosenthal (Ed.), *Skill in nonverbal communication.* Cambridge, MA: Oelgeschlager, Gunn & Hain, 1979.

HALL, V. C., & TURNER, R. R. The validity of the "different languages explanation" for poor scholastic performance by black students. *Review of Educational Research*, 1974, *44*, 69–81.

HALLAM, R. S., & RACHMAN, S. Some effects of aversion therapy on patients with sexual disorders. *Behavior Research and Therapy*, 1972, *10*, 171–180.

HALLAM, R. S., & RACHMAN, S. Current status of aversion therapy. In M. Hersen, R. M. Eisler, & B. M. Miller (Eds.), *Progress in behavior modification*, Vol. 2. New York: Academic Press, 1976.

HAMBURG, D., BIBRING, G., FISCHER, C., STANTON, A., WALLERSTEIN, R., & HAGGART, E. Report of *ad hoc* committee on central fact-gathering data of the American Psychoanalytic Association. *Journal of the American Psychoanalytic Association*, 1967, *15*, 841–861.

HAMMEN, C. L., & KRANTZ, S. Effect of success and failure on depressive cognitions. *Journal of Abnormal Psychology*, 1976, *85*, 577–586.

HAMMER, T. H., & DACHLER, H. P. A test of some assumptions underlying the path goal model of supervision: Some suggested conceptual modifications. *Organizational Behavior and Human Performance*, 1975, *14*, 60–75.

HAMPSTEAD, W. J. The effects of EMG assisted relaxation training with hyperkinetic children: An alternative to medication. Unpublished doctoral dissertation, Western Michigan University, 1977. *Dissertation Abstracts International*, 1978, *38*(10-B), 5017.

HANUSA, B. H., & SCHULZ, R. Attributional mediators of learned helplessness. *Journal of Personality and Social Psychology*, 1977, *8*, 602–611.

HARLOW, H. F. The heterosexual affectional system in monkeys. *American Psychologist*, 1962, *17*, 1–9.

HARLOW, H. F., & ZIMMERMAN, R. R. The development of affectional responses in infant monkeys. *Proceedings of the American Philosophic Society*, 1958, *102*, 501–509.

HARPER, R. A. *The new psychotherapies.* Englewood Cliffs, NJ: Prentice-Hall, 1975.

HARRIS, V. A., & KATKIN, E. S. Primary and secondary emotional behaviour: An analysis of the role of autonomic feedback on affect, arousal and attribution. *Psychological Bulletin*, 1975, *82*, 6, 904–916.

HARTNAGEL, T. F., TEEVAN, J. J., JR., & MCINTYRE, J. J. Television violence and violent behavior. *Social Forces*, 1975, *54*, 341–351.

HARVEY, M. A., & SIPPRELLE, C. N. Color blindness, perceptual interference, and hypnosis. *The American Journal of Clinical Hypnosis*, 1978, *20*, 189–193.

HASS, J. W., BAGLEY, G. S., & ROGERS, R. W. Coping with the energy crisis: Effects of fear appeals upon attitudes toward energy consumption. *Journal of Applied Psychology*, 1975, *60*, 754–756.

HAYNES, S. M., MOSELEY, D., & MCGOWAN, W. T. Relaxation training and biofeedback in the reduction of muscle tension. Paper presented at the Annual Meeting of Biofeedback Research Society, 1974.

HEARNSHAW, L. S. *Cyril Burt, psychologist.* Ithaca, New York: Cornell University Press, 1979.

HEBB, D. O. *Organization of behavior.* New York: John Wiley & Sons, 1949.

HEBB, D. O. Drives and the C. N. S. (conceptual nervous system). *Psychological Review*, 1955, *62*, 243–254.

HEBB, D. O. *Textbook of psychology* (3rd ed.). Philadelphia, PA.: W. B. Saunders, 1972.

HEIDER, E. R. "Focal" color areas and the development of color names. *Developmental Psychology*, 1971, *4*, 447–455.

HEIDER, E. R. Universals in color naming and memory. *Journal of Experimental Psychology*, 1972, *93*, 1, 10–21.

HEIDER, E. R., & OLIVIER, D. C. The structure of the color space in naming and memory for two languages. *Cognitive Psychology*, 1972, *3*(2), 337–354.

HEIN, A., VITAL-DURAND, F., SALINGER, W., & DIAMOND, R. Eye movements initiate visual-motor development in the cat. *Science*, 1979, *204*, 1321–1322.

HEKMAT, H. Systematic versus semantics sensitization and implosive therapy: A comparative study. *Journal of Consulting and Clinical Psychology*, 1973, *40*, 202–203.

HELD, R., & BAUER, J. A. Visually guided reaching in infant monkeys after restricted rearing. *Science*, 1967, *155*, 718–720.

HELD, R., & HEIN, A. Movement produced stimulation in the development of visually guided behavior. *Journal of Comparative and Physiological Psychology*, 1963, *56*, 872–276.

HELSON, H. *Adaptation level theory.* New York: Harper & Row, 1964.

HEMBREE, W. C., NAHAS, G. G., & HUANG, H. F. S. Changes in human spermatozoa associated with high dose marihuana smoking. In G. G. Nahas & W. D. M. Paton (Eds.), *Marihuana: Biological effects.* New York: Pergamon Press, 1979.

HENDRICK, C., & GIESEN, M. Self-attribution of attitude as a function of belief feedback. *Memory and Cognition*, 1976, *4*, 150–155.

HENNEKENS, S. H., WILLETT, W., ROSNER, B., COLE, D. S., & MAYRENT, S. L. Effects of beer, wine, and liquor in coronary deaths. *Journal of the American Medical Association*, 1979, *242*, 1973–1974.

HERMAN, C. P., & POLIVY, J. Anxiety, restraint, and eating behavior. *Journal of Abnormal Psychology*, 1975, *84*, 666–672.

HERMAN, C. P., POLIVY, J., & SILVER, R. Effects of an observer on eating behavior: The induction of "sensible" eating. *Journal of Personality*, 1979, *47*, 85–99.

HERMAN, J. B. Are situational contingencies limiting job attitude–job performance relationships? *Organizational Behavior and Human Performance*, 1973, *10*, 208–224.

HERRMANN, D. J., & HARWOOD, J. R. More evidence for the existence of separate semantic and episodic stores in long-term memory. *Journal of Experimental Psychology: Human Learning and Memory*, 1980, *6*, 467–478.

HERON, W. The pathology of boredom. *Scientific American*, 1957, *196*(1), 52–56.

HERSHMAN, S. Hypnosis in the treatment of obesity. *International Journal of Clinical and Experimental Hypnosis*, 1955, *3*, 136–140.

HESTON, L. L. Psychiatric disorders in foster home reared children of schizophrenic mothers. *British Journal of Psychiatry*, 1966, *11*, 819–825.

HIBSCHER, J. A., & HERMAN, C. P. Obesity, dieting, and the expressions of "obese" characteristics. *Journal of Comparative and Physiological Psychology*, 1977, *91*, 374–380.

HILGARD, E. R. *Hypnotic susceptibility.* New York: Harcourt, Brace, & World, 1965.

HILGARD, E. R., & HILGARD, J. R. *Hypnosis in the relief of pain.* Los Altos, CA: William Kaufmann, 1975.

HILGARD, E. R., & MARQUIS, D. G. Acquisition, extinction and retention of conditioned lid responses to light in dogs. *Journal of Comparative Psychology,* 1935, *19,* 29–58.

HILGARD, E. R., SHEEHAN, P. W., MONTEIRO, K. P., & MACDONALD, H. Factorial structure of the creative imagination scale as a measure of hypnotic responsiveness: An international comparative study. *The International Journal of Clinical and Experimental Hypnosis,* 1981, *29,* 66–76.

HILL, C., & GORMALLY, J. Effects of reflection, restatement, probe, and nonverbal behaviors on client affect. *Journal of Counseling Psychology,* 1977, *24,* 92–97.

HILL, J. H., LIEBERT, R. M., & MOTT, D. E. W. Vicarious extinction of avoidance behavior through films: An initial test. *Psychological Reports,* 1968, *22,* 192.

HINDMAN, M. H. Family violence: An overview. Alcohol Health and Research World (NIAAA, Public Health Service Alcohol, Drug Abuse, and Mental Health Administration, DHEW), Fall 1979, *4*(1). Washington, D.C.: U.S. Government Printing Office, 1979.

HINDS, W. C., & FIRST, M. W. Concentrations of nicotine and tobacco smoke in public places. *New England Journal of Medicine,* 1975, *292,* 844–845.

HIROTO, D. S. Locus of control and learned helplessness. *Journal of Experimental Psychology,* 1974, *102,* 187–193.

HIRSCH, H. V. B., & SPINELLI, D. N. Modification of the distribution of receptive field orientation in cats by selective exposure during development. *Experimental Brain Research,* 1971, *13,* 509–527.

HIRSCHFELD, A. *The world of Hirschfeld.* New York: Abrams, 1970.

HOBBS, S. A., MOGUIN, L. E., TYROLER, M., & LAHEY, B. B. Cognitive behavior therapy with children: Has clinical utility been demonstrated? *Psychological Bulletin,* 1980, *87,* 147–165.

HOBSON, J. A., & MCCARLEY, R. W. The brain as a dream state generator: An activation-synthesis hypothesis of the dream process. *American Journal of Psychiatry,* 1977, *134*(12), 1335–1348.

HOCHBERG, J. Organization and the Gestalt tradition. In E. C. Carterette & M. P. Friedman (Eds.), *Handbook of perception.* New York: Academic Press, 1974.

HOCHBERG, J. Sensation and perception. In E. Hearst (Ed.), *The first century of experimental psychology.* New York: John Wiley & Sons, 1979.

HODGSON, R. J., & RACHMAN, S. An experimental investigation of the implosion technique. *Behavior Research and Therapy,* 1970, *8,* 21–27.

HOFFMAN, E. The idiot savant: A case report and a review of explanation. *Mental Retardation,* 1971, *9,* 18–21.

HOLDING, D. H. Sensory storage reconsidered. *Memory and Cognition,* 1975, *3,* 31–41.

HOLLAND, M. K. *Using psychology: Principles of behavior and your life.* Boston: Little, Brown and Company, Inc., 1975.

HOLLAND, M. K., & TARLOW, G. *Using Psychology: Principles of behavior and your life* (2nd ed.). Boston, MA: Little, Brown, 1980.

HOLLINGWORTH, L. *Children above 180 IQ.* New York: World Book Company, 1942.

HOLLISTER, L. E. Marijuana in man: Three years later. *Science,* 1971, *172,* 21–29.

HOLMES, D. S. Projection as a defense mechanism. *Psychological Bulletin,* 1978, *85,* 677–688.

HOLMES, P. A., & DELPRATO, D. J. Classical conditioning of "hypnotic" arm movement. *Psychological Record,* 1978, *28,* 305–313.

HOLZMAN, P. S., KRINGLEN, E., LEVY, D. L., & HABERMAN, S. J. Deviant eye tracking in twins discordant for psychosis. *Archives of General Psychiatry,* 1980, *37,* 627–631.

HOLZMAN, P. S., KRINGLEN, E., LEVY, D. L., PROCTOR, L. R., HABERMAN, S. J., & YASILLO, N. J. Abnormal-pursuit eye movements in schizophrenia: Evidence for genetic indicator. *Archives of General Psychiatry,* 1977, *34,* 802–805.

HOLZMAN, P. S., PROCTOR, L. R., LEVY, D. L., YASILLO, N. J., MELTZER, H. Y., & HURT, S. W. Eye-tracking dysfunctions in schizophrenic patients and their relatives. *Archives of General Psychiatry,* 1974, *31,* 143–151.

HONIG, W. K. *Operant behavior: Areas of research and application.* New York: Appleton-Century-Crofts, 1966.

HOOKER, E. The adjustment of the male overt homosexual. *Journal of Projective Techniques,* 1957, *21,* 18–31.

HOON, E. F. Biofeedback-assisted sexual arousal in females: A comparison of visual and auditory modalities. *Biofeedback and Self-Regulation,* 1980, *5,* 175–191.

HOPPE, R. B., & DAHL, P. R. Hypermnesia for words in serial learning. *The Psychological Record,* 1978, *28,* 219–229.

HORAI, J., NACCARI, N., & FATOULLAH, E. Effects of expertise and physical attractiveness upon opinion agreement and liking. *Sociometry,* 1974, *37,* 601–606.

HORN, D. Psychological analysis of establishment and maintenance of the smoking habit. In N. A. Krasnegor (Ed.), *Cigarette smoking as a dependence process* (NIDA Research Monograph No. 23, DHEW Publication No. (ADM) 79-800). Washington, D.C.: U.S. Government Printing Office, 1979.

HOROWITZ, M. J., DUFF, D. F., & STRATTON, L. O. Body-buffer zone. *Archives of General Psychiatry,* 1964, *11,* 651–656.

HOUSTON, J. P., SCHNEIDER, N. G., & JARVICK, M. Effects of smoking on free recall and organization. *American Journal of Psychiatry,* 1978, *135*(2), 220–222.

HOVLAND, C. I. The generalization of conditioned responses. I. The sensory generalization of conditioned responses with varying frequencies of tone. *Journal of General Psychology,* 1937, *17,* 125–148.

HUBEL, D. H. The visual cortex of the brain. *Scientific American,* 1963, *209,* 54–62.

HUBEL, D. H. The brain. In *The brain* (Scientific American Book). San Francisco, CA: W. H. Freeman, 1979.

HUBEL, D. H., & WIESEL, T. N. Receptive fields, binocular interaction and functional architecture in the cat's visual cortex. *Journal of Physiology,* 1962, *160,* 106–154.

HUBEL, D. H., & WIESEL, T. N. Brain mechanisms of vision. In *The brain* (Scientific American Book). San Francisco, CA: W. H. Freeman, 1979.

HUBER, D. H. Heroin deaths—Mystery or overdose? *Journal of the American Medical Association,* 1974, *229,* 689–690.

HULL, C. L. *Principles of behavior.* New York: Appleton-Century-Crofts, 1943.

HULL, C. L. *Essentials of behavior.* New Haven, CT: Yale University Press, 1951.

HULL, C. L. *A behavior system.* New Haven, CT: Yale University Press, 1952.

HUNT, L. G. Prevalence of active heroin use in the United States. In J. D. Rittenhouse (Ed.), *The epidemiology of heroin and other narcotics* (NIDA Research Monograph No. 16, DHEW Publication No. (ADM) 78-559). Washington, D.C.: U.S. Government Printing Office, 1977.

HUNT, W. A., & BESPALEC, B. A. An evaluation of current methods of modifying smoking behavior. *Journal of Clinical Psychology,* 1974, *30,* 431–438.

HURVICH, L., & JAMESON, D. Opponent processes as a model of neural organization. *American Psychologist,* 1974, *29,* 88–102.

IACONO, W. G., & LYKKEN, D. T. Comments on "Smooth-pursuit eye movements: A comparison of two measurement techniques" by Lindsey, Holzman, Haberman, and Yasillo. *Journal of Abnormal Psychology*, 1979, *88*, 6, 678–680.

INGLES, T. St. Christopher's Hospice. In M. Hamilton & H. Reid (Eds.), *A hospice handbook: A new way to care for the dying*. Grand Rapids, MI: Wm. B. Eerdmans, 1980.

INGRAM, D. Surface contrasts in children's speech. *Journal of Child Language*, 1975, *2*, 287–292.

INGRAM, I. M. Obsessional personality and anal-erotic character. *Journal of Mental Science*, 1961, *107*, 1035–1042.

INHELDER, B., & PIAGET, J. *The growth of logical thinking from childhood to adolescence*. New York: Basic Books, 1958.

INNES, J. M., & YOUNG, R. F. The effect of presence of an audience, evaluation apprehension and objective self-awareness on learning. *Journal of Experimental Social Psychology*, 1975, *11*, 35–42.

INTRAUB, H. Presentation rate and the representation of briefly glimpsed pictures in memory. *Journal of Experimental Psychology: Human Learning and Memory*, 1980, *6*, 1–12.

JACKSON, D. M. The emerging national and state concern. In A. H. Passow (Ed.), *The gifted and the talented: Their education and development*. The 78th Yearbook for the National Society for the Study of Education. Chicago: University of Chicago Press, 1979.

JACKSON, L. A., & LARRANCE, D. T. Is a "refinement" of attribution theory necessary to accommodate the learned helplessness reformulation? A critique of the reformulation of Abramson, Seligman, and Teasdale. *Journal of Abnormal Psychology*, 1979, *88*, 681–682.

JAFFE, J. H., & KANZLER, M. Smoking as an addictive disorder. In N. A. Krasnegor (Ed.), *Cigarette smoking as a dependence process* (NIDA Research Monograph No. 23, DHEW Publication No. (ADM) 79-800). Washington, D.C.: U.S. Government Printing Office, 1979.

JAFFE, P. G., & CARLSON, P. M. Modeling therapy for test anxiety: The role of model affect and consequences. *Behavior Research and Therapy*, 1972, *10*, 329–339.

JAKOBSON, R. *Child language, aphasia and phonological universals*. The Hague, Netherlands: Mouton, 1968.

JAMES, C. T., & HILLINGER, M. L. The role of confusion in the semantic integration paradigm. *Journal of Verbal Learning and Verbal Behavior*, 1977, *16*, 711–721.

JAMES, W. What is an emotion? *Mind*, 1884, *9*, 188–205.

JARVIK, M. E. Further observations on nicotine as the reinforcing agent in smoking. In W. L. Dunn, Jr. (Ed.), *Smoking behavior: Motives and incentives*. Washington, D.C.: V. H. Winston and Sons, 1973.

JAYNES, J. *The origin of consciousness in the breakdown of the bicameral mind*. Boston: Houghton Mifflin, 1976.

JELLISON, J. M., & DAVIS, D. Relationships between perceived ability and attitude extremity. *Journal of Personality and Social Psychology*, 1973, *27*, 430–436.

JENKINS, H. M., & HARRISON, R. H. Effect of discrimination training of auditory generalization. *Journal of Experimental Psychology*, 1960, *59*, 244–253.

JENKINS, J. G., & DALLENBACH, K. M. Oblivescence during sleep and waking. *American Journal of Psychology*, 1924, *35*, 605–612.

JENSEN, A. R. How much can we boost IQ and scholastic achievement? *Harvard Educational Review*, 1969, *39*, 1–123.

JENSEN, A. R. Can we and should we study race differences? In J. Hellmuth (Ed.), *Disadvantaged child* (Vol. 3). New York: Brunner/Mazel, 1970.

JENSEN, A. R. How biased are culture-loaded tests? *Genetic Psychology Monographs*, 1974, *90*, 185–244.

JENSEN, A. R. Test bias and construct validity. *Phi Delta Kappan*, 1976, *58*, 340–346.

JENSEN, A. R. Cumulative deficit in IQ of blacks in the rural South. *Developmental Psychology*, 1977, *3*, 184–191.

JENSEN, A. R. Can we be neutral about bias? *Contemporary Psychology*, 1980, *25*, 868–871.

JENSEN, A. R., & INOUYE, A. R. Level I and Level II abilities in Asian, white, and black children. *Intelligence*, 1980, *4*, 41–49.

JOHN, E. R., CHESLER, P., BARTLETT, F., & VICTOR, I. Observational learning in cats. *Science*, 1968, *159*, 1489–1491.

JOHNSON, D. M. *Systematic introduction to the psychology of thinking*. New York: Harper & Row, 1972.

JOHNSON, R. F. Q., & BARBER, T. X. Hypnosis, suggestions, and warts: An experimental investigation implicating the importance of "Believed-in efficacy." *The American Journal of Clinical Hypnosis*, 1978, *20*, 165–174.

JOHNSON, S. J. Electromyographic biofeedback as a treatment for Alcoholic abuse. *Dissertation Abstracts International*, 1978, *38*(8-B), 3387.

JOHNSTON, E., & DONOGHUE, J. R. Hypnosis and smoking: A review of the literature. *American Journal of Clinical Hypnosis*, 1971, *13*, 265–272.

JONES, E. E. *Ingratiation: A social psychological analysis*. New York: Appleton-Century-Crofts, 1964.

JONES, E. E. Conformity as a tactic of ingratiation. *Science*, 1965, *149*, 144–150.

JONES, E. E., & NISBETT, R. E. The actor and the observer: Divergent perceptions of causes of behavior. In E. E. Jones et al. (Eds.), *Attribution: Perceiving the causes of behavior*. Morristown, NJ: General Learning Press, 1972.

JONES, J. TV influence revisited, not exactly kid stuff. *APA Monitor*, 1977, *8*.

JONES, R. Human effects. In R. C. Petersen (Ed.), *NIDA Research Monograph 14, Marihuana Research Findings: 1976*. Washington, D.C.: U.S. Government Printing Office, Stock No. 017-024-00622-0, 1977.

JONES, R. A. *Self-fulfilling prophecies: Social, psychological, and physiological effects of expectancies*. Hillsdale, NJ: Lawrence Erlbaum Associates, 1977.

JUST, M. A., & CARPENTER, P. A. A theory of reading: From eye fixations to comprehension. *Psychological Review*, 1980, *87*, 329–354.

KAGAN, J. Family experience and the child's development. *American Psychologist*, 1979, *34*, 886–891.

KAGAN, J., KEARSLEY, R. B., & ZELAZO, P. R. *Infancy: Its place in human development* (Trade ed.). Cambridge, MA: Harvard University Press, 1980.

KALES, A., BIXLER, E. O., TAN, T. L., SCHARF, M. B., & KALES, J. D. Cronic hypnotic-drug use—Ineffectiveness, drug-withdrawal, insomnia, and dependence. *Journal of the American Medical Association*, 1974, *227*, 513–517.

KALES, A., CALDWELL, A. B., PRESTON, A., HEALEY, S., & KALES, J. D. Personality patterns and insomnia: Theoretical implications. *Archives of General Psychiatry*, 1976, *33*, 1128–1134.

KALES, A., TAN, T. L., KOLLAR, E. J., NAITOH, P., PRESON, T. A., & MALMSTROM, E. J. Sleep patterns following 205 hours of sleep deprivation. *Psychosomatic Medicine*, 1970, *32*, 189–200.

KALVEN, H. G., JR., & ZEISEL, H. *The American Jury*. Boston: Little, Brown, 1966.

KAMIN, L. J. *The science and politics of IQ*. New York: Lawrence Erlbaum Associates, 1974.

KANELLAKOS, D. P. Transcendental consciousness: Expanded awareness as a means of preventing and eliminating the effects of stress. *Stress and Anxiety*, 1978, *5*, 261–315.

KANFER, F. H. & MARSTON, A. R. Human reinforcement: Vicarious and direct. *Journal of Experimental Psychology*, 1963, *65*, 292–296.

KANNER, L. Autistic disturbances of affective content. *Nervous Child*, 1943, *2*, 217–240.

KAPLAN, H. B. Gender and depression: A sociological analysis of a conditional relationship. In W. E. Fann, I. Karacan, A. D. Pokorny, & R. L. Williams (Eds.), *Phenomenology and treatment of depression.* New York: Spectrum Publications, 1977.

KAPLAN, L. J. *Oneness and separateness: From infant to individual.* New York: Simon and Schuster, 1978.

KAPLAN, R. M., & SINGER, R. D. Television violence and viewer aggression: A reexamination of the evidence. *Journal of Social Issues,* 1976, *32,* 35–70.

KARABENICK, S. A., & SRULL, T. K. Effects of personality and situational variation in locus of control on cheating: Determinants of the "congruence effect." *Journal of Personality,* 1978, *46,* 72–95.

KARLER, R. Toxicological and pharmacological effects (of marihuana). In R. C. Petersen (Ed.), *NIDA Research Monograph 14, Marihuana Research Findings: 1976.* Washington, D.C.: U.S. Government Printing Office, Stock No. 017-024-00622-0, 1977.

KARLSSON, J. L. *The biologic base of schizophrenia.* Springfield, IL: Thomas Press, 1966.

KATSUKI, Y. Neural mechanisms of auditory sensation in cats. In W. A. Rosenblith (Ed.), *Sensory communication.* Cambridge, MA: MIT Press, 1961.

KATZ, I., & GREENBAUM, C. Effects of anxiety, threat, and racial environment on task performance of Negro college students. *Journal of Abnormal and Social Psychology,* 1963, *66,* 562–567.

KATZ, P. A., & ZALK, S. R. Modification of children's racial attitudes. *Developmental Psychology,* 1978, *14*(5), 447–461.

KAUFMAN, A. S. *Intelligent Testing with the WISC-R.* New York: John Wiley & Sons, 1979.

KAUFMAN, N. L. Excerpt from a case study. In A. Kaufman, *Intelligent testing with the WISC-R.* New York: John Wiley & Sons, 1979.

KAYE, K., & MARCUS, J. Imitation of a series of trials without feedback: Age six months infant. *Behavioral Development,* 1978, *1,* 141–155.

KAZDIN, A. E. *Behavior modification in applied settings.* Homewood, IL: Dorsey Press, 1975.

KAZDIN, A. E., & WILSON, G. T. *Evaluation of behavior therapy: Issues, evidence, and research strategies.* Cambridge, MA: Ballinger Press, 1978.

KEITH, S. J., GUNDERSON, J. G., REIFMAN, A., BUCKSBAUM, S., & MOSHER, L. R. Special report: Schizophrenia 1976. *Schizophrenia Bulletin,* 1976, *2,* 509–565.

KELLOGG, W. N. Communication and language in the home-raised chimpanzee. *Science,* 1968, *162,* 423–427.

KELLEY, H. H. Attribution theory in social psychology. In D. Levine (Ed.), *Nebraska Symposium on Motivation,* 1967, *15,* 192–238.

KELLEY, H. H. Attribution in social interaction. In E. E. Jones et al. (Eds.), *Attribution: Perceiving the causes of behavior.* Morristown, NJ: General Learning Press, 1972.

KELLEY, H. H. Process of causal attribution. *American Psychologist,* 1973, *28,* 107–128.

KENNELL, J. H., VOOS, D. K., & KLAUS, M. H. Parent-infant bonding. In J. D. Osofsky (Ed.), *Handbook of infant development.* New York: John Wiley & Sons, 1979.

KENT, M. A., & PETERS, M. A. Effects of ventromedial hypothalamic lesions on hunger-motivated behavior in rats. *Journal of Comparative and Physiological Psychology,* 1973, *83,* 92–97.

KEPPEL, G., & UNDERWOOD, B. J. Proactive inhibition in short-term retention of single items. *Journal of Verbal Learning and Verbal Behavior,* 1962, *1,* 153–161.

KERNBERG, O. F., BURSTEIN, E., COYNE, L., APPLEBAUM, A., HOROWITZ, L., & VOTH, H. Psychotherapy and psychoanalysis: Final report of the Menninger Foundations psychotherapy research project. *Bulletin of the Menninger Clinic,* 1972, *36,* 1–275.

KERR, N., DAVIS, J., MEEK, D., & RISSMAN, A. Group position as a function of member attitudes: Choice shift effects on the perspective of social decision scheme theory. *Journal of Personality and Social Psychology,* 1975, *31,* 574–593.

KESSLER, S. The genetics of schizophrenia: A review. *Schizophrenia Bulletin,* 1980, *6,* 404–416.

KESSLER, S., & MOOS, R. H. Behavioral aspects of chromosomal disorders. *Annual Review of Medicine,* 1973, *24,* 89–99.

KETY, S. S. The biological substrates of schizophrenia. In T. Fukuda & H. Mitsuda (Eds.), *Schizophrenic psychoses.* New York: Igaku-Shoin, 1979.

KETY, S. S., ROSENTHAL, D., WENDER, P. H., & SCHULSINGER, F. Mental illness in the biological and adoptive families of adopted schizophrenics. In D. Rosenthal & S. Kety (Eds.), *Transmission of schizophrenia.* Oxford: Pergamon Press, 1968.

KETY, S. S., ROSENTHAL, D., WENDER, P. H., SCHULSINGER, F., & JACOBSEN, B. Mental illness in the biological and adoptive families of adopted individuals who had become schizophrenic: A preliminary report based upon psychiatric interviews. In R. Five, D. Rosenthal, & H. Brill (Eds.), *Genetic research in psychiatry.* Baltimore, MD: The Johns Hopkins University Press, 1975.

KIHLSTROM, J. F., & SHOR, R. E. Recall and recognition during posthypnotic amnesia. *The International Journal of Clinical and Experimental Hypnosis,* 1978, *26,* 330–349.

KILMANN, P. R., & AUERBACH, S. M. Effects of marathon group therapy on trait and state anxiety. *Journal of Consulting and Clinical Psychology,* 1974, *42,* 607–612.

KILMANN, P. R., & SOTILE, W. M. The marathon encounter group: A review of the outcome literature. *Psychological Bulletin,* 1976, *83,* 827–850.

KILMANN, P. R., ALBERT, B. M., & SOTILE, W. M. Relationship between locus of control, structure of therapy, and outcome. *Journal of Consulting and Clinical Psychology,* 1975, *43,* 588.

KIMMEL, D. C. *Adulthood and aging: An interdisciplinary view.* New York: John Wiley & Sons, 1974.

KINSBOURNE, M. The ontogeny of cerebral dominance. In D. Aaronson & R. W. Rieber (Eds.), *Developmental psycholinguistics and communication disorders. Annals of the New York Academy of Science,* 1975, *263,* 244–250.

KLAUS, M. H., & KENNELL, J. H. *Maternal-infant bonding.* St. Louis, MO: C. V. Mosby, 1976.

KLEBER, H. D., & SLOBETZ, F. Outpatient drug-free treatment. In R. I. Dupont, A. Goldstein & J. O'Donnel (Eds.), *Handbook on drug abuse* (NIDA, DHEW, and Office of Drug Abuse Policy (Executive Office of the President)). Washington, D. C.: U.S. Government Printing Office, 1979.

KLEE, S., & MEYER, R. G. Prevention of learned helplessness in humans. *Journal of Consulting and Clinical Psychology,* 1979, *47,* 411–412.

KLEINKE, C. L., STANESKI, R. A., & BERGER, D. E. Evaluation of an interviewer as a function of the interviewer gaze, reinforcement of subject gaze, and interviewer attractiveness. *Journal of Personality and Social Psychology,* 1975, *31,* 115–122.

KLEITMAN, N., & ENGLEMANN, T. G. Sleep characteristics. *Journal of Applied Physiology,* 1953, *6,* 269–282.

KLINE, J., STEIN, Z. A., SUSSER, M., & WARBURTON, D. Smoking: A risk factor for spontaneous abortion. *The New England Journal of Medicine,* 1977, *297,* 793–796.

KOEGEL, R. I., & COVERT, A. The relationship of self-stimulation to learning in autistic children. *Journal of Applied Behavior Analysis,* 1972, *5,* 381–387.

KOENIG, K. P., & MASTERS, J. Experimental treatment of habitual smoking. *Behavior Research Therapy,* 1965, *3,* 235–243.

KOHLBERG, L. The cognitive-developmental approach to socialization. In D. A. Goslin (Ed.), *Handbook of socialization the-*

ory and research. Chicago, IL: Rand McNally, 1969.

KOHLBERG, L. From is to ought: How to commit the naturalistic fallacy and get away with it in the study of moral development. In T. Micshel (Ed.), *Cognitive development and epistemology*. New York: Academic Press, 1971.

KOLANSKY, H., & MOORE, W. T. Effects of marijuana on adolescents and young adults. *Journal of the American Medical Association*, 1971, *216*, 486–492.

KOLODNY, R. C., MASTERS, W. H., HENDRYX, J., & TORO, G. Plasma testosterone and semen analysis in male homosexuals. *New England Journal of Medicine*, 1971, *285*, 1170–1174.

KORCHIN, S. J., *Modern clinical psychology: Principles in intervention in the clinic and community*. New York: Basic Books, 1976.

KORIAT, A., MELKMAN, R., AVERILL, J. R., & LAZARUS, R. S. The self-control of emotional reactions to a stressful film. *Journal of Personality*, 1972, *40*, 601–619.

KOSSLYN, S. M. Scanning visual images: Some structural implications. *Perception and Psychophysics*, 1973, *12*, 90–94.

KOSSLYN, S. M. Information representation in visual images. *Cognitive Psychology*, 1975, *7*, 341–370.

KOSSLYN, S. M. Measuring the visual angle of the mind's eye. *Cognitive Psychology*, 1978, *10*, 356–389.

KOTELCHUCK, M. The infant's relationship to the father: Experimental evidence. In M. E. Lamb (Ed.), *The role of the father in child development*. New York: John Wiley & Sons, 1976.

KRASHEN, S. Lateralization, language learning, and the critical period: Some new evidence. *Language Learning*, 1973, *23*, 63–74.

KREBS, D., & ADINOLFI, A. A. Physical attractiveness, social relations, and personality style. *Journal of Personality & Social Psychology*, 1975, *31*, 245–253.

KREEK, M. J. Medical safety and side effects of methadone in tolerant individuals. *Journal of the American Medical Association*, 1973, *223*, 665–668.

KREEK, M. J. Methadone in treatment: Physiological and pharmacological issues. In R. I. Dupont, A. Goldstein, & J. O'Donnell (Eds.), *Handbook on drug abuse* (NIDA, DHEW, and Office of the Drug Abuse Policy (Executive Office of the President)). Washington, D.C.: U.S. Government Printing Office, 1979.

KRUGLANSKI, A. W. The endogenous-exogenous partition in attribution theory. *Psychological Review*, 1975, *82*, 387–406.

KÜBLER-ROSS, E. *On death and dying*. New York: Macmillan, 1969.

KUHL, J., & BLANKENSHIP, V. The dynamic theory of achievement motivation: From episodic to dynamic thinking. *Psychological Review*, 1979, *86*, 141–151.

KUNDEL, H. L., & NODINE, C. F. Studies of eye movements and visual search in radiology. In J. W. Senders, D. F. Fisher, & R. A. Monty (Eds.), *Eye movements and the higher psychological processes*. Hillsdale, NJ: Lawrence Erlbaum Associates, 1978.

KURTINAS, W., & GREIF, E. B. The development of moral thought: Review and evaluation of Kohlberg's approach. *Psychological Bulletin*, 1974, *81*, 453–470.

LABOV, W. The logic of nonstandard English. In F. Williams (Ed.), *Language and poverty*. Chicago: Rand McNally, 1970.

LADER, M. The nature of clinical anxiety in modern society. In C. D. Spielberger & I. G. Sarason (Eds.), *Stress and anxiety* (Vol. 1). Washington, D.C.: Hemisphere Publishing, 1975.

LAFERLA, J. J., ANDERSON, D. L., & SCHALCH, D. S. Psychoendocrine response to sexual arousal in human males. *Psychosomatic Medicine*, 1978, *40*, 166–172.

LAHEY, B. B., GREEN, K. D., & FOREHAND, R. On the independence of ratings of hyperactivity, conduct problems, and attention deficits in children: A multiple regression analysis. *Journal of Consulting and Clinical Psychology*, 1980, *48*, 566–574.

LAHEY, B. B., MCNEES, M. P., & BROWN, C. C. Modification of deficits in reading for comprehension. *Journal of Applied Behavior Analysis*, 1973, *6*, 475–480.

LAHEY, B. B., MCNEES, M. P., & MCNEES, M. C. Control of an obscene "verbal tic" through timeout in an elementary school classroom. *Journal of Applied Behavior Analysis*, 1973, *6*, 101–104.

LAMB, M. E. Paternal influences and the father's role. *American Psychologist*, 1979, *34*, 938–943.

LANG, P. J., & LAZOVIK, A. D. Experimental desensitization of a phobia. *Journal of Abnormal Social Psychology*, 1963, *66*, 519–525.

LANG, P. J., LAZOVIK, A. D., & REYNOLDS, D. J. Desensitization, suggestability, and pseudo-therapy. *Journal of Abnormal Psychology*, 1965, *70*, 395–402.

LANGE, C. G. [*The emotions*] (English translation). Baltimore, MD: Williams & Wilkins, 1922. (Originally published, 1885.)

LANGFORD, G. W., MEDDIS, R., & PEARSON, A. J. D. Awakening latency from sleep for meaningful and non-meaningful stimuli. *Psychophysiology*, 1974, *11*, 1–5.

LANGMAN, B., & COCKBURN, A. Sirhan's gun. *Harper's*, 1975, *250*(1496), 16–27.

LANYON, R. I. *A handbook of MMPI group profiles*. Minneapolis: University of Minnesota Press, 1968.

LARGEMAN, R. R. *The social-emotional effects of age of entry into full-time group care*. Unpublished doctoral dissertation, University of California, Berkeley, 1976.

LATANÉ, B., & DARLEY, J. M. *The unresponsive bystander: Why doesn't he help?* New York: Meredith Corporation, 1970.

LATNER, J. *The Gestalt therapy book*. New York: Bantam Books, 1973.

LAVERE, T. E., MORLOCK, G. W., THOMAS, L. P., & HART, M. D. Arousal for sleep. The differential effect of frequencies equated for loudness. *Physiology and Behavior*, 1974, *12*, 573–582.

LAWLER, E. E. *Motivation in work organizations*. Belmont, CA: Brooks/Cole, 1973.

LAWLER, E. E., & PORTER, L. W. Antecedent attitudes of effective managerial performance. *Organizational Behavior and Human Performance*, 1967, *2*, 122–142.

LAZARUS, A. A. *Behavior therapy and beyond*. New York: McGraw-Hill, 1971.

LAZARUS, R. S. Cognitive and coping processes in emotion. In B. Weiner (Ed.), *Cognitive views of human motivation*. New York: Academic Press, 1974.

LAZARUS, R. S., & ALFERT, E. Short-circuiting of threat by experimentally altering cognitive appraisal. *Journal of Abnormal and Social Psychology*, 1964, *69*, 195–205.

LEAHY, R. L., & EITER, M. Moral judgement and the development of real and ideal androgynous self-image during adolescence and young adulthood. *Developmental Psychology*, 1980, *16*, 362–270.

LEBOW, M. D., GOLDBERG, P. S., & COLLINS, A. Eating behavior of overweight and nonoverweight persons in the natural environment. *Journal of Consulting and Clinical Psychology*, 1977, *45*, 1204–1205.

LEE, P. K., ANDERSEN, T. W., MODELL, J. H., & SAGA, S. A. Treatment of chronic pain with acupuncture. *Journal of the American Medical Association*, 1975, *232*, 1133–1135.

LEFTON, L., NAGLE, R. J., JOHNSON, G., & FISHER, D. Eye movements in good and poor readers: Then and now. *Journal of Reading Behavior*, 1979, *11*, 319–328.

LEHMAN, H. C., & GAMERTSFELDER, W. S. Man's creative years in philosophy. *Psychological Review*, 1942, *49*, 319–343.

LEMERE, F., & SMITH, J. W. Alcohol-induced sexual impotence. *American Journal of Psychiatry*, 1973, *130*, 212–213.

LENIGAN, R. W. The effect of electromyographic biofeedback and relaxation on performance of male alcoholics under stress. Unpublished doctoral dissertation, Temple University, 1977. *Dissertation Abstracts International*, 1977, *38*(4-B) 1889–1890.

LENNEBERG, E. H. *Biological foundations of language*. New York: John Wiley & Sons, 1967.

LEON, G. R. *Case histories of deviant behavior: A social learning analysis*. Boston: Holbrook Press, 1974.

LEON, G. R., & ROTH, L. Obesity: Psychological causes, correlations, and speculations. *Psychological Bulletin*, 1977, *84*, 117–139.

LEPPER, M. R., GREENE, D., & NISBETT, R. E. Undermining children's intrinsic interest with extrinsic reward: A test of the overjustification hypothesis. *Journal of Personality and Social Psychology*, 1973, *28*, 129–137.

LERNER, M. J. The desire for justice and reactions to victims. In J. Macaulay & L. Berkowitz (Eds.), *Altruism and helping behavior: Social psychological studies of some antecedents and consequences*. New York: Academic Press, 1970.

LERNER, R. M., & LERNER, J. V. Effects of age, sex, and physical attractiveness on child-peer relations, academic performance, and elementary school adjustment. *Developmental Psychology*, 1977, *13*, 585–590.

LEVENGOOD, R., LOWINGER, P., & SCHOOFF, K. Heroin addiction in the suburbs—An epidemiologic study. *American Journal of Public Health*, 1973, *63*(3), 209–214.

LEVENTHAL, H. Emotions: A basic problem for social psychology. In C. Nemeth (Ed.), *Social Psychology: Classic and contemporary integrations*. Chicago, IL: Rand McNally, 1974.

LEVERE, T. E., MORLOCK, G. W., THOMAS, L. P., & HART, F. D. Arousal from sleep: The differential effect of frequencies equated from loudness. *Physiology and Behavior*, 1974, *12*, 573–582.

LEVINE, M. Hypothesis behavior by humans during discrimination learning. *Journal of Experimental Psychology*, 1966, *71*, 331–336.

LEVINE, M. *Hypothesis testing: A cognitive theory of learning*. Hillsdale, NJ: Lawrence Erlbaum Associates, 1975.

LEVINSON, D. J. *The seasons of a man's life*. New York: Knopf, 1978.

LEVITT, E. E., & TRUUMAA, A. *The Rorschach technique with children and adolescents: Application and norms*. New York: Grune & Stratton, 1972.

LEWIN, K. K. *Brief psychotherapy*. St. Louis, MO: Warren H. Green, 1970.

LEWINSOHN, P. M. Classical and theoretical aspects of depression. In I. S. Calhoun, H. E. Adams, & K. M. Mitchell (Eds.), *Innovative treatment methods in psychopathology*. New York: Wiley-Interscience, 1974.

LEWINSOHN, P. M., & LIBET, J. Present events, activity schedules, and depressions. *Journal of Abnormal Psychology*, 1972, *79*, 291–295.

LEWINSOHN, P. M., & TALKINGTON, J. Studies on the measurement of unpleasant events and relations with depression. *Applied Psychological Measurement*, 1979, *3*, 83–101.

LEWINSOHN, P. M., YOUNGREN, M. A., & GROSSCUP, J. Reinforcement and depression. In R. A. DePue (Ed.), *The psychobiology of the depressive disorders*. New York: Academic Press, 1979.

LEWIS, J. L. Semantic processing of unattended messages using dichotic listening. *Journal of Experimental Psychology*, 1970, *85*, 225–282.

LEWIS, M., & WEINRAUB, M. The father's role in the infant's social network. In M. E. Lamb (Ed.), *The role of the father in child development*. New York: John Wiley & Sons, 1976.

LEWIS, M. S., HONECK, R. P., & FISHBEIN, H. Does shadowing differentially unlock attention? *American Journal of Psychology*, 1975, *88*, 455–458.

LEWIS, T. L., & MAURER, D. Central vision in the newborn. *Journal of Experimental Child Psychology*, 1980, *29*, 475–480.

LI, C. L., AHLBERG, D., LANSDELL, H., GRAVITZ, M. A., CHEN, T. C., TING, C. Y., BAK, A. F., & BLESSING, D. Acupuncture and hypnosis: Effects on induced pain. *Experimental Neurology*, 1975, *49*, 272–280.

LIBET, J. M., & LEWINSOHN, P. M. Concept of social skill with special reference to the behavior of depressed persons. *Journal of Consulting and Clinical Psychology*, 1973, *40*, 304–312.

LIDZ, T. *The origin and treatment of schizophrenic disorders*. New York: Basic Books, 1973.

LIEBERT, R. M., COHEN, L. A., JOYCE, C., MURREL, S., NISONOFF, L., & SONNENSCHEIN, S. Predispositions revisited. *Journal of Communication*, 1977, *27*, 217–221.

LIEF, H. I., & FOX, R. S. Training for "detached concern" in medical students. In H. I. Lief, V. F. Lief, and N. R. Lief (Eds.), *The psychological basis of medical practice*. New York: Harper & Row, 1963.

LILLY, J. C. Mental effects of reduction of ordinary levels of physical stimuli in intact, healthy persons. *Psychiatric Research Reports*, 1956, *5*, 1–28.

LINTZ, L. M., FITZGERALD, H. E., & BRACKBILL, Y. Conditioning the eyeblink response to sound in infants. *Psychonomic Science*, 1967, *7*, 405–406.

LION, J. On punishing criminals. *Psychiatric Opinion*, 1974, *11*, 23–27.

LIPPERT, S. Travel in nursing units. *Human Factors*, 1971, *13*(3), 269–282.

LIPTON, D., MARTINSON, R., & WILKS, J. *The effectiveness of correctional treatment: A survey of treatment evaluation studies*. New York: Praeger Publishers, 1975.

LITTIG, L. W., & WILLIAMS, C. E. Need for affiliation, self-esteem, and social distance of black Americans. *Motivation and Emotion*, 1978, *2*, 369–374.

LITTLE, R. E. Drinking during pregnancy: Implications for public health. *Alcohol Health and Research World* (NIAAA, Public Health Service Alcohol, Drug Abuse, and Mental Health Administration, DHEW), Fall 1979, *4*(1). Washington, D.C.: U.S. Government Printing Office, 1979.

LLOYD, R. W., JR., & SALZBERG, H. C. Controlled social drinking: An alternative to abstinence as a treatment goal for some alcohol abusers. *Psychological Bulletin*, 1975, *82*, 815–842.

LOBITZ, W. C., & POST, R. D. Parameters of self-reinforcement and depression. *Journal of Abnormal Psychology*, 1979, *88*, 33–41.

LOCKE, E. A. The nature and causes of job satisfaction. In M. D. Dunnette (Ed.), *Handbook of industrial and organizational psychology*. Chicago, IL: Rand McNally, 1976.

LOCKE, E. A., & SCHWEIGER, D. M. Participation in decision-making: One more look. In B. M. Staw (Ed.), *Research in organizational behavior* (Vol. 1). Greenwich, CT: JAI Press, 1979.

LOEHLIN, J. C., LINDZEY, G., & SPUHLER, J. N. *Race differences in intelligence*. San Francisco, CA: W. H. Freeman, 1975.

LOGAN, F. A. Decision making by rats: Delay versus amount of reward. *Journal of Comparative and Physiological Psychology*, 1965, *59*, 1–12.

LOFTUS, E. F. Reconstructing memory: The incredible eyewitness. *Psychology Today*, 1974, *8*, 116–119.

LOFTUS, E. F. The malleability of human memory. *American Scientist*, 1979, *67*, 312–320.

LOFTUS, E. F., & PALMER, J. C. Reconstruction of automobile destruction: An example of the interaction between language and memory. *Journal of Verbal Learning and Verbal Behavior,* 1974, *11,* 585–589.

LOFTUS, G. R., & LOFTUS, E. F. *Human memory. The processing of information.* Hillsdale, NJ: Lawrence Erlbaum Associates, 1976.

LORENZ, K. Ritualized fighting. In J. D. Carthy & F. J. Ebling (Eds.), *The natural history of aggression.* New York: Academic Press, 1964.

LOO, C. M. The effects of spatial density on the social behavior of children. *Journal of Applied Social Psychology,* 1972, *2,* 4, 372–381.

LOTHSTEIN, L. M. The psychological management and treatment of hospitalized transsexuals. *The Journal of Nervous and Mental Disease,* 1978, *166,* 255–262.

LOVAAS, O. I. *The autistic child: Language development through behavior modification.* New York: Irvington Publishers, 1977.

LOVALLO, W. R., & PISHKIN, V. A psychological comparison of type A and B men exposed to failure and uncontrollable noise. *Psychophysiology,* 1980, *17,* 29–36.

LOVATT, F. J., & WARR, P. B. Recall after sleep. *American Journal of Psychology,* 1968, *81,* 253–257.

LOWENSTEIN, O., & FRIEDMAN, E. D. Pupilographic study. I. Present state of pupilography; its method and diagnostic significance. *Archives of Ophthalmology,* 1942, *27,* 969–993.

LOWINSON, J. H., & MILLMAN, R. B. Clinical aspects of methadone maintenance treatment. In R. I. Dupont, A. Goldstein, & J. O'Donnell (Eds.), *Handbook on drug abuse* (NIDA, DHEW, and Office of Drug Abuse Policy (Executive Office of the President)). Washington, D.C.: U.S. Government Printing Office, 1979.

LUBORSKY, L., & SPENCE, D. P. Quantitative research on psychoanalytic therapy. In S. L. Garfield & A. E. Bergin (Eds.), *Handbook of psychotherapy and behavior change: An empirical analysis* (2nd ed.). New York: John Wiley & Sons, 1978.

LUBORSKY, L., CHANDLER, M., AUERBACH, A. H., COHEN, J., & BACHRACH, H. M. Factors influencing outcome of psychotherapy: A review of quantitative research. *Psychological Bulletin,* 1971, *75,* 145–185.

LUBORSKY, L., SINGER, B., & LUBORSKY, L. Comparative studies of psychotherapy. *Archives of General Psychiatry,* 1975, *32,* 995–1008.

LUBORSKY, L., MINTZ, J., AUERBACH, A., CHRISTOPH, P., BACHRACH, H., TODD, T., JOHNSON, M., COHEN, M., & O'BRIEN, C. P. Predicting the outcome of psychotherapy. *Archives of General Psychiatry,* 1980, *37,* 471–481.

LUCHINS, A. S. Mechanization in problem-solving: The effect of Einstellung. *Psychological Monographs,* 1942, *54*(6, Whole No. 248).

LUNDIN, R. W. *Personality: An experimental approach.* New York: Macmillan, 1961.

LYKKEN, D. T. A study of anxiety in the sociopathic personality. *Journal of Abnormal and Social Psychology,* 1957, *55,* 6–10.

LYONS, V. M., & LEVINE, S. M. Correlation between responsiveness to information and vicarious learning. *Perceptual and Motor Skills,* 1978, *47,* 467–474.

MACHOVEC, F. J., & MAN, S. C. Acupuncture and hypnosis compared: Fifty-eight cases. *The American Journal of Clinical Hypnosis,* 1978, *21,* 45–47.

MACKIE, R. P. *Special education in the United States: Statistics, 1948 to 1966.* New York: Teachers College Press, Columbia University, 1969.

MACKINNON, D. W. The nature and nurture of creative talent. *American Psychologist,* 1962, *17,* 484–495.

MACRAE, J. W., & HERBERT-JACKSON, E. Are behavioral effects of infant day care programs specific? *Developmental Psychology,* 1976, *12,* 269–270.

MADDI, S. R. *Personality theories: A comparative analysis* (3rd ed.). Homewood, IL: Dorsey Press, 1976.

MAHONEY, M. J. Reflections on the cognitive-learning trend in psychotherapy. *American Psychologist,* 1977, *32,* 5–13.

MAHONEY, M. J., & ARNKOFF, D. Cognitive and self-control therapies. In S. L. Garfield & A. E. Bergin (Eds.), *Handbook of psychotherapy and behavior change* (2nd ed.). New York: John Wiley & Sons, 1978.

MAIER, N. R. F., & KLEE, J. B. Studies of abnormal behavior in the rat. XVII. Guidance versus trial and error and their relation to convulsive tendencies. *Journal of Experimental Psychology,* 1941, *29,* 380–389.

MANDEL, K. H. Preliminary report on a new aversion therapy for male homosexuals. *Behavior Research and Therapy,* 1970, *8,* 93–95.

MANHEIMER, D. I., MELLINGER, G. D., & BALTER, M. B. Marijuana use among urban adults. *Science,* 1969, *166,* 1544–1545.

MANN, H. Group hypnosis in the treatment of obesity. *American Journal of Clinical Hypnosis,* 1959, *1,* 114–116.

MANN, R., BOWSHER, D., MUMFORD, J., LIPTON, S., & MILES, J. Treatment of intractable pain by acupuncture. *Lancet,* 1973, *2,* 57–60.

MANSTEAD, A. S. R. Role-playing replication of Schachter and Singer's (1962) study of the cognitive and physiological determinates of emotional state. *Motivation and Emotion,* 1979, *3,* 251–264.

MANUSO, J. S. The use of biofeedback assisted hand warming training in the treatment of chronic eczematous dermatitis of the hands: A case study. *Journal of Behavior Therapy and Experimental Psychiatry,* 1977, *8,* 445–446.

MAPES, J. L. An investigation of the relationship between an enhanced theta brain wave condition and visually presented paired associate learning. Unpublished doctoral dissertation, University of Colorado at Boulder, 1977. *Dissertation Abstracts International,* 1977, *38*(5-B), 2418.

MARKS, I. M. *Fears and phobias.* New York: Academic Press, 1969.

MARKS, I. M. Clinical phenomena in search of laboratory models. In J. D. Maser & M. E. P. Seligman (Eds.), *Psychopathology experimental models.* San Francisco: W. H. Freeman, 1977.

MARKS, I. M., & GELDER, M. G. Transvestism and fetishism: Clinical and psychological changes during faradic aversion. *British Journal of Psychiatry,* 1967, *113,* 711–729.

MARKS, I. M., & LADER, M. Anxiety states (anxiety neurosis): A review. *Journal of Nervous and Mental Disease,* 1973, *156,* 3–18.

MARKS, I. M., GELDER, M. G., & BANCROFT, J. Sexual deviance two years after electrical aversion. *British Journal of Psychiatry,* 1970, *117,* 73–85.

MARKS, W. B., DOBELL, W. H., & MACNICHOL, J. R. The visual pigments of single primate cones. *Science,* 1964, *143,* 1181–1183.

MARLAND, S. P., JR. Education of the gifted and talented (Vol. I). Report to the Congress of the United States by the U.S. Commissioner of Education. Washington, D.C.: U.S. Government Printing Office, 1972.

MARQUIS, D. P. Can conditioned responses be established in the newborn infant? *Journal of Genetic Psychology,* 1931, *39,* 479–492.

MARQUIS, J. N., & MORGAN, W. G. *A guide book system for systematic desensitization.* Palo Alto, CA: Veterans Administration Hospital, 1969 (as cited in D. C. Rim & J. C. Asters (Eds.), *Behavior Therapy.* New York: Academic Press, 1979).

MARR, D. Early processing of visual information. *Philos. Trans. R. Soc. London Ser. B,* 1976, *275,* 483–524.

MARSLEN-WILSON, W. D., & TEUBER, H. L. Memory for remote

events in anterograde amnesia: Recognition of public figures from newsphotographs. *Neuropsychologia*, 1975, *13*, 353–364.

MARSTON, A. R., LONDON, P., & COHEN, N. In vivo observation of the eating behavior of obese and nonobese subjects. *Journal of Consulting and Clinical Psychology*, 1977, *45*, 335–336.

MARTENS, R., & LANDERS, D. M. Evaluation potential as a determinant of coaction effects. *Journal of Experimental Social Psychology*, 1972, *8*, 347–359.

MARTIN, R., & HAROLDSON, S. Effect of vicarious punishment on stuttering frequency. *Journal of Speech and Hearing Research*, 1977, *20*, 21–26.

MARTINSON, R. A. Educational programs for gifted pupils. Sacramento, CA: California State Department of Education, 1961. As cited in Marland, S. P., Jr., *Education of the gifted and talented* (Vol. I). Report to the Congress of the United States by the U.S. Commissioner of Education. Washington, D.C.: U.S. Government Printing Office, 1972.

MARTINSON, R. A. Children with superior cognitive abilities. In L. M. Dunn (Ed.), *Exceptional children in the schools* (2nd ed.). New York: Holt, Rinehart, & Winston, 1973.

MASLOW, A. H. *Toward a psychology of being.* New York: Van Nostrand, 1962.

MASLOW, A. H. Toward a humanistic biology. *American Psychologist*, 1969, *24*, 734–735.

MASSARO, D. W., & WARNER, D. S. Dividing attention between auditory and visual perception. *Perception & Psychophysics*, 1977, *21*, 569–574.

MASTERS, W. H., & JOHNSON, V. E. *Human sexual response.* Boston, MA: Little, Brown, 1966.

MASTERS, W. H., & JOHNSON, V. E. *Human sexual inadequacies.* Boston, MA: Little, Brown, 1970.

MASTERS, W. H., & JOHNSON, V. E. *Homosexuality in perspective.* Boston, MA: Little, Brown, 1979.

MATHEWS, K. E., JR., & CANON, L. K. Environmental noise level as a determinant of helping behavior. *Journal of Personality and Social Psychology*, 1975, *32*(4), 571–577.

MATIN, E. Saccadic suppression: A review and an analysis. *Psychological Bulletin*, 1974, *81*, 899–917.

MATIN, E. Saccadic suppression and the stable world. In R. A. Monty & J. W. Senders (Eds.), *Eye movements and psychological processes.* Hillsdale, NJ: Lawrence Erlbaum Associates, 1976.

MATTHEWS, K. A., & ANGULO, J. Measurement of the Type A behavior pattern in children: Assessment of children's competitiveness, impatience-anger, and aggression. *Child Development*, 1980, *51*, 466–475.

MATTHEWS, K. A., & BRUNSON, B. I. Allocation of attention and the Type A coronary-prone behavior pattern. *Journal of Personality and Social Psychology*, 1979, *37*, 2081–2090.

MCADOO, W. G., & DEMEYER, M. K. Personality characteristics of parents. In M. Rutter & E. Schopler (Eds.), *Autism: A reappraisal of concepts and treatment.* New York: Plenum, 1978.

MCCARRON, L. T. Psychophysiological discriminants of reactive depression. *Psychophysiology*, 1973, *10*, 223–230.

MCCARTHY, E. D., LANGNER, T. S., GERSTEN, J. C., EISENBERG, J. G., & ORZECK, L. The effects of television on children and adolescents: Violence and behavior disorders. *Journal of Communication*, 1975, *25*, 71–85.

MCCLELLAND, D. C. *The achieving society.* Princeton, NJ: Van Nostrand, 1961.

MCCLELLAND, D. C. *Power: The inner experience.* New York: Irvington, 1975.

MCCLELLAND, D. C., & WATSON, R. I., JR. Power motivation and risk-taking behavior. *Journal of Personality*, 1973, *41*, 121–139.

MCCLELLAND, D. C., ATKINSON, J. W., CLARK, R. W., & LOWELL, E. L. *The achievement motive.* New York: Appleton-Century-Crofts, 1953.

MCCORMICK, E. J., & ILGEN, D. R. *Industrial psychology* (7th ed.). Englewood Cliffs, NJ: Prentice-Hall, 1980.

MCGAUGH, J. L., & HERZ, M. J. (EDS.) *Controversial issues in consolidation of the memory trace.* New York: Atherton Press, 1970.

MCGHIE, A., & CHAPMAN, J. Disorders of attention and perception in early schizophrenia. *British Journal of Medical Psychology*, 1961, *34*, 103–116.

MCGRATH, M. J., & COHEN, D. B. REM sleep facilitation of adaptive waking behavior: A review of the literature. *Psychological Bulletin*, 1978, *85*, 24–57.

MCKENZIE, B. E., & DAY, R. H. Object distance as a determinant of visual fixation in early infancy. *Science*, 1972, *178*, 1108–1110.

MCKENZIE, B. E., TOOTELL, H. E., & DAY, R. H. Development of visual size constancy during the 1st year of human infancy. *Developmental Psychology*, 1980, *16*, 163–174.

MCNEILL, D. Explaining linguistic universals. In J. Morton (Ed.), *Biological and social factors in psycholinguistics.* London: Logos Press, 1970a.

MCNEILL, D. The development of language. In P. H. Mussen (Ed.), *Carmichael's manual of child psychology* (3rd ed.). New York: John Wiley & Sons, 1970b.

MCNEMAR, Q. Lost: Our intelligence. Why? *American Psychologist*, 1964, *19*, 871–882.

MEADOW, A., PARNES, S. J., & REESE, H. Influence of brainstorming instructions and problem sequence on a creative problem solving test. *Journal of Applied Psychology*, 1959, *43*, 413–416.

MEDDIS, R., PEARSON, A. J. D., & LANGFORD, G. N. An extreme case of healthy insomnia. *EEG in Clinical Neurophysiology*, 1973, *35*, 213–224.

MEDWAY, F. J. Developmental aspects of self and other causal attributions. *Psychological Reports*, 1979, *45*, 155–159.

MEHRABIAN, A. *Nonverbal communication.* Chicago: Aldine-Atherton, 1972.

MEHRABIAN, A. The effects of emotional state on approach-avoidance behaviors. In A. Mehrabian (Ed.), *Basic dimensions for general psychological theory.* Cambridge, MA: Oelgeschlager, Gunn & Hain, 1980.

MEICHENBAUM, D. *Cognitive behavior modification.* Morristown, NJ: General Learning Press, 1974.

MEICHENBAUM, D. Self-instructional methods. In F. H. Kanfer & A. P. Goldstein (Eds.), *Helping people change.* New York: Pergamon Press, 1975.

MEICHENBAUM, D. *Cognitive behavior modification.* New York: Plenum Press, 1977.

MEICHENBAUM, D., & CAMERON, R. Training schizophrenics to talk to themselves: A means of developing attentional controls. *Behavior Therapy*, 1973, *4*, 515–534.

MELAMED, L. E., HALAY, M., & GILDOW, W. An examination of the role of task oriented attention in the use of active and passive movement in visual adaptation. *Journal of Experimental Psychology*, 1973, *98*, 125–201.

MELGES, F. T., TINKLENBERG, J. R., HOLLISTER, L. E., & GILLESPIE, H. K. Marijuana and the temporal span of awareness. *Archives of General Psychiatry*, 1971, *24*, 564–567.

MELTZER, H. Y., & STAHL, S. M. The dopamine hypothesis of schizophrenia: A review. *Schizophrenia Bulletin*, 1976, *2*, 19–76.

MELTZOFF, A. N., & MOORE, M. K. Imitation of facial and manual gestures by human neonates. *Science*, 1977, *198*, 75–78.

MELTZOFF, J., & KORNEICH, M. *Research in psychotherapy*. New York: Atherton Press, 1970.

MELVILLE, J. *Phobias and compulsions*. New York: Penguin Books, 1977.

MELZACK, R. *The puzzle of pain*. London: Penguin, 1973.

MELZACK, R. AND COLLEAGUES. Trigger points and acupuncture points for pain: Correlations and implications. *Pain*, 1977, *3*, 3–23.

MELZACK, R., & LOESER, J. D. Phantom body pain in paraplegics: Evidence for a central "pattern generating mechanism" for pain. *Pain*, 1978, *4*, 195–210.

MELZACK, R., & WALL, P. Pain mechanisms: A new theory. *Science*, 1965, *150*, 971–979.

MELZACK, R., & WALL, P. D. Psychophysiology of pain. *International Anesthesiology Clinics*, 1970, *8*, 3–34.

MERCER, J. R. The struggle for children's rights: Critical juncture for school psychology. *School Psychology Digest*, 1977, *6*, 4–19.

MEYERS, D. G., & KAPLAN, M. F. Group induced polarization in simulated juries. *Personality and Social Psychology Bulletin*, 1976, *2*, 63–66.

MEYER, W., FOLKES, V., & WEINER, B. The perceived informational value and affective consequences of choice behavior and intermediate difficulty task selection. *Journal of Research in Personality*, 1976, *10*, 410–423.

MIDDLEBROOK, P. N. *Social psychology and modern life* (2nd ed.). New York: Alfred A. Knopf, 1980.

MIELE, F. Cultural bias in the WISC. *Intelligence*, 1979, *3*, 149–164.

MILES, C. P. Conditions predisposing to suicide: A review. *Journal of Nervous and Mental Disease*, 1977, *164*, 231–246.

MILGRAM, S. Behavioral study of obedience. *Journal of Abnormal and Social Psychology*, 1963, *67*, 371–378.

MILGRAM, S. Some conditions of obedience and disobedience to authority. *Human Relations*, 1965a, *18*, 57–75.

MILGRAM, S., Liberating effects of group pressure. *Journal of Personality and Social Psychology*, 1965b *1*, 127–134.

MILGRAM, S. The experience of living in cities. *Science*, 1970, *167*, 1461–1468.

MILLER, G. A. The magic number seven, plus or minus two: Some limits on our capacity for processing information. *Psychological Review*, 1956, *63*, 81–97.

MILLER, I. W., III, & NORMAN, W. H. Learned helplessness in humans: A review and attribution-theory model. *Psychological Bulletin*, 1979, *86*, 93–118.

MILLER, L. L., MCFARLAND, D. J., CORNETT, T. L., BRIGHTWELL, D. R., & WIKLER, A. Marijuana: Effects on free recall and subjective organization of pictures and words. *Psychopharmacology*, 1977, *55*, 257–262.

MILLER, N., MARUYAMA, G., BEABER, R. J., & VALONE, K. Speed of speech and persuasion. *Journal of Personality and Social Psychology*, 1976, *34*, 615–624.

MILLER, N. E. Experimental studies of conflict. In J. McV. Hunt (Ed.), *Personality and behavioral disorders* (Vol. I). New York: Ronald Press, 1944.

MILLER, N. E. Liberalization of basic S-R concepts: Extensions to conflict behavior, motivation, and social learning. In S. Koch (Ed.), *Psychology: A study of a science* (Vol. II). New York: McGraw-Hill, 1959.

MILLER, N. E. Some motivational effects of electrical and chemical stimulation of the brain. *Electroencephalography and Clinical Neurophysiology Supplement*, 1963, *24*, 247–259.

MILLER, N. E. Learning of visceral and glandular responses. *Science*, 1969, *163*, 434–445.

MILLER, W. R. Behavioral treatment of problem drinkers: A comparative outcome study of three controlled drinking therapies. *Journal of Consulting and Clinical Psychology*, 1978, *46*, 74–86.

MILLMAN, J., BISHOP, C., & EBEL, R. An analysis of testwiseness. *Educational and Psychological Measurement*, 1965, *25*, 707–726.

MILNER, B. Amnesia following operation on the temporal lobes. In C. W. M. Whitty & O. L. Zangwill (Eds.), *Amnesia*. London: Butterworth, 1966.

MILNER, B. Preface; material specific and generalized memory loss. *Neuropsychologia*, 1968, *6*, 175–179.

MILNER, B., CORKIN, S., & TEUBER, H. L. Further analysis of hyppocampal amnesic syndrome: 14 year follow-up study of H. M. *Neuropsychologia*, 1968, *6*, 215–234.

MISCHEL, W. Toward a cognitive social learning reconceptualization of personality. *Psychology Review*, 1973, *80*, 252–283.

MISCHEL, W. On the interface of cognition and personality: Beyond the person-situation debate. *American Psychologist*, 1979, *34*, 740–754.

MISHLER, E. G., & WAXLER, N. E. Family interaction processes and schizophrenia: A review of current theories. In E. G. Mishler & N. E. Waxler (Eds.), *Family processes and schizophrenia*. New York: Science House, 1968.

MITCHELL, K. R., & ORR, F. E. Heterosexual social competence, anxiety, avoidance and self-judged physical attractiveness. *Perceptual and Motor Skills*, 1976, *43*, 553–554.

MOORE, J. J., & MASSARO, D. W. Attention and processing capacity in auditory recognition. *Journal of Experimental Psychology*, 1973, *99*, 49–54.

MORENO, J. L. *The international handbook of group psychotherapy*. New York: Philosophical Library, 1966.

MORGAN, C. P., & ARAM, J. D. The preponderance of arguments in the risky shift phenomenon. *Journal of Experimental Social Psychology*, 1975, *11*, 25–34.

MORGANSTERN, K. P. Implosive therapy and flooding procedures: A critical review. *Psychological Bulletin*, 1973, *79*, 318–334.

MORGANSTERN, K. P. Cigarette smoke as a noxious stimulus in self-managed aversion therapy for compulsive eaters: Technique and case illustration. *Behavior Therapy*, 1974, *5*, 255–260.

MORRISON, J. R. Changes in subtype diagnosis of schizophrenia: 1920–1966. *American Journal of Psychiatry*, 1974, *131*, 674–677.

MOSKOWITZ, B. A. The acquisition of language. *Scientific American*, 1978, *239*(5), 92–108.

MOTT, T., JR. The clinical importance of hypnotizability. *The American Journal of Clinical Hypnosis*, 1979, *21*, 263–269.

MOVSHON, J. A. The velocity tuning of single units in cat striate cortex. *Journal of Physiology*, 1975, *249*, 445–468.

MOVSHON, J. A., THOMPSON, I. D., & TOLHURST, D. J. Spatial and temporal contrast sensitivity of neurones in areas 17 and 18 of the cat's visual cortex. *Journal of Physiology*, 1978, *283*, 101–120.

MOWRER, O. H. *Learning theory and behavior*. New York: John Wiley & Sons, 1960.

MOWRER, O. H., & MOWRER, W. A. Enuresis: A method for its study and treatment. *American Journal of Orthopsychiatry*, 1938, *8*, 436–459.

MOYER, W. W. Effects of loss of freedom on subjects with internal or external locus of control. *Journal of Research and Personality*, 1978, *12*, 253–261.

MUIR, D. W., & MITCHELL, D. E. Visual resolution and experience: Acuity deficits in cats following early selective visual deprivation. *Science*, 1973, *180*, 430–422.

MULCAHY, R., & KNAGGS, J. F. Effect of age, parity, and cigarette smoking on outcome of pregnancy. *American Journal of Obstetrics and Gynecology*, 1968, *101*, 844–849.

MURDOCK, B. B., JR. The retention of individual items. *Journal of Experimental Psychology*, 1961, *62*, 618–625.

MURDOCK, B. B., JR. *Human memory: Theory and data*. Potomac, MD: Lawrence Erlbaum Associates, 1974.

MURRAY, E. J., & BERKUN, M. M. Displacement as a function of conflict. *Journal of Abnormal and Social Psychology*, 1955, *51*, 47–56.

MURRAY, H. A. *Explorations in personality*. New York: Oxford University Press, 1938.

MURRAY, M., & CRACKNELL, A. Adolescents' views on smoking. *Journal of Psychosomatic Research*, 1980, *24*, 243–251.

MUTER, P. Very rapid forgetting. *Memory & Cognition*, 1980, *8*, 174–179.

NAHAS, G. G. Biomedial aspects of Cannabis usage. *Bulletin on Narcotics*, 1977, *24*, 13–27.

NAHAS, G. G., SUCIU-FOCA, N., ARMAND, J. P., & MORISHIMA, A. Inhibition of cellular mediated immunity in marijuana smokers. *Science*, 1974, *183*, 419–420.

NASH, M. R., JOHNSON, L. S., & TIPTON, R. D. Hypnotic age regression and the occurrence of transitional object relationships. *Journal of Abnormal Psychology*, 1979, *88*, 547–555.

NASSAU, K. The causes of color. *Scientific American*, 1980, *243*(4), 124–156.

NATHAN, P. E., ZARE, N., SIMPSON, H. F., & ANDBERT, M. M. A systems analytic model of diagnosis. I. The diagnostic validity of abnormal psychomotor behavior. *Journal of Clinical Psychology*, 1969, *25*, 3–9.

NATSOULAS, T. Consciousness. *American Psychologist*, 1978, *33*, 906–914.

NELSON, K. Structure and strategy in learning to talk. *Monographs of the Society for Research in Child Development*, 1973, *38*(Serial No. 149).

NELSON, R. E. Irrational beliefs in depression. *Journal of Consulting and Clinical Psychology*, 1977, *45*, 1190–1191.

NEMETH, C., & ENDICOTT, J. The midpoint as an anchor: Another look at discrepancy of position and attitude change. *Sociometry*, 1976, *39*, 11–18.

NEWMAN, R. G. Detoxification treatment of narcotic addicts. In R. I. Dupont, A. Goldstein, & J. O'Donnell (Eds.), *Handbook on drug abuse* (NIDA, DHEW, and Office of Drug Abuse Policy (Executive Office of the President)). Washington, D.C.: U.S. Government Printing Office, 1979.

NICHOLS, W. W., MILLER, R. C., HENEEN, W., BRADT, C., HOLLISTER, L., & KANTER, S. Cytogenetic studies on human subjects receiving marihuana and delta-9-tetrahydrocannabinol. *Mutation Research*, 1974, *26*, 413–417.

NISBETT, R. E. Hunger, obesity, and the ventromedial hypothalamus. *Psychological Review*, 1972, *79*, 433–453.

NISBETT, R. E., CAPUTO, C., LEGANT, P., & MARECEK, J. Behavior as seen by the actor and as seen by the observer. *Journal of Personality and Social Psychology*, 1973, *27*, 154–164.

NOBLE, E. P. (ED.) *Alcohol and health* (Third Special Report to the U.S. Congress from the Secretary of DHEW). Washington, D.C.: U.S. Government Printing Office, 1978.

NODINE, C. F., CARMODY, D. P., & HERMAN, E. Eye movements during visual search for artistically embedded targets. *Bulletin of the Psychonomic Society*, 1979, *13*, 371–374.

NODINE, C. F., CARMODY, D. P., & KUNDEL, H. L. Searching for NINA. In J. W. Senders, D. F. Fisher, & R. A. Monty (Eds.), *Eye movements and the higher psychological processes*. Hillsdale, NJ: Lawrence Erlbaum Associates, 1978.

NORMAN, D. A. *Memory and Attention, an Introduction to Human Information Processing*. New York: John Wiley & Sons, 1969.

NORTH, C., & CADORET, R. Diagnostic discrepancy in personal accounts of patients with 'schizophrenia.' *Archives of General Psychiatry*, 1981, *38*, 133–137.

NOTON, D., & STARK, L. Eye movements and visual perception.

Scientific American, 1971, *224*(6), 35–44.

NOVOTNY, M., LEE, M. C., & BARTLE, K. D. A possible chemical basis for the higher mutagenicity of marihuana smoke as compared to tobacco smoke. *Experienta*, 1976, *32*, 280–282.

NUECHTERLEIN, K. H. Reaction time and attention in schizophrenia: A critical evaluation of the data theories. *Schizophrenia Bulletin*, 1977, *3*, 373–428.

NYE, S. I., & MCLAUGHLIN, S. Role competence and marital satisfaction. In F. I. Nye (Ed.), *Role structure and analysis of the family*. Beverly Hills, CA: Sage Publications, 1976.

OBERLY, H. S. A comparison of the spans of "attention" and memory. *American Journal of Psychology*, 1928, *40*, 295–302.

O'BRIEN, F., & AZRIN, N. H. Symptom reduction by functional displacement in a token economy: A case study. *Journal of Behavior Therapy and Experimental Psychiatry*, 1972, *3*, 205–207.

O'BRIEN, R. M. Hypnosis and task-motivation instructions for "post-experimental"–post-hypnotic suggestions. *Perceptual and Motor Skills*, 1977, *45*, 1274.

O'DONNELL, J. A. Comments on Hunt's estimation procedures. In J. D. Rittenhouse (Ed.), *The epidemiology of heroin and other narcotics* (NIDA Research Monograph No. 16, DHEW Publication No. (ADM) 78-559). Washington, D.C.: U.S. Government Printing Office, 1977.

OLDS, J. Physiological mechanisms of reward. *Nebraska Symposium on Motivation*, 1955, *3*, 73–139.

OLDS, J. The central nervous system and the reinforcement of behavior. *American Psychologist*, 1969, *24*, 114–132.

OLDS, J., & MILNER, P. Positive reinforcement produced by electrical stimulation of septal area and other regions of rat brain. *Journal of Comparative and Physiological Psychology*, 1954, *47*, 419–427.

O'LEARY, K. D., & WILSON, G. T. *Behavior therapy: Application and outcome*. Englewood Cliffs, NJ: Prentice-Hall, 1975.

OMURA, Y. Patho-physiology of acupuncture effects, ACTH and morphine-like substances, pain, phantom sensations (phantom pain, itch, and coldness), brain micro-circulation, and memory. *Acpuncture & Electro-Therapeutic Research Institute Journal*, 1976, *2*, 1–31.

OMURA, Y. Critical evaluation of the methods of measurement of "tingling threshold," "pain threshold," and "pain tolerance" by electrical stimulation. *Acupuncture & Electro-Therapeutic Research International Journal*, 1977, *2*, 161–236.

O'REGAN, K. Saccade size control in reading: Evidence for the linguistic control hypothesis. *Perception and Psychophysics*, 1979, *25*, 501–509.

ORENSTEIN, H., & CARR, J. Implosion therapy by tape recording. *Behavior Research and Therapy*, 1975, *13*, 177–182.

ORNITZ, E. M., & RITVO, E. R. The syndrome of autism: A critical review. *American Journal of Psychiatry*, 1976, *133*, 609–621.

ORNSTEIN, R. E. A science of consciousness. In P. R. Lee, R. E. Ornstein, D. Galin, A. Deikman, & C. T. Tart (Eds.), *Symposium of consciousness, San Francisco, 1974*. New York: Viking Press, 1976.

ORNSTEIN, R. E. *The psychology of consciousness* (2nd ed.). New York: Harcourt Brace Jovanovich, 1977.

ÖSTBERG, O. Circadian rhythms of food intake in oral temperature in "morning" and "evening" groups of individuals. *Ergonomics*, 1973, *16*, 203–209.

OSWALD, I. Drugs and sleep. *Pharmacological Review*, 1968, *20*, 273–303.

PAGANO, R. W., ROSE, R. M., STIVERS, R. M., & WARRENBURG, S. Sleep during transcendental meditation. *Science*, 1976, *191*, 308–310.

PAIVIO, A. Learning of adjective-noun paired-associates as a function of adjective-noun word order and noun abstractness. *Canadian Journal of Psychology*, 1963, *17*, 370–379.

PAIVIO, A. Abstractness, imagery, and meaningfulness in paired-associate learning. *Journal of Verbal Learning and*

Verbal Behavior, 1965, *4*, 32–38.

PAIVIO, A. *Imagery and verbal processes*. New York: Holt, Rinehart, & Winston, 1971.

PAIVIO, A., & YARMEY, A. D. Pictures versus words as stimuli and responses in paired-associate learning. *Psychonomic Science*, 1966, *5*, 235–236.

PAIVIO, A., & YUILLE, J. C. Word abstractness and meaningfulness, and paired-associate learning in children. *Journal of Experimental Child Psychology*, 1966, *4*, 81–89.

PALERMO, D. S. *Language acquisition*. In R. W. Reese & L. P. Lipsitt (Eds.), *Experimental child psychology*. New York: Academic Press, 1970.

PALERMO, D. S. *Psychology of language*. Glenview, IL: Scott, Foresman, 1978.

PAPCUN, G., KRASHEN, S., & TERBECK, D. Is the left hemisphere specialized for speech, language, or something else? *UCLA Working Papers in Phonetics*, 1971, *19* (as cited in D. S. Palermo, *Psychology of language*. Glenview, IL: Scott, Foresman, 1978).

PARKE, R. D. Perspectives on father-infant interaction. In J. D. Osofsky (Ed.), *Handbook of infant development*. New York: John Wiley & Sons, 1979.

PARKE, R. D., & O'LEARY, S. E. Father-mother-infant interaction in the newborn period: Some findings, some observations and some unresolved issues. In K. Riegel & J. Meacham (Eds.), *The developing individual in a changing world*. Vol. 2. *Social and environmental issues*. The Hague, Netherlands: Mouton, 1976.

PARKER, D. E. The vestibular apparatus. *Scientific American*, 1980, *243*(5), 118–135.

PARMELEE, A. H., & STERN, E. Development of states in infants. In C. D. Clemente, T. P. Purpara, & F. E. Meyer (Eds.), *Sleep and the maturing nervous system*. New York: Academic Press, 1972.

PARNES, S. J., & MEADOW, A. Effects of "brainstorming" instructions on creative problem solving by trained and untrained subjects. *Journal of Educational Psychology*, 1959, *50*, 171–176.

PAULUS, P. B., ANNIS, A. B., SETA, J. J., SCHKADE, J. K., & MATTHEWS, R. W. Density does affect task performance. *Journal of Personality and Social Psychology*, 1976, *34*, 248–253.

PAVLOV, I. P. *Conditioned reflexes*. London: Oxford University Press, 1927.

PENDERGRASS, V. E. Time out from positive reinforcement following persistent high rate behavior in retardates. *Journal of Applied Behavior Analysis*, 1972, *5*, 85–91.

PEPLER, R. The thermal comfort of students in climate controlled and non-climate controlled schools. *ASHRAE Transactions*, 1972, *78*, 97–109.

PERIN, C. T. Behavior potentiality as a joint function of the amount of training and the degree of hunger at the time of extinction. *Journal of Experimental Psychology*, 1942, *30*, 93–113.

PERLMUTER, L. C., & MONTY, R. A. The importance of perceived control: Fact or fantasy? *American Scientist*, 1977, *65*, 759–765.

PERLMUTER, L. C., SCHARFF, K., KARSH, R., & MONTY, R. A. Perceived control: A generalized state of motivation. *Motivation and Emotion*, 1980, *4*, 35–45.

PERRET-CLERMONT, A-N. [*Social interaction and cognitive development in children*.] (H. Tajfel, Ed., & C. Sherrard, Trans.). London: Academic Press, 1980.

PERSKY, H. Plasma testosterone level and sexual behavior of couples. *Archives of Sexual Behavior*, 1978, *7*, 157–173.

PETERS, R. H., LUTTMERS, L. L., GUNION, M. W., & WELLMAN, P. J. Ventromedial hypothalamic syndrome: Finickiness? *Physiology and Behavior*, 1978, *20*, 279–285.

PETERSEN, B. H., GRAHAM, J., & LEMBERGER, L. Marihuana, tetrahydrocannabinol and T-cell function. *Life Sciences*, 1976, *19*, 395–400.

PETERSEN, R. C. Marihuana research findings: 1976. In R. C. Petersen (Ed.), *NIDA research monograph 14, marijuana research findings: 1976* (DHEW Publication No. (ADM) 79-501). Washington, D.C.: U.S. Government Printing Office, Stock No. 017-024-00622-0, 1977.

PETERSEN, R. C. *Cocaine*. Statement of Petersen, R. C. (NIDA, Alcohol, Drug Abuse, and Mental Health Administration Public Health Service, DHEW) before the Select Committee on Narcotics Abuse and Control, House of Representatives, Tuesday, July 24, 1979.

PETERSEN, R. C. *Marijuana and health* (DHEW Publication No. (ADM) 80-945, Eighth Annual Report to the U.S. Congress from the Secretary of DHEW). Washington, D.C.: U.S. Government Printing Office, 1980.

PETERSON, L. R., & PETERSON, M. J. Short-term retention of individual verbal items. *Journal of Experimental Psychology*, 1959, *58*, 193–198.

PHILLIPS, D. A., & ZIGLER, E. Children's self-image disparity: Effects of age, socioeconomic status, ethnicity, and gender. *Journal of Personality and Social Psychology*, 1980, *39*(4), 689–700.

PIAGET, J. *Judgment and reasoning in the child*. London: Routledge & Kegan Paul, 1928.

PIAGET, J. *The moral judgment of the child*. London: Routledge & Kegan Paul, 1932.

PINKER, S. Mental imagery and the third dimension. *Journal of Experimental Psychology: General*, 1980, *109*, 354–371.

PITT, B. *Psychogeriatrics*. Edinburgh & London: Churchill Livingstone, 1974.

PITTMAN, T. S., & PITTMAN, N. L. Deprivation of control and the attribution process. *Journal of Personality and Social Psychology*, 1980, *39*, 377–389.

PLOMIN, R., & DEFRIES, J. C. Genetics and intelligence: Recent data. *Intelligence*, 1980, *4*, 15–24.

PLUTCHIK, R., & AX, A. F. A critique of determinants of emotional state by Schachter and Singer (1962). *Psychophysiology*, 1967, *4*, 79–82.

PLYSHYN, Z. W. What the mind's eye tells the mind's brain: A critique of mental imagery. *Psychological Review*, 1973, *80*, 1–24.

POKORNY, A. D. Suicide in depression. In W. E. Fann, I. Karacan, A. D. Pokorny, & R. L. Williams (Eds.), *Phenomenology and treatment of depression*. New York: Spectrum Publications, 1977.

POLIVY, J. Perception of calories and regulation of intake in restrained and unrestrained subjects. *Addictive Behaviors*, 1976, *1*, 237–244.

POLIVY, J., HERMAN, C. P., YOUNGER, J. C., & ERSKINE, B. Effects of a model on eating behavior: The induction of a restrained eating style. *Journal of Psychiatry*, 1979, *47*, 100–117.

POLLAK, J. M. Obsessive-compulsive personality: A review. *Psychological Bulletin*, 1979, *86*, 225–241.

POPKIN, S. J., & SMALL, M. Y. Hyperamnesia and the role of imagery. *Bulletin of the Psychonomic Society*, 1979, *13*, 378–380.

PORTER, J. Suggestions and success imagery for study problems. *The International Journal of Clinical and Experimental Hypnosis*, 1978, *26*, 63–75.

PORTER, L. W., & STEERS, R. M. Organizational, work, and personal factors in employee turnover and absenteeism. *Psychological Bulletin*, 1973, *80*, 151–176.

PORTNOY, F. C., & SIMMONS, C. H. Day care and attachment. *Child Development*, 1978, *49*, 239–242.

POSTMAN, L. History and present status of the law of effect. *Psychological Bulletin*, 1947, *44*, 489–563.

POWERS, P. C., & GEEN, R. G. Effects of the behavior and the perceived arousal of a model on instrumental aggression. *Journal of Personality and Social Psychology*, 1972, *23*, 175–184.

POWLEY, T. L. The ventromedial hypothalamic syndrome, satiety, and a cephalic phase hypothesis. *Psychological Review*, 1977, *84*, 89–126.

PREMACK, D. Language in chimpanzees? *Science*, 1971, *172*, 808–822.

PRINZ, R. J., ROBERTS, W. A., & HANTMAN, E. Dietary correlates of hyperactive behavior in children. *Journal of Consulting and Clinical Psychology*, 1980, *48*, 760–769.

PROPST, L. R. Effects of personality and loss of anonymity on aggression: A reevaluation of deindividuation. *Journal of Personality*, 1979, *47*, 531–545.

PROSHANSKY, H. M., & O'HANLON, T. Environmental psychology: Origins and development. In D. Stokols (Ed.). *Perspectives on Environment and Behavior: Theory, Research, and Applications*. New York: Plenum, 1977.

PROVINS, K. A. Environmental conditions and driving efficiency: A review. *Ergonomics*, 1958, *2*, 63–88.

PRUITT, D. G. Indirect communication and the search for agreement in negotiation. *Journal of Applied Social Psychology*, 1971, *1*, 205–239.

PUTNAM, W. H. Hypnosis and distortions in eyewitness memory. *The International Journal of Clinical and Experimental Hypnosis*, 1979, *27*, 437–448.

QUILITCH, H. R., & RISLEY, T. R. The effects of play materials on social play. *Journal of Applied Behavior Analysis*, 1973, *6*, 573–578.

QUISENBERRY, N. L., WALTHER, R., & REYNOLDS, J. E. Relationship of TV-viewing of violence and aggression. *Childhood Education*, October 1978, pp. 59–64.

RABINOWITZ, J. C., MANDLER, G., & PATTERSON, K. E. Determinants of recognition and recall: Accessibility and generation. *Journal of Experimental Psychology: General*, 1977, *106*, 302–329.

RACHMAN, S., & DESILVA, P. Abnormal and normal obsessions. *Behavior Research and Therapy*, 1978, *16*, 223–248.

RADER, N., BAUSANO, M., & RICHARDS, J. E. On the nature of the visual-cliff-avoidance response in human infants. *Child Development*, 1980, *51*, 61–68.

RAFAELSON, O. J., BECH, P., CHRISTIANSEN, J. CHRISTRUP, H., NYBOE, J., & RAFAELSEN, L. Cannabis and alcohol: Effects on simulated car driving. *Science*, 1973, *179*, 920–923.

RAPPOPORT, P. Divided opinions on the split brain. *APA Monitor*, December 1979, 9–10.

RASKIN, M., BALI, L. R., & PEEKE, H. V. Muscle biofeedback and transcendental meditation. *Archives of General Psychiatry*, 1980, *37*, 93–97.

RAY, O. S. *Drugs, society, and human behavior*. St. Louis, MO: C. V. Mosby, 1972.

REEVES, J. L. EMG-biofeedback reduction of tension headaches: A cognitive skills-training approach. *Biofeedback and Self Regulation*, 1976, *1*, 217–225.

REGESTEIN, Q. R., & REICH, P. Pedophilia occurring after onset of cognitive impairment. *The Journal of Nervous and Mental Disease*, 1978, *166*, 794–798.

REIS, H. T., NEZLEK, J., & WHEELER, L. Physical attractiveness in social interaction. *Journal of Personality and Social Psychology*, 1980, *38*, 604–617.

REITMAN, J. S. Without surreptitious rehearsal, information in short-term memory decays. *Journal of Verbal Learning and Verbal Behavior*, 1974, *13*, 365–377.

RESCORLA, R. A. Pavlovian 2nd-order conditioning: Some implications for instrumental behavior. In H. Davis & H. Herwit (Eds.), *Pavlovian-operant interactions*. Hillsdale, NJ: Lawrence Erlbaum Associates, 1977.

RESTLE, F. Moon illusion explained on the basis of relative size. *Science*, 1970, *167*, 1092–1096.

RHEINGOLD, H. L., GEWIRTZ, J. L., & ROSS, H. W. Social conditioning of vocalizations in the infant. *Journal of Comparative and Physiological Psychology*, 1959, *52*, 68–73.

RICHMOND, J. B. *The health consequences of smoking for women: A report of the Surgeon General* (U.S. Department of Health and Human Services, Public Health Service, Office on Smoking and Health). Washington, DC: U.S. Government Printing Office, 1981a.

RICHMOND, J. B. *The health consequences of smoking: The changing cigarette: A report of the Surgeon General* (U.S. Department of Health and Human Services, Public Health Service, Office on Smoking and Health). Washington, DC: U.S. Government Printing Office, 1981b.

RICKS, D. M. Vocal communication in preverbal normal and autistic children. In N. O'Connor (Ed.), *Language, cognitive deficits, and retardation*. London: Butterworth, 1975.

RING, K., WALLSTON, K., & COREY, M. Mode of debriefing as a factor affecting subjective reaction to a Milgram-type obedience experiment: An ethical inquiry. *Representative Research in Social Psychology*, 1970, *1*, 67–88.

RITTER, B. The group desensitization of children's snake phobias using vicarious and contact desensitization procedures. *Behavior Research and Therapy*, 1968, *6*, 1–6.

ROBINS, L. N. *Deviant children grown up*. Baltimore: Williams & Wilkins, 1966.

ROBINS, L. N. The adult development of the antisocial child. *Seminars in Psychiatry*, 1970, *2*, 420–434.

ROBINS, L. N. Addict careers. In R. I. Dupont, A. Goldstein, & J. O'Donnell (Eds.), *Handbook on drug abuse* (NIDA, DHEW, and Office of Drug Abuse Policy (Executive Office of the President)). Washington, D.C.: U.S. Government Printing Office, 1979.

ROBINSON, H. B., ROEDELL, W. C., & JACKSON, N. E. Early identification and intervention. In A. H. Passow (Ed.), *The gifted and the talented: Their education and development*. The 78th Yearbook for the National Society for the Study of Education. Chicago: University of Chicago Press, 1979.

ROBINSON, N. M., & ROBINSON, H. B. *The mentally retarded child* (2nd ed.). New York: McGraw-Hill, 1976.

ROCK, I., & VICTOR, J. Vision and touch: An experimentally created conflict between the two senses. *Science*, 1964, *143*, 574–596.

RODABOUGH, T. Alternatives to the stages model of the dying process. *Death Education*, 1980, *4*, 1–19.

RODIN, J. Obesity theory and treatment: An uneasy couple? Invited address at the Association for the Advancement of Behavior Therapy, San Francisco, CA, 1979.

RODIN, J. Current status of the internal-external hypothesis for obesity. What went wrong? *American Psychologist*, 1981, *36*, 361–372.

ROGERS, C. R. *Client-centered therapy*. Boston, MA: Houghton Mifflin, 1951.

ROGERS, C. R. A theory of therapy, personality, and interpersonal relationships, as developed in the client-centered framework. In S. Koch (Ed.), *Psychology: A study of a science* (Vol. 3). New York: McGraw-Hill, 1959.

ROGERS, C. R. *On becoming a person: A therapist's view of psychotherapy*. Boston, MA: Houghton Mifflin, 1961.

ROGERS, C. R. The process of the basic encounter group. In J. F. T. Bugental (Ed.), *Challenges of humanistic psychology*. New York: McGraw-Hill, 1967.

ROGERS, C. R. The process of the basic encounter group. In J. T. Hart & T. M. Tomlinson (Eds.), *New directions in client-centered therapy*. Boston, MA: Houghton, Mifflin, 1970.

ROGERS, R. W. Protection motivation theory of fear appeals and attitude change. *Journal of Psychology*, 1975, *91*, 93–114.

ROGERS, R. W., & MEWBORN, C. R. Fear appeals on attitude change: Effects of a threat's noxiousness, probability of occurrence, and efficacy of coping responses. *Journal of Personality and Social Psychology*, 1976, *34*, 54–61.

ROSCH, E. Natural categories. *Cognitive Psychology*, 1973, *4*, 328–350.

ROSENTHAL, D. *Genetic theory in abnormal behavior*. New York: McGraw-Hill, 1970.

ROSENTHAL, D., WENDER, P. H., KETY, S. S., SCHULSINGER, F., WELNER, J., & OSTERGAARD, L. Schizophrenic's offspring reared in adoptive homes. In D. Rosenthal & S. S. Kety (Eds.), *The transmission of schizophrenia*. Oxford: Pergamon Press, 1968.

ROSENTHAL, R., & DEPAULO, B. M. Sex differences in accommodation in nonverbal communication. In R. Rosenthal (Ed.), *Skill in nonverbal communication*. Cambridge, MA: Oelgeschlager, Gunn & Hain, 1979.

ROSS, L., BIERBRAUER, G., & HOFFMAN, S. The role of attribution processes in conformity and dissent. *American Psychologist*, 1976, *31*, 148–157.

ROSSI, A. M., KUEHNLE, J. C., & MENDELSON, J. H. Marihuana and mood in human volunteers. *Pharmacology Biochemistry & Behavior*, 1978, *8*, 447–453.

ROTH, S. A revised model of learned helplessness in humans. *Journal of Personality*, 1980, *48*, 103–118.

ROTHMAN, G. R. The relationship between moral judgement and moral behavior. In M. Windmiller, N. Lambert, & E. Turiel (Eds.), *Moral development and socialization*. Boston, MA: Allyn & Bacon, 1980.

ROTTER, J. B. *Clinical psychology* (2nd ed.). Englewood Cliffs, NJ: Prentice-Hall, 1964.

ROTTER, J. B. Generalized expectancies for internal versus external control of reinforcement. *Psychological Monographs*, 1966, *80*, (1, Whole No. 609).

ROUTTENBERG, A., & LINDY, J. Effects of the availability of rewarding septal and hypothalamic stimulation on bar pressing for food under conditions of deprivation. *Journal of Comparative and Physiological Psychology*, 1965, *60*, 158–161.

RUBENSTEIN, E. A., & COELHO, G. V. Mental health and behavioral sciences: One federal agency's role in the behavioral sciences. *American Psychologist*, 1970, *25*, 517–523.

RUBIN, R., ROSENBLATT, C., & BALOW, B. Psychological and educational sequelae of prematurity. *Pediatrics*, 1973, *52*, 352–363.

RUDMAN, H. C. The standardized test flap. *Phi Delta Kappan*, 1977, *59*, 179–185.

RUMBAUGH, D. M., & SAVAGE-RUMBAUGH, S. Chimpanzee language research: Status and potential. *Behavior Research Methods and Instrumentation*, 1978, *10*, 119–131.

RUMBAUGH, D. M., GILL, T. V., & VON GLASERFELD, E. C. Reading and sentence completion by a chimpanzee (PAN). *Science*, 1973, *182*, 731–733.

RUSH, A. J., KHATAMI, M., & BECK, A. T. Cognitive and behavior therapy in chronic depression. *Behavior Therapy*, 1975, *6*, 398–404.

RUSHTON, W. A. H. The sensitivity of rods under illumination. *Journal of Physiology*, 1965, *178*, 141–160.

RUSSELL, M. A. H. Cigarette smoking: Natural history of a dependence disorder. *British Journal of Medical Psychology*, 1971, *44*, 1–16.

SACHS, J. S. Recognition memory for syntactic and semantic aspects of connected discourse. *Perception and Psychophysics*, 1967, *2*, 437–442.

SAKITT, B., & LONG, G. M. Cones determine subjective offset of a stimulus but rods determine total persistence. *Vision Research*, 1979, *19*, 1439–1443.

SALZBERG, H. C., & DEPIANO, F. A. Hypnotizability and task motivating suggestions: A further look at how they affect performance. *The International Journal of Clinical and Experimental Hypnosis*, 1980, *28*, 261–271.

SALZMAN, L. F., KLEIN, R. H., & STRAUSS, J. S. Pendulum eye tracking in remitted psychiatric patients. In L. C. Wynne, R. L. Cromwell, & S. Matthysse (Eds.), *The nature of schizophrenia: New approaches to research and treatment*. New York: John Wiley & Sons, 1978.

SAMUEL, W., SOTO, D., PARKS, M., NGISSAH, P., & JONES, B. Motivation, race, social class, and IQ. *Journal of Educational Psychology*, 1976, *68*(3), 273–285.

SAMUELS, S. J. Interaction of list length and low stimulus similarity on the Von Restorff effect. *Journal of Educational Psychology*, 1970, *61*, 57–58.

SANDERS, R. W. Systematic desensitization in the treatment of child abuse. *American Journal of Psychiatry*, 1978, *135*, 483–484.

SANTORIOUS, N., SHAPIRO, R., & JABLEWSKY, N. The international pilot study of schizophrenia. *Schizophrenia Bulletin*, 1974, *1*, 24–34 (Experimental Issue No. 11).

SATTERFIELD, J. H., CANTWELL, D. P., SAUL, R. E., & YUSIN, A. Intelligence, academic achievement, and EEG abnormalities in hyperactive children. *American Journal of Psychiatry*, 1974, *131*, 391–395.

SATTLER, J. M. Racial "experimenter effects" in experimentation, testing, interviewing, and psychotherapy. *Psychological Bulletin*, 1970, *73*, 137–160.

SATTLER, J. M. *Assessment of children's intelligence* (2nd ed.). Boston, MA: Allyn & Bacon, 1981.

SCHACHTER, F. F. *Everyday mother talk to toddlers*. New York: Academic Press, 1979.

SCHACHTER, S. Some extraordinary facts about obese humans and rats. *American Psychologist*, 1971, *26*, 129–144.

SCHACHTER, S. Nicotine regulation in heavy and light smokers. *Journal of Experimental Psychology*, 1977, *106*, 5–12.

SCHACHTER, S., & LATANÉ, B. Crime, cognition, and the autonomic nervous system. *Nebraska Symposium on Motivation*, 1964, *12*, 221–275.

SCHACHTER, S., & RODIN, J. *Obese humans and rats*. Potomac, MD.: Lawrence Erlbaum Associates, 1974.

SCHACHTER, S., & SINGER, J. E. Cognitive, social and physiological determinants of emotional state. *Psychological Review*, 1962, *69*, 379–399.

SCHACHTER, S., GOLDMAN, R., & GORDON, A. Effects of fear, food deprivation, and obesity on eating. *Journal of Personality and Social Psychology*, 1968, *10*, 91–97.

SCHACTER, S., SILVERSTEIN, B., KOZLOWSKI, L. T., PERLICK, D., HERMAN, C. P., & LIEBLING, B. Studies of the interaction of psychological and pharmacological determinants of smoking. *Journal of Experimental Psychology: General*, 1977, *106*, 3–40.

SCHALLING, D. Psychopathy—Related personality variables and the psychophysiology of socialization. In R. D. Hare & D. Shalling (Eds.), *Psychopathic behavior: Approaches to research*. Chichester, England: John Wiley, 1978, 85–106.

SCHILLER, P. H., & FINLAY, B. L., & VOLMAN, S. F. Quantitative studies of single-cell properties in monkey striate cortex. III. Spatial frequency. *Journal of Neurophysiology*, 1976, *39*, 1334–1351.

SCHMAUK, F. J. Punishment, arousal, and avoidance learning in sociopaths. *Journal of Abnormal Psychology*, 1970, *76*, 443–453.

SCHMIDT, D. E., & KEATING, J. P. Human crowding and personal control: An integration of the research. *Psychological Bulletin*, 1979, *86*, 680–700.

SCHNEIDER, K. Atkinson's "risk preference" model. *Motivation and Emotion*, 1978, *2*, 333–343.

SCHNEIDERMAN, N., FUENTES, I., & GORMEZANO, I. Acquisition and extinction of the classically conditioned eyelid response in the albino rabbit. *Science*, 1962, *136*, 650–652.

SCHOGGEN, M., & SCHOGGEN, P. Environmental forces in the home lives of three-year-old children in three population subgroups. *JSAS Catalog of Selected Documents in Psychology*, 1976, *6*(1). (Ms. No. 1178).

SCHULSINGER, F. Psychopathy: Heredity and environment. *The Journal of Mental Health*, 1972, *1*, 190–206.

SCHWARTZ, B. *Psychology of learning and behavior*, New York: W. W. Norton, 1978.

SCHWARTZ, S. H., & GOTTLIEB, A. Bystander anonymity and reactions to emergencies. *Journal of Personality and Social Psychology*, 1980, *39*, 418–430.

SCOTT, D. S., & BARBER, T. X. Cognitive control of pain: Effects of multiple cognitive strategies. *Psychological Record*, 1977, *2*, 373–383.

SCOVERN, A. W., & KILMANN, P. R. Status of electroconvulsive therapy: Review of the outcome literature. *Psychological Bulletin*, 1980, *87*, 260–303.

SEELY, J. E., ZUSKIN, E., & BOUHUYS, A. Cigarette smoking: Objective evidence or lung damage in teen-agers. *Science*, 1971, *172*, 741–743.

SEIDENBERG, M. S., & PETITTO, L. A. Signing behavior in apes: A critical review. *Cognition*, 1979, *7*, 177–215.

SEIF, M. N., & ATKINS, A. L. Some defensive and cognitive aspects of phobias. *Journal of Abnormal Psychology*, 1979, *88*, 42–51.

SELIGMAN, M. E. P. *Helplessness*. San Francisco, CA: W. H. Freeman, 1975.

SELIGMAN, M. E. P. *Learned helplessness and depression in animals and humans*. Morristown, NJ: General Learning Press, 1976.

SHAKOW, D. Segmental set: The adaptive process in schizophrenia. *American Psychologist*, 1977, *32*, 129–139.

SHANAB, M. E., & YAHYA, K. A. A cross-cultural study of obedience. *Bulletin of the Psychonomic Society*, 1978, *11*, 267–269.

SHAPIRO, D. A biofeedback strategy in the study of consciousness. In N. Zinberg (Ed.), *Alternate states of consciousness*. New York: Macmillan, 1977.

SHAVER, K. G. *Principles of social psychology*. Cambridge, MA: Winthrop, 1977.

SHEPARD, R. N., & METZLER, J. Mental rotation of three-dimensional objects. *Science*, 1971, *171*, 701–703.

SHERMAN, M., & KEY, C. B. The intelligence of isolated mountain children. *Child Development*, 1932, *3*, 279–290.

SHIFFMAN, S. M. The tobacco withdrawal syndrome. In N. A. Krasnegor (Ed.), *Cigarette smoking as a dependence process* (NIDA Research Monograph No. 23, DHEW Publication No. (ADM) 79-8000). Washington, D.C.: U.S. Government Printing Office, 1979.

SHIMBERG, M. E. An investigation into the validity of norms with special reference to urban and rural groups. *Archives of Psychology*, New York: Columbia University, No. 104, 1929.

SIEGEL, E. F. Control of phantom limb pain by hypnosis. *The American Journal of Clinical Hypnosis*, 1979, *21*, 285–286.

SIEGEL, R. K. Cocaine: Recreational use and intoxication. In R. C. Petersen & R. C. Stillman (Eds.), *Cocaine: 1977* (NIDA Research Monographs No. 13, DHEW Publication No. (ADM) 79-471). Washington, D.C.: U.S. Government Printing Office, 1977.

SIEGEL, R. K. Cocaine hallucinations. *American Journal of Psychiatry*, 1978, *135*, 309–313.

SILVERMAN, L. P., & SPRUILL, N. L. Urban crime and the price of heroin. *Journal of Urban Economy*, 1977, *4*, 80–103.

SKINNER, B. F. Two types of conditioned reflex: A reply to Konorski and Miller. *Journal of General Psychology*, 1937, *16*, 272–279.

SKINNER, B. F. *The behavior of organisms*. New York: Appleton-Century-Crofts, 1938.

SKINNER, B. F. Superstition in the pigeon. *Journal of Experimental Psychology*, 1948, *38*, 168–172.

SKINNER, B. F. A case history in scientific method. *American Psychologist*, 1956, *11*, 221–233.

SKINNER, N. F. Learned helplessness: Performance as a function of task significance. *The Journal of Psychology*, 1979, *102*, 77–82.

SLAIKEU, K. A. Temporal variables in telephone crisis intervention: Their relationship to selected process and outcome variables. *Journal of Consulting and Clinical Psychology*, 1979, *47*, 193–195.

SLONE, D., SHAPIRO, S., ROSENBERG, M. S., KAUFMAN, D. W., HARTZ, S. C., ROSSI, A. C., STOLLEY, P. D., & MIETTINEN, O. S. Relation of cigarette smoking to myocardial infarction in young women. *New England Journal of Medicine*, 1978, *298*(23), 1273–1276.

SLOBIN, D. I. On the nature of talk to children. In E. H. Lenneberg & E. Lenneberg (Eds.), *Foundations of language development: A multidisciplinary approach* (Vol. 1). New York: Academic Press, 1975.

SMIALEK, J. E., MONFORTE, J. R., ARONOW, R., & SPITZ, W. U. Methadone deaths in children: A continuing problem. *Journal of the American Medical Association*, 1977, *238*, 2516–2517.

SMITH, D. E., & ROSE, A. J. LSD: Its use, abuse, and suggested treatment. *Journal of Psychedelic Drugs*, 1967-68, *1*, 117–123.

SMITH, F. J. Work attitudes as predictors of attendance on a specific day. *Journal of Applied Psychology*, 1977, *62*, 16–19.

SMITH, G. M. Personality and smoking: A review of the empirical literature. In W. A. Hunt (Ed.), *Learning mechanisms in smoking*. Chicago: Aldine, 1970.

SMITH, G. M., CHIANG, H. T., KITZ, R. J., & ANTOON, A. Acupuncture and experimentally induced ischemic pain. In J. J. Bonica (Ed.), *International symposium on pain: Advances in neurology* (Vol. 4). New York: Raven Press, 1974, 827–832.

SMITH, G. M., PARRY, W. L., DENTON, J. E., & BREECHER, H. K. Effect of morphine on pain produced in man by electric shock delivered through an annylar-disc cellulose sponge electrode. *Proceedings of the 78th Annual Convention of the American Psychological Association*, 1970, *5*, 819–820.

SMITH, J. C. Meditation as psychotherapy: A review of the literature. *Psychological Bulletin*, 1975, *82*, 558–564.

SMITH, J. C. Psychotherapeutic effects of transcendental meditation with controls for expectation of relief and daily sitting. *Journal of Consulting and Clinical Psychology*, 1976, *44*, 630–637.

SMITH, J. O., & ARKANS, J. R. More than ever: A case for the special class. In R. E. Schmid, J. Moneypenny, & R. Johnson (Eds.), *Contemporary issues in special education*. New York: McGraw-Hill, 1977.

SMITH, M. L., & GLASS, G. V. Meta-analysis of psychotherapy outcome studies. *American Psychologist*, 1977, *32*, 752–760.

SNYDER, S. H. *Madness and the brain*. New York: McGraw-Hill, 1974.

SNYDER, S. H. Brain peptides as neurotransmitters. *Science*, 1980, *209*, 976–983.

SOGIN, S. R., & PALLAK, M. S. Bad decisions, responsibility, and attitude change: Effects of volition, foreseeability, and locus of causality of negative consequences. *Journal of Personality and Social Psychology*, 1976, *33*, 300–306.

SOLOWAY, I. H. Methadone and the culture of addiction. *Journal of Psychedelic Drugs*, 1974, *6*, 91–99.

SOLSO, R. L. *Cognitive psychology*. New York: Harcourt Brace Jovanovich, Inc., 1979.

SONNENFELD, J. Variable values in space and landscape: An inquiry into the nature of environmental necessity. *Journal of Social Issues*, 1966, 22(4), 71–82.

SPACE, L. G., & CROMWELL, R. L. Personal constructs among depressed patients. *The Journal of Nervous and Mental Disease*, 1980, 168, 150–158.

SPANOS, N. P., RADTKE-BODORIK, H. L., FERGUSON, J. D., & JONES, B. The effects of hypnotic susceptibility, suggestions for analgesia, and the utilization of cognitive strategies on the reduction of pain. *Journal of Abnormal Psychology*, 1979, 88, 282–292.

SPANOS, N. P., STAM, H. J., D'EON, J. L., PAWLAK, A. E., & RADTKE-BODORIK, H. L. Effects of social-psychological variables on hypnotic amnesia. *Journal of Personality and Social Psychology*, 1980, 39, 737–750.

SPEARMAN, C. "General intelligence" objective development and measures. *American Journal of Psychology*, 1904, 15, 201–293.

SPENCE, K. W. *Behavior theory and conditioning.* New Haven, CT: Yale University Press, 1956.

SPENCER, J. A., & FREMOUW, W. J. Binge eating as a function of restraint and weight classification. *Journal of Abnormal Psychology*, 1979, 88, 262–267.

SPERLING, G. The information available in brief visual presentations. *Psychological Monographs*, 1960, 15, 201–293.

SPERRY, R. W. Mental unity following surgical disconnection of the cerebral hemispheres. In *Harvey Lectures.* New York: Academic Press, 1968.

SPIELBERGER, C. D. The effects of manifest anxiety on the academic achievement of college students. *Science*, 1962, 46, 420–426.

SPITZ, R. Hospitalism: An inquiry into the genesis of psychiatric conditions in early childhood. *Psychoanalytic Study of the Child*, 1945, 1, 53–74.

SPRAGINS, A. B., LEFTON, L. A., & FISHER, D. F. Eye movements while reading and searching spatially transformed text: A developmental examination. *Memory and Cognition*, 1976, 4, 36–42.

STAATS, A. W., & STAATS, C. K. *Complex human behavior; a systematic extension of learning principles.* New York: Holt, Rinehart, & Winston, 1963.

STANDING, L. Learning 10,000 pictures. *Quarterly Journal of Experimental Psychology*, 1973, 25, 207–222.

STANDING, L., CONEZIO, J., & HABER, R. N. Perception and memory for pictures: Single trial learning of 2500 visual stimuli. *Psychonomic Science*, 1970, 19, 73–74.

STANTON, H. E. A one-session hypnotic approach to modifying smoking behavior. *International Journal of Clinical and Experimental Hypnosis*, 1978, 26, 22–29.

STAW, B. M., CALDER, B. J., HESS, R. K., & SANDELANDS, L. E. Intrinsic motivation and norms about payment. *Journal of Personality*, 1980, 48, 1–14.

STEBBINS, W. C. *Animal Psychophysics: The design and conduct of sensory experiments.* New York: Appleton-Century-Crofts, 1970.

STEELE, C. M. Name-calling and compliance. *Journal of Personality and Social Psychology*, 1975, 31, 361–369.

STEELE, R. S. Power motivation, activation, and inspirational speeches. *Journal of Personality*, 1977, 45, 53–64.

STEIN, M. I. *Stimulating creativity.* New York: Academic Press, 1974.

STENCHEVER, M. A., KUNYSZ, T. J., & ALLEN, M. A. Chromosome breakage in users of marihuana. *American Journal of Obstetrics and Gynecology*, 1974, 118, 106–113.

STEPHENS, J. H., Long-term prognosis and follow-up in schizophrenia. *Schizophrenia Bulletin*, 1978, 4, 25–47.

STERN, L. D. A review of theories of human amnesia. *Memory & Cognition*, 1981, 9, 247–262.

STERN, W. *The psychological methods of testing intelligence.* Baltimore, MD: Warwick and York, 1914.

STERNBACH, R. A. *Pain: A psychophysiological analysis.* New York: Academic Press, 1968.

STERNBACH, R. A. Psychophysiology of pain. *International Journal of Psychiatry in Medicine*, 1975, 6, 63–73.

STEVENS, C. F. The neuron. In *The brain* (Scientific American Book). San Francisco, CA: W. H. Freeman, 1979.

STEWART, M. A., DEBLOIS, C. S., MEARDON, J., & CUMMINGS, C. Aggressive conduct disorder in children. *The Journal of Nervous and Mental Disease*, 1980, 168, 604–610.

STOKOLS, D. On the distinction between density and crowding: Some implications for future research. *Psychological Review*, 1972, 79(3), 275–277.

STOKOLS, D. The experience of crowding in primary and secondary environments. *Environmental & Behavior*, 1976, 8(1), 49–86.

STOKOLS, D., RALL, M., PINNER, B., & SCHOPLER, J. Physical, social, and personal determinants of the perception of crowding. *Environment & Behavior*, 1973, 5(1), 87–115.

STOLZ, S. B., WIENCKOWSKI, L. A., & BROWN, B. S. Behavior modification: A perspective on critical issues. *American Psychologist*, 1975, 30, 1027–1048.

STONE, M. H. *The borderline syndromes.* New York: McGraw-Hill, 1980.

STORMS, L. H. Implosive therapy: An alternate to sytematic desensitization. In V. Binder, A. Binder, & B. Rimland (Eds.), *Modern therapies.* Englewood Cliffs, NJ: Prentice-Hall, 1976.

STOTT, D. H., & WILSON, D. M. The adult criminal as a juvenile. *British Journal of Criminology*, 1977, 17, 47–57.

STRAUSS, J. S., & CARPENTER, W. T., JR. A prediction of outcome in schizophrenia. II. Characteristics of outcome. *Archives of General Psychiatry*, 1972, 27, 739–746.

STRENTZ, T., & HASSEL, C. V. The sociopath—A criminal enigma. *Journal of Police Science and Administration*, 1978, 6, 135–140.

STROBER, M., GREEN, J., & CARLSON, G. Reliability of psychiatric diagnosis in hospitalized adolescents. *Archives of General Psychiatry*, 1981, 38, 141–145.

STRUPP, H. H. On the basic ingredients of psychotherapy. *Journal of Consulting and Clinical Psychology*, 1973, 41, 1–8.

STUNKARD, A., COLL, M., LUNDQUIST, S., & MEYERS, A. Obesity and eating style. *Archives of General Psychiatry*, 1980, 37, 1127–1129.

SUEDFELD, P. Birth order of volunteers for sensory deprivation. *Journal of Abnormal and Social Psychology*, 1964, 68, 195–196.

SULLIVAN, E. V. Can values be taught? In M. Windmiller, N. Lambert, & E. Turiel (Eds.), *Moral development and socialization.* Boston, MA: Allyn & Bacon, 1980.

SURWIT, R. S., & KEEFE, F. J. Frontalis emg feedback training: An electronic panacea? *Behavior Therapy*, 1978, 9, 779–792.

SVEJDA, M. J., & CAMPOS, J. J., & EMDE, R. N. Mother-infant "bonding": Failure to generalize. *Child Development*, 1980, 51, 775–779.

SWENSON, W. M., PEARSON, J. S., & OSBORNE, D. *An MMPI source book: Basic item, scale, and pattern data on 50,000 medical patients.* Minneapolis, MN: University of Minnesota Press, 1973.

SZUCKO, J. J., & KLEINMUNTZ, B. Statistical versus clinical lie detection. *American Psychologist*, 1981, 36, 488–496.

TAGRURI, R. Person perception. In G. Lindzey & E. Aronson (Eds.), *The handbook of social psychology.* Reading, MA: Addison-Wesley, 1968.

TANNENBAUM, P. H., & ZILLMAN, D. Emotional arousal in the facilitation of aggression through communication. In L. Berkowitz (Ed.), *Advances in experimental social psychology* (Vol. 8). New York: Academic Press, 1975.

TANNER, J. M., WHITEHOUSE, R. H., & TAKAISHI, M. Standards from birth to maturity for height, weight, height velocity, and weight velocity: British children 1965. *Archives of the Diseases of Childhood*, 1966, *41*, 455–471.

TARPY, R. M., & SAWBINI, F. L. Reinforcement delay: A selective review of the last decade. *Psychological Bulletin*, 1974, *81*, 984–997.

TART, C. T. States of consciousness and state-specific sciences. *Science*, 1972, *176*, 1203–1210.

TART, C. T. States of consciousness and state-specific sciences. *Journal of Altered States of Consciousness*, 1975, *2*, 87–105.

TART, C. T. Putting the pieces together: A conceptual framework for understanding discrete states of consciousness. In N. Zinberg (Ed.), *Alternate states of consciousness*. New York: Macmillan, 1977.

TAYLOR, J. A. Personality scale of manifest anxiety. *Journal of Abnormal and Social Psychology*, 1953, *48*, 285–290.

TAYLOR, S. E. On inferring one's attitude from one's behavior: Some delimiting conditions. *Journal of Personality and Social Psychology*, 1975, *31*, 126–131.

TEEVAN, R. C., & MCGHEE, P. E. Childhood development of fear of failure motivation. *Journal of Personality and Social Psychology*, 1972, *21*, 345–348.

TERMAN, L. M. *The measurement of intelligence*. Boston: Houghton Mifflin, 1916.

TERMAN, L. M. Intelligence and its measurement: A symposium. *Journal of Educational Psychology*, 1921, *12*, 127–133.

TERRACE, H. S. How Nim Chimpski changed my mind. *Psychology Today*, 1979, *13*, 65–76.

TERRACE, H. S. *Nim*. New York: Alfred A. Knopf, 1980.

THELEN, M. H., & KIRKLAND, K. D. On status and being imitated: Effects on reciprocal imitation and attraction. *Journal of Personality and Social Psychology*, 1976, *33*, 691–697.

THOMPSON, R., & MCCONNELL, J. Classical conditioning in the planarian, *Dugesia dorotocephala*. *Journal of Comparative and Physiological Psychology*, 1955, *48*, 65–68.

THOMPSON, W. R. The inheritance and development of intelligence. *Research Publication Association of Nervous and Mental Diseases*, 1954, *33*, 209–331.

THORNDIKE, E. L. *The measurement of intelligence*. New York: Bureau of Publications, Teachers College, Columbia University, 1926.

THORNDIKE, E. L. *The fundamentals of learning*. New York: Teachers College, 1932.

THURSTONE, L. L. *The primary mental abilities tests*. Chicago, IL: Science Research Associates, 1941.

TINBERGEN, N. Ethiology and stress disease. *Science*, 1974, *185*(4145), 20–27.

TITTLE, C. Prisons and rehabilitation: The inevitability of disfavor. *Social Problems*, 1972, *21*, 385–395.

TOM, G., & RUCKER, M. Fat, full, and happy: Effects of food deprivation, external cues, and obesity on preference ratings, consumption, and buying intentions. *Journal of Personality and Social Psychology*, 1975, *32*, 761–766.

TOMKINS, S. S. *Affect imagery consciousness* Vol. 1. *The positive affects*. New York: Springer Press, 1962.

TOMKINS, S. S. *Affect imagery consciousness*. Vol. 2. *The negative affects*. New York: Springer Press, 1963.

TRACHTMAN, J. N. Biofeedback accommodation to reduce functional myopia. Unpublished doctoral dissertation, Yeshiva University, 1978.

TRAMONTANA, M. G. Critical review of research on psychotherapy outcome with adolescents: 1967–1977. *Psychological Bulletin*, 1980, *88*, 429–450.

TREISMAN, A. M. Strategies and models of selective attention. *Psychological Review*, 1969, *76*, 282–295.

TRITES, D., GALBRAITH, F. D., STURDAVENT, M., & LECKWART, J. F. Influence of nursing-unit design on the activities and subjective feelings of nursing personnel. *Environment and Behavior*, 1970, *2*, 203–334.

TROPE, Y. Seeking information about one's own ability as a de-

terminant of choice among tasks. *Journal of Personality and Social Psychology*, 1975, *32*, 1004–1013.

TULVING, E. Episodic and semantic memory. In E. Tulving & W. Donaldson (Eds.), *Organization and memory*. New York: Academic Press, 1972.

TUNE, G. S. Sleep and wakefulness in 509 normal human adults. *British Journal of Medical Psychology*, 1969, *42*, 75–79.

TURNBULL, C. M. Notes and discussions: Some observations regarding the experiences and behavior of the Bambute pygmies. *American Journal of Psychology*, 1961, *7*, 304–308.

TURSKY, B. The measurement of pain reactions: Laboratory studies. In M. Weisenberg (Ed.), *The control of pain*. New York: Psychological Dimensions, 1977.

TWAIN, D., MCGEE, R., & BENNETT, L. A. Functional areas of psychological activity. In S. L. Brodsky (Ed.), *Psychologists in the criminal justice system*. Chicago, IL: University of Illinois Press, 1973.

TYLER, L. E. *Tests and measurements* (2nd ed.). Englewood Cliffs, NJ: Prentice-Hall, 1971.

ULLMANN, L. P., & KRASNER, L. *The psychological approach to abnormal behavior* (2nd ed.). Englewood Cliffs, NJ: Prentice-Hall, 1975.

UNDERWOOD, B. J. Interference and forgetting. *Psychological Review*, 1957, *64*, 49–60.

USDIN, G., & HOFLING, C. K. *Aging: The process and the people*. New York: Brunner/Mazel, 1978.

VAILLANT, G. E. The natural history of drug addiction. *Seminar in Psychiatry*, 1970, *2*, 486–498.

VALINS, S. Cognitive effects of false heart-rate feedback. *Journal of Personality and Social Psychology*, 1966, *4*, 400–408.

VALINS, S., & BAUM, A. Residential group size, social interaction, and crowding. *Environment & Behavior*, 1973, *5*, 421–435.

VAN DYKE, C., JATLOW, P., UNGERER, J., BARASH, P. G., & BYCK, R. Oral cocaine: Plasma concentrations and central effects. *Science*, 1978, *200*, 211–213.

VAN PRAAG, H. M. Neuralendocrine disorders in depression and their significance for the monoamine hypothesis of depression. *Acta Psychiatrica Scandinavica*, 1978, *57*, 389–404.

VAUGHN, B., EGELAND, B., & SROUFE, L. A. Individual differences in infant-mother attachment at twelve and eighteen months: Stability and change in families under stress. *Child Development*, 1979, *50*, 971–975.

VERNON, P. E. *Intelligence: Heredity and environment*. San Francisco: W. H. Freeman, 1979.

VINACKE, W. E. *The psychology of thinking* (2nd ed.). New York: McGraw-Hill, 1974.

VOGEL, G. W. A review of REM sleep deprivation. *Archives of General Psychiatry*, 1975, *32*, 749–760.

VOLKMANN, F. C. Vision during voluntary saccadic eye movements. *Journal of the Optical Society of America*, 1962, *52*, 571–578.

VOLKMANN, F. C. Saccadic suppression: A brief review. In R. A. Monty & J. W. Senders (Eds.), *Eye movements and psychological processes*. Hillsdale, NJ: Lawrence Erlbaum Associates, 1976.

VON SENDEN, M. *Raum- und Gaestaltauffassung bei operierten. Blindgeborernin vor und nach der Operation*. Leipzig, W. Germany: Barth, 1932.

VROOM, V. H. *Work and motivation*. New York: John Wiley & Sons, 1964.

VROOM, V. H. A new look at managerial decision making. *Organizational Dynamics*, 1974, *5*, 66–80.

VROOM, V. H., & DECI, E. L. (EDS.) *Management and motivation*. Baltimore, MD: Penguin, 1970.

VROOM, V. H., & JAGO, A. On the validity of the Vroom-Yetton model. *Journal of Applied Psychology*, 1978, *63*, 151–162.

VROOM, V. H., & YETTON, P. W. *Leadership and decision-making*. Pittsburgh, PA: University of Pittsburgh Press, 1973.

VYKLICKY, L., RUDOMIN, P., ZAJAL, F. E., III, & BURKE, R. E. Primary afferent depolarization evoked by a painful stimulus. *Science*, 1969, *165*, 184–186.

WAGEMAKER, H., & CADE, R. The use of hemodialysis in chronic schizophrenia. *American Journal of Psychiatry*, 1977, *134*, 684–685.

WAHLER, R. G. Deviant child behavior within the family: Developmental speculation in behavior change strategies. In H. Leitenberg (Ed.), *Handbook of behavior modification and behavior therapy*. Englewood Cliffs, NJ: Prentice-Hall, 1976.

WAID, W. M. Skin conductance response to both signaled and unsignaled noxious stimulation predicts level of socialization. *Journal of Personality and Social Psychology*, 1976, *34*, 923–929.

WALDORF, D. *Careers in dope*. Englewood Cliffs, NJ: Prentice-Hall, 1973.

WALK, R. D., & GIBSON, E. J. A comparative and analytical study of visual depth perception. *Psychological Monographs*, 1961, *75*(15).

WALKER, S. F. Lateralization of functions in the vertebrate brain: A review. *British Journal of Psychology*, 1980, *71*, 329–367.

WALLACE, R. K., & BENSON, H. The physiology of meditation. In *Altered States of Awareness: Readings from Scientific American*. San Francisco: W. H. Freeman, 1972.

WARD, A. J. Early childhood autism and structural therapy: Outcome after 3 years. *Journal of Consulting and Clinical Psychology*, 1978, *46*, 586–587.

WARREN, K. R. Fetal alcohol syndrome: New perspectives. *Alcohol Health and Research World* (NIAAA, Public Health Service Alcohol, Drug Abuse, and Mental Health Administration, DHEW), Summer 1978, *4*(2). Washington, D.C.: U.S. Government Printing Office, 1978.

WATSON, O. M., & GRAVES, T. D. Quantitative research in proxemic behavior. *American Anthropologist*, 1966, *68*, 971–985.

WATSON, S. J., AKIL, H., BERGER, P. A., & BARCHAS, J. D. Some observations on the opiate peptides and schizophrenia. *Archives of General Psychiatry*, 1979, *36*, 35–41.

WAUGH, N. C., & NORMAN, D. A. Primary memory. *Psychological Review*, 1965, *72*, 89–104.

WAXER, P. Nonverbal cues for depression. *Journal of Abnormal Psychology*, 1974, *83*, 319–322.

WEAVER, C. N. Job satisfaction in the United States in the 1970s. *Journal of Applied Psychology*, 1980, *65*, 364–367.

WEBB, W. B., & AGNEW, H. W., JR. Sleep and waking in a time-free environment. *Aerospace Medicine*, 1974, *45*, 617–622.

WEBB, W. B., & AGNEW, H. W., JR. The effects on subsequent sleep of an acute restriction of sleep length. *Psychophysiology*, 1975, *12*, 367–370.

WEBB, W. B., & AGNEW, H. W., JR. Analysis of the sleep stages in sleep-wakefulness regimens of varied length. *Psychophysiology*, 1977, *14*, 445–450.

WEBB, W. B., & KERSEY, J. Recall of dreams and the probability of stage 1-REM sleep. *Perceptual and Motor Skills*, 1967, *24*, 627–630.

WEBSTER, M., & DRISKELL, J. E. Status generalization: A review and some new data. *American Sociological Review*, 1978, *43*, 230–236.

WECHSLER, D. *The measurement and appraisal of adult intelligence* (4th ed.). Baltimore, MD: Williams & Wilkins, 1958.

WECHSLER, D. Intelligence defined and undefined: A relativistic appraisal. *American Psychologist*, 1975, *30*, 135–139.

WEIL, A. T. *The natural mind: A new way of looking at drugs and the higher consciousness*. Boston: Houghton Mifflin, 1972.

WEIL, A. T. The marriage of the sun and the moon. In N. Zinberg (Ed.), *Alternate states of consciousness*. New York: Macmillan, 1977.

WEIL, A. T. Coca leaf as a therapeutic agent. *American Journal of Drug, Alcohol Abuse*, 1978, *5*, 75–86.

WEIL, A. T., & ZINBERG, N. E. Acute effects of marijuana in speech. *Nature*, 1969, *222*, 434–437.

WEIL, A. T., ZINBERG, N. E., & NELSON, J. M. Clinical and psychological effects of marijuana in man. *Science*, 1968, *162*, 1234–1242.

WEINER, B. *Human motivation*. New York: Holt, Rinehart & Winston, 1980.

WEINGARTNER, H., COHEN, R. M., MURPHY, D. L., MARTELLO, J., & GERDT, C. Cognitive processes in depression. *Archives of General Psychiatry*, 1981, *38*, 42–47.

WEINGARTNER, H., RAPOPORT, J. L., BUCHSBAUM, M. S., BUNNEY, W. E., JR., EBERT, M. H., MIKKELSEN, E. J., & CAINE, E. D. Cognitive processes in normal and hyperactive children and their response to amphetamine treatment. *Journal of Abnormal Psychology*, 1980, *89*, 25–37.

WEISENBERG, M. Pain and pain control. *Psychological Bulletin*, 1977, *84*, 1008–1044.

WEISS, A. A. *Mental retardation*. Paper presented at the meeting of the Implementation of Protection and Advocacy Systems, Columbia, SC, April 26, 1978.

WELLER, R. A., & HALIKAS, J. A. Objective criteria for the diagnosis of marijuana abuse. *The Journal of Nervous and Mental Disease*, 1980, *168*, 98–103.

WENDER, P. H., ROSENTHAL, D., KETY, S. S., SCHULSINGER, F., & WELNER, J. Cross-fostering: A research strategy for clarifying the role of genetic and experimental factors in the etiology of schizophrenia. *Archives of General Psychiatry*, 1974, *30*, 121–128.

WESSON, D. R., & SMITH, E. E. Cocaine: Its use for central nervous system stimulation including recreational and medical uses in cocaine: 1977: *National Institute of Drug Abuse Research Monograph Series*, 1977, *13*, 137–152.

WETLI, C. V., & WRIGHT, R. K. Death caused by recreational cocaine use. *Journal of the American Medical Association*, 1979, *241*, 2519–2522.

WHITE, B. L. *Experience and environment* (Vol. II). Englewood Cliffs, NJ: Prentice-Hall, 1978.

WHITE, B. W., SAUNDERS, F. A., SCADDEN, L., BACH-Y-RITA, P., & COLLINS, C. C. Seeing with the skin. *Perception and Psychophysics*, 1970, *7*, 23–27.

WHITE, J. R., & FROEB, H. F. Small-airways dysfunction in non-smokers chronically exposed to tobacco smoke. *The New England Journal of Medicine*, 1980, *302*, 720–723.

WHITE, S. H., DAY, M. C., FREEMAN, P. K., HANTMANN, S. A., & MESSENGER, K. P. *Federal programs for young children: Review and recommendations* (3 vols.). Washington, D.C.: U.S. Government Printing Office, 1973.

WHITMAN, T. L. Modification of chronic smoking behavior: A comparison of three approaches. *Behavior Research Therapy*, 1969, *7*, 257–263.

WHITMER, P. O. EMG biofeedback manipulation of arousal and the test of the overarousal and underarousal areas of childhood hyperactivity. Unpublished doctoral dissertation, University of Miami, 1977. *Dissertation Abstracts International*, 1978, *38*(7-B), 3423.

WHORF, B. L. *Language, thought, and reality: Selected writings of Benjamin Lee Whorf*, in J. B. Carroll (Ed.). New York: John Wiley & Sons, 1956.

WICKER, A. W. Ecological psychology: Some recent and prospective developments. *American Psychologist*, 1979, *34*(9), 755–765.

WICKLUND, R. A., & BREHM, J. W. *Perspectives of cognitive dissonance*. Hillsdale, NJ: Lawrence Ehrlbaum Associates, 1976.

WIG, N. N., & VARMA, V. K. Patterns of long-term heavy cannabis use in North India and its effects on cognitive functions: A preliminary report. *Drug and Alcohol Dependence*, 1977, *2*, 211–219.

WILLERMAN, L. Effects of families on intellectual development. *American Psychologist*, 1979, *34*(10), 923–929.

WILLIAMS, C. D. Case report: The elimination of tantrum behavior by extinction procedures. *Journal of Abnormal and Social Psychology*, 1959, 59, 269.

WILLIAMS, J. I., & CRAM, D. M. Diet in the management of hyperkinesis: A review of the tests of Feingold's hypothesis. *Canadian Psychiatric Association Journal*, 1978, 23, 241–248.

WILLIAMS, L. J., & EVANS, J. R. Evidence for perceptual defense using a lexical decision task. *Perceptual and Motor Skills*, 1980, 50, 195–198.

WILLIAMS, R., KARACAN, I., & HURSCH, C. *EEG of human sleep*. New York: John Wiley & Sons, 1974.

WILLIAMS, R. L. Black pride, academic relevance and individual achievement. *The Counseling Psychologist*, 1970, 2, 18–22.

WILLIS, F. N. Initial speaking distance as a function of the speakers' relationship. *Psychonomic Science*, 1966, 5, 221–222.

WILSON, G. T., & DAVISON, G. C. Processes of fear reduction in systematic desensitization: Animal studies. *Psychological Bulletin*, 1971, 76, 1–14.

WILSON, H. R., & GIESE, S. C. Threshold visibility of frequency grating patterns. *Vision Research*, 1977, 17, 1177–1190.

WILSON, M. A., SEYBERT, J. A., & CRAFT, J. L. Human learned helplessness as a function of sex and degree of control over aversive events. *Bulletin of the Psychonomic Society*, 1980, 16, 209–212.

WINCZE, J. P., & CAIRD, W. K. The effects of systematic desensitization and video desensitization in the treatment of essential sexual dysfunction in women. *Behavior Therapy*, 1976, 7, 335–342.

WINDMILLER, M. Introduction. In M. Windmiller, N. Lambert, & E. Turiel (Eds.), *Moral development and socialization*. Boston, MA: Allyn & Bacon, 1980.

WING, J. K. *Reasoning about madness*. Oxford, England: Oxford University Press, 1978.

WING, L. (ED.). *Early childhood autism* (2nd ed.). London and New York: Pergamon, 1976.

WINTERBOTTOM, M. R. The relation of need for achievement to early learning experiences in independence and mastery. In J. W. Atkinson (Ed.), *Motives in fantasy, action and society*. Princeton, NJ: Van Nostrand, 1958.

WITELSON, S. F., & PALLIE, W. Left hemisphere specialization for language in the newborn: Neuroanatomical evidence of asymmetry. *Brain*, 1973, 96, 641–646.

WOHLBERG, L. R. *The technique of psychotherapy: Part two* (3rd ed.). New York: Grune & Stratton, 1977.

WOHLWILL, J. F. Human adaptation to levels of environmental stimulation. *Human Ecology*, 1974, 2(2), 127–147.

WOLK, R. L., & WOLK, R. B. *Manual: Gerontological apperception test*. New York: Behavioral Publications, 1971.

WOLKIND, S. N. The components of "affectionless psychopathy" in institutionalized children. *Journal of Child Psychology and Psychiatry*, 1974, 15, 215–220.

WOLPE, J. *The practice of behavior therapy* (2nd ed.). New York: Pergamon Press, 1973.

WOODROW, H. Intelligence and its measurement: A symposium. *Journal of Educational Psychology*, 1921, 12, 207–210.

WOODROW, K. M., FRIEDMAN, G. D., SIEGELAUB, A. B., & COLLEN, M. F. Pain tolerance: Differences according to age, sex, and race. *Psychosomatic Medicine*, 1972, 34, 548–556.

WOODRUFF, G., & PREMACK, D. Intentional communication in the chimpanzee: The development of deception. *Cognition*, 1979, 7, 333–362.

WORCHELL, S., HARDY, T. W., & HURLEY, R. The effects of commercial interruption of violent and nonviolent films on viewers' subsequent aggression. *Journal of Experimental Social Psychology*, 1976, 12, 220–232.

WORTHINGTON, T. S. The use in court of hypnotically enhanced testimony. *The International Journal of Clinical and Experimental Hypnosis*, 1979, 27, 402–416.

WYNDHAM, C. H. Adaptation to heat and cold. *Environmental Research*, 1969, 2, 442–469.

WYSZECKI, G., & STILES, W. S. *Color science: Concepts and methods, quantitative data and formulas*. New York: John Wiley & Sons, 1967.

WUNDT, W. *Grundress er psychologie*. Leipzig, W. Germany: Engleman, 1896.

YALOM, I. D., BOND, G., BLOCH, S., ZIMMERMAN, E., & FRIEDMAN, L. The impact of a weekend group experience on individual therapy. *Archives of General Psychiatry*, 1977, 34, 399–415.

YANO, K., RHOADS, G. G., & KAGAN, A. Coffee, alcohol and risk of coronary heart disease among Japanese men living in Hawaii. *The New England Journal of Medicine*, 1977, 297, 405–409.

YATES, A. J. *Practice in behavior therapy*. New York: John Wiley & Sons, 1975.

YOUNG, A. W., & ELLIS, A. W. Asymmetry of cerebral hemispheric function in normal and poor readers. *Psychological Bulletin*, 1981, 89, 183–190.

YOUNG, L. R. Physical characteristics of the eye used in eye-movement measurement. In R. A. Monty & J. W. Senders (Eds.), *Eye movements and psychological processes*. Hillsdale, NJ: Lawrence Erlbaum Associates, 1976.

YOUNG-BROWNE, G., ROSENFELD, H. M., & HOROWITZ, F. D. Infant discrimination on facial expressions. *Child Development*, 1977, 48, 555–562.

ZAIDEL, S., & MEHRABIAN, A. The ability to communicate and to infer positive and negative attitudes facially and vocally. *Journal of Experimental Research and Personality*, 1969, 3, 233–241.

ZAJONC, R. B. Social facilitation. *Science*, 1965, 149, 269–274.

ZAJONC, R. B. Family configuration and intelligence. *Science*, 1976, 192, 227–236.

ZAJONC, R. B., & MARKUS, G. B. Birth order and intellectual development. *Psychological Review*, 1975, 82, 74–88.

ZANGWILL, O. L., & BLAKEMORE, C. Dyslexia: Reversal of eye-movements during reading. *Neuropsychologia*, 1972, 10, 371–373.

ZANNA, M. P., HIGGINS, E. T., & TAVES, P. A. Is dissonance phenomenologically aversive? *Journal of Experimental Social Psychology*, 1976, 12, 530–538.

ZENTHALL, S. S. Behavioral comparisons of hyperactive and normally active children in natural settings. *Journal of Abnormal Child Psychology*, 1980, 8, 93–109.

ZIEGLER, S., & HAMBLETON, D. Integration of young TMR children into a regular elementary school. *Exceptional Children*, 1976, 48, 459–461.

ZIGLER, E., & PHILLIPS, L. Psychiatric diagnosis and symptomatology. *Journal of Abnormal and Social Psychology*, 1961, 63, 69–75.

ZIGLER, E., GLICK, M., & MARSH, A. Premorbid social competence and outcome among schizophrenic and nonschizophrenic patients. *The Journal of Nervous and Mental Disease*, 1979, 167, 478–483.

ZILLMAN, D. *Hostility and aggression*. New York: John Wiley & Sons, 1979.

ZIMBARDO, P. Transforming experimental research into advocacy for social change. In M. Deutsch & H. Hornstein (Eds.), *Applying social psychology: Implications for research, practice, and training*. Hillsdale, NJ: Lawrence Erlbaum Associates, 1975.

ZIMBARDO, P. *The psychological power and pathology of imprisonment*. A statement prepared for the U.S. House of Representatives Committee on the Judiciary (Subcommittee No. 3, Robert Kastenmeyer, Chairman: Hearings on prison reform). Unpublished paper, Stanford University, 1971 (as cited in M. J. Lillyquist, *Understanding and changing criminal behavior*. Englewood Cliffs, NJ: Prentice-Hall, 1980).

ZINBERG, N. E., & WEIL, A. T. A comparison of marijuana users and non-users. *Nature*, 1970, *226*, 119–123.

ZUBIN, J., & SPRING, B. Vulnerability—A new view of schizophrenia. *Journal of Abnormal Psychology*, 1977, *86*, 103–126.

ZUCKERMAN, M. Variables affecting deprivation results and hallucinations, reported sensations and images. In J. P. Zubek (Ed.), *Sensory deprivation*. New York: Appleton-Century-Crofts, 1969.

ZUCKERMAN, M., & GERBASI, K. C. Belief in internal control or belief in a just world: The use and misuse of the I-E scale in prediction of attitudes and behavior. *Journal of Personality*, 1977, *45*, 356–378.

ZUCKERMAN, M., & GERBASI, K. C. Dimensions of the I-E scale and their relationship to other personality measures. *Educational and Psychological Measurement*, 1977, *37*, 159–175.

ZUROFF, D. C. Learned helplessness in humans: An analysis of learning processes and the roles of individual and situational differences. *Journal of Personality and Social Psychology*, 1980, *39*, 130–146.

ZUROFF, D. C., & SCHWARZ, J. C. Effects of transcendental meditation and muscle relaxation on trait anxiety, maladjustment, locus of control, and drug use. *Journal of Consulting and Clinical Psychology*, 1978, *46*, 264–271.

ZWEIGENHAFT, R. L., HAYES, K. N., & HAAGEN, C. H. The psychological impact of names. *Journal of Social Psychology*, 1980, *110*, 203–210.

Indexes

NAME INDEX

SUBJECT INDEX

CREDITS

Chapter 7: CO DUOTONE p.295—Bob Clay/Jeroboam. QUOTE p. 296 —"The bookworm and the boatman." In *Marathi Folk Tales*. London: George G. Harrap and Company, 1938. PHOTO p.298—© Susan Lapides 1981. FIG.7.1, p.300—© 1977, Phi Delta Kappan, Inc. FIG.7.6, p.311—From Guilford, J.P., Three faces of intellect, *American Psychologist*, 1959, *14*, 469–479. Copyright 1959 by the American Psychological Association. Reprinted by permission of the publisher and author. PHOTO p.312—Eric Roth/The Picture Cube. CARTOON p.314—© King Features Syndicate, Inc., 1972. PHOTO p.315—Judith D. Sedgewick/The Picture Cube. PHOTO p.317—Peeter Vilms/Jeroboam. QUOTE p.318—Sattler, J.M. *Assessment of Children's Intelligence and Special Abilities*, 2nd ed. Boston, MA: Allyn and Bacon, 1981. TABLE 7.3, p.319—Adapted with modifications from Sattler, J.M. *Assessment of children's intelligence and Special Abilities* 2nd ed. Boston: Allyn and Bacon, 1981. FIG.7.7, p.320—From Thompson, W.R., The inheritance and development of intelligence, *Research Publication of the Association of Nervous and Mental Diseases*, 1954, *33*, 209–331. PHOTO p.321—Anestis Diakopoulos/Stock, Boston. TABLE 7.4, p.321—Loehlin, Lindsey, and Spuhler, *Race differences in intelligence*, 1975, W.H. Freeman and Company, as estimated from Jarvik and Erlenmeyer-Kimling, 1967. BOX p.323—"Twins: Nazi and Jew," *Newsweek*, Dec. 3, 1979, p.139. Copyright 1979, by Newsweek, Inc. All Rights Reserved. Reprinted by Permission. PHOTO p.324—Jane Scherr/Jeroboam. PHOTO p.325— U.S.D.A. photo by Michelle Bogre. PHOTO p.327—Elizabeth Hamlin/Stock, Boston. PHOTO p.328—© Susan Lapides 1981. QUOTE p.332—Sattler, J.M. *Assessment of Children's Intelligence and Special Abilities*, 2nd ed. Boston, MA: Allyn and Bacon, 1981. PHOTO p.333—© Susan Lapides 1981. QUOTE p.333—Weiss, A.A. An address at the "Implementation of Protection and Advocacy Systems" conference, April 26, 1978, Williams-Brice Stadium, Columbia, S.C., sponsored by the South Carolina Training and Technical Project Assistance.

Chapter 8: CO DUOTONE p.341—Suzzane Arms/Jeroboam. QUOTE p.342—From *A Civil Tongue*, copyright © 1975, 1976 by Edwin Newman, used with permission of the publisher, The Bobbs-Merrill Company, Inc. PHOTO p.343—Daniel S. Brody/Stock, Boston. PHOTO p.343 —Frank Siteman/The Picture Cube. PHOTO p.344—Mariette Pathy Allen/Peter Arnold, Inc. FIG.8.1, p.348—From The acquisition of language by Breyne Arlene Moskowitz. Copyright © 1978 by Scientific American, Inc. all rights reserved. PHOTO p.349—Evan Johnson/Jeroboam. PHOTO p.351—Hazel Hankin/Stock, Boston. PHOTO p.357— N.Y. Zoological Society/EPA (Editorial Photo Archives). FIG.8.3, p.358 —From Premack, D., Language in chimpanzees, *Science*, 1971, *172*, 808–822. Copyright © 1971 by the American Association for the Advancement of Science. FIG.8.4, p.358—From Premack, D., Language in chimpanzees, *Science*, 1971, *172*, 808–822. Copyright © 1971 by the American Association for the Advancement of Science. PHOTO p.359—Ellis Herwig/Stock, Boston. BOX p.360—"Idioglossia," *Time*, Dec. 10, 1979, pp. 119–122. Reprinted by permission from TIME, The Weekly Newsmagazine; Copyright Time Inc. 1979. PHOTO p.362—Barbara Kirk/Peter Arnold, Inc. PHOTO p.364—Jerry Berndt/Stock, Boston. PHOTO p.366— Jerry Berndt/Stock, Boston. BOX p.367—From Morris K. Holland, *Using Psychology: Principles of Behavior and Your Life*. Copyright © 1975 by Little, Brown and Company (Inc.). Reprinted by permission. CARTOON p.376—B.C. by permission of Johnny Hart and Field Enterprises, Inc. PHOTO p.377—Barbara Alper/Stock, Boston. PHOTO p.378— Frank Siteman/The Picture Cube. PHOTO p.381—U.S.D.A. photo by Shepard Sherbell.

Chapter 9: CO DUOTONE p.385—Eugene Richards/The Picture Cube. QUOTE p.386—Frank, I., & Richardson, G. "Epidemic!" In *Penthouse*, 1977, 9(1), p.73. Copyright 1977 by Penthouse International Ltd. and reprinted with the permission of the copyright owner. PHOTO p.389— Charles Gatewood. FIG.9.1, p.390—From Carlson, *Physiology of behavior*, Boston: Allyn and Bacon, 1977. PHOTO p.392—© Rachael Elkins 1981. PHOTO p.398—Donald Dietz/Stock, Boston. FIG.9.2, p.399— Photo by Eric Roth/The Picture Cube. FIG.9.3, p.399—Reproduced from *Some must watch while some must sleep* by William C. Dement, with the permission of W.W. Norton & Company, Inc. Copyright © 1972, 1974, 1976 by William C. Dement. FIG.9.4, p.401—Reproduced from *Some must watch while some must sleep* by William C. Dement, with the permission of W.W. Norton & Company, Inc. Copyright © 1972, 1974, 1976 by William C. Dement. FIG.9.5, p.402—Reprinted by permission from Kales, A., and Kales, J.D., Sleep disorders, *The New England Journal of Medicine*, 1974, *290*, 487–499. TABLE 9.1, p.402—From William, R., Karacan, I., and Hursch, C., *The EEG of human sleep*, John Wiley & Sons, Inc., 1974. FIG.9.6, p.404—From Jenkins, J.G., and Dallenbach, K.M., Oblivescence during sleep and waking, *American Journal of Psychology*, 1924, *35*, 605–612. PHOTO p.406—Philip Jones Griffith/Magnum. PHOTO p.409—T.C. Fitzgerald/The Picture Cube. PHOTO p.411—Nicholas Sapieha/Stock, Boston. BOX p.414—"PCP: A Terror of a Drug," *Time*, Dec. 19, 1977, p.53. Reprinted by permission from TIME, The Weekly Newsmagazine; Copyright Time Inc. 1977. PHOTO p.416— Charles Gatewood. PHOTO p.418—Bohdan Hrynewyck/Stock, Boston. TABLE 9.2, p.420—From Ray, Oakley, *Drugs, society, and human behavior*, 2nd ed. St. Louis, 1978, The C.V. Mosby Co. TABLE 9.3, p.421— From Ray, Oakley, *Drugs, society, and human behavior*, 2nd ed. St. Louis, 1978, The C.V. Mosby Co. FIG.9.7, p.422—Adapted by permission of Harcourt Brace Jovanovich, Inc. from Figure 4-4 in *The psychology of consciousness*, 2nd ed. by Robert E. Ornstein. PHOTO p.424—© Rachael Elkins 1981. TABLE 9.5, p.426—E.C. Hammond, World Conference on Smoking and Health, Sept. 11, 1967. PHOTO p.427—Mike Mazzachi/Stock, Boston.

Chapter 10: CO DUOTONE p.433—Charles Gatewood. QUOTE p.434 —From "The Love Song of J. Alfred Prufrock" in *Collected Poems 1909–1962* by T.S. Eliot, copyright 1936 by Harcourt Brace Jovanovich, Inc.; copyright © 1963, 1964 by T.S. Eliot. Reprinted by permission of Harcourt Brace Jovanovich, Inc. PHOTO p.437—Jerry Berndt/Stock, Boston. PHOTO p.439—Eugene Richards/The Picture Cube. PHOTO p.440 —© Carol Palmer 1980. PHOTO p.443—© Rachael Elkins 1981. PHOTO p.447—Peter Southwick/Stock, Boston. PHOTO p.453—Michael Weisbrot. PHOTO p.454—Cary Wolinsky/Stock, Boston. FIG.10.2, p.455— Albrecht, Thomas, Chadwick, *Social psychology* © 1980, pp. 32, 43. Adapted by permission of Prentice-Hall, Inc., Englewood Cliffs, N.J. FIG.10.3, p.457—Albrecht, Thomas, Chadwick, *Social psychology* © 1980, pp. 32, 43. Adapted by permission of Prentice-Hall, Inc., Englewood Cliffs, N.J. PHOTO p.459—Arthur Grace/Stock, Boston. QUOTE p.461—Berkowitz, L., & LePage, A. Weapons as aggression-eliciting stimuli. *Journal of Personality & Social Psychology*, 1967, *7*, p.202. PHOTO p.461—Bohdan Hrynewyck/Stock, Boston. PHOTO p.462—© Bonnie Griffiths 1981. FIG.10.4, p.463—From Goldstein, J.H., Rosnow, R.L., Raday, T., Silverman, I., and Gaskell, G.D., Punitiveness in response to films varying in content: A cross-national field study of aggression, *European Journal of Social Psychology*, 1975, *5*, 149–165. BOX p.464—"What TV Does to Kids," *Newsweek*, Feb. 21, 1977, pp. 63–70. Copyright 1977, by Newsweek, Inc. All Rights Reserved. Reprinted by Permission. FIG.10.5, p.467—From data presented in Milgram, S., Behavioral study of obedience, *Journal of Abnormal and Social Psychology*, 1963, *67*, 371– 378. Copyright 1963 by the American Psychological Association. Adapted by permission of the publisher and author. PHOTO p.468— Arthur Grace/Stock, Boston. PHOTO p.473—Charles Gatewood. PHOTO p.476—Terry McCoy/The Picture Cube. CARTOON p.477— Copyright, 1978, G.B. Trudeau/Distributed by Universal Press Syndicate. PHOTO p.478—© Cynthia Benjamins 1981. PHOTO p.481— Charles Gatewood. PHOTO p.485—© Harvey Stein 1981. FIG.10.8, p.486—From Altman, I., and Vensel, A.M., Personal space: An analysis of E.T. Hall's proxemics framework, in Altman, I., and Wholwill, J.F., (eds.), *Human behavior and environment: Advances in theory and research*, *2*, 1977, Plenum Publishing Corp. PHOTO p.488—Charles Gatewood.

Chapter 11: CO DUOTONE p.495—Eric A. Roth/The Picture Cube. QUOTE p.496—Friedman, M., & Rosenman, R.H. *Type A behavior and your heart*, pp. 13–14. Copyright © 1974 by Alfred A. Knopf, Inc. Reprinted by permission of the publisher. PHOTO p.497—© Harvey Stein 1979. PHOTO p.503—Jean Claude Lejeune/Stock, Boston. PHOTO p.506 —© Bonnie Griffith 1981. PHOTO p.512—Cary Wolinsky/Stock, Boston. PHOTO p.515—Michael Weisbrot. BOX p.517—"What's In A Name," *Newsweek*, July 9, 1973, p.64. Copyright 1973, by Newsweek, Inc. All Rights Reserved. Reprinted by Permission. PHOTO p.518—Michael Weisbrot. PHOTO p.523—Daniel S. Brody/Stock, Boston. PHOTO p.529—Owen Franken/Stock, Boston.

Chapter 12: CO DUOTONE p.533—Sharon Fox/The Picture Cube. QUOTE p.534—From *Fear of Flying* by Erica Jong. Copyright © 1973 by Holt, Rinehart and Winston. Reprinted by permission of Holt, Rinehart and Winston. PHOTO p.537—© Walter S. Silver 1981. PHOTO p.540— Ken Buck/The Picture Cube. TABLE 12.3, p.544—From Marks, I.M., and Lader, M., Anxiety stress (anxiety neurosis): A review, *Journal of Nervous and Mental Disease*, 1973, *156*, 3–18. QUOTE p.546—From *Abnormal Psychology and Modern Life*, 6th edition, p.209, by James C. Coleman, James N. Butcher, and Robert C. Carson. Copyright © 1980 Scott, Foresman and Company. Reprinted by permission. QUOTE top p.547—Reprinted by permission of Coward, McCann & Geoghegan, Inc., from *Phobias & Compulsions: Their Understanding & Treatment*, p.22, by Joy Melville. Copyright © 1977 by Joy Melville. QUOTE bottom p.547—Reprinted by permission of Coward, McCann & Geoghegan, Inc., from *Phobias & Compulsions: Their Understanding & Treatment*. pp. 72–73, by Joy Melville. Copyright © 1977 by Joy Melville. PHOTO top p.548—Michael Weisbrot. PHOTO bottom p.548—© Harvey Stein 1981. QUOTE p.549—Reprinted by permission of Coward, McCann & Geoghegan, Inc., from *Phobias & Compulsions: Their Understanding & Treatment*, pp. 66–67, by Joy Melville. Copyright © 1977 by Joy Melville. PHOTO p.553—Frank Siteman/The Picture Cube. TABLE 12.4, p.554—From Beck, A.T., "Depression: Causes and treatment," University of Pennsylvania Press, 1972, 69, Philadelphia. QUOTE p.554—Pitt, B. (1974) *Psychogeriatrics*, First Edition. Edinburgh: Churchill Livingstone. QUOTE middle p.555—Beck, A.T., *Depressions: Causes and treatment*. Philadelphia, PA: University of Pennsylvania Press, 1972, p.81. Reprinted by permission of the publisher. TABLE 12.5, p.558—From Beck, *Depression: Clinical, experimental, and the theoretical aspects*, Hober, 1967. BOX p.559—© 1975 United Press International. FIG.12.1, p.562—From *Schizophrenia Bulletin*, 1976, 2 (3). PHOTO p.564—Frank Siteman/The Picture Cube. PHOTO p.567—Steve Malone/Jeroboam, Inc. PHOTO p.571—© Rachael Elkins 1981. TABLE 12.9, p.578—American Psychiatric Association, *Diagnostic and statistical manual of mental disorders*, 3rd ed., Washington, D.C., American Psychological Association 1980. QUOTE p.579—From *Abnormal Psychology and Modern Life*, 6th edition, p.496, by James C. Coleman, James N. Butcher, annd Robert C. Carson. Copyright © 1980 Scott, Foresman and Company. Reprinted by permission. PHOTO p.580—Henry Horenstein/The Picture Cube. QUOTE p.581—Gajzago, C., & Prior, M. Two cases of "recovery" in Kanner syndrome. *Archives of General Psychiatry*, 1974, *31*, 264. Copyright 1974, American Medical Association. Reprinted by permission of the author and publisher.

Chapter 13: CO DUOTONE p.587—Eric Kroll/Taurus Photos. QUOTE p.588—Viorst, J. "Twenty Questions." In *How did I get to be 40 and other atrocities*. New York: Simon and Schuster, 1976, p.48. By permission of The Lescher Agency. Copyright © 1976 by Judith Viorst. PHOTO p.595 —Judith D. Sedwick/The Picture Cube. QUOTE p.597—Wohlberg, L.R. The technique of psychotherapy: Part two, 3rd edition. New York: Grune & Stratton, 1977, p.618. By permission of the author. PHOTO p.600—Eric Roth/The Picture Cube. BOX p.604—"TA: Doing Okay," *Time*, August 20, 1973, p.47. Reprinted by permission from TIME, The Weekly Newsmagazine; Copyright Time Inc. 1981. FIG.13.1, p.605—FIG.16 (p.80) from *I'm OK—you're OK* by Thomas A. Harris, M.D. Copyright © 1967, 1968, 1969, by Thomas A. Harris, M.D. Reprinted by permission of Harper & Row, Publishers, Inc. FIG.13.2, p.605—Fig.10 (p.71) from *I'm OK—you're OK* by Thomas A. Harris, M.D. Copyright © 1967, 1968, 1969, by Thomas A. Harris, M.D. Reprinted by permission of Harper & Row, Publishers, Inc. FIG.13.3, p.609—From Lahey, B.B., McNees, M.P., and Brown, C.C., Modification of deficits in reading for comprehension, *Journal of Applied Behavior Analysis*, 1973, *6*, 475–480. FIG.13.4, p.611—From Ayllon, T., and Azrin, N.H., The measurement and reinforcement of behavior of psychotics, *Journal of the Experimental Analysis of Behavior*, 1965, *8*, 377. Copyright 1965 by the Society for the Experimental Analysis of Behavior. For additional findings and related research see *The token economy: A motivational system for therapy and rehabilitation*, Prentice-Hall, 1968. FIG.13.5, p.612—Reprinted with permission from *Behavior Research and Therapy*, 2. Ayllon, T., and Haughton, E., Modification of symptomatic verbal behavior of mental patients, Copyright 1964, Pergamon Press, Ltd. For additional findings and related research see *The token economy: A motivational system for therapy and rehabilitation*. Prentice-Hall, 1968. FIG.13.6, p.613—From Williams, C.D., Case report: The elimination of tantrum behavior by extinction procedures, *Journal of Abnormal and Social Psychology*, 1959, *59*, 269. Copyright 1959 by the American Psychological Association. Reprinted by permission of the publisher and author. QUOTE p.614—From the book, *Modern Therapies*, by Virginia Binder, Arnold Binder and Bernard Rimland, p.141. © 1976 by Prentice-Hall, Inc. Published by Prentice-Hall, Inc., Englewood Cliffs, N.J. 07632. QUOTE p.618—From *Clinical Behavior Therapy* by Marvin R. Goldfried and Gerald C. Davison. Copyright © 1976 by Holt, Rinehart and Winston. Reprinted by permission of Holt, Rinehart and Winston. FIG.13.8, p.620—From Bandura, A., Blanchard, E.B., and Ritter, B., Relative efficacy of desensitization and modeling approaches for inducing behavioral, affective, and attitudinal changes, *Journal of Personality and Social Psychology*, 1968, *13*, 183. Copyright 1968 by the American Psychological Association. Adapted by permission of the publisher and author. PHOTO p.621—Courtesy of Albert Ellis. TABLE 13.3, p.624—Adapted from: *Modern clinical psychology: Principles of intervention in the clinic and the community* by Sheldon J. Korchin. Copyright © 1976 by Sheldon J. Korchin. Published by Basic Books, Inc., New York. PHOTO p.626—© Harvey Stein 1980. PHOTO p.628—Karen R. Preuss/Jeroboam, Inc. PHOTO p.631—Bruce Kliewe/Jeroboam, Inc.

Chapter 14: CO DUOTONE p.637—Constantine Manos/Magnum Photos. QUOTE p.638—Specified excerpt from p.20 in *The Gulag Archipelago 1918–1956* by Aleksandr I. Solzhenitsyn. Translated by Thomas P. Whitney. Copyright © 1973 by Aleksandr I. Solzhenitsyn. English language translation copyright © 1973, 1974 by Harper & Row, Publishers, Inc. Reprinted by permission of Harper & Row, Publishers, Inc. FIG.14.1, p.643—From *Industrial and organizational psychology*, 4th ed., by Gilmer, B.V.H. and Deci., E.L., Copyright © 1977, McGraw Hill. Used with the permission of McGraw-Hill Book Company. FIG.14.2, p.645—From B.M. Staw (Editor) *Research in organizational behavior 1*, 1979, JAI Press, Inc., Greenwich, Connecticut 06830. PHOTO p.649—Abigail Heyman/Magnum. PHOTO p.650—Charles Gatewood. PHOTO p.651—Andrew Brilliant/The Picture Cube. FIG.14.3, p.653—From Donnerstein, E., and Wilson, D.W., Effects of noise and perceived control on ongoing and subsequent aggressive behavior, *Journal of Personality and Social Psychology*. Copyright 1976 by the American Psychological Association. Adapted by permission of the publisher and author. PHOTO p.654—Mark Antman/Stock, Boston. BOX p.655—Reprinted from *Architecture Australia*, 1979, 67(6), p.61, by permission of the publisher. PHOTO p.657—Peter Menzel/Stock, Boston. PHOTO p.660—Charles Harbutt/Magnum. PHOTO p.663—Leonard Freed/Magnum.

Appendix: CO DUOTONE p.675—Ed Hof/The Picture Cube. QUOTE p.676—Excerpt from *The People's Almanac* by David Wallechinsky and Irving Wallace. Copyright © 1975 by David Wallace and Irving Wallace. Reprinted by permission of Doubleday & Company.

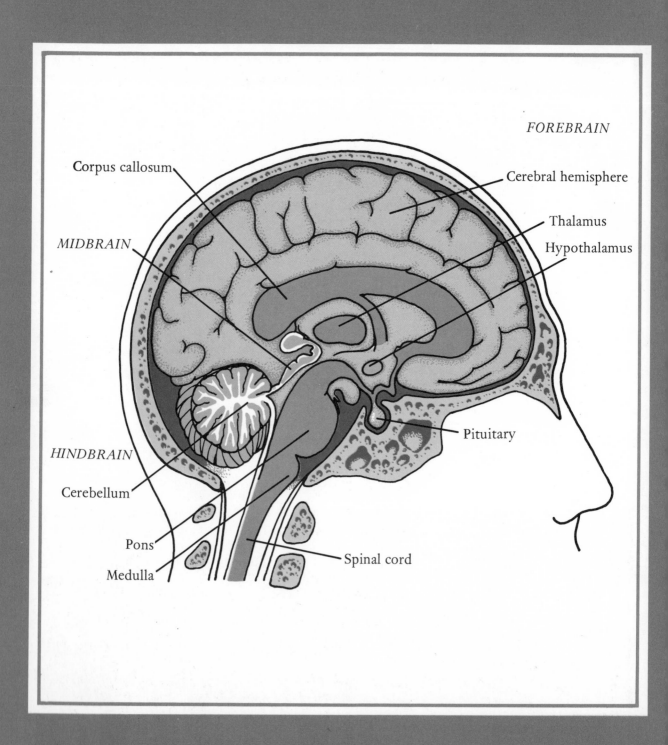

FOREBRAIN

Corpus callosum

Cerebral hemisphere

Thalamus

MIDBRAIN

Hypothalamus

HINDBRAIN

Pituitary

Cerebellum

Pons

Medulla

Spinal cord